Biographical Dictionary of Chinese Women

THE TWENTIETH CENTURY
1912–2000

The second volume in this distinguished series contains some 250 biographies of women active from 1912 until 1990, although many of the biographies contain information current to the year 2000. While the volume includes biographies of such internationally famous Chinese women as the Soong sisters, Lu Gwei-Djen, Jiang Qing, Han Suyin, Anna Chennault, Deng Yingchao, and Ding Ling, because of the enormous amount of historical material and scholarly research that has become available in the last few decades, the editor was also able to include a greater range of women than would have been previously possible. These are Chinese women who have forged careers as scientists, businesswomen, sportswomen, and military officers appearing alongside writers, academics, revolutionary heroines, politicians, musicians, opera stars, film stars, artists, educators, nuns, and traditional good wives. Also included are women from minority nationalities.

Casting a wide net, the editor includes biographies of women from mainland China and Taiwan as well as those of Chinese descent who were born overseas, including famous Americans like Maxine Hong Kingston. More than eighty authors and translators from all over the world have contributed to this indispensable and impressive scholarly undertaking.

The first volume . . .
BIOGRAPHICAL DICTIONARY OF CHINESE WOMEN
The Qing Period, 1644–1911
Edited by Clara Wing-chung Ho
Editors-in-Chief: Lily Xiao Hong Lee and A.D. Stefanowska

"This outstanding volume will stand as a classic reference for decades to come."
— *Asian Studies Review*

"This collaborative work is a most welcome addition to the field of Qing studies. . . . The editors must be congratulated for the wide breadth of profiles encompassing empresses, authors, religious leaders and one pirate. . . . The entries are eminently readable and promise to open many avenues for future research."
— *Pacific Affairs*

中國婦女傳記詞典
二十世紀卷

香港大學圖書館叢書之十四

University of Hong Kong Libraries Publications, No. 14

Biographical Dictionary of Chinese Women

THE TWENTIETH CENTURY
1912–2000

Editors-in-Chief
Lily Xiao Hong Lee
and A.D. Stefanowska

Assistant Editor-in-Chief
Sue Wiles

The Twentieth–Century Period Editor
Lily Xiao Hong Lee

AN EAST GATE BOOK

M.E. Sharpe
Armonk, New York
London, England

An East Gate Book

Library of Congress Cataloging-in-Publication Data

Biographical dictionary of Chinese women : the Qing Period, 1644–1911 / Lily Xiao
Hong Lee and A.D. Stefanowska, editors, Clara Wing-chung Ho, volume editor.
    p. cm.
"An east gate book."
Includes bibliographical references (p.   ).
ISBN 0-7656-0043-9 (cloth : alk. paper)
  1. Women—China—Biography—Dictionaries. 2. China—Biography—Dictionaries.
I. Lee, Lily Xiao Hong. II. Stefanowska, A.D. III. Ho, Clara Wing-chung, 1963–.

HQ1767.5.A3B56 1998
305.4′092′251 dc21   98-11262
CIP

The Twentieth Century, 1912–2000 : ISBN 0-7656-0798-0

Printed in the United States of America

BM (c) 10   9   8   7   6   5   4   3   2   1

Contents

Preface

This English edition of the *Biographical Dictionary of Chinese Women: The Twentieth Century, 1912–2000*, is the second in a multivolume series to be published, *The Qing Period, 1644–1911*, volume having appeared in 1998. The idea for this reference book originated within the then School of Asian Studies at the University of Sydney in Australia in the mid-1980s. Our review of literature in the field revealed the many English-language biographical dictionaries of eminent Chinese that have been published over the years, covering many periods of Chinese history: *Sung Biographies* (ed. Herbert Franke [Wiesbaden: Franz Steiner Verlag, 1976]); *Dictionary of Ming Biography (1368–1644)* (ed. L. Carrington Goodrich and Chaoying Fang [New York: Columbia University Press, 1976]); *Eminent Chinese of the Ch'ing Period (1644–1912)* (ed. Arthur W. Hummel [Washington, D.C.: U.S. Government Printing Office, 1943]); *Biographical Dictionary of Republican China* (ed. Howard L. Boorman and Richard C. Howard [New York: Columbia University Press, 1967]); and the *Biographic Dictionary of Chinese Communism, 1921–1965* (ed. Donald W. Klein and Anne B. Clark [Cambridge, Mass.: Harvard University Press, 1971]). In these biographical works, however, the lives of women have been largely ignored: only nine of the 809 entries in Hummel's work are women; only twenty-three women appear among the 600–odd biographies in Boorman and Howard; and some eighteen women are given individual articles by Klein and Clark, whose dictionary provided biographies of 433 people. Thus, the purpose of the present *Biographical Dictionary of Chinese Women* is to compile under one title biographies of Chinese women throughout history and furnish more complete biographical data on individual Chinese women than presently exists in the general dictionaries that have been published over the past two decades.

The biographical articles in the *Biographical Dictionary of Chinese Women* were not commissioned as original research but as a summary of existing knowledge and information. Even this modest aim has at times been difficult to achieve; until very recently, little material has been available on women from mainland China. However, we consistently view our work as a first step in facilitating further research into the lives and accomplishments of Chinese women.

While the editors-in-chief have worked for many years at The University of Sydney, Australia, this present volume has received the benefit of only limited institutional support. Partly reflecting these financial constraints, we have been able to provide Chinese characters only for the names of the women, not for titles of works or institutions, etc. This omission is rightly lamented, but we believe it is in some measure compensated by the planned publication of a Chinese-language edition of the *Biographical Dictionary of Chinese Women* series, starting with *The Qing Period* volume. All contributors and translators have graciously contributed their time and expertise gratis in support of these projects, and their generosity is keenly appreciated.

The editor of this volume, Lily Xiao Hong Lee, invited sixty-five scholars from

Australia; Canada; China, including Hong Kong and Taiwan; the Netherlands; Southeast Asia; the United Kingdom; and the United States to write the articles in this *Biographical Dictionary of Chinese Women*. The biographees were chosen according to our original criteria of selecting Chinese women of outstanding accomplishment in a field of study, profession, or trade or who had exerted a special influence over their own era or on posterity. All of these women have contributed in some measure to the increasingly globalized world of the twentieth century. Most of them were born and lived or worked in China; some were born of Chinese parents outside China, while others born in China made their mark elsewhere; a few were foreigners who became Chinese citizens and worked in China.

This volume covers the years 1912 to 2000. We should emphasize, however, that the end year of 2000 must be seen as notional. All entries are current to 1990, but many have been updated to 2000, and more than one biography contains information on events that took place in 2001. We have not included women who first emerged onto the public stage in the 1990s because we deemed it prudent to leave a full evaluation of their lives to the editors of a future work. Just over three hundred biographies are gathered in this volume of the *Biographical Dictionary of Chinese Women*, and the range of their collective interests and activities is extensive. By far the largest group comprises women involved to different degrees in politics and government. This is perhaps not surprising in a century that saw the overthrow of the imperial order and the eventual establishment of a people's republic in a China that continues to evolve. Revolutionaries, political activists and reformers, and women's rights activists took center stage in the Republican period during the first half of the twentieth century. Many of the women were early communists but some also fought for democracy, the independence of Taiwan, and the individual rights of women. Some made their way through the hierarchy of government or party posts to wield a degree of authority in China, Hong Kong, and Taiwan; a few won power through other, less legitimate, means.

While no longer being the sole path that educated women in China are expected to take, literature remains a fertile field for female talent. The vast majority of literary women included are fiction writers, re-creating through their works the lives of their less articulate sisters. The poets, essayists, and critics have used their pens to expose what needs to be changed in the lives of women and courageously forged new pathways for all.

Women artists are not novel in China nor are performing artists—opera stars, dancers, singers. What is remarkable about these women in this century is their vigor to generate innovation in their chosen fields. Film and theater spawned a generation of intrepid women performers in the 1930s and 1940s, while local opera saw a blossoming of talent. These women developed and rejuvenated the traditional arts and songs, as well as creating new genres, as the times demanded. Some made happy marriages or made their way alone in a patriarchal world. Others were destroyed by infidelity, intrigue, or politics. In the second half of the century, Chinese women turned to producing and directing film, television, and theater, and actresses who made their name as martial arts and international film stars proliferated.

The professions attracted many women in the era of the twentieth century as their ability to exercise a greater freedom of choice in making a career expanded. History cannot be gainsaid, however, and education remains an area in which women predominate. Some have nevertheless ventured toward stepping into other, more radical, paths, including the law and police enforcement. In line with more traditional pursuits of old China, however, many educated women have become scholars. Some nevertheless extended their interests beyond conventional subjects and entered the newer realms of science and technology. More than one of the scientists in this volume has won international respect in her chosen field. Readers will not be surprised to find nuns appearing in these pages, and even military women. They may wonder a little, however, at the amount of willpower that is required of women to succeed in the harsh worlds of the media, industry, and commerce. Hints of the sacrifices entailed are revealed in their private lives, with many of the women choosing to remain single in order to achieve their goals.

As with *The Qing Period* volume, not all of the biographees are Han Chinese. Included are Tibetan and Manchurian women, as well as Mongolians and other nationalities (Hui, Bai). One is a French woman who lived and died in China as a Chinese citizen. There are women that we would like to have included but were unable to because of lack of information, insufficient time, or our inability to find a suitable contributor. We believe, however, that we have made a reasonable attempt at providing for an English-speaking audience an accurate and informative portrait of the most notable Chinese women of the twentieth century. We hope the *Biographical Dictionary of Chinese Women* forms the basis for further research.

Lily Xiao Hong Lee
A. D. Stefanowska
Sue Wiles

Editors' Note

The style and format adopted in the *Biographical Dictionary of Chinese Women: The Twentieth Century, 1912–2000*, conform to the biographical dictionaries of eminent Chinese mentioned in the Preface as well as to *The Qing Period* volume already published. We have listed the women in a "Finding List by Background or Fields of Endeavor" according to the field of study, profession, or trade for which they are best known; some women will appear in multiple classifications. A Brief Chronology of Twentieth-Century Events and a brief list of Abbreviations and Guide to Chinese Words Used are provided to assist non-specialist readers. Biographical entries are arranged alphabetically in the text. The traditional Chinese name order of surname followed by given names has been preserved throughout except where a biographee, contributor, or translator has chosen to adopt the Western order of given name followed by surname.

As in *The Qing Period* volume, we have used *pinyin* romanization and offer appropriate cross references to alternate spellings of women's names. There are two major exceptions to this rule, however, made only after much thought and discussion. The first is that women who go by or are widely recognized by an English name, e.g., Sally Aw, Anson Chan, and Dame Lydia Dunn, are listed under that name along with a reference from their Chinese name. This exception also extends to non-standard romanization known to be preferred by the woman herself, e.g., Fan Tchun-pi, and commonly accepted usage for well-known people and places, e.g., Chiang Kai-shek, Soong Mayling, Taiwan, and Taipei. The second is that, out of respect for a stated or implicit wish, we have used standard Wade-Giles romanization for the names of women from Taiwan or who spent a significant portion of their lives there. Standard Wade-Giles is also applied to Taiwan place names. Because Taiwan has unofficially adopted a modified Wade-Giles system, dispensing with apostrophes and umlauts—which, when used in conjunction with *pinyin* in a volume such as this, can cause considerable confusion—we have therefore romanized all Chinese words in the biographies of Taiwan-related women in standard Wade-Giles. *Pinyin* equivalents are given in all cases.

The city of Beijing has undergone several name changes over the past one hundred years. To avoid confusion and circumvent difficult decisions, we decided to refer to the city by its current name of "Beijing" regardless of the period under discussion but with two exceptions to this rule. The first is that where "Beiping" appears as part of the name of an institution or entity then that spelling is retained in its translation. The second is when the use of the old post office spelling of "Peking" occurs, that spelling also is retained in a name, e.g., "Peking University."

In translating terms and institutions, we have not had the benefit of any one comprehensive, authoritative reference guide, but we did attempt to follow established authorities. For the People's Republic of China, we consulted the *Chinese-English*

Manual of Chinese Organizations (ed. Xinhua she duiwai bu [Beijing: Jinri Zhongguo chubanshe, 1992; distributed by China International Book Trading Corp.]). Identifying groups and institutions cited in Chinese sources can be quite bewildering: names frequently vary, not only between sources, but within one text. We have nevertheless done our best to maintain internal consistency within our volume, giving the *pinyin* of the original Chinese where possible. We have also attempted to translate in the text the titles of most literary and artistic works produced by the women biographees so as to give English-speaking readers a sense of their content. At times, when the meaning of a title is obscure, we have resorted to an approximate translation. Again, *pinyin* is provided where possible.

   Bibliographies given at the end of each biography are meant not to be exhaustive but to serve as suggestions for additional reading.

Lily Xiao Hong Lee
A. D. Stefanowska
Sue Wiles

Acknowledgments

The editors-in-chief thank The University of Sydney for extending financial support over a number of years to this research project, the *Biographical Dictionary of Chinese Women*.

Our sincere thanks also go to the contributors who gave time and expertise to research and write the articles appearing in this volume and to the translators who rendered into English the articles written in Chinese.

Professor Wang Bing provided advice on scientific matters as well as writing many of the biographies of the scientists; we are greatly indebted to her on both counts.

We must express our special gratitude to Dr. Yu Chien-ming of the Institute of Modern History, Academia Sinica, and Associate Professor Chen Chun-kai at Fu-Jen Catholic University. The time and effort each devoted to the demanding task of coordinating most of the entries on women in Taiwan are greatly appreciated. Their contribution enhanced the breadth and depth of our coverage of the women of Taiwan.

We would also like to acknowledge the unfailingly cheerful and professional assistance we have received over the past three or four years from Magdalen Lee and Sharon Qian at the East Asian Library, The University of Sydney. Without their help, many references would have been incomplete and much information lacking.

Contributors

BAI, Di, Department of Asian Studies, Drew University, Madison, N.J., USA

BI, Xiyan Vivian, Department of Chinese Studies, University of Sydney, Australia

CHAN, H.D. Min-hsi, School of Science and Technology Studies, University of New South Wales, Sydney, Australia

CHAN, Shirley Wai, Department of Chinese Studies, University of Sydney, Australia

CHAN, Sylvia, Centre of Asian Studies, University of Adelaide, Australia

CH'EN Ch'un-ying, Department of General Studies, Police University, Taipei, Taiwan

CHEN Wanjun, Department of Chinese Language and Literature, Peking University, PRC

CHEN, Xiaomei, Department of East Asian Languages and Literatures, Ohio State University, Columbus, USA

CHENG Li-jung, Institute of History, National Chengchi University, Taipei, Taiwan

CHEUNG, Chiu-yee, Department of Asian Languages and Studies, University of Queensland, Brisbane, Australia

CHEY, Jocelyn, Department of Chinese Studies, University of Sydney, Australia

CHU Te-lan, Sun Yat-sen Institute for Social Sciences and Philosophy, Academia Sinica, Nankang, Taiwan

CLARK, John, Department of Art History and Theory, University of Sydney, Australia

CROIZIER, Ralph, Department of History, University of Victoria, Canada

CUI Zhiying, Department of Chinese Studies, University of Sydney, Australia

DENTON, Kirk A., Department of East Asian Languages and Literatures, Ohio State University, Columbus, USA

DING Shoupu, Institute of History, Chinese Academy of Social Sciences, Beijing, PRC

EDWARDS, Louise, School of Arts and Sciences, Australian Catholic University, Brisbane, Australia

FAN Mei-yüan, International Chinese Language Program at National Taiwan University, Taipei, Taiwan

FENG Chongyi, Institute for International Studies, University of Technology, Sydney, Australia; and Department of History, Nankai University, Tianjin, PRC

FERRY, Megan M., Modern Languages Department, Union College, Schenectady, New York, USA

FEUERWERKER, Yi-tsi Mei, Department of Asian Languages and Cultures, University of Michigan, Ann Arbor, USA

FOX, Josephine, Research School of Pacific and Asian Studies, Australian National University, Canberra, Australia

GAO Yuanbao, Department of Chinese, Fudan University, Shanghai, PRC

GILMARTIN, Christina K., Department of History, and Department of Women's Studies, Northeastern University, Boston, USA

GUO Chen, Workers' Publishing House, Beijing, PRC

HE Li, Drama Research Institute, Chinese Academy of Arts, Beijing, PRC

HENDRISCHKE, Barbara, Research School of Pacific and Asian Studies, Australian National University, Canberra, Australia

HO Shu-i, Institute of History, National Taiwan Normal University, Taipei, Taiwan

HO Wah Kam, Regional Language Centre, Singapore

HONG, Rubing, Fisher Library, University of Sydney, Australia

HSIEH, Shih-ying, College of Fine Arts, University of New South Wales, Sydney, Australia

JASCHOK, Maria H.A., Queen Elizabeth House, Oxford University, UK

JEN HWA, Ven, School of Education, University of Sydney, Australia

KAO Yüeh-t'o, Free-lance Writer, Taipei, Taiwan

KING, Richard, Department of Pacific and Asian Studies, University of Victoria, Canada

KINGSBURY, Karen, Foreign Languages and Literature Department, Tunghai University, Taichung, Taiwan

KONG Shuyu, Department of East Asian Studies, University of Alberta, Edmonton, Canada

LAM, Hok-chung, Department of History and Anthropology, University of Tsukuba, Japan

LAM Tung, Department of Chinese Studies, University of Sydney, Australia

LANG, Miriam, School of Languages, Cultures and Linguistics, Monash University, Melbourne, Australia

LEE, Lily Xiao Hong, Department of Chinese Studies, University of Sydney, Australia

LEE, Mabel, Department of Chinese Studies, University of Sydney, Australia

LEE, Sandra, Department of Chinese Studies, University of Sydney, Australia

LIN Ch'ien-ju, Institute of History, National Central University, Taipei, Taiwan

LIU Ying, Department of East Asian Languages and Literatures, Ohio State University, Columbus, USA

LO Chiu-jung, Institute of Modern History, Academia Sinica, Nankang, Taiwan

LO Fu, Free-lance Writer, Sunnyvale, California, USA

McELDERRY, Andrea, Department of History, University of Louisville, USA

NG, Daisy Sheung-yuen, Department of Chinese, National University of Singapore, Singapore

NG Mei Kwan, Department of Chinese Studies, University of Sydney, Australia

NOBLE, Jonathan, Researcher, Shanghai, PRC

PATTON, Simon, Department of Asian Languages and Studies, University of Queensland, Brisbane, Australia

QI Wenying, Women's Studies Center, Peking University, PRC

ROBERTS, Claire, Powerhouse Museum, Sydney, Australia

SHAO Yiyang, Department of Art History and Theory, University of Sydney, Australia

SHUI Jingjun, Academy of Social Sciences, Henan, PRC

SILVIO, Teri, Department of Chinese and Indonesian Studies, University of New South Wales, Sydney, Australia

SU Jui-chiang, National Chang-hua High School, Chang-hua, Taiwan

SUN Ailing, Department of Chinese, Hong Kong Institute of Education, Hong Kong

SUN, Warren, School of Asian Languages and Studies, Monash University, Melbourne, Australia

SWISLOCKI, Mark, Department of History, Stanford University, USA

VAN CREVEL, Maghiel, Chinese Language and Literature, Leiden University, The Netherlands

WADE, Geoff, Centre of Asian Studies, University of Hong Kong, Hong Kong

WANG Bing, Institute for the History of Natural Sciences, Chinese Academy of Sciences, Beijing, PRC

WANG, Jing M., Department of East Asian Languages and Literatures, Colgate University, Hamilton, NY, USA

WANG Jingming, Researcher, Beijing, PRC

WANG, Ping, Department of Chinese and Indonesian Studies, University of New South Wales, Sydney, Australia

WANG, Yiyan, Department of Chinese Studies, University of Sydney, Australia

WILES, Sue, Department of Chinese Studies, University of Sydney, Australia

WILLIAMS, Martin, Institute for International Studies, University of Technology, Sydney, Australia

WONG, Viola Hong Xin Chan, Faculty of Arts and Social Sciences, University of New South Wales, Sydney, Australia

WONG Yin Lee, Department of History, Hong Kong Baptist University, Hong Kong

WU Xiaoli, Museum of Modern Chinese Literature, Beijing, PRC

XI Zezong, Institute of the History of Natural Sciences, Chinese Academy of Sciences, Beijing, PRC

YANG Enhong, Institute of Minority Literature, Chinese Academy of Social Sciences, Beijing, PRC

YANG Ts'ui, Department of Chinese Literature, Providence University, Taichung, Taiwan

YEH, Michelle, Department of East Asian Languages and Cultures, University of California, Davis, USA

YEN Ching-hwang, Department of History, University of Adelaide, Australia

YEUNG, Wai Ling, SoLIE, Curtin University of Technology, Perth, Australia

ZHAO Jinping, All-China Women's Federation Research Institute, Beijing, PRC

ZHU Tianbiao, Department of International Relations, Research School of Pacific and Asian Studies, Australian National University, Canberra, Australia

Translators

CAI, Shirley, MacArthur Girls' High School, New South Wales, Australia

CHAN Yuk Ping, Department of Chinese Studies, University of Sydney, Australia

CHAPMAN, Ian, Department of Chinese Language and Literature, Fudan University, Shanghai, PRC

CHEN, I-Chen, Hsi-lai University, California, USA

CHEN Jinlan, Xinhua News Agency, Beijing, PRC

CHENG, Jeremy Chun Ho, American Express International, Inc., Sydney, Australia

CHEY, Jocelyn, Department of Chinese Studies, University of Sydney, Australia

CUI Zhiying, Department of Chinese Studies, University of Sydney, Australia

EAGLETON, Jennifer, Department of Translation, Chinese University of Hong Kong, Hong Kong

FU, Vivian C.T., Department of Area Studies, University of Tsukuba, Japan

HU Zhuanglin, Department of English, Peking University, PRC

KERR, Katherine, Department of Chinese Studies, University of Sydney, Australia

LAM Hing-hei, Institute of Linguists, UK

LAW, Barbara, Department of Chinese Studies, University of Sydney, Australia

LEE, Lily Xiao Hong, Department of Chinese Studies, University of Sydney, Australia

LI, George, Free-lance Writer and Translator, Sydney, Australia

LI Sheung Yee, Catholic University of Australia, Sydney, Australia

LONG, Laura, AMP Financial Services, Sydney, Australia

NGOK, Yuen Kwan Veronica, Free-lance Translator, Hong Kong

PATON, Michael, Faculty of Economics, University of Sydney, Australia

PRINCE, Tony, Department of Chinese Studies, University of Sydney, Australia

QIAN, Yan, Department of Asian Languages, Macquarie University, Sydney, Australia

ROBERTSON, Malcolm, China and Korea Centre, Faculty of Asian Studies, Australian National University, Canberra, Australia

SONG, Zhongwei, Department of Chinese and Indonesian Studies, University of New South Wales, Sydney, Australia; and Department of Asian Languages, Macquarie University, Sydney, Australia

TAO Naikan, Department of Asian Languages, Macquarie University, Sydney, Australia

WANG Nian'en, Department of Education and Training, New South Wales, Sydney, Australia

WILES, Sue, Department of Chinese Studies, University of Sydney, Australia

WILLIAMS, Martin, University of Technology, Sydney, Australia

WRIGHT, Emily, Guru International, Sydney, Australia

XIN, Qianbo, Institute of Languages, University of New South Wales, Sydney, Australia

YANG Jingqing, Department of Chinese Studies, University of Sydney, Australia

YANG Yi, School of Translation and Interpreting, Beijing Foreign Studies University, PRC

ZHANG, Jan, Capral Aluminium, Sydney, Australia

ZHANG, Jennifer, Free-lance Translator, Sydney, Australia

ZHANG Jinxin, People's University, Beijing, PRC

Finding List by Background or Fields of Endeavor

Academics/Scholars

Archaeology

Zeng Zhaoyu

Economics

Kuo Wan-jung

Education

Chia Fu-ming
Wong, Ruth Hie King

Fine Arts

Pang Tao

History

Chen Hengzhe
Sun, E-tu Zen
Xian Yuqing

International Relations

Li Chung-kui

Law

Han Youtong
Xie Fei

Literature

Chen Ruoxi
Dai Houying

Dai Jinhua
Don-grub Lha-mo
Feng Yuanjun
Su Hsüeh-lin
Xian Yuqing
Xu Guangping
Yang Jiang
Yue Daiyun

Medical Science

Chou Mei-yü
Lin Qiaozhi
Nie Yuchan
Yang Chongrui
Zhu Lian

Sociology

Lei Jieqiong
Zhang Ruoming

Arts

Installation

Wu Mali

Painters

Ch'en Chin
Chen, Georgette
Chen Xingwan
Choi Yan Chi
Chou, Irene
Fan Tchun-pi
Fang Zhaolin
Hu Jieqing

Ch'iung Yao
Chung Ling
Dai Houying
Dai Qing
Ding Ling
Fang Fang
Feng Yuanjun
Han Suyin
Han Zi
Hang Ying
Hsiao Sa
Hsieh Ping-ying
Huang Zongying
Ke Yan
Kingston, Maxine Hong
Li Ang
Lin Bai
Lin Hai-yin
Lin Huiyin
Ling Shuhua
Liu Suola
Liu Zhen
Lu Xing'er
Luyin
Nieh Hualing
Ru Zhijuan
San Mao
Shen Rong
Su Hsüeh-lin
Tan, Amy
Tie Ning
Wang Anyi
Wang Ying
Xiao Hong
Xixi
Yang Jiang
Yang Mo
Yishu
Yü Li-hua
Yu Luojin
Zhang Jie
Zhang Kangkang
Zhang Xinxin
Zhong Xiaoyang

Zhu Lin
Zong Pu

Literary Critics

Chung Ling
Dai Houying
Dai Jinhua
Li Ziyun
Yue Daiyun

Playwrights

Bai Fengxi
Bai Wei
Ding Ling
Li Bozhao
Yang Jiang

Poetry

Bing Xin
Chen Hengzhe
Ch'en Hsiu-hsi
Chung Ling
Fang Fang
Hsia Yu
Jung-tzu
Kang Tongbi
Ke Yan
Lin Huiyin
Ling Yü
Lü Bicheng
Shu Ting
Xian Yuqing
Xixi
Zhai Yongming

Reportage

Bai Wei
Chen Xuezhao
Dai Qing
Hsieh Ping-ying

Huang Zongying
Ke Yan
Peng Zigang
Wang Ying

Media

Journalists

Bai Wei
Chen Xiangmei
Dai Qing
Hou Bo
Hsieh Ping-ying
Lau Emily
Lin Hai-yin
Lin Zongsu
Peng Zigang

Newspaper/Magazine Publishers

Aw, Sally
Kang Tongwei
Lin Hai-yin
Peng Zigang
Shen Zijiu

Photographer

Hou Bo

Radio

Ts'ui Hsiao-p'ing

Television

Ruan Ruolin

Military

Chou Mei-yü
Kang Keqing

Li Jianhua
Li Zhen
Wang Quanyuan
Zhong Yuzheng

Performing Arts

Actors

Bai Fengxi
Bai Yang
Gong Li
Hsü Feng
Hu Die
Huang Zongying
Jiang Qing
Li Lihua
Lin Dai
Liu Xiaoqing
Ruan Lingyu
Shu Xiuwen
Siqin Gaowa
Wang Ying
Yu Shan
Zhou Xuan
Zhu Lin

Circus

Xia Juhua

Dancers, Choreographers

Bai Shuxiang
Dai Ailian
Modegemaa
Yang Liping

Directors, Producers

Bai Yang
Chen Rong
Hsü Feng
Ruan Ruolin

Xie Fei
Xie Xiaomei
Xie Xuehong
Yang Houzhen
Yang Zhihua
Yang Zilie
Ye Qun
Zhang Qinqiu
Zhang Ruoming
Zhang Zhixin
Zhao Yiman
Zhou Yuehua

Foreign Affairs

Chen Xiangmei
Ding Xuesong
Gong Peng
Gong Pusheng
Li Shuzheng

Government

Chan, Anson
Chen Muhua
Chen Xiangmei
Ch'en–Shih Man
Gu Xiulian
Guo Jian
Hao Jianxiu
Hsü Shih-hsien
Kuo Wan-jung
Lau, Emily
Li Chung-kui
Li Jianzhen
Li Shuzheng
Liang–Hsü Ch'un-chü
Liu Yaxiong
Lü Hsiu-lien
Luo Shuzhang
Moss, Irene
Peng Peiyun
Qian Ying
Qian Zhengying

Shi Liang
Song Qingling
Wan Shaofen
Wu Yi
Yü–Ch'en Yüeh-ying
Zhang Qinqiu

Labor Leaders

Chen Shaomin
Liao Siguang
Liu Qunxian
Yang Zhihua

Party Workers

Cai Chang
Chen Congying
Deng Liujin
Hao Jianxiu
Li Jianzhen
Liao Mengxing
Qian Ying
Wan Shaofen
Wang Dingguo
Wang Guangmei
Wang Yizhi
Wei Fengying
Zeng Zhi

Political Activists, Revolutionaries

Chien O
Chi-oang
Dong Zhujun
Lau, Emily
Li Dequan
Lin Zongsu
Liu–Wang Liming
Shi Liang
Wu Mulan
Wu Yifang
Xie Xuehong
Yeh T'ao
Zhang Ruoming

Political Figures

Jiang Qing
Song Qingling
Soong Ailing
Soong Mayling
Wang Guangmei
Yang Kaihui
Ye Qun

Women's Rights

Cai Chang
Cao Mengjun
Ch'en–Shih Man
Ch'ien Chien-ch'iu
Ch'iu Yüan-yang
Deng Yingchao
Kang Keqing
Kang Tongbi
Kang Tongwei
Li Dequan
Lin Zongsu
Lin–Ts'ai Su-nü
Liu Qingyang
Liu–Wang Liming
Lü Hsiu-lien
Shen Zijiu
Wang Huiwu
Wu Mulan
Wu Yifang
Xiang Jingyu
Zhang Mojun
Zhang Ruoming
Zhang Yun

Professional Women

Architecture

Hsiu Tse-lan
Lin Huiyin

Education

Ch'en Ai-chu
Chia Fu-ming
Huang Dianxian
Kang Tongwei
Lin Ch'iu-chin
Lü Bicheng
Mao Yen-wen
Nie Yuchan
Shao Meng-lan
Tao Shufan
Wang Yizhi
Wong, Ruth Hie King
Wu Yifang
Xie Fei
Zhu Lian

Health

Ch'en–Shih Man
Chou Mei-yü
Dbyangs-dgav
Hsü Shih-hsien
Lin Qiaozhi
Nie Yuchan
Yang Chongrui
Ye Gongshao
Zhou Yuehua
Zhu Lian

Law

Ch'ien Chien-ch'iu
Moss, Irene
Shi Liang
Xie Fei

Police

Chao Mo-ya
Ch'en Mei-ch'üan
Ch'eng Hsiao-kuei
Li Li-chüan
Lin Chin-chih

Social Work

Cao Mengjun
Deng Yuzhi
Li Dequan
Mao Yen-wen
Shen Zijiu
Xu Zonghan
Yuen, Susan

Sport/Adventure

Chi Cheng
Lang Ping
Pan-thogs

Religious Women

Ba Jinlan
Cheng Yen, Master
Chi-oang
Deng Yuzhi
Du Shuzhen
Hiu Wan, Ven.
Li Dequan
Longlian, Ven.
Lü Bicheng
Wu Yifang
Yang Huizhen
Zhenhua, Ven.

Romantic Figures

Jiang Biwei
Lu Xiaoman

Scientists

Astronomy

Ye Shuhua
Zou Yixin

Biochemistry

Lu Gwei-Djen

Chemistry

Huang Liang
Jiang Lijin
Zhong Yuzheng

Computer Science

Xia Peisu
Yang Fuqing

Engineering

Qian Zhengying

Geology

Chi Jishang

Medical Sciences

Lin Qiaozhi
Nie Yuchan
Yang Chongrui

Physics

He Zehui
Lin Lanying
Lu Shijia
Wang Chengshu
Wu, Chien-Shiung
Xie Xide

Brief Chronology of
Twentieth-Century Events

1911	October: Xinhai Revolution
1912	1 January: Republic of China established
1912	August: Tongmenghui merges with small political groups to form KMT
1916	Yuan Shikai declares himself emperor
1919	4 May: student demonstrations mark the May Fourth Movement
1921	1 July: CCP formed in Shanghai
1923	1 January: Sun Yat-sen issues manifesto of reorganized KMT
1923–31	Period of the first KMT-CCP united front
1925	30 May: student demonstration in Shanghai in support of striking workers
1926	Northern Expedition sets off from Guangzhou and reaches Shanghai
1927	Chiang Kai-shek purges KMT of CCP members in Shanghai
1931	CCP establishes Jiangxi soviet
1931	18 September: Japan invades Shenyang [Mukden] in Manchuria
1932	28 January: Japan opens fire in Shanghai; a truce is negotiated after the Nineteenth Army puts up stiff resistance
1934–35	The Long March of the CCP Red Army
1936	December: Xi'an Incident (Chiang Kai-shek kidnapped and forced to agree to a second united front with the CCP to fight the Japanese)
1937	Communists move to Yan'an
1937	7 July: Marco Polo Bridge Incident triggers KMT government's declaration of war against Japan
1937–45	Sino-Japanese War
1937	Japan occupies Shanghai (except the foreign concessions)
1941	December: Japan takes over Hong Kong and all foreign concessions in Shanghai
1941	Wannan Incident: CCP and KMT armies clash in southern Anhui
1942	The Rectification Movement in Yan'an
1945	Japan surrenders, handing government over to the KMT; end of Japanese colonization of Taiwan (1895–1945); KMT takes over Taiwan
1946	Beginning of civil war between CCP and KMT
1947	28 February: armed uprising in Taiwan protesting against the KMT government's heavy-handed policies
1949	October 1: Mao Zedong declares the establishment of the People's Republic of China
1949	December: KMT government moves to Taiwan
1950	Promulgation of China's Marriage Law
1957	Anti-rightist campaign
1958	Great Leap Forward, which causes famine over the next few years

1966–76   The Cultural Revolution
1975   Chiang Kai-shek dies, signifying the beginning of the Jiang Jingguo [Chiang Ching-kuo] era in Taiwan
1976   January: Zhou Enlai dies
1976   September: Mao Zedong dies
1976   The arrest of the Gang of Four marks the end of the Cultural Revolution
1978   Third Plenum of the Eleventh CCP Party Congress inaugurates major reforms; the Four Modernizations
1979   The United States recognizes the PRC, breaking off relations with the ROC on Taiwan
1979   Anti-KMT pro-democracy demonstrations in Taiwan mark the birth of the Democratic Progressive Party (DPP)
1988   Jiang Jingguo dies in Taiwan
1989   4 June: Tian'anmen Incident
1996   Taiwan conducts its first direct election
1997   Hong Kong reverts to Chinese rule

Abbreviations and Guide to Chinese Words Used

ACWF   All-China [Democratic] Women's Federation
CCP   Chinese Communist Party
CPPCC   Chinese People's Political Consultative Committee
KMT   Guomindang; Kuomintang; Nationalist Party
NPC   National People's Congress
PLA   People's Liberation Army
PRC   People's Republic of China
ROC   Republic of China
USSR   Union of Soviet Socialist Republics
YMCA   Young Men's Christian Association
YWCA   Young Women's Christian Association

Few Chinese words appear in this volume without explanation or translation. The following have been used, sparingly, because there are no simple and accurate English translations for them:

zi   Courtesy name, used by friends and others
ming   Official personal name
hao   A personal "style," usually revealing one's taste and aspiration

Biographical Dictionary of Chinese Women

THE TWENTIETH CENTURY
1912–2000

Biographies
A

A Jin: *see* **Jin Weiying**

A Xiang: *see* **Xie Fei**

Ah Ch'ing (Hsiang): *see* **Jin Weiying**

Aw, Sally
Sally Aw [Hu Xian], b. 1932, in Penang, belongs to a Hakka family originally from Yongding County, Fujian Province. As head for many years of Sing Tao Holdings and publisher of *Sing Tao*, one of Hong Kong's largest dailies and "the first truly international Chinese-language newspaper," she was long regarded as Hong Kong's richest and most powerful woman.

Her father, Hu Wenhu (Aw Boon Haw, also spelled Har; d. 1954), was famous as a manufacturer of Chinese medicines and the inventor of Wanjinyou medicinal ointment. This aromatic salve, known in English as Tiger Balm, was one of the most widely used patent medicines in East Asia in the early part of the twentieth century. Popular belief had it that Wanjinyou was made from rendered Burmese tigers, but its chief ingredients, carefully guarded secrets, were more likely camphor and eucalyptus oil. Hu Wenhu's father had left China as a young man to settle in Burma, and Hu Wenhu and his brother developed substantial business interests in Singapore and Hong Kong, eventually moving the headquarters of their company from Rangoon to Singapore.

As was the custom among overseas Chinese in Burma at the time, Hu Wenhu had four wives and a large family—nine children, including two daughters. The children were all given rather unusual Chinese names: the two girls were called Xian (Sian, fairy) and Xing (Sing, star). The quixotic choices for the girls' names matched those of Hu Wenhu and his brothers, who had been named Dragon, Tiger, and Panther. Perhaps in reaction, when Xian went to school she chose for herself the plain English name of Sally. Hong Kong people joke that her Chinese personal name sounds like "One Cent" and indicates her miserliness.

Hu Wenhu diversified his business interest in medicines to found several newspapers. Originally, this maneuver may have been partly to help promote Tiger Balm ointment, but the papers were also intended to help modernize the life-style of the overseas Chinese. The *Rangoon Daily* (Yangguang ribao) established in 1909 was one of the first Chinese-language newspapers in the world outside China and soon joined a stable of Chinese-language papers the family launched in Southeast Asia, including the *Chen bao* in Rangoon; *Xingzhou ribao, Xing zhong ribao,* and *Singapore Standard* in Singapore; *Xing hua ribao* in Shantou; *Xing bin ribao* in Penang; the

Sing Tao Daily or *Star Island Daily* (Xingdao ribao) and later the evening paper *Xingdao wanbao* and the English-language *Hong Kong Standard* in Hong Kong. These formed the basis of the *Sing Tao* international newspaper publishing conglomerate.

In the first half of the twentieth century, most of Southeast Asia was divided between European and American powers, which operated benevolent colonial administrations. The Chinese business community was at best tolerated, at worst regarded as subversive and unreliable. China itself was racked by civil war and hardly offered a safe refuge. Chinese intellectuals lived in hope that a strong and uncorrupt government would emerge in China, capable of defending the rights of Chinese people at home and abroad. The Chinese-language newspapers of Hu Wenhu and others helped to spread information and stimulate patriotism.

The Chinese-language press in China and throughout Southeast Asia also played a radical role in promoting social and political reform; it wielded a major influence for change in China through transmitting information on current affairs and molding the opinion of the educated classes. Hu Wenhu had close connections with both the KMT and the CCP and, according to some accounts, gave substantial financial support to their anti-Japanese war efforts. He sent two of his sons to Chongqing during the war years. *Sing Tao Daily* was founded in Hong Kong in 1938, the year after war was declared against Japan. In retrospect this seemed a courageous business decision, perhaps based on a belief that Japan would not dare occupy the British colony. Unfortunately, occupation happened all too quickly. *Sing Tao Daily* was taken over by the Japanese occupying forces and renamed *Xiang Dao Daily*. The Hu family, by then resident in Hong Kong, took refuge in Burma for the duration of the war.

Hu Wenhu was (and still is) admired within the Chinese diaspora of Southeast Asia for his public-spirited and patriotic philanthropy. He donated large sums to China for schools and universities and for setting up hospitals and pharmaceutical factories before the war. In Southeast Asia, he actively promoted Chinese community associations. His daughter Sally Aw was much influenced by his values and social concerns, and they have clearly shaped her own worldview.

The Hu family returned to Hong Kong soon after the war, settling back into their villa on the slopes of the island. The traditionally styled house, with its glazed roof tiles and extensive gardens, has been a local landmark for decades. A section of the Tiger Balm Gardens, featuring statuary and highly colored plaster figures depicting scenes from Buddhist myths and legends, has always been open to the public. The gardens are still maintained by the Aw Boon Har Foundation as a public service. Here, Sally Aw grew up with her brothers, her imagination fed by the monsters and angels surrounding them. The ravening forces of the business world that she met later in life must have seemed tame compared to the garden's vivid illustrations of hell's torments.

Hu Wenhu had earlier created a similar garden in Singapore. There, he also funded a Tiger and Panther Swimming Pool, with a notice restricting its use "For Chinese People Only." At the time, wide revulsion engulfed the Chinese community about a rumor that a park in Shanghai had a notice expressly forbidding Chinese and dogs to enter; so the erection of the notice in Singapore became a very popular move. In both gardens were shrines to the memory of Hu Wenhu's parents to which he paid his respects whenever in residence.

Sally Aw attended St. Stephen's Girls' College, one of the oldest English-language girls' schools in Hong Kong, graduating in 1951. A history of the school was published to commemorate its centenary. It describes how when the school resumed teaching after the war years an intense nationalism pervaded its halls, inspiring a generation of teachers and students, as China and the Western powers defeated Japan and China rebuilt itself after a long period of occupation. The Hong Kong economy had been severely damaged; poverty was widespread. The girls at St. Stephen's were generally from privileged homes and participated in many charitable works, for instance, coaching students from working-class schools. The school was founded on Christian precepts, but many students retained their Buddhist or other religious convictions. The school's spirit of service and dedication transcended religious divides, however, and clearly left a lasting influence on members of the student body. At school Sally excelled at art and craft and was regarded as a serious and quiet student.

Hu Wenhu died suddenly in 1954 while traveling in Hawaii. Undoubtedly, his wish was that the family should continue his newspaper business. By that time, it had become much more important than the manufacture and distribution of patent medicines. Sally had already been assigned responsibility for the management of the press, despite her youth and inexperience. Other parts of the publishing enterprise were taken over by relatives. From that time on, the Hong Kong *Sing Tao* operations developed to become more independent from the rest of the original regional publishing empire. She had worked as a trainee at *Sing Tao* in Hong Kong under her father in 1953. His death and the splitting up of the family conglomerate launched her into prominence in the business field at the relatively young age of twenty-two. Sally Aw's destiny, however, was clear: to succeed to her father's position as head of the company in Hong Kong. In 1960 she was promoted from being company manager to general manager and, when the company was publicly listed as Sing Tao Holdings in 1972, became chair. Still completely under the control of the family at that time, the company saw Sally Aw holding 96.7 percent of its registered capital.

Although one of Hong Kong's more powerful business leaders, she did not use her position to influence political or business decisions in her favor, and this was duly noted in the local press. An interviewer reported that Sally Aw's aim was "to publish a profitable newspaper and to avoid discussion of politics; her ideal was to be a *wugui dianche* [trolley bus]." The goal may have proved elusive, but the newspaper did maintain a relatively independent and unaligned position. The company's annual reports reveal that commercial results always took precedence over political ambitions. For this reason, *Sing Tao* survived while many others folded over time.

In that year the company's staff in Hong Kong numbered 550, including many well-known and experienced editors with a long association with the publishing house. Together with its sister publication *Sing Tao Evening News*, *Sing Tao Daily* became one of Hong Kong's largest daily newspapers. In 1988 its circulation was estimated to be two-hundred-fifty-thousand copies reaching one million readers, roughly one-quarter of Hong Kong's population. The company pioneered the use of technology and used computer-printing systems to produce Chinese-language color dailies in many countries, including Australia, Canada, New Zealand, the United Kingdom, and the United States. Later, the company expanded its publishing business in Canada, especially in Toronto and Vancouver. In 1995 the company introduced *Sing Tao Electronic Daily*, the first electronic daily paper in Hong Kong. However, sales of *Sing Tao Daily* declined after 1996, initially because of a price war launched by other publishers and increased newsprint costs. The business environment in Hong Kong also suffered as a consequence of the Asian financial crisis in 1997/98; the cost of doing business in Hong Kong increased compared with other regional cities whose currency was devalued while the Hong Kong dollar remained pegged to the American dollar. In these external factors lay the seed of the ultimate downfall of Sing Tao Holdings.

Under Sally Aw's stewardship, Sing Tao Holdings diversified its business interests into retailing, tourism, and real estate. To some extent, this diversification was sparked by concerns about Hong Kong's future before the British Government announced an agreement with China on terms for returning the territory. She made extensive investments in 1983 in real estate in Sydney, Australia, and the following year started a local Sydney edition of *Sing Tao Daily*. Sing Tao was the first Hong Kong company to invest in Australia, bringing about a rethinking by other Hong Kong companies of the potential of the Australian market. These investments attracted considerable attention in the Hong Kong and Australian press at the time, including speculation that the family was planning to emigrate to Australia. Sally Aw made it clear, however, that the hub of her business operations was to remain in Hong Kong despite concerns about its political future. In the 1980s and 1990s, these non-core elements of Sing Tao Holdings became major profit centers but lost much of their value following the Asian financial crisis. Hong Kong property values declined by roughly 30 percent in 1998 from 1997 figures, and Sing Tao shares likewise shed much of their value.

Sally Aw has been president of the World Chinese Press Institute and the first female chair of the International Press Institute. In 1988 she was given the Carr Van Anda Award from the E.W. Scripps School of Journalism at Ohio University in commendation for building *Sing Tao* into the first truly international Chinese-language newspaper. According to Sing Tao Holdings's *1996 Annual Report*, Sally Aw's personal business philosophy is that the prime directive is to pick the right business, one of genuine interest, "so that the success can be enjoyed along with the work it takes to achieve it."

In autumn 1992, she and her mother were invited to lead a delegation to Beijing at the time of the Fourteenth Party Congress. Apart from a brief visit to Guangzhou as a small child, this was the first time that Sally Aw had traveled to China. She was received by Party General Secretary Jiang Zemin and Premier Li Peng. While in Beijing, Sally Aw signed an agreement with the *People's Daily* to publish a color magazine to be entitled *Xingguang* (Starlight). She and her mother also traveled to their family's ancestral home in Fujian Province, where they were given a high-level reception.

In 1997 Sally Aw was appointed to the CPPCC, a non-party advisory body, as a delegate from the new Hong Kong Special Administrative Region. Consequently, she spent more time in China and was forced to delegate more of the day-to-day responsibilities of Sing Tao Holdings to others. On reaching her sixties, Sally Aw declared that her priority was to train a team to take over management of the publishing business. In 1999 she sold all her interests in the newspapers and stepped down into retirement. The sale truly marked the end of an era in Chinese newspaper publishing. Unfortunately, her departure was marred by accusations that Sally Aw had used political influence to prevent legal investigation of alleged rigging of circulation figures.

Under her leadership, Sing Tao involved itself in many charitable activities, including community education, homes for the elderly, and disaster relief through the Sing Tao Foundation. Support for education was always a priority and included school and college scholarships and loans to needy pupils in China. Hong Kong journalism schools, for instance, at Hong Kong City University, benefited from generous donations. *Sing Tao* won many international awards for excellence, including from Amnesty International.

Interviewers always noted how the publisher followed a strict daily regimen of work at the office, clearing her desk of papers, ensuring that letters were answered, and following up action taken on office minutes within the week. This was said to have been the reason she preferred to work from a table rather than a desk with drawers. Others noted her simple style of dress and lack of ostentation.

Sally Aw was brought up as a devout Buddhist and is a sincere disciple, devoted to charitable works and the redemption of suffering humanity. She continues to support philanthropy in Hong Kong and overseas and plans to settle eventually in a Buddhist temple in Hong Kong, where she can spend her declining years studying scriptures. Buddhists believe in reincarnation in which the cycle of rebirth is eventually broken through attaining Nirvana.

Sally Aw's personal interests include the companionship of a large bevy of dogs and she enjoys travel for relaxation. When her mother was still alive, the two were often traveling companions. Sally Aw told the author that on one occasion she and some friends drove right across the United States by car, enjoying the freedom of being able to travel where they liked and when they liked.

Jocelyn CHEY

Barker, Kathleen E. *Change and Continuity: A History of Saint Stephen's Girls' College*. Hong Kong: Chinese University Press in conjunction with St. Stephen's Girls' College, 1996.
Chao Jin. "Xianggang Xingdao baoye youxian gongsi dongshizhang Hu Xian." *Haiwai zhuming huaren liezhuan*. Beijing: Gongren, 1988.
Sing Tao Holdings. *1996 Annual Report*. Hong Kong. 1997.
Zhang Yonghe. *Hu Wenhu*. Xiamen: Lujiang chubanshe, 1989.
———. *Hu Wenhu zhuan*. Singapore: Congwen, 1993.

Aw Sian: *see* **Aw, Sally**

B

Ba Jinlan

Ba Jinlan, b. 1922, in Jinzhai village, Xingyang, Henan Province, is a Chinese Muslim *ahong* (religious head of a mosque) of Hui nationality. Ba Jinlan's Islamic name is Fatimah, and she comes from an *ahong* family whose members have held that position for thirteen generations.

Ba Jinlan began her Islamic education at the age of eight, learning scriptures from her father and grandfather. At the age of twelve, she went to the women's mosque to learn Persian scriptures from female *ahong*, continuing her study in the Beixia Street women's mosque in Zhengzhou. After returning home at the age of fifteen, Ba Jinlan helped her mother with housework, studied the Qu'ran in Arabic with her father, and also learned more Persian scriptures from her grandfather. Her devotion and ability motivated her to learn to read Islamic doctrine in both Arabic and Persian languages.

At the age of twenty-two, Ba Jinlan married the son of an *ahong* family named Ma. This was an arranged marriage, her parents believing the most important criteria in selecting a husband for their daughter to be devout belief and religious attainment. Her husband had grown up in mosques, received a traditional Chinese Islamic education, and become an *ahong* after completing his schooling. As the wife of an *ahong*, Ba Jinlan lived in the mosque, counseling and directing the spiritual lives of Muslim women. At the same time, she ran her own household and cared for her children, fulfilling her duty as a wife and mother.

In 1955 Ba Jinlan was invited to become *ahong* of a rural women's mosque in Xingyang, where she and her children remained when her husband was later made *ahong* of the men's mosque in the township of Qinghua in the same province. The women's mosque closed at the start of the Cultural Revolution, and Ba Jinlan and her children returned to her hometown of Jinzhai. After her husband also had to leave his mosque, he became ill; Ba Jinlan then took on responsibility for the family, working in the fields, caring for their eight children, providing their religious education, all the while continuing her own spiritual studies. She was invited to resume the duties of *ahong* in 1983 at the age of sixty-one and subsequently acted as a senior Islamic teacher (*jiaozhang*) in five women's mosques in Xingyang, Zhengzhou, and Wuzhi. Ba Jinlan made two pilgrimages to Mecca, in 1994 and 1998.

She has started up girls' schools, focuses on developing the religious talents of women, chants prayers in households where a death has occurred, and also spends time supervising the construction of women's mosques. Ba Jinlan actively participates in the spiritual education of her children, seven of whom have received special Islamic education. Three of her sons are now *ahong*, one studying at a mosque and another learning modern Arabic at Beijing Foreign Languages University as well as pursuing traditional Islamic studies. Ba Jinlan has also instructed three of her granddaughters, and two of her grandsons study at mosques in Henan and Gansu.

Rare among female Chinese *ahong* of Hui nationality in that her leanings in belief are toward Sufism, Ba Jinlan admires Sufi Muslims who seek communion with God through states of ecstasy. She lives piously, within a simple life devoted to spiritual exercises, and seeks neither fame nor wealth. Her firm belief in the immortality of the spirit has led her to attach great importance to mental training and purity of soul and actions. She is utterly confident of her spiritual fate in the afterlife, having surrendered her heart to Allah through chanting scriptures, prayer, and fasting.

Ba Jinlan was educated in the Islamic faith within her family of male *ahong,* and it instilled in her a conviction that the religious accomplishment and intelligence of men are superior to that of women. She nevertheless believes that a devout woman yearning for Allah is far better than a man of no faith and that a woman who strives to do her best can surpass a man.

While she is considered by some to be uncommunicative and eccentric in disposition, her knowledge, intelligence, perseverance, self-confidence, and self-discipline have earned her the respect and esteem of Chinese Muslims.

Maria H.A. JASCHOK and SHUI Jingjun

Alles, Elisabeth. "Une organisation de l'Islam au féminin: Le personnel des mosquées féminines en Chine." *Lettre d'information.* Paris: Programme de Recherches Interdisciplinaires sur le Monde Müsulman Périphérique, 14 (1994): 1–12.

Dai Jianning. "Shilun huizu funü xinyang yisilanjiaode xinli tezheng." *Huizu yanjiu,* 4 (1992): 67–70.

Etudes Orientales, 13/14 (1994). Contributions by Elisabeth Alles, Leila Cherif, and Constance-Hélène Halfon.

Feng Jinyuan. "Shilun yisilanjiaode funüguan." *Zhongguo musilin,* 4 (1995): 19–24.

Jaschok, Maria, and Shui Jingjun. *The History of Women's Mosques in Chinese Islam: A Mosque of Their Own.* Richmond, Surrey: Curzon Press, 2000.

Nan Wenyuan. *Yisilanjiao yu xibei musilin shehui shenghuo.* Xining: Qinghai renmin chubanshe, 1994.

Pang Keng-Fong. "Islamic 'Fundamentalism' and Female Empowerment among the Muslims of Hainan Island, People's Republic of China." In *Mixed Blessings: Gender and Religious Fundamentalism Cross Culturally,* eds. Judy Brink and Joan Mencher. London: Routledge, 1997, 41–56.

Shui Jingjun. "Lun nüxue nüside xingqi yu fazhan." *Huizu yanjiu,* 1 (1996): 51–59.

Bai Fengxi

Bai Fengxi, b. 1934, in Wen'an, Hebei Province, is a playwright and actress best known for her work in *The Women Trilogy,* depicting the concerns of intellectual women in a transitional time from the Maoist (1949–76) to post-Maoist eras. She is married to Yan Zhongying, a now-retired director and actor formerly with the China Youth Art Theater. They have one daughter, Yan Fanfan, who is an actress in the same theater.

Bai Fengxi enrolled in the North China People's Revolutionary University at the age of fifteen in 1949 and became an actress with the China Youth Art Theater in 1954. Growing up professionally in the first national theater of the PRC under the influence of a generation of renowned artists, she went on to play more than forty diverse dramatic characters. One of her most successful roles was as Liu Hulan (*q.v.*), a fifteen-year-old martyr executed by the KMT in rural Shanxi in 1947, in the 1951 play of the same name. Another important role was as Mingfeng in *The Family* (Jia, 1956), adapted for the stage by Cao Yu from Ba Jin's novel of the same name and a classic of the May Fourth period. In this play, Bai Fengxi created the character of a maid in a traditional patriarchal family who drowns herself after being forced into an arranged marriage to a man her grandfather's age. She reached the peak of her acting career in the title role in the B cast of *Princess Wencheng* (Wencheng gongzhu, 1960), written by Tian Han (1898–1968) and directed by Jin Shan. Other roles ranged from the flirtatious young page Cherubino in *The Marriage of Figaro* (Feijialou de hunyin, 1962) to the lovely Chunni in *Sentry under Neon Lights* (Nihongdeng xia de shaobing, 1962). Chunni is a loyal and understanding wife of rural China who encourages her husband to appreciate his duty as a PLA soldier stationed in newly liberated Shanghai.

In post-Mao China, Bai Fengxi experimented with playwriting. Her first play, *The Lamp in the Cave Brings Light to Thousands of Families* (Yaodong denghuo zhao qianjia, 1977), blended Shaanxi local dialect with poetic language to express the common people's mourning at the untimely death of Premier Zhou Enlai (1898–1976). Her second play, co-authored with Wang Jingyu, *Lift Your Veil* (Liaokai nide miansha, 1979), was also well received in early post-Mao China because of its popular theme of love and true friendship after the Cultural Revolution. Her trilogy of plays about women, however, won her national acclaim as one of the most important women writers of her time.

The first play in this series, *First Bathed in Moonlight* (Mingyue chuzhao ren, 1981), is remarkable for the absence of men on stage. A miniature cultural history of women in the PRC is presented through three generations of women struggling to reconcile their official roles as leaders of women's liberation with their private identities as women who also search for love, happiness, and freedom. After her husband's betrayal, the grandmother of the three women had raised her daughter Fang Ruoming alone; she had supported her daughter not only in the struggle to raise her own family but also in becoming a successful official in the ACWF, a government-sponsored institution in charge of women's affairs. Fang Ruoming, however, meets challenges of a different kind. Although eager to help rural women in arranged marriages to regain their rights of freedom of choice in marriage, she is nevertheless opposed to her own daughter's choice of a lover, a plumber without a college degree. Fang Ruoming does not consider the young man to be a match for her daughter, who teaches English in a college. Fang Ruoming is also confronted with the pain of seeing a second daughter having an affair with a professor in graduate school, a brilliant man that Fang Ruoming had once been in love with herself many years before but whom she had been forced to give up because of his undesirable family background. By the end of the play, Fang Ruoming puts aside her own sorrow to allow her daughters to seek happiness. Although constrained by the political realities of mainstream culture that required the celebration of a new post-Mao regime, Bai Fengxi was the first woman playwright in mainland China to focus on the real-life experiences and problems of women. Her dramaturgy inherited the realist tradition of modern spoken drama that had developed from the time of the May Fourth Movement.

The second play in the trilogy, *An Old Friend Returning on a Stormy Night* (Fengyu guren lai, 1983), probes more deeply into women's many protests against China's sexist society, which glorifies fathers who make women's departure from and staying at home both impossible. The character Xia Zhixian faces a typical dilemma in Maoist China. Conceived in the Maoist discourse that declares "women can hold up half of the sky," women were expected to be the equal of men in their professional careers as well as fulfill domestic duties as loving wives and mothers. Xia Zhixian's successful career as a gynecologist had been achieved at the expense of a family life—she lives alone after her husband found it hard to accept her total devotion to her career. As the play unfolds, Xia Zhixian's daughter confronts a similar dilemma: she ranks first in a graduate school entrance examination to study abroad—her husband comes in second—and is pushed by her mother-in-law to yield her opportunity to him. The older woman tells her that a family with a husband who holds a Ph.D. is more acceptable than a family with a wife who has one. After much soul searching, Xia Zhixian encourages her daughter to pursue her journey abroad, with the now-famous line: "A woman is not a moon. She does not need to depend on someone else's light to glow." Bai Fengxi's play touched a sensitive nerve for many contemporary Chinese women. In Xia Zhixian, the character is drawn with much more complexity and drama than Fang Ruoming's. Bai Fengxi's play exerted such an influence in raising consciousness about women's issues that a number of university students have adopted her famous line about the moon as the title of their M.A. theses.

Her third play, *Where Is Longing in Autumn?* (Buzhi qiusi zai shui jia, 1986), portrays a group of courageous women whose daring and unconventional decisions in marriage and career shocked contemporary audiences. Su Zhongyuan, a teacher who devoted her life to the education of young people, is puzzled by her children's modern choices. Her first daughter divorces her husband for no better reason than that she wishes to take care of herself and has rejected the roles of good wife, mother, and daughter-in-law, while remaining a good worker. Then, a second daughter, in her mid-thirties, is unconcerned about being a spinster and wonders why people are more tolerant of a loveless marriage than of a single woman opting for an independent, meaningful life on her own. Su Zhongyuan's son refuses to take a college entrance examination, preferring a business career, and becomes engaged to a fashion model, a questionable choice of partner at that time. The play ends without closure and does not resolve the mother's anguish. The seemingly irreconcilable dramatic conflicts between mother and daughters suggest the moral tribulations of a nation departing from traditional paths and embarking upon modernization, Westernization, and commercialization. The dilemmas also serve to explicate the feminine conscience of a group of highly educated women who are repositioning themselves, however tentatively, between a private space of their own and a public domain that paradoxically limits that private space while yet approving of it. The emergence and growing awareness of this double bind explains why in 1987 and 1988, at a time of crisis in the theater world when it was considered better than the norm if a new play ran to a dozen performances, *Where Is Longing in Autumn?* played to full houses for more than one hundred performances. The much criticized images of fashion models, millionaires, divorcées, and single women—a population now regarded as conventional in China— accounted for much of the play's popularity but its relevant themes also connected with the historical agencies of audience members.

Bai Fengxi wrote nothing since her trilogy appeared and has been retired for many years.

Xiaomei CHEN

Bai Fengxi. *Bai Fengxi juzuo xuan*. Beijing: Zhongguo xiju chubanshe, 1988.
———. "Shi bei xiaxiang." In *Bai Fengxi juzuo xuan*. Beijing: Zhongguo xiju chubanshe, 1988, 238–50.
———. *The Women Trilogy*, trans. Guan Yuehua. Beijing: Panda Books, 1991.
Chen, Xiaomei. "A Stage of Their Own: The Problematics of Women's Theater in Post-Mao China." *Journal of Asian Studies*, 56, no. 1 (1997): 3–25.
Sheng Ying et al. *Ershi shiji nüxing wenxuan shi*. Tianjin: Tianjin renmin chubanshe, 1994, 967–72.
Tung, Constantine. "Tensions and Reconciliation: Individualistic Rebels and Social Harmony in Bai Fengxi's Plays." In *Drama in the People's Republic of China*, eds. Constantine Tung and Colin MacKerras. Albany: State University of New York Press, 1987, 233–353.

Bai Shuxiang

Bai Shuxiang, b. 1939, in Laiyang, Hunan Province, is a ballet dancer of Man nationality; her ancestral home is Xinbin County, Liaoning Province.

Bai Shuxiang's artistic ability was evident even when very young, and at the age of thirteen she won a prize for her performance in the lead role of *Little White Rabbit*, staged by the Children's Drama Troupe of the Northeast Art Theater. In 1954 Bai Shuxiang was sent to Beijing Dance School to learn ballet, thus becoming one of the first Chinese to receive formal training in that discipline. Physically, she was not ideal for ballet but mastered the difficult routines and rhythms through hard work and enthusiasm. Bai Shuxiang played both Odette and Odile in *Swan Lake* in 1958—acclaimed as the first "white swan" on the ballet stage of China—and played the lead in *The Strait* (Haixia).

Her dancing, while of a high technical standard, is lively and conveys genuine emotion. She was appointed lead dancer upon the establishment of the Central Ballet Ensemble and performed a variety of roles, including Myrtha in *Giselle*, Zarema in *The Fountain of Bakhchisarai*, and Gudule in *The Hunchback of Notre Dame*. Bai Shuxiang danced Qionghua, the leading role in *Red Detachment of Women* (Hongse niangzijun), in 1964 and then danced the lead in several Chinese ballets, including *Hymn to Yimeng* (Yimeng song), *Azalea Mountain* (Dujuan shan), and *Recalling Beloved Premier Zhou* (Mianhuai jing'ai de Zhou Zongli).

Bai Shuxiang has won many prizes for her work and visited other countries with dancers' and artists' delegations. At the 1980 Philippines International Ballet Festival, the group with which she danced won first prize for group performance, and the performer visited North Korea, Burma, the United States, and Japan. She spent 1982 in France on a study tour. Among the professional posts Bai Shuxiang has held are vice-president of the Central Ballet Ensemble, executive director of the Minorities

Foundation, director of the European and American Fellow Students' Association, and director of the Chinese Dancers' Association.

HE Li and Shirley Wai CHAN
(Translated by Yang Jingqing)

Zhongguo dabaike quanshu: Yinyue, wudao. Beijing: Zhongguo dabaike quanshu chubanshe, 1989, 40–41.
Zhongguo wudaojia cidian. Beijing: Wenhua yishu chubanshe, 1994, 15.

Bai Wei

Bai Wei, 1894–1987, was the pen name of Huang Zhang of Zixing, Hunan Province, who also went by other names at various times, including Li, Ying, Su Ru, Chuhong, Laokao, Sufei, Baiwei, Lady Baiwei, Zero, Huang Yufa, and Lady Suru.

Despite enduring a sickly constitution as a child, Bai Wei was known for her strong personality. As a young woman of twenty-four, in 1918, she traveled to Japan to escape a marriage her parents had arranged and there adopted the name Bai Wei. She studied at Tokyo Women's Higher Normal University, majoring first in biology; also training in history, education, psychology, philosophy, Buddhism, and aesthetics; and finally majoring in literature. Bai Wei wrote a three-act play (*Sufei*, 1922), a poetry play (*Lin Li*, 1924), and in 1925 was described by the famous writer Chen Xiying in the well-known review magazine *Xiandai pinglun* as a "shining star of the new literature."

Returning to China in winter 1926, Bai Wei entered into a de facto relationship with the writer Yang Sao. The following spring, Bai Wei acted as a Japanese interpreter for the General Political Department of the Wuhan National Revolutionary Army and lectured at Zhongshan University in Wuchang. She resigned from these positions in September 1927 and went to Shanghai, where several of her works were published in 1928 in the monthly *Benliu*, edited by the renowned writer Lu Xun. Her novel *Fight Your Way Out of the Ghost Tower* (Dachu youlingta) was described by the literary historian Wang Yao as being "like Ibsen's *A Doll's House*, wakening unfortunate women who were puppets in their miserable family lives." Bai Wei also published the new-style poem *Song of the Spring Bamboo Shoots* (Chunsun de ge) and the novel *Bombs and Wild Geese* (Zhadan yu zhengniao) in this period. Appointed in 1929 as a professor at the Zhongguo Public School at Wusong (Wusong Zhongguo gongxue), whose principal was the prominent intellectual Hu Shi, Bai Wei taught foreign literature. In 1930, she added her name along with those of Lu Xun, Yu Dafu, and Tian Han to the "Declaration of the League of the Freedom Movement in China" and joined the League of Left-Wing Writers (Zuo lian), devoting herself from then on to left-wing theater and arts.

Bai Wei separated from Yang Sao in 1931; she was never able to rid herself, however, of the venereal disease she had contracted from him. In spite of illness, Bai Wei continued writing and traveled often between Beijing and Shanghai. Her earlier play *Lin Li* was included in 1935 in the drama section of the Chinese New Literature Series

(Zhongguo xin wenxue daxi), where it was described in Hong Shen's introduction as "a bit hysterical yet full of enthusiasm," and Bai Wei published an autobiographical novel, *A Tragic Life* (Beiju shengya), in 1936. She moved to Wuhan in 1938 after the Japanese occupied Beijing and there became active in the National Resistance Association of Literary and Art Workers (Zhonghua quanguo wenyijie kangdi xiehui). Bai Wei also worked as a special correspondent in Guilin for *New China Daily* (Xinhua ribao) before moving to Chongqing in 1940 to work with the Committee for Cultural Work, under the Political Department, headed by the playwright Guo Moruo.

Soon after the establishment of the PRC, Bai Wei returned to Beijing but published little, although she was still part of the China Federation of Literary and Art Circles (Zhonghua quanguo wenxue yishu jie lianhehui, or Wenlian) and the body that became the Chinese Writers' Association (Zhonghua quanguo wenxue gongzuozhe xiehui, or Wenxie; in 1953 renamed Zhongguo zuojia xiehui, or Zuoxie). She was also appointed to several CPPCC. Bai Wei was persecuted and subjected to torture during the Cultural Revolution, and wrote nothing after 1975. Her "Outside the Great Wall" (Changcheng wai) was selected for the short story section (the second decade) of the Chinese New Literature Series in 1984; in the following year, her *The Third Class Ward* (Sandeng bingfang) and *Fight Your Way Out of the Ghost Tower* were selected for the reportage genre.

Bai Wei died in August 1987 in Beijing Union Hospital at the age of ninety-three.

GAO Yuanbao

(Translated by Laura Long)

Bai Shurong. "Bai Wei." In *Zhongguo xiandai nüzuojia*, vol. 1, ed. Yuan Chunde. Harbin: Heilongjiang renmin chubanshe, 1983.
———. "Yi ge reqing tongku jianqiang linghun—Bai Wei." *Xin wenxue shiliao*, no. 13 (December 1981).
Bai Wei. *Bai Wei zuopin xuan.* Changsha: Hunan renmin chubanshe, 1985.
Fang Ying. "Bai Wei lun." In *Dangdai nüzuojia lun*, ed. Huang Renying. Shanghai: Guanghua shuju, 1933, 59–78.
Li Liming. *Zhongguo xiandai liubai zuojia xiaozhuan.* Hong Kong: Bowen shuju, 1976, 410.
Wang Yingxia. "Wo yu nüzuojia Bai Wei." *Zhuanji wenxue*, 64, no. 4 (1994): 61–63.
Zheng Renjia. "Yisheng kanke de nüzuojia Bai Wei." *Zhuanji wenxue*, 35, no. 1 (July 1988): 107–10.
Zhongguo xin wenxue daxi, 1927–1937, vols. 4, 13, 15. Shanghai: Shanghai wenyi chubanshe, 1984–1989.

Bai Yang

Bai Yang, 1920–1996, born in Beijing, was a film and spoken drama (*huaju*) actress who starred or appeared in over twenty-five films and more than fifty plays throughout a career that began in the 1930s. She is best known for her films, especially those in which she played lower-class working women. Her name was closely associated in the 1930s and early 1940s with the leftist movement in film and drama circles, and she was involved in a series of pro-communist activities. Bai Yang is one of the few actors who remained in China after 1949, survived the Cultural Revolution, and continued acting until an advanced age.

Bai Yang was the youngest of four children; her sister Yang Mo (*q.v.*) is a well-known writer. Her father was a provincial degree holder (*juren*) in late Qing who established a college of which he was president and that was later forced to close because of poor management. Bai Yang's parents cared little about their children, and she was dispatched at the age of five to live in a poor rural area with her wet nurse, not being sent for until she was nine. At the age of eleven, Bai Yang played the minor role of a maid in the film *New Resentments in the Summer Palace* (Gugong xinyuan) and quit junior high school to join a leftist drama troupe. During the next few years, she worked with various professional drama groups, including the Chinese Touring Drama Troupe (Zhongguo lüxing jutuan), and acted in plays by such famous playwrights as Tian Han, Hong Shen, Oscar Wilde, and Eugene O'Neill.

In 1936 Bai Yang was recruited by the Mingxing Film Studio based in Shanghai and co-starred with Zhao Dan, known as the prince of Chinese film, in *Crossroads* (Shizi jietou). This film was an immediate hit, and Bai Yang became quite famous, the media comparing her to Greta Garbo. The characters in *Crossroads*, Zhiying (Bai Yang) and Lao Zhao (Zhao Dan), unwittingly share an apartment; they meet at the bus terminal each day as one goes to work and the other returns from work. These brief encounters are enough for them to fall in love but their lives are interrupted when both lose their jobs in an economic depression brought on by the threat of a Japanese invasion. Inspired by the decision of their friends to fight the invaders, Zhiying and Lao Zhao come to a similar crossroads in their respective lives. Although presented in the style of Hollywood burlesque, the film was not considered to be mere entertainment, as were "soft films" (*ruanxing dianying*), but was lauded for its contribution to the war effort.

The Chinese film industry became badly disrupted when the Sino-Japanese War broke out. Bai Yang joined the Shanghai Film Actors' Drama Troupe (Shanghai yingren jutuan), which staged many plays concerned with the war, as it retreated to the wartime capital of Chongqing. She acted in only three films over the next eight years but performed in over forty plays, including those of Guo Moruo, Cao Yu, Xia Yan, Yang Hansheng, Shakespeare, and Tolstoy, most of which were put on to arouse patriotism. Bai Yang was also considered to be the foremost female drama performer of that period, ahead of Shu Xiuwen (*q.v.*), Zhang Ruifang, and Qin Yi.

Bai Yang returned to Shanghai after the war, the two years from 1946 to 1948 being her most prolific in film. Her two most popular films were *Spring River Flows East* (Yijiang chunshui xiang dongliu) and *Eight Thousand Li of Clouds and Moon* (Ba qian li lu yun he yue). Both dealt with the war, but *Spring River Flows East* is considered a landmark in her career. She played the role of the young worker Sufen, who marries the patriot Zhang Zhongliang in Shanghai as the Japanese invade the northeast. Soon after Sufen gives birth to their child, Zhang Zhongliang decides to go with his medical brigade to Chongqing to be part of the war effort. He is disheartened when rejected for a government position because of his disheveled appearance and turns to a former acquaintance and old admirer, Wang Lizhen, for help. He succumbs to her charms and has an affair with her, gradually forgetting the faithful wife who awaits his return. He returns to Shanghai after the war to take over the factory of

Wang Lizhen's brother-in-law. Sufen, now poverty-stricken, goes to work as a servant in Zhang Zhongliang's new home and is shocked to discover as she serves guests at a party that her new master is in fact her husband. Zhang Zhongliang reproaches her for embarrassing him; in desperation Sufen throws herself into the river and drowns. Reflecting as it does the trauma of a nation viewed through the vicissitudes of an ordinary family, *Spring River Flows East* was acclaimed by some as a Chinese *Gone with the Wind*. The film broke all records for attendance and Bai Yang's performance so moved audiences that they were advised to bring handkerchiefs.

Although assuming several governmental positions after 1949, she continued to act in films and drama, playing Xianglin's wife in *New Year's Sacrifice* (Zhufu, 1955), adapted from Lu Xun's short story of the same name. This film, in which the character is the quintessential suffering woman of May Fourth literary discourse, won a special award in a Czechoslovakian film festival and renewed intense interest in the actor. As with so many actors, her career was disrupted during the Cultural Revolution, but Bai Yang was neither physically harmed nor emotionally scarred. In 1982, she set out to adapt and star in the life story of Madame Song Qingling (*q.v.*), the widow of Sun Yat-sen (1866–1925), founding father of the Republic of China. The story was first broadcast in 1989 as a five-episode television drama, and Bai Yang was crowned that year as one of the ten favorite film stars in the PRC. A grand ceremony was held in 1990 to celebrate her sixty years as an actor. Happily married to the film director and actor Jiang Junchao and the mother of two children, Bai Yang died in September 1996 at the age of seventy-six.

LIU Ying

Bai Yang. *Bai Yang yanyi tan*. Shanghai: Shanghai wenyi chubanshe, 1995.
———. *Wo de yingju shengya*. Beijing: Zhongguo dianying chubanshe, 1996.
Boorman, Howard L., and Richard C. Howard. *Biographical Dictionary of Republican China*, vol. 3. New York: Columbia University Press, 1971, 56–67.
Feng Ming. *Zhongguo dianying shigang*. Tianjin: Nankai daxue chubanshe, 1992.
Lu Xiaokang and Chen Chaoyu. "Bai Yang." In *Zhongguo dianyingjia liezhuan*. Beijing: Zhongguo dianying chubanshe, 1982.
Meng Tao. "Yijiang chushui xiang dong liu." In *Zhongguo dianying juan*. Shanghai: Huadong shida chubanshe, 1993.
———. "Zhufu." In *Zhongguo dianying juan*. Shanghai: Huadong shida chubanshe, 1993.
Zhao Shihui. "Bai Yang." In *Yingtan gouchen*. Shanghai: Dajia chubanshe, 1998.
———. "Shizi jietou." In *Zhongguo zuoyi dianying yundong*. Beijing: Zhongguo dianying chubanshe, 1993.

Bai Yushuang

Bai Yushuang, 1907–1942, of Guye, Luan County, Hebei Province, was a *ping* (local opera of north and northeast China) opera singer and performer specializing in leading female roles (*dan*).

Born as Li Guizhen, the child was given the name Li Huimin after being sold as an adopted daughter to the itinerant entertainer (*lianhua lao*) Li Jingchun and his wife Ms. Bian. Unfortunately, the girl fell out of favor when Ms. Bian gave birth to a son and was forced to learn versified stories, sung to the accompaniment of a small drum and other instruments (*dagu shu*) to earn extra money for the family. At age fourteen, Li Guizhen learned *bengbeng* (another name for *ping*) opera from Dong Faliang (the stage name of Sun Fengming). Li Guizhen adopted Bai Yushuang as her stage name that year and embarked on supporting roles. She became well known around Beijing and Tianjin for her remarkable vocal range, singing notes lower than the lowest note on the *erhu* and soaring straight up to very high ones.

After Li Jingchun died in 1927, his wife bought more girls from impoverished families. Among these was the four-year-old refugee Xiaodezi; Ms. Bian changed her name to Fuzi and ordered her to call Bai Yushuang "Mother," which is how Fuzi's later name of Bai Yushuang the Younger originated. The theatrical troupe in which Bai Yushuang played the lead role was called the Yushun Opera Troupe; it was run by the brother of Ms. Bian. However, because Li Jingchun's widow owned the troupe and her son Li Guozhang played the *erhu* during performances—its public face—the troupe was commonly called Li's Troupe (Lijia ban). Later its name changed to Huabei *Ping* Opera Troupe, however, and in 1935 they went to Shanghai. There, together with such famous stars as Ai Lianjun, Yu Lingzhi, and Zhao Ruquan, they performed the operas *Pan Jinlian*, *Spring in the Jade Hall* (Yutang chun), *The Little Matchmaker* (Hongniang), *Yan Poxi*, and *Lion's Roar East of the River* (Hedong shihou) to large audiences at Enpaiya Theater. The group also toured Suzhou, Wuxi, and Nanjing, so that Bai Yushuang gained quite a following, while northern *ping* opera also began to make a name for itself in the south. The directors of Mingxing Film Studio (Hong Shen, 1894–1955; Tian Han, 1898–1968; and Ouyang Yuqian, 1889–1962) recognized Bai Yushuang's talent as well as the potential of *ping* opera and asked her to play the lead in the film *Red Haitang Flower* (Haitang hong). This was when she began to be widely known as the "Queen of *Ping* Opera" and a movie star.

According to the art critic Ah Ying (Qian Xingcun, 1900–1977), who wrote for the newspaper *Da Wanbao*, *ping* opera improved significantly from the time when Bai Yushuang and the Huabei *Ping* Opera Troupe first brought the genre to Shanghai in performances of *Pan Jinlian* and *Spring in the Jade Hall*. Heavily influenced by *jing* (Beijing) opera, Bai Yushuang also responded to contemporary trends in modern spoken drama (*huaju*). At the peak of her career, she kept busy performing in operas as well as movies. Along with Liu Cuixia, Ai Lianjun, and Xi Cailian, Bai Yushuang was acclaimed as one of "The Four Female *Ping* Opera Singers."

In February 1937, while still at her peak, the opera star fell in love with Li Yongqi, the troupe's cymbal player, and ran off with him to his hometown in Ba County, Hebei Province. Bai Yushuang had suffered many years at the hands of Ms. Bian, who had taken advantage and treated her ward as a slave; when Ms. Bian attempted to thwart Bai Yushuang's affair with the cymbal player, the interference became the final straw and trouble ensued. The employer was not prepared to lose her star performer so easily, however, and followed the couple to Hebei, eventually persuading Bai Yushuang to return to Tianjin. Still acclaimed as the "Queen of *Ping* Opera," she performed in Beijing and Tianjin at the onset of the Sino-Japanese War in July, when Beijing was captured by the Japanese. Bai Yushuang did not feel well, however, and was diagnosed with cancer of the uterus. She continued to perform though, her understudy Bai Yushuang the Younger replacing the star only when she was too ill to go on stage. After a period of treatment in a German hospital in Beijing in 1941, Bai Yushuang returned to Tianjin the following spring to find that her bank account and title deeds to a house in her name had been transferred to Ms. Bian's son. Bai Yushuang collapsed on stage during a performance with Li Yifen of *Understanding after Death* (Sihou mingbai) and died in July 1942, still the "Queen of *Ping* Opera."

Shirley Wai CHAN
(Translated by Cui Zhiying)

Wei Xuan. "Pingju huanghou Bai Yushuang mu-nüqing." *Zhong wai zazhi* (February 1992): 65–68.
Zhongguo dabaike quanshu: Xiqu quyi. Beijing: Zhongguo dabaike quanshu chubanshe, 1989, 8.

Baolian: *see* **Lü Bicheng**

Baolige: *see* **Wulan**

Bin Zhi: *see* **Ding Ling**

Bing Xin
Bing Xin, 1900–1999, of Changle, Minhou County, Fujian Province, was born in Fuzhou. Her original name was Xie Wanying, but it was as Bing Xin that she became recognized as one of the most respected Chinese women writers of the twentieth century. Bing Xin made a name for herself as a writer of fiction, essays, poetry, and children's literature. Her unique literary style inspired some of the best-known contemporary women writers, including Ru Zhijuan (*q.v.*) and Zhang Jie (*q.v.*). Her aesthetic also helped set the standard of literary criticism for modern Chinese literature. However, Bing Xin's literary significance remains largely unexplored outside China, and a formal critical study of her works, from a comparative perspective, is long overdue.

The renowned "Bing Xin literary style" was the product of a normal but privileged upbringing. She spent seven or eight years living by the sea in Yantai, Shandong Province, and recalled her childhood fondly in such autobiographical essays as "The Past" (Wangshi), "My Hometown" (Wo de guxiang), and "My Childhood" (Wo de tongnian). As the daughter of a naval officer and an educated woman from a literary family, Bing Xin had access to both traditional Chinese culture and modern ideas through formal education and daily family interaction. With the help of her mother, Bing Xin became literate at a very young age and read Chinese classics and translations of world literature from the family's library collections. She attended the missionary-run Bridgeman Girls' School in Beijing and in 1918 commenced studies at Union Women's University (Xiehe nüzi daxue), which amalgamated with Yen-ching [Yanjing]

University the following year. After graduating with honors in 1923, the young woman went to the United States, studying English literature at Wellesley College, earning an M.A. in 1926, then returning to China to teach at Yanjing, Tsinghua [Qinghua], and Peking Universities. In 1929, Bing Xin married the eminent socio-anthropologist and ethnologist Wu Wenzao (1901?/1902?–1985).

The May Fourth Movement of 1919 started Bing Xin on her writing career. Her first published piece, "About the Trial on the Twenty-first" (Ershiyiri tingshen de ganxiang) in the *Beijing Morning Herald* (Beijing chenbao) on 25 August, revealed an eyewitness account of the student movement. For the next seventy years, she diligently carved out a productive writing career interrupted only briefly by World War II and the Cultural Revolution, publishing more than 330 essays, some sixty short stories, an almost equal number of poems, a novelette, and several translations. Most of her writings have been collected in thirty anthologies. Her translations include short stories of Rabindranath Tagore and Khalil Gibran's *The Prophet*.

Bing Xin's writing career coincided with the most dramatic political events in the history of modern China. Along with many others, she experienced dispossession, destitution, hardship, and suffering. She had gone to the United States with her husband in 1936 but returned to China via Europe and the Soviet Union at the start of the Sino-Japanese War. Bing Xin spent the years 1938 to 1946 living apart from him in virtual exile in Kunming, Yunnan Province, lecturing at Southwest Union University. Appointed to the KMT People's Political Council (1945), the writer returned briefly to Beijing but went to Japan in 1946. From 1949 to 1950, Bing Xin taught modern Chinese literature at Tokyo University and finally returned to China in the following year. She was appointed as an attaché to many cultural exchange missions and traveled extensively between 1951 and 1965. Some of her essays and travelogues published in those years gave detailed accounts of her overseas experience. Bing Xin spent most of the Cultural Revolution in labor camps, however, after her husband was branded a rightist.

These events became recurring themes in her essays and short stories yet do not seem to have affected the author's positive outlook on life. Nor did they cast a lasting shadow over her unblemished career. On the contrary, Bing Xin was held in high esteem because of her literary achievements. A number of prestigious honorary titles have been bestowed upon her, including deputy to the Fifth NPC, membership in the Standing Committee of the CPPCC, and vice-presidency of the China Federation of Literary and Art Circles. This unusual mix of offices did not draw Bing Xin into political activism, however. Throughout life, she dedicated herself to literary pursuits so that, although participating to some extent in political activities, she remained largely apolitical and free from controversy.

Her encounters with Western culture enabled Bing Xin to appreciate the essence of that civilization as well as her own. When translating this cultural understanding into literary creativity, she produced a style embodying the grace and ingenuity of the Chinese classics and the clarity and ease of Western literature. There is an enduring quality in Bing Xin's writing that appeals to Chinese readers of all ages from all walks of life. Bing Xin wrote about real life experiences, yet she never allowed reality to strip her of a childlike innocence. She wrote about feelings with a directness and lack of pretension that lent her writings, euphemistic though they may have been, spontaneity and ingenuousness. Another famous May Fourth writer, Mao Dun, once made the following insightful comment about Bing Xin: "Of May Fourth writers, Bing Xin is the only one who is forever truthful to herself. When she writes, she inclines to give full expression not to society but to herself. She always strives to express her feelings in the clearest possible way. I therefore venture to suggest that her essays are better than her short stories, and her prose poems are better than her short poems such as *Stars* (Fanxing), and *Spring Water* (Chunshui)." The quality of spontaneous innocence is what Bing Xin's works share with many Chinese literary masterpieces. It also explains why her writing style has been, and will continue to be, a source of inspiration.

Most of the biographical and scholarly studies done on Bing Xin have been in Chinese. The best known biography, written by the renowned biographer Zhao Fengxiang, is part of the Modern Chinese Writers' Biographical Series. Mao Dun's essay "On Bing Xin" (Bing Xin lun) remains by far the best study of her literary achievements. Most critical studies of her writings focus on earlier work (see, for example, the articles cited below by Li Ling and Zhu Chengrong). A detailed study of Bing Xin's later works, including those written in the 1990s and collected in the anthology *About Women and Men* (Guanyu nüren he nanren), will certainly provide valuable data for mapping the literary journey of this prolific writer and will also shed light on the various influences shaping her remarkable literary career.

Wai Ling YEUNG

Bing Xin. "Wo de laoban—Wu Wenzao." In *Guanyu nüren he nanren*, ed. Chen Shu. Beijing: Renmin wenxue chubanshe, 1993, 246–66.
Boorman, Howard L., and Richard C. Howard, eds. *Biographical Dictionary of Republican China*, vol. 2. New York: Columbia University Press, 1971, 103–05.
Li Baochu. "Lüelun Bing Xin de chuangzuo guan." *Wenyi bao*, 7, no. 3 (1993): 245–48.
Li Ling. "Bing Xin xiaoshuo tansuo." *Wenxue pinglun*, no. 2 (1996): 148–55.
Mao Dun. "Bing Xin lun." *Zhongguo xiandai zuojia xuanji*, 2nd ed., ed. Zhuo Ru. Hong Kong: Sanlian shudian, 1986, 217–37.
Snow, Helen. *Women in Modern China*. The Hague and Paris: Mouton Press, 1967, 181–90.
Wu Yanjun. "Minzu chuantong wenxue dui Bing Xin zaoqi sanwen de yishu ziyang." *Neimenggu shida xuebao*, no. 4 (1992): 67–73.
Zhang Wei. "Women Writers through Three Generations." *Beijing Review*, 29, no. 9, 18–20.
Zhao Fengxiang. *Bing Xin zhuan*. Beijing: Shiyue wenyi chubanshe, 1987, 1–81, 227–82.
Zhu Chengrong. "Lun Bing Xin zaoqi sanwen shenmei jiazhi quxiang." *Chengdu xinan minzu xueyuan xuebao zhesheban*, no. 3 (1992): 86–93.
Zhuo Ru. "Bing Xin de shengping he zaoqi chuangzuo." *Minzhong xiandai zuojia zuopin xuanping*, ed. Zhuo Ru. Fujian: Jiaoyu chubanshe, 1982, 3–17.
———. "Mantan Bing Xin de chuangzuo." In *Zhongguo xiandai zuojia xuanji*, 2nd ed., ed. Zhuo Ru. Hong Kong: Sanlian shudian, 1986, 238–47.

Bingxin: *see* **Bing Xin**

C

Cai Chang

Cai Chang, 1900–1990, of Xiangxiang County, Hunan Province, was one of the most prominent women in the communist movement throughout the twentieth century. Famously described by Nym Wales in 1937 as the "Dean of Communist women," Cai Chang was the first woman to become a CCP Central Committee member and for many years after the founding of the PRC in 1949 chaired the ACWF.

Cai Chang's mother, Ge Jianhao (*q.v.*), who was from a once wealthy literati family related by marriage to Zeng Guofan, single-mindedly pursued an education for her children, girls and boys alike. Cai Chang's father, Cai Rongfeng (1862–1932), was a failed businessman who worked initially in his family's chili sauce establishment and then at the Jiangnan Arsenal in Shanghai before returning to the countryside, where he was equally unsuccessful at farming. Cai Chang was the youngest of six children, all of whom were exceptionally close to their mother. Two of the siblings died young (Cai Linxian, 1885–1907, and Cai Shunxi, 1893–1904); her oldest sister, Cai Qingxi (b. 1884), returned home not long after her marriage; and her brothers Cai Hesen (1895–1931) and Cai Luxian (1889–1925) both died as martyrs to the communist cause.

Known as Maomeizi as a child, she took the name Cai Xianxi on entering the lower primary at Xiangxiang County First Girls' School (Xiangxiangxian li diyi nüxiao) at the age of thirteen. The name Cai Chang was adopted in 1915 after she departed to Changsha to avoid a marriage arranged by her father; there, Cai Chang enrolled in music and physical education at Zhounan Girls' Normal School (Zhounan nüzi shifan xuexiao). Graduating in 1916, she then taught physical education at the primary school for two or three years. Cai Chang had grown up hearing her mother speak with great admiration of the late Qing revolutionary martyr Qiu Jin (see *Biographical Dictionary of Chinese Women: The Qing Period*), who had married into a local Xiangxiang family. However, even at eighteen, Cai Chang was apparently considered too young to join the New People's Study Society (Xinmin xuehui) formed in 1918 by her brother Cai Hesen and his close friend Mao Zedong (1893–1976). Xiang Jingyu (*q.v.*), a friend from Zhounan Girls' School and five years her senior, became one of the society's first women members. Cai Chang could only listen in on the lively meetings held at the Cai home. At one stage, she joined with her brother and Mao Zedong in swearing they would never marry, a vow none honored. Cai Chang later said, however, that she did not become politically aware until she became a student in France in the early 1920s.

On 25 December 1919, Cai Chang sailed from Shanghai to France with her mother, a brother, and Xiang Jingyu as part of a work-study program they had organized through the Sino-French Education Society. The women were assigned to Montargis Girls' School southeast of Paris, and Cai Chang actively participated in a series of student movements and protests that eventually resulted in over one hundred Chinese students (including her brother) being deported. At times, she worked in a factory by day and studied at night, but the four years in France were essentially a time of political awakening for her. There she met the Vietnamese revolutionary Ho Chi Minh (Hu Zhiming) and joined the New People's Study Society (1920), the Chinese Socialist Youth League (Zhongguo shehuizhuyi qingnian tuan [1922]), and the French branch of the CCP (1923). That year Cai Chang also married Li Fuchun (1900–1975), giving birth to an only child, a daughter named Li Tete, in early 1924; Cai Chang handed the baby over to Ge Jianhao, who took the child back to China and cared for her granddaughter for many years. At the end of the year, Cai Chang and Li Fuchun set out for the Soviet Union and in February 1925 enrolled at the Communist University of the Toilers of the East (Dongfang laodongzhe gongchangzhuyi daxue).

Returning to China with her husband in August, Cai Chang commenced what was to become a lifetime of work on women and women's labor issues. In Guangzhou, she became secretary of the Women's Committee of the Central Guangdong-Guangxi Area Committee and then worked with He Xiangning (*q.v.*) in the KMT Central Women's Bureau. As a member of the KMT, Cai Chang involved herself for the next year in women's liberation and labor activities. Life did not go altogether smoothly for her during this period. Comparatively Westernized during her time in France—taking to Western dress and also smoking—Cai Chang found that the image she presented in factories alienated her from Chinese women workers; she chose to change her attire rather than lose their faith. Her marriage ran into trouble when Cai Chang discovered that Li Fuchun was having an affair with one of the workers. His betrayal was not taken lightly; she demanded that the affair end, and it was some time before her normally buoyant spirits returned. With the initial success of the Northern Expedition in 1926, however, Cai Chang traveled to Nanchang to join her husband and was appointed head of both the CCP Jiangxi Women's Bureau and the Propaganda Section of the KMT General Political Department. With the collapse of the KMT–CCP alliance in mid-1927, however, she formally resigned from the KMT. Apart from a short period in Moscow (June–July 1928) to attend the CCP's Sixth National Congress and the Sixth Comintern Congress, Cai Chang spent the years 1927 to 1931 doing women's work and underground party work in Wuhan, Wuchang, Shanghai, and Hong Kong.

At the end of the latter year, she was transferred to the newly established Jiangxi soviet to lecture on social history at the Red Army School (Hongjun xuexiao) in Ruijin. In February 1932, Cai Chang headed the Women's Department of the Jiangxi Provincial Central Committee (Zhongyang Jiangxishengwei funübu buzhang) and became acting head of its Organization Department. The marriage regulations (*hunyin tiaoli*) that emerged from the First Soviet Congress held in 1931 had laid down principles of freedom of choice in marriage and the rule of one husband/one wife. Under her direction, the Women's Department worked further toward making women more self-reliant, encouraging them to increase production and participate in the military struggle to establish revolutionary bases. In January 1934, on the eve of the Long March, Cai Chang was elected along with her husband to the Central Executive Committee of the Chinese Soviet Republic. During the Long March, she was in charge of propaganda and civilian organization work; her husband served as a political officer with the First Front Red Army. Her presence on the march is remembered by her colleagues as having been inspirational: she would sing "The Marseillaise" to lift the spirits of the walkers and was patient and optimistic in the face of daily hunger and exhaustion.

The geopolitical stability that the success of the Long March provided the CCP also led Cai Chang and her husband, both fellow provincials of Mao Zedong, to consolidate their positions as party leaders. When the American journalist Edgar Snow met Cai Chang in late 1936, she was already in charge of the work of winning over the local populace in the northwestern Shaanxi-Gansu-Ningxia Border Region. Apart from about eighteen months (autumn 1938 to March 1940) in Moscow studying at the Comintern School (Gongchangguoji Zhongguo zhibu daibiaotuan ban de xuexiban) and receiving medical treatment for an unspecified complaint, Cai Chang spent most of her time between 1936 and 1945 in Yan'an and the northwest. While Li Fuchun chaired the Shaanxi-Gansu-Ningxia Provincial Central Committee in 1936, he also held high-level posts in the Organization Department of the CCP Central Committee from 1935 to 1948. Li Fuchun also held a series of posts in finance and economic planning from the early 1940s and was instrumental in obtaining substantial Soviet aid for China's heavy industry sector in the years immediately after the establishment of the PRC. As chair of the State Planning Commission from 1954, he eventually became responsible for the "day-to-day functioning of the economy."

Cai Chang, for her part, became head (1937) and then secretary (1941–53) of the Women's Committee of the Central Committee and was elected to the Executive Committee of the Shaanxi-Gansu-Ningxia Women's Federation (1940). Her work involved organization and propaganda, the federation's goal being to integrate women into the general programs of the party and set up mechanisms of care for children during wartime, including the National Refugee Children's Association (Zhanshi ertong baoyuhui).

In 1944, during the Yan'an rectification campaigns, she spoke out against the "feminist" (funüzhuyi) stance of some women, stating instead the need for men and women to work together to ensure the success of the revolution. Her response countered the criticisms voiced by Ding Ling (q.v.) regarding the persistence of patriarchal attitudes in Yan'an and revealed her deep loyalty to Mao's party line. In 1945, Cai Chang and her husband were elected as full members to the CCP Central Committee. She was the only woman to hold full membership. Deng Yingchao (q.v.) and Chen Shaomin (q.v.) were elected only as alternate members at that time. That same year marked both the end of the Sino-Japanese War and the beginning of the civil war between the CCP and the KMT. Li Fuchun was assigned to work in the Northeastern Military Region in Manchuria, and Cai Chang was sent to initiate women's work in newly reclaimed areas there in December 1946. For the next two or three years, she was stationed in Harbin but traveled widely throughout the northeast, giving talks, attending conferences, and investigating women's living and working conditions in factories and the countryside.

In anticipation of a communist victory, preparatory committees had been established in the late 1940s to oversee women's organizations. Cai Chang had been elected head of the Preparatory Committee of the Women's Federations of China's Liberated Areas (Zhongguo jiefangqu funü lianhehui) in 1945, a move that led to her election in Paris, in absentia, to the Executive Committee of the Women's International Democratic Federation (WIDF, Guoji minzhu funü lianhehui) the same year. She became its vice-chair in 1948. On behalf of the organization and other responsibilities related to women's affairs, Cai Chang made several trips overseas, to Prague and Paris in 1947 and Budapest and Russia in 1948.

During her time in Russia, Cai Chang's grandson, Li Yong, was born, in December 1948. This was the son of her only daughter of whom she had seen very little since giving the child into her grandmother's care. Even when the party sent then fifteen-year-old Li Tete to Moscow with Cai Chang in mid-1939 for safekeeping, she had occupied herself more with other children, showing no partiality toward her daughter. Cai Chang further alienated Li Tete by explaining that she (Cai Chang) was too busy "driving the Japanese aggressors out of China" to show affection to her. Because Li Tete's grandmother died in 1943, leaving the young woman with no one in China to return to, it is quite possible that she remained in Russia from 1939 on. Li Tete was twenty-four when her son was born; nothing is known of the circumstances. It is unusual that the child bore her surname, that is, that of her father Li Fuchun, rather than that of its own father, who is unacknowledged in any historical sources.

Cai Chang's high profile career continued after the establishment of the PRC in 1949, and she was elected or appointed to a great number and variety of bodies. The most important and apparently influential of these were the CCP Central Committee (1945–77); the presidium of the First CPPCC (1949); the Central People's Government Council (1949) on which she served as the sole female CCP representative; the ACWF (chair, 1949–77; honorary chair, 1978–88); the Women Workers' Department of the All-China Federation of Trade Unions (director, 1948–57); and the Standing Committee of the NPC (1954–80). Maintaining heavy commitments for many years, Cai Chang also continued to attend and speak at International Women's Day (8 March) celebrations, chair and attend meetings and conferences on women and work, publish articles and statements, and receive foreign guests. She virtually ceased traveling overseas but visited Moscow in 1953 for Stalin's funeral and remained there for a short period of recuperation.

Despite carrying a high profile in the 1950s, Cai Chang did not play a significant role in the governing of China and some would say that she appears to have been little more than a cultivated and elegant figurehead for the mass of China's women. Whether for reasons of poor health, poor eyesight (she had gone completely blind by 1984), or, like her husband, because she was a silent critic of Mao Zedong's disastrous economic policies, Cai Chang virtually withdrew from public life from 1961 on, although she continued as a member of the Central Committee and the NPC. Her husband had opposed the Cultural Revolution from the start, and as a veteran Long Marcher she too was in disgrace during that period. From 1978, however, after regaining her status as a model revolutionary, Cai Chang was awarded on International Women's Day in 1989 a Commemorative Medal recognizing her lifelong work for the Chinese people. Because of her blindness, she was unable to attend the ceremony, but a long-time colleague Kang Keqing (q.v.) accepted the medal on her behalf.

Sue WILES

Guo Chen. *Jinguo liezhuan: Hong yifangmianjun sanshiwei changzheng nühongjun shengping shiji.* Beijing: Nongcun duwu chubanshe, 1986, 54, 56–57, 90–94.

Hu Guohua. "Yige weidade nüxing." In *Hongjun nüyingxiong zhuan*, eds. Liaowang bianjibu. Beijing: Xinhua chubanshe, 1986, 7–24.

Klein, Donald W., and Anne B. Clarke. *Biographic Dictionary of Chinese Communism, 1921–1965*. Cambridge, Mass.: Harvard University Press, 1971, 847–50.

Lee, Lily Xiao Hong, and Sue Wiles. *Women of the Long March*. Sydney: Allen & Unwin, 1999.

Salisbury, Harrison E. *The Long March: The Untold Story*. New York: Harper & Row, 1985, 89–90.

Snow, Helen Foster [Nym Wales]. *Inside Red China*. New York: Da Capo Press, 1977, 182–85.

Su Ping. *Cai Chang zhuan*. Beijing: Zhongguo funü chubanshe, 1990.

———. "Cai Chang." In *Nüying zishu*, eds. Jiangxisheng funü lianhehui. Nanchang: Jiangxi renmin chubanshe, 1988, 235–42.

Yang Zilie. *Zhang Guotao furen huiyilu*. Hong Kong: Zilian chubanshe, 1970, 196.

Yingwen *Zhongguo funü*, ed. *Gujin zhuming funü renwu*, vol. 2. Shijiazhuang: Hebei renmin chubanshe, 1986, 420–28.

Cai Lanying

Cai Lanying, b. 1918, of Xianxian County, Hebei Province, is a paper-cut artist. Born to a peasant family, she took up the folk art of papercutting at the age of eight, continuing well into her seventies.

Cai Lanying was also active politically, joining the CCP in 1944 and working as an undercover party member as well as head of her village's Women's Federation. She recounted her accomplishments to a reporter during a 1994 interview, taking evident pride in her history of political activism and emancipation.

Cai Lanying began doing papercuts as New Year decorations of the kind still commonly seen in the countryside, pasted on paper and glass windowpanes and doors. Because she was good at it, Cai Lanying's neighbors would ask her to cut paper patterns for their homes, and gradually she built up a reputation. Unlike recent artists who pre-draw papercuts on paper, then carve them out with a knife, Cai Lanying cut hers out with a small pair of scissors, creating designs as she went along. Strips of white cloth would be wrapped around the handles of the scissors to lessen the friction, but still she developed thick corns on her fingers. In more than sixty years of papercutting, Cai Lanying has cut more than ten thousand pieces and gone through more than one hundred pairs of scissors.

Her works portray various themes, depicting life in the countryside, for example, picking cotton bolls (*zhai miantao*), donkey pulling a mill (*lü la mo*), tending pigs (*fang zhu*), and raking (*pa di*). The images are full of a simple beauty, celebrating farm work. Other scenes depict China's traditions: holidays and festivals, wedding scenes, funerals, and birthdays, all of which reveal her joie de vivre. Other pieces indirectly reflect episodes from legends, folktales, and stories from local operas. Because the latter are performed only once or twice a year in the countryside, papercuts help people recall favorite scenes and characters in the lonely times between performances. Most valuable, however, are the autobiographical papercuts. Cai Lanying once told an interviewer that when she wants to express herself, she turns to her scissors; like many women of her age and circumstances, Cai Lanying cannot read or write. Her autobiographical works record daily activities, for example, going to market (*ganji*) and helping the husband and teaching the kids (*xiangfu jiaozi*). Some are visual narratives revealing innermost feelings. Once offended by her husband's chauvinistic behavior, she created a papercut of a husband bullying his wife. He was so ashamed that when members of the family passed it around, admiring the design, he slipped from the room. Expressing personal emotions through papercutting is unique to Cai Lanying.

The artist has received much recognition for her papercuts. In 1989, she received an award from the China Papercut Grand Competition (*Zhongguo jianzhi dajiang sai*) and the Excellent Creation Award in the first China Folk Art Exhibition (*Zhongguo shoujie minjian meishu jiapin zhan youxiu chuanzuojiang*). Many of the compositions have also been included in recent albums of papercuts. Cai Lanying is a member of several national folk art organizations, such as the Society for Chinese Papercutting (Zhongguo jianzhi xuehui). In 1995, she was invited to Beijing as an outstanding folk artist to perform at the fourth World Women's Conference. Her daughter Deng Yanfang is also a paper-cut artist.

Lily Xiao Hong LEE

Zhang Yunjie. "Yong jiandao jianchu nüren de yisheng." *Zhongguo funü*, no. 2 (1995): 34–35.
Zhongguo renwu nianjian, 1993. Beijing: Huayi chubanshe, 1993, 412–13.

Cai Renzi: *see* **Choi Yan Chi**

Cai Xianxi: *see* **Cai Chang**

Cai Yanci: *see* **Choi Yan Chi**

Can Xue

Can Xue, b. 1953, as Deng Xiaohua in Changsha, Hunan Province, has been described as one of the most interesting and innovative of contemporary Chinese writers.

Can Xue's parents had joined the CCP in the 1930s or 1940s, and after 1949 her father, Deng Junhong (1916–1994), worked as head of *Hunan News* (Xin Hunanbao), where her mother, Li Yin (b. 1923), also was employed. In 1957, Can Xue's father suffered prosecution as leader of an anti-Communist Party group within *Hunan News*, was labeled a right-wing extremist, and was sent to the countryside for two years; her mother was put in the Hengshan Corrective Center. Within a span of ten years, by the start of the Cultural Revolution, her father had been further detained, her mother had been sent to a May Seventh Cadre School, and her brothers and sisters had all been sent down to work in the countryside. Can Xue, at this time thirteen years old, was just finishing primary school and would normally have gone on to secondary school. Instead, unable to continue her schooling, she lived alone in the small shelter that had been allotted to her parents. At seventeen Can Xue got a job in a neighborhood factory as a metalworker and assembly worker, a job she held for ten years. In 1978, she married Lu Yong (b. 1948), who had been sent as a student (*zhiqing*) to work on a farm during the Cultural Revolution and had just returned from the countryside. Two years later, Can Xue resigned from the factory after giving birth to her first child, a son. She and her husband learned to sew and started up a small sewing business. Her husband has managed their shop since 1985, allowing Can Xue to stay at home to write and keep house. She is currently employed by the Hunan Writers' Association as a professional writer.

A slight child, Can Xue was sensitive, nervous, and aloof; she was high strung and said to live in a world of her own. Can Xue remained very close to her maternal grandmother, who brought her up, and whom she described lovingly in the autobiographical piece "A Beautiful Southern Summer Day" (Meili nanfang zhi xiari). In 1959 the nine members of Can Xue's family had moved from the city to Mount Yuelu to live in two small rooms, each only ten yards square. She and her siblings survived the great famine of 1959–61 solely because their grandmother climbed into the mountains to gather mushrooms and wild herbs for them. She had a strong personality—some said she was even deranged—and was a good storyteller. In the eyes of a child like Can Xue, mystery surrounded her grandmother, and from her Can Xue learned to listen to the deep sounds of the night and for many years dreamed about flying. She was eight when her grandmother died (1961) of malnutrition and overwork; only then did Can Xue also learn of her father's heart condition. The strain caused her to become frightened of waking up in the middle of the night, but when morning would come its brilliant sunshine could make her wild with joy. As a teenager, Can Xue often "walked bareheaded and barefoot for long hours under the scorching sun, full of joy and daydreaming." Later, she excelled in telling stories of dark nights and declared that her creativity is stimulated by "the blazing sun of the south, the warm and bright atmosphere." To Can Xue, brightness and darkness, heaven and hell, are opposites that slowly congeal in her to become essences, both abstract and pure.

She describes the activity of her writing as based on "digging her own treasure"; her uniqueness as a gifted writer undoubtedly stems from her childhood experiences and idiosyncratic visual and audio illusions. A privately circulated view is that Can Xue has two souls, or states of consciousness, in which she shifts freely between a real and an imagined world. During the act of writing, she enters into a highly concentrated, creative state, driven by emotions, primitive impulses, and perceptions. This irrational method of writing breaks away from conventional "reality" of ordinary people and becomes a means to explore highly individualistic, inner mental realms. The words "illusion," "nightmare," "absurd," "surreal," and "obscure" appear repeatedly in literary criticism of her work, which remains enigmatic. Can Xue is clearly important and unusual among contemporary Chinese writers.

One short story called "Soap Bubbles on Dirty Water" (Wushui shang de feizao pao), her first published work, came out in 1985 in a little-known magazine *New Creation*. In the story, her mother becomes a basin of dirty, soapy water. In "Yellow Mud Street" (Huangni jie), completed in 1983 and published in *China* magazine in November 1986 and since revised, many strange twists and turns of events happen. Its jargon and scenes from the Cultural Revolution clearly place the piece in a historical setting and, compared to some of her later work, elicit a strong feeling of political allegory.

Between that year and 1987, Can Xue published the novella *Old Floating Cloud* (Canglao de fuyun) and over ten short stories, including "Fog" (Wu), "The Moment When the Cuckoo Crows" (Buguniao jiao de nayi shunjian), "In the Wilderness" (Kuangye li), "Skylight" (Tian chuang), and "Dialogues in Paradise" (Tiantang li de duihua, parts 1 and 2). These unconventional, surrealistic, and dreamlike pieces caused a furor in literary circles but established her literary credentials and gained her work attention and recognition from overseas critics and Sinologists. In 1986 in the United States, *The Intellectual* published "Raindrops between the Tiles" (Wafeng li de yudi), "Amei's Worries on a Sunny Day" (Amei zai yige taiyangtian li de chousi), and "Yellow Mud Street." Her writing has appeared in translation in many languages, including Japanese, English, French, Italian, and Russian. Her first novel, *The Performance of Breaking through the Encirclement* (Tuwei biaoyan), came out in 1988 and is full of ideas and debate, including about artistic creation. This theme continued in the 1990s, explored in such works as "Report on One's Thinking" (Sixiang huibao), "Scar" (Hen), and *A Man and His Neighbor and Two or Three Others* (Yige ren he tade linju ji lingwai liangsan ge ren). This last was originally a novel but was broken up into two novellas when no publisher could be found.

Literary critics in China responded to Can Xue's writings from 1987 on. Some associated her with Lu Xun's critique on the Chinese national character and compared her works with his "true ugly voice." The writer Wang Meng accurately pointed out how her writing describes "the deep layer of humankind's mental world. Like a dagger or a pin, straight away it pricks a very painful spot." Many critics understand the implications of Can Xue's cultural critique; others study her writings through the lens of psychoanalytical theory and feminism.

Overseas Sinologists and literary critics regard Can Xue's style from diverse artistic, philosophical, and cultural reference points. Standing out from her fellow contemporary Chinese literary realist writers, she has made a considerable impact with her novels that, in the words of Charlotte Innes (*New York Times*, 24 September 1998), "remind Westerners of T.S. Eliot's metaphors, Franz Kafka's fantasies, and the nightmare-like paintings of Matisse." Translator Ronald R. Janssen claims that Can Xue explores areas not touched upon by any other contemporary Chinese writer and also "update[s] the long tradition of irrationalism in our own literature." Japanese Sinologist Kondo Naoko considers Can Xue's writings to be the most excellent works written in China since the Cultural Revolution and writes that "the depth, the philosophy, the vivid expression and symbolism and the poetic language are astounding." The Danish Sinologist Anne Wedell-Wedellsborg pointed out the cultural significance of Can Xue in contemporary China, how she expresses individual dilemmas in her own strong, individual voice and "reveals the particularity of the bilateral but oppositional relationship of the self and society."

WU Xiaoli
(Translated by Laura Long)

Can Xue. *Dialogues in Paradise*, trans. Ronald R. Janssen and Jian Zhang. Evanston, Ill.: Northwestern University Press, 1989.

———. "The Huts on the Hill," trans. Michael S. Duke. In *Worlds of Modern Chinese Fiction: Short Stories and Novellas from the People's Republic, Taiwan and Hong Kong*, ed. Michael S. Duke. Armonk, N.Y.: M.E. Sharpe, 1991, 41–44.

———. "Meili nanfang zhi xiari." *Zhongguo*, no. 10 (1986): 75–78.

———. *Old Floating Cloud: Two Novellas*, trans. Ronald R. Janssen and Jian Zhang, with a foreword by Charlotte Innes. Evanston, Ill.: Northwestern University Press, 1991.

Huang Lin. "Chaoyue nüxing: Can Xue de xiaoshuo." *Dangdai zuojia pinglun*, no. 5 (1994): 86–90.

Kondo Naoko. "Can Xue: Heiye de jiang shu zhe," trans. Liao Jinqiu. *Wenxue pinglun*, no. 1 (1995): 76–83.

———. "Chi pingguo de tequan: Can Xue de xiaoshuo," trans. Liao Jinqiu. *Wenxue ziyoutan*, no. 1 (1995): 151–56.

———. "X nüshi huo Can Xue de tuwei," trans. Liao Jinqiu. *Nanfang wentan*, no. 5 (1998): 37–42.

Lu Jingjing. "Dubudong Can Xue: Du Can Xue de *Zai Chunjing de qiliu zhong tui hua*." *Zhongshan*, no. 2 (1993): 167.

Lu Tonglin. "Can Xue: What Is So Paranoid in Her Writings?" In *Gender and Sexuality in Twentieth-Century Chinese Literature and Society*, ed. Lu Tonglin. Albany: State University of New York Press, 1993, 175–204.

Ma Luo. "Tantan Can Xue de xiaoshuo," trans. Chen Chen. *Yalu jiang*, no. 3 (1996): 30–31.

Sha Shui. "Biaoyan rensheng—lun Can Xue de 'Tuwei biaoyan.'" *Wenxue pinglun*, no. 5 (1989): 125–30, 140.

Wedell-Wedellsborg, Anne. "Mo leng liangke de zhuguanxing: Du Can Xue xiaoshuo," trans. Liu Zhi. *Xiaoshuo jie*, no. 3 (1996): 121–25.

Xiao Yuan. "Liang jian yu yizu: Zuowei yige nüxing zuojia de Can Xue." *Furong*, no. 2 (1995): 77–83.

Xiao Yuan, ed. *Shengdian de qingpi—Can Xue zhi mi.* Guiyang: Guizhou renmin chubanshe, 1993.

Cao Mengjun

Cao Mengjun, 1904–1967, of Changsha, Hunan Province, was a social activist and leader of the women's movement, in both KMT-occupied areas before 1949 and the PRC thereafter.

She gained her early schooling in Hunan where she earned a reputation for radical behavior; Cao Mengjun changed schools four times before graduating from high school. She was expelled from both Daotian Girls' Normal School for urging her fellow students to cut off their plaits of hair and Zhounan Girls' School for inciting classmates to hand in blank examination papers at the (presumably provincial) combined examination (*huikao*), which was considered a tool for controlling students' ideology. After entering Hunan First Provincial Normal School as one of its first female students, Cao Mengjun left in disgust at the failure of a student strike. She then transferred to Xiejun High School and became the leader of its students' union. It is thought that Cao Mengjun finished her secondary education there.

Some sources say that Cao Mengjun entered Peking University in 1925, but only one says she graduated. In the late 1920s or early 1930s, she lived in Nanjing and worked in the Agriculture and Mining Department of the Republican government. About this time, Cao Mengjun married Zuo Gong, who is said to have been a protégé of the prominent KMT statesman Sun Fo. Cao Mengjun organized a study group (*dushu hui*) with her friends, including Wang Kunlun and Sun Xiaocun. Although posing as an academic organization, this body was actually strongly influenced by the CCP underground, its aim being to propagate anti-Japanese and national salvation ideas in the Nanjing area. During this period, Cao Mengjun and her friends organized several nonaligned organizations, the first of which were the Women's Society for the Promotion of Culture (Funü wenhua cujinhui, 1931) and Nanjing Women's National Salvation Society (Nanjing funü jiuguohui, 1933). As a leading member in both societies, she established working relations with progressive women in Shanghai and took part in the formation of two national groups: the China National Salvation League of Academic Bodies (Quanguo xueshu tuanti jiuguo lianhehui) and the China National Salvation Association (Quanguo gejie jiuguo hui).

During the period when the call upon the government to discontinue civil war and fight the Japanese arose the loudest among China's intelligentsia in the mid-1930s, many people were arrested for openly agitating for this cause. The most famous group, arrested in Shanghai, was dubbed "the Seven Virtuous Ones" (qijunzi), and included the woman lawyer Shi Liang (q.v.). Cao Mengjun and her friend Sun Xiaocun were arrested at about the same time, but Cao Mengjun was released in mid-1937, at the beginning of the second alliance between the KMT and the CCP.

In 1938, she went to Wuhan where, having divorced Zuo Gong, Cao Mengjun married Wang Kunlun, a fellow graduate of Peking University and a friend from her Nanjing days. She is also said to have established the National Refugee Children's Association (Zhanshi ertong baoyuhui) at the suggestion of the Yangzi River Bureau (Changjiang ju) of the CCP. With other women from Beijing, Tianjin, Nanjing, and Shanghai, Cao Mengjun gathered orphans from among the refugees, as well as children whose parents were devoting themselves to the war, to care for and educate them. In April, when Xuzhou was about to fall to the Japanese, she and her colleagues went to the front to rescue children from the war zone, risking exposure to air raids along the way. In August, Wuhan itself was threatened, and the children had to be evacuated to safer places such as Hunan and Sichuan. Cao Mengjun was with the last contingent of orphans to leave Wuhan, after arranging for others to leave first.

After arriving in Chongqing, she became director of the Geleshan Nursery and Orphanage. The children there were malnourished and undisciplined at first, but Cao Mengjun was patient and managed the school democratically. The children were taught to discuss their differences rather than fight about them. During such discussions, students elected their own chairperson, with teachers standing by to help only if needed. This way, they were taught to think for themselves, and the relationship between teachers and students was harmonious. Students were also encouraged to publish wall newspapers, organize sports events and concerts, keep chickens, build roads, and take part in other activities, which helped to improve their own lives. The orphanage became a well-known model and fostered many children into becoming useful citizens, many of them going on to other schools and receiving higher education.

During the later war years, she took over the editorship of Women's Life (Funü shenghuo) from Shen Zijiu (q.v.) and continued its development. The magazine, after publishing more than one hundred issues, was closed down by the KMT for political reasons in 1941. In order to claim a share of women's public opinion for themselves, the South China Bureau of the CCP supported Cao Mengjun's efforts to create a new magazine, Modern Women (Xiandai funü), in 1943. Publication of a magazine at that time entailed overcoming such difficulties as getting a paper quota approved by the government and submitting manuscripts for censorship. However, with the support of leftist writers such as Mao Dun, Jian Bozan, Lao She, and Xia Yan, the magazine had a good following. After the war, *Modern Women* moved to Shanghai where, despite KMT harassment, the publication continued to appear until March 1949, when it was finally banned.

Cao Mengjun's active role in the China Democratic League (Zhongguo minzhu tongmeng) and China Democratic Revolutionary League (Zhongguo minzhu geming tongmeng), both minority parties, took her to Hong Kong in 1949, but she returned to China in the early part of that year, going first to the northeast, then to Beijing. Cao Mengjun became a leader in the ACWF from its inception in March-April and occupied such important positions as vice-secretary-general and membership in the secretariat in charge of its day-to-day work. She was also elected to the CPPCC and the NPC. Perhaps more important, however, was her membership in the Standing Committee of the Chinese People's Association for Cultural Relations with Foreign Countries (Zhongguo renmin duiwai wenhua xiehui). Cao Mengjun was frequently selected to go abroad with delegations and included in receptions for foreign delegations, always those relating to the women's movement. According to one source, she went abroad on eighteen occasions, visiting sixteen different nations in Asia, Europe, and Africa. In addition to women's organizations, Cao Mengjun was engaged in the international peace movement and the Red Cross Society of China. She became ill and died in Beijing in 1967. Her husband, Wang Kunlun, was associated with the KMT Revolutionary Committee (Guomindang geming weiyuanhui), another minority party in the PRC, and the leftist faction of the KMT. He was at one time a deputy mayor of Beijing. Cao Mengjun is known to have had two daughters, the elder of whom studied foreign languages.

Although Cao Mengjun actively participated in the China Democratic League, she had probably been a covert CCP member since youth. Some sources, in fact, report that Cao Mengjun joined the CCP in 1925, when she was at Peking University, where Wang Kunlun also studied. Klein and Clark are of the opinion that Cao and Wang were both covert CCP members working outside the party for the sake of creating the appearance of the CCP's cooperation with other democratic parties. The case of Song Qingling (*q.v.*) may corroborate this view.

Lily Xiao Hong LEE

Jin Feng. *Deng Yingchao zhuan.* Beijing: Renmin chubanshe, 1993, 227.
Jingsheng and Xiquan, eds. *Xin Zhongguo mingrenlu.* Nanchang: Jiangxi renmin chubanshe, 1987, 14–15.
Klein, Donald W., and Anne B. Clark. *Biographic Dictionary of Chinese Communism, 1921–1965.* Cambridge, Mass.: Harvard University Press, 1971, 857–59.
Yingwen *Zhongguo funü*, ed. *Gujin zhuming funü renwu*, vol. 2. Shijiazhuang: Hebei renmin chubanshe, 1986, 663–69.

Cao Shuying: *see* **Cao Yi'ou**

Cao Yi'ou

Cao Yi'ou, 1903–1991, was born Cao Shuying; her native place is given in official sources as Daxing County, Hebei Province, but she claimed to be a native of Jinan, Shandong Province.

As a student at Shandong Girls' High School when the May Fourth Movement erupted in 1919, Cao Shuying was inspired by the revolutionary ideas that the movement embodied. After graduation she went to Shanghai and enrolled in Chinese literature at Shanghai University, an elite institution that had been established jointly by the CCP and the KMT in 1922 as a revolutionary training ground for professionals. Cao Shuying joined the CCP in 1926 and about the same time changed her personal name to Yi'ou, meaning "anti-Westernization." The university closed down in 1927, and at the end of that year Cao Yi'ou married Zhang Yun (1898–1975), who changed his name to Kang Sheng in 1933. He had been secretary of the CCP's Shanghai University Special Branch. This was a second marriage for both: the name of Cao Yi'ou's first husband is not known, but Kang Sheng had married Chen Yi in 1915. Kang Sheng and his first wife had a son and daughter, while Cao Yi'ou never had children of her own. She became involved in underground activities in Shanghai for a time and then in 1933 accompanied Kang Sheng to Moscow, where he acted as deputy director of the Chinese delegation to the Comintern. The couple may also have studied in Russia between 1930 and 1932.

Returning to China in 1937, Cao Yi'ou and Kang Sheng went to the communist enclave in Yan'an. He was made director of the Social and Central Intelligence Department and president of the Central Party School, eventually rising to membership in the powerful Politburo. It is not known what position Cao Yi'ou held in Yan'an. She was, however, instrumental in the marriage of Mao Zedong (1893–1976) to the former Shanghai actress Jiang Qing (*q.v.*), who was an old acquaintance and fellow provincial of Kang Sheng. With most of the party leaders against the marriage, Kang Sheng aided Jiang Qing's cause by suppressing evidence sent to his department concerning her past sexual liaisons in Shanghai. Cao Yi'ou passed on to Jiang Qing the names of those opposed to the marriage, thus providing her with information that was used to lethal effect during the Cultural Revolution.

Cao Yi'ou was appointed deputy director of the CCP's Organization Department in Shandong Province in 1949 but chose to remain at home with Kang Sheng, who was at that time "recuperating" from an illness. Rumor had it that his illness had more to do with his resentment at being appointed to provincial posts rather than being reappointed to the Central Committee.

After the communists came to power that year, Cao Yi'ou was quick to take advantage of her political connections. In 1952 she served as director of Beijing's Department of Higher Education and the following year was transferred to the Central Party School and placed in charge of training workshops. Cao Yi'ou is believed to have been responsible, directly or indirectly, for much of the turmoil in the Party School from the late 1950s to the 1960s. During the political movements of this period—which included the anti-rightist, the Great Leap Forward, and the "Don't Forget the Conflict between Classes" movements—about 80 percent of the Party School's senior scholars, researchers, and leaders were labeled "rightists" or "counter-revolutionaries." Some were expelled from the CCP, sent to labor camps, or died under torture. Yang Xianzhen (1905–1992), for example, who had been president of the Central Party School and the most authoritative Marxist theorist in China, was imprisoned for twenty years.

In 1966, when Kang Sheng was director of the Central Committee's Organization Department, deputy chair of both the CPPCC and the Standing Committee of the NPC and director of State Security, Cao Yi'ou became his office manager. The position placed her at the pinnacle of her political power as she became involved in planning and initiating the Cultural Revolution. A big-character poster entitled "Just What Are Song Shuo, Lu Ping and Peng Peiyun [Peking University leaders] up to in the Cultural Revolution?" was pasted up on a wall at Peking University on 25 May. This poster is considered to have signaled the beginning of the Cultural Revolution and was written by Nie Yuanzi (*q.v.*), a member of the Philosophy Department at Peking University and an old colleague of Cao Yi'ou from Yan'an days. The latter is generally believed to have been the force behind Nie Yuanzi, supporting her in successful efforts to foment rebellion among university and college students, which soon engulfed the country.

In April 1967, Cao Yi'ou's sister Su Mei (Cao Wenmin, 1912–1967) committed suicide. Su Mei was deputy director of the Political Department at the Beijing Cadres' College of Political Science and Law. She had lived with Cao Yi'ou and Kang Sheng since the 1930s and was widely regarded as his not-so-secret lover. Cao Yi'ou believed that her sister's suicide was the result of political persecution aimed at Kang Sheng and herself. When the doctors investigating the case and staff members of Su Mei's college would not confirm her suspicions, Cao Yi'ou had some of them arrested. Of the rest of those involved, some committed suicide while others developed psychological problems. The case was never formally resolved.

She was a member of the Ninth, Tenth, and Eleventh CCP Central Committees from 1969 to 1983 and retired in 1978 when the Cultural Revolution drew to a close. The posthumous expulsion of Kang Sheng from the CCP in 1980 is said to have unbalanced her, and Cao Yi'ou died in 1991 at the age of eighty-eight. She is considered to have been a political troublemaker with a talent for aggressive action. Yet, as a calligrapher Cao Yi'ou was rated as the best of all the wives of senior Chinese cadres; her painting and calligraphy, practiced as a means of relaxation, displayed delicacy and refinement.

Viola Hong Xin Chan WONG

Byron, John, and Robert Pack. *The Claws of the Dragon: Kang Sheng, the Evil Genius Behind Mao and His Legacy of Terror in People's China.* Taipei: China Times Publishing, 1998.
Lin Qingshan. "Hongdu nüyao—Kang Sheng 'nei zhu' Cao Yi'ou." *Da shidai wenxue*, no. 8 (1997): 16, 53–60.
Ling Yun. "Cong Kang Sheng zhizao 'Mousha Su Mei' yuan'an yinqi de lianxiang yu sikao." *Yan huang chun qiu*, no. 9 (1998): 39.
Pan Xiangchen. *Zhongguo gaogan furen dang'an.* Beijing: Beifang funü ertong chubanshe, 1998.
Xiao Chaoran and Wang Qilai, eds. *A Concise Dictionary of the Chinese Communist Party's History.* Beijing: Jiefangjun chubanshe, 1986.

Caoming

Caoming, b. 1913, in Shunde County, Guangdong Province, is a writer whose subjects are predominantly workers in China's heavy industry in the northeast. One source gives her original name as Wu Xuanwen; in addition to Caoming, she has used the pen name Chu Yaming.

Not a great deal is known about Caoming's childhood except that she and her elder brothers lived on what her mother earned by sewing. Although illiterate herself, Caoming's mother encouraged her daughter to learn to read; thus, Caoming learned needlework from her mother and how to read from her older brothers. When she did eventually go to school, Caoming excelled in language and literature. During her high school days, her favorite authors were Lu Xun and Maxim Gorky. She loved the way the latter described the lives of workers and decided to write about them, too. In 1931, Caoming took part in propaganda work against the Japanese invasion of China's north-east and began to be influenced by leftist intellectuals. She and her comrades edited and published a small magazine, writing in the local dialect about workers' hardships. For this, Caoming was blacklisted by the local KMT government and had to move to Shang-hai. She had begun writing essays and short stories before the age of twenty, but her first published work was the novella *The Fall* (Qingdie), which appeared in *Wenyi* monthly, published by the League of Leftist Writers (Zuoyi zuojia lianhehui) in 1933. The story tells how three silk workers ended up as prostitutes when traditional silk-making meth-ods were made redundant by automation introduced by foreign capitalists.

From 1932 to 1942, Caoming wrote about the trauma of workers and the disillusion-ment and bewilderment of ordinary people toward the old society. At the end of this period, more positive themes were treated, such as workers going on strike and young people seeking a brave new life in areas that, although not openly identified as such, were nevertheless communist. Her style was still clearly influenced by translations of Western literature and incorporated Western sentence structures and vocabulary. Dur-ing the early years of the Sino-Japanese War, Caoming was in Chongqing and joined the CCP in 1940. In May 1942, she was called to the communist enclave in Yan'an and heard Mao Zedong's "Talks at the Yan'an Forum on Literature and Art." She was appar-ently deeply inspired by this event, describing it as earthshaking and epochmaking, and resolved to heed his words and again dedicate herself to writing about peasants, work-ers, and soldiers. Caoming then spent some time in the villages near Yan'an, going from there to Zhangjiakou in Hebei Province. Her works from this period reflect a closer relationship with the masses as she tried to make more use of the colloquial language of the people. Some of these works are *Yan'an People* (Yan'an ren), *He Did Not Die* (Ta meiyou si), and *The New Couple* (Xin fufu).

In 1946, Caoming went to northeast China to work closely with heavy industry workers. She stayed there for eighteen years during which time some of her most important works were written. Initially sent to Jingbohu power plant in Heilongjiang Province to experience the life of workers there, Caoming, for her part, taught them to read and to sing revolutionary songs, told stories about the history of the CCP and the Long March, and organized their families to grow vegetables and raise chickens. Hearing that an old worker named Sun had helped to save the power plant from destruction at the hands of the retreating KMT, she asked him to tell his story. From this came the novel *Power* (Yuandongli), which is lauded as the first Chinese novel on the working class, and it was praised highly by famous writers such as Mao Dun and Guo Moruo. The novel tells how a worker named Sun Huaide saved a power plant, and then struggled to revive it so that dynamic power could beam out to satisfy the needs of the whole city. When she wrote *Power* (1948), Caoming's only criterion was that workers had to be able to read and understand it. Hence, the ideas in the book are straightforward, the language direct and simple. After completing her first draft, she showed it to workers who had gone only to primary school and was ecstatic when they understood.

Caoming next went, in that year, to Huanggutun Railway Works in Shenyang to help establish a CCP organization and the Youth League. While there, she witnessed how workers worked overtime to repair the engine of a train that would enable more PLA soldiers to be transferred to the south to help take over the whole country. She then wrote *The Train Engine* (Huochetou), describing the enthusiasm with which workers repair a train engine and how they learn to apply scientific experimentation to what they are doing. In this novel, revolution stands as the metaphor for the engine of history.

From the small and aging industrial establishments of early PRC days, Caoming moved in 1954 to a shining example of new China's heavy industry: Anshan Steel Works in Liaoning Province. She became deputy party secretary of the First Steel Works of Anshan. As the largest steel works in China, Anshan was the nation's pride and joy, representing as it did the most advanced technology in the country. Caoming wrote *Riding the Wind over the Waves* (Chengfeng polang), a novel in which images of lofty furnaces, gleaming streams of steel, strong blasts of air, and giant flames intertwine in a symphony of vital productivity. At this point in her career, Caoming had reached maturity in her knowledge of the industrial establishment, characterization of workers, and the control of her pen. The main conflicts portrayed in this novel remain relevant today: the conservatism and bureaucracy of management versus the creativity and progressiveness of workers and party leadership versus administrative leadership. *Riding the Wind over the Waves* quickly won wide critical acclaim.

The eighteen years spent in the northeast represent Caoming's most successful and prolific period. Aside from the three novels *Power*, *The Train Engine*, and *Riding the Wind over the Waves*, which are thought to represent the three stages of China's industrial development, she also wrote many short stories, essays, and reports. During her years in Anshan, Caoming also devoted time to teaching writing classes for workers. By the time she left, several of the participants were ready to publish poetry, stories, novellas, and novels themselves.

In 1964, Caoming left Anshan to go to Beijing to "experience life" in a machine tool factory. During the Cultural Revolution that soon descended on China, she was unable to publish anything. When one of her works, "Happiness" (Xinfgu), was finally published in *Liberation Army Literature*, the editorial staff was attacked for letting it see the light of day.

Despite a back problem, Caoming continued to write in the 1980s with the help of a clipboard. Her novel *Sons and Daughters of China* (Shenzhou ernü) published during this period was based on life in an industrial city during the Cultural Revolution. Caoming married the writer Ouyang Shan in 1931 but at some point divorced him. It is not known whether she had any children.

Lily Xiao Hong LEE

Caoming. "Caoming zizhuan." *Zhongguo xiandai zuojia zhuanlüe*, vol.1. Xuzhou: Xuzhou shifan xueyuan, 1981, 499–507.

———. *Chengfeng polang*. Beijing: Zuojia chubanshe, 1959.

———. *Duanpian xiaoshuoji*. Beijing: Zuojia chubanshe, 1957.

———. "Qianyan." In *Caoming xiaoshuo xuan*. Shanghai: Shanghai wenyi chubanshe, 1979, 1–6.

Li Liming. *Zhongguo xiandai liubai zuojia xiaozhuan*. Hong Kong: Bowen shuju, 1977, 333–34.

Yingwen *Zhongguo funü*, ed. *Gujin zhuming funü renwu*, vol. 2. Shijiazhuang: Hebei renmin chubanshe, 1986, 853–57.

Chan, Anson

Anson Chan, b. 1940, whose Chinese name is Fang Ansheng, and twin sister Ninson [Ningsheng] were born in Shanghai on the eve of the Japanese occupation of that city. Their parents gave them names meaning "peace" (Ansheng) and "tranquility" (Ningsheng), no doubt reflecting their hope for an end to war and the restoration of social order and harmony in the family. Anson Chan was Hong Kong's chief secretary in the period of transition from Bristish colonial rule to Chinese sovereignty.

China had suffered decades of upheaval and civil war as well as invasion by Japan. Peace would not finally arrive, however, until after the establishment of the PRC. During their infancy, the twin girls were somewhat protected from the violence and disturbances outside their sheltered family home, but even so their early years must have been colored by national events. Their parents must have wondered whether peace and tranquility would ever return, but eventually those golden years did come back. The forty years after 1950 were a period of relative calm during which China and Hong Kong recovered from the wounds inflicted during the first half of the century.

Anson Chan's grandfather General Fang Zhenwu was a hero in the war of resistance against Japan, and her parents were highly educated modern people. Her father, Fang Xinhao, studied at Jiaotong University in Shanghai, Manchester University in the United Kingdom, and Columbia University in the United States. Her mother, Dr. Fang Zhaolin (*q.v.*), received a traditional education at home but after marrying accompanied Fang Xinhao to Britain and also studied at Manchester University. They had eight children, closely spaced, of whom Anson and Ninson were the only girls.

Because Anson's father was deputy manager of Tianjin Postal Savings Bank, the family divided its time between Shanghai and Tianjin. Anson remembers little of her childhood in China apart from the big house in which they lived in Tianjin and that she spent most of her time playing at home with her brothers. Anson Chan and Ninson started school in Tianjin and learned English and French as well as Chinese; these studies were cut short when the family moved to Hong Kong in 1948 just before the establishment of the PRC. Once in Hong Kong, Anson began to learn Cantonese in place of French.

In 1950 her father died suddenly, but fortunately her mother had support from her mother-in-law and brother-in-law—(Professor Sir Harry Fang [Fang Xinrang], a pediatric specialist at Queen Mary Hospital in Hong Kong)—to help take care of her eight small children. The children were placed in schools in Hong Kong, Anson and Ninson studying at Saint Paul's Convent School. Fang Zhaolin then took the younger boys with her to England, where she returned to study at Cambridge University and attend to some business affairs. Anson Chan recalls that, in addition to her close relationship with her mother, she owed much of her upbringing to the strict discipline of a paternal grandmother, who ensured that the children completed their studies, and to her uncle and his family. Her mother's commitment to the study of Chinese language and literature at Cambridge and later at the University of Hong Kong inspired Anson. In later life, Fang Zhaolin took up watercolor painting and became well known as an artist in Hong Kong; her delicate paintings of landscapes and flowers and birds combine traditional Chinese techniques with Western influences.

Anson Chan worked hard at school, enjoying English, history, and music, although she retains the impression of having been a rather naughty student. At the University of Hong Kong, she studied English literature and lived in Lady Ho Tung Hall, while Ninson studied political science and lived across the road at St. John's College. Anson particularly enjoyed lectures given by Edmund Blunden, who was then on the staff of the English Department. Through the English literature course, she was introduced to the English classics, studying Chaucer, Shakespeare, Jane Austen, and Wordsworth. Anson Chan felt a great affinity with the English language and always felt comfortable reading and writing in English. She spoke Cantonese as well as Mandarin and some Shanghainese and had a tutor for Mandarin but recalls finding abbreviated characters difficult at the time because they were not in common use in Hong Kong.

During the period of British administration, Hong Kong's educational system, cultural life, and governance were dominated by the use of English and reference to British norms and historical precedent. It was in this colonial and post-colonial context that Anson Chan spent her formative years. Having reached eminence in her career during the transition to Chinese rule, she adjusted her perspective on life and is now rediscovering her Chinese roots. The path traveled by her mother, who took up the study of Chinese literature and painting in adulthood, clearly set a pattern. In 1997, the year in which Hong Kong returned to Chinese sovereignty, Anson habitually dressed in an updated version of the Chinese cheongsam to demonstrate her Chineseness. She says that her ambition is to emulate her mother and take up Chinese calligraphy at retirement.

Anson Chan met her future husband, Chan Tai Wing [Chen Tairong] (usually known as Archie Chan), at university, where he was one year ahead of her and active in the student dramatic society, taking part in performances of Shakespeare. At that time, it was compulsory for all students to participate in social services, and Archie Chan joined the Royal Hong Kong Auxiliary Police Force. He remained in the force even when service was no longer required, regarding this as his contribution to society. Archie Chan eventually rose to the post of chief officer, resigning only after Anson became chief secretary. The two married in 1963, shortly after her graduation from university.

Spending university holidays coaching English in order to earn pocket money, Anson Chan was also responsible for assisting her younger brothers with their homework. After graduation she was assisted by her uncle, Harry Fang, in obtaining a job as almoner at Queen Mary Hospital. Finding contact with patients and their families rewarding, Anson Chan considered a career in social work but in 1962 started working with the influential Hong Kong orphanage and social welfare organization Baoliangju (Po Leung Kuk) and undertook a number of other welfare activities. Soon, however, the young woman won a position as a cadet officer with the Hong Kong government. Anson

Chan acknowledges that had her original plan of becoming a social worker been followed, she would not have had the opportunity to extend her influence as widely as she has done in many social welfare and related fields.

Traditionally, the Hong Kong civil service system trained officers to work in as many departments as possible in order to broaden talents and provide greater perspective on the work. Anson Chan's first job was in Economic Services within the Department of Finance, and she was later moved to Agriculture and Fisheries, Trade and Commerce, and New Territories Administration. Anson Chan spent a relatively longer period as head of the Department of Social Welfare (from 1984 to 1987), afterward receiving a promotion, becoming the first Chinese woman policy secretary in charge of Economic Services. Anson Chan feels that her greatest achievements have been in these two posts, one concerned with policy development, the other with social commitment.

As secretary for social welfare in the late 1970s, Anson Chan came to understand the basic concerns of the disadvantaged, sick, and elderly and, within the government's limited resources, had the opportunity to relieve a degree of pain and suffering. The department maintained a fairly large staff, and she was also able to mentor the career development of more junior officers, believing it important to groom successors and develop potential by helping colleagues identify their weaknesses and strengths. Committed to equality for working women and the protection of children from abuse, Anson Chan also tried to spend as much time as possible in the field in order to understand the problems of ordinary citizens. During the 1980s, the department's responsibilities included welfare provisions for the aged and the handicapped, early childhood education, care of orphans, rehabilitation of prisoners, and youth activities. The position of children was then quite vulnerable and child abuse of major concern, so Anson Chan gave priority to instituting proper procedures for child adoption. She was particularly concerned to ensure that there were support procedures for families to care for handicapped children at home so that they could enjoy as normal a family life as possible. Despite her high-minded intentions, Anson Chan's performance came under press scrutiny in 1986 when Welfare Department staff forcibly removed a child from the home of a mentally ill client. Anson did not handle the press skillfully on this occasion, possibly through inexperience, and the press generally attributed her apparent later aversion to publicity to this episode.

While Anson Chan found her unsolicited promotion to secretary of Economic Services pleasing, it was also a very taxing position. For the first time, she had to deal directly with powerful chief executives of major corporations and balance many vested interests in the private sector. The portfolio covered the whole of Hong Kong's infrastructure and was challenging, albeit ultimately satisfying. Anson Chan is most proud of the work done to promote liberalization of the telecommunications market. She says this helped position Hong Kong for development into the twenty-first century. Anson Chan believes that Hong Kong will continue to liberalize its economic structure now that it is a Special Administrative Region (SAR).

Exemplifying many of the characteristics of the perfect public servant, Anson Chan is quick and adaptable, clear thinking, and able to express herself forcefully. She absorbs new knowledge quickly and is dependable and loyal and also understands the limits placed on her authority by the prevailing political and social environment. These abilities, noted by successive chief secretaries and governors, were the reason for her promotion. From April 1980 until May 1984, Anson Chan chaired the Association of Female Senior Government Officers and encouraged the career development of women in government. While gender parity in civil service pay had existed since 1975, a number of gender differences remained, and this association played a leading role in the fight for equal treatment for male and female officers. The association achieved its goal in 1981 when the government brought in a policy of equity in eligibility for fringe benefits, regardless of gender.

In 1984 she was one of six senior civil servants invited by the Chinese government to Beijing to attend ceremonies marking agreement between Britain and China regarding the terms of the handover of Hong Kong. In 1993 Anson Chan played a key role during the crucial handover period after being appointed chief secretary and was able to make the difficult psychological transition from British administration to Chinese rule. Some vignettes will provide an insight into this period. In July 1995, when relations between the British and Chinese governments reached a nadir over arrangements for the handover, she led a secret mission to Beijing to meet the foreign minister Qian Qichen and the director of the Hong Kong and Macau Affairs Office Lu Ping. Although telling the Legislative Council before her departure that this meeting was to be a simple getting-to-know-you exercise and there would be no secret deals, it was in fact an important diplomatic breakthrough. When talks finally broke down, Anson Chan defended the authority and credibility of Hong Kong's Legislative Council against the Chinese decision of March 1996 to establish a provisional legislature. She also defended civil servants against Beijing's threat to disown any who refused to support this provisional body and invited Lu Ping to discuss with her on his next visit to Hong Kong the question of civil service loyalty and other issues.

Anson Chan had enjoyed a good relationship with the last British governor of Hong Kong, Christopher Patten. The first chief executive of the new Hong Kong SAR, Tung Chee Hwa [Dong Jianhua] (or C.H. Tung), persuaded her to remain as chief secretary after the handover, a decision welcomed by the civil service as an assurance of the stability of future administrative policy. But according to one authority, Anson Chan did not initially enjoy as cordial a relationship with Tung Chee Hwa as she had with Patten, being excluded from the decision-making process. By late 1997, however, Anson Chan was able to tell the author in an interview that those difficulties were behind her and now reveled in the challenges of Hong Kong's new era.

Immediately following the handover in 1997, a series of crises beset the Hong Kong government: start-up problems with the commissioning of the new Chek Lap Kok airport, an outbreak of avian flu, administrative mistakes in the public hospital system, continuing environmental problems with air and water quality, attacks by international speculators on the peg between the Hong Kong and US dollars, and, most seriously, fluidity problems resulting from the Asian financial crisis. The common thread in these matters was lack of coordination between various government departments and failure of leadership on the part of senior public servants. Tung Chee Hwa's style was less hands-on than his British predecessors. Anson Chan therefore had to assume leadership of the civil service team, and the outcome revealed both shortcomings in her leadership style as well as difficulties in the transitional political situation.

Early in 2001, Anson announced her retirement for personal reasons. Press speculation centered on personality and policy differences with Tung Chee Hwa, probably sparked by her approval of the use of a government-controlled venue for a meeting of the Falungong religious sect that had been banned in China. On 19 April, Anson gave a last speech in which she restated her views on Hong Kong, stressing the importance of personal and institutional values as guiding principles that "must endure and survive every fad or fashion and paradigm shift that comes our way." In the case of Hong Kong, these values were embodied in the rule of law and personal liberty. She declared her commitment to the notion of a politically neutral civil service and also reminded her audience that Hong Kong's Basic Law provided a timetable for development of full democracy. The latter remark clearly distinguished her position on the subject from that of Tung Chee Hwa, who has avoided comment on when and how the electoral system might be modified. Anson Chan said that Hong Kong was a great international city and "not just another city in China," because the values and institutions in Hong Kong were different.

Her career raises the question as to whether these values and institutions can prevail against those of Beijing.

Jocelyn CHEY

Chan, Anson. Personal communication. Hong Kong, October 1997.
Chan, Mimi. Citation, 151st Congregation, University of Hong Kong, 1996.
Dimbleby, Jonathan. *The Last Governor*. London: Little, Brown, 1998.
Patten, Chris. *East and West*. London: MacMillan, 1998.

Chang Ai-ling: *see* **Chang, Eileen**

Chang, C.H.: *see* **Lu Shijia**

Chang, C.S. Wang: *see* **Wang Chengshu**

Chang, Eileen
Eileen Chang [Zhang Ailing], 1920–1995, childhood name Ying, pen name Liang Jing (used only in 1950–52), married name Eileen Chang Reyher, was born in Shanghai but spent her early childhood in Tianjin. When she was seven years old, her family moved back to Shanghai. Eileen finished high school there, then attended the University of Hong Kong. Immediately after returning to Shanghai in 1942, she established a reputation as a talented writer of fiction and essays.

Eileen Chang left China in 1952 because of changes in the political climate, living in Hong Kong for a few years before emigrating to the United States in 1955. She met her husband, Ferdinand Reyher (1891–1967), in New Hampshire, but their main residences were in San Francisco and Washington, D.C. After Reyher's death in 1967, the writer lived first in Berkeley and then in Los Angeles.

In appearance, Eileen Chang was tall and slender, with a delicate, striking beauty accentuated with clothing that she had designed herself. This instinctive sense of style is evident throughout her oeuvre, which includes short stories, novels, essays, screenplays, translations, and textual annotations. Still, her fame mainly rests on the sensitive, incisive short stories she wrote in Shanghai in the mid-1940s, stories filled with her distinctive quality of *cangliang* (desolate) beauty. Eileen Chang is particularly admired for skillfully blending Chinese and Western narrative techniques (one of her earliest editors, Zhou Shoujuan, remarked that her style reminded him of both *Honglou meng* [Dream of the Red Chamber] and Somerset Maugham). Despite the fact that her career was greatly curtailed by changes in the political climate, Eileen Chang's work resonated deeply throughout the Chinese-speaking world. For many readers and critics, she is, as C.T. Hsia claimed, "the best and most important writer" in mid-twentieth-century China.

Eileen Chang was born into a once-influential family that, after the fall of the Qing dynasty, lost much of its status and wealth. One of her paternal great-grandfathers was the renowned Li Hongzhang (1823–1901), governor of Jiangsu and other provinces and principal architect of the self-strengthening movement that shored up the Qing dynasty in its final years. Her paternal grandfather, Zhang Peilun (1847–1903), was also an official in the Qing court but his political career was less illustrious than his famous father-in-law's and he is often remembered instead for his role in a romantic anecdote that is included in the late Qing roman à clef *Flowers in a Sinful Sea* (Nie hai hua). Her father, Zhang Tingzhong (1896–1953), was well educated in the traditional manner and had read at least some Western literature but never established a career for himself. Zhang Tingzhong appears in Eileen Chang's early autobiographical essays as a decadent family despot but also as the bearer of a vanishing cultural tradition.

Eileen Chang's mother, Huang Yifan (1896–1957), also came from an elite family (from Hunan) but, influenced by the May Fourth cultural trend of the late 1910s, lived her life in increasingly open rebellion against traditional values and decorum. Not surprisingly, given Zhang Tingzhong's conservative ways, their marriage was not happy, although his wife did receive crucial support and encouragement from her sister-in-law Zhang Maoyuan (Zhang Tingzhong's younger sister). When Eileen Chang was about three years old and her brother Zijing still an infant, Huang Yifan endured a tearful parting from her two children and went to Europe on a lengthy sojourn. The concubine that Zhang Tingzhong had kept in a separate residence then moved in with the family; the woman was sometimes generous toward the children but eventually, because of an explosive temper, was sent packing. The family reunited in Shanghai when Eileen Chang was about seven years old, Huang Yifan having returned to nurse her husband, who had overdosed on morphine. She also saw to her daughter's education, and Eileen Chang had lessons in English, art, and piano. This period of domestic harmony was soon destroyed, however, by marital discord. After a series of painful struggles, Huang Yifan obtained a divorce. She then went to France to study art, not returning to Shanghai until 1937. Zhang Tingzhong remarried, this time choosing a woman who shared his opium habit.

In the same year, shortly after graduating from St. Mary's Girls' School, Eileen Chang directly conflicted with her father and stepmother. He beat his daughter, imprisoned her in her room, and denied medical treatment even though she fell seriously ill.

Finally, with a servant's help, Eileen Chang managed to escape to her mother's apartment. Although her mother's home offered physical safety, Eileen Chang was still tormented by an adolescent's sense of insecurity and feared becoming a burden. These traumatic events informed the dramatic center of her early memoir "Whispered Words" (Siyu) and seem to have directly contributed to the tone of penetrating pessimism that so stirs and disturbs readers of her early work.

In 1939 she entered Hong Kong University as an English major and was an excellent student, winning scholarships that improved her finances but did little to increase her confidence, surrounded as she was by much wealthier classmates. Eileen Chang did form a close friendship with Fatima Mohideen (also called Yan Ying), a bold, lively young woman whose mother was from Tianjin and whose father, a Sri Lankan of Arab ancestry, had established a business in Shanghai. Fatima's and Eileen's studies abruptly halted, however, when the Japanese invaded Hong Kong in 1941. Later, in numerous stories and essays, the writer made highly effective use of the colorful colonial Hong Kong milieu and the catastrophe by which it was disrupted.

In 1942, when Eileen returned to Shanghai, that city too was Japanese-occupied but an air of hushed calm prevailed. She moved into her aunt's apartment and began to write and publish rapidly, averaging one essay and one story (or story installment) per month for about eighteen months. At first the writer wrote essays in English and fiction in Chinese, but the public and critical response from Chinese readers was so favorable that she soon stopped writing for the much smaller English-language market. In 1944, the first edition of her collected stories, entitled *Romances* (Chuanqi), sold out almost immediately, and in early 1945 her story of wartime romance in Hong Kong, *Love in a Fallen City* (Qingcheng zhi lian), was produced for the stage. At the age of twenty-five, Eileen Chang was a literary sensation. Although the political uncertainties of the time meant that any kind of public prominence could be dangerous, she exulted in the success, redoubling her efforts. Her first essay collection, *Liuyan* (the meaning of this title for the purposes of translation is unclear), was published that year, and two years later Eileen Chang released the revised edition of *Romances*. By late 1947 she was also writing screenplays (*Unsuccessful Love* [Bu liao qing] and *Long Live the Missus* [Taitai wansui]) that were well received.

During this period, in mid-1944, Eileen Chang and Hu Lancheng (1906–1981) secretly made a common-law marriage agreement, witnessed only by Fatima Mohideen. Hu Lancheng was a minor figure in the world of letters, an ardent admirer of Eileen Chang's writing and, briefly, an official in the collaborationist regime the Japanese had installed in Nanjing. He launched a short-lived literary magazine, *Bitter Bamboo* (Ku zhu), featuring her work and also used his influence to help free Ke Ling, Eileen Chang's friend and editor at *Wanxiang*, when Ke was imprisoned by the Japanese. Eileen Chang's fiction deepened and matured during this time, as can be seen in "A-Xiao's Autumn Lament" (Guihuazheng A-Xiao beiqiu) and "Lingering Love" (Liuqing). By his account, theirs was a union of two free and happy equals who kept separate residences but saw each other a few days each month. (Apparently, the exact nature of their relationship was kept secret in order to shield Eileen Chang from political reprisals.) She, for her part, was very much in love with Hu Lancheng and hoped for a lifelong relationship with him. He, however, was unwilling to give up his ties with other women (Hu had two mistresses during their marriage), and their relationship became increasingly fraught. Nonetheless, Eileen supported him financially while he was in hiding from the KMT after the war. In 1947, when Hu Lancheng seemed to have gained a modicum of security, she broke off the marriage. After the communist victory, he left China and eventually settled in Japan.

Eileen Chang remained in Shanghai during the initial transition to communist rule, publishing two serialized novels, *Eighteen Springs* (Shiba chun) and *Little Ai* (Xiao Ai), that conformed to the political climate by offering happy endings. She later revised *Eighteen Springs* under the title *Half a Lifetime's Romance* (Bansheng yuan) and gave it a sadder but more consistent conclusion. By 1952, however, she realized that her prospects under the new regime were not promising. She entered Hong Kong with little difficulty, but life there was lonely and difficult. Eileen Chang translated American authors (Ernest Hemingway, Washington Irving, and Ralph Waldo Emerson) for the United States Information Agency but had little enthusiasm for the task. Still, it was through this work that she met Stephen and Mae Soong, literary people with whom Eileen developed a lifelong friendship, and Richard McCarthy, the U.S. consular official who sponsored her visa to the United States. Before leaving Hong Kong, Eileen Chang published two novels offering a critical view of life in communist China: *The Rice Sprout Song* (Yangge) and *The Naked Earth* (Chidi zhi lian). Neither work, however, did much to revive her fame, which had tumbled precipitously in the rapidly changing political and cultural climate.

She spent her first few months in America in New York City, living in a spartan hostel run by the Salvation Army. Eileen Chang was cheered by the consideration shown her by the famous May Fourth intellectual Hu Shi (1891–1962), who praised her work, and by a reunion with Fatima Mohideen. In 1956 Eileen Chang obtained a fellowship at the MacDowell Colony, an artists' retreat in New Hampshire, and lived there for the better part of a year during which time she met and married fellow writer Ferdinand Reyher. Reyher, the son of German immigrants, was born in Philadelphia but had pursued a writing career in Europe, New York, and Hollywood. In 1917 he had married Rebecca Hourwich and they had a daughter, Faith, though eventually the marriage ended in an amicable divorce. Reyher was generous, well liked, and enjoyed a wide circle of acquaintances in the literary world. In the mid-1930s, he became a Marxist (although he did not join the Communist Party) and in later years was best known for his role in introducing Bertold Brecht to American audiences in the 1930s and 1940s. By the time Reyher met Eileen Chang, he was sixty-six years old (she was thirty-six), and both his health and career were in decline. Nonetheless, the two provided each other with valuable emotional and practical support throughout their marriage, which lasted until his death.

Eileen Chang's married life was comforting in many ways but entailed considerable travail. She and Reyher moved to the Huntington Hartford Foundation (another artists' colony) in Los Angeles in 1958 and to San Francisco the following year. In 1959, Eileen Chang became a naturalized American citizen. Throughout this period, she tried to write fiction that would appeal to American readers, but her manuscripts were repeatedly turned down by publishers. Disappointed though Eileen Chang was, she had little choice but to plunge into the writing of screenplays for the film market in Hong Kong—a fairly steady source of income, though not conducive to artistic endeavor—in order to support herself and her husband. In 1961 the writer traveled to Taiwan and Hong Kong to gather material, renew contacts in Hong Kong, and work on screenplays there. The trip lasted six months. In Taiwan Eileen Chang was accorded a warm reception by Richard McCarthy, now stationed in Taipei, and also by many of the island's most promising young writers, including Bai Xianyong, Chen Ruoxi (*q.v.*), and Wang Zhenhe. Her tour of Taiwan was cut short by the news that Reyher had suffered a serious stroke, but for financial reasons Eileen could not return to him immediately. Fortunately, her husband's daughter Faith was able to help, and he was admitted to a hospital near her home in Washington, D.C. Eileen went on to Hong Kong, where she could improve their finances by writing screenplays. This was accomplished despite many hardships and difficulties. As always, Stephen and Mae Soong offered encouragement and practical help. In spring 1962, Eileen returned to live with Reyher in Washington, D.C., renting a small apartment not far from the Library of Congress, where he spent a few hours each day. Over the next four years, his health deteriorated and, for reasons entirely beyond her control, she lost the connections that had enabled her to sell screenplays in Hong Kong. In 1966, Eileen Chang obtained a position as resident writer at Miami University in Oxford, Ohio, but the university was disappointed to find that the writer, always reclusive and now busy with the care of a very ill husband, did not participate in seminars or social gatherings. In 1967, she took up a fellowship at Radcliffe College in Cambridge, Massachusetts. Reyher died in October that year.

As Eileen Chang adjusted to her new life as a widow, two trends emerged with particular force. Her reputation as a literary artist began to rise again, especially in Taiwan, where the large and popular publisher Crown was reissuing her work thanks to the tireless efforts of Stephen Soong and the high praise bestowed on her by C.T. Hsia in his influential *A History of Modern Chinese Fiction*. But the greater her fame grew, the more deeply she retreated into seclusion. Eileen Chang received very few visitors and generally corresponded only with a few old friends. In 1969, she accepted an offer for a position as a senior researcher at the Center of Chinese Studies at the University of California in Berkeley. However, the staff at the center rarely saw her because of the writer's well-established habit of working at night.

By 1972 income from royalties finally reached the point of allowing the author a measure of financial independence. Moving to Los Angeles, Eileen Chang spent her remaining twenty-five years in nearly total isolation from anyone who knew her as a writer, even though she never stopped writing. Eileen Chang published her second collection of essays, *As Zhang Sees It* (Zhang kan); a textual study of *The Dream of the Red Chamber*; an annotated Mandarin version of the late-Qing novel *Flowers of Shanghai* (*Lives of Shanghai Beauties* [Haishanghua liezhuan]); and four other compilations of new, revised, or reissued works. In 1991, Crown issued the definitive edition of her collected works; eventually the collection came to sixteen volumes. In 1994, Eileen Chang completed her last book, an annotated album of personal photographs, filled with amusing observations and wry anecdotes. By this time, most of her major stories had been adapted for the screen. She also worked on a novel based on the life of Zhang Xueliang, the "Young Marshall" who had been Chiang Kai-shek's captor in the Xi'an Incident of December 1936.

In the last decade of her life, Eileen Chang was afflicted with various physical ailments and tended to neglect her health. In the mid-1980s, her apartment became infested with fleas, which aggravated her already delicate skin. She chose to move out altogether, and for about four years lived in a series of motel rooms in the Los Angeles area. Eventually her skin inflammation was cured, and she moved back into an apartment. Her style of life, which had always been simple, became almost monastic, and to some observers at least she seemed to have attained a transcendent purity. When word of her death reached Taiwan in September 1995, it was front-page news, but Eileen Chang had asked that no services be held. Her ashes were scattered in a simple ceremony, and her belongings were entrusted to her lifelong friends the Soongs.

Literary fortunes rise and wane, but it seems unlikely that Eileen Chang will again suffer the kind of eclipse that befell her in the middle decades of her life, when censors kept her work off the market in mainland China and the market for literature in Hong Kong and Taiwan was in a relatively early stage of development. By the time of death, Eileen's reputation as a major literary figure had been firmly established, and her writing had become an important influence for many younger Chinese writers, especially those striving for the kind of deep, rich style that she had achieved, with seemingly preternatural power, early in her writing career. After all, there is little doubt that Eileen Chang was an unusually gifted writer. According to Hu Lancheng, the writer never felt any difficulty in transforming her thoughts into written words. In her first published essay, "Dream of Genius" (Tiancai meng), Eileen Chang frankly asserted that she had always been regarded as a person of unusual literary talent. What these early prognostications cannot show, however, is the lifetime of effort she devoted to her art, often amid poverty and hardship. In the end, more impressive than mere talent is the tenacity with which Eileen Chang dedicated herself to writing, whatever the current state of her literary fame.

Karen KINGSBURY

Cai Fengyi [Ts'ai Feng-i], ed. *Huali yu cangliang: Zhang Ailing jinian wenji.* Taipei: Huangguan, 1996.

Chang, Ai-ling [Chang, Eileen]. *Zhang Ailing quanji,* 16 vols. Taipei: Huangguan, 1991–1994.

Chang, Eileen. *The Rice Sprout Song* (1955). Berkeley and Los Angeles: University of California Press, 1998.

———. *The Rouge of the North* (1967). Berkeley and Los Angeles: University of California Press, 1998.

———. "International Shanghai, 1941: Coffee House Chat about Sexual Intimacy and the Childlike Charm of the Japanese." In *Modern Chinese Writers' Self-Portrayals,* eds. Helmut Martin and Jeffrey C. Kinkley. London: M.E. Sharpe, 1992, 295–301.

———. "Sealed Off," trans. Karen Kingsbury. In *The Columbia Anthology of Modern Chinese Literature,* eds. Joseph S.M. Lau and Howard Goldblatt. New York: Columbia University Press, 1995, 188–97.

———, trans. "The Golden Cangue." In *Modern Chinese Stories and Novellas: 1919–1949,* eds.

Joseph S.M. Lau, C.T. Hsia, and Leo Ou-Fan Lee. New York: Columbia University Press, 1981, 530–59.

Chen Bingliang [Ch'en Ping-liang]. *Zhang Ailing duanpian xiaoshuo lunji.* Taipei: Yuanjing, 1985.

Chen Zishan, ed. *Siyu Zhang Ailing.* Hangzhou: Zhejiang wenyi chubanshe, 1996.

Chow, Rey. *Woman and Chinese Modernity: The Politics of Reading between East and West.* Theory and History of Literature 75. Minneapolis: University of Minnesota Press, 1991.

"Eileen Chang." *Renditions: A Chinese-English Translation Magazine,* special issue, no. 45 (1996). Includes translations of essays and fiction as well as recent literary criticism.

Feng Zutai. *Bainian jiazu: Zhang Ailing.* Xindian: Lixu wenhua, 1999.

Gunn, Edward M. *Unwelcome Muse: Chinese Literature in Shanghai and Peking 1937–1945.* New York: Columbia University Press, 1980.

Hsia, C.T. *A History of Modern Chinese Fiction.* New Haven: Yale University Press, 2nd ed., 1971.

Hu Lancheng [Hu Lan-ch'eng]. *Jinsheng jinshi.* Taipei: Yuanxing, 1976.

Hu Xing [Hu Hsing]. *Zuihou de guizu: Zhang Ailing.* Taipei: Guoji cun, 1995.

Lu Zhengheng [Lu Cheng-heng]. *Zhang Ailing xiaoshuo de shidaigan.* Taipei: Maitian, 1994.

Shui Jing [Shui Ching]. *Zhang Ailing de xiaoshuo yishu.* Taipei: Dadi, 1976.

———. *Zhang Ailing wei wan: Jiedu Zhang Ailing de zuopin.* Taipei: Dadi, 1996.

Sima Xin [Ssu-ma Hsin]. *Zhang Ailing yu Laiya,* trans. Xusi [Hsü-ssu] and Sima Xin [Ssu-ma Hsin]. Taipei: Dadi, 1996.

Song Mingwei [Sung Ming-wei]. *Zhang Ailing zhuan.* Zhongguo wenhua mingren zhuangji 27. Taipei: Yeqiang, 1996.

Wang Dewei [Wang Te-wei]. *Zhongsheng xuanhua.* Taipei: Yuanliu, 1988.

Yang Ze [Yang Tse], ed. *Yuedu Zhang Ailing: Guoji yantaohui lunwenji.* Taipei: Maitian chubanshe, 1999.

Yu Bin [Yü Pin]. *Zhang Ailing zhuan.* Taipei: Chenxing, 1998.

Yu Qing [Yü Ch'ing]. *Zhang Ailing zhuan.* Taipei: Shijie shuju, 1993.

Zheng Shusen [Cheng Shu-sen], ed. *Zhang Ailing de shijie.* Taipei: Yunchen wenhua, 1989.

Zhou Fenling [Chou Fen-ling]. *Yanyi: Zhang Ailing yu Zhongguo wenxue.* Taipei: Yuanzun wenhua, 1999.

Chang Hsiu-Chen: *see* **Lu Shijia**

Chang Hsui-Chen: *see* **Lu Shijia**

Chao Fuhuan: *see* **Zhong Yuzheng**

Chao Mo-ya

Chao Mo-ya [Zhao Moya], b. 1915, in Lin-ch'ing [Linqing] County, Shantung [Shandong] Province, is known for her work in the field of fingerprint identification and was the highest-ranking woman in the Taiwan police force when she retired in 1980.

Chao Mo-ya's father had been a teacher of the last emperor of the Ch'ing dynasty (Hsüan-t'ung, r. 1909–12) and opposed her joining the police force. She defied the wishes of her family, however, and enrolled at Che-chiang [Zhejiang] Police Academy (Che-chiang ching-kuan hsüeh-hsiao), specializing in what was then the little known field of fingerprint identification. After graduating in 1936, Chao Mo-ya was assigned to the fingerprint laboratory in the Capital Police Bureau (Shou-tu ching-ch'a-t'ing) in

Nan-ching [Nanjing]. During the Sino-Japanese War, she worked in the crime laboratory in the city of Ch'ung-ch'ing [Chongqing]. After the war, Chao Mo-ya was appointed to teach fingerprint studies in the Special Police Training Program of the Central Police Academy (Chung-yang ching-kuan hsüeh-hsiao). She later returned to the Capital Police Bureau as head of the fingerprint room of the Criminal Identification Department.

During the hotly contested presidential campaign of 1946, the home of one of the candidates, Li Tsung-jen, was robbed. Such were the political implications of this crime that the police were given a deadline to solve the case. Working through the night, Chao Mo-ya took fingerprints and identified them, leading to the apprehension of the culprits within four hours. This remarkable achievement won her the epithet "a female Sherlock Holmes."

At the height of her reputation, in 1948, Chao Mo-ya left the field of criminal investigation to teach at the Central Police College. After retreating to Taiwan with the KMT government, she taught fingerprint studies at the Taiwan Police School, returning to the Central Police College when it was reestablished in Taiwan. Chao Mo-ya was involved in police education for more than thirty years. She was responsible for collating and systematizing a great deal of material on fingerprint studies in Taiwan during the pioneering stages of the field, as well as writing instruction material. Chao Mo-ya devoted her life to fingerprint analysis and related academic studies, one of her great contributions being on differentiating the fingerprints of identical twins.

When she retired from the Central Police College as a two-star, three-stripe officer in 1980, Chao Mo-ya was the highest-ranking woman in the police force. She was also known as the "queen of Taiwan fingerprint studies." Furthermore, the officer was the first person from Taiwan to participate in international fingerprint studies. In 1980, the International Fingerprint Society published in their magazine a story about the life and work of Chao Mo-ya, acknowledging her international importance as a fingerprint specialist.

CH'EN Ch'un-ying
(Translated by Lily Xiao Hong Lee and Sue Wiles)

Chang P'ing-i. "Taiwan chih-wen-hsüeh chih hou, Chao Mo-ya ti ku-shih." *Chung-kuo shih-pao*, 29 June 1992, 17.
"Chao Mo-ya chiao-kuan jung-ying shih-chieh-feng-yün jen-wu." *Chung-ching*, no. 336 (December 1980): 2.
Yü Chao. "Chung keng fang-chieh shu-nü-shih." *Ching-ch'a chih yu*, 33, no. 9 (September 1980): 21.

Chee, Irene Kwong: *see* **Moss, Irene**

Ch'en Ai-chu
Ch'en Ai-chu [Chen Aizhu], b. 1914, in Yi Lan County, Taiwan, actively took part in her local society, particularly in the care and education of children.

Considered clever from childhood, she graduated with top marks in 1932 from Taipei

Third Girls' Senior High School (Taipei ti-san kao-teng nü-hsüeh-hsiao) and then taught at Yi Lan Girls' Public School, Taipei City Jih-hsin Public School, and Lo-tung Girls' Public School. In 1942, Ch'en Ai-chu married Wu Ta-hai [Wu Dahai], a colleague from Yi Lan Girls' Public School, and she immediately resigned from her teaching post to concentrate on bringing up her deceased brother's five children. During that time, Ch'en Ai-chu and her colleagues set up the Yi Lan Young Women's Organization (I-lan nü-tzu ch'ing-nien t'uan) to teach handicrafts and Japanese to local women. With the end of Japanese colonial rule in 1945, she started a career in kindergarten education and then received an appointment as director of Lo-tung County Child Care Center. It had been established at the suggestion of Ms. Ch'en-Shih Man (*q.v.*). Perceiving the need to provide educational opportunities to the community, Ch'en Ai-chu established social education organizations for such activities as dancing, choral groups, music, and flower arrangement. Her dedication to the cultural activities of Lo-tung was lauded, and she was frequently awarded the title "Contributor to Social Education."

Ch'en Ai-chu's social conscience led her to assume responsibility as chair of Lo-tung County Women's Association in 1951. Because mediation committees had not yet been established in villages, the major task of the women's association was to mediate family disputes. In 1964, she stood for Parliament and was elected to the Sixth Session of Yi Lan County. Her move into local politics did not lessen her interest in early childhood education, and in 1969 Ch'en Ai-chu established the Yi Lan County Early Childhood Education Committee. Its task was to facilitate on-the-job training and education exchange for early childhood educators in order to standardize the education of young children. She was dedicated to her work and has always been a role model for career women in Taiwan.

Ch'en Ai-chu did not neglect the education of her own children, all four making outstanding contributions in their chosen fields.

HO Shu-i
(Translated by George Li)

Yu Chien-ming. "Ch'en Ai-chu." In *Tsou-kuo liang ko shih-tai ti Taiwan chih-yeh fu-nü fang-wen chi-lu*. Taipei: Chung-yang yen-chiu-yüan. Chin-tai-shih yen-chiu-so, 1994.

Chen Aizhu: *see* **Ch'en Ai-chu**

Chen Bijun
Chen Bijun, 1891–1959, was born in the town of Tai Ping, Malaya (part of present-day Malaysia), as Chen Bingru; her baby name was Huan. Although born in Malaya, her ancestral place was Xinhui County, Guangdong Province, and when Chen Bijun was still very young her family moved to George Town on Penang.

Her father, Chen Gengji, had left Xinhui as a young man to find work on a rubber plantation in Malaya. He also worked in a tin mine and later formed his own rubber and mining business, eventually becoming famous as "Chen, the Millionaire." Chen Bijun's mother, Wei Yuelang, came from a farming family in Panyu County, Guangdong Province, but was educated and enlightened in her thinking. After marrying, she accompanied her new husband to Malaya and became a capable housewife. Chen Bijun was the second child: she had an elder brother, two younger brothers—Chen Yaozu and Chen Changzu—and a younger sister, Chen Shujun.

As a child, Chen Bijun studied in a local Catholic school known as Mama Tang; English was among the subjects she learned. Her father retained a deep emotional attachment to his native land and in order to instill Chinese cultural tradition in his overseas-born children employed an old teacher from China to tutor them after school in Chinese language, the classics, and history. This sound training in Chinese in her early years gave Chen Bijun a firm foundation that later enabled her to help her husband, Wang Jingwei (1883–1944), draft various documents.

In early November 1907, Sun Yat-sen (1866–1925), Hu Hanmin, and Wang Jingwei traveled from Japan to Penang to promote and expand their anti-Qing Tongmenghui. Chen Bijun was sixteen years old at the time and enrolled at Biru Girls' School. She became very interested in the visiting revolutionaries' democratic ideas and their slogan "Expel the Manchus, Restore Han Rule" and set aside her studies to attend all of their talks. Chen Bijun was also, however, attracted to the elegant and eloquent Wang Jingwei, who was then twenty-four years old, and secretly joined the Tongmenghui, thus becoming its youngest female member. Her father was very angry when he found out, believing that girls should behave circumspectly, not show their faces in public, and most of all not join a revolutionary party that might bring misfortune to the family. Her mother was supportive, however, and in summer 1908 accompanied Chen Bijun to Singapore to meet Sun Yat-sen. Convinced by him of the need for revolution to overthrow the Manchu government, Chen Bijun's mother also joined the Tongmenghui.

Chen Bijun had been engaged to her cousin Liang Yugao with whom she had grown up and got along very well. However, after falling in love with Wang Jingwei, Chen Bijun told her parents to break off the engagement because she would marry no one but Wang Jingwei. Her father refused to allow a marriage to "such a desperado" and her mother was unable to oppose him in this, even though she sympathized with her daughter. Knowing that in reality he was unable to stop her, Chen Bijun's father decided to remove her from temptation by sending her to study in England. Chen Bijun countered that England was too far away should family matters require her speedy return and proposed study in Japan as a compromise. She was supported in this by her mother and left for Japan in spring 1909.

There, Chen Bijun joined the assassination group formed by Wang Jingwei, Huang Fusheng, Yu Peilun, Li Zhongshi, Zeng Xing, and Fang Junying (see *Biographical Dictionary of Chinese Women: The Qing Period*). She did this out of love for Wang Jingwei to whom she wrote, proposing marriage. Wang gracefully declined her proposal by return mail and maintained a distance from the plain and forceful Chen, treating her merely as one of his "revolutionary comrades." Her unrequited love remained just that until a quite separate heroic revolutionary act occurred, which shocked both the government and the public and brought about her marriage to Wang Jingwei.

In March 1910, members of the assassination group gathered in Beijing, planning to kill Prince Regent Chun with a bomb. Wang Jingwei and Huang Fusheng were arrested when the plot was exposed, and Wang was sentenced to life imprisonment. Chen Bijun fled Beijing and returned with her companions to Southeast Asia via Japan to devise a rescue plan with Hu Hanmin. Chen Bijun then went home to Penang, and raised a considerable sum of money for the cause: her father had just died and her mother gave her the family fortune. Her father's third concubine also contributed a substantial amount. Risking exposure, Chen Bijun returned secretly to Beijing with Zeng Xing that winter and bribed a prison guard, asking him to smuggle a letter to Wang Jingwei. Wang, his life in the balance, was extremely touched to receive Chen's letter and composed a poem to the tune "Jinglüqu," indicating his acceptance of her love.

When the Guangzhou Uprising (the Battle of Yellow Flower Mound [Honghua gang]) broke out on 27 April 1911, she immediately set out from Hong Kong with Hu Hanmin, Li Zhongshi, and Zeng Xing. Arriving after the uprising had failed, they were fortunate to escape unharmed. Their hopes were finally realized, however, when the revolution that began in Wuchang on 10 October succeeded in overthrowing the Manchu Qing dynasty. Wang Jingwei was released from prison on 6 November and he went straight to Shanghai to join Chen Bijun. They married in Guangzhou in May 1912; He Xiangning (*q.v.*) acted as the matron-of-honor at their wedding. The newlyweds went to France in July to further their studies, accompanied by Zeng Xing, Zeng Zhongming, Fang Junying, and Fang Junbi (Fan Tchun-pi, *q.v.*); Chen Bijun abandoned her studies during World War I, however, joining the French Women's Red Cross as a nurse.

In April 1913, Chen Bijun gave birth to a son in Montargis, France, naming him Wang Wenying; the *ying* of his name reflected her appreciation of the care and assistance Fang Jun*ying* gave at this time. At the end of 1914, after a long and difficult journey to southwest France to escape the early turmoil of the war, Chen Bijun gave birth to a girl, born prematurely at seven months. She named her daughter Wang Wenxing, the *xing* of her name reflecting her gratitude to Zeng *Xing*.

In early 1915, Chen Bijun left her children in the care of Cai Yuanpei, Fang Junbi, and Zeng Zhongming and returned to China with her husband, whom Sun Yat-sen had recalled when it became clear that Yuan Shikai was planning to betray the revolution and make himself emperor. Such was the popular opposition to Yuan Shikai, however, that he was forced to abandon his plan and died not long after. Returning to France in early 1916, Chen Bijun finally took her children and younger brother home to China in autumn 1917 to be with her husband. She made a further trip overseas in 1923, after receiving a request to raise funds for Sun Yat-sen's newly reorganized KMT and the Whampoa Military Academy. Chen Bijun and her younger brother traveled to the United States, Cuba, and Canada over a period of about six months, and her success in this venture added greatly to her status in the KMT.

In 1924, she attended the first National Congress of the KMT as one of three women representatives (the other two being He Xiangning and Tang Yungong) and was elected to the Central Supervisory Committee; Wang Jingwei was on the Central Executive Committee. He had been at Sun Yat-sen's bedside during his last illness, and when Sun died in Beijing on 12 March 1925 Wang was in charge of such important matters as drafting Sun's will, thus becoming his natural successor. When the KMT government established the Republic of China in Guangzhou on 1 July, Wang Jingwei became its first president and Chen Bijun the first lady. Their status in the party grew rapidly, and they were very active in Guangzhou.

In November 1935, an attempt was made on Wang Jingwei's life in Nanjing. It was later learned that the assassin had been acting alone and his target had been Chiang Kai-shek; the man had apparently attacked Wang Jingwei simply because he was there and Chiang Kai-shek was not. Initially, however, Chen Bijun accused Chiang Kai-shek of organizing the assassination attempt. Wang Jingwei went to Europe to recuperate, leaving Chen Bijun in China. In December 1936, when Chiang Kai-shek was kidnapped by one of his own generals during the Xi'an Incident, Chen Bijun sensed an opportunity to seize power and besieged Wang Jingwei with telegrams asking him to return to China to replace Chiang Kai-shek as leader. Her plan failed, however, because Wang Jingwei no longer held any real power once he had relinquished his position as chairman of the Executive Yuan.

With the outbreak of the Sino-Japanese War in mid-1937, Chen Bijun and Wang Jingwei revealed themselves to be pro-Japanese and opposed any efforts on the part of the KMT to form an anti-Japanese alliance with the CCP. Their stance was to make peace with the Japanese and fight the communists. They left the KMT capital of Chongqing in December 1938 and went via Kunming to the French colony of Hanoi (Vietnam), whence they attempted to induce the KMT government to capitulate to the Japanese. On 1 January 1939, an extraordinary meeting of the KMT Central Executive and Supervisory Committee headed by Chiang Kai-shek permanently expelled Wang Jingwei from the party and dismissed him from all his posts. On 21 March, the KMT sent someone to assassinate Wang in Hanoi but the plot failed, and Zeng Zhongming was killed by mistake. Secret agents from Japan escorted Wang Jingwei and Chen Bijun to Shanghai, and in June the KMT government issued a nationwide order for the arrest of the "traitor to China," Wang Jingwei. In July, Chen Bijun was permanently expelled from the KMT, and an order was issued on 26 August for the arrest of Chen Bijun, Zhou Fohai, and Chu Minyi. Two days later, Wang Jingwei's clique convened the Sixth NPC, claiming to be the "legitimate" KMT and Wang Jingwei to be the real successor of Dr. Sun Yat-sen. As vice-president of the presidium of the congress, Chen Bijun was elected to the Standing Committee of the Central Supervisory Committee; she was later made a member of the Central Political Conference. On 30 March 1940, the pro-Japanese clique headed by Wang Jingwei and Chen Gongbo set up a nationalist government in Nanjing under the pretense of "returning to the capital." Chen Bijin promptly appointed her brothers to important posts: Chen Yaozu became governor of Guangdong Province and Chen Changzu was appointed commissioner of the Aviation Commission.

In November 1944, Wang Jingwei died of illness in Japan; he was sixty-one years old. Chen Bijun was neglected in the reshuffle that followed his death, with Chen Gongbo becoming acting president and head of the Executive Yuan. She returned angrily to Guangzhou and took personal charge of the government for four months. Chen Bijun was still there when Japan surrendered unconditionally on 15 August 1945 and was distraught when she heard the news. Nevertheless, Chen Bijun rejected the proposals put to her the following day by Chen Gongbo, that the Japanese government send a plane to fly her to Japan or wherever she wished to go or that a troop of one hundred Japanese soldiers be sent to guard her house if she did not want to leave Guangzhou. Under the pretext of having a personal talk in Chongqing, Chiang Kai-shek managed to arrest and imprison Chen Bijun on 25 August. She was transferred to Nanjing in November and in February 1946 again transferred, this time to the Suzhou lockup. In March, Jiangsu High Court charged her in a public trial with being a traitor to China, but she refused to capitulate. On 1 July 1949, with major cities under communist control, Chen Bijin was transferred to Tilanqiao Prison in Shanghai.

It is understood that at the CPPCC held in Beijing in September Song Qingling (*q.v.*) and He Xiangning approached Mao Zedong (1893–1976) and Zhou Enlai (1898–1976), seeking a special amnesty for Chen Bijun. Mao indicated that she could be released if she were to write a brief statement admitting guilt; Zhou Enlai nodded his agreement. Chen Bijun rejected this proposal, however, stressing in her letter of reply to Song Qingling and He Xiangning that the real traitor was Chiang Kai-shek, who had been responsible for labeling her and Wang Jingwei "traitors to China." Chen Bijun thanked the two women for their concern and care but said she was prepared to spend the rest of her life in prison.

Suffering from high blood pressure and heart disease complicated by pneumonia, Chen Bijun died in Tilanqiao Prison Hospital, Shanghai, on 17 June 1959; she was sixty-eight years old. Chen Bijun and Wang Jingwei had six children, three sons and three daughters. One son, born in America, died young; the others were Wang Wenying and Wang Wendi. The daughters were Wang Wenxing, Wang Wenbin, and Wang Wenxun. Because her surviving children had escaped abroad or gone to Hong Kong before 1949, Chen Bijun's daughter-in-law's brother, Tan Wenliang, handled her affairs upon her death. Chen Bijun's body was cremated and ashes sent to Guangzhou, where her children claimed them from Hong Kong.

Chen Gongbo, the second most important man in Wang Jingwei's clique, once said of Chen Bijun: "Wang Jingwei could not have achieved what he did without Chen Bijun; yet, had she not been there, he might not have failed." This is thought to be a just and balanced criticism of Chen Bijun, who was "capable" of both good and bad. She came from a rich family and was intelligent and precocious from a young age. Chen Bijun was also proud and unruly as a result of a pampered childhood. She was an enthusiastic and devoted revolutionary in her youth and there was a time when the patriotic heroine had been determined to prove herself the equal of any man. With age, however, Chen Bijun became self-willed and opinionated, unwilling to play second fiddle. Blinded by greed and the desire for power, she gradually relinquished her early aspirations and betrayed her country.

LAM Tung
(Translated by Barbara Law)

Boorman, Howard L., and Richard C. Howard, eds. *Biographical Dictionary of Republican China*, vol. 1. New York: Columbia University Press, 1967, 218–20.

Chen Gongshu. *Henei Wang'an shimo*. Taipei: Zhuanji wenxue chubanshe, n.d.

He Shifu. *Duguo—Wang Jingwei*. Chengdu: Sichuan renmin chubanshe, 1995.

Huang Meizhen. *Weiting youyin lu—dui Wang Wei zhengquan de huiyi jishi*. Beijing: Zhongguo wenshi chubanshe, 1991.

Huang Meizhen and Zhang Yun. *Wang Jingwei jituan panguo toudi ji*. Zhengzhou: Henan renmin chubanshe, 1987.

Huang Yanru. "Tong'e gongji de Chen Bijun." In *Yingxiang Zhongguo lishi de yibai ge nü ren*, eds. Xiao Li, Ma Baozhu, and Lü Yantao. Guangzhou: Guangdong renmin chubanshe, 1992.

Liu Hongwen. "Wang Jingwei yu sige nü ren de enenyuanyuan." *Bolan jinghua* (November 1991).

Nanjingshi dang'an guan, comp. *Shenxun Wang Wei hanjian bilu*. Nanjing: Jiangsu guji chubanshe, 1992.

Tan Tianhe. *Wang Jingwei shengping*. Guangzhou: Guangdong renmin chubanshe, 1996.

Wang Guangyuan and Jiang Zhongqiu. *Chen Bijun yu Wang Jingwei*. Beijing: Zhongguo qingnian chubanshe, 1992.

———. *Wang Jingwei*. Beijing: Zhongguo heping chubanshe, 1995.

Wang Guanxing. *Wang Jingwei zhuan*. Hefei: Anhui renmin chubanshe, 1993.

Wen Shaohua. *Wang Jingwei zhuan*. Changchun: Jilin wenshi chubanshe, 1988.

Zhang Jingxing. *Cong geming nü tongzhi dao tou hao nü hanjian—Chen Bijun zhuanji*. Shanghai: Xuelin chubanshe, 1994.

Zhang Qingjun and Liu Bing. *Xianjing—Wang Jingwei panguo'an tanmi*. Beijing: Zhongguo dang'an chubanshe, 1995.

Chen Bingru: *see* **Chen Bijun**

Ch'en Che: *see* **Ch'iung Yao**

Ch'en Chin

Ch'en Chin [Chen Jin], 1907–1998, born in Hsiang-shan, Hsin-chu County, Taiwan, was an outstanding Taiwanese painter of *bijin* (beautiful women). Her work was exhibited for many years in Taiwan at important *taiten* (Taiwan art exhibitions) and *futen* (Taiwan government exhibitions) and in Japan in *bunten* (Ministry of Education art exhibitions) and *teiten* (exhibitions of the Imperial Academy of Fine Arts) during Japan's occupation of Taiwan. She was popularly recognized as Taiwan's leading woman artist.

Ch'en Chin was born into a wealthy family, the third daughter of Ch'en Yün-ju, who served as an official of the Japanese colonial government; her mother's name is not known. Ch'en Chin received her early education in public school where major courses were taught in Japanese. From 1922 to 1925, she attended Taipei Third Girls' High School and was exposed for the first time to the world of art. Her teacher there, Gohara Koto (1892–1965), taught watercolor and encouraged Ch'en Chin to pursue advanced art training in Japan. She went to Japan in 1925 and started academic art training at Tokyo Women's Art School (Tokyo joshi bijutsu gakko); her teachers included Yuki Somei (1875–1957) and Endo Kyozo. After graduation Ch'en Chin continued her studies with two prominent Tokyo *bijin* artists, Ito Shinsui (1898–1972) and Kaburagi Kiyokata (1878–1972).

In 1927, while still a student at art school, three of her works—*Appearance, Poppy,* and *Morning*—were accepted into the First Taiwan *Taiten* Exhibition. Ch'en Chin was one of only three Taiwanese among the ninety-two artists accepted (the other two were Lin Yü-shan and Kuo Hsüeh-hu); they were dubbed the "Three Youths in *Taiten*." From then on, her works were regularly accepted for *taiten* and *futen*. Ch'en Chin had three times received the special award from *taiten* exhibitions by 1932 and then became one of the first two Taiwanese painters to be elected as *taiten* jurors. She sat on the Eastern-style Paintings Panel for the Sixth *Taiten* Exhibition and served as juror for the Seventh and Eighth *Taiten* Exhibitions.

Once having received the highest honors Taiwanese art circles could offer, Ch'en Chin challenged herself by sending works to Japan. In 1934, *Playing Instruments* was accepted for the Fifteenth *Teiten* [imperial] Exhibition, considered the pinnacle of her art career. Her *Makeup* was accepted for the Spring *Teiten* Exhibition the following year, while an earlier work, *Aboriginal Women of Shanti Gate*, completed in 1936 during her four years (1934–38) as a teacher at P'ing-tung Girls' High School, was accepted for the *bunten* exhibition. One of her reasons for teaching at that school had been to observe and sketch aboriginal people in southern Taiwan.

Bijin-ga (beautiful-women painting) was an important part of Ch'en Chin's art. She portrayed beautiful women in Taiwanese costume against a Taiwanese background, often rendering her subjects with the latest fashion of clothes, hairdress, jewels, and ornaments. In *Playing Instruments*, she depicted two young women playing the flute and the *ch'in* (stringed instrument); they sit on a long bench inlaid with seashells but the background is empty. This type of long bench was common in upper-class Taiwanese families of that period. The fine hair of the women was delicately and painstakingly painted, and their faces, almost identical, were depicted as doll-like, with narrow eyes, fine eyebrows, and small mouths. The dresses were similarly treated, the white lace borders built up with layers of pigment in shallow relief and the drapery folds handled skillfully, giving them a natural look. The decorative effect of the painting was achieved with outlines filled with harmonious colors.

Ch'en Chin returned to Taiwan in 1945 and the following year, at the age of almost forty, married Hsiao Chen-ch'iung. She bore a son, Hsiao Ch'eng-chia, the next year and took over the care of her husband's six children from a previous marriage. Although spending much time with her new family and limiting her involvement in Taiwanese art circles to jurorship for annual national exhibitions, Ch'en Chin continued to paint.

In 1958 she held her first solo exhibition in Chung-shan Hall in Taipei; sixty-two pieces were shown. In 1969 Ch'en Chin went to the United States, where she visited art museums and made many sketches during her travels. Retrospective exhibitions were mounted in the Taipei Fine Arts Museum (1986) and the Taipei National Museum of History (1996); that year she received the Premier's Office National Cultural Achievement Award and donated the prize money to a scholarship for young artists. Ch'en Chin died in 1998 at the age of ninety-two.

Shih-ying HSIEH

Chuang Po-ho. "The Art of Chen Chin." *Hsiung-shih mei-shu*, no. 109 (March 1980): 26–39.
Han Hsiu-jung, ed. *Ch'en Chin hua-chi*. Taipei: Taipei Fine Arts Museum, 1986.
Hsieh Li-fa. "Taiwan mei-shu yün-tung shih." *I-shu-chia* (November 1975): 100–02.
Hsieh Shih-ying. "An Interview with Chen Jin." In *An Anthology of Chen Jin's Art*, ed. National Museum of History. Taipei: The Museum, 1997, 131–50.
———, ed. *The Art of Chen Chin*. Exhibition catalog. Taipei: National Museum of History, 1996.

Hsiung-shih mei-shu, ed. "Introduction of Selected Works of Chen Chin." *Hsiung-shih mei-shu*, no. 72 (February 1977): 70–72.

Huang Ts'un-hsiu. "An Artist with Modern Spirit: Chen Chin." *Hsiung-shih mei-shu*, no. 109 (March 1980).

Lei T'ien. "Kuei-hsiu hua-chia: Ch'en Chin." *I-shu-chia* (March 1976): 102–10.

Shih Shou-chien. "Image of Life's Beauty: Chen Chin's Painting Career." In *Taiwan Art Series 2: Chen Chin*. Taipei: I-shu-chia Publishing, 1992.

T'ien Li-ch'ing. "Kuei-hsiu, shih-tai, Ch'en Chin." *Hsiung-shih mei-shu* (November 1993).

Chen Chin: *see* **Ch'en Chin**

Chen Congying

Chen Congying, b. 1902, in Changsha, Hunan Province, was a dedicated party worker from the early years of the CCP and wife of CCP leader Ren Bishi (1904–1950).

Chen Congying was four months old when her mother died; because her father was a teacher in Beijing, he left her in the care of his sister. The sister, who was married to Ren Yadao, also died young, however, and the grief-stricken husband vowed to keep Chen Congying in the family by marrying her to his son, should he have one with his second wife. Chen Congying was in fact betrothed, when she was twelve years old, to Ren Yadao's son Ren Bishi.

Unlike most child brides, Chen Congying was treated kindly by her adoptive family. In return, when eleven-year-old Ren Bishi passed the entrance examination of the First Normal School of Changsha in 1915, fourteen-year-old Chen Congying went to work at a sock-knitting factory to help pay his school fees. At this school, Ren Bishi made the acquaintance of Mao Zedong (1893–1976) and began his life as a communist revolutionary. Ren Bishi went to Shanghai in 1920 to study Russian, and when he was about to travel to the Soviet Union for further studies told Chen Congying to learn to read "even if just to be able to read the letters I will be sending you." She took his advice seriously and at the age of eighteen began to learn sewing and reading at a vocational school in Changsha.

They were not reunited and married until 1926; Ren Bishi was kept busy with CCP work in Shanghai after returning from the USSR. Chen Congying's thick Hunan accent and drab country clothes were often derided by fashionable Shanghai youth, but her husband considered these qualities a blessing in disguise that enabled her to do the work he wanted done. Ren Bishi entrusted her, now a member of the Communist Youth League of China, with the important task of carrying messages between himself, as secretary of the Youth League Central Committee, and the CCP Central Committee. Her "country bumpkin" image did not arouse the suspicion of enemy agents, and she proved to be cautious, competent, and loyal in carrying out the dangerous work of delivering messages and helping produce stenciled propaganda material. When Ren Bishi was arrested after being sent to Nanling in Anhui Province to inspect work there, Chen Congying boarded an open coal train in freezing weather to go to his rescue, taking their one-year-old daughter Suming along. Her efforts eventually succeeded and he was released the following year; only then did Ren Bishi learn that their daughter had died of pneumonia. Their second child was due to be born when Ren received orders to go to the Jiangxi soviet in early 1931, so Chen Congying remained in Shanghai, alone. The defection of Shanghai party leaders Gu Shunzhang and Xiang Zhongfa in April led to her arrest, and she went to prison with her three-month-old daughter Yuanzhi. They were released toward the end of the year after six months' imprisonment.

About this time, Chen Congying received a telegram from Zhou Enlai (1898–1976) asking her to go to the Jiangxi soviet. She took her daughter to Hunan, placed her in the care of her mother-in-law, and set out for Ruijin, which she reached on International Women's Day 1932. Chen Congying and Ren Bishi lived a comparatively secure and pleasant life for a period during which she worked in the Confidential Materials (*jiyao ke*) Bureau. When he was dispatched to the Hunan-Jiangxi Border Region as secretary of the Provincial Party Committee in 1933, Chen Congying went with him; she was placed in charge of confidential materials of the Provincial Committee. In August 1934, when orders were issued to march west, Chen Congying placed their son, then only a few months old, with a local peasant family. She never saw him again, despite concerted efforts in the 1950s to find the boy. Ren Bishi was in charge of the Red Army's Sixth Regiment and joined in October 1934 with He Long's Second Regiment to form the Second Front Army, with He Long as commander and Ren Bishi as political commissar. The Second Front Army then marched to the Hunan-Hubei-Sichuan-Guizhou Border Area. From there it set off in November 1935 on its own Long March, meeting up with Zhang Guotao's Fourth Front Army in July 1936 in Ganzi, Sichuan.

Throughout the Long March, Chen Congying remained with the Confidential Materials Department. She was pregnant and went into labor when they reached Aba in Xikang Province (part of present-day Sichuan Province). Helped up into the second-story living quarters of a Miao family, she fell through to the sheep pen below and had her baby there. Chen Congying was heart-broken when Ren Bishi suggested that the baby (who was immediately given the name Yuanzheng [Long March]) be left behind with the Miao family. He relented, however, when soldiers interceded on her behalf, volunteering to carry Yuanzheng themselves. Ren Bishi then sewed a cloth bag in which he carried the baby on his back, supporting Chen Congying, still weak from the birth, with one hand and leaning on a staff with the other. Ren Bishi was himself in poor health but struggled on, refusing any help from his soldiers. After the communists arrived in Yan'an, Chen Congying put Yuanzheng in the care of a wet nurse and continued work with confidential materials, this time for the central government. A year later, Chen Congying took the child to Hunan to be raised with her only other surviving child, Yuanzhi. In 1938, Chen Congying went with Ren Bishi to the Soviet Union, where he was the CCP representative to the Comintern. She gave birth in Moscow to another daughter, Yuanfang, probably in 1939, and left her in the international nursery in Moscow when a recall came to head to China in 1940.

After returning to Yan'an, Ren Bishi became one of the five top leaders of the Central Secretariat of the CCP. Then, in a major party shakeup in 1943, he became one of three men in the Secretariat, his standing in the party below only Mao Zedong and Liu Shaoqi (1898–1969). With the end of the Sino-Japanese War in 1945, Chen Congying and Ren Bishi decided to bring their two daughters from Hunan to Yan'an. A boy, Yuanyuan, had been added to the family in 1941, and in 1948 the whole family moved to Beijing, where they lived in a house in the suburbs.

Mao Zedong declared the establishment of the PRC on 1 October 1949, but Ren

Bishi and his family only listened to the ceremony from a radio because he was too ill to stand on the rostrum at Tian'anmen. His health deteriorated, and in November Ren went to the Soviet Union for treatment. He returned to China in April 1950, bringing with him their daughter Yuanfang, who had been left behind in Moscow in 1940. Ren Bishi attempted to disregard his poor health after China became involved in the Korean War in 1950 and again immersed himself in his work. He suffered a stroke, however, on 27 October and died at the age of forty-six.

Chen Congying was thus left to bring up their four children single-handedly. Because of the great contribution Ren Bishi had made to the nation, however, the party and its leaders provided her with a great deal of help. She continued to play a leading role in handling confidential materials with the Central Committee, attaining the position of director of the Bureau of Confidential Materials (Zhonggong jiyaoju chuzhang). Nevertheless, during the Cultural Revolution, Jiang Qing (*q.v.*) labeled Chen Congying a member of the "widows clique" and had her arrested. The fact that she had been arrested by the KMT in the 1930s was used against her as evidence of political unreliability. However, Zhou Enlai vouched for Chen Congying at a public meeting in the Great Hall of the People, thereby shielding her from further persecution.

Chen Congying had been elected a member of the Fourth CPPCC in 1965 and a member of the Standing Committee of the Executive Committee of the ACWF. Her four children all graduated from university and became useful citizens of the PRC.

Lily Xiao Hong LEE

Huaxia funü mingren cidian. Beijing: Huaxia chubanshe, 1988.
Xie Fenghua and Sun Xiwu. *Zhongguo gaogan furen dang'an.* Changchun: Beifang funü ertong chubanshe, 1998, 1–22.
Yingwen *Zhongguo funü*, ed. *Gujin zhuming funü renwu*, vol. 2. Shijiazhuang: Hebei renmin chubanshe, 1986, 640–46.

Chen Derong: *see* **Shen Rong**

Chen, Georgette
Georgette Chen [Zhang Liying], 1907–1992, was a painter. She was born in Paris where her father, Zhang Jingjiang, was a businessman and supporter of Dr. Sun Yat-sen (1866–1925). Georgette Chen returned to China in 1910 but was educated mostly in Paris and New York. In 1930, she took part in the Paris exhibition *Salon d'Automne* with the painter Liu Kang. Georgette Chen taught painting at the Nanyang Academy of Fine Arts in Singapore from 1954 until retirement in 1981.

Her work is based on well-crafted draftsmanship and carefully applied tonal modulations from pure hues typical of the Parisian taste of the late 1920s and 1930s, and reveals a steely resolve to express herself as a woman and Chinese person. Later works in Singapore are well-essayed urban landscapes that are not over-prettified but remain close to late impressionist precursors such as Bonnard and Vlaminck.

John CLARK

Ushiroshō ji Masahiro et al. *Tō nan Ajia—Kindaibijutsu no Tanjō.* Fukuoka: Fukuoka Art Museum, 1997.
Chow Kwok Kian. *Channels and Confluences: A History of Singapore Art.* Singapore: Singapore Art Museum, 1996.

Chen Hengzhe

Chen Hengzhe, 1890–1976, known in the West as Sophia Zen, was born in Changzhou, Jiangsu Province.

Her family was from Hengshan in Hunan, and her paternal grandfather, Chen Zhongying, and her father, Chen Dao, were well-known scholars and poets as well as government officials. Her mother Zhuang Yaofu, an accomplished painter and calligrapher, came from one of the four prominent families in Changzhou with a long tradition of scholarship and public service. Chen Hengzhe was the second child in a family of six daughters and two sons, all of whom received a classical and modern education. As the Chen family's economic circumstances declined, they lived with the Zhuang family in the countryside of Changzhou.

Two major early influences on Chen Hengzhe were her maternal uncle Zhuang Sijian and her paternal aunt Chen Hong, the elder sister of her father. The uncle was an official and later a New Army officer stationed in Liezhou (Haiyang) in southern Guangdong. He was responsible for much of Chen Hengzhe's early childhood education. Well versed in Chinese classical studies, Zhuang Sijian nevertheless had a great interest in Western science and culture. He introduced his niece to Western knowledge, encouraging her to develop her own talents and be a new age independent and knowledgeable woman.

After studying for three years in a modern school in Shanghai where she learned English, Chen Hengzhe went in 1912 to live with her paternal aunt in a small town near Suzhou. Chen Hong was also a scholarly woman, a good calligrapher and knowledgeable about Chinese poetry, history, and traditional Chinese medicine; her aunt supported and encouraged Chen Hengzhe's desire for knowledge and independence. When, in 1914, ten women were permitted, for the first time, to compete for government grants provided by the Boxer Indemnity Fund to assist Chinese students to study in the United States, Chen Hong encouraged her niece to sit for the examination held by Tsinghua [Qinghua] University. She passed the examination and sailed for the United States that same year.

After a year at Putnam Hall Girls' School in Poughkeepsie, New York, Chen Hengzhe entered Vassar College in autumn 1915. She was one of two Chinese women, the other being Lucy Yang. They were joined by only two other Chinese women during Chen Hengzhe's period at Vassar, and she and Lucy Yang were active on the campus speaking about China and teaching Chinese language. At Vassar, Chen Hengzhe majored in history; won the Golden Key Prize as best student of her year, and was admitted to Phi Beta Kappa, the national honor society. She graduated in 1919. Known at Vassar as Sophia Hung-che Chen, Chen Hengzhe was much influenced by Lucy M. Salmon, head of the History Department, and Eloise Ellery, who encouraged her to undertake comparative studies of Chinese and European history. Awarded a fellowship for graduate study, Chen Hengzhe went on to the University of Chicago where she received an M.A. in 1920. Chen Hengzhe returned to China the same year and was appointed as a professor of Western history at Peking University, the first Chinese woman to be appointed a professor in China.

While attending Vassar, she met two men who became her greatest influences. In summer 1916, Chen Hengzhe visited Ithaca, New York, and met Ren Hongjun (aka H.C. Zen), her future husband. In 1917, he then visited her in Vassar and introduced Chen Hengzhe to Hu Shi. The three became lifelong friends. Ren Hongjun and Hu Shi had been classmates in Shanghai and were students at Cornell University, where in 1915 Ren Hongjun had become founding editor of the Chinese scientific journal *Science* (Kexue) and one of the founders of the Science Society of China. A common aim of both *Science* and the Science Society was the dissemination of scientific knowledge in China. In 1916, while Hu Shi and Ren Hongjun were editors of the *Quarterly of Chinese Students in America* (LiuMei xuesheng jibao), they debated Hu Shi's idea of vernacular (*baihua*) literature. Ren, who wrote poetry, was against using the vernacular, and during his editorship *Science* was published in literary Chinese (*wenyan*). Chen Hengzhe sided with Hu Shi and wrote poetry and prose for the *Quarterly of Chinese Students in America* and *New Youth* (Xin qingnian) in the vernacular. Her collection of short stories *Little Raindrop* (Xiao yudian), published in 1928, was also written in that form as was her short story "One Day" (Yiri), published in the *Quarterly of Chinese Students in America* in 1917, and "I Was Said to Be Insane" (Renjia shuo wo fale chi), published in 1918 in *New Youth*. Chen Hengzhe is often regarded, therefore, as the writer who published in the vernacular before Lu Xun.

Chen Hengzhe and Ren Hongjun married in 1920 in Beijing, where they both held professorships at Peking University. In 1924 and 1925, Chen Hengzhe taught Western history at Southeastern University in Nanjing, where Ren Hongjun was vice-president. After also teaching Western history at Peking University for a further year in 1930, Chen Hengzhe devoted herself to family and writing. She was prolific and versatile, producing poetry, short stories, and essays and contributed to most of the leading literary magazines, such as *New Youth, Endeavor* (Nuli zhoubao), *Eastern Miscellany* (Dongfang zazhi), *Short Story Magazine* (Xiaoshuo yuebao), *Contemporary Review* (Xiandai pinglun), and *Independent Review* (Duli pinglun), the magazine of liberal opinion Chen Hengzhe co-founded with Hu Shi and Ren Hongjun in 1932.

In most of her writings, Chen Hengzhe was concerned with the social and political problems confronting China. She published two collections of short stories and essays, *Little Raindrop* (1928) and *Collected Prose Works* (Hengzhe sanwenji) in two volumes (1938), both of which stressed issues concerning women, youth, and education. In 1934, Chen Hengzhe edited a study of Chinese women, *New Life and Women's Emancipation* (Xin shenghuo yu funü jiefang). In December 1935, she went with her family to live in Chengdu after Ren Hongjun was appointed president of the new Sichuan University. Shocked at the poverty, social backwardness, and rampant warlordism in Sichuan, Chen Hengzhe wrote a series of articles in *Duli pinglun* trenchantly and incisively criticizing warlord politics and cultural and social conditions in Sichuan. The local Sichuan press responded vociferously with personal attacks on her and it became one of the reasons why she returned to Beijing in July 1936; Ren Hongjun resigned from his post and returned to Beijing in 1937. As a historian, Chen Hengzhe published three works on

Western history: *A History of the West* (Xiyang shi, 1927); *A Short History of the Renaissance* (Wenyi fuxing xiaoshi, 1925); and *The Influence of Christianity in Europe* (Jidujiao zai Ouzhou lishi shang de diwei, 1922).

From her student days at Vassar, Chen Hengzhe was also an able interpreter of China to the West, publishing two monographs in English. In 1931 she edited *Symposium on Chinese Culture* for the China Institute of Pacific Relations (IPR) to promote better understanding in the West of contemporary Chinese culture. She contributed to this volume a concluding chapter, "Summary of China's Cultural Problems," which also appeared in her other publication in English *The Chinese Woman and Other Essays* (1932). In both publications, Chen Hengzhe advocated the modernization of Chinese culture through the selective adoption and combination of elements in both Western and Chinese cultures, which would eventually lead to a new world civilization. She advocated a cultural hybrid viewpoint that later became fashionable in intellectual circles in China and the West in the 1990s. Chen Hengzhe was active in the IPR and a member of the Chinese delegation to IPR conferences in Honolulu (1927), Kyoto (1929), Hangzhou (1931), and Banff (1933).

During the war years, she lived first in Kunming and then in Chongqing, where Ren Hongjun continued working in science and education administration. Chen Hengzhe became increasingly dismayed at the corruption of the KMT government, her alienation growing after the war. The two lived in Shanghai after their return from a year-long visit to the United States, and for a time, as the communist forces advanced south, considered joining their three children who were studying in the United States. The couple decided to remain in China, however, their growing disenchantment with the KMT regime possibly contributing to this decision. Upon the founding of the PRC in 1949, both Chen Hengzhe and Ren Hongjun were elected to the Shanghai branch of the CPPCC. He attended the Beijing CPPCC as a specially invited delegate and remained active in scientific and educational affairs until his death on 9 November 1961. Chen Hengzhe, however, withdrew from public life after 1949 and made no further public social or political comment. She survived the traumas of the Cultural Revolution, although her second daughter suffered and lost her husband during that period. Her other daughter and son remained in the United States, where her eldest daughter, E-tu Zen Sun (*q.v.*), became a distinguished professor of Chinese history. Chen Hengzhe died in Shanghai on 7 January 1976.

She is regarded as a major modern Chinese woman writer and one of the pioneers of the new literature movement in China in the 1920s. Her literary works have been critically acclaimed by literary historians such as Sima Changfeng in *Zhongguo xinwenxue shi* (1991) and A Ying in *Xiandai Zhongguo nüzuojia* (1931). Although not in support of the politics of the women's suffragette movement in the West, Chen Hengzhe was one of many Chinese women who in their lives and writings before 1949 advocated the liberation and equality of women in China. She admired Marie Curie Sklodowska and the way in which Western women were able to develop their own individuality and abilities; in her writings Chen Hengzhe sought the opportunity for Chinese women to achieve self-fulfillment by following this lead. As a historian, she played a major role in introducing Western history to Chinese readers in an easily understood manner. Her books on Western history became major texts in Chinese schools and universities before World War II and were reprinted several times.

Chen Hengzhe was known in the 1920s as one of China's "female geniuses"; the wife of Ren Hongjun, who founded modern science in China; and the close confidante of Hu Shi, who founded the field of modern humanities in China. Chen Hengzhe linked science and the humanities, China and the West, and was one of the most influential women in China in the three decades before 1949.

H.D. Min-hsi CHAN and QI Wenying

Boorman, Howard L., and Richard C. Howard, eds. *Biographical Dictionary of Republican China.* New York: Columbia University Press, 1967–71.
"Chen Hengzhe." In *Minguo renwu xiaozhuan,* vol. 4. ed. Liu Shaotang. Taipei: Zhuanji wenxue chubanshe, 1989, 297–300.
Chen Zen, Sophia. *The Chinese Woman and Other Essays.* Peiping: n.p., 1933.
Dooling, Amy B., and Kristina M. Torgeson, eds. *Writing Women in Modern China.* New York: Columbia University Press, 1998.
Sun, E-tu Zen. *Ren Yidu xiansheng fangwen jilu.* Taipei: Zhongyang yanjiuyuan jindaishi yanjiusuo, 1993.
Ye Weili. "Crossing the Cultures: The Experiences of Chinese Students in the USA 1900–1925." Ph.D. dissertation, Yale University, 1989.
Zhu Weizhi, ed. *Chen Hengzhe sanwen xuanji.* Tianjin: Baihua wenyi chubanshe, 1991.

Ch'en Hsiang-mei: *see* **Chen Xiangmei**

Ch'en Hsing-wan

Ch'en Hsing-wan [Chen Xingwan], b. 1951, in T'ai-chung, Taiwan, is an artist.

Her father, Ch'en Hsia-yü [Chen Xiayu] (b. 1917), was the distinguished portrait sculptor who first exhibited at the Japanese national salon *Shinbunten* in 1938. Her father's concentration on his art, possibly to deflect traumas suffered in the period after the retrocession period of Taiwan to China in 1945, exercised a lasting impression on the young Ch'en Hsing-wan, as did the severe domestic pressure his seclusion put on her mother. Ch'en Hsing-wan graduated from Taiwan National Academy of the Arts in 1972 and was also taught by the mainlander and surviving surrealist from 1930s Japan Li Chung-sheng [Li Zhongsheng] (1911–1984).

Ch'en Hsing-wan's work was early recognized in Taiwan, and in the 1980s it thematized a woman's relation to her physiological states in technical effects of pictorial abstraction. In the 1990s, however, her work moved away from a sometimes rather simplistic free association toward a grander and more formally calligraphic composition, possibly stimulated by the artist's residence and exhibition in Switzerland and Paris around 1990–92.

John CLARK

Ch'en Hsing-wan. "Ch'en-tien-hou ti tsai-ch'u-fa." *Yen-huang i-shu tsa-chih,* no. 76 (April 1996).
Ch'en Yü-ling, ed. *I-hsiang yü mei-hsü: Taiwan nü-hsing i-shu-chan.* Taipei: Taipei shih-li mei-shu-kuan, 1998.

Ch'in Sung. "Ch'ou-hsiang ti fei-ch'ou-hsiang piao-hsien." In *Taiwan hsin-i-shu ts'e-hou pu-tui-chan ming-lu*, ed. Hsieh Li-fa. Taipei: I-shu-chia, 1995, 253–57.

Clark, John. "Touch Texture and Concept: Three Woman Artists from Taiwan." In *Art Taiwan*, eds. N. Jose and Yang Wen-I. Sydney: Museum of Contemporary Art, 1995.

Ch'en Hsiu-hsi

Ch'en Hsiu-hsi [Chen Xiuxi], 1921–1991, of Hsin-chu County, Taiwan, is considered to be one of Taiwan's most important modern female poets. In her early period, she composed Japanese haiku and tanka poetry but turned her hand after World War II to modern Chinese poetry.

Her tanka poetry is collected in *The Overturned Leaf* (Fu-yeh), while *The Tree's Sorrow and Joy* (Shu ti ai-le) and *The Stove* (Tsao) are poetry collections. *Magnolias* (Yü-lan-hua) contains her poetry and prose. In 1992, her eldest daughter established the "Ch'en Hsiu-hsi Poetry Prize," which is presented each year on Mother's Day. The complete collection of her writings in ten volumes, edited by Li K'uei-hsien, has been published by the Hsin-chu County Center for Literature.

The year of Ch'en Hsiu-hsi's birth saw the establishment of the Taiwan Culture Society, the driving force behind the island's new culture movement. The year of her death marked the completion of Taiwan's long drawn-out democratic movement. Thus, not only did Ch'en Hsiu-hsi's life straddle both Japanese colonial rule and the KMT regime, it experienced and bore testimony to the most intense period of change occurring in the society, economy, and culture of Taiwan. As a Taiwanese poet at this juncture, Ch'en Hsiu-hsi experienced the frustration of having to choose between identifying with Taiwan or the mainland. Her persistence in this struggle drew on the awareness that the final decision weighing in the balance was in reality a question of identifying either with the land or with nationality.

Ch'en Hsiu-hsi's biological father, whose surname was Ch'en, worked in a sugar refinery in Hsin-chu but also enjoyed poetry; nothing is known of her birth mother. A few months after Ch'en Hsiu-hsi was born, a neighboring family of the same surname offered to adopt her. Her adoptive father managed a printing works and the family was quite well off. In her autobiography, Ch'en Hsiu-hsi indicated how she was the "happiest of adopted daughters" and that her new parents treated her extremely well. After graduating from Hsin-chu Women's Public School, Ch'en Hsiu-hsi was appointed as an instructor at Hsin-chu Heijin Japanese Language Institute and also as a relief teacher at Hsin-hsing Public School. Her parents, however, engaged a private tutor to teach her Chinese, and thus Ch'en Hsiu-hsi became educated in both Chinese and Japanese. Full credit must nevertheless be given to Ch'en Hsiu-hsi herself for the effort she devoted to developing her creative skills in both of these languages. By the age of fifteen, in writing her first poem, her destiny as a poet became sealed.

When she was twenty-two years old, in 1942, Ch'en Hsiu-hsi married Chang I-mou [Zhang Yimou] of Yüan-lin, who worked for the Mitsui Trading Company in Shanghai. She went to live with her new husband there, but her writings reveal that from the beginning this traditional marriage in which she had to wait upon her parents-in-law caused her utmost pain. In her middle years, her emotional turmoil was such that Ch'en Hsiu-hsi attempted to hang herself in the T'ien-mu residence. This happened in 1978, when she was fifty-eight years old; the suicide attempt damaged her vocal chords, leaving her with a permanently husky voice. Ch'en Hsiu-hsi tells of this episode in her autobiography: "After a great deal of careful thought, I was determined to end thirty-six years of married life. After thirty-six years of adhering to the Chinese women's three obediences and four virtues, I was exhausted from being a housewife. I no longer had any qualms; I could leave with a clear conscience. I had lived for everybody else, so that I had lost myself. From that time on, however, I determined to live for myself."

Even before the attempted suicide, Ch'en Hsiu-hsi had revealed in her poetry the breakdown of her marriage and thoughts about gender differences and the marriage system. Her 1974 publication *Successive Reflections of My Three Selves* (Lien-ying ch'eng san-ko wo) presents her three "selves" of wife/daughter-in-law, mother, and herself as an individual. *Chains of Thorns* (Ching so, 1975) revealed her thinking on women's cultural and gender roles and expressed even more poignantly the hopelessness that women found in their position within traditional Chinese society:

> Utterly loyal to the family
> While fabricating the beautiful lie of the filial daughter-in-law,
> While fabricating the beautiful lie of the wife,
> While fabricating the beautiful lie of the mother.
> Impaled on the pain of a thorn,
> While mouthing the smiling "Good fortune and long life!"
> Concealing the pain of the wound
> From others.

Despite the failure of her first marriage, in 1985 Ch'en Hsiu-hsi remarried. Not long after, however, she let it be known that this marriage, too, had broken down. It seems that her second family harbored the intent to commit some form of fraud; the court case so burdened Ch'en Hsiu-hsi that she became weary in mind and body, eventually becoming ill. In poetry, Ch'en Hsiu-hsi probed both her marriages with great honesty, recounting episodes as well as states of mind. In the poems *Self Dissection* (Tzu p'o) and *Tears and I* (Lei yü wo), she explains these matters and clarifies her views on the purpose of poetry. In the latter, Ch'en Hsiu-hsi, by then in her twilight years, writes that her own bitterness and suffering were expressed to portray the plight and spiritual depression that women suffer:

> We have had fifty years of rigid patriarchy,
> We are in the habit of acquiescing with women's misfortunes,
> Rarely is battle joined for the rights of wives.
> Tears should not be the monopoly of women,
> Tears should not be the weapon of women.
> To be ridiculed, to be oppressed, a time of dejection,
> The tears squeezed out are
> To defend myself, but they are inadequate as a shield.

In the act of writing poetry, Ch'en Hsiu-hsi discovered a new impetus for life. She often said that poetry writing was her principal motivation to live and that poetry was not simply literature but rather a way of being. In the article "The Heart of Poetry" (Shih ti hsin), Ch'en Hsiu-hsi outlines this attachment, revealing: "I have thought of it in this way: without poetry, perhaps I would not exist in this world." The simplicity of this stark truth prompted her friend Wu Ying-t'ao to draw the poet into the Bamboo Hat Poetry Society (Li shih she) in 1967. Wu presented Ch'en Hsiu-hsi with the following lines, "She is poetry/She is love." Ch'en Hsiu-hsi asked her children to promise to engrave these words as an epithet on her tombstone.

In April 1964, the first issue of *Taiwanese Literature and Art* (Taiwan wen-i) came out, and in June *The Bamboo Hat Poetry Periodical* was published. Thus, for the first time, Taiwanese writers had a forum in which to share their works. Ch'en Hsiu-hsi was elected to the committee of the Bamboo Hat Poetry Society in 1970, and the following year, with the appearance of the forty-first issue of *The Bamboo Hat Poetry Periodical*, was then appointed as director, a position held until her death. In 1981, she became a founding member of The Taiwan Pen (Taiwan pi hui). After joining the Bamboo Hat Poetry Society, Ch'en Hsiu-hsi not only wrote new poems with great enthusiasm but also contributed her own money to publishing poetry in order to encourage younger people. Thus, she became well known in literary circles as Director Ch'en; close acquaintances, however, referred to her as "Auntie Ch'en."

Throughout her long career as a poet, Ch'en Hsiu-hsi was awarded many literary commendations and prizes. These included Most Outstanding Poet, awarded by the Third World Poet's Conference, and Second Place in the American Poetry Society's International Poetry Competition for *My Pen* (Wo ti pi). Besides taking part in poetry conferences in Taiwan, she attended gatherings in the United States, Japan, and Korea; in later years, however, her literary activities were confined to Taiwan. With the break down of her second marriage, Ch'en Hsiu-hsi was already sixty-five, and her health began to deteriorate. She suffered liver, stomach, and kidney problems and finally died of illness in 1991.

Ch'en Hsiu-hsi's poetry is the poetry of a woman. Regardless of the themes or poetic language employed, her poems retained what in traditional literature is termed "feminine tenderness." Poetry critics have always fixed on her gentle but strong images of women, with their focus on motherhood. Overall, however, another traditional term, "masculine toughness," also pervades Ch'en Hsiu-hsi's poetry, especially evident in the social criticism, nationhood, and nature topics touched upon in her poems. Rather than conveying these "masculine" themes in a female voice in the image of a mother, Ch'en Hsiu-hsi skillfully blended the two and in that fusion created her own poetic voice. However, the terms "masculine" and "feminine" cannot fully explain the more profound aspects of Ch'en Hsiu-hsi's poetry. Mechanical discourse inevitably narrows the interpretive space of her poems such that it excises her integrated view of poetry.

Whether discussing feelings associated with parenthood, friendship, love, marriage, nationality, or social topics, Ch'en Hsiu-hsi for much of her poetry employs natural images of earth, land, and native place. She interposes "land" and "mother," and the earth itself becomes a symbol of the womb; it is the foundation of the nation yet also the place of daily existence; and moreover, the native land is an entity that the poet maps spiritually.

Within these tools—images—of the land, Ch'en Hsiu-hsi integrates gender polarities, love, and national identity equally. Her later poetry clearly expresses her identification of "place" and "native Taiwan" as one and within the reference points of personal experience and historical memory. Her point of view and way of thinking differ from that of male poets.

Ch'en Hsiu-hsi was convinced of the limitless power of poetry. Poetry was her device to seek answers to the sorrow she felt as a woman, the helplessness endured as a Taiwanese, and the confusion experienced as to her identity. As she wrote in *Perhaps It Is the Weight of a Poem* (Yeh-hsü shih i-shou shih-te chung-liang):

> Poetry is an intense source of energy, and sincere love.
> Perhaps with one poem you can overturn the earth.
> Perhaps one poem can save the people of the whole world.
> Perhaps one poem has the ability to radiate energy
> And allow us to hear freedom, peace, coexistence and shared glory,
> The echo of the song of angels.

YANG Ts'ui

(Translated by Michael Paton)

Ch'en Hsiu-hsi. *Ch'en Hsiu-hsi ch'üan-chi*, ed. Li K'uei-hsien. Hsin-chu: Hsin-chu shih-li wen-hua chung-hsin, n.d.

"Ch'en Hsiu-hsi." In *Chung-hua min-kuo tso-chia tso-p'in mu-lu*, vol. 23. Taipei: Hsing-cheng-yüan wen-hua chien-she wei-yüan-hui, 1995, 22.

Ch'en Yü-ling. "Taiwan nü-hsing nei-tsai hua-yüan." In *Taiwan wen-hsüeh ti kuo-tu: Nü-hsing, pen-t'u, fan chih-min lun-shu*. Taipei: Po-yang wen-hua, 2000.

Chen Huiqing

Chen Huiqing, 1909–1983, was one of the thirty women who went with the First Front Red Army on the Chinese communists' Long March of 1934–35. She was born in Hong Kong to a family who came from Panyu County, Guangdong Province.

Classed as a "proletariat," Chen Huiqing did piecework at home from the age of eight or nine and worked in a weaving mill at fourteen. She took part in the 1925 Hong Kong strike that spread to the mainland, was elected to the Weavers' Union, and joined the CCP in 1926. Chen Huiqing worked in Guangdong for three years, at one stage as a member of the KMT's Propaganda Department; she also was involved in the Canton Commune Uprising of December 1927. In 1929 Chen Huiqing married Deng Fa (1906–1946) in Hong Kong and worked with him from then on, first in the labor movement and then in the security office. Deng Fa held the post of head of security throughout the Long March. Chen Huiqing was pregnant when she also set out and she gave birth to her baby in April 1935 in Yunnan; the baby was abandoned, as were all the babies born during the Long March. Little is known of Chen Huiqing after this, except that Helen Foster Snow met her in Yan'an; Chen Huiqing had at least one son who lived with her in Yan'an; and in 1962 she had become vice-chair of the Guangdong branch of the All–China Federation of Trade Unions. Chen Huiqing survived the Cultural Revolution and died in 1983.

Sue WILES

Guo Chen. *Jinguo liezhuan: Hong yifangmianjun sanshiwei changzheng nühongjun shengping shiji*. Beijing: Nongcun duwu chubanshe, 1986, 81–84.
Lee, Lily Xiao Hong, and Sue Wiles. *Women of the Long March*. Sydney: Allen & Unwin, 1999.
Snow, Helen Foster. *Inside Red China*, 1977 reprint [with a new preface and biographical notes by the author]. New York: Da Capo Press, 1939, 29–30, 169.

Chen Jin: *see* **Ch'en Chin**

Ch'en Jo-hsi: *see* **Chen Ruoxi**

Chen Liying: *see* **Chen, Georgette**

Ch'en Mei-ch'üan

Ch'en Mei-ch'üan [Chen Meiquan], b. 1914, in Chen-pei [Zhenbei] County, Liao-ning [Liaoning] Province, became one of China's first policewomen when she graduated in 1936 from the twentieth intake of the Ministry of the Interior's Senior Police College (Nei-cheng-pu ching-kuan kao-teng hsüeh-hsiao).

After graduating, Ch'en Mei-ch'üan was assigned to the Capital Police, and in the same year married Chao Ping-k'un [Zhao Bingkun], who also came from the northeast. He had graduated from the college's sixteenth intake and remained there to undertake responsibilities in education, special duties, and police foreign affairs. When Chao Ping-k'un graduated from air defense school in 1934, he was appointed section chief at air defense headquarters. Ch'en Mei-ch'üan accompanied her husband to Ho-nan [Henan], Hu-nan [Hunan], and Kuang-hsi [Guangxi] when the Sino-Japanese War broke out and was assigned to Kuei-lin [Guilin] Police Headquarters. In 1945, Chao Ping-k'un was a major-general and head of the Civil Defense Bureau (Min-fang ch'u) of China's Aviation Committee (Hang-k'ung wei-yüan-hui). Ch'en Mei-ch'üan headed the training unit of the Young Women's Army.

With the defeat of Japan, the KMT government assumed control of the northeast. Because of his close relationship with Wu Huanzhang, governor of Hsing-an Province (present-day Inner Mongolia Autonomous Region), Chao Ping-k'un was appointed to the Provincial Government Committee and as commissioner of police. Ch'en Mei-ch'üan was appointed as a lecturer to the northeast campus of the Central Police College (Chungyang ching-kuan hsüeh-hsiao tung-pei fen-hsiao) was then made an instructor at Liaoning Police College (Liao-ning ching-ch'a hsüeh-hsiao). In 1947, she and her husband were elected to the National Assembly (Kuo-ta tai-piao). Ch'en Mei-ch'üan was not able to take up her appointment until 1949, however, because the KMT government gave her place to a member of a friendly party.

After the KMT moved to Taiwan, Ch'en Mei-ch'üan, Hu Tao-hsing, and four other colleagues sent a joint letter to the minister of the Interior, attaching their resumés and asking to be assigned work. This led to the Office of Police Affairs (Ching-wu-ch'u) appointing Ch'en Mei-ch'üan in June 1951 as head of the Taipei policewomen's branch (Taipei shih ching-ch'a chü nü-tzu ching-ch'a tui tui-chang), a special appointment. The unit, however, consisted of just one person, the head, because it had only just been established and had no budget. Ch'en Mei-ch'üan knew from experience that women had no place in the male-dominated world of the police. She also knew that because no system had been put in place, little had come of the training and recruitment of police-women to date. Therefore, it was up to policewomen themselves to do what had to be done. Ch'en Mei-ch'üan drafted a plan for a team of policewomen and took it up with Commissioner Li Te-yang. In 1952, a policewomen's team was formally established in Taipei, the first such system in Taiwan.

Ch'en Mei-ch'üan requested a transfer to administrative duties in October 1954 be-cause of poor health, and Hu Tao-hsing took over as head of the team. In her new position as a commissioner in the Office of General Affairs, Ch'en Mei-ch'üan contin-ued to stress the recruitment and training of policewomen. This eventually led to a number of policewomen being accepted into the twenty-sixth intake of the Taiwan Po-lice College (Taiwan sheng ching-ch'a hsüeh-hsiao), where she was a team leader. After their graduation in spring 1956, however, recruitment and training of women ceased. In 1967, Ch'en Mei-ch'üan spoke out on the importance of continuing to recruit and train policewomen, and a resolution that "we should recruit more policewomen" was passed at the 1967 National Assembly.

While determined to push for the creation of a system of recruitment and training for policewomen, Ch'en Mei-ch'üan was aware that the full cooperation of both the police and the public was necessary for this police work to happen. She began to study public relations and published articles in various police magazines stressing the need for a public relations system within the police force. In 1959, the Office of Police Affairs was ordered to set up a public relations unit headed by Ch'en Mei-ch'üan. In the beginning, she was a voice in the wilderness, pioneering in laying the foundation for her ideas. She was made deputy director of the Public Relations Office (Kung-kung kuan-hsi shih) in that year, and her book *The Theory and Practice of Police Public Relations* (Ching-ch'a kung-kung kuan-hsi li-lun yü shih-wu) became the standard textbook for police per-sonnel.

Ch'en Mei-ch'üan was instrumental in establishing a system for policewomen and developing police public relations in Taiwan. She retired from her post in 1972 and resigned from the National Assembly in 1991.

CH'EN Ch'un-ying
(Translated by Jennifer Eagleton)

Ch'en Mei-ch'üan. "Chung-kuo nü-ching ti hui-ku yü chan-wang." *Ching-min tao-pao*, no. 251 (August 1956): 9–11.
Hsü Hsüeh-chi and Shen Huai-yü. "Ch'en Mei-ch'üan hsien-sheng fang-wen chi-lu," transcribed by Tseng Chin-lan. Taipei: Chung-yang yen-chiu-yüan. Chin-tai-shih yen-chiu-so, 1996.

Chen Meiquan: *see* **Ch'en Mei-ch'üan**

Chen Muhua
Chen Muhua, b. 1921, in Qingtian County, Zhejiang Province, was a deputy premier of the PRC from 1982 to 1988, as minister of Foreign Trade and Economic Cooperation.

She completed her high school education with the help of an uncle who was an official in the KMT air force. Sympathetic to the communist call to resist the Japanese at the start of the Sino-Japanese War, however, Chen Muhua went to Yan'an in 1938. She told her mother that she would be back in six months but did not return by the time her mother died, seven years later.

In Yan'an, Chen Muhua enrolled in the Anti-Japanese Military and Political University (KangRi junzheng daxue) and studied military science; she joined the CCP at this time. Upon discovering that the university was not admitting any women to its training program for future staff officers, she decided to direct her complaint to Mao Zedong (1893–1976). Chen Muhua presented him with a written request to join the training course as he stood on a podium, giving a talk to encourage women students at the university to learn radio skills, medicine, and nursing. A few days later, Mao approved the intake of personnel to the Staff Officer's Training Course, and twelve women were among the one hundred students admitted. She thus became one of the first people to complete training sponsored by the Central Military Committee. Her teachers included such prestigious leaders as Zhu De (1886–1976), Chen Yun, and the German Comintern advisor Li De (Otto Braun). Chen Muhua and the other women underwent the same rigorous physical and military training as the men. Tall for a woman, well built, and in robust good health, Chen Muhua gained from this year of military training an endurance that later stood her in good stead when, as a busy leader, she was required to work long hours. After training, Chen Muhua became the first female staff officer assigned to General Xiao Jingguang and served in several different capacities during the Sino-Japanese War. She was staff officer of the Fifth Garrison Regiment of the Yan'an Rear Regiment, education staff officer with regiment headquarters, and a researcher with the regiment's Military Research Room. Chen Muhua was, however, criticized during the rectification movement in 1942 because of her KMT uncle. She was pregnant at the time but was nevertheless subjected to investigation day and night; her feet swelled up from stress and fatigue. Only after Zhou Enlai (1898–1976) vouched for her did the ordeal end. During the civil war (1945–49), Chen Muhua accepted the challenge of working in a variety of jobs with Rehe Military Region headquarters, including assignments to a railway office, a coal mine, and as head of a nursing school and a hospital.

With the founding of the PRC, she moved into economic work. In the 1950s, Chen Muhua participated in planning for the nation's communications and transportation network, as head of the Railway Office and the Long-term Planning Office of the Transportation Bureau attached to the State Planning Commission (Guojia jihua weiyuanhui). When the Foreign Economic Relations General Liaison Office (Duiwai jingji lianluo zongju) was set up, Chen Muhua was placed in charge of economic assistance to African countries. During the Cultural Revolution, however, she was branded as a "capitalist roader" and, because she adhered to a "white expert line," was accused of being not "red" and loyal to Mao Zedong. The reason behind the criticism was that Chen Muhua had suggested that those who had economic dealings with foreign countries should learn foreign languages. It was also rumored that she was the niece of KMT leader Chen Cheng; this charge incriminated her brother, who was working in Heilongjiang Province. He was subsequently persecuted to death. In 1970, Chen Muhua became deputy minister of the Foreign Economic Relations Ministry (Duiwai jingji bu), working directly under Zhou Enlai. She was cautious in this position, careful to do her homework whenever she reported to him; he was known to be a demanding superior, attentive to detail. Zhou Enlai was by all accounts pleased with Chen Muhua's work, however.

In 1982, she was promoted to deputy premier of the State Council, the highest position any woman had achieved until then, apart from honorary posts. Chen Muhua also doubled as minister of Foreign Trade and Economic Cooperation. In order to encourage export, she obtained party approval for local governments and trade units to retain 25 percent of the foreign exchange they earned, half for local government and half for the export unit. Overall exports thus increased rapidly, and national exports grew to more than US$30 billion. As minister of Foreign Trade, Chen Muhua frequently negotiated with foreign countries and companies and gained the reputation of being a sharp negotiator who kept the interests of both sides in mind. In 1985, the party decided to give her the additional responsibility of governing the Peoples' Bank (Renmin yinhang), which serves as the central bank of China, controlling and regulating the macroeconomy of the entire nation. As governor, she instituted tighter control of currency and loan approvals. When, for example, high-level leaders sent notes asking that loans be made to certain people as a favor, Chen Muhua would read the requests aloud at meetings; such notes became increasingly rare. By doing this, she took a degree of personal risk of giving offense to those in high position. Chen Muhua also regulated and strengthened the Peoples' Bank's relationship with other banks, thus enabling it to better fulfill its role as a central bank, both in assisting and monitoring the others. Chen Muhua improved the infrastructure of many of the branches and offices of the People's Bank, as well. In the past, village loan departments had operated out of simple lean-tos, transporting money in ordinary jeeps, but Chen Muhua ordered proper branch offices constructed and organized safer ways of transporting money. Most important, however, was her conviction that China must interact with financial sectors of other countries. In 1986, the PRC therefore became a member of the Asia Development Bank and hosted its annual meeting in 1989. She served on the boards of both the Asia Development Bank and the Africa Development Bank.

To acknowledge a long and illustrious career, Chen Muhua was elected chair of the ACWF in September, six months after leaving the People's Bank to become deputy chair of the NPC executive. The honor genuinely surprised her because she had not previously been involved in women's work. However, as always, Chen Muhua not only accepted responsibility in a field with which she was unfamiliar but did her best by learning and studying. Her first move was to relate women's work to economic work. In order to give more opportunities to women in the countryside, she proposed that they learn to read in order to help learn a farming-related skill. The "Learn to Read and Learn a Skill" movement that the proposal spawned resulted in more than ten million women learning to read, and ninety million receiving some form of training related to agricultural skills. Chen Muhua also established liaison groups with the Ministries of Agriculture, Forestry, and Science, as well as with planning and lending authorities, to achieve practical cooperation. She made sure that similar liaison groups were formed at the provincial and local levels. This movement saw peasant women begin to play a more important role in agricultural production and village and township enterprises. Through the entire process of drafting, evaluating, passing, and propagating the Women's Rights Law (Funü quanyi fa), Chen Muhua helped modernize regulations relating to women, following on from the Marriage Law of the 1950s.

So that women scientists and academics could make a maximum contribution, Chen Muhua fought and won the battle to make the retirement age of senior women intellectuals and officials the same as men's. As China's top woman leader, she was only too aware of the small number of women who made their way into leadership positions. Although comprising 43.6 percent of the work force, women constituted only 6.5 percent of ministers and deputy ministers, the percentage of women in the provincial leadership being about the same. The situation was worse within the CCP leadership. Following in the footsteps of predecessors such as Cai Chang (*q.v.*) and Deng Yingchao (*q.v.*), Chen Muhua urged those responsible for recruiting and promoting government and party personnel to train and select more women as leaders. She said that while everyone paid lip service to gender equality, a long road lay ahead before real equality could be achieved. Her crowning achievement in women's work was in hosting the Fourth Women's World Conference in 1995. Responding to criticism that as a mass organization the ACWF simply acts in unison with the government, Chen Muhua declared that because the government was a government of the people, why should the ACWF stand on the opposite side?

In 1940, in Yan'an, she had married Zhong Yi, who graduated from Harbin Industrial University (Harbin gongye daxue) in the 1930s. He had been involved in anti-Japanese activities in the northeast and fled to Yan'an to escape arrest. As participants in the training program for staff officers and serving in the Yan'an Rear Regiment, the two had shared some unforgettable days before being sent to the northeast. Zhong Yi was a military leader in the 1960s but retired early because of poor health—he had a major operation in 1974. He took up painting and calligraphy with the University for the Aged (Laonian daxue) after retiring. Chen Muhua's four daughters and their husbands all work in foreign trade and finance. Because Zhong Yi was stationed across the Yan River and had his hands full with their first daughter when Chen Muhua was being investigated in Yan'an, she was forced to give away her second daughter in 1943. Despite searching immediately after 1949, Chen Muhua did not find her until 1975; they reunited in Beijing. Although the daughter remained with her adopted mother, the two families have formed a close relationship. As of 1995, Chen Muhua had a grandson and granddaughter. Throughout her career, she had little time for housework; her in-laws, and in later years her granddaughter, kept house for her. Chen Muhua's hobby is gardening, and pots of flowers decorate her coffee table and windowsill. Her love of flowers even prompted Chen Muhua to foster China's flower industry, but now in her seventies she has retired from most of her posts.

Chen Muhua reached the position of alternate member of the Politburo, the highest decision-making group of the CCP. Although Jiang Qing (*q.v.*) and Ye Qun (*q.v.*) were full members of the Politburo during the Cultural Revolution and Deng Yingchao later became a member, none of these women had the opportunity to apply their talents to the level of responsibilities and executive positions that Chen Muhua enjoyed. She rode the wave of post-Cultural Revolution reform for women, reaching a political height and decision-making authority few women have achieved.

Lily Xiao Hong LEE

Bartke, Wolfgang. *Biographical Dictionary and Analysis of China's Party Leadership, 1922–1988.* Munich: Saur, 1990, 14.
Huaxia funü mingren cidian. Beijing: Huaxia chubanshe, 1988, 633–34.
Wang Xiaopeng. "Chen Muhua: Yanjing gaosu ni yiqie." *Zhonghua yingcai*, no. 12 (June 1995): 4–10.
Xie Fenghua and Xun Xiwu. *Zhongguo gaogan furen dang'an.* Changchun: Beifang funü ertong chubanshe, 1988, 339–49.
Zhongguo funü guanli ganbu Xueyuan, ed. *Gujin Zhongwai nümingren cidian.* Beijing: Zhongguo guangbo dianshi chubanshe, 1980, 32–33.

Ch'en P'ing: *see* **San Mao**

Chen Ping: *see* **San Mao**

Chen Ran

Chen Ran, b. 1962, in Beijing, is a writer. Hers was an intellectual family, but an unhappy one. Chen Ran's parents divorced when she was in high school, and the writer has lived with her mother ever since. The traumatic memory of an unhappy childhood and lack of a father figure became both an emotional minefield and source of raw material, strongly affecting her writing.

Chen Ran studied Chinese language and literature in Beijing Normal University from 1982 to 1986 and remained with that institution as a teacher after graduation. After a short marriage in the late 1980s she went to Australia in 1988, but soon returned to Beijing, to work as a news reporter and literary editor. In 1995, Chen Ran quit her job to become a professional writer but in 1997 took an editorial position with the Chinese Writers' Association. She now lives and writes in Beijing.

During her years in college, Chen Ran started writing, first poetry, then fiction. Her most representative work of that period is the short story "Disease of the Century" (Shiji bing, 1986), about a rebellious college student. Between 1987 and 1989, she published a series of surrealistic short stories with strong philosophical undertones; her settings and characters are often mysterious and metaphorical. Not until the next year did Chen Ran's writing find its own distinctive form and subject matter. In the stories "Burden of Playing a Role" (Jiaose leizhui, 1990); "Cheers to the Past" (Yu wangshi ganbei, 1991); and "Nowhere to Say Farewell" (Wuchu gaobie, 1992), a female character-narrator takes center stage. By means of monologue, the narrator describes her thoughts and feelings as she tells of her life, past and present, and relations with her lover, female friend, and mother. A lonely melancholy pervades the character of the urban female intellectual, who feels alienated from the world around her. Chen Ran's female monologue narrative has recently become distinctly feminist in her novella *Breakthrough* (Pokai, 1995) and novel *Private Life* (Siren shenghuo, 1996). Declaring itself to be a manifesto of Chinese feminism, *Breakthrough* explores platonic lesbian love between urban intellectual women. *Private Life* utilizes Chen Ran's favorite narrative style—interior monologue—to relate a bleak story about growing from girlhood to womanhood in the mid-1970s to the mid-1990s. The protagonist undergoes a gradual degeneration, becoming ever more paranoid. Her sense of failure results mainly from the tortuous sexual relations she endures and around which the narrative revolves. The character's heterosexual relationships are often either abnormal or unfulfilled, but the relationship between mother and daughter as well as various homosexual liaisons all end in failure. The protagonist is left alone at the end and finds after visiting a mental hospital that her private bathroom is her only refuge.

In the essay "Transsexual Consciousness and My Writing" (Chaoxingbie yishi he wo de chuangzuo, 1994), Chen Ran claims that the dilemma of modern women is that while they might find physical love with males, they can find understanding and spiritual fulfillment only from females. In other words, real love transcends sex and gender. In an interview with Xiao Gang, Chen Ran insists that the reason she writes about private life is to try "to explore deeply the spiritual and emotional dilemma of modern people" because she believes that "the individual is also universal." Chen Ran also tries to express "gender consciousness (*xingbie yishi*), which has accompanied me ever since I was born." A woman writer should "start her thinking where men stop" and voice her thoughts from the standpoint of a female, marginalized, culture. She also believes, however, that only by combining the good qualities of both sexes can a woman writer "express the feelings and thoughts of [human beings] completely."

Chen Ran's unique voice and "female writing" (*nüxing xiezuo*) receive great attention from feminist critics as well as general publishers in the cultural market. Declaring that the author created "a new genre in women's writing and women's culture in the 1990s," Chinese feminist critics praise the gender consciousness of her work and the introduction into literature of the private female experience, including lesbian love, the Electra complex, and the mother-daughter relationship. They also claim that Chen Ran's writing provides a psychoanalytic case study of women's self-identity.

However, for liberal humanist critics such as Wang Xiaobo, who found Chen Ran's work disappointing, "gender consciousness" cannot replace real experience and depth of insight required of a great writer. For Wang Xiaobo, Chen Ran's philosophical ambitions exceeded her literary achievements. He points out the potential dangers of using "cultural relativity" to hide or replace literary judgment, which he claims occurs in feminist writing and criticism. Many other critics also find the private literature (*siren wenxue*) that Chen Ran represents rather narrow and empty. They censure her for using "private life" as an excuse for a lack of understanding of life and the world. Still other general readers are convinced that some women writers such as Chen Ran exploit sex and "privacy" issues to pursue success and fame in a mass consumer market. The hype surrounding the publication of *Private Life* in 1996 and heated debate about privacy literature also occurring around the time of its release certainly contrast ironically with the elitist and anti-social gestures Chen Ran claims to make against a society and cultural market "dominated by men."

KONG Shuyu

Chen Ran. *Siren shenghuo*. Beijing: Zuojia chubanshe, 1996.

———. *Zuicun li de yangguang*. Wuhan: Changjiang wenyi chubanshe, 1992.

———. "Chaoxingbie yishi he wo de chuangzuo." *Zhongshan*, no. 6 (1994): 105–7.

———. "Pokai." *Huacheng*, no. 1 (1995): 63–77.

Dai Jinhua. "Chen Ran: Geren he nüxing de xiezuo." *Dangdai zuojia pinglun*, no. 3 (1996): 47–56.

Wang Xiaobo. "Siren shenghuo yu nüxing wenxue." *Beijing wenxue*, no. 11 (1996): 48–94.

Xiao Gang. "Ling yishan kaiqi de men" [Interview with Chen Ran]. In *Siren shenghuo*, by Chen Ran. Beijing: Zuojia chubanshe, 1996.

Chen Rong

Chen Rong, b. 1929, in Harbin, is a native of Aihui County, Heilongjiang Province; her name is sometimes spelled Chen Yong. She is a drama director.

Chen Rong entered Bridgeman Girls' High School in Beijing in 1941 but soon left to go to the Hebei-Shandong-Henan Liberated Area to take part in the communist revolution. Early the following year, she was assigned to the Friends-in-Arms Drama Group (Zhanyou jushe) and played the lead in such musicals as *The White-Haired Girl* (Baimaonü), *Liu Hulan*, and *Wang Xiuluan*. She also played the role of Zhao's wife in the play *Growing Up Fighting* (Zhandou zhong chengzhang). She was so convincing in playing the young revolutionary martyr Liu Hulan that the soldiers in the audience threw stones at her stage persecutors. When she was about to be executed, they aimed their rifles at the actor playing her executioner, forcing their company leader to shout the order, "All triggers detached!"

After 1949, Chen Rong returned to her studies, enrolling at the Central Drama Academy (Zhongyang xiju xueyuan) to major in opera and graduating in 1952. She was assigned to work in the Research Institute for Chinese Operas (Zhongguo xiqu yanjiuyuan), but in 1954 was sent to the Lunacharskii Academy of Dramatic Arts in Moscow to study directing. During the admission interview, Chen Rong was advised to tell her country that it should not send students like her, who had not completed a university degree. Despite knowing little Russian, she made good use of her dictionary and borrowed lecture notes from her Russian classmates. At the end of her studies, Chen Rong gained the highest mark in every subject. Returning to China in 1959, she joined the Beijing People's Art Theater (Beijing renmin yishu juyuan) and directed *Aesop* (Yisuo) and *Liu Jiemei*. She co-directed *Three Sisters* (San jiemei) with Ouyang Shanzun, and helped the Children's Art Theater (Ertong yishu juyuan) develop *The Malan Flower* (Malanhua). Transferred to the Children's Art Theater in 1960, Chen Rong directed *Yue Yun*. She was then transferred to the China Youth Art Theater (Zhongguo qingnian yishu juyuan), where she spent the bulk of her career and directed more than thirty plays. Some were Chinese plays but most were modern and contemporary dramas from foreign countries, which opened a fresh new window for Chinese audiences. Her production of the German playwright Bertolt Brecht's *Life of Galileo*, based on the life of the scientist, won the Ministry of Culture's Grade One Award for invited performances. Chen Rong's production of *A Late Blooming Flower* (Chikai de huaduo) won the Grade Two Award in 1981, while her modern Chinese play *Page Four of Thursday's Paper* (Benbao xingqisi disiban) won the Ministry of Culture's award for directing. After directing *Cherry Season* (Yingtao shijie), a play by the French playwright Jules Vallès about the Paris Commune, in 1983, Chen Rong was given honorary membership to both the Paris Commune Association and the Jules Vallès Literary Society. Other foreign plays Chen Rong put on include *The Youth of Our Fathers* (Soviet Union) and *Guess Who's Coming to Dinner* (United States). In 1986, in response to an invitation by the Japanese drama guild Haguruma-za, Chen Rong directed Taiwan playwright Yao Yiwei's [Yao I-wei] play *Red Nose* (Hong bizi), to critical acclaim. Some of the important plays she directed in the late 1980s and early 1990s were Brecht's *The Caucasian Chalk Circle* (1985), Friedrich Dürrenmatt's *An Angel Comes to Babylon* (1987), Ma Zhongjun's *The Old Romantic Town* (1989), and Tian Han's classic *Guan Hanqing* (1991).

Chen Rong's directing style is ebullient and her plays possess a strong sense of historical setting. She was elected to the Executive Committee of the League of Chinese Dramatists (Zhongguo xijujia xiehui) and became deputy director of the China Youth Art Theater in 1984. As its leader, Chen Rong does not confine her focus only to performance; she is now more anxious to train a new generation of drama workers to continue her work. Chen Rong is married to Zhou Xinghua (b. 1925), an opera director with the China Opera and Dance Troupe of the Opera House of China. Their son Zhou Xiaopeng (b. 1968) is a graduate of the Acting Department of China Central Drama Academy and an actor with the China Children's Art Theater.

Lily Xiao Hong LEE

Yingwen *Zhongguo funü*, ed. *Gujin zhuming funü renwu*, vol. 2. Shijiazhuang: Hebei renmin chubanshe, 1986, 1104–8.
Zhongguo dabaike quanshu: Xiju. Beijing: Zhongguo dabaike quanshu chubanshe, 1989

Chen Rong, writer: *see* **Shen Rong**

Chen Ruoxi
Chen Ruoxi [Ch'en Jo-hsi], b. 1938, in the rural outskirts of Taipei, Taiwan, during the period of Japanese occupation, is a novelist and essayist.

Her father was a carpenter, and her mother came from a family of farmers. An unusually bright student, Chen Ruoxi graduated from Taipei First Girls' High School and in 1957 enrolled in the Foreign Languages Department at Taiwan University. She began to write while studying literature at university in the late 1950s, then went to the United States in 1962 to study English literature. Chen Ruoxi attended the University of Iowa Writers' Workshop and went to Mount Holyoke College, then completed an M.A. in Modern American Literature at Johns Hopkins University in 1965, continuing to write and publish in both Chinese and English. Chen Ruoxi and her husband, Duan Shiyao [Tuan Shih-yao], a Taiwanese civil engineering graduate she had met at Johns Hopkins, took up residence in Beijing in 1966. They applied for work (teaching and engineering, respectively) and were transferred in 1969 to the Huadong College of Hydraulic Engineering in Nanjing, where Chen Ruoxi taught English. They moved with their two young children to Hong Kong in 1973, migrated to Canada in 1974, and finally returned to the United States in 1979. There, Chen Ruoxi pursued a successful academic career at the University of California's Center for Chinese Studies at Berkeley and published fiction and critical essays in Chinese and English. She took out American citizenship in 1988. In 1994, however, she resigned from Berkeley and the following year returned alone to live in Taipei, Taiwan. In 1996, Chen Ruoxi was professor of Chinese at Central (Chung-yang) University and at the Tz'u Chi College of Medicine. According to a report in a Hong Kong magazine, Chen Ruoxi and Duan Shiyao were divorced in 1998, and she has since found a new partner.

Chen Ruoxi's first published work, "The Weekend" (Zhoumo), appeared in *Literature* (Wenxue zazhi) magazine in Taipei in 1957, when she was nineteen. By the time she migrated to the PRC in 1966, Chen Ruoxi had published in both Chinese—thirteen short stories and a critical essay on Zhang Ailing (Eileen Chang [*q.v.*])—and in English—a collection of stories and a review essay on the state of Taiwanese literature. She had also published a Chinese translation of Francoise Sagan's *Wonderful Clouds*. Chen Ruoxi did not write or publish any material while living in China but resurfaced in Hong Kong with the publication of "Yin Xianzhang" in 1974 in *Mingbao Monthly*. The piece was subsequently published in English, with several of her other short stories, such as "The Execution of Mayor Yin." Chen Ruoxi's novel *Repatriation* (Gui) was inspired, as was the former title, by her experiences and reflections on the Cultural Revolution and published in Chinese in 1979. Excerpts appeared in English in the volume *Two Writers and the Cultural Revolution*, published by the Hong Kong Chinese University Press in 1980. Her fiction after *Repatriation*, while retaining an overall critical realism, focused on the lives and experiences of overseas Chinese rather than on Chinese in China. It includes the novels *Breaking Out* (Tuwei, 1982); *Foresight* (Yuanjian, 1984); *The Erhu* (Erhu, 1984); and *Paper Anniversary* (Zhihun, 1986).

The bulk of Chen Ruoxi's writing since 1974 has been prose fiction, short and long, in Chinese, but she has also written critical commentary on literature, politics, and society, some of it in English and directed at non-Chinese American readers. At Berkeley, she published *Ethics and Rhetoric of the Chinese Cultural Revolution* (with Professor Lowell Dittmer, 1981) and *Democracy Wall and the Unofficial Journals* (1982), both in English. Her Chinese fiction has been published principally in Taiwan and Hong Kong, particularly in Hong Kong's *Mingbao Monthly* and the literary supplements of the Taiwan newspapers *Zhongguo shibao* and *Lianhe bao*. The Mayor Yin stories were considered to be so politically and culturally significant in Taiwan that two of them—"The Execution of Mayor Yin" and "Night Duty"—were published in the KMT newspaper *Zhongyang ribao*. Two collections of her short stories not dealing exclusively with political conditions in the PRC have been translated into English: *The Old Man and Other Stories*, and *The Short Stories of Chen Ruoxi, Translated from the Original Chinese: A Writer at the Crossroads*.

Chen Ruoxi revisited China in 1985 by invitation of the Chinese government in a delegation of Taiwan writers on a lecture tour, which was repeated in 1986 and 1987. After visiting Tibet in 1985, 1987, and 1988, she published in Hong Kong two book-length travelogues and commentaries: *Journey to Tibet* (Xizang xing, 1988) and *The*

Lure of the Qinghai-Tibet High Plateau (Qing-Zang gaoyuan de youhuo, 1990). Her work first appeared in print in the PRC in 1986, thirteen years after the writer and her family had left there, with the publication of *The Erhu* by Sanlian Bookshop. In America in 1990, Chen Ruoxi founded the short-lived journal *The Square* (Guangchang), so named to commemorate the events in Tian'anmen Square the previous year, with ex-mainland writer Kong Jiesheng. Her writing was not interdicted in China, however, and a collection of her essays—*News from Beyond the Wall* (Chengwai chuanzhen)—was published in Beijing in 1996. Chen Ruoxi has recently become particularly interested in the condition of Chinese women throughout the world and in the cultural status of Chinese women writers. In 1988, she was elected president of the Overseas Chinese Women Writers' Association and also published *A Daughter's House* (Nü'er de jia), a collection of short stories about the need for women to be self-reliant "because the only thing there is for them to rely on is, ultimately, themselves."

Chen Ruoxi came to prominence first in overseas Chinese intellectual circles and soon afterward in English as a writer of what was soon to be called "literature of the wounded" (*shanghen wenxue*). This was fiction dealing with the violence and injustice of the Cultural Revolution. She was among the first wave of writers of what was then not a literary genre but a high-risk, life-transforming act of self-exposure, even for expatriate Chinese. Regardless of whether they intended to align themselves with the international champions of cultural anti-communism, by identifying themselves as "anti-Chinese"—a charge inevitable in the political climate of the early 1970s—these writers endangered family and friends in China by political contagion. Only two related titles preceded the publication of Chen Ruoxi's Mayor Yin stories: Gen Ling's *The Revenge of Heaven* published in New York in English in 1972 and a collection of ex-Red Guards' poems and stories *Ganyu geyin dongdi ai* published in Hong Kong in 1974. Neither claimed to be more than political polemics. Like those authors, Chen Ruoxi had lived through the Cultural Revolution. She, however, was a skilled and proven writer of fiction. The convergence in possessing a claim of authenticity through her personal experience and the ability to write convincingly set the foundation of her career as an internationally prominent Chinese writer. The conflict of priorities and interests thus engendered has underlaid her career since that year. Contending interpretations abound between Chen Ruoxi and her supporters, peers, and readers, including English-language readers, as to the motives of her writing.

"The Execution of Mayor Yin" has been translated into English, Japanese, French, German, Swedish, Norwegian, Danish, and Dutch. The political content of her 1970s stories ensured that they would be accorded cultural importance in Taiwan and Hong Kong. Her ability to express her thoughts on society in China with a degree of detachment and sense of tragedy confirmed, for Chinese and non-Chinese readers alike, her status as a writer rather than publicist for a cause. These attributes secured her entrée to American academia at the Hoover Institute and Berkeley, and, paradoxically, increased her value as publicist for the cause. When "The Execution of Mayor Yin" was published, Chen Ruoxi had been only a promising but not exactly celebrated young Taiwanese woman writer; she had not been heard from for eight years and worked in a Vancouver bank. Her sudden international acclaim following the appearance of her stories must have been unexpected; her material evinces a clear sense of critical-realist moral compulsion. Although doing nothing to resist the attention, Chen Ruoxi has since indicated that she finds her status as a "political" writer an undeserved burden, writing in 1985: "The situation of a Taiwanese writer who is concerned about political and social issues is particularly difficult. If your writing criticizes the realities of the Chinese mainland, people sympathetic to that side will be sure to award you with the titles 'anti-Communist' and 'right-winger.' If you say there are signs of progress and hope for the one billion people on the mainland, you'll immediately be capped as a 'small-time leftist who refuses to admit the error of her ways .'"

Pierre Ryckmans, who wrote the introduction to the English edition of *The Execution of Mayor Yin*, considered Chen Ruoxi to be a young idealist deceived by Chinese communist propaganda. Discussing her portrayal of Teacher Wen's doomed loyalty to Chairman Mao in "Jingjing's Birthday" (Jingjing de shengri; rendered in the English edition as Chairman Mao Is a Rotten Egg), Liu Shaoming wrote in 1976: "If the writer of this story had not experienced feelings similar to Teacher Wen's, she would not have been able to write this kind of confession." (Liu Shaoming used the Buddhist term *chanhui* [to confess one's sins and repent]). The female writer and critic Qian Yingying, who belongs to a much younger generation, wrote in 1998 that Chen Ruoxi was "a prisoner of love" who simply followed her husband, Duan Shiyao, to the mainland. Whatever the cost inherent in seeming to be a small-time leftist, or even a right-winger, refusing to admit the error of one's ways, it cannot be pleasant for a contemporary writer wishing to be heard on political and social issues to be regarded as a "dutiful wife." Such is the controversy enveloping Chen Ruoxi's work, the result of her being a writer, a Chinese, and a woman, striving to relate to the human condition from her own point of view, against which her novels, stories, and essays must be read.

Josephine FOX

Chen Ruoxi. *Chen Ruoxi zixuanji.* Taipei: Qianwei Publishing Co., 1993. Contains complete indexes of Chen Ruoxi's publications to 1991 and critical commentaries.
———. *Democracy Wall and the Unofficial Journals.* Berkeley, Calif.: Center for Chinese Studies, Institute of East Asian Studies, University of California, 1982.
———. *The Execution of Mayor Yin and Other Stories of the Great Proletarian Cultural Revolution,* trans. Nancy Ing and Howard Goldblatt. Bloomington: Indiana University Press, 1978.
———. *Gui.* Taipei: Lianjing chuban, 1978.
———. *Nü'er de jia.* Taipei: Tansuo chubanshe, 1998.
———. *The Old Man and Other Stories.* Hong Kong: Research Center for Translation, The Chinese University of Hong Kong, 1986.
———. *The Short Stories of Chen Ruoxi,* translated from the original Chinese: *A Writer at the Crossroads,* ed. Hsin-sheng C. Kao. Lewiston: E. Mellen Press, 1992.
———. *Tuwei.* Taipei: Lianching chuban, 1983.
———. *Yuanjian.* Taipei: Yuanching chuban, 1984.
Dittmer, Lowell, and Chen Ruoxi [Ch'en Jo-hsi]. *Ethics and Rhetoric of the Chinese Cultural Revolution.* Berkeley, Calif.: Center for Chinese Studies, Institute of East Asian Studies, University of California, 1981.
Duke, Michael S. "Personae: Individual and Society in Three Novels by Chen Ruoxi." In *Modern Chinese Women Writers: Critical Appraisals,* ed. Michael S. Duke. Armonk, N.Y.: M.E. Sharpe, 1989, 53–77.

Liu Shaoming [Lau, Joseph S.M.]. "Chen Ruoxi de gushi." In his *Xiaoshuo yu xiju.* Taipei: Hongfan, 1977, 83–98.

Martin, Helmut. *Modern Chinese Writers: Self-Portrayals.* Armonk, N.Y.: M.E. Sharpe, 1992, 187–92.

Chen Shamin: *see* Chen Shaomin

Chen Shaomin

Chen Shaomin, 1902–1977, was a guerrilla leader and administrator in charge of the Hubei-Henan border area (E-Yu bianqu) in the 1930s as well as a trade union leader of the PRC. She was born Sun Yumei (at various times using the names Sun Zhaoxiu, Sun Shamin, and Chen Shamin) to a family of farm laborers in Shouguang County, Shandong Province.

Her father had been a soldier during the 1911 Revolution, which suggests that he was comparatively progressive in his thinking, and literate. Her mother was a Christian, who, having heard from the missionaries that "all men are created equal," believed girls were, too, and that therefore they should go to school and not have their feet bound. Chen Shaomin's brother had been to France as an indentured worker and often talked about the revolution in Russia, led by a "poor man's party." From the age of thirteen (some sources say from 1913) until 1924, when she was twenty-two years old, Chen Shaomin worked in a lace factory. She then attended primary school for two years. In 1927, because of her mother's Christian connection, Chen Shaomin went to Wenmei Girls' High School in nearby Weixian County. There, she became a student leader and fought against the school authorities. That same year, Chen Shaomin joined the Youth League and went with her fellow students to the countryside to disseminate anti-imperialist ideas and foment revolution. Two years later, her membership was transferred to the CCP.

In 1930, Chen Shaomin was sent by the CCP to Qingdao to work among the textile mill workers and over the next two years built up a core CCP membership in the mills of Qingdao, Beijing, and Tianjin. She met and married Ren Guozhen, secretary of the CCP's Shandong Committee, but he was arrested in Taiyuan (Shanxi Province) and executed by the KMT in 1931. Their child (age and gender unknown) died in 1932. Chen Shaomin herself was arrested and imprisoned for a short time in the following year.

The next period in her life is unclear. Some sources report that she took part in the Long March; others leave the period 1933 to 1937 blank. One, however, indicates that Chen Shaomin worked in Henan in 1933–34 as a special agent (*tepaiyuan*) and did women's work as a member of the Henan Provincial Committee. The Yellow River had just then burst its banks and a famine was in the making. Armed with a bible and a book of hymns, she evangelized the religion of women's rights and "borrowing grain from the landlords." Over this period, Chen Shaomin is said to have recruited more than eight hundred party members. It is known that she was in Yan'an in 1937, because of her attendance at the Party School and presence on a delegation from Yan'an to a KMT conference.

In 1939, Chen Shaomin was sent with Li Xiannian (1909–1992) to establish a Hubei-

Henan border area, anti-Japanese, democratic base (E-Yu bianqu kangRi minzhu genjudi). She is credited with commanding guerrilla units during this time in the capacity of political commissar. When the border area government was established, Chen Shaomin was charged with running the base as deputy chair as well as acting and, later, party secretary. Her major duties were to motivate party and government cadres, local militia, and the masses, including women, to work with the regular army in fighting the enemy in the vicinity. This required her to oversee production of food and clothing for those under her jurisdiction as well as to be responsible for their security. Propaganda work, recruitment of party members, and recruitment and arming of Red soldiers were also part of her job. One of Chen Shaomin's achievements during this period was the rescue of a pregnant colleague, Zhang Guangran, from KMT guards in the seat of Jingshan County. Just five days after rescue, the woman gave birth to a boy. Chen Shaomin's reputation among the KMT was legendary. She was said to have been a dead shot with both hands and to have ridden a swift white horse. The KMT were said to have feared and hated her, giving her the nickname "Chen, Big Feet," a reference to her unbound feet. She was one of the few CCP women in full charge of an area for an extensive period of time and led fighters into armed combat. During and after the war with Japan (1937–45), Chen Shaomin served as director of the Organization Department of the CCP Central China Bureau and later became its deputy secretary.

In 1949, at the close of the CPPCC, she was elected to the National Committee of the All-China Federation of Labor (ACFL) and given the task of organizing the All-China Textile Workers' Trade Union (ACTWTU); in 1950 she was elected to the union's chair. Her union work with the textile workers was recognized by her election to the Executive Committee of the ACFL and membership to its important presidium and secretariat, which ran the organization when the Executive Committee was not in session. In 1957, Chen Shaomin became the first woman elected as vice-chair to the All-China Federation of Trade Unions, which replaced the ACFL. Internationally, from 1950 she sat on the Executive Committee of the Trade Union International of Textile and Clothing Workers, affiliated with the World Federation of Trade Unions (WFTU). She led the Chinese delegation to its Second Congress in East Berlin. More importantly, from 1953 to 1957 Chen Shaomin served as an alternate member to the WFTU's Executive Committee.

At the Seventh Congress in 1945, Chen Shaomin had been elected an alternate member of the CCP Central Committee; and in 1956 at the Eighth Congress she was elevated to full membership, one of few women to be so honored. Her continued high standing in the party hierarchy is shown by the fact that Chen Shaomin was named on the Central Control Committee (Zhongyang jiancha weiyuanhui) in 1962. She also enjoyed the distinction of being elected to the First CPPCC (1949) and the Standing Committee in its next two sessions (1954 and 1959) and was a member of the First and Second NPC (1954 and 1959) and the Standing Committee of the Third NPC (1965).

Only one source refers to Chen Shaomin being persecuted during the Cultural Revolution. She died in Beijing in December 1977 after an illness. Two errors are commonly reported about Chen Shaomin's life. The first is that she took part in the Long March from Jiangxi to Shaanxi. The second is that Chen Shaomin was married to Li Xiannian, a misconception probably arising because of their long association in the Hubei-Henan border area.

Lily Xiao Hong LEE

Huaxia funü mingren cidian. Beijing: Huaxia chubanshe, 1988, 594.
Jingsheng and Xiquan, eds. *Xin Zhongguo mingrenlu*. Nanchang: Jiangxi renmin chubanshe, 1987.
Klein, Donald W., and Anne B. Clark. *Biographic Dictionary of Chinese Communism, 1921–1965*. Cambridge, Mass.: Harvard University Press, 1971, 125–27.
Song Ruizhi, ed. *Zhongguo funü wenhua tonglan*. Jinan: Shandong wenyi chubanshe, 1995, 239–42.
Who's Who in Communist China. Hong Kong: Union Research Institute, 1969.
Yingwen *Zhongguo funü*, ed. *Gujin zhuming funü renwu*, vol. 2. Shijiazhuang: Hebei renmin chubanshe, 1986, 625–29.
Yuan Shaoying and Yang Guizhen, eds. *Zhongguo funü mingren cidian*. Changchun: Beifang funü ertong chubanshe, 1989, 294–95.
Zhonggong dangshi renwu zhuan, vol. 14. Xi'an: Shaanxi renmin chubanshe, 1984, 65–105.

Chen Shiman: *see* **Ch'en-Shih Man**

Chen Shuying: *see* **Chen Xuezhao**

Chen Shuzhang: *see* **Chen Xuezhao**

Chen, Sophia Hung-che: *see* **Chen Hengzhe**

Chen Xiangmei
Chen Xiangmei [Ch'en Hsiang-mei], b. 1925, also known by her English married name of Anna Chennault, was born in Beijing of Cantonese parents. She is a journalist and writer active on the political stages of China, Taiwan, and the United States. Chen Xiangmei is generally credited with laying the groundwork, as a private citizen, for establishing informal contacts between mainland China and Taiwan in the 1980s.

Her father and mother both came from distinguished families. Her paternal grandfather, Chen Qingyun, headed the China Merchant Steamship Company (Zhaoshang ju) but committed suicide at a young age because of a failed investment. Her father, Chen Yingrong, only a teenager then, was sent by his mother to study in England and later in the United States, and he did not return to China until just before his marriage. Chen Yingrong received doctorates from both Oxford and Columbia Universities. Chen Xiangmei's maternal grandfather was the well-known diplomat Liao Fengshu (d. 1958); he was the brother of the early KMT leader Liao Zhongkai, who was married to He Xiangning (*q.v.*). Hence, Chen Xiangmei's mother, Liao Xiangci, studied overseas, as did all her siblings. Yet, while the grandfathers Liao Fengshu and Chen Qingyun were comparatively modern in regard to their children's education, the two men adhered to tradition in betrothing Chen Yingrong and Liao Xiangci as unborn babies. When the two Western-educated young people were ordered to marry, some time after World War I, they initially baulked but capitulated in the end.

Chen Xiangmei's early childhood was spent in Beijing with her wealthy grandfather Liao Fengshu, who worked in the Ministry of Foreign Affairs; several members of the family, including her father, Chen Yingrong, became diplomats. When war broke out between China and Japan in 1937, Chen Xiangmei's family moved to Hong Kong. Soon afterward, her father left them to take up the position of consul to Mexico. When her mother died of uterine cancer in 1941 in Hong Kong, her father did not return. Chen Xiangmei and her elder sister Chen Jingyi buried their mother alone. The latter then undertook nursing training, so at the age of fifteen Chen Xiangmei fended for herself and four younger sisters.

When Hong Kong was occupied by Japan that year, she and her sisters were helped by friends to travel to Guilin, where Lingnan University, which she was attending, had moved. Her studies continued in Guilin, and Chen Xiangmei graduated in 1943. Her first job was with the official Chinese news agency Zhongyangshe. After a stint in its Editorial Department, she was ready to become a reporter. Because of her English proficiency, Chen Xiangmei was assigned as a war correspondent to file special reports on American forces fighting in China. Thus did she meet her future husband, General Claire Chennault, who was in charge of the Fourteenth Brigade of the U.S. Air Force. This brigade was initially a group of American volunteers dubbed by the Chinese the "Flying Tigers" (*Feihu dui*), but after the United States declared war on Japan the unit was absorbed into the U.S. Air Force.

After the war, Chen Xiangmei was transferred to Shanghai and met Chennault again. A recent divorcé, he paid her a great deal of attention and, despite initial opposition from her family, they married in July 1947. She was twenty-two-years old and he was fifty-four (one source gives his age then as fifty-seven). Chinese-European intermarriage was rare at that time, so their union became big news. She also created a stir when a photo of them kissing appeared in the media.

After her marriage, Chen Xiangmei resigned from the news agency and went to work for her husband's civilian airline Civil Air Transport (CAT). Together, they developed the company and traveled to the many parts of China the airline served, including the northeast, the northwest, and the southwest. She wrote in her memoirs how the travel gave her an opportunity to see a great deal of China's beautiful scenery but also some of its most backward and poverty-stricken areas. Before long, as the end of the KMT-CCP civil war and the communist takeover became more certain, Chen Xiangmei gave birth to her first daughter (Claire Anna, or Meihua) in Guangzhou in 1949. Her second daughter (Cynthia Louise, or Meili) was born in Hong Kong the following year. When CAT's headquarters were moved from Shanghai to Taipei, they too moved there, although Chen Xiangmei often flew to Hong Kong to see her maternal grandparents.

The humidity in Taipei was not good for General Chennault's health—he was thought to suffer from bronchitis—so they moved to his native Louisiana in the United States. An examination showed that he had lung cancer, however, and he died in July 1958. After his death, Chen Xiangmei was not given a position of any importance by CAT and was asked to sign a legal document relinquishing any future claims. At about this time, she had a falling out with the Taiwan government, the reasons for which were only vaguely hinted at in her memoirs; Chen Xiangmei decided to leave Taiwan and start a new life in the United States.

She settled in Washington, D.C., in autumn 1960. The impetus for participating in politics in order to fight for her rights came about after an unpleasant experience while Chen Xiangmei worked as a chief in the Chinese Section of the Machine Translation Research Center at Georgetown University. She felt discriminated against when her White assistant was given a parking space while Chen Xiangmei was not. She therefore joined the Republican Party to help them win minority votes. In the meantime, Chen Xiangmei read widely on American history and politics. Despite the help she extended to Richard Nixon in his fight for the presidency against John F. Kennedy that year, Kennedy approved the formation of a private committee, the Chinese Refugee Relief, of which she was president. Chen Xiangmei acted in a variety of similar positions under the administrations of later presidents Nixon, Ford, Carter, Bush, and Reagan. From the early 1960s on, she gained entrée to the most exclusive circles of Washington society and the acquaintance of many important American and international personages. In 1962, her autobiography *A Thousand Springs* was published in New York and made the best-seller list on the *New York Times* for almost six months running, bringing in many speaking engagements. Becoming a celebrity no doubt greatly helped her politically. Besides her political activities, she sits on the board or acts as consultant to many enterprises, facilitating their expansion into Asian markets.

However, if Chen Xiangmei is to be remembered by one single accomplishment, then it must be her role as "match maker" between mainland China and Taiwan. From 1949, Chen Xiangmei adopted an anti-communist stance. Chiang Kai-shek and his wife Soong Mayling (*q.v.*) had been good friends to her and General Chennault, who had considerably helped the KMT government during the Sino-Japanese War. Although she appears to have had a falling out with the Chiangs, Chen Xiangmei's name was often connected to the "China lobby." In Washington press circles, she earned the nickname "Dragon Lady." Despite her Taiwan connections, she continued to support Nixon and did not comment adversely on his visit to mainland China in 1972. Chen Xiangmei even made unofficial visits on his behalf to discern the reactions of various Asian leaders to the visit. In 1980, she re-visited Beijing for the first time in thirty years. There, Chen Xiangmei met with Deng Xiaoping, her uncle Liao Chengzhi, and other Chinese leaders. Soon after, Chen Xiangmei visited Taipei and talked with Jiang Jingguo [Chiang Ching-kuo], president of the Republic of China on Taiwan. These visits were generally understood as laying the groundwork for unofficial contacts between Taiwan and the mainland.

Chen Xiangmei was criticized when she led a delegation of Taiwan entrepreneurs to China at the end of 1989 at a time when public opinion was condemning China for the Tian'anmen Incident in June that year. Her pragmatic view of U.S.-China relations was vindicated when many people followed her footsteps to Beijing afterward. Passing through Hong Kong en route to Beijing, Chen Xiangmei told reporters that she would ask Beijing to release and stop further arrests of participants in the democracy movement. With regard to Chinese Americans, Chen Xiangmei encouraged them to "get out of Chinatown" and participate widely in American politics. As a Republican activist, she joined the Democratic activist Wu Xianbiao in calling a meeting of all Chinese Americans to discuss strategies on how to fight for their rights through normal political channels.

Besides *A Thousand Springs*, written in English, Chen Xiangmei authored many other works, including memoirs, novels, and reportage, in Chinese. She donates scholarships for young writers and playwrights in Taiwan as well as setting up educational funds and scholarships on mainland China. Chen Xiangmei has had many political appointments, the most longstanding perhaps being national president of the Minority Committee of the Republican Party in the U.S. Chen Xiangmei also has received a number of honorary degrees from Asian and American universities and is recognized as a tireless and innovative worker toward a number of goals.

Lily Xiao Hong LEE

Chen Xiangmei. *Wangshi zhi duoshao*. Taipei: Shibao wenhua chuban, 1978.
————. *Yongyuan de chuntian*. Taipei: Tianxia wenhua chuban, 1995.
Chennault, Anna. *A Thousand Springs: A Biography of a Marriage*. New York: Paul S. Erikssen, 1962.
Fu Jianzhong. "Chunqu qiulai de Chen Xiangmei." *Huasheng bao*, 15 December 1989, 15.
Hu Weimei. "Chen Xiangmei—yige ba ziwo jiayu de shiquanshimei de nüren." *Funü zazhi*, 152 (1981): 36–39.
Huang Wenxiang. "Meiji Huayi nüqiangren Chen Xiangmei." In his *Haiwai Huayi jingying*. Hong Kong: Wenhui chubanshe, 1992, 19–36.

Chen Xingwan: *see* **Ch'en Hsing-wan**

Chen Xiuqing: *see* **Pan Yuliang**

Chen Xiuxi: *see* **Ch'en Hsiu-hsi**

Chen Xuezhao
Chen Xuezhao, 1906–1991, was born in Ninghai, Zhejiang Province, although her family was originally from Hengchuang, Henan Province. She was a writer of prose and novels. Although originally named Chen Shuzhang and Chen Shuying, the author became known as Chen Xuezhao and used the pen names Ye Qu, Shi Wei, Xue Zhao, and Hui during her writing career.

Chen Xuezhao commenced education at the Girls' Normal School of Nantong County and went to Shanghai Patriotic Girls' College (Shanghai Aiguo nüxue). In 1923, she joined the literary society Qiancao and published her maiden work, "The New Women of My Ideal" (Wo suo qiwang de xin funü), in the Shanghai newspaper *Shibao*. That same year, she taught, moving from Anhui Fourth Girls' Normal School to Shaoxing Girls' Normal School in Zhejiang and then to Beijing Liming High School and Beijing Shicun High School. Her second work, "A Tiring Trip" (Juanlü), was published in 1924, and Chen Xuezhao helped found the magazines *Yusi* and *Xin Nüxing*.

In May 1927, she traveled to Paris to study Western literature. During the course of her studies, between then and 1931, Chen Xuezhao was appointed special journalist for the well-known newspaper *Dagong bao*. She produced a great deal of prose and fiction, including "In Memory of Paris" (Yi Bali), "A Good Dream" (Nanfeng de meng), and "Like a Dream" (Rumeng), and was invited to become a regular contributor to the Shanghai *Shenghuo zhoukan*. Chen Xuezhao returned to China in 1935 after gaining her Ph.D. from Clermont-Ferrand University. She then traveled around China for some time, going from Wuxi to Shanghai to Nanchang and then to Chongqing. In 1938, *Guoxun xunkan* sent her to Yan'an, the communist capital, on special assignment. On Chen Xuezhao's next visit there, in 1940, she stayed and became editor of the fourth section of the newspaper *Jiefang ribao* and a teacher of literacy at the Central Party School (Zhongyang dangxiao). Chen Xuezhao joined the CCP in 1945 and the following year was transferred to the northeast to work as editor-in-chief for the fourth section of the regional newspaper *Dongbei ribao*. After the establishment of the PRC in 1949, she became CCP secretary at Zhejiang University, director of its Political Study Committee, and a part-time professor in the Chinese Literature Department. She held several other positions at the same time, serving on the Zhejiang Political Consultative Committee, as a special member of the CPPCC, an executive member of the Chinese Writers' Association, a member of the Chinese Federation of Literary and Art Circles, and deputy chair of the Zhejiang Federation of Writers and Artists. In 1957, when the CCP launched the "anti-rightist campaign," Chen Xuezhao was among those who were labeled rightists and became a political outcast. Her writing ceased a few years later, with the start of the Cultural Revolution.

After the Cultural Revolution, Chen Xuezhao returned to the political and literary stage from which she had been excluded for ten years. She was elected to the third session of the Chinese Writers' Association and the fourth session of the Chinese Federation of Literary and Art Circles. She also resumed her writing, producing more prose and fiction.

Chen Xuezhao's pre-1949 writing included "A Tiring Trip," "A Small Token of My Heart" (Cuncao xin), "Companions in the Mist" (Yanxia banlü), "In Memory of Paris," "Visiting Yan'an" (Yan'an fangwenji), and "A Trip in the Liberated Areas" (Jiefangqu manyouji). In the latter two, she confessed to evolving from a state of spiritual confusion to an eventual embrace of communism. After 1949, Chen Xuezhao wrote a series of prose and fiction pieces, including *Random Recollections of Life* (Fuchen zayi; translated into English as *Surviving the Storm*); *Unforgettable Years* (Nanwang de suiyue); and *Like Flowing Water* (Ru shui nianhua). Her novels include the autobiographical *It's Beautiful to Be Working* (two volumes with a sequel), *Earth* (Tudi), and *Spring Tea* (Chun cha). She has also written a memoir, *Returning Home from the Remotest Corner of the World* (Tianya guike). Chen Xuezhao translated *Lenin, Literature, and Others* from French into Chinese and Balzac's *La Femme de trente ans* (A woman of thirty) and some of his plays. Chen Xuezhao also helped translate Charles de Gaulle's *L'Appel* (Call to honor).

GAO Yuanbao
(Translated and amplified by Cui Zhiying)

Chen Xuezhao. *Gongzuozhe shi meili de*. Hangzhou: Zhejiang renmin chubanshe, 1979.
———. *Surviving the Storm: A Memoir*, trans. Ti Hua and Caroline Greene, ed. and intro. Jeffrey C. Kinkley. Armonk, N.Y.: M.E. Sharpe, 1990.
"Chen Xuezhao jianli." In *Zhongguo xiandai zuojia zhuanlüe*, vol. 1. Xuzhou: Xuzhou shifan xueyuan, 1981, 415–18.
Huaxia funü mingren cidian. Beijing: Huaxia chubanshe, 1988, 611.
Zhongguo funü guanli ganbu xueyuan, ed. *Gujin Zhongwai nümingren cidian*. Beijing: Zhongguo guangbo dianshi chubanshe, 1980, 42.

Chen Yong: *see* **Chen Rong**

Ch'en Yüeh-ying: *see* **Yü-Ch'en Yüeh-ying**

Chen Yueying: *see* **Yü-Ch'en Yüeh-ying**

Chen Zen, Sophia: *see* **Chen Hengzhe**

Chen Zhe: *see* **Ch'iung Yao**

Chen-Shi Man: *see* **Ch'en-Shih Man**

Ch'en-Shih Man
Ch'en-Shih Man [Chen-Shi Man], b. 1909, in Yi Lan County, Taiwan, as Shih Man, practiced as a medical doctor and played a role in politics as an elected representative of Yi Lan County.

The Shih family originally came from Chang-chou [Zhangzhou] in Fu-chien [Fujian] Province and had accumulated a great fortune over the generations as merchants, thus holding a prominent position in Yi Lan society. Ch'en-Shih Man's parents subscribed to Western ideas on education and therefore sent their daughter to school. After graduating from Taipei Third Girls' Senior High School (Taipei ti-san kao-teng nü-hsüeh-hsiao) in 1926, she studied in Japan at Tokyo Ladies' Medical College. Graduating in 1931, Ch'en-Shih Man then returned to Taiwan to marry Ch'en Ch'eng-hsiang [Chen Chengxiang]. She returned with him to Japan while he finished his medical studies, and the couple went back to Taiwan in 1933 to start their medical practice. Ch'en-Shih Man became the first woman doctor in the Lo-tung area.

With the end of Japanese colonial rule in 1945, the KMT established women's work organizations throughout Taiwan, and Ch'en-Shih Man responded to a call to take charge of women's work in Yi Lan. After considerable preparation, the Yi Lan Women's Association was formally established in 1950, and she was elected chair. At that time, its main task was to offer classes in teaching life skills to women. Attention was also paid to the problem of girls being sold from poor families or given to other families as adopted daughters. Ch'en-Shih Man stood for local government and from that year was elected consecutively three times to Yi Lan County Council. In 1972, she was elected to the National Assembly and retired in 1978, at the age of sixty-nine.

Although Ch'en-Shih Man spent almost thirty years in politics, she continued to practice medicine during that time. In charge of the Ophthalmology Department of

Taipei Po-ai Hospital from 1954 to 1985, Ch'en-Shih Man attended to many patients suffering from eye diseases. Throughout her life, she worked tirelessly for the rights of Taiwanese women and is a fine example of a successful career woman of contemporary Taiwan.

HO Shu-i
(Translated by George Li)

Yu Chien-ming. "Ch'en-Shih Man." In *Tsou-kuo liang ko shih-tai ti Taiwan chih-yeh fu-nü fang-wen chi-lu*. Taipei: Chung-yang yen-chiu-yüan. Chin-tai-shih yen-chiu-so, 1994.

Ch'eng Hsiao-kuei

Ch'eng Hsiao-kuei [Cheng Xiaogui], b. 1959, in Taiwan, is a native of Shu-ch'eng [Shucheng] County, Anhwei [Anhui] Province. She is a graduate of the Central Police College (Chung-yang ching-kuan hsüeh-hsiao) and recognized for her work in fingerprint identification theory and practice.

Upon graduation, Ch'eng Hsiao-kuei was assigned to the Criminal Investigation Corps (Hsing-shih ching-ch'a-chü), where she made a stunning investigative debut by solving the "1230 Special Case," a shocking murder that had puzzled the police for some time. Ch'eng Hsiao-kuei obtained fingerprints from the corpse by amputating the thumbs and subjecting them to a special treatment. This enabled the police to positively identify the corpse as Ling Yung-ch'üan, the assistant manager of a Hua-nan bank who had apparently been killed during a robbery. Cracking the case led her to write a master's thesis for the Police Research Institute (Ching-cheng yen-chiu-so) on her methodology, entitled "Using Amino Acid Coloring to Render Latent Fingerprints Visible" (Li-yung an-chi-suan ch'eng-se fan-ying chien-yen ch'u chi-chung chih-chang shang ch'ien-fu chih-wen chih yen-chiu).

After returning to her unit, Ch'eng Hsiao-kuei gained additional experience with a variety of cases and put it to good use in her research. She also read widely in foreign-language academic journals, reports, and case studies. In summer 1989, Ch'eng Hsiao-kuei passed an examination that was part of the police force's five-year plan and went on to the United States to further her studies at the Connecticut State Police criminal laboratories. There, she gained practical field experience in fingerprint identification, crime scene investigation, crime scene reconstruction, and murder detection using the latest technology—identification through DNA testing. Ch'eng Hsiao-kuei translated into Chinese various manuals on complex scientific identification equipment and shared the fruits of her research with her colleagues in Taiwan upon her return.

She published the results of her systematic techniques for fingerprinting studies, including her unique ANS and MBO- F fingerprint identification methods. Working with fingerprint identification specialists throughout the world, Ch'eng Hsiao-kuei developed the use of lasers to detect latent fingerprints and light bloodstains, thus contributing greatly to the work of fingerprint identification in Taiwan and receiving international recognition.

Her professional achievements in research and practical application demonstrated the multifaceted capabilities of women in the police force. In 1990, she was selected as one of the ten Outstanding Young Women of the Year and a model police officer. Like Li Li-chüan (*q.v.*), who made her name in fieldwork, Ch'eng Hsiao-kuei has also contributed greatly to professional police work. Both of these women tirelessly pursued excellence and in themselves provide important models for the new generation of policewomen in Taiwan.

CH'EN Ch'un-ying
(Translated by Lily Xiao Hong Lee and Sue Wiles)

"Mo-fan ching-ch'a chien-chieh." *Ching-kuan*, no. 407 (June 1990): 15.
Yü Wei-fen. "T'a tsou-chin le chih-wen shih-chieh—chien-chieh shih-ta-chieh-ch'u nü-ch'ing-nien Ch'eng Hsiao-kuei ching-kuan." *Ching-kuan*, no. 405 (April 1990): 54–55.

Cheng Naishan

Cheng Naishan, b. 1946, in Shanghai although a native of Tongxiang County, Zhejiang Province, is a novelist. She spent her childhood in Hong Kong.

While still at high school, like many girls of that age Cheng Naishan lived in a world of fantasy and became infatuated with film stars. She would follow the monthly box office ratings and try to see all the good films listed, watching *Roman Holiday* and *The Million Pound Note* starring Gregory Peck more than twenty times, and knew the dialogue by heart. Cheng Naishan became interested in creative writing through watching these films. A great love of music also expanded her sensitivity and would eventually inform her writing. After graduating from the English Department of Shanghai Education College (Shanghai jiaoyu xueyuan) in 1965, she taught English in a middle school in Shanghai until 1979.

That year, the author embarked on her writing career with publication in the magazine *Shanghai Literature* of her first novel, *Songs My Mother Taught Me* (Mama jiao chang de ge). She joined the Chinese Writers' Association in 1985 and the same year became a professional writer at its Shanghai branch. Since then, Cheng Naishan has published nearly twenty mid-length novels, more than fifty short novels, and many prose essays. Her novels include *The Blue House* (Lan wu), *The Poor Street* (Qiong jie), *The Yellow Silk Ribbon* (Huang sidai), *Daughters' Tribulations* (Nü'er jing), *Death of a Swan* (Tian'e zhi si), and *The Bankers* (Jinrong jia). More than ten of her novels have been translated into English, French, Japanese, German, and Esperanto. *The Blue House*, *The Poor Street*, *Lilac Villa* (Dingxiang bieshu), and *The Yellow Silk Ribbon* have been adapted as television dramas, while *Daughters' Tribulations* was made into a film.

Cheng Naishan specializes in writing about Shanghai, and her stories capture a tangible local flavor that one critic hails as the evocative power to work "Shanghai magic." She was born into an elite family: her grandfather was a banker, and both of her parents were educated at St. John's University in Shanghai. Her earlier writings such as *The Blue House* and *Lilac Villa* focus on the privileged life of merchants in old Shanghai high society rather than the blue-collar workers at the bottom. After twenty years of working as an English teacher in a working-class area, however, Cheng Naishan began to write about ordinary people in Shanghai, the inherent goodness and interdependence of men and women coping with misery and disarray. Publication of her novel *The Poor Street* marked this change in direction to include both sides of Shanghai society. Her latest full-length novel, *The Bankers*, published by Shanghai Art and Literature Publishing House, 1989, is a breakthrough in perception and objectivity, revealing the enormous variety of Shanghai life. The depth of her novels in showing the vicissitudes of modern times to which Shanghai industrialists, intellectuals, and philistines have been subjected confirms that her writing, especially her Shanghai writing, has reached a new threshold.

Cheng Naishan currently sits on the council of the Shanghai Writers' Association, is a member of the Shanghai Federation of Writers and Artists, and director of the Shanghai Christian Women's Society. She visited the Philippines in 1987 with a delegation of Christian women. Cheng Naishan is married to Yan Erchun, who gives her a great deal of support. They have one daughter.

GAO Yuanbao
(Translated and amplified by Cui Zhiying)

Ai Yi. "Xie bu jin de Shanghai tan—Cheng Naishan yinxiang." *Renwu*, no. 2 (1990): 70–74.
Bi Shuowan. "Shanghai Magic: A Day-and-Night Stream." In *The Blue House*, by Cheng Naishan. Beijing: Panda Books, 1989, 8–14.
Cheng Naishan. "Why Parents Worry," trans. Janice Wickeri. *Renditions*, special issue (Spring and Autumn 1987): 235–48.
Pan Yadun. *Shijie huawen nüzuojia sumiao*. Guangzhou: Jinan daxue chubanshe, 1993, 104–10.

Cheng Xiaogui: *see* **Ch'eng Hsiao-kuei**

Cheng Yen, Master
Master Cheng Yen [Zhengyan fashi], b. 1937, in Ch'ing-shui, T'ai-chung County, Taiwan, is a Buddhist nun. Although her name has been romanized several ways in English, e.g., Ven. Cheng-yen, Cheng-yen Shih, Dharma Master Cheng Yen, Ven. Zhengyan, and Zhengyan fashi, the form adopted here—Master Cheng Yen—is preferred in her foundation's publications.

Born Wang Chin-yün [Wang Jinyun], she was adopted as a child by her paternal uncle Wang T'ien-sung. From early childhood, the girl was known for filial obedience and, later after being struck by the impermanence of life when her adoptive father died suddenly in June 1960, for turning to Buddhism. In September the following year, Wang Chin-yün shaved her head and became a nun. She was ordained by Ven. Yin-shun in February 1963 and given the *hao* of Cheng Yen and the *tzu* [*zi*] of Hui-chang. In 1966 Master Cheng Yen founded the Tzu Chi [Tz'u-Chi] Buddhist Compassion Relief Foundation (Fo-chiao k'o-nan tz'u-chi kung-te hui, or Tz'u-chi kung-te hui) in a small hut at the rear of P'u-ming Monastery in Hua-lien. Known as the Tzu Chi Foundation, it had four missions: charity, medical care, education, and culture. Their realization was founded on the four Buddhist ways of being of boundless loving kindness, compassion, joy, and equanimity. From the very beginning of her Buddhist life, Master Cheng Yen abided by Master Pai-chang's rule that "a day without work is a day without food." She accepts neither financial support from her followers nor attends penance rites, officiates at ritual ceremonies, or begs alms. She and her disciples are self-reliant; farming and a variety of handicrafts earn them a frugal and simple Buddhist living.

The incident that prompted Master Cheng Yen to set up the Tzu Chi Foundation was the treatment meted out to an aboriginal woman who had suffered a miscarriage and been sent to hospital. Although she was bleeding profusely, this woman was refused treatment because she was unable to pay the hospital's TW$ 8,000 deposit. Master Cheng Yen, already aware of the solid contribution that Catholics in particular make to social welfare, called upon her followers to join her in helping the poor and saving the world. They financed the cause of the foundation with their own hard-won earnings from making infant's shoes and personal donations of fifty cents a day from savings.

Their charitable work helped the poor and distressed and soon they set up free medical clinics. The foundation went on to build Tzu Chi Buddhist General Hospital and established both Tzu Chi Junior College of Nursing (restructured as Tzu Chi Technical College of Nursing in 1998) and a medical college (restructured as Tzu Chi University in 2000). To consolidate its work, the foundation puts out publications, in English and Chinese, and produces television programs. In recent years, the charity has expanded its activities to include bone marrow donation (since 1993), international relief, environmental protection, and community volunteerism. These voluntary activities, together with the four missions, are called the Eight Footprints. Since its first cash donation to flood victims in Bangladesh in 1991, the foundation has undertaken a great deal of timely relief work, providing aid for flood relief in central and eastern China, the China Airlines plane crash in Ta-yüan, Hurricane George in Central America, and earthquakes in Turkey and Taiwan.

The primary strength of the foundation's charitable work lies in its large number of lay disciples. Master Cheng Yen adopted what is known as the "Tzu Chi spirit": *Wu-yüan ta-tz'u, t'ung-t'i ta-pei* (Great loving kindness needs no reason, great compassion demands genuine identification with those who are suffering). In other words, neither personal relationships are taken into account when offering aid nor is reciprocity expected—the ones in need are treated as one's self: when others go hungry, one feels the hunger; when others are drowning, one suffers as well. Disciples are actively determined to save the miserable and distressed and purify the mind in order to attain a pure land on earth. Master Cheng Yen's words of meditation (*ching-ssu yü*) have become the spiritual mainstay of Tzu Chi followers and a powerful force behind the development of the foundation's charitable work.

Initially, the Tzu Chi Foundation functioned without hierarchy, but the sheer scope of its work has required that a core group of executive members directs the work of subsidiary teams and associations. Their focus includes a wide range of programs, including voluntary workers; "virtuous mothers and elder sisters"; honorary directors; childcare; teachers' associations; and post-secondary youth, writing teams, and foreign language teams. They also run activities such as camps for young people to learn Buddhism, children classes, choirs, regional visiting circles, social workers' groups, and community actions for the protection of the environment. The foundation has branches in Taipei, T'ai-chung, P'ing-tung, and also overseas. The policy-making body is the Center for Tzu Chi's Charitable Work, and Master Cheng Yen is its chief executive.

Though physically weak, Master Cheng Yen initiated the medical and educational charitable work and propagated the spirit of aiding society and saving others. Both her efforts and Tzu Chi Foundation have been widely recognized for their contributions. To commend her "profound compassion and noble inspiration to pursue benevolent deeds," then-President of the Republic of China Lee Teng-hui awarded her with a plaque bearing the inscription "*tz'u-pei chi-shih*" (helping others with loving kindness and compassion) in October 1989. The Philippines's Ramon Magsaysay Award Foundation, sometimes called the Asian counterpart of the Nobel Prize Committee, honored her in July 1991 with the Award of Community Leader. This was for having "succeeded in drawing the attention of modern Taiwanese to the ancient Buddhist dictum that all beings be treated with benevolence." In November, the State of Texas, U.S., bestowed on her medals, declaring her to be an "Honorary Citizen of Texas," "Honorary Mayor of San Antonio," and "Honorary Consul of San Antonio." In September 1994, she became only the second Asian to win the Dwight D. Eisenhower Award for International Peace, the first being given to India's Mother Teresa. In February 2000, her exemplary deeds were incorporated into high school teaching materials in Nova Scotia, Canada.

Master Cheng Yen's compassion for the welfare of others has endured for more than thirty years, and she undoubtedly experiences exhaustion. Nevertheless, she holds that "a tired body and a mind devoid of perseverance belong to the little self, while a body that knows no tiredness and a faith abounding in perseverance belong to the big self. When one allows one's big self to displace one's little self, one gains superhuman strength and can go forward courageously." These words best portray Master Cheng Yen's devotion to her charitable work.

CHENG Li-jung
(Translated by Chan Yuk Ping)

Chao Hsien-ming. *Ta-she wu-ch'iu—Cheng Yen fa-shih yü tz'u-chi shih-chieh*. Taipei: Hsien-chih ch'u-pan-she, 1999.
Ch'en Hui-chien. *Cheng Yen fa-shih ti tz'u-chi shih-chieh*. Taipei: Tz'u-chi wen-hua chih-yeh chung-hsin, 2000.
Chiang Ts'an-t'eng. "Ts'ung fo-chia 'fa-chieh kuan' ti li-shih hsing-ko k'an hsien-tai Taiwan fo-chiao ti shih-chien mo-shih—i Cheng Yen fa-shih ti tz'u-chi shih-yeh wei-li." In *Taiwan fo-chiao pai-nien shih chih yen-chiu*, ed. Chiang Ts'an-t'eng. Taipei: Nan-t'ien shu-chü, 1996.
Ching Yu-ing. *Master of Love and Mercy: Cheng Yen*. Nevada City: Blue Dolphin Publishing, 1995.
K'ang Lo and Chien Hui-mei. "Tz'u-chi kung-te hui." In *Hsin-yang yü she-hui—Taiwan ti fo-chiao t'uan-t'i*, eds. K'ang Lo and Chien Hui-mei. Taipei: Taipei hsien-li wen-hua chung-hsin, 1995.
Yün-ching. *Ch'ien-shou fo-hsin—Cheng Yen fa-shih*. Taipei: Ta-ch'ien wen-hua ch'u-pan shih-yeh, 1995.

Cheng Yueru: *see* **Lin Dai**

Cheng-yen Shih: *see* **Cheng Yen, Master**

Cheng-yen, Ven.: *see* **Cheng Yen, Master**

Chennault, Anna: *see* **Chen Xiangmei**

Chi Cheng

Chi Cheng [Ji Zheng], b. 1944, in Hsin-chu County, Taiwan, pioneered in women's track and field in Taiwan. Described by the International Amateur Athletic Foundation as "Asia's legendary female sprinter," she was the first woman to run the 100-yard dash in 10 seconds flat and set seven world records during her competing career.

Chi Cheng's birth family was poor and as one of eight children she became adopted out at the age of six or seven years. The girl subsequently suffered the typical verbal abuse and beatings to which adopted daughters were subjected but was fortunate to be able to return to her natural parents when she was nine years old. Her father brought in only a meager income as a street hawker, and her mother earned a pittance washing clothes. When they could not afford to send her to school, Chi Cheng would go to a nearby primary school to watch other children learning in class. A kind patron, whose name has never been made public, eventually paid her school fees so that Chi Cheng could attend. She treasured this opportunity, producing outstanding work and winning scholarships.

Chi Cheng was a competitive child and won many prizes, especially in sporting events. Her nickname was "Long-legs," and it soon became obvious that she showed athletic potential. Chi Cheng attended Second Girls' High School in Hsin-chu and the first time she represented the school in a track meet won a gold medal for the high jump. By the end of the 1950s, her performance attracted attention in various provincial meets in Taiwan, and Chi Cheng began to compete in international sporting events in the 1960s. She represented the Republic of China at the 1960 Rome Olympics but did not do well because of a lack of professional training. This did not deter her, however, and Chi Cheng continued to train hard. The American hurdler-cum-track and field coach Vince Reel (1914?–1999?) went to Taiwan in 1962, and under his supervision she improved rapidly. In 1963, he took her to the United States to seek further training. Some American sources suggest that the two were married; one bibliography of athletes lists her as "Chi Cheng, Reel."

In 1966, Chi Cheng won a gold medal for the long jump at the Fifth Asian Games in Bangkok. At the Sixth Asian Games in 1970, also held in Bangkok, she won a gold medal for the women's 100 meters. At the 1968 Mexico Olympics, Chi Cheng won a bronze medal for the women's 80-meter low hurdles. Her most successful year, however, was 1970, when she won twenty medals at twenty-one indoor events and sixty-six medals at outdoor events and also broke five world records for women's events: 100 meters (11 seconds), 200 meters (22.4 seconds), 100-meter low hurdles (12.8 seconds), 100 yards (10 seconds), and 220 yards (22.6 seconds). Her stunning performance brought her many honors the following year. The Associated Press voted her Global Athlete of the Year (1971), *Women's Track and Field World* magazine (later published by Vince Reel) voted her Best Athlete, and *Track and Field News* broke with tradition to honor her, and not a man, as Athlete of the Year. Chi Cheng was one of the winners of the Victor Awards, considered the Oscar of the sporting world, and dubbed "the Flying Antelope," "Yellow Lightning," and "Flying Woman of Asia."

However, at the peak of her career, Chi Cheng injured a leg and had to undergo surgery. Unfortunately, it was not as successful as expected and she was forced to give up competitive athletics. Chi Cheng commenced study at the California State Polytechnic in Pomona and after graduating in 1973 was appointed sports director at Redland University in California (1974–75). She returned to Taiwan in 1976 to take up the position of secretary-general of the Track and Field Association (T'ien-chin hsieh-hui) of the Republic of China. Armed with the most up-to-date methods and equipment, Chi Cheng threw herself into the training of athletes. As secretary-general, she traveled widely in Taiwan to observe training facilities and document the development of various sports and also made innovations to existing systems, organized meets, and invited distinguished overseas athletes to Taiwan. In order to promote sport there, Chi Cheng stood for election to the Legislative Yuan in 1981 and was elected with a clear majority; she returned to stand again two times, and again won with a clear majority. Her mission was to set up a Sports Committee under the Legislative Yuan. The bill Chi Cheng put forward was proposed by sixty-eight members and eventually passed. After becoming president of Taiwan's Track and Field Association, she visited mainland China in 1990. Chi Cheng downplayed the differences between Chinese separated by the Taiwan Strait, saying how proud she was whenever a competitor from either side won international honors.

Chi Cheng is a tall woman, tanned, and modest. In spite of her success in the world of athletics, she was not blessed with a physical constitution best suited for the profession. Chi Cheng won through sheer hard work and persistence, the scars on her legs testifying to the pain she endured as an athlete. Her husband, Chang Po-fu, believes several factors are behind Chi Cheng's almost fanatical dedication: genuinely loving the sport of athletics, overcoming the insults and ridicule she once suffered, and fulfilling a quiet self-respect and national pride. Her husband is also her former coach Chang Po-fu, who is deputy director of Taiwan's Track and Field Association. They have made a harmonious life together and have four children.

Chi Cheng raised the athletic profile of China, a nation not known for the physical prowess of its people nor Chinese women in particular. She was one of the first Chinese women to gain fame in international sport and serves as a role model for generations of Chinese women. In May 2000, Chi Cheng was voted Female Asian Athlete of the Twentieth Century in a poll conducted by the Asian Amateur Athletic Association. Her promotion of sport in Taiwan through political and social channels allows her to extend her life as an athlete and continue making an important contribution.

Lily Xiao Hong LEE

"Asia's 'Athletes of the Century.'" *International Amateur Athletic Federation News*, no. 41 (May 2000): 4.

Chung-hua min-kuo tang-tai ming-jen lu, vol. 3. Taipei: Taiwan Chung-hua shu-chü, 1978, 1297.

Lu Shen-fang. "Shih-chieh shang p'ao te tsui k'uai ti nü-jen Chi Cheng." In *Hsiang shih-tai t'iao-chan ti nü-hsing*. Taipei: Hsüeh-sheng shu-tien, 1977, 9–15.

Sung Jui-chih [Song Ruizhi], ed. *Chung-kuo fu-nü wen-hua t'ung-lan*. Chi-nan [Jinan]: Shantung wen-i ch'u-pan-she, 1995, 716.

Ying-wen *Chung-kuo fu-nü*, ed. *Ku-chin chu-ming fu-nü jen-wu*. Shih-chia-chuang [Shijiazhuang]: Ho-pei jen-min ch'u-pan-she, 1986, 1215–18.

Yü Hsin-pei. "Fang Chi Cheng t'an Ya-yün." *T'ai-sheng* (August 1990): 8–10.

Chi Cheng, Reel: *see* **Chi Cheng**

Chi Jishang

Chi Jishang, 1917–1994, of Anlu County, Hubei Province, was a geologist and petrologist. Her father, Chi Zehui, was a law graduate of Peking University and worked in the Justice Department of the Beijing government.

Because she was the fourth of five children, Chi Jishang's parents put off sending her to school. The girl was so eager to have an education, however, that she did everything she could to learn indirectly through her older siblings; touched by that determination, Chi Jishang's parents relented and sent her to school. This experience convinced Chi Jishang that one's destiny is not immutable. She enrolled in the high school attached to Beijing Normal University (Beijing shifan daxue fuzhong), graduated in 1936, and went on to Tsinghua [Qinghua] University to study physics. There, she became involved in anti-Japanese activities and joined the CCP. Her life turned tragically at this point, however: her father lost his job; her mother, and one of her sisters, became ill and died; her brother died suddenly while on his way to Europe to study; and her other sister developed a mental illness. With no means of support, Chi Jishang went to Hunan as a refugee student (*liuwang xuesheng*) after the outbreak of the Sino-Japanese War. She studied at a "temporary university" there and also joined the Battlefield Corps of Hunan Youth (Hunan qingnian zhandi fuwu tuan). The father of a friend, a geology professor, extended financial help to her in 1938, and it enabled her to study at Southwest Union University (Xinan lianda) in Kunming. At this stage, she changed her area of study to geology because it was more practical, feeling it would equip her with the necessary skills for developing China's mining industry.

Geology was relatively new to China, and, with very few reference works available in Chinese, Chi Jishang worked hard to learn English so that she could read English-language books and journals. Because she and her fellow students undertook surveys in remote areas where bandits roamed, Chi Jishang was given the Ma Yisi Award, named for an early woman geologist killed by bandits while out in the field. Chi Jishang also discovered a quality iron mine in Yunan Province. Graduating from Southwest Union University at the age of twenty-nine, she soon after married a student in a higher class named Li Pu (d. 1967). He later became a researcher at the Geochemistry Institute of the Chinese Academy of Sciences. It is not known whether they had any children.

Only a matter of weeks after her marriage in 1946, Chi Jishang accepted a scholarship to study at Bryn Mawr in the United States. She completed her master's degree within a year and went straight on to do Ph.D. work on scholarship. Her doctoral supervisor was a woman professor, whose name is not known. The woman was clearly learned, a good and caring teacher, and deeply influenced Chi Jishang. Chi Jishang's doctoral dissertation on granitization was published in the *Bulletin of the Geological Society of America* and won the praise of petrologist F.J. Turner, who invited her to be his research assistant at the University of California, Berkeley. Between 1950 and 1951, she and Turner published three papers together. In the meantime, however, Chi Jishang wrote to Professor Yuan Fuli of Qinghua University and Professor Wang Hongzhen of Peking University, seeking a position so that she could return to China. As soon as a suitable response came, Chi Jishang declined a well-paying position in the United States and took up an associate professorship at Qinghua. In 1952, as part of the reorganization of tertiary education within the PRC, she was transferred to Beijing Geological Institute (Beijing dizhi xueyuan) as a professor.

Chi Jishang led and participated in several important geological surveys of China. From 1955 to 1956, she participated on a Sino-Soviet geological survey team to the Qilian Mountain in the northwest and twice traversed that mountain. In 1958, Chi Jishang was team leader and responsible for all technical matters when more than two hundred staff and students of Beijing Geological School undertook a survey of central and western Shandong. Their brief also included a general search for minerals. Within four years, the team submitted fourteen geological maps and accompanying reports covering an area of 89,600 square kilometers. These maps and reports have all been published and laid the foundation for prospecting west of the Qi and Shu (Rivers) Rift in Shandong. The very discovery of this rift was significant for future prospecting and developing the theory of rock structure. In the 1960s, she led the research conducted on the Yanshan granite of the Badaling area near Beijing. She studied the granite in that area in detail and classified it into four types; her analysis and classification became a model for Chinese geology. Such studies were also rare outside China.

Like all industrialized countries, China needs diamonds, but it was not until 1965 that diamonds were discovered in China, in Guizhou and Shandong. The Ministry of Geology immediately formed Shandong 613 Scientific Research Team, assembled from researchers at the China Institute of Geological Sciences, Beijing Geological School, and the Shandong 809 Geological Team; Chi Jishang was placed in charge of technical matters. Her research team went to the Shandong site, where she conducted fieldwork and experiments during the day and searched and studied materials as well as lecturing the technical staff at night. The team reported results promptly to relevant departments and units by means of "research newsletters" (*keyan jianbao*). Within two years, the team completed its study of the first batch of kimberlite that contained diamond, wrote research papers, held training sessions, and provided guidance for more than twenty provinces interested in diamond prospecting. During the Cultural Revolution, the 613 Team was disbanded, but Chi Jishang continued with her research, under extremely difficult conditions.

From 1975 to 1984, she participated in the establishment of the Wuhan Geological Institute (Wuhan dizhi xueyuan) and, in turn, headed its Petroleum Section, Petrology Section, and the Geology Department, and finally became vice-president of the institute. When Chi Jishang went to Wuhan in the 1970s, she investigated Hubei kimberlite and in the following decade presented reports at conferences on kimberlite and diamond prospecting organized by the Ministry of Geology. Her contribution to this field can be summarized as follows. Firstly, she tabulated the characteristics and composition of minerals accompanying kimberlite and diamonds that serve as indicators for prospecting. Secondly, the scientist proposed the scheme that is still in use for the classification and naming of kimberlite in China. Thirdly, she pointed out that kimberlite containing diamond exists in different forms, hence widening prospecting possibilities. Fourthly, Chi Jishang was the first to propose a formula that helped identify kimberlites containing diamonds. These achievements reflect international consensus and confirm her high level of accomplishment in international kimberlite studies.

In the latter half of the decade when China reopened its door to the international community, its earth sciences lagged behind the rest of the world's. Chi Jishang subsequently organized research consortiums on several large geological topics. From 1981 to 1984, she personally took charge of fieldwork in east China involving thirty-odd colleagues and students. Her research *A Study on the Cenozoic Basalt Rocks and Upper Mantle of East China (Including Kimberlite)* (Zhongguo dongbu xinshengdai xuanwuyan ji shangdiman yanjiu) details relevant geological, petrological, and geochemical data and explores related issues. Experts invited by the Ministry of Geology and Mining described her book as a rich resource utilizing advanced methodology, contributing new ideas, and coordinating multiple disciplines and diverse perspectives on basalt and upper mantle studies related to mining. The book set a new standard, extending both theory and applied science in mining and prospecting; in 1989 it won First Prize in the Ministry of Geology and Mining's Achievement in Science and Technology Awards. Throughout the 1980s and 1990s, Chi Jishang was involved in many projects sponsored by the National Natural Sciences Foundation (Guojia ziran kexue jijin), Ministry of Geology and Mining, and State Education Commission, Science, and Technology Foundation (Guojia jiaowei keji jijin), as well as in a key project of China's Seventh Five-Year Plan.

Her fieldwork took her to all parts of China, including Inner Mongolia, Qinghai, Tibet, and Xinjiang. She also played an active role in international academic forums. From 1979 to 1982, Chi Jishang was China's representative at the International Geological Cooperation Plan (IGCP) organized by the United Nations Educational, Scientific, and Cultural Organization. Besides being an outstanding scientist herself, she was aware of the need to train new generations of geologists and undertook heavy teaching and administration loads even while doing research. Chi Jishang encouraged younger scientists to lead projects, attend conferences, and publish research papers and supported their efforts to open up new areas of research. She recognized the need for older geologists to mentor younger scientists as successors to carry on the work. Chi Jishang once said: "My ideal is to construct a ladder for young people." She practiced what she preached: even in her seventies, Chi Jishang insisted on going into the field to check data collected by students. Up to 1990, she had supervised seventeen students, eleven

Ph.D. candidates, and two postdoctoral candidates. She also wrote and edited many textbooks, including *Petrology* (Yanshixue) and *Sedimentary Petrology* (Chenji yanshixue).

Lily Xiao Hong LEE

Song Ruizhi, ed. *Zhongguo funü wenhua tonglan*. Jinan: Shandong wenyi chubanshe, 1995, 356–57.

Yingwen *Zhongguo funü*, ed. *Gujin zhuming funü renwu*, vol. 2. Shijiazhuang: Hebei renmin chubanshe, 1986, 952–56.

Zhao Chonghe and Yang Guangrong. "Chi Jishang." In *Zhongguo xiandai kexuejia zhuanji*, vol. 3. Beijing: Kexue chubanshe, 1992, 347–53.

Zhonghua quanguo fulian. *Zhongguo nüyuanshi*. Shenyang: Liaoning renmin chubanshe, 1995, 333–36.

Chi Li

Chi Li, b. 1957, possibly in Wuhan, Hubei Province, a leading exponent of "new realism" literature, is one of the new young writers emerging on the Chinese literary scene since the "open door policy" of the 1980s.

In many ways, Chi Li typifies her generation. She was born just before the Great Leap Forward (1958), which was followed in the early 1960s by a three-year famine; still a child when the Cultural Revolution started; and she was sent down to the countryside to be "reeducated" immediately after graduating from high school in 1974. Chi Li was fortunate to be accepted into the Wuhan Metallurgy Medical College (Yejin yixueyuan) as a worker-peasant-soldier student in 1976 and graduated in 1980. Although working as a doctor in the hospital of the Wuhan Iron and Steel Plant for three years, she decided on a change of career in 1983 and enrolled in a Chinese language and literature program at Wuhan University. Chi Li was appointed editor to the literary journal *Fragrant Grass* (Fangcao) after graduating in 1987 and by 1990 became a professional writer. In early 1999, she was deputy chair of the Writers' Association of Wuhan and a member of the Writers' Association of China. She married in 1987 (her husband's name is Lü) and gave birth to a daughter in 1988.

Chi Li's experiences as a doctor and editor provided rich source material for her writing. She reveals in her novels the eye of a keen observer, one who ponders deeply the truth and existence of the common people, whose lives are detailed with great sincerity.

Her first work to be published, in 1978, was poetry and prose. Her first novel, *Yue'er Is Nice* (Yue'er hao, 1982), tells the story of a country girl who is truth, kindness, and beauty incarnate. It is much more optimistic, idealistic, and romantic than her later work and reveals Chi Li's yearning for a simple, natural life. She has written about a dozen novels since then, most of which are in the four-volume *Collected Works of Chi Li* (Chi Li wenji, 1995).

The writer remained silent for a time after *Yue'er Is Nice*, finally publishing *A Troublesome Life* (Fannao rensheng), her best-known work, in 1987. This novel had enormous repercussions, not only marking a turning point in Chi Li's writing but also ushering in a new style of writing known as "new realism." The great political, social, and economic changes taking place in China during the 1980s provoked in her and many other writers a need to shift attention away from stereotypical, idealized, and "heroic" protagonists to real people. When Chi Li found herself unable to create the noble characters favored before and during the Cultural Revolution, she depicted instead the difficulties and predicaments of ordinary people long neglected by the literati.

Completing *A Troublesome Life* at one stretch, Chi Li quickly produced two more novels: *Not Talking of Love* (Bu tan aiqing, 1989) and *The Birth of the Sun* (Taiyang chushi, 1990). Called the "trilogy of life," all three became and remain bestsellers; *The Birth of the Sun* has also been made into a film. In *A Troublesome Life*, a worker called Yin Jiahou works hard and does his best to fulfill multiple roles as husband, father, worker, and lover only to find himself in endless trouble with a garrulous and grumbling wife, a troublesome son, low income and awkward living conditions, and complicated human relationships. Mentally and physically exhausted, Yin finds life trivial and tedious, lacking in glory and excitement. Such realism contrasts strongly with many works written in the early part of the "new era" after the Cultural Revolution. *Entering Middleage*, for example, published by Chen (or Shen) Rong (*q.v.*) in 1979 reflects that author's idealism as the novel's protagonists, ordinary intellectuals, worry as much about the fate of the country and the people as they do about their everyday lives.

Chi Li's *Not Talking of Love* is similar in subject matter and style to her *A Troublesome Life*. As the former title suggests, the novel is about love not in the traditional sense but rather about the loss of love in the trivial episodes of life, moments devoid of lofty ideals, poetry, and romance. Chi Li's love is anything but ideal and spiritual and interweaves with social position, money, and the mundane. While she does not glorify life and idealize love, nor is she pessimistic; her pictures are spattered with warmth, tinged with happiness, and dabbed with delight. The third novel in the trilogy, *The Birth of the Sun*, explores the life of a young couple. For them, everyday life, trivial as it is, is significant. The experience of pregnancy and birth of their daughter encapsulates learning, growth, and maturing. Life, and especially married life, is not easy but it need not be a hell on earth; there may be sadness and bitterness, but there is also happiness and joy. It has been said that Chi Li has not so much killed the idealistic splendor of life as she has dignified its long-neglected aspects.

Wuhan, her native city, is the setting for Chi Li's trilogy as well as several of her other novels. Its dialect and ambience are captured wonderfully by the writer and the many "Han flavors" in the city's cultural heritage give her characters an essential authenticity. Chi Li's fiction also touches on such global themes as the effect of modernization on traditional society, especially its detrimental effect on family values.

Although her trilogy and other novels have been generally well received, some critics dismiss her subject matter, criticizing her perceptions of daily urban life as commonplace, dull, and lacking in historical significance. In the early 1990s, Chi Li accepted the challenge implicit in the criticism and shifted her gaze from metropolitan Wuhan to the township of Mianshui Zhen and the surrounding countryside, publishing in 1990 *You Are a River* (Ni shi yi tiao he) and in 1992 producing the collection *Preconceived Murder* (Yumou sharen).

You Are a River is the story of a family centering on a woman called Lala. Spanning two decades from the 1960s to the 1980s, the book reveals the impact of the Cultural Revolution on the lives of the ordinary people. Lala is thirty when she is widowed and left with eight children. Although three of the children's names clearly echo important historical periods, the family knows little about current politics and hears news of shocking events only when they are over. The family does, however, feel the pain of hunger, and all of Lala's efforts are directed at keeping her children from starving. The lovely qualities usually associated with motherhood—gentleness, softness, and tenderness—seem to have little to do with Lala, whose story tears apart the "myth of the mother," showing the tenacity of lives lived separate from yet damaged by historical events.

Preconceived Murder is about revenge. The main character, Wang Liegou, harbors bitter hatred for the family of Ding Zongwan and tries repeatedly to take advantage of political movements to kill his enemy. Each time, however, he is strangely frustrated by circumstances. More than being a simple story of revenge, however, the writing expresses grief over the poverty of education of the Chinese people.

Chi Li drew on a much broader historical background in her stories of Mianshui Zhen so as to show the tremendous changes that have taken place in society as well as in the lives of individuals, as she has written elsewhere: "Mianshui Zhen is my carrier. Whenever I thought and reflected on history, those historic figures from Mianshui Zhen would flow out of my pen, so I wrote stories about them. Although they live on the Jianhan Plains, they epitomize China and mankind."

Artistically, Chi Li's novels embed poetic imagery or create poetic imagery within the story lines. The beach in *The Beach of the Young Lady* (Shaofu de shatan, before 1985), for example, appears and disappears unexpectedly, symbolizing the unusual emotional state of a young married woman when she unexpectedly meets a middle-aged man on the beach. Another example is the image of the sun in *The Sun in the Rain* (Yu zhong de taiyang, before 1985) where rings of hazy sunlight evoke the unpredictable nature of life and, especially, love. Her images infuse a free and natural poetic quality into plain narrative. Chi Li's new realism fiction, as represented by the trilogy, falls into this category. In other pieces, her lyricism breaks from poetic quality to deal with matters of historic significance; the Mianshui Zhen series belongs in this category.

Chi Li's great achievement lies in the realism conveyed in her writing. For a long time, contemporary Chinese literature followed the path of traditional realism, attempting to create myth from reality. As Michael S. Duke observed, however, since the late 1980s "contemporary Chinese fiction has been 'walking toward the world,' a phrase that may be taken to mean approaching the quality of the finest in world fiction." New realism, succeeding as it did "scar" and reform literature, renders daily life realistically and brings a fresh and new vitality to the Chinese literary world. Dai Jinhua (*q.v.*) recently noted:

> What Chi Li presents in her trilogy is the real life of this shore. It is no longer the wading in the bitter sea nor the idealization of the golden shore opposite; it is an embarrassing yet full, trivial yet real picture of the ordinary life of ordinary people. It

is not a filthy picture of society revealed behind the shattered mirage, but a realistic presentation of life emerging from the cracks in the backdrop that has been resolutely torn up.

Chi Li's special charm is her exercise of a simple and unadorned style, employing neither an elaboration of plot nor play of technique. She captures real life accurately and vividly portrays living characters. Her feminine sensibility, insight, and delicacy also add a human touch and artistic appeal to her works. Chi Li is one of several writers who have been cultivating the fertile land of "new realism literature" from which we can surely expect more beautiful flowers. Her new novel *Salute to the Endless Years* (Zhi wujin suiyue) was listed among the top eight novels in a recent public appraisal of literary works published in 1998 in the *Contemporary Era* (Dangdai) magazine.

Ping WANG

Chen Xiaoming. "Fankan weiji: 'Xin xieshi lun.'" In *Zhongguo xin xieshi xiaoshuo jing xuan, xu*. Lanzhou: Gansu renmin chubanshe, 1993.
Chi Li. *Chi Li wenji*. Nanjing: Jiangsu wenyi chubanshe, 1995.
Dai Jinhua. "Chi Li: Shensheng de fannao rensheng." *Wenxue pinglun*, 6 (1995): 50–61.
Duke, Michael S. "Walking Toward the World: A Turning Point in Contemporary Chinese Fiction." *World Literature Today*, Summer (1991): 389.
Lee, Lily Xiao Hong. "Localization and Globalization: Dichotomy and Convergence in Chi Li's Fiction." *Canadian Review of Comparative Literature*, 24, no. 4 (December 1997): 913–26.
Yu Kexun. "Chi Li de chuangzuo ji qi wenhua tese." *Xiaoshuo pinglun*, 4 (1996): 36–40.
Zeng Zhuo. "Postscript." In *Taiyang chushi*. Wuhan: Changjiang wenyi chubanshe, 1992, 325.

Chia Fu-ming

Chia Fu-ming [Jia Fuming], b. 1926, in Ch'ing [Qing] County, Ho-pei [Hebei] Province, was for many years active in educational research in Taiwan and played a leading role in education policy making.

Her father, who was an officer at the local court, profoundly influenced his daughter with his belief that honesty and integrity were fundamental to personal development. The period of her youth coincided with the Sino-Japanese War, and hostilities between the KMT and the CCP. Forced to flee from her home, Chia Fu-ming's schooling was interrupted, and she found it difficult to study on her own. Between 1946 and 1949, Chia Fu-ming attended the education faculty at the national Beiping Normal University (Pei-p'ing shih-fan ta-hsüeh). She left the mainland in 1949 and in 1950 graduated from the Education Department at Taiwan Normal College (Taiwan shih-fan hsüeh-yüan). She gained a Master of Education from Taiwan Normal University (Taiwan shih-fan ta-hsüeh) in 1957 and in the following year went to America to continue studies. Chia Fu-ming was awarded a master's in educational science by the University of Oregon (1960) and a doctorate in education by the University of California, Los Angeles (1964).

Returning to Taiwan after completing her studies, she taught at the Education Research Institute at Taiwan Normal University (Taiwan shih-fan ta-hsüeh chiao-yü yen-chiu-so). Chia Fu-ming headed a team that planned training courses for normal school and senior high school teachers and devised tests for junior high school students. Between 1969 and 1972, she became director of the institute. During her term of office, Chia Fu-ming expanded the library and equipment and enhanced the standard of teaching; she also established a doctoral degree program and increased the number of postgraduate students. Chia Fu-ming accepted requests from the National Salvation Organization (Chiu-kuo t'uan) to hold meetings to discuss national reconstruction and supervised the transfer of the institute to a branch within the university. At the same time, she spent a great deal of time researching and writing about childhood development and guidance, psychology and creativity, education and character development, the philosophy of education, and the fundamentals of education, publishing a total of seven books and almost forty academic papers.

In 1972, Chia Fu-ming received a presidential appointment to the Examination Yuan, a role she filled for eighteen years, participating in policy decisions on examination and selection. In the meantime, Chia Fu-ming continued her education research. After retiring from the Examination Yuan in 1990, she worked part-time at the Education Research Institute at the Normal University and continued to do research and writing.

The educator never wavered in her belief that education is the means for training and developing character to produce "a fundamental person," one who possesses the essential qualities of "honesty" and "benevolence." Chia Fu-ming always advocated universal education and held that school education should play the dual role of developing both knowledge and skill.

CHENG Li-jung
(Translated by Katherine Kerr)

Lu Shen-fang. "Chia Fu-ming ho t'a feng-shou ti chi-chieh." In her *Hsiang shih-tai t'iao-chan ti nü-hsing*. Taipei: Hsüeh-sheng shu-tien, 1977, 195–99.
Wang Ping. *Chia Fu-ming hsien-sheng fang-wen chi-lu*. Taipei: Chung-yang yen-chiu-yüan. Chin-tai-shih yen-chiu-so, 1992. Includes a biography and list of Chia Fu-ming's works.

Chiang Kai-shek, Madame: *see* **Soong Mayling**

Ch'i-chün
Ch'i-chün [Qijun], b. 1917, as P'an Hsi-chen [Pan Xizhen] in Yung-chia [Yongjia] County (present-day Wenzhou), Che-chiang [Zhejiang] Province, is a contemporary writer with a background steeped in classical literature.

Born into a strongly traditional family, she was her parents' only daughter. Her father, P'an Kuo-kang [Pan Guogang], was a military officer, well read in literature, history and the art of warfare; he also loved poetry (*shih*) and lyrics (*tz'u*). When Ch'i-chün was five years old, P'an Kuo-kang employed a tutor named Yeh Chü-hsiung [Ye Juxiong]. Ch'i-chün learned to read the *Book of Songs* and T'ang poetry at the age of seven and knew several Buddhist sutras by heart from listening to her mother's recitations in the family Buddhist hall (*fo-t'ang*). One childhood companion, the family's old farmhand, a man called Uncle A-jung [Arong], taught her nursery rhymes and shared endless stories. She learned a great deal from his tales, and later in life grew nostalgic about this period in her childhood. At the age of fourteen, Ch'i-chün attended Hung-tao Girls' High School (Hung-tao nü-tzu chung-hsüeh), a famous missionary school in Hang-chou [Hangzhou]. Her fellow students dubbed her "a literary general" (*wen-hsüeh ta-chiang*) because she was able to write beautiful classical and modern Chinese, already had studied classical literature, and was versed in the vernacular, martial arts, and romantic fiction.

At seventeen, Ch'i-chün began writing fiction, but her works were returned when she sent them to newspapers. Her first published work and for which Ch'i-chün also received payment, "My friend Ah-huang" (Wo ti p'eng-yu, Ah-huang), appeared in a newspaper when she was nineteen. After passing the combined high schools external examination, Ch'i-chün enrolled at Chih-chiang [Zhijiang] University in Hang-chou to study Chinese literature. Located beside Liu-ho-t'a Tower on the banks of the Ch'ien-t'ang River, the university is said to be one of the most beautiful campuses in the world. Its Chinese Department was at that time quite famous. Ch'i-chün read widely while studying there, including the works of Chang Hen-shui [Zhang Henshui] and Su Man-shu [Su Manshu], which were considered to be new literature. The head of the Chinese Department, Hsia Ch'eng-t'ao [Xia Chengtao], also from Yung-chia, was a specialist in lyrics and profoundly influenced Ch'i-chün's studies and career. He also encouraged her to study the *Lao-tzu* [Laozi], *Chuang-tzu* [Zhuangzi], and other works of Chinese literature and philosophy and taught her to write classical poetry and lyrics. He greatly encouraged her to write. At the same time, a foreign female teacher in the English Department also encouraged Ch'i-chün to major in foreign literature but Hsia Ch'eng-t'ao disagreed, declaring that with Ch'i-chün's talent and a foundation in Chinese literature she should continue in his field. In Hsia's view, learning foreign languages was merely a way to understand foreign literature. In 1940 when Hsia Ch'eng-t'ao returned to his native place to mourn a parent, another famous lyrics specialist, Lung Mu-hsün [Long Muxun], took his place, teaching selected lyrics. Thus, two famous modern lyrics specialists helped Ch'i-chün to build a solid foundation in writing poetry and lyrics.

Graduating in 1941, she went to Shanghai to teach at Hui-chung [Huizhong] Girls' High School. During that period, Ch'i-chün wrote and directed a play that her students performed, among them Lu Yen [Lu Yan], later to become a film star in Taiwan and Hollywood. After the Sino-Japanese War, Ch'i-chün returned to Hang-chou to teach at her old school Hung-tao. She also held a post as a librarian at the Che-chiang High Court, a position that enabled her to read a great many books and magazines.

Ch'i-chün moved to Taiwan in 1949. Through Wu Yüeh-ch'ing [Wu Yueqing], chief editor of the women's and family pages of *Chung-yang jih-pao*, Ch'i-chün met many literary people and began to write and publish literary essays and fiction. Her collections of short stories include *Brother-in-law* (Chieh-fu), *Sister Qing* (Ch'ing chieh), *Lily Root Soup* (Pai-ho keng), *Eight Hours in the Copying and Proofreading Room* (Shan-chiao-shih pa hsiao-shih), and *Sorrow in July* (Ch'i-yüeh ti ai-shang). Among her literary essays are "Soul of the Zither" (Ch'in hsin) and "Misty Sorrow" (Yen ch'ou). She wrote the short essay "Red Gauze Lantern" (Hung sha-teng) and collected others into *Ch'i-chün's Collected Essays* (Ch'i-chün hsiao-p'in). Ch'i-chün won the Chinese

Literary Association (Chung-kuo wen-i hsüeh-hui) Essay-Writing Award (san-wen ch'uang-tso chiang-chang) in 1964. Her children's fiction includes *Selling Cattle* (Mai niu chi) and *The Old Cobbler and the Dog* (Lao hsieh-chiang ho kou).

With roots nourished in Buddhist culture, Ch'i-chün excelled at writing compassionately and lovingly about family, native land, and childhood. By means of straightforward and deceptively plain narratives, her descriptions of people and situations are imbued with deep feeling that is neither melodramatic nor pretentious. Her works, like the *Book of Songs*, express a "mournful but not distressing" (*ai erh pu shang*) quality; sadness resolves; and tranquility comes forth: the author has created a placid but unforgettable style of her own.

From the time she moved to Taiwan, Ch'i-chün worked as an administrator with the Judicial Administration Department, and she also edited and evaluated teaching material for prisoners. In the course of her work, Ch'i-chün visited many prisons and collected a great deal of material for her writing that would have been difficult to obtain in any other way. She retired from her positions in 1969 to teach part-time at several universities, and continued to write and publish. Her favorite works are *Midnight Dreams with Books as My Pillow* (San-ching yu meng shu-tang-chen), *Cassia Rain* (Kuei-hua yü), and *Soft Rain When the Lamp Is Trimmed* (Hsi-yü teng-hua lo). In 1970, she won the Chung-shan hsüeh-shu Foundation Award for Literary Essays.

Ch'i-chün visited Hawaii and the American mainland in 1972 at the invitation of the United States government. She accompanied her husband, Li T'ang-chi [Li Tangji], an accountant, when he went to work in America in 1977, and they lived in New York for three years. Returning to Taiwan in 1980, Ch'i-chün taught in the Chinese Department of the Central University (Chung-yang ta-hsüeh) and the following year published *The Boat of Lyricists* (Tz'u-jen chih chou). In 1983, she journeyed to America again with her husband, and this time they stayed. In 1985, her *Ch'i-chün's Letters to Young Readers* (Ch'i-chün chi hsiao-tu-che) won the Golden Tripod Award for books and writing given by the Government Information Office (Hsin-wen-chü) of the Executive Yuan in Taiwan.

LAM Tung
(Translated by Lily Xiao Hong Lee and Sue Wiles)

Ch'i-chün. "The Chignon," trans. Jane Perry Young. In *Bamboo Shoots After the Rain: Contemporary Stories by Women Writers of Taiwan*, eds. Ann C. Carver and Sung-sheng Yvonne Chang. New York: Feminist Press at the City University of New York, 1990, 26–31.
———. *Huai-ch'ing chiu ching teng*. Taipei: Hung-fan shu-tien, 1987.
———. *San-ching yu meng shu-tang-chen*. Taipei: Erh-ya ch'u-pan-she, 1990.
Wang Chin-ming. *T'ai-Kang-Ao wen-hsüeh tso-p'in ching-hsüan: Shih-ko san-wen chüan*. Kuang-chou [Guangzhou]: Kuang-tung kao-teng chiao-yü ch'u-pan-she, 1998.
Yin-ti, ed. *Ch'i-chün ti shih-chieh*. Taipei: Erh-ya ch'u-pan-she, 1985.

Ch'ien Chien-ch'iu

Ch'ien Chien-ch'iu [Qian Jianqiu], *tzu* [*zi*] Hsiao Ch'en, 1911–1996, was born in Shanghai, although her native place was Chen-chiang [Zhenjiang] County, Chiang-su [Jiangsu] Province. She trained in law and devoted many years to working with women.

After graduating from Shanghai Law University at the top of her class in 1928, Ch'ien Chien-ch'iu went on to study at Northwestern University in the United States. She was supervised in her postgraduate work on evidence law by John R. Wigmore, a world authority in legal studies. She was the first female from the early Republic of China to gain a Doctor of Law degree in the United States. Returning to China in 1931, Ch'ien Chien-ch'iu set up a law practice and taught at Shanghai Institute of Law and Politics (Shang-hai fa-cheng hsüeh-yüan). In 1937, she was appointed to the KMT Committee of Shanghai City and in 1945 was promoted to membership of the Central Women's Movement Committee (Chung-yang fu-nü yün-tung wei-yüan-hui). Ch'ien Chien-ch'iu later held a variety of party positions.

When the CCP came to power, she went to Taiwan with the KMT government. Her talent, especially an outstanding ability to motivate people to work together, was recognized by Soong Mayling [Song Meiling] (*q.v.*), and Ch'ien Chien-ch'iu was appointed director of the Women's Work Committee of the KMT Central Committee. During her term of office, she visited many cities and counties, establishing women's organizations at all levels. Devoted to women's work, Ch'ien Chien-ch'iu counted among her most significant achievements the movement to "Harmonize the Family, Contribute to the Country." From 1954 to 1991, she held several positions, serving on the Standing Committee of the Chinese Women's Anti-Communism Association, the Central Committee of the Ninth to the Twelfth National Assemblies, and as chair of the presidium of the Central Evaluation Committee.

Ch'ien Chien-ch'iu did not abandon her legal career, however, and frequently represented the Republic of China at annual meetings of the International Women's Legal Studies Association. She also sat on its Executive Committee and as convenor of the Association's Education Committee. In 1982, Ch'ien Chien-ch'iu was elected as its first vice-president and honored with a decoration. She also attended the United Nations High Commission of Human Rights Conference on the Status of Women in the Law of Kinship to discuss the parent-child relationship and the exercise of parents' rights. Ch'ien Chien-ch'iu later published her arguments in *A Study of Kinship Law* (Ch'in-shu-fa yen-chiu). She became ill in 1996 and died in Taipei's Keng-hsin Hospital.

Ch'ien Chien-ch'iu committed her life to women's work, carrying out major tasks on behalf of the KMT from the time it moved to Taiwan. Her publications, including *Chinese Women's Movement over Thirty Years* (San-shih-nien lai Chung-kuo fu-nü yün-tung) and *The Social Status of Women in the Republic of China* (Chung-hua-min-kuo fu-nü chih she-hui ti-wei), demonstrate her commitment to the cause of women.

Ch'ien Chien-ch'iu married Huang Pi-ying [Huang Biying], a fellow student at Northwestern University. Their son, Huang T'ien-lai [Huang Tianlai], received a doctorate in environmental studies from the University of Pennsylvania.

HO Shu-i
(Translated by George Li)

Chang K'o [Zhang Ke]. "Ch'ien Chien-ch'iu." *Chuan-chi wen-hsüeh*, 69, no. 5 (1996): 5.
Chung-hua min-kuo tang-tai ming-jen lu, vol. 1. Taipei: Taiwan Chung-hua shu-chü, 1978, 186.

Chien O

Chien O [Jian E], b. 1909, in Hsin-hua, T'ai-nan, Taiwan, was a pioneer in the Peasants' Union (Nung-min tsu-ho) during the period of Japanese colonial rule and played an important role in social reform in Taiwan.

Her father, Chien Chung-lieh, a teacher of Chinese, disappeared during the Chiao-pa-nien Uprising of 1915 in which over two thousand people were arrested by the Japanese police. Eight hundred were executed. He quite probably was among them; his body was never found. Although Chien O was too young to remember, the stories she heard from her elder brother and cousin, who worked as an attendant at Nan-hua Police Station at the time, had an enormous impact on her.

The Chiao-pa-nien Incident started in present-day Yu-chin Mountain, near Hsin-hua, led by Yu Ch'ing-fang, Chiang Ting, and Lo Chün. The event marked the end of the Han people's armed resistance against their Japanese rulers; almost the entire population of the area had been wiped out after the brutal suppression. According to Chien O's cousin, everybody in the village, including the headmen, was involved in the uprising; women provided food and other supplies. Dressed in white and wearing rice-straw hats, the villagers attacked the police station and then set off toward Hsin-hua, where they were overwhelmed by the Japanese army. The Japanese dug a mass grave and pushed every male over the age of sixteen into it.

Her widowed mother was just a little over thirty years old when this happened, and she took her children to Kao-hsiung and supported her family by selling noodles. Chien O proved to be a talented child and, after finishing elementary schooling at Kao-hsiung Third Public School, was selected to go to Kao-hsiung Girls' High School (Kao-hsiung nü-hsiao), quite an achievement. Only seven or eight Taiwanese students were admitted there each year; the school was mainly for Japanese students. The years spent there made Chien O understand the extent of the discrimination that colonized people suffer. At high school, she met Chang Yü-lan. They became close friends and often attended seminars run by the Peasants' Union and the Culture Association (Wen-hua hsieh-hui). Chien O's thoughts about her father and how he must have died were never far from her mind.

Socialist ideology came to Taiwan in the 1920s. Chien Chi, Su Ch'ing-chiang, and Ch'en Te-hsing, leaders of the Peasants' Union, started reading clubs to spread socialism, and Chien O took part in those meetings. Among the many books she read were *The ABC of Communism* (Kung-ch'an-chu-i ABC) and *The Wonders of Capitalism* (Tzu-pen-chu-i ti ao-miao); Chien O later said that what she found in those books became both her motivation and lifelong beliefs.

Her catalyst for leaving high school and dedicating herself to the peasant movement was the forced withdrawal from the school of her classmate Chang Yü-lan. The two friends were final-year students in 1927, but the school and the local police considered them troublemakers: they were known to be in and out of the Peasants' Union seminars. After a spy reported that Chang Yü-lan had attended a peasants' conference in Ch'ao-chou on 12 October, the school asked her elder brother to get her to withdraw from the school. When she rejected the suggestion, the school forced her to withdraw. Chang Yü-lan then wrote and distributed throughout the school "A Letter to My Sisters" in which she attempted to clear herself. The search started by the school and continued by the police developed into a criminal case, with Chang Yü-lan charged with "breaking publishing laws." The case went to trial and appeal three times, and she was sentenced to three months' imprisonment. The episode created an uproar, and Chang Yü-lan received great support from the Peasants' Union and general public. She was eventually sent to prison after a big farewell party thrown by the Peasants' Union.

In response to this incident, Chien O quit school and joined the peasant movement, a blow to her family. They locked her in, but she fled that night. Her mother sued Chien Chi, one of the leaders of the movement, for luring her daughter away; the accusation became the source for the headlines in the media in May 1928 about "the luring event." Chien Chi had been Chien O's teacher at Kao-hsiung Third Public School, and the media accused him of "having an inappropriate relationship with the girl student Chien O that resulted in her leaving school and home." Chien O, however, declared that she had joined the Peasants' Union of her own free will. In her statement she remarked: "You will see from my future actions whether I was lured or not." Because of lack of evidence, Chien Chi was released after being in custody for four days. As the curtain fell on "the luring event," she became even more determined to devote herself to the peasant movement. Working in the P'ing-tung branch of the Peasants' Union, Chien O established a close relationship with local peasants. She fought for their rights and taught them to read simple texts, such as the three-character classic that the Peasants' Union compiled for the peasants.

It was decided at the Central Committee Conference held by the Peasants' Union in T'ai-chung in June that a joint research body should be set up for the newly established Youth Department and the Women's Department. Chien O was selected to be a member of this body, which became a model for every branch on the island. In 1929, however, the Japanese launched a large-scale arrest of members of the Peasants' Union, known as the February Twelfth Incident. Many of the leaders were jailed, and the union was branded as an illegal organization. She took part in underground activities in the Chungli and T'ao-yüan area for about a year, making full use of the grass-roots peasant movement, and forming trusting relationships with the peasants. As soon as the police appeared, a peasant would tell Chien O, and she would don black cotton trousers and jacket, put on a rice-straw hat, and, disguised as a Hakka woman, work in the rice paddies with the local women.

Chien O was arrested many times by the Japanese police. Thirty-five leaders of the Peasants' Union were arrested during the Chung-li Incident of 1928, and twelve were sentenced to death. The T'ao-yüan police noticed that she paid regular visits to the families of those arrested and captured her in June 1929 at a seminar given by the Peasants' Association of T'ao-yüan. She was charged with "having no fixed address and being unemployed." Chien O protested strongly at being held in custody for twenty days and cut her finger in the detention center to write in her own blood an application for a formal trial.

Her case went to trial twice and she was acquitted; her counsel were the famous Taiwanese barrister Ts'ai Shih-ku and Ku-wu, a consultant of the Peasants' Union.

Chien O also took an active role in the Taiwan Home Borrowers Campaign (Chieh-chia-jen yün-tung). From the mid-1930s, rents had risen sharply as the economy deteriorated, and those who could not afford to pay started the Home Borrowers Campaign. This was similar to the Homeless Campaign of the late 1980s. In 1930, following the lead of the city of T'ai-nan, many places in Taiwan established an Association of Home Borrowers, and by 1931 Taiwan Home Borrowers Union had been established. Because of her support to this campaign from its beginning, she was invited to give a seminar speech held by the Kao-hsiung Alliance of Home Borrowers, entitled "The Kao-hsiung Home Borrowers Campaign" (Kao-hsiung chieh-chia-jen yün-tung te chuang-k'uang).

Chien O became deeply involved with the peasant, worker, and proletarian movements. When 185 women workers from six grass-bag factories of Ling-ya dormitory in Kao-hsiung launched a united strike in 1930, she was there to support them on behalf of the Peasants' Union. The colonial government laid the blame for the workers uniting in their strike at the feet of two women—Chien O and Sun Yeh-lan—and two men—Chou Wei-jan and Chang Ts'ang-hai. The union provided the same assistance to the Taiwan Printing Company at the beginning of 1931, sending Chien O north in March to support the strikers there. In May, she attended the second extraordinary conference of the Taiwan Communist Party (TCP) and was recommended as an alternate member of the Central Committee. After the conference, Chien O was appointed liaison officer for Su Hsin and P'an Ch'in-hsin, who were members of the Central Standing Committee. The position was necessary because contact could not be made in public. TCP was an underground organization.

In that year, the Japanese police launched a large-scale search and arrest of the leaders of the Peasants' Union. After one of the main leaders, Chao Kang, was arrested, Chien O and some others moved to the coast of Taiwan with the intention of going to the mainland. They managed to remain hidden in Chi-lung for a time but were finally arrested.

With the end of the Sino-Japanese War, many of the leaders of the Peasants' Union were still engaged in the battle against the new KMT government. Her old comrade-in-arms Chien Chi became secretary of Aboriginal Affairs with the Taiwan Province Work Commission and was killed in 1951 during the White Terror. Chien O's husband, Ch'en Ch'i-jui, who was director of the Ch'ao-chou branch of the P'ing-tung Peasants' Union, was arrested and charged with "financially supporting the bandits," who were his former comrades. Chien O was not politically active at that stage—being married, with children, and suffering poor health—but still feared that she "might be the next target." Chien O suffered greatly on seeing her friends and comrades jailed and murdered by the White Terror.

In the early 1970s, she emigrated to the United States but never forgot her years with the peasant movement in Taiwan. Chien O, Yeh T'ao (*q.v.*), and Chang Yü-lan were the three elite women of the peasant movement.

YANG Ts'ui

(Translated by Jennifer Zhang)

Han Chia-ling, ed. *Po-chung chi—Jih-chü shi-ch'i Taiwan nung-min yün-tung jen-wu chi*. Taipei: Chien Chi Ch'en-Ho wen-chiao chi-chin, 1997.

Taiwan min-pao/Taiwan hsin min-pao (1927–1930): various articles.

Taiwan she-hui yün-tung-shih, vols. 3 and 4. Taipei: Ch'uang-tsao, 1989. This is a translation of *Taiwan tsung-tu-fu ching-ch'a yüan-ke-chih, ti erh pien, Ling-T'ai i-hou ti chih-an chuang-k'uang*.

Ts'ai Wen-hui. *Pu hui chi—Jih-chü shih-ch'i Taiwan nung-min yün-tung*. Taipei: Chien Chi Ch'en-Ho wen-chiao chi-chin, 1997.

Yang Ts'ui. *Jih-chü shih-ch'i fu-nü chieh-fang yün-tung-shih*. Taipei: Shih-pao, 1993.

Chi-oang

Chi-oang, 1871?–1946, was the eldest daughter of a Sedeq chieftain from Taroko Gorge in northeastern Taiwan; her tribal name was Ciwang Iwal (with variant spellings).

To the consternation of her community and despite having many tribal suitors, she took a Chinese husband and moved to the nearby coastal town of Hua-lien. Chi-oang later moved to the T'ai-chung-Chang-hua area on the western plains to live with her Christian mother-in-law. There she met many Christians, Chinese and foreign. When Chi-oang later returned to her homeland, her fellow tribesmen killed her husband.

After Taiwan ceded to Japan in 1895, she was sent by the Japanese authorities to act as an intermediary between them and the Sedeq, which by 1907 was the only aboriginal tribe that had not capitulated to Japanese rule. Chi-oang communicated with local chieftains, and a peaceful resolution was finally reached in 1914. Her success in averting wholesale slaughter raised her profile among her own people as well as with the Japanese and she was consequently allowed a high degree of mobility between the normally segregated mountains and plains. Chi-oang took two other Chinese husbands: the first died from illness and the second was a dissolute man who dissipated her savings and possessions.

She met a Chinese missionary couple, however, who inspired her to learn to read and study the Bible, and in 1924 became the first Sedeq aborigine to be baptized. Five years later, she was invited by James Dickson, famed American missionary working in Tan-shui [Tamsui] for the Canadian Presbyterian mission, to attend Bible classes and formally train as a missionary. Chi-oang eventually agreed to do this, despite her age; she was then fifty-eight. Two years later (some sources say eight months), Chi-oang completed the studies and returned to her homeland, where she labored for years in her mission work, initially to little effect. Chi-oang conducted services in Taiwanese or Japanese with explanations in tribal language. By the beginning of World War II, Chi-oang had become so influential and attracted so many tribespeople to her lessons that she risked arrest by the Japanese, who were deeply suspicious of Christians, missionaries in particular. Harnessing the tribe's earlier resentment toward the Japanese, Chi-oang transformed the persecution of the Sedeq aboriginal Christians into a challenge for upholding individual and community faith. The resistance was taken up by thousands of her fellow tribespeople who worshipped in secret and, with the assistance of non-Christian aborigines, shielded her from the Japanese police. Many stories tell of an infirm Chi-oang being spirited away from danger into the night on the backs of young Sedeq tribesmen.

At the end of the war, missionaries returned from overseas to discover to their astonishment that small churches had sprung up all over the Sedeq and other communities. This "Pentecost of the Hills" was largely attributed to Chi-oang. Many of her followers, including her adoptive daughter, went on to become missionaries who preached the gospel to the Sedeq and other aboriginal tribes.

Chi-oang is venerated by aboriginal Christians to this day and described in histories of the Aboriginal Presbyterian Church as the Mother of Taiwan Aboriginal Faith, or the Mother of the Mountain Church. She symbolizes the tensions of adaptation of aboriginal culture not only to Japanese and Chinese rule and culture but also to Western religious practices. She remains a key figure in the conversion of the great majority of Taiwan aborigines to Christianity in a Chinese society dominated by a non-Christian tradition. Many details of Chi-oang's life are unclear; some dates, as well as the order of many events, are disputed. Of the references listed, the most reliable on primary sources are Covell, Dickson, and the Chinese-language entries.

Martin WILLIAMS

Band, Edward, ed. *He Brought Them Out: The Story of the Christian Movement Among the Mountain Tribes of Formosa*, 2nd ed. London: The British and Foreign Bible Society, 1956.

Covell, Ralph. *Pentecost of the Hills in Taiwan: The Christian Faith Among the Original Inhabitants*. Pasadena, Calif.: Hope Publishing House, 1998.

Dickson, James. *Stranger Than Fiction*. Toronto: Evangelical Publishers, n.d.

Taiwan chi-tu chang-lao chiao-hui tsung-hui li-shih wei-yüan-hui, ed. *Taiwan chi-tu chang-lao chiao-hui pai-nien shih*, 3rd ed. Taipei: Taiwan chi-tu chang-lao chiao-hui, 1995.

Taiwan chi-tu chang-lao chiao-hui tsung-hui yüan-chu-min hsüan-tao wei-yüan-hui, ed. *Taiwan chi-tu chang-lao chiao-hui yüan-chu-min-tsu hsüan-chiao shih*. N.p.: Taiwan chi-tu chang-lao chiao-hui tsung-hui yüan-chu-min hsüan-tao wei-yüan-hui, 1998.

Tong, Hollington K. *Christianity in Taiwan: A History*. Taipei: China Post, 1961.

Vicedom, George. *Faith That Moves Mountains: A Study Report on the Amazing Growth and Present Life Among the Church Among the Mountain Tribes of Taiwan*. Taipei: China Post, 1967.

Wilson, Kenneth L. *Angel at Her Shoulder: Lillian Dickson and Her Taiwan Mission*. London: Hodder and Stoughton, 1964.

Ch'iu Yüan-yang

Ch'iu Yüan-yang [Qiu Yuanyang], b. 1903, in T'ai-nan County, Taiwan, was a fighter for women's rights.

After graduating from P'u-tzu Public School in 1920, she went on to Taipei Third Girls' Senior High School (Taipei ti-san kao-teng nü-hsüeh-hsiao). Ch'iu Yüan-yang graduated from the Teaching Department and was assigned to teach at Chia-i Suant'ou Public School. Not long after, she was transferred to Chu-ch'i Public School and then to Chia-i Girls' Public School. After marriage in 1926 to Lai Yüan-p'ing [Lai Yuanping], Ch'iu Yüan-yang resigned from her teaching job to take care of her aged mother-in-law.

Because of her participation in the paramilitary women's organization during the period of Japanese colonial rule, Ch'iu Yüan-yang was put forward and elected to Parliament after World War II. During her period in office, she paid special attention to local affairs and women's issues. Ch'iu Yüan-yang insisted on speaking Taiwanese in the Parliament and in general established her own unique style in politics.

She believed that women in modern society should be independent and strong, with sufficient conviction to fight for their rights. Through her positive activities and selfless service to the local people, Ch'iu Yüan-yang realized her own belief in herself, while claiming for women in Taiwan a place where they could develop their own talent.

HO Shu-i
(Translated by George Li)

Yu Chien-ming. "Ch'iu Yüan-yang." In *Tsou-kuo liang ko shih-tai ti Taiwan chih-yeh fu-nü fang-wen chi-lu*. Taipei: Chung-yang yen-chiu-yüan. Chin-tai-shih yen-chiu-so, 1994.

Ch'iung Yao

Ch'iung Yao [Qiong Yao] is the pen name of Ch'en Che [Chen Zhe], b. 1938, in Ch'eng-tu [Chengdu], Ssu-ch'uan [Sichuan] Province, of Henan ancestry. A romance writer, Ch'iung Yao is one of the most famous authors of the Chinese-speaking world.

Her books enjoy wide circulation wherever Chinese is spoken, and many have been translated into other languages, including Vietnamese, Indonesian, Korean, and Japanese. In addition to her novels of which she has written over sixty to date, Ch'iung Yao is equally well known for the many films and television dramas that have been based upon her novels. The most recent, *Princess Huan-chu* (Huan-chu ko-ko), was a great success in Taiwan and on mainland China in 1999–2000.

Ch'iung Yao was the eldest of four children (she has a twin brother). After relocating several times during the Sino-Japanese War and the subsequent civil war, her family moved to Taiwan in 1949 when the KMT forces were defeated and the PRC was established. Her father, Ch'en Chih-p'ing [Chen Zhiping], was a distinguished professor in the Chinese Department at Taiwan Normal University; her mother, Yüan Hsing-ju [Yuan Xingru], had been a schoolteacher. At the end of her final year of high school, Ch'iung Yao failed the university entrance examination; on retaking it the following year she was again unsuccessful. Soon afterward, having conceived the desire to be an author, Ch'iung Yao concentrated on writing stories. She married in 1959 and her only child (a son) was born two years later.

Her first story, "Lovers' Valley" (Ch'ing-jen ku), was also published that same year (1961) in *Crown* (Huang-kuan) magazine. Her first full-length novel, *Outside the Window* (Ch'uang wai), was published in 1963 (first in *Crown* magazine, then by Crown Press). Ch'iung Yao's marriage ended soon afterward, but her publishing career flourished. By the age of thirty, she had published more than thirty works of romantic fiction. Her second marriage, in 1979, was to her publisher, P'ing Hsin-t'ao [Ping Xintao], who encouraged and fostered Ch'iung Yao's career since his publication of her first story. Also of mainland origin, P'ing Hsin-t'ao was a well-known figure in the Taiwan literary establishment. He had not only founded *Crown* magazine (in 1954) and Crown Publishing House but also edited *Lien-ho pao*'s influential literary supplement. Ch'iung Yao's autobiography, *My Story* (Wo ti ku-shih, 1989), outlines the events in her life up to the time of her second marriage.

The writer's success has been closely linked to P'ing Hsin-t'ao's publishing enterprises. Ch'iung Yao's work became a selling point for *Crown*, and the magazine established her as a household name for readers of Chinese from the 1960s onward, not only in Taiwan but also Southeast Asia and North America through its two overseas editions. In addition to publishing her novels, P'ing established a film company in the 1970s (later disbanded) to produce film versions of her stories; both he and Ch'iung Yao were responsible for writing the screenplays and scripts. In the early 1980s, her fame and popularity spread to mainland China as pirated editions of her work began to be published and films based on her novels circulated there.

Ch'iung Yao's first novel, *Outside the Window*, has been her most influential. It is the story of a lonely high-school girl coping with the pressures of her final year of school and the impending examinations that will decide her future. The student's middle-aged teacher, a lonely widower, takes an interest, and they fall in love. The girl's mother does her utmost to terminate the relationship, and finally succeeds, forcing the teacher to leave Taipei and take up a job in a country school, where he turns to drink. The girl, meanwhile, fails the all-important university entrance examination. Thus, the mother's attempts to prevent harm to her daughter's future with an unsuitable romantic attachment do not succeed in securing the kind of life she had wished for her daughter. The story is based upon the author's own experiences; according to her autobiography, the first fourteen chapters of the novel closely parallel her own life story.

The book was a critical success, hailed as an important critique of conflicting priorities and expectations between generations in Taiwan in the 1960s. Ch'iung Yao was considered a promising new author. Though this first novel had established her as a serious writer, Ch'iung Yao's literary profile soon changed. The importance of romantic love in her novels—the quest for the perfect heterosexual romance, with either union or epic renunciation as the ultimate focus—combined with her prolific output tended to preclude her work from serious consideration by (predominantly male) literary scholars. Love and romance—stereotypically feminine concerns—have been taken by critics and readers alike to be the paramount features of Ch'iung Yao's writing, and on this basis she has generally been categorized as a romance novelist.

In literary terms, her work has been variously praised and criticized for its prose style and the poems appearing in many of the early novels. The romantic couples central to her stories are always physically beautiful and carry uniquely romantic names and noble (if flawed) personalities. The novels' titles are often literary allusions. Such features hark back to the "mandarin duck and butterfly" genre of commercially successful novels written in the early twentieth century by professional authors for an expanding literate audience of mainly women. They were published in China's coastal cities at a time when the printing and publishing businesses were undergoing rapid transformation and mass circulation was becoming possible for the first time. Parallels between Ch'iung Yao and the "butterfly" authors could be drawn in commercial as well as literary terms, with Ch'iung Yao's romantic fiction representing the first wave of popular, mass-circulating commercial writing in Taiwan. The fact that many of her romantic novels end in tragedy and parting rather than in happy union for the lovers may also have its roots in the mandarin duck and butterfly fiction tradition. There is, however, a vital difference between the novels of Ch'iung Yao and their antecedents in that her fiction is female-centered, while the earlier tradition is male-centered. Almost without exception, the heroine is at the heart of both the plot action and the emotional action of her novels, and it is from her point of view that the story unfolds. It has therefore been suggested that Ch'iung Yao's novels can be read as "a return to the Chinese romantic tradition with a feminized vision for modern readers" which, because of their female focus, "represent very different gender relationships from the traditional love stories."

The Taiwan literary sociologist Lin Fang-mei noted a number of general formulas in the novels of Ch'iung Yao: immediate and certain knowledge on the part of the hero and heroine that their love is "the real thing"; heroes are usually gentle and caring characters from the beginning (rather than proud brutes who become "civilized" into tenderness through the love of the heroine); and romantic dilemmas, obstacles, and difficulties created by external events or situations (such as family circumstances) occur as the rule rather than the exception to the hero's or heroine's own psychological drama. Again, these features are traceable to the mandarin duck and butterfly tradition and contrast with the paradigms of English-language romance as defined in Janice Radway's seminal study. Lin Fang-mei also notes the relatively large quantity of extra-romantic material in Ch'iung Yao's novels (in terms of settings, characters, and plot) as another aspect that sets her work apart from English-language traditions of romance fiction.

The novels written in the 1960s tend to deal with generational conflict, generally pivoting upon the wish of the younger generation to choose their own marriage partner against parental opposition. They also contain elaborate sub-plots connected with the experiences of the parental generation on the mainland before the family moved to Taiwan. Most of these novels do not end happily. In the 1970s, her stories depicted strong and stable families; their endings (with marriage for the central couple and a general scenario of family harmony) showed a comfortable integration of romantic love into familial structures. In response to criticisms of her novels as fantasies of the lives of the rich and beautiful, Ch'iung Yao incorporated a series of social problems into her work in the 1980s, including plot elements of mental illness and sexual abuse. A number of her earlier stories are set partially or entirely in the past (particularly the Republican period), but almost all of her novels in the 1990s are set even further back in time, in the Ch'ing dynasty. Most end tragically. Her work has frequently been criticized for containing "morbid" elements and socially questionable romantic relationships (such as that between teacher and student in her first novel) and an over-emphasis on love. Other aspects of life are only sketchily present in Ch'iung Yao's novels, with scant attention paid, for example, to the heroines' working lives and work environments. This is interpreted by Lin Fang-mei as a reflection of the author's own experience, as Ch'iung Yao's own working life has been spent entirely as a professional writer.

Perhaps her best-loved novel is *Deep Are the Courts* (T'ing-yüan shen-shen), a two-part story of a young woman who returns to Taipei from the United States for a vacation and meets a man who is later revealed to be her former husband. The novel provides two love stories: that of the couple's initial relationship (which had led to marriage despite opposition from his parents and then broke down because of interference from his mother) and the gradual renewal of love between them again, more than a decade later (during which time he has believed her dead and lost his sight). The couple reunite in the conclusion.

Almost all of Ch'iung Yao's novels have been steady bestsellers. Among them, however, *Outside the Window* and *Deep Are the Courts* have been particularly popular and reprinted in more editions than any other. Although the proliferation of other writers in the genre in Taiwan in the 1980s posed a challenge to Ch'iung Yao's supremacy as the "queen of Chinese romance," the popularity of her television series (continuing into the twenty-first century) restored her to prominence in Chinese culture at large as well as in the affections of the millions who are fans of her novels.

Miriam LANG

Ch'en Pin-pin [Chen Binbin]. *Ch'iung Yao ti meng.* Hong Kong: Huang-kuan ch'u-pan-she, 1994.
Ch'iung Yao. *Ch'uang wai.* Taipei: Huang-kuan ch'u-pan-she, 1963.
———. *Fire and Rain* (Yen yü meng-meng), trans. Mark Wilfer. Sydney: Pan MacMillan, 1998.
———. *T'ing-yüan shen-shen.* Taipei: Huang-kuan ch'u-pan-she, 1969.
———. *Wo ti ku-shih.* Taipei: Huang-kuan ch'u-pan-she, 1979.
Fan Ming-ju. "The Changing Concepts of Love: Fiction by Taiwan Women Writers." Ph.D. dissertation. University of Wisconsin-Madison, 1994, 65.
Lin, Fang-mei. "Social Change and Romantic Ideology: The Impact of the Publishing Industry, Family Organization, and Gender Roles on the Reception and Interpretation of Romance Fiction in Taiwan." Ph.D. dissertation, University of Pennsylvania, 1992.
Radway, Janice. *Reading the Romance: Women, Patriarchy and Popular Literature.* Chapel Hill: University of North Carolina Press, 1984.

Choi Yan Chi

Choi Yan Chi [Cai Yanci], b. 1949, in Hong Kong, is an artist. Her work includes color field painting, performance, and installation.

Choi Yan Chi studied at colleges of education in England and at the Art Institute of Chicago, where she gained an MFA in 1978; she then returned to Hong Kong to teach. In her work, Choi Yan Chi uses mirrors to demand viewer participation or the unfamiliar placement of familiar objects, such as books in bubbling, water-filled aquarium tanks. The effect is to make the viewer aware of the uncanny vulnerability of the familiar and its conditioning by physical and cultural environment.

John CLARK

Choi Yan Chi's Painting, 1976–1986, and Works of Art in Dialogue with Poetry and Dance. Hong Kong: Department of Fine Arts, University of Hong Kong, 1987.
Kirker, Anne. Catalog entry on Choi Yan Chi. In *The First Asia-Pacific Triennial of Contemporary Art*, ed. C. Turner. Brisbane: Queensland Art Gallery, 1993.

Senn, Rolf, Th., and Mathew Turner. *Choi Yan-Chi.* Künstler der Welt Series. Stuttgart: Haus der Kulturen der Welt, Edition Cantz, 1993.

Chou Guanghu: *see* Han Suyin

Chou, Irene

Irene Chou [Zhou Lüyun], b. 1924, in Shanghai, is an artist who graduated from St. John's University in Shanghai in 1945 with a degree in economics.

In 1947 Irene Chou married Yang Yanqi (editor of *Peace Daily*) and in 1949 moved to Hong Kong where she studied with Zhao Shao'ang (1905–84). From 1976 to 1984 she was a teacher at the University of Hong Kong's Extramural Studies Department. Also influenced by Lui Shoukun (1919–76), Irene Chou was among the first artists with *traditional* media background to abandon the formal language identifiable as "Chinese" in favor of a highly dynamic abstraction whose psychological basis refers to Jungian archetypes. Her representations also entail spiritual and religious quests and include a series of paintings on silk after themes from Boccaccio's *Decameron*. In 1992, after a stroke, Irene Chou immigrated to Brisbane, Australia, where her son has a medical practice.

John CLARK

Boccaccio's Decameron: Paintings on Silk by Irene Chou. Hong Kong: Faramir, 1976.
Collector's Choice: The Cosmic Vision of Irene Chou. Hong Kong: Cat Street Galleries, 1995.
Kirker, Anne. Catalog entry. In *The First Asia-Pacific Triennial of Contemporary Art*, ed. C. Turner. Brisbane: Queensland Art Gallery, 1993.

Chou Mei-yü

Chou Mei-yü [Zhou Meiyu], b. 1910, in Peking [Beijing], although her native place was Tz'u-hsi [Cixi], Che-chiang [Zhejiang] Province, trained as a nurse in the 1920s and 1930s. She was active in military nursing education, both on the mainland and, from the late 1940s, in Taiwan.

Her father, Chou Ch'un-lin [Zhou Chunlin], worked on the construction project of the Sino-Russian Frontier Telegraph Department. Her mother, née Shih [Shi], was a devout Buddhist and a woman of strong personality. From the beginning, Chou Mei-yü attended Christian missionary schools in Peking: P'ei-yüan [Peiyuan] Primary School, Bridgeman High School, and Yen-ching [Yanjing] University. By the time she graduated from high school, Chou Mei-yü had already determined to pursue a career in nursing and in 1926 was admitted to a course run jointly by Yen-ching University and the Nursing School of Union Medical College. This was one of five such medical training programs that Union Medical College had entered into with missionary universities; the others were with Soochow, Shanghai, Nanjing, and Lingnan. Before returning to continue her nursing training at Union Medical College, Chou Mei-yü did a one-year course at Yen-ching University in the humanities and sciences. In 1930, Union Medical College awarded her a diploma and a Registered Nurse License.

Chou Mei-yü remained at Union for a year as an intern in medical administration and public health. Inspired by Yen Yang-ch'u (also known as James Yen), who had devoted himself to the education of the people, in 1931 Chou Mei-yü joined his Chinese Mass Education Promotion Society in Ting [Ding] County. She was involved in nursing in the society's health clinic but also founded a nursing school and became its principal. Two years later Chou Mei-yü received a Rockefeller Scholarship to further her studies in the United States. She attended the Massachusetts Institute of Technology, studying biology and public health, and earned a bachelor's degree in public health and health education. At some point during the Sino-Japanese War, she was awarded a master's in public health.

At the outbreak of the Sino-Japanese War, Chou Mei-yü put her patriotism to practical use, leaving the Mass Education Promotion Society in Ting County to go to Ch'angsha [Changsha], Hunan Province, where she joined the Chinese Red Cross. There, Chou Mei-yü became part of the headquarters of Chinese Red Cross medical aid and the wartime health personnel training school of which Lin K'o-sheng [Lin Kesheng] was in charge. In Chou Mei-yü's job as nursing director of medical aid, she was responsible for training medical workers for the medical aid corps and the military hospital. Chou Mei-yü also spent two months each year visiting hospitals in the various war zones and inspecting the work of the Red Cross nursing team. When Japanese forces threatened Ch'ang-sha in 1938, medical aid headquarters and the training school retreated to the southwest, finally arriving in T'u-yung-kuan [Tuyonguan], Kuei-yang [Guiyang], in the following year by a circuitous route. In March 1945, British United Aid to China invited Chou Mei-yü to promote Red Cross work in China. Three months later, she traveled first to the United Kingdom to talk to communities of overseas Chinese and raise funds and then to major cities in the United States. Chou Mei-yü gained considerable support for her cause and in January 1946 returned home.

After the war, she held a succession of high-level positions, including director of the Standing Committee of the Chinese Nursing Society. Her military appointments included nursing director of the United Service Headquarters' Shanghai General Hospital, head of the Nursing Section of the Military Medical Office's Special Technical Department, and colonel/technical commissioner of the Military Medical Office. She was also colonel/head of nursing of the National Defense Medical School, which had been formed on 1 June 1947 in Shanghai by amalgamating the army wartime health workers' training school and the former military medical school. The school initially offered an advanced nursing course that ran four and a half years for female high-school graduates.

Chou Mei-yü moved to Taiwan with this school and immediately agitated for a faculty of nursing. A university-level nursing course was finally accredited by the Ministry of National Defense and the Education Department in 1954, the degree of Bachelor of Nursing carrying with it the rank of second lieutenant. This was a considerable achievement on Chou Mei-yü's part. In the years that followed, the Faculty of Nursing of the National Defense Medical School established throughout Taiwan a comprehensive military nursing system. Chou Mei-yü was promoted in 1958 to the rank of major-general (*shao-chiang*), thus becoming the first woman to achieve the rank of general in the

Republic of China (for the first woman general in the PRC, *see* Li Zhen).

Chou Mei-yü remained a devout Christian throughout life. Upright in manner, she neither shirked responsibility nor avoided difficulties. In her early years, it took tremendous courage, devotion, and intelligence for a young woman such as she to commit herself to nursing and public health in a conservative society. During the war years spent in many hospitals in war zones, her strong patriotism sustained her. After the war, when Chou Mei-yü worked persistently to upgrade the field of nursing education and reform the military nursing system, her vision buoyed her up to accomplish what she had set out to do. Chou Mei-yü never married.

LO Chiu-jung
(Translated by Barbara Law)

Chang P'eng-yüan. *Chou Mei-yü hsien-sheng fang-wen chi-lu.* Taipei: Chung-yang yen-chiu-yüan. Chin-tai-shih yen-chin-so, 1993.
Chung-kuo hu-shih chi-k'an, 3, no. 1 (July 1947): 45.

Chou, Rosalie: *see* **Han Suyin**

Chu Yaming: *see* **Caoming**

Chung Ling
Chung Ling [Zhong Ling], b. 1945, in Ch'ung-ch'ing [Chongqing], Ssu-ch'uan [Sichuan] Province, is a poet, novelist, literary critic, and film scriptwriter. She is currently a professor in the Foreign Languages and Literature Department at the National Sun Yat-sen University in Kao-hsiung, Taiwan, and dean of the College of Liberal Arts.

When Chung Ling was three years old, her father, Chung Han-po, took up a position in the Chinese embassy in Japan and she and her mother, Fan Yung-chen, went to live with him in Tokyo. Two years later, however, the family (Chung Ling has one younger brother, Chung Chien) moved again, to Taiwan. Chung Ling grew up and was educated in Kao-hsiung, attending Kao-hsiung Girls' High School. She was obsessed during her high school years with martial arts novels—one summer vacation she read fifty of them—and also loved Chinese classical poetry (*shih-tz'u*) and fiction (such as *Hung-lou meng* [Dream of the Red Chamber]). Chung Ling read eighteenth- and nineteenth-century Western fiction and was active in drama groups, acting in both spoken drama (*hua-chü*) and Peking opera (*ching-chü*). Her maternal uncle and several of her teachers encouraged her literary aspirations.

After graduating in 1966 from the Foreign Language Department of Tung-hai University, Chung Ling took a modern English and American poetry course given at National Taiwan University's Foreign Languages and Literatures Graduate Program (Wai-wen yen-chiu-so) by the famous poet Yü Kuang-chung [Yu Guangzhong]. The following year, Chung Ling published a criticism of Yü Kuang-chung's poetry entitled "The Fire Bath of Yü Kuang-chung" (Yü Kuang-chung ti huo-yü), pointing out certain weaknesses. The criticism improved the poem, and Chung Ling became something of a literary lion. She also established a pupil-friend relationship with Yü Kuang-chung. Chung Ling began to publish fiction at this time, and her short story "One Who Returned to His Native Place" (Huan-hsiang jen) was translated into English. In autumn 1967, she went to the United States and studied comparative literature at the University of Wisconsin. Chung Ling continued to write poetry, in Chinese and English, and one of her English-language poems was selected for inclusion in a high-school textbook in America. She also collaborated with Kenneth Rexroth on translations of the poetry of Chinese women through the ages, as well as the poems (*shih*) and lyrics (*tz'u*) of Li Ch'ing-chao and other classicists. After completing her Ph.D. in Comparative Literature at the University of Wisconsin, Madison, in 1972, Chung Ling taught the subject and Chinese literature at the State University of New York, Albany.

During this period, she published studies on the influence of Chinese poetics on English and American poetry and culture. The academic has since said that the nine years after the 1970 publication of her first collected essays, *Barefoot on the Grass* (Chih-tsu tsai ts'ao-ti shang), were a dark time because she produced very little creative literary work.

In 1977, Chung Ling married King Hu (Hu Chin-ch'üan [Hu Jinchuan], 1932–1997), the well-known Hong Kong director of martial arts films. She became a coordinator (*ts'e-hua*) for his film company and wrote several screenplays, including *Legend of the Mountain* (Shan-chung ch'uan-ch'i, 1979). That year, Chung Ling and King Hu published *Mountain Guest* (Shan-k'o chi), and it appears to have marked the return of her creative force. Chung Ling wrote prose (*san-wen*), fiction (*hsiao-shuo*), and poetry (*hsin shih*), and translated poetry. Her short story "Samsara" (Ta-lun-hui, 1983; in English "The Wheel of Life") was made into a film in 1984. Eventually her marriage foundered, and she and King Hu divorced in 1991; afterward, Chung Ling returned to Taiwan.

In 1980, she had resumed teaching while still married to King Hu, and in 1982 taught translation and creative writing in the Department of Chinese at the University of Hong Kong. She was active in literary circles in Hong Kong, frequently holding poetry meetings and participating in poetry recitals. Chung Ling mentored several new poets of the 1980s, including Wang Liang-ho, Ch'en Chin-ch'ang, and Wu Mei-chün [Mei Kwan Ng], who often met with her to study English and American poetry. Chung Ling herself continued to write, producing the series *Portraits of Beauties* (Mei-jen t'u) during this period. Although not prolific, by the time she returned to Taiwan in 1989 Chung Ling was counted among the important women poets to have emerged since the Chinese regained Taiwan from Japan. Much of the focus of her writing was on love, capturing its sensual imagery and nuanced complexities; her *Portraits of Beauties* is striking for its literary re-creation in poetic form of beautiful women from the past whose lives she had thoroughly researched.

However, Chung Ling herself values her fiction and essays more than her poetry. Her major themes in fiction explore idealism, love, and death, and almost all of it is narrated from a woman's point of view, the characters not only being denizens of modern metropolises but also sometimes women from classical times. Possibly her most unusual piece, and certainly controversial work, is *Crossing the Mountains* (Kuo-shan). The inspiration for this story was a piece of old jade of which she is an amateur collector. It relates a supernatural experience in which the characters move freely backward and forward between ancient and modern times.

Chung Ling is unique among contemporary women poets, not only because of her fiction and essays. She has also written screenplays, teaches academically, writes in both Chinese and English, and is identified as a feminist writer. Her critical work on Chinese women poets has been well received, *Muses of Modern China: A Critical Study of the Works of Taiwan Women Poets* (Hsien-tai Chung-kuo miu-ssu: Taiwan nü-shih-jen tso-p'in hsi-lun), won the 1991 National Literary Award (Kuo-chia wen-i chiang). Her *American Poetry and Chinese Dream: Chinese Cultural Modes in Modern American Verse* received support from the Government Information Office of the Executive Yuan with the Chung Cheng Cultural Prize and has become an important reference work.

Chung Ling became interested in antique jade in the 1980s at which time she collected and studied it. While Chung Ling would discuss poetry with her teacher Yü Kuang-chung, she would discuss ancient jade with his wife, Fan Wo-ts'un [Fan Wocun]. Chung Ling has written two books on her jade collection.

NG Mei Kwan
(Translated by Lily Xiao Hong Lee and Sue Wiles)

Chung Ling. *Hsien-tai Chung-kuo miu-ssu: Taiwan nü-shih-jen tso-p'in hsi-lun.* Taipei: Lien-ching ch'u-pan shih-yeh, 1989.

———. *Mei-kuo shih yü Chung-kuo meng: Mei-kuo hsien-tai shih-li ti Chung-kuo wen-hua mo-shih* [Colophon title in English: American Poetry and Chinese Dream: Chinese Cultural Modes in Modern American Verse]. Taipei: Mai-t'ien ch'u-pan-she, 1996.

———. "Translation, Imitation and Adaptation: Kenneth Rexroth and Chinese Poetry." Ph.D. dissertation, University of Wisconsin, 1972.

———. "The Window," trans. Wendy Larsen. In *Worlds of Modern Chinese Fiction: Short Stories and Novellas from the People's Republic, Taiwan and Hong Kong,* ed. Michael S. Duke. Armonk, N.Y.: M.E. Sharpe, 1991, 221–26.

P'an Ya-tun [Pan Yadun]. "Chung Ling yü Hu Chin-ch'uan pai-pai le." In *Shih-chieh hua-wen nü tso-chia su-miao,* ed. P'an Ya-tun. Kuang-chou [Guangzhou]: Chi-nan ta-hsüeh ch'u-pan-she, 1993, 207–14.

Rexroth, Kenneth and Chung Ling, trans. and ed. *Women Poets of China* [originally published as *The Orchid Boat*]. New York: Published for J. Laughlin by New Directions, 1982, ca. 1972.

Ciwang Iwal: *see* **Chi-oang**

Cong Xuan: *see* **Ding Ling**

Cui Xiaoping: *see* **Ts'ui Hsiao-p'ing**

D

Dai Ailian

Dai Ailian, b. 1916, in Trinidad in the West Indies to a Chinese family that originated in Guangdong Province, is a dancer and one of China's earliest choreographers and dance educators. She contributed greatly to the world recognition of China's cultural heritage through her study and performance of the national dances of the Han and ethnic minorities in China.

Dai Ailian studied dance from the age of five and at ten (one source says twelve) entered a dance school in Trinidad. In 1931, when she was fourteen, Dai Ailian went to London to study at the Jooss School of Ballet at Darington Hall in Devon; she also worked in the studios of Anton Dolin and Margaret Craske. During this period, Dai Ailian created the dances "Flower-Girl in a Persian Square," "The Umbrella," and "Yang Guifei's Dance before the Emperor."

She felt that while modern dance possessed freedom and vitality, it lacked systematic technique; classical ballet, in her view, lacked expressiveness. Dai Ailian therefore boldly proposed that modern dance and classical dance could well learn from and complement one other. Fearful that her radical views would infect other students, the Jooss School of Ballet expelled her. She continued her studies at the Jooss Modern Dance School, however, and won a scholarship. There, Dai Ailian learned the theory of expression and techniques of stage performance developed by dance theorist Rudolf von Laban. More importantly, she learned his method of recording dance steps, known as Labanotation. In the latter half of the 1930s, Dai Ailian became interested in modern dance and studied with a teacher whose name has been transliterated into Chinese as M. Weigeman. All of these influences were to have a great impact on her career as a choreographer.

When China declared war against Japan in 1937, Dai Ailian participated in concerts to raise money for the China Salvation League (Baowei Zhongguo tongmenghui), organized by Song Qingling (*q.v.*), and created and performed dances eulogizing the spirit of the Chinese people in resisting Japan, such as "Awakening" (Jingxing) and "Advance" (Qianjin). After leaving England in 1940 to take up the study of traditional Chinese dance, Dai Ailian met Song Qingling again in Hong Kong. During her brief sojourn there, Dai Ailian made a few professional appearances and appeared in charity concerts to raise funds for China. Her new work "East River," based on Cantonese folk dancing, premiered at one of them in January 1941. When Hong Kong was attacked by the Japanese at the end of that year, she entered China proper through Guilin. In Guilin, Dai Ailian took part in charity concerts for the war effort and created dances such as "The Guerrilla Story," "For Sale," "The Air-Raid," and "Thinking of Home." Her work promoted the anti-Japanese cause and at the same time advanced the development of Chinese dance.

During this period, she also collected dances from various nationalities in order to study and preserve them. Dai Ailian created, for example, "The Drum of the Yao

People" (Yaoren zhi gu), based on the music they played at celebrations, and choreographed "The Old Piggybacking the Young" (Lao bei shao), an adaptation of the traditional Han skit "Ya bei feng."

Dai Ailian arrived in Chongqing in 1942. She taught at the National Opera School (Guoli geju xuexiao) and the National Institute of Social Education (Guoli shehui jiaoyu xueyuan). Later, at the request of the well-known educator Tao Xingzhi, Dai Ailian established a dance class at Tao's Yucai School. She met and was befriended by communists such as Zhou Enlai (1898–1976) and Deng Yingchao (q.v.), who were working in Chongqing during this period. Dai Ailian became excited over a new National Academy performance of the "Rice-Shoot Song" (yangge) performed by a troupe from Yan'an in 1945 and included it among the dances her students in the Yucai School were learning. She also created at this time "Sister Zhu Gives Away Eggs" (Zhu dasao song jidan).

That summer Dai Ailian traveled with the famous painter Ye Qianyu, whom she married in Chongqing, to north Sichuan and Tibet to collect local material. Using Labanotation, Dai Ailian recorded eight dances of the Tibetan nationality. These pieces are now held in library collections in England and the United States. In early 1946, she and her students at the Yucai School presented a concert of dances of Chinese nationalities, including the Miao, Yao, Yi, Uigur, and Tibetan people; these dances were also collected and choreographed. This performance had profound ramifications. Not only did it promote the traditional dances of different ethnic groups and bring them to city stages, it launched a trend among school and university students and other young people to learn folk dance. That autumn, Dai Ailian went with Ye Qianyu to the United States to give dance recitals in New York. On returning to China in 1947, Dai Ailian organized and assumed the role of principal of the China School of Dance (Zhongguo yuewu xueyuan) in Shanghai.

After the establishment of the PRC in 1949, she headed the dance troupe of the Central Academy of Drama (Zhongyang xiju xueyuan wudao tuan) and the Central Song and Dance Troupe (Zhongyang gewutuan). Dai Ailian then became principal of the Beijing School of Dance, the first of its kind in China at the time it was founded in 1953. This school offered a seven-year course for children between the ages of seven and fourteen, incorporating Chinese choreography as well as the rudiments of Western ballet. Much attention was also given to dances of non-Han nationalities and other Asian countries and a concerted effort made to build up a national repertoire drawn from these sources. During the 1950s, she created two award-winning dances based on traditional Chinese culture. The choreography of "The Lotus Dance" (Hehua wu) was based on a Shaanxi folk dance; the pas de deux "Flight" (Feitian) was inspired by dances portrayed on Tang murals. Dai Ailian also established the Central Ballet (Zhongyang baleiwu tuan) and acted as adjudicator for many international dance competitions. Among the foreign countries she visited were England, America, Germany, and Sweden. To commemorate her contribution to exchanges in the field of dance between China and England, the Royal Academy of Dance placed a bust of Dai Ailian in the foyer and invited her to open the display in 1981.

Dai Ailian devoted herself from the 1940s on to the collection and study of Chinese dance, promoting it in China and abroad. Her years as a dance teacher and educator helped China build a generation of dancers, choreographers, and educators. Her contribution is summed up thus in the *Biographical Dictionary of Republican China*: "Tai Ai-lien [Dai Ailian] was a pioneer in her field. Although there had been some experiments in the dance in China before her arrival in 1942, it was only through the thoroughness of her research, her artistic talent, and her choreographic inventiveness that traditional dance forms were developed into a truly national art performed by professionals."

Lily Xiao Hong LEE

Boorman, Howard L., and Richard C. Howard, eds. *Biographical Dictionary of Republican China*, vol. 4. New York: Columbia University Press, 1971, 198–99.
Zhongguo dabaike quanshu: Yinyue wudao. Beijing: Zhongguo dabaike quanshu chubanshe, 1989, 107–08.
Zhongguo wudaojia cidian. Beijing: Wenhua yishu chubanshe, 1994, 72–73.

Dai Houying

Dai Houying, 1938–1996, of Nanzhaoji, Yingshang County, Anhui Province, was a novelist and literary critic.

She grew up in the small hometown of her birth and attended First High School in the nearby County of Fuyang, the regional center of the area. In 1956, Dai Houying was admitted to East China Normal University in Shanghai and graduated in 1960 with a B.A. in Chinese Literature. Upon graduation, Dai Houying was assigned as a literary critic to the Institute for Literary Research of the Shanghai Writers' Association (Shanghai zuojia xiehui), the district branch of the national body. She changed jobs in 1979, taking up a post as a lecturer at Fudan University in Shanghai to teach critical theory. Dai Houying later moved to Shanghai University and taught there until her sudden death—she was murdered by an intruder during a burglary—in 1996. Dai was divorced and had lived in Shanghai with her only daughter since the late 1960s.

Dai Houying was the first woman in her family to receive an education and the first of her entire extended family to graduate from university. Her family had had its share of poverty and political persecution. Her illiterate mother was a housewife who did casual work for low pay in a sewing workshop run by a neighborhood committee. Her father received two years of traditional private tuition and had managed a shop owned by the local municipality before being branded as a "rightist" in the late 1950s; he had mildly criticized the government's trading policy on agricultural produce. His subsequent demotion meant that their family of almost a dozen people (Dai Houying's aunt and two children lived with them after the aunt's husband committed suicide— he had been falsely accused of financial theft) lived on a salary of less than thirty yuan a month. Dai Houying used to send home most of her salary, withholding only the bare minimum for her own sustenance. Extreme poverty was her constant companion until her writing earned steady extra income, in the 1980s.

Primarily a novelist, Dai Houying also wrote literary criticism, prose essays, short stories, and occasional poems. She started her writing career as a literary critic, although her earlier essays, presumably produced under the direction and surveillance of the CCP and presenting the prevailing Chinese Marxist viewpoint, were not widely circulated within or outside of China. Dai Houying herself said that the few dozen theoretical essays published in the two decades from 1960 to 1978 while she worked at the Institute for Literary Research were of little value because she did not think independently or have any original ideas then. Her later essays, many of which are reflections on social conditions, personal experiences, and observations, appeared in various journals and newspapers such as *Random Jottings* (Suibi) and *Ordinary People* (Baixing).

Dai Houying's first novel, *Death of a Poet* (Shiren zhi si), was inspired by the intense emotions she experienced after the suicide of her lover, the poet Wen Jie, in 1971 at the height of the Cultural Revolution. She did not start writing about the experience until 1978, almost seven years later, and finished the book within a year. Because of political complications it was not published until 1981, after her second novel had come out. *Death of a Poet* is based on Dai Houying's personal experience both in terms of her political destiny, emotional life, and intellectual journey under totalitarian control. It presents a true-to-life historiography of the Cultural Revolution and relates the perspectives of individuals of different generations and varied political persuasions. The book belongs within the "wounded literature" genre.

Dai Houying's literary fame was established soon after the publication of her second novel, *Humanity!* (Ren ah, ren!), which portrays the aftermath of the Cultural Revolution and how those participating in it resolved personal guilt and entanglements in efforts to reestablish basic mutual trust and friendship. The novel focuses on how personal integrity was compromised, to what extent people were deprived of dignity, and how difficult it was to talk about humanity and humanism under the political system of the PRC, permeated as it was by a rule of fear lasting for more than three decades. The narrative presents the journeys of individuals rediscovering, despite political pressure, humanist values. The author writes about this soul searching in the book's postcript:

> At one time, I quite piously believed that everything in the world was a question of class struggle. We had to keep class struggle in mind every waking moment. . . . Eventually, I came to see that I had been playing the role of a tragic dupe in what was a mammoth farce. I was a simpleton who believed herself to be the freest creature on earth, when in fact I had been robbed of the right to think. The cangue that weighted heavy on my soul had always seemed to me a beautiful garland of flowers. I had lived out half my life without having come to any understanding of myself. I wrestled free of that role and went in search of myself.
> . . . Gradually a word written in blazing capitals shone before my eyes. That word was HUMANITY! The words to a much-maligned and long-forgotten song welled up in my throat: Humanity, Human Feelings, Humanism.
> —From "The Rebirth of My Humanity," trans. Geremie Barmé and John Minford

Dai Houying's *Humanity!* came out during the heated debate on humanism in China at the beginning of the 1980s, when a number of intellectuals questioned the unrelenting imposition of class struggle on Chinese life since 1949 and defended humanism as a general principle. The writer and her book were subsequently targeted for criticism by CCP ideologues, especially its mouthpiece the *Literary Gazette* (Wenyibao). Her "sin," according to them was her failure to interpret life accurately, misleading readers with vacuous humanistic sermonizing. *Humanity!* remained highly controversial until the end of the 1980s because of its probing examination of humanism as an alternative to the paradigm of "class struggle."

While fulfilling academic responsibilities, Dai Houying continued to produce fiction prolifically. Her other two novels about academia are *Footsteps in the Air* (Kongzhongde zuyin, 1986) and *Brain Splitting* (Nao lie, 1994). These novels are about the plight of intellectuals seeking intellectual independence and academic freedom from ruthless CCP ideology, overpowering bureaucracy, and, increasingly, encroaching commercialization. The frequent use of irony and sarcasm in *Brain Splitting* enables the narrator to speak in a teasing, pseudo-serious, at times capricious voice. Dai Houying was apparently experimenting with narrative styles and focus in an attempt to break new ground in this period just before her untimely death. She also published many short stories and novellas, many of them collected in *Soft Is the Chain* (Suolian shi rouruande, 1982) and *The Fall* (Luo, 1993).

Dai Houying also wrote about her native place—the rural north of Anhui Province, a relatively poor and disadvantaged area compared with the rest of the east coast of China—wishing to raise its profile. She had planned to write a series of novels under the general title *The Sobbing Huai River* (Liulei de Huaihe). She completed two titles in this series published in Hong Kong: *Changed Times* (Fengshui lunliu, 1989) and *Intersection in Air* (Xuankong de shizi lukou, 1992?).

Dai Houying is not included in many anthologies of modern Chinese literature published in the West. Apparently outside of China, she is regarded more as a political activist and phenomenon of only a particular historical moment in time, as can be seen by her entry in *Seeds of Fire: Chinese Voices of Conscience*. However, Dai Houying's writing shows not only depth as a thinker but also sophistication as a novelist and writer in the Chinese language. *Humanity!*, for instance, was a literary experiment with many merits, especially considered within the context of China's political and cultural era of repression in the decades preceding its publication. Its story comprises different narrative angles, the voices of multiple narrators, each telling an aspect, a point of view, in dialogue appropriate to the character. In her last novel, *Brain Splitting*, psychological realism deftly reflects the confusion of the protagonist.

In short, Dai Houying was both a distinguished political activist and a fine, highly productive writer.

Yiyan WANG

Dai Houying. "Dai Houying." In *Dangdai Zhongguo nü zuojia zuopinxuan*, eds. Liu Xicheng et al. Guangzhou: Huacheng, 1982, 631–32.
———. *Dai Houying suiping*. Hong Kong: Xiangjiang, 1990.
———. *Fengshui lunliu*. Hong Kong: Xiangjiang, 1989.
———. *Kongzhongde zuyin*. Guangzhou: Huacheng chubanshe, 1986.

————. *Luo*. Xi'an: Shaanxi renmin chubanshe, 1993.

————. *Nao lie*. Xi'an: Taibai wenyi chubanshe, 1994.

————. *Ren ah, ren!* Guangzhou: Guangdong renmin chubanshe, 1980.

————. *Shiren zhi si*. Xi'an: Taibai wenyi chubanshe, 1996 reprint.

————. *Suolian shi rouruande*. Guangzhou: Huacheng chubanshe, 1982.

————. *Wangshi nanwang*. Hong Kong: Xiangjiang, 1988.

————. *Xingge/mingyun—wo de gushi*. Xi'an: Taibai wenyi chubanshe, 1994.

————. *Xuankong de shizi lukou*. Hong Kong: Xiangjiang, 1992?

————. "The Rebirth of My Humanity." In *Seeds of Fire: Chinese Voices of Conscience*, eds. Geremie R. Barmé and John Minford. New York: Hill and Wang, 1988, 157–60.

Ling, Vivian. "Dai Houying." In *A Reader in Post-Cultural Revolution Chinese Literature: Chinese Texts in Traditional Characters*. ed. Vivian Ling. Hong Kong: Chinese University Press, 1994.

Pruyn, Carolyn S. *Humanism in Modern Chinese Literature: The Case of Dai Houying*. Bochum: Herausgeber Chinathemen, 1988.

Ye Yonglie. "Cong *Shiren zhi si* dao Dai Houying zhi si." *Mingbao yuekan* (September 1996): 47–49; (October 1996): 60–82.

Dai Jinhua

Dai Jinhua, b. 1959, in Beijing, is an avant-garde feminist literary and cultural critic, film critic, film historian, and professor of comparative literature and culture at Peking University.

Her father, Dai Xuezhong (1929–1990), a native of Shandong Province, was orphaned at an early age and brought up in the countryside by his maternal grandmother. In 1944, he joined the Eighth Route army led by the CCP and in 1949 was assigned to work for the Ministry of International Trade in Beijing. Her mother, Jia Huijing, b. 1929, a primary school teacher, was born and raised in Beijing in a traditional family.

Dai Jinhua's father worked much of the time in overseas Chinese embassies, and her mother devoted much of her energy to teaching. Dai Jinhua's first teacher was her maternal grandmother, Zhang Yuying (1902–1978), who was well versed in both classical and modern Chinese literature and lived out her life as an oppressed but defiant daughter-in-law in a feudal family. It was her grandmother who directly influenced Dai Jinhua into becoming an uncompromising feminist. However, her father's passion for literature and mother's devotion to teaching played equally important roles in Dai Jinhua's personal and academic interests.

Her life intertwines with the cultural and political history of China in recent decades. Attending The East Is Red (Dongfanghong) Primary School from 1966 until 1971, she witnessed the outbreak and full force of the Cultural Revolution. In 1971, Dai Jinhua entered 111 Middle School, which had been established during this period, and graduated from high school the year the Cultural Revolution ended. She was criticized at different times, accused of "white professionalism." As a poet and student leader during the April Fifth Movement in 1976 commemorating the death of Zhou Enlai (1898–1976), Dai Jinhua narrowly escaped arrest. In 1978, she was admitted to the Chinese Department of Peking University (Beijing daxue zhongwen xi) and clearly established academic research and teaching as her goals. Upon graduation in 1982, Dai Jinhua accepted a faculty position in the Department of Film Literature at Beijing Film Academy (BFA, Beijing dianying xueyuan dianying wenxue xi).

Teaching literature and art theory there, she also researched film history and criticism. Filling a gap in Chinese film theory, which had been limited to Chinese socialist realism, the academic introduced structuralist and poststructuralist film theory in the late 1980s. In 1987, she collaborated in founding a film theory major at BFA, designed the curriculum, translated and compiled teaching materials, and taught most of the courses on film studies over the next four years.

She began to publish in the late 1980s. Her *Emerging from the Horizon of History: Studies of Modern Women's Literature* (Fu chu lishi di biao: xiandai nüxing wenxue yanjiu, 1989), co-authored with Meng Yue, proved to be a landmark in rewriting modern Chinese literary history and rediscovering Chinese women's writings. Dai Jinhua also published articles on contemporary Chinese film studies, including "The Leaning Tower: Re-reading the Fourth Generation" (Xie ta: chong du di si dai, 1989); "A Wrecked Bridge: Art of the Younger Generation" (Duan qiao: zi yi dai de yishu 1990); "The Red Flag Genealogy: An Ideological Pontoon" (Hongqi pu: Yi zuo yishi xingtai de fu qiao, 1990); and "Encountering an Other: Notes on Third World Theories" (Zaoyu ta zhe: Di san shijie lilun biji, 1991).

Dai Jinhua's academic life is intricately connected with the social and intellectual milieu of contemporary China. In common with most Chinese intellectuals, she experienced the June Fourth Movement of 1989 traumatically, both academically and personally. Between 1991 and 1992, her writings were banned because of a series of accusations against her, including "trafficking Western bourgeois academic theories" and "instigating rebellion." Dai Jinhua consequently published her articles on feminist, third world, and post-colonialist theory under the pseudonyms Ge Hua and Lu Ni. Since then Dai Jinhua has reviewed Chinese literature and culture through the critical lens of Althusser, Foucault, and the Frankfurt school. Dai Jinhua has also become more engaged with the history of Chinese cinema, writing *Mirror and Secular Myths* (Jing yu shisu shenhua, 1993), a textbook of film theory, and *A Handbook of Film Theory and Criticism* (Dianying lilun yu piping shouce, 1993), a collection of essays on Chinese cinema.

The commercialization of Chinese society that started around 1993 further transformed the direction of Dai Jinhua's academic research. Confronted with the impact of transnational capital and consumerism, she incorporated more complexity and flexibility in her cultural critiques. While criticizing quasi-socialist ideological control, Dai Jinhua also expressed disapproval of government-promoted capitalism in China, imperialist cultural invasion, and consumerism. Critically refocusing on Marxism, Dai Jinhua situated film studies within the context of contemporary social discourse and popular cultural production and published on the popular culture industry and cultural market. In that year, Dai Jinhua left BFA to continue her scholarship and teaching at the Research Institute of Comparative Literature and Culture at Peking University (Beijing daxue bijiao wenxue yu bijiao wenhua yanjiu suo). In 1995, Dai Jinhua organized the Research Studio of Popular Culture (Dazhong wenhua yanjiu shi), China's first cultural studies organization. She taught cultural studies as well and advised graduate students in research. Dai Jinhua continued to put out articles on Chinese women's writing, film history, and the current state of Chinese filmmaking. In 1999, her essays on cultural studies were collected under the title *Invisible Writings: Cultural Studies in 1990s China* (Yinxing shuxie: jiushi niandai Zhongguo wenhua yanjiu). In the same year, she finished her book on Chinese women's writings, *A Boat Crossing the River: Women's Culture and Women's Writings in the New Era* (She du zhi zhou: xin shiqi nüxing wenhua yu nüxing shuxie), and her collected interviews were published under the title *Still in the Mirror* (You zai jing zhong, 1999).

From the early 1990s, Dai Jinhua extended her academic presence internationally, attending the International Conference on Asian Avant-Garde and Experimental Films in New Delhi (1990), the Annual Conference of International Comparative Literature in Tokyo (1991), and the International Women's Film Festival in Créteil, France (1993). Her essay "Invisible Women: Women in Films and Women's Films in China" (Bu ke jian de nüxing: dianying zhong de nüxing yu nüxing de dianying), which she delivered at Créteil and published in China in the journal *Contemporary Cinema*, was one of the first scholarly articles on Chinese film written from an explicitly feminist perspective. In 1994, Dai Jinhua was invited to lecture on Chinese cinema, women's culture, and popular culture at Cornell University, Duke University, Ohio State University, Harvard University, and the University of California at Berkeley, Los Angeles, Santa Barbara, and Irvine. Her scholarship on cultural studies and film studies has been translated into English and published in the United States. In summer 1996, she became a visiting professor at Ohio State University and taught a graduate seminar on the history of Chinese cinema. In 1999, Dai Jinhua offered a summer graduate seminar on contemporary Chinese women's writings. A collection of her writings translated into English is *Cinema and Desire: Feminist Maxism and Cultural Politics in the Work of Dai Jinhua.*

Dai Jinhua presently lives in Beijing with her husband Rong Weijing (b. 1961), mother, and cat, Mao Jiaqiu (b. 1988).

Jing M. WANG

Dai Jinhua. Personal interview. Columbus, Ohio, 26 July 1999.
Wang, Jing, and Tani Barlow, eds. *Cinema and Desire: Feminist Marxism and Cultural Politics in the Work of Dai Jinhua.* London: Verso Books, forthcoming [2002].

Dai Qing

Dai Qing, b. 1941, in Chongqing, Sichuan Province, is a prominent Chinese dissident, journalist, writer, and environmentalist.

She was given the name Fu Xiaoqing at birth and used the name Fu Ning when she reached school age. Her mother, Feng Dazhang, and her father, Fu Daqing, were both CCP activists; her father was jailed and eventually executed by the Japanese occupation forces in Beijing. When Dai Qing was four years old, she was adopted by Ye Jianying (1897–1985), who later became one of the ten marshals of the PRC. Dai Qing grew up in Ye Jianying's family.

Dai Qing received her university education between 1960 and 1965 in the Department of Guided Missile Engineering at the Institute of Military Engineering of the PLA, commonly known as the Harbin Institute of Military Engineering. After graduation, she worked in the research institute of Number Seven Ministry of Machinery Industry for a few months, then joined a Red Guard organization at the beginning of the Cultural Revolution. She had joined the CCP in 1965 and spent three years (from 1968) in cadre schools. In 1972, Dai Qing became a technician in a surveillance equipment factory under the Ministry of Public Security in Beijing. She studied English at the PLA Foreign Languages Institute in Nanjing between 1978 and 1979, then worked as a technician in General Staff Headquarters in Beijing.

Dai Qing published her first piece of work—a short story—in November 1979, and it was at this time that she began to use the name Dai Qing. Between 1980 and 1982, she worked as a foreign affairs liaison officer in the Chinese Writers' Association and as an agent for the Intelligence Section of General Staff Headquarters. In the latter year, Dai Qing became a journalist for *Guangming Daily*, one of the largest newspapers in China. Many of her articles were critical of the CCP, and her interviews with leading intellectuals, published periodically in *Guangming Daily*, often exposed political and social problems. Her investigative work on the intellectuals Wang Shiwei, Liang Shuming, and Chu Anping and their relationship to the party and its leaders revealed how they had been repressed and purged. Their freedom of speech had been limited and eventually was taken away entirely by the party.

Dai Qing also took a strong stand against the Three Gorges Dam project to build the world's largest dam on the Yangzi (Yangtze) River. Her 1989 book *Yangtze! Yangtze!* warned of the potential devastation it would cause, including forced population relocation, loss of historic relics, and irreversible environmental damage. She is believed to have organized China's first environmental lobby in opposition to the construction of the dam.

On the day of the June Fourth Incident that year, Dai Qing resigned from the CCP. A month later she was imprisoned for "advocating bourgeois liberalization and instigating civil unrest." After being released in May 1990, Dai Qing accepted research fellowships offered by several leading universities in the West but declined offers of political asylum. Although the Chinese government has since banned her from publishing, she continues to be based in China and still appeals for freedom of the press. Dai Qing is also unrelenting in her efforts to stop the Three Gorges Dam project; see, for example, her latest overseas publication *The River Dragon Has Come!* Dai Qing was awarded the 1992 Golden Pen for Freedom, and in 1993 the Goldman Environmental Prize and the Conde Nast Environmental Award.

Although Dai Qing is widely regarded as a liberal intellectual, her stand on many issues caused controversy in the West and among Chinese dissidents. On the question of U.S.-China trade relations, she argues that granting China permanent normal trade status is a powerful means of promoting freedom in China. On Tibet, her view is that it is a part of China and Chinese government subsidies to Tibet are worth more than what has been extracted from it. On political change in China, Dai Qing believes in evolution rather than revolution. While highly critical of the communist system, she also credits the CCP with initiating and implementing economic and political reforms. While supporting the students' demand for freedom in the 1989 protest movement, Dai Qing also believed that the movement should have had limits. In particular, she worried that the protest movement would be manipulated by factions within the CCP and thus lead to the downfall of the reformers (the political consequences of the June Fourth Incident appear to vindicate her in this).

Perhaps the biggest controversy in which Dai Qing has been involved is her book *My Imprisonment*, published overseas after her release from jail. In it, she criticizes the emotionalism and radicalism expressed by most leading intellectuals of that 1989 protest movement. In particular, she criticizes their belief in using the CCP's methods (i.e., revolution) to bring it down. Dai Qing also indicates that she was treated well in prison, which seems to suggest an improvement in the Chinese government's treatment of prisoners. It could be argued that Dai Qing is one of very few Chinese dissidents dealing pragmatically with the CCP, understanding its strengths and weaknesses, and willing to compromise so long as the party continues to reform itself and the country.

ZHU Tianbiao

Barmé, Geremie. "The Trouble with Dai Qing: 'My Imprisonment,' Before and After." Paper presented at the Association of Asian Studies of Australia Conference, Sydney, July 1991.
———. "Using the Past to Save the Present: Dai Qing's Historiographical Dissent." *East Asian History*, no. 1 (June 1993): 141–81.
Cai Yongmei. "Dai Qing he ta banyan de jiaose." *Kaifang zazhi* (June 1992): 12–14.
Cao Changqing. "Ping Dai Qing—'Wo de ru yu' yu 'Wo de sige fuqin' du hou." *Zhengming* (December 1995): 73–76.
Dai Qing. *Hun.* Shanghai: Shanghai wenyi chubanshe, 1985.
———. *Liang Shuming, Wang Shiwei, Chu Anping.* Nanjing: Jiangsu wenyi chubanshe, 1989.
———. *Wo de ruyu.* Hong Kong: Mingbao yuekan chubanshe, 1990.
———. *Yangtze! Yangtze!* eds. Patricia Adams and John Thibodeau; trans. Nancy Liu, Wu Mei, Sun Yougeng, and Zhang Xiaogang. London and Toronto: Earthscan, 1994.
———. *Wang Shiwei and "Wild Lilies": Rectification and Purges in the Chinese Communist Party, 1942–1944.* Armonk, N.Y.: M.E. Sharpe, 1994.
———, comp. *The River Dragon Has Come! The Three Gorges Dam and the Fate of China's Yangtze River and Its People,* eds. John G. Thibodeau and Philip B. Williams; trans. Yi Ming. Armonk, N.Y.: M.E. Sharpe, 1997.
———. "Keep the Doors to China Wide Open: Solidifying Trade Status Would Keep Pressure on Beijing to Improve on Rights and the Environment." *L.A. Times* (on-line), 20 April 2000: China Trade Relations Working Group.
———. "Wo de sige fuqin—ziji de gushi." *Mingbao yuekan* (January 1995): 86–92.
"Interview with Dai Qing." *Red Flag: Journal of the Communist Party of Aotearoa,* at <http://home.clear.net.nz/pages/cpa/RedFlag/redflat897.html>.
Jin Zhong. "Qidai guashu diluo—Fangwen Zhongguo jizhe xiaojie Dai Qing." *Kaifang zazhi* (February 1993): 42–46.
Ling Feng. "Zhuizong Dai Qing." *Mingbao yuekan,* no. 9 (September 1988): 52–55.
Su Wei. "Xianshuo Dai Qing." *Mingbao yuekan,* no. 4 (April 1992): 109–12; no. 6 (June 1992): 112–15.
Topping, Audrey Ronning. "Dai Qing, Voice of the Yangtze River Gorges." Earth Times News Service, 1997, at <http://weber.ucsd.edu/~dmccubbi/chinadaiqingjan11 97.htm>.
Wang Zheng. "Three Interviews: Wang Anyi, Zhu Lin, Dai Qing." In *Gender Politics in Modern China: Writing and Feminism,* ed. Tani E. Barlow. Durham and London: Duke University Press, 1993.
Xue Ying. "Zai fang Dai Qing." *Mingbao yuekan,* no. 7 (July 1990): 17–19.

Dbyangs-can Lha-mo: *see* **Dbyangs-dgav**

Dbyangs-dgav

Dbyangs-dgav, 1906–1974, whose original name was Dbyangs-can lha-mo, was born in Ri-bo-che in the Cham-mdo region of Tibet; she was a practitioner of Tibetan medicine.

Dbyangs-dgav was born into a noble family: her father, Rje-drong Lama, was a scholar specializing in Wuming (the five traditional categories of Tibetan knowledge) and a famous doctor with a great deal of experience in Tibetan medicine. The practice of polyandry was widespread in Tibet at that time, and Rje-drong Lama was one of two husbands (the other was Dge-rab Lama) of Tshul-khrims, daughter of a headman named Ngo-mo-sgang. Dbyangs-dgav was the second of three daughters born to this family and was considered to be the child of Rje-drong. Although Dbyangs-dgav was her baby name, she retained it into adulthood because so many people called her affectionately by that name.

Educated by her father, Dbyangs-dgav was an intelligent and studious child. She learned Tibetan grammar and poetry and then medicine and was so diligent that Dbyangs-dgav was said to be able to memorize fifteen pages of medical information within a couple of hours. When she was eight years old, Dbyangs-dgav learned that the Tibetan government had charged her father with collaborating with Han Chinese against Tibet and had exiled him. Two years later, in 1916, the newly established Tibetan hospital in Lhasa requested the consent of the thirteenth Dalai Lama to send two doctors to the Stag-lung Temple where Rje-drong was living in order to learn from him how to make up traditional prescriptions. He in turn requested the doctors to pass on to his daughter their eye surgery techniques when they returned to Lhasa.

Dbyangs-dgav was already a capable and independent doctor by the time she was thirteen, able to examine urine and diagnose through feeling the pulse; when she was twenty-four the young woman approached the Tibetan hospital in Lhasa to learn eye surgery. Dr. Qinrenuobu fulfilled his promise to her father and passed his techniques on to Dbyangs-dgav. From that time on, she traveled widely throughout Lhasa and Cham-mdo, specializing in cataract removal. Most of her patients had little money and some were beggars; she asked no payment for her services, instead providing food for the poor and accommodation for non-locals. In this way she earned the respect and affection of the Tibetan people.

Dbyangs-dgav's father had often attended to the family of King Vjigs-med Dbang-phyug of Bhutan, especially when difficult medical problems presented themselves. Therefore, when the king developed cataracts he sent for Dbyangs-dgav. She attended him in 1948 in Thimbu and after the operation remained with the king for three months to ensure a full and complete recovery. Her name became well known throughout the Himalayas from that time on; Dbyangs-dgav made regular visits to Thimbu, taking the opportunity to visit patients in India, Nepal, and Sikkim while she was in the area. In 1951, Dr. Qinrenuobu, then head of the Tibetan hospital, awarded Dbyangs-dgav the first certificate for eye surgery. With another doctor, she traveled throughout Tibet from that year to 1953, providing medical services to the people; the two doctors carried out 300 successful eye operations.

In addition to preeminence in eye surgery, Dbyangs-dgav grew skilled through long practice in other areas of medicine, including gynecology, pediatrics, arthritis, and bone fractures. Returning to her hometown of Ri-bo-che in 1956, she took up the position of chief of public health for the county before transferring to the Hospital for Tibetan Medicine in Lhasa. In 1959 Dbyangs-dgav was recognized by the Chinese government as a cadre at the national level and was a member of the First and Second Lhasa Autonomous Region People's Political Consultative Conference. With the establishment in the hospital of a Gynecology and Pediatric Department in 1962, she was made its inaugural director. The moral code by which Dbyangs-dgav lived dictated that patients were her priority and her obligation was to "cure illness in order to save the lives of patients." She did everything in her power for her patients, regardless of race or social status, and in this way "Dakini" (Goddess) Dbyangs-dgav became well loved in Tibet and the Himalayan region.

In 1964, Dbyangs-dgav recorded her gynecological experience gained over many years' practice and spoke at a conference. During the Cultural Revolution, however, she suffered many tribulations, being deprived of the right to write prescriptions and denied proper medical treatment when she injured her leg in a fall. Many patients nevertheless continued to consult her surreptitiously and Dbyangs-dgav herself lived in hope for the opportunity to pass her knowledge on to the next generation. Repeatedly, she requested the CCP to send her young people as students and taught them with great care.

Dbyangs-dgav was learned and possessed a good memory. Apart from medicine, she was very knowledgable about Buddhism and history and proficient in Tibetan, Hindi, and Sanskrit. Dbyangs-dgav enjoyed writing poetry in the classical Tibetan style, and her Tibetan calligraphy was beautiful. Her nature was optimistic and she retained the desire to learn throughout life. Dbyangs-dgav began learning Chinese at the age of sixty and loved singing and dancing. The doctor knew the popular love songs and folksongs of Cham-mdo and Lhasa and was especially fond of singing any of a dozen or so versions of *The Epic of King Gesar* from the many transcripts she had collected.

Twice married, Dbyangs-dgav had four daughters and one son; only the son and one daughter are still alive. The latter also became interested in folk literature and before retiring worked at the Tibetan Academy of Social Sciences, conducting research on *The Epic of King Gesar*. Dbyangs-dgav's son presently works as a doctor at the College for Physical Education in the Lhasa Autonomous Region.

In Tibetan tradition, women rarely became doctors, and Dbyangs-dgav was one of very few who did. She was a pioneer not only in eye surgery, especially the removal of cataracts, but also in the use of Tibetan medicine in the previously neglected field of gynecology and pediatrics. Dbyangs-dgav contributed significantly to the training of young female doctors, and her integrity and humanity remain a fine example for those entering the Tibetan medical profession. She died at the age of sixty-seven and, after a funeral held by the Public Health Department of Lhasa Municipality, was buried in Lhasa Martyr's Cemetery.

YANG Enhong
(Translated by Jan Zhang)

Personal interviews with Dbyangs-dgav's daughter, August 1996.

Deng Lianru: *see* **Dunn, Dame Lydia Selina**

Deng Lijun: *see* **Teng Li-chün**

Deng Liujin
Deng Liujin, b. 1912, in Shanghang County, Fujian Province, was one of the thirty women who went with the First Front Red Army on the Chinese communists' Long March of 1934–35.

Born into an impoverished peasant family, she was given away when only a few days old to an itinerant barber and his wife. While it is not certain that as a child Deng Liujin was promised in marriage to an adolescent boy who was training to become a Daoist priest, as one source suggests, she did manage to escape an early marriage. Once set on the path of revolution after the Red Army of Zhu De (1886–1976) and Mao Zedong (1893–1976) passed through western Fujian in mid-1929, Deng Liujin determined never to marry, giving as her reason that children would inevitably follow marriage, and a woman with children would be prevented from continuing revolutionary work.

She joined the CCP in 1931 and within a year had become a county inspector in Shanghang and head of the County Women's Department. In 1933 Deng Liujin progressed to the position of head of Fujian Provincial Women's Department and in 1934 was allowed to enroll in the Jiangxi soviet Party School in Ruijin. She was probably selected to go on the Long March because of her strong political convictions; as a "political fighter" Deng Liujin hired bearers, carried litters, undertook propaganda work, and arranged food supplies. Reaching Yan'an, she worked with the Women's Department, then enrolled in the Party School.

At the end of 1938, Deng Liujin was ordered to return to the south with Zeng Shan (1899–1972), who had been chairman of the Jiangxi soviet. This transparent party ploy forced an unwilling Deng Liujin to accept Zeng Shan as her husband; they married in early 1939 on the way south. Over the next few years, she gave birth to four sons and a daughter but managed to continue with her studies at a branch of the Party School. This was accomplished despite substantial opposition from her husband and other male party leaders, including one who threatened to prevent her from going to school if she did not take what he considered to be proper care of her children. Deng Liujin withstood this intimidation, placing her children with relatives while she went out mobilizing the peasantry. In 1949 Deng Liujin was given the task of setting up a nursery in Ji'an for abandoned and orphaned children and in 1960 was made a deputy head in the State Council, working in the children's welfare field and establishing kindergartens and nurseries.

Deng Liujin was criticized during the Cultural Revolution, as were most of those who took part in the Long March, but resumed work in 1976, again in the area of kindergartens and nurseries. Her children have all risen to positions of considerable influence in the PRC, one as a major-general (*shaojiang*) and two as senior colonels (*daxiao*) in the military. Her eldest son, Zeng Qinghong (b. 1940 in Anhui), holds the positions of alternate member of the Politburo, secretary of the CCP Central Committee secretariat, and director of the Central Committee office. Her second son, Zeng Qinghuai, who was ill as a child, became a welder in a Beijing chemical factory after failing to get into university. He was later appointed as a deputy director in the Ministry of Culture and in 1999 was working in Hong Kong. Her third son, Zeng Qingyang, is a military scientist, while her youngest child, Zeng Qingyuan, was a maintenance worker with the Air Force in Gansu before being transferred to the Propaganda Department and posted to Beijing in 1972. Her daughter, Zeng Haisheng, who was born on a boat at sea in 1947, has never wanted to be anything but a soldier. She worked her way up the army hierarchy in Heilongjiang, then studied at Beijing Industrial University before taking part in the construction of the Qinghai-Tibet railway. She was elected to the NPC in 1978 as a representative of the railway engineering corps (*tiedaobing*).

Despite suffering setbacks, Deng Liujin never hesitated to attribute to the support of the CCP her remarkable achievement of rising from illiterate peasant to public administrator. At the time of writing she was believed to be living in Beijing.

Sue WILES

Guo Chen. *Jinguo liezhuan: Hong yifangmianjun sanshiwei changzheng nühongjun shengping shiji*. Beijing: Nongcun duwu chubanshe, 1986, 9–12.
Lee, Lily Xiao Hong, and Sue Wiles. *Women of the Long March*. Sydney: Allen & Unwin, 1999.
Zhao Yining. "Fengxian chu shenhouse mu'ai." In *Hongjun nüyingxiong zhuan*, eds. Liaowang bianjibu. Beijing: Xinhua chubanshe, 1986, 141–52.
Ziping, ed. *Zhonggong zhengyao furen*. Hong Kong: Huanqin shiye, 1999, 192–201.

Deng Liyun: *see* **Teng Li-chün**

Deng Wenshu: *see* **Deng Yingchao**

Deng Xiangjun: *see* **Deng Yingchao**

Deng Xianqun: *see* **Zhong Yuzheng**

Deng Xiaohua: *see* **Can Xue**

Deng Yingchao

Deng Yingchao, 1904–1992, born as Wenshu and known as Yu'ai, Yongtong, and Xiangjun, was a native of Guangshan County, Henan Province; she was born, however, in Nanning in Guangxi Province. Deng Yingchao was one of the most prominent and active women in the Chinese communist movement from its beginnings until her death, and her enduring and apparently happy marriage to Zhou Enlai (1898–1976) was often held up as an inspiring model of affection and loyalty.

Her father, Deng Tingzhong (d. ca. 1910), was a minor official in the Qing government. He died when she was six or seven, and Deng Yingchao was then brought up by her mother, Yang Zhende, who supported them through teaching and practicing medicine. Lacking the support of a husband, her mother, whose strength and independence remained a positive and lifelong influence on her, moved several times before settling in Tianjin.

During the turbulent years following the downfall of the Qing dynasty in 1911, Deng Yingchao was a student at the First Tianjin Women's Normal School (1913–20). She was fifteen years old at the time of the May Fourth Movement of 1919 and immediately plunged into revolutionary activities, becoming a leader of the student movement in Tianjin organized to boycott Japanese goods and arouse patriotic sentiment. Working with Zhou Enlai, Guo Longzhen, Ma Jun, Liu Qingyang (*q.v.*), Zhang Ruoming (*q.v.*), and Chen Xiaochen, Deng Yingchao organized the Tianjin Students' Union, the Tianjin Women's Patriotic Association, and the Awakening Society (Juewushe). She led student demonstrations, orchestrated the release of students who had been arrested, and made fiery patriotic speeches in public places. Deng Yingchao went from door to door to publicize the need for national independence and sovereignty and spoke of gender equality, urging women to revolt against oppressive feudal traditions and seek liberation and independence. When armed police broke up an anti-Japanese, anti-government demonstration of several thousand people at Nankai University on 10 October, she was at the forefront of the female students breaking through the police cordon and handing out leaflets. Deng Yingchao had been one of the organizers of the rally and suffered injury during the confrontation. A strike by Tianjin students exposed the police brutality and aroused nationwide support for the students' cause.

The student movement had always been segregated along gender lines but Deng Yingchao crossed these repeatedly, as when she and other students from First Tianjin Women's Normal School joined with men in the Awakening Society. Deng Yingchao also became deeply involved in the women's patriotic and liberation movements, sometimes going by the code name Yi-hao (Number One) at this time. Deng Yingchao offered practical assistance to women, helping to extricate them from oppressive domestic situations through such organizations as the Tianjin branch of the Women's Rights Alliance (Nüquan yundong tongmenghui), which was re-formed in 1923 as the Guiding Star for Women Society (Nüxingshe). Concerned that poor women should have access to education, she was instrumental in establishing the Guiding Star for Women Adult Education School (Nüxing diyi buxi xuexiao). Deng Yingchao established and helped run progressive newspapers and magazines, some directed at women—*Awakening* (Juewu), *Awakening Post* (Jue you), *The People* (Pingmin), *Guiding Star for Women* (Nüxing), *Women's Daily* (Funü ribao)—to which she contributed articles. Among these were "Victory" (Shengli), "Love and Instruction" (Ai yu jiao), "Mistaken Love" (Cuowu de lian'ai), "A Classmate Chided by Her Mother-in-law" (Shoule popo jiaoxun de yige tongxue), and "Girls under Economic Oppression" (Jingji yapo xia de shaonü).

Deng Yingchao was not slow to put her women's liberation ideals into practice and in late 1920 was among the first group of women to join the staff of a boys' primary school in Beijing. Two years later, she helped organize and spoke at the opening ceremony of the Tianjin branch of the Women's Rights Alliance, whose stated aim was to "extend women's legal rights and status." Deng Yingchao and three other members of this organization presented to the government in Beijing a petition detailing specific legal, educational, and civil rights that women should be granted and demanding that concubinage, prostitution, and footbinding be outlawed. The four young women also exposed to public scrutiny further police violence against demonstrating students.

While Zhou Enlai and several other youth leaders went to France on work-study programs in 1920, Deng Yingchao remained in China and shouldered much of the responsibility for the patriotic and women's movements. She took up a teaching position at Daren Girls' School in Tianjin in 1924 and the same year also joined the Socialist Youth League; she became a member of the CCP in 1925, the year she turned twenty-one. Deng Yingchao concerns were broad. She brought various schools and colleges together as the Tianjin Women's National Congress with the purpose of promoting parliamentary government and acted as its president. She worked on the Publications Committee of the Women's Liberation Association (Funü jiefang xiehui), organized a commemorative meeting for International Women's Day, and established the Tianjin Women's Association in order to encourage women to play their part in societal reform.

Deng Yingchao also played a major role in the demonstrations and rallies held in support of workers and students killed or wounded by the British in Shanghai in the May Thirtieth (1925) Incident. Elected chair of the presidium of a patriotic united front called Tianjin All-Parties Alliance (Tianjin gejie lianhehui), she spoke movingly of the tragedy at mass memorial meetings (one meeting in June attracted one hundred thousand people, another seventy thousand) and demanded that foreign concessions on Chinese soil be repealed and extraterritoriality and unequal treaties be abolished.

After an order was issued in Tianjin for the arrest of Deng Yingchao, she was instructed by the CCP to go to Guangdong, then the center of revolutionary activity and where Zhou Enlai had been working since his return to China in late 1924. They were joined in marriage—without official ceremony or papers, their only concession to tradition being to give a dinner for their friends the following day—in August 1925. They did not have any children throughout their long marriage: Deng Yingchao had an abortion early in their marriage, and, although her next pregnancy, in 1927, went to term, the baby died after a difficult labor. Over the years, however, the couple adopted many children who had been orphaned during the war years.

After marriage, Deng Yingchao continued her active involvement in women's affairs, publishing articles on the direction of the women's movement in Guangdong while acting as head of both the CCP's Regional Women's Department and the KMT's Guangdong Women's Department, the latter under He Xiangning (*q.v.*). She was elected an alternate member of the CCP Guangdong-Guangxi Regional Committee and of the KMT Central Executive Committee, both relatively senior positions, particularly for a woman at that time. However, with the collapse of the KMT-CCP alliance in 1927—coinciding with her difficult labor and the death of her baby—she and her mother made their way to Shanghai. Deng Yingchao spent the next several years in

Shanghai with Zhou Enlai, working undercover as secretary of the Women's Work Committee of the CCP Central Committee, apart from a short period in Moscow where she attended, but was not a delegate to, the Sixth CCP Congress in 1928.

The three years Deng Yingchao spent in the Jiangxi soviet (1931–34) were not entirely peaceful. She involved herself in "doctrinal feuds" with Trotskyites and argued for a greater emphasis on the trade union movement, a view that placed her at odds with Mao Zedong (1893–1976). Nevertheless, Deng Yingchao was appointed to several high-level positions, including secretary-general of the soviet's Central Bureau, secretary of the Judicial Department, and secretary of the Politburo. She was also one of the thirty women taken on the famous Long March of 1934–35 and, suffering from tuberculosis, was carried most of the way on a stretcher.

Once the communists had established themselves in Yan'an, Deng Yingchao resumed her work among women. She was sent to Wuhan and later to Chongqing to work in the CCP offices in those cities, making contact and developing friendships with women across the spectrum of political parties, among them Soong Eiling (q.v.), Song Qingling (q.v.), Soong Mayling (q.v.), Shi Liang (q.v.), and Shen Zijiu (q.v.). Deng Yingchao also met, and deeply impressed, the American journalists Edgar Snow and Helen Foster Snow (Nym Wales). Deng Yingchao was thus instrumental in advancing the war effort as well as the women's movement. She spent most of the period between 1938 and 1943 in the KMT's wartime capital of Chongqing and held a range of official positions. Deng Yingchao was an organizer in the Women's Department of the Eighth Route Army (in Wuhan), served on the Women's Work Committee of both the Yangzi (Yangtze) branch of the CCP Central Committee and the CCP South China Bureau, and was director of the National Refugee Children's Association (Zhanshi ertong baoyu hui). In Chongqing she represented the CCP at the People's Political Participation Conference (Guomin canzhenghui) and continued her "united front" work among influential women.

During the civil war that broke out soon after the Sino-Japanese War ended in 1945, Deng Yingchao worked in Chongqing and Nanjing. In 1946 she was the sole female representative at a multiparty political consultative conference (Zhengzhi xieshang huiyi). Deng Yingchao thereafter replaced Cai Chang (q.v.) as secretary of the CCP Central Committee's Women's Committee and was active in land reform.

With the establishment of the PRC in 1949, she was elected vice-chair of the ACWF, a position held until elected honorary chair in 1978 at the ACWF's first conference held since 1957. In her role as vice-chair, she worked toward gender equality, freedom of choice in marriage, education, career building, and independence for women, as well as raising such issues as the protection of the rights of children and young people. On the national front, although not occupying key positions Deng Yingchao was a member (1945–68) of the Standing Committee of the NPC and the CCP Central Committee (1956–82). She was extremely careful not to appear publicly in the role of Premier Zhou Enlai's wife and never accompanied him on overseas visits in his capacity as Minister for Foreign Affairs. Deng Yingchao did travel overseas herself, however, visiting Burma, Sri Lanka, Iran, Cambodia, Japan, North Korea, Thailand, and France while with the NPC and regularly received foreign visitors.

She was not specifically targeted during the Cultural Revolution but since the ACWF ceased functioning during that period, became sidelined. Deng Yingchao made few public appearances and no public comment. Zhou Enlai died in early 1976 and with the death of Mao Zedong later that year, the Cultural Revolution ended. Deng Yingchao resumed a degree of political activity, even though she was then seventy-two. She was made president (1976–82) of the Standing Committee of the NPC and elected to two posts that signified the esteem in which she was held: chair (1983–88) of the CPPCC and membership (1978–82) of the Politburo, the Central Committee's decision-making body. Deng Yingchao retired in 1988 but continued to receive foreign visitors.

One of her most important contributions in her last years was to work toward improving China's relationship with Taiwan. As head of a Central Committee group (Zhongyang dui Tai gongzuo lingdao xiaozu), she was instrumental in raising the matter of the reunification of Taiwan with the mainland, an initiative that aroused considerable astonishment on both sides of the strait. The group that Deng Yingchao headed formulated suggestions designed to bring the two sides closer together and further the cause of reunification. She made good use of both her considerable diplomatic skills and personal relationships formed in the 1930s and 1940s.

Deng Yingchao died in 1992 in Beijing at the age of eighty-eight. In March 1998, the Zhou Enlai and Deng Yingchao Museum was opened in Tianjin to commemorate the lives and work of these two remarkable people.

WONG Yin Lee
(Translated by Laura Long)

Dong Zhenxiu. *Qingnian Deng Yingchao de daolu.* Tianjin: Tianjin shehuikexueyuan chubanshe, 1992.
Huang Qizao. *Huainian Deng Yingchao dajie.* Beijing: Zhongguo funü chubanshe, 1993.
Jin Feng. *Deng Yingchao zhuan.* Beijing: Renmin chubanshe, 1993.
Klein, Donald W., and Anne B. Clark. *Biographic Dictionary of Chinese Communism, 1921–1965.* Cambridge, Mass.: Harvard University Press, 1971, 838–43.
Snow, Helen Foster. *My China Years.* London: Harrap, 1985.
Snow, Helen. *Women in Modern China.* The Hague and Paris: Mouton Press, 1967, 249–59.
Xu Ming and Jia Xiu. *Zhongguo funü zhishi quanshu.* Beijing: Zhongguo funü chubanshe, 1995.
Zhonggong Tianjinshiwei dangshi ziliao zhengji weiyuanhui and Tianjinshi funü lianhehui. *Deng Yingchao yu Tianjin zaoqi funü yundong.* Beijing: Zhongguo funü chubanshe, 1987.
Zhonghua quanguo funü lianhehui. *Deng Yingchao geming huodong qishinian dashiji.* Beijing: Zhongguo funü chubanshe, 1990.

Deng Yongtong: *see* **Deng Yingchao**

Deng Yuzhi
Deng Yuzhi, b. 1900, a social worker, social activist, and leader of the Chinese YWCA (Zhonghua Jidujiao nüqingnianhui), was born in Shashi, Hubei Province, into a landlord-cum-business family.

Her father was an official of the Qing dynasty. When Deng Yuzhi was eight, her family moved to Changsha in Hunan Province, a city that was comparatively open to modern ideas at that time. She attended the primary school attached to the First Women's Normal School of Hunan Province and to Fuxiang Girls' High School. At Fuxiang she came under the influence of the May Fourth Movement as well as Christian ideas and decided to become a free and independent "new woman."

To realize her aspiration, Deng Yuzhi first had to break free of a traditionally arranged marriage. Betrothed in childhood, the young woman had agreed in high school to get married if she could continue to study and work outside the home after marriage, be a Christian, and not worship other gods. However, her husband's family failed to abide by any of these three conditions, so she left the family and continued her studies. After a painful and extended dispute, the marriage finally ended in divorce. The experience convinced Deng Yuzhi to devote herself to social work and never remarry.

She entered Ginling [Jinling] University probably in 1923 and studied in the Sociology Department, majoring in applied sociology; Deng Yuzhi began working for the YWCA the same year. Even as a student, she had investigated the living conditions of women brocade workers in Nanjing. Upon graduation in 1926, Deng Yuzhi went to the London School of Economics for one year of additional study, after which she did practical work at the International Labour Organization in Geneva, learning about the protection of women and child workers. Back in China in the late 1920s and early 1930s, Deng Yuzhi was in turn head of the Students' and the Workers' Departments and finally appointed as general secretary of the Chinese YWCA. At different times, she served as a consultant to the YWCA in Changsha, Shanghai, Wuhan, Chongqing, Guiyang, Kunming, and Hong Kong. Deng Yuzhi was also responsible for establishing night schools in Shanghai and Guangzhou for women workers.

During the Sino-Japanese War, she organized YWCA workers and volunteers in Shanghai to go to the front to carry stretchers and care for the wounded. In the rear, they established refugee camps and welfare stations for the families of soldiers, writing letters for them and helping solve day-to-day problems. She also wrested from the KMT government the lawful rights of soldiers' families in welfare and compensation. The YWCA established a national office in Wuhan in 1938 during a period of KMT-CCP unity, and Deng Yuzhi worked with Soong Mayling (*q.v.*), the leading KMT figure in women's work, and Deng Yingchao (*q.v.*), her CCP counterpart. Together, they accomplished a great deal in terms of support for the war and relief work. In 1938, Soong Mayling invited Deng Yuzhi to participate in a meeting of well-known women in various fields, including communist women, in an attempt to provide leadership in solidarity.

After the establishment of the PRC in 1949, Deng Yuzhi was one of a group of religious leaders consulted by the government on religious matters. She was vice-chair of a committee that proposed a Chinese Christian Church independent from the control of foreign bodies. In 1950 Deng Yuzhi was made a member of the East China Military and Political Committee (Huadong junzheng weiyuanhui), elected as an executive member of the China Relief Society, and an executive member of the China Red Cross Society (Zhongguo hongshizihui).

Lily Xiao Hong LEE

"Deng Yuzhi." In *Zhonggong renming lu*. Taipei: Guoli zhengzhi daxue guoji guanxi yanjiu zhongxin, 1978.

Jin Feng. *Deng Yingchao zhuan*. Beijing: Renmin chubanshe, 1993, 262–74.

Yingwen *Zhongguo funü*, ed. *Gujin zhuming funü renwu*, vol. 2. Shijiazhuang: Hebei renmin chubanshe, 1986, 597–600.

Dengzhu Lamu: *see* **Don-grub Lha-mo**

Ding Guoxian

Ding Guoxian, 1909–1972, of Donglu, Hebei Province, was the first woman to play *xusheng* (male lead) roles in local *jin* (Shanxi) opera; she performed under the stage name of Guozi Hong.

Her family was poor, and Ding Guoxian was adopted by the Ding family of Taiyuan. At seven, she was apprenticed to *jin* opera performer Sun Zhulin at the Taishan Temple in Taiyuan and earned her keep for three years singing traditional opera ballads. At eleven Ding Guoxian performed in such places as Jianyiyuan with the famous *jin* opera artists Gao "Hot Storyteller" Wenhan (*shuo shu hong*), Wang "SuperStar" Bishan (*gai tian hong*), and Wang "Babydoll" Yunshan (*maomao dan*). By the time, Ding Guoxian was eighteen, her fame had spread to every corner of Shanxi Province. In 1936, when she went to perform in Beijing, Ding Guoxian sought advice from *jing* (Beijing) opera experts concerning the opera *The Dragon Pearl Necklace* (Chuan longzhu). She also adapted the *jing* opera *The Four Scholars* (Si jinshi) with Ma Lianliang, borrowing the best of *jing* opera music and vocal technique and reforming the *xusheng* role in *jin* opera. After a long period of artistic practice and years of honing her craft on stage, she created the unique Ding style that bears her name. Ding Guoxian also cultivated the talents of Ma Yulou, Ma Zhong, and other up-and-coming young artists. She made an outstanding contribution to the development of the *xusheng* role in *jin* opera.

Ding Guoxian possessed a strong, sonorous voice and excellent breath control; her arias were deep and smooth, making her performance seemingly effortless. She was good at all the artistic techniques at her disposal—singing, acting, and diction—and used them to meticulously fashion all kinds of characters. Ding Guoxian was especially adept at using *jieban* and *liu shui* tunes as well as other *sanban* songs to skillfully express the feelings of her characters. She moved her audiences with the *jieban* aria Tian Yunshan sings when he strikes the child in *The Butterfly Cup* (Hudie bei) as well as with the *liushui* aria Bai Maolin sings when he angrily rebukes Hu Lin in *Selling the Painting at the Open Gate* (Maihua pimen). Also acclaimed were the long aria Zhuge Liang sings when he sits on the city tower strumming his zither in *The Empty City Strategy* (Kongcheng ji) and Min Deren's embellished aria (*huacheng shisan*) in *Hearth Flower* (Lu hua).

Ding Guoxian is celebrated for her interpretations of Yao Da in *A Pair of Silk Jackets* (Shuang luoshan); Cao Fu in *Journey to Snow Mountain* (Zou xueshan); Magistrate Yang in *The Eight Robes* (Ba jian yi); Zhuge Liang, Min Deren, Chen Gong in *The Capture and Release of Cao Cao* (Zhuo fang Cao); Xu Da in *The Dragon Pearl Necklace* (Ch'uan longzhu); Magistrate Yang in *Sun-Moon Painting* (Ri-yue tu); and Tian

Yunshan. Her performances as Wang Renhou, Chen Swift Legs, and an elderly lady in the modern operas *A Hatred of Blood and Tears* (Xuelei chou), *Little Son-in-law* (Xiao nüxu), and *After the Harvest* (Fengshou zhi hou) were also outstanding. In 1952 she took part in a nationwide competition and was awarded the rank of First-Grade Performer. In 1955 Ding Guoxian and Niu Guiying, Guo Fengying, Wang Zhengkui, and Liang Xiaoyun performed together in the opera *Striking the Golden Branch* (Da jinzhi), which was made into a film. In the *jin* opera repertoire, Ding Guoxian played *laosheng* and *xusheng* (young and middle-aged male) roles to much acclaim. She imbued all her roles with artistic integrity, but her most successful artistic creations were two: the white-bearded, green-coated old servant, suffering constant humiliation from a sense of justice, and the upright and honest cap-and-gowned scholar whose career suffered many twists and turns as he upheld righteousness.

In 1959, Ding Guoxian became a member of the CCP. She was appointed deputy director of the Shanxi *Jin* Opera Troupe, principal of the Shanxi Traditional Opera School, and a member of the Executive Committee of the Chinese Dramatists' Association. Ding Guoxian was also elected to the Second and Third CPPCC. In 1964, the Cultural Commission organized a celebration of her forty years as a performer.

Ding Guoxian was outspoken by nature and despised evil. Unwilling to curry favor with the enemy during the Sino-Japanese War, she stopped performing and lived in seclusion in a mountain village in Xinxian for a long period. At the start of the Cultural Revolution, Ding Guoxian was so cruelly persecuted that she became very depressed. Ding Guoxian died in 1972 at the relatively young age of sixty-three. It is not known if she married or had children.

HE Li and Shirley Wai CHAN
(Translated by Jennifer Eagleton)

Zhongguo dabaike quanshu: Xiqu quyi. Beijing: Zhongguo dabaike quanshu chubanshe, 1989, 62.
Zhongguo yinyue cidian. Beijing: Renmin yinyue chubanshe, 1984, 82.

Ding Ling

Ding Ling, 1904–1986, is one of modern China's most famous and important writers. Born into an official-gentry family in Changde, Hunan Province, as Jiang Wei (*zi* Bingzhi), she used various pseudonyms, including Bin Zhi, Cong Xuan, Xiao Han, and Man Jia. It is as Ding Ling, however, that she became widely known nationally as well as internationally.

While her reputation was achieved because of the range of writings the author produced from 1927 to the end of her life, her material compelled particular attention because of the way it was shaped by the turbulent times in which she lived. Changing political and ideological contexts caused dramatic reversals of fortune throughout her life, both in the trajectory of her literary career and the interpretation of her works. Recent biographies, reminiscences, and memoirs provide a great deal of new information about Ding Ling, yet uncertainties remain regarding the controversies she experienced.

Ding Ling's father, Jiang Baoqi, who had passed the county examination and studied briefly in Japan, suffered from poor health; he died when she was three, leaving his wife with a daughter, an infant son, and a host of debts. Her once-wealthy extended gentry family already had entered a period of precipitous decline, and her mother, Yu Manzheng (as a widow she changed her name to Jiang Shengmei, *zi* Mutang), enrolled in Hunan First Normal School for Women to become a teacher. Her transition from a traditional to a new society was later to form the basis of Ding Ling's unfinished 1932 novel *Mother* (Muqin). With such an independent and courageous woman as a model, it is not surprising that Ding Ling herself became a precocious activist.

When the May Fourth Movement reached Taoyuan in Hunan Province in 1919, Ding Ling was a high school student, aged fifteen. Influenced by the new ideas, she cut her hair, took part in lectures and demonstrations, and taught in a night school for the poor. In 1921 Ding Ling and six other students, one of whom was Yang Kaihui (*q.v.*), the first wife of Mao Zedong (1893–1976), enrolled at Yueyang Boys' School, thus making it one of the first co-educational high schools in the area. The following year Ding Ling broke off an arranged marriage to a cousin and left for Shanghai with her friend Wang Jianhong. There they studied under leftist intellectuals, first at a girls' school and later at Shanghai University. Moving back and forth between Shanghai and Nanjing, the two led a chaotic and impoverished but emancipated life among radicals and anarchists, sporadically studying painting and literature. In 1924, Wang Jianhong married the Marxist literary theorist Qu Qiubai, who died soon after, from tuberculosis.

Ding Ling moved to Beijing, where she occasionally audited various classes and met the young poet Hu Yepin; they soon lived together. Their life of poverty, young love, and literary aspirations from 1924 to 1930 has been memorably portrayed in the reminiscences of Shen Congwen, another struggling writer who shared their lives during that period. Ding Ling's attempts to support herself by becoming a movie actress in Shanghai provided the material for "Mengke," the story that launched her literary career in 1927. Several months later, "Miss Sophie's Diary" (Shafei nüshi de riji) followed, portraying with unprecedented boldness a young woman's sexual feelings; it soon set its author on her way to becoming China's most famous—or notorious—woman writer.

The three friends moved to Shanghai, which was becoming the center of literary life, and engaged in various short-lived publishing ventures as they continued to write. Most of Ding Ling's stories from the first three years of her career centered on individual young women living alone in a big city. In depicting their rebellion against tradition and authority and problematic quest for identity, the author explored new literary territory, where a woman might search for her own voice. Because the writer focused on the feelings of her female characters, it was often assumed that she was "writing about herself"; but Ding Ling repeatedly denied this author-character identification. This assumption was later used by party ideologues to condemn her morally and politically.

Meanwhile, Hu Yepin was becoming increasingly involved in the activities of the

CCP. On 17 January 1931, a little over two months after Ding Ling gave birth to their son Jiang Zulin, Hu Yepin was arrested by the KMT government while attending a party meeting. Three weeks later, he and twenty-three others were secretly executed. Ding Ling's political radicalization had begun before Hu Yepin's death, but his martyrdom reinforced her commitment to the revolutionary cause. She gave their son into the care of her mother in Hunan and returned to Shanghai where, under CCP direction, Ding Ling assumed editorship of *Big Dipper* (Beidou), the new literary journal of the League of Left-Wing Writers. Over the following three years, her fiction evolved toward a leftist revolutionary genre as she experimented with new subject matter and techniques. Her novella *Flood* (Shui), depicting the suffering that drove peasants to rebellion during the widespread floods of 1931, became serialized in the first three issues of *Big Dipper*. It was hailed by communist critics as being a landmark in the new proletarian fiction. She joined the CCP in 1932.

Government harassment forced *Big Dipper* to close down after seven issues. Ding Ling went into hiding, although continuing to write, but was abducted by KMT agents on 4 May 1933. It is widely suspected that she was betrayed by Feng Da, the man with whom she was then living, but his role in the kidnapping and the story of her detention has never been clarified. During the anti-rightist campaign of 1957, the incident was exhumed, and Ding Ling was accused of surrendering to the KMT and confessing. She was not cleared of these charges until 1984, two years before her death. Her abductors took her in 1933 to Nanjing, placing her under house arrest with Feng Da. Their daughter Jiang Zuhui was born in 1934 and, like her older brother, this baby was given into the care of her maternal grandmother in Hunan. Rumors of Ding Ling's execution occasioned memoirs and reminiscences (including those by Shen Congwen) as well as new collections of her works, all of which added to her fame.

With the help of the CCP, Ding Ling eventually managed to escape her captors and make her way to the party's headquarters in Bao'an, Shaanxi Province. The arrival of this prominent writer in November 1936 was much celebrated, and for the occasion Mao Zedong (1893–1976) composed two poems. In the border regions, Ding Ling became active in several party organizations and was soon elected director of the recently established Literature and Art Association. She wrote reportage and essays as well as fiction for party papers and journals. With the outbreak of the Sino-Japanese War in 1937, Ding Ling also organized and directed the Northwest Front Service Corps (Xibei zhandi fuwutuan), traveling with a troupe of performing artists to arouse anti-Japanese sentiment. The service corps was an experiment in appropriating popular traditional forms—the song and dance "Rice Shoot Song" (*yangge*), for example—for broad audience appeal and propagation of new political messages. One of the members of the troupe was the writer Chen Ming, whom Ding Ling married in 1942.

She edited the first one hundred issues of the literary supplement of the CCP newspaper *Liberation Daily* (Jiefang ribao), publishing articles that became the target of criticism during the rectification campaign of 1942. The campaign's main objective was to apply party discipline, explicitly to literature, indicated when Mao Zedong gave his "Talks at the Yan'an Forum on Literature and Art" in May. He proclaimed that literature and art should be subordinated to collective goals and should emphasize the bright side of reality rather than exposing its dark side. While Ding Ling was not the main target of the campaign, two of her recent stories—"When I Was in Xia Village" (Wo zai Xiacun de shihou) and "In the Hospital" (Zai yiyuan zhong)—and her essay "Thoughts on March 8" (San ba jie yougan), the latter specifically pointing out the discrimination under which women in Yan'an still labored, were criticized. By speaking out against negative conditions in party-controlled regions, Ding Ling fell short of fulfilling literary criteria as prescribed by the party.

At the end of the war, in 1945, she and Chen Ming traveled in north China and in 1946 took part in various land reform movements. These experiences formulated the basis of her one completed novel, *The Sun Shines on the Sanggan River* (Taiyang zhao zai Sanggan he shang), about land reform. Although claiming to be based on personal experience, obligatory for the genre, the novel is not so much historically real, even supposing there is such a thing, as it is a fictionalized account of the Maoist revolution, informed by its ideals and self-images. The novel's theme is about how a raised mass consciousness can transform the world. The book won Ding Ling considerable acclaim, including a Stalin Prize, but it turned out to be her last published work of fiction for almost three decades.

With the establishment of the PRC in 1949, Ding Ling became a prominent member of its cultural bureaucracy. A member of the Standing Committee of the All-China Federation of Literature and Art Circles (Zhonghua quanguo wenxue yishu gongzuozhe lianhehui), she was also vice-chair of the All-China Union of Literary Workers (Zhonghua quanguo wenxue gongzuozhe xiehui; becoming the Writers' Association [Zuojia xiehui] in 1953); editor of *Literary Gazette* (Wenyi bao); and, later, deputy editor of *People's Literature* (Renmin wenxue). Ding Ling organized and directed the Central Literary Institute (Zhongyang wenxue yanjiushuo), a training school for writers in Beijing, and at one stage headed the Literary Bureau of the party's Propaganda Department. She also traveled abroad, for the first time in her life, as leader or a member of official delegations to Hungary, Czechoslovakia, and the Soviet Union. Her writings now included little fiction, consisting for the most part of essays, addresses, and travel accounts connected with public occasions or party functions.

Ding Ling took an active part in some of the earlier (and milder) political campaigns against writers, but as their frequency increased and the scope widened she herself became a target. In 1954, Ding Ling was criticized for her work in *Literary Gazette*. After she resigned as editor in 1952, the publication remained in the hands of her colleague Chen Qixia; in 1955, the "anti-party activities of Ding Ling and Chen Qixia" were criticized in meetings organized by the Writers' Association. Ding Ling appealed to the party's Central Committee, which appointed an investigative group to review the case. But even as the party organization of the Writers' Association appeared about to exonerate her, the anti-rightist campaign swept the country. In August 1957, she was condemned as a rightist, expelled from the party, and relieved of all duties and positions. This signaled the release of further nationwide reports and accusations against her in journals and papers. Ding Ling was attacked for her sexual immorality (her early stories were brought in as "evidence"), maligning the peasant masses in her fiction, traitorous conspiracy against the party, a superiority complex, and setting up literature as an "independent kingdom" in opposition to the party.

Also branded a rightist, her husband Chen Ming was sent to a state farm in Heilongjiang to do "labor under supervision." Ding Ling was granted permission to join him, little realizing they would remain there effectively in exile for almost twelve years. When they left in 1970, it would be to spend five years in solitary confinement. Ding Ling's rightist label was not removed until 1978. Thousands of writers and intellectuals who, like her, were targeted as rightists in 1957 were rehabilitated after the Maoist era. In recent years, documents of those directly involved in the campaigns have become available. They suggest that, while genuine ideological disagreement did indeed exist, factional rivalries dating back to the 1930s, power struggles, and the need for self-protection by demonstrating ideological zeal, as well as the arbitrary nature of the decision-making process, were all factors in the wrongful case against Ding Ling.

In the northern wilderness of Heilongjiang, she was initially assigned to a large state farm in Tangyuan and sent to work on a poultry farm. Later, Ding Ling became a cultural worker responsible for teaching, recreation, and political study and was permitted to return briefly to Beijing in 1960 to attend the Third National Writers' Congress. She and Chen Ming (whose rightist label had been removed in 1961) were transferred to Baoquanling state farm in 1964 and there, with much improved living and working conditions, Ding Ling resumed her writing. Two years later, however, the Cultural Revolution began, and the couple suffered relentless persecution, including the confiscation of her writings, diaries, and letters. She was put in a "cowshed" and beaten, paraded in the streets with a blackened face, and assigned demeaning tasks.

One night in May 1970, Ding Ling was abruptly awakened, handcuffed, and taken by car and train to Qincheng Prison in Beijing. There she was kept in solitary confinement for five years. Ding Ling survived the ordeal, the writer said, only because she decided not to commit suicide. Not until her release in 1975 did she learn that Chen Ming had been kept in the same prison the whole time.

They were then sent to a remote mountain village in Shanxi Province with a monthly allowance and limited personal freedom. Once her rightist label had been removed in 1978, she appealed the following year to be allowed to return to Beijing for medical care. While in the hospital, Ding Ling wrote the essay "Sketches in the Cowshed" ("Niupeng" xiaopin); this became her first published work in twenty-two years. With the ban on her work lifted, she now resumed an active writing career, producing essays, reviews, and reminiscences of her own life and those of her friends, many now dead. Her one piece of fiction, "Du Wanxiang," was based on a model labor heroine. Originally written in 1966, the story was destroyed during the Cultural Revolution and rewritten for publication in 1979. Ding Ling was re-elected vice-president of the Writers' Association and a committee member of the Federation of Literary and Art Circles (Wenlian). In 1980, the Central Committee accepted the Writers' Association's proposal on rectifying the rightist issue and restored to Ding Ling her party membership, original position, and salary. From then on, in spite of increasingly poor health, she was busy with official functions, lectures, and receiving foreign visitors yet found time to continue writing.

In 1981, Ding Ling visited the United States, spending several weeks at the International Writers' Workshop at the University of Iowa and visiting several other universities, giving talks on her life and work. She disappointed those who expected her to use these public appearances to denounce, or at least criticize, the CCP that had so harshly persecuted her. They did not know, however, that Ding Ling was still at that time awaiting full rehabilitation. She spoke out in support of the anti-spiritual pollution campaign in October 1983, again surprising those who saw this position as supporting the party line. In August 1984, the Organization Department of the Central Committee issued a notice on the restoration of Comrade Ding Ling's reputation: she was now, finally, fully rehabilitated.

Ding Ling had also been engaged at that time in a new venture: co-editorship with Shu Qun of the new literary bimonthly journal *China* (Zhongguo). Featuring works by established and new writers, the periodical claimed to be privately published with public help and responsible for its own profit and loss. In the meantime, however, Ding Ling was in and out of hospital because of her many medical problems. She was made an honorary member of the American Academy and Institute of Arts and Letters on 25 February 1986. She died on 4 March, her funeral attended by many state and party dignitaries.

While seeking to be economically self-sufficient, the political status of *China* remained ambiguous. At the end of 1985, with Ding Ling continuing to run editorial meetings from her hospital bed, the decision was made to make the journal a monthly. After her death, however, the Writers' Association announced a shakeup and demanded control of the publication. Two months later, in a bitter memo in the twelfth and final issue, the editorial staff announced that the journal would cease publication.

Two works by Ding Ling that remained unfinished at her death are memoirs covering the most difficult and controversial periods of her life. "World of Demons and Monsters" (Wangliang shijie), an account of her abduction by the KMT in 1933, subsequent detention, and escape to Yan'an, appeared in the last two issues of *China*. "In Wind and Snow" (Fengxue renjian) covers her exile from 1958 to 1970 in the great northern wilderness on state farms as a rightist and during the Cultural Revolution. These two memoirs were published together in 1989 with supplementary material and notes by Chen Ming. Both works narrate Ding Ling's point of view many years after the events and were recounted in a period when she may still have been concerned about unresolved issues between herself and the CCP. Ding Ling's life and work dramatically exemplifies the complex relationship between party politics and literary production in modern Chinese history. More than likely her story will continue to unfold.

Yi-tsi Mei FEUERWERKER

Barlow, Tani E., ed., with Gary J. Bjorge. *I Myself Am a Woman: Selected Writings of Ding Ling*. Boston: Beacon Press, 1989.

Chang Jun-mei. *Ting Ling: Her Life and Work*. Taipei: Institute of International Relations, National Chengchi University, 1978.

Ding Ling. *Ding Ling lun chuangzuo*. Shanghai: Shanghai wenyi chubanshe, 1985.

————. *Ding Ling wenji*, 5 vols. Changsha: Hunan renmin chubanshe, 1982–1984.

————. *Ding Ling zizhuan*, eds. Xu Yangqing and Zong Cheng. Xuzhou: Jiangsu wenyi chubanshe, 1996.

————. *Wanglian shijie. Fengxue renjian—Ding Ling de huiyi*. Beijing: Renmin wenxue chubanshe, 1989. Includes notes and additional material by Chen Ming.

Ding Ling chuangzuo dutexing mianmianguan—quanguo shouci Ding Ling chuangzuo taolunhui zhuanji. Changsha: Hunan wenyi chubanshe, 1986.

Ding Yanzhao. *Zai nanren de shijie li: Ding Ling zhuan*. Shanghai: Shanghai wenyi chubanshe, 1998.

Feuerwerker, Yi-tsi Mei. *Ding Ling's Fiction: Ideology and Narrative in Modern Chinese Literature*. Cambridge, Mass.: Harvard University Press, 1982.

Klein, Donald W., and Anne B. Clark. *Biographic Dictionary of Chinese Communism, 1921–1965*. Cambridge, Mass.: Harvard University Press, 1971, 843–46.

Li Zhilian. "Bugai fasheng de gushi: Huiyi yijiuwuwu-yijiuwuqi chuli Ding Ling deng wenti de jingguo." *Xinwenxue shiliao*, no. 3 (1989): 129–38.

Shen Congwen. *Ji Ding Ling, ji Ding Ling xuji*. Shanghai: Shanghai liangyou fuxing gongsi, 1934. Revised versions of *Ji Ding Ling nüshi*, serialized in *Guowen zhoubao* 10: 29–51 (20 July–18 December 1933).

————. *Ji Hu Yepin*, 3rd edn. Shanghai: 1935.

Sun Ruizhen and Wang Zhongchen, eds. *Ding Ling yanjiu zai guowai*. Changsha: Hunan renmin chubanshe, 1985.

Wang Zhongchen, ed. *Ding Ling shujian*. Changchun: Dongbei shifan daxue chubanshe, 1986.

Yuan Liangjun. *Ding Ling yanjiu wushinian*. Tianjin: Tianjin jiaoyu chubanshe, 1990.

————. *Ding Ling yanjiu ziliao*. Tianjin: Tianjin renmin chubanshe, 1982.

Zhongguo bianjibu, ed. *Ding Ling jinian ji*. Changsha: Hunan renmin chubanshe, 1987. Contains the most detailed chronology of Ding Ling's life.

Zhongguo Ding Ling yanjiu hui, ed. *Ding Ling yanjiu*. Changsha: Hunan shifan daxue chubanshe, 1992.

Zhongguo xiandangdai wenxue yike yaoyan de juxing—Ding Ling wenxue chuangzuo guoji yantaohui wenji. Changsha: Hunan wenyi chubanshe, 1994.

Zhou Fenna. *Ding Ling yu Zhonggong wenxue*. Taipei: Chengwen chubanshe, 1980.

Zhou Liangpei. *Ding Ling zhuan*. Beijing: Shiyue wenyi chubanshe, 1993.

Zong Cheng. *Fengyu rensheng: Ding Ling zhuan*. Beijing: Zhongguo wenlian chubangongsi, 1988.

Ding Xuesong

Ding Xuesong, b. 1918, in Ba County, Sichuan Province, was China's first female ambassador.

She joined the CCP in 1937 and the following year went to Yan'an. Ding Xuesong studied at the Anti-Japanese Military and Political College (Kangda), acting as group leader of the women students' group, and then attended Yan'an Women's University (Yan'an nüzi daxue), where she was vice-chair of the students' association and club director. In 1941, Ding Xuesong was appointed secretary to Li Dingming, vice-chair of the Shaanxi-Gansu-Ningxia Border Region. That year Ding Xuesong married the celebrated Korean composer and revolutionary Zheng Lücheng (d. 1976), who had gone to Nanjing in China at the age of fifteen, eventually making his way to Yan'an in 1937. He is best known for his "Ode to Yan'an" but also composed the "Grand Eighth Route Army Chorus." Their daughter Xiaoti was born in Yan'an; she attended primary school there but was never in good health, so was transferred to Tianjin Music Academy (Tianjin yinyue xueyuan) as a boarder.

During the five years Ding Xuesong spent in Pyongyang, Korea, with her husband (1945–50), she held several prestigious positions: secretary-general of the Korean Workers' Party's Central Committee's Committee on the Affairs of Foreign Nationals (Chaoxian laodongdang zhongyang qiaowu weiyuanhui mishuzhang) and president of the Federation of North Korean Overseas Chinese Unions (BeiChaoxian huaqiao lianhehui zonghui weiyuanzhang). In 1949 she was made a member of a Chinese trade delegation stationed in Korea and accepted the directorship of the Pyongyang branch of Xinhua News Agency. When China decided to open an embassy in Pyongyang in 1950, Ding Xuesong and her husband resolved the difficult situation of their conflicting nationalities by returning to China, where Zheng Lücheng took out Chinese citizenship.

Upon her return, Ding Xuesong was attached to the CCP Central Committee's Liaison Department and sat on its International Activities Guiding Committee. She was transferred in 1964 to the State Council's foreign affairs office, first as head of secretariat, then as secretary-general. Ding Xuesong was closely associated with various friendship associations with foreign nations and in 1971 served as secretary-general and vice-president of the Chinese People's Association for Friendship with Foreign Countries. During the early years of the PRC, Zheng Lücheng was active in his work as a composer; he wrote the music for the Western-style opera *Cloud Gazing*. He and Ding Xuesong were both persecuted during the Cultural Revolution, and he fell into a deep depression. Tragically, when he heard of the fall of the Gang of Four, which signaled the end of the Cultural Revolution, he suffered a stroke and died.

From 1979 to 1984, Ding Xuesong represented the PRC as ambassador extraordinary and plenipotentiary to the Netherlands and later to Denmark. She won praise and admiration of the people in these countries as well as from her diplomatic peers. Ding Xuesong was also extremely successful in initiating cooperation between China and Western European countries in the areas of economics, trade, and technology. Within China, Ding Xuesong was a delegate to the Eighth and Twelfth CCP National Congresses, the Fourth and Fifth NPCs, and a committee member of the Sixth and Seventh CPPCC. Most recently, she was elected president of the Yan'an Women's University Alumni Association.

Despite an illustrious career, Ding Xuesong always felt that she had failed as a wife and mother. Her work absorbed so much of her time and attention that it precluded a warm and normal family life.

ZHAO Jinping
(Translated by Malcolm Robertson)

Cheng Xiangjun, ed. *Nü waijiaoguan.* Beijing: Renmin tiyu chubanshe, 1995, 3–34.
Jiao Nan. "Zhongguo nü dashi." *Zhongguo funü,* no. 1 (1992): 8–9.
Zhongguo funü wushinian. CD-ROM.

Dong Huang: *see* **Dong Zhujun**

Dong Maoyuan: *see* **Dong Zhujun**

Dong Pu: *see* **Wang Guangmei**

Dong Yuying: *see* **Dong Zhujun**

Dong Zhujun

Dong Zhujun, b. 1900, in Shanghai, was a political activist and entrepreneur. Born in a slum as Dong Maoyuan, she later adopted the school name Yuying; in adult life Dong Zhujun became Dong Huang, *zi* Zhujun, and it is by this courtesy name that she is known.

Dong Zhujun's father, Dong Tongqing, and his younger brother were laborers from Nantong, Jiangsu Province, and went to Shanghai. Her father became a rickshaw boy, and her uncle and his family sold newspapers for a living. Her mother, known only in Dong Zhujun's memory as "second sister" (*er ajie*) was illiterate and worked as the equivalent of a "downstairs maid" for rich families. Despite abject poverty, her parents sent her to school with the conviction that education alone would improve their lot.

After a bout of typhoid fever, her father was no longer strong enough to pull rickshaws, and the family lost their main source of income. Her parents thus felt compelled to indenture Dong Zhujun to a courtesan house for three years, with the understanding that she would entertain guests only by singing Beijing opera arias and would return home after three years. Being only thirteen and not yet having reached puberty, she was not to sell her body. However, Dong Zhujun learned from the woman who helped with her makeup that once indentured it was very difficult to get out of prostitution. If within those three years she "became a woman" (i.e., began menstruating), then her "mother," the procuress, would sell her to the highest bidder as his wife or, more likely, concubine.

This troubled Dong Zhujun so much that she decided to pick a man for herself. By all accounts very beautiful and the most popular courtesan of the house, after mentally reviewing her admirers she chose for her future husband a young revolutionary from Sichuan named Xia Zhishi (1887?–1951?), not only because he was debonair but because she vaguely admired him for working for the good of the country. Xia Zhishi and his comrades would meet at courtesan houses to discuss their plans to thwart the ambitions of warlord Yuan Shikai to reestablish the monarchy. Dong Zhujun said she would agree to marry Xia Zhishi under two conditions: first, that she be his wife and not a concubine, and, second, that he would promise to take her to Japan to study. With his wife having died of sickness recently, Xia Zhishi agreed.

He approached her "mother" to negotiate a deal; however, she asked for 3,000 silver dollars but Xia Zhishi could offer only 1,000. Dong Zhujun became incensed that she was being bought and sold like an object; she also had heard that when men paid a price for a courtesan, they did not usually respect her after marriage. Dong Zhujun then told Xia Zhishi to wait for her; she would secure her own freedom. Dong Zhujun eventually managed to dupe her guard and escape to Xia Zhishi's lodgings, where she found him on the point of boarding a steamship to Japan with Yuan Shikai's soldiers on his heels, intent on killing him and his comrades.

Thus, in 1914, at the age of fourteen (in her memoirs, fifteen) she married Xia Zhishi, then twenty-seven, in a civil ceremony. They sailed for Japan soon after. Dong Zhujun attended a Japanese-language school at first, but her husband objected, not wanting her to go out by herself. He then engaged five private tutors to teach her the Ochanomi School syllabus at home. One of Dong Zhujun's teachers then suggested that she change her name from Yuying to the more elegant Huang, with the courtesy name Zhujun. In 1915, Dong Zhujun gave birth to her first child, a daughter named Guoqiong.

Friends would often drop by their home in Japan to discuss Chinese politics, and Dong Zhujun began to show an interest in China's destiny, wishing she could do something to help. Xia Zhishi received a call in early 1916 to provide assistance in overthrowing Yuan Shikai by leading an army from his native Sichuan. Although remaining in Tokyo, Dong Zhujun continued to discuss China's political situation with friends. She returned there in 1917 at the request of her husband, going first to Chongqing and then to his native Hejiang County. Having defeated the enemy of the fledgling Republic, Xia Zhishi was by then in command of three thousand soldiers ready to march against the northern warlords and also effectively his own boss, able to tax the people and use the revenue as he pleased. Dong Zhujun had once believed Xia Zhishi was a true revolutionary but began to doubt his fervor when she saw him behaving no differently than the warlords he had defeated.

Dong Zhujun spent more than a decade of her married life in Sichuan, most of it in Chengdu. During these years, she adapted to a family she later described as "feudal," in the sense, perhaps, of being backward and steeped in the negative aspects of traditional culture. After Xia Zhishi lost military power to other Sichuan warlords, the entire clan lived off their inherited properties and the funds Xia Zhishi had accumulated while in power. Not one member of the clan, man or woman, was productive in any way, which led Dong Zhujun to worry that the family fortune would soon be gone. While she herself managed a large household that included brothers-in-law, stepson, parents (whom she brought from Shanghai), and her own five children, Dong Zhujun decided to do something to bring in extra income. She started two businesses.

The first one was a sock-knitting factory through which Dong Zhujun intended to help women become financially independent by earning an income; the second was a rickshaw company. Remembering the injustices and hardships her father had suffered as a rickshaw boy, she wanted to reform the industry, asking a fair rent from the pullers and providing welfare such as paid sick leave. Her views continued to diverge more and more from those of her husband, and Dong Zhujun urged him to be more progressive and positive. Instead, Xia Zhishi took up opium. Their biggest source of disagreement was about the education of their children, four daughters—Guoqiong, Guoxiu (b. 1919), Guoying (b. 1920?), and Guozhang (b. 1922 or 1923)—and a son named Daming (b. 1926). Their father cared nothing for the girls, even when they were very sick. He opposed the idea of giving them a good education, pointing out with some degree of accuracy that even in the Republican period many highly educated women still ended up as housewives after they married. Indeed, even when their eldest daughter's music teacher suggested that the girl was talented, Xia Zhishi objected to her going to music school in Shanghai. He wanted instead to marry off each one of the girls as soon as they came of age. Dong Zhujun's other source of dissatisfaction about her marriage and home life was the way she felt her husband used and humiliated her as a servant.

Toward the end of her days in Sichuan, Dong Zhujun met and befriended men and women with communist connections. Though she did not consciously attempt to find out about the CCP at this stage, Dong Zhujun was influenced by its ideology. Then, in 1927, when Xia Zhishi was absent in Nanjing and Shanghai, seeking his political fortune, Dong Zhujun decided to leave Sichuan with her parents and daughters. Leaving her infant son behind in Chengdu, Dong Zhujun, who intended to go back for him later, joined her husband in Shanghai. The main reason she planned to stay with her husband was because it might give her girls an opportunity for a better education. However, the couple fought frequently and finally agreed to separate. Dong Zhujun had taken only 400 yuan when she left Sichuan, leaving the remaining cash and deeds to properties with Xia Zhishi's youngest brother. When the couple formally divorced in 1934, Dong Zhujun did not ask for any money.

She and her daughters sank into poverty, often having to pawn or sell their possessions to get by. Dong Zhujun befriended several more members of the CCP, but when she asked a CCP representative, known to her only as Comrade Li, to be admitted to the party, he told her that her first duty was to feed her family. Since Dong Zhujun clearly had a flair for business, Comrade Li suggested she could best help the party through succeeding in business. Dong Zhujun proceeded to found a Qunyi cotton yarn spindle factory. She sold her jewelry and invited others to invest, and with capital of 4,000 yuan started a factory employing almost one hundred workers. Banks would not lend her any money because they had no faith in women's business skills, so in 1931 with the help of some Chinese Filipino friends Dong Zhujun went to the Philippines to raise more capital. By 1932, Qunyi was operating profitably. However, she had been almost ruined in the January Twentieth Incident of that year when the Japanese bombed Shanghai. After reporting the bad news to her overseas shareholders, some accused her of being a shyster. During this period, she kept in touch with the CCP, joining in protests and other activities they sponsored. One day that year, while putting her daughters to bed, Dong Zhujun had a visit from the French concession police. They found a bag of political pamphlets under her bed, and she was arrested. Her eldest daughter, then only fifteen years old, did her best to care for her grandparents and younger sisters while her mother was in jail, but Dong Zhujun's parents died of anxiety and poverty. She offered a bribe to her jailers and was released after a few months on its promise but, unable to raise the bribe money, fled with her daughters to hide in Hangzhou for a year and a half.

At this darkest moment of her life, Dong Zhujun cast about, unemployed and deeply in debt. Then a man named Li Songgao mysteriously appeared. Although he was a stranger to her, Li explained, as a native of Sichuan he had read of her divorce, big news in the newspapers there, and admired her courage and integrity. Li told her that he was a military leader in Sichuan and was going to Japan to purchase ammunition. Learning of her desperation Li was willing to give her 2,000 yuan to start a new business. Dong Zhujun decided to open a Sichuan restaurant in Shanghai. To her mind, even the most famous and popular Chinese restaurants in Shanghai were in need of reform; their decor was old-fashioned, in bad taste, the establishments offered unfriendly service, and most importantly, were dirty. She planned to change the business and create a restaurant in accord with her own ideals. With great care, Dong Zhujun designed the interior, chose the crockery and other implements, and trained the staff. She called the restaurant Jinjiang, after the river on which the city of Chengdu in Sichuan stood. The name was also reminiscent of Xue Tao, a Tang dynasty poet-courtesan who had lived by the river and with whom Dong Zhujun identified. The restaurant opened in 1935 and was an immediate success, so much so that a year later she added the Jinjiang Teahouse. Both establishments remain successful to this day. Today, all over the world, restaurants are named Jinjiang that have no connection with Dong Zhujun's enterprise; their owners hope that some of her success will rub off on them. Jinjiang developed a new formula in the business: retain excellent traditional cuisine, rejuvenate some of its dishes, and provide cordial service in an aesthetic, modern environment.

As Comrade Li had forecast, through Jinjiang Dong Zhujun was able to help the CCP in several ways. She provided a front for members of the underground and a safe house for those escaping from the KMT secret police, including the woman revolutionary Xie Xuehong (*q.v.*). However, the biggest help she gave the CCP in the 1940s, especially the latter part of the decade, was to create several printing houses that enabled the party to print books, magazines, and propaganda pamphlets in the years just before the communist takeover. These included magazines such as *Shenghuo zhishi*, *Renren zhoukan*, *Shidai xuesheng*, *Xin wenhua*, and a series of pocket-sized books under the series title *Dengta xiaocongshu*. The most important document to come out of one of the printing houses, Meiwen Printers, was "A Letter to the Citizens of Shanghai." In it the Shanghai underground CCP Municipal Committee promised a peaceful transition to communist rule and asked assistance in protecting factories from being destroyed by fleeing capitalists.

In the early years of the PRC, in response to a request from the Shanghai authorities, Dong Zhujun turned the Jinjiang Sichuan restaurant and teahouse into a hotel of the same name. It became a safe and well-run concern, catering to visiting government and party leaders as well as foreign dignitaries. The idea behind the move was apparently to capitalize on Jinjiang's international fame and trained personnel. At this point, like many proprietors of private enterprises in China, Dong Zhujun donated her business to the state. She remained chair of the board as well as general manager of Jinjiang Hotel. In 1953, however, the position of general manager was taken from her without consultation. Nevertheless, her contribution was recognized and she was made a delegate to the Shanghai People's Council and a member of the CPPCC.

The Cultural Revolution was not kind to Dong Zhujun. She was arrested in autumn 1967 and jailed for five years without any specific charge being laid against her. Dong Zhujun was continually asked to write her own confession. She spent her seventieth birthday in jail and was not released to receive medical treatment at home until 1972.

Her ex-husband is thought to have been executed by the communist government in 1951, along with several other members of his clan. Her children all finished university, some of them going to the United States for further study and returning to work in the PRC. One by one, however, they went back to the United States, with the exception of her son Daming. In 1981, Dong Zhujun went to America for a family reunion with her children, grandchildren, and great-grandchildren.

Dong Zhujun was one of China's earliest women entrepreneurs. Her success must be attributed to her outstanding ability in public relations, keen instincts, and insight. In the Shanghai of the 1930s and 1940s, no business could hope to survive without the support of gang bosses and KMT officials. Dong Zhujun seems to have enjoyed doing businesss in both worlds without compromising too much of her personal and political integrity.

Lily Xiao Hong LEE

Dong Zhujun. *Wode yige shiji.* Beijing: Sanlian, 1997.
———. "1935 nian wo chuangban le Jinjiang Fandian." *Zhongwai shuzhai*, no. 1 (1998): 4–7.

Don-grub Lha-mo

Don-grub Lha-mo, b. 1918, in Vba-thang County, Ganzi, Tibet (present-day Ganzi-Tibetan People's Autonomous Prefecture in Sichuan Province), worked for many years on the translation and research of Tibetan folk literature. She was the first Tibetan woman to become a professor.

Her father, Deng Kecheng, a native of Jiang'an County, Sichuan Province, had been commander of an artillery company (*lianzhang*) when he arrived in Xikang Province (a region that is now partly in western Sichuan and partly in the eastern part of the Tibetan Autonomous Region). War-weary, he stayed there and married a woman from Vba-thang; Don-grub Lha-mo was the eldest of their three children, two girls and a boy. Her father died of illness when Don-grub Lha-mo was nine years old, and her mother supported the family from then on. Her mother had a happy disposition, however, and remained optimistic in the face of hardship, often telling her children Tibetan folk tales and teaching them folksongs and the Vba-thang folk dance. This happy childhood laid the foundation for Don-grub Lha-mo's later work on folk literature.

In 1927, she entered Huaxi Christian missionary school where, in addition to the usual subjects, she was taught Tibetan, Chinese, and English. Don-grub Lha-mo then enrolled in the high school attached to Ginling [Jinling] Women's University in Nanjing in 1935, thanks to the intervention of an American couple (possibly named Hogden; their surname has been transliterated as *Haogedeng*). While at senior high school, in her leisure time Don-grub Lha-mo taught Tibetan at the Border School (Bianjiang xuexiao) and assisted with copying, proofreading, and translating for the magazine *Mongolian and Tibetan Monthly* (Meng-Zang yuebao). After the outbreak of the Sino-Japanese War, she went in 1938 to Chongqing and there became Tibetan secretary of the Tibetan (Xizang) Office. Her main duty was interpreting; during this period when she acted as interpreter for the Tibetan government's representative she had talks and dined with the KMT leader Chiang Kai-shek (1887–1975). Don-grub Lha-mo was at that time learning a great deal from Tibetan scholars about Tibetan language and literature. She gathered Tibetan folk tales and folksongs, publishing them under the pen name Mingzhu in *Dagong bao* and *Xinmin wanbao* newspapers.

At the end of the Sino-Japanese War, Don-grub Lha-mo returned to Nanjing, where then-minister of Education Zhu Jiahua appointed her as associate professor of Tibetan at Zhengzhi University. As the first Tibetan woman to become a professor, she was a celebrity, and a report entitled "The Oriole of Xikang—Don-grub Lha-mo" (Xikang zhi ying—Dengzhu Lamu) appeared in *Dagong bao*. She was present as a community leader at the 1946 constitutional conference and two years later was a representative at the KMT National Assembly (Guomin daibiao dahui) for propagating the document. During this period, Don-grub Lha-mo befriended many important political leaders, campaigning for Li Zongren and becoming friendly with his wife, Guo Dejie.

When the PRC was established in 1949, Don-grub Lha-mo returned to Ya'an to become Tibetan secretary of the Bureau of Culture and Education. She was later employed as a Tibetan instructor at the Revolutionary University (Geming daxue) and teacher of Tibetan for the Fifty-third Division of the Eighteenth Army. In 1955, Don-grub Lha-mo was transferred to Chengdu, the capital of Sichuan Province, and made responsible in the Provincial Education Bureau for compiling primary textbooks on Tibetan language and mathematics.

In 1957, she was transferred to Sichuan Nationalities Publishing House as an editor in its Tibetan Section. Even as a teacher, Don-grub Lha-mo never stopped learning. She continued to read Tibetan classics, selecting and editing material from the classics and folk literature to use in her teaching. She also translated and compiled many Tibetan and Chinese books, including *A Collection of Tibetan Folksongs* (Zangzu minge ji) and *The Tale of Agudengba* (Agudengba de gushi), both of which she co-authored with bGra-shi tshe-ring (Zhaxi Zeren). Don-grub Lha-mo translated works from Chinese to Tibetan, such as her *Selected Ancient Chinese Fables* (Zhongguo gudai yuyan xuan), Gao Shiqi's *Soil Studies* (Turang xue), and many stories from the *Spring and Autumn Annals* (Chunqiu). She collaborated on thirty-four volumes of translations during this period, twelve of them published in her name.

Don-grub Lha-mo was targeted in the anti-rightist movement of the late 1950s and during the Cultural Revolution and was forced to stop translation work. In 1966, she returned to Kangding and was sent to Ganzi Political School (Ganzi zhengzhi xuexiao). The following year, Don-grub Lha-mo was imprisoned for three months. The case was eventually overturned in 1978, however, and she represented Ganzi on the CPPCC from then on. Don-grub Lha-mo is a member of the prefectural Federation of Literary and Art Circles (Wenlian) and president of its Folk Literature Research Society (Minjian wenyi yanjiu hui). She has also been deputy director of the prefectural film and television association and a member of the Standing Committee of the Nationalities Language Society of Sichuan. At both provincial and prefectural level, she was assessed as a March Eighth Red Flag holder.

In 1981, Don-grub Lha-mo set up the Tibetan Language School (Zangwen xuexiao), which by 1991 had trained up to 400 students. At the age of seventy-one, in 1989,

Don-grub Lha-mo ranked as a senior assessor (*yishen*) for translation, a professorial level classification.

In the 1980s, she became involved in rescuing the Tibetan epic *Gesar*, searching out different editions and co-authoring translations of portions of the epic, including "Battle on Pine Mountain" (Songling zhi zhan) and "Rescuing Mother from Hell" (Diyu jiumu). Don-grub Lha-mo published papers on its dating, language, and images of the female protagonists. Her work on the epic *Gesar* won her recognition by the Nationalities Committee, the minister for Culture, the Federation of Literary and Art Circles, and the Chinese Academy of Social Sciences as an outstanding individual in 1986 and 1997. During this period, apart from legends and folk tales she also translated Tibetan literature and operas: *Saijia's Aphorisms* (Saijia geyan), *Zhimei gengdeng*, and *Prince Nuosang*. Her output, in addition to translation work, included creative pieces in prose and prose poems.

Don-grub Lha-mo married twice. Her first husband, Li Kai, was a student at Whampoa Military Academy. They lived together in Nanjing for nearly ten years and had a son and daughter, but divorced in 1945. Her son died in the famine of the 1960s, and her daughter went to Taiwan in 1949 with Li Kai. Don-grub Lha-mo met her present husband, sKal-bzang (Ge Sang), when she was working at the Nationalities Publishing House in Chengdu. He was originally a scholar of Buddhism in Zhebang Temple and later became abbot of Anjuesi in Kangding. After the establishment of the PRC, sKal-bzang became a Tibetan language editor with the Nationalities Publishing House of Sichuan. He is now retired.

Don-grub Lha-mo came from a Tibetan-Han family in the Xikang-Tibetan region but left her native place at seventeen to make her way in the Han Chinese world. All she had was confidence in herself, persistence, intelligence, and the desire to better herself. Don-grub Lha-mo experienced both political success and a measure of fame, received honors, but also suffered persecution. All of this has been accepted with equanimity. Although at times she must have despaired, Don-grub Lha-mo never deviated from her aim of celebrating Tibetan culture and promoting cultural exchange between Tibet and the Han people.

She retired from all her posts in 1995 but continues to work with great energy. Don-grub Lha-mo continues to write further beautiful chapters in a long life, firm in her belief that "realizing that the evening will soon draw to a close, the elderly mare keeps on walking without waiting to be prodded."

YANG Enhong
(Translated by Lily Xiao Hong Lee and Sue Wiles)

Dengzhu Lamu [Don-grub Lha-mo]. *Turang de gushi*. Chengdu: Sichuan minzu chubanshe, n.d.
————. *Zangzu mingge ji*. Chengdu: Sichuan minzu chubanshe, 1959.
————. *Zhongguo gudai yuyan xuan*. Chengdu: Sichuan minzu chubanshe, n.d.
————. "Gesa'er wang zhuan de 'Songling zhizhan,' 'Diyu jiumu' Han yi wen." *Sichuan Gesa'er yanjiu wenji*, n.d.
Dengzhu Lamu [Don-grub Lha-mo] and bGra-shi tshe-ring [Zhaxi Zeren]. *Agudengba de gushi*. Chengdu: Sichuan minzu chubanshe, 1963.

Renzhen Wangjie. "Zhongguo diyi ge Zangzu nü jiaoshou." *Sichuan ribao*, 13 March 1998, 5.
Yang Enhong. "Xikang zhiyin—Zangzu diyi wei nü jiaoshou Don-grub Lha-mo." *Zhonghua ernü*, no. 1 (1999).

Du Runzhang: *see* **Zhang Yun**

Du Shuzhen

Du Shuzhen, b. 1924, in Kaifeng, Henan Province, is a Chinese Muslim *ahong* (religious leader) of Hui nationality; her Islamic name is Aminah.

Born into a devout Muslim family, Du Shuzhen entered Wangjia Hutong women's mosque (*nüsi*) at the age of eight and studied Islamic scriptures until she was fourteen. Du Shuzhen was twelve when her mother died; her father, an antiquarian, entered a mosque to become an *ahong* after his antique shop was robbed during the Sino-Japanese War. She heeded her father's wishes and married at the age of fifteen. The marriage was not a happy one but she went with her husband, who was also of Hui nationality and then studying Chinese, to Shanxi Province. He fell ill and died within two years of the marriage, and Du Shuzhen returned to Kaifeng. She refused to remarry but instead continued her studies at the women's mosque, intending to become an *ahong*. Du Shuzhen supported herself throughout her studies, studying Islamic doctrine in Persian under a female *ahong* named Hu, and learning the Q'ran in Arabic from her uncle, an *ahong* in Shanghai, and an *ahong* friend of her father's in Henan.

She graduated at the age of twenty-five and in 1949 was invited to be *ahong* of a rural women's mosque in Zhengzhou. Du Shuzhen was transferred to the women's mosque in Xingyang, Henan Province, in 1954; it was during this period that she taught herself enough Chinese to read newspapers. At the start of the Cultural Revolution, Du Shuzhen returned to Kaifeng and lived until its closure in the East Mosque there. She was protected from harm during the Cultural Revolution by local Muslims. In 1981 she was made senior Islamic teacher (*jiaozhang*) of Beida Street Women's Mosque in Zhengzhou and the following year was recalled to Kaifeng women's mosque; so highly respected was Du Shuzhen that in 1983 she was made lifelong *ahong* of Beida Street Women's Mosque. Du Shuzhen made pilgrimages to Mecca in 1992 and 1996, visiting the Kuala Lumpur mosque in Malaysia the latter year.

Du Shuzhen has lived a noble, inspiring life, guided by Islamic spiritual teachings, devoting herself to the service of others, helping the poor and distressed, encouraging self-confidence and strength in Muslim women with her wise counsel and physical help, and promoting Islamic activities, including the construction of women's mosques. The Beida Street Women's Mosque most closely embodies her generous, high-minded character. It had only eighteen rooms when she became senior Islamic teacher in 1983. Working tirelessly with two devout and capable administrators—Dan Ye and Zhang Xiuying—Du Shuzhen created a stable and transparent financial system designed to serve the spiritual and physical needs of Muslim women. The high regard in which she is held by Muslim women ensured generous contributions and strong support for her work, and the mosque is now one of the most beautiful in Zhengzhou, with over eighty new rooms and modern facilities. It is self-supporting and has become influential.

Greatly admired by Muslim women for her independence, strong will, persistence, kindness, selfless devotion to duty, and frankness, Du Shuzhen has become a reliable leader. As an *ahong*, she is widely esteemed for her work in Islamic education and spiritual guidance for women.

Du Shuzhen is now a member of the Henan Islamic Association (Henan yiselanjiao xiehui), vice-director of the Islamic Association of Zhengzhou (Zhengzhoushi yiselanjiao xiehui), and a Guancheng Hui Nationality District member of the People's Political Consultative Conference in Zhengzhou.

Maria H.A. JASCHOK and SHUI Jingjun

Alles, Elisabeth. "Une organisation de l'Islam au féminin: Le personnel des mosquées féminines en Chine." *Lettre d'information*. Paris: Programme de Recherches Interdisciplinaires sur le Monde Müsulman Périphérique, 14 (1994): 1–12.

Dai Jianning. "Shilun huizu funü xinyang yisilanjiaode xinli tezheng." *Huizu yanjiu*, 4 (1992): 67–70.

Etudes Orientales, 13/14 (1994). Contributions by Elisabeth Alles, Leila Cherif, and Constance-Hélène Halfon.

Feng Jinyuan. "Shilun yisilanjiaode funüguan." *Zhongguo musilin*, 4 (1995): 19–24.

Jaschok, Maria and Shui Jingjun. *The History of Women's Mosques in Chinese Islam: A Mosque of Their Own*. Richmond, Surrey: Curzon Press, 2000.

Nan Wenyuan. *Yisilanjiao yu xibei musilin shehui shenghuo*. Xining: Qinghai renmin chubanshe, 1994.

Pang Keng-Fong. "Islamic 'Fundamentalism' and Female Empowerment among the Muslims of Hainan Island, People's Republic of China." In *Mixed Blessings: Gender and Religious Fundamentalism Cross Culturally*, eds. Judy Brink and Joan Mencher. London: Routledge, 1997, 41–56.

Shui Jingjun. "Lun nüxue nüside xingqi yu fazhan." *Huizu yanjiu*, 1 (1996): 51–59.

Duan Anlin: *see* **Siqin Gaowa**

Dunn, Dame Lydia Selina

Dame Lydia Selina Dunn, b. 1940, whose Chinese name is Deng Lianru, was born in Hong Kong. Her family celebrates her birthday on 28 February instead of her actual birth date of 29 February. Lydia Dunn was the first ethnic Chinese to be elevated to the British peerage.

Lydia Dunn's parents were Cantonese but, when the Japanese occupied Hong Kong in 1940, went with their two daughters to Shanghai, where they had business and lived through the tumultuous war years until 1949. Lydia was the second of three daughters: Mamie (1929–1987), who attended school in Shanghai before going to university in the United States, and Gloria (b. 1941), who now lives in Vancouver, Canada.

Lydia's father, Yen Chuen Yih Dunn, had obtained an M.B.A. from the University of Washington but was not rich. He went into the printing business after returning to Hong Kong following the war. Life there was hard even for affluent families as Hong Kong slowly built its shattered economy, but Yen Chuen Yih Dunn placed a high priority on his children's education. He managed to send both Lydia and her younger sister to the long-established Saint Paul's Convent School in the bustling commercial and residential district of Causeway Bay (Tung Luo Wan) on Hong Kong Island. Yen also taught them from an early age to be responsible for their own affairs. Lydia's mother, Bessie Dunn, who came from a well-known family of tea merchants, also strongly influenced her children, instilling in them respect for family and elders and a desire for independence through education.

Lydia Dunn still today vividly remembers the Hong Kong of the early 1950s, a city with shantytowns dotted around its perimeter. The thousands of refugees from China who poured into the colony set up on the steep hillsides makeshift huts that were often swept away by torrential summer rains or destroyed by fire. The squatters soon forced the Hong Kong government to abandon its laissez-faire philosophy and engage in providing subsidized government housing, education, and medical facilities. As a child, Lydia had no interest in politics but her social environment and family's links with China were influential to her later career.

As a boarder at Saint Paul's School, Lydia played the piano with some success, once coming first in a competition. Although the quality of education was important to Hong Kong families, few could afford to send their children overseas for study in the early 1960s; the highest goal for most ambitious students was to gain entrance to the University of Hong Kong. After graduation from high school in 1959, however, Lydia went to the College of the Holy Names in Oakland, California. This small catholic liberal arts college for women, located in the hills, was close to a cousin who had settled in Oakland; Lydia stayed with him and his family. She transferred in 1961 to the University of California, Berkeley, but was not part of the 1960s hippie culture for which this campus later became famous. This was a happy formative time in Lydia's career during which she made many friendships.

The overseas education helped her to hone her English-language skills and acquire an international outlook that became invaluable in enabling Lydia to adapt well to working in foreign trade; it laid a good foundation for the development of her career. She herself later ascribed her success in large part to "luck," which covered such things as a good education and the opportunity to work with a large company, one of Hong Kong's famous "hongs." This comment obscures as much as it reveals about her attitude to herself and work. Upon returning to Hong Kong, Lydia applied to and was offered a position by each of the three top British firms: the Swire Group, Jardines, and the Wheelock Group. She decided to join the Swire Group because she liked the people she met there and was assigned to work with Maclean's, the group's trading subsidiary. The Swire Group, an international company whose headquarters are still in Hong Kong, has diverse interests including sugar refining, packaging, and retail, shipping and associated services, an airline (Cathay Pacific), trading, finance, and property development. Staffed in large part by British expatriates, the group recruited few Chinese graduates and still fewer Chinese women; Lydia was conspicuous among the suits crowding the corridors of the office building. She accentuated her ethnic origin by wearing the Chinese cheongsam and gained some notoriety because of her habit of smoking (which she later gave up). The habit was considered quite daring in that decade, when Hong Kong was still a conservative society.

Lydia's mentor in the firm gave her considerable authority and taught her to appreciate the meaning of the group's Latin motto: *esse quam videre* (to be, not to be seen to be). Before long the firm sent her to a business training course at Urwick Orr Management Centre in England, thereby acknowledging her potential for promotion. She made a name for herself as an active and perspicacious trader and gained a reputation for accuracy and carefulness, which always characterized her business and political activities.

An important part of Swire Maclean's activities was the sourcing and promotion of garments. The textile and garment sector was even then the backbone of Hong Kong industry, with Hong Kong-made garments exported round the world. In the 1970s and 1980s, when the industry faced the problem of adjusting to rising structural costs, Lydia Dunn realized that the reputation of "Hong Kong made" garments had to be enhanced. Working closely with the Trade Development Council (TDC) on the annual Ready-to-Wear Trade Fair upon which the important Hong Kong Fashion Week was based, she was influential in changing overseas buyers' attitudes to the quality of Hong Kong garments. Lydia also supported campaigns to encourage the development of local garment design talent, stressing that designers should draw on Chinese and Western traditions for inspiration.

Not surprisingly as a consequence of her activities in this important field, she was appointed chair of the Hong Kong TDC, a position held from 1983 to 1991. She was its first woman chair, a fact noted by the local press at the time as evidence of the equal status of women in Hong Kong business and industry. A sponsor and coordinator of trade promotion events, the TDC was set up in 1966 as a semi-official body funded from a levy on all goods exported from Hong Kong. The 1970s saw steady growth in Hong Kong industry as it supplied the American and European markets, but in the early 1980s a number of problems emerged that slowed trade growth and increased local manufacturing costs. Lydia encouraged the TDC to develop closer relations with China, a wise move not only in view of Hong Kong's imminent return to Chinese sovereignty in 1997 but also because this was the only way forward for Hong Kong industry and commerce.

Hong Kong trade with and investment in China preceded later political integration. It brought about a complete rethinking of industry and trade promotion priorities on the part of Hong Kong government and business. Lydia Dunn personally led several Hong Kong trade delegations to China in the 1980s. In 1990 she told a local reporter that China was already Hong Kong's second biggest export market and largest source of imports. She proposed that trade with China should be established on the basis of mutual profit, the very principle that lay behind Hong Kong companies' investments in China. While Lydia Dunn was chair, the TDC commissioned and built a large convention center in Wanchai on Hong Kong Island. Its work was so successful that within five years the convention and trade fair facilities had been outgrown, and a new building of double the capacity was commenced.

Lydia Dunn's capacity for hard work was noted in the press at the time. She told a reporter, "One's attitude to work is very important in deciding whether or not one succeeds. I never discriminate between big or small matters, but am always positive and set to with a will, determined to complete them." She also said that work increased her desire to learn and develop and made her life rich and rewarding. Her advice to young people was to follow their own interests and ambitions rather than aim only for financial reward or social position.

Lydia Dunn was popular with her colleagues and was promoted in 1978 on the recommendation of her boss, Sir John Brembridge, to become a director of John Swire & Sons (HK) Ltd., a position she still holds today. She has been a director of Swire Pacific Ltd. since 1981 and executive director of John Swire & Sons Ltd. since 1996. It was Sir John Brembridge who also recommended her to then governor of Hong Kong, Sir John Maclehose, for appointment to the Legislative Council, where she served from 1976 to 1988, with the title of senior member from 1985 to 1988. At that time, the Legislative Council consisted entirely of appointed members who advised the governor on the administration of the territory of Hong Kong. One place had traditionally been reserved for an appointee of the most powerful "hong," Jardines, and another for Jardine's rival and competitor, Swires.

It is interesting to reflect on the different character of these two companies. Jardines has close ties through the Scottish Keswick family with the British aristocracy and the Conservative Party. The Swire family, however, is of more humble Yorkshire origin, even though it is also powerful in commerce and business. There is a definite and identifiable Swire style that reflects the no-nonsense Yorkshire origins of the company. Through John Swire & Sons Ltd., the family still controls most of the interests and activities of the various Swire subsidiaries. Compared with Jardines, which has had more complicated dealings with Beijing because of their closer involvement in British politics, Swires has had better relations with the Chinese government.

Lydia Dunn has been involved in many aspects of Hong Kong industry and commerce through directorships of important companies. These include the Mass Transit Railway Corporation (MTR, 1979–85); Hong Kong and Shanghai Banking Corporation (HSBC, 1981–86); Kowloon-Canton Railway Corporation (KCR, 1982–84); Cathay Pacific Airways (1985–); HSBC Holdings (1990–); Volvo (1991–93); and Christies International (1996–). She was deputy chair of HSBC from 1992 to 1996 and has been non-executive deputy chair since 1992. Hong Kong operates its public utilities through government-franchised companies that must not only be self-financing but return a profit to the government. The MTR and the KCR are two examples of such successful and profitable companies. Through the development of sites over their stations, they have been able to keep fares low and provide public transport services to Hong Kong commuters rivaling those of any other city in the world. The period of Lydia Dunn's association with these two transport corporations coincided with their rapid expansion to new towns in the New Territories of Hong Kong and the uncertainties caused by negotiations surrounding the Sino-British agreement on the terms of the return of the territory to China in 1997. She was therefore involved in many difficult policy considerations. From 1981 to 1987, Lydia Dunn served as chair of the Prince Philip Dental Hospital, a government-funded hospital providing dental services of a high standard to the people of Hong Kong. She was also a member of the General Committee of the Federation of Hong Kong Industries from 1978 to 1983, a member of the Hong Kong/Japan Business Cooperation Committee from the latter year to 1987, and a member of the Hong Kong/U.S. Economic Cooperation Committee from 1984 to 1993. She held these positions because of her experience in commerce and government, which allowed her to comment on and develop policies conducive to the expansion of trade between Hong Kong and two of its most important partners.

From 1982 to 1995, Lydia Dunn was a member of Hong Kong's Executive Council, a cabinet of senior advisors to the governor. This was the time when Britain and China engaged in negotiations regarding the terms and conditions of the handover of Hong Kong. Before the announcement by then British Prime Minister Margaret Thatcher that agreement had been reached with the government of the PRC and the date of the handover would be 1997 much uncertainty floated about in Hong Kong concerning the former colony's future. In 1984 a serious crisis of confidence surfaced, and in 1989, following the Tian'anmen massacre in Beijing, a downturn occurred in the economy. Many people contemplated leaving Hong Kong altogether because of these crises. The government faced a major task in restoring confidence and rallying popular sentiment. Lydia Dunn was intimately involved in all of these events. She worked closely with several governors, including Sir Edward Youde, whose untimely death because of the strain of the negotiations was much regretted by the people of Hong Kong. Lydia was a close associate of the senior Executive Council member Sir S.Y. Chung. While she generally shared his point of view on transitional matters, it is said that Lydia advocated reform of the Hong Kong governor's advisory councils, including the Legislative and Executive Councils, to approximate the British system of ministerial responsibilities, which would have entailed radical reform of the political system.

As an Executive Council member, Lydia Dunn was in frequent contact with then Attorney General Michael Thomas. Executive Council meetings occupied at least one afternoon a week. The stressful time of overseeing the terms of Hong Kong's eventual return to Chinese sovereignty meant that Executive Council members developed great rapport with each other, perhaps baring their souls concerning their most deeply felt fears and concerns in a way that would not have been possible without these extraordinary external factors. However it may have happened, Lydia and Michael fell in love. They are both by nature private people and did not seek publicity, but their romantic attachment quickly became known in the community. Lydia was over forty years old when she married Michael. It was her first marriage, his second. Although now retired from the Hong Kong government, Michael still practices in Hong Kong as a barrister, specializing in commercial company law and spends several months of every year in Hong Kong.

For many years Lydia Dunn said that she had no plans to leave Hong Kong after its return to Chinese sovereignty. Her eventual decision, made public in 1995, that she would move her primary place of residence to London, shocked the general public. Speaking to the press at the time, Lydia emphasized that the decision was based on personal and not political reasons. Commentators speculated that she had become too closely aligned with British interests to feel at ease in the new social environment in transitional Hong Kong. Lydia was perhaps closer to the former governor, Sir David Wilson, than to his successor, Christopher Patten, and this may have had something to do with her decision to relocate. In spite of it, she still maintains close connections with Hong Kong through her position on various company boards and regular visits to the Special Administrative Region.

Lydia Dunn has been honored for her contribution to Hong Kong industry and commerce by several honorary Doctor of Laws degrees: from the Chinese University of Hong Kong (1984), Hong Kong University (1991), the University of British Colombia (1991), and the University of Leeds (1994). She also received an honorary Doctor of Science from the University of Buckingham (1995). She has received numerous awards, including the Prime Minister of Japan's Trade Award (1987) and the Peace and Commerce Award from the U.S. Secretary of Commerce (1988). She was made an Officer of the Order of the British Empire in 1978, a Commander of the Order of the British Empire in 1983, and a Dame Commander of the Order of the British Empire in 1989. She has been a member of the International Committee of the Asia Society since 1986 and a fellow of the Institute of Directors and the Royal Society for the Encouragement of Arts, Manufactures, and Commerce since 1989.

Having been created Baroness Lydia Dunn in 1990, she is active in the House of Lords in Westminster and has made several speeches on subjects connected with the future of the former British colony of Hong Kong, including during the second reading of the Hong Kong Economic and Trade Office Bill on 12 December 1996 and on the second reading of the British Nationality (Hong Kong) Bill on 25 November. Lydia spoke again on Hong Kong on 12 June 1997. Her publications include *In the Kingdom of the Blind*, published by the Hong Kong Trade Research Centre in 1983.

Lydia Dunn's title is Baroness Dunn of Hong Kong Island in Hong Kong and of Knightsbridge in the Royal Borough of Kensington and Chelsea. Her official parliamentary biography lists her recreations as art and antiques. She is a member of the Hong Kong Club and the Hong Kong Jockey Club. She has in the past told reporters that she likes to spend her spare time at home with her family. Her apartment in Hong Kong was furnished in Western style, and it is likely that this also characterizes her new home in London's fashionable Knightsbridge.

Jocelyn CHEY

Chao Jin. "Xianggang shangyejie nüqiangren Deng Lianru." In *Haiwai zhuming huaren liezhuan*, Beijing: Gongren, 1988, 21–23.

Chen Yushan. "Gongzuo shi yizhong lequ." In his *Gang Ao mingren yu jingying*, Hong Kong: Xianda chubanshe, 1990, pp. 80–81.

Dod's Parliamentary Companion. Hailsham, England: Dod's Parliamentary Companion, 1997.

Dunn, Dame Lydia. Personal communication, February 1998.

Tianjin xin jishu chubanshe kaifa jituan. ed. *Huaxia kexuejia, qiyejia.* Tianjin: Kexue chubanshe, 1987, 199–203.

Echo: *see* **San Mao**

F

Fan Ruijuan

Fan Ruijuan, b. 1924, in Huangze zhen, Shengxian County, Zhejiang Province, is also known as Fan Zhushan. She is a performing artist within the *yueju* genre, a form of local opera in which all the roles were traditionally played by females. Fan Ruijuan is a member of the Chinese Association of Folk Opera Performers and artistic consultant to Shanghai *Yueju* Theater.

Fan Ruijuan was apprenticed as a *yueju* performer to the Longfeng Wutai Opera Troupe under Master Huang Bingwen in spring 1935, mainly playing the part of the young male. The following year, she toured with the troupe to Shaoxing, Ningbo, Shenjiamen, and Zhuji, and early in 1938 went to Shanghai to perform with the Yuesheng Wutai Troupe of which Yao Shuijuan and Xing Zhuqin were the principals. When the lead, Zhu Su'e, fell ill in 1941 while performing at Huiquan lou, Fan Ruijuan ensured that the show would go on by stepping into the role herself. From then on, she was entrusted with lead roles, playing opposite Xing Shuqin, Zhi Lanfang, and Jin Xiangqin during the early 1940s and working with Fu Quanxiang (*q.v.*), one of the great female leads, with the Siji Chun Troupe from late 1943 to the summer of 1944. Fan Ruijuan then collaborated for two years with another famous female lead, Yuan Xuefen (*q.v.*), in reforming *yueju*. During this period, in 1945, Fan Ruijuan worked with a musician named Zhou Baocai to create the style known as *xianxia qiang* (literally "singing below the tune" played on the *huqin*) for the "Deathbed of Shanbo" (Shanbo linzhong) scene in *The Sad Story of Liang Shanbo and Zhu Yingtai* (Liang-Zhu aishi). This *xianxia qiang* style is sung at a slower than usual tempo and, with its wider vocal range, allows singers to hold longer notes.

One of her best-known roles was as Young Master Niu in *Xiang Lin's Wife* (Xiang Lin Sao), which she first played in May 1946. When Yuan Xuefen, who was playing the female lead opposite her, fell ill in 1947 Fan Ruijuan invited Fu Quanxiang to take the female role and the group changed its name to the Dongshan *Yueju* Troupe. *Xiang Lin's Wife* was turned into a film in 1948, starring Yuan Xuefen, with Fan Ruijuan playing the two male roles of Young Master Niu and Xiang Lin.

Fan Ruijuan was one of the "ten sisters of *yueju*," the ten most loved performers, who took part in a benefit performance of *Love for Mountains and Rivers* (Shanhe lian) in 1947. In autumn 1948, she performed with Yuan Xuefen in other *yueju*, including Tian Han's (1898–1968) *Coral Prelude* (Shanhu yin) held at the Shanghai Theater.

Fan Ruijuan collaborated with Fu Quanxiang on the reorganization of the Dongshan *Yueju* Troupe in early 1949 but was also required to attend classes organized by the Art Department of the Shanghai government, at that time under military administration, to research folk operas. After this political training, she went on to star in the *yueju King Li Chuang* (Li Chuang wang), *The Sad Story of Liang Shanbo and Zhu Yingtai*, and *A New Look at Families* (Wanhu gengxin) as well as some plays. In response to a request by Tian Han, Fan Ruijuan and her troupe performed in Beijing in 1950 before many distinguished performers and high-level party officials, including Mao Zedong (1893–1976), Zhou Enlai (1898–1976), and Zhou Yang, then extremely influential in literary circles. They staged *Liang Shanbo and Zhu Yingtai* and *New Year's Sacrifice* (Zhufu), and Fan Ruijuan was received after one performance by Zhou Enlai.

With the establishment of the PRC, she was appointed to various posts connected with performance, as deputy director of the Donghua *Yueju* Company in 1951 and also chair of the Shanghai Union of *Yueju* Performers. In this latter position, Fan Ruijuan helped organize a benefit performance for the purchase of an aeroplane, subsequently named "Yueju hao," as part of the Korean War effort. She was elected as a member of the China Youth Federation and special representative of the CPPCC. At the first Chinese Folk Opera Festival held in 1952, Fan Ruijuan shared first prize for acting with Fu Quanxiang and Yuan Xuefen for their performances in *Liang Shanbo and Zhu Yingtai* and *White Snake* (Baishe zhuan, also called *Leifeng Tower*). *Liang Shanbo and Zhu Yingtai* was made into a color film, starring Fan Ruijuan and Yuan Xuefen in 1953, and won a musical film prize in an international film festival the following year. The Chinese Ministry of Cultural Affairs awarded the film the prize of honor as the Best Film of 1949–55.

In winter 1953, Fan Ruijuan co-starred, as Zhang Sheng, with Yuan Xuefen in *Story of the West Chamber* (Xixiang ji); this opera won first prize for performance at the East China Folk Opera Festival in 1954. During her first trip overseas that summer, Fan Ruijuan attended the Eighth International Film Festival in Czechoslovakia and traveled to Geneva to meet Charlie Chaplin. Over the next few years, she traveled to the Soviet Union and the German Democratic Republic to perform *Liang Shanbo and Zhu Yingtai* and *The Magic Needle* (Da jinzhi). Fan Ruijuan moved to Beijing in 1960 with the cream of the Shanghai *Yueju* Theater, when it amalgamated with the newly established Beijing *Yueju* Troupe, but returned to Shanghai the following year when the troupe closed down. She continued to work with the Shanghai *Yueju* Theater, assisting in the development and performance of *Li Xiucheng, Prince Zhong*, and *The Story of the Embroidered Jacket* (Xiuru ji). During the 1960s, Fan Ruijuan also performed in the modern opera *A Person Not Allowed to Be Born* (Buzhun chusheng de ren). Nothing is known of what happened to her during the Cultural Revolution, but it is quite probable that, like many other artists and performers, she suffered harassment and was deprived of work.

After the Cultural Revolution, Fan Ruijuan returned to giving performances and made several overseas trips. She played Mother Yang in *Song of the Loyal Souls* (Zhong hun qu) and appeared in *Southeastern Flight of the Peacock* (Kongque dongnan fei) and *The Story of Li Wa* (Li Wa zhuan). Fan Ruijuan received a Gold Record from the Chinese Record Company and gave several performances in Hong Kong. In 1988, she lectured at the Bell Laboratory in Chicago, in the U.S., and the following year performed *Liang Shanbo and Zhu Yingtai*, and *The Story of Li Wa* with her troupe in the United States. Traveling once more to Europe in early 1990 with a Chinese national arts delegation, Fan Ruijuan, Lu Ruiying, and Zhang Guifeng performed *The*

Magic Needle in the Federal Republic of Germany, France, Belgium, Luxembourg, and the Netherlands. Back in China, Shanghai TV made a three-episode documentary called *The Performance Art of Fan Ruijuan*. Her last performance appears to have been in 1993, when she played the role of Lu You in the TV series *Masterpiece from Shenyuan Garden* (Shenyuan juechang).

During a career spanning more than fifty years on stage, Fan Ruijuan played more than one hundred roles. As a performer, she displayed confidence, naturalness, and lack of pretension and projected masculine strength and excelled in playing virtuous, honest, sincere, and heroic characters. Fan Ruijuan utilized the tunes and vocal techniques of such distinctive male Beijing opera singers as Ma Lianliang and Gao Qinggui, adding the male tune technique (*zhengdiao qiang*) she inherited from traditional *yueju*. Her singing is thus noted for carrying a deep and broad voice, clear and firm enunciation, and natural and smooth tunes. Her acting and singing have come to be known as the Fan School.

Although Fan Ruijuan published two books—a selection of her arias and the tale of her childhood—nothing is known of her personal life, except that she did marry.

Shirley Wai CHAN
(Translated by Cui Zhiying)

Fan Ruijuan. "Wode zhangfu, wode tongyue." In *Sanshi-jiushi niandai Zhongguo shehui xinwen xuanping*, ed. Ding Guwen. Beijing: Zhongguo gongren chubanshe, n.d., 89–95.
Huaxia funü mingren cidian. Beijing: Huaxia chubanshe, 1988, 647.
Zhongguo funü guanli ganbu xueyuan, ed. *Gujin Zhongwai nümingren cidian*. Beijing: Zhongguo guangbo dianshi chubanshe, 1980, 79.

Fan Tchun-pi

Fan Tchun-pi [Fang Junbi], 1898–1986, a native of Fuzhou, was an artist. Her sister Fang Shengtong became one of the famous seventy-two national heroes sacrificed in the Canton Revolution of 1911.

From 1917 Fan Tchun-pi studied at the Académie Julien in Paris and then at the École des Beaux Arts in Bordeaux, where she graduated in 1920. In 1922 in Paris, she married Ceng Zhongming, a poet and politician. During the 1920s, Fan Tchun-pi was active in the Parisian art world and occasionally taught in Canton, where she also had an exhibition in 1925. Fan Tchun-pi published books in China on her oil painting, including one in 1938 with a foreword by Cai Yuanpei, former minister of Education and a classical scholar. She met the painter Qi Baishi in 1943 and had a series of exhibitions in China between 1944 and 1949 before moving back to Paris, eventually settling in Boston, in the U.S., in 1957.

Stylistically, her work depicted a competent modified realism in the earlier twentieth-century French manner, such as Besnard (with whom she studied in 1926). In its accommodation of a "Chinese" sensibility in the 1930s, her artwork established a (rather neglected) ground from which the "realist and popular" neo-traditional painting with transparently legible motifs and themes would arise in the 1950s.

John CLARK

Bobot, Marie-Thérèse. *Fan Tchun-Pi, Artiste Chinoise Contemporaine*. Paris: Musée Cernuschi, 1984.
A Retrospective Exhibition of the Works of Fan Tchun-pi. Hong Kong: Fung Ping Shan Museum, 1978.

Fan Zhenhua: *see* **Yang Zilie**

Fan Zhushan: *see* **Fan Ruijuan**

Fang Ansheng: *see* **Chan, Anson**

Fang Chao-lin: *see* **Fang Zhaolin**

Fang Fang
Fang Fang, b. 1955, as Wang Fang, a native of Pengze County, Jiangxi Province, is a poet and fiction writer. She played an important role in China's literary "new realism" genre in the 1980s.

Both of her parents came from distinguished families of high social status and intellectual fame. Her paternal grandfather, Wang Guozhen, a graduate of Capital University (Jingshi daxue, the predecessor of Peking University), was a scholar of great attainment in traditional Chinese language and literature. He was killed in 1938 during the Sino-Japanese War. Her father, Wang Youde, inherited his father's scholarship and was a gifted linguist. He experienced the political turbulence of the regime of Mao Zedong (1893–1976) and lived with the fear of persecution until his death in 1973. The lives of her father and grandfather greatly influenced Fang Fang's literary interests and understanding of life.

Born in Nanjing, Jiangsu Province, she moved to Wuhan with her parents in 1957 and completed her primary and secondary education there. After graduating from high school in 1974, Fang Fang was assigned to work as a freight loader and remained in that job for four years. She began to write poems during this period and was first published in 1975. Her poetry has continued since then, but it is for her fiction that she is famous. Her *When I Am Pulling My Flatbed Cart* (Wo laqi banche) won the award for Excellent Poem of 1981–82, offered by the major Chinese literary journal *Shikan*.

From 1978 to 1982, Fang Fang studied Chinese language and literature at Wuhan University. In her last year of university, she published her first short story "On a Canvas-Covered Truck" (Da pengche shang). After graduation, she became an editor with Hubei Television but continued her creative writing, publishing a number of short stories, poems, and television screenplays, including "The Story of Seeking" (Xunzhao de gushi), "The Other Side of the River" (Jiang na yi'an), and the novella *White Dream* (Bai meng). Having established her reputation, Fang Fang joined the Hubei Writers' Association in 1989 and became a professional writer. She is now a member of the Chinese Writers' Association, serves on the Executive Council of the Hubei Writers' Association, and is chair of the Wuhan Youth Writers' Association.

Fang Fang has published numerous short stories and novellas and is considered to be an outstanding representative of contemporary Chinese women writers.

It is generally agreed that the writer's work falls into three periods separated by *White Dream* (1986) and the long short story "The Art of Action" (Xingwei yishu, 1993). The early works in the first period of which "On a Canvas-Covered Truck" is representative are mainly about the lives of young people and brim with youthful enthusiasm and optimism. There is in them, however, an immaturity that later led Fang Fang to comment, "I was vague and ignorant about life itself . . . so the superficiality of my stories is apparent."

White Dream, an acrimonious satire on the hidden commercial purposes of friendship, resulted from her disappointment and frustration at a friend's betrayal in 1986. Its publication not only attracted the attention of readers but also made Fang Fang realize she should develop her own writing style. This new understanding of creative writing moved her work into a new phase, and in 1987 she published *The View* (Fengjing), her most successful work. *The View* focuses on the tough lives of a brutish family living in the poorest area of the city of Wuhan. Its calm, objective narrative led many critics to label Fang Fang as a writer within the genre of "new realism." The following year, she published the novella *The White Foal* (Bai ju, 1988), which reflects the attitudes and consciousness of two types of city youth—intellectuals and workers. In 1989, she completed her second successful novella *My Grandfather in My Father's Mind* (Zufu zai fuqin xin zhong). According to its author, 80 percent of this fictionalized family history is true. In this novella, Fang Fang compared the lives and attitudes of her grandfather and father, who represented two different generations of Chinese intellectuals, and posed the question: who should take responsibility for the fate of individuals—society or individuals?

Fang Fang married in the late 1980s. She appears to have taken pains to draw a veil of secrecy over the identity of her husband, however, revealing only that he was an academic and that she lived with him on his university campus for three years. Her vivid descriptions of the frustrations encountered by academics of all ages in "Shifting Clouds and Flowing Water" (Xingyun liushui, 1991) and "Nowhere to Escape to" (Wu chu duntao, 1992) reflect the insights she gained into Chinese academic life. During this period, she wrote another long short story, "Peach Blossoms" (Taohua canlan), telling of a young couple's unattainable but unforgettable love.

Fang Fang is fond of novellas and most of her output is in this genre. She usually starts a story without planning the ending, letting it develop spontaneously, and this the novella allows her to do. Perhaps because of this tendency, many critics find it hard to categorize Fang Fang as belonging to any one literary school. According to the leading "new wave" fiction writer Han Shaogong, this is the secret of Fang Fang's success: life is colorful, complex and ever changing, and a good writer reflects this without losing the complexity. This comment corresponds to Fang Fang's own view.

The 1993 police-crime story "The Art of Action" marks the third and popular phase of her creative writing. The novella *Where Is My Hometown?* (Hechu shi jiayuan?) tells of two women driven into prostitution. Featuring dramatic stories, clever twists of plot, and smooth narratives, they seem to stray from reality. Fang Fang herself admits to their ephemeral nature. However, this is by no means Fang Fang's last phase. In her essay "At Forty, I Am Not Reconciled" (Sishishui, bu baxiu, 1995), the writer expressed the confident hope that she would create more successful novels and plans to write again about her grandfather and father.

Xiyan Vivian BI

Fang Fang. "Postscript." *Fang Fang: Zhongguo dangdai zuojia xuanji congshu.* Beijing: Renmin wenxue chubanshe, 1993.
———. "Preface." *Bai meng.* Nanjing: Jiangsu wenyi chubanshe, 1995.
———. "Preface." *Fengjing.* Nanjing: Jiangsu wenyi chubanshe, 1995.
———. "Preface." *Hei dong.* Nanjing: Jiangsu wenyi chubanshe, 1995.
———. "Preface." *Xiong an.* Nanjing: Jiangsu wenyi chubanshe, 1995.
Han Shaogong. "Preface." *Fang Fang: Zhongguo dangdai zuojia xuanji congshu.* Beijing: Renmin wenxue chubanshe, 1993.
Jin Jianren. "Preface." *Xin xieshi xiaoshuo xuan.* Shanghai: Zhejiang wenyi chubanshe, 1992.
Lian Peizhen. "Lun Fang Fang de beiju xiaoshuo shijie." *Shangshao shizhuan xuebao,* vols. 64–68, 123–27.
Wu Congju. "Huise youmo: Fang Fang xiaoshuo de gexing he pingjia." *Dangdai wentan,* 115 (1997).
Zhou Ke. "Postscript." *Xingyun liushui.* Wuhan: Changjiang wenyi chubanshe, 1992.

Fang Junbi: *see* **Fan Tchun-pi**

Fang Xiao: *see* **Han Zi**

Fang Zhaolin
Fang Zhaolin, b. 1914, in Wuxi, Jiangsu Province, was the eldest daughter of the industrialist Fang Shouyi, who was assassinated in 1925, and Wang Shuying. Fang Zhaolin was educated by private tutors until she attended art college in Wuxi to study traditional flower and bird and landscape painting.

In 1937 Fang Zhaolin went with her new husband Fang Xinhao (d. 1950) to Manchester, England, to study history but returned via America to Shanghai and Hong Kong in 1939. She wandered in southern China with her family during the Sino-Japanese war years, unable to paint, and her first child was born in 1940. When her husband died in 1950 in Hong Kong, Fang Zhaolin took over the family import-export business as well as the support of her eight children, one of whom was Anson Chan (*q.v.*). Fang Zhaolin also began flower and bird painting studies with Zhao Shao'ang (1905–1984). In 1950–51, Fang Zhaolin's work became better known and in 1953 she became a pupil of the famous painter Zhang Daqian (1889–1983). Fang Zhaolin resumed this tutorship in 1961 and again in 1970 after studying Sinological subjects at the Universities of Hong Kong and Oxford and showing her work in various group exhibitions in North America and Europe. Over a number of years, she visited various artists in China such as He Xianning (1961), Wu Zuoren (1972), and Li Keran (1973). Fang Zhaolin also regularly visited old friends in Wuxi, where she exhibited.

Fang Zhaolin's work combines a remarkably plastic sense of line for major motifs and calligraphic forms with zestful human figures and house-types, owing much to a reconstructed notion of Chinese "folk." Her landscape masses are uninhibited by scholarly pretension to display brushstroke repertoires and utilize the effect of color washes on paper, whose dispersion properties she has fully mastered, to model landscape forms directly and expressively. In representations of floods and boat people, Fang Zhaolin displays an unsentimental empathy for the tragic sufferers of twentieth-century history, rare in more ideologically motivated Chinese neo-traditional paintings.

John CLARK

Fang Zhaolin: Painting and Calligraphy. Hong Kong: Fang Zhaolin, 1981. (Exhibition organized by China Exhibitions Agency, Ministry of Culture, Beijing, which toured Beijing, Shanghai, Nanjing, and Wuxi.)

Feng Kai: *see* **Ke Yan**

Feng Yuanjun
Feng Yuanjun, 1900–1974, of Tanghe County, Henan Province, is remembered today as both a creative writer and prolific literary scholar. She belonged to the first generation of modern women writers in the 1920s and authored several volumes of short fiction.

In her unconventional life-style and defiance of patriarchal norms, Feng Yuanjun exemplified the May Fourth spirit of women's liberation. By the late 1920s, when she turned her scholarly attention to classical literature, she had made important contributions to the study of lyric meter (ci) and drama in particular. She is younger sister to the philosopher Feng Youlan (1895–1990) and married the classical scholar Lu Kanru (1903–1978) with whom she collaborated on many scholarly works.

Feng Yuanjun was born into a wealthy literati family. Her father, Feng Shuhou, was a *jinshi* degree holder who served for a time on the staff of the reformer Zhang Zhidong (1837–1909) and also held the position of prefect of Chongyang County in Hubei Province; he died when Feng Yuanjun was very young. Her mother, née Wu, was an educated woman who was relatively open-minded and acted for a time as principal of a girl's elementary school. Feng Yuanjun was allowed to attend her brothers' tutoring sessions, but when they left home to attend school elsewhere; her mother continued Feng Yuanjun's instruction in the Four Books and classical poetry. Influenced by her brothers Feng Youlan and Feng Jinglan and the progressive journals they brought home on visits from study in Beijing, she pleaded with her mother to allow her to attend a modern school. When the Women's Higher Normal School (Nüzi gaodeng shifan xuexiao) opened in Beijing in 1917, Feng Yuanjun took the entrance examination, although not without a struggle with her mother, and passed.

The five years she studied at the school (1917–22) corresponded with the high tide of the May Fourth Movement. Her fellow students included the writers Shi Pingmei, Luyin (*q.v.*), and Lu Jingqing with whom Feng Yuanjun became quite close. When the conservative principal of the school locked the school gates in an effort to prevent students from participating in the May Fourth demonstrations, Feng Yuanjun smashed the lock with a stone and led a procession of schoolmates onto the streets. One of her first published essays was a reminiscence of her participation in these May Fourth demonstrations. While in school, Feng Yuanjun also performed in a "spoken drama" adaptation, which she herself wrote, of the narrative ballad *The Peacock Flies Southeast* (Kongque dongnan fei). Feng Yuanjun played the role of Mother Jiao, the evil matriarch who tries to rid herself of the daughter-in-law she finds so inferior.

Upon graduation in 1922, Feng Yuanjun entered the Chinese studies section of Peking University's Research Institute as a graduate student specializing in classical literature. Influenced by the new fiction and poetry, particularly that of Guo Moruo (1892–1978), Feng Yuanjun's interests veered more toward creative writing than scholarship. Her early fiction, later collected in *Juanshi Grass* (Juanshi), was first published in the journals of the Creation Society (Chuangzao she) and exhibited the "romantic" tenor for which the society's publications were known. The work has been categorized as "problem fiction" (*wenti xiaoshuo*), dealing primarily with family themes, in particular the question of "free love," a central concern of May Fourth modernity. *Separation* (Gejue) is typical. In the form of a letter to her lover, the story tells of the female I-narrator's "incarceration" by her mother on a visit home (the mother demands that the daughter accept an arranged marriage into the Liu family and fears she will flee). The story expresses the narrator's conflict, torn between filial respect for her mother and love for Shizhen and the "modern" life their relationship represents. A traumatic moment of tension between desires for modernity and continued attachments to family and tradition is captured, a common predicament for young people in that period, perhaps even more poignantly for women who felt uneasy about a modernity that was largely forged by male intellectuals.

Journey (Lüxing) follows a student and her lover on a train trip from Beijing to an unnamed southern city where they stay for ten days in an expensive hotel, experiencing intimacy for the first time . The story extensively uses flashbacks to their times at school together. The narrator expresses Feng Yuanjun's defiance of the conventional marital system and makes clear the protagonist's determination to die rather than submit to this system. In dialogue typical of May Fourth iconoclasm, the couple deems the human relations developing from the Confucian marriage system unnatural.

After 1924, perhaps because she became acquainted with Lu Xun (1881–1936) while studying at Peking University, Feng Yuanjun published regularly in the liberal journal *Spinner of Words* (Yusi, 1924–31), founded by Lu Xun and his younger brother Zhou Zuoren (1885–1968). Here she published essays (*zagan*), scholarly articles, and a few short stories. Beixin shuju, which produced *Spinner of Words* and with which Lu Xun was closely associated; published all three of Feng Yuanjun's books of fiction. Lu Xun was also very much involved in the publication of *Juanshi Grass*, a collection whose stories he praised in his preface to the fiction volume of the compendium *Zhongguo xin wenxue daxi*.

Feng Yuanjun graduated with an M.A. from Peking University in 1925 and started her teaching career at Ginling [Jinling] University in Nanjing. The following year she returned to Beijing, teaching at Zhongfa University and continuing scholarly work in the Research Institute at Peking University. She frequently contributed to the institute's monthly journal with articles on lyric meter poetry, etc. At this time, Feng Yuanjun met Lu Kanru, a graduate of Peking University's Chinese Studies Department and a graduate student at Tsinghua [Qinghua] University, three years her junior. Their love and incipient relationship were captured in her epistolary novella *Spring Scars* (Chunhen, 1927). In the autumn, Feng Yuanjun went to Shanghai, where she taught at both Jinan University and the Chinese Engineering University (Zhongguo gongxue daxue). Lu Kanru joined her after he graduated from Tsinghua. In Shanghai they collaborated on their first scholarly project, *History of Chinese Poetry* (Zhongguo shi shi, 1932). Lu Kanru wrote the pre-Tang sections while Feng Yuanjun covered the period from Tang onward. The two married in 1929 after which Feng Yuanjun essentially abandoned her literary pursuits in favor of a scholarly career.

In 1930, she took up a position at Peking University, becoming one of its first female professors. She and Lu Kanru went in 1932 to the Université de Paris to pursue doctoral studies in classical Chinese literature; her dissertation was on lyric meter poetry ("La Technique et l'histoire du ts'eu," 1935). In Paris she also participated in an anti-fascist pacifist movement led by Henri Barbusse by editing a mimeograph newsletter for the Chinese branch of the movement, whose members included the poet Dai Wangshu (1905–1950) and the playwright and critic Li Jianwu (1906–1982). After returning to China in 1935, Feng Yuanjun taught at Hebei Women's Teachers' College in Tianjin until the outbreak of war in 1937. She and her husband spent their spare time during these two years tracking down, compiling, and editing into a collection rare editions of southern dramas (*nan xi*), *A Collection of Neglected Southern Dramas* (Nanxi yishi). Thus began what would be an abiding scholarly interest for the rest of her life: traditional theater.

Recovering from appendicitis and disgusted with the complaisant and stifling atmosphere under occupation, Feng Yuanjun left the north with her husband in 1938 for Kunming via Shanghai, Hong Kong, and Vietnam. Over the next few years, they lived and taught in various parts of Guangdong, Guizhou, Yunnan, and Sichuan, following their makeshift universities as they sought to find havens from Japanese attack. Feng Yuanjun taught throughout most of the war for Zhongshan University, a Guangzhou university that moved first to western Guangdong, then to Yunnan, then back to northern Guangdong. In 1942, she took a teaching position at Dongbei University in Santai in northern Sichuan. There, she and her husband helped establish a local branch of the Literary Resistance Association with their home as its headquarters, holding discussion meetings, lectures, and performances. Even during these difficult times, Feng Yuanjun managed to find time to pursue her interest in classical drama. Ranging from *zhugongdiao* (sometimes translated as "ballads") to Yuan drama (*zaju*), the essays she wrote during this time were collected in *Compilation of Explanations of Ancient Drama* (Gu ju shuo hui, 1945). Feng Yuanjun also pursued study of the *you* (roughly, jester in ancient Chinese) and its connection to the origins of drama and the term *youling* (actor) of later times.

After the war with Japan ended, she accompanied Dongbei University's return to its original location in Shenyang. In 1946, Feng Yuanjun transferred to Shandong

University in Qingdao (it had moved to Jinan in 1958), where she continued to teach for the rest of her life. Feng Yuanjun was a dedicated teacher who spent a great deal of time preparing teaching materials and helping students. She wrote with her husband several histories of classical literature that were used by students as texts, one of which has been translated into several foreign languages, including English. In the 1960s, she was elected to the NPC and earned a host of provincial titles and was vice-chair of the Shandong Women's Federation and in 1963 was appointed as vice-principal of Shandong University.

Not surprisingly, given her research interests, Feng Yuanjun was declared a "reactionary scholar" during the Cultural Revolution. She was criticized, ordered to clean toilets, and made a "living target" at a "destroy the bourgeois educational black line" meeting. She died in 1974 after a long bout of colon cancer. She was survived by her husband, Lu Kanru.

Kirk A. DENTON

Dai Jinhua and Meng Yue. "Yuanjun: Fanpan yu juanlian." In their *Fuchu lishi dibiao*, Taipei: Shibao, 1993, 103–17.
Feng Yuanjun. *Chunhen*. Shanghai: Beixin, 1927.
———. *Feng Yuanjun chuangzuo yiwen ji*. Jinan: Shandong, 1983.
———. *Feng Yuanjun gudian wenxue lunwen ji*. Jinan: Shandong renmin chubanshe, 1980.
———. *Gu you jie*. Chongqing: Shangwu yinshu guan, 1944.
———. *Jie hui*. Shanghai: Beixin, 1928.
———. *Juanshi*. Shanghai: Beixin, 1928.
———. *An Outline History of Classical Chinese Literature*, trans. Yang Xianyi and Gladys Yang. Hong Kong: Joint Publishing Company, 1983. This is a translation of *Zhongguo wenxue shi jianbian*, first published as *A Short History of Chinese Classical Literature*. Beijing: Foreign Languages Press, 1958.
———. *Yuanjun sa qian xuanji*. Shanghai: Nüzi shudian, 1933.
Feng Yuanjun and Lu Kanru. *Zhongguo shi shi*. Shanghai: Dajiang shupu, 1932.
———. *Zhongguo wenxue shi jian bian*. Beijing: Zuojia, 1957.
———. "The Journey." In *Chinese Women Writers: A Collection of Short Stories by Chinese Women Writers of the 1920s and 1930s*, eds. and trans. J. Anderson and T. Mumford. San Francisco: China Books and Periodicals, 1985, 168–78.
———. "Separation," trans. Janet Ng. In *Writing Women in Modern China: An Anthology of Literature by Chinese Women of the Early Twentieth Century*, eds. Amy Dooling and K. Torgeson. New York: Columbia University Press, 1988, 105–13.
Lu Jiyuan. *Lu Yin, Feng Yuanjun, Lü Yi, Ling Shuhua zuopin xinshang*. Nanning: Guangxi jiaoyu, 1988.
Sun Ruizhen. "He fengjian chuantong zhandou de Feng Yuanjun." *Xin wenxue shi liao*, 4 (1981): 165–71.
Yan Shishuo and Yan Rongxian. "Feng Yuanjun xiansheng zhuanlüe." In their *Feng Yuanjun chuangzuo yiwen ji*. Jinan: Shandong, 1983, 336–47.

Feng Zhongpu: *see* **Zong Pu**

Fu Ning: *see* **Dai Qing**

Fu Quanxiang

Fu Quanxiang, b. 1923, as Sun Quanxiang in a village in Shengxian County, Zhejiang Province, is one of China's two most famous *yueju* artists, the other being Yuan Xuefen (*q.v.*). *Yueju* is local opera indigenous to the Shaoxing region of Zhejiang, characterized by romanticism and lyrical melodies; in traditional times all roles were played by females.

Fu Quanxiang was nine years old when she went to a local opera school attached to the Siji Chun Troupe, which performed out of a temple. The fifty or sixty children of both genders who studied with the troupe lived in sheds at the side of the temple, and although three meals a day were provided, the meals were extremely meager. Students trained in voice and martial arts on the grounds of the temple or, if they were touring, in any available open area such as a beach or a field. They would perform at temples in villages and towns while they were still learning, as a way of gaining experience and earning money. Training began every morning before the moon set and continued until after the moon rose again in the evening. Because the students were illiterate, teachers would read out the scripts line by line, the children repeating after them until they had each scene by heart. Fu Quanxiang eventually learned to read, however, by associating the text she could recite with the written words. Her teacher was an experienced actor of the male *yueju* tradition named Bao Jinlong; he was adept at the *laosheng* (mature male) role and knew all the parts of many operas verbatim. Because of him, the school was set on a solid course and the troupe enjoyed a good name. The owner of the troupe willingly paid famous professionals to head a cast made up of students of the school, and they were thus given an opportunity to observe and learn from professionals. Fu Quanxiang acknowledges her debt to such great performers as Shi Yinhua, Yao Shuijuan, and Xiao Bai Yumei.

After three years, Fu Quanxiang was considered to have completed her course of study (*chu shi*), and that year, 1936, went to Hangzhou and Shanghai to perform at the Laozha Grand Theater in Shanghai. During this period, she became known for her role in *Nine-Catty Girl* (Jiu jin guniang). Originally playing *huadan* (lively young woman) roles, Fu Quanxiang changed to the *qingyi* (morally upright female), which allowed a wider choice of parts. In 1940, she was acclaimed for her performance in the new opera *Heng'e*. Fu Quanxiang formed a new troupe in 1941 with Yin Guifang and Zhu Shuizhao. Fu Quanxiang and Zhu Shuizhao both played female leads in such operas as *Questioning the Husband and Searching for the Husband* (Panfu suofu), *The White Snake* (Baishe zhuan), and *The Jade Dragonfly* (Yu qingting). Yin Guifang and Zhu Shuizhao were both established artists who wanted to help Fu Quanxiang along, so they cast her in important roles in the operas they taught her. By the time she returned to her original Siji Chun Troupe in 1943, Fu Quanxiang was enough of a star that they changed the name to the Quanxiang Opera Troupe.

Fu Quanxiang then invited Fan Ruijuan (*q.v.*), who played male roles, to work with her; two of the operas they performed together were *Little Sister's Death Scene* (Xiaomeimei linzhong) and *Wu Family's Slope* (Wujia po). In 1945, however, Fu Quanxiang was diagnosed with tuberculosis and had to rest in Hangzhou for over a year. By the time she was ready to return to the stage, Fan Ruijuan's stage partner,

Yuan Xuefen, had contracted tuberculosis, so Fan Ruijuan invited Fu Quanxiang to form the Dongshan *Yueju* Troupe with her. Together, they performed several newly scripted operas, including *Dreaming of a Distant Place* (Tianya meng) and *King Li Chuang* (Li Chuang wang). They also performed the traditional operas *The Sad Story of Liang Shanbo and Zhu Yingtai* (Liang-Zhu aishi) and *The Four Great Beauties* (Si da meiren). Fu Quanxiang also played opposite Zhang Guilian and Xu Yulan (*q.v.*). One of the famous operas Fu Quanxiang and Xu Yulan performed in was the Qing period costume opera *Six Chapters of a Floating Life* (Fusheng liu ji), based on the famous autobiography by Shen Fu (1762–after 1803).

In the late 1940s, the *yueju* genre underwent a process of revision, or modernization. Fu Quanxiang attributes this to the changing audience at that time. The new operas that were being written dealt with such new themes as nationalism, revolutionary heroes, and the fight for true love, and were created by outstanding playwrights. The form and technique of *yueju*, as well as its ancillary arts of music, dance, stage setting, lighting, costumes, and so on, were also improved, so that *yueju* became extremely popular in and around Shanghai, where troupes flourished. In 1947, the ten most loved performers of *yueju*, the "ten sisters of *yueju*," staged a benefit performance called *Love for Mountains and Rivers* (Shanhe lian) in solidarity against oppressive theater owners, tabloid libels, and gangsters. Fu Quanxiang participated enthusiastically in the reform of *yueju* and was an active member of this group of women, who also raised funds for a *yueju* school and theater.

She and her Dongshan *Yueju* Troupe performed in Beijing in 1950, also giving a special performance in the leadership compound at Zhongnanhai. In 1951, she and several of the group's artists joined the Huadong *Yueju* Experimental Troupe, which traveled to Beijing in 1952 to take part in the first Chinese Folk Opera Festival (*Di yi jie.quanguo xiqu guanmo yanchu dahui*). She won a Performance Award of the First Grade for her portrayal of the tragic lover Zhu Yingtai. In 1954, Fu Quanxiang also won the same honor in the East China Region Folk Opera Festival with the portrayal of a vivacious and clever maidservant Hongniang in *Story of the Western Chamber*. In 1955, Fu Quanxiang was given the opportunity to visit the Soviet Union and East Germany and the following year performed in North Korea for Chinese military volunteers.

She appeared in the film version of Tian Han's (1898–1968) *Spy of Love* (Qing tan) in 1958, which capitalized on the success of its stage premiere the previous year. Modern *yueju* operas appeared in the early 1960s, and Fu Quanxiang performed in *Sister Jiang* (Jiangjie) and *Two Dollars Sixty* (Liang kuai liu). However, despite her eagerness to support the new trend in opera, Fu Quanxiang was accused of three crimes—being a spy, a reactionary academic authority, and a person of the black line—during the Cultural Revolution. She was imprisoned and isolated from her fellow prisoners, but her spirit was not broken: whenever her jailers were not around she practiced her falsetto singing technique.

After the Cultural Revolution, only eight of the ten sisters of *yueju* were able to meet again: one had died before 1949 and another, Zhu Shuizhao, killed herself during the Cultural Revolution. Yin Guifang had barely escaped with her life and was half paralyzed from a stroke. The other seven sisters gave a performance in her honor. Misfortune also dogged Fu Quanxiang in the latter part of her life. Her husband died from heart disease, then she was diagnosed in 1980 with breast cancer. Undaunted, she went straight to Hong Kong after an operation for the cancer and performed for the many *yueju* lovers in Hong Kong.

In 1991, at the age of almost seventy, Fu Quanxiang initiated a new *yueju* opera. Unlike the female protagonists in most traditional operas, the heroine in Fu Quanxiang's opera ages from her late thirties to her seventies during the story. *Thinner than the Chrysanthemum* (Ren bi huanghua shou) is based on the life of the poet Li Qingzhao (1084–ca. 1151). Fu Quanxiang's aim in creating this opera was to give herself, and other artists of her age, a challenging role in which they could still feel comfortable. Her idea was soon taken up by others, and she received personal and financial support. In order to create her lead character, Fu Quanxiang read Li Qingzhao's *shi* and *ci* poetry and went on pilgrimages to her native place. Fu Quanxiang also visited the various localities in which Li Qingzhao had lived at different stages of her life: Jinhua, Lanxi, Tiantai, and elsewhere in Zhejiang Province. As well as seeking historical authenticity for the setting, Fu Quanxiang worked on the transitions in the speaking and singing voice of a character who moves from early middle to old age during the opera. *Thinner than the Chrysanthemum* was innovative in other respects, too, adapting the format of a television series, with its greater flexibility in the use of time and space, instead of adhering to traditional *yueju* style. The series screening generated a great deal of interest, with academics, opera artists, students, and television professionals holding seminars in Beijing and Shanghai. They all affirmed the innovative significance of the series and praised the quality of the production as well as its artistic, literary, and historical scope.

Fu Quanxiang married Liu Jian in 1956, after five years of long-distance courtship and more than one thousand letters from him. Liu Jian had studied in England and served in the KMT navy before working with the diplomatic corps of the PRC. Fu Quanxiang described their relationship as a reversal of traditional gender roles: Liu Jian gave up the opportunity to serve overseas, choosing instead a desk job in China so that he could take care of their baby daughter and leave Fu Quanxiang free to continue with her career. When she was on tour, they kept in touch by telephone, despite the high cost of long distance calls. During the Cultural Revolution, Liu Jian was the first of the couple to be condemned. Charged with having been an international spy, he was beaten, made to wear a dunce's cap, and paraded in the streets. He nevertheless had the presence of mind to hide in a hole in the wall his wife's scrapbook, photographs, and other valuable records of her career. These materials became an integral part of her 1989 book *Beautiful Views after a Rocky Road* (Kanke qianmian shi meijing).

Their daughter works in the shipping business and their son-in-law works for the Chinese customs service; they have given Fu Quanxiang a grandson, born in 1988. Fu Quanxiang continues to be active through her fan clubs and the social and academic activities associated with her Fu school of *yueju* (*Fu pai*).

At the height of her career, lasting for over fifty years, Fu Quanxiang was one of the two most famous *yueju* artists in China. What distinguished her from others was her unending quest for excellence. Among the many improvements to the singing technique of *yueju* female roles, she is known for adapting the Western falsetto singing technique. This required a great deal of work to ensure a seamless transition from the natural *yueju* voice to the falsetto. Fu Quanxiang also adopted techniques from the great *jingju* (Beijing opera) artist Cheng Yanqiu (1904–1958). It is clear from her part in creating *Thinner than the Chrysanthemum* that Fu Quanxiang was determined to continue her professional development into her twilight years. Her creation in old age of the role of Li Qingzhao is inspired and a model for enriching and modernizing traditional opera, which may well turn out to revive the dwindling attendance of audiences. In this may lie the greatest of all Fu Quanxiang's contributions, to *yueju* opera particularly and traditional opera generally.

Lily Xiao Hong LEE

Fu Quanxiang et al. *Kanke qianmian shi meijing—Fu Quanxiang de yishu shengya.* Shanghai: Baijia chubanshe and Shanghai shengxiang chubanshe, 1989.
Fu Quanxiang. Personal interview. Sydney, 22 March 1999.
Ren bi Huanghua shou—Li Qingzhao de yishu xingxiang. Hangzhou: Zhejiang wenyi chubanshe, 1999.

Fu Xiaoqing: *see* **Dai Qing**

G

Gan Tang: *see* **Kan Shiying**

Ge Hua: *see* **Dai Jinhua**

Ge Jianhao
Ge Jianhao, 1865–1943, of Xiangxiang (present-day Shuangfeng) County, Hunan Province, was the mother of Cai Chang (*q.v.*) and Cai Hesen (1895–1931), two of China's earliest and most respected communist revolutionaries.

Born as Ge Lanying, she changed her name to Jianhao (literally, Robust and Bold) when enrolling at the age of fifty at Hunan Women's Short-Course Teacher Training Institute (Hunan nüzi jiaoyuan yangxi suo). She was progressive and independent. Although binding the feet of her first two daughters, Ge Jianhao heeded her youngest daughter's pleas not to bind hers. The mother allowed her daughters the same freedom as her sons and went to great lengths to ensure that all her children enrolled in modern schools. Ge Jianhao remained close to her children throughout life, and Cai Chang carried a picture of her adored mother "as tenderly as a fetish all through the Long March."

Ge Jianhao belonged to a once wealthy literati family and was related by marriage to another local family, that of the famous Qing dynasty scholar-general Zeng Guofan

(1811–1872). Her father, Ge Baowu (1841–1868), was also an officer in Zeng Guofan's Xiang Army but was killed in action when Ge Jianhao was three years old. Nothing is known of her mother, née Chen, except that she raised two children after the death of her husband and died between 1900 and 1908.

Although Ge Jianhao suffered the traditional female disfigurement of bound feet, she had been allowed to attend the family's private school with her older brother, Ge Wangqin, and was literate as a child. However, Ge Jianhao was married out at the age of sixteen to Cai Rongfeng (1862–1932) of Yongfengzhen, some seventy li distant. Their marriage started off well and within twelve years the couple produced two sons (Cai Linxian, 1885–1907; Cai Luxian, 1889–1925) and two daughters (Cai Qingxi, b. 1884; Cai Shunxi, 1893–1904). However, after Ge Jianho's husband left his lucrative family chili sauce business to take up a position with the Jiangnan Arsenal in Shanghai in 1893, the marriage deteriorated. Ge Jianhao went to live with him in Shanghai, where a third son, Cai Hesen, was born in 1895, but returned home to her family after serious personal disagreements surfaced: Cai Rongfeng had taken a concubine and begun to smoke opium. Ge Jianhao attempted to save the marriage when he followed her back to Hunan and the family reunited; but after the birth of Cai Chang in 1900 the marriage appears to have been in name only. Later, Ge Jianhao and her children successfully resisted his proposal to sell Cai Chang in marriage in 1915, and Cai Rongfeng stormed out of the family home. It is not clear how long this split lasted, but he was again part of the family by 1924.

The two decades at the turn of the nineteenth century were a period of great turmoil in China. Anti-Manchu sentiment ran high after the abortive One Hundred Days of Reform in 1898, and the disastrous international consequences of the failed Boxer Uprising of 1900 served only to heighten revolutionary ardor. Ge Jianhao was personally touched by this milieu when the flamboyant revolutionary Qiu Jin (see *Biographical Dictionary of Chinese Women: The Qing Period*) visited Xiangxiang County in 1906. She had married into the third great family of that county, the Wangs, and during a brief visit to raise consciousness and funds for revolutionary activities announced a break with her husband's family. Deeply impressed by Qiu Jin's courage and independence, Ge Jianhao mourned her execution the following year and encouraged her own children to emulate Qiu Jin's heroic spirit.

Ge Jianhao did not simply manage to send her children to school against all odds, she accompanied them. In 1913, when Xiangxiang First Girls' School (Xiangxiangxianli diyi nüxiao) opened, Ge Jianhao sold her jewelry to raise school fees, enrolling Cai Chang in lower primary school, the oldest daughter in an embroidery class, and herself and Cai Hesen in upper primary school. When the money ran out at the end of the year, Ge Jianhao returned with her children to Yongfeng and set up and taught at Xiangxiang Second Girls' School (Xiangxiangxianli di'er nüxiao) until its closure at the end of 1914. First Cai Hesen and then Cai Chang went to the provincial capital of Changsha to attend school in 1915, and by the following year Ge Jianhao and her oldest daughter had joined them there. Ge Jianhao continued to fund her children's studies while enrolling herself at Hunan Women's Short-Course Teacher Training Institute. After graduating in 1917, she and the family remained in Changsha and became active in the New People's Study Society (Xinmin xuehui), started in 1918 by Cai Hesen and his close friend Mao Zedong (1893–1976).

The 1919 May Fourth Movement, galvanizing intellectuals and students throughout China, prompted many of them to travel to Europe on work-study programs through which they hoped to learn how to modernize China. On 25 December 1919, Ge Jianhao sailed from Shanghai for France with one of these groups, Cai Chang, Cai Hesen, and Xiang Jingyu (*q.v.*) among them. Ge Jianhao remained in France for four years, studying French at Montargis Girls' School, some sixty miles southeast of Paris, and reportedly contributed to group finances by selling embroidery work. During this time, Cai Hesen married Xiang Jingyu (1920) and then returned with her to China (1922), while Cai Chang married Li Fuchun (1900–1975), giving birth to her only child (a daughter named Tete, born early 1924), and then set out several months later for the Soviet Union.

By now fifty-eight years old, Ge Jianhao sailed home to China via Singapore with her baby granddaughter. The two returned to Changsha, where they lived for the next few years with Ge Jianhao's husband, eldest daughter, and the two children of Cai Hesen and Xiang Jingyu. Besides caring for her grandchildren in order to free their parents for revolutionary work, Ge Jianhao involved herself in the women's liberation movement. In 1925 she started a public girls' school to provide vocational training (*pingmin nüzi zhiye xuexiao*). The school was closed down in mid-1927 by KMT authorities, and at the end of 1928 Ge Jianhao moved back to Yongfeng, where she remained for the rest of her life, living in straitened circumstances at a place called Shibanchong. Ge Jianhao maintained a garden, growing vegetables, and planted a red bayberry (*yangmei*) tree, still there; she was unable to have a fishpond, however, another pastime in which Ge Jianhao had taken pleasure throughout her life.

The CCP cared for her in her last years by providing a small pension. Ge Jianhao died on 16 March 1943 at the age of seventy-eight, never having been told of the deaths as martyrs of her two grown sons.

Sue WILES

Klein, Donald W., and Anne B. Clarke. *Biographic Dictionary of Chinese Communism, 1921–1965*. Cambridge, Mass.: Harvard University Press, 1971, 847, 851.

Luo Zhaozhi. "Cai mu Ge Jianhao." In *Zhonggong dangshi renwuzhuan*, vol. 6. Xi'an: Shaanxi renmin chubanshe, 1980–, 47–57.

Snow, Helen Foster [Nym Wales]. *Inside Red China*. New York: Da Capo Press, 1977, 183.

Su Ping. *Cai Chang zhuan*. Beijing: Zhongguo funü chubanshe, 1990.

Yingwen *Zhongguo funü*, ed. *Gujin zhuming funü renwu*, vol. 2, Shijiazhuang: Hebei renmin chubanshe, 1986, 434–37.

Ge Lanying: *see* **Ge Jianhao**

Gong Li

Gong Li, b. 1965, in Shenyang, Liaoning Province, is China's most famous film actor, certainly in the West. Her given name, Li, means "clever and bright" and from early childhood, Gong Li loved dancing and singing.

Her father, Gong Lize, was a professor in the Faculty of Economics at Liaoning University; her mother, Zhao Ying, also worked at the university. Gong Li was the youngest child in a family of three boys and two girls. Her father was transferred to Shandong Business College in Jinan when she was a child and that is where Gong Li grew up. In primary school (Jinan sanhe xiaoxue), her singing and performance talents were recognized, and she was chosen to represent the school in the dance performance *Little Sisters of the Grasslands*. In her second year at primary school, the school recommended her to sing at Jinan People's Broadcasting Station. Gong Li remained active with the school's performance troupe during her six years of high school at Jinan Second High School (Jinan erzhong).

Graduating in 1983 and captivated by vocal music, she applied to the Faculty of Art at Shandong Normal College (Shandong shifan xueyuan) and Qufu Normal College (Qufu shifan xueyuan) but was rejected by both institutions. The following year, the young woman was again rejected when she applied to Shandong Art College (Shandong yishu xueyuan) and the PLA Art College (Jiefangjun yishu xueyuan). In 1985, however, Gong Li happened to meet Yin Dawei, former director of drama with the Jinan Military Region Avant-garde Drama Troupe (Qianwei huajutuan). Recognizing her potential as an actress, he devoted his spare time to preparing her for the entrance tests to art colleges; in July that year she gained admission to the Central Drama Academy (Zhongyang xiju xueyuan) in Beijing.

Gong Li played her first role in a film in 1987, while still a student. She was cast as the female lead in the now famous *Red Sorghum* (Hong gaoliang), directed by Zhang Yimou. This marked the start of an extremely successful professional relationship; in time, they became lovers. He was criticized in many quarters after leaving his wife for Gong Li, but their relationship continued for several years, eventually breaking down in 1995.

Red Sorghum, made by Xi'an Film Productions, won international acclaim, including the Golden Bear Award at the thirty-sixth Berlin International Film Festival, Best Picture and Best Director at the fifth Zimbabwe International Film Festival, and the Sydney Film Critics Award at the fifteenth Sydney International Film Festival. In China, it won the eleventh One Hundred Flowers Award of *Popular Movies Magazine* and the eighth Golden Rooster Award.

Having thus achieved considerable recognition outside China, Gong Li was invited by the Hong Kong director Li Hanxiang to star in his film *Temptress Empress* (Yidai yaohou). She attended the Czechoslovakian International Drama Academies Drama Festival in 1988 and was honored as "Most Beautiful Actress." For her 1988 role as a nurse in *Puma Action* (Daihao meizhou bao), Gong Li was named Best Supporting Actress at the twelfth One Hundred Flowers Award. In 1989, she played three separate roles in the Hong Kong film *Terracotta Warrior* (Qin yong), directed by Cheng Xiaodong: a young woman of the Qin dynasty living in third century BCE, a 1930s Shanghai film star, and a young Japanese woman. She was nominated Best Actress at the Hong Kong Film Festival that year.

Gong Li had by this time developed her own style of performance, emphasizing naturalness. Believing that the source of art is real life, she attempts to capture characters drawn from life. In this, Gong Li was very similar to her collaborator and lover Zhang Yimou, who had already won for himself the nickname "artful genius" (*guicai*). The year Gong Li graduated from the Central Drama Academy (1989), she starred in *Judou*, a Chinese-Japanese venture directed by Zhang Yimou, and delivered a brilliant performance as Judou in this visually stunning film; it broke box-office records in Hong Kong for a film starring a mainland actor. Apart from winning the ninth Hong Kong Golden Statuette Award, the film received great attention throughout the world. It was nominated for the Golden Palm at the forty-third Cannes Film Festival in 1990 and Best Foreign-Language Film at the sixty-third Oscars, and won the Spanish Golden Sheaf Award in October 1989 and the Golden Hugo in Chicago that December. Gong Li became recognized outside China, and after *Judou* played in Japan, was referred to as "the Yamaguchi Momoe of China" because of her physical similarity to the popular 1970s and 1980s singer-film star Yamaguchi.

Gong Li's success in *Judou* was cemented with her performance in the award-winning 1990 film *Raise the Red Lantern* (Dahongdenglong gaogao gua), again directed by Zhang Yimou. She did not win any awards for her performance, but the film won the Venice Film Festival Silver Lion Award, the American National Society of Film Critics Award, the New York Film Critics Circle Award, and Best Film in a non-English language at the British Academy Awards. *Raise the Red Lantern* was also nominated for Best Foreign-Language Film at the sixty-fourth Oscars in 1991.

Gong Li's remarkable versatility was revealed in the films made immediately after *Raise the Red Lantern*. She played a gambler's moll in *God of Gamblers II: Back to Shanghai* (Duxia zhi er: Shanghaitan dusheng, 1991) and starred in *Mary of Beijing* (Mengxing shifen, 1992). Gong Li was a determined peasant in *The Story of Qiuju* (Qiuju daguansi, 1992); the wife of an opera star in *Farewell, My Concubine* (Bawang bieji, 1993); the bohemian painter Pan Yuliang in *Soul of a Painter* (Huahun, 1993); a wife in *To Live* (Huozhe, 1994) and *The King of Western Chu* (Xichu bawang, 1994); a gangster's moll in *Shanghai Triad* (Yao'ayao yaodao waipoqiao, 1995); and a young lady from a well-to-do family in *Temptress Moon* (Fengyue, 1996). *The Story of Qiuju* won the forty-ninth Venice Film Festival Golden Lion Award and the American National Society of Film Critics Award, while Gong Li won the Volpi Cup Best Actress Award for her role in the film.

The last film Gong Li made with Zhang Yimou was *Shanghai Triad*. In 1996, Gong Li married Huang Hexiang, a Singapore businessman. She has since continued film work, frequently outside China. Gong Li has been voted as one of the world's most beautiful women by the American magazine *People* and in 1997 starred with Jeremy Irons in the film *Chinese Box*. Gong Li also appeared in Chen Kaige's film *The Emperor and the Assassin* (Jing ke ci Qin wang). In her 1999 film *Breaking the Silence* (Piaoliang mama), Gong Li extended her repertoire by playing a single working mother struggling to raise a deaf son. She is said to have hoped this courageous film would allow Westerners to see Chinese women in a different light.

As China's most famous film star, Gong Li was made president of the International Jury at the fiftieth Berlin International Film Festival in February 2000. This was the first time a Chinese person had been invited to fill such a prestigious position at a major Western film festival. She has also been invited to be the Asian image for a French cosmetics company. In that year, the United Nations Educational, Scientific, and Cultural Organization declared Gong Li an Artiste of Peace for her contribution to cultural diversity and harmony between peoples.

Shirley Wai CHAN

An Yuan and Liu Huilan. *Zouxiang shijie yingtan de huihuang—Yazhou shouwei guoji yingxing Gong* Li. Beijing: Zhongguo huaqiao chubanshe, 1993.
"Gong Li Chairs Jury." *China Daily*, 17 February 2000.
"The Many Faces of Chinese Cinema." *Sydney Morning Herald*, 11 October 2000.
Pu Li. *Lengyan de beihou—Gong Li*. Beijing: Dianshi ribao and Qin Yuan chubanshe, 1993.
Song Ruizhi, ed. *Zhongguo funü wenhua tonglan*. Jinan: Shandong Wenyi Chubanshe, 1995, 641–42.
"UNESCO Names Gong Li Artiste of Peace." *China Daily*, 10 May 2000.
Wang Ge. *Gong Li—Chushi jiushi jiyu*. Nanning: Sanhuan chubanshe, 1993.

Gong Peiyu: *see* **Shu Ting**

Gong Peng
Gong Peng, 1914–1970, pioneered the cause of the CCP among foreigners during World War II and, along with her sister Gong Pusheng (*q.v.*), became an important official in the Foreign Ministry of the People's Republic of China. The Gong sisters were well known in Christian and YWCA circles in Shanghai and later in Chongqing, and both became capable assistants to Zhou Enlai (1898–1976) in foreign affairs during the war.

A native of Hefei city, Anhui Province, Gong Peng was born in Japan (not in Shanghai, as one source claims) as Gong Weihang; the family was Christian. Her father, Gong Zhenzhou, a member of the revolutionary Tongmenghui, escaped to Japan after being put on a wanted list for opposing Yuan Shikai's plan to become emperor of China. When Gong Zhenzhou returned to China in 1917, he received from the revolutionary government of Sun Yat-sen various appointments, which took the family to Guangzhou and Shanghai.

Gong Peng attended an Episcopalian Girls' School in Shanghai, where she learned English, and graduated from the Department of Chinese Language and Literature at Yanjing (Yen-ching) University in Beijing in 1937. Gong Peng continued her English studies at university and while there was also active in the leftist student movement, joining the CCP in 1936. Upon graduation she went to Yan'an and was appointed in 1938 as secretary to the headquarters of the commander-in-chief of the Eighteenth Group Army. During this period, Gong Peng met and in 1940 married a young man named Liu Wenhua, who had studied in Germany and worked in the same headquarters as the secretary of Red Army Commander Peng Dehuai (1898–1974). About a month after marriage, she was transferred to Chongqing. When Zhu De (1886–1976), commander-in-chief of the Red Army, asked Gong Peng whether she would prefer to stay where she was, Gong Peng, ever the loyal party member, chose to go where the party needed her most. That year, Liu Wenhua died of acute appendicitis.

From 1940 Gong Peng worked for Zhou Enlai in Chongqing, first as a journalist with *Xinhua ribao*, then as secretary to the CCP delegation in Chongqing. She invariably acted as Zhou Enlai's English interpreter at news conferences. Gong Peng met her second husband, Qiao Guanhua (b. 1914), when he went to Chongqing in 1943, and they married the following year. Their son, Paris, was born in 1944 or 1945, and they later had a daughter, Songdu. Working with her husband in Zhou Enlai's unofficial Foreign Ministry in Chongqing, Gong Peng was well known to Western diplomats, journalists, and scholars and mentioned favorably in many of their memoirs for the fresh style she brought to diplomatic circles. Like her immediate superior Zhou Enlai, Gong Peng was good at making friends and winning people over to the communist cause through gentle persuasion. In 1946, she established the English-language weekly *New China Weekly*, but it was soon closed down by the KMT. Later that year, Gong Peng traveled to Hong Kong, where she edited another English-language periodical, *China Digest*, under the nom de guerre Zhong Weiluo.

In 1949 Gong Peng joined the foreign service, becoming the first woman department head in the Foreign Ministry, when she was appointed head of the Information Department; Gong Peng held the position until 1964 when she was promoted to assistant minister. Her husband Qiao Guanhua was one of the most active members of the Foreign Ministry, rising from assistant minister to vice-minister and accompanying PRC leaders such as Zhou Enlai, Chen Yi, and Liu Shaoqi (1898–1969) on U.N. delegations and visits to Soviet bloc and third-world countries. Gong Peng went on several of these overseas delegations, including two to Geneva (1954, 1961) and one to Africa (1963–64).

During the Cultural Revolution, she was persecuted by the Gang of Four, who had her home ransacked and notebooks taken away. The Foreign Ministry was controlled by them at that time. With many officers either under attack or in labor camps, the ones left behind carried extremely heavy workloads. Gong Peng fell ill and suffered a cerebral hemorrhage said to have been caused by hypertension as a result of overwork. She died in 1970 at the comparatively young age of fifty-six.

Lily Xiao Hong LEE

Yingwen *Zhongguo funü*, ed. *Gujin zhuming funü renwu*, vol. 2. Shijiazhuang: Hebei renmin chubanshe, 1986, 868–72.
Han Suyin. "Huainian wo zuihaode pengyou Gong Peng." In *Yanjing daxue wenshi ziliao*, vol. 1, trans. Guo Rui. Beijing: Beijing daxue chubanshe, 1988, 61–69.
Klein, Donald W., and Anne B. Clark. *Biographic Dictionary of Chinese Communism, 1921–1965*. Cambridge, Mass.: Harvard University Press, 1971, 181–82.
Zhang Ying. "Jiechu de nü waijiaojia, Gong Peng." In *Yanda wenshi ziliao*, vol. 9. Beijing: Beijing daxue chubanshe, 1995, 134–49.

Gong Pusheng

Gong Pusheng, b. 1913, in Shanghai, was a pioneer diplomat in the field of foreign affairs with the PRC.

Her family was from Hefei city, Anhui Province, and had at some stage converted to Christianity. Her father, Gong Zhenzhou, joined the Tongmenghui and in 1915 fled to Japan after his name appeared on the government's wanted list as an opponent of Yuan Shikai, who planned to install himself as emperor. When he returned to China in 1917, Gong Zhenzhou was appointed to various positions with Sun Yat-sen's revolutionary government, which took the family to Guangzhou and Shanghai. All that is known of Gong Pusheng's mother, Xu Wen, is that she was a native of Guangdong.

In Shanghai, Gong Pusheng and her sister Gong Peng (*q.v.*) attended St. Mary's Episcopalian Girls' School. Gong Pusheng then enrolled in 1932 at Yanjing (Yenching) University, where she studied English. It was at Yanjing that Gong Pusheng first read about Marxism and the Russian revolution and participated in the anti-Japanese student movement, being elected deputy chair of the Student Self-Rule Association. During this period, Gong Pusheng also experienced her first taste of "foreign affairs," when she and her colleagues attempted to win foreigners on Yanjing's faculty to their cause. They also held press conferences for foreign journalists, among whom were such well-known reporters as Edgar Snow and Nym Wales. Gong Pusheng received her B.A. in 1936 and immediately was sent to work in Shanghai, first in the countryside, then among university students. She joined the CCP in 1938. A first opportunity to travel abroad came in 1939 when Gong Pusheng represented China at the World Congress of Christian Youth in Amsterdam. On her way home to China, she attended the League of World Students in Paris.

Gong Pusheng was received in Chongqing on her return to China by Zhou Enlai (1898–1976), who advised her not to contact her sister Gong Peng, who was also working in Chongqing. It appears that this was done so as not to expose Gong Pusheng's identity as a CCP member and allow her to continue to work as an apparently independent agent. Zhou Enlai requested Gong Pusheng to go instead to the United States both to further her studies and attempt to win friends for the CCP. She did so and went to Columbia University from which she received an M.A. in Religion in 1942. The Japanese attack on Pearl Harbor in December 1941 had made the American people more sympathetic to China's plight and Gong Pusheng received many invitations to speak. At one stage, she rushed from city to city to fulfill her engagements and sometimes had to make three or four speeches a day. Gong Pusheng also spoke at well-known colleges and universities and visited more than half of the states in the nation. She was befriended by such famous people as Mrs. Eleanor Roosevelt, Pearl Buck, and the black singer Paul Robeson and remained friends with some of them.

On hearing from her sister of their father's death in 1942, Gong Pusheng undertook a journey under wartime conditions lasting more than three months, traveling to China via Calcutta. Ironically, she was immediately ordered to return to the United States to study for a doctorate. The reason Zhou Enlai gave was that he hoped Gong Pusheng would become a scholar and educator of the caliber of Wu Yifang (*q.v.*) working for the CCP. Gong Pusheng was unable to travel to the United States, however, until 1945, when traffic between Asia and America resumed. By that time, anticommunist sentiment was growing in America, and she found her task much more difficult. Gong Pusheng spoke now in her talks not of cooperating against the Japanese but of what was to become of China after the war.

With the establishment of the United Nations in New York in 1946, she found a job in the Research Department of the Human Rights Commission and worked there until 1948. As a communist victory in China became more apparent, Gong Pusheng was allowed to return to China, going first to Xibaipo in Hebei. In 1949 she accompanied Li Weihan with the first group of CCP party members to enter Beijing and was involved in preparing for the First CPPCC.

Gong Pusheng married Zhang Hanfu (b. 1905) that year, and the couple has at least one son and daughter. That same year she entered the Foreign Ministry as deputy director of the International Organization and Conference Department, rising to the post of director in 1958. Her first major responsibility in the department was to file with the United Nations a complaint against the United States for armed invasion of North Korea. When the U.N. Security Council discussed the issue in 1950, Gong Pusheng attracted a great deal of attention by being the only woman in the Chinese delegation to the discussions. The *New York Times* published a sizeable article on her, including background and experience, thereby raising the profile of the newly established PRC.

The PRC delegation she led to the Nineteenth International Conference of the Red Cross in New Delhi, India, in 1957, also won a resounding victory. Held after the Bandung Conference at which China had gained many friends and at a time when many Third World countries established diplomatic relations with China, the Red Cross's conference was China's opportunity to win the right to be the only legitimate delegation representing the Chinese people. At the gathering, pressure arose from the United States for the conference to accept instead the delegation from the Republic of China; in resistance, the PRC delegation led a collective exit, which also was to include the chair of the conference. This stratagem was successful and the PRC was accepted as the legitimate delegation. This is seen as the PRC's first victory in its protracted struggle for legitimacy, which culminated in winning representation in the U.N. in 1971, some fourteen years later.

From this time on, Gong Pusheng became a member of various Chinese delegations to conferences and visits abroad, for example, as a delegate to the Geneva Conference on Laos in 1961. She traveled throughout Asia and to Europe, Africa, and the Americas, devoting the remainder of her time to studying international issues.

Gong Pusheng suffered persecution during the Cultural Revolution. Her sister died in 1970, her mother in 1971, and her husband was finally persecuted to death on New Year's Day, 1972.

Although China was admitted to the U.N. in 1971, it was not until after the fall of the infamous Gang of Four in 1978 that Gong Pusheng was sent back to work at that international body. Then, in November 1979, she was unexpectedly appointed ambassador to Ireland. Even though she knew little about the country, she gladly accepted the post, and her innate charm soon won her many friends among the Irish people. Ireland also supported China on a number of international issues and offered study scholarships for Chinese students.

As one of China's longest serving diplomats, Gong Pusheng has remained active in a non-governmental capacity since retirement. She was a member of the International Politics Group of the International Committee of the Red Cross, as well as vice-president of China's U.N. Association. Gong Pusheng and her sister Gong Peng both distinguished themselves in the field of foreign affairs through their competence and hard work. They and their husbands were unique in that all four were prominent in the same field. Their combined contribution and influence on the field has been considerable.

Lily Xiao Hong LEE

Klein, Donald W., and Anne B. Clark. *Biographic Dictionary of Chinese Communism, 1921–1965*. Cambridge, Mass.: Harvard University Press, 1971, 29.
Ruan Hong. "Waijiao shengya liushi nian." In *Nü waijiaoguan*, ed. Cheng Xiangjun. Beijing: Renmin tiyu chubanshe, 1995, 429–52.
Ye Zufu. "Congshi waishi shengya shijian zuichangde nü waijiaojia Gong Pusheng." In *Yanda wenshi ziliao*. Beijing: Beijing daxue chubanshe, 1995, vol. 9, 116–33.

Gong Shuting: *see* **Shu Ting**

Gong Weihang: *see* **Gong Peng**

Gu Mei: *see* **Koo Mei**

Gu Shengying
Gu Shengying, 1937–1967, was born in Shanghai, although her ancestral home was Wuxi, Jiangsu Province. A pianist, she excelled at the works of foreign masters and was described by overseas audiences as "a born Chopin performer and a poet of the piano." Her name has also been romanized as Kou Chen Ying.

Gu Shengying began piano lessons at the age of five under the tutelage of Yang Jiaren and Li Jialu and made her debut at the age of fifteen, playing Mozart's Piano Concerto in D Minor with the Shanghai Symphony Orchestra. After graduating in 1954 from Shanghai Third Girls' High School, she auditioned for and was accepted as a soloist with the Shanghai Symphony Orchestra. Gu Shengying demonstrated exceptional musical talent and through diligence created a unique style characterized by great depth of feeling, sensitivity, and poetic expression. In 1955, she gave solo concerts playing the works of Bach, Beethoven, Schumann, Chopin, and Brahms. Gu Shengying was admitted, again by audition, to the Central Music Academy (Zhongyang yinyue xueyuan) at a graduate level in piano and from that year to 1959 studied under Soviet masters. She won a Gold Award at the Sixth Youth Festival. In 1958, Gu Shengying joined the China Federation of Musicians (Zhongguo yinyue xiehui) and that year received the highest honor in piano performance for women, at the Tenth Congress of International Music Competition in Geneva, Switzerland.

In 1960, graduating from the Central Music Academy, she traveled to Poland, Bulgaria, and Hungary to perform. Gu Shengying also gave concerts to great acclaim with younger talents such as Liu Shikun and Guo Shuzhen in Hong Kong and Macao. In 1964, Gu Shengying won an award in the piano section of the Queen Elisabeth International Music Competition of Belgium.

Gu Shengying died on 31 January 1967, in Shanghai, after an illness.

Shirley Wai CHAN
(Translated by Li Sheung Yee)

Jingsheng and Xiquan, eds. *Xin Zhongguo mingrenlu*. Nanchang: Jiangxi renmin chubanshe, 1987.

Liu Bo, ed. *Zhongguo dangdai wenhua yishu mingren dacidian*. Beijing: Guoji wenhua chubangongsi, 1993.

Zhongguo dabaike quanshu: Yinyue wudao. Shanghai: Zhongguo dabaike quanshu chubanshe, 1989.

Gu Xiulian

Gu Xiulian, b. 1936, in Nantong city, Jiangsu Province, has been minister for Chemical Industry in the PRC since 1989 and a member of the CCP Central Committee from 1982 to 1992.

She was born into a peasant family: her father was a worker and her mother did farm work at home. As the eldest of five children, from a young age Gu Xiulian was expected to help her parents make ends meet by doing chores, such as gathering firewood. She was not sent to school until the age of nine and treasured the opportunity to learn, despite the derision she was subjected to because of being much older than most of the other children. Two years later, however, Gu Xiulian had to be taken out of school because her family could no longer afford the one *picul* of rice it paid in lieu of school fees.

After the CCP took over Nantong in 1947, Gu Xiulian entered Primary Three at Nanyuan Primary School, a PLA free school, but soon afterward transferred to Nantong Needlework School (Nantong nühong jianxisuo), where she studied and practiced embroidery. A year later she transferred to the supplementary class (*buxiban*) of Nantong Girls' Normal School (Nantong nüzi shifan), intending to attempt the junior high school entrance examination. She found the studies very difficult but passed with the aid of the headmistress, Ms. Liao, who proffered extracurricular academic help to students like Gu Xiulian. She thus entered Nantong Third High School and was befriended by Li Lihua, who took Gu Xiulian to live with her family and helped with studies. Later in life, Gu Xiulian spoke with gratitude of the warm friendship extended to her by both Headmistress Liao and fellow student Li Lihua.

The Korean War broke out just as Gu Xiulian finished junior high school in 1953 and, like many young women, she responded to the national recruitment drive for military and political cadres. Gu Xiulian went to a police school (*Gong'an ganxiao*) in Shenyang and in October 1954 was assigned to the Police Department of Benxi city. She joined the CCP in 1956. Gu Xiulian then went to night school to finish high school, managing at the same time to succeed in sports: she won trophies in field sports and basketball. During these years, Gu Xiulian worked as a security officer for large industry and mining enterprises but became increasingly aware of a need for further education. Although her family depended on her income (four younger brothers and sisters remained at home with her parents), her father supported Gu Xiulian's desire to attend university. In 1958 she enrolled in Benxi Iron and Steel College (Benxi gangtie xueyuan) and later transferred to Shenyang Technical College of Metallurgy and Mechanics (Shenyang yejin jixie zhuanke xuexiao).

As a model worker, Gu Xiulian continued to receive 70 percent of her salary while studying. Because of a poor academic background, however, she had to work much harder than her fellow students, at times going into the lavatory to study after lights-out, wearing an overcoat to keep warm. Gu Xiulian graduated, in 1961, with full marks in most of her subjects. Instead of returning to the relatively well-to-do area of her native south China, she elected to work with Jinchuan Non-ferrous Metal Company (Jinchuan youse jinshu gongsi) in poverty stricken, northwestern Gansu Province. There, in the largest nickel mine in China, Gu Xiulian was appalled to find no equipment, the buildings in disrepair, and the workers sent away to Anshan for training. It was one of the most difficult periods in the early years of the PRC, when the nation was only just emerging from a catastrophic famine in the late 1950s and early 1960s. She determined to help develop the northwest, however, and remained there as a technician in the Machine Repair Department and deputy secretary of the Communist Youth League. During her three years in Jinchuan, the nickel mine got back on its feet.

By 1964, Gu Xiulian married (the name of her husband and date of the marriage are not known) and had transferred to Beijing, where her husband worked. She was employed in the Information Department of the Ministry of Textile Industry and made good use of her time there to learn about the textile industry. A year later Gu Xiulian was sent to do political work relating to the "Four Cleanups" Movement. This established her political trustworthiness, which later provided protection during the Cultural Revolution. Also because of her political stability, in the 1960s Gu Xiulian was moved to the Planning Drafting Group. During the Cultural Revolution, this group virtually replaced the State Council's National Planning Commission (Guojia jihua weiyuanhui), which became paralyzed when most of its members were incriminated or under investigation. She worked directly under Premier Zhou Enlai (1898–1976), Li Xiannian, and Yu Qiuli, all of whom greatly appreciated her work. In 1973, at the age of thirty-six, Gu Xiulian was made deputy chair of the National Planning Commission, with light industry and textiles her specific portfolios. The old guard often gave her encouragement and asked others to cooperate with her, and Gu Xiulian showed respect for them and learned much in terms of economic planning and administration.

Her tenure as deputy chair of the National Planning Commission coincided with the beginning of economic reform in China. She became involved in projects to increase the production of goods such as textiles, cigarettes, and beer, the supply of which was inadequate to meet domestic demand. To supplement China's great demand for cotton to clothe the population and with a relatively low investment, Gu Xiulian fostered the synthetic fiber industry to alleviate pressure on grain-growing land that might otherwise have been put to growing cotton. She was also responsible for bringing in the technology for manufacturing filter cigarettes to satisfy the sizeable home market. On her initiative, every province established its own beer brewery to make a variety of brands available in order to increase competition, improve quality, and decrease the price. These achievements not only enriched the domestic market and satisfied its needs, they earned the government a sizeable income, which could be used for more important projects. Thus, in 1977, Gu Xiulian was made an alternate member of the CCP Central Committee and has served as a full member since 1982.

Her youth led the government to believe she would benefit from a wider experience in local government. In 1982, she was thus transferred to Jiangsu Province as party secretary and placed in charge of the Economic Commission. In 1983, Gu Xiulian became the first woman ever to become a governor in China, when the Provincial People's Congress elected her to that position in Jiangsu. Most of the province is located south of the Yangzi (Yangtze) River and has always been a rich agricultural area. As governor, she first turned her attention to further improving agricultural yields, especially in the poorer north. Her next task was to develop "village and township enterprises," small or medium businesses sponsored by a village or a town. Jiangsu had the advantage of being close to the big industrial city of Shanghai, whence technology could be easily transferred, and the enterprises rapidly brought wealth and material prosperity to the peasants. In the 1980s, the village and township enterprises of Jiangsu were considered a model for the entire nation. At the same time, Gu Xiulian devoted energy toward key construction projects, overseeing the construction of a series of large-scale plants such as the Qixiashan Chemical Fertilizer Plant and the Yizheng Chemical Fiber Plant, which soon went into production. Generating plants were also constructed at Jiangyin and Nantong, and in the mid-1980s she initiated a number of exchange programs whereby coal brought from Shanxi, Sichuan, and Guizhou was exchanged for clothing, rice, seafood, and technology. When China decided to designate certain coastal cities and areas as special economic zones, Gu Xiulian made sure that two of them, Lianyungang and Nantong, were in Jiangsu. In addition, she created several economic development areas (*jingji kaifaqu*) and high/new technology development areas (*gaoxin jishu kaifaqu*) in Jiangsu with the aim of earning export dollars. Eager to optimize the performance of Jiangsu, Gu Xiulian led a team of experts to Guangdong Province to learn all she could from the experience of Zhuhai and Shenzhen. Gu Xiulian insisted that industry on all levels invest in research and development. In summary, her successful formula in strategic training and use of talent is as follows: use well the talent you now have, nurture future talent, and introduce from outside urgently needed talent.

In 1989, she was brought back to the central government as minister for Chemical Industry. Her intention was to earn the ministry ten billion export dollars, utilize ten billion yuan of foreign capital, and build one hundred export-oriented enterprise groups by the end of the twentieth century. Gu Xiulian promoted modern management methods and cutting-edge technology. In order to raise the standard of the industry, she not only asked the profession to learn from the domestic models in Jilin and Guangdong but also sent staff abroad for training. Determined that China's chemical industry would catch up with the developed world in order to compete with leaders in the field, Gu Xiulian led fact-finding teams to Holland, Mexico, the United States, and Poland and entered into joint ventures with some of the most prestigious companies in the world, including Bayer, DuPont, and Eastman.

Gu Xiulian broke through the glass ceiling in China's political world, advancing to the rank of full minister and membership of the CCP Central Committee as well as governing a large province. Yet, she says that gender discrimination still exists in China and in order to succeed a woman must try harder to prove her worth and gain recognition by showing ability. At every step of her career, Gu Xiulian stood out from her colleagues because of hard work and achievements. She believes that in a Chinese family one party often sacrifices so that the other can succeed, but with mutual understanding and support there is no reason why both cannot do so. Gu Xiulian admits to having a very happy family life. Her husband is said to be a mathematician with the Institute of Atomic Energy Research and, because he could not be transferred to a suitable position, stayed in Beijing when she went to Jiangsu. Their two sons were born probably in the 1970s and only just in high school at that time, so they went with her to Jiangsu. The three did not live together, however; the boys boarded at school and Gu Xiulian took her meals in cafeterias. The boys did not complain, however, and by the 1990s both were at university.

Gu Xiulian is a CCP cadre who rose from the rank and file since the establishment of the PRC. That she survived the political struggles of the Cultural Revolution unscathed can perhaps be attributed to two factors. The first is timing. Had she risen to a high position earlier, she would have become a target of the rebels during the Cultural Revolution. As it happened, however, Gu Xiulian was then merely a medium-level cadre on the way up. The second is that she maintained an independent stance during the Cultural Revolution and did not make an alliance with the rebels for instant fame and power, as did others of her age and situation. Gu Xiulian was not, therefore, adversely affected by the fall of the Gang of Four with whom she had not been involved. On the contrary, because she worked with Li Xiannian and others of the old guard during the Cultural Revolution, Gu Xiulian was favored and no doubt helped along in her career afterward. She got where she is by hard work and a persistence to better herself; however, her timing was fortunate and an ability to retain a clear head during political turmoil certainly did not hurt her career.

Lily Xiao Hong LEE

Bartke, Wolfgang. *Biographical Dictionary and Analysis of China's Party Leadership, 1922–1988.* Munich: Saur, 1990, 49.
Zhongguo renmin dacidian: Xianren dang zheng jun lingdao renwu juan. Beijing: Waiwen chubanshe, 1994, 165.
Zhonghua quanguo funü lianhehui. Zuzhi lianluobu, Jinri nübuzhang. Shenyang: Liaoning renmin chubanshe, 1995, 1–36.

Gu Yuezhen

Gu Yuezhen, 1921–1970, of Shanghai, was a performing artist in the *huju* (Shanghai opera) genre.

Abandoned at birth, she was taken in by a bamboo craftsman who named her Jinmei. Her adoptive family was extremely poor, and the child determined she would sing in order to help support them. At the age of fourteen, Jinmei learned *shenqu* (an earlier form of *huju*) from Gu Quansheng. He was the one who gave Jinmei the name Gu Yuezhen, after the famous female *shenqu* artist Xiao Yuezhen, because of the girl's delicate features and native intelligence.

Originating from the folksongs of Shanghai's rural villages, *shenqu* has a short history and lacks a substantial repertoire. At that time, masters would allow an apprentice to do menial chores of bringing in tea and carrying bags along the way to the story-telling venues and teahouses and only teach a few songs when they felt like it. Apprentices thus often became more acquainted with the low life of Shanghai than with the real techniques of the opera. Gu Yuezhen, however, intended to become a respected performer. Every morning she accompanied her companions to the home of a veteran artist to rehearse: in exchange for learning one or two songs, they would do housework. Gu Yuezhen would also stand behind the curtain during performances and carefully observe the more seasoned actors in order to memorize the lyrics and movements. After a few months as an apprentice, Gu Yuezhen was able to sing with her master, and after about a year she was able to join a troupe and go on stage.

The hard work and early display of talent aroused the jealousy of some of her colleagues and the insults of local ruffians, however. Unwilling to suffer humiliation, Gu Yuezhen, in a fit of anger, sought refuge in the Buddha and vowed to spend the rest of her life in a nunnery. Only with a great deal of trouble and much persuasion did her master manage to get Gu Yuezhen out.

She specialized in playing the roles of gentle and good-natured women, such as Lin Daiyu in *Daiyu Burying Flowers* (Daiyu zang hua), Mei Lan in *A Beautiful Woman in Troubled Times* (Wanshi jiaren), and Zhenfei in *Empress Dowager* (Xi Taihou). When Gu Yuezhen performed the latter, she collaborated with the musician Zhao Kaiwen to create for the song "Resentment in the Cold Palace" (Lenggong yuan) a distinctive reverse yin-yang (*fan yin-yang*) melody that was both sad and plaintive. The song gained immediate popularity and the format became widely adopted, becoming one of the most artistically charming numbers in *shenqu*.

When Gu Yuezhen turned twenty-six, she succumbed to a bout of pleurisy that soon developed into pulmonary tuberculosis. She had no choice but to leave the stage and recuperate at home. By that time, Gu Yuezhen already had a son and daughter; soon after her misfortune in health, however, her husband left her for another woman.

In 1949, Gu Yuezhen organized a new troupe called Nuli (Great Endeavor) Shanghai Opera Troupe. The first opera staged was *Wang Gui and Li Xiangxiang*, based on the long poem of Li Ji (1922–1980). This was the first performance given in the reformed *huju* style and was closely followed by *Good Daughter-in-law*, *Tian Juhua*, and *Red Flag on Green Hills*. Most *huju* performed at that time was period or modern-dress opera. They were novel and served in addition a political function of inspiring the people. Gu Yuezhen experienced considerable hardship in staging these performances because the theater's proprietor intentionally made matters difficult, and changing the viewing habits of the spectators was not easy. Because the new operas were not of the same calibre as traditional operas, audience numbers declined along with the troupe's income. Troupe members sniped at Gu Yuezhen; others made trouble. To cover expenses, Gu Yuezhen quietly sold the few pieces of jewelry and furniture she had left, at one point bringing in her own bed quilt to use in a performance.

After three years' preparation, in 1953, Gu Yuezhen put on the *huju* performance of *Zhao Yiman*, revolutionizing the genre, and was hugely successful. In this opera about the anti-Japanese heroine Zhao Yiman (q.v.), Gu Yuezhen changed the basic tunes and old format, combining them into a venue of new music for voices through which the inner world of the heroine could be revealed.

She herself played a variety of roles throughout her career and sought to understand the souls of the characters, aspiring to true-to-life performances. Even when Gu Yuezhen's tuberculosis relapsed, she insisted on performing, and only when the removal of one of her lungs caused her voice to lose its resonance did the singer reduce the number of her performances and switch to directing.

In her capacity as head of the Nuli Shanghai Opera Troupe, director of the Shanghai branch of the Chinese Theatrical Association, and member of the Shanghai Municipal Administration Committee, Gu Yuezhen was criticized and denounced during the Cultural Revolution. Her health quickly deteriorated but she was denied proper medical treatment. Her body was found at midnight on 12 January 1970; Gu Yuezhen had fallen to her death from a building. She left no letters or notes.

In September 1978, Changning District Committee of the city of Shanghai held a memorial for Gu Yuezhen. In November 1979, Yang Hansheng, vice-chair of the China Federation of Literary and Art Circles, announced at the Fourth National Congress of Literature and Art the names of writers and artists persecuted to death during the Cultural Revolution and called for expressions of condolence and grief. Gu Yuezhen's name was on that long list.

Shirley Wai CHAN
(Translated by Barbara Law)

Jingsheng and Xiquan, eds. *Xin Zhongguo mingrenlu*. Nanchang: Jiangxi renmin chubanshe, 1987.
Xie Bo. "Gu Yuezhen zhuan." In *Zhongguo dangdai wenhua yishu mingren dacidian*, ed. Liu Bo. Beijing: Guojiwenhua chubanshe, 1993, 191–203.

Guo Jian

Guo Jian, b. 1913, as Guo Jian'en in Zhuzhou, Hunan Province, was vice-minister of Communications between 1978 and possibly 1982, in the PRC.

She was active in her high school days in Hunan, taking part in anti-Japanese activities, for example, advocating the boycott of Japanese goods. In 1934, Guo Jian entered Tsinghua [Qinghua] University in Beijing and became active in the student movement there, participating in protest marches as well as heading south with its Propaganda Expansion Group. She also helped initiate the Vanguards for the National Liberation of China (Zhonghua minzu jiefang xianfengdui) and in 1936 was elected vice-president of the Women's National Salvation League of Beijing. Later, as a representative of Qinghua University, Guo Jian joined the Beiping-Tianjin Students' League (PingJin xuelian) and was elected as a member of its Standing Committee, traveling often on its behalf between Tianjin and Shanghai.

She joined the CCP in 1937. At that time, under the direction of Deng Yingchao (q.v.), communist members worked together with the KMT in women's work, associated with the New Life Movement created by Chiang Kai-shek and his wife Soong

Mayling (*q.v.*). Guo Jian joined the Women Cadres' Training Group (funü ganbu xunlianzu) of the Women's Guidance Committee (Funü zhidao weiyuanhui) in 1938 as part of this New Life Movement. Together with other open or underground CCP members and sympathizers, she endeavored to enlist more women in the cities of Wuhan and Chongqing and countryside of Hunan, Hubei, and Sichuan to aid in the war against Japan. Through the efforts of these women, the united front with the KMT and non-aligned elements in society were strengthened, but after the KMT-CCP united front collapsed in 1941 Guo Jian went north to Jiangsu via Hong Kong.

After the establishment of the PRC in 1949, she became director of the Industry and Commerce Department in the North Jiangsu Administrative Office (1950) and later was appointed as director of the Finance and Economic Affairs Office (1951), head of the Commodity Control Bureau, and head of the Food Bureau. Guo Jian moved to Shanghai and in 1953 was appointed vice-president of Financial and Economic Affairs of the Shanghai People's Government and as a member of the Shanghai People's Committee. In 1957, she became director of the Planning Committee. Guo Jian was also prominent in the ACWF at municipal and national levels, being elected secretary of the ACWF secretariat in 1961. She was elected to the Standing Committee of the Third NPC in 1965.

During the Cultural Revolution, Guo Jian was apparently stood down but re-emerged in 1978 as national vice-minister of Communications, a post probably held until she was elected both to the CCP Central Committee's Discipline Investigating Committee at the Twelfth General Congress in 1982 and to the Guidance Committee for Party Consolidation. Membership in these two committees is reserved for retired, long-serving senior party officials. Guo Jian has visited many foreign countries, mostly with women's delegations but also other groups, such as trade unions. She has often been the leader or deputy leader of such delegations. The last known such trip was in October 1978 when Guo Jian led a delegation of civil engineers to the United States, presumably in her capacity as vice-minister of Communications.

Information regarding Guo Jian is tantalizingly scarce, especially regarding her personal life and official performance. However, from what is known, one can deduce that she has been a loyal and dedicated member of the CCP from her early years. The brief record available on her work and positions held indicates that Guo Jian excels in the management of financial and economic affairs and is good at planning and operating large-scale projects, such as those for which the Ministry of Communications would be responsible. Her long years of loyalty and dedication were eventually rewarded with the party's trust, and she has become one of the few women attaining ministerial status in the PRC.

Lily Xiao Hong LEE

Bartke, Wolfgang. *Who's Who in the People's Republic of China*. Munich & New York: K.G. Saur, 1991.
Huaxia funü mingren cidian. Beijing: Huaxia chubanshe, 1988.
Zhonggong renminglu. Taipei: Guoli zhengzhi daxue guojiguanxi yanjiuzhongxin, 1978.

Guo Jian'en: *see* **Guo Jian**

Guo Wanrong: *see* **Kuo Wan-jung**

Guo Xiaozhuang: *see* **Kuo Hsiao-chuang**

Guozi Hong: *see* **Ding Guoxian**

H

Han Shiying: *see* **Kan Shiying**

Han Suyin

Han Suyin, b. 1917, as Zhou Yuebin in Xinyang County, Henan Province, of a Chinese father and Belgian mother, is a world-renowned writer.

Zhou Yuebin was given the name Guanghu when she went to school and also was known to her Western acquaintances as Rosalie Chou; Han Suyin is a pen name adopted when she began writing in English. Han Suyin is from a Hakka family that had moved from north China to Meixian County, Guangdong Province, in the thirteenth century and subsequently moved to Pi County, Sichuan Province, in the seventeenth century. Originally engaged in business, the family gradually transformed themselves into scholar-official gentry. Her father, Zhou Yingtong, won a scholarship in 1904 to go to Belgium to study railway and mining engineering. In Brussels, he married a Belgian woman named Marguerite Denis and returned with her to China in 1913. Zhou Yingtong continued to work in railways and mining in China until he died in 1958. The couple had eight children, only four of whom survived; Han Suyin has one elder brother and two younger sisters.

When Han Suyin was seven, the family moved to Beijing, where she first attended Sacred Heart Girls' School and then Bridgeman Girls' High School, both Western-language institutions. Her mother was reluctant to support further education after Han Suyin turned fifteen, wanting her to get married instead, so she worked as a typist at Beijing Union Hospital to save up for her own education. By 1933, Han Suyin had enough to study pre-med at Yen-ching [Yanjing] University, and three years later, in 1936, her good academic results won a scholarship to study medicine at Brussels University in Belgium. The Sino-Japanese War (1937–45) broke out before she could finish her studies, however, and driven by a desire to share the destiny of her compatriots Han Suyin returned to China in 1938.

On the ship from Marseilles to China, she met a childhood acquaintance named Tang Baohuang, who was then a young officer in the KMT army. They fell in love and married in October 1938. Soon after they reached Wuhan, however, the city fell to the Japanese and the two finally made their way, via Changsha, Guilin, and Guiyang, to Chongqing, arriving at the beginning of 1939. There, Han Suyin adopted a little girl whom she named Tang Rongmei but who is also known in some of her works as May. In 1942, Han Suyin and Tang Rongmei accompanied Tang Baohuang when he was sent to London as a military attaché to the embassy of the Republic of China. Han Suyin soon resumed medical studies, and during their London years the couple drifted apart. When Tang was recalled to China in 1945, Han Suyin did not go with him but remained to take out her medical degree in 1948. She then began a journey with Rongmei to Hong Kong at the end of December, arriving in Hong Kong in January 1949 to start work for Queen Mary's Hospital.

Han Suyin began writing during the Sino-Japanese War, and her first book, *Destination Chungking*, was published in England in 1942. She continued writing while working as a doctor in Hong Kong, and her second book, *A Many-Splendoured Thing*, became a best-selling novel. After it was made into a Hollywood movie that excelled at the box office worldwide, Han Suyin became quite famous, receiving a great deal of media coverage in the United States and Europe as an internationally renowned writer. Works of fiction and non-fiction followed at regular intervals of two to three years.

Her estranged husband Tang Baohuang died in 1947 in China's northeast region during the civil war, and Han Suyin remarried in February 1952. Her new husband, Leon Combre, was an Englishman who worked for the Special Branch of the Malayan police. She went with him to Malaya the year they married and lived in Johore Bahru, across the Johore Strait from Singapore. Besides practicing medicine, Han Suyin continued to write and give lecture tours abroad. In 1959, she taught a course at Nanyang University in Singapore on contemporary literature, attempting to introduce to the predominantly Chinese students the works of writers from Third-World countries.

Han Suyin wanted to go to China to see for herself the changes that had taken place since the founding of the PRC but was not able to get a visa until 1956. Even then, it was achieved only with the help of the British high commissioner to India, Malcolm McDonald, who introduced her to China's ambassador to India and through whom she made the request to visit. Stepping onto Chinese soil again in May, Han Suyin returned to her homeland. The occasion generated wide publicity because of her fame but also because at that time relatively few people wished to visit there. She was warmly received by Chinese leaders such as Zhou Enlai (1898–1976) and Chen Yi and visited her father and other relatives in China. After leaving, Han Suyin gave glowing accounts of the improvements made by the new government. She began writing about China, publishing *Wind in the Tower* (1976), *Lhasa, the Open City* (1977), *The Morning Deluge* (1993), and *The Eldest Son* (1995). From 1966 she wrote an autobiographical series: *The Crippled Tree* (1966), *A Mortal Flower* (1966), *A Birdless Summer* (1968), *My House Has Two Doors* (1980), and *Phoenix Harvest* (1983). In these books, Han Suyin presented more than the events of her personal life; she embedded them within the wider context of the history of modern China. Western readers welcomed these inside views: Han Suyin interpreted China and its people, combining near-native understanding with insight into what the West would be interested in, and wrote in a style accessible to Westerners, that made the Chinese understandable.

From the 1960s, she became an unofficial spokesperson for the PRC abroad, regularly visiting China and after each trip writing and speaking about her latest experience. Controversy followed some of these reports, especially during the great famine around the beginning of the 1960s and the Cultural Revolution. She was criticized for painting a pretty picture of China when thousands suffered from hunger or persecution. Han Suyin admitted later in her own work that she had overstated certain things during the Cultural Revolution period. However, her error might have been caused by an overzealous desire to see China do well. There is little doubt that she loved and identified completely with the country. This can be seen in her efforts to establish a foundation fostering scientific exchange in China in 1986; the foundation funds training for scientific administrators for China, promotes scientific exchange between East and West, and trains women scientists.

Han Suyin's marriage to Leon Combre ended in 1958, and she began living with Vincent Rathnaswamy in 1960. (It is not clear whether they were formally married.) Han Suyin revealed in *My House Has Two Doors* that, in order to be with her, Rathnaswamy—who was said to have been a protégé of Nehru—gave up his career in the Indian Army, where he had attained the rank of colonel. In the 1970s and 1980s, the couple lived in Hong Kong and in Lausanne, Switzerland. Her adopted daughter Rongmei went to live in North America and made her a grandmother in the 1960s. Han Suyin continued to visit China in the 1980s and write about her country.

Her works are written mainly in English and have been translated into many languages. Her five-volume autobiography was translated into Chinese and published in China in 1991. The title of one of her books, *My House Has Two Doors*, captures the essence of her success: she belongs to two worlds, both Chinese and Western. Her mind is open to the influences of each and the way she looks at things is also through both perspectives: it is what makes her writing unique.

Lily Xiao Hong LEE

Han Suyin. *The Birdless Summer*. London: Jonathan Cape, 1968.
———. *The Crippled Tree*. London: Jonathan Cape, 1966.
———. *The Mortal Flower*. London: Jonathan Cape, 1966.
———. *My House Has Two Doors*. London: Jonathan Cape, 1980.
———. *Zai sheng feng huang*. Beijing: Zhonggong zhongyang dangxiao chubanshe, 1991. English title: *Phoenix Harvest*.
Huang Wenxiang. *Haiwai huayi jingying*. Hong Kong: Wenji chubanshe, 1992, 281–315.
Yu Qing. *Han Suyin zhuan: Zhongguo fenghuang*. Changsha: Hunan wenyi chubanshe, 2000.

Han Youtong

Han Youtong, 1909–1985, the foremost woman law scholar in the PRC, was born into a poor Muslim family in Ning'an County, Heilongjiang Province.

In 1927, she entered the School of Law and Commerce in Peking University during a period of extreme political tension, when the fledgling alliance between the KMT and CCP broke down. While at university, Han Youtong participated in various political activities. She met her future husband, Zhang Youyu, who was a member of the underground Beijing CCP Committee, when they were both arrested by the KMT. Although work and study often kept them apart, their love persisted. In 1931, Han Youtong and her fellow students were determined to go to Nanjing to protest against Chiang Kai-shek's refusal to fight the Japanese, and this led to her second arrest. The students camped on the railway line at Beijing Railway Station for three days and nights until the authorities agreed to dispatch a train to take them to Nanjing. Upon reaching their destination, they smashed the signboards at KMT headquarters and the KMT-sponsored newspaper *Central Daily News*. It was only through the intercession of Zhang Youyu, at that stage a law academic but still an underground worker for the CCP, that the dean of her school agreed to rescue Han Youtong from imprisonment. She married Zhang Youyu in 1933 but then went to Japan to pursue postgraduate studies in law, specializing in international law and diplomatic history.

Returning to China in 1937, the year that saw the start of the Sino-Japanese War, Han Youtong began a busy life as a political activist, academic, and editor, actively working with the National Salvation Society, which existed to arouse patriotism among the people. She also taught at Northwest Union University, edited the magazine *Women's Friend* (Funü zhi you), and published prolifically on the constitutional and women's movements.

In 1945, Han Youtong gave up her work as a Japanese-English translator for the U.S. Information Service in Chongqing and traveled several thousand miles to the northeast to work in the field of culture and education. Her commitments again separated Han Youtong from her husband, who had revealed his identity as a CCP worker and become a member of the CCP delegation negotiating with the KMT in Chongqing. Because the transfer was a party decision, however, neither Han Youtong nor her husband complained at the disruption to their married life. In the northeast, she worked in various positions, finally becoming a member of the Northeast Administrative Committee and head of the Department of Education of Songjiang Province. She published her treatise "On Constitutional Rule" during this period.

In the 1950s, Han Youtong received several appointments in the legal field, heading in turn the North China branch of the Supreme Court (1952), the Civil Court of the Supreme Court (1954), and the High Court of Ningxia Autonomous Region (1958). In 1955, she became deputy director of the Institute of Legal Studies of the Chinese Academy of Social Sciences and also group leader of the Legal Studies Group of the CPPCC. Han Youtong stepped down from the High Court of Ningxia Autonomous Region in 1965 at the age of fifty-six in order to return to Beijing to enjoy a modicum of family life with her husband and son (Zhang Xiaoyu, b. 1956). Throughout the 1950s and 1960s, she traveled with official PRC delegations to various Asian and African countries and in 1964 led a delegation to Budapest to take part in the Eighth Congress of the International Association of Democratic Legal Workers.

During the Cultural Revolution, both Han Youtong and her husband were illegally "investigated in isolation" by Red Guards. In such cases, individuals were not arrested but isolated in their workplace—away from family, friends, and colleagues—and then interrogated and investigated. After the Cultural Revolution, she led discussions on democracy and rule by law, which helped liberate scholars in the legal field from political constraints, enabling them to work in areas in which they had formerly felt inhibited. All through her life, Han Youtong published on law, constitutional rule, and international and women's issues.

Lily Xiao Hong LEE

Huaxia funü mingren cidian. Beijing: Huaxia chubanshe, 1988, 119–20.
Yingwen *Zhongguo funü*, ed. *Gujin zhuming funü renwu*, vol. 2. Shijiazhuang: Hebei renmin chubanshe, 1986, 779–83.
Zhonggong renming lu. Taipei: Guoli zhengzhi daxue guoji guanxi yanjiu zhongxin, 1978, 712–13.

Han Zi

Han Zi, b. 1921, as Fang Xiao in Liyang County, Jiangsu Province, is a contemporary writer who had notable success in China from the 1940s to the 1960s.

Han Zi's father, Fang Lizi, was a small-time merchant who was quite well off; he had charge of a rice mill and also raised silkworms. Her mother married into the family as a child but when she failed to deliver a longed-for boy, producing instead Han Zi, both were looked down upon. Han Zi's childhood was not happy; she remembers her mother often being humiliated and beaten by Fang Lizi. Despite the comparatively high social status her family derived from its prosperity, Han Zi was forced to do many household chores from the time she was little and never wore new clothes. That she attended school from the age of nine was solely because of her mother's unstinting efforts to earn money for that purpose. The hardships and discrimination of Han Zi's childhood helped build in her a stubborn fighting spirit as well as an iron determination to overcome adversity.

When Han Zi's father opposed her going on to high school, her mother borrowed money from friends and relatives to enroll her at Suzhou Normal School for Girls. This college had a tradition of pursuing literary excellence and many of the teachers and students held leftist views. The environment decisively set thirteen-year-old Han Zi on the dual paths of revolution and literature. As soon as she enrolled, Han Zi joined an extracurricular "literary group," where she was introduced to the works of Lu Xun (1881–1936). Han Zi wrote a number of essays for the school magazine, most of them expressing longing for her absent mother. There were a great many students from poor families who attended the school, and the sympathy and help they accorded each other meant a great deal to her.

In 1935 Han Zi participated in a student strike called at the school after their negotiations with the school principal failed to prevent the dismissal of four leftist teachers. She and her fellow students boycotted classes and examinations, eventually petitioning higher authorities for support, but the strike ended when Jiangsu education authorities announced instead the expulsion of ten students. Han Zi wrote about it in her autobiography. "After the failure of the school strike in the summer of 1935, the communist student representative said: 'So long as the social system remains the same, we cannot achieve victory on our own.' This really prompted a change in my thinking."

Han Zi persisted in pursuing progressive ideas, even after her revolutionary mentor—the communist student representative—had left the school. A new librarian clandestinely lent her the works of Lu Xun and other leftist writers as well as Russian publications, thus introducing Han Zi to communism, socialism, and the USSR. She began to study Marxist philosophy. In summer 1936, in her compulsory "weekly diary," the student repeatedly accused the school of banning anti-Japanese activities during the undeclared war against Japan and also wrote a story about a progressive female student who became a worker. The principal concluded that Han Zi was "ideologically unsound." Fearing the story would exert a bad influence on the school's non-academic employees, he contrived to expel her without publicizing the fact in the conventional manner.

Han Zi's expulsion brought down upon her her father's wrath as well as a sound beating. She considered leaving home and going to Shanghai to work in a factory or enter a work-study program. Instead, she enrolled in Jingzhi Private School for Girls in Wuxi, where some of her former classmates, also expelled from Suzhou Normal School, lived. The principal of Jingzhi Private School for Girls, Hou Baojian, allowed the students to pursue their own activities, including those related to the war against Japan. Han Zi and the other expelled students soon established a student society, and she and some twenty like-minded individuals also formed a small group within the politically active Wuxi Study Society. Han Zi's time at this school was immensely exciting; she and her classmates exchanged liberal books and periodicals, discussed current affairs fervently, and took to the streets to give speeches for the war effort. Han Zi participated in memorial services for Lu Xun, whom she greatly admired, and looked for inspiration to Maxim Gorky; Han Zi also held the American radical and journalist Agnes Smedley (1893–1950) in high esteem, regarding her as a role model. Han Zi's ambition was to spread revolution by her pen: to become a "red" writer.

After the August Thirteenth Incident of 1937 in Shanghai, she and her classmates immediately went to work at a casualty hospital to help the injured. In November, Han Zi sought out in Nanchang (Jiangxi Province) the headquarters of the communists' New Fourth Army and was directed to join the Jiangxi Youth Services Troupe. In 1938, she went to the New Fourth Army Service Department in south Anhui to work in the peasant movement. In 1939 her story "Portrait of the Masses" (Qun xiang) was published in *Resistance Literature* (Kangdi wenyi). A few years later, Han Zi was appointed editor of *The Vanguard* newspaper, general editor of *The Masses of Huainan* magazine, and director of the Huainan Branch of the Women's Federation Propaganda Bureau, positions she held for a number of years. She wrote many news stories for *The Vanguard*, the *Huainan Daily*, and *New China Daily* and much CCP propaganda work for the party during the Sino-Japanese War (1937–45). Han Zi joined the CCP in February 1943.

Her first novel, *Dispute* (Jiu fen), published in 1945, was selected as an award-winning work in the liberated areas and included in the series "People's Literature" (Renmin wenyi). She joined the Literary Association of Central China in 1946 and for the next few years fought on the battlefields of northern Jiangsu and Shandong. With the liberation of Shanghai in 1949, Han Zi was assigned to work with military units that were supervising three textile factories. She joined the Chinese Writers' Association the same year and in 1950 was elected to the first session of Shanghai Municipal People's Conference in Shanghai. Han Zi was appointed deputy director of the Propaganda Bureau of the Women's Federation of Eastern China.

Her time in Korea in 1952 as a member of the Chinese People's Volunteer Army, including experiences at the Battle of Shangganling, became the background for *Peace Museum* (Heping bowuguan, 1954). Her appointment as deputy director of the Creative Committee of the Chinese Writers' Association and as an Editorial Committee member of the major literary journal *Harvest* (Shouhuo) took her to Beijing in 1956. The following year, Han Zi returned to Anhui when she was appointed director of that province's Propaganda Bureau. In 1960 Han Zi was elected to the Anhui CPPCC and made a committee member of the Provincial Literary and Art Circles. In early 1962, the writer was sent to Yixing and Wuxian Counties in Jiangsu as a Standing Committee member and, going down to the countryside, experienced life at the bottom in a production team. Her collection of essays *On Clearing Up* (Chu qing ji), reflecting peasant life, was published that year. She was also appointed to the council of the Shanghai Writers' Association.

Han Zi stopped writing during the decade of chaos that was the Cultural Revolution but in 1977 revisited the places in southern China where she had seen combat in the 1930s and 1940s. Afterward, Han Zi wrote many memoirs and essays on life with the New Fourth Army on the battlefield as well as essays and short stories on various other subjects. Her work was published in the collections *Unadorned Flowers* (Shuhua ji) and *Wan Niu*, and she continued literary pursuits at the Shanghai branch of the Chinese Writers' Association while sitting on the Editorial Committee of *Shanghai Literature* that year.

Revolution had been Han Zi's way of life since youth, and she had always put the party's needs before her own; it is not known whether she married or had children. As a long-time propaganda cadre at military and provincial level, her work closely follows the historical periods and political movements of the CCP. While this inevitably constrained the range and scope of her writing, Han Zi produced several works of note. Her essays draw the most attention. Most representative of her collections are *I Came from Shangganling* (Wo cong Shangganling lai), *Diary of Huangshan* (Huangshan xiaoji), and *Plum Mountain Poems* (Meiling shiyi). The style of her essays can be likened to that of Bing Xin (*q.v.*) in its feminine delicacy, and her descriptive powers are beautiful and innovative. When the PRC was established in 1949, the CCP insisted that writers should create socialist heroes and deal with the "big issues" of society. Expression of feelings and pursuit of artistic style were seen as incompatible with socialist heroism, and writers faced a difficult task if they were to avoid the tag "petty capitalist" and becoming a target of criticism. Han Zi's extremely fine and well-crafted style brought a breath of fresh air to the literary scene at the time.

Although the output of fiction was small, a number of her works in this genre are also noteworthy. The short story "Wan Niu," written in 1959 to commemorate her staunch friends of the New Fourth Army, is a work of rare achievement. About a peasant woman who raises an orphan of the New Fourth Army, the plot revolves around the contradictory feelings that the woman has when the girl (Wan Niu), raised from babyhood and whom she regards as her own daughter, must be handed back to the army. Han Zi meticulously unfolds the story to reveal the central character's inner spirit and disposition; her depiction of the sincerity and honesty between people is vivid and deeply moving.

It has been suggested that Han Zi was deeply influenced by the works of Lu Xun. The literary simplicity of her stories makes them appear rather plain, yet it is obvious that they are all carefully crafted from her own life experience.

Rubing HONG
(Translated by Yuen Kwan Veronica Ngok and Jennifer Eagleton

Han Zi. "Han Zi." In *Dangdai nüzuojia zuopin xuan*, vol. 2, ed. Liu Xicheng. Guangzhou: Guangdong renmin chubanshe, 1980.
———. "Wo de shaonü shidai." *Wenhui*, no. 10 (1989): 59–61.
———. "Xiao zhuan." In *Zhongguo xiandai zuojia zhuanlüe*, eds. Xuzhou shifan xueyuan. Chengdu: Sichuan renmin chubanshe, 1983.

Hang Ying

Hang Ying, b. 1944, in Dongping, Shandong Province, is a fiction writer and dramatist.

After graduating in 1959 from the First Girls' High School of Tianjin (Tianjin diyi nüzi zhongxue), she was admitted to the stage design class at Tianjin People's Art Theater (Tianjin renmin yishu juyuan). Hang Ying completed a year of advanced study in 1961 after which she returned to Tianjin People's Art Theater to work in stage and costume design.

Her career took a turn in 1970 when, after the successful performance of her comedy *Make Some Plans* (Jihua jihua), Hang Ying became a playwright. She also wrote film scripts and in 1980 joined the Chinese Drama Association. In 1979, Hang Ying published stories and in 1981 transferred to the Tianjin branch of the Chinese Writers' Association, to begin a career as a professional writer. She was appointed director of the Chinese Writers' Association, vice-chair of the Tianjin branch, and a delegate to the Seventh NPC. Among her major works are the short story collections *The Leaning Garret* (Qingxie de gelou) and *Oriental Women* (Dongfang nüxing) and the stage play *Wedding Ceremony* (Hunli). Hang Ying deals penetratingly with social and ethical issues, treating family, marriage, love, and morality with special sensitivity. She excels at depicting the emotional world and fateful circumstances of ordinary women, often blending dramatic technique with a subtle and painstaking style. "Golden Deer" (Jin lu'er) and "Miss Ming" (Ming guniang)—published in the January 1982 issue of *Qingnian wenxue*—won the National Outstanding Short Story Award in 1981 and 1982. "Miss Ming" was adapted into a film of the same name and then translated into Flemish; "Golden Deer" was modified for television drama.

Critics allude to the "worldliness" in Hang Ying's portrayal of good and noble people or events in the context of the prosaic world. One reviewer divides the author's characters into three categories: women possessing traditional "oriental" virtues, as typified by Wang Chunhua in "Former Wife" (Qian qi) and Lin Qingfen in "Oriental

Women"; idealistic modern women searching for love and career, as typified by Golden Deer and Miss Ming; and bad women, such as Han Yuxia in "The Leaning Garret," enacting negative models. Each has a place in Hang Ying's work and contributes to making it a rich tapestry of female lives.

GAO Yuanbao
(Translated by Katherine Kerr)

Hang Ying. *Dongfang nüxing: Lunli daode xiaoshuoji.* Beijing: Renmin wenxue chubanshe, 1985.

Wu Yundong. "Hang Ying xiaoshuo zhong de nüxing xingxiang." *Nanjing daxue xuebao zheshe kan* (February 1986): 132–39.

Yang Guangyu, ed. *Zhongguo dangdai qingnian zuojia mingdian.* Beijing: Zhongguo huaqiao chuban gongsi, 1991, 915–16.

"Zuozhe jianjie." In *Dongfang nüxing.* Taipei: Xin weilai chubanshe, 1991, [4–5].

Hao Jianxiu

Hao Jianxiu, b. 1935, in Qingdao city, Shandong Province, was vice-minister (1978–81) and minister (1981–87) of Textile Industry in the PRC.

Born the daughter of a worker, she received just over one year's primary education as a child. From the age of nine, Hao Jianxiu sat each year for the recruitment test of the local cotton mills but never gained a place. In 1948 when the CCP took over Qingdao, she tried again and was admitted at the age of thirteen to State Number Six Cotton Mill. Hao Jianxiu devoted herself wholeheartedly, some say obsessively, to her work. Determined to find the most advanced and economical sequence of movements for mill workers, she practiced time-motion studies at work, home, and play. First, Hao Jianxiu would learn from certain workers the movements they were especially good at, then rationalize them into a system that could save mill workers a great deal of time and energy. A lot of workers' time was wasted in rejoining broken yarn. Hao Jianxiu tried to figure out why the yarns broke in the first place. She went on to discover that there was substantially less breakage if the room was kept clean and the mills cleared frequently of fluff. Her methodology soon attracted the attention of the Textile Workers' Trade Union. Chen Shaomin (*q.v.*), who organized the All-China Textile Workers' Trade Union in 1950 and was elected its chair, and Zhang Qinqiu (*q.v.*), deputy minister of Textile Industry, recognized Hao Jianxiu's contribution to the industry and propagated it nationally in textile mills. It was called the Hao Jianxiu Work Method or Hao Jianxiu Fine-Yarn Work Method (Hao Jianxiu [xisha] gongzuofa), and she was named a National Industrial Model Worker in 1951.

Hao Jianxiu joined the CCP in 1954 and the same year won a scholarship to the Intensive High School for Workers and Peasants of the People's University (Renmin daxue gongnong sucheng zhongxue) in Beijing. After completing four years of high school, she continued her studies at East China Textile Engineering Institute in Shanghai, graduating in 1962. Hao Jianxiu returned to work as a technician in her old mill, State Number Six Cotton Mill in Qingdao, and two years later, in 1964, was elected to the Central Committee of the Communist Youth League. Her big chance came in

1965 when she was made deputy director of Number Eight Cotton Mill in Qingdao. Once more Hao Jianxiu made innovations, improving the machinery and using a glue made of algae instead of starch on the cotton thread, thus saving a great deal of rice or other cereals to make the starch. Hao Jianxiu also improved the ventilation system of the mill, allowing it to operate at lower temperatures better suited both to the equipment and workers. With the start of the Cultural Revolution, she headed the mill's Revolutionary Committee, effectively taking charge of running mill operations.

During the Cultural Revolution, Hao Jianxiu rose quickly through the political ranks. In 1971 she was vice-chair of the Revolutionary Committee of Qingdao municipality in what was essentially a leadership position. The next year, 1972, Hao Jianxiu was elected chair of the Qingdao Municipality Federation of Trade Unions and only one year later upgraded to the provincial level as vice-chair of the Shandong Province Federation of Trade Unions. In 1975, she headed the Women's Federation in Shandong Province.

After the Cultural Revolution, Hao Jianxiu did not suffer the adverse effects experienced by many of those who had been rapidly promoted during that period. Instead, her rise continued through the 1970s and 1980s. In 1978, she was made vice-minister of Textile Industry and in 1981 promoted to full minister. At the same time, in the arena of mass organizations, Hao Jianxiu also rose in the ACWF, from director of Shandong Province to national vice-chair in 1978. In the party machine she made spectacular advances, being one of an elite of women to be admitted to the CCP Central Committee (1977–92) and, from 1982, made an alternate member and then a member of the powerful secretariat of the CCP Central Committee. In 1987, her career leapt again when Hao Jianxiu was entrusted with the planning of the country: she was made a senior engineer and vice-minister in charge of the State Planning Commission.

Throughout her long career as a labor model and official of the PRC, Hao Jianxiu made frequent visits abroad. Her first trip was to Albania as leader of a delegation of women workers; she later visited Spain, Romania, Yugoslavia, New Zealand, and Australia.

As the creator of the Hao Jianxiu Work Method, Hao Jianxiu symbolized a new breed of workers, intent on inventing new ways to improve production. She was extolled as an illustrious example of how workers could innovate and solve problems relating to their own work. Naturally, this carried profound political significance in the PRC, and her political career no doubt benefited because of what she symbolized. In view of her rapid promotion during the Cultural Revolution, seemingly her story resonated with the times: an illiterate cotton mill worker with little education could manage factories. Her political rise facilitated the plan to empower women and youth. The fact that Hao Jianxiu continued to rise after the Cultural Revolution indicates that she had not closely allied with the rebels. She is one of a few elite women who rose to full ministership and joined the Central Committee of the CCP in the 1980s. Her membership of the secretariat of that committee signifies that Hao Jianxiu was awarded even more power.

Nothing is known of her personal life.

Lily Xiao Hong LEE

Bartke, Wolfgang. *Biographical Dictionary and Analysis of China's Party Leadership, 1922–1988*. Munich: Saur, 1990.

Song Ruizhi, ed. "Hao Jianxiu xisha gongzuofa." *Zhongguo funüwenhua tonglan*. Jinan: Shandong wenyi chubanshe, 1995, 377–79.

Zhongguo renmin dacidian: Xianren dang zheng jun lingdao renwu juan. Shanghai: Shanghai cishu chubanshe and Waiwen chubanshe, 1989, 261.

He Jiesheng: *see* **Zhong Yuzheng**

He Ruijian: *see* **He Xiangning**

He Xiangning

He Xiangning, 1878–1972, born He Ruijian to a wealthy Hong Kong family, also known as Shuangqing Louzhu; she was a painter, poet, and revolutionary.

Her family was originally from Nanhai County, Guangdong Province, but her father, He Binghuan, went to Macao and Hong Kong where he built up a lucrative business in tea and real estate. Unimpressed by the wealth of her surroundings, from a young age He Xiangning cared only for learning. Her father agreed to her request that she be allowed to study in the private school he set up for her brothers, and He Xiangning became a serious student. When her father ordered her feet to be bound, she continued to study on her own, using her brothers' books and asking questions of the tutor through her maid or brothers. He Xiangning fiercely and successfully resisted all attempts to bind her feet, and it was because of her "big feet" that a match was made for her with Liao Zhongkai (1877–1925), a young man from a Chinese American family who wished to marry a woman with unbound feet.

Liao Zhongkai was of Hakka stock, born in California, and educated at Queen's College in Hong Kong. Theirs was a traditional marriage in the sense that it was arranged, but He Xiangning was pleased when Liao Zhongkai supported her pursuit of knowledge, supplying her with books and magazines and often explaining things she did not fully understand. Like her, Liao Zhongkai loved art and passed on to his wife all that he learned from his art teacher. They also shared a love for China and a sense of mission for its salvation. The two married in October 1897 and their first home was a room on the roof of Liao Zhongkai's uncle's house, which they named Shuangqing lou (Terrace of the two pures). He Xiangning called herself Shuangqing Louzhu (Mistress of the terrace of the two pures); her album of poetry and painting also bears that name.

He Xiangning in turn supported her husband's patriotic desire to study in Japan: topping up personal savings with the sale of pieces of her jewelry, she provided more than 3,000 silver dollars for this purpose. Liao left for Japan in November 1902 and He Xiangning followed him in January 1903. Upon arrival in Tokyo, she enrolled in the preparatory school of Tokyo Women's Normal School, and the young couple quickly became involved with other young Chinese committed to the revolutionary movement. After meeting Dr. Sun Yat-sen (1866–1925) in 1903, at his request they established a network among the Chinese students in preparation for the revolution; under the supervision of the young revolutionary Huang Xing they learned how to shoot firearms. He Xiangning rented a house as a respectable "front" for the clandestine operations of Sun Yat-sen's Tongmenghui and embarked uncomplainingly upon the completely new experience of housework, including carrying water. She returned to Hong Kong to give birth to a daughter (Liao Mengxing, *q.v.*), whom she left in the care of her family.

He Xiangning was one of the earliest members of Sun Yat-sen's Tongmenghui, preceding even her husband, who was at that time in Hong Kong, and one of the first women members. Seeing a need for someone to design flags and emblems for the revolutionary army, after she finished her studies at the preparatory school in 1906, He Xiangning entered a Tokyo art school where twice a week she learned painting from an imperial artist named Tanaka (Tianzhong laizhang). During these years in Tokyo as she took part in much of the propaganda work and designed, embroidered, and sewed revolutionary army flags and emblems, He Xiangning also gave birth to her son Liao Chengzhi (1908–1983). She returned to Hong Kong in 1911 after graduation from art school.

Within three years, however, He Xiangning and her husband were back in Japan with Sun Yat-sen, this time in exile following Yuan Shikai's betrayal of the 1911 Revolution. They returned to Shanghai in 1916 to revive the revolutionary cause, and when Sun Yat-sen organized a military government to oppose the northern warlords he appointed Liao Zhongkai to important portfolios in his new Guangdong government. He Xiangning's not insignificant contribution to the war effort was to persuade the commanders of seven navy gunboats to take their vessels to Guangzhou. There, she joined with Song Qingling (*q.v.*) in initiating an association called Women Devoted to the Needs of Soldiers Leaving for War (Nüjie chuzheng junren weilaohui) to raise funds, provide clothing, and supply medicine. As part of her fundraising efforts, she sold many of her paintings, which at that time were greatly influenced by the Lingnan school of painting.

He Xiangning never flinched from danger. When her husband and Sun Yat-sen disappeared after one of Sun's generals started an insurgence in 1922, she sent her children to Hong Kong so as to better work for the rescue of the two men. He Xiangning arranged for Sun Yat-sen, who was safe on a navy ship, to be reunited with Song Qingling, whom she found hiding in a friend's house, recuperating from a miscarriage. With great difficulty, He Xiangning also gained the release of her husband, who escaped re-arrest by the narrowest of margins.

She and her husband were involved at the highest level in Sun Yat-sen's attempts to ally with the Soviet Union: Liao Zhongkai met unofficially with the Soviet representatives Joffe and Borodin and He Xiangning befriended Borodin's wife. As one of three women delegates at the first meeting of Sun Yat-sen's KMT in 1924, He Xiangning initiated a proposal for the "complete equality of women with regard to legal, social, economic, and educational rights." She was later appointed as the minister for Women in the Central Government and in this capacity organized the first International Women's Day rally on 8 March. He Xiangning established hospitals for the poor, especially the delivery of babies and postnatal care, and initiated evening schools for women workers in Guangzhou. After Sun Yat-sen fell ill in Beijing, where he had been invited to form a united government, he instructed Liao Zhongkai to remain in Guangdong with the KMT government. He Xiangning, however, went to Beijing; she witnessed the will of Sun Yat-sen, who asked her to take care of Song Qingling after his death. He Xiangning joined with Liao Zhongkai and Song Qingling in remaining firm to Sun's policies when the right wing of the KMT wished to reverse them. He Xiangning narrowly escaped bullets when her husband was assassinated in August 1925.

Despite the murder, He Xiangning was not intimidated and continued to write articles and give speeches to promote Sun Yat-sen's ideal, often declaring that though neither she nor her husband were communists the KMT must unite with the CCP. He Xiangning confronted Chiang Kai-shek (1887–1975) when he ordered the arrest of communist leaders, including Zhou Enlai (1898–1976), managing to obtain their release. She also spoke passionately against Chiang Kai-shek when he proposed to go against Sun Yat-sen's policies and expel the communists. However, He Xiangning threw her support behind him when Chiang Kai-shek began the Northern Expedition and selected sixteen nurses trained in her nursing school for the families of soldiers (Junren jiashu funü jiuhu chuanxiao) to accompany the army.

As a minister in the KMT government, He Xiangning went to Wuhan when the government moved there and soon found herself once again opposed to Chiang Kai-shek, who broke with the Wuhan government. When, however, its leader Wang Jingwei also joined Chiang Kai-shek in 1931, she went abroad, traveling to Europe via Hong Kong, Singapore, Malaya (part of present-day Malaysia), and the Philippines and spent time in England, France, and Germany. He Xiangning returned to China as a patriotic gesture in response to the Japanese invasion of northeast China (Manchuria), reaching Shanghai in November 1931. But she immediately made her stance clear, contacting Song Qingling, publicizing in the press her determination to resist the Japanese, openly refusing to join Chiang Kai-shek's government (an uncompromising attitude that she retained for the rest of her life), and sending to Chiang Kai-shek and his generals women's clothing accompanied by a scornful poem. He Xiangning also used her home as a base from which to organize help for the military and relief for war refugees after Japan attacked Shanghai in January 1932. She visited army officers known from her Guangdong days on the battlefront and wrote in her inimitable style many poems to encourage them. Her poetry was stirring and forceful, capable of also awakening the masses to patriotic ideas. In cooperation with other well-known artists, she painted many works that sold at high prices to aid the national salvation effort. Her art advanced during this period to a higher level, characterized by great energy and passion, her strokes confident and forceful.

During the 1930s, the KMT government took many political prisoners, some of whom they executed without trial. One of those arrested was He Xiangning's son Liao Chengzhi, who had joined the CCP in Europe and returned to China as an underground worker. In concert with Song Qingling and with the help of many old friends, He Xiangning finally managed to have him and several other political prisoners freed. She participated, along with other members of the KMT left, in political activities aligned to the CCP, for instance, endorsing the latter's declaration calling for the cooperation of all parties to fight against the common enemy and rescue of the "Seven

Virtuous Ones" (see Song Qingling and Shi Liang). During this period, He Xiangning successfully urged the KMT government to re-inter the remains of her husband next to those of Sun Yat-sen in Nanjing.

When war was declared on Japan in July 1937, He Xiangning again opened her home as a center for national salvation efforts and relief activities. Unwell herself, she sent her daughter Liao Mengxing to represent her and make speeches at many meetings. Placing special importance on involving the housewives of Shanghai—looked down upon, they "thought of themselves as useless"— He Xiangning inspired the women to make one thousand quilted vests for soldiers within a few weeks, thereby both realizing duty to their country and demonstrating their own strength. Shanghai soon fell to the Japanese, and she joined those living in the concessions in their escape to Hong Kong. There, He Xiangning wrote a series of articles, some in support and others critically assessing KMT policies, and made constructive suggestions. She joined with Song Qingling in leading the women of Hong Kong in the war effort and also utilized her own tremendous influence among overseas Chinese all over the world to raise funds. Refugees from nearby Guangdong became one of the main focuses of He Xiangning's attention. With the fall of Hong Kong to the Japanese on Christmas Day 1941, He Xiangning and many of her friends found themselves to be among the more than eight hundred people harboring anti-Japanese sentiment that the CCP rescued and evacuated.

For the remainder of the war, she lived in straitened circumstances in Guilin and elsewhere in Guangxi, surviving on the sale of her paintings and whatever her small farm could produce. Chiang Kai-shek sent her a check for one million yuan, but He Xiangning sent it straight back. Despite the harshness of her life, she wrote more poetry, expressing patriotism and confidence in the outcome of the war. With the end of World War II, with China clearly on the verge of civil war, He Xiangning wrote articles promoting peace, rebuking Chiang Kai-shek's provocative stance, and criticizing the Americans for providing Chiang with huge loans for his fight against the CCP. In 1948 in Hong Kong, she and a number of members of the KMT left, including Li Jishen, Zhu Yunshan, Cai Tingkai, and Zhu Xuefan, formed the Revolutionary Committee of the KMT (Guomindang geming weiyuanhui) with the intention of distancing themselves from Chiang Kai-shek while confirming the legacy of Sun Yat-sen and his party. He Xiangning was an important member of this committee from its inception and as a woman of high status was invited by the CCP to go to Beijing in April 1949 to participate in the work of building the new nation.

In the 1950s, as chair of the Committee on Overseas Chinese Affairs (Huaqiao shiwu weiyuanhui), she made broadcasts and speeches and wrote many articles: He Xiangning became known as the "Mother of Overseas Chinese." She pointed out that a stronger China could help the position of Chinese in other countries and that China would support the Chinese outside China—although this position was not taken in later years by the government. During her ten years in the post, He Xiangning initiated several policies: giving returned overseas Chinese and families of overseas Chinese equal treatment with Chinese citizens, ordering no infringement on or interference with the use of money sent from overseas, encouraging overseas Chinese to form investment companies in China. As a result of such policies, the number of overseas Chinese returning to China and their children coming to China for study increased. Many returned overseas Chinese were sent to farms or work in forestry or other collectives. Preparatory schools were also set up for young Chinese returning to China to study, such as Jinan University in Guangzhou and Huaqiao University in Quanzhou.

He Xiangning stopped working in 1959 at the age of eighty, having served as honorary chair of the ACWF, deputy chair of CPPCC, deputy head of NPC, chair of the KMT Revolutionary Committee, and chair of the Association of Artists. Her health deteriorated in her nineties and she died of pneumonia in 1972 at the age of ninety-four. He Xiangning was buried alongside Liao Zhongkai in Nanjing.

Lily Xiao Hong LEE

He Xiangning. *Huiyi Sun Zhongshan he Liao Zhongkai*. Beijing: Sanlian shudian, 1978.
———. *Shuangqing shi hua ji*. Beijing: Renmin meishu chubanshe, 1982.
Huiyi yu huainian—jinian geming laoren He Xiangning shishi shi zhounian. Beijing: Beijing chubanshe, 1982.
Li Yong, Wen Lequn, and Wang Yunsheng. *He Xiangning zhuan*. Beijing: Zhongguo huaqiao chuban gongsi, 1993.
Liao Mengxing. *Wo de muqin He Xiangning*. Hong Kong: Chaoyang chubanshe, 1973.
Liu Shaotang, ed. "He Xiangning." In *Minguo renwu xiaozhuan*, vol. 5. Taipei: Zhuanji wenxue chubanshe, 1982, 68–72.
Qian Jiaju. "Zatan lishi renwu." *Zhuanji wenxue*, 55, no. 6 (1992): 46–48.
Shao Mingxian. *He Xiangning zhuan*. Beijing: Beijing chubanshe, 1994.
Snow, Helen. *Women in Modern China*. The Hague and Paris: Mouton Press, 1967, 99–109.
Soong Ching Ling [Song Qingling]. "Ho Hsiang-ning: A Staunch Revolutionary, 1877–1972)." *China Reconstructs*, 22, no. 1 (January 1973): 4–6.
Zhonggong dangshi renwu zhuan, vol. 36. Xi'an: Shaanxi renmin chubanshe, 1980–96, 287–354.

He Zehui

He Zehui, b. 1914, in Suzhou, Jiangsu Province, was one of China's earliest nuclear physicists.

Her family was scholarly and liberal minded, originally from Lingshi, Shanxi Province. Her grandmother Xie Changda was an enlightened woman who advocated equality for women and established Suzhou Zhenghua Girls' School. Her father, He Cheng, studied in Japan as a youth, joined the Tongmenghui, and actively participated in the 1911 Revolution.

He Zehui attended Zhenghua Girls' School, where she developed a wide range of interests and was an excellent all-around student. In 1932 she enrolled in the Physics Department of Tsinghua [Qinghua] University, a courageous move in a society prejudiced against women. He Zehui worked hard and under the dual supervision of Wu Youxun (1897–1977) and Ren Zhigong (1906–1995) completed an excellent undergraduate thesis. He Zehui then won financial assistance from Shanxi Province to go overseas to pursue further study in Germany in the Industrial Physics Department of Technische Hochschule, Charlottenburg, Berlin. She gained a doctorate in Engineering in 1940, the title of her dissertation being "A New Precise and Simple Method of Measuring the Speed of Flying Bullets."

With the outbreak of World War II, He Zehui remained in Germany where she researched magnetic materials at the Weak Electricity Current Research Office of the Siemens Company in Berlin (1940–42). From there the scientist moved to the Nuclear Physics Research Institute of the Wilhelminische Akademie in Heidelberg (1943–46) and conducted the first observation of the elastic collision between positrons and electrons using a magnetic field cloud chamber. Her research results were reported at an Anglo-French conference on cosmic rays held in Bristol in 1945 and an international conference on basic particles and cryogenics held at Cambridge in 1946.

In spring in Paris, He Zehui married Qian Sanqiang (Tsian San-Tsiang, 1913–1992) with whom she had a son and daughter. He Zehui then worked at the Nuclear Chemistry Laboratory of the French Academy and the Curie Institute (1946–48). At the latter institution, He Zehui, Qian Sanqiang, and two postgraduate students—R. Chastel and L. Vigneron—made an extremely important discovery: ternary and quarternary fission of uranium. After the discovery of nuclear fission in 1938, physicists generally believed that the nucleus of a heavy atom split into two lighter nuclei, and the prediction of the possibility of ternary fission had not attracted a great deal of attention. He Zehui and Qian Sanqiang used a nuclear emulsion technique to study the fission caused by the attack of slow neutrons and proved the existence of ternary fission from the fission traces. They also explained the theory of the mechanics of ternary fission, predicting the mass spectrum of the split pieces. However, it was He Zehui who discovered quarternary fission. Ternary fission and the explanation of how it worked was not recognized by physicists until the late 1960s, that is, more than twenty years after the discoveries of He Zehui and Qian Sanqiang. Multifission was not proved in laboratory experiments until the 1970s.

In 1948 He Zehui and Qian Sanqiang returned to China with their six-month-old daughter. He Zehui was immediately recruited as the only full-time research fellow of the Nuclear Research Institute of the National Peking Research Academy. After the founding of the PRC in 1949, He Zehui worked as a research fellow of the Modern Physics Institute of the Chinese Academy of Sciences (1950–58); research fellow (1958–73) and deputy director (1963–73) of the Atomic Energy Institute; and research fellow (from 1973) and deputy director (1973–84) of the High Energy Physics Institute of the Chinese Academy of Sciences. In 1981, she became an academician of the Chinese Academy of Sciences.

Nuclear emulsion, first developed in the 1940s, is a nuclear measurement technique very useful in experimental particle physics and nuclear physics. The research group that He Zehui led succeeded in 1956 in making nuclear emulsion of a quality comparable to the most advanced in the world, thus making China one of the few countries in the world able to produce it. For this effort, in that year she and her team won Third Place in the Chinese Academy of Sciences Science Award and the First National Science Award, with their "Research into the Process of Preparing Nuclear Emulsoid."

He Zehui led the Neutron Physics Research Office of the Modern Physics Institute (later renamed Atomic Energy Institute) for many years from 1956 on. She made great contributions to the establishment of basic laboratory infrastructure, the design and manufacture of measuring instruments, the supervision of experimental research into neutron physics and fission physics, and to the solution of technical problems encountered in the design and manufacture of nuclear weapons and in on-site tests. From 1973 on, she promoted research on cosmic ray super high energy physics and high energy astrophysics.

He Zehui disappeared from public view during the Cultural Revolution, but in 1978 was appointed to the Fifth CPPCC. That same year she made her first visit to Germany after thirty years when she became a member of a government delegation; He Zehui visited Copenhagen in 1953 as a delegate to the World Democratic Women's Conference. Throughout her career, she published dozens of papers yet placed little value on personal fame. He Zehui is considered to be a patriot who devoted her life to science, living a simple life and always nurturing young researchers.

WANG Bing
(Translated by Yan Qian)

Gu Yifan. "He Zehui." In *Zhongguo xiandai kexuejia zhuanji*, vol. 6. Beijing: Kexue chubanshe, 1994, 1002–12.
Ho Zah-Wei. "Elastic Collisions between Positrons and Electrons and Annihilation of Positrons." *Physical Society of Cambridge Conference Report* (1947): 78.
Tsian San-Tsiang, Ho Zah-Wei, R. Chastel, and L.Vigneron. "Nouveaux Modes de Fission de l'Uranium: Tripartition et quadripartition." *Journal de Physique*, 8, no. 8 (1947): 165, 200.
Zhao Zhongyao, He Zehui, Yang Chengzhong, eds. *Yuanzi neng de yuanli he yingyong*. Beijing: Kexue chubanshe, 1956, rev. edn., 1964.
Zhonghua quanguo fulian. *Zhongguo nüyuanshi*. Shenyang: Liaoning renmin chubanshe, 1995, 363–67.

He Zizhen

He Zizhen, 1910–1984, née He Guiyuan, of Yongxin County, Jiangxi Province, was the second wife of Mao Zedong (1893–1976). She was one of the thirty women who went with the First Front Red Army on the Chinese communists' Long March of 1934–35.

Born into an impoverished gentry family, He Zizhen received an education when her parents sent her to the free missionary school in Yongxin. She was the second of four children, all of whom became active revolutionaries: her younger brother died as a boy while acting as a courier for the communists, and she and her two remaining siblings were early members of the CCP. Her older brother He Minxue (1908–1983?) rose to the position of deputy governor of Fujian Province after 1949; her sister He Yi (d. 1950) was killed in a car accident while trying to locate He Zizhen's first-born son.

He Zizhen joined the Communist Youth League in 1925 and the following year was made a full member of the CCP. Her first official position was head of the County Women's Bureau, and she also acted as assistant secretary of the Youth Bureau. By the age of seventeen, He Zizhen was traveling alone about the countryside as a propaganda worker and fought in the Yongxin Uprising of summer 1927 during which she is believed to have shot and killed two KMT soldiers. He Zizhen fled Yongxin soon after and became a communist partisan, making her way first to Jinggangshan, the mountainous region separating Hunan and Jiangxi Provinces. When Mao Zedong made Jinggangshan his revolutionary base later that year after the failure of his Autumn Harvest Uprising in Changsha, He Zizhen continued to work as a partisan for a time, taking part in daring reconnaissance missions and raids on local landlords. However, after she and Mao became lovers late in the year or early 1928, He Zizhen confined her activities to clerical work, acting as Mao's confidential secretary and sometime nurse until late 1934. As appears to have been the case with the woman still Mao's wife at that time, Yang Kaihui (*q.v.*), He Zizhen also forsook her own revolutionary career and became a childbearing wife to the revolutionary leader known even then as Chairman Mao.

Her first child was a girl, born somewhere in Fujian Province some time in late 1929 and left with a peasant family when the Red Army moved on. Her second child, a boy named Xiao Mao (Little Mao), was born in Changting, Fujian Province, in spring or summer 1932. In early spring 1934, she gave birth to a premature baby boy who died soon after birth. When He Zizhen set out on the Long March in October as part of the General Medical Unit, she was already about five months pregnant. Just before leaving, He Zizhen consigned her son Xiao Mao to the care of her sister He Yi, who was married to Mao's youngest brother, Mao Zetan (1905–1935). Mao Zetan was killed soon after, however, and the child was apparently passed on to someone else; in any event, Xiao Mao was never found despite official and unofficial efforts over many years to track him down.

On the Long March, He Zizhen was not assigned any duties and traveled separately from Mao, having only infrequent contact with him. She gave birth to her fourth baby, possibly a girl, under battle conditions in perhaps February 1935 somewhere in Guizhou. The baby was effectively abandoned, as was the baby of Zeng Yu, the first to be born on the Long March. He Zizhen's baby is said to have been left with an old and desperately poor Miao peasant woman. Two months later, He Zizhen was badly wounded, spattered with shrapnel from a bomb dropped by a KMT airplane, and was carried for some time by stretcher.

She had her fifth baby, a girl whom she named Jiaojiao, in October 1936 in Bao'an, and spent several settled and contented months there before the communists moved to Yan'an. He Zizhen was exempted from work in Yan'an because of her shrapnel wounds and newborn baby. She attempted to follow a university course but soon fell by the wayside; her health was fragile and she and Mao argued with increasing frequency. In summer 1937, Mao is believed to have been in the throes of an affair with Wu Guanghui (Lily Wu), who acted as an interpreter for the American journalist Agnes Smedley (1893–1950). After a humiliating confrontation one night with Mao, Lily Wu, and Agnes Smedley, He Zizhen decided to go to Russia "for medical treatment and to further her studies." Opinions vary as to whether He Zizhen or Mao initiated their divorce, but it is highly probable that He Zizhen was in fact exiled to Russia. Not until the following year did Jiang Qing (*q.v.*) take her place as the wife of Mao Zedong.

He Zizhen was pregnant when she left Yan'an in October 1937 and reached Moscow in January 1938, having traveled from Xi'an with Liu Ying (q.v.), and attended Oriental University (Dongfang daxue) for a short time. In May she gave birth to her sixth and last child, a boy, who contracted pneumonia and died. Jiaojiao, then about four years old, was sent to Moscow to be cared for by He Zizhen, as were Mao's two teenage sons by his former wife Yang Kaihui. They remained safe from German air raids, having been evacuated in 1941 to the textile city of Ivanovo when hostilities broke out between Russia and Nazi Germany. That winter, however, when Jiaojiao nearly died from pneumonia, an extremely agitated He Zizhen became so aggressive toward Russian authorities that she was confined to a sanitarium to undergo "treatment for mental illness." Labeled schizophrenic, He Zizhen spent four years in the institution and was only released in 1946 after repeated requests from a visiting Chinese physician.

After returning to China in summer 1947, she went to southern China, living at various times in Shanghai, Nanchang, and Fuzhou. He Zizhen lived alone, Jiaojiao having become part of the Mao-Jiang Qing household and called Li Min. He Zizhen's mental health remained under a cloud and she was not appointed to any official posts, receiving instead comfortable financial support from the state. He Zizhen was not harmed during the Cultural Revolution, and is said to have been summoned by Mao to a clandestine meeting on Lushan in 1959 or 1961, the first time since 1937; they never met again.

In 1973 He Zizhen's first child, the daughter born in Fujian in 1929, was said to have been found. Desultory attempts were made to bring together He Zizhen and this woman, Yang Yuehua, but they never met. Although He Zizhen suffered a stroke in 1977 that left her partially paralyzed and bedridden, she was able to travel to Beijing in 1979 to acknowledge her election to the Fifth CPPCC and view the embalmed body of Mao Zedong. He Zizhen spent her last years in hospital in Shanghai and died on 19 April 1984. Her ashes—and the piece of shrapnel found when her body was cremated—were interred in Babaoshan Revolutionary Cemetery in Beijing.

He Zizhen's was the saddest of the Long March women's lives, and her misfortune may well be said to lie in her having been the object of Mao Zedong's desire. She gave birth six times and appears to have suffered repeatedly from postnatal depression; late in life He Zizhen revealed that she had also had four miscarriages. The wounds received during the Long March caused her lifelong pain, and the unsubstantiated diagnosis of schizophrenia that dogged her from the time she was thirty reeks of expediency. Worse, however, was her inviolable status of "first wife": having belonged to Mao Zedong, He Zizhen was unapproachable by any other man and thus condemned to a lifetime of loneliness after he tired of her. In this, He Zizhen epitomized the traditional chaste widow.

Sue WILES

Gao Shuli. "Yang Yuehua fangwen ji." *Qianshao yuekan* (September 1995): 49–50.

Guo Chen. *Jinguo liezhuan: Hong yifangmianjun sanshiwei changzheng nühongjun shengping shiji.* Beijing: Nongcun duwu chubanshe, 1986, 193–201.

Lee, Lily Xiao Hong, and Sue Wiles. *Women of the Long March*. Sydney: Allen & Unwin, 1999.
Liu Fulang. *The Analysis of Mao Tse-tung's Personality*. Hong Kong: Union Press, 1973.
Qiu Zhizhuo. "Guangrong er kankede yi sheng." In *Hongjun nüyingxiong zhuan*, eds. Liaowang bianjibu. Beijing: Xinhua chubanshe, 1986, 83–101.
Salisbury, Harrison E. *The Long March: The Untold Story*. New York: Harper & Row, 1985.
Snow, Helen Foster. *Inside Red China*. 1977 reprint [with a new preface and biographical notes by the author]. New York: Da Capo Press, 1939, 167–91.
Zhonggong dangshi renwu zhuan, vol. 45. Xi'an: Shaanxi renmin chubanshe, 1980–96, 281–301.

Hiu Wan, Ven.

Ven. Hiu Wan [Xiao Yun (Hsiao-yün fa-shih)], b. 1913, in Kuang-chou [Guangzhou], Kuang-tung [Guangdong] Province, is a Buddhist nun, artist, and educator.

Her family name was Yu [You] and pet name was A-sung [Asong]. When starting school, she was given the name Wan-fen and also used the name Yün-shan [Yunshan], with variant characters, one meaning "graceful coral," the other "cloudy mountain." Yün-shan was the eldest daughter and had eleven brothers and sisters (including the children of her father's concubine), five of whom died young. At around the age of five or six, Yün-shan was enrolled in an old-style private school to begin formal studies, reading the Four Books of Confucianism and classical literature, both poetry and prose.

Her father was a merchant who also wrote plays, and the family was quite well off. When Yün-shan was still quite young, their circumstances changed suddenly, however, and her mother's evident distress moved her. Conscious now of the transience of worldly things, Yün-shan would sit at night on the flat roof of their house, pondering the inscrutabilities of life. Although having lost interest in her studies by the time of junior high school, at the age of eighteen she accepted the opportunity to take a full-time course at the Li-ching [Lijing] College of Art in Hong Kong. The young woman did, however, continue studying classical literature with prominent teachers. Yün-shan went on to do postgraduate research and at the same time took lessons from Kao Chien-fu [Gao Jianfu], founder of the Ling-nan school of painting, and taught at St. Paul's and Li-tse [Lize] junior high schools. After seven years of teaching and studying painting, Yün-shan set off alone for Kuei-lin [Guilin], seeking landscapes to paint; she also wanted to see for herself the hardships caused by the Sino-Japanese War (1937–45).

In Kuei-lin the artist admired the magnificent landscape and sketched from life despite frequent air-raid warnings. She was still in Kuei-lin when the Japanese captured Hong Kong in 1941, and so remained in China to embark on a period of traveling. Yün-shan went first to Ch'ü-chiang [Qujiang] and paid respects to Ch'an [Chan] Master Hsü Yün [Xu Yun] at Nan-hua Monastery. She then went to Ch'ang-sha [Changsha], climbing Chu-jung [Zhurong] Peak on Mt. Heng to see the sun rising over a boundless sea of clouds. While in Ch'ang-sha she painted *Three Great Victories at Ch'ang-sha* as a contribution to the war effort. Yün-shan went to Ssu-ch'uan [Sichuan], where the Overseas Chinese Association in Ch'ung-ch'ing [Chongqing] organized an exhibition of her work, which was favorably received. Through high-level personal contacts, she was able to obtain the transport necessary for her to paint *Climbing Mt. Emei to Paint the Ice and Snow* and to climb Mt. Ch'ing-ch'eng [Qingcheng].

In Ch'eng-tu [Chengdu], Yün-shan formally embraced Buddhism, spending time in the monasteries on Mt. Ling-yüan [Lingyuan]. At daybreak one morning, she took a chronological account of the life of Ch'an Master Han Shan (1546–1623) and climbed to the Thousand Buddha Pagoda to meditate to the sounds of the temple gong and chanting. Yün-shan wanted to take monastic vows and devote her life to education, cultural, and artistic work. She decided to travel through Southeast Asia to India, the homeland of Buddhism, and after traveling the world to become a nun.

Yün-shan returned home at the end of the war in early summer 1945 to reunite with her family. Overwhelmed at the devastation caused by wartime bombing, she painted a large picture with the following inscription: "Despite the wind and rain they seek their old home—/Where will returning swallows find the traces of their nest?"

While the people were anxious to rebuild their lives and earn a living, as an artist Hiu Wan (then still known as Yu Yün-shan) thought only of continuing to paint and journey on to India. She was, however, obliged to accept an offer of employment with Kuang-tung Provincial Archives for a time. Hiu Wan then went to P'an-yü [Panyu] County, painting *Empress Yang's Ancestral Shrine*, *Curious Rocks on Mt. Ya-men*, and other sites associated with the decline of the Sung dynasty. She gave her mother the money she received when Kuang-tung Archives Press published the paintings in 1945 as a special volume.

In early summer 1946, Hiu Wan worked as head teacher in the Third High School for Overseas Chinese in Lung-chou [Longzhou], Kuang-hsi [Guangxi] Province. Grateful for the assistance during those early days of the civil war, members of the school assisted Hiu Wan on her way through the Chen-nan Pass, whence she traveled by plane to Saigon via Hanoi. An exhibition of her paintings was held while Hiu Wan was in Saigon. Traveling to Cambodia, she joined a research team from the Museum of Far Eastern History in Paris, which gave her the chance to study the remarkable ruins of Angkor Wat and sketch some of the ancient Buddhist sculptures there. From Cambodia Hiu Wan made her way to Singapore and Malaysia and thence by steamboat to Calcutta to spend four years at Tagore University, the first two researching Indian art. Her study of the Buddhist art of India took her to Ajantå to make copies of the murals, and she visited many other ancient Buddhist sites. (Her book *Indian Art* is in its third edition.) During her last two years at Tagore University, Hiu Wan was a visiting lecturer and once traveled up to Darjeeling, where she painted *In the Mountains of Snow*, a large horizontal scroll depicting the Himalayas.

In winter 1951, Hiu Wan returned to Hong Kong and taught at Pao-chüeh [Baojue] Junior High School and established Yün-men [Yunmen] College. Together with the lawyer Chao Ping [Zhao Bing] and the director of the New Asia Academy T'ang Chün-i [Tang Junyi], Hiu Wan founded the magazine *The Source* (Yüan-ch'üan [Yuanquan]). This effort, which sought to harmonize literature and art with Buddhist and Confucian precepts, ran for four years. Then in 1955, wanting to gain a better understanding of cultural education in other countries, Hiu Wan set off to travel the world.

Her plan was to visit universities, museums, convents, and monasteries. During the three years traversing Europe and America, she visited the major universities, talking with teachers and students. Hiu Wan thus learned much that proved to be extremely valuable in planning her own educational projects. She passed through more than thirty countries, extending her range of contacts with local educational and cultural circles by arranging exhibitions of her paintings. The letters of introduction she carried secured her the assistance of a number of scholars in staging an extremely successful exhibition of her work at Freiburg University. Hiu Wan made several visits to Germany, where she met the philosopher Martin Heidegger, who gave her a copy of his booklet *The Pathway* (Der Feldweg).

Hiu Wan spent about a month in Greece investigating the ruins of ancient culture there. She visited the birthplace of Homer and the site of Plato's Academy, with its remarkable petrified forest. On an island in the Aegean Sea, Hiu Wan painted *Ancient Moon above the Bay*, and arranged for an exhibition of her paintings, this time through the Greek Department of Education. The artist stayed with the Chinese ambassador and made the acquaintance of many young people as well as scholars. Hiu Wan was intrigued one day in Athens to see someone in the street carrying a rosary. Thinking the person must be a follower of the Pure Land School, she made inquiries, only to discover that Greek people use rosaries simply as a means of calming or focusing their minds.

After this period of traveling, Hiu Wan returned to Hong Kong for the third time in her life, content with what she had experienced and learned. In 1958, after the return to Kowloon, Hiu Wan stayed once again in the Tz'u-hang [Cihang] Monastery in Shatin, this time to renounce worldly attachments and become a nun under the Ven. T'an Hsü [Tan Xu], forty-fourth patriarch of the T'ien-t'ai [Tiantai] School of Chinese Buddhism. From that time on, Ven. Hiu Wan devoted herself to a deeper study of Buddhist scripture and practiced T'ien-t'ai meditation, reflecting deeply on the idea that profound understanding of a single teaching can lead to an understanding of all teachings. This approach was very different from the contemplation of the apothegms (*hua-t'ou [huatou]*) and case histories (*kung-an [gong'an]*) of the Ch'an School that she had practiced previously. At this time, Ven. Hiu Wan often climbed the hill on Lantau Island, the birthplace of Buddhism in Hong Kong, for brief periods of secluded meditation. It is her custom still to come to Lantau Island every New Year's Eve and spend time in seclusion. When not on retreat, she helps her co-religionists with welfare work. Ven. Hiu Wan also worked to set up the T'ien-t'ai (heavenly terrace, the latter word as in a flat rooftop) Buddhist School for children fleeing the mainland after it had fallen to the communists.

Ven. Hiu Wan also founded two primary schools at this time: Hui-ch'üan [Huiquan] and Hui-jen [Huiren]. Eight years later, she took charge of the Hui-hai [Huihai] English Language High School in Shatin. At the same time, Ven. Hiu Wan set up the Association for Buddhist Art and Culture in Kowloon and gave regular monthly talks on Buddhism for the government radio station.

In 1966, she accepted an offer of employment from the Chinese Culture University (Chung-kuo wen-hua ta-hsüeh [Zhongguo wenhua daxue], at that time the College of Chinese Culture) at Huakang [Huagang] on Mt. Yang-ming, Taiwan. The founder of the university treated her with exceptional kindness, appointing her as a fully tenured professor after only two years. Ven. Hiu Wan was obliged to resign from the position in 1986, however, for by then she was busy with plans to establish her own fully accredited Buddhist university on Mt. Ta-lun [Dalun].

The more than thirty years that Ven. Hiu Wan has since lived in Taiwan have been spent on three mountains—Yang-ming, Kuang-ming [Guangming], and Ta-lun—working in education, culture, and art. She has continued to study Buddhism, emphasizing the equal importance of doctrine and meditation, believing that it is only through quiet and steady practice of meditation that one develops the ability to become truly spiritually beneficial to others. This message is disseminated through such publications as *The Source of Buddhist Meditation* and *Ch'an Poems and Ch'an Masters*.

Her first seventeen years in Taiwan (1966–83) were spent in the postgraduate Departments of Philosophy and Art at the Chinese Culture University, where she both taught and acted as supervisor for more than twelve theses. From 1968, however, Ven. Hiu Wan was involved in the training and education of young women studying Buddhism at the Lotus Buddhist Ashram, an institution attached to Yung-ming [Yongming] Temple on the lower slopes of Mt. Yang-ming. In the thirty years of its existence, this ashram has been so highly respected that it has never had to advertise for students. After managing the ashram for ten years, she received permission to register it with the Department of Education as the Sino-Indian (Hua-fan [Huafan]) Buddhist Research Institute. Ten years later, Ven. Hiu Wan went on to found Hua-fan University, the first Buddhist university in Buddhism's history in China. A technical college for the first three years of its existence, Hua-fan University then became a college of the humanities and sciences for a further three years, and finally is now a fully accredited university.

Hua-fan University is located on Mt. Ta-lun in Shih-ting [Shiding], Taipei County. Some 550 meters high, the mountain offers fresh air and spectacular views. On the hill in front of the university, Ven. Hiu Wan created the Lotus of Compassion College, where she also established the Sino-Indian Buddhist Research Institute. She thus kept her lifelong vow to neither build temples nor act as an abbess, devoting her energies instead to opening up new areas in Buddhism, education, and culture, especially in the field of Buddhist education. Ven. Hiu Wan and her students worked together to help build the University. She traveled to Singapore and Malaysia to raise funds to purchase the land while her students subsequently raised funds for building construction.

In the decade or so since the founding of Hua-fan University, Ven. Hiu Wan accomplished a great deal. Her guiding principle is "education for enlightenment," and she has shown commitment to her ideals by the work the educator has expended in realizing them. Hua-fan is well regarded throughout the world and has sister links with five universities in Japan, Australia, and the United States. Hua-fan University seeks to embody the cultural and educational spirit and ideals of five thousand years of Chinese culture and two thousand years of Chinese Buddhism. This is the significance of its name, *hua* referring to China and *fan* referring to India and Buddhism.

Many promising scholars have graduated from the Sino-Indian Buddhist Research Institute, becoming heads of monastic institutions or Buddhist colleges of their own and pursuing postgraduate research around the world. In accordance with the T'ien-t'ai attitude to education, teachers and students are expected to develop their innate nature to comprehend Buddha-dharma. Particularly, they are urged to ensure that daily conduct is not affected inappropriately by the modern world. Ven. Hiu Wan and the teachers appointed have spent more than ten years creating the "Exemplification of the Sutras," distinguishing the Lotus Ashram and the Sino-Indian Buddhist Research Institute. Their creative effort is somewhat analogous to the scriptural illustrations (*ching-pien t'u [jingbian tu]*) visible at Tun-huáng [Dunhuang].

Under the auspices of the Department of Education, a major exhibition of Buddhist art entitled *Cool Purity* (Ch'ing-liang [qingliang]) was displayed in 1998 in Taipei, T'ai-nan, and Kao-hsiung, including both modern scriptural illustrations and Ch'an paintings, and served as a retrospective exhibition commemorating Ven. Hiu Wan's seventy-one years of painting. More than eighty volumes of her writings have been published in the Flowing Light Series and another twelve volumes of her poems have been set to music. That year also saw the publication of *In Praise of the Four Sages*, an important poetic work dealing with Hsüan Tsang [Xuan Zang] (602–664), Chih I [Zhi Yi] (538–597), the Bodhisattva Avalokiteśvara (Kuan-yin), and the teachings of the Pure Land School. A second volume published the same year contains a set of ten poems under the title *Reflections on a Better World*. The poetry relates to people's feelings and the endeavor to raise the level of wisdom and compassion in the individual, a mission that is intimately connected with Ven. Hiu Wan's ideal of education for enlightenment. The poems in these two recent volumes have been set to music by the well-known composers Huang Yu-ti [Huang Youdi] and Li Chung-ho [Li Zhonghe].

On Mt. Ta-lun, Ven. Hiu Wan now calmly settles in to fulfill her destiny. Deeply moved by the landscape on her arrival long ago, she realized then that there was no further need to repeat an earlier lament on her life: "I want to flee the world but have no way to flee;/I long to enter the mountains but can find no mountains deep enough." In composing the poetry in the collection *Limpid Melodies*, Ven. Hiu Wan expressed happiness and deep sincerity for her aspirations for realizing education and the welfare of all beings. Strolling among the flowing streams, in the green groves, on the banks of the Armored Tortoise Pond, or in front of Pai Chang's [Bai Zhang] Hut, immersed in a state of Ch'an far removed from worldly thoughts, facing Mt. Ta-lun's panorama of mountain peaks among massive rocks, Ven. Hiu Wan has written: "It is not that one is deep among the mountains—the mountains themselves are deep."

On the peaks of this mountain, Ven. Hiu Wan can surely view the achievement of her goals and has at last found a place where she can rest content.

Ven. JEN HWA
(Translated by Tony Prince)

Hiu Wan. *Fo ch'an chih yüan*. Taipei: Yüan-ch'üan ch'u-pan-she, 1998.

———. *Fo-chiao lun-wen-chi*. Taipei: Yüan-ch'üan ch'u-pan-she, 1997.

———. *Hiu Wan shan-jen hua-chi*, 1, 2, 3. Taipei: Yüan-ch'üan ch'u-pan-she, 1987.

———. *Huan-yü chou-hsing ch'ien hou*, 5 vols. Taipei: Yüan-ch'üan ch'u-pan-she, 1998.

———. *Huan-yü chou-hsing san-chi*. Taipei: Yüan-ch'üan ch'u-pan-she, 1998.

———. *San-shan hsing-chi*. Taipei: Yüan-ch'üan ch'u-pan-she, 1998.

———. *Tao-hsü sui-yüeh*. Taipei: Yüan-ch'üan ch'u-pan-she, 1998.

———. *Tung-hsi-nan hsing san-chi*. Taipei: Yüan-ch'üan ch'u-pan-she, 1998.

————. *Yin-tu i-shu.* Taipei: Yüan-ch'üan ch'u-pan-she, 1994.
Tenzin Yeshe, *bhiksuni.* "Nuns in Contemporary Taiwan and Tibet." Ph.D. dissertation. Canberra: Australian National University, 2000.

Ho Zah-Wei: *see* He Zehui

Hong, Maxine Ting Ting: *see* Kingston, Maxine Hong

Hongxian Nü

Hongxian Nü, b. 1927, as Kuang Jianlian in Kaiping County, Guangdong Province, is a Guangdong (Cantonese) opera performer who specialized in *dan* (female lead) roles. Her stage name Hongxian Nü means Red-Thread Girl, that is, in folklore one who plays a role in matchmaking.

Hongxian Nü attended schools in Guangzhou and Macao as a child but, because her uncle owned an opera troupe, at the age of thirteen became apprenticed to her maternal aunt He Fulian. Hongxian Nü made her stage debut under the name Xiao Yanhong (Little Red Sparrow; red is associated in Guangdong opera tradition with success and fame).

Her fame grew after Hongxian Nü performed throughout Guangdong and Guangxi with an opera troupe under the direction of Ma Shizeng, whom Hongxian Nü later married. By the age of sixteen she played the female lead opposite him and was under instruction from the *jingju* (Beijing opera) master Wang Fuqing. Hongxian Nü adopted techniques from other regional operas, also studying older opera genre called *kunqu* and *huaju* (spoken drama); she also learned to play the piano and became interested in Western music. After 1945, the year the Sino-Japanese War ended, the opera troupe took its performances to Hong Kong, Macao, Vietnam, Singapore, Malaysia, and the Philippines. She and Ma Shizeng were in Hong Kong from the late 1940s to the early 1950s and performed *The Feisty Princess and the Ingenious Prince* (Diaoman gongzhu han fuma) and *Mad About You* (Wo wei qing kuang). Hongxian Nü organized an opera troupe called The True, the Good, and the Beautiful (Zhen shan mei) and was involved in several film productions, including one of Ba Jin's trilogy *Family*, *Spring*, and *Autumn* (Jia, Chun, Qiu). Hongxian Nü returned to Guangzhou in 1955 to join the Guangdong Opera Ensemble, the forerunner of Guangdong Province Opera Academy.

Between 1956 and the start of the Cultural Revolution, Hongxian Nü performed in *Princess Zhaojun* (Zhaojun chusai), *Guan Hanqing*, and *Li Xiangjun* and the contemporary dramas *Liu Hulan* and *Storm over a Mountain Village* (Shanxiang fengyun). In these operas, she played a variety of roles, bringing to life many different female characters of ancient and modern times. After the Cultural Revolution, Hongxian Nü remained active as a performer but also helped revise, script, direct, and perform in *Princess Zhaojun*. She was still able, at the age of fifty, to convincingly portray a nineteen-year-old princess.

Hongxian Nü courageously initiated reforms in Guangdong opera. As a performer, she carried a unique tonal quality, an extended vocal range, and a crisp and rounded tone; the unique timbre of her voice gave rise to the terms "Hong tone" and "Nü tone" (from Hongxian Nü). The Hong tone became the most popular and influential skill emulated by singers of Guangdong opera throughout Guangdong, Hong Kong, and Southeast Asia. Frequent changes in key and the peculiarities of the Cantonese dialect both present challenges to the Guangdong opera performer. Hongxian Nü changed key very naturally by means of a vocal equivalent of the cadenza, without the need for a short instrumental interlude. Because Cantonese has eight or nine tones and many words ending in gutturals and nasals—extremely difficult to hold as long notes—Guangdong opera lyrics use more words and short staccato pieces than other operas. Hongxian Nü was skillful in this regard, enunciating clearly and lightly, making fluent key changes, and creating correct rhymes, always managing to end on the right note and the right syllable even after a long and complex improvisation on a nasal or guttural sound. By trailing the last note out seemingly everlastingly, she conveyed emotion in a most satisfying way. Critics described Hongxian Nü's voice as full and strong and said she was a "dragon head with a phoenix tail," meaning that her performances were outstanding from beginning to end. Her best-known performances were in *Search Warrant for the Imperial College* (Sou shuyuan), *Guan Hanqing*, *Li Xiangjun*, *Princess Zhaojun*, and *Storm over a Mountain Village*.

Hongxian Nü attended the Sixth World Congress of Youth Festivals in 1957 and was awarded a Gold Medal. She also traveled abroad several times to perform. She has been deputy director of Guangdong Opera Academy, general art director of the Guangdong Opera Ensemble of Guangzhou, and vice-chair of the Guangdong branch of the Chinese Opera Federation. She was elected to the CPPCC and the NPC.

In 1984 Hongxian Nü gave a solo concert that was extremely well received but has appeared only occasionally on stage since her retirement in the 1990s. She now lives in Guangzhou.

Shirley Wai CHAN
(Translated by Li Sheung Yee)

Yingwen *Zhongguo funü*, ed. *Gujin zhuming funü renwu*, vol. 2. Shijiazhuang: Hebei renmin chubanshe, 1986, 1062–65.
"Hongxian Nü jiehou dai fozhu hushen." *Hong Kong Apple Daily*, 13 November 2000.
Zhongguo dabaike quanshu: Xiqu quyi. Beijing: Zhongguo dabaike quanshu chubanshe, 1989, 116.

Hou Bo

Hou Bo, b. 1924, in Xiaxian County, Shanxi Province, is a prominent official photographer, senior journalist, and member of the CCP. Hou Bo's photographs have been widely published in government newspapers and journals and acknowledged as icons of China's twentieth-century political and revolutionary history. Most of her photographs are housed in Beijing's State Archive.

Hou Bo joined the communist movement in 1938 at the age of fourteen, having become a member of the League for Self-Sacrifice and National Salvation (Xisheng jiuguo tongmenghui) in Shanxi at the age of twelve. In September, the party underground arranged for her to travel to Xi'an to join the Eighth Route Army, where she studied with the Anwu Fortress Training Group (Anwu bao qingnian xunlianban) and joined the CCP. Later that year, she traveled to Yan'an and was assigned to the Public Security Office (bao'an chu) under the supervision of Kang Sheng. Between 1939 and 1944, while working there Hou Bo also attended the Yan'an Border Region Middle School (Yan'an bianqu zhongxue), Yan'an Women's University, and Yan'an University. After graduation she was assigned work as a nurse at the Yan'an Central Hospital.

Hou Bo married Xu Xiaobing (b. 1916) in late 1942. He is a renowned photographer and documentary filmmaker who, from the late 1930s, made many seminal films for the party in Yan'an, the northeast, and Beijing, including *Yan'an and the Eighth Route Army* (Yan'an yu balujun), *The Democratic Northeast* (Minzhu dongbei), and *Land Reform* (Tudi gaige). Xu Xiaobing introduced Hou Bo to the medium of photography.

At the end of the Sino-Japanese War in 1945, the two were sent to the Northeast China Liberated Area. Hou Bo was made head of the Photography Department of the Northeast Film Studio (formerly, the Manchurian Film Company [Man ying dianying gongsi]) in Changchun. Soon after the communists occupied Beijing, she and Xu Xiaobing moved to what was to become the capital of the new PRC. Xu Xiaobing as the leading official photographer recorded the meetings and activities of party leaders, and from mid-1949 Hou Bo developed and printed many of these photographs.

After her arrival in Beijing, she was appointed section chief of the Department of Photography at the Beijing Film Studio (formerly, Number Three Central Film Studio [Zhongyang dianying disan zhipianchang]). Hou Bo herself was also one of the official photographers who recorded the founding ceremony of the PRC on 1 October. Soon after, she was formally transferred to Zhongnanhai, the residential compound of party and state leaders in Beijing, and given the job of establishing a Photography Department. Required to live at Zhongnanhai, she was allocated a residence in Qinzhengdian. Her husband and their two children eventually joined her there, and the latter were reared in the Zhongnanhai nursery.

As resident photographer, Hou Bo's primary duty was to compile a photographic archive relating to the activities of CCP Central Committee leaders, notably Mao Zedong (1893–1976), Liu Shaoqi (1898–1969), Zhou Enlai (1898–1976), and Zhu De (1886–1976). The photographs remained secret and their circulation was strictly controlled. In particular, publication of photographs of the daily lives of the leaders was prohibited during the early decades of the PRC. Hou Bo would submit one print of a photograph to the senior officer at Zhongnanhai and retain one copy for archival purposes. She was not allowed to place them with the press and had no contact with external news agencies.

During the 1950s, Mao Zedong often spent from six to eight months of every year traveling outside Beijing. Whenever he was on the road, Hou Bo would be on hand to document his activities. In accordance with the stringent security requirements of the day, her whereabouts remained a secret even from her family. According to Hou Bo, many of the leaders disliked having their photograph taken, and she had to be careful to remain as unobtrusive as possible; nonetheless the photographer was always on call. When not out on a job, Hou Bo had to wait by the telephone for her next assignment. She worked on her own until 1951, when her one-woman department was considerably expanded. Prior to 1957, the Zhongnanhai Photography Department was under the control of the Central Security Bureau (Zhongyang jingweiju). After government restructuring that year, the department came under the control of the New China News Agency.

Hou Bo took many photographs of Mao Zedong: with cadres, workers, farmers, soldiers, intellectuals, and foreign visitors. Selected images were published to illustrate or emphasize larger ideological or policy shifts. The government recognized photography as a powerful visual medium through which it was possible to communicate with, and influence, a mass audience. Among her most famous works are *The Founding of the PRC* (1949), *Mao Zedong Swimming across the Yangzi [Yangtze] River* (1955), *Chairman Mao at Work in an Aeroplane* (1957), *We Have Friends All over the World* (1959), and *Mao Zedong with Students from Latin America* (1959), the latter awarded First Prize in the National Photography Exhibition of that year.

In her memoirs, Hou Bo discusses photographing Mao Zedong swimming across the Yangzi River. She recalls that he loved swimming, which for him was an important form of relaxation; he swam in many rivers throughout China. On one occasion after inspecting a textile mill in Hankou, Mao decided to have a swim in the mighty Yangzi River. For Hou Bo, this was an important photo opportunity. Despite the fact that she could not swim, Hou Bo jumped into a small boat that had been prepared for Mao to rest in and with the help of an oarsman kept pace with Mao. She stood on the prow of the boat buffeted by the choppy waters, snapping photographs.

Hou Bo was also interested in showing Mao at work. An opportunity arose in spring 1957 when he was flying south after an inspection in Shandong Province. Hou Bo noticed that Mao, who was sitting at the front of the aeroplane, had not taken off his overcoat and was intently reading a document. Such was his concentration that his cigarette had burned down almost to his fingers. Hou Bo took an impromptu photograph. After the image was published, the poet and man of letters Guo Moruo was inspired to write a verse in praise of what he characterized as Mao's untiring work spirit.

Hou Bo developed an uneasy relationship with Mao Zedong's wife Jiang Qing (*q.v.*), who was also a keen amateur photographer, and in 1961 Hou Bo was transferred to the New China News Agency. During the early to mid-1960s, she traveled extensively throughout China on agency photo assignments and in 1964 accompanied Song Qingling (*q.v.*) on an official visit to Ceylon. In September 1968, during the Cultural Revolution, Hou Bo was denounced by Jiang Qing and endured harsh criticism. Hou Bo was sent to the May Seventh Cadre School to do manual labor and not allowed to return to Beijing until 1974. It was not until 1978, however, that she was allowed to go back to work with the New China News Agency.

Since the late 1970s, Hou Bo has undertaken a number of large photographic projects. In 1979 she traveled to her native Shanxi Province to photograph mural paintings at the Yongle Temple, which were later published as a large format book. In 1985 Hou Bo and Xu Xiaobing made a photographic tour of Xinjiang, and in the late 1990s they documented the construction of the controversial Three Gorges Dam at Sandouping in Hubei Province.

Since 1986 Hou Bo has held many exhibitions of her photographs including *The Great Record of History* (Weidade lishi jilu), which toured over ten cities in China. In 1989, *Road: Photographs by Xu Xiaobing and Hou Bo* (Lu: Xu Xiaobing, Hou Bo sheying zuopin ji) was published, featuring 187 of their photographs, many of them appearing in public for the first time. In 1999, as part of the celebrations to mark the fiftieth anniversary of the founding of the PRC, a large retrospective exhibition of the photographs of Hou Bo and Xu Xiaobing was held at the Museum of the Chinese Revolution (Zhongguo geming bowuguan) in Beijing and traveled to various cities throughout China.

Hou Bo currently chairs the China Women's Photography Association (Zhongguo nüsheyingjia xiehui) and is a member of the Standing Committee of the China Photographers' Association (Zhongguo sheyingjia xiehui changwu lishi). Her career spans the revolutionary history of the CCP since its rise to power. She was a key figure in creating the photographic record of official China and has pursued a role as a propagandist and patriot to the end of her career.

Claire ROBERTS

Ba Yi'er. "Shunjian zhujiude yongheng: Ji sheyingjia Xu Xiaobing, Hou Bo fufu." *Minzu tuanjie*, 11 (1996): 39–42.

Deng Fuchang. "Fengjing zhebian du hao: Ji zhuming lao sheyingjia Xu Xiaobing, Hou Bo Xinjiang zhixing." *Huabao tupian tongxun*, 12 (December 1985), 2.

Hou Bo. "Xingfude suiyue." In *Zhongguo nü jizhe*, ed. Zhongguo nü jizhe bianji weiyuanhui. Beijing: Xinhua chubanshe, 1989, 330–36.

Hou Bo and Xu Xiaobing. *Dai chibangde sheying ji: Hou Bo, Xu Xiaobing koushu huiyi lu*. Beijing: Beijing daxue chubanshe, 1999.

Li Qi and Liang Pingbo, eds. *Lu: Xu Xiaobing, Hou Bo sheying zuopin ji*. Hangzhou: Zhejiang renmin meishu chubanshe, n.d.

Maass, Harald. "Mao: Wie eine legende entstand." *Die Zeit magazin*, 25 (June 1996): 12–24.

Quan Yanchi. "Jingtou qiande lingxiu si shenghuo: Zhongnanhai sheyingshi Xu Xiaobing, Hou Bo shouci 'baoguang.'" In *Lingxiu lei*. Beijing: Qiushi chubanshe, 1989, 121–87.

Xu Zheng. "Liuzhu weidade lishi shunjian: Ji zhuming sheyingjia Xu Xiaobing, Hou Bo fufu." *Beijing ribao*, 13 November 1994, 1.

Yingwen *Zhongguo funü*, ed. *Gu jin zhuming funü renwu*, vol. 2. Shijiazhuang: Hebei renmin chubanshe, 1986, 1052–56.

Yu Wentao. "Album of 1937–66 History." *China Daily*, 11 September 1989, 5.

Hsia Pei-Su: *see* **Xia Peisu**

Hsia Yu

Hsia Yu [Xia Yu], b. 1956, in Taipei, Taiwan, although her parents were from Guangdong Province, is a poet. She graduated from the National Arts College, majoring in film and drama, and worked for a short time in television and theater. A professional song lyricist and translator, the poet now divides her time between Paris and Taipei.

Hsia Yu started writing poetry in 1980. Her first book of poetry, *Memoranda* (Peiwang lu), was self-published in 1984; she designed it and all of her later published works. Although distributed only through limited, non-commercial channels, the book was well received, especially among readers of the younger generation, and established her reputation as one of Taiwan's most promising poets. Her second book of poetry, *Ventriloquy* (Fu-yü shu), published in 1991, was followed by *RUB.INEFFABLE* (Mo-ts'a.wu-i ming-chuang), a collection of a Dadaesque montage of "found poems" made from cut-up words and phrases from the poems in *Ventriloquy*. Her newest book of poetry, *Salsa*, came out in 1999.

Critics have studied Hsia Yu's poetry in terms of feminism and postmodernism. Needless to say, these generalizing concepts highlight only certain aspects of her work and hardly do justice to its richness. Many sources of inspiration and influence can be detected in her pieces, from Confucian and Taoist classics to modern Western art and music as well as to her fellow poets Shang Ch'in (b. 1930) and Yang Mu (b. 1940). Above all, however, it is important to situate Hsia Yu's work within the literary-historical milieu in which it is written, published, and read.

When the poet started out, the Modern Poetry Debate (1972–73) and the Native Literature Movement (1977–79) had recently transformed Taiwan's poetry scene. Both charged modernist literature with being the product of irresponsible individualism and American cultural colonialism of the 1950s and 1960s, turning its back on the society of Taiwan on one hand and Chinese heritage on the other. Critics and many poets therefore advocated a "return" to native tradition and local social reality. Realism was championed as the cure for the modernist malaise. Under the nativist influence, many established poets changed direction and a new generation eagerly embraced realism to address social and political themes in their work, whether to voice discontent with the ruling regime, critique the negative impact of rapid modernization and urbanization, or express sympathy for the marginalized and the oppressed (women, aborigines, and blue-collar workers, for example). Unfortunately, the noble sense of mission rarely translated well into literary representations. With few exceptions, the nativist-realist poetry of the 1970s and 1980s tended to be one-dimensional, repetitive, and predictable.

The nativist-realist reaction to modernism also manifested in its various attempts to make poetry more accessible. In the mid-1970s, the "campus folksong" movement was born. Poems by Cheng Ch'ou-yü (b. 1932) and Yü Kuang-chung (b. 1928), among others, were turned into melodious, folksy songs sung by young non-professional singers, many of whom were college students. The difference between these campus folksongs and popular music at the time was refreshing and made them instantly successful. Ironically, however, as their popularity spread, campus folksongs were absorbed into the market, and the distinction that originally set them apart from commercial music became blurred.

Thus, within this historical context, the emergence of Hsia Yu took on great significance. The fact that she shunned commercial venues for publication and distribution of her first book of poetry was a personal statement against the mass market and commercialization of modern poetry in the early 1980s. In contrast to the nativist-realist mainstream, *Memoranda* is defiantly individualistic, urban, ironic, and deconstructive. The book presents a woman's private world rather than the public domain; but at the same time it breaks the narrowly personal-lyrical mode that has confined most Chinese women poets, traditional and modern. Although patriarchy, as evident in traditional and contemporary culture, is subjected to witty satire and deconstruction (for example, her rewrites of Chinese myths and Western fairytales), social and political themes are absent from her poetry. Her poems are grounded in urban quotidian experience, filled with the sights and sounds of contemporary Taiwanese culture, which blends local and cosmopolitan, pop, and elite elements. By the same token, the poetic language is refreshingly hybrid: by and large colloquial, it freely mixes clichés, slang, proverbs, tongue twisters, commercials, and classical Chinese. Most of the poems are cast in minimalist form, and the tone combines the childlike and whimsical with the pensive and confessional. Together, these characteristics make *Memoranda* the most iconoclastic work in decades.

An oft-quoted—and probably still the best-known—poem from the collection is *Sweet Revenge*, written in 1980:

> I'll take your shadow and add a little salt
> Pickle it
> Dry it in the wind
>
> When I'm old
> I'll wash it down with wine.
> —*Memoranda*, 1984; translated by Andrea Lingenfelter

A powerful dramatic effect is created through the minimalist form, economy of language, projection of the future, and, perhaps most importantly, the use of the familiar (the culinary activity of marinating) and classical images (the image of the poet drinking wine harking back to the Chinese poetic tradition) in a completely unexpected context—revenge (the title itself is a borrowing of a cliché in English). The interplay between forgetting and remembering, between erasure and preservation, was to play a more prominent role in her second book of poetry.

Compared to *Memoranda*, *Ventriloquy* is at once more abstract, more fantastical, and more self-reflexive. Some of the titles reveal her bent for fantasy: *Secret Talks with Animals*, *The Yarmidiso Family of Languages*, *The Hidden Queen and Her Invisible City*, and *Séance*. The recurrent motif of travel or passing through parallels the theme of remembrance, which, in retracing footsteps in time, is essentially a reverse trip. Further, remembrance always presupposes loss—of childhood or love, for instance—and the act of remembering is paradoxically inseparable from that of forgetting. One can only recall that which is temporarily or partially forgotten, and the harder one tries to forget, the more painfully vivid a memory becomes (as can be seen in *Sweet Revenge*). The tension between remembrance and forgetting unfolding in time, with their concomitant emotions, underscores much of the book. *Memory* provides a good example:

> Forget. Two syllables
> inside two lightly puffing cheeks
> tongue-tip pressed to palate gently aspirated:

Forget. Plant some daylilies
Boil soup. Forget.
—*Ventriloquy*, 1991; translated by Andrea Lingenfelter

In traditional Chinese medicine, daylilies, or "gold-needle flowers" in Chinese, are believed to relieve anxiety. But after attempting in five ways to forget "you" in the next five stanzas, the poet concludes with these lines:

Or perhaps take a stroll on the bridge
May one carry a picnic basket?
Walking along the edge of the steel wall
hopping on one foot & step by step getting close
close to you and the sea. Is it enough to use an entire sea?
Somersault three times in the air
and then fall
and then die.
—*Ventriloquy*, 1991; translated by Andrea Lingenfelter

Ventriloquy is more complex than *Memoranda* for another reason. Increasingly, the poet is interested in exploring the multiple facets of language, whether the materiality—the visual and musical attributes—of the Chinese language or the polysemy and ambiguity of the languages with which the poet is familiar: Chinese, French, and English. Her ability to create original images and figures of speech from the hackneyed, quotidian language continues to surprise and delight the reader. A short but brilliant example is *Sadness of Autumn*:

The person whom I don't love any more is sitting across from me watching me
Like an empty plastic bottle that cannot be easily recycled or destroyed.
—*Ventriloquy*, 1991; translated by Michelle Yeh

Like much of Hsia Yu's work, there is a simplicity about this poem that is both disarming and deceptive. Underneath the transparent language, the poem is rich in nuances. The exact parallel structure, which juxtaposes the signified and the signifier of the pedestrian analogy, captures the mixture of pity, reticence, impatience, and boredom at the end of a relationship.

As is true with all strong poets, poetry for Hsia Yu is in the final analysis a lasting love affair with language. Language is not just a means of expression or representation; it molds and intervenes in the process of what gets to be expressed or represented. There is constant negotiation and mutual transformation between the semantic capacity of language and its purely material attributes (with their numerous variations and associations). As Hsia Yu suggested in a 1988 interview, reality is "refracted" through words and every narrative presents "the possibility of a new world." The challenge for the poet, then, is to establish a personal relationship through words, not only with reality but also with the infinite parallel worlds that are opened up by words. Some of the most radical works result from this exploratory process, such as the completely unintelligible graphs made up with fragments of Chinese characters in

Séance III and a whole book of "found poems" in *RUB.INEFFABLE* produced in the mode of chance, à la surrealism and John Cage.

With beautiful miniature watercolors also painted by the poet, *Salsa*, Hsia Yu's latest book of poetry, continues to explore the above themes and issues: time, remembrance and forgetting, chance, repetition, reality, and possible realities and their relationships to language. The poems, including quite a few prose poems, tend to be longer, more diffuse, and punctuated by stream-of-consciousness. In the relationship between words and reality, words now occupy the dominant position to which reality is subordinated. According to the poet, "even a simple sentence is ambiguous, indeterminate, and uninterpretable." These same qualities are projected onto reality. More than any of the earlier collections, *Salsa* celebrates the dance of words—their rhythm and energy, their potentiality and actuality. Perhaps the poet's own words best describe the collection: "What makes it fascinating is not its architecture / but its paralysis."

Michelle YEH

Chung Ling. *Hsien-tai Chung-kuo ti miu-ssu*. Taipei: Lien-ching ch'u-pan-she, 1989, 252–73.

Groppe, Alison McKee. "Reading the Poetry of Xia Yu: Following a Talking Dummy through a Lost-and-Found Museum." M.A. thesis. Cambridge, Mass.: Department of East Asian Languages and Civilizations, Harvard University, 1995.

Hsi Mi [Michelle Yeh]. "Hsia Yü ti nü-hsing shih-hsüeh." In *Chung-kuo wen-hsüeh yü fu-nü lun-chi*, vol. 1, ed. Yenna Wu. Taipei: Tao-hsiang ch'u-pan-she, 1999, 273–305.

———. "Yü-i mai-i yüan: Hsia Yü chin-tso ch'u-t'an." *Ch'eng-p'in yüeh-tu*, 22 (June 1995): 72–75.

Hsia Yu. *Fu-yü shu*. Taipei: Hsien-tai-shih chi-k'an she, 1991.

———. *Mo-ts'a.wu-i ming-chuang*. Taipei: Hsien-tai-shih chi-k'an she, 1995.

———. *Pei-wang lu*. Taipei: Hsia Yu, 1984.

———. *Salsa*. Taipei: Hsia Yu, 1999.

———. "Interview with Wan Hsü-t'ing." In her *Fu-yü shu*. Taipei: Hsien-tai-shih chi-k'an she, 1988, 105–21.

Liao Hsien-hao. "Wu-chih-chu-i ti p'an-pien: Ts'ung wen-hsüeh-shih, nü-hsing-hua, hou-hsien-tai chih mai-lo k'an Hsia Yü ti yin-hsing shih." In *Ai yü chieh-kou: tang-tai Taiwan wen-hsüeh p'ing-lun yü wen-hua kuan-ch'a*. Taipei: Lien-ho wen-hsüeh, 1995, 32–68.

Lin Yao-te. "Chi-mu wan-t'ung—lun Hsia Yü ti shih." In *1949 i hou*, ed. Lin Yao-te. Taipei: Erh-ya ch'u-pan-she, 1986, 127–40.

Yeh, Michelle. "The Feminist Poetic of Hsia Yu." *Modern Chinese Literature*, 7, no. 1 (Summer 1993): 33–60.

Hsia Yü: *see* **Hsia Yu**

Hsiao Ch'ing-yü: *see* **Hsiao Sa**

Hsiao Hung: *see* **Xiao Hong**

Hsiao Sa

Hsiao Sa [Xiao Sa], b. 1953, in Taiwan, is a native of Nan-ching [Nanjing]; her original name was Hsiao Ch'ing-yü. She is a writer of fiction.

Hsiao Sa attended the Taipei Girls' Normal College (Taipei nü-shih-chuan) where, by her own admission, she rebelled against school regulations that prohibited students from growing their hair long, wearing miniskirts, or having boyfriends. Nevertheless, after graduating in the 1970s Hsiao Sa became a primary school teacher. While still in college, she started writing stories. Her first collection, *Long Dyke* (Ch'ang ti), contained stories written at seventeen and eighteen years of age, and was published in 1972, when the writer was almost twenty. Hsiao Sa has said that her first experience of fiction was listening as a child to radio broadcasts of fiction—romantic, detective, and historical stories—and traditional story-telling (*shuo-shu*) based on classical novels, such as *Dream of the Red Chamber* (Hung-lou meng). As she grew older, Hsiao Sa read and admired the literary magazines created by the young men and women of Taiwan in the 1960s and 1970s—*Hsien-tai wen-hsüeh*, edited by Pai Hsien-yung, and *Wen-hsüeh chi-k'an*, edited by Wei T'ien-ts'ung. Hsiao Sa also read translations of Western and Japanese fiction. She acknowledges a proximity to Japanese writers such as Kawabata Yasunari, Mishima Yukio, and Natsume Soseki, feeling closer to the Asian ethos of the works of these authors. However, Hsiao Sa denies being inspired by any one author, emphasizing the complexity of her heritage.

After her first collection was published, she stopped writing for five years. Her novella *My Son, Han-sheng* (Wo erh Han-sheng, 1981), which first appeared in a newspaper in 1978, is generally considered a quantum artistic leap. It shows a broadened vision and concern for the social issues of her time. Her penetrating observation and scalpel-sharp pen expose invidious social conditions as well as their effect on idealistic young people. As in most of her works, Hsiao Sa does not preach but simply presents the story poignantly from several viewpoints and lets readers draw their own conclusions. For example, *My Son* is narrated from the mother's point of view, while the views of her son Han-sheng come from his own mouth, in direct speech. Readers might empathize with either Han-sheng or his mother and yet, in the end, even Han-sheng's strongest critic could not fail to see that society has not offered much of an alternative for such an idealistic youth. Most of Hsiao Sa's stories are similarly openended so that there is ample space for readers to use their own imagination and finish the story however they would like. In *My Son*, Han-sheng is so disillusioned that he drives a taxi for a living and cohabits with a dance-hall girl. At the very end of the story, however, he declines the comfortable future his parents offer him and leaves again to find his own way.

My Son, Han-sheng was followed by several stories about young people. The novel *The Young Man A-hsin* (Shao-nien A-hsin, 1984) is a chilling account of how an innocent and seemingly normal teenager ends up as a kidnapper and murderer. The short story "The Aftermath of the Death of a Junior High Coed" (Ssu-le i-ko kuo-chung nü-sheng chih hou) details the accidental death of a teenage girl. These works expose the cold homes and indifferent society from which these unfortunate young people come and uncover the troubled existence of the young who do not seem to have anywhere to turn for understanding and love.

Hsiao Sa's desire to write about young people may have sprung from her profession as a teacher. Although her career as a primary school teacher does not entail daily dealings with the kind of young people she writes about, Hsiao Sa nevertheless has the capacity to understand how children and young adults think and is compassionate about their inner struggles. Other authors do not seem to be able to fathom in the way that she can the problems of juveniles that splash across the headlines of local newspapers every day.

Hsiao Sa also writes about adults who are victims of an avaricious and materialistic society, men and women who covet the materialistic rewards of a capitalist society but are unwilling or incapable of working toward obtaining them. Sometimes she reveals their weakness through love. Many of her characters are not only failures in life but have, through their own self-interest, lost the capacity to love. These are often little people in the urban jungle. Unlike most women writers, Hsiao Sa creates male protagonists who are as convincing and possess as much depth as her female ones. However, from the mid-1980s Hsiao Sa became increasingly concerned with the destiny of women in the half-old–half-new society of Taiwan in the 1970s and even the 1980s. During that period, gender equality appeared to have received general recognition, yet deep down women still suffered unspoken discrimination. In the novel *Walking through the Past* (Tsou-kuo ts'ung-ch'ien, 1988), she portrays a typically good wife who is unable to comprehend why her husband has deserted her for an obviously much less attractive woman. Hsiao Sa records the wife's humiliation as she tries to get him back, but what makes the story even more compelling is the complete lack of support the woman receives from her in-laws and members of her natal family. Only a sister, who finds herself in the same situation, has any sympathy for her; society in general simply offers scorn. Mercifully, Hsiao Sa provides the protagonist with a resolution—a change in life: she finally wakes up to the futility of trying to win back her husband and begins to build a new life for herself. The woman also becomes a paradigm of sisterly support when she begins to give lectures to encourage other women like herself to overcome marriage problems and discover self-worth. In an even later novel, *The Single Woman I-hui* (Tan-shen I-hui, 1993), Hsiao Sa delineates the struggle of a single mother who eventually succeeds in giving herself and her daughter a meaningful life. At the end of the story, however, when the daughter leaves to study in the United States, the woman is alone once more.

Hsiao Sa's own marriage ran into trouble around 1985 and she, too, had a daughter. Because Hsiao Sa published an emotional letter to her (former) husband, Chang I, in a local newspaper, the incident became well known to the public. A film director, he had fallen in love with Yang Hui-shan, the lead actress in his film *I Spent My Whole Life Just Like This*, based on one of Hsiao Sa's stories. Naturally, the event had deeply affected Hsiao Sa's life. Interviewed a year later, however, she told Chi-chi, editor of *Chung-kuo shih-pao*'s literary page "Jen-chien," that she (Hsiao Sa) had come to terms with her broken marriage and realized a new awareness about change: that she was still able to change, not only in her life but in her writing as well and it could only benefit her as a writer.

Most of Hsiao Sa's characters seem to be victims of circumstance, and she writes about them compassionately. In *Hsia-fei's Home* (Hsia-fei chih chia, 1981), for example, the simple but kind Kuei-mei, who single-handedly and uncomplainingly brings up her husband's children by his previous wife, is a positive model. Another resilient woman who overcomes suffering and loss to reach a calm and comfortable old age is the protagonist in *Diaries of Homecoming* (Fan-hsiang cha-chi, 1987). This novel also marks a first in mainlanders' writing about their Taiwanese neighbors. The period covered—1945 to 1947—was one that writers had touched upon but little until then. Hsiao Sa spent an entire year doing interviews and collecting material before actually beginning to write the novel.

Critics have frequently praised the simplicity of the writer's language; its precision and expressiveness lend the work a characteristic poignancy. Other reviews, however, consider that her stories and novels are filmic in their reliance on dialogue, and characterization is given with little psychological analysis or monologue. Hsiao Sa's fiction is often expressed in different formats: *The Young Man A-hsin*, for example, takes the form of a compilation of juvenile records in a police file, while *Diaries of Homecoming* appears in the form of a diary. Chi-chi has said about Hsiao Sa: "In real life, like you and me, Hsiao Sa has her ups and downs and her emotional problems. In her writing, however, Hsiao Sa always stands cool and aloof at a point from which she regards the world below, like an eagle. She captures the rapidly changing scenes with agility, and then makes them reappear in slow motion in her writing by means of her succinct language."

Hsiao Sa writes prolifically and has published more than fifteen novels and collections of short stories dealing with a wide spectrum of themes and topics. She has the sensitivity usually attributed to women writers but possesses additionally a depth and breadth that is the envy of many. Her artistry is also widely recognized and celebrated. Hsiao Sa has received many honors, including prizes awarded by the two major newspapers *Lien-ho pao* and *Chung-kuo shih-pao* and the Chung-hsing Literary Medal. Several of her stories have been made into films, including *My Son, Han-sheng*, *Hsia-fei's Home* (as the film *I Spent My Whole Life Just Like This* [Wo chiu che-yang kuo le i-sheng]), and *Wei-liang's Love* (Wei-liang ti ai). She has also won a Golden Horse Award for scriptwriting.

Lily Xiao Hong LEE

Chan Hung-chih. "'Hsiao yeh': Fu-lu." In *Liu-shih chiu nien tuan-p'ien hsiao-shuo hsüan*, ed. Chan Hung-chih. Taipei: Erh-ya ch'u-pan-she, 1981, 214–17.
Chang Hsi-kuo. "Hsü." In *Ssu le i-ko kuo-chung nü-sheng chih hou*, Hsiao Sa. Taipei: Hung-fan shu-chü, 1984, i–iv.
Ch'i Pang-yuan. "Moving Beyond the Boudoir." *Free China Review* (April 1991): 26–32.
Chi-chi. "Chan tsai leng-ching ti kao-ch'u: Yü Hsiao Sa t'an sheng-huo yü hsieh-tso." In *Tsou kuo ts'ung-ch'ien*, Hsiao Sa. Taipei: Chiu-ko ch'u-pan-she, 1988, 373–86.
Chou Ning. "P'ing chieh 'Ssu le i-ko kuo-chung nü-sheng chih hou.'" In *Ssu le i-ko kuo-chung nü-sheng chih hou*, Hsiao Sa. Taipei: Hung-fan shu-chü, 1984, 131–35.
Hsiao Sa. "The Aftermath of the Death of a Junior High Coed." In *Bamboo Shoots After the Rain: Contemporary Stories by Women Writers of Taiwan*, eds. Ann C. Carver and Sung-sheng Yvonne Chang. New York: Feminist Press at the City University of New York, 1990, 171–86.
———. "My Son, Han-sheng," trans. Eve Markowitz. In *Worlds of Modern Chinese Fiction: Short Stories and Novellas from the PRC, Taiwan, and Hong Kong*, ed. Michael S. Duke. Armonk, N.Y.: M.E. Sharpe, 1991, 227–45.
Li Ang. "'Wo erh Han-sheng': Fu chu." *Liu-shih ch'i nien tuan-p'ien hsiao-shuo hsüan*. Taipei: Erh-ya ch'u-pan-she, 1979, 183–87.

Ma Sen. "P'ing *Hsiao-chen i-sheng ti ai-ch'ing.*" In *Tang-tai Taiwan wen-hsüeh p'ing-lun ta-hsi*, ed. Cheng Ming-li. Taipei: Cheng-chung shu-chü, 1993, 445–54.

Yindi. "P'ing-chieh 'Hsiao-yeh.'" In *Ssu le i-ko kuo-chung nü-sheng chih hou*, Hsiao Sa. Taipei: Hung-fan shu-chü, 1984, 58–60.

Hsiao Yün: *see* **Hiu Wan, Ven.**

Hsiao-yün fa-shih: *see* **Hiu Wan, Ven.**

Hsieh Ah-nü: *see* **Xie Xuehong**

Hsieh Chia-nü: *see* **Xie Xuehong**

Hsieh Fei-ying: *see* **Xie Xuehong**

Hsieh Hsi-teh: *see* **Xie Xide**

Hsieh Hsüeh-hung: *see* **Xie Xuehong**

Hsieh Ping-ying

Hsieh Ping-ying [Xie Bingying], 1906–2000 (her year of birth is given in some sources as 1903), of Hsin-hua [Xinhua] County, Hunan Province, was an activist writer and journalist. She is best known for her autobiographical work *War Diaries* (Ts'ung-chün jih-chi), which documents her exploits as a soldier as a young woman.

Her father, a provincial degree holder (*chü-jen*) of the Qing dynasty, was devoted to education and principal of the local high school for over twenty-five years. He was also a learned classical scholar and taught Hsieh Ping-ying the rudiments of classical literature. Her mother was a strict disciplinarian who bound her daughter's feet and pierced her ears to conform to tradition. Hsieh Ping-ying later described herself as a rebellious daughter who unbound her feet and studied at a boys' school. In her youth, she also went to a missionary school for girls at I-yang in her native province, and there her rebellious nature again emerged when she organized a demonstration against Japanese imperialism in May 1922. Having been expelled from the missionary school in September of the same year, Hsieh Ping-ying enrolled in the First Women's Normal School of Hu-nan at Ch'ang-sha (Hu-nan ti-i nü-tzu shih-fan). In the more open atmosphere of Ch'ang-sha, the student developed an interest in Chinese and world literature. By her own account, she read widely in classical Chinese fiction, including novels such as *Romance of the Three Kingdoms* (San-kuo yen-i) and *Water Margin* (Shui-hu chuan), about rebellion and war, and translations of French and Russian works. She also looked at the works of Kuo Mo-jo [Guo Moruo] and Ch'eng Fang-wu [Cheng Fangwu], both considered progressive writers of the Creation Society.

Before graduating from the First Women's Normal School of Hu-nan, Hsieh Ping-ying interrupted her studies in favor of more military exploits. In 1926, she entered the Central Academy of Military and Political Studies as a member of its Women Students Brigade. The academy had been established in Wu-han by the Northern

Expedition army of the coalition KMT-CCP government. After what was said to be rigorous military training, she became part of the National Revolutionary Army (Kuo-min ko-ming chün) and marched in 1927 to serve in the front. It was her experience in the army that prompted her to write *War Diaries*, which was published in the national newspaper *Chung-yang jih-pao* at the same time as its English translation came out by the well-known writer Lin Yutang. This work, with Hsieh Ping-ying's unique experience and fresh and direct style, captured the imagination not only of the Chinese public but of people throughout the world. It was reprinted as a monograph and translated into French, German, Russian, Japanese, Korean, and Esperanto. Her military life was brought to an end, however, when the Women's Corps to which she belonged was disbanded, presumably after the KMT and the CCP split that year.

After leaving the army, Hsieh Ping-ying returned to Hu-nan. In danger of being forced into marriage, she went to Shanghai to try to make a living from her writing. This was a great struggle, and Hsieh Ping-ying lived in abject poverty. The prominent literary figure Ch'ien Hsing-ts'un (Ah-ying [Qian Xingcun, Aying] 1900–77) came to know of her, however, and admired her courage and literary talent. He therefore arranged for her to study at the Shanghai University, a left-wing private institution where she met Wang Ying (*q.v.*), who became a close friend. After the KMT closed Shanghai University, with the financial help of her third brother Hsieh Ping-ying enrolled in the Chinese Department of the Pei-p'ing Normal University (Pei-p'ing shih-fan ta-hsüeh) in 1928. In the four years before her graduation in 1931, she also taught part-time at two high schools in Beijing. During this period, Hsieh Ping-ying married Fu Hao, a fellow student from her Wu-han days who had also gone on the Northern Expedition with her. Fu Hao left Hsieh Ping-ying soon after the birth of their daughter Fu Ping [Fu Bing] (1930–1966).

Thanks to an advance payment for two manuscripts, in 1931 Hsieh Ping-ying followed in the footsteps of many modern Chinese intellectuals and set sail for Japan to pursue further study. On the ship she was startled to hear of the Japanese invasion of Manchuria and once in Japan joined other Chinese students in protest against the Japanese action. Several months after her arrival in Tokyo, Hsieh Ping-ying was given three days by the Japanese police to leave the country. When she returned to Japan in 1935 under a different name, Hsieh Ping-ying was determined to avoid contact with other Chinese students. Enrolling in Waseda University, she became friendly with her teacher Professor Saneto Keishu and moved among progressive Japanese writers and editors of both genders. Hsieh Ping-ying was also acquainted with the woman editor Takenaka Shegeko of the newspaper *Asashi shimbun*. Friendship with authors such as Hayashi Fumiko and Takeda Taijun, who were suspected of being leftists, may have brought Hsieh Ping-ying once more to the attention of the Japanese police. Be that as it may, she was arrested and incarcerated for three weeks in April 1936 after refusing to participate in a welcome for the puppet emperor P'u-i [Puyi], whom the Japanese had installed in Man-ch'u-kuo (Manchuria). Considering him a traitor to China, she remained in her lodgings in defiance of a Japanese government order that all Chinese students welcome P'u-i upon his arrival at Tokyo airport. During imprisonment, Hsieh Ping-ying was tortured and interrogated and her release was obtained only after diplomatic intervention through the Chinese embassy. She left Japan soon afterward.

In the time between her two sojourns in Japan, Hsieh Ping-ying wrote *Autobiography of a Woman Soldier* (I-ko nü-ping ti tzu-chuan), which came out in 1936. After the Japanese attack on Shanghai in January 1932, she had tried to mobilize the women of Shanghai. On her second return to China, however, Hsieh Ping-ying was in ill health and after her brother sent money for her to go to Kuei-lin in Kuang-hsi Province did little more than rest and recuperate. At some stage, she returned to teaching, and in 1935, while in Fu-chien, met and married Wang Yü-ch'en [Wang Yuchen].

When China eventually declared war on Japan in July 1937, Hsieh Ping-ying was in Hu-nan in mourning for her mother. Despite poor health, within days of hearing the war news she had organized a team of women to go to the front and help. This Hunan Women's Service Group in the Battlefields comprised sixteen women from Hunan. They were later joined by eight women from Shanghai and Su-chou. A lone male high-school student also insisted on going with them. They left Ch'ang-sha in September with General Wu Ch'i-wei's [Wu Qiwei] Fourth Army to care for the wounded around Shanghai, Chia-ting, and Su-chou. All this time, Hsieh Ping-ying was writing prolifically about what she saw and publishing her articles in newspapers. These writings were gathered together in the book *New War Diaries* (Hsin ts'ung-chün jih-chi, 1938). Her stories told in simple language about the excitement and sadness she experienced on the battlefield, but they also revealed bureaucratic corruption and the cowardice and selfishness of the people. In one article, Hsieh Ping-ying called upon the Chinese people to send food and warm clothes to the soldiers and money to buy medicine for hospitals. Her second stint on the battlefield was as a war correspondent. She visited the Fifth War Area south of the Huai River in Chiang-su and Ho-nan and interviewed commanders Li Tsung-jen and Pai Ch'ung-hsi in Hsü-chou, as well as visiting the site of a famous victory at Tai-erh-chuang in Ho-nan. Hsieh Ping-ying sent back several interviews and many stories from the front. The third time on the battlefield, Hsieh Ping-ying led a corps of volunteer women university and high school students who were training to work at the front as nurses' aides. During this period, Hsieh Ping-ying noted down her impressions in tiny handwriting in small diaries measuring only four inches by two inches. She never found time to transcribe them, however, and by the time she was eventually able to return to them in her old age, her eyesight was too poor to read the tiny characters. Only a few articles emerged from this third and final phase of her work at the front. Her husband, Wang Yü-ch'en, was with her during her war years and is said to have collaborated in writing the dispatches sent from the front. Their marriage broke up in 1939, however, and she was left with their two children, a son and daughter.

Besides working at the front, in the war years from 1937 to 1945 Hsieh Ping-ying edited "Tide of Blood," the literary supplement of *Hsin-min pao* newspaper, and set up and edited (1940–43) the new Hsi-an [Xi'an] literary magazine *Yellow River Literature and Art Monthly* (Huang-ho wen-i yüeh-k'an). Returning to Ssu-ch'uan, she taught at the Provincial Higher Vocational School in Chengdu, presumably from 1944 to 1945. After the war, Hsieh Ping-ying became chief editor of *Ho-p'ing jih-pao* newspaper in Wu-han before being made a professor at Pei-p'ing Normal University and North

China Cultural College (Hua-pei wen-hua hsüeh-yüan). Around 1946, she married Chia I-chen [Jia Yizhen]; this, her third marriage, was happy and lasting.

In 1948, Hsieh Ping-ying went to Taiwan and taught at Taiwan Normal College (Taiwan shih-fan hsüeh-yüan), later to become Taiwan Normal University (Taiwan shih-fan ta-hsüeh). The numerous articles and prose essays written during her years in Taiwan form part of the volume *Collected Prose of Hsieh Ping-ying* (Hsieh Ping-ying san-wen chi), and in 1963 her *How I Write* (Wo tsen-yang hsieh-tso) was published.

While traveling by ship to visit her daughter in the United States in 1971, Hsieh Ping-ying fell and fractured her right leg. By then sixty-five years old, she retired from teaching and lived in San Francisco with her husband Chia I-chen from then on. (The *New York Times* reported that she died in that city on 5 January 2000.) Hsieh Ping-ying continued to write there and put her early works in order. Her *My Sojourns in Japan* (Wo tsai Jih-pen), published in 1984, is based on her 1940 *In a Japanese Prison* (Tsai Jih-pen yü chung) but with additional material relating her first visit to Japan and reminiscences about Japanese friends. She also expanded her *New War Diaries*, including her experiences the second and third times she served at the battlefront, publishing it in 1981 as *Diaries from the War of Resistance* (K'ang-chan jih-chi).

Hsieh Ping-ying's first daughter, Fu Ping, remained with her paternal grandmother when Hsieh Ping-ying went to Taiwan. Fu Ping worked at the Central Academy of Drama in Beijing but became one of the first victims of the Cultural Revolution when she was persecuted to death in 1966. Hsieh Ping-ying's other two children grew up in Taiwan.

The fame of Hsieh Ping-ying was built on her combined role as female activist and writer. In the world of the 1920s, the image of a young girl soldier fascinated people inside and out of China. Her plain and direct style suited the subject material, and her stories were poignant and stimulating. She wanted "to be one hundred percent faithful, to never write one word of falsity." Hsieh Ping-ying became famous outside China because her work attracted the attention of famous writers and intellectuals such as Romain Rolland and Lin Yutang, the latter translating her first work; his daughters published in America their translation of Hsieh Ping-ying's autobiography. Throughout her long life, she wrote more than ten million words and published more than seventy titles. Her works include autobiography, fiction, prose essays, children's literature, and reminiscences. *Autobiography of a Woman Soldier* has been reprinted in Taiwan and on the mainland, nineteen times all told.

Lily Xiao Hong LEE

Ch'en Ching-chih. "Hsieh Ping-ying," *Hsien-tai wen-hsüeh tsao-ch'i ti nü-tso-chia.* Taipei: Ch'eng-wen ch'u-pan-she, 1980, 169–94
Chung-hua min-kuo tang-tai ming-jen lu, vol. 3. Taipei: Chung-hua shu-chü, 1978, 1384.
Hsieh Ping-ying. *Autobiography of a Chinese Girl*, trans. Tsui Chi, with a new introduction by Elizabeth Croll. London: Pandora, 1986.
———. *Girl Rebel: The Autobiography of Hsieh Pingying, with Extracts from Her New War Diaries*, trans. Adet Lin and Anor Lin, with an introduction by Lin Yutang. New York: Da Capo Press, 1975.
———. *Hsieh Ping-ying san-wen hsüan.* Hong Kong: Shan-pien-she, 1983.

——. *K'ang-chan jih-chi.* Taipei: Tung-ta t'u-shu, 1981.

——. *Wo tsai Jih-pen.* Taipei: Tung-ta t'u-shu, 1984.

"Hsieh Ping-ying." In *Biographical Dictionary of Republican China,* ed. Howard Boorman and Richard C. Howard. New York: Columbia University Press, 1970, 102–03.

P'an Ya-tun [Pan Yadun]. *Shih-chieh hua-wen nü-tso-chia su-miao.* Kuang-chou: Chi-nan ta-hsüeh ch'u-pan-she, 1993, 332–42.

Ying-wen *Chung-kuo fu-nü,* ed. *Ku-chin chu-ming fu-nü jen-wu,* vol. 2. Shih-chia-chuang: Ho-pei jen-min ch'u-pan-she, 1986, 748–53.

Hsiu Tse-lan

Hsiu Tse-lan [Xiu Zelan], b. 1925, in Yüan-ning [Yuanning] County, Hunan Province, was an architect.

Keenly interested in mathematics and physics while in high school, she listed architecture as her first choice when it came to selecting a university course. Hsiu Tse-lan was admitted to the Architectural Engineering Department at the Central University (Chung-yang ta-hsüeh) in Nan-ching [Nanjing] and graduated in 1947. She immediately commenced work at Nan-ching Railway Bureau's general machine factory. When, two years later, the KMT government transferred its offices to Taiwan, Hsiu Tse-lan chose to go to Taiwan rather than remain on the mainland. She worked first in the Communications Department and later transferred to the Taiwan Railway Bureau.

By September 1950, it had become clear that the old Pan-ch'iao Station was no longer able to handle the heavier demands made on it, and Hsiu Tse-lan was given the task of designing a new station. It was this design that first brought her to the attention of the public. She then set up a firm called Tse-ch'ün Architecture and won many design contracts. Her works include the teachers' clubs at Jih-yüeh T'an Lake and T'ai-chung, Hua-lien Normal College Library, and the elegant library and science building at Yi Lan Lan-yang Girls' High School. Then-president Chiang Kai-shek was greatly impressed by her talent and in the 1960s commissioned her to design the Chung-shan building on Yang-ming-shan. This building became a symbol of modern Chinese architecture.

Hsiu Tse-lan and her husband, Fu Chi-k'uan [Fu Jikuan], were responsible for building the New Garden City (Hua-yüan hsin-ch'eng) in suburban Taipei in 1968, which became recognized as an ideal new community center. At the same time, the two actively expanded their architecture markets overseas and became involved in many construction projects in Saudi Arabia. Although generally successful, they are known to have had financial difficulties in the 1980s.

Through her own efforts, Hsiu Tse-lan managed to change the perception that women's talents are limited to purely literary achievements. She created a unique architectural style, that of a woman, based on attention to detail and artistic sensitivity and became a role model for women seeking success in the field of architectural engineering.

HO Shu-i
(Translated by George Li)

Chung-hua min-kuo ming-jen lu. Taipei: Chung-yang t'ung-hsün she, 1998.

Chung-hua min-kuo tang-tai ming-jen lu, vol. 3. Taipei: Taiwan Chung-hua shu-chü, 1978.

Hsü Ch'un-chü: *see* **Liang-Hsü Ch'un-chü**

Hsü Feng

Hsü Feng [Xu Feng], b. 1950, in Taipei, Taiwan, has figured prominently in the development and internationalization of Chinese cinema. As the swashbuckling heroine of the swordplay films of King Hu (Hu Chin-ch'üan [Hu Jinquan]), she was Taiwan's first international film star in the 1970s. As head of Tomson (T'ang Ch'en) Motion Picture Company, Hsü Feng produced some of the most internationally successful Chinese films of the 1980s and 1990s, bringing artists from the PRC, Taiwan, and Hong Kong together.

Her parents were emigrés from Chiang-su [Jiangsu] Province, but her father died when she was a child, leaving the family quite poor. At sixteen, Hsü Feng passed a screen test for United Motion Picture Company (Lien-pang) and joined their acting troupe. One year later, she made her screen debut playing a minor role in King Hu's now classic *Dragon Gate Inn* (Lung-men k'o chan, 1967). The film was a hit and marked the beginning of her productive cooperation with the director.

Hsü Feng had her first starring role in her next film with King Hu, the two-part *Swordswoman* (Hsia-nü, 1971; also called *A Touch of Zen*). That year, she won the Best New Performer Award at the Taipei Golden Horse Film Festival for her performance in T'u Chung-hsün's [Tu Zhongxun] *Ten Days in Dragon City* (Lung-ch'eng shih-jih), which came out while *Swordswoman* was in post-production. *Swordswoman* started a revival of the swordplay (*wu-hsia*) genre, and Hsü Feng went on to star in many other films of this type made by King Hu and other Taiwanese directors (*The Fate of Lee Khan* (Ying-ch'un-ko chih feng-p'o, 1973); *Rain on the Mountain* (K'ung-shan ling-yü, 1979). In 1975, *Swordswoman* won the Grand Prix at the Cannes International Film Festival, propelling Hsü Feng to international fame. Her face was on the cover of *Film Comment* and *Positif* that year. The next year she won awards for Best Leading Actress at the Taipei Golden Horse Festival and the Asian Film Festival. Hsü Feng also won acclaim for her roles in literary and patriotic films, being awarded a second Golden Horse Award for Best Leading Actress for her role as the persevering wife in the historical epic *The Pioneers* (Yüan, 1980). That year, as the Taiwanese *wu-hsia* film boom faded, Hsü Feng retired from the cinema to raise a child and work with her husband, the successful businessman T'ang Chün-nien [Tang Junnian].

In 1984, she returned to the film industry, this time to work behind the camera. With initial capital provided by her husband, Hsü Feng started the Tomson Film Company. Her plan was to produce an entertainment film in tandem with an art film, one providing financial security for the other. Throughout the 1980s, Tomson produced several commercially successful entertainment films, including several starring the Taiwanese comedian Chu Yen-p'ing [Zhu Yanping] and the Hao Hsiao-tzu series. This series of seven films about a trio of child kungfu experts did extremely well at the box office in Taiwan as well as in Japan, Hong Kong, and Southeast Asia.

Their commercial success allowed Hsü Feng to produce during the 1980s several films that were more daring, including some exploring the themes of women's sexuality and oppression. These included an adaptation of the controversial feminist novel

The Butcher's Wife (Sha-fu, 1986; also called *Woman of Wrath*) by the Taiwanese author Li Ang (*q.v.*) in which the heroine finally murders her brutish husband. *Hsin So* (1986) is a tale of sexual infidelity, also based on a banned novel, and *Starry Is the Night* (Chin-yeh hsing-kuang ts'an-lan, 1988) was directed by Ann Hui. Tomson also produced the "native soil" films *Mei jen t'u* (1985), a comedy by the satirist Wang Chen-ho about an innocent from the countryside in Taipei, and *Unending Lovestories* (Chiu ch'ing mien-mien, 1988), about the rise and fall of the Taiwanese-dialect film industry in the 1950s and 1960s. Although none of these was a great success, commercially or critically, they did provide the Taiwanese cinema with a middle ground between the emerging Taiwanese New Wave cinema, which did well at international festivals but was too avant-garde for the general Taiwanese public, and generic entertainment films.

In 1989, Hsü Feng moved to Hong Kong. The following year, she produced *Red Dust* (Kun-kun hung-ch'en), a film directed by Hong Kong's Yim Ho about a Chinese woman writer (based loosely on Eileen Chang, *q.v.*) living through the Sino-Japanese War and the Chinese civil war. The film swept the Golden Horse Awards, winning Best Feature Film, Best Director, Best Leading Actress, Best Supporting Actress, Best Cinematography, Best Art Design, and Best Music. With the success of *Red Dust*, Hsü Feng decided that Tomson could now focus primarily on art films.

In 1991, the company released *Five Girls and a Rope* (Wu-ko nü-tzu ho i-ken sheng-tzu) (directed by Yen Hung-wei), about five girls who commit suicide rather than submit to arranged marriages. Although the film won awards at five international film festivals, it was banned in Taiwan because one of its stars was from the PRC. Hsü Feng battled the Government Information Office (GIO) both by donating money to the Golden Horse Festival to establish a special fund to invite film people from the mainland to participate and also by filing a lawsuit. The GIO relented a year later, allowing the film to premiere at the Golden Horse Festival and giving Hsü Feng an award for recognizing her efforts in bringing Chinese cinema to an international audience.

Hsü Feng met mainland director Ch'en K'ai-ko [Chen Kaige] at the 1988 Cannes Festival and was impressed by his entry *King of the Children* (Hai-tzu wang). They decided to cooperate on *Farewell, My Concubine* (Pa-wang pieh chi [Bawang bie ji]), which was released in 1992. *Farewell* was a truly international project, based on a novel by Hong Kong writer Lilian Lee, starring actors from the PRC and Hong Kong. It was also the most internationally successful film of the decade, winning many awards, including the Palme d'Or at Cannes and with worldwide distribution. After *Farewell*, Hsü Feng and Ch'en K'ai-ko collaborated on *Temptress Moon* (Feng yüeh, 1996). Hsü Feng has continued to produce art films with directors from the PRC and featuring international casts, including Ho P'ing's [He Ping] *Red Firecracker, Green Firecracker* (P'ao-ta shuang-sheng [Paoda shuangsheng], 1994). Tomson has also distributed independents from the PRC that were more experimental, including Chang Yüan's [Zhang Yuan] *Beijing Bastards* (Pei-ching tsa-chung [Beijing zazhong], 1993). Hsü Feng is currently working on another film with Ch'en K'ai-ko and on a screen adaptation of Nien Cheng's family history *Life and Death in Shanghai*. In 1998, Hsü

Feng received a Lifelong Achievement Award from the Cannes International Film Festival. She remains happily married to T'ang Ch'ün-nien; they have two sons.

Teri SILVIO

On the Internet, at <http://ray.com.hk/tomson/company.html>.
Tien-ying tang-an: Chung-kuo tien-ying tzu-shen ying-jen: Hsü Feng. Issue 7. Taipei: Chin-ma ying-chan chih-hsing wei-yüan-hui, 1992.
Zhang Yingjin and Xiao Zhiwei. *Encyclopedia of Chinese Film.* New York: Routledge, 1999, 191.

Hsü Shih-hsien

Hsü Shih-hsien [Xu Shixian], 1908–1983, was born in T'ai-nan city, Taiwan. Her father, Hsü Huan-ch'ang [Xu Huanchang], was a "cultivated talent" (*hsiu-ts'ai*) of the former Ch'ing [Qing] dynasty; her mother's name was Ch'en Fu.

At the age of six, Hsü Shih-hsien studied the Chinese classics at the behest of her father. She enrolled in T'ai-nan Public School for Girls (now Ch'eng-kung Elementary in T'ai-nan) in 1914, graduated in 1920, and went on to the Second T'ai-nan Prefectural Girls' Senior High School (now T'ai-nan Girls' High School). Extremely talented, she made regular contributions to campus publications, but on one occasion refused to compose a celebratory piece on the life of Prince Showa. Because Taiwan was at that time under Japanese colonial rule, Hsü Shih-hsien was disciplined and narrowly avoided expulsion from the school. Nevertheless, after graduating from high school in 1925, she went to Japan to complete her tertiary education. Hsü Shih-hsien enrolled in Tokyo Women's Medical College (now Tokyo Women's Medical Science University) and graduated in 1930. Upon returning to Taiwan, she was first appointed as a physician to T'ai-nan Hospital but soon acceded to her elder brother's request to take charge of both T'e-t'ai Hospital and Shih-hsien Hospital. The benevolence and kindness Hsü Shih-hsien exhibited in these positions were greatly appreciated by the public.

She married Dr. Chang Chin-t'ung [Zhang Jintong], a graduate of Kyushu Imperial University's School of Medicine in Japan, in a ceremony in Hsi-k'ou, Chia-i County in 1933. After their marriage, the couple returned to medical school to pursue advanced studies, firstly in surgery, then in pharmacology, gynecology, and obstetrics. Her husband, however, did not specialize but studied general medicine, receiving his doctorate in medicine in 1938. Hsü Shih-hsien received her doctorate in medicine the following year. They returned in 1940 to Taiwan, where they were frequently referred to as "Dr. and Dr. Lovebird." They immediately established a practice at Shun-t'ien-t'ang Hospital in Chia-i.

In November 1945, the Taiwan Provincial Executive Administrative Office appointed Hsü Shih-hsien principal of Chia-i Provincial Girls' High School (now Chia-i Girls' High School). She thus became the first woman to be appointed after the war as a principal in Taiwan. During her tenure, Hsü Shih-hsien increased the number of classes in the school and established a senior high, thus laying solid foundations for today's Chia-i Girls' High School.

Chia-i City Women's Association, which Hsü Shih-hsien organized in February

1946, was the earliest post-war women's association to be established in Taiwan; she served as its chair. Hsü Shih-hsien formally entered politics in March of the same year with her election as councillor in the first Chia-i City Council, where she was in coalition with the female councillors Hsieh O and Ch'iu Yüan-yang (*q.v.*). When the anti-KMT government February Twenty-eighth Incident erupted across Taiwan the following year, Hsü Shih-hsien took part in negotiations at the besieged Shui-shang Airport in her capacity as councillor. Tragically, several of her colleagues were murdered, but Hsü Shih-hsien fled into the night with her infant daughter Chang Po-ya under her arm and was fortunate enough to avoid trouble.

Hsü Shih-hsien ran in the elections for mayor of Chia-i County and the First Provisional Provincial Assembly in 1951 but lost on both occasions. It should be mentioned that Hsü Shih-hsien applied at this time to drop her married name, a very unusual action during that period. Three years later she returned to the fray and was elected to the Second Provisional Provincial Assembly. Throughout her term, Hsü Shih-hsien frequently appealed to the government to take women's rights seriously, particularly the social problems of adopted daughters and prostitutes; she advocated the safeguarding of the rights of the former and assistance for rehabilitating the latter. In 1956, Hsü Shih-hsien resigned from the KMT after the party refused her permission to interpellate at the council the suspension of the mayor of Chia-i County, Li Mao-sung. This was the start of Hsü Shih-hsien's political activities as an independent. In 1953, she had been reelected to the Third Provisional Provincial Assembly (which, in 1959, became the First Provincial Assembly). Hsü Shih-hsien and Kuo Kuo-chi, Wu San-lien, Li Yüan-chan, Kuo Yü-hsin, and Li Wan-chü, who had also been elected to office but who had moved in the direction of reform, became known as the "Five Dragons, One Phoenix." They gradually moved down the road of organizing an opposition party.

The fortnightly journal *Free China*, edited by Lei Chen, had begun publishing frequent critiques of current government affairs in the early 1950s and led the way in pushing for political reform. A further step toward coalescing native Taiwanese political figures took place in the latter half of the decade with the planning for the formation of an opposition party. The "Five Dragons, One Phoenix" became passionate players in this movement to form a party. In April 1960, Hsü Shih-hsien was elected as a Taiwan provincial assemblywoman for the third time, and at the same time the Lei Chen-devised movement to form the "Chinese Democratic Party" was developing formidably. Hsü Shih-hsien served as one of sixteen convenors of this party-in-preparation. However, with the arrest of Lei Chen in September, the movement to form the party aborted. Hsü Shih-hsien's determination to participate in democratic reform was in no way lessened by this setback, however. Early the next year, she played a role in forming a national body that assisted independent candidates for county and city council, touring Taiwan to assist with local campaigning. This resulted in independent candidates winning 347 seats, which was 37.4 percent of the total number of seats on offer.

Hsü Shih-hsien was reelected in 1963 and served as provincial assemblywoman for the fourth time. With her election as the sixth mayor of Chia-i City (a city at a county administrative level) in 1968, she became Taiwan's first popularly elected city mayor and performed her duties enthusiastically, notably with the widening of Chung-shan Road and the construction of a seven-colored fountain. Citizens in the area often talked about the things she had done. However, despite Hsü Shih-hsien's conspicuous achievements in administration, the government resorted to a law that stipulated: "Those older than sixty years of age may not act as candidates for heads of local autonomous areas." In this way, they deprived Hsü Shih-hsien, by then over sixty, of the opportunity to serve another term as city mayor. All she could do was fight instead for a legislative seat.

When Hsü Shih-hsien was elected supplementary legislator in 1972, she gained the largest vote in Taiwan for that poll. The legislator renewed her term three years later. Hsü Shih-hsien was active in politics at that time and cultivated candidates to succeed her: her daughters Chang Wen-ying and Chang Po-ya both ran for various official posts but were unsuccessful. In 1982, the government repealed electoral restrictions on age, and Hsü Shih-hsien took advantage of this to contest the mayoralty of Chia-i City once again. Thus, after ten years, she finally satisfied her ambition to serve again as Chia-i City mayor. In July, Chia-i City's administrative status was upgraded so that Hsü Shih-hsien became Taiwan's first female mayor of a provincial-level city. During her term, she was active in promoting the city, as well as expanding international links, forging a sister-city relationship with Jackson, capital of Mississippi, in the U.S.

Hsü Shih-hsien died of cirrhosis of the liver on 30 January 1983. In December, her fourth daughter, Chang Po-ya, won a by-election for mayor, thus beginning the political line of the "Hsü Family Group." Hsü Shih-hsien had borne two sons and four daughters, but her sons Chang Po-yen and Chang Po-ming both died at a young age. Her eldest daughter, Chang Kuei-ying, graduated in medicine from Kagoshima University in Japan and married Hsü Po-ying. Her second daughter, Chang Po-ying, graduated from Ch'eng-kung University's Architecture Department and married Chung Wen-i. Her third daughter, Chang Wen-ying, graduated from Kao-hsiung Medical College and married Lai Ch'iung-hsün. Her youngest daughter, Chang Po-ya, graduated from Kao-hsiung Medical College, National Taiwan University's Public Health Research Institute, and the Johns Hopkins University's School of Public Health and married Chi Chan-nan.

The decades of hard work that Hsü Shih-hsien devoted to administering Chia-i won her the respectful nickname "the [Goddess] Matsu of Chia-i." After Hsü Shih-hsien's death, her daughters Chang Po-ya and Chang Wen-ying each received support from the people of Chia-i in mayoral elections and cemented the unwavering political status of the Hsü Family Group. Chang Po-ya went on to serve as interior minister in Ch'en Shui-bian's Democratic Progressive Party (DPP) government, elected in 2000.

SU Jui-chiang
(Translated by Martin Williams)

Chia-i-shih yü-shan wen-hsieh-hui, ed. *Hsü Shih-hsien po-shih chi-nien chi*. Chia-i: Chang Chin-t'ung Hsü Shih-hsien wen-chiao chi-chin-hui, 1997, 5–14, 40–42.
Hsieh Te-hsi. "Chia-i ma-tsu-p'o—Hsü Shih-hsien." In *Taiwan chin-tai ming-jen chih*, vol. 2,

eds. Chang Yan-hsien, Li Hsiao-feng, and Chuang Yung-ming. Taipei: Tzu-li wan-pao-she, 1991, 37–235.

"Hsü Shih-hsien nü-shih shih-chi." In *Kuo shih-kuan hsien-ts'ang min-kuo jen-wu chuan-chi shih-liao hui-pien*, no. 13, ed. Kuo Shih-kuan. Taipei: Kuo Shih-kuan, 1995, 286–89.

Huang Ying. *Hsü ku shih-chang huai-ssu lu.* N.p., n.d.

Kuo Chung-chih, Ch'en Pin-t'ien, and Yeh Ch'ang-keng. "Chia-i-shih: Hsü Chia-pan i-li pu-yao, Kuo-min-tang li-cheng shang-yu." In *Ti-fang p'ai-hsi yü Taiwan cheng-chih*, eds. Chang K'un-shang and Huang Cheng-hsiung. Taipei: Lien-ho-pao she, 1996, 219–29.

Li Wang-t'ai. "Hsü Shih-hsien ti ch'uan-ch'i chi ch'i shih-tai pei-ching." In *Taiwan fan-tui shih-li, 1976–1986*, ed. Li Wang-t'ai. Taipei: Wu-ch'ien-nien ch'u-pan-she, 1993, 203–08.

Lien-ho-pao, 7 January 1983, 3.

Lin Tzu-hou. "Hsü Shih-hsien." In *Min-kuo jen-wu hsiao-chuan*, vol. 10, ed. Liu Shao-t'ang. Taipei: Chuan-chi wen-hsüeh ch'u-pan-she, 1988, 259–61.

Taiwan-sheng i-hui kung-pao, 3, no. 18 (10 April 1960): 719.

Hu Baojuan: *see* **Hu Die**

Hu Dachang: *see* **Wu Mulan**

Hu Die

Hu Die, 1908–1989, a native of Heshan County, Guangdong Province, was the "Film Queen of China" in the 1930s. She enjoyed fame not only for the dozens of films made and the length of her screen career but also for her beauty, especially her smile, revealing two bewitching dimples. Born Hu Baojuan in Shanghai, Hu Die acquired the name Ruihua when she went to school. Hu Die was the name she chose for herself as a nom de guerre; it is a homophone for "butterfly," hence her sometime English name Butterfly Wu.

Hu Die's father, Hu Shaogong, was a chief inspector with the Peking-Fengtian Railway, so the family frequently moved up and down the railway line. This meant that Hu Die had to adapt to new environments and quickly learn to speak with different accents, skills she later said had probably been useful preparation for her work as an actress. Her mother, who was from a big family and had little education, was nevertheless wise in the ways of the world. Hu Die was for many years an only child, and while her father spoiled her, her mother was strict, teaching Hu Die to work diligently without worrying too much about a reward. This was a lesson she held on to all her life. In 1917, the whole family moved back to Guangdong and lived there for seven years. Hu Die had gone to Christian schools in Tianjin and Guangzhou, and in those days when film stars were hardly literate, her formal education stood her in good stead.

In 1924, when she was sixteen, the family moved back to Shanghai and there Hu Die saw in a newspaper that the Zhonghua Film Academy (Zhonghua dianying xueyuan) was advertising for students. She was interviewed and selected. The teachers and many of the students were part-time, so classes were held in the evenings. The school was strict regarding attendance, however, and students learned the basics of film history and theory as well as technical aspects such as cinematography, makeup, and directing. After completing the course, the young woman got a small part in a film called *Merit of War* (Zhangong, 1925?). Hu Die played a leading role in her second film, *Deserted Fan in Autumn* (Qiushan yuan, 1925), which not only won an audience but also introduced her to Lin Xuehuai, who co-starred in the film and with whom she fell in love. However, the relationship did not work out, and when they broke off their engagement the entertainment pages of newspapers were filled with reports and rumors. This made Hu Die vigilant of the pitfalls of being a female star and reminded her to heed her mother's precept of leading a blameless life.

Hu Die's next break came when the Tianyi Film Company signed her up in 1926 as a long-term artist. Shao Zuiweng, the eldest of the Shaw brothers who later made their fame in Hong Kong and Southeast Asia, was at the helm of Tianyi. His policy was to cater to the tastes of the common people and have rapid turnover in films. In the less than two years that Hu Die was under contract to him, she made fifteen films. Some of these—*The Traumatic Romance of Liang and Zhu* (Liang Zhu tongshi, 1926); *Mengjiangnü* (1926); and *The New Camille* (Xin Chahua, 1927)—were quite popular, but none were considered to have any artistic merit. Hu Die later confessed to having reservations about continuing her career with Tianyi but waited for a suitable moment to leave the company. Hu Die also said, however, that while at Tianyi she familiarized herself with the workings of the industry and the exposure helped her to advance.

The opportunity Hu Die was waiting for came in 1928 when Tianyi had to restructure and all contracts had to be renegotiated. She tactfully declined to sign hers and in that year joined the Mingxing Film Studio. Of the three people who operated this company, Zheng Zhengqiu (1888–1935) distinguished himself by a talent for writing good scripts and adapting pieces from the work of others. From Zheng Zhengqiu, Hu Die learned a great deal about what constituted good films. Also, under the direction of Zhang Shichuan (1889–1953), her acting improved. At this time, she was earning a monthly salary of $1,000, a considerable sum at that time. Her first film with Mingxing was *Tower in the White Clouds* (Baiyun ta, 1928). Her co-star in this film was Ruan Lingyu (*q.v.*) with whom she forged a lasting friendship, and the two became the biggest stars in Chinese film in the 1930s. In that same year, Hu Die first played a role for which she would become known to thousands of fans: Red Girl (Honggu) in the film series *Burning of the Red Lotus Temple* (Huoshao Hongliansi). This series was based on a popular martial arts novel. The first film met with such success that between 1928 and 1931 a total of eighteen films of the same title were made. Ironically, Hu Die had joined Mingxing in the hope of acting in films of a higher standard, but in the first three years all she had to her credit was a string of popular martial arts films. *Burning of the Red Lotus Temple* also had an unexpected social impact. Its success at the box office was such that it spawned dozens of shoddy imitators that led to a martial arts craze. Children ran away from home to seek out a master of special skills, and schoolwork was cast aside in favor of martial arts comics and fiction. As a result, intellectuals criticized the films and publications, and Hu Die, the shining star of *Burning of the Red Lotus Temple*, was indirectly affected by the negative criticism.

In 1930, Mingxing worked toward producing sound films. They signed a contract with Pathé in a joint venture in which the dialogues were pre-recorded. Hu Die had the honor of starring in the first sound film made in China using this method. Although *The Singing Girl Red Peony* (Genü Hong Mudan) was not excellent either artistically or technically, it was welcomed by fans as a novelty. Because many of the early film stars were southerners, from Guangdong, they had difficulty speaking standard Mandarin (*guoyu*) and were forced either to quit the industry or strive to learn the correct pronunciation. Hu Die, however, was fortunate in that she had learned the Beijing accent from her Manchu "Nannan," her father's concubine's mother, who had lived with them for many years. Hu Die was happier with the next two films she made because, not only were they real sound films, they were of a much higher quality. Moreover, Hu Die had a chance to sing a folksong in *The Flower of Freedom* (Ziyou zhi hua) and in the traditional storytelling genre *dagu* in *A Marriage of Tears and Laughter* (Tixiao yinyuan). Mingxing also hoped that these two films would improve its image as a maker of serious films. The company was even willing to film on location in Beijing. So it was that in 1931 the directors Zhang Shichuan and Hong Shen set off with the location unit by train for Beijing. Just as they arrived in Tianjin on 18 September, China exploded with the news of the Japanese occupation of Shenyang (Mukden) in the northeast (Manchuria). Hu Die not only heard the news but saw in Tianjin the disgruntled soldiers who were being withdrawn from the northeast. With great difficulty, the team finally reached Beijing, where they stayed for two months before receiving another piece of bad news. The Shanghai filmmakers Dahua were also filming *Marriage of Tears and Laughter*. It seems that copyright at that time did not include film rights, so that although Mingxing had the support of Zhang Henshui, the author of this famous opus of the romantic fiction genre known as the Butterfly School, they were not covered legally. Because the decision to film *Marriage of Tears and Laughter* was made suddenly in order to save money in shooting on location, they had set out before actually receiving the permit they had applied for. Zhang Shichuan and Hong Shen therefore quickly wound up their work in Beijing and returned with the whole team to Shanghai in the middle of November.

Hu Die had two concerns after the return to Shanghai. The first was the legal case involving *Marriage of Tears and Laughter*. Mingxing was adamant that they obtain the film rights in view of its investment already made. When they could get no satisfaction through legal channels, the studio asked the help of Du Yuesheng, one of Shanghai's biggest gangsters, promising 100,000 yuan to Dahua. Dahua was supported by Huang Jinrong, the gangster mentor of Du Yuesheng, and the quarrel was thus peacefully resolved.

Hu Die's second worry was more personal. She was rumored to have danced in Beijing with the "young marshal" Zhang Xueliang on the evening Shenyang was lost to the Japanese. He had inherited his warlord father's northeastern army and allied it to the KMT army of Chiang Kai-shek. He was said to have been in hospital in Beijing when the invasion took place, but instead of ordering his troops to fight the Japanese Zhang told them not to resist. Years later, the truth came out: when Zhang had reported the Japanese action, Chiang Kai-shek ordered him not to resist. Without the support of the central government, Zhang had not wished to fight and lose his army. Many people hated him for not resisting and were willing to believe the worst.

Hu Die thus by association became an innocent victim in this incident. She was publicly attacked for enjoying herself at the time of an enemy attack. These were serious charges that could harm the actress personally and damage the reputation of Mingxing. Hu Die therefore bought space in Shanghai's biggest newspaper, *Shen bao*, to tell her side of the story, pointing out that when Shenyang was attacked on 18 September, she and the Mingxing team had just arrived in Tianjin. Hu Die suggested that the rumor had been created as part of a conspiracy by the Japanese news media to discredit Zhang Xueliang. The staff and actors of Mingxing substantiated her story in a separate advertisement in the same paper that day. These countermeasures helped reduce the harmful effects of the rumor. When various memoirs of people involved with Zhang Xueliang were published in the 1970s, it became clear that he had never met Hu Die in his life. Her biographer pointed out that despite these disturbing incidents in 1931, Hu Die remained calm and performed her duties as usual, revealing an inner strength of character.

Mingxing hoped that the legal troubles *Marriage of Tears and Laughter* had encountered would attract sufficient public attention to make it a box office success. However, although the film did reasonably well, it fell short of its creators' expectations. For Hu Die, however, the cinema piece was a personal triumph. For the first time, she was recognized for her acting talent. At the peak of her career, Hu Die earned the title "film queen" through a well-publicized newspaper ballot of all film viewers. This title, which she was too modest to accept, gave her the clout to be the leader of the film world; the prestige further increased her already considerable popularity.

Leftist dramatists and film workers were increasingly influential in the 1930s. When Mingxing faced financial difficulties after the *Marriage of Tears and Laughter* incident, they looked around for new blood to give them a new dimension. The success of some left-wing films prompted the company to approach three left-wing scriptwriters: Aying (Qian Xingcun, 1900–1977); Xia Yan (Shen Duanxian, b. 1900); and Zheng Boqi (1895–1979). It gave them entrée into China's mainstream film industry. Xia Yan contributed two scripts: *The Flood* (Hongshui) and *The Cosmetics Market* (Zhifen shichang), both starring Hu Die. The former was a feature film about the Yangzi [Yangtze] River flood with documentary footage skillfully edited into it. Its realism impressed the audience and clear social message also won praise from critics. *The Cosmetics Market* was tailored to Hu Die's personality and on the surface was not too different from Mingxing's usual stories of a good little woman. However, it took a deeper look at the life of a working woman to reveal the hypocrisy of women's economic independence and the prevailing rhetoric of gender equality. As the humiliated and exploited working woman, Hu Die won popularity at the box office and critical acclaim. In the years that followed, she made films advocating class struggle as well as films of the Butterfly School. The film in which Hu Die took special pride was *Sisters* (Zimei hua, 1934); in it she played a pair of twin sisters with different personalities. The film was extremely popular and is generally recognized as her best film.

In February 1935, Hu Die received a personal invitation to participate in a film festival being held in the Soviet Union. For various reasons, she did not arrive in Moscow until 10 March, ten days after the festival had closed, yet she was warmly welcomed by the Soviet government and film industry. Her films *Sisters* and *Orchid in a Remote Valley* (Konggu lan) premiered in Moscow and Leningrad, and she had the opportunity to visit studios and talk to well-known personalities of the Soviet film industry. From Moscow Hu Die went on to Berlin, Paris, London, Geneva, and Rome, enjoying VIP treatment wherever she went, studying the film industry and exchanging ideas with film workers. Along the way, Hu Die took careful notes and photographs for a travelogue that was published on her return by Liangyou Publishing House.

After the unpleasant experience of her broken engagement and subsequent lawsuit, together with the accompanying troublesome press coverage, Hu Die was very careful in her personal life. In 1931 through her cousin Hu Shan, the actress had met a young man named Pan Yousheng who worked for a Shanghai trading company. He did not seem to conform to the negative image of being a comprador or businessman and their relationship progressed slowly and cautiously, partly because Hu Die was worried how marriage might affect her popularity. However, the two grew closer when she came back from her European tour, and in autumn 1935 they announced their intention to marry. The wedding was the social event of the year in Shanghai: the bridesmaids, groomsmen, flower girls, and page boys were all well-known film and child stars. Hu Die's decision to marry meant that she was ready to retire, at least partly, from the film world. She wanted to leave at the peak of her popularity. However, because Pan Yousheng had no objection to her making films, she contracted with Mingxing to make one film a year after marriage. When war broke out between China and Japan in mid-1937, Hu Die made only one more film for the studio before Shanghai fell to the Japanese and Mingxing ceased to exist.

Hu Die and her husband left Shanghai for Hong Kong. Pan Yousheng had a high-salaried position in a trading firm, while Hu Die busied herself with social and family responsibilities. She gave birth to a daughter and son, the former probably born in 1939, the latter in 1941. In the meantime, she also made a couple of films to pass the time. Then Hong Kong fell to the Japanese in December 1941. Although Hu Die was on the list of Chinese to be protected, she still lived in anxiety and fear because such special treatment was bound to come with conditions. And indeed, the Japanese tried to make her work for them. This drove Hu Die and her husband to feel that they had to leave Hong Kong quickly: she entrusted her luggage to the underground and walked out of her home one morning as if going to visit relatives, being guided by partisans from the New Territories to inland China. She stayed at Qujiang (also known as Shaoguan) in Guangdong for a year and a half and from there went to Guilin in Guangxi Province, arriving in Chongqing at the end of 1943. On her arrival there, Hu Die let it be known through the press that she would like to contribute to the war effort by taking part in films that would help national salvation. She was soon invited to star in a film entitled *The Road to Nation Building* (Jiangguo zhi lu) about the building of a railway from Guangxi to Guizhou to aid the war effort. Location work in Guilin coincided with a ferocious attack by the Japanese along the Hunan-Guangxi Railway and the film unit lost all its equipment, becoming part of the tens of thousands of refugees caught on foot in the crossfire of war. Hu Die said in her memoir that *The Road to Nation Building* "is my only unfinished film and this incident is the most tragic moment of my life."

Her life in Chongqing became the source of yet another controversy, one that has not yet reached a satisfactory conclusion. Hu Die's name was connected with Dai Li, the KMT spy master who was dangerously powerful during the war years. Shen Zui, a former staffer of Dai Li's, described Hu Die in his memoirs as Dai Li's mistress. This was confirmed by accounts published on the mainland during the 1980s. Most accounts from Taiwan did not mention the affair, yet no evidence to disprove it was offered, even by those critical of Shen Zui's memoirs. Dai Li was killed in an accident in March 1946 at a moment when all eyes were on the civil war and the subsequent CCP takeover, which may explain why little was known of the affair.

After the war, Hu Die returned to a Shanghai troubled by inflation and unrest. Pan Yousheng, who always seemed able to remain one step ahead of trouble, moved his family to Hong Kong again in 1946. He started a trading company and factory, manufacturing thermos flasks under the brand Butterfly, named after Hu Die. She took an active part in promoting the product, appearing at trade fairs in Hong Kong and Southeast Asia. The couple had some happy years together, but then Pan Yousheng was diagnosed with cancer of the liver in 1958 and died a few months later. His company and factory were taken over by others, and Hu Die and her family lived on savings. Some sources mention the appearance during this period of a secret admirer (named Zhu Fangkun or Song Kunfang) who had known her in the 1920s and later made a fortune in Japan. He is said to have extended financial assistance to Hu Die after hearing that her husband had died. The two are said to have married in 1967; Zhu Fangkun died in the United States in 1986.

Hu Die returned to the silver screen in 1959 and made several films for the Shaw brothers of Hong Kong. This time she had to take roles as a middle aged or older woman. To begin with, Hu Die was uncomfortable with such parts but soon improved and gave creditable performances. One of these was in *Rear Door* (Houmen), directed by the young director Li Hanxiang who had to his credit two successful period films replete with beautiful young stars and colorful costumes. *Rear Door*, however, featured only a simple plot with two mature actors as the leading characters. Nevertheless, when it premiered at a gala charity function in Hong Kong at the end of the year, the film commanded great crowds. The following year (1960) at the Seventh Asian Film Festival in Tokyo, it won Best Film Award and Hu Die won the Best Actress Award. She finally retired in 1966 at the age of fifty-six, more than forty years after debuting in 1925.

Hu Die migrated to Canada in 1975 and lived in Vancouver, where her son and family lived. She tried to live the life of an ordinary woman and, to avoid undue attention, enrolled in an English class as Pan Baojuan. In 1986 she began dictating her memoirs, which were serialized in the Taiwan newspaper *Lianhe bao* and appeared as a monograph at the end of that year; mainland editions appeared in 1987 and 1988. Hu Die had a stroke in April 1989 and died on 23 April. She was survived by her daughter, who lived in the U.S., and her son, living in Vancouver.

During her long career, Hu Die met many interesting people, including the Hollywood stars Mary Pickford and Charlie Chaplin. Her great ambition had been to go to Hollywood one day, but when she finally made it to the studios, the occasion was after her retirement and only as a private individual in a multitude of tourists. Also of interest is her friendship with the famous *jingju* (Peking opera) actor Mei Lanfang. They first met when Hu Die went to Beijing to film *Marriage of Tears and Laughter* on location and met again when the two were both invited to the Soviet Union. They traveled to Russia together by boat and train, and on that trip Hu Die learned to sing *jingju* from the master and became his informal pupil.

Hu Die's film career extended over a period during which China was embroiled in political turmoil. She always remained aloof from politics, however. Hu Die saw herself as simply a tool in the hands of her directors and produced the same quality work in left-wing films, which the KMT authorities hated, as in films that incurred attack and criticism from left-wing film workers. Her personal life was also comparatively comfortable and happy. In all her dealings, Hu Die retained a balanced attitude and revealed an innate wisdom that enabled her to escape the tragic destinies and short-lived success that seemed to accompany many of the female stars of her era.

Lily Xiao Hong LEE

Hu Die. *Hu Die huiyilu.* Beijing: Wenhua yishu chubanshe, 1988.
Shen Zui. "Wo suo zhidao de Dai Li." *Wenshi ziliao xuan*, 22. Beijing: Zhonghua shuju, 1961.
Yu Yiqi. "Hu Die yu Dai Li." *Zhuanji wenxue*, 55, no. 3 (September 1989): 35–38.
Zheng Renjia. "Hu Die." *Zhuanji wenxue*, 54, no. 6 (June 1989): 146–51.
Zhu Jian. *Dianying huanghou Hu Die.* Lanzhou: Lanzhou daxue chubanshe, 1996.

Hu Feipei: *see* **Zhong Yuzheng**

Hu Jieqing

Hu Jieqing, b. 1905, in Beijing into a Manchu Plain Red Banner Clan, is a painter in traditional Chinese style, specializing in flowers and birds.

Although the expectation that women behave according to tradition gradually lessened after the establishment of the Republic in 1911, He Jieqing's family still adhered closely to the old traditions of the Qing dynasty and expected their daughter to grow up, following traditional standards of feminine behavior. She loved literature, painting, and calligraphy from a young age and enjoyed a classical literary education as part of her upbringing. Hu Jieqing also learned painting and calligraphy from the well-known painter Wang Kongqi (*zi* Caibai) for four years.

Like many other women of her time, Hu Jieqing wanted to pursue higher education and become independent; the young woman managed to overcome family opposition and was allowed to study Chinese literature at Pei-p'ing Normal University (Beiping shifan daxue) on the condition that she would not fraternize with male students. During her university years, Hu Jieqing took courses in painting and calligraphy and formed the Truth Society (Zhen she) with students who shared a love for literature. When the famous writer Lao She (Shu Qingchun, 1899–1966) came back to Beijing from England in 1930, members of the society asked Hu Jieqing to extend an invitation to him on their behalf to give a talk. They chose her, perhaps, because Lao She also was of Manchu descent. In this way, Hu Jieqing met her future husband.

Because her family remained bound to tradition, however, a matchmaker for the two was necessary, and Lao She's old friend, the philosopher Luo Changpei, volunteered to perform the role. The couple married after Hu Jieqing graduated from Pei-p'ing Normal University in 1931, and the two then moved to Shandong where Lao She taught at universities in Jinan and Qingdao, and Hu Jieqing taught in high schools. They had three children while they lived there.

With the outbreak of the Sino-Japanese War (1937–45), most intellectuals moved to the rear, in southwest China. Hu Jieqing was aware of Lao She's mounting personal struggle in wanting to follow suit. Because of his filial responsibilities—three young children and his elderly mother, in her eighties and living alone in Beijing—he did not join his friends and colleagues, who had already left. Hu Jieqing offered to shoulder the responsibility of rearing the children and caring for his mother. Deeply grateful, Lao She took the last train leaving Jinan (probably in 1938) and headed for Chongqing, where he worked hard at writing, bringing together writers of different political persuasions under the unified aim of national salvation. Hu Jieqing stayed in the Japanese-occupied area. Going to Beijing that year, she earned a living by teaching at the Girls' High School attached to Pei-p'ing Normal University (Beiping shifan daxue nüfuzhong). In this way, she fulfilled the role of being a model wife and mother in the Chinese tradition.

After her mother-in-law died in 1942, Hu Jieqing traveled with her children through enemy-occupied areas and across enemy lines to Chongqing to reunite with her husband. What Lao She earned from writing, however, was not enough to feed a family of five to which they soon added a daughter. Hu Jieqing found work as an editor in a unit providing reading material for the community and also popular readers under the National Editing and Translating Bureau (Guoli bianyiguan, shehui tongsu duwuzu), thus assuming a double burden of work and domestic duties. During this period, the couple barely managed to make ends meet, but Hu Jieqing contributed greatly to Lao She's writing career. She not only provided him with a trouble-free environment in which to work but also valuable writing material. Through her keen observation of people and events, Hu Jieqing passed on to Lao She what she had seen and experienced in occupied Beijing and during her trip to the west; on the basis of what she told him, Lao She wrote his famous trilogy *Four Generations under the Same Roof* (Si shi tong tang). He acknowledged her contribution, thanking his wife for "bringing me this novel series." After the war, Hu Jieqing continued to work and support the family while Lao She went in 1946 to the United States as a visitor of the State Department. Hu Jieqing stayed in Chongqing, teaching at Beipei Normal College (Beipei shifan xueyuan) and working as an associate professor at the Teaching and Research Department of Rural Studies.

In 1950, Hu Jieqing and her husband reunited in Beijing, where Lao She became a professional writer with a salary, and their circumstances became more comfortable. At this time, Hu Jieqing was finally able to do something she had always wanted to do. She began studying painting formally with the famous painter Qi Baishi (1863–1957). Building on the foundation of skills gained when young, Hu Jieqing progressed rapidly. Her flowers show Qi's influence but clearly bear her own style, characterized by attention to detail and a tendency toward realistic portrayal in contrast to the bold

and highly idealized form of her master. She strove always for freshness and originality in a genre that had a tradition of over one thousand years. The large painting on
which she collaborated in 1957 with Yu Feiyin, Chen Banding, and Sun Yongzhao,
Blooms in Red and Purple, was later presented by the PRC to the Vietnamese leader
Ho Chi Minh. In 1958, Hu Jieqing was appointed as a professional painter with the
Beijing Academy of Painting. She also designed a series of chrysanthemum stamps,
and this and some of her other work won several awards.

In 1966, at the very beginning of the Cultural Revolution, Lao She was attacked by
young Red Guards. His body was found in Taiping Lake on 24 August 1966. It is
generally believed that, unable to bear the humiliation meted out to him, Lao She
drowned himself. In his writings, his son Shu Yi draws a parallel between the death of
his father and that of Qu Yuan, whose own suicide by drowning over two thousand
years ago was intended to draw attention to the political injustice he and others had
suffered. Hu Jieqing, however, believed that Lao She was murdered, and there were
others who were of the same mind. Left feeling angry and vengeful by Lao She's
sudden death, his persecutors then incriminated Hu Jieqing and her children. For
twelve years, she endured the pain of a broken family and political persecution until
she and her children were finally exonerated in 1978.

In the 1970s and 1980s, despite her age, Hu Jieqing devoted time and effort to two
things: the editing of Lao She's works and her own career as a painter. She edited *Lao
She's Autobiographical Writings on His Life and Literary Creation* (Lao She de
shenghuo yu chuangzuo zishu) and *The Complete Dramatic Works of Lao She* (Lao
She juzuo quanji). Hu Jieqing also wrote memoirs about him, such as *Random Memories of Lao She* (Sanji Lao She) on which she collaborated with her son Shu Yi. For
herself, Hu Jieqing published paintings and calligraphy and often used them as a
means of winning goodwill for the PRC. She inscribed a painting for the people of
Taiwan and mounted an exhibition in Hong Kong. Hu Jieqing wrote essays, articles,
and poetry, some but not all related to Lao She. One book of her paintings was published in 1980—*The First Album of Jieqing's Paintings* (Jieqing huace chuji)—and
her pieces can also be seen in albums such as *Zhongguo nühuajia zuopinxuan*,
Zhongguo funü huaxuan, and *Zhongguo hua*. Her paintings and calligraphy in both
cursive and regular style can be viewed at various museums throughout China.

Hu Jieqing is one of many Chinese women who, having fulfilled their role as a
"good wife and wise mother" in the traditional sense, created in their later years
something purely for themselves. Such women demonstrated extraordinary dedication and a capacity for long years of hard work. Surely, Hu Jieqing exemplifies the
Chinese woman in transition from housewife to career woman.

Lily Xiao Hong LEE

Huaxia funü mingren cidian. Beijing: Huaxia chubanshe, 1988.
Yingwen *Zhongguo funü*, ed. *Gujin zhuming funü renwu*, vol. 2. Shijiazhuang: Hebei renmin
   chubanshe, 1986, 726–29.
Zhongguo funü guanli ganbu xueyuan, ed. *Gujin Zhongwai nümingren cidian*. Beijing:
   Zhongguo guangbo dianshi chubanshe, 1980, 142–43.

Hu Ruihua: *see* **Hu Die**

Hu Xian: *see* **Aw, Sally**

Huang Dianxian
Huang Dianxian, fl. early twentieth century, born in Singapore, was a forerunner for education of Chinese women in overseas Chinese communities in Southeast Asia, and one of the earliest female educationists in modern Chinese history.

Huang Dianxian was born into a wealthy Cantonese family; her father Huang Yafu (Wong Ah Fook) was a famous merchant banker and leader of the Cantonese communities in Singapore and Johore in the late-nineteenth and early-twentieth centuries. She received a traditional Chinese education but was influenced by reformers such as Kang Youwei and Liang Qichao, who were concerned about raising the status of Chinese women. In June 1899, two ardent followers of these reformers—Dr. Lim Boon Keng (Lin Wenqing) and Khoo Seok Wan (Qiu Shuyuan)—founded the Singapore Chinese Girls' School with seven students. In two months, the number increased to thirty. English was the medium of instruction at the school, and its curriculum catered to the daughters of Straits Chinese families whose principal language was English.

In 1905 Huang Dianxian founded Huaqiao Girls' School (Huaqiao xuexiao) in Singapore. Chinese was the medium of instruction, but nothing is known about the school's curriculum, staff, or students, except that Huang Dianxian herself assumed the role of principal. The school operated for almost ten years.

As a dedicated educationist and individual of honesty and integrity, Huang Dianxian was known during her lifetime as "the first good person in the overseas Chinese communities in Southeast Asia." She was probably influenced by the efforts of Lim and Khoo in educating her Chinese students, but Huang Dianxian herself apparently perceived a need to provide a school for girls from Chinese-speaking backgrounds. She may also have been influenced by her elder brother Huang Jingtang, who was sent back to China to receive a Chinese education, and enthusiastically promoted the value of education. Of the three schools he founded in Canton, one was for girls.

YEN Ching-hwang

Li Guan Kin [Li Yuanjin]. *Lin Wenqing de sixiang: Zhong-Xi wenhua de huiliu yu maodun.* Singapore: Singapore Society of Asian Studies, 1990.
Song Ong Siang. *One Hundred Years' History of the Chinese in Singapore.* Singapore: University of Malaya Press, 1967 reprint.
Tay Lian Soo [Zheng Liangshu]. "Xin-Ma huashe zaoqi de nüzi jiaoyu." *Malaixiya huaren yanjiu xuekan,* 1 (August 1997): 47–58.
Xu Suwu. *Xinjiapo huaqiao jiaoyu quanmao.* Singapore: Nanyang shuju, 1949.

Huang Liang
Huang Liang, b. 1920, in Shanghai, although her family was from Ningbo County, Zhejiang Province, is an organic chemist who has undertaken considerable research in medicinal chemistry.

Her parents divorced early in her childhood, and she was brought up by both her mother, Xu Jingfen, a nurse, and her unmarried aunt. Huang Liang was always diligent and single-minded in pursuing her purpose in life. She graduated from McTyeire Girls' School (Zhongxi nüxue) in Shanghai in 1938, and because of her excellent results was recommended to St. John's University, Shanghai, without having to sit the entrance examination. In 1942, Huang Liang graduated from its Chemistry Department at the top of her class.

From that year to 1944, she worked at Shanghai Biochemical Pharmaceutical Company. The company reluctantly employed her at first because she was a woman, but later they commended her for being the first person to manufacture Vitamin C in China. By nature proud and stubborn, Huang Liang worked hard to show what a Chinese could do, as well as what a woman could do. In 1944, she left Shanghai, which was then under Japanese occupation, for Chongqing. Huang Liang taught and carried out research at Chongqing University, Central Industrial Laboratories, and other places. In 1946, the head of the Chemistry Department of St. John's University recommended her for further studies at Cornell University in the United States. The year she received her Ph.D. from Cornell, she also married Liu Jinxu, who had gained his Ph.D. in Livestock Nutrition. In the first half of the 1950s, Huang Liang did research at the laboratories at Bryn Mawr University (1949–50), Cornell University (1950–52), Wayne State University (1952–54), and Iowa University (1954–56), working with such well-known chemists as A.T. Blomquest, C. Djerassi, and E. Wenkert. During this period, Huang Liang published articles on organic theory, organic synthesis, steroid chemistry, and the determination of the chemical structure of natural bodies.

In 1956, she returned to China with her husband and their five-year-old daughter, giving up a comfortable life in America to use her knowledge to serve her country, despite the far from ideal conditions and research facilities in China. Huang Liang was already an experienced organic chemist with good training in chemical synthesis, extraction of plant matter, and determining the chemical structures of compounds. In response to China's needs, however, she changed her field of research to pharmaceutics and joined the Department of Medicinal Chemistry in the Institute of Materia Medica at the Chinese Academy of Sciences in that same year. In the 1950s, when China still had to import hypertension drugs, Huang Liang developed China's first anti-hypertension drug, *jiangyaling*, whose active principle, alkaloid reserpine, was extracted from the trees of the native genus *Rauwolfia* (also spelled *Rauvolfia*). She also initiated the study of steroids at the Institute of Materia Medica; the project Huang Liang headed extracted hecongenin from agave waste to obtain an anti-inflammatory cortisone drug. For this achievement, she received the National Science Congress Award (Quanguo kexue dahui jiang) in 1978.

Huang Liang next turned her attention to anti-cancer and anti-virus drugs, contraceptives, and natural products. Carcinogens are necessary for the study of anti-cancer drugs and so Huang Liang first studied nitrosamine, which came from mold-affected food. In a crudely equipped laboratory she and her team finally succeeded in making the carcinogen nitrosamine. In the 1970s, researchers at a hospital in Hainan (formerly part of Guangdong Province) discovered a valuable rare botanic species—

Cephalotaxus hainanensis Li—containing harringtonine, which has anti-carcinogenic properties. Huang Liang and her colleagues isolated more than twenty alkaloids from this tree, among them hailin alkaloid or harringtonine, five of which were found to possess anti-carcinogenic properties. Because natural harringtonine did not occur in sufficient quantity to satisfy clinical needs, they decided in 1973 to synthesize it from a similar but not anti-carcinogenic alkaloid found in a large number of trees of the *Cephalotaxus hainanensis Li* species. Their efforts succeeded the following year, and the product has been used clinically to treat acute monocyclic leukemia, acute granulocyclic leukemia, and erythroleukemia. The achievement won a prize from the Ministry of Health in 1980 and also comprised the major body of research for the project "A Study of the Anti-Carcinogenic Properties of the Harringtonine from *Cephalotaxus hainanensis li*," which won First Prize in the National Award for Advances in Science and Technology (Guojiaji keji jinbu jiang). Huang Liang also directed research into synthesizing derivatives of indirubin, an anti-carcinogenic element of the Chinese medicinal herb indigo. A new drug, *yidianjia*, was developed from this and has been used clinically to treat chronic granulocyclic leukemia with better and less toxic results than indirubin.

In the 1980s, Huang Liang devoted herself to research into contraceptives; her main interest was in the male oral contraceptive gossypol. Extracted from cottonseed, in the 1970s gossypol was found to act as a contraceptive but had not been successfully isolated before the 1980s. Huang Liang was instrumental in Chinese scientists finally being able to split the compound into optically active enantiomers, an important international advance of research in this area. In the latter half of the decade, Huang Liang directed research on the chemical constitution of *Clausena lansium*, a plant of the Rutaceae family.The drugs they identified and isolated from it are used to treat icteric viral hepatitis. Some of the drugs Huang Liang and her colleagues found have been patented in China, Germany, and Japan.

As an academic, Huang Liang trained many students in the field of medicinal chemistry. She has also been active at conferences throughout the world to raise standards in the field and contributed chapters in textbooks, including "Advances in the Study of Tumors: Chemical Treatment" (Zhongliuxue jinzhan: Huaxue zhiliao), edited by Wu Huanxing. Her own work, *The Application of Ultraviolet Spectroscopy in Organic Chemistry* (Ziwaiguangpu zai youji huaxue zhong de yingyong) and the fascicle "Pharmaceutics and Pharmacology" (Yaowuxue yu yaolixue) in the *Medical Encyclopedia* (Yixue baike quanshu) were published in 1988. In 1980, Huang Liang presented a paper at the Fourth International Conference on Family Planning in Genoa on the male contraceptive gossypol. In 1985, she spoke to the Chemistry Conference of the Pacific Region in Hawaii regarding the contribution of chemistry to family planning. Moreover, Huang Liang keeps countries such as Denmark, France, Mexico, and the United States abreast of advances made in China in the study of harringtonine. She also contributed articles or chapters in books to overseas academic publications. In 1984, Huang Liang was elected deputy director of the China Cancer Research Fund; from 1986 to 1989 served as consultant to the All-China Family Planning Committee; and in 1990 served as consultant to the All-China Tumor Prevention and Treatment Office. On the political side, she was a member of the Fifth, Sixth, and Seventh CPPCC.

Huang Liang trained as an organic chemist but shifted her teaching and research interests to medicinal chemistry to enable China to produce its own drugs and not rely on imports. To do this, she taught herself the pathology and study of tumors, biochemistry, and immunology and offered herself for clinical tests of her drugs. Huang Liang's hard-working, persistent nature has served her well in her life's work, and her contribution covers many fields, including anti-hypertension, anti-viral and anti-cancer drugs, as well as male oral contraceptives.

While researching harringtonine in the early 1970s, Huang Liang was diagnosed with rectal cancer. She underwent radiation treatment and surgery and resumed her work, seeking cures for cancer through pharmaceutics, as soon as she was able. Huang Liang appears to have had no recurrence of the disease.

Lily Xiao Hong LEE

Yingwen *Zhongguo funü*, ed. *Gujin zhuming funü renwu*, vol. 2. Shijiazhuang: Hebei renmin chubanshe, 1986, 1000–1005.
Zhongguo xiandai kexuejia zhuanji, vol. 2. Beijing: Kexue chubanshe, 1991, 269–74.
Zhonghua quanguo fulian. *Zhongguo nü yuanshi*. Shenyang: Liaoning renmin chubanshe, 1995, 263–76.

Huang Luyin: *see* **Luyin**

Huang Ying: *see* **Luyin**

Huang Zhang: *see* **Bai Wei**

Huang Zonghan: *see* **Xu Zonghan**

Huang Zongying

Huang Zongying, b. 1925, in Beijing although her family originated from Rui'an, Zhejiang Province, achieved fame as both an actress and writer.

Her literati family enjoyed high social standing; Huang Zongying's great-grandfather and grandfather were both metropolitan graduates (*jinshi*), while her father, Huang Cengming, was an engineer. He held enlightened democratic views and studied in Japan in the closing years of the Qing dynasty. Her mother, Chen Cong, was a housewife, intelligent and well-read, kind, and loving. Huang Zongying thus grew up in an atmosphere of liberty, enlightenment, and affection. Her parents adopted a democratic attitude toward family affairs, allowing Huang Zongying and her siblings to pursue their interests and choose freely their path in life.

Of greatest influence on Huang Zongying's artistic career was her eldest brother, Huang Zongjiang, four years senior. Precociously talented, while at secondary school he wrote on a wide range of topics in forms as diverse as poetry, fiction, prose essay, and drama and went on to win a place in Chinese theater history as a writer of drama and film. Huang Zongying also developed an early interest in the arts. As a child, she read passionately, an interest facilitated by the family home's impressive library encompassing classical and modern, Chinese, and foreign books. Huang Zongying was particularly captivated by "To Young Readers" (Zhi xiao duzhe) by Bing Xin (*q.v.*) and in imitation penned the prose essay "Under a Big Tree" (Zai dashu xia). This marked Huang Zongying's first excursion into print, at the age of nine, in the weekly *Huangjin shidai*, edited by Huang Zongjiang. Soon afterward Huang Zongying published the Essay Series Scribblings of a Solitary Student (Hanchuang zoubi).

At the age of sixteen, in 1941, Huang Zongying accompanied her eldest brother to Shanghai, where she became an actress in the professional theater company run by Huang Zuolin. Her stage debut in *Metamorphosis* (Tuibian) was soon followed by *Mandarin Duck Sword* (Yuanyang jian), *The King of Chu and His Concubine* (Bawang bieji), and *Sweet Sister* (Tian jie'er). Her skills as a performer matured greatly during these years on stage.

She devoted her energies to film art in 1946. Chinese theater, flourishing during the Sino-Japanese War (1937–45), had gradually fallen into decline, leading large numbers of playwrights, directors, and performers to look for opportunities in the newly emerging world of film. At the invitation of the renowned scriptwriter Shen Fu, Huang Zongying made her film debut in *Pursuit* (Zhui). In 1947 she was doubly fortunate to win the leading role in the film *Rhapsody of Bliss* (Xingfu kuangxiangqu), an important turning point both artistically and personally. This film boasted an impressive array of talent, including the writer Chen Baichen, known for such comedies as *Wedding March* and *Blueprint for Official Promotion*. The director Chen Liting also enjoyed considerable fame at the time. In the male lead role was China's greatest screen star, Zhao Dan, whose 1930s hits *Crossroads* and *Street Angel* had spellbound millions of film goers.

At that time Huang Zongying was caught in an unhappy marriage, being at odds with her husband and a mother-in-law intent on exercising her full powers; Huang Zongying was forbidden to continue the performance career she so loved. Huang Zongying fled her marriage in Beijing to go to Shanghai, hub of the national film industry, to work on *Rhapsody of Bliss*. The male lead, Zhao Dan, famous for his film and stage accomplishments, had also been a founder and most active organizer of the left-wing theater movement. He had been imprisoned for five years from 1938 by the anti-communist warlord Sheng Shicai; Zhao Dan's wife, believing a rumor that he had already been martyred, had remarried. Huang Zongying was won over by Zhao Dan's unconventional character, friendliness, and lack of pretension at this, their first collaboration. By the end of filming, their fledgling love had grown.

Rhapsody of Bliss was the catalyst for Huang Zongying and Zhao Dan's romance; it is also a fine film etched in Chinese film history. Its narrative of the lives and fates of a group of ordinary city dwellers authentically portrays post-war life in KMT-ruled areas. Zhao Dan plays the silver-tongued Wu Zhihai, intent on making his fortune but not at the price of moral degradation. Wu, narrow but good-natured and equipped to survive in a big city, is brought to life with great subtlety by Zhao. Huang Zongying plays a prostitute, deceived and toyed with by a hustler and forced into selling drugs. Huang's portrayal of the heroine is also of unprecedented artistic quality, capturing with authenticity, naturalness, and control the prostitute's degeneracy and fierce temperament as well as goodness and integrity. Zhao Dan and Huang Zongying married on New Year's Day 1948, their wedding presided over by the famous director Zheng Junli and attended by many people from the film industry.

Shortly afterward, Zhao and Huang joined the Kunlun Film Studio, run by the CCP. Underground CCP organizations were active in Shanghai, and many leading film industry figures such as Chen Baichen, Xia Yan, Yang Hansheng, and Cai Chusheng were either members or closely associated with the party. They made many films outstanding for artistic merit and political content, ushering in a masterpiece-studded era of unprecedented richness for the Shanghai film industry. Huang Zongying and Zhao Dan devoted themselves to the work with enormous zeal. In a little over a year, Huang worked on such outstanding films as *In the Streets and Alleyways* (Jietou xiangwei), *The Cock Crows at Dawn* (Jiming zao kan tian), *Ballad of a Beauty* (Liren xing), and *The Crow and the Sparrow* (Wuya yu maque). She created a series of characters that included an official's mistress, a prostitute, a revolutionary, and a teacher, confirming her status as a character actor of rare skill and depth. The films to which Huang and Zhao contributed in this period represent a milestone in Chinese film history; some foreign critics believe they reached an unprecedented peak of achievement and rank at the forefront of world cinema.

Huang Zongying was also an exemplary wife and mother. Despite a demanding schedule of producing five films per year, she maintained a highly organized household, catering always to Zhao's culinary and other needs and caring for two children from his previous marriage. She later also volunteered to take on the burden of raising two children of the 1930s film star Zhou Xuan (*q.v.*).

Huang Zongying was the youngest member of China's delegation to the Second World Peace Convention, held in Poland in autumn 1950. In the same year, she attended a National Youth Delegates Convention and worked on the film *A Life of Wu Xun* (Wu Xun zhuan). Her visits to Warsaw and Moscow left such deep impressions that when invited by Premier Zhou Enlai and his wife Deng Yingchao (*q.v.*) for an interview on her return Huang Zongying excitedly related her experiences and thoughts. Zhou Enlai suggested she commit her account to writing, and the actress did so in a number of short articles. He also recommended her articles for publication in the *People's Daily* (Renmin ribao).

In 1951 Huang Zongying published the prose collection *Onward Moves the Peace Train* (Heping lieche xiangqian xing). Later, between the prose collections *Stories of Love* (Ai de gushi) and *A Girl* (Yige nühaizi), she starred in the film *Blessings for the Children* (Wei haizimen zhufu), probably her last film. One reason she switched from film to writing, which had also been a love of hers since childhood, was the astute realization that under the direction of Mao Zedong's policy that "the arts must serve the workers, peasants and soldiers, they must serve proletarian politics," PRC theater and film roles would become stereotypical worker, farmer, and soldier "heroes," leaving very few roles suited to her breadth of talent.

Huang Zongying worked creatively in film literature in 1954. The following year, her film script "Working Wherever the Motherland Needs Me" (Zai zuguo xuyao de gangwei shang) was filmed by the Shanghai Film Studio as *An Everyday Occupation* (Pingfan de shiye). In 1958 she co-wrote the script "Striving Together" (Ni zhui wo gan), the narrative for *The First Spring of the 60s* (Liushi niandai diyi chun), and the long documentary *Symphony for the Heroes of Shanghai* (Shanghai yingxiong jiaoxiangqu). In 1963 and 1964, Huang Zongying began to write in the reportage genre. Her works "An Unusual Girl" (Tebie de guniang) and "A Big Flag over Her Shoulder" (Xiaoya kang daqi) are based on the lives of the young urban intellectuals Xing Yanzi and Hou Juan, who were later made national youth study models. Both pieces received unanimous acclaim.

Although Huang Zongying had become a member of the CCP in 1956, with the start of the Cultural Revolution her fate was sealed because of her prominence as an actress in KMT-ruled China. Also, while Zhao Dan had been a peer of Mao Zedong's wife, Jiang Qing (*q.v.*), herself a former actress, Zhao Dan had been a core member of the left-wing theater alliance. Purportedly targeting the "black line" of the 1930s arts world, Jiang Qing disposed of anyone intimate with her secrets from that period. Zhao Dan, first in the firing line, was duly imprisoned. Many of the couple's friends from that decade, including Zheng Junli, Cai Chusheng, Xu Tao, and Wang Ying (*q.v.*), were hounded to death in chilling circumstances. Zhao Dan, however, miraculously endured five years in jail and another five with criminal status after his release. During these ten years, Huang Zongying was subjected to enormous mental pressures. At the beginning of the Cultural Revolution, she faced daily criticism as well as physical abuse and humiliation by Red Guards. For the five years of Zhao Dan's incarceration, Huang Zongying had no idea if her husband was alive or dead. Her family, numbering more than ten, were sent to live in one tiny room, with a meager allowance of thirty yuan per month. What pained her most was that her own children had sought to "draw the line" between themselves and their "anti-revolutionary" family, exposing the "anti-party criminal activities" of their parents in order to prove their own innocence.

Huang Zongying did not resume creative writing until the end of the Cultural Revolution when Zhao Dan was rehabilitated and returned to her side. In 1979, she took part in the Fourth National Delegates Convention for the Arts, was elected a member of the Executive Committee of the Chinese Writers' Association, and made special research fellow of the Research Center of the National Science Committee. In the next three years, Huang Zongying wrote over thirty reportage essays, prose essays, and poems, as well as the film scripts "Wen Yiduo" and "Red Candle" (Hong zhu). Both quantitatively and qualitatively, her literary output during this period well surpassed what she had done in the seventeen years before the Cultural Revolution.

Huang Zongying's literary achievement lies mainly in the reportage genre. For articles such as "Feelings of the Wild Geese" (Dayan qing), "Mandarin Oranges" (Ju), and "The Wooden Cabin" (Xiao muwu), she received the National Award for Outstanding Reportage Literature. Her work is characterized by a depth of emotional response, lyrical intensity, and use of inner monologue. Her descriptions take as their subject not the successful but the unsung common folk; in particular, she shows a concern for intellectuals facing hardship. Her three prize-winning articles all focus on such people. "Feelings of the Wild Geese" tells of the beleaguered Qin Guanshu, an assistant researcher at Xi'an Botanic Gardens. Qin works determinedly to improve the biological stock of poplars but is resisted by a web of ignorance and prejudice. "Mandarin Oranges" tells of the loneliness and sadness of Zeng Mian, an aging expert on mandarins. Too aloof and unconventional to compromise with the world, he has to forfeit work entitlements and is labeled mentally abnormal. "The Wooden Cabin" is the story of female forestry expert Xu Fengxiang who, drawn to exploring the mysteries of the wilderness, exchanges city comforts for the primeval forests of Tibet. She makes countless appeals to the authorities for the construction of a "wooden cabin," a mountain forest observation post, but her pleas fall on deaf ears. The intellectuals Huang Zongying describes are solitary battlers striving for their ideals with the fanaticism of martyrs to science but they lack recognition by society. Such stories demonstrated the prejudice and belittlement intellectuals had faced, their lack of opportunity to make use of knowledge, and society's continuing indifference toward their selfless attempts to benefit the country. Intellectuals had been discredited with such notions as "knowledge is useless" and debased by being called "stinking number nine." As this was the fate of an entire generation, her stories evoked considerable empathy. Huang Zongying uses in her reportage writing a writer's sense of justice and responsibility to inspire concern for the suppression of values and lend whatever power a voice may have to summon support for the oppressed.

Huang Zongying's reportage can also lay claim to considerable literary achievement. She often uses a first-person narrator, enabling the writer to appear directly within the work, pouring her deepest and most genuine feelings into her characters and amplifying their power. They are at once real people from real life and also moving artistic images endowed with universality, faithful to both life and art. Of special interest are her filmic techniques, the legacy of earlier work as a screen actress and scriptwriter; her writing is strengthened by such techniques as switches and flashbacks. Also remarked on and invariably acclaimed by critics are her detailed but fluid descriptions, scenes full of poetic lyricism and cadence, the simplicity of her language, and rich evocation of human life.

Rubing HONG
(Translated by Ian Chapman)

Beijing yuyan xueyuan. Zhongguo yishujia cidian bian weihui. *Zhongguo yishujia cidian: Xiandai, diyi fence.* Changsha: Hunan renmin chubanshe, 1981.

Cheng Jihua, ed. *Zhongguo dianying fazhan shi*, 2nd edn. Beijing: Zhongguo dianying chubanshe, 1980.

Huang Zongying. "Ye suan shi jianli." In *Zhongguo zuojia xiehui: Quanguo youxiu baogao wenxue pingxuan huojiang zuopin ji, 1981–1982.* Beijing: Renmin wenxue chuban she, 1984.

Jiang Hong. "Ta zhongxia yipian shengming zhi shu—Huang Zongying baogao wenxue de renwu suzao." *Dangdai zuojia pinglun* (Shenyang), no. 6 (1985).

Li Hui et al., eds. *Zhongguo xiandai xiju dianying yishujia zhuan.* Nanchang: Jiangxi renmin chubanshe, 1981.

Xu Guorong. "Huang Zongying, Zhao Dan de buxiu aiqing." *Renwu*, no. 4 (1992).

Hui: *see* Chen Xuezhao

Hui Wan: *see* Hiu Wan, Ven.

Huizhu: *see* Yan Huizhu

J

Jen I-tu: *see* Sun, E-tu Zen

Ji Zheng: *see* Chi Cheng

Jia Fuming: *see* Chia Fu-ming

Jian E: *see* Chien O

Jiang Bingzhi: *see* Ding Ling

Jiang Biwei

Jiang Biwei, 1899–1978, of Yixing in Jiangsu Province, was born Jiang Tangzhen (*zi* Shumei). Twice in her life, she had the courage to choose love at the risk of being ostracized and stigmatized by society. She was important also because her life entwined with two men—Xu Beihong (1895–1953) and Zhang Daofan (1896–1968)— each of whom in his own way was important in modern Chinese history.

While Jiang Biwei does not appear to have been judged a beauty by her contemporaries, photographs reveal the young woman as attractive and stylish. Constantly surrounded by friends and the object of attention of two talented men, she must have been possessed of a vibrant personality. Hers was an old and distinguished family, which not only owned the largest mansion in Yixing but could also boast of many scholars and poets. Jiang Biwei's father, Jiang Meisheng (1871–1942), was the author of a book on the *Zhuangzi*, a collection of essays, and a collection of poetry. Her mother, Dai Qingbo (1874–1943), was also a poet and published with Jiang Meisheng a joint collection of poems entitled *Yinfenglou shi cao*. In 1911, when Jiang Biwei was fourteen years old, her family gave her in marriage to Zha Zihan, son of a distinguished family of Haining County, Zhejiang Province.

In 1916, Jiang Biwei's family moved to Shanghai to escape disturbances in their native Yixing, and her father became a professor at Fudan University. Xu Beihong, a student at Fudan, was introduced to the family at that time by a mutual friend called Zhu Liaoweng. Xu was well liked by the whole family and became a frequent guest of the Jiang house, at times staying overnight. Jiang Biwei's father, particularly, admired

Xu's talent as a painter and expressed regret that his daughters were either married or betrothed for he would have been happy to marry either one of them to Xu. Up until then, Jiang Biwei had led a fairly cloistered life with little opportunity to meet young men of her own age. She found Xu attractive and admired his ideals of wishing to study and advance his station in life. Jiang Biwei grew worried in 1917 as the time approached for the Zha family to come to take her away, and Xu Beihong, through his friend Zhu Liaoweng, asked her to elope. Since it was virtually impossible to get out of a marriage agreement without good reason at this time, elopement was their only way out. After an inner struggle and at the urging of Zhu Liaoweng, Jiang Biwei agreed to the plan of action. Xu had received a gift from a rich foreign friend, which would enable him to study art abroad, and his first planned destination was France. Because the world was at war, however, passage to Europe was closed, and Xu took Jiang to Japan. He bestowed on her at this time the name Jiang Biwei by which she was thenceforth known in order to prevent her whereabouts from being discovered.

Jiang Biwei's parents were more worried than angry when they discovered the letter she had left behind. To avoid the embarrassment of facing the Zha family when they came for their daughter, Jiang Biwei's parents announced that Jiang Biwei had died of a sudden illness. Some believed the story, others were skeptical; all manner of rumors circulated. The entire family was greatly troubled, and her parents were angry but eventually accepted the affair as a fait accompli when she wrote from Japan asking forgiveness.

The young couple left for Japan in May. He was not good at managing money, however, and the sum given to him was soon spent on paintings and other art works he could not resist buying. After about six months, the fund was gone, and they returned to Shanghai. At the end of 1918, however, Xu Beihong received a government scholarship to go to France, and Jiang Biwei went with him. While Xu visited museums and art galleries, Jiang Biwei studied French in order to deal with daily living in Paris. They moved to Berlin for a time to take advantage of the cheaper living conditions. During this period, the couple formed a close circle with a few good friends, among them Xie Shoukang, Zhang Daofan, Shao Xunmei, and Guo Youshou. When the scholarship money stopped in 1925, Xu Beihong returned to China to raise funds, leaving Jiang Biwei in Paris with little money to survive on. After realizing that she was pregnant, Jiang Biwei returned to China.

Her first child, a boy named Boyang, was born in 1927; her daughter, Lili (later changed to Jingfei) was born in 1929. By this time, Xu Beihong's reputation as a painter had grown, and he was appointed professor in the Fine Arts Department at Zhongyang University in Nanjing. Some of his important friends raised funds to build a house for them in Nanjing with a big studio for Xu. However, financial security did not bring happiness, and their marriage deteriorated. It would appear that there were disagreements over money: while Xu Beihong would spend his on art works, Jiang Biwei would oppose him, possibly because she kept in mind the needs of the family and children. In 1930, Xu Beihong told her that he was in love with one of his students, Sun Yunjun, also known as Sun Duoci, whose talent Xu said he wanted to foster. Jiang was, of course, devastated, but kept her pain to herself, as she thought that news of the affair would harm his reputation and make him lose his position. In her memoirs, Jiang Biwei wrote how she had hoped that their relationship could be mended and asked to accompany Xu on a European tour of his exhibition *Chinese Contemporary Paintings*. He, for his part, took her along because he needed Jiang Biwei's organizational skills. They traveled to France, Belgium, England, Holland, Italy, Greece, Austria, and Germany and returned home through the Soviet Union. The exhibition was a great success, but because of constant disagreements their relationship continued to deteriorate.

Before Xu Beihong left for Guangxi in 1935, they agreed to separate. Jiang Biwei decided to find work to help support herself and the children; she had no faith in the support Xu promised and gained a position with the Sino-France Friendship Society. When the Japanese threatened to bomb Nanjing in 1937, Jiang Biwei managed to escape to Chongqing by boat with the help of Zhang Daofan, one of her friends from Parisian days. He had been in love with Jiang Biwei since the time they had moved in the same circles in Paris in the 1920s. Zhang did not reveal his feelings, however, until a rift appeared in her marriage, when she had been left behind in Paris by her husband; Jiang at that time had not been willing to give up on her marriage. Zhang in turn married a French woman in 1928; the couple had a daughter, Lilian. Although Zhang Daofan went to France to study art, he entered politics when back in China and soon became a vice-minister in the KMT government. He was therefore in a position to give Jiang Biwei a great deal of help.

Jiang and Zhang began exchanging love letters just before their last days in Nanjing: the letters make up a large part of the second section of Jiang's memoirs, which was devoted to her life with him. Their correspondence continued when they both lived in Chongqing, when Jiang was teaching French at Fudan University. With Zhang's help, she got a second job as reader/assessor at the Division for Reading Material for Young People (qingnian duwu zu) with the Education Department. Yet, although Jiang and Zhang fell hopelessly in love, they could only see each other when a legitimate reason presented itself, such as if he, as vice-minister of Education, came to give a talk or inspect one of the institutions where she worked.

Many changes occurred in her family circumstances during Jiang Biwei's Chongqing years. In 1938, Xu Beihong, now one of the most successful painters in China, put an advertisement in the Guilin daily newspaper *Zhongyang ribao* announcing that he and Jiang Biwei had ended their cohabitation (they had presumably never formally married) and that henceforth she would be responsible for herself. A similar advertisement appeared in the same newspaper in Guiyang in February 1944. Three days later another advertisement appeared, announcing his engagement to a Ms. Liao Jingwen. That same year, eighteen-year-old Xu Boyang (the son of Jiang Biwei and Xu Beihong), who was studying at high school, enlisted in the army. Jiang Biwei was unhappy at this and blamed herself for having been a severe mother who did not show sufficient love and care for her son. She concluded that a child from a broken home like theirs would be more likely to act radically. It was also during this period that her father and mother died in quick succession in Chongqing in 1942 and Shanghai in 1943, respectively. This was clearly one of the lowest points in Jiang Biwei's life. Zhang Daofan offered her comfort and support, however.

When the war ended in 1945, Jiang Biwei finally accepted the fact that her marriage with Xu Beihong was really over and decided to begin a new life. She asked him for one million yuan in *fabi* (which she said in her memoirs was equivalent to one year's salary of an ordinary civil servant, enough for three fares from Chongqing to Nanjing); one hundred Chinese paintings; and monthly alimony of 20,000 yuan. Xu signed the agreement that was drawn up but, according to Jiang, what he paid was actually worth very little because of the devaluation of the currency.

She then went back to the house in Nanjing where they had once lived before the war. Jiang Biwei was nominated as a delegate, representing community leaders, to a congress that was drafting a constitution. Zhang Daofan continued to play an important role in the KMT government in Nanjing and was a frequent visitor at her house. As in Chongqing, Jiang Biwei made many friends in literary and art circles. She was saddened, however, during a trip back to her native Yixing in seeing the deterioration of the city as a commercial center and especially the decline of her own clan. Jiang Biwei reunited with her son Xu Boyang, who was no longer in the army, and tried to interest him in further studies. But mother and son did not hit it off, and Boyang went to live with his father. She and Zhang Daofan had always been close to her daughter Lili, but when the young woman finished high school and went to Ginling [Jinling] Women's University (Jinling nüzi daxue) she drifted away from them. One day Lili disappeared. Jiang Biwei never saw her again and believed that her daughter had been "lured away" by communists.

When the KMT government moved to Taiwan, Jiang Biwei went with it. Zhang Daofan joined her later, his French wife having gone to live in New Caledonia with her mother and brother. After taking pains to hide their love for years, in their fifties Jiang Biwei and Zhang Daofan finally began living together. Zhang became head of the Legislative Yuan, the equivalent of prime minister, and Jiang still played the role of the "other woman," never appearing in public with him as his partner. They had ten happy years but were not able to end their lives together. When Zhang's wife wanted to come back to Taiwan, Jiang went away to see her nephew in Penang and visit Singapore. The two lived apart from then on. Zhang Daofan died in 1968, and Jiang Biwei survived him by ten years. Besides being a successful politician, Zhang dabbled in writing plays and painting, and Jiang Biwei fulfilled his wish to have his plays and paintings published after his death. Three years before Zhang's death, she had published her own memoirs in serial form in the magazine *Huangguan zazhi*. In a postscript to these, Jiang said that the idea of writing her memoirs had been Zhang's: many years ago, he had once suggested that their love story could be written into a great romantic novel based on their packet of love letters. When friends admonished her for publishing the memoirs, saying it would harm his reputation, Jiang replied: "I do not believe that true love will be detrimental to people's character, that it will make people feel guilty or wrong."

Jiang Biwei died in Taipei in 1978 of a cerebral hemorrhage. The last ten years of her life were peaceful and perhaps even reasonably happy. Xu Beihong and the two children she had with him remained in China. Her former husband became president of the Central Fine Arts Institute (Zhongyang meishu xueyuan) at its inception in 1950 and died in 1953. Jiang Biwei heard in a roundabout way that Lili had married and produced many children.

Jiang Biwei loved and was loved by two geniuses of modern China and was the object of much envy. The pain she endured for love testifies to the fact that in China, as perhaps elsewhere, to follow your heart does not necessarily lead to happiness. Because her partners were such highly visible men, her story may have served as some sort of mirror to ordinary women. Her memoirs, apart from providing rich social reference helpful to reconstructing the history of an era, might also help shift public opinion toward and strengthen people's faith in love.

Lily Xiao Hong LEE

Jiang Biwei. *Jiang Biwei huiyilu*. Taipei: Huangguan zazhishe, 1966.
Zheng Renjia. "Xu Beihong de san qi ji qi zinü." *Zhuanji wenxue*, 58, no. 3 (March 1991): 32–41.

Jiang Lijin

Jiang Lijin, b. 1919, in Beijing, is from Hangzhou, Zhejiang Province. She is an organic chemist.

Plagued by poor health from childhood, Jiang Lijin often had to remain at home but compensated for the seclusion by working hard at her schoolwork, thus gaining consistently outstanding marks. Her dream was to become a doctor and help remove pain and sickness from the world. Jiang Lijin studied at the well-known Bridgeman (Beiman) Girls' High School in Beijing and took physical exercise seriously in order to become strong enough to undertake the rigors of earning a medical degree. After graduating in 1938, she was admitted by recommendation to Yen-ching [Yanjing] University without having to sit the entrance examination. The student completed the pre-med course at Yanjing and enrolled in 1941 in Peking Union Medical College. With realization of her dream of becoming a doctor in sight, Jiang Lijin's hopes were dashed when the Japanese forced the college to close its doors that year. She then transferred to the medical school of St. John's University in Shanghai, but sickness brought her back to Beijing. Jiang Lijin therefore decided in 1943 to transfer to the Chemistry Department of Fu Jen University in Beijing. She graduated in 1944 but continued with postgraduate work and took out a master's degree two years later. Jiang Lijin then tutored at Pei-p'ing Medical School (Beiping yixueyuan) while carrying out research.

In 1948, she went to study pharmaceutics at the University of Minnesota in the United States, supporting herself by working as a research assistant while preparing for her Ph.D. After receiving a doctorate in 1951, Jiang Lijin undertook postdoctoral work at the University of Kansas and Massachusetts Institute of Technology (MIT). She was on the verge of a breakthrough in her research at MIT on Vitamin D when the opportunity to return to China presented itself. Ignoring the advice of her supervisor and friends, Jiang Lijin abandoned the work almost completed and returned to China, heeding her innate patriotism.

Arriving back in China in 1955, she was assigned to the Chemistry Institute of the Chinese Academy of Sciences and tackled research on the highly flammable and explosive compound boron. Fully aware of the risks inherent in such research, Jiang Lijin always placed herself at the front line and insisted on strict security measures. In 1965 she was assigned to a mission that was highly significant to China's defense. Her task was to analyze for high-altitude photography a film that was highly light sensitive, and her results finally enabled the Chinese to produce their own film. For this, Jiang Lijin won the National Science Congress Award (Quanguo kexue dahui jiang). In 1985, her research won her the National Award for Advances in Science and Technology (Guojiaji keji jinbu jiang).

During the Cultural Revolution, Jiang Lijin's right to work was taken away for several years. In 1975, however, she was transferred to the newly established Institute of Photographic Chemistry. Already over sixty years old by then and suffering from severe glaucoma, Jiang Lijin plunged into another difficult field to undertake pioneering work in photobiology. Under her leadership, the phototherapeutic properties of hypocrellins were discovered around 1980 and have since been used clinically to treat certain skin diseases and cancers. Jiang Lijin and her team have continued to study the mechanism of the phototherapeutic effects of hypocrellins. Her paper "The Phototherapeutic Mechanism of Hypocrellins" won Second Prize in the Natural Science Award of the Chinese Academy of Sciences (Zhongguo kexueyuan ziran kexue erdengjiang) in 1990. The team has also made progress in the study of structures and light energy transfers among the phycobiliproteins of marine algae, and in 1993 their publications on phycobiliproteins won Second Prize in the Natural Science Award.

Jiang Lijin has written over 150 scientific papers and in 1987 was made an academician of the Chinese Academy of Sciences. She was also a member of the Standing Committee of the Chinese Chemical Society and the CPPCC. Age has by no means diminished her appetite for work: even in her seventies, she participated in a large research project on "Important Chemical Problems in the Life Process."

It is not clear if Jiang Lijin married or has children.

Lily Xiao Hong LEE

Song Ruizhi, ed. *Zhongguo funü wenhua tonglan*. Jinan: Shandong wenyi chubanshe, 1995, 360–61.

Yanjing daxue renwuzhi, vol. 1: Shiyinben. Beijing: Yanjing yanjiuyuan, 1999, 74–75.

Yingwen *Zhongguo funü*, ed. *Gujin zhuming funü renwu*, vol. 2. Shijiazhuang: Hebei renmin chubanshe, 1986, 976–79.

Zhonghua quanguo fulian. *Zhongguo nü yuanshi*. Shenyang: Liaoning renmin chubanshe, 1995, 307–14.

Jiang Qing

Jiang Qing, 1914–1991, was born Li Shumeng in Zhucheng County, Shandong Province; she was also known at various times as Li Yunhe, Lan Ping, and Li Jin. An actress in the 1920s and 1930s who became the third wife of Mao Zedong (1893–

1976) in Yan'an, she was the architect of the Cultural Revolution, a political movement that affected the lives of millions of Chinese.

Her father was a carpenter who owned a cartwright shop. Her mother was the
daughter of a literati family of the same province; she is said to have been a concubine, however, and as such often abused by her husband, just as Jiang Qing was also
often bullied by her half-brothers and sisters, the children of her father's official wife.
When Jiang Qing was about five years old, her mother left Zhucheng after a particularly bad family row and began working as a domestic to support herself and her
daughter. Jiang Qing started school about this time, but the unfortunate family circumstances made her a difficult child and she was often bullied by other children.
Not one to endure insults, Jiang Qing fought back at school, at one stage earning
expulsion. In 1928, at age fourteen, she and her mother went to live with her grandparents in Jinan, where Jiang Qing attended the Experimental Arts Academy, a training ground for actors of both traditional opera and modern plays. At this school, she
was influenced by teachers and other young intellectuals as well as by books and
publications disseminating radical ideas in politics and art. There, Jiang Qing first
read a translation of Ibsen's *A Doll's House* and started to think of herself as the lead
character, Nora. When the school closed because of lack of funds, Jiang Qing married
a young man named Fei. Their marriage soon dissolved because of incompatibility.

Jiang Qing went to Qingdao to seek assistance from a former teacher; his wife, Yu
Shan (*q.v.*), herself an actress, introduced Jiang to her brother Yu Qiwei (1911–1958;
he was also known as Huang Jing and David Huang). Although from a prominent
family, Yu Qiwei was an underground student worker for the CCP. The two fell in
love and lived together. He became her political mentor and with his support Jiang
Qing joined the League of Left-Wing Theater Workers and the League of Left-Wing
Writers. In 1933, she joined the CCP in Qingdao and participated eagerly in many
CCP-inspired cultural activities there. Yu Qiwei was at one point arrested by the KMT
but rescued by his uncle, who held an important position in the Nanjing KMT government. After being released, Yu Qiwei was sent by the party to work in Beijing
among university students.

Armed with introductions from people she had known in Qingdao, Jiang Qing
went to Shanghai and moved among left-wing theater workers and writers such as
Tian Han, Hong Shen, and Liao Mosha. Her entry to the theater and film world of
Shanghai was nevertheless not easy. As a newcomer not particularly blessed with
talent or beauty (she is said to have been attractive but not beautiful), Jiang Qing
suffered, or thought she suffered, rejection and humiliation. But being resourceful
and persistent, Jiang Qing gradually carved a profile for herself, starting with small
parts in left-wing theater to a breakthrough to her dream role as Nora in Ibsen's *A
Doll's House*. The modicum of fame Jiang Qing enjoyed enabled her to gain parts in
Shanghai movies. She was first employed by the left-wing Diantong company and
then by Lianhua, a company with a broader agenda. Jiang Qing starred in *Fighting on
Wolf Mountain* (Langshan diexue, 1936) and *Old Bachelor Wang* (Wang Laowu, 1936),
receiving fair reviews for both. During this period, she had several brief affairs with
men in the theater and film world and a long and dramatic love affair and marriage

(1936–1937) with the film critic and scriptwriter Tang Na. Their marriage and separation were widely publicized in the media, so that those who did not know her from the movies would have known of her because of her private life.

In the early years in Shanghai, Jiang Qing had also been active in political work, not as a member of the CCP, which she claimed to be unable to contact, but with the Communist Youth League. Her political mentor at that time was a woman named Xu Yiyong (also known as Xu Mingqing). Jiang Qing handed out leaflets and delivered documents for the party as well as taught at the evening school for working women set up by leftists in the YWCA. At the end of 1933, she went to Beijing, wanting to resume her relationship with Yu Qiwei; in early 1934 Jiang Qing returned to Shanghai, apparently failing in the attempt and later that year was arrested by the KMT police and imprisoned. Her account of the experience is that she put up such stiff resistance and made such a nuisance of herself that they let her go. Another version has it that Jiang Qing befriended the prison guards—entertaining them with arias from Peking opera and giving them autographed photographs of herself—and was released after signing a good behavior bond. She stopped active political work after that.

With Shanghai about to fall to the Japanese in 1937, Jiang Qing went first to Wuhan and then chose to go to the communist base of Yan'an rather than Chongqing, the KMT capital during the Sino-Japanese War. Xu Yiyong and Yu Qiwei vouched for her, and Jiang Qing was accepted back into the party and assigned to study at the Party School in mid-1937. She soon made an important acquaintance in Kang Sheng (1899–1975), a fellow native of Shandong. With his help, Jiang Qing became an assistant teacher at the Lu Xun Academy of Literature and Art, where Mao Zedong, chairman of the CCP, first noticed her. He was at that time living alone, his second wife, He Zizhen (*q.v.*), having left him in October 1937 because of his affair with Wu Guanghui (known in the works of Western writers as Lily Wu or Wu Kuangwei), the interpreter-secretary of the American journalist Agnes Smedley. Jiang Qing filled a vacuum in Mao's life. She was soon transferred to the archive near Mao's office, and the two began living together in his cave dwelling, probably in 1938.

In spite of the allegedly relaxed sexual atmosphere at Yan'an, Mao's political position made his relationship with Jiang Qing more than a private affair. According to most reports except Jiang Qing's own, Mao had not yet divorced He Zizhen when Jiang Qing moved into his cave. Perhaps out of sympathy for and camaraderie with He Zizhen, top leaders of the party raised objections to the new relationship. They were not objecting to the legality of the liaison; rather, they had problems with Jiang Qing's checkered past. Mao, however, was adamant that despite party opposition he would marry the woman he loved, even threatening to leave the party and go back to Hunan. The party elders met several times over the matter and finally granted him a divorce from He Zizhen. However, they are said to have imposed conditions on Mao's marriage to Jiang Qing, including one that required her to devote herself solely to the care of Mao and another placing a thirty-year ban on her taking part in any political activity.

Jiang Qing's first two decades with Mao were characterized by passivity. She did not hold high official position in either the party or government and even looked on without raising any objections when Mao had an affair with her old acquaintance Yu Shan. Jiang

Qing was twice sent to Russia "for treatment in Moscow" (1949 and 1952), a fate common to leaders' wives during this period when their presence was not desired in China. Inevitably, a comparison could be drawn between Jiang Qing in this period and He Zizhen. He Zizhen had made a scene when Mao had had an affair, for example, whereas Jiang Qing chose to remain quiet and not cause the chairman to lose face. He Zizhen was broken by her traumatic experience in Moscow, whereas Jiang Qing, although her situation was much better than He Zizhen's had been, retained her sanity and vented bitterness on those around her, mostly the small number of staff living with her in Moscow.

However, Jiang Qing was not totally inactive during this period. Her experience in the film world led to an appointment in 1949 to the Film Guidance Committee of the Ministry of Culture, and she attempted in this capacity to make a few marks as an arbiter of films and, later, literature. Her initial effort criticized the bourgeois ideas of a popular film made in Hong Kong but, lacking political backing, Jiang Qing was soon silenced by more heavyweight personalities in film and literature. Her second attempt was more successful: Mao supported her 1951 criticism of a film from Jiang Qing's native Shandong entitled *Wu Xun zhuan*, the story of a do-gooder beggar named Wu Xun who used "reformist" methods rather than class struggle to improve society. Mao's condemnation of the ideological confusion apparent in cultural circles allowed Jiang Qing to lead an investigation in Shandong to find materials detrimental to Wu Xun's image. Then, in 1954, Jiang Qing initiated a debate on the classic novel *Honglou meng* (Dream of the Red Chamber), which Mao also supported, and she enjoyed a degree of success. From this, Jiang Qing learned how to gain Mao's confidence and support in campaigns and make her initiatives a success.

During the 1950s, Jiang Qing engaged in grass-roots party work, doing land reform work in the countryside in Jiangsu and Hubei. Perhaps in recognition, her political work led to an appointment at the end of 1951 as head of the secretariat of the General Office of the CCP Central Committee. This was not only a confidential but also an exceedingly influential post; however, the position seems to have been more than she could handle. After accepting it, she fell ill. One source reports that her immediate superior recommended that Jiang Qing resign from the appointment in early 1952, adding as a reminder that it was Jiang Qing's duty to take care of the chairman on the party's behalf.

In 1959, Mao was openly criticized by General Peng Dehuai, the defense minister, and over the next few years Mao's personal prestige suffered as a result of the disastrous failure of the Great Leap Forward (1958–60). Perhaps in casting about for a trusted and loyal political ally, the chairman welcomed to that role a willing Jiang Qing. The timing of the alliance certainly coincided with an improvement in his wife's health, although one cannot but suspect the reverse may have been the case: that her health improved *because* Mao reached out to her in time of need. Together, going to Shanghai, they fostered a group of supporters. In 1963 came the first major attack on art and literature, the target: a play by Tian Han. This is usually considered the onset of the Cultural Revolution, although it officially began in 1965 with the manifesto—the May Seventeenth Circular—formally passed by the CCP Politburo. Tian Han's play had as its theme the praising of a conscientious official who remonstrated with the emperor for the sake of the people. It was seen as a veiled attack on Mao for his demotion of Defense Minister Peng Dehuai. Jiang Qing extended the range of her supervision beyond Chinese opera, plays, and films to Western ballet, orchestral music, and composition, demanding reform that emphasized politics rather than art.

She and Mao Zedong encouraged young people from their teens to early thirties to become Red Guards and utilized them as a force of destruction. Under Jiang's direction, the leadership of all work units, whether economic, political, educational, or cultural, was removed and in its place a new, extreme leftist, leadership was installed. Power was thus removed from established bureaucrats and put in the hands of people loyal only to Jiang and Mao. For the first half of the Cultural Revolution, from the mid-1960s to the end of that decade, Jiang Qing's activities mainly focused on destruction: all old elements and institutions, Mao's political enemies, her personal enemies. In the name of *chu si jiu* (getting rid of the Four Olds), many historical sites and relics such as temples, images, and inscriptions were destroyed. Liu Shaoqi (1898–1969), Deng Xiaoping (1904–1997), and almost all members of the Old Guard of the party, with the exception of Zhou Enlai (1898–1976) and Jiang's own ally Lin Biao (1907–1971), were toppled and persecuted. Many died of ill health; others took their own lives, unable to endure the humiliation and wrongs meted out to them. People in theater and film circles whom Jiang Qing had known in Shanghai and she felt had slighted her were charged with serious crimes and endured tragic fates.

The toll on the nation of the Cultural Revolution toward the end of the 1960s was heavy. The Red Guards split into warring factions, which sometimes took to weapons such as knives and spears as well as guns. The economy was savaged, prompting Mao, who had learned from the food shortage caused by the Great Leap Forward and foresaw another crisis looming, to empower Zhou Enlai to clean up the mess. Although Zhou had never been singled out for attack as were other members of the Old Guard, his work on governing the nation had been greatly hampered by the leftists. Their rapid rise to power had made it necessary for him to retain a low profile. Mao's move to Zhou was therefore seen as a move away from Jiang Qing, who now looked upon Zhou as a deadly enemy.

Early in the Cultural Revolution, Jiang Qing had allied herself with Lin Biao, the new defense minister, and his wife Ye Qun (*q.v.*). Through Lin Biao, Jiang Qing got the support of the military and through Ye Qun was able to arrange for the air force chief Wu Faxian to execute some of her secret revenge operations. Lin Biao was named Mao's official successor in 1969 just as Jiang Qing was elected to the Politburo. For the next two years, Jiang Qing and Lin Biao competed for the number two position in the nation. What happened next is not totally clear, but in 1971 it was reportedly discovered that Lin Biao had planned an unsuccessful coup against Mao and was attempting to escape by plane to Russia. An announcement was then made that his plane had crashed in Mongolia and all on board were killed. If it was indeed Jiang Qing's ambition to succeed her now very frail husband Mao Zedong, then Zhou Enlai remained the only obstacle in her path. She immediately unleashed a campaign against Zhou under the cryptic rubric *"pi Lin pi Kong"* (Criticize Lin and criticize Kong). Lin obviously referred to Lin Biao, but Kong, ostensibly a reference to Confucius (Kong fuzi), was generally taken as code for Zhou Enlai.

Since her election to the Politburo, Jiang Qing had been a political force to be reckoned with so that, despite her growing alienation from Mao and his ever-failing health, she was able to operate as an independent agent. The Tenth Party Congress of 1973 in which many of her cronies had been elected to the Politburo gave an appearance of a feminist victory because of the number of women included. Jiang Qing moved out of Mao's house in Zhongnanhai to an apartment at the Diaoyutai Guesthouse. There, she was constantly surrounded by her loyal supporters, particularly Zhang Chunqiao, Yao Wenyuan, and Wang Hongwen, whom Mao referred to collectively as the "Gang of Four"; but no longer sure of Mao's protection, Jiang Qing felt increasingly vulnerable. Zhou Enlai, however, even though in and out of hospital, could rely on his old staffer Deng Xiaoping and other bureaucrats who had been quietly brought back from labor camps and imprisonment. Jiang Qing was greatly relieved when Zhou died of cancer in January 1976, but a popular riot broke out in April as she (probably with Mao's consent) tried to take down mourning posters and drive away the more than one hundred thousand mourners gathered in Tian'anmen Square. Once again, Mao moved closer to his wife and dismissed Deng Xiaoping, whom the chairman suspected of orchestrating the riot. Mao died that September.

Jiang Qing and the other members of the infamous Gang of Four were arrested on 6 October in a coup jointly executed by Hua Guofeng (Mao's successor, appointed just before his death) and Wang Dongxing (Mao's head bodyguard) with the cooperation of Ye Jianying and Li Xiannian, two surviving members of the Old Guard. The Gang of Four was tried in 1980 according to Chinese law and found guilty in January 1981 of a series of crimes including treason. They were sentenced to death and deprivation of political rights for life, with two years' reprieve. Jiang Qing's sentence was commuted in 1983 to life, and she was later released under house arrest. Jiang Qing went to hospital for treatment of throat cancer and hanged herself there in May 1991. The news of her death was broken by the United States news magazine *Time* but not confirmed by official Chinese media until June. Jiang Qing was survived by her daughter Li Na, who has married twice. Li Na's first husband was a security guard named Xu with whom she had a son, Li Xiaoyu. In 1985 Li Na married Wang Jingqing, and the two visited Jiang Qing regularly while she was in jail.

Jiang Qing was an ambitious woman who wanted to make a mark on history. She wanted fame and political status but was unwilling to expend the necessary hard work, gaining political power instead through illegitimate means. Jiang Qing demonstrated in marriages prior to the one with Mao that she was not a "good wife and wise mother," but, in order to be allowed to marry the chairman, had been cast into that mould by party elders. Any positive significance for breaking out of those constraints was ruined, however, by her vindictiveness and abuse of power. Jiang Qing also lacked the administrative genius and broad vision of her role model, Empress Wu Zetian (624–705). Women who dare to be ambitious have always been stigmatized, and Jiang Qing, with many obvious faults, did not escape condemnation as a "white-boned demon." This appellation nevertheless reveals how deeply entrenched in the Chinese psyche remains the patriarchal custom of demonizing women.

Lily Xiao Hong LEE

Bai Xuechun. "Rezhong quanshi, haowu jianshu, nanbi Wuhou." *Huasheng bao*, 21 June 1991, 13.
Bonavia, David. *Verdict in Peking*. New York: Putnam, 1984.
Cui Wanqiu. *Jiang Qing qianzhuan*. Hong Kong: Tiandi tushu gongsi, 1988.
"A Great Standard-Bearer, a Dauntless Warrior: A Chronicle of Comrade Jiang Qing's Activities in the Field of Literature and Art." *Issues and Studies* (October 1975): 88–95.
Ihara, Kinosuke. "Kō Sei hyōdenkō." *Tezukayama Daigaku ronshu*, no. 14–31 (1963–1966).
Lin Qingshan. *Jiang Qing chenfulu*, 2 vols. Guangzhou: Zhongguo xinwen chubanshe and Guangzhou wenhua chubanshe, 1988.
Terrill, Ross. *Madame Mao, the White-Boned Demon: A Biography of Madame Mao Zedong*. New York: Simon & Schuster, 1992.
Witke, Roxane. *Comrade Chiang Ch'ing*. London: Weidenfeld and Nicolson, 1977.
Ye Yonglie. *Jiang Qing shilu*. Hong Kong: Liwen chubanshe, 1993.
———. *Jiang Qing zai Shanghai tan*. Hong Kong: Mingxing chubanshe, 1988. Contains text of Jiang Qing's extant writings.
———. *Jiang Qing zhuan*. Beijing: Zuojia chubanshe, 1995.
Zhong Huamin. *Jiang Qing zhengzhuan*. Hong Kong: Youlian yanjiusuo, 1967.
Zhu Shan. *Jiang Qing mizhuan*. Hong Kong: Xingchen chubanshe, 1987.

Jiang Tangzhen: *see* **Jiang Biwei**

Jiang Wei: *see* **Ding Ling**

Jin Weiying
Jin Weiying, 1904–1941?, also known as A Jin, of Daishan County, Zhejiang Province, was one of the thirty women who went with the First Front Red Army on the Chinese communists' Long March of 1934–35. She was mistakenly called Ah Ch'ing (Hsiang) by Helen Foster Snow in Yan'an, having been confused in this instance with Xie Fei (*q.v.*), who was known as A Xiang.

Jin Weiying was born into the gentry. Hers was a progressive family that did not bind a daughter's feet, and they provided Jin Weiying with an education. After moving with her father to the Zhoushan Islands off the coast of Zhejiang, she attended Dinghai County primary school. Then Jin Weiying went to Ningpo Women's Normal School, where she was deeply influenced by the principal Shen Yi, a patriot who worked closely with many active communists. Jin Weiying returned to teach at Dinghai County primary school after graduation and for the next few years was involved in revolutionary work. She joined the CCP in late 1926 and was made one of three leaders of a CCP cell in Dinghai. Jin Weiying agitated among workers in various industries to form a labor union federation and became a militant leader in the burgeoning labor movement, earning herself the sobriquet "the Girl General of Dinghai."

She moved to Shanghai after the infamous KMT massacre of striking workers in 1927 and worked as a teacher in a primary school while continuing union involvement. In 1930 Jin Weiying set up a night school and preached revolution to silk factory workers. She shared their harsh life and was appointed that year as secretary to the Shanghai Silk Workers Party Group and also led a committee for joint union action, which initiated a strike of silk workers.

In 1931 Jin Weiying was ordered to leave Shanghai and go to the Jiangxi soviet. Over the next three years, she was appointed secretary to two county committees and head of the Central Organization Department. Jin Weiying was elected as a delegate to the Soviet Republic of China National Congress and rose in February 1934 to the unusually high position (for a woman) of being a member of the Executive Committee of the central soviet government in Ruijin. Her outstanding work in the Jiangxi soviet in recruitment and grain collection was reported several times that year in *Red China* (Hongse Zhonghua); it listed her name along with Lo Man and Mao Zetan (1905–1935) on the Honor Roll of Recruitment Shock Brigade Leaders.

At some stage, Jin Weiying married Deng Xiaoping (1904–1997), who in 1978 succeeded Mao Zedong (1893–1976) as China's paramount leader. She had divorced Deng by 1934, however, and married Li Weihan (1896–1984; aka Luo Mai and Lo Man), secretary to the party's Central Organization Unit. Their son, Li Tieying (b. September 1936), has achieved prominence in the party, becoming a member of the Central Committee in 1985 and a Politburo member in 1987.

During the Long March, Jin Weiying was a political instructor with the convalescent unit, which also involved doing local work and organizing food supplies. Initially, she worked in the Central Committee's Organization Department when the marchers reached the northwest, but in Yan'an Jin Weiying attended the Anti-Japanese University. She became ill and began coughing up blood, however, and by spring 1938 her marriage to Li Weihan appears to have been over. It was then that she traveled to Moscow with a group that included Cai Chang (*q.v.*); the purpose of her visit was stated as being for medical treatment and "to further her studies." It has been suggested that in fact she was exiled to Russia, where she was what was termed "a difficult student" who frequently challenged her Russian lecturers on matters of principle. Jin Weiying is believed to have been committed to an institution in Russia and died in German air raids toward the end of 1941. Her death in exile at the age of thirty-six or thirty-seven was a truly tragic end for a young woman who had contributed so much, at enormous cost to her health and well-being, to the young communist movement.

Sue WILES

Bartke, Wolfgang. *Who Was Who in the PRC*. Munich: K.G. Saur, 1997, 243.
Guo Chen. *Jinguo liezhuan: Hong yifangmianjun sanshiwei changzheng nühongjun shengping shiji*. Beijing: Nongcun duwu chubanshe, 1986, 138–43.
Lee, Lily Xiao Hong, and Sue Wiles. *Women of the Long March*. Sydney: Allen & Unwin, 1999.
Snow, Helen Foster. *Inside Red China*. 1977 reprint [with a new preface and biographical notes by the author]. New York: Da Capo Press, 1939, 175.
Yingwen *Zhongguo funü*, ed. *Gujin zhuming funü renwu*, vol. 2. Shijiazhuang: Hebei renmin chubanshe, 1986, 684–88.

June-Nikel, Renée: *see* **Wang Henei**

Jung-tzu

Jung-tzu (sometimes spelled Yung-tzu or Yungtze), b. 1928, as Wang Jung-chih, is a native of Chiang-yin [Jiangyin] County, Chiang-su [Jiangsu] Province. She has been writing poetry for more than forty years and incorporates a wide range of subjects in her work.

The daughter of a clergyman, Jung-tzu attended school in Chiang-yin, Nan-ching [Nanjing], and Shanghai. She commenced work in Nan-ching in 1949 with International Radio but transferred to Taiwan. After completing a course at the Center of Education for Public Administration and Business Management at Chengchi University (Cheng-chih ta-hsüeh), Jung -tzu gained employment with the Telecommunications Bureau (Tien-hsün chü).

She loved poetry from early childhood and recalls admiring the poetry of Ping-hsin [Bing Xin (*q.v.*)]. Jung-tzu later became fond of the Chinese poets of the 1920s–40s, Hsü Chih-mo [Xu Zhimo], Ho Ch'i-fang [He Qifang], and Feng Chih [Feng Zhi]. Jung-tzu was especially fond of the sonnets of Feng Chih and wanted to write poetry herself. Her earliest poems were published in poetry magazines in Taiwan: *Muse* (Miu-ssu) appeared in the August 1952 issue of *Shih-chih* and *Blue Bird* (Ch'ing-niao) and *Image* (Hsing-hsiang) appeared in *Hsin-shih chou-k'an* in 1953. Jung-tzu soon joined the Blue Star Poetry Society (Lan-hsing shih-she), whose *Lan-hsing shih-k'an* she edited for ten years. Jung-tzu thus was a part of the development of modern Chinese poetry in Taiwan as both a writer and editor.

In 1953, she published her first poetry collection, *Blue Bird* (Ch'ing-niao chi), which brought her recognition as a poet and also won an admirer, the poet Lo-men (b. 1929). They married in 1955, but because Lo-men's income was not enough to support a family Jung-tzu continued to work as well as take care of the housework. Laden with this double burden, she tried, not very successfully, to find time for her own creativity. A further reason why Jung-tzu wrote less poetry from the mid-1950s to the early 1960s could have been her ambivalence toward the avant-garde and experimental poetry trends of that time. She finally decided to go her own way, however, and her next collection, *The South in July* (Ch'i-yueh ti nan-fang, 1961), displayed maturity and a richer and more varied voice. Above all, it displayed the "classicism" that remains one of her most felicitous characteristics.

One of Jung-tzu's themes is revelation of the internal world of modern women. In a group of poems entitled *Verna Lisa Suite* (Wei-na li-sha tsu-ch'ü), she describes the stages of a woman's life. Each of the twelve individual poems is about one aspect of Verna Lisa's life, her maturing, strength, self-reliance, and ability to withstand loneliness. Verna Lisa is perhaps an ideal woman, and one that Jung-tzu wishes to become, that is, an independent modern woman. The reason for the Western name is perhaps that in Jung-tzu's eyes Chinese women had to look to the West to find a model for liberation and independence. The *Verna Lisa Suite* collection was published in 1969, well before feminism became a popular topic in the West. The poem may not possess strong feminist ideology, but it does suggest the awakening of Chinese women that began during the May Fourth (1919) period in China. The poem *My Makeup Mirror Is Like a Cat with an Arched Back* (Wo ti chuang-ching shih i-chih kung-pei ti mao) records the gradual transition of an inquisitive, expectant young girl into a woman living within a closed and restricted life. As an adult, finally realizing that she has become as indolent as the cat with its arched back that is trapped in the mirror, devoid of light and shadow, only a puzzling dream, comes the desire to break out of the mirror. The women in Jung-tzu's poetry are usually a mixture of the traditional and modern, reserved, but with faith in their own value, and independent.

Jung-tzu was also an early critic of urban decay and pollution. In her eyes, the city is rampant with materialism and moral degeneration. In the 1962 poem *The Wind No Longer Blows Flower Petals in Our City* (Wo-men ti ch'eng pu tsai fei hua), she likens buildings to sphinxes crouching in the desert and cars to ferocious "city tigers," while sooty rain and thunderous noise tear people's time and lives to shreds. This was written at least twenty years before concern for the environment became a global issue. Along with distress over the city is a love of nature. Her three collections *The South in July*; *Collection of Jung-Tzu's Poetry* (Jung-tzu shih-ch'ao, 1965); and *The Afternoon of the Flute and the Harp* (Heng-ti yü shu-ch'in ti hsiang-wu, 1974) contain many poems about nature, not only imbued with its colors and sounds but also highlighting the procreative power of mother earth by showing nature's abundance. Her nature poems are most representative of the elegance and harmony of classical Chinese poetry, where nature is often a metaphor for the poet's own ideals of purity, vitality, and integrity. Her poetry, too, provides philosophical insights. In the poem *Time* (Shih-chien), Jung-tzu contrasts the transcendence of human life with the constancy of the passing of time. Gems of wisdom are embedded even in her poems about everyday life and nature.

For children, she wrote the collection *The City of Fairy Tales* (T'ung-hua ch'eng), published in 1967. Jung-tzu also writes essays, and a collection of her impressions of Europe was published in *European Notes* (Ou-yu shou-chi, 1982). Her latest work, *As Long as We Have Roots* (Chih-yao wo-men yu ken), deals with the roots of overseas Chinese people.

Jung-tzu and her husband Lo-men have participated in several international poetry meetings and won joint honors. In 1966, they won the Koret Award from the United Poets Laureate Internationale and a gold medal from President Marcos of the Philippines. The following year they were again honored as "the distinguished literary couple from China." They appear to have children, but no information is readily available on them. Jung-tzu's poetry has been translated into English, French, Japanese, Korean, and Turkish. Angela Jung Palandri's English translation of Jung-tzu's and Lo-men's poetry was published in 1968 as the *Sun Moon Collection*.

Jung-tzu, Chang Hsiu-ya, Li Cheng-nai, and Lin Ling all began writing poetry in Taiwan in the 1950s, but Jung-tzu, who has continued writing for over forty years, enjoys the longest writing career of all Taiwanese women poets. The poet Yü Kuang-chung has called her "the longest flowering chrysanthemum of the poetic world," and others have often alluded to her as the "mother," the "grandmother," and the "premier poetess" of Taiwan.

Lily Xiao Hong LEE

Chung Ling. *Hsien-tai Chung-kuo miu-ssu: Taiwan nü-shih-jen tso-p'in hsi-lun*. Taipei: Lien-ching ch'u-pan, 1989, 139–55.
Jung-tzu. *Chih-yao wo-men you ken*. Taipei: Wen-ching she, 1989.
———. *Jung-tzu tzu hsüan chi*. Taipei: Li-ming wen-hua, 1978.

———. *Wei-na li-sha tsu-ch'ü*. Taipei: Ch'un-wen-hsüeh ch'u-pan-she, 1969.

Li Yüan-chen. "Tzu-yu ti nü-ling: T'an Taiwan hsien-tai nü-shih-jen ti t'u-p'o." *Fu-nü hsin-chih* (May 1987): 2–5.

Lin, Julia C. "A Woman's Voice: The Poetry of Yongtzu." In *Women Writers of Twentieth-Century China*, ed. Angela Jung Palandri. Eugene, Oregon: Asian Studies Program, University of Oregon, 1982, 137–62.

———. "Women's Voices in Modern China." In *Women and Literature in China*, eds. Anna Gerstlacher et al. Bochum, Brockmeyer, 1985, 429–53.

Lo-men and Jung-tzu. *Sun and Moon Collection: Selected Poems of Lomen and Yungtze*, trans. Angela Jung Palandri. Taipei: Mei Ya Publications, 1968.

P'an Ya-tun. *Shih-chieh hua-wen nü-tso-chia su-miao*. Kuang-chou: Chi-nan ta-hsüeh, 1993, 185–97.

K

Kan Shiying

Kan Shiying, 1910–1971, of Nanxi County, Sichuan Province, was one of the thirty women who went with the First Front Red Army on the Chinese communists' Long March of 1934–35.

Born into a family of merchants, she was taught calligraphy and painting by her father and went to school from the age of seven. At age fourteen, Kan Shiying's father disowned her, displaying notices to that effect in public places after she resisted a marriage he had arranged to the son of a landlord. Kan Shiying had by this time entered a prefectural middle school in Yibin and there was exposed to communist groups; her older brother had also become a communist. She joined the Communist Youth League and then the CCP in 1926 and at the end of that year went to university in Chongqing. After being injured by KMT troops during the patriotic demonstrations of 31 March 1927, she fled to Wuhan but three months later was sent by the party to Shanghai. There, Kan Shiying attended Wenzhi University and in early 1928 was assigned to liaison work. To facilitate this work, she assumed the identity of a married woman; this sham marriage soon became real, however, and Kan Shiying soon had her first child. It is not known what became of the baby, but Kan Shiying's lover turned out to be a traitor. Kan Shiying moved on to the Jiangxi soviet base, traveling through Hong Kong. In Ruijin, she worked in the secretariat of the General Party Liaison Section for two years from 1930 and also became involved in setting up and running a smelting works in which valuables captured from landlords were melted down into gold and silver ingots. Kan Shiying's health suffered, however, and she became sick. After recovering somewhat, the young woman was enrolled in national economy classes at the soviet university and then transferred at the end of 1933 to the Central Party School in Ruijin.

Immediately before setting off on the Long March, Kan Shiying was in the secretariat of the Central Women's Department. At the start of the march, she worked as a political fighter but was soon made head of Propaganda with the Convalescent Company's Political Department. In February 1935, Kan Shiying was instructed to drop out of the main Long March in Yunnan with Li Guiying (*q.v.*), along with about one hundred male comrades, to act as partisans and work with local guerrilla groups: Kan Shiying was placed in charge of the unit's Women's Department. The unit suffered great hardship in extremely harsh conditions, and when Li Guiying became pregnant the two women journeyed alone to Sichuan in early 1936 for the birth, rejoining the unit soon afterward. Kan Shiying and Li Guiying were eventually captured by the KMT at the end of 1936 and held for several months until a general amnesty had been declared as part of the 1937 KMT-CCP united front. Upon release in May, Kan Shiying was placed in the custody of her father, but she was able to escape from the virtual house arrest under which he kept her and made her way to Chongqing. There, Kan Shiying worked as a primary school teacher and several months later had renewed contact with the CCP. She married fellow worker Zou Fengping in 1938, and in 1940 the couple was sent to Yan'an. After a short period of convalescence, Kan Shiying attended the Marx-Lenin College and then spent five and a half years at the Party School. Despite her obvious devotion to the CCP, she and her husband were criticized during the 1942 rectification movement. After 1949, Kan Shiying was appointed to several official bodies in Sichuan: as secretary of Chongqing Women's Committee; member of the Municipal Committee; member of the Southwest ACWF; deputy head of the Southwest Region Women Workers' Department; deputy secretary of the Southwest Women's Committee. She was also elected as a delegate to the Third NPC, deputy director of Sichuan People's High Court, and deputy secretary of the Party Organization.

Kan Shiying suffered greatly during the Cultural Revolution, however, and was persecuted to death. She was labeled a traitor, publicly humiliated and bullied, and required to report all visits and contacts made. The stress Kan Shiying was placed under triggered bronchial problems that possibly had their genesis during her time in the smelting works in the Jiangxi soviet. She was also sent to a labor camp and made to do menial physical work. Upon returning home to Chengdu, she was ill and depressed but refused hospital treatment for breathing difficulties and died at home on 28 November 1971. She was posthumously rehabilitated in 1978.

As one of comparatively few well-educated and politically committed young women, Kan Shiying was of great value to the CCP during the 1920s and 1930s, and she devoted herself to the cause of communism at the cost of her health and, finally, her life. Had the revolution not erupted during her youth, Kan Shiying would probably have lived a comfortable and secluded middle-class life as a wife and mother.

Sue WILES

Guo Chen. *Jinguo liezhuan: Hong yifangmianjun sanshiwei changzheng nühongjun shengping shiji.* Beijing: Nongcun duwu chubanshe, 1986, 150–57.
Lee, Lily Xiao Hong, and Sue Wiles. *Women of the Long March.* Sydney: Allen & Unwin, 1999.
Snow, Helen Foster. *Inside Red China.* 1977 reprint [with a new preface and biographical notes by the author]. New York: Da Capo Press, 1939, 175.

Kan Siying: *see* **Kan Shiying**

Kan Tang: *see* **Kan Shiying**

Kang Keqing

Kang Keqing, 1912–1992, of Wan'an County, Jiangxi Province, was one of very few women of peasant origin who rose through the communist ranks to fill a leadership role in the PRC. Born as Kang Guixiu to a poor fisherman and his wife who lived on a fishing boat on the Gan River, Kang Guixiu changed her name to Kang Keqing in 1930.

Kang Keqing once gave the poverty she had lived in as a child as her reason for becoming a revolutionary. Kang Keqing had her first contact with roving communist organizers in 1926, at the age of fourteen, and by the following year had become a communist youth inspector in her local district. Kang Keqing soon joined the Communist Youth League and was made a captain of the Young Pioneers but did not become a member of the CCP until 1931. Kang Keqing did, however, join the Fourth Red Army commanded by Zhu De (1886–1976) in 1928, and the two nicknames famously given to her—the Girl Commander and the Red Amazon—reflect the military interests of her youth. Kang Keqing was never to become a soldier, however, and it was as a partisan organizer that she followed the army onto Jinggangshan late in the year. The young woman had already successfully resisted a marriage arranged by her parents, but when the forty-two-year-old Zhu De asked her to become his partner Kang Keqing was too shy to refuse; she was then only sixteen. Kang Keqing remained with him from then on, and the two were rarely apart. Their enduring, but childless, marriage came to be seen as a comradely and loving union of two outstanding revolutionaries and has always been held up as a model in much the same way as the marriage of Deng Yingchao (*q.v.*) and Zhou Enlai.

As a partisan, Kang Keqing was not involved in day-to-day guerrilla fighting but followed the Zhu-Mao Red Army as it fought its way across several provinces seeking to establish a secure base. Once the Jiangxi soviet was established in 1931, she continued to do propaganda work and partisan organizing, assiduously avoiding women's work. Kang Keqing clearly preferred working with military men than with women and admitted to the American journalist Helen Snow (who dubbed her the Red Amazon) in 1937 that she was not qualified to discuss "the woman problem" because she had never been a part of women's life in the soviets. Kang Keqing and Wu Zhonglian (*q.v.*) trained local peasant women at the Red Military Academy in 1932 for a short period, and it was during this period (1934) that Kang Keqing led a small band of men into battle, successfully fighting off KMT forces.

On the Long March of the First Front Red Army that left the Jiangxi soviet in October 1934, Kang Keqing carried out similar duties to several of the other women, such as recruiting soldiers; confiscating grain, valuables, and cash from landlords; and rounding up stragglers and the wounded at the end of the day's march. In August 1935, however, she was assigned to the section of the Red Army placed under the dual command of Zhang Guotao and Zhu De. Zhang Guotao challenged Mao Zedong's control of the CCP by splitting his forces off and taking a different route from those under Mao's command. During the year that Kang Keqing spent in Sichuan and Tibet, she and her husband were virtual prisoners of Zhang Guotao; at the very least, Kang Keqing claimed they were continually under suspicion. She was assigned to work with the Women's Bureau and finally reached Bao'an in November 1936. Kang

Keqing then moved with the communists to Yan'an. She spent only a few months there at this time and attended the Anti-Japanese University (Kang-Ri junzheng daxue, commonly referred to as Kangda). Upon the outbreak of the Sino-Japanese War in July 1937, Kang Keqing sought and was granted special permission to go to the war zone in the Taihang Mountains, where Zhu De had established the headquarters of the Eighth Route Army.

For the next two years, until 1939, Kang Keqing was an organizing cadre with the Eighth Route Army headquarter's Political Bureau and in this capacity worked among the local people in support of the war effort, helped set up literacy groups, and organized local miners' and other workers' unions. She was assigned to women's work that same year as honorary chair of the Southeast Shanxi Women's National Salvation Confederation (Jindongnan funü jiuguo lianhehui), but in reality her duties remained those of an organizer with headquarters.

Kang Keqing returned to Yan'an in May 1940 and was enrolled as a cadre at the Party School. In September 1945, as the Sino-Japanese War drew to a close, she was appointed to the CCP Central Committee's Women's Council and two years later assigned to the group preparing for the first National Women's Congress. Her unique relationship with the military formally ceased in late 1947 or early 1948 when Kang Keqing was refused permission to work with army veterans and instead directed to work with the Women's Council. Then in September, she was appointed acting director of the Council for Children and Welfare in the Liberated Areas.

The All-China Democratic Women's Federation (later changed to the All-China Women's Federation [ACWF], Quanguo funü lianhehui) was established at the first National Women's Congress in 1949. There, Kang Keqing was elected to the Standing Committee, a position held until 1983. She worked with its Children's Welfare Department and traveled overseas to present papers on women and peace (Warsaw, 1950) and children's welfare (Vienna, 1953). She was made secretary-general to the Chinese People's Council for the Protection of Children (Zhongguo renmin baowei ertong quanguo weiyuanhui) in 1955 and in September 1957 elected deputy chair of the ACWF.

Kang Keqing did not fare well, however, in the two decades of political turmoil that began with the One Hundred Flowers Movement of 1956. The ACWF was accused of "demonstrating little concern for the continued oppression of women" and, with the launching of the anti-rightist campaign in early 1957, Kang Keqing was placed in charge of a rectification movement within the ACWF. She was thus partly responsible, to her later chagrin, for allowing the famous writer Ding Ling (*q.v.*) and several other well-known women, including Liu-Wang Liming (*q.v.*), to be criticized and severely "struggled." To subject someone to "struggle" involved verbal and physical humiliation and, sometimes, violence against their person. Two years later, Kang Keqing found herself labeled as "a rightist with capitalist tendencies" after Zhu De was accused of having turned against Mao Zedong (1893–1976).

Then, in the early years of the Cultural Revolution, both Kang Keqing and Zhu De were persecuted. She was subjected to a big character poster attack, paraded as a "capitalist roader" and "struggled" at a large meeting of cadres. The ACWF soon went into recess and Kang Keqing remained idle, but unmolested, until 1977.

Zhu De died in July 1976, six months after Zhou Enlai and two months before Mao Zedong. In March the following year, Kang Keqing was reappointed to leadership of the ACWF, holding the position of chair from 1978 until she was made honorary chair in 1988. The end of the Cultural Revolution saw a genuine revival of the ACWF. Kang Keqing traveled overseas as its representative, presenting a paper at the U.N. Women's Conference in Copenhagen in 1980 and representing China at the signing of the U.N. charter on eliminating all forms of discrimination against women. A new Marriage Law was brought down in 1981; birth control became a national priority; a clause outlawing the concept of male superiority was inserted into the new Chinese Constitution in 1982; the Inheritance Law of 1985 guaranteed women the right to possess, inherit, and bequeath property; and regulations issued in 1988 guaranteed equal pay for equal work.

Kang Keqing's health and sight gradually deteriorated in the 1980s, and she made her last overseas trip (to Yugoslavia and Romania) in 1984. She died in 1992 in Beijing. Kang Keqing had attended the Sixth NPC as a delegate and been deputy chair of several CPPCC, but it is for her work with the ACWF that she is best remembered. Kang Keqing remains a fine example of the early generation of women communists whose lives acted as a bridge between traditional and modern China.

Helen Snow commented when she met her in 1937 in Yan'an: "I am sure she has never had a dress, and probably never will." This was indeed a prescient remark, for Kang Keqing never appeared in public in anything other than the unisex Red Army uniform or, later, the unisex Mao-style suit favored in the first few decades of the PRC. She was described in her obituary in the *People's Daily* as a "proletarian revolutionary."

Sue WILES

Bartke, Wolfgang. *Who Was Who in the PRC*. Munich: K.G. Saur, 1997.

Bi Fang. "Hongjunli de nü siling." In *Hongjun nüyingxiong zhuan*, eds. Liaowang bianjibu. Beijing: Xinhua chubanshe, 1986, 25–37.

Guo Chen. *Jinguo liezhuan: Hong yifangmianjun sanshiwei changzheng nühongjun shengping shiji*. Beijing: Nongcun duwu chubanshe, 1986.

Kang Keqing. *Kang Keqing huiyilu*. Beijing: Jiefangjun chubanshe, 1993.

Lee, Lily Xiao Hong, and Sue Wiles. *Women of the Long March*. Sydney: Allen & Unwin, 1999.

Salisbury, Harrison E. *The Long March: The Untold Story*. New York: Harper & Row, 1985.

Snow, Helen Foster. *Inside Red China*. 1977 reprint [with a new preface and biographical notes by the author]. New York: Da Capo Press, 1939, 167–91.

Wales, Nym [Helen Snow], "K'ang K'ê-ching: A Peasant Partisan." In *Red Dust: Autobiographies of Chinese Communists*, Stanford, California: Stanford University Press, 1952, 211–18.

Kang Tongbi

Kang Tongbi, 1881–1969, *zi* Wenpei, of Nanhai County, Guangdong Province, was a woman activist, poet, and painter.

She was the second daughter of the well-known Qing reformer Kang Youwei (1858–1927), a metropolitan graduate (*jinshi*) of 1895 who memorialized Emperor Guangxu on the subject of reform. After the reforms that Kang Youwei and others proposed were quashed by Dowager Empress Cixi (see *Biographical Dictionary of Chinese*

Women: The Qing Period: Empress Dowager Xiao Qin Xian), Kang Youwei fled to Japan into exile. Kang Tongbi's elder sister (there were eight daughters in the family), Kang Tongwei (*q.v.*), pioneered in publishing women's newspapers and advocated education for women. Both were influenced by the reformist ideas of their father and consciously set an example for other Chinese women in not piercing their ears or binding their feet. The daughters also enjoyed an excellent education that combined the Chinese classics with what was thought to be the best of European and Japanese culture. Both sisters knew several foreign languages; Kang Tongwei focused on writing while Kang Tongbi was able to give public speeches in English. Their mother, Zhang Yunzhu (1856–1922), was also from a literati family and had received a good classical education. During her husband's absence in Beijing as an examination candidate, she resisted pressure from clan elders to bind the feet of her eldest daughter, Kang Tongwei.

In 1901, when her father was in exile, Kang Tongbi went to Penang, then part of British Malaya, to look after and then stay with him as he traveled to India, the first of several such trips together. In a poem written after a pilgrimage to Vulture Peak, a Buddhist shrine, Kang Tongbi claimed to have been the first Chinese woman to visit the Western Heaven, as India was sometimes called. In the winter of 1902–3, when she was twenty, her father sent her to the United States to study and then on a speaking tour of Europe and the U.S. Kang Youwei clearly expected a great deal from his daughter: in a poem dated in the latter year, he wrote of his hope that in her speaking tour she would contribute to his reformist cause as well as to the women's cause and have the opportunity to meet famous statesmen. Kang Tongbi later went to a high school in Hartford, Connecticut. She joined her father in Paris in 1906 for a tour of several European countries during which he bought an island in Sweden. The king of Sweden, who happened to have a villa nearby, was one of their visitors. Kang Tongbi returned to the U.S. to continue her studies at Barnard College at Columbia University but returned the following year, 1908, to Sweden to join several members of her family there. One memorable interlude was her trip to Lyngseidet in Norway with her father to see the rising midnight sun. In the two years before Kang Youwei's death in 1927, Kang Tongbi spent a great deal of time with her father, traveling to Qingdao to view the cherry blossoms in 1925 and inviting him to stay in her home in Beijing after a visit in 1926.

Kang Tongbi and her father had been accompanied on their 1906 tour of Europe by a young man named Lo Chong (Luo Chang, 1883–1955). Born in Honolulu, Lo Chong had studied at Waseda University in Japan but was then studying at Oxford University. It is not clear when Kang Tongbi married Lo Chong, but their first child, a son, was born in 1911.

Not a great deal is known about Kang Tongbi's activities after her return to China, some time before 1925. She did, however, become vice-president of an International Women's Association (Wanguo funühui), president of the Moral Society of Shandong (Shandong daodehui), and president of the CCP-sponsored China Women's Association (Zhongguo funü lianyihui). In 1948, Kang Tongbi acted as a women's representative when General Fu Zuoyi called a meeting in Beijing, just before its fall in January 1949 to the communists, to discuss the peaceful transition of power to the PLA. After that year, she was a member of the Literature and History Research Institute (Wen shi guan) in Beijing and a member of the People's Representative of Beijing (Beijingshi renmin daibiao) as well as the CPPCC. In her last years, Kang Tongbi devoted herself to putting her father's writings in order and edited *Sequel to the Chronological Record of Master Kang of Nanhai* (Nanhai Kang xiansheng nianpu xubian) and *Posthumous Manuscripts from Wanmu Caotang* (Wanmu caotang yigao). She inherited her father's love of the arts and is said to have been a skilled calligrapher as well as adept at flower painting. As was her father, Kang Tongbi was a talented poet in the classical style, receiving praise from Liang Qichao in his *Shihua*.

Both Kang Tongbi and her sister Kang Tongwei helped their father and his cause and were living examples of his ideas regarding women on such matters as footbinding, the value of a good education, and living independently. They were also Kang Youwei's means of liaising with his disciples and others in China during the time he was in exile and with the Western community in Hong Kong. Because he was unable to speak or write in Western languages, his daughters were especially useful to him in this way. More than once, he wrote asking them to speak to the wife of the governor of Hong Kong and other Westerners on his behalf. They were, however, important in their own right. Kang Tongbi went abroad on her own at the age of twenty and spoke about the necessity for reform in China and women's causes. She acted as a role model for Chinese women not only to concern themselves with these issues but in having the courage to speak out in public about them. Kang Tongbi continued to work in the women's movement later in her life.

Her husband, Lo Chong, became a successful academic whose interests included international law, world history, Chinese history, and the ancient literature of Greece and Rome. He taught at such well-known institutions as Women's Normal University of Beijing (Beijing nüzi shifan daxue), Beijing Normal University (Beijing shifan daxue), and Peking University and also served as a diplomat in Singapore, London, and Canada. Kang Tongbi had one son and daughter. Her son, Lo Jung-pang (Luo Rongbang, b. 1911), is an academic in the U.S. and has edited and translated Kang Youwei's biography. Her daughter, Luo Yifeng (1914–1977), is said to have known six languages and been well versed in literature.

Lily Xiao Hong LEE

Kang Tongbi. "Qingmo de Buchanzu hui." *Zhongguo funü*, no. 5 (1957): 12.
Kang Youwei. "Song nü Tongbi wang Mei, Ou yanshuo guoshi jian huan Gang xingqin zhao nü Tongwei lai bing shi zhu tongmen." In *Jindai Zhongguo nüquan yundong shiliao, 1842–1911*, eds. Li Youning and Zhang Yufa. Taipei: Zhuanji wenxueshe, 1975, 390.
Lo Jung-pang, ed. *Kang Yu-wei: A Biography and a Symposium.* Tucson: University of Arizona Press, 1967.
Minguo renwu dacidian. Shijiazhuang: Hebei renmin chubanshe, 1991.
Pang Lian. "Kang Youwei de jiashi he wannian shenghuo." In *Jinian Kang Youwei danchen 130 zhounian, Wuxu weixin yundong 90 zhounian zhuanji*, comp. Nanhai xian zhengxie, Wenshi ziliao yanjiu weiyuanhui. Nanhai: Nanhai xian zhengxie, Wenshi ziliao yanjiu weiyuanhui, 1988, 96–112.
Qin Bangxian. "Kang Youwei de wannian." *Dacheng*, no. 234 (1993): 4–13.
Yin Gang and Yin Changjian. *Zhonghua diyi ren.* Jinan: Shandong youyi shushe, 1989, 416–17.

Kang Tongwei

Kang Tongwei, 1879–1974, *zi* Wenxian, of Nanhai County, Guangdong Province, pioneered in the publication of women's newspapers and advocated women's education.

She was the eldest of eight daughters (nine including a niece adopted into the family) of the well-known Qing reformer Kang Youwei (1858–1927), a metropolitan graduate (*jinshi*) of 1895 who memorialized Emperor Guangxu on the subject of reform. After the reforms that he and others proposed were quashed by Dowager Empress Cixi (see *Biographical Dictionary of Chinese Women: The Qing Period*: Empress Dowager Xiao Qin Xian), Kang Youwei fled to Japan into exile. Kang Tongwei's next younger sister, Kang Tongbi (*q.v*), was also a political and women's movement activist. Both were influenced by the reformist ideas of their father and consciously set an example for other Chinese women in not piercing their ears or binding their feet. They also enjoyed an excellent education that combined the Chinese classics with what was thought to be the best of European and Japanese culture. Both sisters knew several foreign languages; Kang Tongwei focused on writing while Kang Tongbi gave public speeches in English. Their mother, Zhang Yunzhu (1856–1922), was also from a literati family and had received a good classical education. During her husband's absence in Beijing as an examination candidate, she resisted pressure from clan elders to bind Kang Tongwei's feet.

Kang Tongwei was a diligent student who mastered both English and Japanese. At the age of fifteen, her father assigned her to the task of helping him in a project in which he claimed to have restored the original text of the ancient historical record *Guoyu*. In the same year, 1894, Kang Tongwei wrote *Customs and Institutions* (Fengsu zhi), which looks at the progress of humankind through the twenty-four official histories of China. She also translated many of the Japanese books her father had used as sources for his *A Study of Political Reform in Japan* (Riben bianzheng kao) and *A Japanese Bibliography* (Riben shumuzhi), both seminal works on Japanese studies in China. In 1897, Kang Tongwei worked as a translator in the newly established newspaper *Zhixin bao*, thus becoming one of the first Chinese women to work for a newspaper. The following year, she joined with several others, including Li Huixian (see *Biographical Dictionary of Chinese Women: The Qing Period*), the wife of Liang Qichao, to establish a school for girls in Shanghai. This was one of the earliest schools of its kind initiated by Chinese women, schools for women having previously been established only by foreign missionaries. The same group also published a women's magazine, released three times a month, called *Guanhua nüxuebao*. Usually known simply as *Nüxuebao*, it promoted women's education and the opportunity to lead a self-reliant working life. This magazine was one of the earliest published by women for women in China.

After the failure in late 1898 of the One Hundred Days Reform, an order was issued for the arrest of Kang Youwei and his family. Kang Tongwei went with her mother to live in exile in Portuguese Macao, although the family later moved to Hong Kong. As did her next younger sister, Kang Tongwei frequently accompanied her father on his travels. In 1897, they toured the West Lake of Hangzhou; when Kang Youwei was living in exile in Darjeeling, India, in 1903, he sent for her to come and care for him. In 1908, she joined her father and sister Kang Tongbi in Sweden and visited the University of Uppsala.

Kang Tongwei married Mai Zhonghua (1876–1955) in 1898; he was a younger brother of Kang Youwei's disciple Mai Menghua and had himself studied under Kang Youwei. Mai Zhonghua studied in Japan and England and was at one stage head of the Hong Kong Telegraph Company. One source says that Kang Tongwei organized the Yokohama Girls' School in Yokohama in 1899 for the Chinese living in Japan; this may have coincided with the time when Mai Zhonghua was studying in Japan. Kang Tongwei and Mai Zhonghua were based in Hong Kong, however. They had eleven children, who now live in places as far apart as North America, Australia, Hong Kong, and China. In her old age, Kang Tongwei's legs were paralyzed, and she seldom went out. She died of illness in Hong Kong in 1974.

In her writings, Kang Tongwei argued for the education of women on the ground of gender equality. In an article published in *Zhixin bao* in 1898, she pointed to Chinese antiquity as well as to Japan and the West as models for gender equality, criticizing the customs of her own time as debasing women. She argued that the reason why China was so weak was because it had enslaved one-half of its population and made them unproductive. Similarly, the reason why Chinese men were weak and ignorant was because they had been brought up by mothers who were uneducated and therefore unable to give them the appropriate training and family education. Not surprisingly, perhaps, her ideas on women were similar to her father's and those of his pupil and comrade-in-reform Liang Qichao.

Kang Tongwei's involvement in setting up more than one school for women and her writings on women's education made important contributions to the development of women's education in China around the beginning of the twentieth century. She was also very helpful to her father in his writings, both in classical studies and political reform in Japan. Unfortunately, perhaps because raising eleven children devoured her time and energy, little is known of Kang Tongwei's work in the later part of her life.

Kang Tongwei had eight younger sisters and two younger brothers by six of Kang Youwei's wives and concubines. Only three of the sisters lived to adulthood, three dying in infancy and two others dying young. Kang Tongfu (1903–1979) married Pan Qixuan (1898–?), whose father, Pan Zhibo, had been a follower of Kang Youwei; as he neared death, Pan entrusted his fifteen-year-old son to Kang Youwei. Pan Qixuan grew up to be an able assistant to Kang Youwei and editor of his magazine *Buren zazhi*. Kang Tongfu bore eight children who are now scattered throughout the world. Another daughter, Kang Tonghuan (b. 1907), married He Zichao (Yongle), a businessman operating in Vietnam and Hong Kong, and emerged in Hong Kong in the 1960s. She published magazine articles in Taiwan and Hong Kong interpreting her father's later political thought in an attempt to exonerate his role in the infamous restoration movement of 1917, which attempted to restore the Qing emperor. She was said to be still living in Hong Kong in 1987. Kang Tongwei's younger brother Kang Tongqian (1908–1961) was an engineer who died in poverty in Taiwan. Her other younger brother Kang Tongning stayed in China after 1949 and worked in business. He possessed some family documents and letters that his wife, Pang Lian, donated to the Committee for the Safekeeping of Cultural Relics in Shanghai in 1980, after his death in 1978. These documents include letters from Kang Youwei to Kang Tongwei and Kang Tongbi that provide insight into their role in his work.

Kang Tongwei's daughter Mai Jiazeng (Nina Mai Chang) and her son Mai Xinzeng (Mark Mai) provided some of the information in this biography.

Lily Xiao Hong LEE

Huaxia funü mingren cidian. Beijing: Huaxia chubanshe, 1988, 973.

Kang Tongwei. "Nüxue libi shuo." In *Jindai Zhongguo nüquan yundong shiliao, 1842–1911*, eds. Li Youning and Zhang Yufa. Taipei: Zhuanji wenxueshe, 1975, 562–66.

Kang Youwei. "Song nü Tongbi wang Mei,Ou yanshuo guoshi jian huan Gang xingqin zhao nü Tongwei lai bing shi zhu tongmen." In *Jindai Zhongguo nüquan yundong shiliao, 1842– 1911*, eds. Li Youning and Zhang Yufa. Taipei: Zhuanji wenxueshe, 1975, 390.

Lo Jung-pang, ed. *Kang Yu-wei: A Biography and a Symposium*. Tucson: University of Arizona Press, 1967.

Pang Lian. "Kang Youwei de jiashi he wannian shenghuo." In *Jinian Kang Youwei danchen 130 zhounian, Wuxu weixin yundong 90 zhounian zhuanji*, comp. Nanhai xian zhengxie, Wenshi ziliao yanjiu weiyuanhui. Nanhai: Nanhai xian zhengxie, Wenshi ziliao yanjiu weiyuanhui, 1988, 96–112.

Qin Bangxian. "Kang Youwei de wannian." *Dacheng*, no. 234 (1993): 4–13.

Song Ruizhi, ed. *Zhongguo funü wenhua tonglan*. Jinan: Shandong wenyi chubanshe, 1995, 275.

Zhongguo funü guanli ganbu xueyuan, ed. *Gujin Zhongwai nümingren cidian*. Beijing: Zhongguo guangbo dianshi chubanshe, 1980, 182.

Ke Yan

Ke Yan, b. 1929, in Zhengzhou, Henan Province, is a poet and writer specializing in reportage and children's literature.

Her original name was Feng Kai, and her family was originally from Nanhai, Guangdong Province. Ke Yan's father, an educated man who loved literature, is said to have translated French works into Chinese; one source also said he worked for the railroads.

Ke Yan was a student activist while at high school and normal school in Hubei and Yunnan. She passed the entrance examination for the Drama Department of Suzhou Social Education College (Shehui jiaoyu xueyuan) and enrolled in 1948. As the CCP swept to victory, Ke Yan was assigned in May 1949 as a playwright to the Beijing Youth Art Theater (Beijing qingnian yishu juyuan) and sent to factories, army garrisons, rural areas, and women's production and education centers to collect first-hand material. In 1955, she wrote the children's poem *The Story of Xiao Bing* (Xiaobing de gushi), which won the Chinese Second Children's Literature Award. This work made her name as a poet. Ke Yan joined the CCP the following year and became resident playwright of the Chinese Children's Art Theater, producing a series of children's poems and plays, including *Big Red Flower* (Da honghua), *Here Is What I Would Say to Uncle Lei Feng* (Wo dui Lei Feng shushu shuo), *To Tell the Young Pioneers* (Jiang gei shaoxianduiyuan ting), *Aunt Muddle-head* ("Xiao Mihu" ayi), *A Children's Shop* (Wawa dian), *Shuangshuang and Her Grandma* (Shuansghuang he laolao), *Flying Off the Earth* (Feichu diqiu qu), and *A Crystal Cave* (Shuijing dong). She started to work as a professional writer for the Creation Workshop of the Chinese Ministry of Culture in 1962 and also that year joined the Chinese Writers' Association and the Chinese Playwrights' Association.

Ke Yan's writing career halted during the Cultural Revolution, however. But as the period ended, she wrote a few long poems, *Where Are You, Premier Zhou?*, *At the Dawn of September Nine*, and *Please Let Me* . . . , in praise of persecuted leaders such as Zhou Enlai. She attracted considerable, but temporary, attention with her speech at the third Chinese Writers' Association Conference in November 1979 in which she called on writers to break away from ultra-leftist ideology and strive for freedom of thought. That year, Ke Yan was elected to the third and fourth sessions of the Executive Committee of the Chinese Writers' Association, acting as general secretary, and the fourth China Federation of Literary and Art Circles.

After China opened its door to the West in the early 1980s, Ke Yan turned her attention to morality, traditional values, love, life, and young people. She spent most of her time giving lectures at universities in Beijing, Shandong, and Shenzhen in discussion forums with university students; visited youth rehabilitation schools; and gathered material from grass-roots areas. Ke Yan's writing style altered when she returned to writing in the late 1970s. The range of projects changed from poems and plays to reportage, novels, prose, and film and television scripts, applying to these formats the poetic touches and dramatic effects for which she was known. Her experiment has been well received; many of her post-1979 works have won prizes. These include the novel *Finding the Lost World* (Xunzhao huilai de shijie; translated into English as *The World Regained*), written after spending two years in a Beijing youth rehabilitation school. Between 1985 and 1987, the novel won the Flying *Apsaras* (Feitian jiang), the Golden Eagle (Jin ying jiang), and the National Education Council Prizes (Guojia jiaowei jiang), as well as the Madame Sun Yat-sen Prize for Children's Literature (Song Qingling ertong wenxue jiang). Ke Yan's reportage pieces "Captain" (Chuanzhang), "A Special Representative" (Teyao daibiao), and "Cancer Does Not Equal Death" (Aizheng bu dengyu siwang) won the National Award for Excellence in Reportage (Quanguo youxiu baogao wenxue jiang) between 1977 and 1980. She edited the volume on reportage writing in the anthology *Zhongguo xin wenyi daxi, 1976–1982*.

After being diagnosed with cancer in the early 1980s, Ke Yan became increasingly bedridden. In her writings, she started to explore the themes of life and death, which produced reportage pieces on cancer (see above) and "The High Pressure Oxygen Cabin" and "Facing Death." These musings on cancer patients express a tranquil attitude toward life and death, and her condition was clearly responsible for the writer's thematic evolution from portrayals of heroism and political enthusiasm to serene reflection on universal love. Her latest works tend to concentrate on the latter, in particular the novel *The Bright Moon on a Strange Land* (Taxiang mingyue), which describes two Chinese girls pursuing different dreams and experiencing different fates in America. Her works have been translated into many foreign languages.

Ke Yan is currently deputy editor-in-chief of the magazine *Poetry*. She also serves on the Chinese Children's Protection Committee and the Editorial Committees of various literary magazines.

GAO Yuanbao
(Translated and expanded by Cui Zhiying)

Huaxia funü mingren cidian. Beijing: Huaxia chubanshe, 1988, 782–83.

Ke Yan. *The World Regained,* trans. Wu Jingshu and Wang Ningjun. Beijing: Foreign Language Press, 1993.

"Ke Yan xiao zhuan." *Zhongguo xiandai zuojia zhuanlüe,* vol. 2. Xuzhou: Xuzhou shifan xueyuan, 1981, 371–73.

Sheng Ying. "Zai lun Ke Yan." *Wenxue pinglun,* no. 5 (1994): 32–41.

Zhongguo funü guanli ganbu xueyuan, ed. *Gujin Zhongwai nümingren cidian.* Beijing: Zhongguo guangbo dianshi chubanshe, 1980, 182–83.

Kingston, Maxine Hong

Maxine Hong Kingston, b. 1940, as Maxine Ting Ting Hong in Stockton, California, in the U.S., is a Chinese American writer.

Her parents came from the Say Yup dialect region near Canton, Guangdong Province. Her father, Tom Hong (d. 1991), was a native of Sun Woi village and, although the youngest son of a peasant family, received a classical education. One source says he left China after failing to obtain a government position; others mention that Tom Hong was a teacher in China before emigrating to the United States in 1924. Maxine Hong's father worked in a laundry in New York for many years but never learned to speak or read English with any degree of fluency. Tom Hong had left his wife, Chew Ying Lan (who came to be known in the U.S. as Ying Lan Hong), behind in China, and their two children died before she was able to join him in New York in 1939. Chew Ying Lan had been educated in China and trained in midwifery and Western medicine at a medical college in Canton. Like her husband, she never learned to speak or read English because they continued to live very much within the Chinese community. The couple moved form New York to California, where he worked in a gambling house for a time before setting up a family laundry business. Maxine is the eldest of their six American-born children, three girls and three boys.

From 1954 to 1958, Maxine Hong attended Edison High School in Stockton and won a journalism scholarship to the University of California, Berkeley (UCB). She enrolled in engineering but soon switched to English literature, graduating in 1962 with a B.A. In November she married Earll Kingston, an actor she met at UCB; their son Joseph Lawrence Chung Mei Kingston was born in 1964. Maxine Hong Kingston gained a teaching qualification in 1965 and taught in California. For the next two years, she was active in the free-speech movement and anti-Vietnam War protests, then in 1967 moved with her husband and son to Hawaii and continued teaching for another ten years or so. Although brought up in a literate household where books, writing, and storytelling were considered important, Maxine did not start writing until she went to school. "I started writing, actually writing, when I learned English," she said in a 1989 interview. "I have all kinds of miraculous feelings about the English language." Her first essay, "I Am an American," appeared in *American Girl* magazine in 1955, and she worked for the *Daily Californian* student newspaper while at UCB. Her first book, however, was not published until 1976. The book *The Woman Warrior: Memoirs of a Girlhood among Ghosts* won the National Book Critics Circle Award in non-fiction that year and in 1979 was rated by *Time* magazine as one of the top ten non-fiction works of the decade. *China Men* (1980)—her companion volume to *The Woman Warrior*—won the National Book Award for non-fiction in 1980 and was runner up for the Pulitzer Prize in 1981.

In these two memoirs, Maxine Hong Kingston uses the Cantonese tradition of "talk-story" that she says is inherited from her mother, an inveterate and inspired teller of myths and stories. Talk-story was also part of the local oral traditions of Hawaii where she was writing and teaching in the late 1960s and 1970s. In the words of Wendy Ho, Kingston adapted talk-story to "retell traditional stories and/or invent subversive stories to account for the varying social, economic, cultural, and historical circumstances of Chinese women, families, and communities in the United States."

Weaving myth with reality, *The Woman Warrior* and *China Men* are Kingston's accounts of growing up as a Chinese American. She told an interviewer in 1986 that the two pieces were originally conceived as "one huge book. However, part of the reason for two books is history. The women had their own time and place and their lives were coherent; there was a woman's way of thinking. My men's stories seemed to interfere. They were weakening the feminist point of view. So I took all the men's stories out, and then I had *The Woman Warrior*." The unnamed young girl who narrates *The Woman Warrior* names the unspeakable by relating her mother's stories of the dreadful things that had befallen the women of their family, cautionary tales intended to silence Chinese girls. But she also relates and is liberated by the heroic tales her mother told of swordswomen such as the famous warrior woman Fa Mu Lan (Hua Mulan). *China Men* tells the stories of the men of her family who emigrated and created a new life in the Unites States. In locating the psyche and experience of Chinese Americans within American literature, Maxine Hong Kingston was deliberately "claiming the English language and the literature to tell our story as Americans." To capture the rhythms of Chinese-American English, she would translate Chinese into English as she wrote and then find English words for Chinese ways and dialogue, developing a unique style with a Chinese-American voice.

Thus, at a time when the face of the United States was purely European, Maxine Hong Kingston began writing individual Chinese Americans and their culture into the texture of American history and society. In this, her work paralleled that of other ethnic women writers such as the African Americans Alice Walker and Toni Morrison and prefigures the Asian American writers Amy Tan (*q.v.*), Hisaye Yamamoto, Steven Lo, Ruth-Anne Lumm McKunn, Jessica Hagedorn, and Bharati Mukherjee. However, Maxine Hong Kingston always acknowledged her own debt to Jade Snow Wong, the "Mother of Chinese-American literature," whose autobiographical *Fifth Chinese Daughter* inspired her and, as she put it, made it possible for her to be a writer.

Maxine Hong Kingston has not been spared criticism, however; her arch critic, the Chinese American playwright Frank Chin, branded her as a "race traitor" for tampering with the authentic literary and mythological heritage of China. Her work (and Amy Tan's) has been dismissed as Orientalist, presenting (in the words of Gloria Chun) a "detrimental, self-hating, assimilationist view of Chinese American" for predominantly White audiences. Kingston's response to such criticism is that she is neither an archivist nor an anthropologist, much less a historian. She changes myths and legends, stating that her "new stories should not be seamlessly traced back to ancient, scholarly stories derived from a 'high culture' or a purist classic Chinese tradition or past." For her, there are many authentic versions that differ from person to person: "I am writing about real people, all of whom have minds that love to invent fictions. I am writing the biography of their imaginations."

The commercial success of her first two books enabled Maxine Hong Kingston to give up teaching and write full time. She did, however, continue teaching part time and from 1977 to 1981 was a visiting professor of English at the University of Hawaii. The literary recognition that followed the success of her books led to other honors, including several honorary doctorates and her induction in 1992 into the American Academy of Arts and Sciences. She was the Thelma McAndless Distinguished Professor in the Humanities at Eastern Michigan University in 1986 and the Chancellor's Distinguished Professor in the English Department at UCB in 1990. In 1984 Maxine Hong Kingston and her husband moved back to California (Los Angeles), somewhat regretfully leaving their musician son in Hawaii. That year she also made her first trip to China. As a guest of the Chinese Writers' Association, she traveled with seven other writers, including Toni Morrison, Allen Ginsberg, and Gary Snyder, visiting her native village and meeting some of her relatives for the first time. She published *Hawai'i One Summer, 1978*, a volume of essays, in 1987; and her first novel—*Tripmaster Monkey: His Fake Book*—came out two years later. *Tripmaster Monkey* is about the United States in the 1960s, when the Tripitika Monkey King of Chinese Buddhist mythology is reincarnated as Wittman Ah Sing, an English major. Many readers found this book difficult and much less accessible than her earlier works, while critics accused her of having written a vengeful roman à clef about Frank Chin, a claim she dismisses.

Maxine Hong Kingston and her husband moved in 1987 to Oakland, not far from her birthplace; during this late 1980s period, she began to attend Buddhist retreats led by the Vietnamese Buddhist monk Thich Nhat Hanh. She had become increasingly active since 1980 in the anti-draft movement in Hawaii and by 1991 her aesthetics and politics had become inseparable, making her a "very political writer." The writer has long held pacifist views and said that she wants "to change the world through artistic pacifist means." Two of her brothers served in Vietnam, and Maxine was aware that, for many, this had been an inconclusive war, so in 1996 she started giving writing workshops with Vietnam veterans. Her work-in-progress, *The Fourth Book of Peace*, was among the manuscripts that were lost when her home was destroyed in the Oakland Hills firestorm of 1991, just three weeks after the death of her father. She immediately made plans to start again, renaming it *The Fifth Book of Peace*.

Sue WILES

Chen Xuanbo. "Cong Lin Yutang dao Tang Tingting: Zhongxin yu bianyuan de wenhua xunshi." *Waiguo wenxue pinglun* (Beijing), 4, no. 92–99 (1995): 249–56.

Ho, Wendy. In *Her Mother's House: The Politics of Asian American Mother-Daughter Writing*. Walnut Creek: AltaMira Press, 1999.

Huang Wenxiang. *Ou-Mei jiechu huayi nüxing*. Hong Kong: Shanghai shuju, 1992, 157–83.

Kingston, Maxine Hong. *China Men*. New York: Knopf, 1980.

———. *Hawai'i One Summer, 1978.* San Francisco: Meadow Press, 1987.

———. *Tripmaster Monkey: His Fake Book.* New York: Knopf, 1989.

———. *The Woman Warrior: Memoirs of a Girlhood among Ghosts.* New York: Knopf, 1976.

———. "Precepts for the Twenty-first Century." In *Engaged Buddhist Reader,* ed. Arnold Kotler. Berkeley, Calif.: Parallax Press, 1996.

Lau, Joseph S.M. "Kingston as Exorcist." In *Modern Chinese Women Writers: Critical Appraisals,* ed. Michael S. Duke. Armonk, N.Y.: M.E. Sharpe, 1989, 44–52.

Skenazy, Paul, and Tera Martin, eds. *Conversations with Maxine Hong Kingston.* Jackson: University Press of Mississippi, 1998.

Soderstrom, Christina K. "Maxine Hong Kingston." In *Voices from the Gaps: Women Writers of Color,* at <http://voices.cla.umn.edu/authors/MaxineHongKingston.html>, July 2000.

Wong, Sau-ling Cynthia. "'Sugar Sisterhood': Situating the Amy Tan Phenomenon." In *The Ethnic Canon: Histories, Institutions, and Interventions,* ed. David Palumbo-Liu. Minneapolis/London: University of Minnesota Press, 1995, 174–205.

Koo Mei

Koo Mei [Gu Mei], b. 1934, in Canton, is a painter.

Her father was also a painter, her brother a musician. She had a successful career as a singer and film actress in Hong Kong and later started painting studies with Zhao Shao'ang (1905–84) in 1962, as well as with Hu Nianzi in 1969. She began exhibiting in 1971. Her notion of imaginary landscape has also been strongly influenced by Lui Shou-kwan (1919–76) and Liu Guosong (b. 1932), representing a nocturnal world of almost inconceivable spaces, twisted in on themselves with engroined trees and mountains. These eschew traditional brushwork convention as much as they refer to abstracted "Chinese" spatial conventions for ink landscape, also in the domain of other modernist Hong Kong painters like Wang Wuxie (Wucius Wong, b. 1936).

John CLARK

Koo Mei. Hong Kong: The Artist, 1979.

The Painting of Koo Mei. Hong Kong: Arts Centre, 1981.

Kou Chen Ying: *see* Gu Shengying

Kuang Jianlian: *see* Hongxian Nü

Kuo Hsiao-chuang

Kuo Hsiao-chuang [Guo Xiaozhuang], b. 1951, in Taiwan but a native of Hua-hsien [Huaxian], Ho-nan [Henan] Province, is renowned as a *ching-chü* (*jingju* [Peking opera]) performer as well as a reformer of the genre.

Her father was a *ching-chü* aficionado and enrolled his daughter when she was eight years old at the Ta-p'eng Drama School. This marked the end of Kuo Hsiao-chuang's childhood for the next few years were harsh. Every day she practiced singing and martial arts exercises, including weapon fights, to the point of exhaustion and endured corporal punishment. After this basic training, Kuo Hsiao-chuang was trained in the various *tan* (female leads) roles of *ching-chü*, beginning with the *hua-tan* (lively young women). Body movements and postures are the essence of this role, so Kuo Hsiao-chuang learned how to walk, walk and run on stilts, and use her eyes in an expressive and lively way. She learned to sing her roles in the traditional manner: repeating words line by line, sometimes singing a single line over and over for weeks on end until she had timing, delivery, and intonation by heart.

Her father continued to be ambitious for her and supported his daughter's development by seeking out famous teachers. He initially sought someone who could train her in both artistic and martial (*wen-wu*) skills but finally accepted Su Sheng-shih as Kuo Hsiao-chuang's martial arts teacher and engaged Pai Yü-wei as coach for non-fighting roles. Kuo Hsiao-chuang would practice martial arts under the hot midday sun while everyone else rested. Wearing a thick padded coat with four big flags attached to her back, she would do ten fast laps around the exercise ground in preparation for the ritual actions of getting ready for battle. Wielding her large sword, Kuo Hsiao-chuang had to be careful not to hit the flags on her back and had to be able to toss the sword in the air and whirl around to catch it on the way down, remaining graceful and lithe all the while. These basic skills necessary for the *tao-ma-tan* (young warrior woman) roles developed in her a resilience and bodily strength that marked her performance throughout her career.

Her other teacher was the well-known mainlander actress Pai Yü-wei, who had also taught Hsü Lu. Pai Yü-wei was the mistress of willowy pliancy in both body and facial expression. The latter, while seemingly natural, was perfectly controlled down to the finest detail. In her acting, Pai Yü-wei coined the maxim "stillness in control of movement." By this she meant that the eyes should always move before any other part of the body.

In the opera *Love at First Sight* (Ma-shang yüan), Kuo Hsiao-chuang embodied her teachers' theories in her performance as the female lead. Given the opportunity to display her artistic (*wen*) and martial arts (*wu*) skills, she convinced the teachers of her prodigious talent. They therefore gave her the chance to play Tou Hsien-t'ung (the immortal page, Tou) in the famous Ta-p'eng opera *Chessboard Mountain* (Ch'i-p'an shan). With the experience of performing in *Love at First Sight* behind her, Kuo Hsiao-chuang made a vivacious and witty pageboy. She was by this time fifteen years old. Su Sheng-shih also taught her the role in the opera *The Hu Family Village* (Hu-chia-chuang) that Hsü Lu had made her own. No one had dared play the part after her, but Kuo Hsiao-chuang absorbed everything she could from her teacher and was able to make every single movement tug at her audience's heart strings in the role. This established Kuo Hsiao-chuang as a *ching-chü* performer. The first phase of her career ended when she graduated from the Ta-p'eng Troupe in 1970 as a leading lady.

Aware of her lack of formal education to round out becoming a complete performer, Kuo Hsiao-chuang took courses in lyrics (*tz'u*) and songs (*ch'ü*) at Tan-chiang University (Tan-chiang ta-hsüeh) from the well-known dramatist and literary personage Yü Ta-kang. Kuo Hsiao-chuang went on to graduate from the Drama Department of the Fine Arts Faculty of Wen-hua University (Wen-hua ta-hsüeh i-shu hsüeh-yüan hsi-chü hsi). One particular piece of Professor Yü's advice influenced her deeply: "Find your own way through life and be true to yourself." He also encouraged her to ask questions and be thorough in planning, thereby guiding her toward greater reflectivity.

In this, the second stage of her career, Kuo Hsiao-chuang learned to observe from life, thus broadening her artistic horizons and establishing a rich background for understanding people. She was able to incorporate these perceptions into her acting. Yü Ta-kang wrote a script for her entitled *Wang K'uei Betrays Kuei-ying* (Wang K'uei fu Kuei-ying) that marked a new development in her career. She had previously been known for her *hua-tan* and *tao-ma-tan* roles, but this script required her to play the *ch'ing-i* (young or middle-aged women of rectitude) role. However, the part Yü Ta-kang created for her was not a traditional *ch'ing-i*, but a more complex character, with equal stress on singing and movement. Kuo Hsiao-chuang's interpretation was outstanding, especially in the changes of mood, and her singing was very moving. This performance seems to have marked a broadening in the scope of her *ching-chü* performance. Under Yü Ta-kang's guidance, Kuo Hsiao-chuang pioneered a new era in *ching-chü*. Yü wrote several scripts for her, including *Eighth Sister Yang* (Yang pa-mei), *A Heroic Couple* (Erh-nü ying-hao), and *The Princess of One Hundred Flowers* (Pai-hua kung-chu), and adapted old operas for her to perform.

Kuo Hsiao-chuang was much in demand for her martial arts skills in 1972, when such films were in vogue. After her first martial arts film, *Ch'iu Chin*, she was dubbed the "Queen of Martial Arts Films." Kuo Hsiao-chuang went on to appear in the television series *A Long Reputation* (Wan-ku liu-fang) and came to realize the value of a good script and story above all the ancillary things that go to make up good entertainment. From experience, she understood the difference between acting for opera and acting for film and television. Further, Kuo Hsiao-chuang knew instinctively that if opera were to survive in the modern world it would need to adopt the newer film and television style of acting. She therefore went about inserting new techniques of acting into *ching-chü*.

Yü Ta-kang had supported her desire to reform *ching-chü*, and after he died in 1977 Kuo Hsiao-chuang set about realizing her dream of organizing an opera troupe to be known as the Ya-yin Ensemble (Ya-yin Hsiao-chi). She chose this name because it meant a collection of like-minded people called together by Hsiao-chuang to accomplish the mission of renewing *ching-chü*. The Ya-yin Ensemble was formed in March 1979. The artist Chang Ta-ch'ien and his eldest son, Chang Pao-lo, hand-painted a design from Tun-huang on the curtain for her Ya-yin Ensemble. Their first opera was *The White Snake and Hsü Hsien* (Pai-she yü Hsü Hsien). Yü Ta-kang had revised *Excursion on the Lake* (Yu-hu) especially for her, and his new words provided new ideas for the opera, causing considerable controversy as well, however. Another controversial opera they produced was *Tou O Yüan*, but in this case they were forced to change the plot. Chang Ta-ch'ien designed Kuo Hsiao-chuang's costumes for *Liang Shan-po and Chu Ying-t'ai* (Liang Shan-po yü Chu Ying-t'ai). He used light and elegant hues instead of the traditional more stark colors and painted and inscribed a fan for her to use in the production. Kuo Hsiao-chuang also introduced classical Chinese music to *ching-chü*, which had been accompanied by music of the popular folk tradition. She would frequently visit universities and colleges to give talks and seminars, because she wanted to understand how young people felt about opera. Kuo Hsiao-chuang believed that only by involving the young would it be possible for a traditional art such as opera to continue.

The 1980s were a time of wider recognition of Kuo Hsiao-chuang's talents. She lectured at Taiwan Art College (Taiwan i-shu chuan-k'o hsüeh-hsiao) from 1980 to 1981, taught at the World Journalism School at Ch'eng-kung University and at Central University, and served on the Executive Committee of the China National Drama Society from 1981 to 1984. Selected as one of the year's Ten Most Outstanding Young Women in 1982, the following year Kuo Hsiao-chuang was voted Asia's Most Outstanding Performer. Among her other awards are the International Media Medal (Government Information Office) and membership of the China–Taiwan Association of Film (Chung-kuo liang-an ying-i hsieh-hui). She has been chief executive officer of her own company (Kuo Hsiao-chuang wen-hua kung-ssu) since 1985.

Kuo Hsiao-chuang spent a year (1983) at the Juilliard School of Music in the United States and learned a great deal about the differences between Chinese and Western operas with the intention of introducing new elements into traditional Chinese opera. The first opera she performed after returning to Taiwan was *Madam Han* (Han fu-jen), which incorporated Western techniques and designs. Between 1979 and 1997, the Ya-yin Ensemble performed eleven operas, each well received by the younger generation because the productions were innovative and of professional quality.

Although hers was a childhood without dolls, a childhood of endless practice and suffering, Kuo Hsiao-chuang feels a responsibility to opera as well as to society and culture to extend the life of the art form. She would like the world to see the Ya-yin Ensemble and plans to establish scholarships and establish a college to encourage young people into the profession, thereby enriching the tradition. In recent years, Kuo Hsiao-chuang has performed several times in mainland China.

KAO Yüeh-t'o
(Translated by Lily Xiao Hong Lee and Sue Wiles)

Clendenin, Mike. "Opera in the Age of Pop." *Taipei Times*, 24 October 1999, at <http://taipeitimes.com/news/1999/10/24/story/0000008007>.
Kuo Hsiao-chuang. *T'ien ya hsiang i.* Taipei: Chiu-ta wen-hua ku-fen yu-hsien kung-ssu, 1987.
Liu T'ien-i. *Kuo Hsiao-chuang Ya-yin liao-jao.* Taipei: T'ai-shih wen-hua, 1998.

Kuo, Shirley: *see* **Kuo Wan-jung**

Kuo Wan-jung

Kuo Wan-jung [Guo Wanrong], b. 1930, in T'ai-nan County, Taiwan, is also known by her English name Shirley Kuo. She became the first woman minister in the Republic of China in Taiwan with her appointment as minister of Finance, a post held from 1988 to 1990.

Born into a comfortable home—her father was a doctor—Kuo Wan-jung was an outstanding student from childhood. She studied economics at Taiwan University and specialized in mathematical economics, graduating in 1952. Kuo Wan-jung performed so well academically that she was asked to stay on at the university and by 1966 had become a professor. In 1959, Kuo Wan-jung went to the United States to begin post-graduate studies at the Department of Economics at the Massachusetts Institute of Technology (MIT). She earned her M.E.c. degree in 1971 (under the name Kuo Wanyong) and from then to 1972 was a visiting professor at MIT. Kuo Wan-jung then undertook doctoral work at the National Kobe University, Japan, and received her Ph.D. in Economics in 1984. During this period, she focused on analyzing data from developing countries to study their economic development. This experience equipped her to combine economic theory with economic reality.

When Kuo Wan-jung returned to Taiwan from the United States, the government of Taiwan was in the process of including more local Taiwan people in leadership roles. She was appointed deputy chair (1973) of the Economic Planning Committee (Ching-chi she-chi wei-yüan-hui), which the head of the Legislative Yuan, Chiang Ching-kuo, had just established. Kuo Wan-jung was kept on as deputy chair when the committee changed its name in 1977 to the Economic Reconstruction Committee (Ching-chi chien-she wei-yüan-hui). Two years later (1979), after being appointed vice-president of the Central Bank of the Republic of China, she liberalized finances in Taiwan and pushed for freeing interest rates from government control and opening up foreign exchange.

Her academic work on general economics includes *Selected Papers on Mathematical Economics* (Shu-li ching-chi-hsüeh hsüan-lun); *Individual Economics* (Ko-t'i ching-chi-hsüeh, 1984); and *Integrated Economics* (Tsung-t'i ching-chi-hsüeh, 1976). She has, however, published specifically on Taiwan issues, and these better known works are internationally considered basic references. They include *The Ramifications for Taiwan's Foreign Trade and Commodity Prices of Changing Foreign Exchange Rates and How to Handle Them* (Hui-lü pien-tung tui Taiwan tui wai mao-i yü wu-chia chih ying-hsiang chi tui-ts'e, 1973); *Growth with Equity: The Taiwan Case* (with John C.H. Fei and Gustav Ranis, World Bank, 1979); and *The Taiwan Economy in Transition* (Westview Press, 1983).

In 1988, Kuo Wan-jung was appointed by President Li Teng-hui [Lee Teng-hui] to succeed Ch'ien Ch'un as minister of Finance. During her tenure, she tackled such difficult issues as taxing the trading of stocks and stock exchange companies. The government had previously avoided doing this, and Kuo Wan-jung encountered great resistance in the Legislative Yuan when she tried to push these reforms through. Kuo Wan-jung succeeded, however, compromising only on the rate of the taxes. Kuo Wan-jung also made her ministerial mark in recruiting non-KMT people to influential positions in her ministry. In contrast to the elderly members who had got there because of party politics, these new people were professionals in their forties who were eager to improve Taiwan's economy and accelerate its growth.

In May 1989, Kuo Wan-jung became the first high-level official from Taiwan to visit mainland China. She went there not as minister of Finance but as a board member of the Asia Development Bank to attend the annual general meeting held in Beijing. It appears, because the original board member from Taiwan was asked to resign to make way for her, that Li Teng-hui handpicked her for this mission. It has been suggested that Kuo Wan-jung was selected, firstly, because she had never displayed any anti-communist tendencies and, secondly, to counter the common view that people of Taiwanese origin were in favor of independence and opposed reunification with China. Her visit attracted great attention from the international media. At her first press conference at the Great Wall Hotel, she was almost mobbed by reporters and asked to answer questions in both Chinese and English, sometimes having to repeat her answers in both languages. Few remained unimpressed by her poise and friendliness. In 1990, Kuo Wan-jung was made head of the Economic Reconstruction Committee, a position held until 1993. She has since become a minister without portfolio and returned to teaching at Taiwan University. As a minister, Kuo Wan-jung made visits abroad, including one visit to Australia in 1993 to attend the Asia-Pacific Insight Conference.

Kuo Wan-jung met her first husband, Liu Ch'ing-jui (1923–before 1968), a specialist on constitutional law, at Taiwan University. They married despite the fact that he had been diagnosed with cancer, and they had three daughters. In 1968, Kuo Wan-jung married Ni Wen-ya, a former head of the Legislative Yuan. He is said to have influenced Kuo Wan-jung in her change of academic direction (from the study of economic theory to its practical application in Taiwan) and her subsequent entry into politics.

Although sometimes referred to in the Taiwan media as the "Iron Lady," after the former British Prime Minister Margaret Thatcher, Kuo Wan-jung also appears to have her soft spots and has been described as gentle but principled. She was once on the verge of tears when grilled by members of the Legislative Yuan, yet Kuo Wan-jung never deviated from her stance in important matters. Her role in freeing up Taiwan's economy, first as vice-president of the Central Bank and then as minister for Finance, has exerted a great influence on the country's economic development.

Lily Xiao Hong LEE

Ch'eng Ming-hao. "Kuo Wan-jung fu Pei-ching ti ch'ien-yin hou-kuo." *Chiu-shih nien-tai* (May 1989): 39–41.
Chung-hua min-kuo ming-jen lu. Taipei: Chung-yang t'ung-hsün-she, 1999.
Chung-hua min-kuo tang-tai ming-jen lu. Taipei: Taiwan Chung-hua shu-chü, 1978, 126.
Kuo, Shirley W.Y., Gustav Ranis, and John C.H. Fei. *The Taiwan Success Story: Rapid Growth with Improved Distribution in the Republic of China, 1952–1979.* Boulder, Colo.: Westview Press, 1981.
"Kuo Wan-jung tuan-jan chüeh-ting ch'üan-ch'eng ts'an-yü." *Lien-ho pao,* 4 May 1989, 2.
Kuo Wanyong. "Technological Change, Foreign Investment, and Growth in the Non-Agricultural Sector of Taiwan, 1952–1969—With Emphasis on the Manufacturing Sector." Master's thesis, MIT, Department of Economics, 1972.
Liu Hsing-jen. "Kuan pu liao sheng: Kuo Wan-jung li-yüan shou ch'ü." *Chung-wai tsa-chih* (May 1990): 16.

Kuo Wanyong: *see* **Kuo Wan-jung**

Kwong Wai Lin: *see* **Moss, Irene**

L

Lai Chunchun: *see* **Lai, Jun T.**

Lai, Jun T.
Jun T. Lai [Lai Chunchun], b. 1953, in Taipei, Taiwan, is an artist and sculptor.

Her family had just survived the purge of Japanese-trained intellectuals under the KMT when she was born, and her father became active in the postwar Taiwanese film industry. Jun T. Lai graduated from the Chinese Culture College (Chung-kuo wen-hua hsüeh-yüan, later University) in 1974, gained her M.F.A. at Tama Art University near Tokyo in 1978, and studied graphics at the Pratt Institute in New York from 1980 to 1982. She had a notable solo exhibition at Lungmen Gallery in 1983 that seemed to concretize the arrival in Taipei of a minimalism with a "Chinese" sensibility. Her exhibition was also associated with the work of Lin Shou-yü [Lin Shouyu] (Richard Lin, b. 1933), who had trained as an architect in London, and Chuang P'u [Zhuang Pu] (Ts'ong Pu), who had studied painting in Madrid. Jun T. Lai has pursued her minimalist and conceptualist vision, which owes much to Japanese *mono-ha* with its sensibility to materials and the viewer's placement toward the artist's action on them. She has carried this forward with great intelligence toward the privileging of tactility in dialogue between levels of spiritual reference and the viewer's own touch.

John CLARK

Being and Transformation, 1983–1988. Taipei: Taipei Fine Arts Museum, 1988.
Ch'en Yü-ling, ed. *I-hsiang yü mei-hsu: Taiwan nü-hsing I-shu-chan*. Taipei: Taipei shih-li mei-shu-kuan, 1998.
Clark, John. "Touch Texture and Concept: Three Woman Artists from Taiwan." In *Art Taiwan*, eds. N. Jose and Yang Wen-i. Sydney: Museum of Contemporary Art, 1995.
Jun Lai: New Works on Canvas. Taipei: Lungmen Gallery, 1983.
Jun T. Lai: Sculpture Natural. Taipei: The Artist, 1995.
Lai Chunchun. Taipei: Cherng Pin Gallery, 1992.

Lan Ping: *see* **Jiang Qing**

Lang Ping
Lang Ping, b. 1960, in Tianjin, grew up in Beijing. In the early 1980s, she was recognized as the world's best female volleyball player.

Despite also having academic potential and artistic talent, Lang Ping had been obsessed by volleyball since 1975, after watching an international women's volleyball match in Beijing. She lived quite close to Beijing Workers' Stadium and walked past it on her way to school every morning, longing to one day play volleyball there herself.

Her father was a sports fan and saw in his daughter the makings of a volleyball player. Lang Ping was the tallest girl in school, and when she was fourteen her father sent her to an after-school sports school. After two years of training, Lang Ping was selected for the Beijing Youth Team; she was then 1.83 meters tall. A childhood dream came true when Lang Ping was made a member of the Women's Volleyball Team of Beijing at the age of seventeen. She then set her sights on making the national team, and within six months Yuan Weiming, then its coach, included her on the team. Yuan Weiming subjected the Chinese women's volleyball team to extremely strict and arduous training. As one of the top players and possessed of a mighty smash, Lang Ping often had extra exercises to do. Every step of her long and hard journey to the world championships meant sweat, injury, and not a few tears.

The 1980s were the golden age of Chinese women's volleyball and marked the peak of Lang Ping's career. Between 1981 and 1986, the Chinese women's volleyball team won five consecutive international championships, and Lang Ping was one of the best players in all five matches. The year 1981 was unforgettable for the team. This was when they showed the world how far they had come, proving the team was strong enough to stand up to the toughest opponents in the world by winning the Third Women's Volleyball World Championship Cup. This was also the first time that Chinese teams had won world championships in the three big-ball sports (basketball, football, and volleyball). The Chinese women, with their courage, energy, skill, and court appeal, became the focus of the world's media. Commentators described Lang Ping's prodigious smash as an "iron hammer," and as far afield as Germany admirers stopped her in the street. In 1982, the Chinese women won their Second World Championship at the Ninth Women's World Volleyball Championship, following this with a Third at the 1984 Olympic Games. They won their Fourth Championship in 1985, and Fifth in 1986. For her outstanding performances in international volleyball, Lang Ping was awarded many medals and prizes, including "Best Smash" and "Outstanding Player." Within China, she was chosen as one of the Ten Best Sports Stars for five years running from 1980.

After so long in the limelight, Lang Ping longed for an ordinary life. She retired from volleyball after the 1986 world championship to rest from years of hard training and competition, which had fatigued and injured her body. However, not content to rest on her laurels, Lang Ping decided to continue her education. She started learning English at Beijing Normal School and six months later became the first recipient of the Education Foundation of New China Scholarship offered by American Chinese living in San Francisco.

After studying English in Los Angeles for some time, Lang Ping moved to New Mexico and enrolled as a postgraduate, majoring in sports management at New Mexico University. Her life as an overseas student was not easy, however. From the time she had entered the after-school sports school in Beijing at the age of fourteen, Lang Ping had only had to play volleyball, everything else being provided and arranged by the government. Now for the first time, far away from home, she needed to look after and support herself. Lang Ping earned money doing a variety of jobs, including teaching volleyball to schoolchildren at summer camps. Life took a turn for the better in 1989, when an Italian volleyball club employed her. This helped financially and made her eligible for permanent residency in the United States.

In 1995, however, Lang Ping and her three-year-old daughter left their comfortable home in the United States to return to face a new challenge in China. In Beijing, she took up the post as main coach of the Chinese women's volleyball team, no easy task. After winning five successive championships, the Chinese team had gradually gone downhill as its senior players—Cao Huiying, Sun Jinfang, Chen Yaqiong, Chen Zhaodi, Zhou Xiaolan, and Lang Ping—retired one after another. Lang Ping started the young women of the volleyball team back on the long and difficult journey to the championships but resigned in 1998 for health and family reasons.

Ping WANG

Lang Ping and Lu Xing'er. "Lang Ping zizhuan." Dongfang chuban zhongxin, 1999.
Song Ruizhi, ed. *Zhongguo funü wenhua tonglan*. Jinan: Shandong wenyi chubanshe, 1995, 664–68.
Yingwen *Zhongguo funü*, ed. *Gujin zhuming funü renwu*, vol. 2. Shijiazhuang: Hebei renmin chubanshe, 1986, 1224–29.

Lau, Emily

Emily Lau, or Lau Wai-hing [Liu Huiqing], b. 1952, in Hong Kong, was a most prominent liberal, government critic, and populist politician in Hong Kong both before and following the 1997 return of the colony to China. Her life reflects a new pattern arising among Chinese women in the late twentieth century, where education abroad, a wide range of professional positions, and political aspirations were all achievable goals.

Emily Lau's early years in Hong Kong were little different from those of many of her contemporaries. Her Cantonese parents moved there in 1948 during a period of great turmoil on the mainland. As in many immigrant families, education of the children was paramount and in 1962 the Lau family transferred Wai-hing to the then new English-language Maryknoll Sisters' School in Happy Valley, where she studied until 1972. While still in primary school, Wai-hing was given the English name Emily, which was to remain with her, by her aunt. When an opportunity arose that year to study abroad, Emily Lau traveled to the United States to embark on undergraduate studies. From 1973 to 1976 she pursued journalism studies at the University of Southern California and graduated with a B.A. in Broadcast Journalism. She later cited the Watergate scandals and the investigative journalism by which they were revealed as having had a major formative effect on her views on the role and potential of the press.

Returning to Hong Kong, Lau worked between 1976 and 1978 as a reporter with the *South China Morning Post*, the major English-language newspaper in Hong Kong, then moved into television journalism with the commercial broadcaster Hong Kong TVB News. Through the years 1978 to 1981, she advanced from being a reporter to senior producer. A desire to further her studies saw her moving to the United Kingdom in the early 1980s, and in 1982 she completed an M.Sc. in International Relations at the London School of Economics and Political Science within the University of London. Then followed a position as an assistant producer within the BBC (1982–84), while concurrently working as the London correspondent of Hong Kong TVB News. It was at this time that discussions between China and Britain over the political fate of Hong Kong (the lease on the major part of which was due to expire in 1997) began in earnest. Lau noted later: "My passion for politics began to develop in 1982, when China told Britain that it would impose a settlement on Hong Kong if the two sides could not reach an agreement by 1984. From that moment, politics began to matter."

Emily Lau married John Ball in 1983, and in 1984 she returned again to her home and began work as Hong Kong correspondent of the Hong Kong-based *Far Eastern Economic Review*, a position that allowed her access to and insights into the politics of what was still the British Crown Colony of Hong Kong. During the time Lau worked with this magazine (1984–91), she was also involved in teaching, taking up a position with the Journalism and Communication Department within the Chinese University of Hong Kong in 1987 and subsequently with the Extra-Mural Department at the University of Hong Kong. She married again in 1989, to the Hong Kong lawyer Winston Poon, QC. She was also extensively involved during this period with the Hong Kong Journalists' Association serving as an Executive Committee member, vice-chair, and eventually chair.

When direct elections for Hong Kong's legislature were first introduced in 1991, Lau resigned from her posts and ran for office, campaigning for five months as one of a new breed of politicians in Hong Kong: the populist politician, one who appealed to a wide range of the Hong Kong populace. She won the seat for New Territories East in 1991 and was returned in the elections in 1995 by popular vote, winning with 58.51 percent of votes cast, the highest figure among all the geographic constituencies.

In this period, Lau Wai-hing (or Emily Lau) became a household name in much of Hong Kong, and the legislator came to be both a champion of her constituents and a perceived thorn in the side of the Hong Kong administration. There was almost no major issue on which Emily Lau did not speak, but it was in the political reform realm that her voice was loudest. Equally a critic of Britain and the People's Republic of China (PRC), Lau's political aims were essentially threefold: to ensure that Britain treated its Hong Kong subjects (British Nationals Overseas and British Dependent Territories Citizens) with decency, ensure that Hong Kong people ran their own affairs as promised by the Basic Law, and ensure that Hong Kong people were free to elect those who would govern them.

The political future of Hong Kong engaged her continually. During 1992, she was constantly critical of China's attempts to expand its influence in Hong Kong affairs and refusal to allow an increase in the number of directly elected legislators before the 1997 takeover. In June 1994, Lau introduced a private bill, which would have allowed for all sixty Legislative Council seats to be directly elected in 1995. The bill failed in the Legislative Council when members voted 21–20 against. Beyond the debating chamber Lau also participated in street protests, and in December 1996 she was arrested with twenty-nine others while demonstrating outside the closed-door meeting where Hong Kong's post-handover leader was being chosen. Over the following several months leading up to the July 1997 handover, Lau urged this leader, Tung Chee-hwa, to stand up against China, following his "unreserved support" for its decision to abolish or modify some Hong Kong laws covering human rights and civil liberties. In March, Lau also called for a boycott of Hong Kong's future first elections under Chinese rule if the voting system was unfair and the proportional representation favored pro-Beijing candidates.

Equally important to her was the British government's treatment of its British Dependent Territories Citizen "nationals." In October 1994, as Anglo-Chinese cooperation foundered, Lau led legislators in urging Britain to grant full citizenship to 3.5 million native Hong Konger British Dependent Territories Citizens. As the situation intensified, in November 1996 she led a cross-party delegation of Hong Kong legislative councillors to Britain to lobby government and opposition politicians ahead of a parliamentary debate on the territory. The five councillors met the British foreign secretary and other senior officials, but achieved little.

Growing disillusionment with the Democrats and other liberal forces impelled Lau to found a new political grouping—The Frontier (Qianxian)—in August 1996. This organization, which she was elected to head, aimed to catalyze mass opposition to Beijing's plans for Hong Kong after its reversion to Chinese sovereignty. Lau remained in the Hong Kong legislature until the body was disbanded by the PRC government following Chinese resumption of sovereignty on 1 July 1997.

The Hong Kong Legislative Council elections in May 1998, the first to be held under the Hong Kong Special Administrative Region, saw major changes in the methods by which legislators were elected. One of these required that Lau relinquish her British passport and adopt Chinese citizenship in order to be eligible to run for election in a geographical constituency. Despite these changes, the pro-democracy group won 63 percent of the popular vote, and Lau was returned again as a Hong Kong lawmaker, a position she remained in until the end of the twentieth century.

In the 1990s, some of the more conservative members of Hong Kong society depicted Emily Lau as an agitator, a rebel, and impractical, while the Chinese government found her abrasive. She was characterized in the media, however, as "fiercely independent" and a defender of the interests of Hong Kong people against both the British and Chinese governments. Lau described herself as a freedom fighter and the people of her Hong Kong constituency showed through their votes that they believed her to be the best representative of their interests. It can be truly averred that Emily Lau and Martin Lee Chu-ming were the two most important figures in Hong Kong politics during this period. While the mainland slogan "Don't Underestimate the Power of the People" may have been the catchcry of the CCP, in Hong Kong it was Emily Lau's creed.

Geoff WADE

Dyja, Marina and Dorian Malovic. *Hong Kong: Un destin chinois.* Paris: Bayard Éditions, 1997, 226–33.
Far Eastern Economic Review. Hong Kong, 1984–91.
Lau, Emily. "The News Media." In *Hong Kong in Transition*, ed. Joseph Y.S. Cheng. Hong Kong: Oxford University Press, 1986, 420–46.
Liu Huiqing. *Liu Huiqing miandui Xianggang.* Hong Kong: Open Magazine, 1991.
———. *Xianggang keyi shuo bu.* Hong Kong: Hongye shudian, 1998.

Lau Wai-hing: *see* **Lau, Emily**

Lee Ang: *see* **Li Ang**

Lei Jieqiong

Lei Jieqiong, b. 1905, a native of Taishan County, Guangdong Province, is a Western-educated sociologist and academic highly regarded by the CCP.

Her grandfather went to America during the Gold Rush and became well known among overseas Chinese as a businessman; her father, Lei Zichang (1875–1926), was his third son. Abiding by the wishes of his own father, Lei Zichang undertook traditional Chinese studies in Guangdong instead of going to America to enter the family business. He passed the imperial examination just before the 1911 Revolution and was appointed to the reserve list for the mayor of Suzhou. Subsequent changes in the national administrative system wrought by the revolution, however, meant that he was no longer required to take up the position, and Lei Zichang went instead to Beijing, to take a one-year course at the Beijing Institute of Politics and Law. Upon return to Guangzhou, Lei Zichang worked in the Guangzhou Railway Office; in addition to this official position, however, he was also a part-time lawyer and chief editor of the magazine *Mass Rule* (Qunzhi). Lei Jieqiong's mother, Li Peizhi, was a native of Guangdong. After marriage she unbound her feet and started to learn to read.

Lei Jieqiong was much influenced by her father, an enlightened man who allowed his daughter to study from an early age alongside the boys in their private school and took her with him when he went among the laboring people. He then sent Lei Jieqiong to a well-known progressive public school—the primary school attached to Guangdong Women's Normal School—where she was exposed to new ideas such as democracy and science and first read the important radical magazine *The New Youth* (Xin qingnian), all of which laid the foundation for later studies and her political involvement.

At the age of nineteen, in 1924, Lei Jieqiong went to high school in California in the United States to learn English. She then attended the University of Southern California and in 1931 completed an M.A. in Sociology there before taking up a position as lecturer in the Sociology Department at Yen-ching University (later to become Peking University). Here Lei Jieqiong took her first steps as a revolutionary when in 1935 she and her students launched the patriotic December Ninth Movement opposing the Japanese invasion of north China and the KMT's lack of resistance to it. When Japan occupied Beijing in 1937, Lei Jieqiong continued her anti-Japanese stance and joined the National Salvation Movement in Nanchang, Jiangxi Province. She was appointed as an advisor in the reform movement for the advancement of women in Jiangxi and served as a colonel, carrying out administrative duties in a group caring for wounded soldiers in Nanjing. Lei Jieqiong was in charge of a women's training class in 1938 in the famous Jiangxi Political Movement Institute. Its president was Xiong Shihui (1893–1974) and two of the deans were Xu Dehen (1890–1990) and Jiang Jingguo [Chiang Chingguo] (1910–1988; a son of Chiang Kai-shek and later to become KMT president on Taiwan). When the Japanese occupied Nanchang the following year, Lei Jieqiong moved to Ji'an, meeting and becoming friends with Zhou Enlai (1898–1976).

Lei Jieqiong published her work in 1933, advocating policies and methods for family planning in her article "Social Work and Birth Control" (Shehui fuwu yu jiezhi shengyu), which appeared in the "Population" supplement of *Morning Daily* (Chenbao). She published more than ten works in the magazine *Women of Jiangxi* (Jiangxi funü) between 1938 and 1941, including "Country Women during the Anti-Japanese War" (Kangzhan zhong de nongcun funü), "Female Students and Women's Work" (Nüxuesheng yu funü gongzuo), "Women's Careers during the Anti-Japanese War" (Kangzhan zhong de funü zhiye), and "Seminars on Women" (Funü wenti jiangzuo). Her research papers include "A Study of the Chinese Family" (Zhongguo jiating wenti yanjiu taolun), "Reviewing the Women's Movement of the Past Thirty-six Years" (Sanshiliunian lai funü yundong de zong jiantao), "A Survey of Marriage and the Family" (Hunying yu jiating wenti de yanjiu diaocha), and "Aging and Its Impact on Social Development" (Laonian wenti jiqi dui shehui fazhan de yingxiang). All of her essays are gathered in the two-volume *The Selected Works of Lei Jieqiong* (Lei Jieqiong wenji).

In 1940 Lei Jieqiong helped establish Zhongzheng University in Jiangxi, doubling as supervisor of the Jiangxi Provincial Women's Office. The following year she was engaged as a professor at Soochow University in Shanghai but also lectured at St. John's University, Shanghai [Hujiang] University, Huadong University, and Aurora College of Arts and Science. Lei Jieqiong was one of twenty-six people who attended the opening ceremony in Shanghai of the China Association for Promoting Democracy (CAPD, Zhongguo minzhu cujinhui), which she had helped establish in 1945; forty-seven years later, in 1992, she was appointed chair of the Central Committee of CAPD.

Lei Jieqiong was one of eleven people (nine public figures and two students) sent to Nanjing in June 1946 by the Shanghai Union of People's Associations to petition the KMT government not to start a civil war. Upon arrival at Xiaguan railway station in Nanjing, they were physically attacked and had to be taken to hospital because of the injuries sustained. This incident, which became known as the Xiaguan Massacre, sent shockwaves throughout Nanjing, Shanghai, and Yan'an and aroused support and sympathy for the injured participants from women's associations, literary and artistic groups, industrial and commercial circles, and students. Newspapers carried sympathetic comment from Mao Zedong (1892–1976) and Zhu De (1886–1976), as well as from Zhou Enlai, who visited them in hospital. At the end of that year, Lei Jieqiong returned to Yen-ching University as an academic and a revolutionary and was made a professor in the Sociology Department.

When she was thirty-six, in 1941, Lei Jieqiong married Yan Jingyao (1905–1976), a native of Yuyao, Zhejiang Province. They did not have children. A scholar of social science and Marxism-Leninism, Yan Jingyao had completed his Ph.D. in America before working in England and Russia. He was on good terms with many leaders of the CCP and was a co-founder of the CAPD. In December 1948, the couple visited the liberated areas in northern China and were known to Mao Zedong, Zhu De, Liu Shaoqi (1898–1969), and, of course, Zhou Enlai. At one stage during the Cultural Revolution, Lei Jieqiong and her husband were sent together to Su County, Anhui Province, for labor reform; however, a comment written by Zhou Enlai on a report enabled Lei Jieqiong to escape long-term labor reform.

After 1949, apart from being elected in various capacities to the standing committees of several CPPCC and NPC national committees over a period of forty years, Lei Jieqiong held a variety of administrative and academic posts. She was vice-dean of studies, Beijing College of Political Science and Law (1956–67); deputy director,

Bureau of Foreign Experts Administration under State Council (1952–73); professor of law, Peking University (1978); vice-mayor of Beijing Municipality (1977–83); vice-president, ACWF (1978); vice-chair, China Sociology Society (1986); vice-chair, Legislative Affairs Committee of the Sixth NPC (1983); vice-chair, Committee for Drafting the Basic Law of Macao Special Administrative Region (SAR) of the PRC (1985); member of the Committee for Drafting the Basic Law of Hong Kong SAR of the PRC (1985); vice-chair, CAPD Sixth and Seventh Central Committees (1978, 1982); and chair, CAPD Eighth and Ninth Central Committees (1988, 1992).

Viola Hong Xin Chan WONG

Chen Yutang, ed. *Zhongguo jindai renwu mingbao da cidian*. Zhejiang: Guji chubanshe, 1993.
Lei Jieqiong. "Dang yindao wo zuo xiang jinbu." *Renmin ribao*, 23 June 1991, 3.
Who's Who in China: Current Leaders. Beijing: Foreign Language Press, 1994, 280–81.
Zhonghua quanguo funü lianhehui zuzhi lianjie bu, ed. *Lei Jieqiong*. Shenyang: Liaoning renmin chubanshe, 1995, 5–95, 144–48.

Li Ang

Li Ang (original name Shih Shu-tuan), b. 1952, in Lu-kang, Taiwan, is one of Taiwan's most popular and controversial writers.

The youngest of three literary sisters—Shih Shu-nü (Shi Shunü), a critic, and Shih Shu-ch'ing (Shi Shuqing, b. 1945), a novelist—Li Ang began writing fiction at the age of thirteen under their influence. Her first piece of fiction, "Ang K'o's First Loveletter" (Ang K'o ti ti-i feng ch'ing-shu), has not been published. Li Ang's first published story was "The Flowering Season" (Hua-chi, 1968). To date she has published numerous volumes of fiction and prose and a biography of the famous Taiwan dissident Shih Ming-te (b. 1941) and edited two collections of stories and a collection of articles. Translations of her fiction have appeared in English, German, French, and Japanese.

Li Ang's literary apprenticeship began in the heyday of the modernist movement in Taiwan. Her early fiction was heavily influenced both by modern Western writers such as Kierkegaard, Camus, and Kafka and Freudian psychoanalysis. The following short stories were all published while she was still in high school in Lu-kang (1968–69): "The Flowering Season," "The Wedding Ceremony" (Hun-li), "Choral Singing" (Hun-sheng ho-ch'ang), "Looking Back at Point Zero" (Ling-tien ti hui-ku), "The Curvaceous Doll" (Yu ch'ü-hsien ti wa-wa), "A Journey to the Sea" (Hai-chih lü), and "The Long Distance Runner" (Ch'ang-p'ao che).

In 1970 after becoming a student at the Chinese Culture University (Chung-kuo wen-hua ta-hsüeh) in Taipei, Li Ang's writing underwent a marked change in subject matter and style. Inspired by study in Chinese philosophy, she made use of material from the Chinese classics and mythology in two short stories—"Song of Ospreys" (Kuan-sui) and "Moon Hunting" (Chui-yüeh)—which are regarded by critics as aberrations. From 1973 her writing echoed the growing interest of Taiwanese intellectuals in native culture and tradition that by the mid-1970s had become the Indigenous Literature Debate. *Stories of Lu-ch'eng* (Lu-ch'eng ku-shih), a series of nine stories published in 1973–74, is a product of this prolific period.

At this time Li Ang also published *The Human World* (Jen-chien shih), a series of four stories whose explicit depictions of sex and attacks on sexual taboos provoked vitriolic criticism. While the series made Li Ang famous as a writer committed to social concerns, it incited so much moral outrage about its handling of sex that she left Taiwan for Canada in 1975. From there she went to the United States and studied drama at Oregon State University, gaining her M.A. in 1977. Since her return to Taiwan in 1978, Li Ang has been teaching in the Drama Department at the Chinese Culture University.

Her social concerns are not only revealed in fiction but also surface in her column "Women's Opinions" (Nü-hsing ti i-chien) in *Shih-pao* (China Times) and her journalistic writings. Her article "Do Not Pity Me, Please Educate Me" (Pieh k'o-lien wo, ch'ing chiao-yü wo) won First Prize in *Shih-pao* journalistic literature in 1981.

Yet, Li Ang is best known for her writings about sex, which has been the recurrent motif throughout her writing career. In her early fiction, Li Ang explores women's experience through sexuality, considering sex "a form of self-affirmation" and a vital part in the process of growth. Her series The Flowering Series explores the psychological dimension of sex, portraying sexual awareness as a teenager's rite of passage. The Human World Series deals with the social aspect of sex, unveiling the hypocrisy of the educational system and how traditional conservative attitudes toward sex oppress young people, especially girls. Sex also provides the grounds for Li Ang's literary feminism: it is the basis upon which she exposes the inequality between the genders and women's oppression within patriarchal society.

Her most famous feminist fiction, *The Butcher's Wife* (Sha-fu), was written out of a desire "to investigate the relationship between men and women and to articulate the role and status of women in a traditional society." *The Butcher's Wife* was awarded First Prize in the annual fiction contest sponsored by *United Daily* (Lien-ho pao) in 1983. This novella, which won acclaim for its artistry and criticism for its gruesome treatment of sex, firmly established Li Ang as a feminist writer whose work transgressively breaks away from what are conventionally considered to be appropriate subjects and style for women writers.

In "Protest of a Woman Author against Reckless Accusations: Another Self-Interview, This Time from Taipei," Li Ang challenges the notion that female writers can only write about romantic feelings and subjects like "the wind, the clouds, and the moon." She believes that women's literature should not be limited to "the realm of proper ladies and their personal essays" but that "there should be a way to write something great as well as female." She defends her writing about sex as an expression of truth, which to her is a writer's most fundamental moral obligation. Li Ang's conscious, serious, and flagrant depictions of sex have earned her a unique place among contemporary Chinese writers.

Howard Goldblatt, the translator of *The Butcher's Wife*, observed that Li Ang must be regarded as "the most consistent, successful, and influential writer of sexual fiction in Chinese." Following the controversial success of this novella, Li Ang has continued to explore the relationship between the sexes in four epistolary stories in the series A Loveletter Unsent (I feng wei-chi ti ch'ing-shu) and further examined the relationship between sex and power in the novella *Dark Night* (An-yeh) and the novel

The Labyrinth (Mi-yüan). The sexual textual politics in Li Ang's fiction really peaked, however, in her most recent work *Everyone Sticks It in Pei-kang's Incense Pot* (Pei-kang hsiang-lu jen-jen ch'a). The story that gives this collection its name generated immense controversy over whether it was based upon a real sexual relationship between actual political figures in Taiwan's contemporary political scene. The sound and fury surrounding the story affirmed once again Li Ang's standing as the most controversial woman writer in Taiwan.

Daisy Sheung-yuen NG

Chang Hsi-kuo. "Hsiao-lun *Sha-fu.*" *Hsin-shu yüeh-k'an*, no. 12 (September 1984): 30–31.

Ch'en Ying-hsiang. "Tang-tai Chung-kuo tso-chia ti k'ao-ch'a: ch'u-lun Li Ang." *Chung-wai wen-hsüeh*, 5, no. 8 (January 1977): 80–81.

Cheng Jung-chin. "Mo-jan hui-shou: Shih-lun Li Ang ti 'Hun-li.'" *Chung-hua wen-i*, 12, no. 1 (September 1976): 74–82.

Goldblatt, Howard. "Sex and Society: The Fiction of Li Ang." In *Worlds Apart: Recent Chinese Writing and Its Audience*, ed. Howard Goldblatt. New York: M.E. Sharpe, 1990, 150–65.

Ho Sheng-fen. "Cheng-ch'ing shih-i: Li Ang yü Yang Ch'ing-shu tui-t'an." In *Fu Li Ang ti Ch'ing-shu*, Yang Ch'ing-shu. Taipei: Tun-lu wen-k'u, 1987, 139–51.

Hsi Mi. "Hei-an chih hsing: T'an *An-yeh* chung ti hsiang-cheng." In *Pei-kang hsiang-lu jen-jen ch'a*, Li Ang. Taipei: Mai-t'ien, 1997, 249–72.

Ku T'ien-hung. "Tu Li Ang ti *Sha-fu*: Chüeh-kuei, tui-teng, ho funü wen-t'i." *Chung-wai wen-hsüeh*, 14, no. 10 (March 1986): 41–49.

Kuo Feng. "P'ing-hsi Li Ang hsiao-shuo *An-yeh.*" *Hsiang-kang wen-hsüeh*, no. 34 (October 1987): 34–39.

Li Ang. "Butcher," trans. Fan Wen-mei and John Minford. *Renditions*, special issue (Spring and Autumn 1987), 61–75.

———. "Curvaceous dolls," trans. Howard Goldblatt. *Renditions*, special issue (Spring and Autumn 1987), 49–60.

———. "Flower Season." In *Bamboo Shoots After the Rain: Contemporary Stories by Women Writers of Taiwan*, eds. Ann C. Carver and Sung-sheng Yvonne Chang. New York: Feminist Press at the City University of New York, 1990,125–33.

———. "Protest of a Woman Author against Reckless Accusations: Another Self-Interview, This Time from Taipei." In *Modern Chinese Writers: Self-Portrayals*, eds. Helmut Martin and Jeffrey Kinkley. New York: M.E. Sharpe, 1992, 254–60.

Lin I-chieh. "P'an-ni yü chiu-shu." In *T'a-men ti yen-lei*, Li Ang. Taipei: Hung-fan, 1984, 203–28.

Liu, Joyce C.H. "From Loo Port to Taipei: The World of Women in Lee Ang's Works." *Fu Jen Studies*, no. 19 (1986): 65–85.

Lu-kang-jen. "T'an tui *Sha-fu* ti chi ko wu-chieh." *Hsin-shu yüeh-k'an*, no. 5 (February 1984): 77.

P'eng Hsiao-yen. "Nü tso-chia ti ch'ing-yü shu-hsieh yü cheng-chih lun-shu: Chieh-tu *Mi-yüan.*" In *Pei-kang hsiang-lu jen-jen ch'a*, Li Ang. Taipei: Mai-t'ien, 1997, 273–301.

P'eng Jui-chin. "Hsien-tai chu-i hsia ti Lu-ch'eng ku-shih." *Shu-p'ing shu-mu*, no. 54 (October 1977): 23–36.

Shih Shu. "Wen-chi mi-kung: *Hua-chi* p'ing-hsi." In *Pei-kang hsiang-lu jen-jen ch'a*, Li Ang. Taipei: Mai-t'ien, 1997, 221–34.

———. "Yen-wu." In *Hua-chi*, Li Ang. Taipei: Hung-fan, 1985, 5–18.

Ts'ai Ying-chün. "Nü tso-chia ti liang chung tien-hsing ho ch'i k'un-ching." *Wen hsing*, no. 110 (August 1987): 96–101.

Wang Te-wei. "Hsing, ch'ou-wen, yü mei-hsüeh cheng-chih: Li Ang ti ch'ing-yü hsiao-shuo." In *Pei-kang hsiang-lu jen-jen ch'a*, Li Ang. Taipei: Mai-t'ien, 1997, 9–42.

Wei-chih. "Ts'ung 'Tso-yeh' tao 'Mo-ch'un'—p'ing Li ang ti liang p'ien hsiao-shuo." *Chung-hua jih-pao*, 8 March 1975, C9.

Wu Chin-fa. "Lüeh-lun Li Ang hsiao-shuo chung ti hsing fan-k'ang—*Ai-ch'ing shih-yen* ti t'an-t'ao." *Tzu-li wan-pao*, 12/13 July 1983.

Yeh, Michelle. "Shapes of Darkness: Symbols in Li Ang's *Dark Night.*" In *Modern Chinese Women Writers: Critical Appraisals*, ed. Michael S. Duke. New York: M.E. Sharpe, 1989, 78–95.

Yü T'ien-ts'ung. "Taiwan fu-nü wen-hsüeh ti k'un-ching." *Wen hsing*, no. 110 (August 1987): 96–101.

Li Bozhao

Li Bozhao, 1911–1985, of Chongqing, Sichuan Province, was one of the most important women playwrights in modern Chinese spoken drama and a pioneering educator in theatrical art. She is best remembered for her *geju* (folk opera) *The Long March* (Changzheng), an epic play premiered by the Beijing People's Art Theater (Beijing renmin yishu juyuan) in 1951 and in which Mao Zedong (1893–1976) appeared for the first time as a dramatic character on stage. In addition to plays and folk operas, Li Bozhao also wrote fiction, including *A Female Communist* (Nü gongchandang yuan, 1948) and *Birch Gully* (Huashu gou, 1955). Along with He Zizhen (*q.v.*), Kang Keqing (*q.v.*), and Deng Yinchao (*q.v.*), Li Bozhao was highly respected for her endurance and bravery as one of the thirty Red Army women who undertook the communists' Long March of 1934–35.

Her father, Li Hanzhou, had passed the civil service examinations at the county level during the Qing dynasty and later worked as a government official in Yonglin County. He died when Li Bozhao was only four years old and she was brought up by her mother, Yang Fengxian, who told her traditional tales. Li Bozhao enrolled at Second Women's Normal School of Sichuan Province, where she was influenced by Xiao Chunü, her Chinese instructor and a leader of the CCP youth movement, to join the Marxist Study Group organized by the Common People's Study Group (Pinmin xueshe). In 1925, Li Bozhao joined the Communist Youth League. She published progressive, or leftist, new poetry in the school newspaper and acted in school drama productions. After being expelled from school for her involvement in student demonstrations, Li Bozhao was sent to Shanghai by the CCP to study at Shanghai University and taught literacy to workers at night school. She was detained in prison for three months at the tender age of fifteen after which the CCP sent her to the USSR to pursue studies in Moscow at what became known as the Sun Yat-sen University.

In Moscow, Li Bozhao acted in *huaju* (spoken drama). Together with Zhang Hanfu and Sha Kefu, two pioneers of modern Chinese spoken drama, Li Bozhao educated herself in Western dramatic classics, frequented theaters, and performed at Moscow University and several factories in the city the plays the three of them had written. Upon graduation from Sun Yat-sen University in summer 1928, she worked as an interpreter at the Ninth Congress of the International League of Communist Leagues and in 1929 married Yang Shangkun (1907–1998).

Li Bozhao returned to China in 1930, having spent five years in the USSR. She joined the CCP in the following year and played a leading role in promoting education and performing arts in the Red Army in the soviet areas of western Fujian Province (Minxi geming genjudi). In celebrations of Labor Day (1 May), Li Bozhao was instrumental in producing songs, dances, reportage drama, and spoken drama such as *Tomorrow* (Mingtian) and *The Song of the Cavalry* (Qibing ge). *Tomorrow*, originally performed when Li Bozhao studied in Moscow, told how CCP members revived their spirits after the failure in 1927 of the CCP-KMT united front. The drama was warmly received by the local audience; many of them could relate to the difficulties and hardships depicted in the play, because they had undergone similar trials in establishing the new soviet. In *The Song of the Cavalry*, Li Bozhao borrowed plots and characters from a Soviet Union play in which the Soviet Red Army mobilized the masses with its determination to "fight for land, bread, and freedom." The official version of the drama's history from the PRC claims that although this play was set in the civil war period of Russia, the local audience responded with enthusiasm because they were going through the same kind of struggles to win their own land. Deng Fa (1906–46), the CCP provincial secretary who played the role of the protagonist, won high praise for his excellent performance.

In autumn 1931, Li Bozhao arrived in Ruijin, Jiangxi Province, where she worked in several capacities, as political instructor in the Central Red Army School (Zhongyang hongjun xuexiao), editor of *Red China* (Hongse Zhonghua), president of the Gorky Drama School (Gao'erji xiju xuexiao), and head of the Art Bureau attached to the central soviet government's Ministry of Education. On the occasion of the first Worker-Peasant-Soldier Congress (Diyijie gong-nong-bing daibiao dahui) in Ruijin in the winter, Li Bozhao, Hu Di, and Qian Zhuangfei produced the spoken dramas *The Last Supper* (Zuihou de wancan) and *Peasant Slaves* (Nongnu). Li Bozhao adapted *Peasant Slaves* from Harriet Beecher Stowe's novel *Uncle Tom's Cabin*, translated by Lin Shu and Wei Yi in 1901 as *Heinu yu tian lu*, and first performed by the Spring Willow Society (Chunliu she) in Tokyo in 1907. Li Bozhao's adaptation, however, was different: it was in four acts and had a happy ending where the oppressed slaves won out over the slave owners. She also played the role of Black Sister (Heiren mei). Performances often ended with the audience applauding and shouting: "Down with slave owners!" and "Down with the landlords!" To further promote dramatic performance in the soviet areas, Li Bozhao was instrumental in founding the August First Drama Troupe (Bayi jutuan). She served as president of the Blue Shirt Theater School (Lanshan jutuan xuexiao) in which she trained younger performers and produced reportage drama.

In autumn 1934, Li Bozhao set off on the Long March. She crossed the grasslands, one of the most difficult sections of the Long March, three times after being caught up in Zhang Guotao's split with the army of Mao Zedong (1893–1976). In 1939, Li Bozhao served as president of the Lu Xun Art School (Lu Xun yishu xuexiao) in Yan'an, CCP headquarters during the anti-Japanese war. She wrote *Song of the Countryside* (Nongcun qu), a folk opera that depicted the peasants' struggle against spies and traitors. It was later performed in other parts of China and warmly received by audiences of diverse backgrounds for its folkloric and local styles.

After the founding of the PRC in 1949, Li Bozhao founded the Beijing People's Art Theater and served as president during its first two years. She was instrumental in recruiting artists from various fields in the performing arts and produced a variety of folk dances, folk opera, and spoken drama. Her folk opera *The Long March* ran for forty-five sessions at the Beijing People's Art Theater and met with great success. Among other achievements, Li Bozhao encouraged the eminent playwright Lao She to write *Longxu gou*, a play that became a classic of modern Chinese spoken drama, upon his return from the United States. When Beijing People's Art Theater specialized in spoken drama in 1952 after Cao Yu took over as president, Li Bozhao devoted herself to drama education while serving as party secretary and vice-president of the Central Drama School (Zhongyang xiju xueyuan).

During the Cultural Revolution, Li Bozhao was persecuted and relocated with her husband and son to Linfen, Shanxi Province, where they lived under difficult conditions. She continued to devote herself to writing drama concerned with the Red Army's experience during the Long March. The result of this became the spoken drama *March Northward* (Beishang), which premiered in 1981 by the Soldiers Theater of the Guangzhou Military District (Guangzhou budui zhanshi huajutuan). The character Kang Xiaomei, a female Red Army soldier from a propaganda team (*xuanchuan yuan*) who had reported Zhang Guotao's behavior during the Long March to He Long and Ren Bishi of the Second Army, shows how playwriting reflected personal experiences. Li Bozhao died of illness at the age of seventy-four on 14 July 1985, in Beijing.

Xiaomei CHEN

Bai Shurong and Liang Huaqun. "Lixiang zhihuo yongbu ximie." In *Zhongguo huaju yishujia zhuan*, vol. 1, comp. Zhongguo yishu yanjiuyuan huaju yanjiusuo. Beijing: Wenhua yishu chubanshe, 1984, 104–23.

Klein, Donald W., and Anne B. Clark. *Biographic Dictionary of Chinese Communism, 1921–1965*. Cambridge, Mass.: Harvard University Press, 1971, 987.

Lee, Lily Xiao Hong, and Sue Wiles. *Women of the Long March*. Sydney: Allen and Unwin, 1999.

"Li Bozhao." In *Zhongguo xiandai wenxue cidian*. Shanghai: Shanghai cishu chubanshe, 1990, 252–53.

"Li Bozhao tongzhi shengping shiji." *Renmin ribao*, 25 April 1985, 4.

Li Shangzhi. "Li Bozhao: Changzheng ren pu Changzheng ge." In *Hongjun nüyingxiong zhuan*, comp. Liaowang bianjibu. Beijing: Xinhua chubanshe, 1986, 66–73.

Liu Shaotang, ed. "Li Bozhao." In *Minguo renwu xiaozhuan*, vol. 9. Taipei: Zhuanji wenxue chubanshe, 1987, 65–71.

Li Chün-chen: *see* **Li Jianzhen**

Li Chung-kuei: *see* **Li Chung-kui**

Li Chung-kui

Li Chung-kui, b. 1938, in T'ai-hsing [Taixing] County, Chiang-su [Jiangsu] Province, is an international relations academic and high-level government official in Taiwan.

She was a brilliant student from childhood, and when her family moved to Hsinchu in Taiwan Li Chung-kui attended local primary and junior high schools. After her family moved to Taipei, she entered the prestigious First Girls' High School of Taipei (Taipei i-nü-chung) and received solid academic training. At the suggestion of her father, Li Chung-kui entered the Foreign Affairs Department (Wai-chiao hsi) at

Chengchi University. She continued to excel in her studies and took part in extracurricular activities. Li Chung-kui remained at Chengchi University as a tutor after graduation and passed the examination to study abroad at her own expense. In order to ease the financial burden on her parents, however, the graduate waited until she won a scholarship to France in 1961 before embarking on further studies. In 1964 Li Chung-kui received a doctorate in Law from the University of Paris.

After returning from France, she taught full time at Chengchi University, part-time at Taiwan University, and became a part-time research fellow at the Institute of International Relations. In 1966 Li Chung-kui was honored as one of the Ten Outstanding Young Women in Taiwan. During this period, she renewed her friendship with Shih Ch'i-yang (b. 1935), a colleague from Taiwan University whom Li Chung-kui had met while studying in France and he in Germany. They fell in love and married in 1969. Two years later, Li Chung-kui was made head of the Foreign Affairs Department at Chengchi University. She taught international law and treaty studies and was frequently invited by the media and commuity groups to comment on international developments and current affairs. Li Chung-kui thus became one of the most popular young academics in Taiwan.

From being a rank-and-file member of the KMT, she advanced quickly through the hierarchy. In 1969 Li Chung-kui became a member of the KMT Central Committee and in 1988 was appointed by the KMT Central Committee as director of its Women's Work Committee (Fu-nü kung-tso hui), a position retained until 1993. During her tenure, she updated the organization's image and developed new directions of work. By 1993 Li Chung-kui had reached the top leadership of the KMT, becoming deputy secretary-general of the KMT Central Committee. She also worked extensively in the area of education and culture and was appointed head of the Division of International Cultural and Educational Affairs in the Ministry of Education in 1972 and in 1977 as executive director of the Pacific Culture Fund (T'ai-p'ing-yang wen-hua chi-chin), which awarded grants to overseas academics researching China and its culture. Li Chung-kui also headed the Association for the Promotion of Asia Culture (Ya-chou wen-hua t'ui-chan lien-meng) from 1990 to 1998. In 1995 she went to mainland China in her capacity as president of the Anti-Communist Women's League to take part in the Fourth World Women's Conference held in Beijing. Despite the strongly anti-communist stance of her organization, she was accorded VIP status, a clear statement of the PRC's desire for peaceful reunification with Taiwan. Li Chung-kui is also involved in Taiwan's professional basketball league as chair of the board of the China Professional Basketball Company from 1995 to 1997 and as president of the China Professional Basketball League from 1997 to 1998.

Her husband has led a parallel career in the KMT, holding several positions in the KMT Central Committee in the 1970s and acting as undersecretary of Education in 1976. Unlike Li Chung-kui, he is a native of Taiwan Province. Their union is but one of many similar relationships that ignore differences in provincial and native places of origin and demonstrates how people from Taiwan and the mainland may live together happily.

Lily Xiao Hong LEE

Chung-hua min-kuo ming-jen-lu. Taipei: Chung-yang t'ung-hsün-she, 1999.
Chung-hua min-kuo tang-tai ming-jen-lu, vol. 2. Taipei: Taiwan Chung-hua shu-chü, 1978, 665.
Lu Fang-shen. "Chieh-ch'u nü ch'ing-nien Li Chung-kuei." *Hsiang shih-tai t'iao-chan ti nü-hsing.* Taipei: Hsüeh-sheng shu-tien, 1977, 1–8.

Li Dequan

Li Dequan, 1896–1972, of Tongxian County, Hebei Province, became famous as a social activist and leader of the feminist movement.

Born into a poor family but eager from a very young age to learn, Li Dequan was sent to school by her parents on money borrowed from the local Christian missionaries. After graduating from Huabei Women's Liberal Arts College (Huabei nüzi wenli xueyuan) in 1923, she worked as a teacher at Bridgeman Girls' High School before becoming a secretary and later secretary-general of the Peking YWCA.

In 1924 Li Dequan married the famous KMT general and patriot Feng Yuxiang (1882–1948). During the first six years of their marriage (1924–30), she bore five children, two boys and three girls. Li Dequan also assumed responsibility for at least three of her husband's children from his first marriage. After accompanying her husband to the Soviet Union in 1926, she first became acquainted with Marxism. With her husband's support, on their return to China Li Dequan established the Qiuzhi School in Beijing in 1928: with a primary school and kindergarten attached, the school offered free admission for women and girls from poor families. In 1932, she and her husband set up fifteen primary schools in the Mount Tai area to provide educational opportunities for children of local peasants.

After moving to Nanjing in 1935, Li Dequan established the Women's Association for Academic Studies in the Capital (Shoudu nüzi xueshu yanjiuhui). Because war with Japan appeared to be imminent, she wanted to study social and women's issues and arouse in women a spirit of nationalism. At the 1936 celebration in Nanjing commemorating 8 March (International Women's Day), Li Dequan spoke out against the traditional "virtuous woman" role upheld by KMT representatives, pointing out that only by joining the national liberation movement and transforming society could Chinese women hope for a genuine future. With the outbreak of the Sino-Japanese War in July 1937, Li Dequan declared her support for the anti-Japanese stance of the CCP and took an active part in the resistance movement. She established a progressive women's organization called the Chinese Women's Association (Zhongguo funü lianyihui) and acted as its chair. This association united women from different democratic and non-aligned parties in the KMT-ruled areas and played a positive role in the movement against civil war and dictatorship. Her work extended to the protection and rescue of children in war zones, and Li Dequan took on the role of vice-chair of the National Refugee Children's Association (Zhanshi ertong baoyu hui), which helped establish and raise funds for operations. The organization rescued over 30,000 children during the war, setting up more than twenty branches and fifty orphanages. Along with her husband, in 1945 she joined with the democratic movement opposing KMT General Chiang Kai-shek.

In autumn 1946, Li Dequan traveled to the United States and represented Deng

Yingchao (*q.v.*) at the World Congress of Women in New York. The proposals she put to the Congress—that women throughout the world should unite to achieve democracy and peace and oppose American aid enabling Chiang Kai-shek to start a civil war in China—were supported.

Tragedy struck, however, on Li Dequan's return to China via the Soviet Union in summer 1948. A fire broke out on the ship she was traveling on, and both her husband and one of their daughters were killed. Grief did not prevent her from continuing with her work, however, and, as Feng Yuxiang would have wished, Li Dequan formally supported the CCP war effort as soon as she reached Harbin.

The following year Li Dequan was appointed head of the delegation from the previously KMT-ruled areas, and at the First National Women's Congress she reported on the women's movements there. Li Dequan was elected vice-chair of the ACWF in 1949, a position held until the Cultural Revolution. She attended the First CPPCC that year and was elected to the Third CPPCC. Li Dequan was the first woman to become a full minister in the newly established PRC as minister of Public Health. She was also appointed to membership in the Culture and Education Committee under the Government Administration Council (1949–54) and acted as president of the Chinese Red Cross Society (1950–65).

ZHAO Jinping
(Translated by Laura Long)

Guo Xuyin and Chen Xingtang. *Aiguo jiangjun Feng Yuxiang*. Zhengzhou: Henan renmin chubanshe, 1987.
Klein, Donald W., and Anne B. Clark. *Biographic Dictionary of Chinese Communism, 1921– 1965*. Cambridge, Mass.: Harvard University Press, 1971, 531–34.
Liu Jucai. *Li Dequan de gushi*. Shijiazhuang: Hebei shaonian ertong chubanshe, 1995.
Snow, Helen. *Women in Modern China*. The Hague and Paris: Mouton Press, 1967, 85–90.
Yingwen *Zhongguo funü*, ed. *Gujin zhuming funü renwu*, vol. 2. Shijiazhuang: Hebei renmin chubanshe, 1986, 495–98.
Zhongguo funü wushinian, CD-ROM.

Li Guiying

Li Guiying, 1911–1997, of Xunwu County, Jiangxi Province, was one of the thirty women who went with the First Front Red Army on the Chinese communists' Long March of 1934–35.

Li Guiying was of peasant origin. Her father died when she was four years old and the girl was married out at the age of seven to a twenty-year-old man. Li Guiying was eighteen when she took up the cudgel of revolution, inspired by the Red Army commander Zhu De (1886–1976), who addressed her fellow villagers in early 1929. Li Guiying joined the Communist Youth League in 1930 and was sent for military education to Huichang in 1931. In 1932. she became secretary to the Mazhou District Party Committee, placed in charge of a Red Army guerrilla unit, and made head of Huichang County Women's Department. The following year Li Guiying joined the CCP and just before the Long March was deputy head of the Guangdong-Jiangxi Women's Department.

She carried out the same duties on the Long March as other women of peasant origin, such as Liu Caixiang and Zhong Yuelin: political instruction, hiring of bearers, occasional litter bearing. At the start of the Long March, Li Guiying was married to Dai Yuanhuai, who held the title of special commissioner of south Sichuan. In February 1935, Li Guiying and her husband were instructed to remain behind in Yunnan to act as partisans and work with local guerrilla groups; Kan Shiying (*q.v.*) and about one hundred men were left behind with them. Dai Yuanhuai was soon killed, and Li Guiying married one of the other men, Yu Zehong, but he too was killed. Li Guiying went to Sichuan and gave birth to a child in the beginning of 1936. She left the baby with relatives of Kan Shiying so that she could return to revolutionary work. She was imprisoned by the KMT that winter but upon release in October 1937 was contacted by the party and soon made contact with Deng Yingchao (*q.v.*).

Li Guiying undertook further guerrilla work in the southwest and in 1939 married Luo Xiangtao, who was attached to the New Fourth Army in Anhui as deputy head of a supply section and with whom she worked in central China until 1949. Li Guiying too was attached to the New Fourth Army, working with its Women's Committee, Political Department, and in Logistics. It is not known whether she had any more children.

After 1949, Li Guiying held various mid-level posts, including organizational section head of Military Supplies, head of the Organization Department of the War Industries Union, director of the Political Office in the Huadong Military Region, and deputy head of a convalescent hospital in Qingdao. During the Cultural Revolution, however, she was labeled a traitor because of her imprisonment by the KMT in the late 1930s. Her name was removed from the party register at that time and Li Guiying was not rehabilitated until July 1978 by which time she was totally blind and unable to work. Li Guiying spent the last decade or so of her life in a military hospital in Nanjing. She faced many difficulties in her life, not least among them the death of two of the men with whom she formed relationships under wartime conditions and the placing of her child in the care of others so that she could resume her revolutionary work. After 1949, however, Li Guiying was able to work for at least fifteen years in responsible positions that afforded her unprecedented financial security and status, given her peasant origin.

Sue WILES

Guo Chen. *Jinguo liezhuan: Hong yifangmianjun sanshiwei changzheng nühongjun shengping shiji*. Beijing: Nongcun duwu chubanshe, 1986, 154–57.
Lee, Lily Xiao Hong, and Sue Wiles. *Women of the Long March*. Sydney: Allen & Unwin, 1999.
Wu Dongfeng. "Zai qianglin-danyu zhong lixian jingnan." In *Hongjun nüyingxiong zhuan*, eds. Liaowang bianjibu. Beijing: Xinhua chubanshe, 1986, 153–62.

Li Guizhen: *see* **Bai Yushuang**

Li Huimin: *see* **Bai Yushuang**

Li Jianhua

Li Jianhua, 1915–1936, of Gao'an County, Jiangxi Province, was one of the thirty women who went with the First Front Red Army on the Chinese communists' Long March of 1934–35. She did not reach Bao'an, and was the first of the women to die.

Li Jianhua was born into a family of merchants who rented out small plots of land to peasants. She was educated to the upper primary school level, a valuable asset for a young woman in the early days of the communist movement. Born as Tu Xiugen, the young woman adopted the name Li Jianhua, meaning National Reconstruction Li, when she and a female friend joined the Red Army after Peng Dehuai (1898–1974) led his division to her village in 1930. Li Jianhua became one of only three women among Peng Dehuai's soldiers: the other two were her friends Li Chihua and Qiu Yihan (*q.v.*). The following year Li Jianhua joined the Communist Youth League and then the CCP.

At first she carried out clerical duties with the Red Army, but after a wireless was captured in January 1931 Li Jianhua was sent to train as a telegraphist. She was then assigned to general headquarters as an apprentice wireless operator and served at the front in the Jiangxi soviet. In early 1934, Li Jianhua was promoted to wireless operator and by August that year had married her superior officer, twenty-seven-year-old telegraphist Yue Xia. The young couple worked in separate units for the first few months of the Long March, then Li Jianhua was assigned to her husband's unit as his assistant. She became pregnant and is said to have attempted to induce a miscarriage by tying musk to her waistband, an old folk remedy, but it was unsuccessful. The time and place of the birth of her baby is not known, and it is assumed that the baby was abandoned, as were all the babies born during the Long March.

Li Jianhua and her husband were assigned in summer 1935 to the Fourth Front Army under the command of Zhang Guotao (1897–1979), and Li Jianhua remained in contact with Kang Keqing (*q.v.*) during their year in Tibet. Zhang Guotao suspected the allegiance of Li Jianhua and her husband, however, and disabled their broadcast capability, allowing them only to receive messages. Li Jianhua is believed to have crossed the Yellow River with the Western Wing (the Western Route Army) of the Fourth Front Army and been killed by Moslem cavalry.

Sue WILES

Guo Chen. *Jinguo liezhuan: Hong yifangmianjun sanshiwei changzheng nühongjun shengping shiji.* Beijing: Nongcun duwu chubanshe, 1986, 79, 85, 178–79.
Lee, Lily Xiao Hong, and Sue Wiles. *Women of the Long March.* Sydney: Allen & Unwin, 1999.

Li Jianzhen

Li Jianzhen, 1906–1992, was born in Fengshun County, Guangdong Province, to a family of impoverished coolies. One of the thirty women who went with the First Front Red Army on the Chinese communists' Long March of 1934–35, she was immortalized in Helen Snow's *Inside Red China* as typifying the Cantonese "Fighting Irishwomen of China." Snow interviewed Li Jianzhen in Yan'an in 1937, transcribing her name as Li Chün-chen. From the age of twenty, Li Jianzhen was an active revolutionary and by 1960 had risen to the comparatively powerful position of secretary to the party's Guangdong Provincial Committee.

Li Jianzhen told Helen Snow that her parents had been brick carriers. She was one of twelve children; an only sister had died, and Li Jianzhen was given away as a child bride to a merchant family named Zhu. She was well treated by her adoptive family, and at the age of seventeen became the wife of one of their three sons. This man's name is given as Zhu Riquan in one later source, which also says he was seven (not ten, as she told Helen Snow) years older. Li Jianzhen gave birth to a son in 1925; she appears not to have had any other children. The Zhu family lived in the Dongjiang District near Hailufeng, site of the first Chinese soviet in August 1927, and was sympathetic to the revolutionary movement spreading through Guangdong and Fujian. Li Jianzhen's husband joined the CCP in 1926, the year before she did, and was killed in battle at Taipu in 1930; his brothers also died fighting for the revolution. Li Jianzhen joined the revolution after a peasant uprising at the time of the Dragon Boat Festival, in May 1927, apparently led by her brother-in-law, who died in the attempt. She said that she was attracted to the revolutionary slogans demanding equality of men and women and individual choice in marriage instead of the old family contract. Li Jianzhen led a propaganda team during this uprising and when it was defeated fled with her fellow insurgents to join the Eleventh Red Army led by Gu Dacun. Li Jianzhen did not take part in the Hailufeng Uprising but spent a year with the guerrillas of the Eleventh Army during which time she did propaganda work, organized workers, and took charge of the Coolies' Union. Li Jianzhen told Helen Snow that the women of Guangdong were "the most revolutionary in China and not afraid to fight," simply because their lives were so bitter. Most of their men went abroad to find work, leaving the women to do all the low-paid coolie work.

Described by Helen Snow as "a tall, square-shouldered, strong-looking woman of obvious courage, intelligence and determination," Li Jianzhen spent the next few years in the border region of western Fujian. She left her son with his paternal grandparents in Dongjiang to more easily pursue her revolutionary activities. Sources provide a dazzling array of titles for the positions Li Jianzhen held during this time but, essentially, she worked at the county level with the soviet government, sometimes as party committee secretary and head of several women's departments. After coming to the attention of party leaders Deng Yingchao (q.v.), Zhou Enlai (1898–1976), and Mao Zedong (1893–1976), Li Jianzhen was transferred to the Jiangxi soviet at the end of 1933 to attend the Central Party School. No mention is made of when she became literate, but it seems likely that Li Jianzhen was exposed to some form of education within her merchant adoptive family. Whether learning to read as a child or picking up what she could as the party trained her in administration, Li Jianzhen was placed in the senior class of the Party School's second intake. She roomed during this short period with two other young women soon to take part in the Long March—Kan Shiying (q.v.) and Wei Gongzhi (q.v.). In January 1934, Li Jianzhen represented Fujian at the Second National Congress of the Soviet Republic of China held in the Jiangxi soviet. Li Jianzhen was elected to the governing Central Executive Committee and made head of the Central Women's Department.

During the Long March, which left Ruijin in October 1934, she was a political instructor and propaganda worker responsible for raising food supplies and confiscating money and valuables from landlords. A touching glimpse of her humanity is revealed by her obvious attachment to a young boy who was her animal handler for the first half of the march. After he was wounded, fatally as it turned out, during the marchers' desperate dash to cross the Yangzi [Yangtze] River at Luding Bridge, Li Jianzhen carried the boy on her back until it became clear that he would not survive. She finally placed him in a hut near a shrine, leaving salt and silver dollars in his pocket.

At the end of 1935, after the communists reached Wayaobu in the northwest, Li Jianzhen married fellow Long Marcher Deng Zhongming (?–1943); his name is transcribed in Helen Snow's account as Teng Chün-hsiung. Li Jianzhen spent only two years in the northwest, as director of the Provincial Women's Department and deputy head of the Organization Department of North Shaanxi, and head of the Shaanxi-Gansu-Ningxia Border Region Women's Department in Yan'an (1937). In 1938, however, she and her husband were sent back to the south to work in the New Fourth Army region of Jiangxi, Zhejiang, and Guangdong. Li Jianzhen continued to work with women as head of the Southeastern Region Women's Department but was also on the Party's Jiangxi Provincial Committee. She told a journalist in the early 1990s that while attending the wedding celebrations of a colleague one night she received news of her husband's death in 1943. She does not appear to have remarried.

As party secretary of Changting County in Fujian in 1945, Li Jianzhen continued to work on Central China and Shandong Party Committees during the civil war period from 1945 to 1949. She was also deputy head of the Central China Propaganda and Organization Department, head of the Shandong Women's Federation, secretary of Shandong Women's Committee, and head of Shandong Provincial Women's Federation. With the establishment of the PRC in 1949, Li Jianzhen became an integral part of the administration of the new nation, participating in the First CPPCC in 1949 as a delegate to the East China Liberated Areas and elected the same year to the Executive Council of the ACWF. She filled a multitude of party and government posts in the first years of the PRC, most of them Guangdong-based. The most noteworthy, however, were her appointments as an alternate member of the CCP Central Committee (1956) and to the key position of a secretary of the party's Guangdong Provincial Committee (1960). As a deputy to the Guangdong Provincial People's Congress (GPPC), Li Jianzhen was elected to the nation's first three sessions of the NPC (1954, 1959, and 1965). She also served from its inauguration in 1955 on the Guangdong Control Commission, holding the position of senior secretary from August 1957. This led to her appointment to the Central Committee's Central Control Commission in 1963.

During the Cultural Revolution, Li Jianzhen disappeared from public view, having apparently been removed from all the positions she held. Most veteran party members who had been part of the Long March were similarly treated. Li Jianzhen does not appear to have been mistreated as some were, however, and by 1973 regained a measure of authority, serving as vice-chair of the Guangdong Provincial Revolutionary Committee. Full rehabilitation came in 1977 with her appointment as an alternate member of the Central Committee and resumption of her position as secretary to the party's Guangdong Provincial Committee. Other appointments followed, including chair of the GPPC (1979) and deputy for Guangdong to the NPC (1978, 1981, and 1988). It is not known when Li Jianzhen retired. She was re-appointed in 1982 to the Central Committee's Central Control Commission but was reported as being in the senior cadres ward of a Beijing hospital in 1984 and is believed to have died in 1992.

Li Jianzhen held a lifelong love of folksongs and during the Long March gained a reputation as one of the most popular of the women folksingers. She is one of very few women to have held the position of provincial party secretary, a remarkable achievement for one born to a family of illiterate poor peasants.

Sue WILES

Bartke, Wolfgang. *Who Was Who in the PRC*. Munich: K.G. Saur, 1997, 223.
Guo Chen. *Jinguo liezhuan: Hong yifangmianjun sanshiwei changzheng nühongjun shengping shiji*. Beijing: Nongcun duwu chubanshe, 1986, 23–26, 36–40.
Klein, Donald W., and Anne B. Clark. *Biographic Dictionary of Chinese Communism, 1921–1965*. Cambridge, Mass.: Harvard University Press, 1971, 482–84.
Lee, Lily Xiao Hong, and Sue Wiles. *Women of the Long March*. Sydney: Allen & Unwin, 1999.
Liu Zhuo'an. "Cong nüzhanshi dao shengwei shuji." In *Hongjun nüyingxiong zhuan*, eds. Liaowang bianjibu. Beijing: Xinhua chubanshe, 1986, 53–65.
Wales, Nym [Helen Foster Snow]. *Inside Red China*. 1977 reprint [with a new preface and biographical notes by the author]. New York: Da Capo Press, 1939, 178–81, 191–96.
Yang Qijun. "Li Jianzhen." In *Nüying zishu*, ed. Jiangxisheng funü lianhehui. Nanchang: Jiangxi renmin chubanshe, 1988, 162–70.
Yingwen *Zhongguo funü*, ed. *Gujin zhuming funü renwu*, vol. 2. Shijiazhuang: Hebei renmin chubanshe, 1986, 735–42.

Li Jin: *see* **Jiang Qing**

Li Kuntai: *see* **Zhao Yiman**

Li Li Hua: *see* **Li Lihua**

Li Li-chüan
Li Li-chüan [Li Lijuan], b. 1955, in T'ai-nan County, Taiwan, was one of the first female graduates of the Central Police College in Taiwan and rose to the rank of inspector in the Taipei Municipal Police Station.

Because her father, Li Yao-tseng, had been a policeman for nearly forty years, Li Li-chüan knew what that life was like. After graduating from Hsin-ying High School, she applied to and was accepted by both Fu-jen University and the Central Police College (Chung-yang ching-kuan hsüeh-hsiao) but chose to enroll in the latter. Li Li-chüan was thus in the first wave of female students to be accepted into the college since its relocation to Taiwan. She graduated in 1978 and, having majored in criminal investigation, was assigned to criminal work at a police station. Li Li-chüan was enthusiastic and ambitious in carrying out fieldwork and neither wanted nor expected preferential treatment because of her gender. She worked alongside her male colleagues on overnight stakeouts and surveillance, as well as in tailing and interrogating suspects, proving to be calm and brave, with an eye for detail.

Li Li-chüan won her nickname—Brave Sister (Yung-sao)—in 1987 for her crucial role in capturing the cunning and ruthless murderer Wu Hsin-hua. The police had been unable to apprehend him and eventually assigned Li Li-chüan to pose as an underground arms dealer by the name of Brave Sister. She managed to contact Wu Hsin-hua and penetrated to the very heart of his criminal organization and was lauded as a heroine when he was finally captured. For her role in the operation, Li Li-chüan was honored as one of the Ten Outstanding Young Women of the Year and became responsible for creating a "tough policewoman" image throughout Taiwan. Knowing the extra effort that she, as a woman, had had to exert in the male-dominated sphere of police work, Li Li-chüan was determined to pave the way for other women who would follow her.

The success in the Wu Hsin-hua case led to an appointment as head of a women's criminal investigation team, and she spent the next ten years in the field. Li Li-chüan was then transferred to administrative work as team leader of the Taipei policewomen's branch (T'ai-pei-shih nü-ching tui-chang) and finally promoted to three-stripe, one-star inspector at Taipei Municipal Police Station. Her husband, Wei Chan-t'ang, who is also a police officer, has provided considerable support and understanding throughout his wife's career.

Although the mainlander Hu Tao-hsing had been head of Taipei policewomen's branch for some twenty-one years, native Taiwanese women had found it difficult to gain promotion in the police force because of the limited roles available to them. Li Li-chüan's excellent work in every field of police work served to break down these barriers, however, and showed how extremely capable women were, by no means mere ornaments. The timing of Li Li-chüan's career was such that she saw a great development in women's roles in Taiwan's police force, from striving for equal opportunity to creating positive images in society of policewomen. The part she played in normalizing women's participation is considerable.

CH'EN Ch'un-ying
(Translated by Laura Long)

Li Ch'un-ying. "San-tz'u ssu-wang chih lü hou ti Yung-sao—Ling tui ch'uang hsin chü." *Hsien-ch'in ching-ch'a hsin-wen*, no. 6 (March-May 1993): 15–16.
Sung Ya-tzu. "P'i-li chiao-wa hua chia-ch'ang." *Fu-nü tsa-chih* (July 1982): 50–52.
Yang Tzu-wei and Chung Chih-ning. *Ching-ch'a feng-yün-pang*. Taipei: T'ien-hui wen-hua shih-yeh, 1997, 103–6.
Yü Wei-fen. "Nü chiao-wa—Li Li-chüan." *Ching-kuang*, no. 379 (1988): 54–55.

Li Lihua

Li Lihua, b. 1923 (some sources give 1925), in Shanghai, is a film star who was prominent for more than thirty years, from the late 1930s, in the Mandarin film industry of China, Hong Kong, and Taiwan. She is known to friends and fans alike by her baby name Xiaomi (kitten), a reference to her diminutive size at birth.

Both parents were *jingju* (Beijing opera) actors: her father, Li Guifang, played *xiaosheng* (young and teenaged male) roles, while her mother, Zhang Shaoquan, played *laodan* (middle-aged or older female) roles. After her husband died, Li Lihua's mother sent her teenaged daughter to Beijing to study *jingju* under Zhang Eyun. When Li Lihua returned to Shanghai for a visit in 1939, the husband of one of her two elder sisters, Yao Yiben, recommended Li Lihua to his friend Yan Chuntang. He was head of Yihua Film Studios and looking for a new face to play the role of Guanshiyin (Guanyin, the Goddess of Mercy) in a new film. Because he was a Buddhist, Yan Chuntang was determined that a virgin should play the part. Soon after meeting Li Lihua, he signed her on for five years and prepared to have her play the role. This was not to be, however, for several people convinced Yan Chuntang that Li Lihua was too small in stature and thus lacked the presence necessary for the part; he ended up using a more mature actress in the film.

In the meantime, having signed a five-year contract with Li Lihua, Yan Chuntang had to find a role for her. Her second assignment—*The Heroes* (Yinglie zhuan)—also turned sour when the director stopped filming after only one day, saying that the lead actress, i.e., Li Lihua, was unsatisfactory. Deciding then that she would be suitable as a maid, the studio cast her in *Three Smiles* (San xiao), a story of the famous Ming painter and writer Tang Ying (*zi* Bohu, 1470–1523) and his pursuit of the maid of a rich and powerful family. It so happened, however, that another studio, Guohua, also planned to film this story. In the race that ensued, Yihua finished its film in six days and six nights, while Guohua took just one more day to wrap up theirs. In 1930s Shanghai, then under Japanese occupation, literature and art were tightly controlled and people were starved for good entertainment. Films based on folk stories and with no political undertones, however, could pass Japanese censors and enjoyed tremendous popularity. Both versions of *Three Smiles* screened in 1940 and did well at the box office. Riding on this wave, Li Lihua became famous with her first film.

After *Three Smiles*, she made more than ten films in the three years from 1940 to 1942, including *Accompanying Jingniang for One Thousand Li* (Qianli song Jingniang), whose theme song was recorded and became popular. Another was a second attempt at *The Heroes*, successful this time even though it had the same director and female lead. Nevertheless, Li Lihua felt vindicated by its success. With the outbreak of the Pacific War in December 1941, the Japanese took over the concessions in Shanghai, and the major film studios merged as China United Film Industry Company (Zhongguo lianhe yingye gongsi, or Hualian). It gained the patronage of the Japanese military and was therefore able to continue making movies without interference. Li Lihua made *Rainy Night on a Cold Mountain* (Hanshan yeyu) and *Autumn Crabapple Blossoms* (Qiu haitang), both directed by Ma Xu Weibang, and the musical *Gorgeous Reds and Purples* (Wanzi qianhong), directed by Fang Peilin, who specialized in musicals. It was during this period that Li Lihua met Zhang Xupu, the young owner of Zhang Yu Winery in Qingdao, and they married.

With the end of the war in 1945, Shanghai's film industry gained new life. Li Lihua, who held a responsible attitude toward her work and tried wherever possible to oblige the studios, was still a much sought-after film actress. After repeated late nights filming *My Dream Ceases at the End of Spring* (Chun can meng duan) that year, she collapsed on the set. Her husband persuaded her to take a respite from work and go to his vineyards in Qingdao, but just as Li Lihua almost decided to go she was prevented from doing so by a new development. A new studio with considerable financial backing, Wenhua, announced that it was recruiting elite actors. Wenhua wanted to begin filming *The Imposters* (Jia feng xu huang) straight away and had Li Lihua in mind as the female lead. She had little choice but to put off her trip to Qingdao. *The Imposters* was about a male hairdresser and a female manicurist who both pretended to be rich and wanted to marry the other for money. The hairdressers' union became incensed with what they saw as a negative portrayal of hairdressers and appeared en masse at the cinema where *The Imposters* was showing, scuffling with security guards and demanding that copies of the film be burned. This unexpected turn of events forced the studio to secure the services of powerful people to mediate, and the studio eventually issued a public apology to the hairdressing profession. The controversy generated a great deal of free publicity, however, and the film was a big box office success when it was finally screened. Li Lihua even won a cover story in the American magazine *Life*.

A new film studio—Da Zhonghua—was established in Hong Kong around 1946 and offered to pay Li Lihua thirty billion yuan if she would go there to make *Shanghai Ladies* (Shanghai xiaojie; later changed to *Three Females*, San nüxing). Despite the high rate of inflation at that time, thirty billion yuan was still an extraordinary amount of money for one film, indeed, the most ever paid to a film star. Li Lihua's husband, Zhang Xupu, tried to stop her from going to Hong Kong, but he was in a parlous financial situation himself. Li Lihua claimed she went in order to make money to pay his debts. After completing *Shanghai Ladies*, the actress returned to Shanghai to make *A Bright and Sunny Day* (Yanyang tian), a screenplay by China's most famous playwright, Cao Yu. This was clearly a quality production because, apart from its famous screenwriter and female lead, the rest of the cast was drawn from the much more prestigious world of stage. This film further advanced Li Lihua's reputation.

In 1947, she left Shanghai for good after going to Hong Kong to make *A Marriageable Age* (Nü da dang jia) and deciding to stay there. Zhang Xupu went to Hong Kong to see her but before long he left; they never saw each other again and formally divorced in 1949. In the meantime, Li Lihua had grown closer to the actor Tao Jin, who co-starred with her in *Sworn to the Sea* (Haishi) in 1948 and *A Cultivated Family* (Shi li chuan jia) in 1950. They parted at the beginning of 1951, however, after repeated calls from Tao Jin's wife that he return to Shanghai. In the early 1950s, another new studio appeared in Hong Kong called Changcheng. Li Lihua made two films with this one: *The Whole World Is Lying* (Shuohuang shijie) and *New Dream of the Red Mansion* (Xin Honglou meng).

Because most of the pre-1949 film stars stayed on the mainland, during the early 1950s Li Lihua was practically the only one who remained active in film making in Hong Kong. Indeed, for a time, she appeared to monopolize Hong Kong's silver screen. From 1952, Li Lihua made a number of films for Xinhua Studio and Nanyang Studio (Shaw Brothers), including two based on the stories of late Qing/early Republican women: *Xiao Fengxian* and *Qiu Jin*, both directed by Tu Guangqi. Others were

The Song of the Cold Cicada (Han chan qu), directed by Tao Qin; *Wind in the Trees* (Feng xiaoxiao), directed by Tu Guangqi; *The Fisherman's Song* (Yu ge), directed by Bu Wancang; and *Blind Love* (Mang lian) and *Xiao Baicai*, both directed by Yi Wen. Li Lihua also went to Japan where she made *Love in the Cherry Blossom City* (Ying du yanji) and *Madame Butterfly* (Hudie furen).

Around the mid-1950s, however, new stars appeared on the horizon who at least partially eclipsed Li Lihua. These fresh young talents included Lin Dai (*q.v.*) and You Min. Then, about 1955 or 1956, the film actor and director Yan Jun began to figure in Li Lihua's life. They had known one another many years previously, when she first entered the film world, and Yan Jun, too, had started as an actor. They had been attracted to each other then, but Li Lihua extricated herself from their relationship because he was already married. Yan Jun had initially received recognition in Shanghai as a stage actor before switching to film and getting his first break as a director in 1951 at Yonghua Studio in Hong Kong. He and his lover Lin Dai (his wife had by this time returned to the mainland) became a successful team in Hong Kong films, proving his talent as a director. After Yan Jun broke up with Lin Dai, however, he renewed his friendship with Li Lihua. Although divorced since 1949, she had resisted the many men who had tried to win her hand and remained single. Li Lihua and Yan Jun not only felt an emotional need for one another, they also saw the advantage of teaming up in making films. Yan Jun could replace his lost star Lin Dai with the dependable asset Li Lihua, while she would have the help of a good director and co-star in remaining a strong contender in the new galaxy of younger stars. The two married in 1957 at St. Teresa Cathedral in Kowloon.

Because their relationship was based on long years of friendship, Li Lihua and Yan Jun enjoyed a stable and happy married life. At the same time, they cooperated in a series of successful historical color films. In time, they joined Shaw Brothers and with its backing—it had made a fortune in films—made even bigger and more lavish productions. Li Lihua reached the peak of her film career in the color historical movies *Empress Wu* (Wu Zetian) and *Precious Consort Yang* (Yang Guifei), both suitable roles for the mature actress she had become by then. After that, Li Lihua played middle-aged women parts. She won the Golden Horse (Jin-Ma) Best Actress Award for her role in *Guarding Every Inch of Our Land with Our Blood* (Yicun shanhe yicun xue) but rarely appeared on screen from then on except in special roles. The actress starred as a Ming loyalist leader in the 1972 martial arts blockbuster *Crises at Yingchun Pavilion* (Yingchunge zhi fengbo), directed by King Hu (Hu Jinchuan, 1932–1997), and as Empress Cixi in *The Siege of Peking* (Ba guo lianjun, 1975). After Yan Jun was diagnosed with diabetes and heart disease in the early 1970s, the couple moved to the United States and lived on Long Island, New York. Yan Jun died in 1980. Li Lihua has two daughters, one born during her first marriage, the other with Yan Jun. Her second daughter, Yan Delan, had been born in 1961. Li Lihua is said to be frugal, good at managing her finances, and in the 1970s, for example, invested in Chinese television in New York.

Although best known for her beauty and staying power in the world of films rather than acting, she was a competent and responsible actress. Li Lihua took a serious attitude toward her work, was always punctual and cooperative, and maintained a prominent position in the Mandarin film world for more than three decades. Her only venture into international film was in 1958 when she co-starred with Victor Mature in the Hollywood movie *China Doll*, directed by Frank Borzage.

Lily Xiao Hong LEE

Chen Dieyi. "Xiaomi qingshi—Li Lihua beizhuan zhi yi." *Zhongwai zazhi*, 46, no. 1 (July 1989): 60–74; 46, no. 2 (August 1989): 37–43.
China Doll, on the Internet at <http://us.imdb.com>.
Lu Shenfang. "Yingtan changqingshu Li Lihua." In *Xiang shidai tiaozhan de nüxing*. Taipei: Xuesheng shudian, 1977, 117–23.

Li Lijuan: *see* **Li Li-chüan**

Li Shude: *see* **Li Shu-te**

Li Shumeng: *see* **Jiang Qing**

Li Shu-te
Li Shu-te [Li Shude], b. 1929, in Wan-tan District, P'ing-tung County, Taiwan, is a violinist and teacher of violin.

Her father, Li Ming, was a medical practitioner who graduated from Taipei Medical College (now Taiwan University Medical School), and her mother, Lin Sen-sen, was the daughter of a translator at Ta-tao-ying Tea Wholesalers in Taipei. The Li family was the wealthiest in P'ing-tung during the period of Japanese colonial rule.

Born into a rich family, Li Shu-te enjoyed a good education, and because both of her parents liked music she grew up in an environment that ensured hers would be a life of music making. At the age of seven, Li Shu-te started piano lessons with Li Chih-ch'uan [Li Zhichuan], a graduate of the Imperial Music University in Japan. However, having difficulty reading music, she later changed to the violin.

After finishing primary school, Li Shu-te was admitted into P'ing-tung Girls' High School. She enjoyed a wide range of interests, excelling both at her studies and in physical education, while continuing to learn violin with Li Chih-ch'uan. Li Shu-te was good at sports, representing P'ing-tung County in javelin throwing at the Provincial Games and setting a new record. What she most enjoyed at that time, however, was painting. Li Shu-te took lessons from Yang Tsao-hua [Yang Zaohua] and was admitted to her first choice for tertiary study—the Art Department at the Normal College (now Normal University). The Art Department was all but destroyed during the April Sixth Incident of 1948, however, and Li Shu-te had to transfer to the Music Department. Although her dream of being an artist may have been shattered, the life of a musician opened to her.

Li Shu-te learned violin under Tai Ts'ui-lun [Dai Cuilun], dean of the Music Department, and was well on her way to becoming a professional violinist. After graduation, she joined the Taiwan provincial government's Education Department's symphony orchestra as first violin. Li Shu-te yearned to learn more, however, and overseas study became her next goal. In 1957, she traveled alone to the United States, a move not supported by her parents, and was admitted to the New England Music College in Boston, studying violin under Professor Alfred Krips and, later, Professor Ruth Posselt. Li Shu-te became the first person from the Republic of China to hold a master's degree in violin, awarded in 1964.

The government of Taiwan then encouraged students to come back to serve the country after graduation, and Li Shu-te heeded the call. She was employed to teach at the Normal College, thus commencing her career of teaching and training good violinists. Li Shu-te had by this time developed her own understanding of teaching violin: that learning must commence at an early age and professional training should be laid as a good foundation. At the same time, she believed that children's potential should be awakened by acknowledging the unique talent of the individual. Working with these principles, Li Shu-te accepted responsibility for training T'ai-nan 3B Children's Orchestra, T'ai-chung Youth and Children's Orchestra, Chung-hua Youth Symphony Orchestra, and the High School Symphony Orchestra affiliated with the Normal University. She also held many recitals for children's performances. Among her students were the famous violinists Hu Nai-yüan [Hu Naiyuan], Lin Chao-liang [Lin Zhaoliang], and Ch'en T'ai-i [Chen Taiyi]. Nevertheless, Li Shu-te did not abandon her own performance career and from 1964 gave successful concerts highly praised by music critics.

Li Shu-te is easygoing and carefree, loves her homeland dearly, and has devoted her life to teaching children to play the violin. She has fulfilled her obligation to pass on her art, reaping the harvest of Taiwanese string musicians from the seeds the musician herself has sown.

HO Shu-i
(Translated by George Li)

Ch'ien Li-an. "Wei hsiao t'i-ch'in fu-yü i-sheng—Taiwan hsüan-yüeh chih mu Li Shu-te." *Piao-yen i-shu*, no. 36 (1995): 10.
Ts'ai Tung-yüan. *T'i-ch'in yu-meng—Li Shu-te liu-shih-wu hui-ku*. P'ing-tung: P'ing-tung hsien-li wen-hua chung-hsin, 1995.

Li Shuzheng

Li Shuzheng, b. 1929, of Dangtu County, Anhui Province, is head of the CCP Central Committee's International Liaison Department, the arm of the party responsible for foreign affairs.

She once went by the name Wang Zhiying and probably grew up in Shanghai. Her grandfather was a big landlord and wealthy businessman, and her father lived the sensual life typical of a rich man's son. Her mother was from a wealthy family from Wuhu in the same province. As a child, Li Shuzheng lived in a grand mansion with extended gardens and decorative pavilions of the kind featured in old novels. The family's fortunes rapidly declined, however, and Li Shuzheng was eager to break free from the hated old traditions. Of her parents' six children, only she and an elder sister survived. The status of her mother, who had failed to produce a male heir, deteriorated to the point that her father took a maid as his unofficial concubine. Li Shuzheng's mother was a high school graduate and knew her legal rights, so sued her husband for bigamy. The lawsuit dragged on interminably, and at one stage Li Shuzheng's mother was so demoralized that she tried to kill herself. The case was eventually decided in the wife's favor, and Li Shuzheng's mother was awarded almost 50,000 yuan to cover living and educational expenses for the girls. Seemingly a considerable sum at the time, with galloping inflation in China in the 1930s and 1940s the money was quickly eaten away, however.

Li Shuzheng's sister, Li Wei, studied at a high school where underground CCP activities were carried out and became involved in them early in life. She and her friends would meet at home to read progressive books and magazines and sing anti-Japanese songs. Under such influence, Li Shuzheng became aware of communist ideology. In 1941, Li Wei discreetly joined the CCP; four years later (in 1945) she sponsored her fifteen-year-old sister into the party. Li Shuzheng later admitted that at that stage she had little understanding of what communism and Marxism represented and was merely anti-imperialist and anti-tradition, seeing that China must change and reform.

Li Shuzheng went to the high school attached to Aurora Women's College of Arts and Science (Zhendan nüzi wenli xueyuan), a Catholic institution known for strict discipline and high academic standards. The girls who went there were mainly from upper class, well-to-do families, but Li Shuzheng won a scholarship. Her first mission for the party was to spread revolutionary ideas in this exclusive girls' school. At the conclusion of the Sino-Japanese War, Shanghai was taken over by the KMT. The CCP organization there had to go underground, and in order to maintain a good front, Li Shuzheng had to continue to do well in her studies. At Aurora, not only did she succeed in disseminating progressive ideas and winning active supporters for the CCP, Li Shuzheng learned useful skills of her own. One was English, which later came in handy in her work at the International Liaison Department. In 1947, the party needed Li Shuzheng to work in a different high school, so she transferred to the First Women's High School of the Shanghai municipality. There, Li Shuzheng incited the students to demand that a rough-mannered Girl Guide instructor be fired and later in the same year was expelled after leading leftist students in Shanghai to organize the "Anti-Starvation, Anti-Civil War, and Anti-Persecution" Movement against the KMT government. Also in that year, Li Shuzheng transferred to the Minli Women's High School but because of her political activities was expelled again. Eventually, she stopped going to school and became a full-time political worker. When Shanghai came under CCP rule in May 1949, twenty-year-old Li Shuzheng revealed her CCP membership and welcomed the party to Shanghai. In those early days, she worked in various positions with the Shanghai Communist Youth League.

In December 1950, Li Shuzheng received notice that she was to study in the Soviet Union and was among the first batch of youths from big cities to be sent to the Youth League School of the Soviet Union. While there, Li Shuzheng worked hard at learning Russian, and because of her proficiency in the language was asked to work at the Communist Youth League's Central Committee after her return to China in 1951. She had been deputy head and head of several sections in the Communist Youth League and in time became a standing member of the League's Central Committee and head of the Juvenile Department (Shaonianbu).

During the Cultural Revolution, the Communist Youth League's Central Committee came under scrutiny. First, it was reorganized, then moved outside Beijing. Li Shuzheng was subjected to the different stages of maltreatment meted out to officials of the party and the government: stepping aside (*kaobian zhan*), investigation (*jiancha*), and criticism and attack (*pidou*). In 1973, she was recalled from the countryside and in early 1974 sent to the United Nations to act as an advisor to the Chinese delegation to a meeting on the status of women. In 1975, during the World Conference of the International Women's Year in Mexico, Li Shuzheng put forward the Chinese view that a woman's lot is closely tied to national liberation. From 1978 on, she proceeded from being director of a bureau in the International Liaison Department of the CCP Central Committee to deputy head, then to head. After China's reform and opening up, the CCP developed its relations with political parties all over the world. The work of the International Liaison Department is guided by the principle of not basing association on ideology. In its pursuit of friendly relations with other political parties, the International Liaison Department follows four principles: (1) maintenance of independence and autonomy; (2) complete equality; (3) mutual respect; and (4) non-interference with one another's domestic affairs. Through Li Shuzheng's energetic work, by the mid-1990s the CCP had established relations at various levels with more than three hundred political parties in more than 120 countries. In her capacity as a party diplomat, she visited all five continents and entertained dignitaries from all over the world.

Li Shuzheng is said to be approachable and considerate, leading a simple life and with an amazing capacity for work. Music is one of her few ways of relaxing: she plays the piano and the piano accordion. Li Shuzheng believes that women still have many hurdles to overcome to succeed in their chosen career: they must pay a higher price than men. On the one hand, they cannot completely ignore housework and children; on the other, they still have to overcome doubts regarding their ability. She maintains there is no point to women just shouting slogans about gender equality; they must improve themselves and show real worth, fighting for equality every step of the way. The important thing for women is to be willing to take on responsibility, confront hardship, and keep on urging themselves forward. Li Shuzheng married, probably during the 1960s, and has at least one daughter and one granddaughter.

Lily Xiao Hong LEE

Huaxia funü mingren cidian. Beijing: Huaxia chubanshe, 1988.
Liu Jinxiu. "Zhonglianbu diyiwei nübuzhang." *Zhongguo funü*, August (1993): 4–5.
Zhongguo funü guanli ganbu xueyuan, ed. *Gujin Zhongwai nümingren cidian*. Beijing: Zhongguo guangbo dianshi chubanshe, 1980, 219.
Zhonghua quanguo funü lianhehui. Zuzhi lianluobu, ed. *Jinri nübuzhang*. Shenyang: Liaoning renmin chubanshe, 1995, 189–216.

Li Xikai: *see* **Zhong Yuzheng**

Li Yijie: *see* **Zhao Yiman**

Li Yunhe: *see* **Jiang Qing**

Li Zhen
Li Zhen, 1908–1990, of Liuyang County, Hunan Province, was the first woman to be promoted to the rank of major-general in the Chinese military. For thirty-three years, from 1955, she remained the only woman to hold this status; a further five women were promoted to equivalent rank in 1988 (*vide* Zhong Yuzheng).

Li Zhen in many ways typified peasant women who joined the early communists. Born of poor parents, for the first eighteen years of her life she was known as Danwazi, that is, simply Girl. Her father died when she was ten years old, and Danwazi and all five of her sisters were given away at about the age of six. Danwazi went to the family of a doctor but remained in close contact with her natal family. By the mid-1920s, Hunan had become one of the centers of revolutionary activity, and in spring 1926 she joined a district women's organization (funü xiehui), signing up as Li Zhen, the name by which she was known from then on. She acted as a scout (*zhenchayuan*) for the local communists, passing with her short-cropped hair as a boy or girl as circumstances required, and joined the CCP in March 1927. Soon after, Li Zhen severed all connection with her adoptive family and, with the full support of her birth mother, who is said to have died at the hands of Japanese soldiers during the Sino-Japanese War, devoted herself to revolutionary work.

By 1928, Li Zhen was a member of the District Committee and deputy secretary of the party branch of the Pingliu guerrillas. During this period, she embarked on a military career by becoming head of the Soldiers Committee (Shibing weiyuan zhang) of the Liudong Guerrilla Unit (Liudong youjidui), which later became Liuyang County Party Committee (Liuyang xianwei). While her duties included washing other soldiers' clothing and dyeing hemp, she also saw battle, as did most of the women who joined guerrilla and partisan groups at this time. Li Zhen later said, however, that in the beginning no one in her unit knew how to fire the rifles they were given by Red Army General Peng Dehuai. In the spring, she initiated and participated with Wang Shoudao (*vide* Wang Quanyuan) in the rescue of Zhang Qilong (1900–1987), secretary of a Special Agent's Committee and one of her sponsors into the CCP. Li Zhen was four months' pregnant the following autumn when she and a handful of guerrillas managed to survive an engagement with the enemy; however, Li Zhen suffered a miscarriage, which apparently left her unable to have children. It cannot be discerned from sources to whom Li Zhen was married at that time, although it is possible that Zhang Qilong, whom she officially married in 1932, was the father of her child. He had entered into an arranged marriage in his youth, but his wife (Huang Guangju) and daughter were killed by the KMT in 1930.

Despite early direct military involvement and a period in late 1934 relaying information about vanguard activities to General Xiao Ke, from the end of 1928 Li Zhen held political posts within the Red Army. She worked with the newly established Hunan-Hubei-Jiangxi soviet government and three years later (winter 1931) was transferred to the Hunan-Jiangxi Border Region soviet government based in Yongxin. There, Li Zhen appears to have worked closely until early 1933 with Zhang Qilong, who held a range of high-level provincial party and political posts. Li Zhen was appointed to leading positions with provincial women's committees and as political commissar to a Yongxin women's team (funü tuan) in 1932. The focus of women's work at that time was on supporting the Red Army, recruiting soldiers, and organizing local women to step into the civilian breach when their men joined the army. She was also political commissar to a medical school in the Hunan-Jiangxi Military Region (Xiang-Gansheng junqu yiwu xuexiao). The vast majority of students were women, indicating that it was perhaps a training ground for nurses.

In mid-summer 1933, Li Zhen was transferred to Anfu County as deputy secretary and head of military affairs (Anfu xianwei fushuji jian junshi buzhang) and then sent to study for three months in Ruijin at the School of Marxist Communism (Makesi gongchanzhuyi xuexiao; described generically in one source as a central party school, *zhongyang dangxiao*). This transfer coincided with the political maneuvering now damned by the CCP as the "Wang Ming leftist line" that saw Zhang Qilong stripped of party membership and imprisoned for fourteen months. To protect her, Zhang chivalrously divorced Li Zhen; both later remarried others but remained close throughout their lives.

After returning to the Hunan-Jiangxi base area, Li Zhen headed the Political Department of its Red Army School. As the military prepared to abandon the base in July-August 1934, one of her superiors suggested that because "fighting was so hard for women," Li Zhen should remain behind. In spite of her position and proven political and fighting ability, he suggested that she should consider staying with her younger sisters, one of whom was about to give birth. Appalled at the idea of being left behind simply because she was a woman, Li Zhen appealed to the highest level and was allowed to continue her work. She thus took part in the famed Long March, her unit first joining the Sixth Corps under Ren Bishi and Xiao Ke and then amalgamating with General He Long's forces in November 1934 to form the Second Front Red Army. The Second Front Army remained in western Hunan until November 1935, then marched northwest to join Zhang Guotao's forces in Tibet (*vide* Wang Quanyuan and Kang Keqing), reaching Shaanxi in October 1936. Li Zhen's duties on the Long March included party and cadre work as well as taking in wounded soldiers.

On New Year's Day 1935, Li Zhen married Gan Siqi (1903–1964). She had been working with him for several years, since his return from studying in the USSR in 1930. At the time of their marriage, Li Zhen headed the Organization Department; he headed the Political Department of the Hunan-Hubei-Sichuan-Guizhou Soviet Military Region. They appear to have continued to work in close proximity from then on. They had no children of their own but adopted and cared for a number of orphaned youngsters over the years.

In Yan'an, Li Zhen attended the Anti-Japanese University for a short time before being assigned in late 1937 to the post of principal of the Eighth Route Army Girls' School (Balujun funü xuexiao). By spring 1941, however, as director of the Political

Office (Zhenzhichu zhuren) attached to the 120th Division, Li Zhen took part in the great production movement in Nanniwan. From 1945 to 1949, she was secretary-general with the Political Department, first of Shanxi-Suiyuan Military Region and then of the Northwest Field Army.

By the time the PRC was established, Li Zhen was forty-one years old but remained active in the PLA. She served in Korea as secretary-general of the Political Department of the Chinese People's Volunteer Army and upon her return in 1953 was appointed head of the Cadres Department of the Air Defense Forces's Political Department. This was a prestigious post attached to the Military Commission of the CCP's Central Committee. In September 1955, Li Zhen was promoted to major-general (*shaojiang*), her promotion a direct result of the short-lived modernization process of China's military instituted by Peng Dehuai and completed that year. A system of ranks and awards for officers was introduced at that time as a step toward professionalization, and the PLA's command structure was reorganized. Two years later, in 1957, Li Zhen was appointed deputy procurator in the Military Procuratorate and helped lay valuable ground rules for this newly established area of the military.

Li Zhen's husband, by then Colonel-General Gan Siqi, had been one of Lin Biao's political targets as early as 1960 (Gan Suqi died in 1964), and Li Zhen herself suffered persecution during the Cultural Revolution. She was stood down in 1967 because of her long and close association with Red Army Generals He Long and Peng Dehuai and held in detention for four years. In March 1971, Li Zhen was released and sent back to Hunan, but not until 1976 was she rehabilitated and allowed to return to Beijing; however, the case fabricated against her was not overturned until 1979. During the 1980s, Li Zhen was rewarded for her long and faithful service with appointment to several high-level positions, including deputy for the PLA to the Fifth NPC and membership to the Advisory Committee of the Central Committee (Zhongyang guwen weiyuanhui). She resigned from all her posts in 1985 and died in March 1990; her ashes were interred alongside those of Gan Siqi.

Li Zhen remained throughout life proudly grounded in her peasant origins. Although not in good health in later years, she persisted in growing her own vegetables and almost to the end wore her old army uniform, patched but clean, in Red Army tradition.

Sue WILES

Bartke, Wolfgang. *Who Was Who in the PRC*. Munich: K.G. Saur, 1997, 252.

Cui Xianghua et al., eds. *Zhongguo nü jiangjun*. Beijing: Jiefangjun wenyi chubanshe, 1995, 1–36.

Gu Lanying. "Jiefangjun weiyi de nü jiangjun." In *Hongjun nüyingxiong zhuan*, eds. Liaowang bianjibu. Beijing: Xinhua chubanshe, 1986, 207–15.

Jiangxisheng funü lianhehui. *Nüying zishu*. Nanchang: Jiangxi renmin chubanshe, 1988, 114–23.

Klein, Donald W., and Anne B. Clark. *Biographic Dictionary of Chinese Communism, 1921–1965*. Cambridge, Mass.: Harvard University Press, 1971, 424.

Xiao Li et al., eds. *Yingxiang Zhongguo lishi de yibai ge nüren*. Guangzhou: Guangdong renmin chubanshe, 1992, 386–90.

Yingwen *Zhongguo funü*, ed. *Gujin zhuming funü renwu*, vol. 2. Shijiazhuang: Hebei renmin chubanshe, 1986, 774–78.

Li Zhonggui: *see* **Li Chung-kui**

Li Ziyun

Li Ziyun, b. 1930, in Beijing although her native place is Xiamen, Fujian Province, is a literary critic who writes under the pen name Xiao Li.

She was active in her youth in student patriotic movements and studied in Shanghai at Aurora College of Arts and Science (Zhendan wenli xueyuan) in 1949 but did not graduate. From 1950 on, Li Ziyun worked in various agencies, including the East China Bureau of the Central Committee of the CCP and the Propaganda, Art, and Literature Departments of Shanghai Municipal Council. She became a member of the CCP (1951) and the Chinese Writers' Association (1958) and between 1961 and 1966 researched contemporary Chinese literature, working at the modern Chinese Group of the Shanghai Literature Institute. During the Cultural Revolution, she was the first of the Shanghai Writers' Association members to be singled out to "stand aside," a phrase usually meaning that she was deprived of all positions as well as the right to work. She was not allowed to return to work until 1976. Since 1977, when she was transferred to the magazine *Shanghai Literature* (Shanghai wenxue), she has worked as deputy chief editor and literary assessor. She continues to reside in Shanghai.

Li Ziyun began in 1952 to publish many reviews and research articles on Chinese writers, including overseas Chinese writers, especially women. Her critiques of Wang Meng, Wan Anyi (*q.v.*), Zhang Xinxin (*q.v.*), and Shi Shuqing considerably influenced literary circles. In her reviews, which are considered fresh and straightforward, Li Ziyun sets forth her own opinion and yet empathizes with writers; her comments are precise, appropriate, and candid. She has been invited frequently on cultural exchanges all over the world by Chinese writers and feminist organizations.

Her own published work includes *Comments on Contemporary Women Writers* (Dangdai nüzuojia sanlun), *Purify One's Soul* (Jinghua ren de xinling), and *Streams* (Juanliu ji), and Li Ziyun has edited several selections of contemporary literature, such as *Watching the Tide on the Other Shore* (Ge hai guan lan). In recent years, she has been the leading executive of the Shanghai Writers' Association's Literature and Art Fund. As chief editor, Li Ziyun organized and published the large series literary collections of *Echo of the Century* (Shiji de huixiang), which included many works from writers, critics, thinkers, and scholars who have been ignored or forgotten since 1949. Li Ziyun won praise in publishing and scholarly circles for her work in thus filling in gaps in academic and cultural history. She herself is a diligent writer of prose: her articles of reminiscences and assessments of writers of the older generation are interesting, well written, and retain value academically.

GAO Yuanbao
(Translated by Laura Long)

Li Ziyun. *Dangdai nüzuojia sanlun*. Hong Kong: Sanlian shudian, 1984.
———. *Jinghua ren de xinling*. Hong Kong and Beijing: Sanlian shudian, 1984.
Li Ziyun et al., eds. *Shiji de huixiang*. Zhuhai: Guangdong Zhuhai chubanshe, 1988–1999.
Pan Yadun. *Shijie huawen nüzuojia sumiao*. Guangzhou: Jinan daxue chubanshe, 1993, 45–47.

Liang Danfeng: *see* **Liang Tan-feng**

Liang Jing: *see* **Chang, Eileen**

Liang Tan-feng

Liang Tan-feng [Liang Danfeng], b. 1935 in Nan-ching [Nanjing], is an artist, best known for her sketches made during world-wide travels but especially in mainland China. During the Sino-Japanese War, from the age of three or four Liang Tan-feng traversed half of the provinces of China with her family before they settled in Ch'ung-ch'ing [Chongqing]. She returned with her family to live and study in Shanghai and Hangzhou until 1948, when her father moved the family to Taiwan.

The Liang family of Shun-te [Shunde] in Kuang-tung [Guangdong] Province has produced two generations of painters. Liang Tan-feng's father, Liang Ting-ming [Liang Dingming] (b. 1897), was a painter as were his two younger brothers Liang Yu-ming [Liang Youming] (b. 1906) and Liang Chung-ming [Liang Zhongming] (b. 1907), and his sister Liang Hsüeh-ch'ing [Liang Xueqing] (b. before 1907). Liang Tan-feng was the second of three daughters: her elder sister, Liang Tan-mei [Liang Danmei], is an art academic who specializes in painting plum blossoms, while her younger sister, Liang Tan-hui [Liang Danhui], excels at water colors and oils. Their cousin Liang Hsiu-chung [Liang Xiuzhong] is a painter of portraits and has headed the Fine Arts Department of Taiwan Normal University (Taiwan Shih-fan ta-hsüeh). Liang Tan-feng studied art under her father from childhood. He and his brothers were skilled at traditional Chinese painting and Western painting, both of which Liang Tan-feng studied. She is best known, however, for her life and nature studies.

Liang Tan-feng has mounted exhibitions annually since her first one-woman exhibition in 1956. She has traveled around the world several times in pursuit of her art, visiting busy cities and remote villages from the North Pole to the deserts of Jordan. Her numerous trips have taken her to more than sixty countries in Asia, the Americas, and Europe; in the 1970s she would travel alone, unusual for a single woman from Taiwan at that time. Liang Tan-feng is never without her sketchbook when she travels. Her sketches have been published as *Travels around the Globe* (Huan-ch'iu chih lü, 1974?), *European Tour* (Ou-chou chih lü, 1977), *Journey to the Arctic Circle* (Pei-chi-ch'üan chih lü, 1977), *Journey to* "Arabian Nights": *Eighty Days in Turkey* (T'ien-fang yeh-t'an chih lü: T'u-erh-ch'i pa-shih t'ien, 1984), and *Crossing the Grand Canyon* (Chu'an yueh Ta-hsia-ku, 1984). The artist has held exhibition in many of the countries she has visited and her works are collected by museums and universities throughout the world. Her work projects a strong sense of Chinese aesthetics, representations of scenes and people of other parts of the world clearly seen through Chinese eyes.

In 1989, the Taipei newspaper *Lien-ho pao* sponsored Liang Tan-feng on a six-month journey to mainland China. From that trip came a series of articles under the general title *Traversing the Vast Land of China* (Tsou-kuo Chung-kuo ta-ti), published in *Lien-ho pao*. Some of her four hundred artworks from this trip illustrated articles on the physical appearance of the land, the many cultural sites, and the people, their pains and their hopes. These articles offered more than her insights into Chinese culture and how mainland Chinese lived; they revealed her patriotic passion and the profound anxiety she felt for her compatriots on the other side of the Taiwan Strait. The artist proved an equally eloquent writer and the articles were published as a monograph later that year. Two volumes of art works also resulted from this trip: *Sketching China* (Su-hsieh Shen-chou, 1991) and *Watercolors of China* (Ts'ai-hui Chung-kuo, 1991).

From 1964, Liang Tan-feng has taught art in high schools and colleges; she has also taught art in the Philippines and at St. John's University, New York. She created her own studio—the Happy Studio (K'uai-lo hua-hui)—in 1969 and has held annual exhibitions of both her own work and the work of her students.

Liang Tan-feng has received many honors, including the Golden Bell Award (Chin-to chiang) in 1970, and the Ministry of Education's Literature and Art Award (Wen-i chiang) in 1976 for her achievement in art as well as for her "citizen diplomacy." Her appointment in August 2000 to the Interparty Task Force on Cross-Strait Relations, an advisory body to President Ch'en Shui-pien, was possibly in recognition of her experience trekking across mainland China. Liang Tan-feng has published technical works, including *An Introduction to Sketching* (Hsieh-sheng kai-shuo), *Landscape Sketching* (Feng-ching hsieh sheng), and *Studies on the Brush Techniques of Water and Ink Paintings* (Shui-mo hua pi-ch'u te yen-chiu). Pencil drawings, Chinese paintings, and Western-style paintings, in addition to her travel sketches, are among the more than ten published collections of her drawings and paintings.

Liang Tan-feng's significance to Taiwan is threefold: as a painter, as a writer, and as a single woman traveling the world. Her art and literature are treasured for themselves but they have also been able to broaden the vision of Chinese people in Taiwan and elsewhere, enhancing their love for their motherland and their cultural origins.

Lily Xiao Hong LEE

Chung-hua min-kuo tang-tai ming-jen lu, vol. 3. Taipei: Taiwan Chung-hua shu-chü, 1978, 1327.
Fu-nü wei-yuan-hui. *Chung-hua min-kuo lien-ho-kuo t'ung-chih-hui san-shih chou-nien chi-nien t'e-k'an: San-shih nien lai wo kuo funü tui kuo-chia chien-she chih kung-hsien yü ch'eng-chiu*. Taipei: Fu-nü wei-yuan-hui, 1979?, 109.
Lai Ying-ying. "Historical Development of Women's Art in Taiwan." *In Catalog for Mind and spirit—Women's Art in Taiwan, Taiwan Fine Arts Museum, 18 April–9 August 1998—A Major Exhibition of Women Artists in Taiwan in the 20th Century*. Online at <http//web.ukonline.co.uk/n.paradoxa/lai.htm>
Liang Tan-feng. *Tsou-kuo Chung-kuo ta-ti*. Taipei: Lien-ching ch'u-pan, 1989.

Liang-Hsü Ch'un-chü

Liang-Hsü Ch'un-chü [Liang-Xu Chunju], 1918–1997, born Hsü Ch'un-chü in P'eng-hu County, Taiwan, was the first woman ever to be elected to the Legislative Yuan in Taiwan.

Her early education was undertaken during the period of Japanese occupation after she gained admission by examination to the Second Girls' High School in T'ai-nan. After graduating, Liang-Hsü Ch'un-chü studied in Japan, first at Nara Teachers' Training College and then at Tōyō University, obtaining a master's in Law. Returning to Taiwan, she was given a teaching post at her old school in T'ai-nan.

In 1940, Hsü Ch'un-chü married Liang Ping-yüan [Liang Bingyuan], son of a prominent T'ai-nan family. The young couple went to mainland China to explore prospects for their future but returned to Taiwan in 1946. Liang-Hsü Ch'un-chü started teaching at Hsin-hua Junior High School, assuming the additional responsibility of running the school office. Elected coordinator of T'ai-nan Women's Council, in 1951 she began her forty-year political career in earnest after being elected unopposed to the recently restructured First Provisional Provincial Council. Liang-Hsü Ch'un-chü served six consecutive terms, totaling eighteen years. In 1969 she became the first Taiwanese woman ever to be elected to the Legislative Yuan and the first member from Hsin-hua to serve in the legislature. Her achievement is all the more remarkable because Liang-Hsü Ch'un-chü won her place on her own merit, not through the quota allocated to female candidates.

Her main concern during her career as a legislative councillor was education. Throughout six terms on the Provincial Council and twenty-two years in the Legislative Yuan, she coordinated the Board for the Study of Education, sat on the committee that implemented the nine-year universal education program, and served as consultant to various education and sports boards, including the Fifth Asian Games and the Mexico Olympic Games. Liang-Hsü Ch'un-chü proposed that, in order to improve teacher-student ratios in schools, funds for local education should come from the central government. She also drafted several bills on welfare for teachers, including the Research Study Fund for Teachers, and established a teachers' club and the channels necessary to allow teachers to go abroad. Through sound management at a grass-roots district level and careful attention to providing services to her constituency, Liang-Hsü Ch'un-chü maintained both her power base and influence. She was dubbed the Dollar Councillor because any members of her constituency who found themselves in difficulty could seek her help for the price of a dollar postage stamp (to stick on the letter to her).

When the issue of the retirement of senior members to the Legislative Yuan exploded in 1991, Liang-Hsü Ch'un-chü's status became a further source of controversy because she was neither a senior member nor a supernumerary. After forty years of public service, Liang-Hsü Ch'un-chü chose to bow out of politics. Despite her retirement and ill health, however, her enthusiasm for service remained undiminished, and she continued to devote a great deal of time and effort to the betterment of underprivileged social groups. Liang-Hsü Ch'un-chü died from colon cancer in April 1997, at the age of eighty years.

LIN Qianru
(Translated by Li Sheung Yee)

Chung-hua min-kuo tang-tai jen-ming-lu. Taipei: Taiwan Chung-hua shu-chü, 1978, 372.

Liang-Xu Chunju: *see* **Liang-Hsü Ch'un-chü**

Liao Mengxing

Liao Mengxing, 1904–1988, also known as Liao Xianlin and Liao Shaofen, was born in Hong Kong, although her native place was Huizhou, Guangdong Province. She joined the CCP in 1932 in Hong Kong and for several decades from the mid-1930s worked closely with Song Qingling (*q.v.*) as a translator and private secretary. In this capacity she was able to give substantial help to the communist cause.

Her father, Liao Zhongkai (1877–1925), was born in America but at the age of seventeen went to Hong Kong and studied at Wah Yan College (one source gives Queen's College). He traveled to Japan nine years later and soon joined the Tongmenghui established by Dr. Sun Yat-sen (1866–1925). Liao Zhongkai acted as an external affairs organizer and became Sun Yat-sen's most capable lieutenant. After the Tongmenghui reorganized into the KMT in 1924, Liao Zhongkai served as deputy minister of Finance, director of Industry and Agriculture, and general director of Military Supplies. He had been at Sun Yat-sen's side guiding the revolutionary cause for more than twenty years until he was assassinated in Guangzhou in 1925, the same year Sun Yat-sen died.

Liao Mengxing's mother, He Xiangning (*q.v.*), came from a rich Hong Kong business family. She studied natural science and fine arts in Japan, and was both one of its earliest members and one of the first women to join the Tongmenghui. Well respected by both the KMT and the communists, He Xiangning held several high-ranking positions during her long life. Although she had been director of the KMT Women's Department (1927) and chair of the KMT Revolutionary Committee of China from 1960, He Xiangning was made honorary chair of the ACWF (1949) and deputy chair of the CPPCC (1954) after the communists gained power in 1949.

The eldest child in her family, Liao Mengxing was taken to Japan by her father when she was one and grew up in Tokyo with her brother Liao Chengzhi (1908–83). Both siblings returned to China at high school age. Liao Chengzhi later took part in the communists' famous Long March of 1934–35 from the Jiangxi soviet to northern Shaanxi Province and went on to fill various important posts. In later years, he was made director of the Beijing Foreign Languages Institute and honorary chair of the All-China Federation of Returned Overseas Chinese.

The daughter of revolutionaries, Liao Mengxing committed herself to the cause at an early age. At twenty-one, she was the only female student from Lingnan University in Guangzhou to participate in demonstrations in support of the May Thirtieth Incident of 1925, thus earning expulsion from the university. At the age of twenty-six, Liao Mengxing married Li Shaoshi (Li Guojun, aka Li Monong and Li Juezhen, 1906–1945) in Hong Kong. They had a daughter, whose name is Li Mei, in 1932. The young couple assumed aliases—she went by the name Liao Shaofen and he, as head of an underground CCP contact organization, was Li Juezhen—to facilitate their clandestine work of arranging safe travel for CCP leaders into and out of Hong Kong, among them Deng Xiaoping (1904–1996).

In 1934 Liao Mengxing accompanied her husband to Shanghai when he was assigned to propaganda work in Jiangsu Province and made director of the Chinese Workers' News Agency (Zhongguo gongren tongxunshe), responsible for providing articles in English to foreign news agencies along with translating and publishing foreign-language material into Chinese. Liao Mengxing had learned English in Japan (from her American-born father) and translated English-language works into Chinese. Li Shaoshi was arrested by the KMT in Shanghai in 1934 because of his communist affiliation and imprisoned for four years. During this time, Liao Mengxing lived for two years in Shanghai and Hong Kong but when her husband was released in 1938, after KMT and the CCP had joined forces to oppose the Japanese, went with him to Chongqing. There, he was appointed as secretary to the office of the Eighth Route Army and became private English secretary to Zhou Enlai (1898–1976). The reason for Li Shaoshi's assassination in 1945 is not known, but he was held in high esteem by the CCP leaders; Mao Zedong (1893–1976) wrote of his grief at Li Shaoshi's untimely death.

Before her marriage, Liao Mengxing had acted as interpreter and private secretary to her mother and had also taken part in many fundraising activities and drives to rouse moral support for soldiers, initiated by her mother and Madame Song Qingling, the widow of Dr. Sun Yat-sen. During the Sino-Japanese War, Liao Mengxing remained in Chongqing and managed the office of the China Defense League, also acting as its Chinese secretary. This association operated under the leadership of Song Qingling and was supported by many international figures. Liao Mengxing's work involved researching and translating information for the *China Defense League Newsletter*. She also acted as Song Qingling's private secretary and in that capacity attended many meetings. Liao Mengxing liaised with Zhou Enlai, for instance, to arrange for donations of money and equipment to be sent to communist-held areas.

Liao Mengxing returned to Shanghai after 1945 and continued to work with Song Qingling and the China Defense League, which had changed its name to the Chinese Welfare Foundation. Its activities between 1945 and 1949 focused on getting supplies to the communists, raising funds, and providing education for the women and children of Shanghai.

With the establishment of the PRC in the latter year, Mao Zedong and Zhou Enlai personally invited Song Qingling to come to Beijing to "give advice on how to organize a new China." Liao Mengxing facilitated the ensuing discussion, which took place by mail, and six months later, when Song Qingling finally agreed, Liao Mengxing accompanied her to Beijing. She again acted as Song Qingling's secretary but also held the positions of deputy director of the International Department of the ACWF and director of the Liao Zhongkai and He Xiangning Museum. In recognition of her revolutionary activities before 1949, Liao Mengxing was elected to the First (1954), Second (1959), and Third (1963) NPCs and made a member of the Fifth (1978) and Sixth (1982) CPPCC.

Viola Hong Xin Chan WONG

Guan Guoxuan. "Liao Mengxing sui mu He Xiangning di Chengzhi er qu." *Zhuanji wenxue*, 25, no. 3 (July 1974): 39–40, 42–45.
Jiang Hongbin. *Song Qingling*. Nanjing: Jiangsu renmin chubanshe, 1986.
Li Qing and Sun Sibai, eds. *Zhongguo renming da cidian: Minguo renwu zhuan*, vol. 2. Beijing: Zhonghua shuju, 1980.
Liao Chengzhi. "Yi qing-shao nian shidai." In *Liao Chengzhi wenji*, vol. 1. Hong Kong: Sanlian shudian, 1990, 4–7.
Shang Mingxuan. *He Xiangning zhuan*. Beijing: Beijing chubanshe, 1994.
Xu Youchun, ed. *Minguo renwu da cidian*. Baoding: Hebei renmin chubanshe, 1991.

Liao Shaofen: *see* **Liao Mengxing**

Liao Siguang

Liao Siguang, b. 1911, née Liao Jiao, of Huiyang County, Guangdong Province, was one of the thirty women who went with the First Front Red Army on the Chinese communists' Long March of 1934–35.

After the death of her father left the family poverty stricken, Liao Siguang was sold as a child bride at the age of four. By the time she was eight, Liao Siguang was working in the fields alongside her stepmother. However, at age sixteen an epidemic of dysentery swept through Huiyang County and many people died, including her betrothed and one of his brothers. As preparations were just then being made for her marriage, Liao Siguang was held responsible for the deaths of the brothers. Labeled unlucky and no longer welcome in the family to which she had been sold, Liao Siguang returned to her natal family.

The area in which she lived had for several years been the site of much peasant activism, and Liao Siguang soon became part of a women's group. By 1928 she was involved in underground revolutionary work in the Dongjiang area of Guangdong and joined the Communist Youth League in 1929. Liao Siguang was sent to Hong Kong in spring 1930 to work with the Guangdong branch of the Youth League and there entered into a sham marriage with Kai Feng (He Kequan, 1906–1955), secretary of the branch. In time, however, they became lovers and established a lasting relationship. They were arrested in Hong Kong in 1930, but party authorities intervened and managed to have them deported rather than incarcerated. In September the two made their way to Shanghai, where Kai Feng became head of the Youth League's Propaganda Department and Liao Siguang took on the dangerous work of political liaison, receiving secret documents and propaganda material.

When the CCP's Political Department evacuated from Shanghai in spring 1933, Kai Feng was transferred to the Jiangxi soviet, leaving Liao Siguang to continue underground work in Shanghai. She was pregnant at the time. In the summer Liao Siguang gave birth to a daughter and placed the baby in the care of another liaison worker after the party ordered the new mother to make the difficult journey to the Jiangxi soviet three months later. The liaison worker deposited the baby girl in the Red Cross hospital, and the child was never traced. Liao Siguang worked as an inspector with the Youth League in Ruijin and joined the CCP in 1934. About four months pregnant with her second child, she set off with the Red Army's Convalescent Company on the Long March. Liao Siguang gave birth prematurely, at seven months, in Guizhou and abandoned her baby boy after wrapping him in a blanket, pinning a note on it giving the time and date of his birth. It is not known if Liao Siguang had any more children. For the rest of the march, she carried out the same propaganda work and organizing of food supplies and funds as the other women.

At the end of the Long March, Liao Siguang was appointed deputy secretary of the Youth League in Wayaobao and head of the Organization Department. She worked several years in the Shaanxi-Gansu-Ningxia Border Region and with Deng Yingchao (*q.v.*) in developing the women's movement and anti-Japanese activities. In 1938 Liao

Siguang was sent to Wuhan with Liu Qunxian (*q.v.*) on union work and also became involved with orphaned and abandoned children in central China, especially in Wuhan and Chongqing. Liao Siguang returned to Yan'an in 1941 and for a period attended the elite Party School and then from 1946 worked in land reform and the labor movement in the northeast. She was a delegate to the First National Women's Congress in Beijing in 1949 after which Liao Siguang returned to the south. After being chair of the newly established Wuhan Federation of Trade Unions, she was transferred to Guangzhou, holding several municipal and provincial posts, including deputy secretary of Guangzhou Municipal Committee, first chair of the Guangzhou Trade Unions Federation, director of Guangdong's Department of Industry, and deputy head of the Provincial Organization Department.

During the Cultural Revolution, Liao Siguang was imprisoned and interrogated, as were many of those who took part in the Long March, but she steadfastly refused to incriminate anyone with written "confessions." Liao Siguang was rehabilitated after the Cultural Revolution and in 1986 was made deputy chair of the Guangdong CPPCC. At the time of writing she was believed to be living in Guangdong.

Sue WILES

Bianco, Lucien, and Yves Chevrier, eds. *Dictionnaire Biographique du Mouvement Ouvrier International: La Chine*. Paris: Les Éditions Ouvrières, n.d.

Chen Wanwen. "Xiangwang he xunqiu shuguang." In *Hongjun nüyingxiong zhuan*, eds. Liaowang bianjibu. Beijing: Xinhua chubanshe, 1986, 129–40.

Guo Chen. *Jinguo liezhuan: Hong yifangmianjun sanshiwei changzheng nühongjun shengping shiji*. Beijing: Nongcun duwu chubanshe, 1986, 48–52.

Lee, Lily Xiao Hong, and Sue Wiles. *Women of the Long March*. Sydney: Allen & Unwin, 1999.

Snow, Helen Foster. *Inside Red China*. 1977 reprint [with a new preface and biographical notes by the author]. New York: Da Capo Press, 1939, 175.

Liao Wenhai: *see* **Zhong Yuzheng**

Liao Xianlin: *see* **Liao Mengxing**

Lin Bai

Lin Bai, b. 1958, as Lin Baiwei in Beiliu County, Guangxi Province, is a writer.

After her father died of cancer when she was three, Lin Bai experienced an insecure and lonely childhood. She was sent to the countryside as an "educated youth" at seventeen and started writing poems then. Her first experience with publishing, however, was a disaster—one of her four poems published in *Guangxi Literature and Art* (Guangxi wenyi) had actually been plagiarized from another writer and it was soon discovered. Lin Bai was fortunate to pass the college entrance examination, which had just resumed that year (1977), and studied at Wuhan University from 1978 to 1982, majoring in library science. During college years, she lived under the shadow of her past and stopped writing completely. After graduation, Lin Bai first worked as a librarian in Guangxi Provincial Library, and it was not until autumn in the latter year, after a trip across China, that she regained her enthusiasm both for life and writing. Lin Bai has published prolifically since then, first in the field of poetry, then fiction. She worked in Guangxi Film Studio from 1985 to 1990 as an editor and screenwriter. This direct contact with the world of cinema also inspired and enriched her fiction writing. That year, Lin Bai was transferred to Beijing, where she worked for the newspaper *Chinese Cultural Forum* (Zhongguo wenhua bao), and also married a senior cultural official; their daughter was born in 1991. However, the marriage was not happy and Lin Bai is now separated from her husband. In spring 1996, she became one of thousands who were laid off as part of the reform and downsizing of government institutions, and Lin Bai now works at home as a full-time writer.

Two aspects of her writing distinguish it from her contemporaries: its autobiographical nature and thematic focus on female sexual desire and experience. In her novel trilogy *A War of One's Own* (Yigeren de zhanzheng, 1994); *Watching the Empty Years Pass By* (Shouwang kongxin suiyue, 1995); and *Speaking, My Room* (Shuoba, fangjian, 1997), frequent juxtapositions occur of fictional figures with "real" people and there is great similarity between Lin's personal life and that of the narrator/heroine in the story. Also, she adopts a first-person narrator voice and incorporates reflective psychological perspective, both of which further display the intense involvement of the writer in the material. Lin Bai's writing also deserves attention for exploring the problems that women face in maturity. Women's sexual identity and private experiences, such as masturbation, abortion, lesbian relationships, adultery, and narcissistic love for themselves, have never before been so fully exposed and sincerely examined.

The heterosexual relationships in Lin Bai's fiction, however, are all rather desperate. The female characters' longing for true love frequently clashes with harsh reality, and the hostility between and mutual exploitation of the sexes often leads to deadends, as in *Fatal Flight* (Zhiming de feixiang, 1995). In Lin Bai's most recent novel *Speaking, My Room*, domestic sexual oppression interweaves with social discrimination, and women's situation in the commercialized China of the 1990s takes an even bleaker turn. In terms of narrative language, Lin Bai developed a set of sophisticated narrative strategies as well as use of sensory, poetic language. Her construction of parallel-development structure, double-persona characters, and fluid female voices alternating between "I" and "we" demonstrate a unique *écriture feminine* based on bodily experience.

In the cultural market of 1990s China, Lin Bai's work enjoys a certain commercial success but also suffers from reductive reading, both because of its "sexual appeal" and bowdlerization by her publishers. *A War of One's Own*, for example, has been crudely edited to emphasize its sexual content, and several different editions now circulate. The more explicit parts of this book also caused much controversy among critics and the general public. While ordinary readers debate from a moralistic point of view about the propriety of recording "abnormal" sexual experiences, some critics read her work as a revival of gendered writing in the post-Mao era. Also, while some feminist critics may applaud Lin Bai for breaking taboos and telling the truth about women's experience and psychological reality, others criticize her explicit "exhibition" of women's sexual experience as satisfying voyeurism and confirming traditional ideas about gender difference. Clearly, Lin Bai's writing has become a contested field, where a multilayered audience with conflicting ideological agendas meet to thrash out differences.

KONG Shuyu

Chen Sihe. "Lin Bai lun." *Zuojia*, no. 5 (1998): 107–11.
Lin Bai. *Lin Bai zixuanji*. Gulin: Lijiang chubanshe, 1999.
———. "Shouwang kongxin suiyue." *Huacheng*, no. 4 (1995): 4–80.
———. "Shuoba, fangjian." *Huacheng*, no. 3 (1997): 6–72.
———. "Yigeren de zhanzheng." *Huacheng*, no. 3 (1994): 4–80.
Xu Kun. *Shuangdiao yexingchuan*. Taiyuan: Shangxi jiaoyu chubanshe, 1999, 72–88.
Yue Yue. "Jiushiniandai nüxing sixiaoshuo xingbie ruoshi." *Zhongguo wenhua yanjiu*, no. 3 (1999): 108–12.

Lin Baiwei: *see* **Lin Bai**

Lin Chin-chih
Lin Chin-chih [Lin Jinzhi], b. 1928, in Taipei, Taiwan, was one of the first women to undergo police training in Taiwan. She spent more than forty years in the police force and worked hard to gain training opportunities for women that would enable them to gain promotion.

Lin Chin-chih was born into a police family, her father and elder brother being policemen during the period of Japanese occupation. After the Japanese left in 1945, however, many people saw the police simply as an extension of the Japanese colonial government and constantly attacked them. Lin Chin-chih's brother was permanently disabled as the result of one such attack, and her grieving father died soon after, from illness. Feeling sure that a new era was dawning with the departure of the Japanese, Lin Chin-chih studied standard modern Chinese (*kuo-yü*) and looked for a means to support her family. One aftermath of the February Twenty-eighth Incident of 1947 was that, in December, women were admitted for the first time to basic training at the Taiwan Police Training Institute (Taiwan sheng ching-ch'a hsün-lien-so). This was because police authorities felt that the force was severely understaffed and needed a new image. At the suggestion of her brother-in-law, who worked in Hsin-tien Police Station, Lin Chin-chih registered for the force. After taking an examination, she became one of the students in the first group of women to be trained as policewomen in Taiwan in a three-month, junior cadres training class. Sixty-one women were accepted into that initial training class; after the institute underwent a name change (i.e., Taiwan Police School [Taiwan ching-ch'a hsüeh-hsiao]) in April 1948, the training was extended to a six-month course. After graduation, Lin Chin-chih was assigned to the third division at Chi-lung Harbor Police Bureau, a criminal investigation unit concerned mainly with ships, travelers, and anti-smuggling activities.

Smuggling was rife in the initial post-occupation period, and in 1955 Lin Chin-chih cracked a major drug case that was extensively covered in the media. The performance brought her work to the attention of the police commissioner, who could have promoted the officer despite her limited experience. However, because of her limited educational background and nonexistence of a channel for women's promotion, many years passed before Lin Chin-chih was transferred to administrative duties.

She worked with Chi-lung Harbor Police Bureau for twenty-one years and then requested a transfer to Taipei, where she served in the Inspectors' Office and the Personnel Office before being appointed deputy team leader of Taipei policewomen's branch (Taipei shih nü-ching tui) in 1977. Because the branch leader was at that time also team leader of the Security Unit, the bulk of leadership duties fell to Lin Chin-chih.

She put a great deal of effort into fighting for the provision of further training for women in the lower ranks. Although Lin Chin-chih herself had returned for extra training with the eighteenth intake of women many years after the initial junior cadres training class, there was no further opportunity for training. Formal education facilities were limited and promotions were difficult to gain, which left women at the bottom of the hierarchy with little incentive to perform well. When taking part in the KMT women cadres' training course, Lin Chin-chih strove to bring to the attention of the authorities the fact that the constable classes of the Central Police College (Ching-kuan hsüeh-hsiao hsün-kuan pan) had not recruited any female students. If policewomen did not have a channel through which they could receive further training, or a means by which they could be promoted, the best they could aspire to was remaining a cop on the beat. Lin Chin-chih therefore suggested that women be admitted to the Central Police College (Chung-yang ching-kuan hsüeh-hsiao) and, apart from the four years' formal training, women in the lower ranks be allowed to study for a degree or attend shorter training courses.

In 1967, Lin Chin-chih was accepted into the second intake of the Central Police College. She had to wait, however, until the sixth intake in June 1971 before commencing her studies, simply because there was no women's dormitory. Along with Hsiao Hsiu-feng (from the junior cadres training class) and Chih Hsiang-hua (from the twenty-sixth intake), Lin Chin-chih became one of the first women to train as an inspector in Taiwan. In 1974, the Central Police College started a formal training program, a two-year additional training course for women police officers.

Lin Chin-chih retired from the Inspectors' Office of Taipei Municipal Police Station (Taipei shih ching-ch'a-chü tu-ch'a-shih) in 1989. She and her husband, Ch'en Tai-chou, had both attended the Police Training Institute and had a good and loving marriage. Theirs was indeed a "police family." They had three sons and a daughter, and several of their sons and daughters-in-law became members of the force. Lin Chin-chih always considered herself blessed in her career because she had a mother and a sister-in-law to look after her children and the understanding and support of her husband. Lin Chin-chih therefore had few worries in her attempt to carry forward the torch lit by her father and brother.

CH' EN Ch'un-ying
(Translated by Jennifer Eagleton)

Ch'en Ch'un-ying. "Lin Chin-chih k'ou-shu fang-wen chi-lu." Unpublished transcript. 21 September 1995.
"Taipei-shih ko-chieh piao-yang mo-fan nü-ching." *Tzu-li wan-pao*, 7 March 1983, 2.

Lin Ch'iu-chin

Lin Ch'iu-chin [Lin Qiujin], b. 1909, in T'ai-nan County, Taiwan, was a coloratura soprano and a pioneer of vocal music education in Taiwan.

She grew up in a Christian family and was educated at the Presbyterian High School in T'ai-nan, acquiring there considerable knowledge and understanding of Western music in the church school musical environment. In 1929 Lin Ch'iu-chin was admitted to the Music College in Nakano, Japan, and majored in voice. Japanese music critics praised her as having "a distinguished and admirable voice" when she performed in Tokyo in 1933.

Soon after graduation, Lin Ch'iu-chin returned to Taiwan. In 1934, the Tokyo Taiwanese Compatriots' Association requested students who had returned from studies in Japan to form a minstrel group to tour Taiwan and introduce Western music to the local people. Lin Ch'iu-chin joined the group and was placed in charge of its vocal section. She was thus responsible for promoting Western music to the great bulk of the population.

In 1933, Lin Ch'iu-chin began teaching at T'ai-nan Presbyterian High School, and this marked the start of her six decades as a music educator. She went to Taiwan Normal University in 1951 to teach at the Music Department, soon becoming prominent as a core member in Taiwan's music circles. From the 1950s to the 1980s, Lin Ch'iu-chin treated the school as her home and devoted herself to teaching and training many excellent Taiwanese vocalists.

Lin Ch'iu-chin formally retired in 1980 and reoriented her professional focus as a vocalist and university professor to teaching vocal music to the wider community. She acted as choirmistress of Ch'ang-jung Girls' High School Alumni Choir, Chung-shan Church, and the combined Ch'eng-chung and T'ien-mu Japanese Presbyterian Church Choir.

For Lin Ch'iu-chin, music and religion were her whole life, her aim being to spread melody into the hearts of all. Her achievement was not simply to be a senior coloratura soprano in the early development of music in Taiwan but that she also pioneered vocal music education in Taiwan. Her life of performing and teaching paralleled the development of Taiwanese vocal music.

HO Shu-i
(Translated by George Li)

Yu Chien-ming. "Lin Ch'iu-chin." In *Tsou-kuo liang ko shih-tai ti Taiwan chih-yeh fu-nü fang-wen chi-lu.* Taipei: Chung-yang yen-chiu-yüan, Chin-tai-shih yen-chiu-so, 1994.

Lin Dai

Lin Dai, 1934–1964, born in Nanning, Guangxi Province, as Cheng Yueru, became in her short life a celebrated Hong Kong film star and four-time winner of the Best Actress Award at the Asian Film Festival.

She also used the English name Linda but adopted the name Lin Dai on entering films. According to some, the name was a transliteration of Linda, but others say it originated from two lines of Chinese poetry. Lin Dai's father, Cheng Siyuan, was an important political figure in Guangxi Province before 1949, and her mother, Jiang Xiuyun, came from an old family. Her parents divorced when Lin Dai was young and for a time she stayed with her father, who gave her little love and attention. When her father decided to remain in China and cooperate with the CCP, Lin Dai chose to go with her mother to Hong Kong in 1948. Lin Dai attended Sun Yat-sen Memorial Elementary School (Zhongshan jinian xiaoxue) in Guilin and Huiwen High School in Nanjing. In Hong Kong she studied at the New Asia College, but the money and jewelry her mother had brought from the mainland soon ran out and Lin Dai left school at seventeen to earn a living.

Yuan Yang'an, head of Changcheng Studios, was struck by Lin Dai's beauty when he saw her photograph in a photographer's window. Yuan got her name and address and set up an interview. He then offered the young woman a one-year contract, which she signed not so much to become an actress but because it included a basic allowance. Changcheng did not use Lin Dai in any of their films that year, instead requesting that she and many others, including famous film stars Li Lihua (q.v.), Huang He, and Yan Jun, attend study classes. However, these "study classes" were in effect classes in Marxist-Leninist thought. When Lin Dai refused to renew her contract, the studio threatened her with a large debt, which they claimed had been incurred on clothes, photography, etc. According to the contract, an actress was obliged to repay these expenses if she did not extend the contract. Lin Dai registered her protest by swallowing a large number of sleeping pills. She was found in time, but her name was splashed all over the newspapers and magazines in Hong Kong. This incident alerted the Hong Kong government to the political activities of the studio and a number of people were expelled from the colony. The stars who had attended the "study classes" with Lin Dai were then also free to join other studios.

The actor Yan Jun (d. 1980) had made a name for himself on stage and in film and had tried his hand at directing. When he joined Yonghua Studio, he asked its head, Li Zuyong, to give him a chance to make Lin Dai famous. She therefore formed an association with Yonghua Studio and starred in a film adapted from *Border Town* (Bian cheng), by the well-known novelist Shen Congwen. Yan Jun put a great deal of effort into this new film—entitled *Cuicui*—and played two different characters as well as directing it. *Cuicui* made Lin Dai an instant star in 1953, and she made several more pictures for Yonghua Studio; however, apart from *Jinfeng*, which was Taiwan's highest-grossing film, none of them were out of the ordinary. After the Yonghua Studio burned down, putting Li Zuyong virtually out of business, Lin Dai and Yan Jun were free of their commitments to him.

In negotiations with other studios, Lin and Yan offered themselves as a package, with Lin Dai as the female lead and Yan Jun as either the director or the male lead. Because they had begun living together, Lin Dai felt an obligation to Yan Jun, who had taken her as an unknown and made her into a star. The arrangement, however, reduced her chances of getting new roles. The couple nevertheless made two more films together: *The Fisherman's Song* (Yuge) for Xinhua Studio and *Love at Apricot Flower Stream* (Xinghua xi zhi lian) for Longfeng Studio.

Next, Lin Dai signed a three-year contract with Shaw Brothers Studio for three films per year, at the same time agreeing to make three films a year for Dianmao Studio. Perhaps because of an oversight, Shaw Brothers had not included in her contract a clause prohibiting her to make films for other companies. Lin Dai therefore entered into secret negotiations with Dianmao Studio, financed by Singapore tycoon Lu Yuntao. Dianmao offered her the highest pay per film, HK$45,000, and guaranteed to increase this the following year to HK$55,000. Her Dianmao contract was signed without the knowledge of Yan Jun.

When Shaw Brothers learned of the Dianmao arrangement, they asked Lin Dai to sign another three-year contract, matching the figure Dianmao had offered. Thus assured of six films a year for three years at the highest pay in Hong Kong, Lin Dai was offered by both studios the best scripts and the best backup for her films. All this left Yan Jun somewhat out in the cold. Lin Dai was the first of the new stars fostered in Hong Kong in the mid-1950s. Although many of them lacked experience, their audiences welcomed them, especially the younger generation, and the old stars of the Shanghai period who had dominated the silver screen began to fade away. Lin Dai still tried to include Yan Jun in her films, but increasingly the studios wanted to team her up with new male leads. Yan Jun made a couple of films with her in this period but then renewed his friendship with Li Lihua, whom he married in 1957, despite the fact that he had a wife in Shanghai.

Lin Dai made a series of quality films with Shaw Brothers and Dianmao in those three years and these were also box office successes. For the 1955 musical *Happy Years* (Huanle niannian), she practiced feverishly to become competent in the many dances that had to be performed, from *Meng Jiangnü* in the classical Chinese style to the cancan, the cha-cha, and the flamenco. For other films, she learned to ride and studied ikebana and the tea ceremony. The 1957 *Gold Lotus Flower* (Jin lianhua) in which Lin Dai played two women with different personalities won her the Best Actress Award at the fourth Asian Film Festival, which in turn earned her the title of "Asian Film Queen." She won again the following year with her performance in the period film *Diaochan*, directed by Li Hanxiang with whom Lin Dai collaborated in a series of lavish period films, including *Empire or Love* (Jiangshan meiren), which won twelve awards at the 1959 Asian Film Festival. These films also used the *huangmeidiao* folk tunes from Jiangsu and Zhejiang, thus creating a *huangmeidiao* craze in Hong Kong, Taiwan, and Southeast Asian Chinese communities.

After completing all the films under contract, Lin Dai went to the United States in 1959 to visit Hollywood studios and audit film and drama courses at Columbia University. She had planned to stay three months, but at the end of her studies a childhood friend offered to show her the sights of America. This was Long Shengxun, whom she had met again briefly in Hong Kong. The fifth son of the Yunnan warlord Long Yun, Long Shengxun was more popularly known as Long Wu Gongzi (Fifth young master Long), or Long Wu for short. Though Long Yun had remained in mainland China after 1949, the warlord had sent his favorite son Long Wu to study in the United States.

Fabulously wealthy, he was said to be a playboy who loved fast cars and women. Lin Dai could not have known this, but she toured America with him and extended her stay to eight or nine months. When Lin Dai finally returned to Hong Kong, Long Wu followed not long after. It is said that he had so many traffic offenses that the U.S. government gave him the choice of going to jail or leaving the country, and he opted for the latter. The romance of Lin Dai and Long Wu swept the Hong Kong media, and its political implications came as a complete surprise, even to them. Lin Dai belonged to the Free Film Workers' Association, closely associated with the KMT government of Taiwan. Long Wu's courtship raised speculation that he might lure Lin Dai to the mainland, however. The veteran actor Wang Yuanlong, who was head of the association, alerted Lin Dai to the implications of her affair, using the case of Zhou Xuan (*q.v.*), who had died in mainland China apparently from CCP persecution, as a warning. In an article written for a film magazine, Lin Dai refuted her close relationship with Long Wu and reconfirmed her loyalty to Taiwan. She then went on a tour to entertain its soldiers during the New Year holiday of 1959–60.

Despite her protestations, Lin Dai married Long Wu in 1961. The same year she won Best Actress Award at the Asian Film Festival for the third time, given for her performance in the musical *Charming Ladies* (Qian jiao bai mei). Cries of unfair were heard from other contenders, but when Lin Dai won the same award for the fourth time, for the romantic tragedy *Endless Love* (Buliao qing), praise for her acting came from all quarters.

Meanwhile, her marriage with Long Wu showed signs of strain for a number of reasons. While she continued to make films, Long Wu attended business dinners and other social activities alone, which increased his chances of meeting other women. Although he told Lin Dai they meant nothing to him, she could not put these dalliances totally out of mind. Moreover, their marital life was often complicated by the presence of Long Wu's old wet nurse, who came from Yunnan ostensibly to serve them but often created conflict. In addition, Long Wu started to criticize Lin Dai's film roles, especially in *Daji*, based on a well-known and lascivious queen of ancient China. He was further infuriated by a rumor circulating in the media about her alleged affair with Lu Yuntao, chairman of Dianmao Studio. The birth of a son, Long Zonghan, in 1963 does not seem to have improved the situation. In the meantime, Lin Dai felt the pressure of new stars who, at least to her mind, were gradually becoming more popular. These enormous family and career pressures clearly depressed Lin Dai, and she was found dead, at home, on 17 July 1964. She had had a row with her husband the previous evening and swallowed a lethal dose of sleeping pills before turning on the gas in her room. Her husband and friends argued that she had only meant to frighten Long Wu. The coroner, however, declared that because Lin Dai had taken an overdose of sleeping pills the case could not be categorized as an accident, and legally her death was suicide. Lin Dai's funeral was attended by thousands of fans, who also sent hundreds of wreaths and flowers. She was interred in Happy Valley Catholic Cemetery and fans continue to visit her gravesite, praying and saying rosaries; there were even reports that her death caused madness and suicide among them.

Lin Dai was not yet thirty years old when she died. In her thirteen years as a film star, the actress made more than forty pictures and won the Asian Film Festival Best

Actress award four times. Although perhaps gaining popularity initially because of her beauty, Lin Dai worked hard at her art and was recognized as a competent and many faceted actress. Suicide seems to have been the fate of many female stars, the best-known being Ruan Lingyu (*q.v.*), who preceded her, and Ledi and Weng Meiling, who followed. These women were all in their mid- to late twenties and had been catapulted to stardom while lacking the resilience to face setbacks. In love and marriage, they had relied heavily on the approval and support of men; once this was lost they did not have the courage to face life as single women. Such suicides continued unabated until urban women internalized feminist ideas.

Lily Xiao Hong LEE

Jingsheng and Xiquan, eds. *Xin Zhongguo mingrenlu.* Nanchang: Jiangxi renmin chubanshe, 1987, 195–96.
Liu Shaotang, ed. *Minguo renwu xiaozhuan,* vol. 8. Taipei: Zhuanji wenxue chubanshe, 135–42.
Qi Chengcun. "Tian du hongyan yun yanxing: Yinghou Lin Dai zhi si." *Zhongwai zazhi,* 36, no. 3 (September 1973): 130–34.
Zhang Yali. *Yidai yinghou Lin Dai.* Taipei: Xidai shuban, 1993.

Lin Hai-yin

Lin Hai-yin, b. 1918, in Osaka, Japan, as Lin Han-ying, is a Taiwanese author, editor, and publisher who played a significant role in the development of Taiwanese literature after World War II.

Her father, Lin Huan-wen, was a native of Miao-li County, Taiwan, while her mother was from the town of Pan-ch'iao near Taipei. Her father taught at Hsin-pu Public School, one of his students being Wu Chuo-liu, who became a well-known writer. Her parents went to live in Japan before Lin Hai-yin was born, and when she was five they moved to Beijing, settling in the area known as South City (Nan-ch'eng). Lin Hai-yin spent a significant period of her life in Beijing, where she grew up, was educated, worked, married, and had children.

When Lin Hai-yin was thirteen (1931), her father died, an event that signaled the end of her childhood. After graduating from Ch'un-ming Girls' High School in 1934, she passed the entrance examination for Pei-p'ing School of Journalism (Pei-p'ing hsin-wen chuan-ko hsüeh-hsiao), established by Cheng She-wo, and started as an apprentice journalist with *World Daily* (Shih-chieh jih-pao). Lin Hai-yin was promoted to journalist in 1937 and given the women's news section. The following year she married Hsia Ch'eng-ying (Xia Chengying, pen name Ho Fan [He Fan]), an editor with *World Daily.* Although her new husband came from a typical traditional literati family consisting of some thirty or forty members, Lin Hai-yin managed to remain on good terms with all of them. For a time, she attended Pei-p'ing Normal University (Pei-p'ing shih-fan ta-hsüeh) and worked in the library as a cataloger but soon returned to *World Daily* as editor of the women's page.

After the Japanese withdrew from Taiwan in 1945, Lin Hai-yin's relatives in Taiwan expressed a desire for her family's return. She and her husband finally decided to move there in 1948, not long before the communists won the mainland from the KMT. That autumn, at the age of thirty and with three children, Lin Hai-yin first set foot on Taiwanese soil, bringing with her her mother. Her mother's native land, however, was in reality foreign to Lin Hai-yin, and she has revealed in her work as well as in later interviews the complex thoughts she had at the time.

Lin Hai-yin's husband was invited by Hung Yen-ch'iu to work at the *Chinese Daily* (Kuo-yü jih-pao) on their arrival, but Lin Hai-yin remained a housewife. She began writing in her spare time and published works in newspapers such as the *Central Daily* (Chung-yang jih-pao) and *Chinese Daily*. In 1949, however, Lin Hai-yin became an editor with *Chinese Daily*, responsible for the weekend edition, and held the position until 1955. During this period, she met and befriended many women writers, including Ch'i-chün (*q.v.*), Liu Fang, Wang Yen-ju, and Liu Hsien-ssu. All writers for the *Central Daily* supplement; they became lifelong friends. Lin Hai-yin's writings at that time were mainly prose and have been collected in *The Ilex Tree* (Tung-ch'ing shu) and *Silhouettes from the Literary World* (Chien-ying hua wen-t'an). She wrote mainly about everyday family stories, but readers welcomed her work because she also pondered life's questions.

Lin Hai-yin gave birth to her fourth child in 1953, at the age of thirty-five, and within a month of the birth accepted the position of editor of *Lien-ho-pao*'s literary supplement, a position held for ten years. This period when she was at her most creative also featured an important stage in the post-war development of Taiwanese literature. Lin Hai-yin excelled in her role as editor of a literary supplement; she allowed mainland writers to continue placing their works in the publication and also provided a space for Taiwanese writers, who had had few opportunities to publish. When the KMT took over Taiwan from the Japanese in 1945, they did away with the Japanese-language pages in all the newspapers. The sudden change in language policy did not allow sufficient time for the Taiwanese people, who had until then been reading Japanese, to familiarize themselves with modern Chinese. Additional factors relating to the almost complete disappearance of Taiwanese writers were the occurrences of a serious post-war economic crash and political terrorism that began with the February Twenty-eighth Incident of 1947. Taiwanese writers were later deprived of any chance of publication when the government endorsed a period of "anti-communist literature."

Many Taiwanese writers remember with gratitude Lin Hai-yin's efforts on their behalf. Her first step as editor in 1953 was to increase the literary and artistic content of the supplement. The work of such writers as Ho Hsin, Hung Yen-ch'iu, Hsieh Ping-ying (*q.v.*), Ch'i-chün, Chang Hsiu-ya, Kuo Liang-hui, and Meng Yao appeared frequently on its pages. At the same time, Lin Hai-yin opened a window for the people of Taiwan by publishing news of foreign literature and extracts from foreign works and also initiated a series of columns, each written by a different writer. Ho Fan's column "Glass-topped Desk" (Po-li tien-shan) critiqued society and culture and struck a chord with many people.

Lin Hai-yin was the first to value the work of Taiwanese writers such as Chung Chao-cheng and Chung Li-ho, and Lin Hai-yin discovered a new generation of fiction writers typified by Huang Ch'un-ming, Chang Hsi-kuo, Lin Huai-min, and Ch'i-teng-sheng. Wen Hsin's novella *Ch'ien-sui kuei* was published in Lin Hai-yin's supplement, as was Chung Chao-cheng's famous novel *Lu-ping hua* and Chung Li-ho's *Ts'ang-yin* and *Tso-t'ien*. Lin Hai-yin's championing of authors neglected by the post-war media in Taiwan was a great encouragement to them. Chung Chao-cheng later recalled his reaction when he read Wen Hsin's *Ch'ien-sui kuei* in the supplement: "This was a great shock and stimulation to us Taiwanese writers. People like us can also have things published in the supplement? The surprise, joy and envy we felt [that the writer had been published] was a complex experience."

In addition to this work, in 1957 Lin Hai-yin and Ho Fan joined in the work of establishing *Literary Star* (Wen-hsing tsa-chih) for which they assumed editorial responsibility for four years. They put together *Introducing Taiwanese Literary Writers* (Pen-sheng wen-i tso-chia chieh-shao), which featured eleven writers, including Chung Li-ho, Chung Chao-cheng, Cheng Ch'ing-wen, Liao Ch'ing-hsiu, and Wen Hsin. Chung Li-ho was grateful for the interest Lin Hai-yin took in his writing as well as his personal life. The night he died, in 1960, Lin Hai-yin wrote an elegy mourning this brave friend in literature who would not allow even tuberculosis to stop his writing. In the harsh political environment of that period, Lin Hai-yin's concern for Taiwanese writers induced the birth of many a worthwhile work. The writer Cheng Ch'ing-wen has said: "Even now, I miss Ms. Lin Hai-yin, who was the editor of the literary supplement to *Lien-ho-pao* in those days. She pushed open a stout city gate, thereby liberating an area that had long been prohibited to certain writers."

In 1967 January, Lin Hai-yin was among those who created *Pure Literature Monthly* (Ch'un-wen-hsüeh yüeh-k'an), which was followed the next year by the establishment of Ch'un-wen-hsüeh Publishing House. She wrote more than one hundred personal invitations to literary friends to submit work. The *Monthly* provided a valuable literary venue, and the work of many writers who were published in it eventually gained positive critical attention. The publication carried foreign literature as well as the work of Chinese writers of the 1930s and was an important literary venue at a time when the journals *Hsien-tai wen-hsüeh*, *Wen-hsüeh chi-k'an*, *Taiwan wen-i*, and *Li shih-k'an* were also active. Retaining a focus on literature, however, meant that the *Monthly*'s sales were low and funds were always problematic; the publication finally ceased in 1972 after running for five years and two months and putting out sixty-two issues. Ch'un-wen-hsüeh Publishing House continued to publish literary books and magazines and in its later period turned more toward history and nostalgia. Lin Hai-yin also spent many years editing the complete works of Ho Fan in twenty-five volumes. For her editorial work, Lin Hai-yin won the Golden Tripod Prize given by the Government Information Office of the Executive Yuan for contributions to the field of publishing and editing of books (*ch'u-pan-lei t'u-shu chu-pien*).

Lin Hai-yin remains enthusiastic about literary creation, editing, and publishing and has received kudos in all three areas. Her daughter, writer Hsia Tsu-li [Xia Zuli], said: "Writing is her love; editing was her work; publishing was her ideal." In the field of creative writing, Lin Hai-yin published 437 works in the twenty years since she began writing in 1948. Her fiction, prose, and children's literature have been well received. Some of her short stories are collected in *Green Seaweed and Salty Eggs*

(Lü-tsao yü hsien-tan), but her short story collection on her Beijing childhood is what established her literary fame.

The many years she lived in Beijing imbued in Lin Hai-yin's works the special atmosphere of the city, and in 1960 her reminiscences of childhood were gathered into the collection *Old Stories from the South City* (Ch'eng-nan chiu-shih), which also came out in an illustrated edition and was later made into a film (*Memories of Old Beijing*). Her Ying-tzu character is the young Lin Hai-yin, through whose early eyes and heart we experience the people and events of Beijing. The stories encompass the cultural history and memory of the city as well as the daily life of its ordinary people, their feelings, loves, life, and laughter rippling through the lines. Sustaining naturalness and great tenderness, the stories convey a special compassion and sensitivity. Since it was first published, *Old Stories from the South City* has been critically acclaimed.

In addition, Lin Hai-yin wrote a series of stories depicting women in traditional Chinese marriages, revealing in them a woman writer's concern for feminist topics. Her story "Candle" (Chu), for example, tells of a woman who could not accept her husband's taking a concubine and finally becomes paralyzed. The critic Yeh Shih-t'ao commented that it is a story with a horrific theme but perfect technique. Lin Hai-yin's story "Chin Li-yü's Pleated Skirt" (Chin Li-yü ti pai-chien ch'ün) presents the sad fate of a concubine who gave birth to a son and heir but who had no status herself, even in death. Ch'i Pang-yüan pointed out that what makes this story unforgettable is its lingering aftertaste, when one dwells on what has been left unsaid. Women protagonists of different generations who experience the conflict between love and marriage people her novels *Hsiao Yün*, *Spring Wind* (Ch'un-feng), and *The Journey of Meng-chu* (Meng-chu ti lü-ch'eng). All three end with "the other woman" choosing to retreat from an illicit romantic attachment and journeying on to a distant place.

When Lin Hai-yin talked about the principles of writing, she said that a writer must write about the familiar. As to technique, Lin Hai-yin used brief and simple words to express ideas. She worked hard at being author, editor, and publisher in order to put her literary ideals into practice and received many awards and praise for her efforts. In 1994, for example, Lin Hai-yin was recognized by her peers in the World Chinese Language Writers' Association and the Asian Chinese Writers' Literary Fund for her "contribution as a long-time Chinese-language writer" and in 1998 received a Lifelong Achievement Award from the World Chinese Language Writers' Association. In 1999 she received the May Fourth Award and the Literary Contribution Award, while the year 2000 brought the Honorary Literature and Art Medal, awarded by the Chinese Writers' Association (Chung-kuo wen-i tso-chia hsieh-hui). Her complete works in twelve volumes were published in May 2000, and an audiovisual rendition of her memoirs was published at the same time. In the literary world of Taiwan, Lin Hai-yin's contribution and achievement are outstanding in every field.

YANG Ts'ui
(Translated by Lily Xiao Hong Lee and Sue Wiles)

Hsia Tsu-li. *Ts'ung ch'eng-nan tsou-lai—Lin Hai-yin chuan*. Taipei: T'ien-hsia wen-hua, 2000.

Lin Hai-yin. "The Candle." In *Bamboo Shoots after the Rain: Contemporary Stories by Women Writers of Taiwan*, eds. Ann C. Carver and Sung-sheng Yvonne Chang. New York: Feminist Press at the City University of New York, 1990, 17–25.

———. *Ch'uan-kuo lin-chien ti hai-yin—Lin Hai-yin ying-hsiang hui-i-lu*. Taipei: Yü-mu-tsu, 2000.

———. *Lin Hai-yin tso-p'in-chi*. Taipei: Yü-mu-tsu, 2000.

———. "Memories of Old Peking," trans. Cathy Poon. *Renditions*, special issue (Spring and Autumn 1987): 19–48.

"Lin Hai-yin." In *Chung-hua min-kuo tso-chia tso-p'in mu-lu*, vol. 2. Taipei: Hsing-cheng-yüan wen-hua chien-she wei-yüan-hui, 1995, 39–41.

Lin Han-ying: *see* **Lin Hai-yin**

Lin Huiyin

Lin Huiyin, 1904–1955, of Minhou, Fujian Province, was modern China's foremost woman architect, an expert in the history of ancient buildings, an artist, a famous poet during the 1930s, a novelist, and a writer.

She changed the character "yin" in her name to a homophonic character in 1935 to avoid confusion with a contemporaneous writer of the Shanghai school named Lin Weiyin. Lin Huiyin's grandfather Lin Xiaoxun was a Hanlin graduate at the end of the Qing period; an innovative thinker, he held office in various prefectural counties in Jinhua and Shimen, Zhejiang Province. Her father, Lin Changmin, graduated from Waseda University in Japan, majoring in politics and law; he was also a competent poet and writer. As head of the committee drafting a national constitution, Lin Changmin became a famous figure after the 1911 Revolution and served as a senator on the State Council of the Chinese Republic and as head of the judiciary.

Having thus grown up in a literary family of officials, Lin Huiyin received an excellent education, an eclectic mix of old and new, East and West. Between 1920 and 1921, she accompanied her father on a fact-finding tour of Europe. While Lin Huiyin was in London, she was influenced by her landlady, an English architect, to study architecture. During this period, Lin Huiyin also came to know two of her father's friends: the famous poet Xu Zhimo (1897–1931) and Liang Sicheng (b. 1901). Xu Zhimo became an intimate, lifelong friend whom she admired and he helped her to develop her own literary creativity. Liang Sicheng, the eldest son of the reformer Liang Qichao and subsequently China's greatest specialist in the history of architecture, became her husband and lifelong collaborator.

When the Indian poet/philosopher Tagore visited China in 1925 in response to an invitation from Liang Qichao and Lin Changmin, Lin Huiyin was thoroughly involved in the welcome and, together with Xu Zhimo, acted as interpreter. She even played the leading lady in Tagore's play *Chitra* and was a celebrity for a time. In June of that year, Lin Huiyin accompanied Liang Sicheng to America, where she was admitted to the College of Fine Arts at the University of Pennsylvania and chose to major in architecture. After graduation, she studied stage design at the Yale University Drama Institute, eventually becoming the most qualified person in China in this field.

In March 1928, she and Liang Sicheng married in Ottawa, Canada. After their wedding, they traveled to Europe and explored architecture and art for several months.

Together with her husband, in 1929 she accepted an offer of employment in the Architecture Department of Dongbei University in Shenyang, where she lectured on the history of carved ornaments and taught professional English. Her daughter Liang Zaibing was born in 1929; the following year Lin Huiyin succumbed to pulmonary tuberculosis and returned to Beijing to recuperate.

Both Lin Huiyin and her husband joined the Chinese Society of Building Sciences in 1931. She worked with them as a proofreader and co-editor, often assisting with identifying ancient architecture in the field in China's northern region. Alone and in collaboration with her husband, she wrote many innovative treatises and investigative reports, including "Special Features of Chinese Architecture" (Lun Zhongguo jianzhu zhi jige tezheng), "Summary of a Preliminary Investigation into the Ancient Architecture of Shanxi" (Jinfen gu jianzhu yucha jilüe), and "Jottings on Suburban Architecture of Beijing" (Pingjiao jianzhu zalu). These works established the foundation for the history of contemporary Chinese architecture.

Also that year, Lin Huiyin wrote poems in quantity (she was subsequently to become a poet of significance in the New Moon school) and as well published fiction, plays, and prose. In the short novel *Ninety-nine Degrees* (Jiushijiu du zhong), Lin Huiyin used an extremely modern montage technique. She ingeniously strung together the lives of forty-odd figures from different strata of Beijing society living in 99 degrees Fahrenheit heat, making distinct and vivid contrasts between them and demonstrating acute insight and sensitivity. In her prose "Inside and Beyond the Window" (Chuangzi nei wai), Lin Huiyin employed a subtle technique to demonstrate the entrenched lack of understanding between the two strata of the elite and intellectual and the working masses. This work was listed among the national textbooks of Southwest Union University. She was at that time involved in various literary activities with the Beijing school of scholars. She compiled "Selected Fiction from *Dagongbao*'s Literary and Arts Supplement" (Dagongbao wenyi fukan xiaoshuo xuan) and adjudicated literary and art awards for their journal. After the formation of the New Moon Society by Zhou Zuoren, Shen Congwen, Zhu Guangqian, and others, Lin Huiyin sat on the Editorial Committee of the Beijing school's important publication *Literary Magazine* (Wenxue zazhi). She joined the Poetry Reading Society of Northern Poets, enthusiastically promoting the younger generation, and during the 1930s became a central figure of the literary world in the north. She bore her second child, a boy named Congjie, in 1932.

At the outbreak of the Sino-Japanese War, the whole family headed south. Although they lived under unsettled and difficult circumstances and Lin Huiyin was ill, she nevertheless persevered with her research into ancient architectural history. At the end of the war, they returned to Beijing, and she and her husband established the Architecture Department at Tsinghua [Qinghua] University. In preparation for the entry of the Red Army into the city of Beijing in 1948, she and her husband completed "An Index to the Cultural Relics and Ancient Architecture of the Nation" (Quanguo wenwu gu jianzhu mulu).

From the establishment of the PRC in 1949 to her death in 1955, Lin Huiyin was very active. She strongly advocated the preservation of Beijing's city walls and ancient architecture and was adamant that contemporary architecture incorporate the tradition of a national style. She assisted in the renovation of Huairentang within Zhongnanhai and participated in the designing of the national emblem of the PRC and the design and construction of the Monument to the People's Heroes in Tian'anmen. She was appointed as a professor (Grade A) in the Architecture Department of Qinghua University and held a series of other positions. She sat on the Beijing Metropolitan Planning Committee, acting as its engineer, and was also an Executive Committee member of the Architectural Society of China and member of the Beijing Municipal People's Congress. Lin Huiyin wrote a series of articles in 1952 on ancient Chinese architecture for the column "Our Capital" in the *New Observer* (Xin guancha) and was editor of the *Journal of Architecture*. She was a reader for and wrote the preface of the large reference work *Colored Designs in Chinese Architecture*, published after her death, and co-authored "Historical Stages in the Development of Chinese Architecture" for the *Journal of Architecture*.

As she grew weaker—the cause of her death is not specified but it would seem that she never fully recovered from tuberculosis—Lin Huiyin spent increasingly longer periods in bed. At one stage, she was giving half of her lectures to her students from her sickbed. She died in hospital on 1 April 1955. The design Lin Huiyin had helped create for the Monument to the People's Heroes was used on her grave, which read: Grave of Architect Lin Huiyin.

GAO Yuanbao
(Translated by Katherine Kerr)

Chen Xuenan. "Guanyu Lin Huiyin xiaozhuan de xie buchong." *Zhuanji wenxue* (November 1991): 73–74.
Chen Zhongying and Chen Yuhe, comps. *Lin Huiyin shiji*. Beijing: Renmin wenxue chubanshe, 1985.
Liang Sicheng wenji. Beijing: Zhongguo jianzhu chubanshe, 1982.
Lin Zhu. "Liang Sicheng yu Lin Huiyin (2)." *Zhuanji wenxue*, 71, no. 1 (July 1997): 59–67.
Song Ruizhi, ed. *Zhongguo funü wenhua tonglan*. Jinan: Shandong wenyi chubanshe, 1995, 346–47.
Zhongguo xiandai zuojia xuanji, Lin Huiyin ji. Hong Kong: Sanlian shudian and Renmin wenxue chubanshe, 1990, 1–10, 325–41.

Lin Jinzhi: *see* **Lin Chin-chih**

Lin Lanying
Lin Lanying, b. 1918, in Putian County, Fujian Province, is an eminent physicist who has worked in the PRC in the area of semiconductor physics.

Her father, Lin Jianhua, served in the local government before becoming a high school teacher; her mother, Zhou Shuixian, devoted herself in the traditional manner to managing the household. Although the value of education was recognized in principle at that time, women rarely had access to it. Lin Lanying never wavered, however, in her determination to learn, and in the face of her daughter's insistence her mother gave permission for Lin Lanying to attend school.

She was admitted to the Physics Department at Fuzhou Union University at the age of eighteen and in 1940 joined the staff, first as a teaching assistant, then as a lecturer. Lin Lanying taught physics and mathematics and compiled a coursebook for optical experiments that was approved by the Ministry of Education as a university text. She was extremely talented but had been denied a university scholarship to study abroad on the grounds that the lecturer had refused to take part in religious activities. One of the professors recommended in 1948, however, that Lin Lanying undertake advanced training in mathematics at the Dickinson Institute in Pennsylvania, in the U.S.; the following year she transferred to Pennsylvania University majoring in solid physics and was awarded a master's degree in 1951 and a Ph.D. in 1955.

At this time, Lin Lanying, who never married, decided to focus on the new field of semiconductor physics. Her work as a senior engineer with a prominent American private company was the start of a lifelong commitment to studying semiconductor, mono-crystal materials in which she eventually became a recognized specialist in China. At this company, Lin Lanying headed the study of the physical properties of materials and components and proposed the method by which they successfully produced silicon mono-crystals, gaining wide respect for her scholarship and talent from both colleagues and employers. However, upon learning through her family that the leaders of the young PRC had expressed the wish that she put her talents to the service of her country, Lin Lanying decided to return home. Not without difficulty in that early Cold War period, she arrived back in China in 1957.

By autumn, Lin Lanying and her colleagues had produced China's first germanium mono-crystal, and in 1958 they produced the first silicon mono-crystal. At the beginning of the 1960s, she developed a new type of mono-crystal oven and in one year produced non-dislocation silicon mono-crystal as well as semiconductor gallium-arsenic (GaAs) mono-crystal. As head of the Materials Section of the Semiconductor Research Institute of the Chinese Academy of Sciences, Lin Lanying oversaw the development of various semiconductor materials in the first half of the decade, a period when much inspiring research was done.

She fared rather better during the Cultural Revolution than many of her fellow scientists and in the second half of the 1970s pioneered the study of several techniques. These include an improvement in the quality of silicon mono-crystals, technological methods for improving the quality of GaAs mono-crystals through the growth of gas and liquid phase epitaxy, the creation of ion-beam film technique, the development of SOS-CMOS integrated circuit materials, and the production of GaAs mono-crystal materials in space. Lin Lanying was awarded the State Science and Technology Progress Award and the Science and Technology Progress Award of the Chinese Academy of Sciences several times and published many papers in science journals both at home and abroad. In 1981 she was elected as an academician of the Chinese Academy of Sciences.

As a physicist, her research work has been rigorous and meticulous and her perseverance and realism have been rewarded by a string of distinguished academic achievements. This, together with Lin Lanying's social activism, serves as a fine example of female self-respect and independence for the women of China.

WANG Bing
(Translated by Hu Zhuanglin)

He Chunfan and Wang Zhanguo. "Lin Lanying." In *Zhongguo xiandai kexuejia zhuanji*, vol. 3. Beijing: Kexue chubanshe, 1992, 844–57.

Yingwen *Zhongguo funü*, ed. *Gujin zhuming funü renwu*, vol. 2. Shijiazhuang: Hebei renmin chubanshe, 1986.

Zhonghua quanguo fulian. *Zhongguo nüyuanshi*. Shenyang: Liaoning renmin chubanshe, 1995, 121–35.

Lin Qiaozhi

Lin Qiaozhi, 1901–1983, of Gulangxu Island near Xiamen, Fujian Province, was one of China's pioneers in gynecology and obstetrics.

When Lin Qiaozhi was only five years old, her mother died of cervical cancer, and the child. went to live with her eldest brother and his wife. This sad event planted in her the desire to become a doctor, in particular a gynecologist. Lin Qiaozhi's father, Lin Liangying, had received ten years of English education as a boy in Singapore, and his daughter also learned English, beginning in kindergarten. An English teacher at Xiamen Girls' High School (Xiamen nüzi zhongxue) introduced Lin Qiaozhi to English literature, so she formed the habit of reading.

After graduating from high school in 1921, the young woman went with her friend Yu Qiongying to Shanghai to sit the entrance examination for Peking Union Medical College. Halfway through the last paper, her friend fainted, and Lin Qiaozhi was called to assist. Because of this mishap, she did not complete her own paper but was admitted nevertheless, reportedly because of the calmness and efficiency she displayed in helping her friend. As a student, Lin Qiaozhi achieved high marks but also engaged in extracurricular activities such as basketball, oratory, and editing the student wall-paper. She graduated in 1929 as a doctor of medicine with the highest mark of her year, winning the Wenhai Award.

Lin Qiaozhi was appointed as a resident doctor of the Gynecology and Obstetrics Department of Peking Union Hospital. After six months, she acted as chief resident doctor and ten months after that, in 1931, was appointed formally to the position. A condition of being a chief resident at Union Hospital was that one remain single, so Lin Qiaozhi put thoughts of love and marriage aside. She felt that the role of a good wife and mother would be in conflict with the time and energy devoted to her work. In 1932, Lin Qiaozhi was offered the opportunity to further her studies in England, first at Manchester and then in London. She also went to Austria before returning to Beijing in 1933. Two years later, Lin Qiaozhi became a specialist in gynecology and obstetrics and in 1937 was associate professor. In 1939, with the assistance of the hospital she went to Chicago where, because of her excellent work, Lin Qiaozhi received admission to the Honorary Society of Natural Sciences. Not long after her return to Peking Union Hospital, she was appointed head of the Gynecology and Obstetrics Department, the first Chinese woman ever to head a department at Peking Union Hospital.

After the Pacific War broke out in December 1941, Union Hospital was forced by the Japanese to close its doors. Lin Qiaozhi therefore opened a private clinic but was invited to plan and establish Zhonghe Hospital's Gynecology and Obstetrics Department of which she became head. After the war, Lin Qiaozhi became part-time professor at the medical school at Peking University and from 1945 head of its Gynecology and Obstetrics Department. When Peking Union Hospital and its medical college reopened in 1947 and 1948, Lin Qiaozhi became professor in charge of gynecology and obstetrics. At the same time, she worked toward reestablishing the Gynecology and Obstetrics Department at Union Hospital. Just before the communists took over Beijing, a KMT official offered Lin Qiaozhi a plane ticket out of Beijing, but she chose to remain with her work and patients.

Peking Union Hospital was taken over by the new PRC government in 1951, and during the Cultural Revolution the hospital was renamed Capital Hospital (Shoudu yiyuan). Throughout the pre-Cultural Revolution period, Lin Qiaozhi remained head of the department. She was also instrumental in establishing a gynecology and obstetrics hospital in Beijing, and Peng Zhen, mayor of Beijing, consulted her every step of the way in its planning, which was completed in 1959.

Lin Qiaozhi was consequently named honorary director of the Beijing Gynecology and Obstetrics Hospital and made sure she spent time there every week. During the Cultural Revolution, Lin Qiaozhi was condemned as a "reactionary academic authority" and ordered to stand down from her position as head of gynecology and obstetrics. She even lost the right to see patients and later was demoted to doing the work of interns because of an unsubstantiated accusation of being an American spy. After the Cultural Revolution, however, Lin Qiaozhi resumed her previous titles and responsibilities.

She worked at her job as a gynecology and obstetrics doctor and teacher for more than half a century. There are three main aspects to her contribution. First, Lin Qiaozhi was an outstanding clinician. Her years of experience and insistence on seeing patients personally worked to her advantage. The doctor was known for her astute observations, the high standards she demanded of herself and others, and cautiousness. Lin Qiaozhi had an uncanny ability for accurate diagnosis and was bold in taking calculated risks. Where normal procedure might be to perform a hysterectomy, she would suspect other reasons for cancer-like symptoms; through careful monitoring and removal of only the collateral appendage, the doctor saved the uteruses of several young women. Lin Qiaozhi also initiated a cure for the hemolytic condition in newborn babies by a total blood transfusion; this procedure saved more than one hundred babies born at Union Hospital with this condition. In her many years of clinical practice, the doctor also tried different ways to enable infertile women to conceive. She was therefore often called "the Goddess of Mercy who gives children" (*songzi guanyin*).

Second, Lin Qiaozhi achieved excellent results in her research into many problems in her field. When going to Chicago for further study, she worked on the contraction of the uterus and in utero fetal respiration. Lin Qiaozhi also studied tuberculosis of the pelvic organs and the mechanism of labor and miscarriage. Because early detection of cervical cancer saves the lives of many women, Lin Qiaozhi proposed in 1958 a general survey of the population of women in Beijing. With the help of her colleague Zhang Caifen, she undertook a pilot study in the eastern area of Beijing and obtained data from fifty thousand cases. The area was extended when Beijing Gynecology and Obstetrics Hospital became involved, and another ninety thousand cases were studied. The results of this study were published in the *Journal of Chinese Gynecology and Obstetrics*. Treatment was given at the same time as the women were examined, which prevented many cases of cervical cancer. The Beijing study inspired a national survey of twenty cities in which over 1.1 million women over twenty-five years of age were examined; it was found that 145 women out of every one hundred thousand had the disease. The results published in the *Journal of Chinese Medicine* drew international attention because a study with such a large sample and treatment was unprecedented. The data enabled researchers to find the causes of the disease, which in turn led to proposals for prevention, so that the death rate from cervical cancer was greatly lowered. According to statistics from the Beijing area, the incidence of this disease in 1972–76 was 14.3 percent of the 1958–59 figure. The rate of detection increased eight times, so that the rate of cure was also higher.

Another tumor that seriously threatened women's lives was chorioepithelioma. Its high rate of malignancy, rapid deterioration, and shifting meant that surgery was unsatisfactory, and the death toll from the disease was high, with tens of millions of women dying from it in China alone. Lin Qiaozhi proposed that chorioepithelioma be put on the national scientific research plan, and a study group for this purpose was established at Peking Union Hospital, with Liang Hongchao as its head. After more than twenty years' work, researchers were finally able to effect a cure in most cases, the success rate rising from 10 percent in 1959 to over 80 percent in 1978. This research also allowed the recovery rate of those afflicted with hydatidiform mole (grape mole) to reach almost 100 percent. In the case of metastatic encephaloma, the chemical treatment they developed was more effective than the radiation treatment used abroad and had fewer side effects. Their research received several national awards. The summation of Lin Qiaozhi's research and clinical experience appeared in a book that she edited entitled *Gynecological Tumors* (Fuke zhongliu, 1982), which won First Prize in a National Scientific Book Award. On a more populist level, her works *Family Health Adviser* (Jiating weisheng guwen) and *Child Rearing Encyclopedia* (Yu'er baike quanshu) have been welcomed by the public.

Third, Lin Qiaozhi contributed greatly to China's family planning policy. As early as 1956, she seized an opportunity when Mao Zedong (1893–1976) was recuperating in Qingdao to talk to him about the need to control population growth. This was, of course, before the famous incident in 1957 in which the economist Ma Yinchu raised the issue with the CCP. In their brief, arguing from the medical point of view for family planning, Lin Qiaozhi and her colleague Wang Shuzhen supported Ma's proposal and included practical measures and methodology that could be put into action. In the 1950s, Lin Qiaozhi led a team to the suburbs of Beijing and other parts of Hebei and Henan to undertake surveys and promote family planning. In the 1960s, she set up a research group in her department to undertake specialized research evaluating types of contraceptives that were then available. With the cooperation of Beijing Gynecology and Obstetrics Hospital, the group designed an intra-uterine device made of metal and plastic, calling it the Beijing intra-uterine contraceptive ring (*Beijingxing gongnei jieyuhuan*). Lin Qiaozhi also worked on the detection of deformed fetuses. For a variety of reasons, every year in China 260,000 babies were born with congenital deformities, a source of heartache to the parents and a burden to the nation. Working in a research group under the leadership of Wang Niangu, Lin Qiaozhi developed cell genetics, enzyme studies, and molecular biology in order to improve prenatal diagnosis. The group also made use of advances in acoustics and optics to aid in the examination of the fetus. She and her colleagues gained several national honors for their work.

Lin Qiaozhi's contribution to her profession won her the recognition of the PRC government as well as the scientific community. She joined the NCP in 1955 and later became a member of its Standing Committee. In that year, Lin Qiaozhi became the first woman elected as an academician of the Chinese Academy of Sciences. She was elected deputy president of the Chinese Medical Association (Zhonghua yixuehui) in 1956, the year its Gynecology and Obstetrics Association was formed. Lin Qiaozhi was also elected chair and chief editor of the *Journal of Chinese Gynecology and Obstetrics* and in 1957 was appointed to membership of the Medical Section of the State Council's Scientific Planning Committee and from 1973 to 1977 was a consultant to the World Health Organization's Medical Research Advisory Committee. She was active as a distinguished woman in the ACWF, progressing from deputy chair of the Beijing association to deputy chair of the national organization in 1978.

Lin Qiaozhi is said to have been straightforward and upright in her dealings with people. She was kind and sensitive toward patients but applied strict standards for doctors and nurses. In her almost sixty years of professional life, Lin Qiaozhi delivered more than fifty thousand babies, many of whom would not have lived but for her skill and patience. The impact this wonderful doctor had is clear from the number of men and women all over China and abroad who bear names such as Nianlin (remembering Lin), Silin (thinking of Lin), Yilin (relying on Lin), and Ailin (loving Lin): she delivered all of them. Therefore, although Lin Qiaozhi never married or had children of her own, she was never lonely and also remained close to her nephews and nieces. Lin Qiaozhi contributed to the discovery of cures to many diseases detrimental to women's life and health and was one of the engineers of China's family planning program. Her funeral was attended by almost a thousand people, among them political leaders such as Kang Keqing (*q.v.*), Deng Yingchao (*q.v.*), and Peng Zhen, as well as scientists, former patients, and those whom Lin Qiaozhi had brought into this world. Her body was donated to medical research.

Lily Xiao Hong LEE

Ma Yunong and Wang Wu. *Lin Qiaozhi zhuan*. Beijing: Guangming ribao chubanshe, 1985.
Wu Chongqi and Deng Jiarong. *Lin Qiaozhi*. Beijing: Zhongguo qingnian chubanshe, 1985.
Yingwen *Zhongguo funü*, ed. *Gujin zhuming funü renwu*, vol. 2. Shijiazhuang: Hebei renmin chubanshe, 1986, 800–06.
Zhongguo xiandai kexuejia zhuanji. Beijing: Kexue chubanshe, 1994, vol. 6, 628–40.
Zhonghua quanguo fulian *Zhongguo nüyuanshi*. Shenyang: Liaoning renmin chubanshe, 1995, 137–60.
"Zhuidao weida yixuejia Lin Qiaozhi." *Renmin ribao*, 8 May 1985, 1.

Lin Qiujin: *see* **Lin Ch'iu-chin**

Lin Zongsu

Lin Zongsu, 1878–1944, a native of Fujian Province, was one of China's most important feminist political revolutionaries of the late Qing-early Republican period. She became one of China's first woman newspaper editors and journalists and, through her positions on various newspapers, published widely on women's rights. Lin Zongsu assumed a leadership role in significant women's organizations until 1913, when the women's political lobby was suppressed by Yuan Shikai as part of his crackdown on democracy.

Lin Zongsu began revolutionary activities when she joined her elder brother, journalist Lin Baiyong (1873–1926), in Hangzhou around 1898. While there, Lin Zongsu socialized with the revolutionary young intellectuals of the Zhejiang Education Society (Zhejiang jiaoyu hui). During this period, she met Qiu Jin (see *Biographical Dictionary of Chinese Women: The Qing Period*), China's most famous female revolutionary martyr. Lin Zongsu and Qiu Jin were both dedicated to principles of republicanism and gender equality and the necessity of using physical force as a means to achieve these goals. In 1902 Lin Zongsu continued her involvement with the burgeoning anti-Qing groups by attending classes at the Shanghai Patriotic Women's School (Aiguo nüxuexiao), when it opened as a wing of the Patriotic Schools; the latter were radically anti-Qing and functioned briefly with the protection of the foreign concessions where they were housed. The founder of these schools, Cai Yuanpei (1868–1940), intended that they become centers for discussion of revolutionary theory and political activism: the radical paper *Subao* became their semi-official organ. During a Qing government clampdown on revolutionary activities in 1903, however, both *Subao* and the Patriotic Schools were closed.

Lin Zongsu's brother Lin Baiyong remained constant in his support for his sister's revolutionary activities. Not only did he encourage her participation in the Patriotic Girls' School but also traveled with her in 1903 to Japan. Like many young revolutionaries of the time, the two intended to develop their political and revolutionary skills outside of Qing government control while furthering their knowledge of the modernization process. During her year in Japan, Lin Zongsu studied at the Tokyo Women's Higher Normal College. Throughout this time, brother and sister were both active in the Chinese students' associations that fomented anti-Qing sentiment. Lin Baiyong had worked closely with Cai Yuanpei in the establishment of the Patriotic Study Society (Aiguo xueshe) and the Patriotic Schools, and his enthusiasm for republicanism led him to political positions in the republican parliament after the 1911 Revolution. He remained active in journalism and politics until his execution, at the age of fifty-three, during the chaotic period of warlord rule.

In 1903, a preface that Lin Zongsu wrote for one of China's earliest feminist treatises, Jin Songcen's *A Tocsin for Women* (Nüjie zhong), was published. The book-length manuscript called upon the women of China to liberate themselves and their nation from oppression. As was common during late Qing, the weakness of women was perceived to be a major cause of the weakness of China, and Jin Songcen, like

Kang Youwei before him, advocated improvement in the status of women as a key to strengthening China. Lin Zongsu's contribution resoundingly endorsed this "wake-up" call to the women of her nation. She wrote of the importance of women's participation in revolutionary military action and stressed that they must fight for equal rights because men would not concede them. Gender equality in all aspects of life—social, economic, and political—were advocated in Jin Songcen's *Tocsin* but so also was women's responsibility to participate in the overthrow of the Qing government. Over the next few years, Lin Zongsu applied herself to these dual revolutionary tasks.

On returning to Shanghai in 1904, she immersed herself in the newspaper industry. Her brother Lin Baiyong was at that time editing the revolutionary newspaper *China Vernacular News* (Zhongguo baihua bao), and Lin Zongsu contributed to it many articles calling for revolution. *China Vernacular News* was among the earliest publications to promote through practical demonstration the use of vernacular Chinese; the articles in its twenty-four issues were written in this "democratic" grammar. Later that year, Lin Zongsu herself assumed the position of associate editor for Cai Yuanpei's revolutionary paper *Warning Bell Daily* (Jingzhong ribao). The daily survived in Shanghai until March 1905, when it was closed by the Qing government. Like other radical Shanghai papers, *Warning Bell Daily* covered a range of material including current affairs, political debate, theoretical criticism, and commentary on democratic activities around the globe. The publication demonstrated its support for use of the vernacular by using this style in its articles, but the paper was also unique because of its inclusion of cartoons and pictures.

The Lin family's revolutionary commitment manifested in military action as well as in journalism. Lin Zongsu's sister Lin Zongxue gained fame as one of China's "Amazons" during the battles to defeat Qing government forces in 1911. She was active in the Women's Recovery Army (Nüzi guangfu jun) led by the youthful Yin sisters (Yin Ruizhi and Yin Weijun); this force conducted numerous daring bombing raids around Zhejiang. The army regrouped and under its new name of Zhejiang Women's Army took part in the battle to liberate Nanjing. A few months later, Lin Zongxue organized in Shanghai the Women's Citizen's Army (Nü guomin jun), which became the preeminent lobby group for women's participation in the military.

Lin Zongsu's commitment to revolutionary activism was formalized with party membership in 1905 when she joined Sun Yat-sen's Tongmenghui. As was common at that time, political party membership was fluid and far from exclusive, and Lin Zongsu also joined the Socialist Party of China, headed by Jiang Kanghu, when it formed in 1911. It was from her base in the Socialist Party that Lin Zongsu's major activities concerned with women's rights were conducted. After the collapse of the Qing dynasty in October, she established China's first women's suffrage organization, the Women's Suffrage Comrades' Alliance (Nüzi canzheng tongzhi hui); the organization formed in Shanghai on 12 November as a sub-branch of the Socialist Party, which itself had been formed the previous week.

The Women's Suffrage Comrades' Alliance was committed to educating women about the effect politics had on their status in society. It organized study sessions and public addresses as well as a host of publishing activities for which Lin Zongsu had already proven ability. In 1911 she had opened a journal titled *Women's Times* (Funü shibao), which was specifically for women and became the Alliance's organ for disseminating information on the important topic of women's suffrage. The specific goals of the Alliance typified women's suffrage organizations around the globe: to enhance women's knowledge of politics, nurture women's political strengths, and win for women their rights as full citizens to participate in politics. Men were limited to honorary membership and only women over the age of sixteen could become full members.

The Alliance made a tremendous impact with its first foray into official national politics. On 5 January 1912, only five days after the establishment of the interim parliament, Lin Zongsu made an appointment with Dr. Sun Yat-sen, provisional president of the new republic, to discuss the issue of women's suffrage and gender equality. She hoped that their amicable meeting in which Dr. Sun reportedly affirmed women's right to vote would succeed in swaying political opinion in favor of gender equality. A practiced political operator, Lin Zongsu immediately published in *Women's Times* details of her conversation with Dr. Sun. Her article caused a furor among conservative supporters of the republic, and Dr. Sun's apparent unequivocal support for women's suffrage attracted inconvenient criticism. The conservative Zhang Binglin, for example, noted in a formal written complaint that, in making ill-considered comments to the women's suffrage activists, Dr. Sun was stepping beyond his brief. Lin Zongsu's article clearly had the desired effect of putting women's suffrage on the mainstream political agenda. Between January and March, while the Constitution was under debate, other suffrage groups formed, the largest being the Alliance for Women's Participation in Politics (Nüzi canzheng tongmenghui), founded by Tang Qunying (*q.v.*); it absorbed Lin Zongsu's Women's Suffrage Comrades' Alliance in late February. (For details of Lin Zongsu's activities as part of this larger women's suffrage group, *vide* Tang Qunying.)

Lin Zongsu was forced to cease her political activities when Yuan Shikai suppressed democracy in 1913. The Socialist Party of China was ordered to disband, as was the Alliance for Women's Participation in Politics. Lin Zongsu's activities from this point on are unclear. One source (Gao Kuixiang and Shen Jianguo) states that she went to Nanjing to engage in education and commercial activities to subsidize her brother's newspapers. The editors of *Funü cidian*, however, state that the activist was forced into hiding in the Jiangsu region, but no further detail is provided.

Lin Zongsu died of illness in Kunming in 1944 at the age of sixty-six.

Louise EDWARDS

Funü cidian. Beijing: Qiushi chubanshe, 1990.
Gao Kuixiang and Shen Jianguo, eds. *Zhonghua gujin nüjie pu*. Beijing: Zhongguo shehui chubanshe, 1991.
Jing Shenghong. "Xinhai geming hou de zhengqu nüzi canzheng yundong." *Nanjing shizhi*, no. 6 (1996): 13–15.
Lin Zongsu. "Houguan Lin nüshi xu." In Jin Songcen, *Nüjie zhong*. Shanghai: Datong shuju, 1903.

————. "Nüzi canzheng tongzhi hui xuanyan shu." *Funü shibao*, no. 5 (1912): 17–19.

Shang Hai et al., eds. *Minguo shi da cidian*. Beijing: Zhongguo guangbo dianshi chubanshe, 1991.

Wang Jiajian. "Minchu de nüzi canzheng yundong." In *Zhongguo funü shi lunwenji*, eds. Zhang Yufa and Li Youning. Taipei: Shangwu yinshuguan, 1988, 577–608.

Zhejiangsheng xinhai geming shi yanjiu hui. *Xinhai geming Zhejiang shiliao xuanji*. Hangzhou: Zhejiang remin chubanshe, 1981, 483–91.

Zhou Yaping. "Lun Xinhai geming shiqi de funü canzheng yundong." *Lishi dang'an* (Jing), no. 2 (1993): 118–23, 125.

Lin Zongxue: *see* **Lin Zongsu**

Lin-Cai Sunü: *see* **Lin-Ts'ai Su-nü**

Lin-Ts'ai Su-nü

Lin-Ts'ai Su-nü [Lin-Cai Sunü], born Ts'ai Su-nü in 1902, in Pei-kang, Taiwan, devoted considerable time and effort to community work and women in Taiwan.

The daughter of a rich family, she benefited from the enlightened views of her father, who had been among the first batch of graduates from Taiwan Governor's Grammar School. Lin-Ts'ai Su-nü did not have to suffer the trauma and pain of bound feet and enjoyed the privilege of an education. After graduating at the age of thirteen from Pei-kang Public School, she went on to study at Taipei Third Girls' Senior High School (Taipei ti-san kao-teng nü-hsüeh-hsiao). Lin-Ts'ai Su-nü gained excellent results and continued her studies in the Education Department within the Normal School. She then returned to Pei-kang Public School to teach but left after becoming engaged to Lin Li-ming, thus bringing her short teaching career to a close.

Lin Li-ming had graduated from Taipei Medical College and after his marriage to Ts'ai Su-nü went back to Pei-kang to start a practice. At that time, he was under surveillance by the Japanese government because of his active participation in the Cultural Association. When he later became too busy at his clinic to take part, he continued to support the association financially. Lin-Ts'ai Su-nü helped at his clinic during that period but also began to do community work. She started free classes in setting up cottage industries and taught local women how to knit.

In 1946, Lin-Ts'ai Su-nü responded to the suggestion of Hsieh O to join the local Women's Association and thus began her service to the community. At that time, the association's focus was to improve the level of education for women: it planned to start with changing social attitudes and have as a final goal the enhancement of women's status and achievement of gender equality. When Hsüeh Jen-yang was mayor of T'ai-nan County in 1950, Lin-Ts'ai Su-nü was elected chair of T'ai-nan County Women's Association. She was later placed in charge of the newly established Yün-lin County Women's Association. During her term of office, Lin-Ts'ai Su-nü worked hard to obtain government funding and started a child care center to respond to the needs of farming women during busy agricultural times. In the meantime, she called on the government to establish a women's welfare center and overall made a considerable contribution to the women of Yün-lin County. From 1966 to 1972, Lin-Ts'ai Su-nü served as ninth chair of the Taiwan Women's Association. In contrast to her predecessors, she focused on establishing an efficient internal structure for the association, particularly, scrutinizing the systems for the signing-on and signing-off of staff, daily work journal records, finance and property records, and financial management.

Besides working specifically for women, Lin-Ts'ai Su-nü ran for Yün-lin County Council in 1950. Her election marked the beginning of her career in politics, and she was elected to the Provincial Assembly in 1957. During her term of office, Lin-Ts'ai Su-nü managed to obtain funds for local infrastructure and promoted the establishment of tourist facilities at Ch'ao-t'ien-kung in Pei-kang, which brought considerable prosperity to the area. In 1973, she was appointed as a representative of Taiwan Province to the Control Yuan. Although retiring in 1981, Lin-Ts'ai Su-nü continued to take an active part in Red Cross activities and continues to be concerned for society.

HO Shu-i
(Translated by George Li)

Ts'ai Hsiang-hui, ed. *Lin-Ts'ai Su-nü nü-shih chiu-chih sung-shou chi-nien chi.* Taipei: N.p., 1992.
Yu Chien-ming. "Lin-Ts'ai Su-nü." In *Tsou-kuo liang ko shih-tai ti Taiwan chih-yeh fu-nü fang-wen chi-lu.* Taipei: Chung-yang yen-chiu-yüan, Chin-tai-shih yen-chiu-so, 1994.

Linda: *see* **Lin Dai**

Ling Ruitang: *see* **Ling Shuhua**

Ling Shuhua
Ling Shuhua, 1900–1990 (some sources indicate b. 1904), was born Ling Ruitang in Beijing; her family came from Panyu, Guangdong Province. She was a writer of modern Chinese fiction as well as a painter and calligrapher in the traditional style.

As the daughter of a family of officials, Ling Shuhua received an excellent classical education, which included training in the arts of painting and calligraphy. She used the pen names Shuhua and Suxin but is best known by the name Ling Shuhua. Her father, Ling Fupeng, was provincial administration commissioner (*buzhengsi*) of Zhili and prefect of Shuntian (*shuntian fuyin*), which was equivalent to being mayor of Beijing, so Ling Shuhua spent most of her youth in the north. Her mother was the fourth of six wives, which means she was most probably a concubine. To screen their mother from oppression in their old-fashioned family because she had not produced a son, all four of her daughters did their utmost to succeed in life.

Ling Shuhua's father, besides being an accomplished literary man (he passed the metropolitan examination [*jinshi*] in 1895), loved painting and calligraphy. In addition, one of his six fathers-in-law, Xie Lansheng (1760–1831), was a famous Guangdong painter. Ling Shuhua, however, was the only child to show any interest in realizing her father's hopes to follow in Xie Lansheng's footsteps. She was therefore tutored from the age of six by Miao Jiahui (see *Biographical Dictionary of Chinese Women: The Qing Period*), a painter who had served Empress Dowager Cixi (see

Biographical Dictionary of Chinese Women: The Qing Period: Empress Xiao Qin Xian) at the turn of the twentieth century. Ling Shuhua also enjoyed many opportunities to view and make copies of the art collection in the Forbidden City. For English and classical Chinese poetry, she studied under Gu Hongming (1857–1928), a professor at Peking University. Later, Ling Shuhua also learned painting from Wang Zhulin and Hao Shuyu.

Ling Shuhua had been a student at Hebei First Women's Normal School (Hebei diyi nüzi shifan) in Tianjin before entering Yen-ching [Yanjing] University in Beijing in 1922 to study in its Foreign Languages Department. Her first short story, "After Drinking" (Jiu hou), was published in *Xiandai pinglun* in 1925 and won instant fame. This story was adapted into a one-act play by the famous playwright Ding Xilin, thus adding to the luster of her success. Ling Shuhua had at some stage met the editor and academic Chen Yuan (Xiying) at a welcome party for the Indian poet Tagore, and in 1927 the couple married. Their friends viewed them as an ideal literary couple, both enjoyed popular success and critical acclaim. The many short stories Ling Shuhua wrote in the 1930s were collected in *Temple of Flowers* (Hua zhi si, 1928); *Women* (Nüren, 1930); and *Children* (Xiaohai; later renamed *Two Little Brothers* [Xiao ger lia], 1935).

Chen Yuan became dean of the Faculty of Arts at Wuhan University in 1929, but during the Sino-Japanese War the university moved to Leshan in Sichuan Province. Ling Shuhua accompanied her husband to both places and, according to her friend Su Xuelin (*q.v.*), the couple enjoyed an ideal married life of shared academic and literary interests. The Luojiashan campus in Wuhan was set in idyllic surroundings, and they spent their summers in mountain retreats at Lushan or the seaside at Beidaihe. Ling Shuhua wrote and painted during leisure time. During this period, she published stories and essays in newspapers and magazines but seemingly not in any collections. Ling Shuhua devoted three years (1936–38) to editing the literary supplement "Wuhan wenyi" for *Wuhan ribao* publishing in it the works of writers living in central China. A collection entitled *Liu Huiying* seems to have appeared in 1943, but this title is not reported in all sources.

In 1947, Ling Shuhua went with Chen Yuan to Europe where he represented China at the United Nations Educational, Scientific, and Cultural Organization. Because Paris was so expensive to live in, they made their home in London; there, Ling Shuhua learned to cook and do housework. She had begun writing in English after corresponding with the English writer Virginia Woolf, having read her novel *A Room of One's Own* in Sichuan during the war. Being troubled by the chaotic and extremely difficult life of wartime China, Ling Shuhua wrote to Woolf for advice. The latter reportedly told her that only by steady working could one endure such an enormous disruption as war. Their correspondence continued until Woolf's death in 1941. When Ling Shuhua went to London, she sought the help of Woolf's friend and fellow writer Vita Sackville-West to retrieve her letters from Virginia Woolf's husband; these were published in 1953 as *Ancient Melodies*, enjoying a degree of success, and translated into French, German, Russian, and Swedish. While in England, Ling Shuhua also lectured on Chinese drama and art.

In her middle years, her accomplishment in painting reached new heights. Refined and exquisite before, her pieces now acquired the power that comes with maturity and experience. In the mid-1950s, Ling Shuhua exhibited in London, Paris, New York, Singapore, and Penang to critical acclaim. Chinese literati painting being still relatively unknown in the West, her works introduced a different world of art. In 1956, she went alone to Singapore to teach at Nanyang University, staying there for six years to lecture on modern Chinese literature. Ling Shuhua published her selected works (*Ling Shuhua xuanji*) in Singapore in 1960 as well as a collection of literary essays and critiques entitled *Shadows of Dreams from the Mountain Loving Cottage* (Aishanlu mengying), written there. She was called back to England in 1961 when her husband became ill, and throughout the 1960s taught modern Chinese literature in Canada, also giving seminars in various English universities on modern Chinese literature, Chinese painting, and calligraphy. Although her husband died in 1970, Ling Shuhua continued to live in England. She was unable to care for herself after hurting her back in a fall but chose to be cared for by social workers rather than living with her daughter in Edinburgh. Ling Shuhua made many visits to China from the 1970s on, the last one at the end of 1989 to seek treatment for her back. Only a few days before dying in May 1990, she visited old haunts in Beijing on a stretcher. Her ashes were buried alongside those of her husband's, in his native Wuxi in Jiangsu Province. Ling Shuhua is survived by her only daughter, Chen Xiaoying.

Ling Shuhua and Bing Xin (*q.v.*) were China's earliest women writers of the May Fourth period. Ling Shuhua is best known for her early works, especially *Temple of Flowers*. Her intimate portrayal of women and the insidious suffering they endure reflects the awakening of a generation of Chinese women. The famous poet Xu Zhimo (1897–1931) compared Ling Shuhua to the New Zealand writer Katherine Mansfield in the portrayal of extremely detailed psychological descriptions. Ling Shuhua was also one of the earliest women writers to effectively challenge patriarchal values in traditional Chinese culture, not by shouting slogans but by depicting in her writings the injustice and cruelty inherent in social attitudes and practices. Michael Holloch accurately points out that Ling Shuhua had the confidence to do so because she too belonged to the elite. Rey Chow argues that the fact that she was assigned to the *guixiu* school reflects her good breeding, implying that her works are engrossed by the triviality of women's lives. With women destined to live trivial existences circumscribed by their cultural confines, however, such criticism is unreasonable, demanding as it does that they then produce works on things outside that experience. Ling Shuhua's writings, in Chow's opinion, call attention in their own way to patriarchal oppression by mimicking closed ideological structures. Her style is said to have inherited its elegance from classical literature, yet her language has the simplicity and directness as well as the liveliness of the modern Beijing dialect.

Ling Shuhua's painting and calligraphy sit squarely in the literati tradition (*wenren hua*). Her paintings are characterized by strong technique and exquisite execution and are deeply poetic. She was especially skilled at painting flowers and birds, but her landscapes show the influence of the painters Shi Tao (seventeenth-eighteenth century) and Bada Shanren (1626–1705), two of the Eight Eccentrics of Yangzhou. Ling Shuhua inherited from them something of their unconventional spirit. She was also a collector of Chinese painting, her collection including the works of Ni Zan, Shi Tao, and Zheng Banqiao.

A controversy arose after the death of Ling Shuhua regarding a novel, written by a woman named Hong Ying, that was implicitly based on an alleged affair between Ling Shuhua and Julian Bell, Virginia Woolf's nephew. Julian Bell taught at Wuhan University during the 1930s and he alluded to their relationship in letters published in 1937. The incident received wide exposure in the media when Chen Xiaoying, Ling Shuhua's daughter, threatened to take Hong Ying to court.

Lily Xiao Hong LEE

Chen Jingzhi. "Ling Shuhua." In *Xiandai wenxue zaoqi de nüzuojia*. Taipei: Chengwen chubanshe, 1980, 79–93.

Chow, Rey. "Virtuous Transactions: A Rereading of Three Stories by Ling Shuhua." *Modern Chinese Literature*, 4 (1980): 71–86.

Cuadrado, Clara Yu. "Portrait of a Lady: The Fictional World of Ling Shuhua." In *Women Writers of 20th Century China*, ed. Angela Jung Palandri. Eugene: The Asian Studies Program at the University of Oregon, 1982, 41–62.

Holloch, Michael. "Everyday Feudalism: The Subversive Stories of Ling Shuhua." In *Women and Literature in China*, eds. Anna Gerstlacher, Ruth Keen, et al. Bochum: Brockmeyer, 1985, 379–89.

Huang Wenxiang. "Xiangyu Zhongwai wentan de Ling Shuhua." In *Ou-Mei jiechu huayi nüxing*, ed. Huang Wenxiang. Hong Kong: Xianggang Shanghai shuju, 1992, 100–13.

Jingsheng and Xiquan, eds. *Xin Zhongguo mingrenlu*. Nanchang: Jiangxi renmin chubanshe, 1987, 604–05.

Li Qizhi. "Ling Shuhua xiaoshuo 'wenwan danya' de yishu fenge." *Zhongguo xiandai wenxue yanjiu*, no. 2 (1992): 95–108.

Ling Shuhua. *Ling Shuhua xiaoshuoji*. Taipei: Hongfan shudian, 1984.

———. *Ling Shuhua xuanji*. Singapore: Shijie shuju, 1960.

Patton, Simon. "The Julian Bell affair." Unpublished article, 2000.

Qian Xingcun. "Guanyu Ling Shuhua chuangzuo de kaocha." In *Dangdai nüzuojia lun*, ed. Huang Renying. Shanghai: Guanghua shuju, 1933, 259–64.

Qin Xianci. "Ling Shuhua nianbiao." In *Ling Shuhua xiaoshuoji*. Taipei: Hongfan shudian, 1984, 471–87.

Yanjing daxue renwuzhi. Beijing: Yanjing yanjiuyuan, 1999, 217–18.

Ling Yü

Ling Yü, b. 1952, in Taipei County, Taiwan, is a writer and poet.

She received a B.A. in Chinese from Taiwan University and an M.A. in East Asian Languages and Literatures from the University of Wisconsin, Madison, in the U.S. In 1991, Ling Yü was invited by Professor Helen Vendler to Harvard University as a visiting scholar for that academic year. Ling Yü lives in Taipei and teaches at the National Yi Lan Institute of Technology in Yi Lan, Taiwan.

She wrote fiction initially but developed an interest in poetry in 1982–83, with the encouragement of the poet-editor-journalist Mei Hsin (pen name of Chang I-hsin, 1937–1997), then director of the Modern Poetry Quarterly Publishing Company. Ling Yü took over the editorship of the revived *Modern Poetry Quarterly* in 1984 and served as chief editor until the early 1990s. To date she has published four collections of poetry: *Compositions of the City* (Ch'eng ti lien-tso, 1990); *Names That Have*

Disappeared from the Map (Hsiao-shih tsai ti-t'u shang ti ming-tzu, 1992); *A Family of Acrobats* (T'e-chi chia-tsu, 1996); and *Odes to Winter Woods* (Mu-tung yung-ko chi, 1999). These collections established her as a leading poet in Taiwan in the 1990s.

When asked about the spiritual genealogy of her poems, Ling Yü indicates the influence of a number of traditional Chinese poets, including Ch'ü Yüan (343?–278 BCE), T'ao Yüan-ming (365–427), Li Po (701–762), Tu Fu (712–770), Li Shang-yin (813?–858), and Li Yü (937–978). Other writers such as Chuang-tzu, the Taoist philosopher of the third century BCE, and Ts'ao Hsüeh-ch'in (1715?–1763), author of the classic novel *Dream of the Red Chamber* (Hung-lou meng), are also important sources of inspiration. Among non-Chinese poets, Ling Yü has a strong affinity with Paul Celan (1920–70), Gabriel Garcia Marquez (b. 1928), and Jorge Luis Borges (1899–1986). Ling Yü said in a 1996 interview: "Celan is my sorrowful brother, Marquez is a distant relative whom I miss, Borges is a fatherly figure, a teacher whom I can never hope to approximate."

Critics note that Ling Yü's poetry gives little indication of her being a woman and resists inclusion in any category titled as "feminist" or even "female." The poet admits that she did not develop a strong awareness of gender until quite late into her writing career. Further, Ling Yü also feels that such labels serve a sociological purpose but are not useful aesthetically. Nor does she consider herself an "intellectual" poet, which many consider her to be. For her, concrete poetry, conceptual poetry, collage, and the like are intellectually based, but Ling Yü has never written any of these. Formally, her work to date consists of free verse and prose poems. The closest she comes to concrete poetry is *A Family of Acrobats*, the first section of which suggests the motion of the somersaulting acrobat.

The word "winter" probably best describes the tenor of Ling Yü's poetry. A recurrent image in her work, winter conjures up solitude, adversity, and contemplation. The poet's preface to her first book is entitled "Winter's Prisoner," and winter appears frequently in her work, including as the title of her most recent book. In the preface, Ling Yü envisions herself embarking on a solitary journey through a snowy wilderness in the night. Those who come to see her off give her presents: a black coat, an alms bowl, a pair of cuffs, and shackles. Losing her way, she is caught up by the dark, fights with it, and is left with deep wounds. Halfway through the journey she builds a snow castle, puts on the cuffs and shackles, and incubates seeds in the bowl. The preface ends with these hopeful words: "Next spring, or in a month and year with unknown names, I will nurture the growing flowers; they will open the record book and cross out my crimes. Lowering my head to look at my scars, I keep walking. I wait for another winter." The violent struggle, the building of a snow castle, the growing of flowers from seeds, and their eventual blossoming compose an allegory to the creative process. It suggests Ling Yü's experience as a novice poet, confronting the uncertainty, trepidation, and even guilt involved in poetry writing; yet in persisting and, having overcome the initial difficulty, she confidently looks forward to fruition.

The care with which the poet tends to the flowers in the allegory also suggests the craft going into her poetry. Her prior experience as a fiction writer may account for the sketchy plot that we often find in her poems, conjured up by various characters (in addition to the singular "I"), and the physical details and actions, often presented in an elliptical and abstracted manner. Ling Yü derives scenes and plots from modern life or ancient Chinese myths and history. In the series *Names That Have Disappeared from the Map*, for example, Zhao Pass evokes the legend of Wu Zixu of the Spring and Autumn Period (722–479 BCE). A fugitive in his own land, Wu must cross Zhao Pass to escape his unjust king, who has murdered Wu's father. Spending the night in an inn near the pass, Wu racks his brain trying to think of a plan to cross without being identified by the guards. By dawn, he still has not come up with one, but when Wu looks in the mirror he sees that his hair has turned completely white, overnight. The guards do not recognize him, and Wu successfully escapes and wreaks revenge on the king. Ling Yü tells us in the subtitle that the poem is based on an association between her riding a bus and the Wu story. By comparing her bus ride to Wu crossing the pass, Ling Yü turns a mundane experience into an allegory.

The somber tone of her work stems from two kinds of discontent. One is with modern life, entailing alienation of individuals from the world and each other. Human relationships are characterized by distance, distrust, and indifference, a theme often expressed in images of enclosure, such as the square box (which is the title of a serial poem) and the room. The other type of discontent underscores the poet's quest for transcendence of life's limitations. Images of the ladder (leading to heaven), flying, and the mirror (a Taoist symbol for the eternal Way) invoke this idea. In the final analysis, poetry does not just record but embodies this endless quest. These lines from the last poem of the sequence *Our Room* in her most recent book, *Odes to Winter Woods*, aptly sum up her belief in the power of poetry to go beyond life's limitations:

> An entity with a pair of wings, gradually
> Grows—from an infant to an old man
> And back to an infant again . . .
> Or—(take a pledge on the wings)
> Choose an alien name—call it poetry
> Or not call it poetry, with the heart of Heaven and
> Earth, God and Man, interconnected
> . . . Recognize it with teary eyes . . .
> As if smiling (or not smiling) . . .
> Walk into our room
> And, beyond the room.
>   —Translated by Michelle Yeh

Michelle YEH

Huang Liang. "Hsiang-hsiang ti tui-hua: Ling Yü shih-ko ching-yen mo-shih fen-hsi." In *Hsiang-hsiang ti tui-hua*, ed. Huang Liang. Taipei: T'ang-shan ch'u-pan-she, 1997, 72–85.

Ling Yü. *Ch'eng ti lien-tso*. Taipei: Hsien-tai-shih chi-k'an-she, 1990.

———. *Hsiao-shih tsai ti-t'u shang ti ming-tzu*. Taipei: Shih-pao wen-hua shih-yeh ch'u-pan-she, 1992.

———. *Mu-tung yung-ko chi*. Taipei: T'ang-shan ch'u-pan-she, 1999.

———. *T'e-chi chia-tsu*. Taipei: Hsien-tai-shih chi-k'an-she, 1996.

———. "Interview with Yang Hsiao-pin." In *T'e-chi chia-tsu*. Taipei: Hsien-tai-shih chi-k'an-she, 1996, 161–70.

Liu Chien-hsien: *see* **Liu Qunxian**

Liu Fulan: *see* **Liu Hulan**

Liu Huiqing: *see* **Lau, Emily**

Liu Hulan

Liu Hulan, 1932–1947, was born Liu Fulan in west Yunzhou village, Wenshui County, Shanxi Province. She is revered by the communists as a young peasant heroine who became a martyr to their cause.

The older daughter of a peasant family, Liu Hulan was just four when her mother died of illness. After Liu Hulan's father remarried, she and her sister went to live with their grandparents. The village in which Liu Hulan lived was well known as a guerrilla base from the time of the Sino-Japanese War right through the civil war (1945–49). It was called "little Yan'an," a reference to the communist capital in north China during that period, and many of the villagers were CCP members. Meetings conducted by CCP leaders were often held there, and when anti-Japanese troops passed through they would leave their wounded. Because almost the entire village was involved in provisioning troops, raising funds, and making shoes and clothes for soldiers at the front, Liu Hulan was from a young age exposed to revolutionary ideas and patriotic activities. At the age of ten, in 1942, she began acting as a courier, delivering mail to guerrilla groups and standing sentry during village meetings.

The turning point for Liu Hulan came in 1945 when she went against her grandmother's wishes and attended a training course for women. This course, which was conducted by Wenshui County Women's Department in the neighboring village of Guanjiabao and lasted for forty days, was designed to instruct women in the revolutionary policies of the CCP. They were also exposed to some of the writings of Mao Zedong, such as "How to Analyze the Classes in the Countryside," "An Introduction to *The Communist*," and "The Chinese Revolution and the Chinese Communist Party." Upon returning to the village, Liu Hulan was made secretary of the village branch of the Women's Anti-Japanese and National Salvation Federation. Over the following few months, the women running the federation were held up as models for their work supporting soldiers at the front, making shoes and caring for the wounded. In May 1946, Liu Hulan was also appointed secretary in charge of the District Women's National Salvation Federation. She applied to join the CCP two months later, but because she was not yet fourteen the County Party Committee was only able to grant admission to her as an "alternate member" until she turned eighteen.

Liu Hulan worked in the land reform movement, helping allocate land seized from the landlords to the peasants, denouncing landlords at public meetings, and mediating disputes between the people. By the time this movement came to a successful conclusion at the end of 1946, the civil war had gained such momentum that the local government decided to move leading cadres, including Liu Hulan, to safety at the famous guerrilla base of Lü Liangshan. She did not leave her village, however, believing that her extreme youth would be her safeguard. KMT troops entered the village at dawn on 12 January 1947 and learning that Liu Hulan was a member of the CCP publicly executed her with a hand hay cutter in the village square. She was not yet fifteen years old.

Liu Hulan was posthumously admitted to full membership of the CCP, and Mao Zedong wrote that hers had been "a great life and an honorable death." He also asked the national Xinhua News Agency to publicize widely Liu Hulan's heroic deeds and issued a call to the people of the liberated areas to organize classes about her. Liu Hulan was declared a national hero after the communists came to power in 1949 and her story has been kept alive in poems, short stories, picture books, and primary school textbooks.

Viola Hong Xin Chan WONG

Huaxia funü mingren cidian. Beijing: Huaxia chubanshe, 1988.
Tang Ning. *Liu Hulan*. Beijing: Zhongguo heping chubanshe, 1992.
Zhang Guizhong. "Liu Hulan: Laisheng xianghui zai bai tou." *Dongfang youbao*, 27 April 1995, 23.

Liu Lianqing: *see* **Liu Zhen**

Liu Qingyang
Liu Qingyang, 1894–1977 (some sources give b. 1902), from a wealthy Muslim family of the northeastern coastal city of Tianjin, was a feminist, patriot, and an intellectual.

Liu Qingyang studied at Beijing Normal College (Beijing nüzi shifan xueyuan) and was involved peripherally with the Tongmenghui, possibly after the 1911 Revolution. She became active in May Fourth Movement demonstrations in Tianjin in the late 1910s as a leading figure in various patriotic groups, including the Tianjin Association of Women Patriots (Tianjin nüjie aiguo tongzhi hui). After graduating from Beijing Women's Normal College, Liu Qingyang took part in student protests in that city against China's signing of the Versailles Peace Treaty and was one of a handful of students arrested and imprisoned for several weeks in August 1919. The following month, she joined with Zhou Enlai (1898–1976), Deng Yingchao (*q.v.*), and eighteen others to found the Awakened Society (Juewu she) in Tianjin; her code name, derived from drawing numbers from a hat, was "Twenty-five."

Liu Qingyang left for France in November 1920 as part of a work-study program and in 1921 was accepted as a member of the CCP in Paris on the recommendation of Zhang Shenfu (Zhang Songnian, 1893–?), a philosopher, mathematician, and logician and one of the founders of the CCP. He also recommended Zhou Enlai for party membership at that time. Liu Qingyang and Zhang Shenfu married in France and remained in Europe until 1923. Upon their return to China, Liu Qingyang resumed her involvement in revolutionary feminist activities, helping set up patriotic women's groups in Guangzhou, Shanghai, and Beijing. She joined the KMT and worked in its Women's Department in Wuhan with He Xiangning (*q.v.*) during the first CCP-KMT united front (1923–27). However, when the united front collapsed, Liu Qingyang withdrew entirely from revolutionary work, resigning in quick succession from the KMT and the CCP.

The return of Liu Qingyang and Zhang Shenfu to active participation in politics was triggered by the September Eighteenth Incident of 1931, known in the West as the Mukden Incident, which marked the start of Japan's military takeover of Manchuria. Liu Qingyang set up several anti-Japanese national salvation associations and chaired the Beiping Women's National Salvation Association (Beiping funü jiuguo hui). Suspected of clandestine CCP activities in north China, she and Zhang were arrested in 1936 but soon released. In her travels around the region agitating against the KMT's lack of resistance to the Japanese, Liu Qingyang visited Wuhan, Chongqing, Hong Kong, and Guilin. The July Seventh Incident of 1937 (the Marco Polo Bridge Incident) further strengthened her anti-Japanese resolve. At this time, she was separated from her husband and had left their two-year-old child (born in 1935) in the care of others to continue with her work. Liu Qingyang was made a director of a children's welfare association and for two years, until early 1940, headed in Wuhan and Chongqing a training group for women that was part of the New Life Movement. In this latter capacity, she worked closely with Soong Mayling (*q.v.*) as well as many communist women, including Deng Yingchao.

In 1941, after reclaiming her child, Liu Qingyang went to Hong Kong, where she established a Chinese girls' school. Liu Qingyang returned to Chongqing when the Japanese occupied the island in 1941. At this stage, she and Zhang Shenfu became reunited in their commitment to democracy when Liu Qingyang joined the Democratic Political League (Minzhu zhengtuan tongmeng). He was a co-founder of this group, which was reorganized in 1944 into the China Democratic League (Minzhu tongmeng), and she served on its Central Committee as director of the Women's Committee. Working in conjunction with Liu-Wang Liming (*q.v.*) and several other women, Liu Qingyang also helped establish the Chinese Women's Association (Zhongguo funü lianyi hui) in 1945. By 1948 she and Zhang Shenfu drifted apart again, and in that year Liu Qingyang obtained a formal divorce; whether the timing of it was linked to a campaign of criticism directed against Zhang Shenfu at the time is not clear. He was also criticized in 1957 and labeled a rightist during the Hundred Flowers Movement.

Liu Qingyang took an active part in the political life of the new nation from 1949 on and was elected to various committees, many of these to do with women. She served on the Executive Committee of the ACWF (1949–66) and chaired its Beijing branch (1957). In 1953, Liu Qingyang was elected to the Government Administration Council's Standing Committee for the implementation of the Marriage Law. Appointed principal of the New China Women's Vocational School (1949), she was also a member of the Government Administration Council's Cultural and Educational Committee (1949–54). Liu Qingyang served with the Chinese Red Cross as deputy secretary-general (1955–65), vice-president (1961–66), and president (1966). On the political front, she represented Hebei at the NPC (1954, 1958, 1964); served on the Standing Committee of the CPPCC (1959, 1965); sat on the Standing Committee (1956) of the Chinese Democratic League; and chaired its Hebei branch (1958).

Readmitted to party membership in 1961, Liu Qingyang eventually fell from grace early in the Cultural Revolution. She was imprisoned, her history of fringe involvement with the KMT apparently carrying more weight than her longstanding patriotic and feminist commitments. Liu Qingyang died in 1977, just after the end of the Cultural Revolution but before she had been rehabilitated.

Sue WILES

Jin Feng. *Deng Yingchao zhuan.* Beijing: Renmin chubanshe, 1993, 36–40.

Schwarcz, Vera. "Liu Qingyang." In *Dictionnaire Biographique du Mouvement Ouvrier International: La Chine,* eds. Lucien Bianco and Yves Chevrier. Paris: Les Éditions Ouvrières, n.d.

———. "Zhang Shenfu." In *Dictionnaire Biographique du Mouvement Ouvrier International: La Chine,* eds. Lucien Bianco and Yves Chevrier. Paris: Les Éditions Ouvrières, n.d., 751–53.

Yingwen *Zhongguo funü,* ed. *Gujin zhuming funü renwu,* vol. 2. Shijiazhuang: Hebei renmin chubanshe, 1986, 482–87.

Zhonggong renmin lu. Taipei: Guoli zhengzhi daxue guoji guanxi yanjiu zhongxin, 1978, 629–30.

Liu Qunxian

Liu Qunxian, 1907–1941?, of Wuxi, Jiangsu Province, was one of the thirty women who went with the First Front Red Army on the Chinese communists' Long March of 1934–35.

Liu Qunxian belonged to a family of workers; she started work at the age of nine and by the time she was thirteen, put in sixteen-hour days in a silk factory. She joined the CCP in 1926 and was soon active as a labor leader among the women factory workers in Wuxi, taking part both in the Workers' Strike and attending the National Workers' Congress in Wuhan in 1927. Toward the end of that year, the young woman was sent to Moscow. While studying there at Sun Yat-sen University, Liu Qunxian met and married fellow student Bo Gu (Qin Bangxian, 1907–1946), who also acted as her interpreter when Liu Qingyang represented China in 1927 at the Moscow World Workers' Congress. Bo Gu was one of the "28 Bolsheviks," young students who seized control of the CCP when they returned from the Soviet Union about 1930. When he usurped control of the party, possibly in 1932, he won the enmity of Mao Zedong (1893–1976), whom he considered too politically unorthodox. As party secretary, Bo Gu was, with Zhou Enlai (1898–1976) and Otto Braun, one of the three de facto leaders of the CCP. Mao Zedong removed him and Otto Braun from power during the Zunyi Conference of 1935 in the early months of the Long March, but Bo Gu continued to hold high-level party posts.

Upon returning to China in 1930, Liu Qunxian headed the Women Workers' Department of the All-China Federation of Trade Unions in Shanghai and continued this work when she moved to the Jiangxi soviet in 1933. At the Second National Congress of the Soviet Republic of China in 1934, Liu Qunxian was elected to the relatively high position of member of the Central Executive Committee. She had given birth in Shanghai in May 1933 to a daughter, whom she dispatched for safekeeping to relatives in Wuxi. Liu Qunxian was recovering from a miscarriage when the Long March began in October 1934, and she may also have had a child in Moscow. During the Long March, Liu Qunxian captained the Independent Women's Unit for a time, was a political worker with the General Political Department, organized local workers in Guizhou, and carried out propaganda work as head of the Women Workers' Group. After reaching the northwest, she resumed her All-China Federation of Trade Unions duties with women workers and in Yan'an was director of National Mines and Factories and was also made assistant director of the Shaanxi-Gansu-Ningxia Border Region Federation of Trade Unions. Liu Qunxian gave birth to a son in Bao'an in 1936.

After becoming friendly with the American reporter Helen Foster Snow in Yan'an the following year, Liu Qunxian asked Helen to "take the baby to bring up" because she was too busy to look after him. Helen Snow referred to her as "Miss Liu Chien-hsien, Leader of the Proletariat."

Leaving Yan'an in late 1937, Liu Qunxian went with her husband to Wuhan, where she headed the Yangzi (Yangtze) Regional Trade Unions Office. While there, Liu Qunxian and Liao Siguang (*q.v.*) worked with the Chinese Labor Association. However, Liu Qunxian became ill and was sent to the southern port city of Amoy to recuperate; her marriage had broken down by early 1939, and her illness may have been exacerbated by personal difficulties. She was sent to Moscow in March 1939 for medical treatment but there is speculation that Liu Qunxian was in fact exiled. She is said to have been admitted to a lunatic asylum in Moscow and disappeared, presumed killed during German air raids on Moscow in mid-1941. Liu Qunxian's husband, who had already formed a de facto relationship with another woman in Yan'an before Liu Qunxian reached Moscow, died in a plane crash in 1946.

Sue WILES

Bianco, Lucien, and Yves Chevrier, eds. *Dictionnaire biographique du mouvement ouvrier international: La Chine*. Paris: Les Éditions Ouvrières, n.d.

Guo Chen. *Jinguo liezhuan: Hong yifangmianjun sanshiwei changzheng nühongjun shengping shiji*. Beijing: Nongcun duwu chubanshe, 1986, 128–38.

Lee, Lily Xiao Hong, and Sue Wiles. *Women of the Long March*. Sydney: Allen & Unwin, 1999.

Salisbury, Harrison E. *The Long March: The Untold Story*. New York: Harper & Row, 1985, 87–88.

Snow, Helen Foster. *Inside Red China*. 1977 reprint [with a new preface and biographical notes by the author]. New York: Da Capo Press, 1939, 185–86.

Yingwen *Zhongguo funü*, ed. *Gujin zhuming funü renwu*, vol. 2. Shijiazhuang: Hebei renmin chubanshe, 1986, 769–73.

Liu Sola: *see* **Liu Suola**

Liu Suola

Liu Suola, b. 1955, in Beijing, is a writer, musician, and musical producer; her name is also romanized as Liu Sola.

Her uncle, Liu Zhidan, was the famous revolutionary hero of Shaanxi of the Long March period, and both her father, Liu Jingfan, and mother, Li Jiantong, were at one time influential members of the CCP. Liu Suola therefore grew up in a privileged environment, beginning piano lessons at the age of five. However, in the early 1960s her mother wrote a biography of Liu Zhidan that angered Mao Zedong (1893–1976). Subsequently, while still a teenager, Liu Suola went with her parents to a cadre school (a euphemism for a labor reform camp) in Jiangxi in 1969; she returned to Beijing the following year, however.

Being too young to work, Liu Suola was left to her own devices, reading whatever she wanted to, listening to Western classical music and the Beatles, and viewing the paintings of Picasso. In short, Liu Suola enjoyed the privileges available only to the children of high cadres, even disgraced cadres. Those years of self-study, although not disciplined, greatly affected her outlook. In 1973, she taught music at a high school. When universities and institutions of higher education reopened their doors, Liu Suola passed the entrance examination of the Central Conservatorium of Music (Zhongyang yinyue xueyuan) in 1976 and studied composition. After graduation, she chose to be assigned to the Central Institute for Nationalities and worked in the Theory and Composition Section of the Dance Department. Liu Suola began publishing her writings in 1982 and by 1985 had become famous for her novella *You Got No Other Choice* (Ni bie wu xuanze), first published in *Renmin wenxue*, which won the National Outstanding Novella Award that year. This piece is considered a first in "new wave" literature and exercised considerable influence at the time. Her other main works of this period are "In Search of the King of Singers" (Xunzhao gewang) and *Blue Sky, Green Sea* (Lantian lühai). Her works mainly reflect the frustration of educated youth of the 1980s and their idealism. "In Search of the King of Singers," for instance, portrays a tormented woman torn between pragmatism and idealism, between down-to-earth realistic considerations and the yearnings of her soul. Written in deceptively simple language, the piece is full of self-mockery and irreverence. Liu Suola's works are avant-garde in their anti-social, anti-tradition consciousness, and she has been called China's first true modernist writer, "who appeared out of nowhere" (*hengkong chushi*). Her music is also so innovative that Liu Suola is sometimes spoken of as the first rock'n'roll musician of mainland China. In 1987, she composed a rock opera based on her novella *Blue Sky, Green Sea* but was not allowed to have it performed in China.

In 1988, Liu Suola traveled to England to work with musicians. The following year, she went to the United States and spent time with blues musicians from Memphis, developing a Chinese blues style. Liu Suola continued to work in the British and American music industry and in the early 1990s composed and performed with Hong Kong music groups such works as *Chronicle of Women* and *Snow in June*. During this period, her music metamorphed into world music as she searched for a syncretic genre combining Asian, African-American, and rock'n'roll music. Her album *Blues in the East* (Landiao zai dongfang) got a great response in New York and was on the CD best-seller list. In two concerts in New York in 1995, Liu Suola debuted her work *China Collage* (Zhongguo pintie) and performed her already well-recognized *Blues in the East*. One critic maintains that Liu's music synthesizes a rich heritage of Asian folk and avant-garde world music and is not simply a Chinese response to the blues or a novelty. Liu Suola took some of her American colleagues with her to Beijing in 1999 to perform at the Beijing Jazz Festival. She has also set up her own recording company, named Also Productions; among its new releases are two CDs of relaxation music designed "to help *qigong* practitioners to be one with the universe."

Busy with her musical activities, Liu Suola stopped writing for several years. However, in 1992 she had the opportunity to participate in the International Writing Program at the University of Iowa initiated by Nieh Hualing (*q.v.*). Her novella *Hundun jia ligeleng* (Chaos and All That) was first published in *Guangchang*, a magazine commemorating the 1989 Tian'anmen Incident.

Liu Suola uniquely holds outstanding successes in literature and music. In both, she radiates rebelliousness toward tradition, preferring the directness and elemental approach of folk traditions. Fittingly, then, through her new project entitled *New Folk Project* Liu Suola hopes to bring Chinese musicians and musicians from other countries together.

GAO Yuanbao
(Translated by Lily Xiao Hong Lee)

Cheung, Martha. "Introduction." *Blue Sky, Green Sea and Other Stories*, Liu Sola. Hong Kong: Chinese University of Hong Kong, 1993, ix–xxv.
Kong Jiesheng. "Liu Suola yu Dongfang landiao." *Mingbao yuekan* (November 1995): 72–73.
Liu Sola. *Blue Sky, Green Sea, and Other Stories*. Hong Kong: Chinese University of Hong Kong, 1993.
———. *Chaos and All That*, trans. Richard King. Honolulu: University of Hawaii Press, 1994.
———. "In Search of the King of Singers," trans. Martha Cheung. *Renditions*, special issue: Contemporary Women Writers (Spring and Summer 1987): 208–34.
Olesen, Alexa. "Liu Sola Making Worlds Collide," at <http://virtualchina.org/archive/leisure/music/060900-liusola-alo.html>.

Liu Xiaoqing

Liu Xiaoqing, b. 1955 (sometimes given as 1950, 1952, or 1953), in Fuling, Sichuan Province, is a film actress.

Her parents separated before she was born so Liu Xiaoqing has always gone by her maternal surname rather than her father's, which was Feng. Liu Xiaoqing's mother became a teacher at Chengdu College of Physical Education, where she met and married her second husband, an associate professor in the Department of Medicine; this marriage also produced a daughter.

At the age of eleven, Liu Xiaoqing enrolled in the middle school attached to the Sichuan Conservatory of Music, majoring in the *yangqin*, a stringed instrument similar to the lute or dulcimer. She first performed with a propaganda team during the Cultural Revolution, playing a Red Guard, a worker, a peasant, and a PLA soldier. Liu Xiaoqing was in the wave of graduates sent, both before and after the Cultural Revolution, to work in the countryside as peasants. Before long, she joined the regional propaganda team in a division of the Daxian Army in Sichuan. When that team disbanded, Liu Xiaoqing applied to join a theatrical company in Chengdu Military District. In 1975, she appeared in the stage play *Dujuan Mountain* (Dujuanshan). That same year Liu Xiaoqing played the leading role in *The Great Wall on the South China Sea* (Nanhai changcheng), the first film produced by the August First Film Studio. The film received excellent reviews, and Liu Xiaoqing went on to appear in several other movies, including *Four Crossings of the Red River* (Sidu chishui) and *Thank You, Comrade* (Tongzhi ganxie ni). Although none of these enjoyed great success, they served to hone Liu Xiaoqing's skills.

In 1978, Beijing Film Studio shot *Little Flower* (Xiao hua), known then as *Cedar Heroes* (Tongbai yingxiong). Liu Xiaoqing's portrayal of He Cuigu in this film won her the Chinese film industry's Hundred Flowers Award for Best Actress, as well as the Wenhui Award for Best Supporting Actress. Her exceptional performance earned the praise of Wang Yang, head of Beijing Film Studio, and an invitation to remain with the studio: this officially launched Liu Xiaoqing's film career. She went on to make such films as *Wedding Ceremony* (Hunli), *Hidden Net* (Qian wang), and *Mysterious Big Buddha* (Shenmi dafo). Her talent was evident from the start, and Liu Xiaoqing was considered the most outstanding actress on the mainland, receiving the Hundred Flowers and the Golden Rooster Awards on several occasions.

Throughout her career, the actress portrayed a variety of screen figures. These include a valiant young girl; daughter of a fisherman; daring guerrilla leader (He Cuigu); vulgar shop assistant Zhang Lan in *Look at This Family* (Qiao zhe yi jiazi); shrewish and sexy Hua Jinzi in *The Wilderness* (Yuanye); affectionate, sensitive teacher Luo Xian in *Hidden Net*; honest volunteer soldier Ouyang Lan in *Deep in the Heart* (Xinling shenchu); illiterate village girl Lu Xuezhi in *A Northern Country Love Affair* (Beiguo hongdou); brave, wild Tibetan girl Nuomei Qincuo in *The Heartless Lover* (Wuqing de qingren); clever Feng Jie in *Dream of the Red Chamber* (Honglou meng); rice tofu shop owner Hu Yuyin, with a soft exterior but a resolute heart, in *Hibiscus Town* (Furongzhen); and scavenging Beijing pauper Chuntao in the film of that name. Many of the films in which Liu Xiaoqing starred received acclaim overseas as well, and festivals devoted to her films have been held in the United States, France, Japan, and Singapore. The famous playwright Cao Yu commended Liu Xiaoqing for her superb performance in the film version of his *The Wilderness* with an impromptu eight-character verse: "Your sincerity is convincing and your labor effortless. You have sought depth and achieved worldly wisdom."

In addition to convincingly portraying a variety of characters, Liu Xiaoqing endeavored to extend her skill to also playing women of various ages. In the films *Burning Yuanmingyuan* (Huoshao Yuanmingyuan), *Governing from Behind the Screen* (Chuilian ting zheng), *Empress Dowager of the Western Palace* (Xitaihou), and *Grand Eunuch Li Lianying* (Dataijian Li Lianying), she played Empress Dowager Cixi from a young girl right through to being an old woman. In 1992, Liu Xiaoqing accepted an invitation to appear in the forty-part television series "Unrivaled Beauty" (Fenghua juedai) as Chun Ni, whom she portrayed from the age of eighteen up to sixty. This was the first time a mainland actor had played a lead role in a Taiwanese television series. Liu Xiaoqing subsequently starred in the television series *Empress Wu* (Wu Zetian), which received good reviews in China, Hong Kong, and Taiwan. The actress set out to become an independent producer in 1985 when she filmed *Qing Artillery* (Da Qing paodui) and *The Heartless Lover*. Although Liu Xiaoqing had difficulty releasing the films, they allowed her to strengthen her organizational and administrative abilities and laid the foundation for later entrepreneurial activities.

Liu Xiaoqing's artistic talent stretched to playing the *yangqin*, the xylophone, and the piano. Her first record was released in Hong Kong during the filming of *The Wilderness*, followed by *Cixi Suite* (Cixi zuqu), also recorded in Hong Kong. She became the first film star to win a prize for the recording of individual voice when her *Songs of Liu Xiaoqing* (Liu Xiaoqing zhi ge), produced by Pacific Audiovisual Recording Company, won the Lark Award.

As a celebrity, Liu Xiaoqing—who was frequently involved in disputes, rumors, and lawsuits—generated widespread interest. Her autobiography *My Way* (Wo de lu, 1983), written after her first divorce, was seen as both a justification and an explanation to her audience. She once made a celebrated and widely quoted remark that seems to summarize her life: "To be a man is hard. To be a woman is hard. To be a famous woman is harder. And to be a single famous woman is hardest of all." In her autobiography, Liu Xiaoqing encouraged individual struggle, stressing that one must seize destiny with both hands. Never, under any circumstances, must one be seen to lose confidence. This became an inspiration to many young people at that time. She later wrote pieces that revealed her individual views and appeared in influential publications, including *Popular Films* (Dazhong dianying). Liu Xiaoqing also published more autobiographical works: *These Eight Years of Mine* (Wo zhe ba nian), *A Portrait of Liu Xiaoqing* (Liu Xiaoqing xiezhen), and *My Vindication—From Filmstar to Billionairess* (Wo de zibai—cong dianying mingxing dao yiwan fuji'er). She married her second husband, a film director with Beijing Film Studio, in 1986. They divorced in 1989, and she has since remained single. At the time of writing, Liu Xiaoqing had no children.

By being courageous in speech and writing and candidly pursuing her individual dream, Liu Xiaoqing carved out for her audience a unique image of a strong and independent woman. People have not only been interested in her performances and screen image but in her story as a person in society, and her example has created what has been called "the Liu Xiaoqing phenomenon."

At the beginning of the 1990s, the actress began withdrawing from artistic circles. She started to use her name for commercial investment and real estate and also set up a beautician school and invested in films. Liu Xiaoqing is currently a member of the CPPCC and the Chinese Writer's Association.

Shirley Wai CHAN
(Translated by Katherine Kerr)

Chen Guojun. *Wo he Liu Xiaoqing . . . budebu shuo de gushi*. Guangzhou: Guangdong renmin chubanshe, 1997.
Cheng Shu'an and Wu Qirong, eds. *Wo de kulian—Liu Xiaoqing*. Beijing: Nongcun duwu chubanshe, 1989.
Liu Xiaoqing. *Liu Xiaoqing xiezhen*. Beijing: Huaxia chubanshe, 1995.
———. *Liu Xiaoqing zizhuan: Wo de lu*. Hong Kong: Yuanfang chubanshe and Xianggang Zhong-wai fazhan chubanshe, 1983.
———. *Wo zhe ba nian*. Beijing: Renmin ribao chubanshe, 1992.
Ma Huiqin. *Xuanwo zhong de gongheguo redian renwu*. Beijing: Tuanjie chubanshe, 1993, 1–46.
Song Ruizhi, ed. *Zhongguo funü wenhua tonglan*. Jinan: Shandong wenyi chubanshe, 1995, 639–41.
Zhang Zuomin. "Diyi laoban Liu Xiaoqing." In *Diyi laoban Liu Xiaoqing*. Changchun: Shidai wenyi chubanshe, 1993, 1–42.

Liu Yaxiong

Liu Yaxiong, 1901–1988, of Xingxian County, Shanxi Province, was a revolutionary and political leader in the PRC.

Her father, Liu Shaobai, was a liberal man who supported Liu Yaxiong's desire for an education; nothing is known of her mother. Liu Yaxiong was the first girl in her county not to have her feet bound, and she went to the provincial capital, Taiyuan, to study at the Provincial Women's Normal School of Shanxi (Nüzi shifan xuexiao) about 1917. Liu Yaxiong and her fellow students were greatly influenced by the May Fourth Movement of 1919, immersing themselves in progressive books and journals, organizing a students union, and traveling to the countryside to publicize anti-footbinding ideas. After graduating in 1923, she passed the entrance examination to the Beijing Women's Normal University (Beijing nüzi shifan daxue) and won two scholarships, one from Shanxi and one from her county; her teachers were such masters as Lu Xun and Xu Shouchang. Liu Yaxiong could have graduated without incident but was not one to stand on the sidelines in the turmoil of the 1920s. She continued to be socially and politically active at university and fought against university authorities who were supported by the warlord government, winning the approval of the famous literati Lu Xun. In 1926, the warlord government fired on students protesting against the Japanese attack on Dagu, killing some of them. CCP members noticed that Liu Yaxiong was in the thick of all this and recommended her for membership into the party. She was among the first eight party members to join the CCP in this way. At about the same time, Liu Yaxiong was expelled from the university.

In September 1926, she was sent by the CCP to Moscow to study at Sun Yat-sen University and then returned to China in 1928 to work in the Propaganda Department of Jiangsu Provincial Party Committee. Liu Yaxiong married Chen Yuandao, a fellow student from Moscow, in 1931, and was immediately sent to Hebei as director of the CCP secretariat of the Provisional Committee. She was soon arrested in Tianjin but released because of lack of evidence. After joining her husband in Jiangsu in 1933, Liu Yaxiong was appointed director of the secretariat of the CCP Committee of Jiangsu Province. Chen Yuandao was arrested that year, however, after a betrayal by former members of the party, and executed by the KMT in Nanjing. Liu Yaxiong was pregnant at the time and returned to Shanxi to give birth; she named her son Jiyuan (commemorating Yuandao).

Entrusting her son to her father, Liu Yaxiong went back to Beijing to try to contact the party organization but was unable to do so for a long time. This was one of the darkest periods of her life. According to the reminiscences of Bo Yibo, the party did not give her assignments until he had traveled from Taiyuan to Beijing and invited Liu Yaxiong to work in Shanxi. She re-surfaced in October 1935 working openly in the leadership of the Shanxi League for Self-Sacrifice and National Salvation (Shanxi xisheng jiuguo tongmenghui) and the Shanxi New Army. An alliance formed by the CCP with the warlord Yan Xishan enabled the communists to work openly in Shanxi at that time.

In 1937, Liu Yaxiong organized the Women's Militia Company (Nü minbing lian) within the Shanxi Military and Political Training School (Shanxi junzheng xunlianban) and became the political instructor (*zhidaoyuan*). This training school had been formed to train anti-Japanese fighters and was a joint CCP-Yan Xishan operation in which the CCP provided political instructors while Yan Xishan provided military trainers. More than one hundred women in the militia company flocked to the training school from all over China. Liu Yaxiong was a serious and demanding teacher, but the women found that she had a soft side as well. Many of the young women, who were further steeled by war and political struggle, became reliable and capable cadres of the CCP. Later that year at Wutaishan, Liu Yaxiong organized a Partisan Commando Unit of which she was political instructor. It subsequently became the basis of the First Regiment of the Partisans, led by Liu Yaxiong.

In 1939, she was transferred to eastern Shanxi as both chair of the Women's National Salvation Association (Funü jiuguo zonghui) and party secretary. In 1940, Liu Yaxiong became the first commissioner (*zhuanyuan*) of Taiyue base when she was appointed to the Third Administrative Office (Disan zhuanshu). Soon after becoming commissioner, her district was frequently targeted by the Japanese. Liu Yaxiong ensured that no grain was left in the fields and protected her area with land mines, thus making the Third District a most unattractive prospect for attack. At the same time, she mobilized the people to build Linzhang Dam in Wuxian County to aid agriculture. The stone tablet that bears an inscription in her calligraphy still stands near the dam.

During the Rectification Movement of 1942, Liu Yaxiong went to Yan'an to study and take part in the political movement. However, she was accused of being a "traitor," and it was more than two years before her name was cleared. Liu Yaxiong regained her standing in the party in 1945, when she took part in the CCP Seventh Congress. After the Sino-Japanese War, Liu Yaxiong was sent to the northeast and given a number of responsible positions, including CCP secretary in the city of Shuanliao, head of the Organization Department of Nenjiang Province, and membership of Shenyang Municipal Committee.

In 1949, Liu Yaxiong attended the first ACWF National Congress and was elected to the Standing Committee. She was also appointed first secretary of Changchun municipality in the same year. In 1953, Liu Yaxiong was one of few women given a ministerial position, when she became vice-minister of Labor (Laodongbu fu buzhang). Liu Yaxiong was elected to the CCP Supervising Committee in 1963, and the following year the committee sent her to the Ministry of Transportation. She later, probably in the 1980s, became an advisor to that ministry.

It was Liu Yaxiong who influenced her father and all of her siblings to join the CCP. During the Cultural Revolution, however, she was branded as a renegade and persecuted severely. Because of her, her whole family was incriminated. By the time Liu Yaxiong was rehabilitated at the end of the Cultural Revolution, she was already in her seventies and had come to the end of her career. Liu Yaxiong was a delegate to the CCP Seventh and Eighth Congresses and a member of the NPC and CPPCC. She died in February 1988 in Beijing at the age of eighty-seven. Her son, Chen Jiyuan was for a long time a "black child." This was because in the eyes of the KMT he was the son of rebels, so his name could not appear on his grandparents' household register. Liu Yaxiong was said to have been a good mother to him later in his life.

She was one of the lesser-known women cadres who for periods of time wielded real military and political power on the local level and rose to become a vice-minister. Although maintaining a low profile and not acquiring many fancy titles, Liu Yaxiong was probably one of a few women silently making a real difference in China.

Lily Xiao Hong LEE

Bo Yibo. "Liu Yaxiong jinianji xu." *Renmin ribao*, 17 February 1989, 5.
"Liu Yaxiong tongzhi shengping." *Renmin ribao*, 4 March 1989, 4.
Yingwen *Zhongguo funü*, ed. *Gujin zhuming funü renwu*. vol. 2. Shijiazhuang: Hebei renmin chubanshe, 1986, 611–15.
Zhongguo renwu nianjian, 1989. Huayi chubanshe, 1989, 91.

Liu Ying

Liu Ying, b. 1905, in Changsha County, Hunan Province, to a gentry-landlord family; her original name was Zheng Jie. A fellow provincial of Mao Zedong (1893–1976), Liu Ying became active in revolutionary work in the early 1920s and was one of the thirty women who went on the Long March of 1934–35. She worked mainly with the Communist Youth League until the late 1940s and then was assigned to work more closely with her husband, Zhang Wentian (aka Luo Fu, 1900–1976). Liu Ying was widely respected in the CCP.

She had nine siblings. Her traditionalist father ensured that his sons received an education but denied the same right to his daughters. The widowing of an older sister within a year of entering into an arranged marriage and subsequent death from tuberculosis, contracted from her husband, deeply affected Liu Ying. Her mother managed to send her to private school. When the family moved to Changsha city, Liu Ying joined the Chinese Socialist Youth League (its name was later changed to the Communist Youth League) in 1924, even before enrolling in Changsha Women's Normal School (Changsha nüzi shifan xuexiao). She joined the CCP in 1925 in Changsha and the following year was one of only two women among the forty students selected to study at the Hunan-Hubei Party School in Wuhan. Elected head of Hunan Women's Bureau and an alternate member of the Provincial Party Committee in 1927, Liu Ying was already an underground CCP worker when the party assigned her to a live-in partnership with Lin Wei. The two had become close after he had returned from his studies in France in 1926. Lin Wei was killed in 1927, however, and one source says that Liu Ying gave birth to his child, although no further details are offered. After working for some time in Shanghai, Liu Ying was sent in 1929 to Moscow to study at Sun Yat-sen University and later transferred to the International Wireless School (Guoji wuxiandian xuexiao). While a student in Russia, she met her future husband, then known as Luo Fu, who taught at Sun Yat-sen University. After returning to China in 1932, Liu Ying was involved with Youth League work, mainly in Fujian Province. In early 1934, however, she attended a conference in Ruijin, capital of the Jiangxi soviet, and remained there as the Youth League Central Committee's head of Propaganda. Liu Ying was working in the field on a massive recruitment drive on the eve of the Long March but was alerted by Mao Zedong to return quickly to Ruijin in time to join.it, an act of kindness that may be explained by their status as fellow provincials.

During the Long March, Liu Ying was classed as a student and assigned the duties of a political fighter, which included propaganda work and acting as political instructor, fundraiser, and scout for food and laborers. Initially assigned to logistics, she hired bearers and occasionally helped carry litters. Possibly because Liu Ying was what has been described as a "political protégée" of Mao Zedong, she was appointed in mid-May 1935 (about the time of the Zunyi Conference) to succeed Deng Xiaoping to the position of secretary-general to the Central Committee. This post had been held previously by a woman—Deng Yingchao (*q.v.*)—in the Jiangxi soviet, but it passed again into male hands (Wang Shoudao) toward the end of the Long March, and Liu Ying went back to her work as a political fighter.

Toward the end of the Long March, she finally married Zhang Wentian (still then known as Luo Fu). She had steadfastly refused to marry him before then because she did not want to become pregnant during the march nor did she want children to interfere with her work. In Yan'an, Liu Ying and her husband lived next door to Mao Zedong. She worked as head of a propaganda team with the Youth League. Helen Snow described Liu Ying at that time as "Lo Fu's 'pocket wife' . . . the tiniest little creature conceivable. How she could possibly have kept from being blown away during the Long March I can't imagine." Indeed, Liu Ying's nickname in Yan'an was "Little Sparrow" (Xiao maque). Her work with the Youth League came to an end, however, when she was assigned to her husband as his political secretary and worked closely with him from then on. One source says that Liu Ying gave birth in Yan'an, but the baby became ill and died.

Liu Ying became ill in Yan'an as well, catching pneumonia and suffering gastric troubles and chronic high fever. Suffering from nervous exhaustion—and possibly tuberculosis, like so many of her comrades—she was sent to Russia for medical treatment. Liu Ying was pregnant when she traveled there by train with Mao's estranged (but pregnant) wife He Zizhen (*q.v.*) at the end of 1937 (one source gives this as November 1938). The child Liu Ying gave birth to in Moscow died, however, and she returned to Yan'an in March 1939 and then became head of the secretariat of the Central Committee. Liu Ying was sent in 1942 to the northwest on investigative research but returned to attend the CCP's Seventh Congress in 1945. She and her husband worked together in the northeast between that year and 1949; Liu Ying served as head of Hejiang Provincial Organization Department. She served on the Harbin Municipal Standing Committee and as head of the Harbin Organization Department in 1948 and filled similar positions at provincial level in Liaoning Province in 1949.

With the establishment of the PRC that year, Zhang Wentian was transferred to foreign affairs. When he was appointed ambassador to the USSR, Liu Ying went with him to Moscow, where she spent nearly four years (1951–54) in charge of party affairs. In October 1954, Zhou Enlai (1898–1976) recalled her to Beijing to work in the Foreign Ministry. Five years later, Zhang Wentian, then a vice-foreign minister, voiced criticism of the Great Leap Forward and Mao Zedong's leadership. Saying he would rather die telling the truth than live in misery, he spoke up for democracy and free speech. He was immediately labeled a "right opportunist." Inevitably, as his wife, Liu Ying was also smeared; her punishment for her husband's words was a demotion to a modern history work unit. When her husband was accused of treachery—spying for the USSR—in the early days of the Cultural Revolution, Liu Ying was also subjected to harassment, being confined under guard for over a year, before she and her husband were exiled, under house arrest, in Guangdong, for six years. Zhang Wentian died in exile on 1 July 1976, just a few months before the end of the Cultural Revolution. Liu Ying was allowed to return to Beijing in September.

Initially resentful at the treatment she and her husband had received since the late 1950s, Liu Ying demanded redress. She demanded that the wrongful charges against her in 1959 be reversed; she requested that Zhang Wentian's ashes be brought to Beijing and placed in Babaoshan Revolutionary Cemetery; and she asked to be provided with money to buy books. She was rehabilitated in 1977 and, in 1978, was appointed to the CCP's Central Commission for Discipline Inspection. Zhang Wentian was also rehabilitated that year.

Once all three of her demands had been met, Liu Ying appears to have put the past behind her and reaffirmed her commitment to the party. At the time of writing, she was believed to be living in Beijing.

Sue WILES

Guo Chen. *Jinguo liezhuan: Hong yifangmian jun sanshiwei changzheng nü hongjun shengping shiji*. Beijing: Nongcun duwu chubanshe, 1986, 77, 92–93, 99–104, 138.
———. "Shengming zhi shu changqing." In *Nü bing liezhuan*, vol. 1, ed. Han Zi. Shanghai: Shanghai wenyi chubanshe, 1985, 119–33.
Li Zhisui. *The Private Life of Chairman Mao*, trans. Professor Tai Hung-chao. New York: Random House, 1994.
Salisbury, Harrison. *The Long March: The Untold Story*. New York: Harper & Row, 1985.
Sun Xiaoyang. "Fengyu zhengcheng liushizai." In *Hongjun nüyingxiong zhuan*, ed. Liaowang bianjibu. Beijing: Xinhua chubanshe, 1986, 38–52.
Wales, Nym [Helen Foster Snow]. *Inside Red China*. New York: Da Capo Press, 1977, 178.
Zeng Zhi. *Changzheng nü zhanshi*. Changchun: Beifang funü ertong chubanshe, 1987, 13–27.

Liu Zhen

Liu Zhen is the pen name adopted by the contemporary writer Liu Lianqing, b. 1930, in Xiajin County, Shandong Province.

Her father, Liu Shaotang, was a peasant who received only a few years of primary education. Although Liu Zhen herself appears not to have had her feet bound, young girls in that area were still subjected to the torture of footbinding, and females did not receive an education of any kind. There was no school in her village, and the women generally worked at weaving in their homes and helped in the fields during the summer and autumn harvest periods.

Liu Zhen's older brother Liu Qingfang joined the Communist Youth League in 1927 and later worked in the communist enclave at Yan'an. Whether influenced by him or because of the presence of a very active communist network in Shandong, the entire Liu family was sympathetic to the communists; they became part of the CCP underground in the mid-1930s. To escape the encroaching Japanese army, the family fled in 1938 to the CCP base in Qinghe County, Hebei Province, where Liu Zhen became a member of a CCP anti-Japanese propaganda team in the south of Hebei Province. She learned performance skills and went to school for the first time, learning reading, writing, and communism. Liu Zhen undertook the extremely dangerous work of carrying messages for the underground in 1942 when she was twelve years old, shaving her hair to pass as a boy. Liu Zhen was arrested three times by Japanese military police and once was nearly mauled to death by police dogs. Her remarkable bravery led the CCP to accept her as a candidate for membership, and she was assigned to training classes in the communist base in the Taihang Mountains.

Liu Zhen then worked as an actress in the Pingyuan Theatrical Troupe affiliated with the southern Hebei military area command in 1945 and in the following year was formally recognized as a CCP member. She was promoted to group-head of the troupe and assigned at the front during the 1945–49 civil war, caring for the wounded, performing for soldiers, and publicizing the communist message to the masses. Liu Zhen commenced her writing career in 1946 when she produced some literary reports and prose pieces.

After Liu Zhen's troupe reached Sichuan in 1949 and became involved in pacifying the region, she was made director of the Troupe Writers' Office. In 1951 Liu Zhen studied at the Lu Xun Institute of Literature and Arts in northeastern China and wrote the short story "Good Aunty" (Hao daniang), which was published in the journal *Dongbei Literature and Arts* (Dongbei wenyi). The story is realistic and touching, telling of a rural woman who gave her life to save a young soldier of the Eighth Route Army; it received Third Prize in a Children's Literature Award. In winter 1952, the institute recommended Liu Zhen for a period of study at the Central Institute for Literature of Beijing, which was presided over by the renowned woman writer Ding Ling (*q.v.*). There Liu Zhen wrote several short stories as well as prose and folk stories and in 1956 was made a member of the Chinese Writers' Association. That year she also lived for a time among ethnic minorities in Yunnan Province and wrote novels with minority settings, such as *The Thick Forest* (Mimi de da senlin) and *Yes, I Am Jingpo* (Dui, wo shi Jingpozu).

Like many other writers, Liu Zhen found herself a victim of the political movements launched by Mao Zedong (1893–1976) after 1949. The CCP call of 1958 that "writers should enter deeply into the lives of workers, peasants and soldiers and go to the class struggle and production battlefront," for example, saw her assigned to Xushui County in Hebei Province as deputy CCP secretary. She undertook various tasks there during the Great Leap Forward (1958–60), but when Liu Zhen reported to the Provincial CCP Committee that tallies of agricultural production were being falsified at all levels she was accused of being a "counter-party opportunist and an anti-Great Leap Forward rightist." Liu Zhen was dismissed from her post; her party membership was reduced to probationary status for a year; and she was sent to work on a pig farm.

Her novel *The Heroes' Sonata* (Yingxiong de yuezhang) was also criticized as revisionist. Contrary to the Maoist edict that art and literature should serve the revolution, Liu Zhen had explored instead the significance and beauty of humanity and love and approached war, peace, and life philosophically rather than politically. An article published in the journal *The Bee* (Mifeng) said: "In *The Heroes' Sonata*, revolutionary war and love are looked at from the bourgeois viewpoint of humanitarianism, and individual happiness is contrasted with the revolutionary cause. What it reveals is weariness with revolutionary war and illusory peace and happiness . . . The characters in this novel are clothed as revolutionary soldiers but have the mentality of decadent capitalists." Liu Zhen was blacklisted as a counter-revolutionary writer, together with such celebrities as Hu Feng and Ding Ling, until 1962, when Liu Zhen was rehabilitated by Zhou Yang, minister of Culture.

A collection of her novels titled *Water Flowing On and On* (Changchang de liushui) was published in 1963 by the Writers' Publishing House. Soon after the start of the Cultural Revolution (1966–76), however, Liu Zhen was again accused of conspiring against the revolution. She was detained, criticized, and publicly humiliated, then sent to a farm for labor reform. Liu Zhen was not allowed to write anything at all during the Cultural Revolution. Between 1976 and the early 1980s, however, she produced the short story "The Black Flag" (Hei-qi); the prose poem *Mourning You, Commander-in-Chief Peng Dehuai* (Ku ni, Peng Dehuai zongsiling); and the novelette *A Little Spark* (Xiao huohua).

Liu Zhen married at some stage and had at least one son. After she migrated to Sydney, Australia, in 1988, Liu Zhen wrote several memoirs, including "Around the Imperial Tombs" (Zai huangling de zhouwei) and "I'll Beat You to Death If You Don't Say It Clearly" (Shuo bu qing, wo da si ni), both published in Hong Kong journals. She has not been a prolific writer, having spent her life more as a professional activist. Her work as a cadre certainly absorbed much time that could have been devoted to writing. More destructive in this regard, however, was the hardship and frustration Liu Zhen suffered during the onslaught of various political movements and her being forbidden to write for many years.

Liu Zhen's finest novels are *Xiao Rong and I* (Wo he Xiao Rong) and *Water Flowing On and On*, both of which are children's fiction based on the "little devils" of the Eighth Route Army and other groups of adolescents fighting during the 1930s and 1940s. These novels contain glimpses of her own childhood experiences, full of innocence and originality, while the children she follows through wartime are presented vividly and with delicacy.

Liu Zhen's reputation within China rests as much on her legendary life as it does her literary achievements. A revolutionary from the age of nine, accepted into the CCP at thirteen, and acquainted with many senior party officials, both civil and military, she shared with many communists the lofty revolutionary ideal of the emancipation of humanity. However, Liu Zhen became suspicious of the party she had devoted her life to after Mao Zedong established what was in reality a dictatorship and set in train a series of disastrous economic and social policies. Liu Zhen was one of the few communists who dared to criticize Mao, and her sense of justice, conscience, and sensitivity as a writer led her to expose for all to see the catastrophic results of those events.

In the late 1990s, Liu Zhen became a practitioner of Falungong in Sydney and wrote many articles defending and promoting the movement.

Rubing HONG
(Translated by Tao Naikan)

Hsu, Kaiyu. *Literature of the People's Republic of China*. Bloomington: Indiana University Press, 1980, 592–605.

Jin Han. *Zhongguo dangdai xiaoshuo shi*. Hangzhou: Hangzhou daxue chubanshe, 1990, 83–85.
Liu Zhen. *Changchang de liushui*. Beijing: Zuojia chubanshe, 1963.
———. "Shuo bu qing, wo da si ni." *Kaifang* (December 1992): 64–69.
———. "Yi pi ma de yuan'an." *Kaifang* (April 1993): 8–11.
———. "Zai huangling zhouwei." *Kaifang* (March 1993): 95–98.
Zhongguo wenxuejia cidian: Xiandai, 1. Chengdu: Sichuan People's Press, 1979, 213–14.
Zhongguo xiandai zuojia zhuanlüe, vol. 2. Chengdu: Sichuan People's Press, 1983, 104–08.

Liu Zhihua

Liu Zhihua, b. 1940, in the countryside near the city of Xinxiang, Henan Province, is one of the women from villages and small towns who have emerged as entrepreneurs in the economic reform period that began in the late 1970s in the PRC.

Her company, Jinghua Industries, grew from being a small production team (equivalent to a village) of seventy-two households comprising 353 people. The villagers in this poor village had difficulty feeding themselves. Having no money to buy chemical fertilizer with which to produce more food and despite freezing weather, Liu Zhihua once led the villagers to collect wastewater from a ditch near a chemical fertilizer factory and cart it to their fields. That year, they had a bumper harvest. With that success behind her and the economic environment in the country becoming freer, Liu Zhihua thought about markets.

Local conditions convinced her that it would be best to start a business in processing agricultural by-products and food. In 1979, she headed the production team of her fellow villagers again, and this time had them using rope-making machines to weave rope from rice straw. Two years later, Liu Zhihua set up a factory to manufacture dried beancurd rolls (*fuzhu*), taking advantage of the large local production of soybeans. This factory turned a profit the same year its doors opened for business. Production then snowballed in different directions, into a series of food-processing factories—including two canned-food factories, a soybean by-products factory, a soybean-milk factory that produced granules for soy drinks, and a factory for processing a variety of animal husbandry products. Other ventures associated with these efforts set up a paper-carton factory and an amusement park.

Liu Zhihua marketed these companies' products in eleven provinces and cities; profits were re-invested into mechanizing the production team's farm and opening its own market. She had effectively parleyed the small production team's effort into the beginnings of a conglomerate. In 1993, this entity had a fixed capital of 31 million RMB, a circulating fund of 11 million RMB, and an annual profit of around 10 million RMB. Average income of each member was 4,800 RMB; while not a large amount, even for those times, the sum brought with it many fringe benefits. Each of the seventy-two households in the team lived in its own house, at thirty square meters per person. Architecturally, the houses copied diverse styles from around the world, and all had modern plumbing, heating, and hot water. The company provided furnishings for each house, a gas stove, as well as basic foods such as rice, oil, and salt; it also assumed financial responsibility for weddings, funerals, births, sickness, and injuries. Jinghua Gardens, combining the functions of a hotel, sanatorium, and tourist attraction, was completed in 1992. The company also concerns itself with the arts and sports, establishing an orchestra, art group, and gymnastics and table tennis teams.

Liu Zhihua summarizes the principle by which she runs her business as one ensuring outstanding quality, new products, cheap prices, considerate service, and a trustworthy reputation. She sets aside 25 percent of pre-tax profit for remuneration for staff and workers, while 45 percent of after-tax profit goes to expansion and development of the company; the remainder acts as circulating capital. Liu Zhihua believes in continuous expansion and therefore starts up a new factory or branch every year to increase annual productivity and profit. Her company has won awards for food sanitation and excellence in management. Liu Zhihua won the title of Contemporary China's Outstanding Peasant Entrepreneur (Dangdai youxiu nongmin qiyejia) and received the National Award for Talent for Economic Reform (Quanguo jingji gaige rencai jiang). These honors acknowledge her hard work in creating a unique peasant-type enterprise from her own peasant background.

Lily Xiao Hong LEE

Song Ruizhi. *Zhongguo funü wenhua tonglan*. Jinan: Shandong wenyi chubanshe, 1995, 48–49.
"Xiangcun dushi nüdangjia—Liu Zhihua." *Zhongguo jiaoyubao*, 8 March 1993, 4.

Liu-Wang Liming

Liu-Wang Liming, 1897–1970, whose original name was Wang Liming, was a native of Taihu in Anhui Province. She was a prominent women's rights activist and left-leaning democratic campaigner and played a leading role in the women's suffrage campaigns of the 1920s and 1930s. During the war against Japan, Liu-Wang Liming participated as a women's leader in the People's Political Participation Conference. After 1949 the activist remained in China and assumed numerous official posts until she fell into disfavor during the 1957 anti-rightist campaign. Her contributions to the Chinese women's movement and the nation's democratic parties were exceptional.

Liu-Wang Liming's father, a doctor servicing the villages around Taihu, died when she was nine years old. His death plunged the family into financial hardship, and they survived only through the generosity of relatives and her mother's needlework. Despite the impecunious state of the household, Liu-Wang Liming was able to start school at the age of ten by attending Fuyin Elementary (Fuyin xiaoxue), which was a free school. She excelled in her studies and was sent on to Jiujiang Confucian College (Ruli xueyuan), where her excellent grades won a scholarship and relieved her of the worry of finding money for school fees. This college was one of the few middle schools in the region that accepted female students. At this time, Liu-Wang Liming demonstrated a characteristic strength of will and independent spirit when she was one of the first girls in her district to refuse to have her feet bound. After graduating four years later, Liu-Wang Liming was invited to remain at the college as a teacher and stayed at Jiujiang until 1916, when she won a scholarship to study in America. There Liu-Wang Liming enrolled at Northwestern University and studied biology. Like many of her contemporaries, she believed that science was the discipline that would enable her to help rebuild her ailing nation.

Liu-Wang Liming's time at Northwestern University stimulated her interest in women's rights, and on returning to China in 1920 after graduation she immersed herself in publishing in order to propagate the importance of women's liberation for strengthening the nation. During this period, Liu-Wang Liming became active in the women's suffrage movement. She took a leadership role in the Shanghai branch of the Progressive Association for Women's Participation in Politics (Nüzi canzheng xiejinhui), established on 15 October 1922, which, echoing its parent body in Beijing, called for provisions guaranteeing gender equality in the national and provincial constitutions. The goals of the association included reforming the marriage system (arranged marriages and concubinage), eliminating the practice of buying and selling slavegirls, and generally promoting women's rights within marriage. The Shanghai branch published a short-lived journal entitled *Women Citizens* (Nü guomin).

As well as maintaining an interest in women's rights, Liu-Wang Liming was active in philanthropic and welfare societies around Shanghai; she founded refuge places for beggar girls and escaped slavegirls in Shanghai and established numerous women's industrial schools, women's culture societies, and women's handicraft cooperatives throughout urban areas, including Shanghai, Hong Kong, Chengdu, and Chongqing. Liu-Wang Liming was a member of the Protestant Church; president of the Chinese Women's Christian Temperance Union (Zhonghua funü jiezhi hui, WCTU); and vice-president of the Far Eastern Section of the World WCTU. Women's suffrage organizations worldwide had been supported, if not dominated, by the WCTU, and Liu-Wang Liming provided this link between Protestantism and women's suffrage in China. She was concurrently president of the Birth Control League in a further intersection of her Protestant and feminist convictions. One of her several books, *The Chinese Women's Movement* (Zhongguo funü yundong), published by Commercial Press in 1934, explores the importance of women's political and economic independence and the need to reform the family and marriage customs.

The war against Japan interrupted her work in Shanghai dramatically. In 1938, her husband Liu Zhan'en (1895–1938) was assassinated by the Japanese secret police. He had been president of Shanghai University (Hujiang) and an active member of the YMCA, but his involvement, as president, in the Anti-Japanese United Association (KangRi lianhehui) of Shanghai universities and the United National Salvation Association (Shanghai gejie jiuwang xiehui) targeted him for attention by the Japanese military. Liu-Wang Liming was also blacklisted by the Japanese. With her two daughters, she fled Shanghai, going first to Wuhan then to Chongqing to escape the Japanese occupation.

During the time in Chongqing, Liu-Wang Liming was selected as a councillor to the People's Political Participation Conference (Guomin canzheng hui) in mid-1938. In this semi-democratic forum, she pushed for a guaranteed set minimum quota of seats for women in the nation's legislative bodies, a campaign that was won when the Constitution of 1946 set a 10 percent minimum for women. Liu-Wang Liming was so outspoken in her demands for the implementation of constitutional rule in China that in September 1943 she was removed from the Third People's Political Participation Conference. The following year Liu-Wang Liming joined the China Democratic League (CDL, Zhongguo minzhu tongmeng), a coalition that occupied the middle ground between the CCP and the KMT, and was elected to its Central Committee.

Between 1944 and 1949, Liu-Wang Liming continued to work for women's rights and democracy. She and fellow women activists Li Dequan (*q.v.*), Shi Liang (*q.v.*), and Liu Qingyang (*q.v.*) established the Chinese Women's Association (Zhongguo funü lianyi hui) in 1945. This group aimed to mobilize women to promote democracy in the face of Chiang Kai-shek's continued dictatorial rule. With the assassination of the poet Wen Yiduo (1899–1946) by KMT hitmen in July, Liu-Wang Liming organized outraged citizens into the League for the Protection of Human Rights (Zhongguo renquan baozhang weiyuanhui). This was despite clear threats to her personal safety. However, the increased suppression of democratic sentiment in China forced her to leave for Hong Kong, where she continued her work as part of the Central Committee of the CDL. The CDL and the League for the Protection of Human Rights had both been declared illegal by the KMT and were forcibly disbanded in early 1947.

The founding of the PRC in 1949 allowed Liu-Wang Liming to return to China in safety. As a representative of the CDL, she participated in discussions on the formation of the new government and continued to support it while retaining her membership in the CDL. Liu-Wang Liming was elected to the CPPCC's Second, Third, and Fourth National Committees (Quanguo zhengxie weiyuanhui). She also maintained her passion for women's issues and sat on the Standing Committee of the ACWF. From this position, Liu-Wang Liming represented China at the International Asian Women's Conference held in Beijing in 1954. Two years later, as president of the Chinese WCTU, she led a delegation to West Germany to attend the WCTU Congress and was elected vice-president.

Liu-Wang Liming's support for CCP rule in China in those early years was not sufficient, however, to protect her from persecution. In 1957 she was labeled a rightist and her political career abruptly ended. Her troubles resurfaced in 1966 with the advent of the Cultural Revolution (1966–76). Jailed for unspecified "political crimes" and having barely recovered from a broken arm (the result of a fall), Liu-Wang Liming spent three and a half years in prison, where she died in 1970 at the age of seventy-four.

On 18 March 1981, the CPPCC National Committee, the CDL, and the ACWF held a memorial meeting honoring Liu-Wang Liming. Although her death had passed without official recognition in 1970, she was posthumously honored by these associations to which Liu-Wang Liming had dedicated so much of her life. She was an outstanding feminist and democrat whose contribution to China remains undisputed.

Louise EDWARDS

Funü cidian. Beijing: Qiushi chubanshe, 1990, 100.
Gao Kuixiang and Shen Jianguo, eds. *Zhonghua gujin nüjie pu*. Beijing: Zhongguo shehui chubanshe, 1991, 147–48.
Jingsheng and Xiquan, eds. *Xin Zhongguo mingrenlu*. Nanchang: Jiangxi renmin chubanshe, 1987.
Liu Guanghua. "Wo de muqin Liu-Wang Liming." *Renwu*, no. 6 (1981): 143–49.
Liu Shaotang, ed. "Wang Liming." In *Minguo renwu xiaozhuan*, vol. 9. Taipei: Zhuanji wenxue chubanshe, 1987, 11–15.
Wang Xin, ed. *Zhongguo minzhu dangpai mingrenlu*. Nanjing: Jiangsu renmin chubanshe, 1993, 220–22.

Wang Zheng. *Women in the Chinese Enlightenment: Oral and Textual Histories*. Berkeley: University of California Press, 1999, 135–43.
Yuan Shaoying and Yang Guizhen, eds. *Zhongguo funü mingren cidian*. Changchun: Beifang funü ertong chubanshe, 1989, 129–31.

Longlian fashi: *see* **Longlian, Ven.**

Longlian, Ven.
Ven. Longlian [Longlian fashi], b. 1909, as You Yongkang in Leshan County, Sichuan Province, is a Buddhist nun and scholar.

Her paternal grandfather had gained the degree of cultivated talent (*xiucai*) in the Qing civil service examination. Her maternal grandfather was a Tribute Student (Second Class) who became principal of a primary school that boasted such famous students as the poet Guo Moruo. Her father was a graduate of Chengdu Normal College and taught school all his life. While he could not afford to provide a full education for all seven of his children, Ven. Longlian's father believed in home education. After leaving school at the age of twelve, Ven. Longlian studied at home both under his tutelage—completing the high school syllabus—and by herself and under the guidance of specialists, learning English, painting, calligraphy, and traditional medicine. At the age of twenty, she started teaching at Chengdu Women's Normal School. In the meantime, Ven. Longlian had published her first book, *The First Book on My Dedication to Learning* (Zhi xue chuji). She was known, deservedly, in her province as a talented woman and was given the sobriquet "Female Principal Scholar" (Nü zhuangyuan).

In 1939, the government of Sichuan set three examinations for those aspiring to be educational administrators, civil servants, and senior civil servants. Ven. Longlian's father encouraged her to sit for them and his daughter not only passed but came first in all three. She was appointed as an editor-translator at the Provincial Editing and Translating Bureau but surprised everyone four years later by relinquishing her prestigious position to become a Buddhist nun in the Aidao Buddhist Convent. The governor of the province, Deng Xiting, was so concerned at her decision that he visited her on the day of her ordination to make sure it was her own wish and her parents had consented. Speculation was rife at the time that Ven. Longlian had become a nun because she was disillusioned with her career or disappointed in love. Ven. Longlian later maintained that her decision came about because of her belief that she could contribute little to society as a civil servant and because of the Buddhist influence of her family. Thenceforth, she has devoted herself to the study of Buddhist thought and headed the Nuns' Department (ni zhong bu) at the Lotus School Academy in Sichuan (Lian zong yuan) in which capacity Ven. Longlian has trained generations of female Buddhist scholars.

Her family had indeed been deeply involved with Buddhism: Ven. Longlian's maternal grandfather was president of the local Buddhist association, maternal grandmother and mother were devout Buddhists, and father also knew a great deal about Buddhism. When young, Ven. Longlian had recited sutras with her grandmother; after starting work in Chengdu, both as a teacher and in the provincial government, Ven. Longlian went to the Aidao Buddhist Convent to study sutras in her spare time. When her first work on Buddhism appeared—*A Brief Discussion on She Dasheng* (She Dasheng lun lüeshu)—specialists thought it was the work of a senior Buddhist master.

After the establishment of the PRC in 1949, Ven. Longlian continued to work in Buddhist studies and teaching within the guidelines of the new government. She was president of the Buddhist Association of Sichuan and deputy secretary-general of the Buddhist Association of China. In the 1970s, Ven. Longlian established the Buddhist College for Nuns at the site of the Ming dynasty Temple Tiexiang si. This was the first institution of higher education devoted to the training of female Buddhist scholars. She was president of the college and taught courses such as Buddhist knowledge and law and sutras in classical Chinese.

As a Buddhist scholar, Ven. Longlian was the only woman invited by the chief editor and the Ministry of Culture of Sri Lanka to contribute to the section on Chinese Buddhism in a Buddhist encyclopedia they were compiling. She was also proficient in the Tibetan language and one of the compilers of the *Great Chinese-Tibetan Dictionary* (Han-Zang dacidian) in the 1950s. Ven. Longlian has said that in her remaining years she wishes to make the Buddhist College for Nuns an institution for fostering women Buddhist leaders in China; Ven. Longlian also looks forward to putting in order the ten or more works she has compiled and translated in the past for publication and distribution as soon as possible. In addition to *A Brief Discussion on She Dasheng*, she has published *Ru pusha xinglun*.

Lily Xiao Hong LEE

Huaxia funü mingren cidian. Beijing: Huaxia chubanshe, 1988.
Yingwen *Zhongguo funü,* ed. *Gujin zhuming funü renwu,* vol. 2. Shijiazhuang: Hebei renmin chubanshe, 1986, 790–93.

Lu, Annette: *see* **Lü Hsiu-lien**

Lü, Annette: *see* **Lü Hsiu-lien**

Lü Bicheng
Lü Bicheng, 1883–1943, of Jingde County, Anhui Province, was a woman of high scholarly attainment who became active in the movement to promote women's education during late Qing and converted to Buddhism in later life. She was known by various names at different times of her life: Lü Lanqing, *zi* Duntian, Lü Mingyin, Lü Shengyin, and Baolian (her Buddhist name).

Her father, Lü Fengqi (d. 1895), was a provincial education commissioner (*xuezheng*) in Shanxi. When both of his sons died young, he devoted his attention to his four daughters, who became proficient in poetry and prose writing and gained a measure of fame. Lü Bicheng was the third daughter, and she and her two elder sisters (Lü Huiru and Lü Meisheng) were dubbed "the three Lü of west of the Huai River" (*Huaixi san Lü*). Lü Bicheng was exceptionally talented and cherished by her parents for her intelligence; she was well versed in literary writing, calligraphy, painting, seal engraving, music and, in particular, the lyric genre (*ci*). Lü Bicheng enjoyed a comfortable and happy childhood and studied the classics and the histories, being able to write poems at the age of five and paint at the age of seven.

After her father died of a stroke in 1895, Lü Bicheng went to live with her mother, née Yan, in Jingde. She studied with her maternal uncle Yan Langxuan, who was a government official in Tanggu, and by the time Lü Bicheng was fifteen or sixteen her poems and lyrics received praise from scholars such as Fan Zengxiang. Soon afterward, Lü Bicheng traveled alone to Tianjin, where she was recruited by Ying Lianzhi, general manager of the newspaper *Dagongbao*, as an assistant editor. Lü Bicheng also studied Western logic with the famous scholar Yan Fu [Yen Fu], who was known for his translations of Western scientific works and philosophy of enlightenment. Lü Bicheng frequently communicated with celebrated scholars in Beijing and Tianjin, exchanging poems with some of them, and contributed to *Dagongbao* as well as the women's newspapers *Zhongguo nübao* and *Nüzi shijie*.

At this time, about 1900, many scholars and reformers called for the establishment of schools for women, and in the wake of the abortive One Hundred Days of Reform of 1898 both Yuan Shikai, then governor of Zhili, and Tang Shaoyi of Tianjian implemented new policies. Yuan Shikai made available to Fu Zengxiang the sum of 1,000 silver dollars to establish schools for women; Lü Bicheng became actively involved in formulating educational objectives as well as the curriculum of one of them, Beiyang Women's School (Beiyang nüzi gongxue). She believed that the work of strengthening and saving the nation should start with education, and developing people's minds and changing customs and beliefs were the first steps in this process. Thus, the educational curriculum of Beiyang Women's School followed the prevailing reformist ideology of that era; it also emphasized women's moral education. The school was officially inaugurated in 1904 with Lü Bicheng, then twenty-one years old, acting as head teacher; she subsequently became principal. Her contribution to the founding and running of women's schools extended to Hedong Girls' Academy (Hedong nüxuetang), which she also helped run that year.

During this period, Lü Bicheng became acquainted with the revolutionary Qiu Jin (see *Biographical Dictionary of Chinese Women: The Qing Period*), a forerunner of the feminist movement. Qiu Jin invited her to go to Japan to pursue the revolution but Lü Bicheng declined: although she endorsed Qiu Jin's revolution, Lü Bicheng attached greater importance to educational reforms. She therefore remained in China and channeled her enthusiasm into running schools in a bid to fulfill the reforms for which the campaign for women's schools had pressed. Lü Bicheng asserted that women should be bold enough to aspire to personal independence, self-determination, patriotism, and strengthening the nation, yet she also believed that women lacking knowledge and intelligence would "harm the nation" if they interfered in politics. Her attitude toward the women's liberation movement was cautious, and Lü Bicheng kept an open mind on the topic of women's participation in politics. Despite these substantial philosophical differences from Qiu Jin, however, Lü Bicheng found her contact with another woman on this level deeply inspiring.

In spring 1907, a normal school was attached to the Beiyang School to train women teachers, but with the founding of the Republic of China in 1912 the latter school closed. Recruited by Yuan Shikai as secretary to his office, Lü Bicheng was highly regarded as a scholar with national standing, but she was quick to distance herself from Yuan Shikai when he embarked on an abortive attempt to become emperor. Lü Bicheng resigned from her position and went to live in Shanghai with her mother. Over the next few years, Lü Bicheng traveled widely within China, touring scenic spots and historical sites and writing about them in many of her poems. She worked hard at learning English, French, German, and Japanese and became acquainted with a great many celebrities and scholars. She also "ran a business" in order to amass funds for her planned overseas study, but the nature of the business is not known.

Lü Bicheng had at some stage joined the revolutionary literary body of the Southern Society (Nanshe)—established in 1909 for the purpose of using literature to promote social reform and revolution—and attended one of its gatherings of literati in Xuyuan, Shanghai, in August 1914. It was not for another six years, however, that she was able to enroll, in 1920, at Columbia University in the United States to undertake further study at her own expense. Lü Bicheng studied literature and fine arts, working at the same time as a special correspondent for the Shanghai newspaper *Shibao*. After graduating, she traveled to England and Europe, visiting France, Italy, and Switzerland. During this period, Lü Bicheng wrote many poems praising the scenery of her motherland and also the travelogue *Traces on the Snow* (Hongxue yinyuan) edited by Zhou Shoujuan and published in *Banyue zazhi*.

In the meantime, however, Lü Bicheng had been studying Buddhist doctrine deeply. Ever since she had discussed Zen principles with Master Dixian during an earlier period of residence in Beijing, Lü Bicheng had harbored a desire to become a Buddhist. In 1922, during a trip back to China, she delivered addresses on Buddhism at several universities; after settling in the Swiss Alps in 1926, Lü Bicheng devoted herself to Buddhist teachings and the propagation of Buddhist doctrine. Her article "The Road to the Lotus Land" (Lianbang zhi lu), published in *Fragrance and Light* (Xiangguang xiaolu), is an account of her Buddhist studies in the United Kingdom. Lü Bicheng had long advocated vegetarianism, abstention from killing, cessation of slaughter, and protection of animals. The central philosophical imperative of her *Wanderings in Europe and the Americas* (OuMei manyou lu, 1929) was the precept "Do No Harm"—which she expressed thus: "human beings [must] not harm fellow human beings, and human beings [must] not harm other beings." In this work, which underwent many reprintings and enjoyed wide circulation, she also championed the cardinal significance of "beauty" and "goodness." Lü Bicheng sponsored the publication of books by a British person (whose name has been transliterated as Fu Huade) on abstaining from killing and attended seminars with other philanthropists to initiate a "movement for the protection of beings and abandoning slaughter." Her translations into English of a number of Buddhist scriptures aroused the attention of Westerners, and she herself converted to Buddhism in Geneva in spring 1930. Lü Bicheng produced no literary works from then on, maintaining that all earthly things were but dreams and illusion, wisdom being all. She returned to Hong Kong by way of America when World War II erupted in 1939. Lü Bicheng died of illness, in Lianyuan Buddhist Sanctuary, on 24 January 1943 at the age of sixty.

As a prolific writer, she wrote many works extolling the beauty of China's landscape and reflecting her patriotism, including *Lü Bicheng's Collected Works* (Lü Bicheng ji), *Xinfang Collection* (Xinfang ji), *Xiaozhu Lyrics* (Xiaozhu ci), *Wanderings in Europe and the Americas* (also known as *Traces on the Snow*), *The Protection of Life* (Husheng ji), *The Light of Europe and the Americas* (OuMei zhi guang), and *Miscellaneous Recollections of Touring Lushan* (You Lu suoji). Lü Bicheng confessed that she "often had strange dreams," and dreams were indeed one of her favorite themes. Her *Groping for Minnows* (Mo yu'er) and *Clear Moonlight: Inscription on a Painting of Dreams of Rushes by the Lay Disciple Baijia* (Yuehua qing: Wei Baijia jushi ti jiameng tu) projected a bewildering sense of illusion and reality; evocative, diffuse, sublimated, her scenes and images shattered barriers in describing people, objects, and emotions. Boasting an original style and profound sincerity as well as an intriguing and elegant form of composition, Lü Bicheng's writing style was mellow and deep, expansive in conception, and demonstrated exquisite artistry, including mastery of various literary forms and rules of rhyme and rhythm.

Lü Bicheng exhibited great courage in leaving home to pursue studies, taking up residence alone abroad and remaining unmarried. Entirely through her own efforts, she achieved preeminent social status and led an independent, affluent, and self-sufficient life. Her travel and residence outside China enhanced her knowledge and enriched her observations. The full range of Lü Bicheng's life—education, spiritual journey, celibacy, setting up a business, overseas studies, international travels, conscious integration of Chinese and Western cultures—was a testament to the late Qing and early Republican "modern woman." There is no doubt that she played a crucial role in the reform, patriotic, and women's movements of late Qing.

WONG Yin Lee and CHEN Wanjun
(Translated by Chan Yuk-ping)

Fang Hao. "Ying Lianzhi bixia de Lü Bicheng sizimei." *Zhuanji wenxue*, 6, no. 6 (June 1965): 44–50; 7, no. 1 (July 1965): 44–50; 7, no. 2 (August 1965): 41–46.

Gao Baishi. "Lü Bicheng chen'ai ningyuan." In *Gu chunfenglou suoji*, vol. 3. Jianshi. Taipei: Taiwan xinsheng baoshe, 1963, 118–24.

Li Yu-ning [Li Youning]. "Lü Bicheng shi zenyang kaishi xinfo de." In *Guan wuliangshou fojing shilun*, Lü Bicheng. Taipei: Tianhua chuban shiye gufen youxian gongsi, 1986, 1–4.

Liu Egong. "Shejiao xueren. Lü Bicheng." In *Zhongguo xiandai mingnüren bieji*. Taipei: Ziyoutan, 1962, 44–46.

Liu Na. *Qingmo Minchu wenren congshu—Lü Bicheng pingzhuan, zuopinxuan.* Beijing: Zhongguo wenshi chubanshe, 1998, 3–45.

"Lü Bicheng." In *Jin sanbainian mingjia cixuan*, ed. Long Yusheng. Shanghai: Shanghai gudian wenxue chubanshe, 1956, 231.

"Lü Bicheng." In *Zhongguo foxue renming cidian*, ed. Ven. Mingfu. Beijing: Zhonghua shuju, 1988, 135.

Shao Yingwu. "Lü Bicheng." In *Nanshe renwu yinping*. Beijing: Shehui kexue wenxian chubanshe, 1994, 41–42.

Wong Yin Lee. "Lü Bicheng yu Qingmo Minchu funü jiaoyu." In *Zhuangtai yu zhuangtai*

yiwai—Zhongguo funüshi yanjiu lunji, Jianshi. Hong Kong: Oxford University Press, 1999, 122–40.
Xie Kunshu. "Dongya nüzi Lü Bicheng." *Dacheng*, 148 (March 1986): 37–39.

Lü Duntian: *see* **Lü Bicheng**

Lü Fan: *see* **Zong Pu**

Lu Guizhen: *see* **Lu Gwei-Djen**

Lu Guo: *see* **Yishu**

Lu Gwei-Djen
Lu Gwei-Djen [Lu Guizhen], 1904–1991, was born in Nanjing, Jiangsu Province, although her ancestral home was Jichun County, Hubei Province. She trained as a medical biochemist at Cambridge University, served on the Division of Natural Sciences for the United Nations Educational, Scientific, and Cultural Organization (UNESCO), and collaborated closely with Joseph Needham on his influential history of Chinese science and technology, particularly the sections on traditional medicine and pharmacology.

Her family had practiced medicine for generations, and her father, Lu Maoting (*zi* Shiguo), was both a practitioner and herb merchant; he was also a political progressive. Her mother, Chen Xiuying, was barely literate. Lu Gwei-Djen was an adored child who received a good education within her family. She completed her secondary education at Nanjing Mingde Girls' High School and studied for four years in the Chemistry Faculty at Ginling [Jinling] College in Nanjing, graduating in 1930.

In 1931 Lu Gwei-Djen commenced her study of pathology and pharmacology at Beiping (Peking) Union Hospital (Xiehe yiyuan). After moving to Shanghai, she lectured in biochemistry and physiology in the medical school of St. John's University before undertaking medical research at the Henry Lester Institute into the physiological functions of Vitamin B1. When the Japanese began bombing Shanghai in 1937, Lu Gwei-Djen left by ship for Britain. She was one of three students traveling to Cambridge University to study for their doctorates in biochemistry, the other two being Shen Shizhang and Wang Yinglai. They profoundly influenced the biochemist Joseph Needham (1900–1995), who completely redirected his academic research after coming into contact with the graduate students. He became a universally respected expert on the history of Chinese science and technology and was one of the first foreign academics admitted to Academia Sinica. In the introduction to the first volume of his groundbreaking work *Science and Civilisation in China*, Needham wrote that it was to these three students, and especially to Lu Gwei-Djen, that "the credit of being the hormone or evocator of the present book should be accorded." He also dedicated the first volume to Lu Gwei-Djen's father, Lu Shiguo, "a distinguished pharmacist of the city of Nanking . . . [who] had brought up his daughter to appreciate and understand modern science" as well as to value traditional Chinese materia medica.

Lu Gwei-Djen was granted her doctorate in 1939, the year that saw the beginning of a long-term collaboration between herself and Joseph Needham. The article they wrote together, "A Contribution to the History of Chinese Dietetics" (Zhongguo yingyangxue shi shang de yige gongxian), was not published until 1951, in *Isis*, however, because of wartime restrictions. In August 1939, Lu Gwei-Djen and Zhao Yuanren (1892–1982) were sent by the Chinese Academy of Sciences to the Sixth Pacific Science Conference in the United States. Before leaving Britain, however, Lu Gwei-Djen came to an agreement with Joseph Needham that they would co-author a book on the history of Chinese science. The outbreak of World War II forced Lu Gwei-Djen to remain in the United States, and during her six-year sojourn there she was involved in various short-term research projects. Lu Gwei-Djen worked in the medical school at the University of California; the medical center of Columbia University, New York; and in the biochemistry laboratory of the University of Birmingham, Alabama.

The British government sent Joseph Needham to China in 1942 to assist the war effort as a representative of the British Royal Academy. Knowing of his presence there, Lu Gwei-Djen returned to China in 1945 after the war. She reunited with him and his wife and then took up the position of professor of nutrition at Ginling [Jinling] College. The following year, however, Joseph Needham went to Paris to make preliminary plans for the establishment of the Division of Natural Sciences for UNESCO. Once again they discussed their project and confirmed their commitment to setting it in motion in Cambridge.

In 1948, Lu Gwei-Djen went to Paris where she took over Joseph Needham's post while he went on to Cambridge to do preliminary work for and begin writing *Science and Civilisation in China*. Lu Gwei-Djen finally resigned her United Nations position in 1957 and returned to Cambridge, where she was engaged from then on in assisting Needham in this monumental work. Lu Gwei-Djen was directly involved with volume 4 (Physics and Physical Technology), volume 5 (Chemistry and Chemical Technology), and volume 6 (Biology and Biological Technology). Together, she and Needham published many essays and books over the years on the history of Chinese science and technology. Lu Gwei-Djen also published under her own name, but it was the great collaboration of Lu Gwei-Djen and Joseph Needham that made such an enormous contribution to introducing arcane aspects of China's ancient civilization to the West.

Lu Gwei-Djen remained single, preferring to devote her life to academic work. However, two years after the death from illness of Joseph's wife, Dorothy Mary Moyle Needham (1898–1987), Lu Gwei-Djen and Joseph married (in 1989). Neither of them lived to see the completion of the seven volumes, with thirty-four parts, of the great *Science and Civilisation in China*, which they had begun half a century before.

WANG Bing
(Translated by I-Chen Chen)

He Bingyu. "Lu Guizhen boshi jianjie." *Zhongguo keji shiliao*, 11, no. 4 (1990): 25–27.
Lu Gwei-Djen and Joseph Needham. *Celestial Lancets: A History and Rationale of Acupuncture and Moxa*. Cambridge: Cambridge University Press, 1980.
———. "A Contribution to the History of Chinese Dietetics." *Isis*, 42 (1951): 17.
Needham, Joseph. *Science and Civilisation in China*, vol. 4, part 3: Civil Engineering and

Nautics, with the collaboration of Wang Ling and Lu Gwei-Djen; vol. 5, parts 2, 3, 4, 5: Spagyrical Discovery and Invention, with the collaboration of Lu Gwei-Djen. Cambridge: Cambridge University Press, 1954–99.

Pan Jixing. "Jiechu de nüxing Lu Guizhen boshi." *Zhongguo keji shiliao*, 14, no. 4 (1993): 55–61.

Lu Hsih-Chia: *see* Lu Shijia

Lü Hsiu-lien

Lü Hsiu-lien [Lü Xiulian] (aka Annette Lu or Lü), b. 1944, in T'ao-yüan County, Taiwan, is a prominent women's rights leader and vice-president of Taiwan, representing the Democratic Progressive Party (DPP). She is the first woman to hold this position.

Lü Hsiu-lien was born into a merchant's family. At one stage, her parents gave their daughter away to another family because of financial difficulties in the immediate post-World War II period. They relented, however, and decided to keep her after Lü Hsiu-lien's brother Lü Ch'uan-sheng spirited his sister away, hiding her in the home of relatives in the countryside for a day.

Lü Hsiu-lien was always an excellent student and after graduating from Taiwan University Law School (Taiwan ta-hsüeh fa-lü-hsi) went overseas to further her studies. She gained a Master of Comparative Law from the University of Illinois in 1974. While studying in the United States, Lü Hsiu-lien first made contact with women's movements around the world. After returning to Taiwan, she worked for the Regulations Committee of the Executive Yuan and taught at the Ming-ch'uan Business College. Lü Hsiu-lien also published a series of newspapers and magazines articles on traditional gender roles, introducing new feminism and thereby opening a new field in Taiwanese academic circles. She had also actively contacted international women's organizations and received invitations from them to visit such countries as the United States, Japan, and Korea. Lü Hsiu-lien then established Pioneer (T'o-huang-che) Publishing House, which did indeed attract many activists in the women's movement. During this "pioneer" period, Lü Hsiu-lien wrote and published fifteen volumes in the Women's Series, including *The New Feminism* (Hsin nü-hsing-chu-i), *In Search of Another Window* (Hsün-chao ling-i shan ch'uang), *The Destination of the New Woman* (Hsin nü-hsing ho-ch'ü ho-ts'ung?), and *Count the Footsteps of the Pioneers* (Shu-i-shu t'o-huang ti chiao-pu). In the meantime, she established a "Protect-You Direct Line" (hotline) and a Women's Information Center in Kao-hsiung and Taipei, effectively creating a rescue resource center in the women's movement organizations in Taiwan.

Taiwan was a very dangerous environment for movements of any kind in the 1970s, with its government exceedingly sensitive to any political dissent. The women's movement, which had been the first to discuss gender topics after World War II, was just one of the anti-establishment movements to be muted. Realizing the difficulty of promoting the status of women in a Taiwan ruled by "male politics," Lü Hsiu-lien believed her only choice was to obtain more resources through active involvement in those politics. She ceased working with the women's movement and went overseas again to study. Other members of the women's movement she had come to know through Pioneer, such as Li Yüan-chen, Ku Yen-ling, and Cheng Chih-hui, continued the fight and played important roles in the women's movement in the 1980s.

Some saw Lü Hsiu-lien's views on new feminism and gender roles as ambiguous. She had coined the slogan "First Be a Person, Then Be a Female Person" to criticize traditional gender roles, arguing for the expansion of women's roles. Yet, she also called on women to "Act and Look Like Who You Are." This clearly left women trapped in traditional roles: women must be feminine, gentle, and ready to please. Lü Hsiu-lien was criticized because her ideal woman seemed to be a middle-class working woman who successfully maintained a career and a happy family. The leftist feminist Su Ch'ing-li stated bluntly that Lü Hsiu-lien's women's movement was nothing but a bunch of middle-class women fixated on gender.

Lü Hsiu-lien completed her Master of Law at Harvard in 1977 and was about to do her doctorate when the United States announced it was breaking off diplomatic ties with Taiwan. She gave up her scholarship and left for Taiwan immediately. Because its government had gagged the media on the subject, Lü Hsiu-lien gave public addresses to let people know that the United States had established formal relations with communist China. She stood for election to the National Assembly representing T'ao-yüan County but, because of the diplomatic crisis, the elections were not held. Not long after this, Lü Hsiu-lien joined the fledgling democratic opposition, known as the *tang-wai* (lit. outside the [KMT] party) movement.

In 1979 she became deputy director of the company that published the magazine *Beautiful Island* (Mei-li-tao) and secretary-general of the Association of Non-KMT Candidates (Tang-wai hou-hsüan-jen lien-i-hui). In December, however, Lü Hsiu-lien was arrested in the aftermath of the Kao-hsiung Incident. Initially peaceful, this celebration of human rights turned nasty when police closed in and used tear gas on the gathering. Some ninety civilians and forty police were injured in the melee and three days later the KMT government arrested almost every well-known opposition leader. The movement that grew out of this incident became the basis for the formation in September 1986 of the Democratic Progressive Party (DPP). Because she had given a speech on the night of the incident, Lü Hsiu-lien was among those arrested and sentenced to twelve years' imprisonment for sedition. Adopted by Amnesty International as a prisoner of conscience, Lü Hsiu-lien was released on medical bail (for parathyroid cancer) in March 1985, after serving five years and four months in prison. She took the opportunity to go to the United States for treatment, but this also marked the commencement of her second life in politics. Lü Hsiu-lien spent some time at Harvard University and traveled around Europe and the United States, calling for international recognition of human rights for the people of Taiwan and international status for Taiwan. She and Ch'en Chü, another woman who had been arrested in the Kao-hsiung Incident, are both examples of women who have been active in the fight against KMT injustice and suppression.

Lü Hsiu-lien ended her overseas exile in 1988 and returned to Taiwan to participate in the democratic movement that erupted with the end of martial law. In 1991, she organized the group promoting Taiwan's joining the United Nations and went to

New York to discuss these views. This was separate from the KMT's lobby that promoted the cause of Taiwan's joining the United Nations.

In December 1992, Lü Hsiu-lien was nominated by the DPP and elected to the Legislative Yuan with a majority of votes. She was also at that time hosting international women's conferences and inviting women leaders in politics and the military from all over the world to discuss women, war, and peace from a feminist stance. In 1997, Lü Hsiu-lien was elected as a T'ao-yüan county magistrate. During her term in office, she initiated much local construction and reform, one such being the establishment of T'ao-yüan County Women's and Children's Safety Center. In early December 1999, however, Lü Hsiu-lien formally announced that she was standing as a DPP candidate and runningmate of Ch'en Shui-pien [Chen Shui-bian] for the position of vice-president of Taiwan. Their election in March 2000 signaled the end of the long rule of the KMT in Taiwan, saw Lü Hsiu-lien become the first female vice-president in the history of the Republic of China, and wrote a new page in the history of Chinese women's struggle for social status.

Because both Lü Hsiu-lien and Ch'en Shui-pien clearly favor separatism, their election has become a destabilizing factor in the various issues of the Taiwan Strait. However, since taking office, Lü Hsiu-lien insisted that she is not a "silent second-in-command" and has expressed many opinions that differ from those of Ch'en Shui-pien's. This has led some to suspect that the two politicians are playing "good cop, bad cop." Lü Hsiu-lien has even been accused of being "the hen crowing in the morning in place of the rooster." It is widely believed that her words and deeds will continue to be controversial.

FAN Mei-yüan
(Translated by George Li)

Hsin Taiwan yen-chiu wen-chiao chi-chin hui. Mei-li-tao shih-chien k'ou-shu li-shih pien-chi hsiao-tsu, ed. *Chen-ts'ang Mei-li-tao—Taiwan min-chu li-ch'eng chen chi-lu, Vol. 1: Tsou hsiang Mei-li-tao: Chan-hou fan-tui i-shih ti meng-ya.* Taipei: Shih-pao wen-hua ch'u-pan-kung-ssu, 1999.
Li Wen. *Tsung-heng wu-shih-nien: Lü Hsiu-lien ch'ien-chuan.* Taipei: Shih-pao wen-hua ch'u-pan-kung-ssu, 1996.
Lü Hsiu-lien. *Ch'ung-shen Mei-li-tao.* Taipei: Ch'ien-wei ch'u-pan-she, 1997.
———. *Hsin nü-hsing-chu-i.* Taipei: Ch'ien-wei ch'u-pan-she, 1990.
Yang Tse, ed. *Ch'i-ling nien-tai: Li-hsiang chi-hsü jan-shao.* Taipei: Shih-pao wen-hua ch'u-pan-kung-ssu, 1994.

Lu Hsui-Chen: *see* **Lu Shijia**

Lü Lanqing: *see* **Lü Bicheng**

Lu Lin: *see* **Wulan**

Lu Mei: *see* **Lu Xiaoman**

Lü Mingyin: *see* **Lü Bicheng**

Lu Ni: *see* **Dai Jinhua**

Lü Shengyin: *see* **Lü Bicheng**

Lu Shih-Chia: *see* **Lu Shijia**

Lu Shijia

Lu Shijia, 1911–1986, whose original name was Lu Xiuzhen, was born in Beijing, although her native place was Xiaoshan County, Zhejiang Province. She was a scientist, trained in modern fluid mechanics, and contributed to the field of Chinese aeronautics both as a theorist and educator.

Her father, Lu Guangxi, was a Hanlin academician of the Qing dynasty who had studied in Japan. He was associated with the revolutionary Dr. Sun Yat-sen (1866–1925) and lost his life while participating in the Xinhai Revolution of 1911 that overthrew the Qing. Lu Shijia was only a few months old when her father died, and her superstitious mother (née Shi) blamed the child for his death. Lu Shijia was therefore brought up in the household of a paternal uncle and financially supported by friends of her father. She grew up to be a strong-willed and independent young woman accustomed to enduring hardship.

Lu Shijia spent her formative years in the primary school, high school, and women's high school affiliated with Peking Normal University. Because her uncle did not provide financial support for her studies beyond the women's high school, she had to sit the entrance examination for Peking Normal University, which did not charge tuition fees. Lu Shijia was the only female student in the Physics Department and from her second year until graduation (1933) supported herself with part-time work and tutoring children. She very much wanted to conduct research in the National Academy of Beiping, but it did not employ females. Lu Shijia therefore started teaching at the Fifth Women's Normal School of Hebei Province at Daming (Hebei Daming diwu nüzi shifan) and later taught at the private Zhicheng High School. She was at this time also supporting her mother.

Lu Shijia borrowed money with the help of her maternal uncle, Shi Jinmo, and in 1937 went to study in Germany at her own expense. She was awarded a von Humboldt Scholarship because of her excellent academic results. Lu Shijia decided at this time not to pursue the study of physics, however, changing instead to fluid mechanics; her decision was said to have been influenced by the outbreak of the Sino-Japanese War (1937–45). Her supervisor was Professor Ludwig Prandtl (1875–1953) of Göttingen University, one of the founders of modern fluid mechanics. She was his last, and only female, student. Experimental work was highly classified in Nazi Germany and thus inaccessible to Lu Shijia; she was constrained to restrict her research approach to solely theoretical methods. Her results, however, were confirmed when she was later able to conduct appropriate experiments. Her 1942 doctoral dissertation "Aufrollung eines zylindrischen Strahles durch Querwind," written under the name Chang Hsui-Chen, was translated in 1973 for the United States Aerospace Research Laboratories under the title "The Roll-up of a Cylindrical Jet in a Cross Flow."

In 1941, Lu Shijia married Zhang Wei (b. 1913) in Germany. A graduate of Jiaotong University in Tangshan, he had won a Sino-British Boxer Indemnity Scholarship to study in the United Kingdom. Zhang Wei had gone to Germany to conduct research on shell structure theories in Berlin and, when war broke out in 1939 was forced to remain there. As a woman, Lu Shijia experienced considerable difficulty finding employment after finishing her Ph.D. When World War II ended, the couple went first to Switzerland and later to France, where they boarded a ship for China. They arrived in Shanghai in July 1946.

Upon her return to China, Lu Shijia taught at Tongji University, moving from there to Beiyang University and then to Tsinghua [Qinghua] University. A husband and wife were not both permitted to be professors in Tsinghua University at that time, so Lu Shijia worked as a research fellow in the Hydraulic Engineering Laboratory. Not until 1949 did she receive an appointment as a professor in the Aeronautics Department of Tsinghua.

A national restructuring of universities in 1952 saw the Aeronautics Departments of eight universities amalgamated as the Aeronautics College of Beijing (Beijing hangkong xueyuan). Lu Shijia was appointed to a professorship and remained there until the end of her working life. In addition to a heavy teaching load, she collaborated on the building of educational and scientific equipment, including low-speed, high-speed, and supersonic wind tunnels. Lu Shijia encouraged the development of branch sciences within hydraulic engineering, compiled lecture notes, initiated new courses, and translated important works. She also supervised the research of many postgraduate students. Lu Shijia was unfailingly serious and diligent in all that she did and maintained a meticulous attitude toward science; her contribution to the development of Chinese aeronautics has been significant.

Lu Shijia also played a part in the international society of scientists. In the 1950s, she went overseas with a variety of delegations, visiting Germany twice after 1980 to facilitate academic exchange. After the Chinese Academy of Sciences increased its intake of academicians that year, Lu Shijia was twice nominated. She declined the honor, however, insisting that the academy "give this opportunity to outstanding middle-aged scientists." Lu Shijia was an honest and highly moral woman, willing to help others, and widely respected.

WANG Bing
(Translated by George Li)

Chang, C.H. [Lu Shijia]. "Aufrollung eines zylindrischen Strahles durch Querwind." Ph.D. dissertation, Göttingen University, 1942; trans. K.S. Nagaraja and H.O. Schrade, as "The Roll-up of a Cylindrical Jet in a Cross Flow," Interim Scientific Report ARL-73–0131, U.S. Department of Energy, Aerospace Research Labs, Hypersonic Research Lab. (Wright-Patterson AFB, OH), September 1973.

Lu Hsih-Chia [Lu Shijia]. "On the Surface of Discontinuity Between Two Flows Perpendicular to Each Other." Ph.D. dissertation, Göttingen University. *Engineering Reports of National Tsing Hua University*, 4, no. 1 (December 1948): 40–62.

Wang Renhui and Li Fulin. "Woguo diyi wei nü liutilixuejia Lu Shijia." *Renwu*, no. 4 (1990): 73–84.

Zhu Ziqiang. "Lu Shijia." In *Zhongguo xiandai kexuejia zhuanji*, vol. 3. Beijing: Kexue chubanshe, 1992, 28–32.

Lu Xiaoman

Lu Xiaoman, 1903–1965, born Xiaomei, also used the name Mei but it is under her *zi* Xiaoman that she is mostly known. A native of Wujin County, Jiangsu Province, but born in Shanghai to a family of officials, Lu Xiaoman was a minor writer and painter. She was probably one of the best known women in China in the 1920s, however, because of her love affair with the famous poet Xu Zhimo (1897–1931). Both Lu Xiaoman and Xu Zhimo were said to have been beautiful and talented, and their love story was widely known and followed by the Chinese public, most of whom were envious, others sharply critical. Lu Xiaoman exemplified by her life the courage and determination to pursue the freedom to love.

Lu Xiaoman's father, Lu Ding, passed one of the last civil service examinations of the Qing dynasty (1644–1911), but the qualification soon had little relevance when the civil service examination system was abolished. Because of this, he went to Japan to study politics and law and became known as a diplomat and scholar. Nothing is known of her mother except that, according to one source, it was she who selected Lu Xiaoman's first husband.

Lu Xiaoman not only received training in traditional Chinese accomplishments—among them Chinese painting, calligraphy, singing, acting, and *jingju* (Peking opera)—as a girl but was also fluent in English and French. She first made her appearance in Beijing social circles at the age of eighteen. In painting, Lu Xiaoman specialized in flowers, birds, and light ink landscape (*danmo shanshui*), while her calligraphy was demonstrated in the small regular style (*xiaokai*). She was trained well enough in *jingju* to appear on stage as an amateur singer (*piaoyou*); in addition, Lu Xiaoman was a famous beauty. As soon as she made her debut, the young woman was much sought after by young men from rich and famous families. Her mother, however, had her eye on Wang Geng (1895–ca. 1945), a graduate of Princeton and West Point. The two married in 1920, a month after they met, and were thought to be a good match.

Among Wang Geng's patrons was the famous reformer and scholar Liang Qichao. He had also befriended the young poet Xu Zhimo, who thus moved in the same circles as Wang Geng and Lu Xiaoman. A native of Haining, Zhejiang Province, Xu Zhimo was the best known poet in China during the 1920s. He had been educated in America, with a B.A. from Clark University and an M.A. from Columbia. The poet had then gone on to Cambridge to attend literature courses there. He married Zhang Youyi, a young woman from a distinguished family from Baoshan near Shanghai, but they were already divorced by the time Xu met Lu Xiaoman. In what has been described as China's first modern divorce, it is understood that the poet divorced his wife in order to be free to pursue Lin Huiyin (*q.v.*), who, however, rejected him. Xu then fell in love with Lu Xiaoman while her husband was working away from home. From Lu Xiaoman's diary, published in the 1930s, it is clear that she had fallen in love with Xu Zhimo, too, but they both realized that their love was forbidden. Xu Zhimo traveled to Europe in 1925, one source speculating that he might have been attempting to forget Lu Xiaoman. However, according to Zhang Youyi, the poet ran away because Wang Geng had threatened to kill him (this recollection was published in Natasha Chang Pang-mei's book about her great aunt Zhang Youyi).

In the 1920s, the love between Lu Xiaoman and Xu Zhimo fired the imagination of liberal intellectuals, even the middle-aged Hu Shi, who was most sympathetic. One of Xu Zhimo's friends, the painter Liu Haisu, eventually took it upon himself to try to negotiate for Lu Xiaoman a divorce from her husband. From all accounts, Wang Geng was a reasonable man and saw the futility of continuing a loveless marriage, so he consented to a divorce. In 1925, the happy couple chose the seventh day of the seventh lunar month as their engagement day. This date is generally considered to be for lovers because legend has it that it is the one day in the year when the shepherd and weaver-maid meet in the heavens. The engagement of Lu Xiaoman and Xu Zhimo was the biggest social news of the year, and three months later they married. At the ceremony, Liang Qichao, who served as a witness, startled the guests by giving a very stern speech in which he criticized the couple for their past unfaithfulness and admonished them to make sure that this would be their last marriage.

Marriage did not end the couple's problems, however. Xu Zhimo's parents had been attached to his former wife, Zhang Youyi, and opposed the second marriage. In an attempt to make them accept Lu Xiaoman, Xu Zhimo took his bride back to his native village in Jiashi, Haining County, but she was cruelly humiliated and found the first experience of village life harsh. Lu Xiaoman is also believed to have contracted tuberculosis during this period. The couple returned to Shanghai, where Lu Xiaoman felt liberated. Perhaps to compensate for the unhappy life she had led in the country-side, Lu Xiaoman then adopted a luxurious and carefree style of life.

She led a busy social life; among her many friends was a man named Weng Ruiwu to whom she was especially close because he alone, Lu Xiaoman said, could lessen her pain when she was ill. The two shared a love of *jingju* and often appeared on stage together. Under Weng's influence, however, Lu Xiaoman became addicted to opium. They would spend the whole night lying together on a bed smoking, and when Xu Zhimo returned from teaching he would join them on the bed. Despite the inevitable rumors, Xu Zhimo chose to believe that Weng Ruiwu was nothing more than a close friend. Xu Zhimo soon found himself in dire financial straits, however, because of his wife's opium habit. Hu Shi offered his young friend a job at Peking University, but Lu Xiaoman was unwilling to go and live there. Xu Zhimo then arranged to commute between Beijing and Shanghai. In November 1931, he was killed when his plane crashed on a mountain near Jinan, Shandong Province.

Lu Xiaoman thus became widowed at the age of twenty-nine. After Xu Zhimo's death, for which, predictably, she was blamed, Lu Xiaoman ceased all social activities and devoted her time to collecting, editing, and publishing her husband's works. At the same time, she worked hard to improve her painting skills. Lu Xiaoman held a personal exhibition in Shanghai and supported herself by teaching and selling paintings. It is said, however, that she was also supported to some extent by Weng Ruiwu, who was forced to sell antiques and his family's collection of calligraphy and paintings to keep them both in opium.

Lu Xiaoman stayed in Shanghai after the establishment of the People's Republic in 1949. When Chen Yi, the mayor of Shanghai, heard that she was still alive and in his city, he gave her a position in the Shanghai Institute of Culture and History (*Shanghai wenshi guan*). This institute had been established to provide a place in socialist China for non-communist celebrities such as Lu Xiaoman. Later, she also became a paid artist of the Shanghai Academy of Chinese Painting. According to one source, Lu Xiaoman did not have to go out to work but had only to produce works for the academy. By this time, she had overcome her opium habit, but still her income from two jobs was not sufficient to afford her expensive life-style. Lu Xiaoman appeared to be healthy and in good spirits in those years and worked with a young man named Wang Yiling, translating works from Western languages. He grew quite close to Lu Xiaoman in her later life and described it as reasonably secure and peaceful throughout the political movements of the 1950s and early 1960s.

Lu Xiaoman's one regret at the end of her days was that the complete works of Xu Zhimo had not been published. Although the collection had been typeset and made into paper molds ready to be printed just as the Sino-Japanese War broke out in 1937, the molds were lost in transit when the publisher, Shangwu yinshuguan, moved inland. In 1954, Lu Xiaoman was notified that the molds had been found but the material was not suitable for the times. During the Hundred Flowers Movement (1956), control over literary activities seemed to be more relaxed and plans were then again made to publish the writings, but the anti-rightist movement that followed in 1957 dashed Lu Xiaoman's hopes once more. Weng Ruiwu remained with her during her PRC years. He is thought to have died in the early 1960s.

The only literary work of Lu Xiaoman extant is a volume of her and Xu Zhimo's diaries entitled *Love Letters to Mei* (Ai Mei xiaozha) and two prefaces, one written for that volume and one for *Zhimo riji*. She is also said to have worked with her husband on a play entitled *Bian Kungang* and on translations. These works appear in the fourth volume of *Xu Zhimo quanji* published by Zhuanji wenxue chubanshe in Taiwan, but no credit is given to Lu Xiaoman. She is also said to have written prose, poetry, and fiction, but these have not been collected and published. In Zhejiang Museum, one of her painting scrolls can be found with inscriptions by famous literati such as Hu Shi, Yang Xingfo, and He Tianjian (Lu Xiaoman's painting instructor) praising her talent and achievement. This work is dated spring 1931.

Apart from those submitted to the Academy of Chinese Paintings to fulfill obligations, the few paintings Lu Xiaoman did in the 1960s sold out quickly at Duoyun Zhai. The artist suffered from asthma and pulmonary emphysema but still managed to paint a series of ink paintings depicting ideas expressed in Tang poetry. These were for Du Fu's Thatched Hut, a historical site in Sichuan commemorating the Tang poet and open to the public. In early spring 1965, Lu Xiaoman was hospitalized for the last time and told friends she wished to be buried with Xu Zhimo. This proved to be impossible, however, because Xu Zhimo's son by his first wife objected. Lu Xiaoman died that year, just before the outbreak of the Cultural Revolution (1966–76), a timely death in the opinion of many people, given the controversial life she had lived. None of her friends escaped attack during the Cultural Revolution, and so no one was able to take care of her ashes, which, according to one source, were buried in a mass grave. The same source says that Lu Xiaoman's nephew returned from Taiwan and built in Suzhou a tomb for her that contains some of her personal effects (*yiguanzhong*).

Lu Xiaoman embodied the liberated modern woman of the May Fourth period. Her story fascinated and scandalized contemporaries. Whatever they might have thought of her, they could never be the same again. Lu Xiaoman's act of breaking the fetters of tradition may have served as an example to women, but her tragic end might also have warned others of the perils in fighting tradition.

Lily Xiao Hong LEE

Chang Pang-mei, Natasha. *Xiaojiao yu xifu*, trans. Tan Jiayu. Taibei: Zhiku chuban, 1996.

Liu Shaotang, ed. "Lu Xiaoman." In *Minguo renwu xiaozhuan*, vol. 6. Taipei: Zhuanji wenxue chubanshe, 1984, 338–43.

Lu Xiaoman. "Preface to *Zhimo riji*." In *Xu Zhimo quanji*, vol. 4. Taipei: Zhuanji wenxue chubanshe, 1980, 479–82.

Lu Xiaoman and Xu Zhimo. "Ai Mei xiaozha." In *Xu Zhimo quanji*, vol. 4. Taipei: Zhuanji wenxue chubanshe, 1980, 249–472.

Wang Jueyuan. "Xu Zhimo yu Lu Xiaoman." *Zhongwai zazhi*, 37, no. 5 (May 1985): 86–90.

Wang Yiling. "Lu Xiaoman yu wo." *Zhongwai zazhi*, 42, no. 5 (April 1990): 127–31.

Wang Yingxia. "Wo yu Lu Xiaoman." *Zhuanji wenxue*, 55, no. 6 (December 1989): 57–61.

Xu Zhimo and Lu Xiaoman. *Ai de xinyue*, ed. Fengzhou. Nanjing: Jiangsu wenyi chubanshe, 1996.

Zhao Qingge. "Lu Xiaoman youyuan nanmin." *Xinwenxue shiliao*, no. 2 (1999): 36–40.

Lu Xiaomei: *see* **Lu Xiaoman**

Lu Xing'er

Lu Xing'er, b. 1949, in Shanghai, although her family is from Nantong, Jiangsu Province, is a novelist.

She had just graduated from high school at the age of nineteen when the Cultural Revolution (1966–76) began. In 1968, Lu Xing'er was sent to northeast China to work on a farm. Over the course of five years, she worked as a tractor operator, secretary, clerk, and political propagandist. Lu Xing'er published her first novel, *Ox Horn* (Niujiao), in 1974 in the magazine *Heilongjiang wenyi*. In 1978, however, she passed the entrance examination to Beijing Central Drama Institute (Zhongyang xiqu xueyuan) and studied drama literature. After graduating in 1982, Lu Xing'er became a scriptwriter at Beijing Chinese Children's Art Theater, then moved to Shanghai to work as a professional writer for the Shanghai branch of the Chinese Writers' Association and as editor-in-chief of the *Shanghai Literary Arena* (Hai shang wentan). During this period, she divorced her husband, Chen Kexiong, a journalist with the newspaper *Guangming ribao*, and resumed life as a single parent, looking after her only son.

Because Lu Xing'er herself endured many tribulations typical of her generation, her feelings in her novels convey these experiences readily, vividly reflecting within a graceful and lyrical style an authenticity of the lives of Chinese people. While her earlier writing mainly captured youthfulness in its lust for life, love, and success, her later works are more profound and thought provoking. Lu Xing'er shifted her attention to depicting women of all social ranks, revealing exquisite sensitivity and deep concern for the fate of contemporary Chinese women embroiled in a time of rapid social change.

Over a period of nearly twenty years, Lu Xing'er produced more than ten collections of short stories and three full-length novels. Her short stories include "The Structure of Beauty" (Mei de jiegou; co-authored with Chen Kexiong); "Oh! Blue Bird" (A Qingniao); "The Mountain Flowers Have Bloomed Quietly" (Dazixiang qiaoqiaode kai le); "The Unremembered Stone Tablet in the Wilderness" (Yiliu zai huangyuan shang de bei); and "Born a Woman" (Bu ken shiluo de xingbie). Her novels are *The Kiss for the Century* (Liu gei shiji de wen), *Fairytales in a Grey Building* (Huilou li de tonghua), and *Surgeon* (Waike yisheng). In her 1987 short story "The Sun Is Not Out Today" (Taiyang jintian mei you chulai), Lu Xing'er touches upon the controversial subject of a woman's right to refuse an abortion ordered by the Chinese government.

GAO Yuanbao
(Translated and expanded by Cui Zhiying)

Lu Xing'er. *Oh! Blue Bird*. Beijing: Chinese Literature Press, 1993.
———. "The Sun Is Not Out Today." In *The Serenity of Whiteness*, ed. and trans. Zhu Hong. New York: Ballantine, 1991.
Roberts, Rosemary. "Body, Individual, and State: Abortion in Lu Xing'er's 'The Sun Is Not Out Today.'" Paper presented at the "Women, Modernity, and Opportunity in Twentieth-century China" Workshop, University of Sydney, 27–28 April 2000.
Zhao Lihong. "Preface." In *Oh! Blue Bird*, Lu Xing'er. Beijing: Chinese Literature Press, 1993, 7–9.

Lü Xiulian: *see* **Lü Hsiu-lien**

Lu Xiuzhen: *see* **Lu Shijia**

Lü-i: *see* **Su Hsüeh-lin**

Luo Caoming: *see* **Caoming**

Luo Feiya: *see* **Zhang Mojun**

Luo Jiang: *see* **Yishu**

Luo Shuzhang
Luo Shuzhang, b. 1898 (some sources give 1899 or 1907), was a native of Yueyang County, Hunan Province. She was an underground worker for the CCP for many years and was appointed as a vice-minister to the ministries of Labor, Food Industry, and Light Industry upon the establishment of the PRC.

Her doctor father practiced Chinese herbal medicine and did not allow Luo Shuzhang to attend the family-run private school with her brothers. Her mother, however, introduced her to such traditional elementary primers as the *Three Character Classic* (Sanzijing) and *Names of the Hundred Families* (Baijiaxing) and poetry and prose selections. When Luo Shuzhang was fifteen, around 1913, friends and relatives supported her desire to attempt the entrance examination of Yueyang Girls' School, which had recently been established in her hometown. She passed the examination and enrolled and a year later entered the First Normal School of Changsha. In 1916, Luo Shuzhang joined in a protest organized by her schoolmates against Yuan Shikai's plan to become emperor of China and began to absorb progressive ideas.

Luo Shuzhang graduated from Changsha First Normal School in 1919 and went to Chuxian County in Anhui Province and where she taught for three years. She suffered persecution because of her leftist politics and decided in 1922 to go to the Dutch Indies to teach at Chinese community schools. Luo Shuzhang taught at Zhonghua School in Dutch Borneo (present-day Kalimantan, Indonesia) and three years later moved to Batavia (present-day Jakarta), where she taught at the Huaqiao School. Luo Shuzhang returned to China in 1928 with three Chinese students from Batavia and enrolled in the Politics and Economics Department of Jinan University in Shanghai. There, she attended lectures by several leftist intellectuals and began to study Marxist-Leninist ideas. After the Mukden (Shenyang) Incident of September 1931 in Manchuria, China's northeast, anti-Japanese feeling ran high in Shanghai, and Luo Shuzhang performed plays on such themes as national salvation, advocated by leftist literary and art circles in Shanghai. She joined the CCP in 1935 and began underground work.

After the war against Japan broke out in July 1937, Luo Shuzhang established a vocational school as a cover for communist activities. Most of the students who trained there joined teams that went to the front to care for and support the soldiers. When Japan invaded Shanghai on 13 August, Luo Shuzhang housed in her school women workers who had fled the Japanese-occupied areas and either helped them find jobs or organized the women into service teams to go to the front. She also worked with Song Qingling (*q.v.*) and He Xiangning (*q.v.*) on the Committee of the Shanghai Women's National Salvation Association, organizing short courses in nursing, mobilizing middle-class women to raise funds, making gifts, and caring for the wounded. Only on the eve of Shanghai's fall to the Japanese did Luo Shuzhang leave for Wuhan via Hong Kong.

In Wuhan, she worked with Deng Yingchao (*q.v.*) to unite women of all social backgrounds and political persuasions under the banner of national salvation. Deng Yingchao was a council member of the National Refugee Children's Association (Zhanshi ertong baoyuhui) and recommended Luo Shuzhang for the position when the Junxian County Home was without a director. To reach Junxian, Luo Shuzhang traveled over a month behind enemy lines, across mountains, and down the Han River. When she finally arrived, Luo Shuzhang found the five hundred children and one hundred or so staff of the home hungry, cold, and living in a deserted temple. With a letter from Song Qingling, Luo Shuzhang went to see General Li Zongren, who helped them out with food and clothing. In just a few months, Luo Shuzhang had her charges fed, clothed, and attending class. When the Chinese army eventually retreated from Junxian, she led the six hundred children and staff on a circuitous journey to safety. They traveled up the Han River to northern Sichuan then down the Jialing River to the town of Yunmen, where they built their new home. During this journey, taking more than two months, they met bandits and wounded soldiers who tried to steal their wooden boats from them. Luo Shuzhang was able to reason and appeal to their sense of common decency, however, and led the children out of these crises unscathed. After the Wannan Incident when the KMT killed CCP members, the KMT-CCP coalition existed in hardly more than name. The KMT again adopted a harsh attitude toward communist and leftist elements, and the orphanage was ordered to disband because it was making "little communists."

With the help of the National Salvation Association (Jiuguohui) and local gentry, in 1939 Luo Shuzhang started the Diyi Pharmaceutical Production Cooperative in Chongqing. Under cover of this cooperative, she became active in industrial and commercial circles. Just before the end of the Sino-Japanese War in 1945, Luo Shuzhang worked hard to establish a political group called the China Democratic National Construction Association (Minzhu jianguohui) of which she was an executive member. Luo Shuzhang was also elected as an executive member of the communist-led Chinese Women's Association (Zhongguo funü lianyihui) and did all she could in this capacity to win over upper-class women and professional women to the communist cause.

After the war, Luo Shuzhang returned to Shanghai and opened a branch of her pharmaceutical concern. In 1946, she left Shanghai for the northeast to manage Harbin Yuchangyuan Flour Mill and the Dongbei Medical and Pharmaceutical Corporation. Luo Shuzhang was given a number of important posts in 1949, including secretary-general of the China Democratic National Construction Association, a minor party she helped establish in 1945. Luo Shuzhang was also made a member of the Financial and Economic Committee of the Government Administrative Council (Zhengwuyuan caijing weiyuanhui weiyuan) and deputy director of the General Office of the Central People's Government (Zhongyang renmin zhengfu bangongting fuzhuren). That same year, she helped organize the All-China Democratic Women's Federation and was active thenceforth in its successor, the ACWF. In the early 1950s, Luo Shuzhang was instrumental in organizing China's industrial and commercial sectors into a federation supporting the government. As a member of the Preparatory Committee of the All-China Federation of Industry and Commerce (Gongshanglian), she worked toward its establishment and was a member of its Central Standing Committee in 1956. In 1959, Luo Shuzhang became vice-chair of the Coordinating Committee jointly set up by the China Democratic National Construction Association and the All-China Federation of Industry and Commerce.

In the early years of the PRC, she was vice-minister of a number of ministries. Her first portfolio was in the Ministry of Labor (1954–1957), where she succeeded Liu Yaxiong (*q.v.*). Luo Shuzhang was subsequently moved to the Ministry of Food Industry (1957–58). Her final assignment before retirement was to the Ministry of Light Industry (1958–65). She was also elected to the CPPCC and the NPC, rising to the position of deputy secretary-general of both in 1954 and 1965, respectively.

Nothing is known of Luo Shuzhang's experiences during the Cultural Revolution (1966–76), but it is reasonable to suggest that, because of her advanced age and the fact that her tenure as vice-minister for Light Industry terminated in March 1965, she was probably not targeted. All that is known about the period after her retirement is that in 1988 Luo Shuzhang was invited to become honorary vice-chair of the All-China Federation of Industry and Commerce. Nothing is known of her personal life, whether she married or had children.

As were a number of underground CCP members, Luo Shuzhang was responsible before 1949 in helping to establish and operate a minor political party that was sympathetic to the CCP yet worked independently from it. The identity of these people as members of the CCP was not revealed until after the establishment of the PRC. Because of her considerable experience in industry and commerce, Luo Shuzhang was entrusted with important work in this field after 1949. However, although she was vice-minister in three different ministries, Luo Shuzhang never became a full minister, perhaps because she was active in the very early period. We would be justified in concluding from this that, as a woman, Luo Shuzhang was not able to break through the glass ceiling.

Lily Xiao Hong LEE

Huaxia funü mingren cidian. Beijing: Huaxia chubanshe, 1988, 676–77.
Who's Who in Communist China. Hong Kong: Union Research Institute, 1969.
Yingwen *Zhongguo funü,* ed. *Gujin zhuming funü renwu,* vol. 2. Shijiazhuang: Hebei renmin chubanshe, 1986, 512–16.
Zhongguo renming dacidian: Xianren dang zheng jun lingdao renwu juan. Shanghai and Beijing: Shanghai cishu chubanshe and Waiwen chubanshe, 1989, 236.

Luyin

Luyin, 1898–1934, also known as Huang Luyin, was born Huang Ying in Fuzhou city, Fujian Province, to an upper middle-class family. She was a writer of fiction and essays during the May Fourth era of the early twentieth century.

Her father, Huang Juren, was magistrate of Changsha but died when Luyin was seven; the family had to go to Beijing to live with an uncle who was an official in the Qing government. Luyin's mother disliked her daughter because on the day she was born her maternal grandmother died; the baby was therefore considered to be a curse to the family. Luyin grew up in the care of servants and developed a close bond with her wet nurse.

While her elder brother and younger sister went to regular schools in Beijing, Luyin studied the *Three Character Classic* (Sanzi jing) under the tutelage of her aunt, who had also been educated at home. Luyin's deep resentment at the unfair treatment seems to have driven her to study much harder when she finally got a chance to go to school, at the age of nine. At Muzhen School, a missionary school for poor children, Luyin displayed a talent and diligence that both surprised her family and earned her the opportunity to continue studies in the preparatory school attached to Beijing Women's Normal School (Beijing shifan xuexiao yuke). She passed the entrance examination and began her studies in 1912. After graduating from the preparatory school in 1917, the young woman worked as a schoolteacher in Beijing, Anqing, and Kaifeng until enough money had been saved up to return to Beijing in 1919. There, Luyin at first audited classes in the Chinese Studies Department of Beijing Women's Higher Normal School (Beijing guoli nüzi gaodeng shifan xuexiao) but was allowed to become a regular student after performing well in examinations.

The year 1919 is a significant date in Chinese history and culture, because it was the beginning of the May Fourth Movement, both a patriotic and a cultural movement. Luyin threw herself into the spirit of the times and busily attended meetings, gave speeches, and wrote articles. She was one of the first to join the Literary Studies Society (Wenxue yanjiuhui), initiated in 1921 by Mao Dun and other famous writers. During this period, Luyin's first literary works were written.

She graduated from the Higher Normal School in 1922 and returned to teaching. However, Luyin sought not only to break traditional literary conventions under the influence of the May Fourth Movement, but also pursued a personal liberation that opposed arranged marriages and advocated free love. Her convictions led her to renounce an arranged marriage, thus offending her mother. At the same time, in defiance of prevailing social attitudes in 1923 she married Guo Mengliang (d. 1925), who had already entered into an arranged marriage but left that wife in his native Fuzhou. Ostracized by family and society, they put on a brave front, but after only two years of marriage Guo died of tuberculosis (some say enterogastritis), leaving Luyin with a ten-month-old daughter named Weixuan. The loss had a serious effect on Luyin: she started to drink and chain smoke and generally abused her health, displaying extremes of moods, laughing one minute and weeping the next. Nevertheless, Luyin continued working to maintain her sanity as much as to support her daughter. Besides teaching at several schools in Shanghai and Beijing, Luyin persisted with her writing. Her first collection was published in 1925 under the title *Old Friends from the Seaside* (Haibin guren).

In 1928 at a friend's home, Luyin chanced to meet Li Weijian, a student in the Foreign Language Department of Tsinghua [Qinghua] University. Nine years her junior, he nevertheless fell in love with Luyin. They corresponded frequently (their letters were later published in a joint collection), and after much soul searching Luyin finally accepted his love. They left together for Tokyo in August 1930 as a married couple but spent only a few happy months there before straitened finances made a longer stay impossible. Back in China by the end of the year, the couple lived in Hangzhou briefly before moving to Shanghai, where they remained until 1934. In those few short years, Luyin published the short story collection *The Thorns of the Rose* (Meigui de ci) and the novels *A Woman's Heart* (Nüren de xin) and *Flame* (Huoyan). But just as she seemed to have reached a safe haven, Luyin's bad fortune struck again. She died in childbirth in a Shanghai hospital in May. Her death precipitated a series of reports, reminiscences, and critiques in contemporaneous newspapers and literary magazines. Luyin was survived by her second husband, Li Weijian, and two daughters: Weixuan from her first marriage and Yingxian from her second.

It is generally recognized that Luyin's voice expressed the experience of female Chinese intellectuals who had awakened from their submissive and dependent roles in society in the 1920s and 1930s. Committed though they were to breaking free from traditional constraints, the women found the problems they then confronted much harder to deal with. Many sank into despair; others oscillated between the insoluble conflict of their romantic idealism and the harsh reality of twentieth-century China.

Luyin's early works, though not quite mature in form and thinking, were nevertheless valuable for their pioneering contribution. Critics judge that her later pieces cover the same themes and portray the same characters as the earlier ones but are more refined in language and structure. It is true that Luyin was only partially successful in her attempts to broaden her writing from conveying a purely subjective perspective and that at times it sank into sentimentality; but had she lived beyond thirty-six she might have had a much better chance of succeeding.

Nevertheless, Luyin made a substantial contribution to modern Chinese literature with the ten volumes produced in her fourteen years of literary creation. She voiced the helplessness and hopelessness of women like herself and, most importantly, dared to reveal an inner self to the world when the autobiographic genre appeared rarely in Chinese literature.

Lily Xiao Hong LEE

Anderson, Jennifer, and Theresa Munro, trans. *Chinese Women Writers: A Collection of Short Stories by Chinese Women Writers of the 1920s and 30s.* Hong Kong: Joint Publishing, 1985, 84–94.

Boorman, Howard L., and Richard C. Howard, eds. *Biographical Dictionary of Republican China*, vol. 2. New York: Columbia University Press, 1971, 201–03.

He Yubo. "Luyin nüshi ji qi zuopin." In *Dangdai nüzuojia lun*, ed. Huang Renying. Shanghai: Guanghua shuju, 1933, 223–45.

Junkers, Elke. *Leben und Werk der chinesichen Schriftstellerin Lu Yin (ca. 1899–1934) anhand ihrer Autobiographie.* Munich: Minerva Publications, 1984.

Junwei, "Luyin de guiyan." In *Dangdai nüzuojia lun*, ed. Huang Renying. Shanghai: Guanghua shuju, 1933, 246–50.

Liu Dajie. "Huang Luyin." In *Luyin*, ed. Xiao Feng. Hong Kong: Sanlian shudian, 1983, 250–52.

Liu Shaotang, ed. "Huang Luyin." In *Minguo renwu xiaozhuan*, vol. 1. Taipei: Zhuanji wenxue chubanshe, 1981, 223–25.

Su Xuelin. "Guanyu Luyin de huiyi." In *Luyin*, ed. Xiao Feng. Hong Kong: Sanlian shudian, 1983, 254–58.

Weiming [Mao Dun]. "Luyin lun." In *Zuojia lun*, ed. Mao Dun. Shanghai: Shenghuo shudian, 1936, 75–87.

Xiao Feng. "Luyin de shengping yu chuangzuo daolu." In *Luyin*, ed. Xiao Feng. Hong Kong: Sanlian shudian, 1983, 259–65.

Yingwen *Zhongguo funü*, ed. *Gujin zhuming funü renwu*, vol. 2. Shijiazhuang: Hebei renmin chubanshe, 1986, 522–27.

M

Man Jia: *see* **Ding Ling**

Mao Yanwen: *see* **Mao Yen-wen**

Mao Yen-wen

Mao Yen-wen [Mao Yanwen], 1898–1999, was a native of Chiang-shan [Jiangshan] County, Che-chiang [Zhejiang] Province. In her youth, she engaged in philanthropy as an administrator of orphanages and later was active as a kindergarten educator and journalist.

Her father, Mao Hua-tung, ran the family's Yü-ch'ang Fabric Store after gaining the cultivated talent (*hsiu-ts'ai*) degree in the late Ch'ing [Qing] dynasty. Her mother, Chu Ch'iung-p'ei, described as wise and elegant, suffered persecution in her marriage because she did not give birth to a son. The eldest of four daughters, Mao Yen-wen was taught to read and write at home by a family teacher from the age of seven and at thirteen went to the comparatively modern Hsi-ho Girls' School. Three years later, the provincial authorities sent her to the training course run by Hang-chou [Hangzhou] Women's Normal School (Hang-chou nü-tzu shih-fan hsüeh-hsiao) to train as a primary school teacher. She graduated at eighteen and taught for a year at a women's training course in Yung-k'ang [Yongkang] County before enrolling in 1918 at Hu-chün Girls' School in Wu-hsing [Wuxing] County. After gaining the highest mark of the Che-chiang candidates in the entrance examination, Mao Yen-wen was admitted to the English Department of the Women's Higher Normal School (Nü-tzu kao-teng shih-fan hsüeh-hsiao) in Peking. In 1922, she transferred to Ginling [Chinling (Jinling)] Women's University in Nan-ching [Nanjing], majoring in education with sociology as a minor.

Mao Yen-wen had been betrothed as a child to Fang Yao-t'ang, the son of a friend of her father's. As she grew older, however, Mao Yen-wen rebelled against this idea and at the age of seventeen shocked the entire county seat by publicly rejecting the arranged marriage. Instead, Mao Yen-wen accepted the proposal of her cousin Chu Chün-i [Zhu Junyi]. He had gone to Columbia University in the United States to study educational statistics after graduating from a preparatory class at Tsinghua [Qinghua] University. When Chu Chün-i returned to China in 1917, he taught at Tung-nan [Dongnan] University. Their engagement was broken off in 1924, however, when Chu Chün-i fell in love with someone else, leaving Mao Yen-wen in great distress.

After graduating from Ginling in 1925, the young woman taught at Chiang-su [Jiangsu] First High School in Nan-ching. When the school closed in 1926 because of the Northern Expedition, she returned with her sister Mao T'ung-wen [Mao Tongwen] to Che-chiang. There, Mao Yen-wen worked in the Judicial Section of the Che-chiang provincial government in Hang-chou, acting at the same time as secretary to the Che-chiang branch of the KMT Women's Bureau. She proved to be highly efficient and confident in her work and was transferred to the Political Department. Within a short time, however, Mao Yen-wen was offered a Barbour Scholarship to the University of Michigan, Ann Arbor, and in 1929 enrolled in a graduate program of secondary school education administration, again taking sociology as a minor. She was awarded a master's degree in the summer of 1931 and returned to China via Europe. Mao Yen-wen then taught at Fu-tan [Fudan] University, where she also acted as a counselor for women students, and at Chi-nan [Jinan] University.

In 1935, Mao Yen-wen married Hsiung Hsi-ling [Xiong Xiling], who was thirty-five years her senior. Their Christian ceremony held in Shanghai and attended by celebrities from the fields of literature, education, and politics was widely reported in the press, particularly, the status of the groom, the beauty and intelligence of the bride, and the difference in their ages. Hsiung Hsi-ling (*tzu* Ping-san) was a native of Feng-huang County, Hu-nan [Hunan] Province, and had been a child prodigy later famous for his calligraphy and painting. He reached the pinnacle of his political career when made prime minister by Yüan Shih-k'ai in July 1913, at the beginning of the Republican period. After retiring from politics, Hsiung Hsi-ling threw himself into philanthropic works, establishing the Pei-p'ing Fragrant Hills Orphanage (Pei-p'ing hsiang-shan tz'u-yu yüan) and donating all of his property to a children's welfare foundation (Hsiung-Chu i-chu erh-t'ung fu-li chi-chin-she) that he and his first wife had set up. This woman, Chu Ch'i-hui (Zhu Qihui, d. 1931), had been the aunt of one of Mao Yen-wen's school friends. The young woman had visited the Hsiung home as a student in Peking. So clearly of a younger generation, Mao Yen-wen was startled when her friend made an approach on behalf of her uncle in October 1934 to ask for Mao Yen-wen's hand in marriage. She had never recovered from the disillusionment of her broken engagement and, uninterested in seeking love, finally agreed. The marriage, though short, turned out to be a happy one.

Even though she realized that Hsiung Hsi-ling's purpose in seeking her as his wife may have been to secure a successor to run his philanthropic establishments, Mao Yen-wen devoted herself to the day-to-day administration of the orphanage. Their peaceful life lasted only three years, however, before the couple had to flee Peking with the outbreak of the Sino-Japanese War. Moving first to Shanghai, Hsiung Hsi-ling immediately became involved in relief work of the Red Swastika Society (Hung wanzi hui), helping war refugees. After Nan-ching fell to the Japanese in February 1938, however, the couple set off for Hong Kong, intending to go by a roundabout route to Ch'ang-sha in Hunan. However, Hsiung Hsi-ling suffered a stroke and died on 25 December that year, leaving Mao Yen-wen to continue on the journey alone.

During the Sino-Japanese War, she took charge of the orphanage in Japanese-occupied Peking for a time; set up branches in Kuei-lin [Guilin], Liu-chou [Liuzhou], and Chih-chiang [Zhijiang]; and also opened kindergartens and started a training school for kindergarten teachers. Mao Yen-wen was elected to the Provisional Assembly in 1939 and in 1945 returned to Peking to revive the Fragrant Hills Orphanage. Elected to the Peking Municipal Council in 1947, she was then nominated for the National Assembly and was elected without having to campaign.

In April 1949, Mao Yen-wen went to Taiwan, leaving a large estate behind in China.

In order to earn a living, she went to America and worked as an editor with Chinese newspapers, first with the New York *Hua-mei jih-pao* and then the San Francisco *Shao-nien Chung-kuo ch'en-pao*. Mao Yen-wen also spent time at the University of California, Berkeley, as a counselor for women students. She returned briefly to Taiwan in 1954 for the National Assembly meeting at which Chiang Kai-shek (1887–1975) was elected president, but returned to the United States to undertake research at the University of Washington in Seattle on Chinese communism. She finally moved permanently to Taiwan in 1958. Besides sitting on the National Assembly, Mao Yen-wen taught English at Fu-tan High School and Shih-chieh Home Economics College (Shih-chieh chia-cheng chuan-ko hsüeh-hsiao). Retiring in 1966, she then made two visits to the United States and in 1981 traveled to Singapore to visit her cousin. Mao Yen-wen died in 1999 after being bed-ridden for a month because of circulation problems in her legs.

She was a strong and independent "new woman" of the May Fourth generation. During her long life, Mao Yen-wen experienced happiness and sadness and witnessed the enormous changes that affected the lives of Chinese women in the twentieth century.

LO Chiu-jung
(Translated by Lily Xiao Hong Lee and Sue Wiles)

Chung-hua min-kuo tang-tai ming-jen lu, vol. 3. Taipei: Chung-hua shu-chü, 1978, 215.
Hsü Yu-ch'un, ed. *Min-kuo jen-wu ta-tz'u-tien*. Shih-chia-chuang [Shijiazhuang]: Ho-pei jen-min ch'u-pan-she, 1991, 117.
Mao Yen-wen. *Wang shih*. Taipei: The author, 1989.

Meifeng: *see* **Yishu**

Meiqian: *see* **Yishu**

Mingzhu: *see* **Don-grub Lha-mo**

Modegemaa
Modegemaa, b. 1941, in Ulaancabu Aimeg, Inner Mongolia, became famous as a Mongolian dancer.

Born into a poor herdsman's family, she was fostered out to a woman named Ningbu. Ningbu's family was not well off, and when her husband and son died one after the other, she was left penniless. With a blind mother-in-law to support as well, Ningbu was forced to put Modegemaa to work herding other people's sheep. Still very young then, even the sheep taller than she, Modegemaa would run after them rain, hail, or shine, winter and summer, staying close so that not a single one would be taken by a wolf. The harsh life she endured in this difficult period firmed her will, while the continual running about developed her physical prowess and the beauty of the grasslands spoke to her artistic soul.

Inner Mongolia was won by the communists in 1947, and about this time both

Ningbu and her blind mother-in-law died. Modegemaa returned to her own family and attended primary school in the grasslands. She was bright and became known as an excellent student and was able to skip a year. Life at home was not easy, however; her father was ill and Modegemaa had to help with the housework as well as look after her siblings. Although only ten years old, she assumed these domestic responsibilities at the same time as her artistic talent was becoming apparent. Modegemaa was elected head of cultural activities in her school's student association.

The Inner Mongolia Song and Dance Troupe (Nei-Menggu gewu tuan) offered the young woman a position in May 1956, and at the age of fifteen she left her hometown forever. Modegemaa traveled to Huhhote, the capital of Inner Mongolia Autonomous Region, to embark on a career as an artist. She received training in elocution, dancing, and literacy and studied music, drama, and dance under famous Mongolian artists, finally choosing dance as her artistic medium.

Dance is an extremely hard profession that demands a sound technical foundation. When still just fifteen years old, Modegemaa would get up at 3:00 o'clock every morning and quietly make her way into the gym to stretch and press her legs and bend and stretch her body. Day after day, she welcomed the dawn in a lather of sweat, not realizing that these were just the first steps on a long road to her artistic peak. Such great effort achieved results, however, and after six months' training Modegemaa was formally accepted into the troupe as a dancer. When she started to perform, Modegemaa received additional training from a professional Mongolian dancer, especially in using her shoulders. In Mongolian folk dancing, the many shoulder movements must be practiced relentlessly in order to attain the necessary toughness, softness, tremulousness, and bounce. Training is very tiring, and Modegemaa was often reduced to tears because of the pain. Her chest and back would ache, and she would feel nauseous, as if her organs had been scrambled, yet the young dancer never gave up. She performed in the countryside with the troupe, and the difficult living conditions served only to strengthen her mentally and improve her skills. Within two years, Modegemaa had become the featured performer in the Inner Mongolian Song and Dance Troupe.

During this period, she took part in a rehearsal of the "Big Wine Cup Dance" (Da zhongwan wu), which formed the basis for her famous "Wine Cup Dance" (Zhongwan wu). The "Big Wine Cup Dance" in which one male dancer is accompanied by sixteen female dancers, draws on the folk customs of the Ordos highlands in the Yehezoo region of Inner Mongolia. People dance at feasts there with chopsticks or a bowl of wine in their hands. Most of the female dancers' movements in the dance based on this ritual are executed on their knees. They sway with the music, bowing their faces to the ground in front and bending right back, all the while rhythmically clicking two wine cups held in each hand. It is an extremely difficult and strenuous maneuver. After learning and performing the routine, Modegemaa added the further challenge of balancing on her head a stack of bowls: this was her "Wine Cup Dance." Wearing a long Mongolian dress and balancing the bowls on her head, she would begin with an innovative forward lunge (a bow step). When the music was slow, the dancer resembled a sculpture, while in the fast sections her shoulders shimmered and her body seemed to float around the stage. For the finale, Modegemaa would tip the bowls from her head and catch them. The difficulty of the movements and the speed at which they were performed vividly manifested the dignity and passion of Mongolian women.

The "Wine Cup Dance" won the Award for Outstanding Dance, and Modegemaa won the Outstanding Actress Award at a solo song and dance concert in Inner Mongolia in November 1959, signaling the beginning of the fame of both dance and dancer. Premier Zhou Enlai (1898–1976) subsequently requested that she be transferred to the newly established Oriental Troupe of China (Zhongguo dongfang gewu tuan). Modegemaa and her dance went on to receive a Gold Award at the Eighth World Peace and Friendship Festival of Youth and Students in August 1962, the "Wine Cup Dance" causing a sensation. The chairman of the jury described Modegemaa as "rhythm incarnate." The dance has remained a staple in the repertoire of the Oriental Troupe. Modegemaa has always been ready to include new elements to the steps, adapting Chinese traditional opera and foreign ballet to her purposes.

She is grateful to her teachers in the Mongolian troupes, who guided her transformation from shepherdess to dancer. Other works for which Modegemaa is famous are "Single Drum Dance" (Dangu wu), "Dawn at the Lake" (Hupan chenxi), "Enchantment at an Ancient Temple" (Gumiao shensi), and "Lady Gada" (Gada furen). In all her many travels throughout Asia, Europe, and America, where her performances are well received, she has not forgotten the people of her native place—the Inner Mongolia steppes. Modegemaa has returned nine times to her hometown since the early 1980s and performed to great acclaim.

In 1980, she started teaching and writing, passing on to younger dancers the experience she accumulated over several decades. A Mongolian dance research school was opened in 1985, and thirty-eight students from Inner Mongolia and Xinjiang enrolled. After graduating, these students became leading dance figures in Tianshan and the steppes of Inner Mongolia. In order to create a systemic training method for the physical positions required by Mongolian dance, Modegemaa studied anatomy. Her *Sectional Training Method* (Buwei xunlianfa) crystallizes her art. In December 1993, she published *The Development of Mongolian Nationality Dances* (Menggu buzu wudao zhi fazhan).

Modegemaa currently holds the rank of First-Grade Dancer in the Oriental Troupe of China and is also a member of the CPPCC.

DING Shoupu
(Translated by Jan Zhang)

Caoyuan de nü'er [film]. Zhongyang xinwen dianying zhipianchang, 1983.
Modegemaa. *Menggu wudao wenhua.* Beijing: Zhongguo funü chubanshe, 1990.
———. *Shiyue wuyun.* Beijing: Zhongguo qingnian chubanshe, 2000.
Renqin Dao'erji. "Chuangye yongwu zhijing." *Wudao,* no. 5 (2000).
Zhang Yongchang, Gu Yingbin, and Hu Dade. *Dongfang yijue—Modegemaa wudao zhi lu.* Beijing: Zhongguo wenlian chubanshe, 1987.
Zi Huayun. "Sixiangzhe de wudaojia." *Zhongguo wenhuabao,* 5 October 2000.

Moss, Irene

Irene Moss, b. 1948, in Sydney, Australia, as Kwong Wai Lin and known in girlhood as Irene Kwong Chee, gained prominence in Australia for her commitment to anti-discrimination and has served with distinction in several high-level state and federal government posts. Her most recent appointment (October 1999) was as commissioner to the New South Wales (NSW) Independent Commission Against Corruption (ICAC).

Irene Moss is of southern Chinese descent, her paternal forebears having gone to Australia during the Gold Rush of the 1850s, and she was brought up in a traditional Chinese family by Cantonese-speaking parents (her father's English was rudimentary, her mother's non-existent). Not a great deal is known about the origins and history of Irene Moss's parents because, as she later said, "no one spoke of it." However, Irene Moss's father, William Chee (1892–1978), was born in Australia, the youngest of at least four brothers. He apparently married and had a son (Reggie Chee) and then decided to leave Australia for Hong Kong some time in the 1930s. According to Reggie Chee, this decision was prompted by the "Anti-Asian White Australia" policy that had come into effect in 1901. It convinced Chinese people that "Australians did not like them." William Chee spent some fifteen years in Hong Kong. He bought a cinema, which was lost to the Japanese when they occupied the area in the early 1940s, and over time "acquired another two families." One of the women he married there was Irene's mother, Poy Kin (Ann, d. 1984). Assisted back to Australia by the government at the end of World War II, William Chee used the £20 grant to which his Australian birth entitled him to start a tomato business in Sydney's Haymarket (Chinatown). He eventually became known as "Willie, the Tomato King."

Irene was born in Dixon Street in Chinatown but moved with her sisters to the suburbs in 1953, at about the age of four; her parents remained in the city to carry on the tomato business. The first intimations of racial difference came when Irene Moss was sent to the local primary school (Belmore Public School); she was the only Chinese girl and spoke no English. Irene Moss matriculated from nearby Wiley Park Girls' High, a state high school, and won a Commonwealth Scholarship to the University of Sydney (1966). There, she first gained a B.A., then studied law because of her interest in human rights, and throughout confronted the realities of race and class in Australia: she was "small, Chinese and female, from the western suburbs, and hung around with other Asians." At the university, however, Irene Moss also met her future husband, Allan Edward Moss (b. 1949), son of the Jewish financier Alfred Moss and currently managing director and CEO of the influential Macquarie Bank.

After graduating with an LLB, Irene Moss found it difficult to find work in a law firm and remained convinced that being Chinese, female, and from a poor family background militated against her. She finally gained employment with a law firm in Chinatown. Irene married Allan Moss in 1973 and moved with him to Canberra. Three years later, in 1976, they went to the United Stated to do postgraduate study at Harvard. Irene completed a master's of tax law (LLM), and the couple returned to Australia in 1978. Her time at Harvard provided the impetus for the career that she would soon embark upon. Irene's mother had always believed that injustices are simply how the world works and that no one, least of all the government, could do anything about it. At Harvard, however, Irene befriended women who were among the most active feminists in America and returned to Australia with "a willingness to do battle to get things done." She immediately took a job as conciliation officer with the NSW Anti-Discrimination Board, whose head, Carmel Niland, acted as her mentor. Niland once described Irene Moss as made of "stainless steel," adding that she was very persuasive in putting across alternative points of view.

In 1984, only days after accepting the deputy chair position of the Ethnic Affairs Commission, Irene Moss was offered a job she believed would allow her to make a difference at the federal level: a position as race discrimination commissioner with the Human Rights and Equal Opportunity Commission. She was well equipped for this post, as a comment made during a 1986 interview reveals: "To tell the truth, I feel more Chinese than Australian, even though I speak with a broad Australian accent. Well, I can't change the way I look." As race discrimination commissioner, Irene Moss chaired the National Inquiry into Racist Violence (1989–91), which she described as "the first national stocktaking of racism in Australia." Acknowledging that Aborigines suffer worse and more consistent racism than any other group in Australia, Irene Moss recommended an overhaul of police training, a nationwide racist violence databank, and, controversially, a national racial vilification law. Racial extremists did not take kindly to this last recommendation and even during the hearings of inquiry bomb threats were made.

Other official committees or boards on which Irene Moss served include the multicultural broadcaster SBS (1992–97); the Fulbright Commission of the Australian-American Education Foundation (since 1993); the Australian Honours and Awards Committee (since 1994); the National Breast Cancer Centre (chair, 1995–98); and the Powerhouse Museum (trustee, since 1999). In 1995 she was awarded an Order of Australia (AO) for her services to multiculturalism.

After her term as race discrimination commissioner drew to a close in 1994, Irene Moss returned, briefly, to the law; she became the first Asian woman to be appointed as a magistrate to the Children's Court. The following year, Irene Moss was appointed to a six-year term as NSW ombudsman. She exhibited a deep commitment to mediation and conciliation in this position and actively directed the efforts of her office toward the prevention of corruption. Setting up a Police Integrity Commission was an important step in that direction.

Soon after Irene Moss was appointed ICAC commissioner in October 1999, a merging of the roles of the ombudsman and the ICAC commissioner was mooted as a means of ensuring better, more effective, and efficient administration. This maneuver caused such public consternation, however, that the proposal was immediately squashed. The controversy, centered as it was on her, annoyed Irene Moss, but she is quoted as saying that it did not in any way lessen her resolve to lead ICAC as effectively as she knows she can. While her family, as many migrants have done over the ages, may have lived out their lives in a "meek and mild role of continual gratitude," Irene Moss is accustomed to controversy, believing that when justice demands, it is necessary to rock the boat.

Sue WILES

Conde, Sara. Interview. *The Sydney Morning Herald*, "Spectrum." Saturday, 31 May 1997, 2.

Fitzgerald, Shirley. *Red Tape, Gold Scissors: The Story of Sydney's Chinese*. Sydney: State Library of NSW Press, 1996.

Ricketson, Matthew. "Slaying the Dragons of Racism." *Time Australia*, 6, no. 17 (29 April 1991): 50–52.

Sung, Rosetta. "Australian Chinese. A Collection of Personal Histories and Family Photographs from Descendants of Earlier Chinese Settlers to New South Wales." 25 September 1989. Draft typescript held in the Mitchell Library, State Library of NSW, Sydney. Interview 52 (1986), 8–11.

Totaro, Paola, and David Humphries. "Gathering Moss."*The Sydney Morning Herald*, "News Review." Saturday, 20 November 1999, 42.

Who's Who in Australia 1999, 35th ed. Melbourne: Information Australia Group, 1998.

Mo-te-ko-ma: *see* **Modegemaa**

N

Ni Yishu: *see* **Yishu**

Nie Hualing: *see* **Nieh Hualing**

Nie Li: *see* **Zhong Yuzheng**

Nie Ou
Nie Ou, b. 1948, of Shenyang, Liaoning Province, is a contemporary artist whose paintings have been exhibited in many countries, including the United States, Canada, the United Kingdom, France, Switzerland, Australia, Denmark, and Japan. Her direct appreciation of nature, humanity, and landscape transcends cultural barriers.

When she was five years old, Nie Ou moved with her family to Beijing, where the little girl learned to paint at a municipal children's center after school. She was sent down to the countryside with other educated youth during the Cultural Revolution and returned to Beijing in 1975. Nie Ou passed the entrance examination to the Central Academy of Fine Arts (Zhongyang meishu xueyuan) in 1978 and majored in Chinese ink painting. After completing postgraduate work at the same institution, she was assigned to the Beijing Painting Academy (Beijing huayuan). Nie Ou's graduation piece, *The Bronze Age*, is ink and color on paper in the grand manner, within a wide rectangular format. She aimed in this work to show the skill, wisdom, and enthusiasm of the Chinese people during the period known as the slave society (2000–475 BCE), which included the Confucian Golden Age. This large narrative work depicts the process of making bronze vessels, beginning with mining the metal, transporting it, casting the vessels, using the vessels in sacrificial ceremonies, and, finally, burying the human sacrifice. In the space normally occupied by the sky is an enormous monster mask that symbolizes the world of another age.

Nie Ou learned academic anatomical rendering from Xu Beihong. Her work has a powerfully human element and while she draws upon socialist realist roots, Nie Ou inserts ideal heroes from the world of real people. Her figures have warmth and humanity with none of the sentimentality of the official propaganda style. Combining outstanding brush skills with personal observations of remote areas, Nie Ou selects from real life to create genuinely human scenes.

In 1982 the artist married fellow artist Sun Weimin (b. 1946 in Jinan), an oil painter who also attended the Central Academy of Fine Arts; he genuinely understands her art and commitment to it. Although her main medium is ink painting, Nie Ou paints in oil as well, her style suiting both mediums. The artist's work exemplifies the merging of past and present, continuity and change, the weight of tradition, and the emergence of fresh individual genius. The modern style she has created in her work shows the influence of China's rich history and culture, combining formal art training and a close association with the people.

Since the late 1980s, Nie Ou has created in her work a direct and lively rural environment peopled by villagers and typified by freer brush strokes. The change was marked by *Sorghum*, painted for the Bezel International Fair, and other 1985 works. In the lower left-hand corner of *Sorghum*, a cluster of sorghum in different shades takes up almost half the picture; the other half shows a young peasant woman kissing her baby. The flowing brush strokes and unrestrained composition are unique in traditional ink painting. While the images in this work appear to derive from Han dynasty (206 BCE–CE 220) stone rubbings, the artist's experience of rural life may also be an important source. Her work in this genre demonstrates a personal style and natural genius alongside a feminine sensitivity, meticulous detail, and ordered calm. Her academic training has provided an appreciation of past and present, yet her work is neither restricted nor moribund.

SHAO Yiyang

Nie Ou. *Catalogue of Nie Ou's Work*. Taipei: Xiongshi hualang, 1988.

Nie Yuanzi

Nie Yuanzi, b. 1921, in Hua County, Henan Province, was prominent in the early days of the Cultural Revolution.

From a wealthy family, she was the youngest in the group of four brothers and two sisters. Her eldest brother, Nie Zhen, joined the communists at a young age and his siblings followed his example. Nie Zhen's wife, Wang Qian, was a senior CCP cadre and the third wife of Liu Shaoqi (1898–1969).

In July 1937, at the outbreak of the Sino-Japanese war, sixteen-year-old Nie Yuanzi took part in a military training course organized at the National Teachers' College in Taiyuan by the Shanxi League for Self-sacrifice and National Salvation (Shanxi xisheng jiuguo tongmenghui). This was a community organization led by the CCP and supported by the Shanxi warlord Yan Xishan (1883–1960). Her part in the community signaled the start of Nie Yuanzi's anti-Japanese activities, and she joined the CCP in 1938. After studying in Taiyuan at the Institute for Military and Political Cadres of North China, Nie Yuanzi went in the 1940s to the communist enclave in Yan'an, where she met Kang Sheng (1898–1975) and his wife Cao Yi'ou (*q.v.*). Nie Yuanzi was appointed deputy secretary of the first branch of Qiqiha'er municipality in Heilongjiang Province in 1946 and the following year served as head of the Theory Section of the Harbin Propaganda Department.

A turning point came in her personal and political life in 1964 when she was transferred to Peking University. Nie Yuanzi became deputy head of the Economics Department and was then made secretary to the CCP branch in the Philosophy Department. On 25 May 1966, she and six of her colleagues wrote and pasted up on a wall at Peking University a big-character poster entitled "Just What Are Song Shuo, Lu Ping, and Peng Peiyun [Peking University leaders] up to in the Cultural Revolution?" Song Shuo was deputy director of the Department of Higher Education within the Beijing Municipal Party Committee; Lu Ping was a CCP president and secretary at Peking University; and Peng Peiyun (*q.v.*) was a CCP secretary at Peking University. Ten days after the poster appeared, Lu Ping and Peng Peiyun had been dismissed from their posts and the university leadership reshuffled; soon after that Song Shuo was also dismissed and investigated.

It is generally believed that Kang Sheng and Cao Yi'ou were the forces behind the poster that Nie Yuanzi wrote and that caused huge repercussions throughout the country. The debate it stirred began with words but ended in violence. A week after the poster was pasted up, the Central People's Broadcasting Station and the *People's Daily* (Renmin ribao) published the text, together with "commentaries." Because these organizations were the major official CCP mass media outlets, their commentaries were tacitly recognized as conveying official CCP policy. In a speech to teachers and students at Peking University not long afterward, Kang Sheng stated: "Nie Yuanzi's big-character poster is a declaration in the style of the Paris Commune; it is the declaration of the Beijing Commune of the 1960s." Two months later, Mao Zedong (1892–1976) praised Nie Yuanzi's poster as the first Chinese Marxist-Leninist big-character poster, and with his support it kindled the flames of the Cultural Revolution that soon consumed China.

Nie Yuanzi's wall poster was a crucial event within this era, and opinions vary as to how and why it was composed. One theory is that Kang Sheng and Cao Yi'ou provided Nie Yuanzi with the poster's theme, including details of the wrongdoings of Song, Lu, and Peng, and that Nie Yuanzi and her colleagues expanded on the message before signing their names to it. The background to this theory is that because Kang Sheng was not on good terms with Peng Zhen, long-time secretary of Beijing Municipal Party Committee, Kang wanted to destroy the committee in order to overthrow Peng Zhen. This committee was also administratively and geographically close to the Central Committee and therefore close to Mao Zedong, who from time to time had shown support for Peng Zhen. To do this, Kang Sheng decided to attack obliquely. Because Song Shuo and Lu Ping were capable administrators under Peng Zhen, Kang Sheng lit his fire under them, at Peking University, in order to consume the Beijing Municipal Party Committee. He gained the support of Nie Yuanzi in his plan because she was his and his wife's friend and had been unhappy with the leadership of the university, where she worked.

Another theory has it that Nie Yuanzi nursed a grievance about the attitudes of Peking University's leadership toward the incipient Cultural Revolution and, dissatisfied with her post, hoped to improve her position by displacing the current leaders. She passed their comments and statements on to Cao Yi'ou who, together with Kang Sheng, capitalized on the situation and encouraged Nie Yuanzi to put up a big-character poster to stimulate revolutionary change.

Once the poster was up and publicized, Nie Yuanzi was lionized by revolutionary groups. In November 1966, she led groups of rebels to Shanghai and attended and gave keynote addresses at all the congresses held by the major factories—Shanghai Shipbuilding Works, National Number Seventeen Cotton Mill, Yangshupu Power Station, and Lianggong Valve Company—and the tertiary institutions—Fudan University, Tongji University, Jiaotong University, and Huadong Normal College. That same month, a large rally to criticize the leadership of Shanghai Municipal Committee was held in Shanghai People's Square. Nie Yuanzi worked hard to ensure that the criticism was effective; leaders of the committee were persecuted and she is credited with rendering the leadership ineffective in the 1960s. Nie Yuanzi has disagreed with this interpretation of events, however, in the record she wrote in prison in 1980, claiming that the plan of emasculating the Shanghai Committee originated with Mao Zedong, who wanted workers and students in Shanghai to rebel. Nie Yuanzi said she simply followed orders issued by Mao's wife, Jiang Qing (*q.v.*).

Between 1966 and 1969, Nie Yuanzi served as chair of the Cultural Revolution Committee at Peking University and the New Peking University Commune. She was also head of the core group of the Red Guard Congress of Universities and Colleges in the capital, vice-chair of the Beijing Municipal Revolutionary Committee, and a member of the CCP Ninth Central Committee.

After 1969 Nie Yuanzi was investigated repeatedly and spent time in labor reform camps: the Cadres School of Peking University in Liyuzhou, Jiangxi Province; Xinhua Printery, Beijing; and Peking University Equipment Factory. She was arrested in April 1978 for "counterrevolutionary propaganda and inciting crime and slander" and sentenced in March 1983 to seventeen years in jail plus deprivation of political rights for four years.

Nie Yuanzi had married twice. She left her first husband, Wu Hongyi, in 1959 because he was labeled a rightist while her own political career was in ascendancy; they had a son and daughter. Nie Yuanzi divorced her second husband, Wu Gaizhi (1898–1968), in 1968 after two years of marriage. A peer of Kang Sheng, Wu Gaizhi was on the powerful Standing Committee of the Central Committee's Control Commission. Many people thought Nie Yuanzi had married him to further her own political career. Others believed the marriage to be merely a preparatory step to leaving Peking University, where she had never been happy.

Nie Yuanzi was released in 1995 at the age of seventy-four and now lives in seclusion in her home, shunning any contact with the outside world. Her political activity as one of the passionate instigators of the Cultural Revolution lasted only three years, but she and the nation paid a high price. Nie Yuanzi is seen in various ways by observers. Some consider her to be a political opportunist, her desire for power being at the root of her personal misfortune: because she chose to exacerbate the catastrophe that was the Cultural Revolution, all responsibility for losing everything must rest on her own shoulders. Others see her as a victim. In this script, Nie Yuanzi gained a sense of superiority in her early years through being the youngest and favorite child and a young revolutionary, but her confidence was shaken by an unsuccessful marriage. Searching for political power as a substitute, Nie Yuanzi allowed herself to become a tool at the beginning of the Cultural Revolution. Because she lost political power, career, husband, and family, Nie Yuanzi is as much a victim of the Cultural Revolution as the millions of others she was instrumental in harming. A third view of her is that Nie Yuanzi was merely a puppet. That she participated actively in the rebellion at Peking University and was a key figure in destroying the Shanghai Committee is undeniable. However, while these were catastrophic events, it is unjust to attribute too many wrongdoings to her alone.

Viola Hong Xin Chan WONG

Ai Qun. *Luanshi kuangnü*. Zhengzhou: Huanghe chubanshe, 1986.
Byron, John, and Robert Pack. *The Claws of the Dragon: Kang Sheng—the Evil Genius Behind Mao—and His Legacy of Terror in People's China*. Taipei: China Times Publishing Co., 1998.
Gao Hualun and Fang Xuechun, eds. *Zhonggong renming lu*. Taipei: Zhonghua minguo guoji guanxi yanjiusuo, 1968.
Lin Qingshan. *Kang Sheng waizhuan*. Hong Kong: Xingchen chubanshe, 1988.
Wang Nianyi. "Nie Yuanzi de Shanghai zhi xing." In *Mengya xilie: Shijianjuan: Bingbian! Bingbian!* Sichuan: Renmin chubanshe, 1994.
Who's Who in Communist China. Hong Kong: Union Research Institute, 1969.
Zhao Wumian. *Wenge dashi nianbiao: Yuanyuan, geming, yubo*. Hong Kong: Mingjing chubanshe, 1996.

Nie Yuchan

Nie Yuchan, b. 1903, of Funing, Hebei Province, was a pioneer both in nursing education and administration in China. Earlier in her life, she wrote her personal name with variant characters.

Nie Yuchan came from a family of intellectuals, and her father, Nie Jixun, was an open-minded man who realized the value of education to his children and society. At the age of thirteen, Nie Yuchan and her older sister left their hometown to attend the Sino-Anglo Girls' School (Zhongxi nüzi zhongxue) in Tianjin. Nie Yuchan was such an excellent all-round student that upon graduation the Nankai University waived its entrance examination and offered her a place. However, inspired by the humiliating epithet of "the sick man of East Asia" then applied to China, the young woman had already resolved to study medicine and gained admission to Union Medical College in Beijing.

Once enrolled there, Nie Yuchan became aware that the greatest lack in medical personnel in China at that time was qualified nursing staff and nursing and management staff with higher educational credentials in particular. With her father's support, the young woman sought and gained permission to transfer to the college's Nursing School, from which she graduated in 1927. Nie Yuchan commenced work as a nurse at Union Hospital but was then selected to be sent to Toronto University in 1929 to undertake further studies in public health and nursing. From there she went to Columbia University in the United States to continue further studies in nursing education. In 1931, Nie Yuchan was awarded a bachelor's degree.

Upon returning to China, she took up the position of director of nursing at the First Office of Public Health (Beiping diyi weisheng shiwusuo) in Beijing. In 1935, Nie Yuchan was appointed secretary of the Nursing Education Committee jointly set up by the Central Public Health Bureau and the Ministry of Education. At that time, nursing schools throughout the country each followed their own syllabus, teaching programs, and management systems, resulting in great disparity in the quality of the students produced. A survey undertaken by the Nursing Education Committee on which Nie Yuchan also served provided sufficient information to allow public health and education authorities to formulate regulations standardizing and improving the nursing profession.

She then returned to the United States in 1936, this time to study at the University of Michigan. Nie Yuchan was awarded a master's in 1938 and offered a scholarship for a doctorate. Uppermost in her mind at that time, however, was China's need for medical and nursing personnel—the Sino-Japanese War had broken out in 1937—and she decided to go back to China instead. Nie Yuchan was appointed principal of the Nursing School at Union Medical College in 1940, the first Chinese person to fill that post, and head of the Nursing Department at Union Hospital. As principal, she rigorously selected and tested teachers for the Nursing School and demanded a lot from her students. By ensuring the high quality of the teaching staff and raising the standard of students, Nie Yuchan transformed Union Nursing School into a model of nursing education in China. As director of the Nursing Department at the hospital, she paid particular attention to management, setting up comprehensive rules and regulations, strictly enforced, and thereby raised the quality of nursing to the point where the work of Union Hospital received special recognition in China and abroad.

Union Medical College had been forced to close down when Beijing fell to the Japanese in mid-1937, but Nie Yuchan determined to re-open the Nursing School elsewhere in order to provide badly needed qualified nursing personnel. In 1943, she and her younger brother Nie Guochen traveled together to the interior of China, where, tragically, he was shot and killed. Nie Yuchan continued on alone to Xi'an, Lanzhou, Chongqing, and, finally, Chengdu, where under extremely difficult conditions she re-opened the school. Three years later, at the end of the Sino-Japanese War, Nie Yuchan moved the school back to Beijing and resumed teaching, again in the face of much hardship. She was principal of the Nursing School during its most difficult two decades, but it never ceased producing qualified personnel, with Nie Yuchan herself training many nursing specialists.

The school was closed in 1953 and she was transferred as deputy director to the PLA General Hospital. Nie Yuchan suffered badly, however, in the many political movements that swept the PRC in its early years, being at various times criticized, isolated, and investigated. In 1958, she was branded a rightist and sent to a village in Anhui Province for labor reform. Despite this, Nie Yuchan never allowed bitterness to prevent her from contributing her best in whatever circumstances she found herself. Appointed head of the Nursing Department at Anhui Provincial Hospital in 1960, Nie Yuchan was responsible for a great improvement in nursing work throughout the hospital. Yet, during the Cultural Revolution, she again suffered persecution and was not exonerated till 1979 when her reputation was restored. She was then re-appointed to her position as deputy director of the PLA General Hospital.

Wanting to recognize Nie Yuchan's contribution to nursing education in China, Guo Huanwei and other graduates from Union Nursing School, who were then living in the United States, raised funds to set up the Nie Yuchan Prize for specialized nursing teachers from their alma mater. Then, in 1988, Nie Yuchan was appointed honorary head of the Faculty of Nursing at Union Medical University.

Nie Yuchan never married, preferring instead to devote herself to the establishment and development of the nursing profession. She is much loved and deeply respected by her students.

WANG Bing
(Translated by Emily Wright)

Ferguson, M.E. *China Medical Board and Peking Union Medical College.* New York: China Medical Board of New York, 1970.
Gu Fangzhou et al. *Zhongguo xiehe yikedaxue xiaoshi.* Beijing: Beijing kexue jishu chubanshe, 1987, 121–42.
Li Yixiu. "Ji Nie Yuchan." *Zhonghua huli zazhi*, 23, no. 8–10 (1988).
———. "Nie Yuchan." In *Zhongguo xiandai kexuejia zhuanji*, vol. 2. Beijing: Kexue chubanshe, 1991, 675–82.
Wang Xiuying. *Huli fazhan jianshi.* Shanghai: Shanghai kexue jishu chubanshe, 1987.

Nieh Hualing

Nieh Hualing, b. 1925, in Yichang, Hubei Province, is an American Chinese writer whose life and career have been enriched by the experience of living in mainland China, Taiwan, and the United States. She is also known, however, for her role in promoting international cultural exchanges, and her name is closely associated with the International Writing Program at the University of Iowa. This literary organization, established in 1967, has benefited hundreds of writers throughout the world.

Nieh Hualing spent her early years in the city of Wuhan, Hubei Province. She had just entered high school when Japan invaded China in mid-1937 and fled the city with her family. Nieh Hualing enrolled in the United High School (Lianhe zhongxue) in Enshi, Hebei Province, but this school also constantly retreated before the Japanese advance. After finally graduating from the National Eleventh High School (Dishiyi zhongxue) in Changshou, Sichuan Province, she was recommended for admission to Southwest Union University (Xinan lianda). Her family could not afford to send her there, however, so Nieh Hualing enrolled instead at National Central University (Zhongyang daxue) in Chongqing, Sichuan Province. In 1948, she graduated from its Foreign Language Department, which had by then moved to Nanjing. There, Nieh Hualing's writing talent revealed itself, and she started publishing under the pen name Yuan En.

Nieh Hualing migrated to Taiwan in 1949 with her mother and three siblings; her father, a KMT administrative commissioner in Guizhou Province, had been killed by the communists in 1934. Nieh Hualing started working as an editor with the fortnightly *Free China* (Ziyou Zhongguo) soon after arrival and remained with the journal until 1960 by which time she had established herself as a writer. *Free China* was well known in the 1950s for its advocacy of democracy and reform; some of its articles enraged the authorities. The journal's founder, Lei Zhen, was imprisoned for ten years, and other staff members were persecuted in 1960. Nieh Hualing was kept in isolation and, when the journal closed down, lost her means of financial support. She later recalled that, despite teaching creative writing in the Chinese Department at Taiwan University and Tung-hai University, she did not even have enough money for a burial service when her mother died of cancer in 1963. She wrote the article "Lei Zhen Said: 'What Crime Did I Commit?'" in 1996 as a memorial to Lei Zhen and the dreadful times *Free China* had experienced.

Nieh Hualing first started writing while still a university student in Nanjing. *Amoeba* (Bianxing chong, 1948), which was a satire in prose on political speculators during the civil war, was published under a pen name and must be considered her maiden work. Her 1950s writings in Taiwan include *Kudzu Vine* (Geteng, a collection of short stories); "The Jadeite Cat" (Feicui mao); "A Small White Flower" (Yiduo xiao baihua); "A Few Joyous Things for Wang Danian" (Wang Danian de jijian xishi); and *Shanshan, Where Are You?* (Shanshan, ni zai nar?). Many of these stories are about people who had gone to Taiwan from mainland China and focus on their predicaments, frustrations, and feelings of homesickness. For example, *Kudzu Vine*, ostensibly a love story, is really about an encounter between mainlanders in Taiwan who are very depressed. Again, Nieh Hualing considers *Shanshan, Where Are You?* a romantic novel. The main character is a middle-aged man on his way to see a girlfriend whom he met in mainland China many years previously. As the bus reaches the terminal, however, he discovers that the fat lady sitting opposite with several young children at her knees is none other than the girl he has always dreamed of and is on his way to see! His dream is shattered, and all he is left with is emptiness.

Nieh Hualing became famous with the publication of her first novel, *The Lost Chinaberry* (Shiqu de jinlingzi, 1960; first appeared in Taiwan in *Lianhebao*). Based on stories her mother had told her, this novel describes the "solemn and painful" experience of a girl coming to maturity during the Sino-Japanese War. Her best-known work, however, is *Mulberry and Peach: Two Women of China* (Sang Qing yu Tao Hong). Both of these novels are generally considered semi-autobiographical. Sang Qing and Tao Hong are the names of the split personalities of the main character in *Mulberry and Peach*. Written in the form of letters and diaries, the story tells of the frustrations of a Chinese woman who left the mainland for Taiwan and then went to the United States. Some critics see the protagonist's turmoil in China, vagrant life overseas, and subsequent schizophrenia as epitomizing the plight of many overseas Chinese, uprooted and living aimless lives. Others maintain that the significance of the novel lies in its symbolism: the main character's split personality symbolizes the nation's political divisions and the trauma caused to its people. Herein lies the reason why the Taiwanese authorities were not impressed when the novel appeared in serialized form in *Lianhebao* and why they refused to allow the rest of it to be published (the novel was later serialized in full in Hong Kong in *Mingbao Monthly*). *Mulberry and Peach* is a complex exploration of fiction writing that fuses Western technique with Chinese tradition. In form, it resembles Robert Louis Stevenson's *The Strange Case of Dr. Jekyll and Mr. Hyde*, with its syndrome of split personality.

The year 1962 marked a turning point in Nieh Hualing's career and personal life when she met her future husband, the American poet Professor Paul Engle (1908–1991), at a cocktail party given at the American consulate in Taipei. He had been appointed professor of English and director of the Writers' Workshop at the University of Iowa in 1937. Established the previous year, the workshop had become increasingly prestigious because of the involvement of such renowned academics and writers as Tennessee Williams, Saul Bellow, Flannery O'Connery, and Robert Penn Warren. In 1964, Nieh Hualing went to America to work with the workshop's program. Engle at first dismissed as financially unfeasible her suggestion that it be turned into an international writing program but finally agreed to try. Working together, they set up the International Writing Program in 1967 and in 1971 married. Engle retired from the directorship in 1977, at the age of sixty-nine, and Nieh Hualing took his place.

Each year, the International Writing Program houses thirty to forty writers from all over the world for up to a year, enabling them to write and engage in cultural exchange. Chinese writers first participated in the program in 1979 when Xiao Qian and Bi Shuowang were invited to a "Chinese Weekend" seminar. The renowned mainland Chinese writers Ai Qing and Wang Meng were invited for a similar seminar the following year, along with Wu Sheng and Yuan Kejia from Taiwan. In her opening remarks in 1980, Nieh Hualing said: "Today, three generations of Chinese writers have come together. We have Ai Qing representing the first generation, Wang Meng representing the middle generation, and Wu Sheng representing the younger generation; Yuan Kejia straddles the old and middle generations." Nieh Hualing observed that modern Chinese history "reflects social change in twentieth-century China, the vicissitudes of human life as much as the rise and fall of the nation." She continued: "The fact that these four Chinese writers have come here today proves one thing: that no matter where we are—on the mainland, in Taiwan or overseas—Chinese blood runs in our veins, and this blood relationship is inviolable."

After thirty years, Nieh Hualing went back to mainland China for a visit in 1978. She had previously married and divorced while living in Taiwan; this marriage produced two daughters: Wang Xiaowei, born in 1950, and Wang Xiaolan, in 1951. They joined their mother in the United States in 1965. Nieh Hualing was accompanied by Paul Engle and her two daughters during the month-long tour of China during which she visited many relatives and friends. Nieh Hualing also met such famous writers as Ai Qing, Xia Yan, Yang Mo, Cao Yu, and Bing Xin (*q.v.*). She visited China again in 1980, going to fifteen cities, including Guangzhou, Guilin, Xi'an, Shanghai, Nanjing, and Hangzhou during a two-month stay. On one occasion at that time, Nieh Hualing was warmly received by Mao Dun, one of China's greatest writers. Visiting China again in 1984 at the invitation of the Chinese Writers' Association, Nieh Hualing was received by Zhou Yang (then president of the All-China Federation of Literature and Art Circles), Xia Yan (vice-president of the Association of Foreign Relations), Ba Jin (president of the Chinese Writers' Association), and Huang Hua (vice-director of the Standing Committee of the NPC).

In January 1985, Nieh Hualing's novel *Beyond a Thousand Mountains, Water Forever Flows* (Qianshan wai, shui changliu) was published in Hong Kong. Centering on a Chinese woman named Liu Fenglian, this three hundred thousand-word masterpiece tells the story of modern China and unfolds on a magnificent scale. Shortly before the communist takeover in 1949, Liu Fenglian, a university student, falls in love with William Brown, an American journalist working in China. They marry and have a daughter, Lian'er. After her husband dies, in 1949, Liu Fenglian marries a communist cadre who is falsely accused in the late 1950s of being a rightist. When the Cultural Revolution ends, Lian'er Brown goes to America, not just to study but to seek out her father's family. She experiences culture shock, racial prejudice, and misunderstanding in her new country but in the end is accepted by her paternal grandmother. At the novel's end, Lian'er is writing a letter to her mother in mainland China, a copy of *The History of Modern China* on her lap. *Beyond a Thousand Mountains, Water Forever Flows* is not just about China or a Chinese woman. It is a story of love and understanding between people from different cultures.

A longing for the mainland, accompanied sometimes by disappointment and disillusionment, is a dominant theme in Nieh Hualing's writings, particularly in *The Lost Chinaberry*, *Mulberry and Peach*, and *Beyond a Thousand Mountains, Water Forever Flows*. The African novelist and critic Peter Nazareth pointed out an apparent contradiction between Nieh Hualing's life and her writing. Although she left mainland China, she has always yearned for the land and its people, and these feelings are why she wrote about mainlanders living in Taiwan. Nieh Hualing also made it clear how impossible it was for those people to return to the mainland. The author responded to Nazareth's comment:

> That is not really a contradiction. In fact, I'm always sympathetic to those people. It was for historic reasons that many people left the mainland for Taiwan, yet in Taiwan their hopes were shattered. Some of them went to Taiwan because they had nowhere else to go. It was with sympathy that I portrayed these sorts of people, who were truly aimless and had bleak prospects. They knew that unless the political situation changed, there was no hope whatsoever for them to go back. Although the Taiwanese government always threatened to "fight back to the mainland," it was very clear to these people that there was no way to "fight back," but who dared

speak their mind? They had to have a goal in order to go on living, so they dreamed of "returning to the mainland"—their own wishful thinking.

Since the 1980s, Nieh Hualing's work has been published in mainland China. Among these are *Anecdotes from Taiwan* (Taiwan yi shi), *The Lost Chinaberry*, *Mulberry and Peach*, and *Black, Black, the Most Beautiful Color* (Heise, heise, zui meili de yanse). Shanghai Film Studio plans to make *The Lost Chinaberry* into a movie.

Nieh Hualing's prose writings have been collected in *Collection of the Dream Valley* (Menggu ji). Her published essays include "A Critical Biography of Shen Congwen" (Shen Congwen pingzhuan) and "Thirty Years Later—the Reading Notes of the Returned" (Sanshinian hou—guiren zhaji). She has also undertaken translation work, translating many foreign works into Chinese, including *A Selection of American Short Stories* (Meiguo duanpian xiaoshuo xuan), *One Hundred Flowers Blossom* (Baihuiqifang ji), and *Black, Black, the Most Beautiful Color.* In the early 1970s, she and Paul Engle started translating the poems of Mao Zedong (1893–1976) into English. *The Poetry of Mao Tse-tung* was published by Wildwood House, London, in 1973. Nieh Hualing has translated many Chinese works into English, two volumes having been published by Columbia University.

Nieh Hualing's outstanding achievements in literature and promoting cultural exchange have been widely acknowledged and won her many honors and prizes. In 1981, she received honorary doctorates from two American universities, and the fifty governors in the United States awarded her and Paul Engle the prize for Outstanding Achievement in Literature and Arts.

Nieh Hualing may not be the most prolific of writers, but beautiful language, fresh images, and emotional richness characterize her work. Her writing harmoniously blends Chinese tradition and Western technique. Most importantly, however, there is in her work, as well as in her heart, always a feeling of "that which cannot be cut, and still remains tangled after brushing"—a feeling of nostalgia. This "special taste in one's heart" evokes a response in her readers similar to eating olives; a little bitter to start with but the longer you chew, the better the taste.

Ping WANG

Huang Wenxiang, *Haiwai Huayi Jingying*. Hong Kong: Shenghuo wenhui chubanshe, 1992.
Nieh Hua-ling. *Feicui mao*. Taipei: Minghua shuju, 1959.
———. *Geteng*. Taipei: Ziyou Zhongguo zazhishe, 1953.
———. *Mulberry and Peach: Two Women of China*, trans. Jane Parish Yang with Linda Lappin. New York: Feminist Press at the City University of New York, 1998.
———. *Qianshan wai, shui changliu*. Hong Kong: Sanlian shudian, 1985.
———. *Shiqu de jinlingzi*. Taipei: Xuesheng chubanshe, 1960.
———. *Yiduo xiao baihua*. Taipei: Wenxin shudian, 1963.
———. "Lei Zhen shuo: 'Wo fanle shenme zui?'" *Mingbao Monthly*, no. 7 (1996).
———. "Nieh Hualing he Feizhou zuojia tan xiaoshuo chuangzuo." *Mingbao Monthly*, no. 9 (1983).

Ouyang Quanyuan: *see* **Wang Quanyuan**

P

Pan Baojuan: *see* **Hu Die**

Pan Duo: *see* **Pan-thogs**

P'an Hsi-chen: *see* **Ch'i-chün**

Pan Xizhen: *see* **Ch'i-chün**

Pan Yuliang

Pan Yuliang, 1895?–1977, original name Chen Xiuqing and later known as Zhang Yuliang, was a painter. She was born in Yangzhou but after being orphaned was sold to a prostitution teahouse in the Anhui River port city of Wuhu. On the basis of this history and the fact that her husband Pan Zanhua was from Anhui, that province now claims her as a native daughter.

Pan Yuliang rose from such humble and socially unrespectable circumstances to become one of modern China's first female oil painters and, for a brief period in the mid-1930s, professor of oil painting at National Central University in Nanjing. Most of her artistic career, however, was spent abroad; after studying in Europe from 1920 to 1928, she returned there in 1937 and remained until her death. Virtually forgotten in her native land, Pan Yuliang was rediscovered in the early 1980s and became in China's new "open-country" era nationally celebrated as an example of cultural cosmopolitanism and artistic achievement.

Even without recent dramatizations in print, film, and on television, Pan Yuliang's life has a highly dramatic, almost mythic, quality. Her escape from the brothel echoes traditional tales of virtuous and culturally talented courtesans finding respectability in marriage to a worthy scholar-official, but her benefactor and husband was a modern-minded Republican government official who possessed strong ties to the revolutionary movement through his early membership in the Tongmenghui. Also, Pan Zanhua did not bring her into the household of his first wife but took her to the modern world of Shanghai. There, Pan Yuliang became interested in Western-style painting and entered the pioneering Shanghai art school of Liu Haisu (1896–1994), which at that time was scandalizing conservative opinion by providing nude models to coeducational classes. Pan Yuliang graduated in 1921 and through her husband's official connections got a government scholarship to study in France.

She remained in Europe for eight years, thus decisively breaking with the traditional pattern of the liberated courtesan who chooses domestic respectability, and pursued instead the distinctly modern career of professional artist. After studying briefly in Lyons, Pan Yuliang went to Paris and graduated from the prestigious but artistically conservative l'École des Beaux-arts before undertaking further study of oil painting and sculpture at the Academy of Rome.

In 1928 she returned to China as one of the very few first-generation Chinese women artists thoroughly trained in Western art. Pan Yuliang taught the subject at her old school in Shanghai before obtaining the post of professor at the new Art Department of the National Central University. There she was somewhat overshadowed by her already famous, Paris-trained fellow artist Xu Beihong (1895–1953). More seriously, gossip and scandal about her past persisted to the extent that one of her paintings in an exhibition was defaced with the scrawled graffiti: "a prostitute's tribute to her patron." Although remaining intensely grateful to Pan Zanhua throughout her life, Pan Yuliang may also have experienced difficulty in her relationship with his traditional first wife. In any event, Pan Yuliang decided to go back to Paris, where opportunities for artistic development were greater and her past would not follow. While the artist may have intended to return home to China, the Sino-Japanese War and the Second World War intervened, and then the revolution; by that time, both her husband and teacher, Liu Haisu, were branded rightists. By the end of the Cultural Revolution, Pan Yuliang had become quite old and died the following year.

Her artistic career in Paris from 1937 to 1977 has been celebrated in recent Chinese publications, but it appears that her life in Paris was a struggle. The ink paintings in a syncretic Western-Chinese style that Pan Yuliang produced after World War II gained more critical recognition than the more conventional oils. The artist's sensitive and delicate rendering of the nude female form, combined with her rather rough and "masculine" demeanor in later years, has led to speculation about her sexuality. Pan Yuliang held a well-reviewed solo exhibition at the Gallerie d'Orsay in 1957, which featured these works. The Musée Cernuschi (City of Paris's Museum of Oriental Art) acquired a number of them, plus prints and sculpture. The more prestigious Musée Guimet (France's National Museum of Oriental Art) commissioned her to do a bust of the famous ink painter Zhang Daqian. Such recognition did not, however, translate into commercial success, and Pan Yuliang died in poverty with a large number of unsold works still left in her shabby Montmartre flat.

Her substantial body of work consisting of hundreds, if not thousands, of canvases, ink paintings, and sketches became one of the sources for rediscovering the artist in a China that was just starting to reawaken to the outside world and modern Western art. One of her former students from the 1930s—Yu Feng—traveled to Paris in 1978 and learned of the collection. An influential artist and art critic in her own right, Yu Feng used her connections at the Chinese embassy to have the artworks returned to China. A few were accessioned by the National Gallery of Art in Beijing, but the vast majority did not find a home until a second woman—Shi Nan, a much younger schoolteacher and aspiring writer—played the decisive role in the rediscovery and rehabilitation of Pan Yuliang.

Shi Nan discovered the artist through letters still in the possession of her husband's family in the small provincial Anhui town of Anqing. Shi Nan wrote a dramatized biography entitled *The Soul of Painting* (Hua hun), which was first serialized in a popular Shanghai literary magazine and then published in 1983 by People's Press. It became a national bestseller. At symposia convened by art scholars recently liberated from the dogma of the Cultural Revolution and eager to reaffirm international art contacts, Pan Yuliang was praised even while the historical accuracy of Shi Nan's romanticized heroine was questioned. But historical accuracy was not the real issue in the China of the early 1980s. A new generation was eager to discover the outside world and pursue its own dreams of personal self-realization. Pan Yuliang's Paris paintings were shown to large and enthusiastic audiences in Shanghai, Guangzhou, and many smaller cities. The Anhui Provincial Museum in Hefei was glad to claim her for the province and take all those works for its otherwise very uncosmopolitan collection.

In the next few years, modern media—television and film—further spread the artist's reputation, although traveling exhibitions of her works continued to be shown, mostly in smaller cities. In 1988 the Fujian Provincial Television Studio in Fuzhou produced an eight-part special on her life that generally adopted Shi Nan's approach of dramatizing Pan Yuliang's conflict between romantic love and domestic happiness on the one side and personal self-realization through dedication to artistic pursuits on the other. The dilemma resonated with the lives of many Chinese women who had themselves probably received an education. The television director was an early middle-aged woman named He Ailin who was a graduate of the Shanghai Film Academy.

The posthumous celebrity status brought Pan Yuliang to the attention of Gong Li (*q.v.*), the most prominent actress in China's new post-Mao cinema. She played the role of the artist in a 1994 film directed again by a woman, the older and well-established filmmaker Huang Shuqin. By that time, however, the craze for things new and foreign had passed, and the film, which also used Shi Nan's title of *The Soul of Painting*, was a box-office flop. Critics were also unkind, one calling a nude scene where Gong Li serves as her own anatomy model (and there is some reason to believe Pan Yuliang actually did this) as nothing more than a "cheap trick" in a dull film. The cinematic version of *The Soul of Painting*, this critic complained, had no soul, which may have been less a comment on the competently directed and acted film than a sign that the 1980s had already become the 1990s. As a bestseller and symbol of the new, modern, and cosmopolitan woman, Pan Yuliang's decade was the 1980s, especially its early years.

Her relatively brief period of acclaim, however, does not mean that the artist has disappeared into historical obscurity. The works that had survived outside China now command five-figure prices (in U.S. dollars) at international art auctions. The new histories of twentieth-century art being written both inside and outside China give Pan Yuliang an important, if modest, acknowledgement in her introduction of Western oil painting to China and modernized Chinese ink painting to the West.

Perhaps the historical verdict on this remarkable figure will be that she played two roles. In her lifetime, Pan Yuliang was a forerunner, opening new paths for women in the new art and culture coming out of China's early twentieth-century opening to the modern world. Soon after her death, and thus too late for her to witness personally, she then became an even more potent symbol of personal and artistic self-expression for the country's new generation. Pan Yuliang's place in modern China's art history, as well as its gender and international cultural histories, seems secure.

Ralph CROIZIER

Hu Yinghong. "'Hua Hun' wu hun." *Dianying zhoubao*, 21 August 1994.
Huang Chunxiu. "Kan xin wu mei yi Hua Hun." *Xiong shi meishu*, 198 (August 1987): 57–70.
Pan Yuliang. *Pan Yuliang meishu zuopin xuanji*. Nanjing: Jiangsu meishu chubanshe, 1988.
Quartre Artistes Chinoises Contemporaines: Pan Yu-Lin, Lam Oi, Ou Seu-Tan, Shing Wai.
   Paris: Musée Cernuschi, 1977.
Shi Nan. *Hua Hun: Zhang Yuliang zhuan*. Beijing: Renmin wenxue chubanshe, 1983.
Zhou Zhikan. "Yiwei zhide zunjing de nühuajia." *Zhongguo meishu*, 13 (February 1986): 1–5.

Pang Tao

Pang Tao, b. 1934, in Shanghai, is an artist, researcher, and teacher of painting.

She is the daughter of well-known modernist artists Pang Xunqin (1906–1985) and Qiu Di (1906–1958). Pang Tao held her first show in Guangzhou Provincial Library in 1947, at the age of thirteen, with her younger brother Pang Jun; the following year they again exhibited their oil paintings together, this time at the Yili Art Gallery in Shanghai.

Pang Tao graduated from the Beijing Central Academy of Fine Arts (Zhongyang meishu xueyuan) with a bachelor's degree in 1953 and a master's degree in 1954 and taught painting at that institution for over thirty years. In 1986 she became professor of oil painting when the Fourth Studio was established at the academy in response to modern art. Pang Tao was one of the first professors there to research art materials and contemporary painting in Paris; the results of her research are contained in the valuable *Art Materials in Contemporary French Paintings* (Xiandai Faguo huihua cailiao, 1992) and *Modern Materials and Techniques of Painting* (Huahua cailiao yanjiu, 1996).

After many years of political turmoil, she began a series of paintings related to designs on Chinese bronzes in 1981. Employing expressive brush strokes full of strength and energy, Pang Tao transformed their shapes into flat pattern-oriented surfaces in bold colors. The series marked a turning point in her artistic journey from realism to semi-abstraction.

The artist was awarded an Excellent Work Commendation at the National Art Exhibition in 1979 and won First Prize at the Beijing Art Exhibition in 1980. The volume *Recent Works by Lin Gang and Pang Tao* was published in 1983, and in 1986 her Chinese Bronzes Series was presented in a solo show at the Museum of the Central Academy of Fine Arts. Pang Tao's work has been included in more than fifty major art exhibitions.

The artist is married to the oil painter Lin Gang, who studied in Leningrad between 1954 and 1960 and is a professor at the Central Academy of Fine Arts. Their daughter Lin Yan is also an artist; she graduated from the academy and is currently living in the United States, practicing contemporary art.

SHAO Yiyang

Sullivan, Michael. *Jue Lanshe hou yishu xianxiang*. Taiwan: Jinxiu Art Press, 1996.

Pan-thogs

Pan-thogs [Pan Duo], b. 1938, in vJo-mdav, Tibet, is a mountaineer of Tibetan nationality.

According to her husband and biographer, Deng Jiashan, Pan-thogs was originally a serf who from childhood tended sheep, spun wool, and wove cloth for her master.

When deprived of even that lowly livelihood, she turned to begging and slept in a beggar's hovel. Pan-thogs became a worker on a farm in 1959 after Tibet was brought under Chinese administration but was selected to join a mountaineering expedition. She climbed Mount Mushitage, 7,546 m, and for this achievement was awarded the title of Outstanding Sportswoman that year.

Two years later, Pan-thogs attempted a peak of 7,595 m with a group of male and female mountaineers. Taking part in the climb was her future husband, whom she had first met in 1959. He had studied surveying before joining the mountaineering team and was a group leader on the attempt. Halfway into the ascent, Deng Jiashan had to take a sick member of the team back to base, where he waited for news of the climbers still on the mountain. The team was overjoyed to hear that Pan-thogs and another Tibetan woman named Shes-rab had reached the top, thus creating a new height record for women mountaineers.

The crowning moment in Pan-thogs's career, however, was climbing Mount Everest (Qomolangma) in 1975. As deputy team captain, she and eight men conquered the world's highest peak (8,848.13 m) from the northern approach. The northern face is the most difficult one on Mount Everest, and only one team, comprising three Chinese men, in 1960, had ever reached the summit from that aspect. Pan-thogs was the first Chinese woman to reach the Mount Everest summit and only the second woman ever; she was beaten to this honor by the Japanese climber Junko Tabei, who had reached the peak eleven days before. Pan-thogs made great sacrifices to make this climb. She was thirty-seven years old and had three children by then. Pan-thogs and her husband sent their children to his brother and sister in Wuxi so that Pan-thogs could focus on her training, which included a demanding fitness regimen that her coach had designed to help the mountaineer lose the weight gained since giving birth to her children.

The climb was extremely dangerous. At about the 8,000 m mark, for example, there is a platform called the "road to death"—virtually unclimbable. Pan-thogs knew she would experience severe headaches and nausea and that wind velocity at the peak is 800 m/second. It was fine on the day of her climb, so the support team had a clear view of the climbers. At the summit, where the air is four times thinner than at sea level, the team surveyed the precise height of the peak—8,848.13 m. This superseded the figure Chinese authorities had previously used, of 8,882 m, and the other eight figures different international surveyors had used. Pan-thogs also performed an experimental distance electrocardiogram, which is essentially an electrocardiogram taken on the world's highest peak.

Between 1959 and 1978, she received three Medals of Honor from China's State Sports Committee (Guojia tiwei), and Pan-thogs has been deputy chair of the China National Sports Association (Zhonghua quanguo tiyu zonghui) since 1979. In 1984, and again in 1989, she was honored as Most Outstanding Sportsperson since the establishment of the PRC.

Pan-thogs had married Deng Jiashan in 1963. To begin with, she was not sure that their marriage would work, because of cultural differences, but Pan-thogs later said that a holiday in Wuxi with her Han nationality husband and his family allayed her fears. In 1981, she moved from Tibet to Wuxi to be close to her children and took up the post of head of the Wuxi Sports Association.

Lily Xiao Hong LEE

Song Ruizhi, ed. *Zhongguo funüwenhua tonglan.* Jinan: Shandong wenyi chubanshe, 1995, 702.

Wang Yanyu. "Zhumulangma fengding shang de nüxing." In *Titan zhengxiong renwu,* eds. Kang Jie, Wei Bing, and Liu Shuang. Xi'an: Taibai wenyi chubanshe, 1995.

Yingwen *Zhongguo funü,* ed. *Gujin zhuming funü renwu,* vol. 2. Shijiazhuang: Hebei renmin chubanshe, 1986, 1193–98.

Zhongguo dabaike quanshu: Tiyu. Beijing: Zhongguo dabaike quanshu chubanshe, 1991, 239.

Zhongguo dangdai wenhua mingren dacidian. Beiijing: Zhongguo guangbo dianshi chubanshe, 1992, 673.

Peng Gang: *see* **Zhong Yuzheng**

Peng Peiyun

Peng Peiyun, b. 1929, in Liuyang, Hunan Province, is a member of the State Council and director of the State Birth Control Commission of the PRC.

Not a great deal is known about her family background and early life. Because she later studied at some of China's most prestigious universities, however, Peng Peiyun must have come from a reasonably well-to-do-family and been a good student. During the later years of the Sino-Japanese War, she studied at Southwest Union University in Kunming. After the war, presumably from 1946 to 1949, Peng Peiyun studied at Ginling [Jinling] University in Nanjing and Tsinghua [Qinghua] University in Beijing. She joined the Democratic Youth League in 1945 and became a member of the CCP in 1946, at the age of seventeen, working in the underground throughout her university years. Peng Peiyun graduated from the Sociology Department of Qinghua University in 1949; one source says that she studied (*yiye*) at Qinghua but does not mention graduation.

No longer having to work underground after China came under communist rule in 1949, Peng Peiyun became a party administrator in higher education from 1950 to 1978. Her first position was as secretary to the CCP general branch at Qinghua University; her second one was as standing member of the Beijing Municipality Higher Education Working Committee. At the outbreak of the Cultural Revolution, she was deputy secretary of the CCP at Peking University. In 1966, a "big character poster" appeared at Peking University, attacking Song Shuo, Lu Ping, and Peng Peiyun, all three party secretaries with the Higher Education Working Committee of Beijing Municipality and Peking University. Lu Ping and Peng Peiyun were dismissed from their posts some two weeks later. This big character poster is said to have been initiated by Nie Yuanzi (*q.v.*), working under the direction of Cao Yi'ou (*q.v.*). Both women were followers of Jiang Qing (*q.v.*), who was intent on destroying the leadership of higher education in Beijing. It was probably not until the end of the Cultural Revolution that Peng Peiyun regained some of her status and became head of the Revolutionary Committee of the Beijing Chemical Industry College (Beijing huagong xueyuan).

After the fall of the Gang of Four in 1976, her career entered a new phase when she was transferred to the State Science and Technology Commission and headed its first bureau (Guojia kewei yi ju, 1978–79). In 1980, Peng Peiyun went to another ministry of the central government, this time to head the Policy Study Room in the Ministry of Education. She was promoted in 1982 to vice-minister of Education, and when the ministry was renamed the State Education Commission Peng Peiyun became its deputy director. Although having spent most of her career in education, in 1988 she was assigned and appointed as director to a ministry whose work was entirely new to her: the State Birth Control Commission. At the same time, Peng Peiyun advanced to be the only woman on the State Council and became a member of the Supervisory Committee of the CCP Central Committee.

In order to perform her responsibilities better, she read widely on family planning and birth control and made fact-finding trips to talk to experts and grass-roots workers. Her advice to the 290,000 workers in the birth control field was to broaden the vision and tactics of their outreach. Peng Peiyun recommended that birth control be linked with the many benefits it provides indirectly to the people, such as wealthier, more comfortable, and happier families. In the meantime, the director stabilized and supported continuity in birth control policies generally in order to avoid fluctuations in her workers' caseloads. She also expected that enforcement of the one-child policy would vary with changing conditions and special needs in certain areas. Most important of all, Peng Peiyun has made birth control the responsibility of various levels of officialdom, not just of birth control workers. This strategy appears to be working, with the birth rate falling every year since 1988; the 2000 census cited a figure of 16.12, down from 17.70 in 1994.

Peng Peiyun is said to be an active, energetic, down-to-earth, and modest person. Not surprisingly, she also takes her work seriously. Peng Peiyun is married to Wang Hanbin, whom she met during her Southwest Union University days, and he is also an official of the PRC. It is not clear if they have any children.

Lily Xiao Hong LEE

Bowen. *Zhongguo gaoceng xin zhenrong*. Hong Kong: Guanxiong, 1993, 183–85.
Huaxia funü mingren cidian. Beijing: Huaxia chubanshe, 1988, 999.
Zhongguo renming dacidian: Xianren dang zheng jun lingdao renwu juan. Shanghai and Beijing: Shanghai cishu chubanshe and Waiwen chubanshe, 1989, 341.

Peng Xuezhen: *see* **Peng Zigang**

Peng Zigang
Peng Zigang, 1914 (or 1916)–1988, born Peng Xuezhen in Beijing, is a native of Suzhou, Jiangsu Province. She is a journalist who won acclaim in the 1930s and 1940s for injecting literary quality into journalistic writing but is also known as an editor of newspapers and magazines.

After graduating from Zhenhua Girls' School (Zhenhua nüxiao) in Suzhou in 1934,

Peng Zigang enrolled at Zhongguo University in Beijing. She studied there for only one year, however, and in 1936 started working with the Shanghai magazine *Women's Life* (Funü shenghuo) run by the women's movement activist Shen Zijiu (*q.v.*). That same year Peng Zigang married Xu Ying, a journalist with the newspaper *Dagong bao*. While working as an editor with *Women's Life*, Peng Zigang was assigned to interview Shi Liang (*q.v.*), one of seven prominent intellectuals arrested by the KMT government for advocating China's resistance to Japan. The report that Peng Zigang subsequently wrote for *Women's Life* is believed to have influenced public opinion and assisted in the release of the seven intellectuals.

She joined the CCP in 1938, and during the Sino-Japanese War and the civil war that followed (1945–49), was a reporter with *Dagong bao*, stationed in Chongqing and Beijing. Her reports filed during this period on social activities and family life and her hospital and literary interviews became popular with readers. Peng Zigang developed an innovative style of writing news with a literary touch; it became her personal trademark and was not only accepted but acclaimed. Indeed, her style was even imitated, which helped create a new genre of reportage literature. Peng Zigang's report on the visit of Mao Zedong (1893–1976) to KMT-controlled Chongqing in 1945, entitled "Mr. Mao Zedong Comes to Chongqing," was memorable. Another article, in 1946, during the civil war, on a prison interview with CCP officials arrested by the KMT exposed the arrests and brought the victims a speedy release. Thus, Peng Zigang wielded her pen as a weapon to aid the CCP's struggle against the KMT.

After the establishment of the PRC in 1949, she worked with *Jinbu ribao* in Tianjin and *People's Daily* (Renmin ribao). Peng Zigang went to Hungary in 1950 to take part in the World Youth Congress, was accepted as a member of the Chinese Writers' Association (Zuojia xiehui) in 1951, and later was made chief editor of *The Traveler* (Lüxingjia) magazine (date unknown). Her reportage works are collected in *Old Postal Worker* (Lao yougong) and *Clear Vision* (Xueliang de yanjing), and her travelogues appear in *Brief Letters from the Soviet Union and Hungary* (Su Xiong duan jian). In the anti-rightist movement of 1957, both Peng Zigang and her husband Xu Ying were accused of being rightists. She was rehabilitated in 1979 and resumed chief editorship of *The Traveler*. Even though in poor health in the 1980s, Peng Zigang continued to write, producing among other pieces lyrical essays such as "The Beginning of Humanity" (Ren zhi chu), and "The Sculpture" (Suxiang). It is not known if Peng Zigang and Xu Ying have any children.

Peng Zigang is one of China's early women journalists. She is also one of the few women who edited newspapers and magazines catering not just to traditional women's issues but addressing matters of general interest.

Lily Xiao Hong LEE

Li Liming. *Zhongguo xiandai liubai zuojia xiaozhuan*. Hong Kong: Bowen shuju, 1977?, 427.
Yingwen *Zhongguo funü*, ed. *Gujin zhuming funü renwu*, vol. 2. Shijiazhuang: Hebei renmin chubanshe, 1986, 891–95.
Zhongguo funü guanli ganbu xueyuan, ed. *Gujin Zhongwai nümingren cidian*. Beijing: Zhongguo guangbo dianshi chubanshe, 1980, 318.
Zhongguo renwu nianjian, 1989. Beijing: Huayi chubanshe, 1989, 14.

Phantog: *see* **Pan-thogs**

Ping-hsin: *see* **Bing Xin**

Q

Qian Jianqiu: *see* Ch'ien Chien-ch'iu

Qian Xijun

Qian Xijun, 1905–1990(?), one of the thirty women who took part in the Chinese communists Long March of 1934–35, was born in Zhuji County, Zhejiang Province, to poor peasants who sold her as a child bride. Her betrothed, Zhang Qiuren, was an enlightened boy who rejected their arranged marriage and became one of the founders of the Communist Youth League. Qian Xijun later married Mao Zemin (1896–1943), a younger brother of Mao Zedong (1893–1976).

Qian Xijun joined the Youth League in 1924 and the CCP in 1925. Moving to Shanghai, she attended the same free school run by the communists as the writer Ding Ling (*q.v.*) and went on to further schooling, doing underground work (publishing revolutionary materials) between 1926 and 1931. During this time, Qian Xijun worked with and married (in 1926) Mao Zemin. Qian Xijun and Mao Zemin looked after three nephews for several months after Mao Zedong's wife, Yang Kaihui (*q.v.*), was executed by a warlord at the end of 1930; however, upon being assigned to the Jiangxi soviet in 1931, the aunt and uncle left the boys in Shanghai. Qian Xijun became a branch secretary of the central government and assisted Mao Zemin in his work as treasurer of the soviet bank. As an organizer and inspector during the Long March, she did propaganda work, hired bearers, and organized grain supplies and cash funds. Qian Xijun also conducted an assignment with Wei Gongzhi (*q.v.*) to smuggle a large sum of international aid money from Shanghai to Xi'an in 1937, a dangerous job that took four months. She then spent four years (1938–42) with her husband in Xinjiang in the northwest. After Mao Zemin was executed there by a warlord who betrayed the communists, Qian Xijun returned to Yan'an and studied at various party schools. In 1945 or 1946, she married Zhou Xiaoding and went with him to Shanghai to organize strikes among the workers. No mention is made of her having had children.

After 1949 Qian Xijun was made deputy head of the Food Bureau and General Office of the Bureau of Light Industry, as well as being elected to the CPPCC (1959, 1965, 1978). It is not known what happened to her during the Cultural Revolution. She is believed to have died in 1990.

Sue WILES

Guo Chen. *Jinguo liezhuan: Hong yifangmianjun sanshiwei changzheng nühongjun shengping shiji.* Beijing: Nongcun duwu chubanshe, 1986, 28–34, 149, 194.

Liu Jinghui and Mao Shucheng. "Jiechu de Hongjun xuanchuanyuan." In *Hongjun nüyingxiong zhuan*, eds. Liaowang bianjibu. Beijing: Xinhua chubanshe, 1986, 102–17.

Qian Ying

Qian Ying, 1903–1973, of Xianning County, Hubei Province, was born in Qianjiang County, Hubei Province. She is known for her supervisory and disciplinary work with party and government officials of the CCP and the PRC.

Her parents, Qian Chenxun and Peng Zhenghao, operated a Chinese herbal shop in Qianjiang County, and Qian Ying's early education consisted of attendance at various family-run private schools in Qianjiang and Xianning. While still a teenager, she opposed an arranged marriage by attempting suicide and thus won her freedom, making clear her determination to study and have a career "like a man." In 1923, at the age of twenty, Qian Ying went to Wuhan and enlisted the aid of her uncle, Qian Jiapan, who was a communist activist and educator, to enroll at Hubei Women's Normal School (Hubei nüzi shifan xuexiao). There, she met women students such as Xia Zhixu and Yang Zilie (*q.v.*) under whose influence Qian Ying cared for wounded soldiers during the Northern Expedition and distributed propaganda leaflets for the revolution. She joined the CCP in 1927 after the KMT-CCP united front disintegrated and communist members were pursued and persecuted.

Qian Ying took part in some of the most important events organized by the CCP. She first displayed ability and leadership in 1927 during preparations for the Nanchang (August) and the Canton Commune (December) Uprisings. When both of them failed, Qian Ying was transferred to Shanghai and made secretary of the General Union. It was at this time that she married Tan Shoulin, a colleague there. The following year Qian Ying traveled to Moscow to study at the Communist University of the Toilers of the East (Dongfang laodongzhe gongchangzhuyi daxue), even though the young woman had just learned she was pregnant. Qian Ying gave birth in Moscow to a baby girl whom she placed in a crèche. Deciding that her concentration on work would be affected if the baby came back with her to China in 1931, Qian Ying left the infant in Moscow. Nothing is known of what became of the child, and it is assumed that Qian Ying's daughter was killed during the Nazi bombing of Moscow in the early 1940s. Qian Ying's husband was executed soon after his arrest in Shanghai in April 1931; she resolved not to remarry and devoted herself thenceforth to the communist revolution.

Upon return to China that year, Qian Ying was sent with a small group of CCP members to Hubei, with orders to establish a base. When the KMT army moved toward this poorly defended area the following year, Qian Ying led a few hundred militia to the enemy's rear, thus contributing to the base's defense. This operation was later immortalized in the 1960s film *Red Militia of Honghu* (Honghu chiweidui). Eventually, however, so overwhelming was the KMT attack that the base had to be abandoned. In September 1932, Qian Ying broke through enemy lines disguised as a peasant and made her way to Shanghai. She was reassigned to Jiangsu Province and made secretary to the Women's Committee of the Provincial Party Committee. Qian Ying and others on the committee were arrested, however, after being betrayed.

During the four years spent in the KMT prison in Nanjing, Qian Ying clandestinely contacted all the female political prisoners jailed there. They organized a succession of hunger strikes and each time won concessions from the prison management. Qian Ying kept herself alert in mind and body by trying to exercise regularly. She also asked that women prisoners be allowed to study English with the American Gertrude Noulens-Ruegg, who held a Swiss passport and was in prison for spying. Qian Ying's purpose in doing this was to get news of the outside world from the English-language newspapers they studied. One of the Chinese women's hunger strikes was nevertheless undertaken to secure the release of the American and her husband, Paul Noulens-Ruegg.

In 1937, all political prisoners were let go when a second alliance between the KMT and the CCP was negotiated, and for the next few years communists were able to work openly. Qian Ying was sent to her native Hubei and appointed to the significant positions of head of the Organization Committee of the CCP's Provincial Committee and, later, became its secretary. She revived the membership and organizational structure previously established with her colleagues when they were working in the base area and expanded party influence by recruiting new members. From that time on, Qian Ying held a series of party positions in Hubei and Hunan.

In line with united front policy, she established friendly relations with KMT generals such as Li Zongren and Bai Chongxi. These men requested the help of CCP political instructors to stir up anti-Japanese sentiment in their soldiers and local officials in areas under their control. Qian Ying was transferred to the South China Bureau in 1941 and appointed to responsible positions until she went to Yan'an, to study and participate in the Rectification Movement. During this movement, many CCP members who had worked in KMT-controlled areas were wrongly accused of being traitors and spies, and Qian Ying risked her unblemished name to vouch for the ones she knew to be loyal party members. In 1945, Qian Ying was elected as a delegate to the Seventh CCP Congress.

At the end of the Sino-Japanese War that year, moving to east China, she was appointed head of the Organization Committee of the CCP in Chongqing, Nanjing, and Shanghai. When the second united front officially ended in 1946, the CCP's Central Committee directed that work in all KMT-controlled areas come under the control of the Shanghai Bureau. Qian Ying was then in charge of underground work in Sichuan, Yunnan, Guizhou, and Hunan, as well as the student movement in Beijing and Tianjin. She followed party directives to go under cover, win the trust and support of the general population, and wait for a suitable opportunity to start the next initiative. The opportunity came with the unfortunate rape of a female university student in Beijing by an American serviceman that year; the attack provided the spark that set off an explosion of protests and demonstrations by university teachers, students, and other notables. Qian Ying directed CCP members to lead students from other parts of China in support of the Beijing movement and thus launched the first nationwide student movement of the post-war period, followed in 1947 with the "Anti-Starvation, Anti-Civil War, and Anti-Persecution" Movement. From then on until the CCP takeover in 1949, over ten student movements were organized, all of them eventually resolved in the CCP's favor.

Qian Ying's policy was to seize the moment when the KMT government was in the wrong, choose a time and place most favorable to her own party, and not prolong a movement once the climax had been reached. She instructed her subordinates to make the transition from demonstrations and protests to an attempt to "unite all elements that can be united." Qian Ying also identified people in the middle ground as special targets and issued instructions to instigate defection among KMT military and political officials, emphasizing the importance in the last days of KMT rule of preventing the retreating KMT government from destroying factories, transportation facilities, schools, etc. Because of her successful maneuvering and negotiations, Hunan Province came under CCP rule without a single shot being fired.

After the establishment of the PRC that year, Qian Ying continued to fill regional-level party positions centered in Wuhan. She was a member of the Central China Bureau and head of its Organization Department and in December was identified as a standing member of the Central-South Bureau and head of its Women's Work Committee. With the establishment in 1950 of the regional government of the Central-South Military and Administrative Committee (Zhongnan junzheng weiyuanhui), Qian Ying was appointed a member. Two of the posts held were vice-chair of the People's Supervision Committee and director of its Personnel Department. At the same time, her work for the party also complemented these positions in government: she was promoted in 1952 from deputy party secretary of the Central-South Bureau's Discipline Inspection Committee to secretary of the Bureau.

Qian Ying's outstanding ability at the regional level saw her called to Beijing early that year to work in the central government and the Central Committee, perhaps not coincidentally because in both cases the work was related to inspecting discipline. She was first appointed vice-chair of the Supervision Committee of the State Council and later the minister of the Control Commission (Jianchabu) of the PRC government. In the party context, Qian Ying became deputy secretary of the Central Disciplinary Inspection Committee, and when the Central Control Commission replaced it she was appointed vice-secretary. During her tenure, Qian Ying led work parties to the northeast, Anhui and Gansu, where there were problems of discipline. She is said to have brought down just rulings regarding wronged officials, exposed those who acted against the law, and saved the people of Gansu from starvation by requesting grain to be shipped there urgently. Qian Ying is credited with accelerating the process in 1962 of rehabilitating most people who had been accused since 1957 of being rightists. It required courage to do that because, in order to liberate these individuals, Qian Ying would have been unable to avoid offending numerous others. She was therefore praised by top leaders such as Liu Shaoqi (1898–1969) and Zhou Enlai (1898–1976) and given the sobriquet "a Female Judge Bao."

During the Cultural Revolution, the cliques surrounding Jiang Qing (*q.v.*) and Lin Biao (1907–71) claimed that the Central Control Commission had been simply a tool for the restoration of capitalism, even though it appeared to promote the anti-revolutionary line. They therefore ordered that Qian Ying be examined under guard, and during this time she endured all kinds of humiliation and cruelty. Even when diagnosed in 1972 with lung cancer and sent to hospital to undergo "treatment under guard," Qian Ying was attended by two guards only and no medical personnel. She died from the cancer the following year, at the age of seventy. In 1978, party leaders

Deng Yingchao (*q.v.*) and Liao Chengzhi spoke at an interment ceremony for her ashes, describing her as a "woman cadre who possessed leadership and prestige."

Throughout life, Qian Ying wrote important articles on the history and development of the CCP and the issue of the discipline of members. As early as 1931, one report on "How to Establish Workers' Unions in the Countryside" elaborated on the importance of uniting farm workers and educating them in revolutionary ideas and action. A later and broader work is her historical essay on the role of the CCP in Central-South China. In 1953, she wrote "A Brief Summary of the Party's Discipline Inspection Work in the Last Two Years and Views on the Work in the Future."

Qian Ying was one of few communist women who exercised real power from the 1930s to the 1960s. She started at the local level and moved gradually to the party's Central Committee and the central government in the capital. Qian Ying was a rare example of a woman who may be said to have had a real chance of holding up half the sky had her career not been interrupted by the Cultural Revolution.

Lily Xiao Hong LEE

Huaxia funü mingren cidian. Beijing: Huaxia chubanshe, 1988, 852.
Klein, Donald W., and Anne B. Clark. *Biographic Dictionary of Chinese Communism, 1921–1965.* Cambridge, Mass.: Harvard University Press, 1971.
Who's Who in Communist China. Hong Kong: Union Research Institute, 1969.
Yingwen *Zhongguo funü,* ed. *Gujin zhuming funü renwu,* vol. 2. Shijiazhuang: Hebei renmin chubanshe, 1986, 653–57.
Zhonggong dangshi renwuzhuan, vol. 30. Xi'an, Shanxi renmin chubanshe, 1986, 242–72.
Zhongguo funü guanli ganbu xueyuan, ed. *Gujin Zhongwai nümingren cidian.* Beijing: Zhongguo guangbo dianshi chubanshe, 1980, 325–26.

Qian Zhengying

Qian Zhengying, b. 1923, is a native of Jiaxing, in Zhejiang Province, although she grew up in Shanghai. Qian Zhengying is an engineer and was China's vice-minister, then minister, of Water Resources from 1952 to 1988.

Her father, Qian Shizeng, studied engineering in the United States and encouraged his daughter to take up civil engineering at Datong University in Shanghai during the Sino-Japanese War. Her political involvement as secretary of her CCP branch (she had joined the CCP in 1941) forced Qian Zhengying to leave Shanghai in 1942, however, just six months before completing her degree. She went to the communist base north of the Huai River that had recently been established by the New Fourth Army in central China and did two years of propaganda and education work. Qian Zhengying thought she would never have an opportunity to work as an engineer but was moved to river management and read up on the subject before carrying out field surveys and investigations. Her greatest happiness was that she was not discriminated against or belittled because she was a woman.

When the dams on the Huai River were breached in 1944, Qian Zhengying was asked to join a dam-building team working between Bangfu and Linhuai guan. After the Jiangsu-Anhui Border Government (Su-Wan bianqu zhengfu) was formed in 1945, she became part of the Department of Water Resources and built dams up and down the Grand Canal to prevent flooding. Her ability and reputation as an engineer grew as Qian Zhengying was given increasingly important missions. In 1947 she was transferred to Shandong to help combat the "ice floods" of the Yellow River. These were caused by the action of the river as it froze at various points in the winter; at some point, as the ice melted it would break up, piling up great chunks, which in turn stopped the flow of the river water. The location of these ice jams could never be predicted, and they always caused gigantic floods. Working with the people and the army, which blew up the ice with strategically placed explosives, Qian Zhengying helped prevent flooding that year.

With the establishment of the PRC in 1949, she was made deputy department head of the Department of Water Resources of the Military and Administrative Council of East China (Huadong junzheng weiyuanhui) and was transferred to the Yellow River Water Resources Commission (Huanghe shuili weiyuanhui) the same year. Qian Zhengying was promoted to deputy director and chief engineer of Huai River Harnessing Commission in Shandong (Shandong Huaihe hewuju) in 1950; her title later changed to deputy head of the Department for Harnessing the Huai River, Shandong Province.

Qian Zhengying's long tenure in the Central Government's Ministry of Water Resources and Electric Power (Shuili dianli bu; the name of this ministry alternated between Water Resources and Water Resources and Electric Power) began in 1952. She remained a minister until receiving a promotion in 1988 to deputy chair of the CPPCC. In 1957, the position of deputy director of the Committee for the Management of Haihe River and Its Tributaries (Haihe shuixi zhili weiyuanhui) was added to her ministerial responsibilities.

As vice-minister and then minister of Water Resources and Electric Power, Qian Zhengying was actively involved in water conservancy in China. She frequently traveled to different parts of China to examine the work of others and provide guidance on flood prevention. In 1953, for example, Qian Zhengying led an inspection of the work at Dahuofang Dam on the Hun River in northeast China. She was also entrusted with some of China's largest projects of water conservancy, some of them involving grave technical problems, e.g., the dams on the Huai River and the Miyun Dam near Beijing, the hydraulic power station at Liujiaxia on the upper reaches of the Yellow River, and Gezhou Dam on the Yangzi [Yangtze] River.

The Gezhou Dam was a fine example of how she worked. The project took forty thousand workers five years to complete. Although she was fifty-eight years old when the dam was completed, Qian Zhengying went on inspection tours that took her up and down more than one thousand steps and saw her sloshing through wet tunnels. Her colleagues considered the minister efficient, resolute, and willing to take responsibility. In January 1981, for example, opinions differed about when the final gap of the Gezhou Dam should be sealed. After meticulously checking every stage of the project, Qian Zhengying ran through a trial sealing of the dam on 3 January, a procedure that was supposed to take one day. She and her engineers on hand checked the velocity of the water flow at the narrowing gap and on the basis of their new figures decided at an emergency meeting that the gap should be sealed in one go. The nation, watching on television, held its collective breath as the gap filled, not in the planned seven days, but in just thirty-six hours. Qian Zhengying was there the whole time, right behind the workers and their bulldozers. The evening after the gap was sealed, it snowed. The arrival of the snow, which lasted for several days and would have caused a most unwelcome delay, vindicated Qian Zhengying's decisiveness. During the debate on the building of the Three Gorges Dam on the Yangzi River in the 1990s, Qian Zhengying was a strong advocate for its construction.

On the political front, Qian Zhengying was a leader of the CCP during her student days and in 1950, at the age of only twenty-seven, was appointed to membership of the powerful Military and Administrative Council of East China. Since then, she rose steadily through the hierarchy. Qian Zhengying was elected to membership of the First NPC in 1954 and addressed that body on water conservancy in 1962. After stepping down as minister for Water Resources and Power in 1988, she was elevated to deputy chair of the CPPCC until 1993. From 1973 on, Qian Zhengying was a member of the CCP's Central Committee.

She has also provided leadership in the women's movement, sitting on the Executive Committee of the ACWF since 1949 and leading a delegation of women to Moscow in 1957 to take part in the celebrations of the fortieth anniversary of the October Revolution. Qian Zhengying also traveled to Albania and Sri Lanka in the 1970s and visited more than twenty countries in Asia, Africa, Europe, South America, and North America in the late 1970s and 1980s.

Said to be of a larger build than most women from southern China, Qian Zhengying is straightforward in her manner. She is married to Huang Xinbai, who was once the vice-minister for Education, and they have three children. The family enjoys swimming, and Qian Zhengying is proficient in English.

One of the earliest women ministers of the PRC, she is unusual for being entrusted with a portfolio not traditionally in the purview of women. If one seeks examples of women who truly succeeded in the men's world of the PRC, Qian Zhengying is clearly one.

Lily Xiao Hong LEE

Bartke, Wolfgang. *Biographical Dictionary and Analysis of China's Party Leadership, 1922–1988*. Munich: Saur, 1990, 169.
Bowen. *Zhongguo gaoceng xin zhenrong*. Hong Kong: Guanxiong, 1993, 255–57.
Chang Jialong. "Sidelight on a Woman Minister." *Women in China*, no. 1 (January 1982): 6–8.
Who's Who in China: Current Leaders. Beijing: Foreign Languages Press, 1994, 501.
Who's Who in Communist China. Hong Kong: Union Research Institute, 1969, 143.
Zhongguo funü guanli ganbu xueyuan, ed. *Gujin Zhongwai nümingren cidian*. Beijing: Zhongguo guangbo dianshi chubanshe, 1980, 326.

Qiao Peijuan: see Zhong Yuzheng

Qiao Yin: *see* **Xiao Hong**

Qijun: *see* **Ch'i-chün**

Qiong Yao: *see* **Ch'iung Yao**

Qiu Yihan

Qiu Yihan, 1907–1956, one of the thirty women who took part in the Chinese communists Long March of 1934–35, was born in Pingjiang County, Hunan Province. Nothing is known of her early life, but she received an education and was therefore classed as an intellectual. Qiu Yihan joined the Youth League in 1926 and the CCP in 1929.

She and another Long Marcher, Li Jianhua (*q.v.*), were part of the division of the Red Army led by Peng Dehuai (1898–1974) in 1930; they worked with young people. Qiu Yihan was appointed in 1931 to head the Hunan-Jiangxi Women's Bureau and became an inspector in 1932 for the Public Health Unit. She also taught at the Red Army University in the Jiangxi soviet. Just before the Long March, Qiu Yihan was branch secretary of the Youth League at the Red Army University and a political instructor. When she set out on the Long March, she suffered from a poisoned hand, and her glasses (she was very shortsighted) were broken quite early on. Her husband, Yuan Guoping (1905–1941), contracted acute tuberculosis in Guizhou, and Qiu Yihan was assigned to care for him in a separate medical unit. She was nevertheless given the title of secretary and is said to have done political work.

After reaching Yan'an safely, Qiu Yihan returned south with her husband to work with the New Fourth Army, as head of the Political Department of the Military University of East China. After 1949 she held the important posts of head of the Organization Department of the City of Nanjing and head of the Organization Department of Jiangsu Province. Qiu Yihan died in 1956, apparently from illness.

Sue WILES

Guo Chen. *Jinguo liezhuan: Hong yifangmianjun sanshiwei changzheng nühongjun shengping shiji.* Beijing: Nongcun duwu chubanshe, 1986, 12, 73, 178.

Qiu Yuanyang: *see* **Ch'iu Yüan-yang**

R

Ren Yidu: *see* **Sun, E-tu Zen**

Reyher, Eileen Chang: *see* **Chang, Eileen**

Rongzi: *see* **Jung-tzu**

Ru Zhijuan

Ru Zhijuan, b. 1925, in Shanghai, is, of all prominent Chinese women writers, the one whose career is perhaps most closely linked to the fate of the CCP. The course of her personal life is tied to the stages of the party's development, and the messages conveyed in her writings can be seen as programmatic.

The autobiographical novella *Which Way Has She Come?* (Ta cong na tiaolu shang lai, 1982) describes the fast-moving events of Ru Zhijuan's childhood. She was the youngest of five children who, after the death of their mother and disappearance of their father, were parceled up among various relatives. Two-year-old Ru Zhijuan and a slightly older brother were raised by a grandmother, who supported herself on casual work. They moved continuously between Shanghai and Hangzhou. Ru Zhijuan attended several schools, among them a Christian orphanage, where she learned to fear and abhor the Christian belief in guilt and sin, as Ru Zhijuan remarked in the autobiographical short story "The Night of Separation" (Shiqu de ye, 1963). The schools she attended taught the girl how to read and write, but her knowledge of literature was self-taught. Ru Zhijuan studied *Dream of the Red Chamber* (Honglou meng) and passages translated into Chinese from Tolstoy's *War and Peace.*

In 1943 Ru Zhijuan worked briefly as a primary school teacher and published her first literary works. The same year, she followed her brother to Jiangsu to join the Propaganda Division of the New Fourth Army in the fight against the Japanese. In 1944 Ru Zhijuan married Wang Xiaoping, an overseas Chinese from Singapore who had returned to China to help fight the Japanese; in 1947 she joined the CCP.

Ru Zhijuan became editor of the prestigious *Monthly for Literature and Art* (Wenyi yuebao) in 1955 and was promoted a year later to a position in the Chinese Writers' Association. The famous author Mao Dun (1896–1981) spoke openly of how impressed he was by her short stories "Lilies" (Baihehua, 1958) and "Tall White Poplars" (Gaogao de baiyangshu, 1959). Ru Zhijuan became one of the most popular writers of the 1950s. Her texts of this period depict scenes from the wars of the 1940s and were meant to show the people's enthusiasm for the revolutionary cause and solidarity with the communist army. To move her readers, the author focused on giving her characters striking individual gestures whose symbolism was easy to decipher. In "Lilies," for example, a young woman shows her concern for the revolutionary cause by covering the dead body of a heroic young peasant soldier with the lily-ornamented blanket she had embroidered in preparation for her own wedding. In "On the Banks of Cheng River" (Chenghe bian shang, 1959), an old peasant offers to flood his fields, which are just ready for harvesting, to enable revolutionary troops to cross the river.

For Ru Zhijuan, writing was a political and propaganda mission, and her choice of topics and approach were in tune with official discourse. She reminded her readers of the revolutionary wars not just in the stories above but also in "Mother Guan" (Guan dama, 1955) and "Among Comrades" (Tongzhi zhi jian, 1961). Ru Zhijuan also wrote "Before Daybreak" (Liming qian de gushi, 1957) in memory of the risks taken by those working clandestinely in enemy territory. Such writings glorified the history of the party and became her best-known works. However, she also tackled the conditions of the 1950s, writing about the new role attributed to women as if to exemplify the radical changes advanced by the governing CCP. "Sisters-in-law" (Zhouli, 1955) deals with the restructuring of the family by pointing to the conflict between the younger and older generations. The entry of women to the labor market became another important topic ("The Warmth of Spring" [Chunnuan shijie], 1959; "A Wish Fulfilled" [Ru yuan], 1959). "On the Way" (Licheng, 1959) and "A Shu" (1961) contrast a younger, progressive, and enlightened woman with an older one who continues to subscribe to traditional values.

Ru Zhijuan survived the Hundred Flowers Campaign of 1956 untouched because she was too much of a party writer to engage in any outspokenness. She fell silent, however, during the course of the socialist education campaign (1962–65) when her work was criticized for its preoccupation with small people with their worries over what were seen as the big issues dominating the language of the propaganda apparatus. This argument led to the accusation that Ru Zhijuan's work lacked political orientation: she was censured severely for avoiding full and clear-cut accounts of contradictions and, particularly, for not attributing a major role to the depiction of class struggle. While these accusations were not without foundation, they were directed against precisely those elements of Ru Zhijuan's work that had gained the respect of colleagues and admiration of readers. Class struggle, for instance, served in her stories as the background rather than the topic. Her popularity had largely rested on an ability to recreate some reflections on the "big issues" within the world experienced by average readers, thereby arousing in them familiar feelings. She avoided the stark contrast between characters that were either all black or all white and concentrated instead on the shades in-between, creating plausible figures who were both interesting and sympathetic. Ru Zhijuan's response to her critics took the form of a story dealing with the continued relevance of class struggle—"The Sergeant Turns Around" (Huitou zou, 1964)—but it was not well received, and she produced nothing except a few essays and the draft of a film script in the next decade. During the Cultural Revolution, Ru Zhijuan spent some years in the countryside.

She became a popular and influential writer during the first years of the reform period after the Cultural Revolution. As before, her choice of topics corresponded closely to the new official discourse, which was a general criticism of Cultural Revolution policies. "Household Affairs" (Jiawushi, 1980) depicts city dwellers who were forced to move to the countryside. "Ice Lanterns" (Bingdeng, 1978); "Winter Landscape in Warm Colors" (Zhao nuanse de xuedi, 1981); and "Boats without Steering" (Diule duo de xiao chuan, 1981) deal with the persecution of intellectuals during the "ten chaotic years." "A Story in Wrong Order" (Jianji cuole de gushi, 1979) describes the difficulties caused by the Great Leap Forward (1958–60), another subject of great importance in the new discourse. There were, however, new social problems that deserved attention. "A Path on the Grass Land" (Caoyuan shang de xiao lu, 1979) criticizes certain Cultural Revolution victims who abused the privileges they obtained through rehabilitation. "Honors List" (San bang zhi qian, 1980) warns against a new spirit of competition replacing the old solidarity and willingness to cooperate. In "Parental Love" (Ernüqing, 1980), a mother dies a solitary death unheeded by a son to whom she has dedicated her life; he has been spoiled with her unwise, family-centered, and egoistic love. This last story invites readers to shed tears, just as some of her stories from the 1950s did.

Throughout her career Ru Zhijuan did not venture into genres other than the short story. However, despite such continuity, her writing underwent certain changes. In line with new literary trends of the early 1980s, her reform era stories give more room to protagonists' reflections and thoughts. Occasionally, as in "Search" (Xunmi, 1982), these become so powerful that they alone drive the narrative forward. In 1981 Ru Zhijuan told the Hong Kong journalist Li Li that writers of her generation had not learned to write without restriction or guidance or, in other words, without regard for political aims and propaganda needs. Ru Zhijuan welcomed the new individualism and freedom of expression but also admitted that she still had to learn how to live with them. Her learning process has not been in vain. "Search" is an attempt to show how an individual under duress comes to term with existence, and "Boats" and "Winter Landscape" also strike a new tune. These are well written stories. As often in Ru Zhijuan's work, landscape plays a big part in visualizing human attitudes and emotions. Characters are painted in pastel colors, their feelings and reactions moderate, as if they, as well as the author, had to learn how to live in a new world.

An interview in 1981 with Ru Zhijuan was devoted to the relationship of mother and daughter, that is to Ru Zhijuan as well as to her daughter Wang Anyi (*q.v.*), who has since become a successful author. Seemingly, Ru Zhijuan faded from the public eye as her daughter entered it.

Barbara HENDRISCHKE

Cheng Ying. "Ru Zhijuan lun." In *Dangdai nüzuojia sanlun*, ed. Li Ziyun. Hong Kong: Joint Publishing, 1984, 393–416.

Hegel, R.E. "Political Integration in Ru Zhijuan's 'Lilies.'" In *Reading the Modern Chinese Short Story*, ed. T. Huters. Armonk: M.E. Sharpe, 1990.

Hendrischke, B. "Ru Zhijuan: Chinas sozialistische Revolution aus weiblicher Sicht." In *Moderne Chinesische Literatur*, ed. W. Kubin. Frankfurt: Suhrkamp, 1985, 394–411.

Hsu, Kaiyu. *Literature of the People's Republic of China*. Bloomington: Indiana University Press, 1980, 257–64.

Li Li. "Zhong shengdai yu xin shengdai." *Qishi niandai*, 5 (1981): 100–05.

Ru Zhijuan. *Lilies and Other Stories*. Beijing: Panda, 1985.

———. *Ru Zhijuan xiaoshuo xuan*. Chengdu: Sichuan renmin chubanshe, 1983.

Sun Luxi and Wang Fengbo, eds. *Ru Zhijuan yanjiu zhuanji*. Hangzhou: Zhejiang renmin chubanshe, 1982.

Ruan Fenggen: *see* **Ruan Lingyu**

Ruan Lingyu
Ruan Lingyu, 1910–1935, was born Ruan Fenggen in Shanghai, although her native place was Xiangshan County (present-day Zhongshan), Guangdong Province. Her baby name was Agen, and she used the name Yuying at school. Ruan Lingyu became famous in early Chinese silent films as the "Queen of Tragedy."

Ruan Lingyu's father, Ruan Yongrong (*hao* Dichao), was the son of a very poor peasant and went to Shanghai to escape poverty. He got a job in the Machine Section of the Asian Kerosene Distribution Centre of Pudong but died of illness when Ruan Lingyu was six years old. Because an older sister had died of malnutrition four years previously, Ruan Lingyu thus became the sole dependent of her mother, who was a servant with the well-known and wealthy Zhang family of Shanghai.

Ruan Lingyu was a beautiful child, intelligent and sensitive. She attended Chongde Girls' School, and her artistic talent was already evident when she performed in school dramas. Ruan Lingyu began her acting career in summer 1926 when she appeared in the film *Husband and Wife in Name Only* (Guaming fuqi).

Opinions differ as to how Ruan Lingyu took up acting. Some say she had to give up school because her mother became ill from overwork and was in dire financial straits. To help out, Ruan Lingyu sat for and passed a screen test with Mingxing Film Studio for a part in *Husband and Wife in Name Only*; later on she met the playboy Zhang Damin and married him. Another version has it that Ruan Lingyu had known Zhang Damin since childhood because he was a member of the Zhang family for whom her mother worked. He was a spoiled and pampered son but attracted to Ruan Lingyu and wanted to marry her. The family's fortunes declined dramatically during the early Republic period (immediately after the 1911 Revolution), however, and the love between the young couple soured because Zhang Damin would not work. When he went overseas, out of loneliness Ruan Lingyu decided to support herself, sat for the screen test, and was signed up.

Over the next two years, the actress attracted attention with her performances in *The Tablet of Blood and Tears* (Xuelei bei), *Yang Xiaozhen*, *White Cloud Pagoda* (Baiyun ta), and *Scholar Cai Builds Luoyang Bridge* (Cai Zhuangyuan jianzao Luoyangqiao). She moved to Dazhonghua baihe, which was later taken over by the Lianhua Film Company. She played leading roles in *The Pearl Crown* (Zhenzhu guan), *A Guide to Love and Desire* (Qingyu baojian), *The Sole Surviving Swan* (Jiehou guhong), *Conquering Nine Dragon Mountain* (Dapo Jiulongshan), *Burning Nine Dragon Mountain* (Huoshao Jiulongshan), *A Woman's Heart* (Furen xin), and *Flower of the Silver Screen* (Yinmu zhi hua), and became famous as a film star.

It was while she worked with Lianhua that Ruan Lingyu reached the pinnacle of her career. She played the leads in *Spring Dream in the Ancient Capital* (Gudu chunmeng), *Girls to Be Picked Up* (Yecao xianhua), and *Love and Obligation* (Lian'ai yu yiwu), each film more popular and profitable than the last. Praise came from all quarters for her performances in *Wintersweet* (Yijian mei); *The Peach Blossom's Tears of Blood* (Taohua qixueji); *Yutang Chun*, *Spring Dream in the Ancient Capital II*; *Three Modern Women* (Sange modeng nüxing); *City Nights* (Chengshi zhi ye); *Life* (Rensheng); *Doodad* (Xiaowanyi); *Homecoming* (Guilai); *Goodbye, Shanghai* (Zaihuiba Shanghai); *Sweet Scent of Wintersweet* (Xiangxuemei); *New Women* (Xin nüxing); and *Women of the Night* (Shennü).

Ruan Lingyu put to good use in her acting all the experiences of her short life: hardship and impoverishment in childhood, flamboyance and decadence of Shanghai's wealthy families, the misery and sorrow of marriage. She was talented and worked hard, her brilliant successes driving the developing film industry to greater levels of professionalism. Ruan Lingyu played to perfection a great variety of characters: headstrong rich girls, coquettish concubines, bewitching dancing girls, charming society girls, dignified young ladies, shy young girls, chaste students. She made an unprecedented contribution to Chinese films, playing twenty-seven different roles in twenty-seven films and bringing each one to life.

In her personal life, however, Ruan Lingyu was not so successful. She was unhappy about her husband's idleness, and although repeatedly trying to save the marriage the couple finally divorced in 1933. Ruan Lingyu then moved in with the playboy Tang Jishan, manager of Shanghai Chinese Tea Company, taking an adopted daughter with her.

Upon its release just after Chinese New Year 1935, Ruan Lingyu's film *New Women* created a furor. The film told about a scandal involving reporters and, while doing well at the box office, drew howls of protest from Shanghai newspapers. The actress, the innocent target of this protest, was crucified in the tabloid newspapers for divorcing Zhang Damin and setting up house with Tang Jishan. Zhang Damin also turned on her, tearing up their divorce agreement and demanding that the court issue a summons. Extremely sensitive about her reputation, Ruan Lingyu found the prospect of further gossip unbearable and poisoned herself on the night of 7 March 1935. She was taken to hospital the next day but died; Ruan Lingyu was twenty-six years old. The day she died was, coincidentally, International Women's Day.

The famous writer Lu Xun (1881–1936) recognized the real tragedy of Ruan Lingyu when he pointed out that public opinion had been the main cause of her death and the incident revealed how little respect society had for women. He wrote the article "Public Opinion Is a Fearful Thing" (Renyan kewei) soon afterward. The irresponsibility and corruption of the press and legal system also came in for their share of blame. Lu Xun publicly reprimanded the Chinese media for the unhealthy way it had developed in recent times. However, that was not the last word about Ruan Lingyu's death. In July 2001 a writer named Shen Ji revealed to the Sydney (Australia) publication *Dajiyuan* that, while researching for a script on Ruan Lingyu, he found in what appeared to be a small college publication an article by two sisters. One of these sisters was Tang Jishan's mistress. The article told of Tang's conspiring with the sisters to falsify Ruan Lingyu's last letters, which were published in the media immediately after her death. Two letters purporting to be Ruan Lingyu's real letters appeared alongside the sisters' article. In one of the letters, addressed to Tang Jishan, Ruan Lingyu gave the real reason for her suicide as being Tang Jishan's obsession with another woman and his repeated abuse of her. Thus, it is ironic that the furor that leftist intellectuals created following her death appears to have been based on falsified evidence.

Shirley Wai CHAN

Huang Weijun. *Ruan Lingyu zhuan*. Changchun: Beifang funü ertong chubanshe, 1986.
Jiang Deming. "Ruan Lingyu de beiju." *Suibi*, 21 (1982): 65–67.
Liu Shaotang, ed. "Ruan Lingyu." In *Minguo renwu xiaozhuan*, vol. 5. Taipei: Zhuanji wenxue chubanshe, 1982, 125–28.
"Ruan Lingyu siwang zhenxiang jiemi." *Daijiyuan*, 27 July 2001, 12.
Shangdu. "Hongyan boming mingling lei: Ruan Lingyu." *Nüxing* (1987): 86–89.
Shu Qi. *Ruan Lingyu shenhua*. Hong Kong: Xianggang chuangjian chuban gongsi, 1992.
Tang Yu. "Sanbajie yu Ruan Lingyu." *Kaifang zazhi*, March (1996): 75.
Yingwen *Zhongguo funü*, ed. *Gujin zhuming funü renwu*, vol. 2. Shijiazhuang: Hebei renmin chubanshe, 1986.
Zhang Huochi. "Ruan Lingyu de ai yu hen." *Zhongwai zazhi*, 9 (1970): 16–20.

Ruan Ruolin

Ruan Ruolin, b. 1925, of Zigoubao in Zhangjiakou city, Chahar Province (present-day Hebei), is a writer and television producer.

At the age of four she moved to Beijing with her mother and two years later was enrolled in the Primary School attached to Beijing Normal University. In mid-1937 Ruan Ruolin was accepted into the Girls' Middle School, attached there as well. Her father, Ruan Muhan (1902–1964), was a professor at a political science and law institute and active as an underground worker with the communists. Her oldest sister, Ruan Ruoshan, also took part in student movements. Ruan Ruolin was thus nurtured in revolutionary ideas and exposed to progressive literature; her mother taught her classical Chinese prose and poetry.

Not long after the July Seventh Incident of 1937 (known in the West as the Marco Polo Bridge Incident), which marked the beginning of the Sino-Japanese War, Ruan Ruolin's father and sister went to a revolutionary base leaving the rest of the family, six in all, in Beijing. It was not long before the city fell to the Japanese, but her mother was eventually able to arrange for Ruan Ruolin (then aged fourteen) and one of her younger brothers, Ruan Congwu (then aged nine), to make the dangerous journey to the comparative safety of the communist enclave in Yan'an. An underground worker named Cui Yueli sent them by train to the Shanxi-Chahar-Hebei Region where the children stayed for several months before walking on with a group of eleven people. Chaperoned by armed underground workers, the sister and brother skirted blockades, crossed the Hutuo River, and trekked beyond Tongpulu; the journey took three months and covered a distance of 2,500 li (about 1,200 km). In the northwest, Ruan Ruolin studied in the Border Region Normal College, the start of what she described as "a life of study, producing, and laboring." Ruan Ruolin was then sent to Ganquan County Winter School to teach literacy and there met Liu Shicang, commissar of a Moslem detachment, who was to become her lifelong partner. He was then working in an educational brigade but eventually rose to the position of commissar of a division in the military. They have two sons and a daughter.

At the end of the Sino-Japanese War in 1945, Ruan Ruolin went to work in the northeast, first in Shenyang, and then as a guerrilla and land reform worker in Kailu, Tongliao, Naimanqi, Kangping, and Qingkang. She gave birth to her first child, a girl, in the Naimanqi desert but continued to serve with the CCP as a district magistrate and secretary to a District Workers' Committee. Moving with the Red Army from Shenyang across to Tianjin, Ruan Ruolin worked there for over a year with the People's Court.

After the establishment of the PRC in 1949, she went to the south, in Jiangxi Province, for several years, undertaking various tasks. She worked with the Land Reform Committee, as head of production with the Provincial Rural Administration Department, "surveyed the one hundred villages," founded the Communist Labor University, and reclaimed land. Ruan Ruolin also found time to write short stories and other prose and became an Executive Committee member of the Jiangxi Writers' Association.

From 1959 to 1971, she lived in Guangdong Province, having transferred there with the PLA. During this period, Ruan Ruolin held several positions: member of Guangzhou Municipal Committee, deputy principal of the Party School, secretary of the Guangzhou Municipal Youth League, and deputy chief editor of *Guangzhou Daily*. She was active in mass movements of that period, including the Three Criticisms and Four Clean-Ups (*san-pi-si-qing*), and later claimed to have learned a great deal from experiencing something of the hardships of the life of the peasants. In the early years of the Cultural Revolution, Ruan Ruolin was sent to do labor reform at the Huangpi Cadre School near Yingde in the mountains of north Guangdong, but a change in policy saw her appointed in 1969 as head of Guangdong Television Broadcasting Station and then, in 1971, deputy head of the Shaanxi Broadcasting Bureau. Ruan Ruolin found her five years in the north very difficult. The "Learn from Dazhai" Movement in which she participated, for example, accomplished little because no infrastructure had been created to compensate for the harsh environment there. In order to survive, the local people were forced to work illegally at other jobs, thereby developing "black households," "black contract labor," and black markets.

Ruan Ruolin moved to Xi'an and was transferred in 1976 to the Central Television Station in Beijing as head of the Chief Editorial Office and deputy head of the station. Again, this was a difficult period, this time because of the many problems inherent in establishing such a station. In 1985 she was transferred to the TV series' production center, and during her five years there produced *Journey to the West* (Xiyouji), *Dream of Red Chambers* (Honglou meng), *The Last Emperor* (Modai huangdi), *The Rediscovered World* (Xunzhao huilai de shijie), and *Romance of the Three Kingdoms* (Sanguo yanyi) as well as the large-scale documentary *Story of the Yangzi [Yangtze]* (Huashuo changjiang). In 1991 Ruan Ruolin transferred to the Television Arts Committee and the Television Artists Society. Since her retirement in 1997, she has continued to review manuscripts for the Big Issues Team.

WANG Jingming
(Translated by Jan Zhang)

Huaxia funü mingren cidian. Beijing: Huaxia chubanshe, 1988, 316–17.
Personal interview. Beijing, July 1999.

S

San Mao

San Mao, 1943–1991, is the pen name of the writer Ch'en P'ing [Chen Ping]. Also known as Echo, San Mao came to prominence as a writer in the mid-1970s in Taiwan and Hong Kong with best-selling stories about her adventures in the Sahara Desert. Her fame spread to the mainland when pirate editions of her books began to appear in the mid-1980s. She remained a well-known public figure until her suicide in 1991, and continued to be acclaimed even after death. Such was the influence on her readers (predominantly female, mostly young) that her death reportedly prompted more than one suicide in imitation. San Mao was one of the first mass media celebrities in the Chinese-speaking world, achieved through her engagement with magazine and newspaper columns and interviews, public lectures and recordings, radio and television appearances, as well as her published collections of quasi-autobiographical stories.

The words "legend" and "legendary" are used often to describe the writer's life. Paradoxically, the facts of Ch'en P'ing's personal history are inextricably entangled with the literary persona of San Mao that Ch'en P'ing created in her stories. Most of the narratives are told in the first person and supposedly are based on the author's own experience. Biographies (not of Ch'en P'ing but of "San Mao") are largely based upon the character's own narratives, incorporating events recounted in the stories to construct a quasi-history and personality. The biographical San Mao, as well as the San Mao of self-presentation, reveals a playful, ironic, capable, and kind woman: she roams the world freely, speaks several European languages, understands and appreciates European as well as Chinese art and literature, found her "twin soul" in a foreign husband whose personality complemented hers perfectly, is full of concern for humankind, attaches herself passionately to her Chinese motherland, does not care for possessions except insofar as they intimate human feeling, and is loved by all.

Ch'en P'ing was born in Ch'ung-ch'ing [Chongqing], Ssu-ch'uan [Sichuan] Province, where her family (of Che-chiang [Zhejiang] origin) had moved to escape the Japanese invasion. Some accounts place her birth in 1945 rather than 1943, and various other dates in her life are also contested. Her father, Ch'en Ssu-ch'ing, was a lawyer and her mother, Mu Chin-lan, was a recent high school graduate. Ch'en P'ing was the second of four children. With the communist defeat of the KMT, the family moved to Taiwan in 1948 or 1949.

The first defining event in what would become the "legendary" life of Ch'en P'ing/San Mao was the girl's withdrawal from the educational system at the age of fourteen in her second year of junior high school. Having proved her academic ability by being accepted into Taiwan's most prestigious girls' school, she refused to continue there, according to her own account, after being accused of cheating and unfairly punished by a teacher. Biographers identify this resistance to the pressures inherent in Taiwan's education system as an important factor in the writer's appeal to young readers. From the age of fourteen to seventeen, Ch'en P'ing remained at home, tutored by her father in Chinese literature and foreign languages, and read widely. She began taking painting classes in her late teens, and her art teacher encouraged Ch'en P'ing to begin writing creatively. She did and her first published story, "Doubt" (Huo), the tale of a young woman who believes she has become possessed by a character in a film, appeared in the journal *Modern Literature* (Hsien-tai wen-hsüeh) in 1962. Several more of her short stories on adolescent life and love in Taiwan subsequently became published in the literary pages of Taiwan newspapers.

In 1964, Ch'en P'ing audited philosophy classes at Taipei's Chinese Culture Institute (Chung-kuo wen-hua hsüeh-yüan); she would later return there as a teacher. In 1967, at the age of twenty-four, Ch'en P'ing left Taiwan to spend three years abroad. She claimed to have studied languages and philosophy in Spain and Germany but did not complete any degree courses. Biographies state that after returning to Taiwan in 1971 she prepared to marry a German academic, but his sudden death shortly before the marriage took place caused her to flee back to Spain. Thus began the stage of life's episodes upon which San Mao's/Ch'en P'ing's fame was built. From Spain she traveled to what is called the "Spanish Sahara," a Spanish colonial territory in the western Sahara Desert. There, Ch'en P'ing married the Spaniard Josémaria Quero Ruiz, a diver and, she claimed, an engineer. In October 1974, Ch'en P'ing's first story of life in the Sahara was published in Taiwan's *United Daily News* (Lien-ho pao) under the new pen name: San Mao.

The writer later explained the pesudonym's selection by stating that San Mao was an unremarkable name, commonly used as a nickname for children (although generally for male children), thus conveying a self-image for herself as a common, everyday young person and a teller of simple tales rather than elegantly mannered literary creations. The name also could signal that her work is modest and unassuming (supposedly worth only *san mao*, or thirty cents) or insinuate that she herself is a "little" person with no great wealth, only thirty cents in her pocket. San Mao also was the name of a cartoon character from the late 1940s of a small homeless boy who roamed the streets of Shanghai and found adventure, created by Chang Lo-p'ing [Zhang Leping] in *The Wanderings of San Mao* (San Mao liu-lang chi). Ch'en P'ing/San Mao claimed that had been the first book she had read as a child.

The new, female, adult "San Mao" was widely acclaimed. A collection of San Mao's Saharan material, *Stories of the Sahara* (Sa-ha-la ti ku-shih), was published in 1976 and in the same year the early (pre-San Mao) work *The Rainy Season Won't Come Again* (Yü-chi pu tsai lai) was republished to capitalize on the success. San Mao's Saharan stories describe adventures in the desert and interactions with Sahrawi people, including tales of exoticized customs (public bath-house behavior), social practices (child marriage and slavery), and the supernatural (a cursed amulet), as well as descriptions of the daily life of a Chinese woman in the desert (cooking Chinese food, procuring water, taking a driving test). In the collection *The Crying Camels* (K'u-ch'i ti lo-t'o, 1977), San Mao's final and most dramatic Saharan stories appear and reveal connections between herself and the major players who struggled in the desert for western Saharan independence. The "desert period" in San Mao's literary life ended when the author moved to the Canary Islands in late 1975, as Spain prepared to withdraw from its desert colony. Critics claim that none of her later writing equals the stories from the Sahara.

San Mao's literary career still flourished, however, with pieces about her life in the Canaries and previous experiences in Europe (*Diary of a Scarecrow* [Tao-ts'ao jen shou-chi], 1977; *The Tender Night* [Wen-jou ti yeh], 1979). When her husband died in a diving accident in 1979, she published the collection *How Many Flowers Fell While I Slept?* (Meng-li hua-lo chih to-shao, 1981) to commemorate their life together, and *Rear View* (Pei-ying, 1981) contained more stories about José.

In 1982 Ch'en P'ing returned to settle permanently in Taiwan, and the subject matter of her material next turned to home and family, childhood, and life in Taipei. Two collections were produced, devoted to specific accounts of additional travel into foreign countries: a six-month journey to Central and South America in 1981 (*Over the Hills and Far Away* [Wan-shui ch'ien-shan tsa-pien], 1982) and a spell at a community college in Seattle (*Stirring Up the School* [Nao-hsüeh chi], 1988), about the English-language classes she attended and relationships with classmates and teachers. In addition, San Mao/Ch'en P'ing presided over two magazine "problem pages" (collected into the monographs *Heart to Heart* [T'an-hsin], 1985, and *Dear San Mao* [Ch'in-ai ti San Mao], 1991). She gave public lectures around Taiwan (drawing enormous crowds); participated in seminars and talks in Singapore and Hong Kong; wrote song lyrics (the eponymous *Echo* album of 1985 as well as the enormously popular song "The Olive Tree" [Kan-lan shu], from the 1970s); and published a book of photographs and stories of souvenirs (*My Treasures* [Wo ti pao-pei], 1987). In 1990 she claimed to have won a Spanish Literary Prize for a novella written in Spanish, but no such work has been published. The catalog of San Mao's complete works lists twenty-six items, mostly short story collections but also including cassette tapes of public story readings and several translations.

San Mao's trips to China in 1989 and 1990 attracted much attention from the press, particularly her filial rituals at her ancestors' graves and meetings with Chang Lo-p'ing, the "father" of her namesake cartoon character. San Mao produced several stories about her mainland travels, which were included in the posthumous collection *My Happy Paradise* (Wo ti k'uai-le t'ien-t'ang, 1991). Her final work—and only piece of writing that was longer than a short story or novella—was a screenplay for the 1990 film *Red Dust* (Kun-kun hung-ch'en), directed by Hong Kong director Yim Ho and produced by Hsü Feng (*q.v.*). The film depicts a love story set in the period of Japanese occupation and civil war in China and was judged critically successful. However, San Mao was criticized for creating too positive a picture of the leading male character, who was sympathetic to the Japanese occupying force and hence a traitor to the Chinese nation. The film won a number of Taiwan's Golden Horse Film Awards in late 1990, including Best Film, but San Mao conspicuously did not win the Best Screenplay Award.

San Mao's suicide in early 1991—she hanged herself in the bathroom of a hospital after having minor surgery—generated intense public interest and speculation. Obituaries appeared in major newspapers in Taiwan and China, along with conjecture about the reasons for the suicide. There was speculation about San Mao's loneliness, illness (both mental and physical), distress about not having won a screenplay award for *Red Dust*, belief that she would be reunited with her husband in the afterlife, despair about having nothing new to write about that could match the exotic appeal of her Saharan stories, and inability to continue meeting readers' and society's expectations in living up to the persona of the character created in her books. While reasons for her death can never be known, a history of suicide attempts coupled with apparent manic episodes of sociability and withdrawal suggest that the writer suffered from bipolar disorder. Ch'en P'ing was at the time of her death being treated for a hormone imbalance that caused mood swings. Along with obituaries to San Mao and reports on the death, many newspapers carried discussions about the significance of a writer who elicited such an extraordinary level of emotional response among her readers; some even ran cautionary articles discouraging copycat suicides.

San Mao's life, writing, and celebrity have been discussed in several biographies, which dwell particularly upon her emotional life and humanistic philosophies of living, romantic encounters, and frequently articulated love for "China" and all Chinese people. Biographers suggest that the reasons for her enormous success, a virtual "San Mao fever" lasting at least fifteen years, were many: her early resistance to the education system; the "exotic" nature of her writing about foreign countries; the human concern and feeling that supposedly imbued her writing; and her simple, direct style. Certainly, the appeal of the exotic was an important factor at a time when few in Taiwan (and, a decade later, the mainland) had the means to travel. Many readers noted how they derived some kind of personal message of love and concern for the world and the individual from San Mao's writing, often drawing analogies between the stories of San Mao and the intimacy of reading a personal letter. Ch'en P'ing had the ability to differentiate herself from her audience while at the same time creating a sense of union with them.

While her experiences are presented as exotically different from anything her readers could hope to emulate, San Mao persistently claimed unexceptionality, her choice of pen name reflecting this wish to identify herself as ordinary. Although her life was somewhat unusual for a woman of her time and place (in that she traveled and lived abroad, married a non-Chinese, and remained childless), the author nonetheless reaffirmed her commitment to traditional feminine obligations, presenting herself as happily serving her husband as a model housewife, providing a welcoming environment for him and his friends, creating leisure time for him, and taking sole responsibility for domestic labor. Although the exterior of San Mao's life may have been unconventional, the values expressed in her books remained relatively conservative, posing little threat or challenge to the reader. Described as an "old-fashioned new woman" who sought beauty and feeling in the everyday world despite the conflicts increasingly brought about by the changing roles of women and their quest for independence, San Mao projected a stable feminine identity that may have contributed to her popularity among young women readers who similarly faced the demands of the modern world.

In addition to biographical works, the "San Mao phenomenon" also generated several books of evaluation and discussion and many magazine interviews and feature articles. A measure of criticism and skepticism is evident in public evaluations of the events in San Mao's life, and several writers questioned the veracity of the seemingly autobiographical stories. Such doubt focuses particularly on her Spanish husband. Questions have been raised as to whether the story of his romantic six-year wait for her to marry him was true, whether he had actually died an early death, and indeed whether he had ever existed at all. Among those writers "following in San Mao's footsteps," attempting to challenge or defend the truthfulness of her stories, the consensus is that although details may have been fabricated, characters aestheticized, and time sequences blurred, the general outlines of her stories are based on San Mao's/Ch'en P'ing's life.

Miriam LANG

Ku Chi-t'ang [Gu Jitang]. *P'ing-shuo San Mao*. Beijing: Chih-shih ch'u-pan-she, 1991.
Lu Shih-ch'ing, Yang Yu-li, and Sun Yung-ch'ao. *San Mao chuan*. Taipei: Ch'en-hsing ch'u-pan-she, 1993.
P'an Hsiang-li [Pan Xiangli]. *San Mao chuan*. Fuzhou: Hai-hsia wen-i ch'u-pan-she, 1991.
San Mao. *Ch'ing ch'eng*. Taipei: Huang-kuan ch'u-pan-she, 1985.
———. *K'u-ch'i ti lo-t'o*. Taipei: Huang-kuan ch'u-pan-she, 1977.
———. *Pei-ying*. Taipei: Huang-kuan ch'u-pan-she, 1981.
———. *Sa-ha-la ti ku-shih*. Taipei: Huang-kuan ch'u-pan-she, 1976.
———. *Wen-jou ti yeh*. Taipei: Huang-kuan ch'u-pan-she, 1979.
———. *Yü-chi pu tsai lai*. Taipei: Huang-kuan ch'u-pan-she, 1976.
———. "Kun-kun hung-ch'en" (screenplay). Taipei: Huang-kuan ch'u-pan-she, 1990.
Ts'ui Chien-fei [Cui Jianfei] and Chao Chün [Zhao Jun]. *San Mao chuan*. Beijing: Wen-hua i-shu ch'u-pan-she, 1995.

Shao Meng-lan

Shao Meng-lan [Shao Menglan], 1909–2000, of Ch'un-an [Chun'an] County, Che-chiang [Zhejiang] Province, devoted her life to teaching and made an outstanding contribution to education for sixty-four years.

Her father, Shao Hung-lieh, was a Ch'ing dynasty "Graduate for Preeminence" (*pa-kung*) and well known as a poet and essayist. Her traditional family was well off and generous to those less blessed. As a child, Shao Meng-lan learned from her mother, whose name is not recorded, studying the *Kung-ho kuo-wen*, which was an eight-volume language textbook. Shao Meng-lan entered fourth class at Shih-hsin Girls' Primary School in Ch'un-an County when she was eleven (1919) and went on to Hangzhou Junior High School for Girls, graduating in 1926. Shao Meng-lan was immediately offered the position of head of Shih-hsin Girls' Primary School, a post held for three years (1926–29). She subsequently went on to further education, graduating from the experimental high school at Fu-tan [Fudan] University in 1931 and from that university's Politics Department in 1936.

Shao Meng-lan's commitment to the world of education began that year. Before and during the Sino-Japanese War, she worked as a teacher at several high schools in Che-chiang Province and at the National Third Wartime High School. After the war, Shao Meng-lan taught for one year at Hang-chou [Hangzhou] Municipal Tsung-wen

High School and one year at Che-chiang National Reconstruction High School, then moved to Hai-nan District to teach at Hai-nan University from 1947 to 1949. In 1949, she went to Taiwan and taught at Hsin-chu High School (1950–51), Chi-lung Girls' High School (1951–53), and Taipei First Girls' School (1953–56). In February 1956, Shao Meng-lan was appointed principal of Shih-lin Junior High School in Taipei County (Yang-ming-shan Administrative Bureau). This school was later restructured as Shih-lin High School, then subdivided into Shih-lin Senior and Shih-lin Junior High Schools. In 1975, Shih-lin Senior High School changed its name to Taipei Chung-cheng Senior High School, and in that year she was permitted to retire from the public school system.

At the age of sixty-six, Shao Meng-lan responded to a call from Soong Mayling (*q.v.*) in June 1975 to become head of Hua-hsing High School and director of Hua-hsing Kindergarten. During her term of office, Shao Meng-lan led the Chinese Youth Baseball team when they successfully defended the International Youth Baseball Championship in the United States. She resigned from office the following year to become a full-time associate professor at Chinese Culture University (Chung-kuo wen-hua ta-hsüeh), became part-time in 1990, and in 1993 resigned. Shao Meng-lan also worked concurrently as a part-time associate professor at Soochow University (Tung-wu ta-hsüeh) and taught at the University for the Aged (*Sung-pai hsüeh-yüan*) until she died.

In 1931, Shao Meng-lan had entered into a uxorilocal marriage with Yü Hsüeh-jen [Yu Xueren]. Of their three children (a daughter and two sons), only the second son, Shao Jen-chieh [Shao Renjie], accompanied her to Taiwan. Shao Meng-lan's husband died in 1944.

Shao Meng-lan was fond of music and literature and as a woman of integrity, led a principled and regulated life. She once said: "Let me be the first to grieve for the sorrows of the world and the last to bask in . . . [its] joys." These lofty ideals dominated her life. While teaching, Shao Meng-lan held firmly to the principles of "Chinese language and literature first." She insisted that her students recite works from memory and spot-checked weekly journals and compositions. For many years, Shao Meng-lan regarded the school as her home. Her mind focused on guiding youth; the motivating force in her life was education; and she left her students with a lasting impression of rigor and benevolence.

CHENG Li-jung
(Translated by Katherine Kerr)

Taipei shih-lin chung-cheng kao-chi chung-hsüeh, eds. *Shao hsiao-chang Meng-lan chiu-chih hua-tan sung-shou chuan-chi*. Taipei: N.p., 1999.
Taipei shih-lin chung-cheng kao-chi chung-hsüeh, eds. *Shao hsiao-chang Meng-lan pa-chih hua-tan chu-shou chuan-chi*. Taipei: N.p., 1989.
Yu Chien-ming. "Shao Meng-lan fang-wen chi lu." August 2000. Unpublished manuscript.

Shen Rong

Shen Rong, b. 1936, in Hankou, Hubei Province, as Chen Derong, grew up in Chengdu and Chongqing. She is a novelist and adopted Shen Rong as her pen name. Although the standard Chinese pronunciation of the assumed surname is "Chen," she prefers the Sichuan pronunciation of "Shen," as given here. Many publications and library catalogers, however, keep to the standard spelling of Chen Rong.

Shen Rong entered the Beijing Institute of Russian Studies in 1954 and after graduation was assigned to the positions of music editor and Russian translator at the Central Broadcasting Bureau in Beijing. She then contracted an illness, which caused her to faint frequently at her desk, and had to leave work and stay at home. Eventually, the condition forced Shen Rong to change jobs and become a high school teacher.

However, it was precisely this pathological condition that provided her with ample leisure time. She tried many activities to fill her time, including stamp collecting, painting, attending the theater, reading, and even dancing. However, a feeling of social rejection and strong sense of social responsibility finally urged Shen Rong to reinvent herself in the 1960s. A friend found a place for her to stay in a village in Shanxi in the northwest about five hundred kilometers from Beijing, and there Shen Rong started to write.

Like many Chinese writers engaged in literary creativity in the mid-1970s, Shen Rong found herself writing about rural communist heroes and miniature class struggles, approved subjects in the prevailing political climate of the era. Inevitably, the dominant theme for her first two novels was village scenes of class struggle: *Everlasting Youth* (Wannianqing, 1975) and *Brightness and Darkness* (Guangming yu hei'an, 1978). With the Cultural Revolution drawing to an end, Shen Rong joined other Chinese writers in creating "wounded literature" as a means of reassessing the past ten years of political catastrophe and their tragic human cost. The best of her stories produced from the first half of the 1980s were published in *Collected Works of Shen Rong* (Shen Rong ji, 1986).

Starting from *Spring Forever* (Yongyuan shi chuntian) in 1980, Shen Rong's writing focused on the victims of the Cultural Revolution, especially intellectuals and revolutionary veterans who had endured public humiliation and persecution. Conspicuously, many of the "wounded" and those suffering the most in Shen Rong's works were women. *Spring Forever* is among the earliest writings to explore the dilemma women faced after the establishment of the PRC, caught between having a career and family life and between what they achieved and the progress of the Chinese revolution.

Shen Rong's most successful, and perhaps only influential, work so far is the novella *At Middle Age* (Ren dao zhongnian), which won the First National Prize for Novellas also in 1980. The prize brought with it membership into the prestigious Chinese Writers' Association (Zhongguo zuojia xiehui), which in turn allowed Shen Rong to become officially acknowledged as a full-time writer with a monthly stipend.

At Middle Age tells the story of a woman ophthalmologist, Lu Wenting, her life unfolding retrospectively while she lingers near death in hospital after a heart attack. She goes back to her university days when she was young, beautiful, and full of life. Lu has been working in the hospital for nearly twenty years since graduation and is the best eye surgeon there, both in terms of operating skill and sense of vocation. Middle-aged, married, and with two school-age children, she nevertheless spends most of her time at the hospital, leaving her husband, a metallurgist, to take care of the children and the housework. Lu Wenting is burdened with guilt over depriving her husband time for his own research as he becomes increasingly anxious to make up for time lost during the Cultural Revolution. Constantly torn between the needs of her family and those of the hospital, the wife/mother and doctor inevitably chooses her patients.

Despite the dedication, Lu Wenting and her family live in extreme poverty. Their salaries are so low that they can barely afford the necessities. All they have is one eleven-square-yard room, holding only two beds and a desk at which all four members of the family must take turns when they want to study. With neither time nor money to spend on her children, Lu Wenting's deathbed wishes are to buy her son a pair of white sneakers and to plait her daughter's hair. Only with the approach of death does Lu Wenting feel justified in lying down and taking time to rest.

The character's integrity and dignity are highlighted by a contrast with another woman in the story, the wife of a revolutionary veteran, dubbed "Mrs. Marxist-Leninist," whose frequent declarations of the political capital she and her husband have accumulated are mocked. Twice, under extremely difficult conditions, Lu Wenting operates on and saves the eyes of this woman's husband, who has been persecuted during the Cultural Revolution and just restored to power. Yet, Lu, who could easily exploit the veteran's gratitude, demands no favors and refuses privileges bestowed upon her by his influential, self-righteous wife. Lu Wenting eventually survives her illness and walks out of the hospital, an image no less heroic than that of the revolutionary veterans.

The novella thus sings high praise for the sacrifice that intellectuals, in their characteristically low-profile way, have made for country and the people, a sacrifice all the more powerfully represented in the form of a slim, frail, quiet woman. The work was an appeal to the authorities to rectify the poor treatment intellectuals received. *At Middle Age* was later adapted into an enormously successful film. Both Lu Wenting, as the modest, tenacious, and capable female intellectual, and Mrs. Marxist-Leninist, wife of the revolutionary veteran, have become lasting images in contemporary Chinese culture.

Commenting in 1989 on Shen Rong's works, Wendy Larson noted the author's focus on three important issues: the contradictory demands reform placed on intellectuals, the characterization of an ideal woman, and the writer's identity and role of writing in society. Indeed, Shen Rong's quietly suffering, enduring women captured the hearts of her readers. Despite portraying their ambiguous relationship with the authorities, the characters' loyalty and commitment to what they identify as a worthy cause never fluctuates. Hence, Shen Rong's ideal women hardly ever question social or party hierarchy or express doubt about their own social placement.

However, as Shen Rong's literary depictions gradually shifted to looking at the problems of family and marriage, especially the difficulties encountered by professional women, her characters did consider and challenge their commitment to marriage and family. In portraying the tension that working women experience between conflicting needs for professional career development and responsibilities as daughter, wife, and mother, Shen Rong's characters always respect and are willing to make sacrifices for the institutions of family and marriage.

However, this convention is no longer retained in the attitudes of her male or female characters in the short story collection *Too Lazy to Divorce* (Lande lihun). The six stories explore self-development and growth, complexity of marriage life, male-female relationships, social bias, and the disillusion of love and romantic ideals in the face of the encroaching power of commercialization fast eroding Chinese society. *Too Lazy to Divorce* reveals marriage as a mutual entrapment in which both partners feel helpless. The collection presents both social satire and in-depth analysis of the status of many marriages in Chinese society.

Shen Rong also expends considerable effort in writing satirical social commentaries within the limits of political censorship. *Stories of Humor* (Shen Rong youmo xiaoshuo ji), a collection of short stories mimicking and commenting on social phenomena and bureaucracy, is a fine example of this style of humor. The collection is made more interesting by the inclusion of a good number of illustrations done by the best-known artists of contemporary China.

Yiyan WANG

Larson, Wendy. "Women, Writers, Social Reform: Three Issues in Shen Rong's Fiction." In *Modern Chinese Women Writers: Critical Appraisals*, ed. Michael Duke. Armonk, N.Y.: M.E. Sharpe, 1989, 174–95.

McDougall, Bonnie S., and Kam Louie. *The Literature of China in the Twentieth Century*. Gosford, NSW: Bushbooks, 1997, 381–83.

Shanghai cishu. *Zhongguo xiandai wenxue cidian*. Shanghai: Shanghai yishu chubanshe, 1990, p. 464.

Shen Rong. *At Middle Age*. Beijing: Chinese Literature, 1987.

———. *Guangming yu hei'an*. Beijing: Renmin wenxue chubanshe, 1978.

———. *Lande lihun*. Beijing: Huayi chubanshe, 1991.

———. *Ren dao zhongnian*. Beijing: Baihua wenyi chubanshe, 1980.

———. *Shen Rong ji*. Fuzhou: Haixia wenyi chubanshe, 1986.

———. *Shen Rong xiaoshuo xuan*. Beijing: Beijing chubanshe, 1981.

———. *Shen Rong youmo xiaoshuo ji*. Hong Kong: Xiangjiang chubanshe, 1987.

———. *Taizicun de mimi*. Beijing: Renmin wenxue chubanshe, 1973.

———. *Wannianqing*. Beijing: Renmin wenxue chubanshe, 1975.

———. *Yang Yueyue yu Sate zhi yanjiu*. Beijing: Zhongguo wenlian chuban gongsi, 1984.

———. *Yongyuan shi chuntian*. Beijing: Renmin wenxue chubanshe, 1980.

———. *Zange*. Chengdu: Sichuan renmin chubanshe, 1983.

———. *Zhongnian kutuan: Shen Rong suibi*. Shanghai: Dongfang chuban zhongxin, 1994.

———. "Tongku de jueze." In *Lande lihun*. Beijing: Huayi chubanshe, 1991, 5–10.

Shen Zijiu

Shen Zijiu, 1898–1989, of Deqing County, Zhejiang Province, was a social activist, a leader of the women's liberation movement, and a long-time member of the CCP.

Her father was an accountant with a silk company and provided a middle-class lifestyle for his family. Shen Zijiu gained an education as a child and attended Zhejiang Normal School. Her parents arranged a marriage for her, while she was still at school, with Zhang Jialu; the two had a daughter, Zhang Lüyi. Zhang Jialu died in 1921, however.

After graduating with distinction, Shen Zijiu was given a teaching post in the primary school affiliated with Zhejiang Normal School. She studied art in Japan at the Japanese Higher Normal School for Women for several years from 1921 and on returning to China in 1925 undertook a series of teaching appointments at Zhejiang Normal School for Women, Jiangsu Songjiang Girls' High School, and Nanjing Huiwen Girls' High School. Not until the summer of 1932, however, did Shen Zijiu have more than passing contact with the CCP. At that time, she was recruited as assistant editor for *Current Affairs Journal* (Shishi leibian), published by the Shanghai sub-bureau of the Zhongshan Culture and Education Bureau. For a short period, from February 1934 until its suppression by the KMT, Shen Zijiu edited the women's supplement of the progressive *Shenbao Daily* and publicized such ideas as the liberation of women, anti-Japanese activities, national liberation, and social reform. Supported by the communist Du Junhui and others, in 1935 Shen Zijiu took up the position of founding editor of *Women's Life* magazine (Funü shenghuo). This CCP-run publication had an anti-Japanese agenda and attacked the KMT for its betrayal of the Chinese people, internationally as well as domestically. Shen specifically addressed Chinese women, calling upon them to participate in anti-Japanese resistance and the National Salvation Movement. She herself organized the Association of Shanghai Women's National Salvation Movement, serving as deputy general secretary of its Executive Committee, and sat also on the Executive Committee of the Federation of National Salvation Movements.

During this period Shen Zijiu published a who's who of world-famous women and collaborated with Luo Qiong in translating *On Being a New Woman* by the Russian woman revolutionary Alexandra Kollontay, their purpose being to inspire Chinese women to revolution. Shen Zijiu also became active in the movement led by Song Qingling (*q.v.*) and He Xiangning (*q.v.*) to "go to jail" in protest at the arrest on 22 December 1936 of the "Seven Virtuous Ones," one of whom was Shi Liang (*q.v.*). With the outbreak of the Sino-Japanese War in mid-1937, Shen Zijiu worked under He Xiangning as a public relations officer with the Shanghai women's "moral support for our boys at the front" Propaganda Group (Shanghai funü weilao fenhui). Toward the end of that year, Shen Zijiu withdrew to Wuhan, where she worked as a Standing Committee member of the Committee for the Protection of Children in Wartime and in 1938 as leader of the Cultural Affairs Group of the Women's Guidance Committee of the New Life Movement, also taking charge of publishing their *New Women's Movement Journal*, working in Wuhan and Chongqing.

In 1939 Shen Zijiu joined the CCP and the following year worked first with command headquarters of the New Fourth Army in Anhui and then in Shanghai. Traveling a roundabout route, she went to Singapore in 1941 to assist the journalist Hu Yuzhi (1896–1986), whom she married soon afterwards; they had no children. Her anti-Japanese work in Singapore involved becoming active in various associations formed to mobilize overseas Chinese in support of China. However, with the fall of Singapore in 1942 Shen Zijiu fled with her husband and the writer Yu Dafu to Sumatra, where they lived for almost four years under assumed identities. Shen Zijiu wrote of the hardship they endured under occupation in her book *Fugitives along the Equator*

(Liuwang zai chidao xianshang), which was published when the Pacific War ended.

She returned to Singapore then and worked with Hu Yuzhi to expand the China Democratic League through Southeast Asia by uniting overseas Chinese in patriotism and democracy. They set up Nanyang Publishing Company, and Shen Zijiu became editor of several magazines, including "South Wind" (a supplement to *Nanqiao ribao*), *Downwind Weekly*, and *New Women's Monthly*. She helped found a branch of the China Democratic League in Malaya in 1947, served on its Standing Committee, and acted as director of its women's group. The following year Shen Zijiu traveled back to northeast China via Hong Kong and was in Xibaipo in 1949 to take part in preparations for the first national All-China Women's Congress; she attended the congress held in Beijing toward the end of that year.

In the early years of the PRC, Shen Zijiu held a series of appointments with the ACWF—Standing Committee member, director of Propaganda and Education, editor of *Women of New China*—and also became director of the *Women of China* publishing house. She attended the NPC and was a member of the first three CPPCC. Her work with the China Democratic League continued, and Shen Zijiu held various posts on its Central Committee. She and her husband were both stood down from their positions during the Cultural Revolution.

Shen Zijiu died at the age of ninety-one on 26 December 1989.

ZHAO Jinping
(Translated by Li Sheung Yee)

Nüjie wenhua zhanshi Shen Zijiu. Beijing: Zhongguo funü chubanshe, 1991.
Yingwen *Zhongguo funü*, ed. *Gujin zhuming funü renwu*, vol. 2. Shijiazhuang: Hebei renmin chubanshe, 1986, 535–40.
Zhongguo funü wushinian. CD.

Shi Liang

Shi Liang, 1900–1985, a native of Changzhou, Jiangsu Province, was a leading figure in the women's and human rights movements in China in the 1930s and 1940s. She was the PRC's first minister of Justice, and held the post from 1950 until the abolition of the ministry in 1959.

Shi Liang was born into an impoverished scholar family. Both of her grandfathers had been successful in the civil service examination of the Qing dynasty (1644–1911), but her father earned a living as a private tutor because he objected to the antiquated examination system. Shi Liang had eight siblings, some of whom are said to have died of malnutrition and lack of medical care. To alleviate their straitened circumstances, her mother tried to betroth her to a rich family but relented when Shi Liang offered strong resistance. Her father taught her the Chinese classics and histories, and by the time Shi Liang was fourteen the family could afford to send her to school. She started at fourth grade, completed primary school within two years, and later in 1915 entered Changzhou Women's Normal School. During the May Fourth Movement of 1919, Shi Liang represented students of her native Changzhou at a

Nanjing meeting, convened in support of students in Beijing who had been jailed and beaten by the warlord government there. The young woman devoured progressive books and magazines and dreamed of achieving a just society for China.

After graduating from the Women's Normal School, probably in 1921, Shi Liang first taught at school, then enrolled in 1923 at Shanghai University of Law and Politics (Shanghai fazheng daxue), established by the well-known jurist Xu Qian. Shi Liang was one of the first, woman or man, to be trained in this field. She remained politically active, however, and in May 1925 took part in a three thousand-strong student demonstration in support of striking workers. Shi Liang was arrested but released the following day. Back on campus, she edited the student magazine *Erasing the Shame* (Xuechi), which had considerable influence among Shanghai students.

By the time Shi Liang graduated in 1927, the first KMT-CCP united front had been declared. She took part in the Northern Expedition, working in the Personnel Training Department of the KMT Revolutionary Army's General Political Department (Guomin gemingjun zong zhengzhibu gongzuo renyuan yangchengsuo). Later, Shi Liang was taken into a training course for district heads (*quzhang*) in Jiangsu and sat the Jiangsu provincial examination for county mayors (*xianzhang*). However, because of what she considered unfair treatment during its physical examination, Shi Liang left in anger and returned to Shanghai.

In 1931, she began practicing law in Shanghai, enjoying the career for the next sixteen years. One of only two women to be admitted to the Shanghai bar, Shi Liang first started off in the law office of Dong Kang, a former teacher at Shanghai University of Law and Politics. Then she opened her own office, specializing in marriage and political cases. The cases Shi Liang handled allowed her to gain insight into the great social injustices of the time, and she became known as a spokeswoman for her gender. Despite some success with political cases, Shi Liang experienced at least one painful failure. The KMT secret police's constant infringement of civil liberties led her and others in the China League for the Protection of Civil Rights (Zhongguo minquan baozhang tongmeng) to attempt to provide legal aid to political prisoners. Song Qingling (*q.v.*) was also involved in this work. Shi Liang successfully defended an underground communist worker named Liao Chengzhi, the son of Liao Zhongkai and He Xiangning (*q.v.*), winning him his freedom. Shi Liang was unable, however, to prevent the transfer of Deng Zhongxia, an eminent communist labor leader and close friend of Song Qingling, to Nanjing, where he was out of reach of the law of the concessions. Not long after his transfer, Deng Zhongxia was summarily executed.

Shi Liang said later that she realized that the law in those days was simply an ornament, a sham. Seeking an alternative, Shi Liang gravitated toward the CCP. After the Japanese occupation of northeast China in September 1931, she became increasingly involved in women's and political activities. While speaking at the rally on International Women's Day in March 1932, Shi Liang witnessed police intervention and saw many women hurt. From then on, she sat on the committees of several women's organizations in Shanghai and Jiangsu and in 1934, with several other women, including Shen Zijiu (*q.v.*) and Hu Ziying, formed the Women's National Salvation Association of Shanghai (Shanghai funüjie jiuguo lianhehui). In 1935 it became part of the national body called the National Salvation Association (Quanguo gejie jiuguo lianhehui), headed by Song Qingling and with Shi Liang serving on its Standing Committee. The organization called for a national effort to resist the Japanese, stop the civil war, and ensure people's civil rights.

That year, she and Shen Junru joined the people's front and took an active part in politics. To mark the fifth anniversary of the Japanese invasion of the northeast, in September 1936 Shi Liang marched with the National Salvation Association alongside students and workers. In the ensuing clash with the military and police, she was hurt; however, a group of workers formed a human wall to shield her from attack and helped her to escape. The Chinese writer Lu Xun died in October, and, with Shi Liang as one of the pallbearers, the National Salvation Association took advantage of his funeral to further promote its aims.

All of these activities brought Shi Liang into a degree of prominence, and on the night of 22 November 1936 she was arrested at her home. Six other writers, academics, and professionals were seized at the same time, all of them men: Shen Junru, Zou Taofen, Wang Zaoshi, Zhang Naiqi, Sha Qianli, and Li Gongpu. At the time, the seven were dubbed *Qi junzi*, a term which is unfortunately often translated as "the Seven Gentlemen," thus rendering Shi Liang's gender invisible. Because *junzi* is non-gender specific in Chinese, it is perhaps more appropriate to translate the epithet as "the Seven Virtuous Ones." The seven were released on bail the next day, but an order was issued the day after for their arrest.

Shi Liang, however, evaded the police and went into hiding. She revealed in 1981 that this was done to give herself time to deal with the many documents in her possession that might incriminate others. Seeing posters offering 10,000 yuan for her arrest, Shi Liang with great daring had herself photographed in front of one. After completing her work, at the end of that year she walked into Suzhou Police Station (where the others had been taken from Shanghai) and gave herself up. Imprisoned in the women's prison with criminals and murder suspects, Shi Liang proceeded to befriend them, offering legal advice to help their defense cases. Through her exposure to these unfortunate women, the attorney gained deeper insight into the unfair situations that women often found themselves in, especially in marriage.

The Seven Virtuous Ones had been accused of endangering the Republic of China and promoting an ideology incompatible with the republic's basic philosophy, nominally Sun Yat-sen's Three Principles of the People (Sanmin zhuyi). In June 1937, the KMT offered a deal: it would give each of the seven a sentence of five years that would be waived as soon as they were delivered to the Self-Examination Institution (Fanxingyuan), a prison for elite political prisoners. When they refused this offer, the government proceeded with prosecution. In June, Song Qingling and He Xiangning went with sixteen others to Suzhou to ask to be imprisoned with the Seven Virtuous Ones, giving as their reason that if it was a crime to be patriotic then they had all transgressed. However, the political situation in China then turned dramatically; after the KMT government declared war on the Japanese on 7 July the second KMT-CCP united front was declared. Shi Liang and her comrades were released at the end of the month. She immediately threw herself into the war effort and went to Hong Kong and

Macau to promote the war against Japan. The activist joined the committee of Soong Mayling's Women's Guidance Committee of the New Life Movement (Xinshenghuo funü zhidao weiyuanhui) and also headed its Liaison Committee. Also in that year, Shi Liang married Lu Diandong (*zi* Chaohua), also a Shanghai lawyer. It is said that she had lived with him for some time and that they only consented to hold a formal ceremony because of Soong Mayling's middle-class moral qualms.

In 1938, Shi Liang was appointed as a delegate to the First People's Political Participation Conference (Guomin canzhenghui), a consultative group operating during the war years. She attended its meetings in Wuhan in July and moved to Chongqing after the fall of Wuhan in October. Shi Liang was active in the conference until the Wannan Incident of January 1941 in which the KMT killed communist soldiers with whom they were supposedly in coalition. She and other members belonging to the National Salvation Association refused to attend further meetings of the conference and their names were therefore dropped from the list of delegates for later conferences. She was also forced to withdraw from the Women's Guidance Committee. Shi Liang then returned to law practice, this time in Chongqing; in conjunction with another woman activist, Cao Mengjun (*q.v.*), Shi Liang formed the Association of Democratic Women (Minzhu funü lianyihui). In 1944, she was elected to the Central Committee of the China Democratic League (Zhongguo minzhu tongmeng, or Minmeng) at its inaugural meeting.

At the end of the Sino-Japanese War in 1945, Shi Liang met Mao Zedong (1893–1976) in Chongqing. She had worked before with underground communists and others who were openly communist, including Zhou Enlai (1898–1976) and Deng Yingchao (*q.v.*). Shi Liang soon returned to her previous base of Shanghai to practice law, however. The Democratic League continued to move closer to the CCP, and in 1946 two of its members, Li Gongpu and Wen Yiduo, were assassinated in Kunming. In October 1947, the KMT government outlawed the Democratic League, which reformed in Hong Kong the following year with Shi Liang still working underground in Shanghai. In May 1949, she learned that the Shanghai police had decided to arrest and kill her; Shi Liang and her husband hid in the home of her sister Shi Long. It was not long before Shanghai fell to the communists, however, and Shi Liang went to Beijing to take part in the first meeting of the ACWF and the CPPCC. She was elected to the Executive Committees of both organizations.

After attending the opening ceremony of the PRC, Shi Liang was appointed both as minister of Justice and to the Political and Legal Affairs Committee (Zhengzhi falü weiyuanhui); later she was made a member of the Law Commission. In 1953, Shi Liang was elected deputy chair of the ACWF and concurrently appointed deputy chair of the Committee for the Enforcement of the Marriage Law (which had been promulgated in 1950). Her role on this committee was probably not purely symbolic. The law was intended to erase many of the injustices women suffered, and Shi Liang knew something about these conditions, even if only because she had once shared a jail cell with women prisoners in the 1930s. From 1954 to 1956, Shi Liang was also vice-president of the Central Political and Legal Cadres' Academy (Zhongyang zhengfa ganbu xueyuan), working directly under Politburo member Peng Zhen.

After the Ministry of Justice was abolished in 1959 and she lost her ministerial portfolio, Shi Liang took a more active interest in the ACWF and the work of the China Democratic League. Since 1954, she had also been a member of the NPC; in 1959, she was made a member of the CPPCC. According to one source (and not corroborated elsewhere to date), she had once made revelations in a self-criticism meeting during the Anti-Rightist Movement of the late 1950s incriminating her colleagues Zhang Bojun, Luo Longji, and Wang Zaoshi. During the Cultural Revolution, Shi Liang is said to have been taken to the Great Hall of the People for criticism and to be "struggled"; Zhou Enlai came to her rescue and shielded Shi Liang from further attacks. In 1978, she was reappointed deputy chair of the ACWF and received two new titles: deputy president of the CPPCC and deputy chair of the NPC Standing Committee (1979). Shi Liang had been an active member of the China Democratic League from its inception in 1944 and advanced quickly through the hierarchy to deputy chair (1953) and chair (1979) of its Central Committee. The Democratic League had been the largest of the non-communist parties in the PRC but over the years had offered little opposition to the CCP.

Shi Liang maintained an interest in politics until shortly before her death. In 1983, she said that the British attempt to substitute the right to rule for the sovereignty of Hong Kong was not acceptable. Her memoirs, "The Road I Traveled" (Wo de shenghuo daolu), were published in the magazine *Renwu* the same year. She died of illness in September 1985 in Beijing. Her funeral was attended by top leaders of the PRC and the CCP, and her ashes were interred at the Babaoshan Revolution Cemetery.

Throughout a long official career, Shi Liang often represented China overseas on women's and legal delegations. She led the former on missions to France (1949), Czechoslovakia (1956), India (1956 and 1967), and Ceylon (1958) and headed a delegation of jurists to Russia (1950). In 1957, Shi Liang took part in a preparatory meeting of the International Jurists Conference in Syria and in 1952 accompanied Song Qingling to the World Peace Congress in Vienna, Austria. Shi Liang also frequently met with visiting dignitaries from foreign countries in Beijing.

In spite of the serious nature of her work in politics and the women's movement, as a person she appears to have been vivacious and also exercised an independent turn of mind. The former French Premier Edgar Faure, who visited China in 1956, described Shi Liang as "very beautiful and very chic." Her unconventional attitude is evident from her cohabiting with Lu Diandong before marriage; however, her modernity was also flexible. A more sensitive side was revealed when she gave her mother a full Buddhist funeral in 1945, observing all the traditions in response to her mother's last wish. One source says Shi Liang's marriage to Lu Diandong seems to have ended just before the communist takeover of China. Another reports that he died in 1976 of cerebral hemorrhage. Edgar Faure reports that when he met Shi Liang in 1956 she was accompanied by a polyglot husband but does not give any name. Shi Liang and Lu Diandong had no children but they adopted Lu Yang, the son of her sister Shi Long. Lu Yang entered Shanghai's prestigious Jiaotong University, and when the higher education system was restructured he transferred to and graduated from Shanghai's equally prestigious Fudan University. Lu Yang was assigned to the Research Institute of Nuclear Physics (Hezi wuli yanjiusuo) after graduation. In 1957, however, he was named a rightist; Lu Yang killed himself during the Cultural Revolution.

Shi Liang was one of two of the earliest women to practice law in China. The other was Zheng Yuxiu who, after marrying a KMT minister, no longer practiced law, adhering instead more closely to the idea of being a traditional good wife. Shi Liang, on the other hand, led a brilliant career of political activity until the end of the 1950s and again in the 1980s. However, one biographer points out that in spite of the impressive positions and titles Shi Liang held after 1949, she wielded considerably less actual authority in the councils of government than may have been expected. This is probably true given the weak role that the judicial branch has played in the PRC up to the present. This is regretful. With her potential, Shi Liang could have accomplished far more.

Lily Xiao Hong LEE

Hoe, Susanna. "The Seventh Gentleman: Shi Liang." In *Chinese Footprints: Exploring Women's History in China, Hong Kong and Macau*, Susanna Hoe. Hong Kong: Roundhouse Publications (Asia), 1996, 92–130.

Hu Yuzhi and Shen Zijiu. "Daonian 'qi junzi' de zuihou yige—Shi Liang tongzhi." *Renmin ribao*, 13 October 1985, 5.

Klein, Donald W., and Anne B. Clark. *Biographic Dictionary of Chinese Communism, 1921– 1965*. Cambridge, Mass.: Harvard University Press, 1971, 764–66.

Minguo renwu xiaozhuan, vol. 10. Taipei: Zhuanji wenxue chubanshe, 1988, 68–82.

Shi Liang. "The Road I Traveled." *Women of China* (1981): 18–20, 25.

———. "Wo de shenghuo daolu." *Renwu*, no. 22 (September 1983): 22–33, no. 23 (November 1983): 76–90.

Wang Xin, ed. *Zhongguo minzhu dangpai mingrenlu*. Nanjing: Jiangsu renmin chubanshe, 1993, 177–78.

Who's Who in Communist China. Hong Kong: Union Research Institute, 1969, 569–70.

Xi Zhongxun. "Chentong daonian Zhongguo gongchandang de qinmi zhanyou—Shi Liang tongzhi." *Renmin ribao*, 16 September 1985, 4.

Yingwen *Zhongguo funü*, ed. *Gujin zhuming funü renwu*, vol. 2. Shijiazhuang: Hebei renmin chubanshe, 1986, 576–81.

Shi Wei: *see* **Chen Xuezhao**

Shih Man: *see* **Ch'en-Shih Man**

Shih Shu-tuan: *see* **Li Ang**

Shu Ting

Shu Ting, b. 1952, was born in Jinjiang, Fujian Province. Her original name was Gong Peiyu; at school she was also known as Gong Shuting. Shu Ting is one of the most celebrated poets in the PRC today and probably the most significant female poet to emerge on the literary scene since Bing Xin (*q.v.*). Originally associated with "misty poetry" (*menglongshi*), Shu Ting continues to evolve in developing her style, which harmonizes introspective musings with a profound concern for public issues.

She was the second of three children, having an older brother and a younger sister. In 1957, her father was denounced as a rightist and sent to a mountain village for re-education. According to Shu Ting's own account of this period in her life, her mother divorced him in order to minimize for their three children the potentially disastrous political consequences of the denunciation. After the divorce, Shu Ting moved to Xiamen with her mother, grandmother, brother, and sister. As a child, Shu Ting was extremely precocious. In the essay "The Mist of My Heart" (Xin yan), she recalls memorizing, at the age of four, two lines (in classical Chinese) from a poem by Du Mu and, as a result, was allowed to accompany her grandmother to literacy classes. The grandmother was an important figure in Shu Ting's early life and stimulated her granddaughter's imagination with bedtime stories from classics such as *The Journey to the West* (Xiyou ji), *Romance of the Three Kingdoms* (Sanguo yanyi), and Pu Songling's *Strange Tales from a Chinese Studio* (Liaozhai zhiyi). The fact that her grandmother was a Christian also no doubt exposed Shu Ting to certain aspects of this religious tradition. Despite traces of Christian imagery in her writing, however, the poet has made it clear that she does not believe in God.

In third grade at school, Shu Ting developed a passion for reading that was to a large degree encouraged by close relatives with accessible collections of Chinese literature. By the time she was in middle school, Shu Ting turned to foreign books for the simple reason that she claimed to have "read all the Chinese books." Composition was a subject in which Shu Ting excelled at school, although she once failed a final examination in it because of what the examiner called "petty bourgeois sentimentality." At the age of thirteen, Shu Ting wrote what she describes as her first poem for publication in her school magazine.

Shu Ting's education was cut short by the outbreak of the Cultural Revolution. She had completed only two years in junior high school and was sent in 1969 to a commune in remote western Fujian, an experience she—like many others of her generation—describes as both debilitating and in some ways liberating. Shu Ting kept a diary during her three years in the countryside and continued reading (she mentions a fascination with Tagore and records her eclectic interest in the work of poets such as He Qifang, Byron, Keats, and Zhu Ziqing). Poems she wrote in letters to friends were copied and circulated at this time; anecdotal evidence suggests that Shu Ting enjoyed a substantial reputation based on such hand-copied texts.

In 1972, she returned to Xiamen but a lack of stable employment left her feeling "stranded." Shu Ting continued writing while working at various odd jobs; in 1973, she had a series of temporary jobs, assigned first to work at a construction company and later as a propaganda writer, statistician, furnace operator, guide, and bricklayer. In 1974 Shu Ting came into contact with the older male poet and teacher Cai Qijiao (b. 1918), a former student of the Lu Xun Academy of Arts and recipient of a prize for poetry in 1941. Cai, with whom she corresponded, served as a mentor to her; it was he who first introduced her to the work of certain innovative young writers from Beijing. In 1975, Shu Ting found work in a textile factory. In 1977, she worked as a solderer in a factory making light bulbs. In her prose writing of this period, Shu Ting makes it clear that she took considerable pride in her ability to relate to her fellow workers despite a lack of aptitude for physical labor. The experience of solidarity certainly informs the public dimension of her writing.

In the course of the Democracy Wall Movement, the unofficial literary journal *Today* (Jintian) was launched. The inaugural issue, appearing on 23 December 1978, featured two poems by Shu Ting, one of which was *To an Oak* (Zhi xiangshu). Representative of her early style, this poem is noteworthy for its poetic argument against the traditional notion of feminine dependence on the male. By means of extended metaphors drawn from nature, the text argues for a fundamental independence within relationships:

> If I really loved you
> I would never imitate that infatuated bird
> caroling monotonously in your leafy-green shade;
> nor would I merely resemble a spring
> comforting you the year long with refreshing water;
> nor be a sheer precipice
> enhancing your grandeur, complementing your majesty.
> Nor even your sunlight.
> Nor even your spring rain.

Her work also appeared in the third and eighth issues (both poetry specials) of the journal and an early example of her prose writing—a short story entitled "Piano Music in the Church" (Jiaotangli de qinsheng)—was published in its fifth issue. Despite the obvious lack of opacity in her writing, her publication in *Today* established Shu Ting as one representative of a new generation of linguistically adventurous poets who were later branded by conservative critics as "obscure." (Shu Ting herself has described *Today* as the single most important influence on her work.) Links with this group were consolidated by two events: Shu Ting's participation in a poetry reading organized by the editorial board of *Today* on 20 October 1979 (reportedly attracting an audience of approximately one thousand people) and involvement in a conference on new poetry organized by *Poetry* (Shikan) in 1980.

At this point, Shu Ting's popularity accelerated rapidly. Like other *Today* poets such as Bei Dao and Gu Cheng, her connection with the literary mainstream consolidated her standing. In January, the early poem *A Poem Sent to Shanghang Town* (Ji Hangcheng) was published in the first issue of *Fujian Literature*. Starting in the February edition, the magazine established a special section ("Issues Concerning the Creation of New Poetry") as a forum for discussing Shu Ting's work and post-Mao poetry in general, thus contributing to the vigorous debate on "misty poetry" that filled the pages of mainland literary publications. The section continued right through until the end of the year. *Poetry* republished *To an Oak* in its April issue and in October also ran a brief (and, typically, self-deprecating) statement "Please understand me, you people" (Ren a, lijie wo ba) by Shu Ting explaining what poetry meant to her:

> Oh, you people. Please understand me.
> I have never considered myself to be a poet. I also know that I will never be a thinker (even if I really wished to). My experiences have taught me that today people are in

urgent need of respect, trust, and warmth. In my poetry, I strive to express my deep concern for the "human."

Obstacles must be cleared away; masks should be removed. I believe people are capable of mutual understanding because a way leading to another's heart can always be found.

Shu Ting's status as a poet was confirmed in 1981 when she was assigned to the Fujian Writers' Association. In the same year, her *A Boat with Two Masts* (Shuangwei chuan) was published by the Shanghai Art and Literature Press. This, her first volume of poetry, contained forty-seven poems written between 1971 and 1981. It later won a prize in the category of poetry collections given by the Chinese Writers' Association (1979–82). Shu Ting was also awarded a prize by the association for her poem *Homeland, My Dear Homeland* (Zuguo a, wo qin'aide zuguo), a fluent example of the more publicly engaged aspect of Shu Ting's poetry.

Her fortunes took a dramatic turn at the end of 1981. Her sixteen-part poem *The Singing Iris* (Hui changgede yuanweihua) was attacked as "pornographic" because of lines such as "Take your broad palm / and cover me / for now." In retrospect, however, the poem represents an intensification of Shu Ting's singular blending of the personal and the political:

> Love, lift your lamp
> light my way
> Let me be scattered far and wide with my poems
> the bell of ideals strikes beyond the marshland, so gentle the night
> villages and towns cluster in the circle of my arms, let lamplight
> nudge my poems along as I trudge on my way
> the road brandishes its tentacles and shouts: you shall not pass.

The Assembly Line (Liushuixian), a poem based on her long years of factory work, was interpreted as a slight on socialist labor for equating such activity with dehumanizing monotony. In her poignant essay "Penetrating Silence with the Clarity of Sadness" (Yi youshang de mingliang touche chenmo), Shu Ting attributes her decision to withdraw into a self-imposed, three-year period of literary silence because of the personal attacks that accompanied the so-called "critical" appraisal of her poetry. Her personal life also underwent important changes at this time; she married poetry critic and college teacher Chen Zhongyi in 1982. Because of difficulties with her first pregnancy, Shu Ting was forced to spend a long period in hospital but finally gave birth to a son. Despite her declaration not to publish any new writings, another selection of her poetry appeared in 1982 in a joint volume containing work by Gu Cheng.

Shu Ting's silence was not really broken until 1984, however, her re-emergence coinciding with the end of the anti-spiritual pollution campaign. In that year, she was elected to the board of the Chinese Writers' Association and in the spring began publishing her work again. With the poet's re-entry into public life, the journal *Dangdai wenyi sichao* organized a discussion of Shu Ting's poetry in 1985. At this time, she was involved in an innovative project combining poetry with television. Although it never came to fruition, a brief twelve-part "screenplay" entitled *Twelve Nights of the Milky Way* appeared in English translation. Her third collection, entitled *The Singing Iris*, appeared in 1986. Also in the same year, in recognition of her stature as the preeminent female poet of her generation, Shu Ting was one of the few Chinese poets invited to speak at an international conference on modern Chinese literature held in Shanghai. With the consolidation of her poetic career, she turned to the preparation of a book of essays, which appeared in 1988 under the title *Mist of the Heart* (Xin yan).

Despite the voluntary or enforced exile of many of her contemporaries and the rise of a new generation of challenging poets, which included several remarkable women (Zhai Yongming (*q.v.*) and Zhang Zhen), Shu Ting remained in China and continued to develop as a writer. A fourth collection of poetry—*Archaeopteryx* (Shizu niao)—was published in 1992, a volume that included poems exploring explicitly Buddhist themes, such as *Where Zen Is Cultivated* (Chanzong xiuxidi) and *Guanyin, Drop by Drop* (Di shui Guanyin). A second collection of essays, entitled *A Carefree Life*, came out in 1994. In 1996, she was invited by DAAD (Deutscher Akademischer Austauschdienst) to spend a year in Berlin, pursuing her writing. Despite what she describes as difficulties in returning to poetry, new and challenging work continues to appear in leading mainland journals.

Considered critical responses to Shu Ting's poetry have come out since the publication in 1980 of an exploratory article by critic and poet Liu Denghan entitled "Beginning from the Search for One's Self." Liu stresses the important role of the Cultural Revolution in shaping the practices of post-Mao poets. Shu Ting's emphasis on the poet's subjective world and self-expression (a discourse that recuperates the individual) is interpreted as a direct response to the Gang of Four's "philosophy of struggle and the philistine influence it brought with it." Liu notes the recurrent manifestations of love and tender concern in Shu Ting's work but criticizes her for a certain narrowness of subject matter.

Wang Guangming's chapter-length essay provides one of the most extensive discussions of Shu Ting's poetry up to and including the work contained in *Archaeopteryx*. He describes her as a Romantic and discerns three principal stages to her poetic evolution. Wang reads her early work as grounded in collective experience and attributes its broad readership appeal to its "typicality." With the advent of the 1980s, he detects a growing social awareness in Shu Ting's poetry, exemplified by texts such as *Goddess Peak* (Shennü feng). At the same time, Wang is highly critical of ultra-personal poems in her œuvre, such as *The Singing Iris*, for failure to illuminate a reality beyond that of the individual. In the poetry Shu Ting wrote after her three years of silence, the critic discerns another shift accompanied by a concentration on exclusively personal themes and the presence of urban motifs. Unlike earlier work, however, the personal in Shu Ting's poetry of the late 1980s captures the life circumstances of contemporary China. Wang interprets this development as a transcendence of self and notes the emergence of Buddhist concerns in her work as evidence for his view.

The absence of gender awareness in both these responses is redressed by Li Yuanzhen in a perceptive article specifically focusing on the feminine and the feminist in Shu Ting's writing. Li regards Shu Ting's faith in the social order and conservative maternal voice of her early poetry as characteristics distinguishing her work from that of her contemporaries. In later pieces starting with *The Singing Iris*, Li perceives a shift away from the ungendered "humanity" assumed in her best-known writing toward a form of feminine thought (*nüxing siwei*), one based on an affirmation of so-called "essential" feminine qualities such as tenderness, intuition, and love. In Li's view, Shu Ting's rejection of philosophy is a strategy that enables her to avoid the self-deception in much masculinist reasoning, but it also deprives women of a powerful tool with which to explore the world and critique masculine knowledge. In conclusion, Li finds that while Shu Ting's œuvre is impressive in terms of its considerable powers of description and emotion, the poetry ultimately lacks the critical force necessary to make a significant impact on the inequality between the sexes.

Wolfgang Kubin also explored Shu Ting's poetry in terms of gender. Relying on analyses by American theorists, he argues that it is "the bodily aspect" that establishes Shu Ting within an international tradition of feminine literature. Within it, writing is experienced as a kind of "injury," manifesting itself both in the poet's conception of poetry as well as certain metaphorical tendencies in the work. In this article, Kubin also reveals that a number of poems published in the volume *Selected Lyric Poems of Shu Ting and Gu Cheng* (Shu Ting Gu Cheng shuqing shixuan) and usually ascribed to Shu Ting were in fact written by Gu Cheng.

Simon PATTON

Hong Zicheng and Liu Denghan, eds. *Zhongguo dangdai xinshi shi*. Beijing: Renmin wenxue, 1993.

Kubin, Wolfgang. "Writing with Your Body: Literature as a Wound—Remarks on the Poetry of Shu Ting." *Modern Chinese Literature*, 4 (1988): 149–62.

Lao Mu, ed. *Qingnian shiren tanshi*. Beijing: Beijing daxue wu si wenxueshe, 1985, 3–21.

Li Yuanzhen. "Lun Shu Ting shi zhong de nüxing siwei." *Lianhe wenxue*, 5, no. 9 (1988): 60–64.

Liu Denghan. "Cong xunzhao ziji kaishi—Shu Ting he tade shi." *Shitansuo*, 1 (1980): 67–74.

Shu Ting. *Hui changge de yuanweihua*. Chengdu: Sichuan wenyi chubanshe, 1984.

———. *The Mist of My Heart: Selected Poems of Shu Ting*, ed. William O'Donnell; trans. Gordon T. Osing and Dean Wu Swihart. Beijing: Panda Books, 1995.

———. *Ni diushi le shenme*. Changchun: Jilin renmin chubanshe, 1996.

———. *Shizuniao*. Fuzhou: Haixia wenyi chubanshe, 1992.

———. *Shu Ting: Selected Poems*, trans. Eva Hung, et al. Hong Kong: The Research Centre for Translation, Chinese University of Hong Kong, 1994.

———. *Shuangwei chuan*. Shanghai: Shanghai wenyi chubanshe, 1981.

———. *Xin yan*. Shanghai: Shanghai wenyi chubanshe, 1988.

———. *Yinggu lingxiao*. Zhuhai: Lujian chubanshe, 1994.

Shu Ting and Gu Cheng. *Shu Ting Gu Cheng shuqing shixuan*. Fuzhou: Fujian renmin chubanshe, 1982.

Wang Guangming. *Jiannan de zhixiang: "Xin shichao" yu ershi shiji Zhongguo xiandaishi*. Changchun: Mingdai wenyi chubanshe, 1993.

Yeh, Michelle. *Anthology of Modern Chinese Poetry*. New Haven: Yale University Press, 1992.

Zhang Xuemeng et al. "Qing tingting women de shengyin." *Shitansuo*, 1 (1980): 56–57.

Shu Xiuwen

Shu Xiuwen, 1915–1969, of Yi County, Anhui Province, was one of the better-known actresses in Chinese cinema of the 1930s and 1940s.

She was born into a family that had known better times, her grandfather having apparently been a famous Confucian scholar. Her father traveled to Beijing to teach at a secondary school but lost his job when Shu Xiuwen was in high school; she had to quit school to help her mother with household chores. Depressed by the financial circumstances and the bleak future ahead for their four daughters, Shu Xiuwen's parents turned to opium and became addicts. Debt finally forced her father to sell Shu Xiuwen but she escaped before it happened and became an escort dancing-girl in a dance club on East Chang'an Street in Beijing. Humiliated by the work, she sought her fortune in Shanghai, looking for better opportunities.

There, Shu Xiuwen was introduced by a friend to Chen Yumei, a Mandarin tutor and wife of the owner of Tianyi Film Studio; she soon got Shu Xiuwen a minor role in the film *Ms. Yunlan* (Yunlan guniang). The acting experience, although limited, enabled Shu Xiuwen to join the Jimei Song and Dance Troupe (Jimei gewu jushe), where she became acquainted with Wei Heling, later a famous film actor. Performing on stage was challenging, touring was harsh, and the troupe disbanded because of lack of funds after performances in Jiading and Changzhou. The Jimei Troupe proved to be a formative period in Shu Xiuwen's acting career, however.

She spent time with Wei Heling, Gui Jiangong, and Liu Yumin before becoming acquainted with Tian Hong, brother of famous leftist playwright and director Tian Han (1898–1968). At Tian Hong's suggestion, Shu Xiuwen joined the May Flower Drama Troupe (Wuyuehua jushe), then under the direction of Tian Han. Shu Xiuwen was exposed to leftist ideas and performed plays with obvious leftist slants such as *Disordered Bell* (Luan Zhong), *Comrades-in-arms* (Zhanyou), and *SOS*. The troupe was soon disbanded by the KMT government, and her friend Gui Jiangong was arrested. These events marked a political turning point for Shu Xiuwen, who then became more actively involved in the leftist movement.

She soon joined Tian Han's other performing organization, the Spring and Autumn Troupe (Chunqiu jushe), which had been formed to give benefit performances for disaster relief when the Yangzi [Yangtze] River flooded. It was not long before Shu Xiuwen became the troupe's key actress. Among the many stage dramas in which she acted during this period were *Death of a Star* (Mingyou zhi si), *Seven Women in the Storm* (Baofengyu zhong de qige nüxing), and *Killing of an Infant* (Shalu ying'er).

Shu Xiuwen went with Tian Han when he joined the Yihua Film Studio in 1932, and this studio launched her career as a film actress formally. She starred in two of the studio's films: *National Survival* (Minzu shengcun), directed by Tian Han, and *Raging Tide in the China Sea* (Zhongguo hai de nuchao), directed by Yang Hansheng. Shu Xiuwen was a versatile actress; while steadily establishing her reputation as a film star, she never gave up stage performance. In 1933 and 1934 Shu Xiuwen toured with the Chinese Touring Drama Troupe (Zhongguo lüxing jutuan) between Nanjing and Shanghai. In 1934, the Mingxing Film Studio offered her a three-year contract. Her time with Mingxing was the most productive: she starred or co-starred in at least fifteen films from that year to 1937. Two films, *Peach Flowers after Calamity* (Jie hou taohua) and *Fragrant by Night* (Ye lai xiang), both co-starring Hu Die (*q.v.*), received favorable attention in the film world. Shu Xiuwen continued to be a responsible daughter and sister. As soon as she was able to earn a secure income, the actress moved her parents and three sisters from Beijing to Shanghai and supported them financially.

After the outbreak of the Sino-Japanese War, Shu Xiuwen left Shanghai to go inland with her husband, whose name is not given in source material. She joined the government-sponsored China Film Studio (Zhongguo dianying zhipian chang) and in 1938 had leading roles in several films, including *Defend Our Land* (Baowei women de tudi), *A Good Husband* (Hao zhangfu), and *Frontier Storm* (Sai shang fengyun). While traveling to Inner Mongolia to shoot a scene on location, Shu Xiuwen passed through Yan'an. In this communist base area, she was warmly welcomed by the people and received by Mao Zedong (1893–1976). From 1941 to 1946, Shu Xiuwen essentially abandoned film and devoted herself to performing anti-Japanese stage dramas. Her vivid and moving performances in such plays as *Long Live China!* (Zhongguo wansui), *Thunderstorm* (Leiyu), and *Sunrise* (Ri chu) established her reputation as one of the four best stage actresses in the interior.

After the war, she returned to Shanghai to resume her film career with several film studios. Among her best-known works of this period are *The River Flows East* (Yijiang chun shui xiang dong liu) and *Killer* (Xiongshou), with the Guotai Studio, and *Weakness, Your Name Is Woman* (Ruozhe, nide mingzi shi nüren), with Datong. In 1948 and 1949, Shu Xiuwen was invited to Hong Kong to star in *Flowers Fall in Spring City* (Chun cheng hua luo), *Way of Love* (Lian'ai zhi dao), and *Wild Fire, Spring Wind* (Yehuo chunfeng).

The successful actress is best known for her love of acting and ability to portray a range of characters. When she played the part of a rural woman who had to kill her newborn infant in order to survive (*Killing of an Infant*), so complete was her concentration on the role that she cried aloud on stage. Her emotionally charged performance moved the audience to such an extent that they cried with her throughout the play. Shu Xiuwen's versatility is evidenced by realistic presentations of a simple, good-hearted girl in *Killer* and a grasp of the slick, cruel, and shrewish social butterfly Wang Lizhen in *The River Flows East*. In *Flowers Fall in Spring City*, she played two characters of different generations, a mother and daughter, each with a distinct personality. The mother was once a poor village girl; life for her in the city was full of insults and sufferings. The daughter, on the other hand, was brought up in affluence; she was a kind young woman and carried some politically progressive ideas. Shu Xiuwen brought both characters to life convincingly.

After the founding of the PRC in 1949, she went to Beijing and continued to be active on stage and screen. Besides acting in such films as *Female Driver* (Nü siji) and *Li Shizhen* and dramas such as *Camel Xiangzi* (Luotuo Xiangzi) and *Guan Hanqing*, Shu Xiuwen was active in dubbing foreign films. The political persecution she suffered during the Cultural Revolution cut her life short, however, and she died on 17 March 1969 at the age of fifty-four.

Di BAI

Hsiao Kuo. *Zhongguo zaoqi yingxing*. Guangzhou: Guangdong renmin chubanshe, 1987.
Zhang Yingjin. *Encyclopedia of Chinese Film*. London & New York: Routledge, 1998.
Zhuming biaoyan yishujia Shu Xiuwen. Beijing: Zhongguo wenshi chubanshe, 1986.

Shuai Mengqi

Shuai Mengqi, 1897–1987?, a native of Hanshou, Hunan Province, was an early revolutionary and communist.

Her father passed the county imperial examination during late Qing, thus becoming a "cultivated talent" (*xiucai*); he joined the revolutionary Tongmenghui in the early years of the twentieth century and pioneered the "Anti-Qing, Restore Han" Movement in Hunan Province. When she was twenty, Shuai Mengqi married her cousin, Xu Zhizhen (1893–1964; also known as Xu Hao), who graduated from Jiazhong Industrial College in Changsha in 1919 before studying at Shanghai Foreign Languages Institute. In Shanghai he met Chen Duxiu (1880–1942) and Li Da (1890–1966), two of the founders of the CCP, and joined the party himself in 1922, the year after its formation. It was Xu Zhizhen who awakened in Shuai Mengqi a spirit of revolution when he sent copies of revolutionary magazines home to her. Xu returned to Hunan in summer 1926 and became secretary-general of the Hunan Peasants' Association. Shuai Mengqi joined the CCP that year, became a member of the Party's County Committee of Hanshou, and, as acting head of its Organization Department and head of the Women's Department, organized several women's rallies.

When the CCP-KMT united front collapsed in 1927, as a party leader Shuai Mengqi was in great danger of arrest and so left Hanshou and joined her husband in Wuhan. There, she worked with the Hubei party branch as head of the Organization and Propaganda Departments as well as being director of the Hubei Workers' Movement Institute. However, Shuai Mengqi was unable to get to her husband, who was ill in an underground hospital, for fear of leading the KMT to him. They never reunited; an official plan that he would join her in Moscow where she was sent to study that year, did not eventuate. Xu was sent to another city in Russia (possibly Bikin; the Chinese transliteration is Boli).

After Shuai Mengqi returned to China in 1930, she continued her revolutionary activities, becoming head of the Jiangsu Women's Department; attended an anti-Japanese mass rally in Jiangsu both to support volunteer fighters in the northeast and oppose an armistice in Shanghai; and organized a women's movement in a Shanghai cotton mill. While engaged in this last work, Shuai Mengqi was informed on and arrested at the end of 1932. In March 1933, the activist was sentenced to life imprisonment and transferred to the KMT "model prison" in Nanjing where important political prisoners were held. Over the next five years there, from that year to 1937, she was tortured, her right eye blinded and right leg crippled from multiple fractures. It was reported incorrectly that she had died in prison, and her name was mistakenly included among the revolutionary martyrs named by Zhang Wentian (1900–1976) in his opening message to the Soviet Bases Congress in Yan'an in May 1937. Other catastrophes followed for Shuai Mengqi: her husband remarried in Russia; her membership in the CCP caused local government authorities to expel her father from Hunan

after which he wandered about as an itinerant teacher; her mother developed schizophrenia; and her only daughter was poisoned in an orphanage; she had just turned
thirteen years old.

Shuai Mengqi was released from prison after the second CCP-KMT united front
was formed in 1937 when a friend of her father's spoke up for her. She returned to her
hometown and worked as secretary-general of the Workers' Committee and Hunan
Provincial Party Committee and as secretary to the county governments of Changde,
Yiyang, and Zhongxin. Two years later, Shuai Mengqi attended the Seventh NPC in
Yan'an, then worked there until the central government moved to Beijing in 1949. In
Yan'an she served over the years as minute secretary and general branch secretary of
the Central Committee's Agricultural Committee, member of the Party Committee
Shaanxi-Gansu-Ningxia Border Region government, and as secretary-general of the
Central Committee's Women's Committee. Between 1949 and 1966, Shuai Mengqi
held the following positions: deputy head of the Central Committee's Organization
Department, standing member of the ACWF First National Congress, director of the
ACWF Organization Department, and standing member of the Central Committee's
Supervisory Committee.

In 1966, at the start of the Cultural Revolution, she was isolated for investigation
because her father had been a member of the Tongmenghui (the revolutionary party
that became the KMT) and her coming out alive from imprisonment by the KMT
suggested Shuai Mengqi might have betrayed the party. Some time during this investigation and in the following seven years spent in jail, her left eye was blinded. She
was sent to work in a village in Pingxiang County, Jiangxi Province, and expelled
from the party in 1975.

Shuai Mengqi became rehabilitated and reinstated as a party member in 1978,
later serving as a member of the Central Committee's Commission for Inspecting
Discipline, a member of the Central Committee's Advisory Committee, and an advisor to the Central Committee's Organization Department. She retired in 1985 at the
age of eighty-eight.

Shuai Mengqi never remarried but had many "children," many of them orphans of
revolutionary martyrs. She began taking care of them when living in Shanghai and
continued to do so in Yan'an, also looking after children of CCP leaders and orphaned
children there. Some of these youngsters to whom she devoted such care became
third and fourth generation CCP leaders: Li Tieying (b. 1936), for example, the son of
Jin Weiying (*q.v.*) and Li Weihan, is currently a member of the State Council, a high-
ranking minister, and a member of the Politburo and the Central Committee.

Viola Hong Xin Chan WONG

Bartke, Wolfgang. *Biographical Dictionary and Analysis of China's Party Leaders (1922–
    1988).* Munich: Saur, 1990, 185.
Chen Yutang, ed. *Zhongguo jindai renwu minghao da cidian.* Zhejiang: Guji chubanshe, 1993,
    227.
Klein, Donald W., and Anne B. Clark. *Biographic Dictionary of Chinese Communism, 1921–
    1965.* Cambridge, Mass.: Harvard University Press, 1971, 770–71.

Liu Shaoru. *Zhongnanhai guike*. Hong Kong: Shangtai chubanshe, 1997, 155–57.

Liu Ying. "Dang kaimo, nü zhongyang hao—wo suo zhidao de Shuai dajie." *Renmin ribao*, 12 December 1987.

Niu Zhiqiang. "Shiji zhi ai: Ji Shuai Mengqi tongzhi." In *Zhongguo Gongchangdang di yi dai nü gemingjia de gushi*. Beijing: Renmin chubanshe, 1997, 312, 316–21.

Who's Who in Communist China. Hong Kong: Union Research Institute, 1969.

Yingwen *Zhongguo funü*, ed. *Gujin zhuming funü renwu*, vol. 2. Shijiazhuang: Hebei renmin chubanshe, 1986.

Shuangqing Louzhu: *see* **He Xiangning**

Shuhua: *see* **Ling Shuhua**

Siqin Gaowa

Siqin Gaowa, b. 1949, as Duan Anlin in Guangzhou, Guangdong Province, of a Han Chinese father and Mongolian mother, is a film actress of the Mongolian nation.

Her father, who came from Shanxi Province, was an officer in the Red Army stationed in Guangzhou when she was born. He died of illness in the early 1950s, however, and her mother took her back to Inner Mongolia, where Siqin Gaowa grew up.

Life was hard and material comforts rare in Ningcheng in Zhaowuda League (Zhaowuda meng) where she lived, but from a very young age Siqin Gaowa displayed a talent for dancing. At the age of thirteen, she choreographed and performed a version of the "Wine Cup Dance" (Zhongwan wu). In 1965 (one source says 1964), Siqin Gaowa was selected to join the song and dance troupe in Huhhot, the capital of Inner Mongolian Autonomous Region, as a dancer. After she left her hometown and mother to embark on a new life alone, Siqin Gaowa gave herself the name by which she is known presently; in Mongolian Siqin Gaowa means "beauty and wisdom." The young dancer performed at the combined music and dance programs of minority groups (*shaoshu minzu wenyi huiyan*) in Beijing in 1964 as a dancer and as an announcer. Not long before the Cultural Revolution, she encountered a serious problem with her foot; no longer being able to dance, Siqin Gaowa decided to try her luck in films.

Fortunately, the young woman possessed talent as an actress. In the feature film *Eagerly Homebound* (Guixin sijian), she played the role of a young widow called Yuzhen and won the Ministry of Culture's Youth Creativity Award in 1979. The role that brought her wide acclaim, however, was Huniu in *Camel Xiangzi* (Luotuo Xiangzi, 1982), the film based on the novel by Lao She (1899–1955) of the same title, translated into English as *Rickshaw Boy*. This film won her the double honor in 1983 of receiving China's Golden Rooster Award for Best Leading Actress and the One Hundred Flowers Award given by the film magazine *Dazhong dianying* for Best Actress. For her portrayal of Azhen in *Time and Tide* (Sishui liunian, 1984), Siqin Gaowa won Best Actress in the Hong Kong Golden Statuette Award (Jinxiang jiang) in 1985. Other films she has appeared in are *Xu Mao and His Daughters* (Xu Mao he tade nü'ermen, 1981), *Dragons and Snakes of the Big Lake* (Daze long she, 1982), and

Genghis Khan (Chengjisihan, 1986). Siqin Gaowa also sat as an executive member of the Film Workers' Association of China.

In 1987, the actress married Chen Liangsheng, a Swiss-Chinese music professor and conductor, and migrated to Switzerland. However, she continued to make films in China, Hong Kong, and Taiwan. In 1989 she appeared in *A Story of Three Women* (Sange nüren de gushi), also known as *Living in New York* (Ren zai Niuyue). This film is about three Chinese women in New York, one coming from Hong Kong, another from Taiwan, and the third from mainland China. One of the other actresses in the film, Zhang Manyu from Hong Kong, won Best Actress at the Golden Horse Awards in Taiwan, but as a Swiss national Siqin Gaowa was not eligible to compete for it. She visited Taiwan in 1990 and received a warm reception, especially from the Mongolian community there. Her 1992 film directed by Xie Jin entitled *Woman with a Fragrant Soul* (Xianghun nü) won the Golden Bear Award at the 43rd Berlin Festival (1993). With the Hong Kong director Yim Ho she made the controversial film *The Rebellious One in Heaven* (Tianguo nizi, 1995), which explores women's sexuality and the complex issue of a son's moral duty to his father and gratitude to his mother. In the 1990s Siqin Gaowa also appeared in the successful television series *Mother of Party Member Erleng* (Dangyuan Erleng ma) and *The Empire of Kangxi* (Kangxi diguo), and in 2000 she performed in *The Big Manor* (Da zhaimen). In these series she played older women with complex characters and won acclaim as a talented and experienced leading actress.

Lily Xiao Hong LEE

Huaxia funü mingren cidian. Beijing: Huaxia chubanshe, 1988, 1000.
Qian Shiying. "Menggu yinghou Siqin Gaowa fang Tai ji." *Zhongwai zazhi*, January (1990): 27.
Zhongguo funü guanli ganbu xueyuan, ed. *Gujin Zhongwai nümingren cidian*. Beijing: Zhongguo guangbo dianshi chubanshe, 1980, 358–60.

Song Ailing: *see* **Soong Ailing**

Song Meiling: *see* **Soong Mayling**

Song Qingling
Song Qingling [Soong Ching-ling], 1893–1981, also known as Madame Sun Yat-sen, was born in Shanghai, although her native place was Wenchang in present-day Hainan Province. As the wife of Dr. Sun Yat-sen (Sun Zhongshan, 1866–1925), she is often referred to as the "Mother of Modern China." An active participant in politics, Song Qingling helped bring together Chinese people of all political persuasions throughout the world. For Chinese and non-Chinese alike, she symbolizes the democratic modern Chinese woman: liberated yet not aggressive, tactful yet candid, always standing firm in her beliefs.

Song Qingling's father, Song Yaoru (1866?–1918), was born as Han Jiaozun into a Hakka family in Wenchang but was adopted at the age of nine by his maternal uncle; Song Yaoru later became known in the West as Charlie Soong. He was taken to Boston in the United States when still very young to work for his uncle but ran away; Song Yaoru then was taken under the wing of the Carr family, devout Christians who cared for the boy and put him through school. He attended university while working part-time and after graduating in 1885 returned to China to work as a missionary before turning to business and making a fortune in Shanghai. Song Yaoru gave financial support to the anti-Manchu cause of Sun Yat-sen and joined the revolutionary Tongmenghui. Song's wife, Ni Guizhen, was also modern and educated; she had unbound feet and came from a distinguished Christian family in Shanghai.

Song Qingling was the second of their six children and the middle of the famous three Soong sisters, the other two also were linked to prominent statesmen: Soong Ailing (*q.v.*) married H.H. Kung (1880–1967) and Soong Mayling (*q.v.*) married Chiang Kai-shek (1887–1975). Her three brothers became well-known financiers: T.V. Soong (Song Ziwen, 1894–1971); Song Ziliang (1899–mid-1980s); and Song Zi'an (?–1969).

The three Soong sisters attended missionary schools in Shanghai before going on to the United States for further education. Song Qingling spent six years from 1907 in Wesleyan College, Macon, Georgia, graduating in 1913. She was an excellent student and deeply patriotic. In 1914 when her sister Ailing left her position in Japan as English secretary to her father's old friend Sun Yat-sen, Song Qingling agreed to take her place. She and Sun Yat-sen grew close as they worked together and finally married in Japan, in the office of Sun's Japanese lawyer friend Wada (Hetian Rui). The marriage was conducted despite the opposition of Song Qingling's parents, who felt that the much older Sun Yat-sen had betrayed their trust.

Song Qingling returned to China with her husband in 1916 to continue his revolutionary work, living in the French concession in Shanghai. Theirs was a close partnership. She moved to Guangzhou with him in 1918 when Sun Yat-sen agreed to establish a provisional government to which he was elected president. Pregnant in June 1922 when they fled a military coup, Song Qingling suffered a miscarriage, which affected her health, and she remained childless. Song Qingling helped Sun Yat-sen restructure the Tongmenghui into the KMT and returned with him to Guangzhou when he decided to launch the Northern Expedition from Shaoguan.

Sun Yat-sen's ideas remained a profound influence on Song Qingling throughout her life. Disillusioned with the West, he sought assistance instead from the new revolutionary government of Soviet Russia, having discussions with Comintern and Soviet Union representatives A.A. Joffe and Mikhail Borodin at which Song Qingling was present. Sun's aim was to ally the KMT with the Soviet Union and the CCP while fostering the peasants and the workers. With Soviet help, the Guangzhou government established the famous Whampoa Academy to train its own army; with Soviet encouragement the KMT and the CCP formed their first united front. Song Qingling also accompanied her husband to Beijing, via Japan, in October 1924 where he had been summoned to discussions by the northern warlord Feng Yuxiang.

Poised to finally unite the nation, Sun Yat-sen was tragically struck down with liver cancer. He died on 12 March 1925 in Beijing. Not one to wallow in personal tragedy, Song Qingling quickly rose to the demands of the time and determined to make her voice heard. She issued statements condemning the actions of Japanese and

British police who had fired upon Shanghai workers (May Thirtieth Incident) and organized fundraising to aid workers in Hong Kong and Guangzhou; they had gone out on strike in support of their Shanghai colleagues. The assassination by the KMT right of her husband's long-time friend and comrade Liao Zhongkai at this time is seen by some as the decisive event that crystallized Song Qingling's leftist sympathies for the CCP.

In January 1926, she was elected in Guangzhou to the Central Executive Committee of the KMT, the first political position held in her own stead. After participating in the committee's Second Congress, Song Qingling became involved in preparations for the Northern Expedition of 1926–27. She made the long and arduous journey from Guangzhou to Wuhan when the left-dominated Republic government was established there in 1926, bravely withstanding family pressure after her future brother-in-law Chiang Kai-shek (who married Soong Mayling in late 1927) established an alternative capital at Nanjing. Song Qingling further exhibited her independence and courage by adding her name to a telegram condemning Chiang's large-scale assassination of communist leaders and members that year. Song Qingling made it clear in an article in the *People's Tribune* (Hankou) that she would no longer carry out KMT policies of the Nanjing government.

Perhaps to extend Sun Yat-sen's work of forging an alliance with Russia, perhaps to see for herself what this socialist country was like, or perhaps because her life was in danger, as one source suggests, Song Qingling went to Moscow in August. She undertook a series of fact-finding tours and speaking engagements and in company with Deng Yanda and Chen Yuren (Eugene Chen) met with Soviet officials, including Josef Stalin. Despite a heated exchange of telegrams with Chiang Kai-shek who wanted her to return to China, Song Qingling left for Europe after six months in Moscow. She later wrote to her biographer Israel Epstein that her stay was not long "because Stalin didn't want to continue to help us but wanted to let Chiang have his way." Just before Song Qingling left, Stalin nevertheless urged her to return to China to lead the revolution, indicating that he would pass information on to her through Comintern messengers.

Between 1928 and 1931, Qingling sojourned in Europe, mainly in Berlin. She returned to China briefly in 1929 for the re-interment of Sun Yat-sen's body in a tomb built in Nanjing. While in China, Song Qingling was re-elected to the Central Executive Committee of the KMT. She made it clear, however, that her return should not be seen as a change in her stance or capitulation to Chiang. When an old friend of her husband's visited her, ostensibly to persuade Song Qingling to go to Nanjing but in reality to warn her not to make public statements against Chiang's government there, Song Qingling revealed her contempt for Chiang Kai-shek's manipulations by publishing in a Beijing student newspaper an account of the meeting. The death of her mother in July 1931 brought Song Qingling home to China for good, again passing through Moscow where she met once more with Josef Stalin. Barely a month after her mother's funeral, her old comrade Deng Yanda was arrested by the KMT and secretly executed.

When the Japanese invaded the northeastern provinces of China then known as

Manchuria on 18 September 1931 and Chiang Kai-shek refused to respond to the national outcry to declare war, Song Qingling issued a statement entitled "The Guomindang Is No Longer a Political Power." In this article, she effectively called an end to her relationship with the KMT, the unspoken message being that her sympathies now lay with the CCP.

Chinese soldiers defended Shanghai valiantly against a Japanese attack on 28 January 1932 and continued to gain victories, yet within a month Chiang Kai-shek had capitulated to Japan by signing an agreement to withdraw all Chinese troops from Shanghai. He sent those troops, the Nineteenth Army, to fight the Red Army in Fujian instead. With the Japanese attack, Song Qingling plunged herself into fundraising, organizing care and relief for the wounded and refugees in Shanghai, as well as visiting the front and hospitals.

An important aspect of her work during this period was her promotion of human rights and the rescue of political prisoners. With Cai Yuanpei and Yang Xingfo, Song Qingling formed the China League for the Protection of Civil Rights (Zhongguo minquan baozhang tongmeng) in 1932, succeeding through this means to free leftist students, foreign visitors later identified as Comintern officers, and even communists from KMT jails. The assassination in June 1933 of Yang Xingfo, then secretary-general of the league, not far from her residence was no doubt a covert warning to Song Qingling and the league was disbanded. Its work continued in different forms, however. She asked help from her many friends of other nationalities in shielding communist fugitives, providing secret meeting places, and chaperoning people to safety.

Song Qingling was prepared to go to great lengths on this account, as her dramatic attempt to "go to jail" in 1936 attests. This affair began when in November 1935 the seven leaders of the National Salvation Association (Quanguo gejie jiuguohui) were arrested by the Shanghai police and imprisoned for six months in Suzhou without trial. Song Qingling led a small group of people to Suzhou to join the seven, stating: "If it is a crime to love our country, then we are as guilty as they." Thousands of ordinary Chinese responded to this very public stance by also clamoring to go to jail with the "Seven Virtuous Ones" (the usual translation the "Seven Gentlemen" is clearly inappropriate, as one of them was a woman). The prisoners were eventually released.

She was unable to accept a prestigious invitation to an international congress in Geneva against war and Japanese aggression in China but agreed to lend her name to the gathering. Song Qingling was, however, able to preside over an international congress held secretly in Shanghai in September 1933, attended by over three hundred delegates: the Far East Congress of the World Committee against Imperialist War.

Ignoring public opinion in China, which was overwhelmingly in favor of fighting the Japanese invaders, Chiang Kai-shek sought instead to "exterminate the bandits," in other words, the communists. When the communists issued a stirring call on 1 August 1935 for an end to civil war and asked the KMT to join them in fighting the Japanese, Song Qingling was one of several important KMT members to respond. The two others were Sun Fo, Sun Yat-sen's son by his first wife, and Yu Yuren.

Song Qingling may also have played a key role in a related event that was to have a momentous effect on the future of China: the Xi'an Incident of 12 December 1936.

This drama unfolded when Chiang Kai-shek was kidnapped by one of his own generals, Zhang Xueliang, who demanded that a call be issued to stop fighting the communists and form instead a coalition with them against the Japanese. The result of this event was the formation of the second KMT-CCP united front. Song Qingling's role in the incident is still not entirely clear. There are strong indications, however, that she transmitted to the CCP a secret message from Stalin demanding that Chiang's life be spared so as to avoid civil war and engage the Japanese in China. It is known, for example, that Song Qingling was twice mentioned in a report that Zhou Enlai (1898–1976) wrote at the time. The memoirs of Liao Chengzhi published in 1982 also confirm that Song Qingling was a trusted liaison between the Comintern and the CCP. It was she who later chose Dr. George Hatem (Ma Haide) and the journalist Edgar Snow as the Americans who would go to Yan'an. While this particular request came directly from the CCP, one source suggests that many of Song Qingling's activities during this period—shielding refugees and involvement in the Xi'an Incident—were carried out at the request of the Comintern or even Stalin himself.

After the second KMT-CCP united front was declared, Song Qingling was elected to the Central Committee of the KMT. During its Fifth Congress in February 1937, she and her leftist colleagues gained a majority decision for re-establishing Sun Yatsen's three important policies of allying with Russia and the CCP and fostering the peasants and workers. Official talks soon began in Nanjing between the KMT and the CCP, represented by Zhou Enlai and other leaders invited by Song Qingling to her home. Six months later, however, the Japanese invaded Shanghai (August), and she slipped secretly out of the city with the help of her New Zealand friend Rewi Alley. After traveling by boat to Hong Kong, Song Qingling formed the China Defense League (Baowei Zhongguo tongmeng) to garner help and support for China's struggle against Japan. She was assisted in her work by many Hong Kong women from prominent families; money and materials poured in from all over the world, thus enabling the league to provide medicine, medical equipment, and much needed provisions to the battlefield. Her "A Letter to the World" published at this time was influential in obtaining much valuable assistance for China.

In 1940, Song Qingling began appearing in public with her sisters, first in Hong Kong, then in Chongqing, where they toured bomb sites, air-raid shelter systems, and hospitals and also attended dinners and exhibitions. Although no doubt prompted by the common enemy of a puppet Japanese government led by the defector Wang Jingwei, these signs of Soong unity were no more than a political veneer. Song Qingling soon returned to her real work in Hong Kong rather than endure the efforts of Chiang Kaishek and her own family to draw her into his circle. Song Qingling remained in Hong Kong until 8 December 1941, the day after Japan began its attack on the island, and reportedly left for Chongqing on the last plane from Kai Tak Airport.

Staying initially with her sister Ailing and brother-in-law H.H. Kung, now the wartime minister of Finance for the Republic's government, Song Qingling continued to appear with Ailing and Mayling. Song Qingling moved to a house of her own outside the VIP area and was soon sought out by journalists, foreign visitors, and expatriates. Her Defense League work was severely affected by the loss of support from Southeast Asia, which quickly fell to the Japanese; however, one of the advantages of Chongqing was the opportunity it afforded to meet and influence international figures. U.S. General Joseph Stilwell, for example, allowed supply planes to deliver provisions to Yan'an toward the end of the war. The league's presence in Chongqing also facilitated its claiming on behalf of the communists a share of foreign agencies' relief money and materials. It is said that a well-built American would act as a "chaperone" when cash was withdrawn from a certain bank and passed to a waiting car, sent by Zhou Enlai; the car then proceeded to the International Peace Hospital in Yan'an established by the Canadian Dr. Norman Bethune. With supporters like Anna and Eleanor Roosevelt, the Defense League was immune from Chiang Kai-shek's interference.

Despite surveillance on her person and home, Song Qingling remained courageous and outspoken. She maintained close contact with official representatives of the CCP, including Dong Biwu, Zhou Enlai, and Deng Yingchao (*q.v.*) and harbored political fugitives. Song Qingling met with Mao Zedong (1893–1976) and other communist leaders whom Chiang Kai-shek had invited to Chongqing in August 1945 to discuss the preservation of unity after the war. When in the following year Chiang Kai-shek broke an agreed ceasefire and resumed his attack on the communists, Song Qingling issued a statement of protest and continued raising funds for hospitals, pharmaceutical factories, and orphanages in communist areas. She had by this time moved back to Shanghai and had also renamed the league the China Welfare Foundation (Zhongguo fuli jijin hui), stating that its focus would now be on helping the children of China.

When Chiang Kai-shek resigned as president of the Republican government in early 1949, Vice-President Li Zongren approached Song Qingling with an offer that she lead the Republican government. Song Qingling declined, choosing instead to remain in Shanghai despite the personal danger this decision placed her in. Invited to a celebration of the anniversary of the founding of the CCP after Shanghai was taken over by the communists in May, she gave a speech entitled "A Salute to the Communist Party" and that September was accompanied to Beijing by Deng Yingchao to provide guidance on the construction of the new nation. Song Qingling attended the First Political Consultative Conference and was elected vice-president of China and an executive member of the First CPPCC. On 1 October, Song Qingling stood on the rostrum at Tian'anmen Square as one of the leaders of the new nation.

In the early years of the PRC, she became the nation's foremost diplomat and symbol of unity of the Chinese people. Song Qingling frequently met with visiting foreign dignitaries, made several overseas visits, and attended international conferences. She was the only non-communist member of the delegation to Moscow for the fortieth anniversary of Russia's October Revolution. When receiving the International Stalin Peace Prize, Song Qingling donated the money part of the award to the China Welfare Institute to set up the International Maternity and Child Health Hospital.

During this period, she lived mostly in Beijing, in a tranquil residence that had once belonged to a Qing dynasty prince. With secretarial and household staff provided by the state, Song Qingling often entertained Chinese and foreign dignitaries with characteristic simplicity. She also visited from time to time her Shanghai house, which she maintained with her own staff. In 1958 Song Qingling applied to become a party member but was told that her work would be more effective if she remained an outsider. Song Qingling is said to have been extremely saddened by this decision.

In 1948 she was invited to be honorary chair of the All China Federation of Democratic Women and confirmed in that position when it was renamed the ACWF in 1949. Taking an even greater interest in women's issues than before, Song Qingling also continued to show an active concern for the welfare of children, from that year on, serving as president of the Association for the Protection of Children (Baowei ertong quanguo weiyuanhui). She established the magazine *China Reconstructs* as a means of promoting China internationally. With Jin Zhonghua, Israel Epstein, and his wife Elsie Fairfax-Cholmeley acting as editors, *China Reconstructs* reported the achievement of the Chinese people in the fields of literature, the arts, education, and sports, winning a great deal of sympathy and admiration worldwide for China. In addition to the original editions in Chinese and English, later issues were published in French, Spanish, Arabic, Russian, and German.

Despite her name being at the top of Zhou Enlai's list of people to be protected during the Cultural Revolution, Song Qingling was not completely spared from attack and all but disappeared until 1971. She refused to yield to an anonymous demand to stop wearing her hair in a bun, defending it as "a traditional style of the Chinese people," but was willing to make other changes in her life. Quotations of Mao were hung up on the walls of her residence and plaques bearing classical names to the rooms in the old palace where she lived were taken down. Song Qingling contemplated killing the doves she kept as pets but was dissuaded only when her secretary pointed out that, favorites of her late husband, the birds were symbols of peace. When the tomb of her parents in Shanghai was violated and their remains exposed, Zhou Enlai ordered its immediate restoration. While the work of the China Welfare Institute came to a virtual standstill, Song Qingling was able to retain the integrity of its offshoot, the Shanghai Children's Art Drama Troupe.

It would seem from her public pronouncements and private letters that she was at first supportive of the Cultural Revolution. Her later grave concerns are evident, however, from the fact that Song Qingling wrote notes to her friends Anna Louise Strong, the Epsteins, and George Hatem and had them hand delivered with the request that the notes be destroyed after reading. Their contents have never been revealed. Yet, Song Qingling continued to help others in more precarious situations than herself. She remained in communication with the children of the discredited president of state Liu Shaoqi (1898–1969) with whom Song Qingling had worked closely from the 1930s in Shanghai, and she forwarded to Mao Zedong their written request for assistance in locating scattered family members. Song Qingling also vouchsafed in writing the loyalty to China, and in particular to the CCP, of her old New Zealand comrade Rewi Alley.

During this period, Song Qingling lived a lonely life. She did not go out or entertain and was afflicted by arthritis and a distressing skin condition that caused insomnia. The suicide in Shanghai of her cousin's daughter and the death of her brother

Song Zi'an added to her suffering. Song Qingling saw Edgar Snow in 1970 on his last visit to China, but he remained silent about the content of their conversation.

In 1966 Song Qingling made a resounding speech on the occasion of the centenary of Sun Yat-sen's birth, affirming the correctness of his revolutionary line and praising his lasting contribution to the cause. She did not break her silence again until 1972, just before President Nixon's visit to China, with the publication of an article in *China Reconstructs* entitled "The Beginning of a New Era." She was, however, not included in the receptions for Nixon. As the political atmosphere in China relaxed from then onward, foreign visitors started to appear on her doorstep again. With the end of the Cultural Revolution in 1976, Song Qingling resumed her place in the public eye, expressing great pleasure in the reforms and more open policies of the late 1970s. On the eve of the thirtieth anniversary of the establishment of the PRC, she wrote "The Will of the People Is Unconquerable" in which she outlined the damage done by the Cultural Revolution to China and its people.

With the opening up of international relations, Song Qingling tried to re-establish ties with relatives outside China, but with mixed success; her older sister Ailing had died in 1973, and efforts to bring Mayling to China came to nothing. Song Qingling's health deteriorated from the late 1970s as she lost much of the use of her legs, suffered from back pain, and had four falls in close succession. Song Qingling prepared clear instructions that when she died her body was to be cremated and buried with her faithful lifelong maid and companion Li Yan'e, near her parents' tomb in Shanghai rather than with her husband Sun Yat-sen in Nanjing. Song Qingling was accepted as a member of the CCP on her deathbed and was also informed that the Central Committee intended to confer on her the terminal title (i.e., the last title bestowed before death) of honorary president (*zhuxi*) of the People's Republic. At her last public appearance, in the Great Hall of the People, Song Qingling received an honorary LLD from Victoria University in Canada and made an acceptance speech from a wheelchair. She died on 29 May 1981 surrounded by family members, old friends, and colleagues. Condolences poured in from around the world and over one hundred thousand people viewed her body as she lay in state in the Great Hall of the People. A memorial service presided over by Hu Yaobang, secretary-general of the CCP, was held on 3 June at which Deng Xiaoping delivered the eulogy.

Song Qingling was a modest woman and did not share the love of luxury of which her sisters were accused. Her favorite relaxation was playing the piano, which she did every evening and whenever her heart was not at peace. Song Qingling was a faithful correspondent who retained friendships for decades and kept abreast of the world by reading avidly; over the years, she had counted among her friends writers such as Lu Xun, Guo Moruo, Maxim Gorki, Romain Roland, and George Bernard Shaw. Song Qingling had been a young and attractive woman when she was widowed and probably not surprisingly throughout her life was dogged by rumors linking her to various men, Chinese and foreign. Reports, clearly erroneous, were once printed by such well-respected establishments as the Associated Press and *The New York Times* of an impending marriage to Chen Yuren, but Song Qingling never remarried.

In recent years, questions have been posed, particularly in Hong Kong and Taiwan, about her unquestioning loyalty to the CCP. Why, for instance, did she remain silent about the clearly wrong policies of the late 1950s and especially the madness of the Cultural Revolution, when in earlier times Song Qingling had been such a fearless and outspoken critic of Chiang Kai-shek? The answers to such intriguing questions may soon be found in material that came to light in the mid-1990s through the Editorial Committee of the History of the CCP. Not yet made public, this material is said to contain a series of letters written by Song Qingling to Mao Zedong and the CCP Central Committee from 1955 on in which she expresses puzzlement and dissent from party policies. Whatever these letters reveal, Song Qingling will be remembered as one of the few women who, through their bold participation in politics, made an indelible mark on Chinese history.

Lily Xiao Hong LEE

Bi Wanwen. "Sidalin, Song Qingling yu Xi'an shibian." *Shehui kexue zhanxian*, 5 (1994): 143–49.

Boorman, Howard, and Richard C. Howard, eds. *Biographical Dictionary of Republican China*, vol. 3. New York: Columbia University Press, 1970, 142–46.

Chen Shuyu. *Song Qingling zhuan*. Changchun: Beifang funü'ertong chubanshe, 1988.

Deng Shulin. "Commemorating the Centennial of Soong Ching Ling's Birth." *China Today*, 4 (1993): 26–32.

Epstein, Israel. *Women in World History: Soong Ching Ling (Mme. Sun Yat-sen)*. Beijing: New World Press, 1993.

Eunson, Roby. *The Soong Sisters*. New York: Franklin Watts, 1975.

Hahn, Emily. *The Soong Sisters*. London: R. Hale, 1942.

"In Memory of Song Qingling." *China Reconstructs*, distributed with the September 1981 regular issue.

Klein, Donald W., and Anne B. Clark. *Biographic Dictionary of Chinese Communism, 1921–1965*. Cambridge, Mass.: Harvard University Press, 1971, 782–87.

Lestz, Michael. "The Soong Sisters and China's Revolution." In *Women, Religion and Social Change*, ed. Yvonne Yazback Haddad. Albany, N.Y.: State University of New York Press, 1985.

Liu Jiaquan. *Song Qingling zhuan*. Beijing: Zhongguo wenlian, 1988.

Liu Shaotang, ed. "Song Qingling." In *Minguo renwu xiaozhuan*, vol. 5. Taipei: Zhuanji wenxue chubanshe, 1982, 78–90.

Luo Bing. "Song Qingling yu Mao Zedong de en'en yuanyuan." *Zhengming*, no. 1 (1995): 12–18.

Shang Mingxian and Tang Baolin. *Song Qingling zhuan*. Beijing: Beijing chubanshe, 1990.

Shikawa Teruko. "Sōkeirei kenkyū no genjō to kadai." *Tsuda juku Daigaku Kokusai kankeigaku kenkyū*, no. 12 (1986): 47–58.

Snow, Helen Foster. *Women in Modern China*. The Hague: Mouton, 1967, 109–57.

"Song Qingling jianguo hou de jingli: Zhonggong neibu wenjian zhaiyao." *Kaifang*, 4 (1997): 24–25.

Song Qingling. *Song Qingling xuanji*. Hong Kong Zhonghua shuju, 1967.

Song Qingling yanjiu wenxian lu. Beijing: Zhongguo heping chubanshe, 1993.

Xia Wensi. "Jiquan xia tousheng de 'guomu': Cong zuixin ziliao kan Song Qingling he Zhonggong guanxi." *Kaifang*, 4 (1997): 26–29.

Yang Yaojian. *Songshi jiemei zai Chongqing*. Beijing: Renmin ribao chubanshe, 1986.

Zhonggong dangshi renwu zhuan, vol. 28. Xi'an: Shaanxi renmin chubanshe, 1980–96, 1–71.

Zhuang Zheng. "Tan Song Qingling." *Zhongwai zazhi*, 30, no. 3 (1981): 80–85.

Soong Ailing

Soong Ailing [Song Ailing], 1890–1973, was the eldest sister of Song Qingling (*q.v.*) and Soong Mayling (*q.v.*). Soong Ailing married H.H. Kung (Kong Xiangxi [K'ung Hsiang-hsi], 1880–1967), head of the Executive Yuan and minister of Finance of the Republic of China in the 1930s and 1940s. Soong Ailing was a businesswoman and financier in her own right who, with the help of her children, built a family fortune of fabulous proportions. She became a controversial figure, however, when her business deals attracted media criticism for insider trading and unscrupulous practices.

Soong Ailing's father, Charlie Soong (Song Yaoru, 1866?–1918), had worked hard as a young man to gain a university education in America and achieved a measure of fame as a self-made wealthy Shanghai merchant. Her mother, Ni Guizhen, came from a distinguished Shanghai Christian family and was an educated, modern woman with unbound feet. Soong Ailing's two sisters also married prominent statesmen, while her three brothers—T.V. Soong (Song Ziwen, 1894–1971); Song Ziliang (1899–mid-1980s); and Song Zi'an (d. 1969)—became well-known financiers.

Determined that all of his children should have both a Chinese and an American education, Charlie Soong employed a private tutor to teach them Chinese at home and sent them to American schools in Shanghai. Ailing was enrolled at McTyeire Girls' School when she was five years old, and her sisters followed in her footsteps in later years. At the age of fourteen, Soong Ailing traveled to America with the missionary couple William and Addie Burke but was initially prevented by immigration authorities from landing in San Francisco. Only through the help of friends did Ailing manage to evade being quarantined along with third-class passengers and eventually allowed to enter the United States. Soong Ailing studied at Wesleyan College in Macon, Georgia, where she became popular; her generosity in sharing with classmates the food and dress materials sent from home was widely appreciated. Soong Ailing was described as a serious student and somewhat reserved but also clearly of an independent mind and rather audacious. When, for example, her uncle B.C. Wen (Wen Bingzhang) was invited to the White House by President Theodore Roosevelt, Ailing accompanied him. In response to the president's question as to what she thought of America, Ailing recounted her experience at the hands of the immigration officers and reportedly embarrassed Roosevelt by asking: "Why should a Chinese girl be kept out of a country if it is so free?"

After returning to China, Soong Ailing worked in her father's Huamei Print Shop where Chinese-language Bibles were produced. Charlie Soong was a patriot who provided financial support to the anti-Manchu cause of Dr. Sun Yat-sen (1866–1925) and a member of the Tongmenghui. Ailing handled secret coded messages sent to Charlie and accompanied him to banquets and dances that served as a front for secret meetings. She sought donations for the revolutionary cause from the wealthy in Shanghai and was at times more successful than her father in raising funds. When Sun Yat-sen returned to China immediately after the 1911 Wuchang Uprising, Soong Ailing became his secretary, a position in which she was efficient and resourceful, although many saw in her a tendency to be dictatorial and ruthless. Soong Ailing and her father followed Sun Yat-sen to Japan in 1913 when it became apparent that Yuan Shikai had betrayed the Republican revolution. It was there that Ailing was introduced by her father to H.H. Kung, who was working for the YMCA in Yokohama. They fell in love and married in a small Christian church in the city in 1914.

Soong Ailing's husband came from Shanxi, but his origins are unclear. Kung claimed to be a descendant of Confucius and to have inherited a profitable business, but information made available in China in the 1970s and 1980s has thrown doubt on these claims. Kung came, apparently, from a literati family whose fortunes were in decline, and he had gained a good foundation in classical Chinese from his father, who tutored in a private school. Kung entered missionary schools, was secretly baptized, and sent by the missionaries to the United States for further education. He returned to China with a bachelor's degree from Oberlin and a master's degree from Yale, carrying the intention of starting an "Oberlin in China," to be called Mingxian School, with donations collected from America. Kung made his first fortune, however, when he obtained the sole agency for Shell (or perhaps Mobil) kerosene, a product in great demand as a replacement for candles and oil lamps as lighting.

Soong Ailing returned with her new husband to his native Taigu County in Shanxi in 1915. Initially, she played the role of model wife of country gentleman-cum-liberal educator and was also drafted into teaching English. Soon, however, her husband responded to a summons from the Shanxi warlord Yan Xishan to be his consultant, which marked the start of his political career. Soong Ailing's connections with Sun Yat-sen, now her brother-in-law, and many prominent members of his party placed her in a potent position that would help her husband to build a successful political career as well as create an enormous family fortune herself. When Sun Yat-sen asked H.H. Kung to join him in Guangzhou in 1922, Soong Ailing went instead, leaving her husband to continue negotiations with the northern warlords Zhang Zuolin and Feng Yuxiang. After a short period in Guangzhou in 1924, H.H. Kung returned to Beijing on behalf of Sun Yat-sen. Kung and Soong Ailing were at Sun Yat-sen's side during his last illness in Beijing and played an important part in managing his affairs and funeral in 1925.

In the days after Sun Yat-sen's death, the couple transferred their loyalty to Chiang Kai-shek, and Soong Ailing is said to have tried to persuade her sister Song Qingling to do the same. In the meantime, Soong Ailing brought Chiang Kai-shek and her youngest sister, Soong Mayling, together and probably planned their wedding, which was a major social event in Shanghai and reported worldwide. This marriage alliance gained for Chiang Kai-shek the support of Jiangsu and Zhejiang magnates and the Americans and for the Kung and Soong families opportunities to amass wealth.

When the Japanese attacked Shanghai on 28 January 1931, Soong Ailing threw herself into the work of helping the wounded and refugees; she and her friends also donated two hospitals for wounded soldiers. Soon after Chiang Kai-shek capitulated to the Japanese by signing a ceasefire, however, Soong Ailing left China to accompany her husband, then minister of Industry and Commerce for the KMT government, on a fact-finding tour of Europe and America. The prestige of her family and her diplomatic skills were an enormous asset to the mission, and everywhere they went they were received with great cordiality. While visiting her alma mater, Wesleyan, Soong Ailing donated money to establish scholarships.

Her brother T.V. Soong was at that stage minister of Finance, but H.H. Kung replaced him in 1933 after T.V. fell out with Chiang Kai-shek. In 1936, Kung was appointed head of the Executive Yuan, the highest position under the president in the Republic of China. At the same time, Ailing formed the Sandai Company (also known as Sanbu Company) and proceeded to make her fortune on the strength of information to which she as wife of the minister of Finance was privy. By this time, their four children—Lingyi (Rosamond, b. 1916); Lingjun (or Lingwei; Jeanette, d. 1998?); Lingjie (Louis); and Lingkan (David, b. 1923)—were already being criticized by the press for their arrogant and lawless behavior.

When war with Japan broke out in 1937, Soong Ailing and her husband did much good work for the country and the people. She sat on the Committee of the National Friends of the Wounded Soldiers and, after moving to Hong Kong at the fall of Shanghai, also became the local chair of the Association of Friends of the Wounded Soldiers. Soong Ailing continued her patriotic work, raising large sums of money and donating quilts, warm clothing, three ambulances, and thirty-seven trucks. She worked with the National Refugee Children's Association (Zhanshi ertong baoyuhui), making a personal pledge to support one hundred children. Ailing and her two sisters met and made public appearances together in Hong Kong in 1940 for relief work in China. After Japanese radio predicted the Soong sisters would evacuate rather than endure the danger and hardship of wartime Chongqing, the three women demonstrated their commitment to the war effort by flying together to that city and remaining there until the end of the war. In spite of political differences, they presented a united front, touring hospitals, air-raid shelter systems, and bombsites together. All three sisters, but especially Ailing, played important roles in the establishment of Indusco (Chungkuo kung-yeh ho-tso she [Kungho, or Gonghe], popularly known in English as "Gungho"), an organization dedicated to ensuring that China's industry was able to continue despite difficult wartime conditions at the rear. Toward the end of the war, however, Soong Ailing and her children were accused of graft and corruption, blackmarketeering, and compiling huge sums of money by playing the bond and foreign exchange markets with insider information.

In later years, Ailing stepped from the limelight as her son Kong Lingkan with his Yangtze Company and her daughter Kong Lingjun with her Jialing Company took over the family business. Large profits continued to be made through illegal means and privilege continued to be abused. When, for example, Lingkan was arrested by his stepcousin Jiang Jingguo (Chiang Ching-kuo, 1919–1988; this was Chiang Kaishek's son by his first wife) for illegally hoarding foodstuffs and cotton, Lingkan was freed after his aunt Soong Mayling intervened. Leftist writers and academics had been attacking Soong Ailing and her family for some time and in 1944 Chiang Kaishek finally asked for H.H. Kung's resignation as minister of Finance. The following year, Kung resigned from almost all of his important portfolios, and the couple hurriedly wound up business in China and transferred their immense wealth abroad. Thus, by sheer good luck Soong Ailing and her husband managed to move their investments before China was lost to the communists; many other KMT officials got out too late. In the late 1940s, the Federal Bureau of Investigation claimed it was unable to discover the total worth of the Kung family in America, but the fortune would certainly have been in the billions of U.S. dollars, an astronomical sum in those days.

Living in retirement in New York, Soong Ailing and her family continued to involve themselves in politics. They supported Richard Nixon in his bid for political greatness in exchange for his support for the KMT. The family is also reported to have financed the China lobby that for many years has influenced America's policies toward China. H.H. Kung died in New York of heart disease in 1967 at the age of eighty-seven; Soong Ailing died six years later in 1973 at the age of eighty-three. The cause of death was not given, but one source reports that she "suffered intermittently from a kind of cancer."

Soong Ailing and H.H. Kung had long been the target of criticism in the Chinese and American press for corruption and unscrupulous business practices, and reports of their private wealth have fascinated people. Kung's answer to such accusations and speculation was that the charges were CCP propaganda aimed at bringing down the KMT government. He claimed his wealth came from family business in Shanxi and that, having lost most of it when he left the mainland, he and his family lived on modest savings. Nevertheless, because the Shanxi family fortune seems to have been a myth and the life-style of the Kungs in America can hardly be described as modest, the controversy remains.

Lily Xiao Hong LEE

Coble, Parks. *The Shanghai Capitalists and the Nationalist Government, 1927–1937.* Cambridge, Mass.: Council of East Asian Studies, 1980.
Croizier, Brian. *The Man Who Lost China.* N.p.: The Author, 1978.
Eunson, Roby. *The Soong Sisters.* New York: Franklin Watts, 1975.
Hahn, Emily. *The Soong Sisters.* London: R. Hale, 1942.
Hu Huaigu. *Kongshi chaodai.* Taipei: Qunlun chubanshe, 1988.
Liu Shaotang, ed. "Song Ailing." In *Minguo renwu xiaozhuan,* vol. 8. Taipei: Zhuanji wenxue chubanshe, 1987, 74–81.
Seagrave, Sterling. *The Soong Dynasty.* London, Corgi Press, 1985.
Snow, Helen Foster. *Women in Modern China.* The Hague: Mouton, 1967, 109–16, 157–73.
Yan Su. "Kong Xiangxi he Song Ailing." *Renwu,* no. 2 (1996): 172–84.
Zhang Jianping and Li An. *Kongshi jiazu quanzhuan.* Beijing: Zhongguo wenshi chubanshe, 1997.
Zhen Tingyi. *Song Ailing quanzhuan.* Qingdao: Qingdao chubanshe, 1994.

Soong Ching-ling: *see* **Song Qingling**

Soong E-Ling: *see* **Soong Ailing**

Soong Mayling
Soong Mayling [Song Meiling; her name is also spelled as Soong Mei-ling and Sung Mei-ling], b. 1897, in Shanghai, was influential in the history of modern China as the wife of Chiang Kai-shek (1887–1975), head of the KMT government from 1927 until

his death. She was his advisor, English interpreter, and personal representative in dealings with foreign heads of state and other dignitaries and thus served often as a crucial figure in the Republican government's relations with the United States.

Soong Mayling's father, Sung Yao-ju (Song Yaoru, 1866?–1918), was born Han Chiao-tsun into a Hakka family in Wen-ch'ang [Wenchang], Hai-nan Island, which was then part of Kuang-tung [Guangdong] Province. He was adopted at the age of nine by his maternal uncle and became known in the West as Charlie Soong. He was taken to Boston in the United States when still very young to work for his uncle but ran away and was taken under the wing of the Carr family, devout Christians who cared for the boy and put him through school. Charlie Soong attended university while working part-time and after graduating in 1885 returned to China where he worked as a missionary before turning to business and making a fortune in Shanghai. He gave financial support to the anti-Manchu cause of Sun Yat-sen and joined the T'ung-meng-hui. His wife, Ni Kuei-chen [Ni Guizhen], was also modern and educated; she had unbound feet and came from a distinguished Christian family in Shanghai.

Soong Mayling was the fourth of six children and the youngest of the famous three Soong sisters; the other two were also linked with prominent statesmen: Soong Ailing (*q.v.*) married H.H. Kung (1880–1967), and Song Qingling (*q.v.*) married Sun Yat-sen (1866–1925). Her three brothers became well-known financiers: T.V. Soong (Sung Tzu-wen [Song Ziwen], 1894–1971); Sung Tzu-liang (Song Ziliang, 1899–mid-1980s); and Sung Tzu-an (Song Zi'an, ?–1969).

The Soong children had a private Chinese tutor to teach them the Chinese classics, but they all went on to obtain a Western education. The three girls attended missionary schools in Shanghai before going to the United States for further education. Soong Mayling was only eight when she arrived in America with her sister Song Qingling in 1907. They spent some time together at Miss Potwin's Preparatory School in New Jersey, but when Qingling went on to Wesleyan College in Macon, Georgia, Mayling went to Piedmont School in Demorest, also in Georgia. After a year at Piedmont, she was still far too young to be enrolled at Wesleyan, but rules were bent to accommodate her as a special student. Therefore, of the six years Mayling spent at Wesleyan, only one (1912) was counted as college education. When Song Qingling graduated from Wesleyan in 1913, Mayling transferred to Wellesley College in Massachusetts in order to be closer to her brother T.V. Soong, who was studying at Harvard.

In her four years at Wellesley, Soong Mayling grew from being a chubby adolescent to a graceful young woman serious about her studies. She majored in English literature, taking philosophy as a minor and elocution as an elective. One of her fellow students remembered her as sociable and popular, an independent thinker, and a person possessing "interior forces." Perhaps at one point, Soong Mayling felt she also should take marriage into her own hands because of her parents' strong opposition to her sister Qingling's marriage to Sun Yat-sen. Mayling is said to have chosen a Chinese student and made a verbal commitment to marry him, but that promise came to nothing.

She returned to China in 1917. Within a year, her father had died of stomach cancer (May 1918). The responsibility of comforting her mother and helping to put the family's affairs in order fell on Mayling because her sisters and brother T.V. Soong were all engrossed in politics in Kuang-chou. Mayling curtailed her social activities and settled down quietly in the house she and her mother had moved to. Conscious of her own inadequacies in Chinese culture, Mayling took lessons, learning to speak, read, and write Chinese well. Later, when she finally became China's first lady, Mayling was able to produce reasonably respectable literary Chinese for any occasion. In the meantime, she accepted work with the Film Censorship Board and, at the invitation of the French Concessions, sat on a Child Labor Committee. Not only had such a position never been offered to a Chinese woman, it had never been offered to a Chinese before. Mayling also did charity work for the YWCA in Shanghai, a contact she was later to value.

Possibly in 1922, Soong Mayling first met Chiang Kai-shek, at a Christmas party organized by her brother T.V. Soong at the residence of Sun Yat-sen and Song Qingling, who were also present. Chiang Kai-shek had recently divorced his first wife Mao Fu-mei by an arranged marriage and sent away his concubine Yao I-ch'eng (Yao Yicheng; also known as Yao Chih-ch'eng and Yao I-ch'in) so that he could marry a young student named Ch'en Chieh-ju [Chen Jieru]. In spite of that commitment, Chiang enlisted the help of his mentor Sun Yat-sen to make a match with Soong Mayling. Knowing from experience how difficult it would be for a man with a past to be accepted by a Christian family like the Soongs, Sun Yat-sen promised Chiang Kai-shek only that he would try, counseling him to be prepared to wait. In fact, Sun Yat-sen did not pursue the matter, probably because his wife was against it.

However, in an interview published in 1927, Soong Mayling revealed that her courtship with Chiang Kai-shek had started five years previously (i.e., 1922). Although busy at that time with the Northern Expedition, he had corresponded with Soong Mayling. When Chiang Kai-shek stepped down temporarily from the post of commander-in-chief of the KMT army in 1927 and retired to his native Feng-hua, he wrote to her again asking for her hand. It appears that both Song Qingling and T.V. Soong opposed the marriage but her eldest sister, Soong Ailing, who had already formed an alliance with Chiang Kai-shek, was favorably disposed. However, the person whose agreement was critical was Mayling's mother, Madame Ni Kuei-chen.

Predictably, Madame Ni was set against the alliance because Chiang Kai-shek was well known in Shanghai and Canton for his dalliances; also, she wanted her daughter to marry a Christian. Madame Ni went to Japan to avoid Chiang Kai-shek's persistent entreaties but, undaunted, he followed her and put the question to her in person. Chiang Kai-shek showed Madame Ni evidence that he had divorced his wife and sent away his concubine (his marriage to Ch'en Chieh-ju was a well-kept secret), and promised to study the Bible and learn about Christianity. In the meantime, Chiang Kai-shek had sent Ch'en Chieh-ju to study in the United States, bestowing on her a generous severance fee, said to be US$100,000 or silver dollars. Madame Ni could raise no more objections.

The marriage of Soong Mayling and Chiang Kai-shek may not have been, as is generally suspected, based purely on money and power. It is true that he was placed to gain enormously useful allies in the Soong and Kung families. Through them Chiang Kai-shek could further hope to gain the support of the capitalists based in Chiang-su [Jiangsu] and Che-chiang [Zhejiang] as well as the favor of the American government and people. It is perhaps also true, however, that he had fallen in love with this beautiful, vivacious, and accomplished young woman. On Soong Mayling's side, she would have been at least twenty-eight (if she was born in 1899), or even thirty, and had not yet met a man to whom she was willing to give herself. Chiang Kai-shek, who had emerged in 1927 as the most powerful man in China, must have appeared to be a good choice. Even Song Qingling, who was initially against the marriage, later thought they genuinely loved each other.

After the marriage, Soong Mayling was ready to give up her comfortable life in Shanghai and share the hardship of her husband's busy life in Nan-ching [Nanjing], a city that was still rather primitive materially. The newlyweds lived on the campus of the Central Military Academy while a residence was built for them. While Chiang Kai-shek was busy governing China, Soong Mayling occupied herself with what might best be described as community work. Firstly, she took in orphans of the soldiers who had died and provided the children with a home and an education, the quality of which she saw to personally. Soong Mayling tried to bring to China modern ideas on education, such as training students to reaching conclusions through practical experience. She also encouraged students to think independently and creatively. Secondly, Soong Mayling organized the Li-chih Club (Li-chih she [Lizhi she]) for military personnel where they could enjoy healthy leisure activities such as sports, music, and literature instead of spending time in red-light districts. Though in the beginning the soldiers showed resistance, they eventually took to it, and Soong Mayling was praised for creating an environment in which young military personnel could study and rest. The Li-chih Club became the best-run mass organization of the KMT on the mainland.

At the end of 1933, she joined her husband in his campaign against the CCP. They traveled to the border of Fu-chien [Fujian] and Chiang-hsi [Jiangxi] Provinces where Soong Mayling experienced the most primitive conditions and saw for herself the poverty and backwardness that existed in many parts of China. She recorded this experience in an article entitled "At the Fu-chien Border" (Min pien hsün-li), which describes the desolation of some of the villages and the hardships of the people. In a sense, these places and the people the first lady met during this trip influenced her so much that Soong Mayling sought a way to help improve China's situation. To her mind, the country had been isolated from the modern world for so long that its people still lived in the Middle Ages. She became convinced that they must be shown a new way of life so that they would follow the most basic rules of cleanliness, obedience to the law, and moral integrity. In consultation with foreign missionaries in China, Soong Mayling designed the principles of the New Life Movement (NLM [Hsin sheng-huo yün-tung]), which stipulated that the Chinese should have a strong sense of right and wrong and clearly distinguish between the private and the public domains. The NLM aimed to sweep away all old habits that stood in the way of moving China to modernity.

Chiang Kai-shek also believed that the morality of the Chinese people had degenerated because of the recent war and disturbances and that a new spiritual movement was required to revive it. The NLM thus gained her husband's patronage, and he promoted it through all levels of government and mass organizations. Critics of the movement pointed out that fundamental problems of hunger and civil strife had not yet even been solved, and the NLM, or at least the way it was promoted at the grassroots level, appeared trivial and insignificant. Another criticism was that the movement lacked new ideology, clinging instead to traditional virtues of "civility, righteousness, incorruptibility, and a sense of shame" (*li-i-lien-ch'ih*). One important achievement of the NLM, however, was its success in practically wiping out opium smoking and trade in opium because of strict enforcement. While the movement may have been unable to solve all of China's problems, it was a first step in making ordinary Chinese aware that some of their habits and ways of thinking must change if their nation was to take its place in the modern world.

In 1934, Soong Mayling and Chiang Kai-shek toured some of the poverty-stricken provinces of China's north and northwest. They traveled by plane to Ho-nan [Henan], Shensi [Shaanxi], Kan-su [Gansu], Ning-hsia [Ningxia], and Shan-tung [Shandong]. After resting for a few days in Beijing, the two sent a delegation to Inner Mongolia while traveling on to Chahar, Sui-yüan, and Shan-hsi [Shanxi]. This brief tour was important to the KMT ruling clique because it consolidated the power of the remote provinces and rallied them around Chiang Kai-shek. During the tour, Soong Mayling talked to the wives of officials and other women leaders, urging them to fight against poverty, filth, and harmful old customs and to play an active role in welfare work for women and children.

This trip convinced her even more of the importance of establishing a modern airforce in a country as vast as China. Such was his wife's interest that Chiang appointed Mayling as secretary-general to China's Aviation Committee (Hang-k'ung wei-yüan-hui). She took her appointment seriously and proceeded to read up on aviation theory and aeronautic design as well as the merits and deficiencies of various aircraft. The entire Chinese airforce at that time comprised a few outdated American planes and new Italian planes that proved to be of inferior quality. Soong Mayling chose her husband's fiftieth birthday in 1936 as the occasion to ask the Chinese people to donate money to buy planes. Enough funding was eventually raised to buy one hundred second-hand planes from England and the United States. She then went to America to request personnel to help train pilots, technicians, and administrators in China. Soong Mayling was received by President Franklin Roosevelt and also given one hundred brand new planes as well as a team of U.S. volunteers. This was the first hint of her talent for diplomacy with the United States.

The American Volunteers Group (AVG) led by General Claire Chennault came into being the following year with the outbreak of the Sino-Japanese War. The Chinese dubbed his air force unit the "Flying Tigers" for their bravery in battle. During the war years, the AVG protected the Chinese rear from the ferocious bombing of Japanese planes and saved thousands of lives. General Chennault went back to China after the war and started a civil airline called CTA. He married a young Chinese journalist named Anna (Chen Xiangmei, *q.v.*) and the newlyweds' fate continued to be tied to that of Chiang Kai-shek and Soong Mayling.

As China suffered humiliation at the hands of the Japanese attackers, Chiang Kai-shek stopped short of resisting them, calling instead for the extermination of the CCP before the foreign invaders. This proved to be an unpopular suggestion. Marshal Chang Hsüeh-liang [Zhang Xueliang], who had obeyed Chiang Kai-shek's order to retreat from his home territory in northeast China, was but one of many who doubted the rectitude of fighting compatriots—the communists—but not the Japanese. In 1936, Chiang Kai-shek went to Hsi-an [Xi'an] to see for himself why Marshal Chang Hsüeh-liang would not lead his men to fight the communists. In the meantime, the marshal had made an alliance with General Yang Hu-ch'eng and the communists, however, and on 12 December kidnapped Chiang Kai-shek. The marshal's aim was to force Chiang Kai-shek to form a united front with the communists to fight the Japanese. Unfortunately, this incident provided pro-Japanese elements in Nan-ching the opportunity to seize power and the hope of ridding themselves of Chiang Kai-shek. A proposal was put forward to bomb the "rebels" in Hsi-an. Realizing the danger this maneuver placed her husband in, Soong Mayling mobilized her relatives in the Nan-ching government and gained permission to fly to Hsi-an to rescue him. In doing this, she exhibited great courage and the ability to think clearly under pressure. Accompanied by her brother-in-law H.H. Kung and her brother T.V. Soong, Soong Mayling first of all negotiated with Marshal Chang Hsüeh-liang. Then, she convinced her husband to agree to Chang Hsüeh-liang's conditions. Her intervention in this incident may not have been the one factor that secured her husband's release and averted civil war, but the rescue did reveal Mayling as a woman of character. Documents that came to light in the 1980s indicate that her sister Song Qingling may in fact have been instrumental in securing the release of Chiang Kai-shek when she acted as a messenger from Stalin (*vide* Song Qingling).

During the first half of the Sino-Japanese War, Soong Mayling worked tirelessly for the war effort. The central government was located in Wuhan for a short period, and during that time she held a meeting at Lushan to which she invited women from all walks of life and every political color. She headed the Women's Guidance Committee of the NLM (Hsin sheng-huo fu-nü chih-tao wei-yüan-hui [Xinshenghuo funü zhidao weiyuanhui]) that was formed at that time, its mission being to organize Chinese women and release their energy to aid the war effort. Lacking a network of cadres, Mayling entrusted some tasks to communist members and also, perhaps unwittingly, to members of the communist underground. As head, Soong Mayling empowered the National Refugee Children's Association (Chan-shih erh-t'ung pao-yü hui) to save tens of thousands of refugee children and provide them with food, shelter, and an education. After the KMT capital moved to Ch'ung-ch'ing [Chongqing] in May 1939, the Japanese bombarded the city, killing and injuring thousands of civilians and destroying their homes. Through her NLM Women's Guidance Committee, Soong Mayling did a great deal of good helping the homeless, providing drinking water and simple meals, and organizing accommodation for refugees and orphans.

In 1940, she went to Hong Kong to seek treatment for an allergy. A more important mission, however, was to try to persuade her sisters, who had flown to Hong Kong when the Chinese part of Shanghai fell to the Japanese in 1937, to return with her to Ch'ung-ch'ing. During their three years in the British colony, Soong Ailing and Song Qingling had devoted themselves to raising money for the war against Japan. They heeded their sister's entreaty, however, at least partly to put the lie to the Japanese propaganda rumor that the Soong family had abandoned China in its darkest hour. The three sisters created quite a stir in Ch'ung-ch'ing. The appearance of Song Qingling particularly gave a great deal of substance to the slogan for a united front because she had always been such a stern critic of Chiang Kai-shek and his government. Two of the projects the three sisters put their combined weight behind were the Home for Wounded Soldiers (Shang-ping chih chia) and Indusco (Chung-kuo kung-yeh ho-tso she, or "Gung-ho"). The latter was an attempt to maintain the industrial power of China and manufacture of such basic commodities as paper, matches, and soap.

Throughout the war, all three Soong sisters broadcast messages to the people of the United States, and sometimes to Canada and Australia, presenting China's case and warning Western governments of the consequences of not stopping Japan's military activities in Asia. Soong Mayling also published articles in English on the same topic in American newspapers and magazines. As China's first lady, she practiced what is known in Chinese as "first lady's diplomacy." In 1942, Mayling visited India (February) and America (November) in this capacity. Chiang Kai-shek had been invited to visit India, then still a British colony, as head of the Far East Theater when British forces in the Far East were under his command. During this visit, Soong Mayling and her husband offended their British hosts by meeting with Gandhi and Nehru and speaking out for Indian independence.

Chiang Kai-shek wrote to President Roosevelt in November informing him that Soong Mayling would be going to the United States for medical reasons. He wrote that she would also be his personal emissary in the hope of improving the friendship between the two leaders and developing a better relationship between the two republics. This made it obvious that Soong Mayling's visit to the United States included diplomatic responsibilities. About the middle of February 1943, when her medical treatment had been completed, she began her diplomatic activities, that month speaking to both the U.S. Senate and the House of Representatives. In the meantime, four radio stations broadcast her speeches to the people of America. She was only the second woman ever to have addressed the U.S. Congress, the other being Queen Wilhelmina of Holland.

In her speech, Soong Mayling praised Sino-American cooperation and expressed hope that the two countries would continue to fight against invaders in order to create a lasting peace. She exhorted "China's [fellow] brave allies" to continue to uphold their principles even when the time came to discuss peace. This seems to have been a reminder to the allies not to abandon China when the war was over and the country was no longer needed to defeat the common enemy, Japan. The following day, accompanied by Mrs. Eleanor Roosevelt, Soong Mayling met the press in the oval office of the White House, where she was a guest of the president and the first lady.

After visiting Washington, Soong Mayling went on to New York, Boston, Chicago, and San Francisco, and called on her alma maters, Wesleyan College in Georgia and Wellesley in Massachusetts, before crossing the border to Ottawa, Canada. She spent about six weeks on the road, and her diplomatic visit was a success, her beauty, talent, and dedication impressing the American people immensely. Soong Mayling worked hard to achieve the success, however, revising her scripts seven or eight times to perfect both theme and diction. Mayling's fluent spoken English and poise and charm were potent additives in achieving the desired effect. Her diplomatic triumphs continued in Cairo later in the same year when she accompanied her husband to the Cairo Conference. Chiang Kai-shek attended it as one of the three powers, that is, on an equal footing with Franklin D. Roosevelt and Winston Churchill. As his interpreter, Soong Mayling helped make China's voice heard in this meeting among world leaders.

During the war years in the 1940s, she reached the zenith of her power and influence. It was also in this period, however, that negative reports about Mayling and her relatives surfaced at home and abroad. She did not have children but had treated her sister Soong Ailing's children as her own. The arrogant and unruly behavior of these youngsters had from time to time brought criticism of their parents and aunt. As the young people grew older and more adept at using their special status, their mischief became much more serious in nature. Soong Ailing's second daughter, Kung Ling-wei [Kong Lingwei] also known as Kung Ling-jun, angered the public during an evacuation of artists, intellectuals, and party elders by plane from Hong Kong. She insisted that her maidservant and pet dog be given two of the limited number of seats, thereby displacing an important intellectual. The Kung offsprings' later financial dealings also incurred criticism when exposed by the media. Even Soong Mayling herself was accused of having asked U.S. volunteers to fly luxury goods across the Himalayas from India to Ch'ung-ch'ing under the pretext that they were provisions for government departments under the control of her relatives. When word of the inefficiency and corruption of the Chiang Kai-shek government reached America, President Roosevelt sent his own observer to Ch'ung-ch'ing. Wendell Wilkie arrived in August 1942. Soong Mayling and Soong Ailing manipulated the emissary's itinerary in his tour there, making sure he had no chance to meet people who might offer him divergent opinions, and Wilkie went home with nothing but praise for Chiang Kai-shek and his wife.

General Joseph Stilwell, America's highest military commander in China, never saw eye to eye with Chiang Kai-shek, however. Stilwell wanted the CCP to receive American aid and be given a more prominent role in the war against Japan. The two men frequently came into open conflict, and Chiang Kai-shek very much wanted Stilwell recalled from China. Soong Mayling and Soong Ailing played an important role in the long struggle between the two military men, and it was a combined effort of the Chiang Kai-sheks, the Kung family, and T.V. Soong that finally saw Stilwell replaced, in October 1944, by Albert C. Wedemeyer.

Although the Stilwell affair ended to the satisfaction of Chiang Kai-shek and Soong Mayling, 1944 was not a good year for Soong Mayling. Her brother-in-law H.H.

Kung was forced by the weight of public opinion to resign as minister of Finance. She also experienced difficulty in her marriage. In 1927, Chiang Kai-shek had sent his legal wife Ch'en Chieh-ju to the United States so that he could marry Soong Mayling. But Ch'en Chieh-ju returned to China and, with her adopted daughter, lived a reclusive life in Shanghai. However, one day in a department store Ch'en Chieh-ju ran into Ch'en Pi-chün [Chen Bijun (q.v.)], who tried to involve her in the pro-Japan government that her husband Wang Ching-wei [Wang Jingwei] headed. Whether out of loyalty to Chiang Kai-shek or an unwillingness to collaborate with the enemy, Ch'en Chieh-ju quietly left the city for the rear. She contacted her former husband through a former student of Whampoa Military Academy and was taken secretly to Ch'ung-ch'ing. Chiang Kai-shek set her up in the home of a close friend and saw her frequently. This caused fights between Chiang Kai-shek and Soong Mayling, who finally left the city in 1944, ostensibly for health reasons. She went to Brazil, to her and the Kung family's holiday house and made a number of investments. Soong Mayling and her relatives then went to New York City later that year, and she stayed in a hospital there for a month before moving to the Kung residence in Riverdale, New York. Toward the end of World War II (July 1945), with victory in sight, Soong Mayling returned to Ch'ung-ch'ing. Her marital problems seemed to have blown over, and she reappeared as the unshakeable first lady.

As one of the Allies, China enjoyed the benefits of victory at the end of World War II. Chiang Kai-shek and Soong Mayling moved back to the former capital, Nan-ching. Within three years, however, in 1948 they were on the run again, this time fighting the CCP. Bowing to U.S. pressure, Chiang Kai-shek invited Chinese communist leaders to Ch'ung-ch'ing to hold a political consultative meeting to discuss powersharing among all the contending parties. But the insoluble conflict between the two biggest ones, each supported by their respective allies—the United States and the Soviet Union—made full-scale civil war inevitable. One by one, the KMT-held cities fell. Their failure was fueled by crippling inflation, caused partly by the stockpiling of commodities by a few capitalists. The Chiang government came under attack from all directions, until finally Chiang Kai-shek felt bound to curb the profiteering. He appointed his son Chiang Ching-kuo [Jiang Jingguo] commissioner extraordinary of Economic Affairs in Shanghai, where the stockpiling was especially bad. He received information that Kung Ling-k'an [Kong Lingkan], a nephew of Soong Mayling, had used his Yangtze Trading Company to stockpile more than twenty thousand tons of cotton materials, food stuffs, and other goods. Chiang Ching-kuo arrested Kung Ling-k'an in September. Soong Mayling immediately flew to Shanghai and secured her nephew's release. The fact that even Chiang Kai-shek's own son did not have enough power to put order into the country's economy was a strong message to the Chinese people. Through this one act, Soong Mayling might have saved her nephew but possibly contributed to her husband's loss of China.

In order to gain U.S. support in the civil war against the CCP, Soong Mayling visited America in November 1948. Because Chiang Kai-shek had supported the unsuccessful election campaign of Thomas Dewey, she could not have expected as warm a welcome from Harry Truman and his wife as the one she had had with the Roosevelts. Soong Mayling's hope of obtaining aid through the intercession of George C. Marshall also came to nothing during this trip. After more than a year's effort, a disappointed Soong Mayling joined Chiang Kai-shek, now in Taipei, in January 1950. Before leaving the U.S., she made a broadcast from Riverdale thanking the American people for hospitality but criticized their leaders for abandoning their former ally Chiang Kai-shek.

Soong Mayling returned to Taiwan to find her husband at his lowest ebb. Chiang Kai-shek likened himself to Ho-lu, king of Wu in the Warring States Period (475–221 BCE), who was vanquished by the king of Yüeh. Instead of losing hope, Ho-lu worked harder to regain power and eventually defeated the king of Yüeh to reclaim the state. She adjusted her life to this new role. They lived simply while Chiang Kai-shek put reforms in place. He rid his government of the Ch'en brothers and Soong Mayling's relatives, both groups having been accused of graft and corruption, monopolizing the KMT government on the mainland, and ruining the economy. Soong Mayling restricted herself to organizing the women of Taiwan, seldom becoming involved in public affairs. In 1950, the China Women's Anti-Communist Anti-Russia League (Chung-hua fu-nü fan-kung k'ang-O lien-ho hui) was formed under her leadership to work for the education of war orphans, sew for soldiers, and undertake other community projects.

With the outbreak of the Korean War in the early 1950s, Taiwan's status changed from a regime deserted by its friends to an ally again. The U.S. needed Taiwan as a base for transporting provisions to Korea, and even after the Korean War Taiwan remained an important link in America's chain of defense against communism in Asia. She quietly visited the U.S. in 1952, 1953, and 1958 to lend support to a group of Chinese and Americans known unofficially as the "China lobby." People close to the Chiang government on Taiwan hoped to exert influence through this group on U.S. policies relating to China and promote the anti-CCP and anti-Russia cause. Back in Taiwan, however, signs of a power struggle grew between Soong Mayling and her stepson Chiang Ching-kuo. She emerged as the loser, signifying a decline in her power.

As Taiwan lost its seat in the United Nations and the U.S. moved toward recognizing the PRC, Chiang Kai-shek's health deteriorated, his death in 1975 virtually marking the end of Soong Mayling's political life. She went to New York and lived on Long Island, close to her nephews and nieces. When Chiang Ching-kuo took the helm in Taiwan, Soong Mayling was treated with deference but had no real influence in the KMT. Ironically, she outlived her stepson, and at Chiang Ching-kuo's death in 1988 attempted to influence the choice of his successor at the request of the conservative faction in the KMT. Her bid was not successful, however, and Soong Mayling retired again to her residence on Long Island. Blessed with longevity, she is now over one hundred years old and surfaces from time to time to make comments. Her latest was an expression of regret that Chang Hsiao-yen [Zhang Xiaoyan], one of Chiang Ching-kuo's illegitimate sons, had not consulted with her before going to Feng-hua to register his name on the Chiang clan record in April 2000. When the new president from KMT's rival Democratic Progressive Party went to New York in May 2001, he and his wife did not forget to send flowers to Soong Mayling.

In the 1980s, PRC leaders attempted to establish friendly relationships with Taiwan with a view toward peaceful unification. On the death of Song Qingling in 1981, they invited Soong Mayling to China. Perhaps regarding it as a propaganda ploy, she flatly refused their offer. Soong Mayling also replied to letters from the CCP leaders Liao Ch'eng-chih [Liao Chengzhi] and Teng Ying-ch'ao [Deng Yingchao] (*q.v.*) confirming her firm anti-communist stance.

Like her famous sisters, Soong Mayling influenced the history of modern China but, because of her longevity, her influence far outlasted theirs. During the Sino-Japanese War, the first lady helped bring the destiny of the Chinese people to the attention of the world and won many friends for China. Her beauty, charm, poise, and talent were admired internationally. From the beginning, Mayling counseled Chinese women to be independent and concerned with state affairs. Throughout a long life, she also devoted herself to the care of others, especially orphans, wounded soldiers, and refugees. On the other hand, critics argue that her selfish and pampered behavior and complicity in allowing relatives to operate above the law angered many of her compatriots. Nevertheless, later in life in Taiwan during the 1960s and 1970s, Soong Mayling was content to live simply and devoted her days to painting, becoming a reasonably accomplished painter. Her flowers and landscapes are said to retain a distinctive style.

Lily Xiao Hong LEE

Chiang fu-jen hsieh-chen. Taipei: Ch'ün-lun ch'u-pan-she, 1985.

Croizier, Brian. *The Man Who Lost China*. N.p.: The Author, 1978.

Eunson, Roby. *The Soong Sisters*. New York: Franklin Watts, 1975.

Hahn, Emily. *The Soong Sisters*. New York: Doubleday, Coran, 1941.

Hsü Han. *Sung Mei-ling—Chung-kuo ti-i fu-jen*. Taipei: K'ai-chin wen-hua shih-yeh, 1994.

Lestz, Michael. "The Soong Sisters and China's Revolution." In *Women, Religion, and Social Change*, ed. Yvonne Yazback Haddad. Albany: State University of New York Press, 1985.

Li Huan. *Sung Mei-ling chuan*. Taipei: T'ien-yüan t'u-shu kung-ssu, 1985.

Lin Chia-yu and Li Chi-k'uei. *Sung Mei-ling chuan*. Cheng-chou [Zhengzhou]: Ho-nan jen-min ch'u-pan-she, 1995.

Seagrave, Sterling. *The Soong Dynasty*. London: Corgi Press, 1985.

Snow, Helen Foster. "Madame Chiang Kai-shek and Madame H.H. Kung." In *Women in Modern China*. The Hague: Mouton, 1967, 157–73.

———. "The Soong Daughters." In *Women in Modern China*. The Hague: Mouton, 1967, 109–16.

Soong Mayling [Sung Mei-ling]. *This Is Our China*. New York: Harper, 1940.

———. *War Messages and Other Selections*. Ch'ung-ch'ing: Free China Press, 1938.

———. "Shu mien ch'üan-t'i kuo-jen." In *Sung Mei-ling chuan*, ed. Li Huan. Taipei: Tien-yüan t'u-shu kung-ssu, 1985.

Sung Jui-chih [Song Ruizhi], ed. "Sung Mei-ling ti cheng-chih." In *Chung-kuo fu-nü wen-hua t'ung-lan*. Chi-nan [Jinan]: Shan-tung wen-i ch'u-pan-she, 1995, 141–42.

Wang Feng. *Mei-li yü ai-ch'ou: i-ko chen-shih ti Sung Mei-ling*. Beijing: T'uan-chieh ch'u-pan-she, 1998.

Soong Mei-ling: *see* **Soong Mayling**

Su Hsüeh-lin

Su Hsüeh-lin [Su Xuelin], 1896–1999, was a native of T'ai-p'ing County, Anhui Province, although she was born in Jui-an [Rui'an] County, Che-chiang [Zhejiang] Province. Her original name was Su Mei; her *tzu* was Hsüeh-lin; and her pen name was Lü-i. Su Hsüeh-lin was a writer and academic best known for her innovative research into the classical Chinese poetry collection *Songs of the South* (Ch'u-tz'u).

Su Hsüeh-lin was born to a family of officials during the late Ch'ing [Qing] dynasty. Because her grandfather Su Chin-hsia acted as a magistrate in several counties in Che-chiang, she was born in that province instead of the family's native Anhui. Her mother, née Tu, had no formal name but simply went by the nickname of To-ni, which Su Hsüeh-lin implied had derogatory connotations in her native dialect. Su Hsüeh-lin's mother was one of many Chinese women determined to be a perfect person (*wan-jen*), sacrificing her own happiness for the sake of others in order to be the perfect daughter-in-law, wife, and mother. She served her mother-in-law with utter devotion and managed the household of an extended family with meager resources. Su Hsüeh-lin's mother died at the relatively young age of fifty-four, perhaps from sheer exhaustion. Su Hsüeh-lin said she inherited nothing of her mother's talent for needlework, cooking, and household management. Her mother's laborious and thankless life probably convinced her daughter not to follow in her mother's footsteps but to go in a completely different direction. Su Hsüeh-lin's father held a minor official post during the last years of the Ch'ing dynasty and after the changeover to the Republic continued to work as a civil servant.

Su Hsüeh-lin had three brothers, who were all sent to school in big cities, and two sisters. As granddaughters of an official, she and her sisters had the privilege of studying under a private tutor for a few years; their texts inculcated them with the traditional virtues of womanhood. When the Ch'ing dynasty was overthrown in October 1911 and the Republic of China established, Su Hsüeh-lin's grandfather lost his magisterial post but Su Hsüeh-lin benefited, as she could now go to school.

Su Hsüeh-lin first went to P'ei-yüan Girls' School in An-ch'ing, Anhui Province, where part of her extended family lived. Although she was not happy with the teaching and the curriculum there, the schooling served as a beginning to a formal education. When Su Hsüeh-lin heard in 1914 that the First Women's Normal School of An-ch'ing was holding an entrance examination for new students, she went with her younger sister to sit for it, and both were admitted. Su Hsüeh-lin met some resistance from her grandmother because of expenses, but that objection was overcome when it was understood that not only did the school not charge fees but free room and board were provided. Su Hsüeh-lin studied at the school from that year to 1917, showing outstanding performance as a student and winning a reputation as a talented girl. After graduation, she was invited to stay and teach at the primary school attached to the school.

Then, when Su Hsüeh-lin heard that the Peking Women's Higher Normal School (Nü-tzu kao-teng shih-fan hsüeh-hsiao; later to become Peking Women's Normal University) was ready to admit students in 1918, she was eager to pursue further studies. Two obstacles stood in the way, however. The first was that, because Su Hsüeh-lin had been sending a portion of the money she earned as a primary teacher home, her grandmother was unhappy about losing the income and thus objected to the idea. The second was that her grandfather had promised her in marriage to Chang Pao-ling [Zhang Baoling], a merchant's son from Chiang-hsi; the Chang family was just then urging the Su family to set a date for the event. By the time Su Hsüeh-lin had won her right to advance her education, she missed the admission examination and had to enroll as an auditing student in the Chinese Department.

Her old classmate from First Women's Normal School of An-ch'ing, Huang Ying, who later wrote under the name Luyin (*q.v.*), was in the same situation. After submitting a few excellent essays (and some say doing well at examinations), however, the two students received their teacher's recommendation to be admitted as regular students; this standing exempted them from being liable for the boarding expenses charged to auditing students. Among the well-known intellectuals teaching at Peking Higher Women's Normal School were Hu Shih, Ch'en Tu-hsiu [Chen Duxiu], and Chou Tso-jen [Zhou Zuoren], and some, especially Hu Shih, left an indelible impression on Su Hsüeh-lin. The young woman also read many of the literary magazines published by different literary groups in China at the time, saying later that although accepting many ideas of the May Fourth period, she did not agree with those that advocated the total rejection of traditional culture.

After two years of study and just one year to go before graduation, consideration of Su Hsüeh-lin's career prospects loomed close; with academic preparations almost in hand, the young woman knew she could probably look forward to obtaining a senior teaching position in a girls' normal school or high school. But Su Hsüeh-lin decided to seize the opportunity to study in France instead. Aside from academic interests, another reason propelled her choice to study abroad. She had had a war of words with certain male critics in the newspapers over her criticism of a poetry collection and the incident had attracted national attention, which Hsüeh-lin wished to escape. She then applied for and received a place at the Institut Franco-Chinois (IFC) de Lyon (Li-ang Chung-Fa hsüeh-yüan; one source gives the name of the institution as Université d'Outre-Mer de Lyon). In her bid to go to Europe, Su Hsüeh-lin was encouraged and supported by her father, who paid the 600 silver dollars required for a year's expenses. Su Hsüeh-lin set sail for France in 1921.

The IFC had been newly established by Wu Chih-hui, Li Shih-tseng, and others, who felt that an earlier work-study program they had started was a failure; it was a preparatory program for Chinese students to live in Franch and study French for two years before enrolling in French institutions. Su Hsüeh-lin had never studied French before, so the classes were difficult. When several of her friends, including P'an Yü-liang [Pan Yuliang (*q.v.*)], enrolled in an academy of fine arts attached to the University of Lyon, Su Hsüeh-lin joined them. After a few months, she decided to study the history of art. The subject, however, required far greater proficiency in French than Su Hsüeh-lin possessed, so she moved away from her Chinese-speaking friends to live at a boarding house set up by the Catholic church for single women, many of them from French colonies in Asia and Africa. Su Hsüeh-lin's language skills improved dramatically. In addition, she came to admire the Catholic sisters who devoted themselves so selflessly to others. This was undoubtedly why Su Hsüeh-lin later became involved with Catholic organizations in China and is also said to have converted to Catholicism in 1924 when her mother fell ill.

Returning to China in 1925 to see her, Su Hsüeh-lin obeyed her mother's last wish to finally marry. Su Hsüeh-lin had managed to defer this arranged marriage for more than a decade. Chang Pao-ling was a marine engineer graduate of the Massachusetts Institute of Technology in the United States, but Hsüeh-lin found him "cold, narrow-minded and chauvinistic," clearly unsuitable as a husband for a woman who had studied in France and held certain modern and perhaps romantic expectations. Chang admitted that he, too, had been forced into the marriage and would much prefer the life of a bachelor. Thus, apart from their first year in Su-chou, where Chang Pao-ling built his dream house and the couple lived together, for most of their married life the two lived in different cities. The couple's relationship was from all accounts not a happy one.

Between 1926 and 1928, Su Hsüeh-lin taught at both Soochow (Tung-wu ta-hsüeh) and Shanghai (Hu-chiang ta-hsüeh) Universities. While she was at Soochow, her husband took a long leave from his position at Jiangnan Shipbuilders in Shanghai and taught for a year at the same university. This was the only happy time of their marriage. In the latter year, Chang Pao-ling decided to return to his job in Shanghai; Su Hsüeh-lin followed him and started teaching in the city.

However, during her time at Soochow, she lectured on the poetry of Li Shang-yin, which inspired her to write and publish her first academic work, "Research on Li Shang-yin's Love Affairs" (Li Shang-yin lien-ai shih-chi k'ao-cheng) in which she proposed to give her own interpretation on the enigmatic poems of this T'ang dynasty poet, offering evidence of his romantic relationships. This was followed by a series of additional papers, including further innovative studies on Li Shang-yin, the love life of a man and a woman, both Ch'ing dynasty lyric (*tz'u*) poets, and the sacrificial significance of a poem in *Songs of the South*. In this period, her first literary works appeared: *The Green Heaven* (Lü t'ien), a semi-autobiographical novel about a newly wed couple; *The Rose and the Spring* (Mei-kuei yü ch'un), an allegory of sacred and profane love; and *The Heart of the Thornbush* (Chi-hsin), a description of a Chinese woman's three troubled years in France. Su Hsüeh-lin also contributed poems, short stories, and articles to the contemporary literary magazines *Yü-ssu*, *Hsin-yüeh*, and *Hsien-tai p'ing-lun* as well as *Ch'en-pao fu-k'an*. *The Heart of the Thornbush* was her most successful work during this period.

As a university teacher, Su Hsüeh-lin was disadvantaged in not having completed her college degree, a requirement at the missionary-run institutions of Soochow and Shanghai if she wanted to ensure progress in her career there. This stricter policy contrasted the standards, generally speaking, of the university system at large in China. The reality then was that relatively few universities existed in the country, and a high demand arose for the small number of degree-holders available to meet the needs of the new universities continually being set up. Most academics teaching in the Chinese departments of universities were engaged because of their reputation or the recommendation of reputable people rather than solely for their academic qualifications. Universities run at various levels of the Chinese government also paid less attention to degrees than reputation. In any event, Su Hsüeh-lin decided to move her teaching career to Anhui University in 1930 and then in 1931 to Wu-han University, where she stayed for seventeen years.

Wu-han was a new university built on top of a mountain called Lo-chia shan. Su Hsüeh-lin was happy there, and her previously poor health improved. She worked on several articles on *Songs of the South* and discovered Indian and Buddhist literature. Su Hsüeh-lin wrote a play entitled *The Eyes of Kunala* (Chiu-na-lo ti yen-ching), based on a story in the Buddhist anthology *Fa-yüan chu-lin*, which received critical acclaim but sold few copies.

She later claimed that during the 1920s and 1930s she experienced discrimination against her writing; leftist writers and editors boycotted her works after Su Hsüeh-lin befriended the liberals Hu Shih and Ch'en Yüan [Chen Yuan (Xiying)] and published articles in *Hsien-tai p'ing-lun*. When Lu Hsün [Lu Xun] died in 1936, Su Hsüeh-lin wrote to Ts'ai Yüan-p'ei [Cai Yuanpei], the president of Peking University, emphasizing Lu Hsün's leftist associations and urging Ts'ai not to put his name to serve on the committee responsible for arranging Lu Hsün's memorial service. Someone got hold of the letter and published it in a Wu-han magazine; Su Hsüeh-lin then became the target of attacks from all over China, becoming a pariah in a literary world dominated by leftists.

After the Sino-Japanese War broke out in 1937, the Chinese government moved to Ch'ung-ch'ing [Chongqing], Ssu-ch'uan Province, as did most other institutions. In 1938 Wu-han University moved to Lo-shan County, between Ssu-ch'uan's two largest cities of Ch'ung-ch'ing and Ch'eng-tu [Chengdu], and staff members followed. Su Hsüeh-lin relocated there, too, until 1946 and was among the last of the Wu-han University teachers to return to Wu-han. While in Lo-shan, she wrote creative works such as the patriotic *Biographies of Southern Ming Loyalists* (Nan-Ming chung-lieh chuan) and short stories later collected under the title *The Cicada's Shell* (Ch'an-t'ui chi), reprinted in Taiwan as *Night Words at Yanshan* (Yen-shan yeh-hua). The primitive conditions in Lo-shan and dearth of consumer goods during the war years forced people to improvise and become self-sufficient. During those years, Su Hsüeh-lin grew her own vegetables, made furniture, and repaired and added small improvements to her rented home. Su Hsüeh-lin's elder sister came to live with her from 1931, and Chang Pao-ling also joined Su Hsüeh-lin in Lo-shan for two years after the fall of Shanghai in 1941, once again gaining employment at the same university.

Su Hsüeh-lin's most important undertaking in Lo-shan in terms of scholarly work started in 1943, with her serious analysis of the Chinese classic anthology *Songs of the South*. Concentrating on the poem *T'ien-wen*, which had puzzled scholars and commentators for almost two thousand years, Su Hsüeh-lin followed clues of an earlier scholar who had suggested that the wooden or bamboo slips upon which *T'ien-wen* was written had been strung together in the wrong order when compiled into a book. After poring over much resource material on *Songs of the South* and Chinese mythology to lay down a foundation of knowledge, she wrote the lines of *T'ien-wen* onto cards made from old cardboard boxes and re-arranged their order. Su Hsüeh-lin was able to determine the pattern by which *T'ien-wen* had been structured and set the poem in what she considered to be its correct order.

Her other discovery, which elicited a strong personal response, was the realization that the mythology section of *T'ien-wen* had cognates with the mythologies of both West Asia (the Hebrews, Assyrians, and Egyptians) and the European antiquity of Greece and Rome. She later described the moment of this discovery as a religious experience that put her in a trance for a good ten days. From then onward, Su Hsüeh-lin dedicated her academic efforts to advancing research on *Songs of the South* along these lines.

The Sino-Japanese War ended in 1945, and 1946 found her back in her old home in Wu-han, teaching at Wu-han University. However, civil war moved ever closer to the city and communist-occupied areas expanded with alarming speed. Not wishing to live under communism, Su Hsüeh-lin accepted the offer of the Catholic Church in 1948 to work in Hong Kong as a writer and editor for their Chinese publications *Kung-chiao pao* and *Shih-tai hsüeh-sheng*. After the move, she received letters and visits from friends and colleagues trying to persuade Su Hsüeh-lin to return to China, but the scholar demurred. She was saving up to go to Europe, ostensibly for a pilgrimage to the Vatican but really to search for materials on the mythology of ancient cultures, related to her *Songs of the South* project.

Su Hsüeh-lin spent two years in France (1950–52) and during this period scoured libraries and bookstores for relevant literature, all the while continuing to write for the Catholic publications in Hong Kong to earn living expenses. She and her friend Fan Tchun-pi (*q.v.*) also attended classes at French universities, including a course on Babylonian and Assyrian mythology and one by the French Sinologist Paul Demiéville on Buddhism. In the latter year, Su Hsüeh-lin received a letter from her elder sister, who had moved to Taiwan with her son, telling her that she had been diagnosed with heart disease. Su Hsüeh-lin sailed for Taiwan via Hong Kong, arriving in the summer.

Ensconced in Taiwan, unlike on the mainland where she had been ostracized, the academic was sought after by literary circles and other publications. Su Hsüeh-lin accepted a teaching post at Taiwan Normal College (Taiwan Sheng-li shih-fan hsüeh-yüan; later to become Taiwan Normal University [Sheng-li shih-fan ta-hsüeh]), offering a third-year course on *Songs of the South*. In her research during this period, she made additional discoveries linking the deities in *Songs of the South* to mythological figures in diverse cultures. Su Hsüeh-lin remained at the college for over three years, until 1956, and also republished in Taiwan a selection of her creative works from the 1920s and 1930s.

In 1956, she was appointed head of the Chinese Department of the newly established Ch'eng-kung University in T'ai-nan. Although declining that position, Su Hsüeh-lin accepted a teaching post. She was assigned a spacious home by the university and again invited her elder sister to live with her. They planted trees, grew vegetables, and kept chickens, making the place as comfortable as the one they had left in Ssu-ch'uan. Academically, Su Hsüeh-lin continued research on *Songs of the South* and wrote articles with the assistance of grants from the Organization for the Long-term Development of the Sciences (Ch'ang-ch'i k'o-hsüeh fa-chan hui). This organization had been proposed by Hu Shih, who also oversaw the disbursal of the funds, and Su Hsüeh-lin's work received steady support. In 1968, she redirected her research to also include another Chinese classic, the *Book of Songs* (Shih-ching).

The main thrust of Su Hsüeh-lin's interpretation of *Songs of the South* was that early contacts were evident between China and the West, particularly influencing the Ch'u [Chu] culture, and, more specifically, revealed in *Songs of the South*. She believed that in order to understand the ancient anthology fully, it was imperative to understand and utilize the mythology of the West. To her great disappointment, her innovative work on *Songs of the South* met either apathy or controversy, being looked upon as heresy in the field of Chinese studies. Her work raised little academic debate and received little recognition.

After retiring from Ch'eng-kung University in 1973, Su Hsüeh-lin concentrated on publishing in book form the results of her research, *Ch'ü Yüan and the Nine Songs* (Ch'ü Yüan yü *Chiu-ko*), *The Correct Arrangement of T'ien-wen* (T'ien-wen cheng-chien), and finally *The New Interpretation of Ch'ü Yüan's Li-sao* (Ch'ü Sao hsin-ku) and *Collected Essays on Ch'ü Yüan's Rhapsodies* (Ch'ü fu lun-ts'ung). Apart from *The Correct Arrangement of T'ien-wen*, these books were published with the assistance of academic or government bodies. Su Hsüeh-lin retained deep gratitude toward Hu Shih, whose support had enabled her to carry on her research over an extended period. In addition, in 1981 Su Hsüeh-lin received Taiwan's Sixth Literature and Art Award, offering a cash prize of 100,000 Taiwan yuan, and in 1990 the Cultural Award of the Executive Yuan (Hsing-cheng yüan wen-hua chiang), with a cash prize of 400,000 yuan. She used these funds and the royalties from her books to help relatives on both sides of the Taiwan Strait.

In 1960, Su Hsüeh-lin received news that Chang Pao-ling had died in Peking. She explained in her autobiographical writings that she had not divorced her husband, despite their unhappy marriage, because she was bound by certain religious principles, presumably a reference to her nominal Catholic faith. Su Hsüeh-lin also added that to her mind, a divorced woman was not reputable. Also, because she had enjoyed a certain degree of success in the literary world, Su Hsüeh-lin did not want her name to be sullied. She felt that perhaps because of her unhappy marriage, her capacity for romantic love had been sublimated into the energy that had been devoted to her creative writing and research endeavors. In 1972, Su Hsüeh-lin lost the elder sister who had shared a home with her for more than thirty years. In many ways, her sister had been the person closest to Su Hsüeh-lin throughout her life.

In 1991, students and colleagues from Wu-han and Ch'eng-kung Universities and old friends gathered at a conference held in Su Hsüeh-lin's honor to celebrate the scholar's ninety-fifth birthday, and she was asked to write her memoirs. A journalist who interviewed her in 1995 noted that Su Hsüeh-lin had become extremely hard of hearing, but they conversed on paper. Preparations were in place for writers and academics in Taiwan to celebrate her one hundredth birthday on 24 April 1996, but Su Hsüeh-lin fell and fractured a hip, which necessitated going to hospital. However, she proved to be blessed with longevity and, despite being immobilized by the fall, visited in 1999 her native T'ai-p'ing County in a wheelchair at the age of one hundred and three. During this trip to China, Su Hsüeh-lin died.

Her one regret in old age was that of all the creative and academic work produced over her lifetime, she was still best known for an excerpt from a piece written in the 1920s, published in the literature textbook for junior high school students in pre-1949 China, Taiwan, and elsewhere (perhaps it is still being used). What Su Hsüeh-lin failed to see, however, is that to be included in a junior high school textbook is proof of the vitality of her creative work. Her groundbreaking discoveries in her analysis of *Songs of the South* were probably ahead of her time. One day, new archeaological findings may well substantiate her theories and arouse new interest in them. In the meantime, Su Hsüeh-lin should be remembered as a woman who dared to tread outside traditional scholarship and worked tirelessly to turn out solid research publications in order to prove her theories.

Lily Xiao Hong LEE

Boorman, Howard L., and Richard C. Howard, eds. *Biographical Dictionary of Republican China*, vol. 3. New York: Columbia University Press, 1970, 155–56.
Chung-hua min-kuo tang-tai ming-jen lu, vol. 2. Taipei: Chung-hua shu-chü, 1978, 1111.
Fang Ying. "Lü-i lun." In *Tang-tai Chung-kuo nü-tso-chia lun*, ed. Huang Jen-ying. Shanghai: Kuang-hua shu-chü, 1933, 131–49.
Huang Chung-shen. *Ku-chin wen-hai ch'i-ching k'o: Su Hsüeh-lin chiao-shou*. Taipei: Wen-shih-che ch'u-pan-she, 1999.
Shih Nan [Shi Nan]. "Su Hsüeh-lin yü P'an Yü-liang." *Jen-wu*, no. 9 (1998): 116–24.
Shu I. "Fang pai-sui lao tso-chia Su Hsüeh-lin." *Jen-min jih-pao*, Hai-wai-pan, 11 April 1995.
Su Hsüeh-lin. *Fu-sheng chiu-ssu*. Taipei: San-min shu-chü, 1991.
———. *Su Hsüeh-lin tzu-chuan*. Nan-ching: Chiang-su wen-i ch'u-pan-she, 1996.
Yen Ch'un-te. "Su Hsüeh-lin: Ts'ung *Chi-hsin* tao Ch'ü-fu yen-chiu." *Jen-wu*, no. 12 (1999): 71–80; no. 1 (2000): 108–24.

Su Mei: *see* **Su Hsüeh-lin**

Su Xuelin: *see* **Su Hsüeh-lin**

Sun, E-tu Zen
E-tu Zen Sun [Ren Yidu], b. 1921, in Beijing, is the eldest daughter of Ren Hongjun and Chen Hengzhe (*q.v.*), both famous veterans of the May Fourth Movement of 1919.

E-tu Zen Sun was extremely well educated, receiving a classical Chinese education comprising the Four Books, the Five Classics, and classical poetry, as well as a Western education. The latter was undertaken at a mission school in Beijing—Peihua Girls' School—which she attended from 1927 to 1937. Growing up in Beijing, through her family E-tu Zen Sun knew such famous academics as Hu Shi, Ding Wenjiang, and the linguist Y.R. Chao (Zhao Yuanren).

After the July Seventh Incident in 1937 (known in the West as the Marco Polo Bridge Incident), marking the start of the Sino-Japanese War, E-tu Zen Sun's whole family moved to Shanghai and lived for a time at Lushan in Jiangxi Province. As the Japanese army approached, however, E-tu Zen Sun traveled to Hong Kong via Hankou and Guangzhou to resume studies at St. Stephen's Girls' College. After being accepted into Southwest Union University, she returned to China, traveling by sea to Vietnam and then to Kunming in Yunnan Province. While at Southwest Union University, the young woman joined the Chinese Christian Students' Union and made speeches, attended meetings, and organized publications in support of the student movement. In July 1941, E-tu Zen Sun went to the United States for further study and enrolled in the History Department at Vassar College. After graduating, she went to the Radcliffe Institute and undertook postgraduate work. Her doctoral thesis was on railways in modern China; in 1954 E-tu Zen Sun published a book on a similar topic, *Chinese Railways and British Interests, 1898–1911*. During her years of study in the United States, many restrictions were still in place on women's education. Some of her teachers appear to have been racist as well; one reason given for E-tu Zen Sun's not being permitted to take a course on American social history was that she was Chinese.

Between 1949 and 1950, she assisted John King Fairbank at Harvard University with his *Trade and Diplomacy on the China Coast: The Opening of the Treaty Ports, 1842–1854* (1953) and *China's Response to the West*. She contributed to *The Cambridge History of China* (volume 13) with an article on academic community groups during the Republican period, and also assisted Owen Lattimore at the Johns Hopkins University to record interviews with people from Inner Mongolia between 1950 and 1952. E-tu Zen Sun took up her first teaching post at Goucher College. Since the latter year, she has taught at Pennsylvania State University, where in 1970 E-tu Zen Sun initiated the establishment of the School of East Asian Studies.

Her husband, Shiou-chuan Sun [Sun Shouquan], obtained his doctorate from the Massachusetts Institute of Technology. They have two sons, and E-tu Zen Sun took leave from her teaching position between 1956 and 1964 to look after her family. She continued research work at home, however, through grants from the American Council of Learned Societies and the Radcliffe Institute. Her best-known work is possibly *Ch'ing Administrative Terms*. As a specialist in the socioeconomic history of modern China, however, E-tu Zen Sun has published on a variety of topics, including the Chinese mining industry and labor, the silk trade, and technology.

CHENG Li-jung
(Translated by Emily Wright)

Sun, E-tu Zen. *Selected Essays in Chinese Economic History*. Hong Kong: Institute of Advanced Chinese Studies and Research, New Asia College, 1981.
———, trans. and ed. *Ch'ing Administrative Terms: A Translation of the Terminology of the Six Boards with Explanatory Notes*. Cambridge, Mass.: Harvard University Press, 1961.
Sun, E-tu Zen, and John De Francis. *Chinese Social History: Translations of Selected Studies*. Washington: American Council of Learned Societies, 1956.
Teng Ssu-yu. *China's Response to the West: A Documentary Survey, 1839–1923* [by] Ssu-yu Teng [and] John K. Fairbank, with E-tu Zen Sun, Chaoying Fang, and others. Cambridge: Harvard University Press, 1954.

Zhang Pengyuan et al. *Ren Yidu xiansheng fangwen jilu zhilu* [title also given as *The Reminiscences of Prof. E-tu Zen Sun*]. Taipei: Zhongyang yanjiuyuanbu jindaishi yanjiusuo, 1993.

Sun Quanxiang: *see* **Fu Quanxiang**

Sun Shamin: *see* **Chen Shaomin**

Sun Weishi

Sun Weishi, 1921–1968, of Nanxi County, Sichuan Province, was the first woman director of modern spoken drama (*huaju*) in the PRC.

Educated in the Soviet Union in the Stanislavsky system (generally known as the system), she successfully transplanted the acting methodology onto the modern Chinese stage. Sun Weishi was instrumental in building up the China Youth Art Theater (Zhongguo qingnian yishu juyuan), the first national theater in the PRC, and the Central Experimental Theater (Zhongyang shiyan huajuyuan).

Sun Weishi's father, Sun Bingwen (d. 1927), was a close friend of Zhu De (1886–1976) and Zhou Enlai (1898–1976). Upon return from the Soviet Union in 1924, her father held a key position at the famous Whampoa Military Academy but was executed by the KMT in April 1927, when the CCP-KMT united front disintegrated. Sun Weishi's mother, Ren Rui, then took her children into exile, raising them alone under difficult circumstances while still participating in CCP underground work. Ren Rui had four children, two boys and two girls.

Sun Weishi's brother Sun Yang was twelve years old when he was imprisoned with his father but was released and later served for many years as Zhu De's personal assistant. Sun Yang eventually became deputy party secretary and vice-president of the People's University (Renmin daxue). He was persecuted to death during the Cultural Revolution. Her other brother, Sun Mingshi, died in combat in the civil war between the CCP and KMT. Her sister, Sun Xinshi, taught in the Foreign Languages Department at Peking University and, in 1975, after the death of Sun Weishi, married her brother-in-law Jin Shan when he was released from prison.

Legend has it that at the age of sixteen, in 1937, Sun Weishi went to the Eighth Route Army Liaison Office in Wuhan seeking permission to go to the CCP enclave in Yan'an but was refused, because of her youth. Her father's old friend Zhou Enlai, who was childless, came upon her crying outside the Liaison Office and adopted her as his own daughter. Thus, with the help of Zhou Enlai, in 1938 Sun Weishi finally fulfilled her dream of going to Yan'an. She joined the CCP at the age of seventeen and together with her mother attended the Yan'an Anti-Japanese Military and Political University. Sun Weishi also played a minor role in the play *Reunion* (Tuanyuan), written by Sha Kefu and directed by Zuo Ming. In summer 1939, Sun Weishi accompanied Zhou Enlai to the Soviet Union, where he underwent medical treatment; she worked as his personal assistant and learned Russian in her spare time. Sun Weishi remained in Moscow to pursue her directing and acting studies when Zhou Enlai returned to China in 1940. She graduated from Moscow Oriental University and Moscow Drama School with flying colors.

Returning to China in September 1946, Sun Weishi first participated in the land reform movement in the CCP liberated areas in Shanxi Province. She then joined the performing troupe of United University (Lianda wengongtuan) and toured in Shaanxi, Shanxi, and Hebei Provinces. In December 1949, Sun Weishi was head of the interpreting team for Mao Zedong (1893–1976) during his state visit to the Soviet Union.

In spring 1950, Liao Chengzhi, then general secretary of the Central Committee of the Communist Youth League and founding president of China Youth Art Theater, invited Sun Weishi to become its artistic director. She enthusiastically embraced the opportunity to build the first professional theater of spoken drama in the new nation. The first play Sun Weishi directed, *How Steel Is Made* (Kak zakalyalas' stal; translated into Chinese as Gangtie shi zenyang lianchengde), was based on the novel of the same title by the Soviet writer Ostrovsky. This book, based on the author's own experience, told of a devoted revolutionary named Pavel Korchaghin who had been crippled and paralyzed in the revolutionary war but overcame unimaginable difficulties to become a successful writer. Premiered in September, the play was regarded as the first piece of PRC spoken drama. Thanks to the popularity of the novel and the stage production by Sun Weishi, Pavel became a household name in the early 1950s and a role model for many young people of the time.

Although Stanislavsky had been introduced to the Chinese stage in the 1930s, his system had not yet been seriously studied or practiced. Combining it with the realist tradition of modern Chinese spoken drama, Sun Weishi created a way of directing that utilized the creativity of acting and stage design crews. After researching the cultural and historical conditions that had produced the original novel, she wrote backstories, biographical (fictionalized) sketches of the characters, including their motives, personalities, and past experience. The second step entailed script reading and preliminary rehearsals with makeshift props to help the actors achieve a balance between Stanislavsky's "inner experiencing of the role" (*perezhivanitye*; translated into Chinese as *neixin tiyan*) and physical and vocal expression most appropriate to the characters. The last step was the dress rehearsal in which the acting crew familiarized themselves with the stage setting to achieve the best dramatic effects.

The success of Sun Weishi's play became legendary: during one production in Beijing, Jin Shan (who played the role of Pavel) was delayed on his way from Tianjin, where he had been invited to give a lecture on Pavel's life and his own experience in recreating him on stage. The audience in Beijing declined the theater's offer of a ticket refund and waited uncomplainingly for two hours, watching a Jin Shan film until the actor himself arrived and the play began at 10:00 P.M. Even those who missed the last bus home because the performance ended at 1:00 A.M. were said to have had no regrets at having to walk home. The creation of Pavel also inspired a romance in real life when Sun Weishi and Jin Shan fell in love. They were not able to marry, however, until Jin Shan divorced Zhang Ruifang, a famous actress who played the lover of the young Pavel.

In 1952, Sun Weishi produced the most successful foreign classic ever mounted on the PRC stage. *Qinchai dachen*, adapted from Gogol's *The Inspector-General*, featured a combined cast from the China Youth Art Theater and the Beijing People's Art Theater (Beijing renmin yishu juyuan). The same year, she directed another Soviet play, *Little Rabbit* (Xiao baitu), in celebration of the founding of the Children's Art Theater attached to the China Youth Art Theater. To familiarize herself with children, she took child actors to the zoo where they observed animals and to the forest to experience nature. The production was warmly received and in 1953 was made into a film of the same title by the Beijing Film Studio (Beijing dianying zhipianchang). It remains one of the earliest and best children's plays in the PRC.

In 1954, the fiftieth anniversary of Anton Chekhov's death, Sun Weishi co-directed his *Uncle Vanya* (Wanniya jiujiu) in collaboration with a Soviet expert. The distinguished cast of Jin Shan, Wu Xue, Ji Shuping, and Lu Xi ensured the performance was an instant success and another classic production of Chinese spoken drama and the China Youth Art Theater was put on the international map. From that year to 1956, Sun Weishi continued to work in the China Youth Art Theater as well as being principal instructor of directors with the China Central Drama College (Zhongyang xiju xueyuan), in which capacity she helped produce the leading drama directors of the future.

In 1956, Sun Weishi became artistic director and vice-president of the new China Central Experimental Theater (Zhongyang shiyan huaju yuan); Ouyang Yuqian, a formally trained operatic actor and playwright of spoken drama in his own right, was president. Inspired by such excellent performances in traditional operatic theater as the older *kunqu* opera genre version of *Fifteen Strings of Cash* (Shiwu guan), Sun Weishi attempted to develop a new brand of socialist art by combining Stanislavsky's system with Chinese operatic traditions. *Joys and Sorrows* (Tonggan gonghu) centered on a romantic triangle between a CCP official and two women. The drama unfolds when the protagonist realizes he is more attracted to his ex-wife from an arranged marriage in the countryside, once divorced because she was "ignorant and unlovely," than to his educated wife, with whom he fell in love and married after realizing they had shared similar experiences during the revolutionary war. In the course of the play, the protagonist is able to work things out with his wife and maintain a deep friendship with his ex-wife, who has grown into a new socialist woman and is a leader of the collective movement in rural China. Premiered in July, the play was warmly received for creating flesh and blood characters, presenting CCP officials who were as prone to human weakness as other people. However, the play's probing look into the private life of a CCP leader made it an easy target during the Anti-Rightist Movement in 1957.

Peach Flower Fan (Taohua shan), the second play Sun Weishi produced for the China Central Experimental Theater, was a period play in which she developed a Chinese style through introducing elements of operatic theater and folk dance. In further experiments, Sun Weishi directed in 1957 *Portrait of One Hundred Clowns* (Bai chou tu), which was comic, even farcical, so as to appeal to a broader audience in spite of its shallow theme of promoting the Anti-Rightist Movement. In her 1961 production of *The Hatred of Black Slaves* (Heinu hen), adapted from Harriet Beecher Stowe's *Uncle Tom's Cabin*, Sun Weishi experimented with performance techniques from Chinese operatic theater (that had inspired Brecht's concept of "alienation effects") in an effort to break down what was known as the "fourth wall." She experimented with expanding the dramatic action beyond the confines of the stage to, for example, the orchestra pit.

The last play Sun Weishi ever produced was *The Rising Sun* (Chusheng de taiyang), in collaboration with Jin Shan. In response to Zhou Enlai's directive to produce a play portraying the heroic deeds of oil workers in the northeast, Sun Weishi and Jin Shan moved to the Daqing oilfields where for several years they worked side by side with the oil workers and their spouses. The play focused on the contribution spouses made, from agricultural production to the construction of the oilfield. Most ingeniously, the cast was made up entirely of locals. The play was warmly received in Daqing, Beijing, and Shandong Province in particular. Encouraged by the play's success, the couple returned to Daqing to create more plays based on oil workers.

However, they were recalled to Beijing at the beginning of the Cultural Revolution. Jin Shan was imprisoned for seven years; he did not receive the heart-breaking news of Sun Weishi's untimely death in 1968, after more than seven months' imprisonment and torture, until his release in 1975. She had been arrested on 1 March and died in prison on 14 October. When *The Rising Sun* re-staged in the post-Mao period, the piece became part of the political theater that critiqued the Gang of Four, held responsible for persecuting Sun Weishi. The solemn occasion of its performance celebrated the artistic career of a woman who helped shape the direction and development of modern Chinese spoken drama.

Xiaomei CHEN

Du Gao. "Sun Weishi." In *Zhongguo da baike quan shu, xiju juan*. Beijing: Zhongguo da baike quan shu chubanshe, 1989, 358–59.
Sun Bin. "Wode guma Sun Weishi." *Zhuanji wenxue*, 64, no. 5 (1994): 32–39.
Xian Jihua and Zhao Yunsheng. *Huaju huangdi Jin Shan*. Beijing: Zhongguo wenlian shubanshe, 1987.
Zhongguo yishujia cidian, vol. 5. Changsha: Hunan renmin chubanshe, 1985, 18–19.
Zuo Lai and Liang Huaqun. "Sun Weishi zhuanlüe." In *Zhongguo huaju yishujia zhuanlüe*, eds. Zhongguo yishu yanjiu yuan huaju yanjiusuo. Beijing: Wenhua yishu chubanshe, 1986, 71–104.

Sun Yat-sen, Madame: *see* **Song Qingling**

Sun Yumei: *see* **Chen Shaomin**

Sun Zhaoxiu: *see* **Chen Shaomin**

Sung Ai-ling: *see* **Soong Ailing**

Sung Ch'ing-ling: *see* **Song Qingling**

Sung Mei-ling: *see* **Soong Mayling**

Suxin: *see* **Ling Shuhua**

T

Tai Ai-lien: *see* **Dai Ailian**

Tan, Amy

Amy Ruth Tan, b. 1952, in Oakland, California, in the U.S., and given the Chinese name An-mei Tan, is a writer. Of Chinese descent, she describes herself as "an American writer—my sensibilities, my obsessions are American." As did Maxine Hong Kingston (*q.v.*), who burst onto the bestseller lists a decade before her, Amy Tan has explored to great effect the cultural and personal conflicts she experienced growing up in America as an Asian American.

Her father, John Yueh-han Tan (d. 1967), was from Guangzhou but had trained in Beijing as an electrical engineer. He migrated to the United States in 1947 and became a Baptist minister "by avocation"; it is from him that Amy Tan believes she inherited her storytelling ability. Her mother was from a wealthy Shanghai family and endured an arranged marriage before fleeing China in 1949. She had trained as a nurse and left behind not only an abusive husband but also three daughters. The details of Amy Tan's mother's origins remained a mystery until shortly before she died in 2000; her mother by then had Alzheimer's disease. She was born Li Bingzi in 1916; after her own mother (Amy's grandmother) had committed suicide in 1925, Li Bingzi was adopted by a family named Tu, who gave her the name Tu Lian Zen. However, she was known as Tu Ching at school and throughout her first marriage. Then, after marrying John Tan, she settled on Daisy (Tu) Ching Tan, the name by which her American-born children knew her. Amy was her parents' second child and only girl. The Tan family moved several times during her childhood, and Amy grew up in Fresno, Oakland, Berkeley, and the San Francisco Bay Area, frequently finding herself the only Chinese girl in her school. Chinese (Mandarin) was spoken at home, but Amy refused to speak it any longer at about the age of five, when she started school.

With her habitual wry humor, Amy Tan has said that her parents expected a good deal of her: ideally, she would be a neurosurgeon by trade and a concert pianist in her spare time. Her family was not literary and her migrant parents did not speak English well, but they hoped their children would excel in their adopted country. When Amy Tan was fifteen, however, her father and slightly older brother died in quick succession, both from brain tumors. Her mother immediately took her daughter and the younger brother to Europe. Amy completed high school in Montreux, Switzerland, in 1969, and then went to several different colleges after returning to America. From Linfield College in Oregon, she went to San Jose City College, earning a B.A. in English and Linguistics (1973), and then an M.A. in Linguistics (1974) at San Jose State University. Amy Tan also undertook postgraduate work at the University of California at Santa Cruz and Berkeley between 1974 and 1976.

Contrary to her parents' expectations, Amy did not embark on an academic or professional career but worked as a language development consultant for children with developmental disabilities (1976–81) and as a reporter (1981–83). Amy Tan then became a free-lance business writer and was so successful that she was soon working up to ninety hours per week. She did not start writing fiction until the age of thirty-three, and only then as therapy to cure herself of being a workaholic. Amy Tan is best known for her novels in which she writes about human connections: ethnicity, family history, and the articulation of female voices. Her main themes are mother-daughter relationships and the contrast between the Chinese past and the American present.

Amy Tan traveled in China with her mother in 1987, recalling this as a turning point in her understanding of herself as well as her mother and her heritage. Amy met her three half-sisters and discovered what she describes as a spiritual sense of geography, a sense of finally belonging to a period of history to a degree that she had never felt with American history. Her first novel, *The Joy Luck Club* (1989), grew from a series of short stories written during a writers' workshop. The material describes the journey of four young American-born Chinese women as they come to an understanding and acceptance of their "embarrassing" migrant mothers and the culture they brought with them from China. The novel was an immediate success, remaining on *The New York Times* hard-cover bestseller list for thirty-four weeks, and nominated for the National Book Critics Circle Award and a *Los Angeles Times* Book Award. The novel was made into a film, directed by Wayne Wang, for which Amy Tan co-wrote the screenplay with Ron Bass.

Amy Tan wrote her second novel, *The Kitchen God's Wife* (1991), only after her mother begged her to write her story down. Amy's grandmother, who as a young woman had been raped, forced to become a concubine, and died tragically, also figures in the story. Like its predecessor, the book was very successful, making the number one bestseller spot on *The New York Times* hard cover list and appearing on bestseller lists in Canada, Europe, and Australia.

In her third novel, *The Hundred Secret Senses* (1995), Amy Tan turns away from the mother-daughter relationship, creating for her sophisticated American-born Chinese heroine a subversive half-sister who has "yin eyes." This young woman from mainland China, whose hilariously fractured English Tan clearly delights in rendering, is able with her "yin eyes" to see dead people who dwell in the "World of Yin." This book deals with love, and the supernatural, and takes some liberties with historical time frames as the heroine reclaims her Chinese mainland heritage. It reached *The New York Times* hard-cover bestseller list but was not so well received, certainly by critics, as her previous two novels.

The Bonesetter's Daughter, Amy Tan's fourth novel, published in early 2001, returns to the mother-daughter theme and clearly has autobiographical overtones. She had been working on this novel for five years but rewrote it immediately after the death of her mother. She did this, she said, "remembering what scared me: the ghost, the threats, the curse. I wrote of wrong birth dates, secret marriages, the changing place one has in a family, the names that were nearly forgotten."

Amy Tan has written two children's books—*The Moon Lady* (1992) and *The Chi-*

nese Siamese Cats (1994), both illustrated by Gretchen Schields—and her stories have appeared in various anthologies and magazines. Her work has been translated into more than twenty languages and is on various high school and college reading lists.

Certain Asian American critics have been vitriolic in their criticism of Amy Tan. Describing what she calls the "Amy Tan phenomenon," Sau-ling Cynthia Wong situates Tan's writing in the "quasi-ethnographic, Orientalist discourse." Sau-ling Wong takes the writer to task for her "profound ignorance of the Chinese kinship system," lists various erroneous details in Tan's work dealing with things Chinese, and says she has "failed as a cultural guide." Wong coins the term the "sugar sisterhood" to describe the (White) "nonintellectual consumer of Orientalism [who] can find much in *The Joy Luck Club* and *The Kitchen God's Wife* to satisfy her curiosity about China and Chinatown." This sugar sisterhood comprising Tan's vast army of readers is, according to Sau-ling Wong, mainly White middle-class women who find her work comforting in its "reproduction of stereotypical images." Male critics such as Frank Chin also condemn Amy Tan and Maxine Hong Kingston as "fakes" and "White racists." According to them, women lack the traditionally masculine qualities of originality, daring, physical courage, and creativity, and the "mere fact that four of the five American-born Chinese American writers are women reinforces this [womanly, effeminate] stereotype" of the Asian, to the clear detriment of the less popular male writers. Amy Tan dismisses these criticisms, saying that her works are intended neither to be scholarly texts and/or tourist guides nor "cultural lesson plans." She does not want her work to be seen as "representative" of Chinese American or Asian American experiences and has never claimed to be an expert on China. She writes to discover what is true for her alone.

In 1974, Amy Tan married Louis DeMattei, now a tax lawyer, whom she met while at college in Oregon. Amy has chosen not to have children, she once said, so as not to repeat her mother's mistakes. Amy Tan and her husband live in San Francisco and New York, sharing their lives with their Yorkshire terriers and at least one cat. She takes her two little dogs with her for company and as mini-guard dogs; when traveling alone in the United States, Amy carries them in a large holdall. For some years, she has been a member (a "Rockette") of the Rock Bottom Remainders, a "vintage garage" rock band formed by several well-known writers. Other members include Stephen King, Robert Fulghum, Dave Barry, Ridley Pearson, and Matt Groening.

Sue WILES

"Amy Tan. Best-Selling Novelist." The Hall of Arts, American Academy of Achievement. Interview, 28 June 1996, at <http://www.achievement.org>.

Ho, Wendy. *In Her Mother's House: The Politics of Asian American Mother-Daughter Writing.* Walnut Creek: AltaMira Press, 1999.

"An Interview with Amy Tan." *Mosaic, Penn's Asian American Literary Magazine*, University . of Pennsylvania, at <http://dolphin.upenn.edu/~mosaic/fall94>.

"North Suburban Library Foundation Presents: Amy Tan," at <http://www.nslsilus.org/Foundation/Archive/981itcirc/amy.html>.

Powell, Sian. "Unravelling Amy." *The Weekend Australian*, 10–11 March 2001, R4–5.

"The Salon Interview: Amy Tan. The Spirit Within." *Salon, an Electronic Magazine*, at <http://www.salon.com/12nov1995/feature/tan.html>.

Tan, Amy. "Ghosts Writing." *The Sydney Morning Herald*, "Spectrum," 10 March 2001, 6–7 (from *The New York Times*).

Wong, Sau-ling Cynthia. "'Sugar Sisterhood': Situating the Amy Tan Phenomenon." In *The Ethnic Canon: Histories, Institutions, and Interventions*, ed. David Palumbo-Liu. Minneapolis/London: University of Minnesota Press, 1995, 174–205.

Tan An-mei: *see* **Tan, Amy**

Tang Qunying

Tang Qunying, 1871–1937, original name Gongyi, *hao* Xi Tao, a native of Hengshan, Hunan Province, was one of China's foremost female political activists in the early twentieth century. She was an active member of the anti-Qing Tongmenghui and established and headed a variety of women's rights groups, particularly those struggling for women's suffrage and gender equality in political rights and educational opportunities. Tang Qunying was one of the most important and best-known women activists in modern Chinese history. She also earned the reputation of being a radical among women's rights activists of her time.

Tang Qunying was born in a village just north of Hengshan and was the third of seven children: three sons and four daughters. Her father, Tang Xingzhao, retired from the Qing army to devote himself to educating his children. From him, Tang Qunying received a traditional education in the Confucian classics, poetry, and history. She learned to write the formal eight-legged essay as well as various forms of poetry. Her exceptional talent for poetry composition won respect throughout her lifetime. In all, Tang Qunying was an intelligent woman and an exceptional student. From her classical base, she developed an interest in the more radical intellectual trends of the time, including Kang Youwei's *Datongshu*.

After the death of her father in 1891, Tang Qunying complied with her mother's instructions and married Zeng Zhuangang, a cousin of the famous Qing official Zeng Guofan. The marriage was brief as her husband died within two years; the only child of the marriage also died. Breaking with the tradition that widows should serve their husbands' parents, Tang Qunying returned to her natal home to join her mother. During these years, Tang Qunying developed a close friendship with other politically minded women, including Qiu Jin (see *Biographical Dictionary of Chinese Women: The Qing Period*) and Ge Jianhao (*q.v.*), the mother of Cai Chang (*q.v.*). They corresponded, visited, and exchanged books, poems, and ideas on politics and China's place in the world. In 1904 Tang Qunying and Qiu Jin resolved to go to Japan for further study and develop the skills that would enable them to strengthen the nation.

In the autumn, Tang Qunying arrived in Japan, and initially as a self-funded student at Aoyama Vocational Women's School (Aoyama Jissen Jogakkō), along with Qiu Jin. After two years study, Tang Qunying earned sufficiently high grades to enter the Higher Normal School for Girls (Jokōtō jogakkō shihanka) as a scholarship student funded by the Hunan Provincial Education Department. Here, she formed close friendships with three other Hunanese women: Zhang Hanying (see *Biographical Dictionary of Chinese Women: The Qing Period*), He Bulan, and Liu Yalan. These relationships provided the support of many of Tang Qunying's later political groups that fought for gender equality.

Typical of the women who ventured to Japan endeavoring to discover methods to modernize China's social and political system, Tang Qunying soon joined the radical anti-Qing revolutionaries based in Tokyo, including such prominent figures as Sun Yat-sen, Liu Daoyi, and Huang Xing. Her direct participation in anti-Qing politics began in 1905 when Tang Qunying joined the Awaken China Society (Hua xing hui) with the support of Zhao Hengti from her hometown. Tang Qunying quickly gained prominence in the society as a leader of women's activities. In August, the Awaken China Society and the China Awakening Society (Xing Zhong hui) amalgamated to form the Tongmenghui. The Tongmenghui, led by Sun Yat-sen, was to become the major anti-Qing group in the years leading to the collapse of the Qing dynasty in 1911. Tang Qunying was the first woman to sign up as a member of the new political party. He Xiangning and Qiu Jin followed her lead; because Tang Qunying was the eldest of the three, she became known to her revolutionary comrades as Big Sister Tang. As part of her anti-Qing political activities, she contributed articles to the Tongmenghui's organ *Minbao*, translated articles for the revolutionary journal *Dong ting bo*, and, in 1906, founded the Association for Women Studying in Japan (LiuRi nüxuesheng hui), initially assuming the office of secretary and then became president.

In 1907, when news of Qiu Jin's failed uprising and subsequent execution reached Tokyo, in grief Tang Qunying resolved to return to China to carry on the struggle. As soon as she had graduated at the end of the year, Tang Qunying carried back to China messages from the Tokyo base of the Tongmenghui from Sun Yat-sen's close ally Chen Shuren. Once in Hunan, Tang Qunying maintained secret contact with Chen Shuren and engaged in underground propaganda work for the Tongmenghui. The disparate and intermittent nature of these underground tasks did not engage her energies sufficiently, so Tang Qunying returned to Japan to study music and continue her republican activism. She encouraged interest in the anti-Qing cause among the many Chinese students at various universities and colleges in Japan at the time, particularly among the women students. After the suppression of the Guangzhou Uprising in April 1911, Tang Qunying began publishing the periodical *Journal of Women Students Studying in Japan* (LiuRi nüxuesheng zazhi), which included revolutionary news and comment on events in China as well as items advocating women's rights. She saw republicanism and women's rights as inextricably intertwined, and her activities in China and Japan during these years demonstrated those twin commitments.

In the summer of 1911, Tang Qunying returned to China and moved between Shanghai, Hunan, and Hubei, organizing a military organization called the Women's Northern Attack Brigade (Nüzi beifa dui). This group was formed with the assistance of He Bulan and Liu Yalan, two of the Hunanese women Tang Qunying had befriended during her student days during her first stint in Japan. The army became famous as a "women's army" for its participation in the Wuchang Uprising when

Tang Qunying led the women in battle to take over Nanjing. In November, her military activity expanded to include "troop support," when she formed the Women's Reinforcement Association (Nüzi houyuan hui) in Shanghai with Zhang Hanying, whom Tang Qunying had known in Japan. Zhang also had become a prominent activist. This group coordinated a host of other women's organizations and arranged for the provision of medical and liaison support for the republican troops still suppressing Qing resistance. Of considerable importance in the months after the establishment of the republic was their work in raising funds to pay troops' wages. For Tang Qunying and other radical women's rights advocates, it was crucial that women demonstrate their commitment to full participation in all aspects of the military and political transformation of China.

With the collapse of republican forces in October 1911, Tang Qunying's political activism developed along fresh lines. As an advocate of democracy from her early days in the Tongmenghui, she took for granted the notion that women would have equal voting and political rights with men in the new China. However, soon after the establishment of the Republic, there was clearly considerable opposition to female suffrage from conservatives from whom the Tongmenghui required cooperation. Ensuring that women were given equal treatment in the political arena thus became the focus of Tang Qunying's activities. Indignantly, she declared: "During the armed uprisings women assumed responsibilities as secret agents, organized bombing squads, and undertook a whole host of dangerous tasks—risking both their lives and their properties—just like the men. How is it that now the revolution has been achieved women's interests are not taken into account!"

Not content to sit idle while the fruits of the revolution were denied to women, Tang Qunying began an intensive and widely publicized campaign to ensure that gender equality was enshrined in the Constitution of the new Republic. The interim Parliament was due to debate a constitution in March 1912 under the guidance of the provisional president Sun Yat-sen, and in preparation for this debate Tang Qunying called to Nanjing representatives from a host of women's groups from around the nation to form a national lobby. As a result, the Alliance for Women's Participation in Politics (Nüzi canzheng tongmenghui) formed on 20 February, heralding the beginning of what was to be the first, albeit brief, wave of suffrage activism on a national level in China. The Alliance comprised the Women's Suffrage Comrades' Society (Nüzi canzheng tongzhi hui), the Women's Reinforcement Association (Nüzi houyuan hui), the Hunan Women's Citizens' Association (Hunan nüguomin hui), the Women's Society for the Esteem of Military Affairs (Nüzi shang wu hui), and the Women's Revolutionary Alliance (Nüzi tongmenghui). It brought together under Tang Qunying's leadership an impressive array of women activists, including Wang Changguo, Zhang Hanying, Cai Hui, Wu Mulan (*q.v.*), and He Xiangning (*q.v.*). Their manifesto promulgated at a major meeting convened in Nanjing on 8 April maintained as key tenets gender equality and women's suffrage.

During February and March, Tang Qunying and the various women's groups supporting her stance publicly promoted the notion that the Constitution should unambiguously include a statement guaranteeing the equality of men and women in all aspects of political life. A republic is not a republic, they declared, unless both men and women participate equally. To the dismay of the women's suffrage activists, the provisional Constitution promulgated on 11 March failed to include stipulations regarding equality of the sexes. In protest, Tang Qunying led a group of more than twenty women into the Parliament on 19 March, the women moving from the public gallery into the chambers to sit among the parliamentarians. When advised by the president of the Parliament, Lin Sen, to wait until the formal Parliament convened later in the year before requesting an amendment to the national Constitution, the women were furious and let fly a hail of abuse. The following day they returned to press their case but found their path into the Parliament blocked by security guards. For five hours, Tang Qunying and her supporters staged a noisy demonstration protesting Lin Sen's refusal to speak to them. During the fracas, the women smashed the windows of the parliamentary building, a security guard was kicked to the ground, and minor injuries were sustained on both sides. These radical actions were in direct imitation of the British suffragettes who had conducted extensive window-smashing raids in central London only days before.

Alternating between physical force and persuasion, on 21 March the women sent a delegation to Sun Yat-sen hoping he would intervene on their behalf. While he expressed support for the principle of gender equality, his influence on the Parliament was minimal and no change was effected. By 30 March, Tang Qunying and her militant group lost all patience. They stormed the parliamentary chambers again, raging noisily at the men housed inside. Blows were exchanged, and threats of further violence were made before security guards subdued the women, dragging them from the chambers. In the face of such consistent resistance, Tang Qunying's activists retired to consider less militant tactics.

At the April inaugural meeting of the Alliance for Women's Participation in Politics, an eleven-point manifesto was sent by telegram around the nation to generate support and interest for the cause of women's suffrage. When the electoral laws were being promulgated in July, however, they explicitly stated that "men" had the right to vote and stand for election. Tang Qunying declared this to be a "great crime," and she and her supporters wrote a bill, called the "Women's Suffrage Law," to put before Parliament. This too was ignored. When the electoral laws were announced on 10 August 1912, Tang Qunying led a group of more than sixty women past the security guards into the parliamentary chambers to register their disgust. Tang Qunying made three legal requests to the Parliament regarding gender equality during the course of the year, the final one on 6 November, when only a handful of votes were cast in favor of her amendments.

Compounding these disastrous laws was the dismantling of the support of Tang Qunying's own political party for the principle of gender equality. The Tongmenghui had adhered to the principle since its inception but, with the increasing need for a formal merger with more conservative parties taking shape in the formation of the Nationalist Party (KMT), support for this founding principle weakened. At a meeting of the Tongmenghui on 14 July, Tang Qunying and other female members had questioned their male comrades about the likely consequences on the status of women in

the impending merger. When it became clear that gender equality was indeed a nego-
tiable point to the men, Tang Qunying and her supporters declared in frustration that
the women of the Tongmenghui opposed the amalgamation plans. As only a minority
within the alliance, however, their opposition carried little weight.

On 25 August, the KMT held its inaugural conference in Beijing, binding conservatives and radicals together in the hope of creating a viable broad-based democratic
party. When gender equality was excluded from the new party Constitution, the women
delegates from the Tongmenghui expressed strong objections. At the height of this
intensely emotional debate, Tang Qunying slapped the faces of both Song Jiaoren and
Lin Sen because of their betrayal. The entire auditorium was stunned by the vehe-
mence of her actions. Nonetheless, the Constitution excluding the principle of gender
equality was passed.

On 2 September, Sun Yat-sen wrote to Tang Qunying expressing his support for
women's suffrage but advising her that the goal was a long-term one. He exhorted her
to engage in activities that would prepare women for their eventual gaining of the
right to political participation. Promoting women's education and broad social awareness, he argued, would facilitate women's preparedness for suffrage. Few options
were open to Tang Qunying and her activist friends, and, in any case, they had never
ceased being involved in these sorts of "preparatory" activities.

During that year, Tang Qunying maintained her publishing and educational commitments on behalf of China's women, and these became her sole focus once the
KMT effectively barred women from equal political participation. She helped establish in Beijing two newspapers: *East Asia Times* (Yadong cong bao) and *Women's
Vernacular Chronicle* (Nüzi baihua xunbao, later Nüzi baihua bao). Tang Qunying
also established the Central Girls' School (Zhongyang nüxuexiao) and the Girls Craft
Factory (Nüzi gongyi chang). Returning to Changsha with Zhang Hanying in December, Tang Qunying continued her activism on the issue of suffrage through the
Hunan branch of the Alliance for Women's Participation in Politics of which she was
also president. From here the first Hunanese women's newspaper—*Women's Rights
Daily* (Nüquan ribao)—was published, calling for women to leave the confines of the
family, enter the public realm, and overthrow feudal customs. Tang Qunying also
established the Girls' Art School (Nüzi meishu xuexiao) and the Girl's Occupational
School (Nüzi zhiye xuexiao) and strove in earnest to "awaken Hunan's women."

However, after returning to Hunan, further setbacks to Tang Qunying's goal of
reforming China by winning concessions for Chinese women were only months away.
In March 1913, the newly appointed president, Yuan Shikai, began suppressing potential opponents to his rule and curtailing their activities. A warrant was issued for
Tang Qunying's arrest, and her newspapers in Hunan and Beijing were closed. The
Alliance for Women's Participation in Politics was ordered disbanded, and Tang
Qunying was forced to flee Changsha, seeking refuge in her home village with her
elderly mother. Over the following few years, Tang Qunying largely focused on local
affairs and concentrated on organizing schooling for local girls. In 1918 her mother
died, and Tang Qunying observed the three-year mourning period.

In 1924, at the height of the New Culture Movement, Tang Qunying returned to

Changsha, where she and Wang Changguo established a new suffrage organization called Hunan Women's Suffrage Circle (Hunan nüjie canzheng lianhehui) and made preparations for the Women's Political and Legal University (Nüzi zhengfa daxue). Despite the acknowledgement of the equal legal status of women in Hunan's provincial Constitution, which had come into effect in January 1922, Tang Qunying clearly felt the need to continue asserting the importance of gender equality and ensure that women were well placed to make full use of their political rights. It is she who must be given most of the credit for Hunan's achievements with regard to its provincial Constitution because her individual efforts in lobbying for suffrage and women's rights in Hunan had been preeminent since before the inception of the Republic in 1911.

Tang Qunying's prominence as a senior member of the KMT is acknowledged by the recognition the party granted to her. In 1928 she was invited to sit on its Party History Committee but declined. In spring 1935, Tang Qunying returned to Nanjing to visit friends and while there came across her old sparring partner Lin Sen, now KMT government chairman. He invited Tang Qunying to assume the position of national advisor to the KMT but, preferring to work in Hunan, she soon returned to her home village.

Tang Qunying died at the age of sixty-five in spring 1937 in her hometown, apparently having lost none of the strength of her resolve.

Louise EDWARDS

Funü cidian. Beijing: Qiushi chubanshe, 1990, 94.

Gao Kuixiang and Shen Jianguo, eds. *Zhonghua gujin nüjie pu.* Beijing: Zhonghua shehui chubanshe, 1991.

Jiang Ping and Tang Cunzheng. *Tang Qunying pingzhuan.* Changsha: Hunan chubanshe, 1995.

Lü Meiyi and Zheng Yongfu. *Zhongguo funü yundong (1840–1921)*: Zhengzhou: Henan renmin chubanshe, 1990.

Sheng Shusen, Tan Changchun, and Tao Zhisun. "Zhongguo nüquan yundong de xianqu, Tang Qunying." *Renwu,* no. 4 (1992): 82–90.

Xu Huiqi. "Tang Qunying yu 'Nüzi canzheng tongmenghui.'" *Guizhou shehui kexue,* no. 4 (1981): 30–37.

Yingwen *Zhongguo funü,* ed. *Gujin zhuming funü renwu,* vol. 2. Shijiazhuang: Hebei renmin chubanshe, 1986, 443–46.

Tang Tingting: *see* **Kingston, Maxine Hong**

Tang Tiyin

Tang Tiyin, b. 1916, into a merchant family in Suzhou, Jiangsu Province, is a successful businesswoman and pen manufacturer.

She attended only primary school—finishing Wanzhu Primary School in Shanghai in 1931—because her parents did not consider it important for a girl to have an education and did not send her on to high school. Tang Tiyin's father later deserted the family, so she was forced to find a way to make her own living. At the age of fourteen, in 1930, Tang Tiyin sat for and passed a test to join a stationery company named Shanghai Yixin Educational Goods Company. Her first job was selling fountain pens, which in those days were widely used. Her hard work and good business sense were rewarded by a promotion in 1932 to head of the Buying Department, with an increase in pay from 16 to 24 silver dollars. Tang Tiyin took pride in being the family's breadwinner, a burden that would normally have been her older brother's. However, when her employer wanted to transgress their business relationship and take her as a concubine, Tang Tiyin was forced to leave Yixin.

After suffering many indignities in working for others, Tang Tiyin decided to be her own boss. She opened a small stationery store in her home in 1933, at the age of seventeen, calling it Modern Articles Store (Xiandai wupinshe). The contacts Tang Tiyin had made while working with Yixin enabled her to start up a business with little difficulty. She kept prices slightly below those of Yixin, and customers transferred their business to her. This store was destroyed, however, when Shanghai became ravaged during the Sino-Japanese War. Tang Tiyin's fiancé, Bi Zigui, who was manager of Shenghuo Book Store in Kunming, Yunnan Province, assisted her in re-opening her Modern Articles Store there. Her stock had to be bought in Shanghai and transported to Kunming via Hai Phong in Vietnam. In 1940, however, she was devastated when Bi Zigui, with whom she had enjoyed an eight-year romance, died of illness. Then, more than one hundred crates of stationery were stolen in transit by Japanese soldiers. Tang Tiyin returned to Shanghai in 1942 with a broken heart.

There, she opened another small stationery shop—Modern Educational Goods Store (Xiandai jiaoyu wupin she)—in 1944. This time, her policy was to charge cheaper prices in order to attract students. Then, as her experience grew, she gained the confidence to branch out into manufacturing. Because the "Blue Spot" Parker pen was difficult to get during the war, Tang Tiyin made a fountain pen with a gold nib called "Green Spot" Gold Pen in order to cash in on the Parker name. Initially, she contracted a small factory to produce the Green Spot pen. Using a lifelong guarantee as a selling point, Tang Tiyin soon made Green Spot a recognized brand. After the war, she bought a small factory of her own to manufacture the Green Spot pens, thus winning for herself the sobriquet "Gold Pen Tang."

In order to be more competitive, Tang Tiyin paid special attention to the design and packaging of her product. In addition to plain black pens for office use and tri-color pens for school children, for example, she developed a slimmer "Happiness" pen for ladies and a thicker "Longevity" pen for men, then offered them gift-packaged as a set. Relying on cheaper prices, comparable quality, and new styles, Green Spot gradually claimed the lower end of the market for fountain pens after the war, leaving the higher end to imports and Chinese name brands.

Besides retailing pens in Shanghai, Tang Tiyin explored the wholesale market in other cities and provinces as well as in communist-occupied areas. The staggering inflation spiral of the late 1940s and the chaotic economy, however, pushed Green Spot to the brink of collapse. Then, with the communist takeover in 1949, people of every class were given the opportunity to learn to read and write, and demand for pens rose rapidly. That winter, the state put in an order for the entire production output of Green Spot; banks provided loans; and the factory's gold, silver, and platinum supplies for making pen nibs were guaranteed. Green Spot quickly regained its vitality and expanded. Tang Tiyin and her family vacated the first floor of the site and moved to a bungalow, and she acquired a car to take her to work. In 1955, the entire pen manufacturing trade in Shanghai agreed to a wholesale joint venture with the state, and Green Spot Gold Pen Factory merged with Huafu Gold Pen Factory to become Hero Gold Pen Factory. It was not long before Hero was the most popular brand in the PRC. Tang Tiyin was appointed manager of the private factory as well as Shanghai Pen Manufacturing Company.

During the Cultural Revolution, Tang Tiyin suffered the indignity of being sent down to the factory as a fitter. When recalled in 1979, she was given back all the property that had been taken from her and received all the back pay owed to her. Tang Tiyin was also assigned a new flat. That same year, she was made a member of the CPPCC, having been a member of the NPC since 1964. Tang Tiyin has long been involved in minor party politics and attained the position of member of the Central Committee of the Democratic Reconstruction Party (Minjian) as well as deputy chair of its Shanghai Committee.

Tang Tiyin is president of the China Pen Manufacturers' Association and has remained an innovative force in the industry. In 1981, in conjunction with Wu Meimei, an expert in the production of pencils and fellow member of the CPPCC, Tang Tiyin put forward a proposal for an increase in the production of fine body pencils. This proposal, which was adopted nationally, saw a savings of approximately 20 percent in timber, which was worth a great deal of foreign exchange annually. When Tang Tiyin saw that economic reform was not resulting in a sufficient increase of professionals to fill the needs of new enterprises, she took an active part in planning and establishing Shanghai College for Further Studies in Commerce and Industry. In spite of her age and bad health, Tang Tiyin also took on the position of president. The college offered courses in accounting, English, and management, and the student population soon numbered in the thousands. The college was followed by a technical high school for industry and commerce workers and the private Gongshang School in Shanghai. Her autobiographical *The Gold Pen Story* (Jinbi yuan) records the long and tortuous road she traveled.

After the death of Bi Zigui in 1940, Tang Tiyin did not marry. She lives in her old age with her nephew Tang Qiliang, his wife and daughter, and enjoys a happy family life.

Lily Xiao Hong LEE

Song Ruizhi, ed. *Zhongguo funü wenhua tonglan*. Jinan: Shandong wenyi chubanshe, 1995, 31–32.
Xin Ru. *Jinbi nüwang Tang Tiyin*. Beijing: Jiefangjun chubanshe, 1995.
Yingwen *Zhongguo funü*, ed. *Gujin zhuming funü renwu*, vol. 2. Shijiazhuang: Hebei renmin chubanshe, 1986, 930–35.
Zhongguo funü guanli ganbu xueyuan, ed. *Gujin Zhongwai nümingren cidian*. Beijing: Zhongguo guangbo dianshi chubanshe, 1980, 379.

Tao Shufan

Tao Shufan, b. 1898, of Qiqiha'er city in Heilongjiang Province, was a primary educator who worked in the same school for more than sixty years.

Significantly for Tao Shufan's later career, her mother died when Tao Shufan was very young; because she did not get along with her stepmother, Tao Shufan always felt that she had never had a mother's love. In 1918, with the help of her elder brother, Tao Shufan enrolled at the Women's Higher Normal School of Beijing (Beijing nüzi gaodeng shifan xuexiao; later to become Beijing Women's Normal University). At that time, she took part in the student activities of the May Fourth Movement. At her graduation in 1921, Tao Shufan was invited to teach in the Second Primary School attached to the Higher Normal School, and she remained there until retirement in 1965. Through this period, Tao Shufan progressed from being a teacher to deputy headmistress and was promoted to headmistress of the Second Experimental Primary School of Beijing (Beijing di'er shiyan xiaoxue), when her school was renamed. Asked to be a consultant after retiring, she continued to sit in on classes and offer teachers constructive opinions.

From the very beginning, Tao Shufan tried to implement in her teaching a number of policies and innovations that are now recognized as characteristic of her teaching and administration style. They can be divided broadly into three aspects. The first and most important one is what her admirers describe as Tao Shufan's principle of "educating through love." Because of her childhood experience and perhaps never having had children herself, she decided to give her students what amounted to motherly love and did not discriminate between children of different backgrounds, abilities, and behavior patterns. In an era when bodily punishment was still common in China, Tao Shufan abstained from it completely.

Secondly, she opposed testing in any sort of external examination that pitted schools against one another; such competition encouraged schools within a city or province to chase high marks and high standing. To her mind, this kind of examination put unnecessary pressure on students and made schools pursue wrong aims.

Thirdly, Tao Shufan placed importance on teaching students life skills appropriate to age and ability. Primary one students were taught to wash their handkerchiefs and make beds; primary two students were taught to plait their hair and sew on buttons, and so on. In higher classes, students learned to operate machine tools modified for their use. In short, all students were encouraged to undertake some form of manual work as a balance to traditional emphasis on book learning. The motto of her school was to train students who were "happy with their work, love their work, and constantly improve their work."

Although Tao Shufan's ideas were not unique, she put them into practice consistently throughout her long career as an educator. Her example made such an indelible impression on generations of students and the general public that she was recognized as a leader in the field of primary education. Tao Shufan was elected to the Chinese People's Association for the Protection of Children (Zhongguo renmin baohu ertong weiyuanhui) and the All-China Educators' Union (Quanguo jiaoyuzhe gonghui) and designated a Model Teacher. She also served as a member of the NPC and CPPCC.

Her greatest honor, however, was to be praised by former students who rose to distinguished positions. One student wrote to her: "Of all the education I received in my life, what I received at your school influenced me most deeply and benefited me most. Thus, when I went to university and furthered my studies in the United States, I chose teacher education as my field of study." Tao Shufan is the author of *My Memories of Sixty Years in Beijing Second Experimental School* and *The Women's Higher Normal School during the May Fourth Period*.

Lily Xiao Hong LEE

Huaxia funü mingren cidian. Beijing: Huaxia chubanshe, 1988, 917.
Yingwen *Zhongguo funü*, ed. *Gujin zhuming funü renwu*, vol. 2. Shijiazhuang: Hebei renmin chubanshe, 1986, 552–56.
Zhongguo funü guanli ganbu xueyuan, ed. *Gujin Zhongwai nümingren cidian*. Beijing: Zhongguo guangbo dianshi chubanshe, 1980, 385.

Teng Li-chün

Teng Li-chün [Deng Lijun], 1953–1995, was possibly the most famous female singer among Chinese communities throughout the world. She was also known by the English name Teresa Teng, and her original name was Teng Li-yun. She was born in Yun-lin County, Taiwan, although her native place was Ho-pei [Hebei] Province, China.

Hers was a military family, and Teng Li-chün had three elder brothers and one younger brother. As a child, Teng Li-chün often accompanied her father when he went to see *ching-chü* (*jingju*, or Beijing opera) of which he was an aficionado. At the age of only five or six, Teng Li-chün would dress up in her father's gown and, standing in front of a "microphone" made from a shoe-polish can, start singing "on stage." She started performing at informal parties and evening gatherings at primary school age and in 1964, at the age of eleven, took part in the Huang-mei song contest held by CTS (Chung-hua tien-t'ai). Teng Li-chün won First Prize with the song "Visiting Ying-t'ai" (Fang Ying-t'ai). She gave up formal education in her third year of secondary school in order to perform in floorshows.

In 1965, Teng Li-chün enrolled in a vocal training class and won First Prize at a singing competition put on by the Golden Horse Record Company. Her television career commenced in 1967 as host of the television show *One Star a Day*, and she went on to appear in television dramas and to play the lead in the film *Thank You, General Manager* (Hsieh-hsieh tsung-ching-li). After she began recording songs, Teng Li-chün was invited to perform at a charity concert in Singapore. In 1970, she performed with the K'ai-sheng Variety Troupe (K'ai-sheng tsung-ho i-shu-t'uan) in Hong Kong and did a concert tour of Southeast Asia the following year. Her popularity grew in Taiwan, Hong Kong, and Southeast Asia, and after being crowned as Hong Kong's Pai-hua-yu Arts Auction Charity Queen Teng Li-chün became one of the most popular singers in Hong Kong.

In 1973, the singer went to Japan for further vocal training after signing a contract with Polydor Records. It was there that she started on the path to international stardom. Before then, Teng Li-chün had been known as a singer of folksongs and romantic ditties with cute little voice inflections. In Japan, she performed more demanding ballads and improved her singing technique, not only in learning to speak Japanese with correct pronunciation but also in expressing nuances of feeling in each word and gesture. Teng Li-chün won the prize for Best New Singing Star in Japan's famous Red and White Singing Competition. Her popularity grew in the country, and her first Japanese album, released in 1974, was a smash hit. The next year she won Japan's eighteenth Album Award and the Award of Best New Artist.

Teng Li-chün signed up with Polygram Records in Hong Kong in 1975 and released the first volume in her series of albums, *Love Songs of an Island Nation* (Tao-kuo ch'ing-ko). The following year, she gave her first concert in Hong Kong, which was well received. Her popularity in Japan climbed, and her 1977 Taiwan television show *The Songs of Teresa* (Teng Li-chün chuan-chi) won a prize there.

In 1979, Teng Li-chün gave her first concerts in the United States and Canada. She stayed in America for a time studying English and recording albums and in 1980 performed at Lincoln Center in New York and the Los Angeles Music Center in California. Teng Li-chün was the first Chinese singer to perform in the place where the Academy Awards are held.

She performed in Southeast Asia, Hong Kong, and Taiwan and released a number of albums in the 1980s. Among these were *Faded Feelings* (songs based on poems of the T'ang and Sung dynasties, 1983); the Cantonese album *The Road of Life* (Man-pu jen-sheng lu, 1983); *I Am in Your Debt* (Ch'ang-huan, 1984); *I Only Care About You* (Wo chih tsai-hu ni, 1987); and *The Unforgettable Teresa* (Nan-wang ti Teng Li-chün, 1992). Although rarely performing in public from the early 1990s, Teng Li-chün spent most of her time traveling the world until finally settling in Paris. However, as a child from a military family, she often returned to Taiwan to sing for the troops; Teng Li-chün was known as "the Soldiers' Sweetheart." She continued to do this until 1994, the year before she died.

The performer's singing was sweet and emotional. Her voice won fans not only among overseas Chinese but also in mainland China, where her popularity came in the early 1980s as Little Teng (in contrast to Old Teng, the paramount leader Teng Hsiao-p'ing [Deng Xiaoping]). Her gentle qualities and friendliness and lightness were disarming and refreshing to mainlanders just recovering from the Cultural Revolution. Despite the best efforts of the authorities to ban the music of Little Teng, considered the worst of bourgeois sentimentalism, Teng Li-chün's voice wafted across the mainland. The concurrent rising popularity of Teng Hsiao-p'ing (1904–97) as the "engineer of reform" in China gave birth to the saying "Teng Hsiao-p'ing rules by day, Teng Li-chün rules by night."

Teng Li-chün died of an asthma attack in May 1995 while on holiday in Chiang Mai, Thailand. She had just turned forty-one years old, and her death triggered an outpouring of grief among her fans throughout the world. Teng Li-chün was posthumously awarded the Ministry of Defense's highest honor for civilians, the KMT Hua-hsia Grade One medal (Hua-hsia i-teng chiang), and the president's Commendation. The national flag of the Republic of China and the KMT party flag were draped across the coffin at her funeral.

Teng Li-chün never married and did not have any children.

Shirley Wai CHAN

"Ch'ing-ch'üan-kang i-pieh, ho jih chün tsai lai." T'ai-sheng (July 1995).

Reuters. "Teresa Teng Lives on Via the Internet," at <www.taipeitimes.com/news/11/23/story/0000062616>.

Sung Jui-chih [Song Ruizhi], ed. *Chung-kuo fu-nü wen-hua t'ung-lan*. Chi-nan: Shan-tung wen-i ch'u-pan-she, 1995, 609–10.

"Teng Li-chün chih ko." K'ai-fang tza-chih (July 1995): 77–78.

"Teng Li-chün Forever." *Sinorama* (Kuang-hua) (July 1995): 7–17.

Teng, Li-yun: *see* **Teng Li-chün**

Teng, Teresa: *see* **Teng Li-chün**

Teng Ying-ch'ao: *see* **Deng Yingchao**

Tie Ning

Tie Ning, b. 1957, in Zhaoxian County, Hebei Province, is a writer of fiction.

Her parents, who were officials in Hebei Province, went to cadre schools (a euphemism for labor reform camps) during the Cultural Revolution when Tie Ning was only a child. She went to live with her grandmother in Beijing and lived in a courtyard house shared by many families; although crowded, Tie Ning had an opportunity to observe in close proximity a microcosm of life in Chinese society.

She found solace from her lonely childhood in books and began writing in high school. After graduating in 1975, Tie Ning went to work on a production team in the countryside. Later, she said her motive as a writer was to observe society and life, as a writing mentor had once advised her to do. Four years later, Tie Ning was transferred to the Editorial Department of *Huashan*, sponsored by the Federation of Literature and Art Circles (Wenlian) of the Baoding Region, and appointed fiction editor.

She started publishing her work while still in high school and in 1980 released a short story collection entitled *Night Path* (Ye lu), which brought her to the attention of the literary world. In 1982 her story "Oh! Fragrant Snow" (O, Xiangxue), originally appearing in the May issue of *Qingnian wenxue*, won the National Short Story Prize. This story tells of the experiences of a high school student, Xiang Xue, who lives in a remote mountain village where the train stops for only one minute. One day she is selling eggs on the train and does not have enough time to step down before it leaves. The student gets off at the next stop and walks the thirty li home. The story describes the girl's adventures and her wonderment along the way, evoking both her pleasure at the world outside her village and the innocence of the daydreams that world inspires.

During that same year, Tie Ning joined the Chinese Writers' Association. Two years later, she produced the novella *Red Shirt without Buttons* (Meiyou niukou de hong chenshan)—subsequently adapted as the film *The Girl in the Red Shirt*—and the short story "About June" (Liu yue de huati), which were awarded the National Prize for Best Novella and the Short Story Excellence Award (Quanguo youxiu zhongpian/duanpian xiaoshuo jiang), respectively. In 1999, her essay collection *Women's White Night* (Nüren de baiye) won the First Lu Xun Literary Prize. Films based on her fiction also won many awards: *The Girl in the Red Shirt* won the Golden Rooster (Jinji) and One Hundred Flowers (Baihua) Award as well as the Outstanding

Feature Film Award from the Ministry of Culture. *Fragrant Snow*, based on the short story of the same name, won an award in the Berlin Film Festival in 1991.

Tie Ning's early works are mainly about the Chinese countryside. Her closeness with peasants enabled her to depict them with profound feeling and understanding. Subsequent works shifted to urban dwellers, usually insignificant people. Their lives were skillfully revealed in stories that portrayed their emotional world as well as the spirit of the times, through subtle nuances in personality. Tie Ning is good at exploring unique perspectives, discovering inner conflicts in characters in a changing world, and creating spirituality, a cultured artistic style, and a subtle implicit beauty. Her narrative language is clear and terse, rhythmic, and poetic.

Recent works include "Haystacks" (Maijie duo) and the novels *Rose Gate* (Meigui men), *Rainless City* (Wu yu zhi cheng), and *Big Bath Girl* (Da yu nü). These later works display deeper engagement with the darker side of human nature. The writer tends to question China's cultural institutions, yet never appears to despair. These later pieces also show a deeper concern with the dilemma of the "new woman" who seems to have gained something but is at a loss as to how to move forward. One critic says that Tie Ning is the least likely of the women writers of today to be described as feminist, yet she is the one who writes with the strongest feminine consciousness and is searching intensely for answers to the questions concerning the innermost core of women's fate.

In a 1999 interview, the author said that the work she was most happy with was *Rose Gate*. This novel about three generations of women probed the inner world of ordinary yet individualistic women. Through studying their relationships, Tie Ning attempts to point out the vicious circle potentially repeated from generation to generation in women's lives. In the same interview, she stressed the importance of magnanimity (*baorong*). Little wonder her latest novel, *Big Bath Girl*, ends with the protagonist finding in her own heart a beautiful garden where she finds peace, peace with all of her friends and peace with her relatives, despite the fact of their having hurt, betrayed, and left her. The character has even made peace with herself for what she did in childhood—letting her baby half-sister walk into a well and drown.

Tie Ning is presently vice-chair of the Chinese Writers' Association and chair of its Hebei branch. She sees these positions as a way of doing something for her colleagues. She has led a fundraising drive to build a museum to hold both the literature of Hebei Province and display items relating to the literati of Hebei from the past five thousand years. Tie Ning accepted an invitation from the Columbia University Chinese-American Arts Exchange Center to visit America and in 1985 went to Norway for an international exhibition of the work of women writers. Her other published collections include *Red Roof* (Hong wuding), *Red Shirt without Buttons*, and *The Tie Ning Short Story Collection*. Her short stories and essays are collected in a five-volume *Collected Works of Tie Ning* (Tie Ning wen ji). "Oh! Fragrant Snow," *Red Shirt without Buttons*, "Haystacks," "About June," and "Night Bell" (Wan zhong) have been translated into several languages: English, French, Russian, German, Japanese, Spanish, and Esperanto.

GAO Yuanbao
(Translated by Katherine Kerr)

Dai Jinhua. "Zhenchunzhe de zhi yi—chong du Tie Ning." *Wenxue pinglun* (May 1994): 5–14.
Li Yang. "Wenhua yu xinli, *Meigui men* de shijie." *Zhongguo wenxue yanjiu congkan*, no. 1 (1989): 8–11.
Lin Jianfa et al., eds. *Dangdai zuojia mianmian guan*. Changchun: Shidai wenyi chubanshe, 1991.
Meng Xiaoyun. "Yu wenxue yiqi chengshou: Tie Ning fangtanlu." *Renwu*, no. 2 (1999): 77–92.
Tie Ning. *Da yu nü*. Shenyang, Chunfeng wenyi, 2000.
———. "Haystacks." Beijing: Chinese Literature Press, 1989.
———. *Nüren de baiye*. Shanghai: Shanghai wenyi chubanshe, 1992.

Ts'ai Su-nü: *see* Lin-Ts'ai Su-nü

Ts'ui Hsiao-p'ing

Ts'ui Hsiao-p'ing [Cui Xiaoping], b. 1922, in the city of Chi-nan [Jinan], Shan-tung [Shandong] Province, played a significant role in broadcasting and performing arts in Taiwan.

Her father worked for the post office in Chi-nan, and their family life was comfortable. She was very interested from a young age in the performing arts. When the Marco Polo Bridge Incident led to the outbreak of the Sino-Japanese War, Ts'ui Hsiao-p'ing fled with her mother and sister while her father decided to remain behind to defend their home. Then fifteen years old, Ts'ui Hsiao-p'ing attended Ssu-chuan [Sichuan] Sixth Middle School, second campus, at Te-yang [Deyang], and next enrolled in the National Drama School (Kuo-li hsi-chü chuan-k'o hsüeh-hsiao). When the Japanese were defeated in 1945, the KMT government dispatched Ch'en I [Chen Yi] to handle the takeover of Taiwan. However, the officials sent there were corrupt, and the administration performed poorly; the people expressed their opposition to the KMT in the February Twenty-eighth Incident of 1947.

In October 1947, Ts'ui Hsiao-p'ing went to Taiwan to tour with the Shanghai Audience Company. The standard of the company's drama performances was very high and garnered good reviews. When mainland China fell to the communists in 1949, Ts'ui Hsiao-p'ing was alone in Taiwan, and she came to the attention of Ch'iu Nan [Qiu Nan], who recommended her to the China Broadcasting Company (CBC) as a director of radio drama.

Because of the war, 1950s Taiwan was quite poor, in cities as well as in the villages. There was no television, and for recreation and entertainment people mostly looked forward to the CBC *Broadcast Drama*, broadcast on the radio nationally from 8:10 to 9:00 P.M. on Sunday nights. The show would pour out from the radio of every family and home onto every street corner and alleyway as if it were the only program on the air. Ts'ui Hsiao-p'ing gradually became a household name, and her talents enriched many lives.

Not only did Ts'ui Hsiao-p'ing gain renown in broadcasting circles, she also developed consummate skills in the performing arts by directing, writing, and acting in films and on stage. In 1959, she received an award for Best Supporting Actress at the Sixth Asian Film Festival for her role in *Precipice* (Hsüan-ya), thus contributing in a sense to the battle for recognition of Taiwan. Ts'ui Hsiao-p'ing also taught at several institutions: the National College of the Arts (Kuo-li i-shu chuan-k'o hsüeh-hsiao), World College of Journalism (Shih-hsin chuan-hsiao), the Political Warfare Academy (Cheng-chan hsüeh-hsiao), Kuo Kuang Drama College (Kuo Kuang chü-hsiao), the Actors' Training School at the Central Motion Picture Corporation (Chung-ying yen-yüan hsün-lien-pan), Taipei First Girls' Middle School, and Chien-kuo Middle School. As a teacher, she cultivated several outstanding and famous talents in broadcasting, film, and performing arts.

However, the national security campaign of the Chiang Kai-shek regime was under way and at its peak from the 1950s until the 1970s. In the wake of his defeat in China's civil war and subsequent loss of the mainland, his campaign furiously sought to eliminate communist spies, calling for the people to "hate communists," "fear communists," "oppose communists," and "defend against communists." The policy ran under the slogan "Better to Kill One Hundred People in Error than Release One Person by Mistake"; and it cultivated an ideal ground for opportunists and individuals bearing grudges and led to countless people becoming sacrificial objects of the White Terror. Ts'ui Hsiao-p'ing was one of these.

In 1968 she was tricked by Taiwan's Bureau of Investigation into going to a detention center for an interview. There, Ts'ui Hsiao-p'ing was held and interrogated over a long period, simply disappearing from the CBC. Investigators resorted to humiliation and threats to force Ts'ui Hsiao-p'ing to write a confession. On the basis of this coerced document, the military authorities brought three charges against her. The first one was that, in 1937, she had joined the "Northwest Front Service Corp" and received two weeks of training in a "[Communist] Bandit Training Class." This had indeed taken place when, as a fifteen-year-old, she had gone with an older sister to An-wu-pao [Anwubao] in Shen-hsi [Shaanxi] Province to search for her sister's displaced husband. The second charge was that, in 1939, Ts'ui Hsiao-p'ing had received instruction from "Communist Bandit" Fu Kuo-liang [Fu Guoliang] and participated in a "reading group." This had taken place at the age of seventeen when she studied at Ssu-chuan Sixth Middle School. Ts'ui Hsiao-p'ing was accused of recruiting others (including classmate Lü Tao-hsin [Lü Daoxin]) to join the reading group, which frequently gathered to discuss "bandit literature" and national affairs. The third charge was that, in 1947, Ts'ui Hsiao-p'ing participated in the Audience Company formed by the National Drama School's Liu Hou-sheng; Ts'ui Hsiao-p'ing was then twenty-five. The charge involved the plays *Unofficial History of the Ch'ing Palace*, *Thunderstorm*, *The Second Wife*, and *The Eternal Paragon*, which the company had brought to Taiwan to perform at the end of October. Her accusers described these plays as "left-leaning" concealed attacks on the darkness of the ruling class, speaking of a bright future under the CCP and inciting workers to class struggle. It was therefore "Bandit" propaganda. A military court sentenced Ts'ui Hsiao-p'ing to life imprisonment at its first hearing for the crime of "attempting to overthrow the government by direct action" under Clause 2, Paragraph 1, of the Regulations for the Punishment of Sedition.

Ts'ui Hsiao-p'ing did not admit to these charges. Her response was that during her childhood the KMT and the CCP had been cooperating to resist the Japanese, so how could it have been against the law to go to Shen-hsi? Further, the plays mentioned had been examined and passed by the Government Information Office for performance, so that they could, in fact, be staged at the time. How could plays that were legally performed more than twenty years previously now be illegal? She appealed to have the decision overturned, but the court finally settled upon a fourteen-year jail sentence. With this decision, Ts'ui Hsiao-p'ing's career in the performing arts came to an end just as it had reached its peak.

When President Chiang Kai-shek died in 1975, the government declared a general amnesty. Ts'ui Hsiao-p'ing's sentence was reduced, and nine years and four months after her imprisonment she became free again. Ts'ui Hsiao-p'ing was a fervent Christian and after her release attended church regularly, leading a simple life. In 1998, the Legislative Yuan passed the "Compensation Measures for Inappropriate Trials for [Communist] Bandit Agent Sedition During the Martial Law Era" to allow innocent victims of the martial law era from 1949 to 1987 to restore their reputations and claim compensation. A grey-haired Ts'ui Hsiao-p'ing submitted an application but has yet to see a result. One source of comfort for Ts'ui Hsiao-p'ing was that at the ceremony of the Golden Bell Awards for broadcasting in 2000, President Ch'en Shui-pien presented the performer with a Special Lifetime Achievement Award, reaffirming her contribution to Taiwanese society. Ts'ui Hsiao-p'ing's specialist publications include *Wasted Years* (Fang-hua hsü tu, 1961); *The Victim's Lament* (Shou-nan ch'ü, 1965); *The Second Dream* (Ti-erh meng, 1967); and *Performing Arts and Method* (Piao-yen i-shu yü fang-fa, 1994).

CHU Te-lan
(Translated by Martin Williams)

"Kuo-fang-pu p'an-chüeh shu. 2 July 1968." Document #57 nien fu-p'u shan-tzu ti 093 hao. Taipei: Ministry of Defense.

"Pei-kao-jen Ts'ui Hsiao-p'ing ta-pien shu. 25 October 1968." Taipei: Ministry of Defense.

"Taiwan ching-pei tsung ssu-ling pu. Chien-hsing ts'ai-ting. 14 July 1975." Document #64 nien chien-chien-tzu ti 343 hao. Taipei: Taiwan Police Headquarters.

"Taiwan ching-pei tsung ssu-ling pu. Chün-shih chien-ch'a kuan ch'i-su-shu. 14 September 1968." Document #58 nien ching-chien su-tzu ti 037 hao. Taipei: Taiwan Police Headquarters Military Prosecutor.

"Taiwan ching-pei tsung ssu-ling pu. Keng-shen p'an-chüeh shu. 20 May 1970." Document #59 nien keng-tzu ti 2 hao; #57 nien ching-hsü tzu, ti 3725 hao. Taipei: Taiwan Police Headquarters.

Ts'ui Hsiao-p'ing. *Fang-hua hsü tu*. Taipei: Huang-kuan ch'u-pan-she, 1961.

———. *Shou-nan ch'ü*. Taipei: Cheng-chung shu-chü, 1965.

———. *Ti-erh meng*. Taipei: Li-chih ch'u-pan-she, 1967.

T'ung Ch'ing-feng. "Hui-shou t'ien-o pei-ko, yen-yi ch'ü-che jen-sheng." *Ya-chou chou-k'an*, 27 August–2 September 2001, 46-47.

Tsui Hsiao-ping: *see* **Ts'ui Hsiao-p'ing**

W

Wan Shaofen

Wan Shaofen, b. 1930, is a native of Jiangxi Province. She was born into a family of primary school teachers in a village not far from Nanchang, the provincial capital. It is said that one of her ancestors served as defense minister (*bingbu shangshu*) during the Song dynasty (960–1279). Chinese tradition would have it that because of this blood connection the family produced Wan Shaofen, another famous politician, more than one thousand years later.

Wan Shaofen joined the CCP underground in 1948, when she was a student of economics at Zhongzheng University in Jiangxi, and soon abandoned her studies to become a professional revolutionary. Wan Shaofen was accepted into the CCP in 1952 and started her career as a cadre by becoming a local leader of the Chinese Communist Youth League (CCYL) and a trade union sponsored by the CCP. In the 1950s and 1960s, she served in various capacities with Nanchang city: office manager and deputy secretary of its CCYL Committee, director of its Youth Work Department, and director of the Trade Union Youth Work Department. Wan Shaofen was secretary of the CCYL, chair of the trade union of Number 514 Factory in Shaanxi Province, and alternate member of the CCYL Eighth Central Committee. During this period, she became acquainted with Hu Yaobang (1915–1989), who successively held the positions of secretary to the CCYL Central Committee and secretary of the Shaanxi Provincial Committee of the CCP.

Her friendship with Hu Yaobang was not to Wan Shaofen's advantage during the Cultural Revolution, when she was detained and physically abused after being accused of being a "capitalist roader" and "young follower of the line of Liu [Shaoqi], Deng [Xiaoping], and Hu [Yaobang]." However, this same friendship helped Wan Shaofen emerge as an important politician during the reform era that followed. She was rehabilitated in 1974 and appointed deputy chief of Jiangxi Provincial Office for Educated Youth. This was followed by appointment to deputy directorship to the Jiangxi Provincial Labor Bureau (1982–83), chair of Jiangxi Provincial Women's Federation, and membership in the Executive Committee of the ACWF (1983–84). Her party positions were as director of the Organization Department and member of the Standing Committee of the CCP Jiangxi Provincial Committee (1984–85). Wan Shaofen was then appointed secretary to the CCP Jiangxi Provincial Committee, one of the first women to hold such a position since the establishment of the PRC. In the meantime, she became a member of the Twelfth and Thirteenth CCP Central Committees. Largely because of the downfall of Hu Yaobang in January 1987, Wan Shaofen was unable to complete her term as provincial party secretary. She left Jiangxi for Beijing in June 1988 and acted as deputy secretary of the CCP Leading Group of the All-China Federation of Trade Unions for several months. Since late 1988, Wan Shaofen has served as deputy director of the United Front Work Department of the CCP Central Committee.

She attracted worldwide attention as one of the first female provincial party secretaries in the PRC but did not achieve much in that capacity. First of all, her extensive experience as an official of the CCYL and the trade union and women's associations was of little help in running a provincial economy. Secondly, despite having been an extremely hard-working individual, her populist style did not work well with the new reform polity, which demanded flexibility, openness, and a certain degree of money worship. During her time as secretary to the CCP Jiangxi Provincial Committee, Wan Shaofen developed a reputation for maintaining close contact with the people and solving practical local problems, such as inadequate public toilets and buses. She was also popular at that level among old communist revolutionaries and some villagers for paying much attention to the poverty release projects in areas known as "old revolutionary bases." However, reform and economic development in Jiangxi during that period did not keep pace with its neighboring provinces, particularly with Guangdong, Fujian, and Zhejiang to the south and east.

Her current assignment as deputy director of the United Front Work Department of the CCP Central Committee does not suit Wan Shaofen any better. She is in charge of liaison and conducts the business of making friends with Taiwan, Hong Kong, Macao, and overseas countries. It is not an important position, involving as it does mainly courtesy visits and social receptions. Wan Shaofen does not speak any foreign languages nor did she receive any special training in foreign affairs before taking up the post.

Her most remarkable achievement lies in her contribution to women's work. As a high-ranking female official, Wan Shaofen exerted great influence on women's affairs in Jiangxi. She took several major measures to improve the life of women when she was serving as chair and secretary to the Leading Party Group of the Jiangxi Provincial Women's Federation. Wan Shaofen helped set up a provincial women's cadre school to train women personnel and organized hundreds of public lectures around the theme of "the Four Selves" (self-respect, self-love, dignity, and self-improvement) to raise the level of awareness in protecting women's rights in the province. She took the lead in drafting regulations protecting the legitimate rights and interests of women and children in Jiangxi and set up women's legal advisory offices at city and county level throughout the province to oversee implementation of these regulations. Thousands of women have benefited from her endeavor. Wan Shaofen's achievements in this area have been so impressive that in February 1984 the ACWF issued a circular entitled "Learn from Wan Shaofen to Become an Outstanding Woman Cadre"; this was the first circular of this sort in the PRC. In her capacity as party boss of Jiangxi, Wan Shaofen devoted much time and energy to women's affairs, particularly to the appointment and promotion of women cadres, throughout the province.

Wan Shaofen has been a single mother (of one daughter) since the late 1960s, after a failed marriage.

FENG Chongyi

Feng Chongyi. "Jiangxi in Reform: The Fear of Exclusion and the Search for a New Identity." In *The Political Economy of China's Provinces: Comparative and Competitive Advantage*, eds. Hans Hendrischke and Feng Chongyi. London and New York: Routledge, 1999, 249–76.

Gong Yin. "Zhonggong diyige shengwei shuji Wan Shaofen." In *Zhongguo dangdai mingren lu*, vol. 2, ed. Li Guoqiang. Hong Kong: Wide Angle Press, 1988, 172–81.

Guo Chen and Guo Haiyan. "Wan Shaofen: Gongheguo diyi wei nü shengweishuji." In *Jin ri nü buzhang*, ed. Zhonghua quanguo funü lianhehui. Shenyang: Liaoning renmin chubanshe, 1995, 230–88.

Liang Xing and Jiang Xiusheng. "Wan Shaofen he ta de shenghuo ri." *Liao Wang*, 5 August 1985.

Song Ruizhi, ed. *Zhongguo funü wenhua tonglan*. Jinan: Shandong wenyi chubanshe, 1995, 173–74.

Wang Anyi

Wang Anyi, b. 1954 in Nanjing, is a well-known and innovative writer. She is presently deputy chair of the Shanghai branch of the Chinese Writers' Association and sits on the council of the Chinese Writers' Association.

Wang Anyi possibly inherited her literary talent from her mother Ru Zhijuan (*q.v.*), who was one of the outstanding literary talents to emerge after the founding of the PRC. Wang Anyi went to Shanghai with Ru Zhijuan in 1955 and spent her childhood and youth there; she graduated from primary school the year the Cultural Revolution was launched and was assigned to Xiangming Middle School. Her three years of high school coincided with the most intense period of the Cultural Revolution when all classes were suspended in schools throughout China in order to encourage young people to make revolution. This was a time of extreme leftist ideology, with young Red Guards "sweeping away the dregs of the old world," "attacking capitalist roaders and their ox and snake devils," "writing big-character posters," "launching thorough criticisms," and "making visits to other centers of revolutionary activity." In 1970, Wang Anyi was one of many young people to go to the countryside to live and work in a village. She was assigned to the Toupu Commune in Huaibei Wuhe County, Anhui Province. Coming from a comfortable family of intellectuals and growing up in Shanghai, Wang Anyi found her new and difficult life in this poverty-stricken village a stark contrast. However, the harshness of the environment in which she found herself was no match for her youth and enthusiasm, and she became an advanced activist representative in the study of Mao Zedong thought, first for the county, then for the district, and finally for the province of Anhui. In 1972 she joined the Communist Youth League.

That same year, Wang Anyi escaped from the hard life of the village when she joined the Cultural and Art Troupe of Xuzhou District, Jiangsu Province. She played the accordion and string bass with its music ensemble, traveling through Anhui, Shanxi, and Henan provinces, performing "revolutionary model operas." Although her lifestyle was unsettled at this time, it provided rich material for her later writing.

Wang Anyi produced her first literary work, an essay entitled "Marble" (Dalishi) in 1975; it was edited by Zhang Kangkang (*q.v.*) and included in *Fly, Rocs of This Age* (Fei ba, shidai de kunpeng), a collection of essays by educated youth. This essay is juvenile and bears the stamp of the "Gang of Four" period when literature had to serve politics. Other essays Wang Anyi wrote in the mid-1970s were "Advance" (Xiang qian jin) and "Teacher" (Laoshi).

After returning to Shanghai in April 1978 as part of a large-scale resettlement of educated youth from the countryside, she became editor of *Children's Era* (Ertong shidai), a magazine that had recently resumed publication. During this time, Wang Anyi concentrated on children's writing and visited many schools. In 1979 her novel *Who Will Be the Future Squadron Leader?* (Shui shi weilai de zhongduizhang?), published in *Youth Literature* (Shaonian wenyi), won that publication's annual Best Literary Work Award and the 1980 National Second Prize for Children's Literature.

In 1980, on the recommendation of *Children's Era*, Wang Anyi enrolled in the fifth literary study course of the Chinese Writers' Association. This was her first opportunity since primary school to undertake formal study of literature, and she studied literary theory and principles of literary creation fairly systematically. Wang Anyi rapidly progressed with her writing in these six months, producing a series of novels, including *Rain, Rustling* (Yu sha-sha-sha) and *The Junior Middle School Student in the Class of '69* (Liujiu jie chuzhongsheng).

These books were later described by literary critics as the "Wenwen Series" and as representative of Wang Anyi's early artistic style. Based on the subject of educated youth, the works bear all the hallmarks of Wang Anyi's own experience and feelings, her emotional and pure nature beautifully conveyed through her prose-poetry. She had gone to the countryside and to work in a village at the age of sixteen, full of dreams and ideals. This was a formative period and an important turning point in her life. Forced to leave her parents for the "wider world" at a young age, Wang Anyi left the city to which she was accustomed and faced a grim, gray life. In her series of novels, Wang Anyi endowed the girl Wenwen with delicacy and sensitivity and described in minute detail the emotions experienced by the girl. The development of the novels in the series centers on drawing out the emotional qualities of the main character. Speaking about her early work, Wang Anyi said, "I described my own feelings, the path in life that I followed and my own experiences and emotions. In this period, I did not admit that a novel has two parts, ideology and substance, because at that time I was in a childlike state of mind and wanted to describe feelings in a naturalistic way."

This Train's Final Destination (Benci lieche zhongdian) won the 1981 National Novella Award, and *Rush* (Liushi) won the 1982 National Medium-Length Novel (Novella) Award. With the latter, Wang Anyi's writing had matured. Through detailed description and finely tuned emotion, she successfully depicts the female character Ouyang Duanli, from a wealthy Shanghai family and with a typically aristocratic air, as the Cultural Revolution shifts the woman's life onto another track and forces her to become an overworked and harried urban worker. In this novel, Wang Anyi abandoned writing from her own experience and cultivated the art of perception, measuring everything as a novelist and investigator. This opened up wider social subjects for her analysis, and she searched for archetypal characters reflecting all strata of society. Her traditional techniques in realism were raised to a new height.

In 1983 Wang Anyi accompanied her mother when she accepted an invitation to participate in a four-month international writing program at the University of Iowa in the United States. During this period, Wang Anyi also got to know writers from various countries, exchanging experiences and exploring issues of writing. This greatly stimulated her ideology, emotions, and worldview, as well as views on life and art. She took stock of her own creative direction and stopped writing for a year, saying later, "During that decade, this was my most active year with regard to thinking and feeling. It was a very rich period. In fact I carried out a kind of reconstruction of my worldview."

In order to collect new material and develop new ways of expression, Wang Anyi traveled throughout China upon her return. Staying in a remote village in north Jiangsu for two days, she was inspired to write a work that eventually saw the light of day after a year's preparation. *Xiaobao Village* (Xiaobao zhuang) won the 1984 National Award for a Medium-Length Novel. A number of critics, as well as Wang Anyi herself, see *Xiaobao Village* as important in marking her change to incorporating a simple aesthetic style. *Xiaobao Village* is loosely structured and written in natural, flowing language; it describes a small village and tells the story of its twenty-odd inhabitants. None of them is the main character, and even those described in comparative detail, such as Old Aunt (Dagu), Xiao Cui, Shilai, and Second Aunt, leave only fragmentary impressions. The events described revolve around the minutiae of the characters' lives and there is no essential connection between them; the author adopts a flexible and shifting point of view throughout. She explores the conflict between modern and primitive impulses and provides deep, historically and philosophically reliable evidence for pessimism in revealing the elements of destiny in the characters' lives.

In 1986 Wang Anyi published three medium-length novels—*Love on Wild Mountain* (Huangshan zhi lian), *Love in a Small Town* (Xiaocheng zhi lian), and *Love in Brocade Valley* (Jinxiugu zhi lian)—all about "sexual love." Their bold description and analysis of the psychology of sex and sexual behavior shook the literary world and generated controversy from a number of critics. These works were labeled typical "sex literature" and dubbed the "Three Loves." With the special sensitivity and endowment of a female writer, Wang Anyi thoroughly analyzed the complicated transaction of sexual love and deliberately diluted historical and social elements. None of the main characters has a name; they are all simply a "he" or "she" to the other characters. Through her naturalistic lens, Wang Anyi reveals an important aspect of human nature: the primeval desire of humankind. The main characters, both male and female, demonstrate the complexities of attraction, pursuit, and satiation of sexual love and the joy and bitterness in relationships attending that experience. Wang Anyi continued with this theme in her medium-length novel *Time at the Hilltop* (Gang shang de shiji, 1989). The works mark a development in Wang Anyi's plain and direct style and reveal an understanding of human nature in all of its naturalistic facets.

In 1988 Wang Anyi continued writing novels while studying related artistic issues. She started a literary theory column in the magazine *Literary Angle* (Wenxue jiao) under the title "Stories and Telling Stories." The same year, when the Hanse Press in Munich translated and published a volume incorporating her novels *Love in a Small Town* and *Love in Brocade Valley*, Wang Anyi traveled to Germany to participate in the Frankfurt Book Fair. In 1990 she published a full-length work called *Stories of Traveling in Germany* (Lü De de gushi). It became another bumper year of recognition for her novels, her main ones being the medium-length novel *Uncle's Story* (Shushu de gushi), the full-length novel *Minnie* (Mini), and *Thirty Episodes of Running Water* (Liu shui sanshi zhang).

The writing in these works represents a further development to Wang Anyi's style. A number of critics said that *Uncle's Story* particularly signaled a new turn in her narratives. The narrating "I" was no longer the "I" appearing in earlier works, which had simply passed through the story as a narrator, but rather had become an integral part of the story. The characters and plots do not open up through natural development from within but are organized according to the needs of "I." The point of Wang Anyi's stories does not lie in their dramatic and detailed descriptions, but that they cannot exist apart from the narrator.

Thirty Episodes of Running Water is a novel uniquely reflecting Wang Anyi's view of fate. Old questions are posed about fate, can it be known? Through the state of mind of a newborn infant, the author expresses the mysticism individuals feel toward the workings of destiny. The descriptive device she employs of using many long and vague allegorical stories is considered by many people to be abstruse, but Wang Anyi believes that it conveys precisely the theme. It expresses the mysterious psychological world of an infant's extrasensory experiences and a mysterious consciousness of life and fate. Her latest novel, *Song of Eternal Sorrow* (Chang hen ge, 1999), a penetrating and sensitive portrayal of an urbane Shanghai woman, is reminiscent of Eileen Chang (*q.v.*) and won the Mao Dun Prize for Literature in 2000.

Wang Anyi's work at this time indicates a complete discarding of her own personal experience and an understanding and control of the highest reaches of creating fiction as well as her own creative process. She is a talented writer with considerable achievement. In her art, Wang Anyi dares to break out of a mold, striving ceaselessly to realize new forms and the innate rules of creation. She explores a wide range of subjects illustrating the richness and variety of the human condition and the psychological states of her characters and issues that are also socially significant. The depth of her writing derives from her value that literature's highest goal is to give voice to humanity, and she is dedicated to exploring those experiences that are most innate and primal. This gives her artistic spirit particular durability in society and history. Wang Anyi's work has won attention not only among contemporary Chinese women writers but also from the international literary stage. Her creative achievements should occupy an important place in the history of Chinese literature.

Wang Anyi is married to Li Zhang; they do not appear to have any children.

Rubing HONG
(Translated by Jocelyn Chey)

Fang Keqiang. "Wang Anyi lun." *Wenyi zhengming*, no. 5 (1992): 50–64.
Jiao Tong. "Tiansheng shi ge nüren—tan Wang Anyi." *Xiaoshuo pinglun*, no. 3 (1993): 34–39.
McDougall, Bonnie S., and Kam Louie. *The Literature of China in the Twentieth Century*. Gosford: Bushbooks, 1998, 410–12.
Peng Bing. "Lun Wang Anyi yishu fengge de yanbian." *Shehui kexuejia*, no. 6 (1989): 74–78.
Wang Anyi. *Baotown*, trans. Martha Avery. New York: Viking, 1989.

———. *Brocade Valley*, trans. Bonnie S. McDougall and Chen Maiping. New York: New Directions, 1992.

———. *Lapse of Time*. San Francisco: China Books, 1988.

———. *Love in a Small Town*, trans. Eva Hung. Hong Kong: Renditions, 1988.

———. *Love on a Barren Mountain*, trans. Eva Hung. Hong Kong: Renditions, 1991.

———. "Jinri chuangzuo tan." *Zhengming*, no. 5 (1992): 62.

———. "Xie xiaoshuo de lixiang." *Dushu*, no. 1 (1991).

Yang Guangxin, ed. *Zhongguo dangdai qingnian zuojia mingdian*. Beijing: Zhongguo huaqiao chubanshe, 1991, 69–70.

Zhang Zhizhong. "Wang Anyi xiaoshuo jin zuo manping." *Wenxue pinglun*, no. 5 (1992): 47–62.

Wang Chengshu

Wang Chengshu, 1912–1994, also known in the United States as C.S. Wang Chang, of Wuchang, Hubei Province, was a nuclear scientist.

She commenced her studies in the Physics Department of Yen-ching [Yanjing] University in Beijing in 1930 and graduated with a Bachelor of Science in 1934 and a Master of Science in 1936. Wang Chengshu held the position of assistant lecturer in the Physics Department from 1934 to 1937 while studying for her master's and from 1938 to 1939 was a lecturer at Xiangya Medical College in Changsha, Hunan Province.

In September 1939, she married physics professor Zhang Wenyu (1910–92) of Southwest Union University in Kunming. He had graduated from Peking University; Zhang later studied in the United Kingdom under the famous physicist Ernest Rutherford (1871–1937) and gained his Ph.D. from Cambridge University in 1938.

Wang Chengshu went to the U.S. in 1941 and became a top student, working under the eminent statistical physicist G.E. Uhlenbeck (b. 1900) and with whom she later wrote several papers. Wang Chengshu gained her Ph.D. at the University of Michigan and worked from 1946 to 1956 as an assistant researcher and later a research fellow, including two periods of research with the Advanced Research Institute of Princeton (summer of 1945, 1948–49). During her stay in the United States, Wang Chengshu conducted research into statistical mechanics and the kinetics of inert gases. She is credited with an adjustment to the Boltzmann equation (L.E. Boltzmann, 1844–1906) in polyatomic gases that resulted in its being renamed the WC-U equation. Wang Chengshu published more than ten research papers, some of which were collected in the multivolume *Studies in Statistical Mechanics*, in which she is referred to as "Mrs. Chang."

Wang Chengshu's husband was invited to Princeton University as a research professor (1943–50) and subsequently appointed to a professorship at Purdue University (1950–56). She and her husband wished to return to China after the People's Republic was established in 1949. However, because of American regulations in force during the early years of the Cold War, forbidding Chinese nationals from leaving the country, several years went by before they succeeded in gaining permission to return. They did so in 1956, with their American-born infant son.

Wang Chengshu was appointed researcher with the Institute of Physics of the Chinese Academy of Sciences in Beijing (1956–64), at one stage concurrently holding a professorship at Peking University (1957–58). She worked at the Third Research Institute of the Ministry of Nuclear Industry between 1964 and 1978, first as a research fellow and later as deputy director. Appointed to a professorship at Qinghua University in 1978, Wang Chengshu continued her association with the Ministry of Nuclear Industry, acting as chief engineer in the Technology Department from then until 1986. She was instrumental in planning the plasma and thermonuclear fusion laboratories of the Research Department of Atomic Energy, where a research team of theoreticians had been trained. Wang Chengshu conducted research into the separation of uranium isotopes, which included initiating and running the cascade theory analysis of the diffusion plants, and an economic analysis of the project. She was also involved in making improvements to diffusers and designing new models, as well as research into uranium isotopes separation by using centrifugation and laser. Overall, Wang Chengshu contributed greatly to the development of nuclear technology in China, not least through the research theoreticians she trained in uranium isotopes separation studies.

WANG Bing
(Translated by Jeremy Chun Ho Cheng)

Wang Chang, C.S., and G.E. Uhlenbeck. "The Kinetic Theory of Gases." In *Studies in Statistical Mechanics*, vol. 5, eds. J. de Boer and G.E. Uhlenbeck. Amsterdam: North-Holland, 1970, xi–100.

Wang Chang, C.S., G.E. Uhlenbeck, and J. de Boer. "The Heat Conductivity and Viscosity of Polyatomic Gases." In *Studies in Statistical Mechanics*, vol. 2, eds. J. de Boer and G.E. Uhlenbeck. Amsterdam: North-Holland, 1964, 241–68.

Yanjing renwuzhi. Beijing: Yanjing yanjiuyuan, 1999, 43–44.

Yingwen *Zhongguo funü*, ed. *Gujin zhuming funü renwu*, vol. 2. Shijiazhuang: Hebei renmin chubanshe, 1986, 843-47.

Zhonghua quanguo fulian, ed. *Zhongguo nüyuanshi*. Shenyang: Liaoning renmin chubanshe, 1995, 31–33.

Wang, C.S. Chang: *see* Wang Chengshu

Wang Dingguo

Wang Dingguo, b. 1913 as Yi Xiang in Yingshan County, Sichuan Province, belongs to the first generation of twentieth-century communist women revolutionaries.

She grew up in desperate poverty in a mountainous region of Sichuan; her ancestors were believed to have been porters from Hubei Province who had become stranded there at some unspecified time. Wang Dingguo was given as a child to a Li family who attempted to bind her feet; the girl managed to return to her widowed mother and along with a maternal uncle became involved in revolutionary activities in her teens. Wang Dingguo adopted this name after joining the CCP in 1933 and being elected to the newly established Yingshan County Committee Soviet.

She was a courageous young woman, unafraid to fight, and headed the local women in a Self-Defense Corps called Yingshan Independent Women's Battalion (Yingshan funü duli ying). The party then sent her to the Bazhong Soviet School in northeastern Sichuan in early 1934 and from there to Hongjiang County, where Wang Dingguo first met Zhang Qinqiu (*q.v.*); Wang Dingguo was absorbed into the Fourth Front Red Army under the command of Zhang Guotao. Wang Dingguo took part in propaganda and recruiting work, collecting grain, and providing supplies for the fighting men; at one stage she was involved in a skirmish with the enemy and either seriously wounded a man or speared him to death. By 1935 Wang Dingguo had been assigned to the headquarter's cultural troupe (zongbu wengong tuan), a group of young women and children, some only eleven years old, who wrote and performed morale-boosting songs and dances but also transported ammunition to the front and fetched the wounded.

As a member of the Fourth Front Red Army's Cultural Troupe, Wang Dingguo marched from Sichuan to the Tibetan border to join the First Front Red Army under Mao Zedong (1893–1976) in June 1935. It was there that she first met, albeit briefly, her future husband, the veteran communist Xie Juezhai (1883–1971). When the two armies split soon afterward, Wang Dingguo remained with the Fourth Front Red Army as head of the Wardrobe and Props Section of the Advance Theatrical Troupe under the General Political Department (Zongzhengzhibu qianjin jutuan). After spending another year in Sichuan and Tibet, she became part of the ill-fated Western Route Army that crossed the Yellow River in October 1936. As one of the few to survive its massacre by Moslem cavalry sympathetic to the KMT, Wang Dingguo was captured in early December and sent with other young survivors of the performing troupe to Xining in Qinghai. There, they were re-formed into a theatrical troupe (*xin jutuan*) to entertain former enemies.

Wang Dingguo is particularly remembered for her part in rescuing Western Route Army survivors during this period. She was instrumental in extricating a very ill Zhang Qinqiu from the factory where she had been sent to work. After being moved to Zhangye in Gansu, Wang Dingguo worked undercover in a hospital, seeking out and speeding on their way to Lanzhou hundreds of her comrades. She escaped from Gansu in September 1937 and made her way to the Eighth Route Army office in Lanzhou, which was under the command of Xie Juezhai. They married in October 1938, and by the time they left Lanzhou in 1940 had two children.

Despite their thirty-year age difference, Wang Dingguo and Xie Juezhai made a happy marriage. Xie Juezhai was a poet and scholar, described as one of the "elders" of the communist movement. He kept detailed diaries covering a period of some sixty years and these later became valuable historical source material. During the Yan'an period, Xie was director of the Departments of Interior and Justice and made minister of Internal Affairs in 1949 with the establishment of the PRC. He held this post until 1959 at which time Xie became president of the Supreme People's Court. After their marriage, Wang Dingguo worked with her husband—she was deputy head of the Party Committee Office in the People's Supreme Court, for example—and devoted herself to his care.

Xie Juezhai became paralyzed, possibly because of a stroke, in 1963, and was completely dependent upon his wife. He was not personally harmed during the Cultural Revolution, but in early 1969 Wang Dingguo was arrested and kept for over a month, her movements carefully scrutinized from then on. Little is known of her activities after Xie Juezhai died in 1971 except that she was elected to the Fifth and Sixth CPPCC after the Cultural Revolution. Wang Dingguo is held in high regard for her devotion to the communist cause.

Sue WILES

Guo Chen. *Jinguo liezhuan: Hong yifangmianjun sanshiwei changzheng nühongjun shengping shiji.* Beijing: Nongcun duwu chubanshe, 1986, 176–77.

Han Zi, ed. *Nübing liezhuan,* vol. 3. Shanghai: Shanghai wenyi chubanshe, 1987, 143–60.

Klein, Donald W., and Anne B. Clarke. *Biographic Dictionary of Chinese Communism, 1921–1965.* Cambridge, Mass.: Harvard University Press, 1971, 330.

Wang Dingguo. "Fendou zhongsheng—Yi Xie Juezhai tongzhi de wannian shenghuo." In *Hongqi piaopiao.* Beijing: Zhongguo qingnian chubanshe, 1981, 152–63.

Yingwen *Zhongguo funü,* ed. *Gujin zhuming funü renwu,* vol. 2. Shijiazhuang: Hebei renmin chubanshe, 1986, 848–52.

You Yan, ed. *Zhongguo nübing dang'an,* vol. 2. Beijing: Changcheng chubanshe, 1999, 339–58.

Yun Shan. "Nanwang de licheng." In *Hongjun nüyingxiong zhuan,* eds. Liaowang bianjibu. Beijing: Xinhua chubanshe, 1986, 275–86.

Wang Fang: *see* **Fang Fang**

Wang Guangmei

Wang Guangmei, b. 1921 in Beijing, is a native of the city of Tianjin; she was once known as Dong Pu. An activitist working for the communist cause as a student, she later married Liu Shaoqi (1898–1969), one of the top CCP leaders and head of state of the PRC. Caught up in the power struggle between Mao Zedong (1893–1976) and her husband, she was severely persecuted during the Cultural Revolution.

Some sources claim that Wang Guangmei was born in America (Mei guo), pointing as evidence of this to the "mei" element in her given name. Her father, Wang Zhichang (1877–?; also known as Wang Huaiqing), taught at Tianjin Women's Normal College after graduating from the Commerce Department at Waseda University in Japan. He later became a government official in the warlord period (1912–27), serving as head of the Bureau of Industry and Commerce in the Ministry of Agriculture and Commerce and as acting minister of Agriculture and Commerce. Sources also differ as to her father's position, some saying he was an officer in the Beijing Police, others that he headed the Bureau of Mining in the Ministry of Agriculture and Mining in the warlord period. Wang Guangmei's mother came from a wealthy Tianjin family and graduated from Tianjin Women's Normal College. Wang Guangmei was one of ten brothers and sisters: her eldest brother died at an early age and two elder brothers lived overseas, while the remaining six siblings all joined the CCP and became prominent in various fields.

In 1939 Wang Guangmei enrolled at Fujen Catholic University in Beijing, completing an undergraduate degree in the Physics Department in 1943 and then a master's in physics in 1945 before becoming a teaching assistant at the university. She was ideologically left wing and became involved with the Beijing underground organization of the CCP. Wang Guangmei acted as English interpreter in Beijing for CCP representatives Ye Jianying (1897–1986), Luo Ruiqin (1906–1978), and Li Kenong (1899–1962) on the Military Mediation Executive Commission, an organization formed jointly in January 1946 by the CCP, the KMT, and representatives of the U.S. government. The commission's purpose was to carry out surveillance on Japan while implementing the truce agreement with that country.

At the end of 1946, it was arranged that Wang Guangmei would be transferred to Yan'an, where she worked initially as a translator in the Foreign Affairs Department of the CCP Central Committee and then in land reform in the Jin-Sui (i.e., Shanxi-Suiyuan) liberated areas. In 1948 Wang Guangmei moved with the Military Commission of the Central Committee to Xibaipo in Hebei Province and became an editor and translator on *Neibu cankao*, a digest of news stories from around the world, intended for the eyes of designated personnel only. That same year, she joined the CCP and married fifty-year-old Liu Shaoqi, head of the Central Committee's Organization Department, chair of the All-China Federation of Trade Unions, and in 1958 China's head of state. Their twenty-year marriage produced one son and three daughters; Liu Shaoqi already had five children from previous marriages. Wang Guangmei was transferred to the General Office of the Central Committee and worked as her husband's private secretary for nearly twenty years, until she was imprisoned in 1967 at the start of the Cultural Revolution. Wang Guangmei also had been elected to the Executive Committee of the ACWF in 1957.

In 1963, as part of his "socialist education movement" (1962–65), Mao Zedong launched the "Four Clean-Ups"—of politics, the economy, organization, and ideology—in the countryside in accordance with his view that a clear line of demarcation should be drawn between socialism and capitalism. This view, however, was not shared by Liu Shaoqi, who believed instead that a distinction should be made between "ourselves" and "the enemy" and that opposing sides of the CCP should be clearly defined, as should any contradictions existing among the people.

At the end of 1963, Liu Shaoqi instructed Wang Guangmei to go to Hebei Province under the guise of being a secretary to the Provincial Public Security Bureau and under the assumed name of Dong Pu. Over a period of two months, she transformed Taoyuan (Peach garden) Production Brigade, which was within the Luwangzhuang Commune in Funing County, into a model "Four Clean-Ups" brigade. Upon returning to Beijing, Wang Guangmei wrote up her research data into a report entitled "The Taoyuan Experience," which was publicized throughout the country. Soon afterward, Liu Shaoqi formulated his "Policies and Regulations for the Socialist Education Movement in the Countryside," basing his thoughts on Wang Guangmei's research report. Mao was critical of "The Taoyuan Experience," and this became the first public airing of political differences between the two leaders.

Liu Shaoqi took charge of the day-to-day affairs of the Central Committee in early 1966 while Mao Zedong recuperated in southern China from an illness. However, in May the big-character posters that signaled the start of the Cultural Revolution appeared at Peking University (*vide* Nie Yuanzi), and students ceased attending classes, devoting their energies instead to rebellion. In early June, Liu Shaoqi convened the Standing Committee of the Politburo, which decided to send work teams to all high schools and universities in Beijing. A few weeks later, Wang Guangmei was sent as an advisor to such a work team at Qinghua University. Many students and teachers at Qinghua opposed the teams (some students registered their protest by committing suicide). When Mao returned to Beijing at the end of August, he recalled all of the work teams. He censured Liu Shaoqi, describing him as "the leading person in authority taking the capitalist road," and criticized Wang Guangmei's "The Taoyuan Experience" as "left in form but right in essence." She was isolated for investigation on the grounds of putting her husband's views into practice; Liu Shaoqi never appeared in public again.

On 10 April 1967, Qinghua University was the site for what is believed to have been the largest rally ever held during the ten years of the Cultural Revolution, convened for the purpose of criticism and denunciation. Attended by three hundred thousand people, the rally's focus was Wang Guangmei. She was made to wear the very tight cheongsam (*qipao*) once worn a few years previously when accompanying her husband on a visit to Southeast Asia. With a string of table tennis balls strung around her neck in mockery of the pearl necklace that had also been worn, Wang Guangmei was forced to make a public exhibition of herself. Five months later, she was placed in Qincheng Prison in west Beijing, where high officials of the Central Committee were kept if imprisoned. Her children were not allowed to visit her for another five years; it has been said that they had rejected her during this period, not wanting anything to do with her. Wang Guangmei spent twelve years all told in jail, the charge against her being that she was a spy on behalf of America, which wanted strategic information. Wang Guangmei is said to have been sentenced to capital punishment but that Mao Zedong did not think it an appropriate sentence, writing on her file "Spare her."

Meanwhile, having been expelled from the CCP and dismissed from every post once held, Liu Shaoqi finally died in prison in November 1969 in Kaifeng, Henan Province. The cause of his death is often cited as pneumonia, but he was diabetic and it is generally believed his death was caused by guards "forgetting" to ensure his access to insulin. Wang Guangmei was not told until her release from prison nearly ten years later that her husband had died.

Wang Guangmei's status was restored following the posthumous rehabilitation of Liu Shaoqi in 1979 after which she served in the following positions: director of the Foreign Affairs Bureau in the Academy of Social Sciences; Executive Committee member of ACWF; and director of the Birth Control Association of the Central Committee. Wang Guangmei also sat on the Twelfth National Congress of the CCP, the CPPCC (1979), and the Standing Committee of the CPPCC (1983–93). She was invited to fill many community organization positions after retirement, including president of Fujen Alumnus University, director of the Combined Alumni Associations of Institutions of Higher Education, and honorary director of the Beijing International Friendship Society.

Apart from the fact of being caught up in the power struggle between Mao Zedong and her husband, two additional reasons have been put forward as to why Wang Guangmei suffered so deeply during the Cultural Revolution. The first turns on the issue of conflict with Mao's wife, Jiang Qing (*q.v.*), with whom Wang Guangmei had been on good terms in Yan'an; each of the women's status was equivalent to that of First Lady. However, while Jiang Qing was constrained to play an exclusively offstage role in the 1950s and early 1960s, Wang Guangmei accompanied her husband on many overseas trips and often appeared in public. Jiang Qing's resentment over this visibility is said to have been fueled by Wang Guangmei rejecting advice that Jiang Qing had given her on grooming, and the two women drifted apart. As a leading figure of the Cultural Revolution, Jiang Qing's charge labeling Wang Guangmei as an American spy because of what was perceived as her American education carried weight; ardent revolutionaries accepted the accusation because Wang Guangmei's unusual clothes indicated to them that she was as decadent as Westerners.

The second reason is concerned with Wang Guangmei's alienation from the common people and springs from her wealthy background, which allowed her to gain a good education, especially in Western culture. This meant that not only her clothes but also her very way of being differed greatly from the people of an economically backward China. She had traveled incognito to observe ordinary people closely while researching "The Taoyuan Experience," but it appears even then that Wang Guangmei was reproached about her different life-style. Unfortunately, these remarks were later compiled and appeared on the desks of people in high places as facts proving her guilty of leading a capitalist life-style.

Viola Hong Xin Chan WONG

Guo Hualun and Fang Xuechun, eds. *Zhonggong renming lu.* Taipei: Zhonghua minguo guoji guanxi yanjiusuo, 1968, 121–23.

Liu Shaoru. *Zhongnanhai guike.* Hong Kong: Shangtai chubanshe, 1997, 155–57.

Pan Xiangchen. *Zhongguo gaogan furen dang'an.* Beijing: Beifang funü ertong chubanshe, 1997, 78–80.

Ren Jian. *Gongheguo yuanshou zhi si.* Hong Kong: Haiming wenhua shiye gongsi, 1994, 21–29, 46.

Rong Zi. "Wang Guangmei: Libian renjian beixiju." *Xinbao,* 25 May 1993, 5.

Wang Guangmei. "Yu jun tongzhou, fengyu wuhui." *Yan huang chunqiu,* 10 (general 79, 1998): 13.

Zhang Xiaolin, ed. *Lingxiu yizu: Gongheguo xinshengdai jishi.* Beijing: Tuanjie chubanshe, 1993, 156.

Wang Henei

Wang Henei was the Chinese name adopted by the contemporary sculptor Renée June-Nikel, 1912–2000. Born in France, she married a Chinese man and lived in China for over sixty years, becoming a naturalized Chinese citizen in 1955. Their marriage did not produce children.

Wang Henei loved art from childhood as much as she loved animals. Enrolled in l'Ecole des Beaux-arts in Nice in 1929, the artist specialized in sculpture. Five years later, in 1934, Wang Henei moved to Paris to study sculpture at l'Institut Supérieur des Beaux-arts. She married Wang Linyi, a young Chinese man studying sculptural art in France, and went with him to China in 1937 at the start of the Sino-Japanese War. They arrived in Shanghai, then traveled westward to Chongqing in Sichuan Province under very difficult conditions via Hunan and Yunnan. After the war, the couple moved to Beijing.

For several years after arriving in China, Wang Henei had considerable difficulty settling down. She moved constantly because of the war, and language difficulties made it easier at first for her to remain at home rather than getting on with her work.

Once the couple had moved to Beijing, however, Wang Henei set up a small studio in her home and began working on sculptures of animals. Not long afterward, she was invited to teach sketching and sculpture in the Arts and Craft Department of Beijing Normal University (Beijing shifan daxue, Gongyi xi). Her spoken Chinese was still not fluent, but her obvious achievement in art and responsible attitude toward teaching quickly won over students. Wang Henei was appointed professor-sculptor at the Central Academy of Fine Arts (Zhongyang meishu xueyuan) after the establishment of the People's Republic in 1949 and taught sculpture, sketching, and French, doing her own creative work after class.

Wang Henei's sculptures fall into two main categories: animals and people. For her animal sculptures, she often went to the zoo to observe living animals. These small sculptures, exhibited in 1957 with the work of Xiao Shufang, Zong Qixiang, and Li Hu, have been praised for their natural beauty and vividness. China's famous painter of horses, Xu Beihong (1895–1953), had already singled out Wang Henei's powerful and awe-inspiring *Big Tiger* (Da hu) for special praise. Her *Snow Leopard* (Xuebao) was selected to be part of the Exhibition of Plastic Arts of the Socialist State in 1958, while *Deer* (Xiao lu) resides in the collection of the Art Gallery of China. Wang Henei's animals, however, capture more than simple likenesses; each reveals an individual spirit. Her famous work, the disarming *Cat* (Mao, 1963), is the piece most often shown of her animal sculptures. The influence of both Western art and ancient Chinese sculpture can be detected in her work, and Wang Henei devoted considerable time to studying Chinese traditional sculpture. She traveled to the ancient capitals of Luoyang and Xi'an, as well as to various places in Yunnan Province. The journeys enabled her to develop a unique style of realism tempered with exaggeration and decorativeness. The artist emphasized the characteristics of the animals she sculpted but added certain human qualities to them.

At the request of the Palace of Nationalities in Beijing, Wang Henei created a large decorative relief sculpture in 1958. She later took part in several cooperative projects creating large reliefs for Beijing Observatory and the Norman Bethuen Memorial Museum and an exhibition devoted to the life of Jiao Yulu, a model official promoted during the Cultural Revolution. Working as an individual artist, she created sculptures of people, including *The Children's Corps Keeping Watch* (Ertongtuan fangshao) and *Head of the Women's Team* (Funü duizhang). After the reform period that began in 1978, Wang Henei sculpted the likenesses of women revolutionaries, such as Yang Kaihui (*q.v.*) and Xiang Jingyu (*q.v.*), highlighting their elegance and kindness.

Because this blond, blue-eyed woman called Wang Henei adopted China as her country and incorporated strong Chinese themes in her art, it is appropriate that she be known as a Chinese sculptor. She is buried in Babaoshan cemetery in Beijing.

Lily Xiao Hong LEE

Li Qian and Yang Rongsheng. "À la Mémoire de Wang Henei, Professeur de Sculpture—Une Artiste Éprise des Beaux-arts et Captivée par l'Art Oriental." *China Today*, at <http://

www.chinatoday.com.cn/ChinaToday/Today/ChinaToday/ct2000f/07/ct2000–7f-10.html>, accessed 1 January 2001.
Song Ruizhi, ed. *Zhongguo funü wenhua tonglan.* Jinan: Shandong wenyi chubanshe, 1995, 625.
Zhongguo dabaike quanshu: Meishu. Beijing: Zhongguo dabaike quanshu chubanshe, 1991, 832.

Wang Huiwu

Wang Huiwu, 1898–1993, of Jiaxing County, Zhejiang Province, was an early CCP women's organizer, a staunch proponent of women's emancipation, and the wife of Li Da (1890–1966), one of the founders of the CCP and a noted Marxist philosopher.

Wang Huiwu was educated by her father, Wang Yanchen, who ran a local school. His untimely death impoverished the family, but Wang Huiwu was able to continue her education at Jiaxing Women's Normal School and later at the Hujun Academy for Girls, run by Christian missionaries. While at Hujun, she became fluent in English and knowledgeable about the iconoclastic ideas of the May Fourth Movement, particularly relating to women's emancipation.

After graduation, Wang Huiwu went to Shanghai and became acquainted with various fledgling Marxists through her cousin, Shen Yanbing (later known by his pseudonym Mao Dun [1896–1981]), who became one of China's most prominent twentieth-century writers. In autumn 1920, Wang Huiwu married Li Da, who had recently returned from study in Japan and was working closely with Chen Duxiu (1880–1942), a prominent May Fourth intellectual, to establish a communist party in China. Both Wang Huiwu and Li Da shared a strong interest in the emancipation of women and published articles on the subject in the flourishing periodical press of the post-World War I era. Wang Huiwu's best-known early treatise on women's issues, entitled "The Chinese Woman Question: Liberation from a Trap," was published in *Young China* (Shaonian Zhongguo) in 1919. In this essay, she bitterly attacked parentally arranged marriages as a form of lifelong imprisonment for women. In her view, women were blinded to the real nature of their subjugation because of their acceptance of certain traditional norms about womanhood. These included the Confucian ideal of female obedience to male authority figures in the family, the notion that wives should blindly obey their husbands, and the belief that women should aspire only to become virtuous wives and excellent mothers and consciously strive to shun acquisition of knowledge.

Wang's marriage to Li Da placed her at the center of the Chinese communist movement, which was run out of the apartment they shared with Chen Duxiu, first general secretary of the party, and his wife, Gao Junman. Initially, Wang Huiwu assisted her husband in party-building work. Through her efforts, for instance, a site was secured for the party's First Congress in July 1921 at the Bowen Girls' School in the French Concession of Shanghai, which was closed for the summer. When suspicious strangers started snooping around the clandestine gathering, it was Wang Huiwu who organized the reconvening of the congress on a houseboat on a lake in Zhejiang.

Before long, she assumed a leadership role in developing the party's first Women's Program, which consisted of running the Shanghai Pingmin Girls' School and editing the journal *Women's Voice* (Funü sheng). Although the school was in operation for less than a year, it attracted outstanding women to the communist cause, including Ding Ling (*q.v.*), Qian Xijun (*q.v.*), Wang Jianhong, and Wang Yizhi (*q.v.*). Under Wang Huiwu's management, *Women's Voice* aimed to become a forum for women to express political views, in contrast to the numerous journals that served primarily as organs for men to express their ideas about women's emancipation. An important theme in Wang Huiwu's own writings for this publication was the need for "conscious" women to become involved in organizing women workers. She argued that the recent outbreak of a large strike at the British-American Tobacco Company in Hankou (more than three thousand women had been involved) signaled that a new trend had commenced in China by which working-class women's activism would soon overshadow the middle-class women's movement.

Reproduction was another issue that Wang Huiwu addressed in her writings. When Margaret Sanger, the American birth control advocate, came to China in 1922, Wang Huiwu published an article supporting her position despite the general negative stance voiced by male communists in other journals. Shen Yanbing, for instance, argued that it was not excessive population but rather the unequal distribution of wealth and services that caused poverty. In his view, the issue of birth control diverted women from engaging in the more important struggle of instituting socialism.

Wang Huiwu's leadership position in the communist Women's Program ended with the Second Party Congress in June 1922 as Li Da's relationship with party leader Chen Duxiu deteriorated. The two projects she had overseen were terminated, but the party's commitment to women's work continued through the establishment of a Central Women's Bureau and the appointment of another capable woman, Xiang Jingyu (*q.v.*), as its director. Wang Huiwu moved with Li Da to Changsha, where she gave birth to her second child, a son, in 1924 and her youngest daughter in 1925. After the violent rupture between the Chinese communists and the KMT in 1927, Wang Huiwu and Li Da lived in Shanghai and then in Beijing, where she was active in the women's movement. When the Japanese invaded north China in July 1937, the whole family fled south, living in Guilin and Guiyang. Their eldest daughter died because of inadequate medical services, and they finally moved to the KMT wartime capital of Chongqing.

After the establishment of the PRC in 1949, Wang Huiwu lived in Beijing, working for the Legal Committee of the central government. She also attended important events such as celebrations for the sixtieth anniversary of the founding of the CCP and published essays on her recollections of the founding of the party.

Christina K. GILMARTIN

Gilmartin, Christina K. *Engendering the Chinese Revolution: Radical Women, Communist Politics, and Mass Movements in the 1920s.* Berkeley: University of California Press, 1995.

[Shen Yan] Bing. "'Shengyu jiezhi' de shengjia." *Funü pinglun,* no. 40 (10 May 1922): 2–3.

[Wang] Huiwu. "Dui bagong nügongren shuo jijuhua." *Funü sheng,* no. 10 (20 June 1922): 3.

———. "'Yida' zai Nanhu kaihui de qingkuang." In *'Yida' qianhou: Zhongguo gongchandang di yici daibiao dahui qianhou ziliao xuanbian,* ed. Zhongguo shehui kexueyuan xiandaishi yanjiushi, Zhongguo geming bowuguan dangshi yanjiushi, 2. Beijing: Renmin chubanshe, 1980, 58–60.

Wang Jinyun: *see* **Cheng Yen, Master**

Wang Jung-chih: *see* **Jung-tzu**

Wang Keqin: *see* **Wang Ying**

Wang Liming: *see* **Liu-Wang Liming**

Wang Quanyuan

Wang Quanyuan, b. 1913 as Ouyang Quanyuan in Aocheng, Ji'an County, Jiangxi Province, was one of the thirty women who took part in the Chinese communists' Long March of 1934–35.

Of peasant origin, she became an activist in the CCP after moving in March 1930 to the nearby village of Chayuan to marry Wang Zhaodou (b. 1897). It was an arranged marriage, and in accordance with local custom Wang Quanyuan took and retained her husband's surname. She soon left him, however, and over the next few years devoted herself to revolutionary work, joining the Young Pioneers (as deputy leader), the Youth League (responsible for local women's affairs and head of Ji'an County Women's Bureau) and, in 1934, the CCP. She represented Ji'an County at the 1933 Women's Congress held in Yongxin, became a member of the Hunan-Jiangxi Women's Bureau, which Wang Quanyuan then represented at a national congress held in Ruijin in 1934. She attended the Communist Marxist University in Ruijin for several months and was assigned to the massive recruiting drive that immediately preceded the Long March; Wang Quanyuan worked with Wang Shoudao (1906–97), whom she married in Zunyi during the Long March. Her duties as a political fighter with the Women Workers' Group of the General Medical Unit of the First Front Red Army included organizing food supplies, hiring bearers, and organizing and performing at propaganda meetings.

In August 1935, Wang Quanyuan was assigned for a year to the newly formed Cadres Convalescent Company of the Fourth Front Red Army commanded by Zhang Guotao (the Left Column), a taint that later would mark the beginning of the injustice and misery she suffered for the rest of her life. Zhang Guotao was eventually branded as a traitor because he unsuccessfully contested Mao Zedong for leadership of the party. During this time, Wang Quanyuan worked as head of the Sichuan Women's Bureau and did propaganda work among Tibetan people. In October 1936, she was made regimental commander of the Women's Anti-Japanese Vanguard Regiment with Wu Fulian (*q.v.*) serving as her political commissar. This women's army crossed the Yellow River with the doomed soldiers of what became known as the Western Route Army; it was annihilated within three months by local Moslem Ma clan cavalry. Most of the women were killed.

Wang Quanyuan, however, was captured by the Moslems and in November 1937 given as a concubine to an engineer named Ma Zhengchang (or Jinchang). Women who were caught by the Moslems in the Gansu corridor then knew that their capture meant the virtual impossibility of returning to the lives they had once known. Comrades would suspect that they had traded survival for the death of others; families would be humiliated by community perceptions of the women's collaboration with the enemy, politically, possibly sexually. Most of the captured women submitted to their fate as concubines or found a man to live with and settled down in the northwest. Yet, Wang Quanyuan escaped eighteen months later and made her way to the office of the communists' Eighth Route Army in Lanzhou. There, she was told that because more than two years had elapsed since losing contact with Mao Zedong's Long Marchers (in other words, because of her assignment to the army of Zhang Guotao), Wang Quanyuan could not be accepted back into the Red Army. The gross unfairness of the decision dogged her for more than forty years.

She took up with an itinerant named Wan Ling and returned in 1941 to Yunnan Province; after he left for military service in Burma, Wang Quanyuan made her way back to her native village in Jiangxi. There she was branded as a "bandit's whore," a traitor, and deserter. She eventually (in August 1948) married a local man named Liu Gaohua, and they moved to neighboring Taihe County.

After the communists came to power in 1949, Wang Quanyuan was placed in charge of women's affairs and then transferred to responsibilities as production team leader in charge of land reform. Then, during one of the often vindictive campaigns of the early 1950s, her husband was imprisoned, and Wang Quanyuan was dismissed from her position, labeled with the damning verdict "political history unclear." She was eventually able to call on her fellow Long Marcher Kang Keqing (*q.v.*), who went guarantor for her in 1962, but Wang Quanyuan was not given work until 1968. She was then placed in charge of the district's Old People's Home and also elected to the local council of the CPPCC.

Wang Quanyuan was fortunate in not being physically harmed during the Cultural Revolution, as many women of her generation were; like them she was rehabilitated in the early 1980s through the efforts of the ACWF. Her Long March husband Wang Shoudao, who had risen to great political heights, finally spoke up for her at that time, and Wang Quanyuan was portrayed as a Red Army heroine in a film called *Echoes of Qilian Mountains*. She was readmitted to membership of the CCP in 1985 and elected the same year to the county and provincial committees of the CPPCC.

Asked during a 1990s interview if she had any regrets at being unable to fulfill the dramatic promise of her experiences with the Red Army, she replied: "No, I have no regrets. It is the greatest honor of my life that I was able to go on the Long March. I am very content just to have been a part of it." Such loyalty is somewhat vindicated by the practical support the Long March women were finally able to extend to Wang Quanyuan. At the time of writing, she was said to be living in her village in Jiangxi Province.

Sue WILES

Dong Hanhe. *Xilujun nüzhanshi mengnan ji.* Beijing: Jiefangjun wenyi chubanshe, 1990, 17–59.
Guo Chen. *Jinguo liezhuan: Hong yifangmianjun sanshiwei changzheng nühongjun shengping shiji.* Beijing: Nongcun duwu chubanshe, 1986, 24–5, 42, 180–90.
Hu Yang. "Yige nühongjun tuanzhang de chuanqi rensheng." *Jinan yuebao*, reprinted in *Beijing qingnian bao*, 5 August 1996, 5.

Lee, Lily Xiao Hong, and Sue Wiles. *Women of the Long March.* Sydney: Allen & Unwin, 1999.

Luo Guojun. "Xueyu-xingfeng yi nüjie." In *Hongjun nüyingxiong zhuan*, eds. Liaowang bianjibu. Beijing: Xinhua chubanshe, 1986, 188–206.

Wang Xia. *Moran: Xilujun nü hongjun tuanzhang de chuanqi.* Beijing: Jiefangjun chubanshe, 1999.

Wang Rong: *see* **Yang Huizhen**

Wang Rongzhi: *see* **Jung-tzu**

Wang Xiaotang: *see* **Zhong Yuzheng**

Wang Ying

Wang Ying, 1915–1974, original name Yu Zhihua, of Wuhu County, Anhui Province, was one of the leading actresses of leftist spoken drama (*huaju*) and film during the 1930s. Along with Chen Bo'er and Ai Xia, Wang Ying is celebrated as a "writer-star" (*zuojia mingxing*) and garnered high praise for her literary and journalistic writings. These included essays, travel reportage, and autobiographical novels, many of which were based on experiences in Singapore, Japan, and America.

Wang Ying's father, Yu Youren, was a banker in Nanjing. Her mother, Ms. Wang, was an aficionado of music and literature who had nurtured her daughter in literature and the performing arts. Wang Ying's joyful childhood ended abruptly, however, shortly after her tenth birthday when her mother died; her stepmother mistreated Wang Ying and forced her to board at a strict Christian high school. Soon thereafter, the young girl was betrothed to the Xue family in exchange for funds to pay off her father's banking debt. Wang Ying escaped to Changsha and enrolled in Xiangya Nursing School as Wang Keqin. She participated in revolutionary activities organized by the CCP during the Northern Expedition of 1926–27 and in 1928, aged thirteen, volunteered to deliver messages for the CCP. She was captured by the KMT but escaped and eventually fled to Shanghai, again changing her name, this time to Wang Ying.

In Shanghai, she acted in spoken dramas, many of which put forward progressive or leftist ideas. Wang Ying joined the Shanghai Arts and Drama Society (Yishu jushe), one of the leading progressive theaters, in 1929, and also enrolled at Fudan University, acting with the Fudan Drama Society (Fudan jushe) and performing in such plays as Ding Xilin's *Oppression* (Yapo). In 1930, at fifteen, she joined the CCP and devoted herself to leftist activities, which resulted in repeated incarceration by the KMT. After the formation in 1931 of the League of Left-wing Dramatists, Wang Ying starred in a number of leftist dramas, including *Man of the Tarpit* (Tankang fu); *Missus' Fan* (Shaonainai de shanzi, adapted from Oscar Wilde's *Lady Windemere's Fan*); and *Marco Polo Bridge* (Lugouqiao).

Her film career began with the Mingxing Film Studio, which was increasingly guided in the mid-1930s by the CCP's promotion of leftist concerns in the arts. Her first three films, all silent, revealed these concerns as well as class solidarity but had also a tendency toward the melodrama of "soft" entertainment films. *Protest of Women*

(Nüxing de nahan, 1933; directed by Shen Xiling) depicted the harsh conditions of disenfranchised laborers. *Red Tear Chronicles* (Tieban honglei lu, 1933; directed by Hong Shen) told of class conflicts and struggles of rural peasants. *Common Enemy* (Tongchou, 1934; directed by Cheng Bugao) combined domestic intrigue with a call for national solidarity against the Japanese, depicting a woman forgiving her philandering lover because he has joined the front line of the anti-Japanese resistance.

After a short period in Japan studying film and drama, Wang Ying returned to China in 1935 and played the lead in *Goddess of Freedom* (Ziyou shen, 1935; Diantong Films). Critics credited this film with depicting in a fresh manner women's quest for independence from a feudal family and dedication to national salvation. The actress played Chen Xingsu who, encouraged by the ideals of the May Fourth Movement, runs away from family and fiancé with an impoverished fellow student. They marry and devote themselves to revolutionary activities; her husband eventually dies a heroic martyr's death in Canton. Although Xingsu is separated from her child during the Northern Expedition, the character devotes herself to helping war orphans.

During the mid- to late 1930s, Wang Ying dedicated herself to dramatic productions promoting the CCP's cultural policies and China's national salvation efforts. Defense drama (*guofang xiju*) was established at that time under the "Declaration of Defense Drama" statement of the Association of Shanghai Dramatists (Shanghai juzuozhe xiehui). Wang Ying took the lead in the 1936 Shanghai premiere of Xia Yan's historical romance *Sai Jinhua*. This is the story of the famous Qing dynasty courtesan of the same name (see *Biographical Dictionary of Chinese Women: The Qing Period*), who negotiated a peace agreement favorable to China during the Boxer Rebellion through her lover, a prominent German count. Seen as impugning the KMT's policy of non-resistance to the Japanese, *Sai Jinhua* created such a sensation in Shanghai that the KMT banned the film.

. In 1937, war against Japan erupted. Wang Ying toured fifteen provinces with the Shanghai Salvation Troupe Number Two (Shanghai jiuwang yanju erdui) led by Hong Shen, performing for both the soldiers and the people in an effort to fire patriotism and boost morale. A staple of her repertoire in the defense drama genre was Chen Liting's *Put Down Your Whip* (Fangxia ni de bianzi), which she performed throughout China and later in Singapore and the United States. Frequently re-appearing outdoors as street theater (*jietou ju*), this drama about the cruelty of the Japanese invaders of Manchukuo involved audience participation as a means of arousing patriotic awareness in audiences. Renamed New China Troupe (Xin Zhongguo jushe) in 1939, the group traveled to Southeast Asia; Wang Ying was the lead actress and assistant troupe leader. During this tour to win moral and financial support, she also wrote a column about their work for the Singapore *Nanyang Commerce News* (Nanyang shangbao).

Wang Ying went to the United States in 1942 to study. As director of the East-West Cultural Association (Dongxi wenhua xiehui), she put on many national defense dramas and was invited to the White House—meeting the Roosevelts, various congress members, and dignitaries—and performed *Put Down Your Whip*. Wang Ying also wrote several social critiques for overseas Chinese papers such as *New York Newspaper* (Niuyue xinbao) and *Overseas Chinese Daily* (Huaqiao ribao). In 1946 she assisted Agnes Smedley in writing the classic biography *The Great Road: The Life and Times of Zhu De.*

Wang Ying became an acclaimed writer of what is known as "miscellaneous essays" (*sanwen*); mainland critics frequently point to her recurrent themes on the pursuit of freedom and love as a universal right. Yet, significantly, she writes from a personal female perspective about the fate of women in a swiftly changing social landscape. Some of her best pieces are "Spring Rain" (Chun yu), "Girls from Xi'an" (Xi'an de nü'ermen), "Recommendation of a New Woman" (Xin nüxing de tuijian), "A Christmas Present" (Shengdanjie de liwu), and "Expunging the Darkness of Film Circles" (Chongchu hei'an de dianying quan).

While living in America, Wang Ying wrote her autobiographical novel *Precious Girl* (Baogu), tracing the vicissitudes of the first twenty years of her turbulent life. She and her husband Xie Hegeng (b. 1912) were imprisoned during the McCarthy communist purges of 1952, and the couple was finally deported, returning to Beijing at the beginning of 1955. Wang Ying was assigned to the Beijing Film Studio and worked on film scripts. When her husband was denounced as a "rightist" and sent for labor reform to the northeast, Wang Ying retreated to the Fragrant Hills just west of Beijing. There, she wrote her second autobiographical novel, *Two Types of Americans* (Liang zhong Meiguoren), based on her experiences in America and entanglement with the McCarthy purges.

On 1 July 1967, Wang Ying became one of the earliest victims of the Cultural Revolution; she was imprisoned by order of Jiang Qing (*q.v.*) for having played the role of Sai Jinhua. Wang Ying died in prison on 2 March 1974.

Jonathan NOBLE

Chen Ye et al., eds. "Wang Ying." In *Zhongguo dianyingjia liezhuan*, vol. 2. Beijing: Beijing dianying chubanshe, 1982, 31–38.
Li Runxin. *Jiebai de mingxing—Wang Ying.* Beijing: Zhongguo qingnian chubanshe, 1987.
Sheng Ying, ed. "Yanyuan zuojia: Wang Ying." In *Ershi shiji Zhongguo nüxing wenxueshi*, vol. 1. Tianjin: Tianjin renmin chubanshe, 1995, 433–40.
Wang Ying. *Baogu.* Beijing: Zhongguo qingnian chubanshe, 1982.
———. *Liang zhong Meiguoren.* Beijing: Zhongguo qingnian chubanshe, 1980.

Wang Yingchun

Wang Yingchun, b. 1942, of Taiyuan, Shanxi Province, is a traditional Chinese painter.

She began painting at a very early age and was admitted in 1957 to a high school attached to Xi'an Fine Arts Academy (Xi'an meishu xueyuan), where she took Chinese ink painting (*guohua*) and sculpture. Wang Yingchun graduated with a bachelor's degree from its Chinese Ink Painting Department, having specialized in figure painting; her other subjects included flower and bird painting, landscape, and calligraphy. Wang Yingchun learned much from Zheng Naiguang and fondly portrayed rural life in northwest China, influenced in this by Professor Liu Wenxi.

After graduating, Wang Yingchun returned to Shanxi, devoting herself to print design oil painting, traditional Chinese painting, and engraving. Many of her oil paintings were exhibited in the 1970s. In 1978 she undertook graduate studies in the Chinese Ink Painting Department of the Central Academy of Fine Arts (Zhongyang meishu xueyuan), specializing again in figure painting. Among her teachers were the influential artists Jiang Zhaohe, Ye Qianyu, and Liu Lingcang. From 1980 Wang Yingchun was employed by the Traditional Chinese Painting Research Society (Zhongguohua yanjiuyuan) to work on traditional Chinese painting and academic research.

Wang Yingchun excels at large-scale paintings whose themes are social concern, which is rare in her field. Her graduation ink painting *Roar Yellow River* (Huanghe zai paoxiao) won her the Ye Qianyu Scholarship that year and *Taihang Wall of Iron* (Taihang tiebi) won a Gold Award in the Sixth National Fine Arts Exhibition of 1984. The latter is a large-scale work featuring brusque, choppy brush strokes; it glorifies the indomitable spirit of the Chinese during the Sino-Japanese War. With a mountainscape as a backdrop that draws the line of sight across the canvas, the piece unconventionally frees the vision of viewers, slamming them into a ringside seat at a time of historic struggle. Her comic book "Marriage of Xiao Er'hei" won Second Prize in the Third National Comic Book Appreciation Competition of 1984. Another of her works, *Golden Dream*, won a Bronze Award in 1989 in the National Fine Arts Exhibition.

SHAO Yiyang

Wang Yizhi

Wang Yizhi, 1901–1991, née Yang, of Zhijiang, Hunan Province, was the first woman to be formally admitted to the CCP. She was a leader in the national revolutionary upsurge of 1925–27, an underground communist member in the "White areas" in the 1930s, and principal of Number 101 High School in Beijing from the early 1950s until the early 1980s.

Wang Yizhi was born in the remote township of Zhijiang in western Hunan into the prosperous Yang family. She escaped footbinding because her father, while studying in Japan in the first decade of the twentieth century, realized that the practice was archaic and should not be continued. When he finally returned after many years, however, he became frustrated by his wife's inability to produce a male heir and decided to take a concubine. Deeply offended, his wife returned to her natal family in the countryside outside Zhijiang. After several months, a very melancholy Wang Yizhi was allowed to join her mother and the large Tan family.

In 1915 Wang Yizhi passed the highly competitive entrance examination for the Second Provincial Girls' Normal School in Taoyuan. This success was somewhat marred by the sudden death of her beloved mother. At the Taoyuan boarding school, she met Ding Ling (*q.v.*) and Wang Jianhong, two friends who were to have a major impact on her life. It was also at Taoyuan that Wang Yizhi came under the influence of May Fourth iconoclasm and participated in student efforts to reform the curriculum, particularly the moral conduct (*xiushen*) course that extolled the Confucian virtues of female chastity and subservience to male authority.

After graduating in late 1920, she secured a teaching position at a coeducational school in Xupu, Hunan, which had been founded by Xiang Jingyu (*q.v.*), a young woman of extraordinary talent who had recently left Hunan to participate in a work-study program in France. Before long, however, Wang Yizhi felt compelled to leave the province in order to avoid the arranged marriage her father was intent on forcing upon her. Her good friends Wang Jianhong and Ding Ling invited her to come with them to Shanghai, where they planned to attend the Shanghai Pingmin Girls' School, which was being set up by Wang Huiwu (*q.v.*) and her husband Li Da, a founding member of the CCP. When Wang Yizhi enrolled in the school, she opted to abandon her father's surname of Yang as a rejection of the patriarchal kinship system. At first Wang Yizhi wanted to be called simply Yizhi, but the difficulties of trying to function without a surname quickly became apparent (a conventional greeting was the question "What is your surname?"), so she decided to use the name Wang because it was common and written with only a few uncomplicated strokes.

Wang Yizhi's life as a communist began in early 1922 when she fell in love with Shi Cuntong (also known as Shi Fuliang, b. ca. 1895), one of the founding members of the party. Wang Yizhi stated in personal interviews in 1979 and 1980 that she became the first woman to be formally admitted to the Shanghai communist organization when introduced to it in mid-1922 by Liu Shaoqi (1898–1969); he was one of the most important leaders of the party and a man with whom she formed a close and lasting political affiliation. While no published source supports her contention, a careful examination of historical records reveals nothing to the contrary. Xiang Jingyu, the most important woman communist of the period, appears to have entered into the Shanghai communist organization in early 1922 *without any procedures*, as an automatic extension of the membership status accorded her husband, Cai Hesen.

During the next few years, Wang Yizhi attended Shanghai University and focused on women's work for the party, which consisted primarily of providing strike support for women workers, writing for women's journals, especially the *Women's Weekly* (Funü zhoubao), and joining a women's suffrage group. When the Shanghai branch of the Women's Rights League was established, she took a strong stand in one of her published articles on the significance of suffrage for women.

Wang Yizhi's relationship with Shi Cuntong dissolved in 1925, she took her small daughter from the union and in that same year entered into a relationship with Zhang Tailei (1898–1927), who had distinguished himself in party circles for excellent Russian language skills and knowledge of the Soviet Union. Like many communist men of that era, he already had a family by an arranged marriage. Zhang chose not to divorce his first wife at this time, but Wang Yizhi considered herself to be his wife and accompanied him to Guangdong, where Zhang served in a prominent role as translator for Comintern advisor Michael Borodin. Wang Yizhi's primary political activity while in Guangzhou was to serve as chief editor of *Light* (Guangming), the journal of the Guangdong Women's Emancipation Association. In late 1926, she and Zhang Tailei moved to Wuhan, the new capital of the revolutionary effort.

After the alliance between the CCP and KMT ruptured in April 1927 and the Wuhan government collapsed in July, her husband commenced communist insurrectionist activities and Wang Yizhi went back to Shanghai to prepare for the birth of their child.

A son was born in mid-October, and a month later Zhang Tailei left for Guangzhou, where he staged an uprising in December. This insurrection, which came to be known as the Canton Commune, was easily crushed and Zhang Tailei lost his life. For the next few years, Wang Yizhi engaged in communist underground work in Shanghai, marrying Liu Shaowen in 1928 and giving birth to a daughter in 1929. When this relationship broke apart under the inordinate pressures of underground work, Wang Yizhi married Li Zaiyun and then Gong Yibing in 1937.

After the Japanese invasion of north China in 1937, Wang Yizhi stayed in the White areas rather than going to Yan'an where Mao Zedong (1893–1976) had established a communist rural base area. When an underground radio station where she worked in Shanghai was raided by police, Wang Yizhi narrowly avoided arrest but lost contact with the underground CCP in Shanghai. In 1942 she undertook the difficult trek to Chongqing, the wartime capital, and worked at the Sichuan Hejiang Girls' School as a Chinese-language teacher.

After 1949 Wang Yizhi became an educator, serving as principal at a number of schools before assuming the position of principal at the coeducational Number 101 High School in Beijing in 1955. Under her guidance, this school became well known for its revolutionary curriculum and excellence in education. Red Guards ravaged it in the Cultural Revolution, however, and subjected Wang Yizhi to harsh treatment. She survived the ordeal and remained principal until her retirement in 1982.

Christina K. GILMARTIN

Cai Bo. Personal interview. Beijing, 23 July 1983.

Gilmartin, Christina K. *Engendering the Chinese Revolution: Radical Women, Communist Politics, and Mass Movements in the 1920s.* Berkeley: University of California Press, 1995.

Huaxia funü mingren cidian. Beijing: Huaxia chubanshe, 1988.

Wang Yizhi. Personal interviews. Beijing, 1979 and 1980.

———. "Wusi shidai de yige nüzhong." In *Wusi yundong huiyilu.* Beijing: Zhongguo shehui kexue chubanshe, 1979, 518.

[Wang] Yizhi. "Zimeimen kuailai gan nüquan yundong ba." *Funü pinglun,* no. 60 (27 September 1922): 1.

Wang Zhiying: *see* **Li Shuzheng**

Wang Zuling: *see* **Zhu Lin (writer)**

Wei Fengying

Wei Fengying, b. 1934? (sometimes given as 1933 or 1935), probably in Shenyang, Liaoning Province, was widely known in the 1960s as "Chairman Mao's Good Worker." During the Cultural Revolution, she rocketed to such high positions as the vice-chair of the Revolutionary Committee of Liaoning Province and member of the CCP's Ninth and Tenth Central Committees.

Wei Fengying was born into a worker's family. One source says that her father was a miner who died when she was only three; she and her mother had to beg for food, and they later earned a living by gathering firewood. In 1953, Wei Fengying got an apprenticeship with Northeast Machinery Works in Shenyang and, grateful for a new life as a worker, became determined to make the best of the opportunity. She carefully observed where technical improvements could be made and, although having no training of any kind, taught herself to make technical drawings from library books, trying to find new ideas from exhibitions of machinery. By repeated experimentation, Wei Fengying improved the machine tools of her own and neighboring shops. It was said that she made further innovations at amazing frequency and speed. She soon organized a group of sixteen workers who devoted their leisure time to solving production problems. Wei Fengying was appraised as a Model Worker of the city of Shenyang in 1954 and joined the CCP the same year. In 1959, she was appraised as a Model Worker of Liaoning Province and represented it in the NPC. She is said to have completed 109 separate improvements up to that year, some of them increasing productivity 100 percent. From the 1950s on, she won many model worker titles at local, provincial, and national levels, and it became commonplace for her to receive medals, flowers, and applause.

During the Cultural Revolution, Wei Fengying became a National Model Worker and an engineer at her plant. More than once, she represented the mass organizations for her province in Beijing. Her prestige rose considerably, however, after she was granted an audience by Mao Zedong (1893–1976) in 1964. The photograph of the chairman shaking her hand appeared on the front page of *People's Daily*, and shortly afterward she was given the sobriquet "Chairman Mao's Good Worker." Wei Fengying was promoted everywhere in China by the media. As a high-profile symbol of Mao's faithful workers, Wei Fengying found herself courted by all factions of the Cultural Revolution period, including Jiang Qing (*q.v.*) and her clique. Consequently, Wei Fengying catapulted to the leadership of Liaoning Province and the CCP Central Committee and from 1968 to 1977 was vice-chair of the Revolutionary Committee of Liaoning Province and full member of the CCP's Ninth and Tenth Central Committees. From that year to 1982, however, during the Eleventh Committee her status was lowered to alternate member. In the women's movement, Wei Fengying was chair of Liaoning Women's Federation and deputy section head of the ACWF.

After the death of Mao Zedong in 1976, Wei Fengying revealed uncertainty about her position in the political arena, declaring that she felt more at ease as a worker. She requested a transfer back to Liaoning. After working at the Provincial General Trade Union for some time, Wei Fengying was appointed as deputy manager of Xinyang Machinery Plant, a large-scale war industry plant in Shenyang. Reportedly, a leader of the party made the following comment to her: "There is no case against you at the Party's Central Committee. You have no problems. You did not cause harm to the old guard, neither did you join any gangs." With this comment from the highest level, Wei Fengying felt greatly relieved and reportedly responded that, in the special political climate of the Cultural Revolution, she had reached heights in political leadership beyond her wildest dreams. Now returned to her rightful place and doing what she did best, Wei Fengying felt relaxed and unpressured. Her performance in the new job gradually won her universal trust in the plant, and she was elected head of the Trade Union and a member of the Party Committee. In 1987, she was again elected as representative of the Huanggu District of Shenyang. Although the latter position hardly compares with those of her heyday in the 1960s, it may be more indicative of the road she would have traveled had the Cultural Revolution not wrenched her from her own context. By the 1990s, Wei Fengying had retired and enjoys a peaceful life with her husband, Lu Qichang, a former colleague from Northeast Machinery Works, whom she married in 1958. They have two daughters. A 1998 published article reported that she is writing her memoirs.

Lily Xiao Hong LEE

Bartke, Wolfgang. *Biographical Dictionary and Analysis of China's Party Leadership, 1922–1988.* Munich: Saur, 1990, 232.
Huaxia funü mingren cidian. Beijing: Huaxia chubanshe, 1988, 990.
Who's Who in Communist China. Hong Kong: Union Research Institute, 1969, 709.
Yifei. "Mao zhuxi de hao gongren." *Jinri mingliu,* no. 4 (1998): 48–51.

Wei Gongzhi

Wei Gongzhi, 1908–1973, of Xinyang County, Henan Province, was one of the thirty women who went with the First Front Red Army on the Chinese communists' Long March of 1934–35.

Born into a gentry family, Wei Gongzhi was subjected to footbinding as a young girl but "liberated" her feet in her early teens. She attended Kaifeng Middle School, becoming involved in its patriotic, anti-imperialist student movement, and was elected as a student representative at the time of the May Thirtieth Movement of 1925. The following year, Wei Gongzhi passed an examination that enabled her to enroll in the Women's Training Course at the Wuhan branch of the prestigious Whampoa Military Academy. There she studied military matters, one of her classmates being Zhou Yuehua (*q.v.*) who also took part in the Long March, and joined the CCP. Possibly during this period, she met and married Ye Jianying (1898–1986), who was an instructor at Whampoa Military Academy. He later became, during the 1970s, the most powerful military figure in the PRC.

Sent by the party to Guangzhou, Wei Gongzhi worked as a nurse during the famous Canton Commune of December 1927; then she became an editor on the magazine *Red Army Life*, while living in the first Chinese soviet in Hailufeng in Guangdong Province. Wei Gongzhi studied in Moscow for two years (1929–30) and upon return was appointed to various positions in charge of artistic and cultural activities in the Jiangxi soviet. She composed many plays, dances, and songs and was credited, along with Li Bozhao (*q.v.*), with developing the artistic life of the early soviet. During 1931 Wei Gongzhi worked in the secretariat of the Central Government Office in Ruijin and was that year expelled from the party as a suspected Trotskyite; her name was ordered removed "forever" from party records.

Despite the suspect political standing, Wei Gongzhi was included among the few women permitted to retreat from the Jiangxi soviet with the Red Army and party headquarters, probably because as an intellectual she was valuable and also because she was the wife of Ye Jianying. Wei Gongzhi went as an "ordinary person" (*laobaixing*), however, not as a cadre; even though walking with the cadres unit, she undertook the same duties as the women political workers. At the end of the Long March, Mao Zedong (1893–1976) directed that everyone who had completed the march be awarded party membership, and Wei Gongzhi was reinstated as a party member.

When Edgar Snow met her in Bao'an in 1936, Wei Gongzhi was director of the Chinese People's Anti-Japanese Dramatics Society; she had just had a baby when Helen Foster Snow met her in September 1937 in Xi'an. Wei Gongzhi must therefore have been pregnant during the four dangerous months she spent with Qian Xijun (*q.v.*), smuggling a large sum of international aid money from Shanghai to Xi'an in that year. Wei Gongzhi returned to Hunan on party business in 1939; she served there as head of the Henan secretariat, head of the Organization Department, and represented Henan at the CCP's Seventh National Congress. Wei Gongzhi attended the Party School in Yan'an in 1943 and was again accused of political misbehavior. Working in extremely harsh conditions in the northeast from 1945 to 1949, she contracted tuberculosis and was unable to work after the latter year. Her death on 8 February 1973 "from natural causes" was no doubt hastened by her being sent, in 1969, to Hubei during the Cultural Revolution. She was not provided proper medical care.

Sue WILES

Guo Chen. *Jinguo liezhuan: Hong yifangmianjun sanshiwei changzheng nühongjun shengping shiji.* Beijing: Nongcun duwu chubanshe, 1986, 32–33, 143–49.
Lee, Lily Xiao Hong and Sue Wiles. *Women of the Long March.* Sydney: Allen & Unwin, 1999.
Snow, Helen Foster. *Inside Red China.* 1977 reprint [with a new preface and biographical notes by the author]. New York: Da Capo Press, 1939, 296–97.
Song Ruizhi, ed. *Zhongguo funü wenhua tonglan.* Jinan: Shandong wenyi chubanshe, 1995, 235–37.
Zhao Heping. "Wei Gongzhi." In *Zhonggongdangshi renwuzhuan.* Xi'an: Shaanxi renmin chubanshe, 1988, 239–67.

Wei Xiuying

Wei Xiuying, b. 1910, of Ruijin County, Jiangxi Province, was one of the thirty women who went with the First Front Red Army on the Chinese communists' Long March of 1934–35.

A peasant, Wei Xiuying was sold as a child bride to a merchant in neighboring Xingguo County when she was five; she never remarried after running away from her husband's family to join the Red Army in 1930. The seventeen year old joined the CCP in 1932 and for the next year headed the Women's Department of Xingguo County, going on in the following year to the Women's Department of Jiangxi Provincial Committee. She was designated as a "political fighter" on the Long March, doing political propaganda and hiring bearers. Many times Wei Xiuying carried litters herself when bodyguards refused to and hired laborers had fled, this despite a diminutive build that earned her the nickname "Shortie." After reaching Yan'an, Wei Xiuying was attached to the Women's Bureau and then in mid-1938 sent back to the south to carry out women's work and guerrilla activities in the dangerous Jiangxi-Guangdong region. She was recalled in late 1940 to Yan'an and attended the Marx-Lenin School and the elite Party School. Wei Xiuying was elected in 1945 to the Seventh Party Congress and between that year and 1949 held various posts in Jilin Province in the northeast, including membership of the Standing Committee and head of the Organization Department of Dunhua County, as well as secretary to the Provincial Women's Committee.

After 1949, she was appointed to the Jiangxi Provincial Party Committee, became secretary to its Women's Committee, deputy head of the ACWF's Rural Work Team Department, and a member of the Standing Committee of Jiangxi CPPCC. Wei Xiuying suffered criticism during the Cultural Revolution but was not physically harmed and became rehabilitated in 1978. She retired in 1983, retaining her seat on the Jiangxi CPPCC. Wei Xiuying was in good health when interviewed by American and Chinese journalists in 1986 and at the time of writing was believed to be living in Jiangxi. Even the malicious behavior that surfaced during the Cultural Revolution did not destroy her loyalty to the CCP, which she regarded as responsible for rescuing her from a life of poverty, illiteracy, and an unhappy marriage.

Sue WILES

Guo Chen. *Jinguo liezhuan: Hong yifangmianjun sanshiwei changzheng nühongjun shengping shiji.* Beijing: Nongcun duwu chubanshe, 1986, 13–15.
Huang Qizhuang. "Yige nüzhanshide zuji." In *Hongjun nüyingxiong zhuan*, eds. Liaowang bianjibu. Beijing: Xinhua chubanshe, 1986, 163–74.
Lee, Lily Xiao Hong and Sue Wiles. *Women of the Long March.* Sydney: Allen & Unwin, 1999.
Salisbury, Harrison E. *The Long March: The Untold Story.* New York: Harper & Row, 1985, 32, 36, 81, 88, 206, 237, 265–666.

Wong, Ruth Hie King

Ruth Wong Hie King, 1918–1982, was a dedicated and highly respected educator in Singapore and Malaysia.

Born in Singapore, she began her working life there as a schoolteacher during the days of British colonial rule and later trained teachers at both the University of Singapore and the University of Malaya. The academic awards (with attendant responsibilities) from around the world with which Ruth Wong was honored acknowledged the contributions she made during her career that spanned more than thirty-seven years. She received a visiting fellowship under the Commonwealth Scholarship and Fellowship Plan (Australia) and was elected to fellowship of the College of Preceptors (London) and the World Academy of Arts and Sciences. Ruth Wong served in 1968 as a consultant to the Malaysia-based Regional Centre for Science and Mathematics and was appointed to the governing board of the United Nations Educational, Scientific, Cultural Organization's Institute of Education, based in Hamburg (1972–75); the board of directors to the International Council on Education for Teaching, based in Virginia, in the U.S.; and the Research Review Advisory Committee of the International Development and Research Council of Canada.

Dr. Wong's beliefs and educational convictions are best understood in the light of the evangelical Christian home she grew up in. Her father, Wong Kai Seng (1888–1977), a highly respected lay preacher who came to Singapore from Fuzhou in China in 1916, made sure his children were fully aware of the teachings of Christ and did not lack spiritual guidance. Ruth Wong's understanding of her father's values manifested early in her life by her own filial behavior: when her father's "limping business failed miserably," she gave up a scholarship after successfully completing her Senior Cambridge examinations in 1935 and "took to teaching in a private school for the lordly sum of $26 a month," before entering Raffles College in Singapore.

Ruth Wong gained a Diploma of Arts and Diploma of Education there, studying from 1935 to 1939, and her outstanding performance won her an Exhibition. She then taught at the Singapore Methodist Girls' School for a while just before and soon after World War II; Ruth Wong was also a teacher during the Japanese occupation of Singapore. In early 1950, she went abroad and studied at Queen's University in Belfast, winning the Sir John Porter Scholarship and the Isabella Tod Memorial Prize, and graduated in 1954 with an honors degree in mathematics. Returning to Singapore, Ruth Wong taught at the Anglo-Chinese School for a year, then became head (1955–56) of the Mathematics Department of the Teachers' Training College before being seconded as a lecturer to the Education Department at the University of Malaya in Singapore. In 1959, she spent time at the Educational Testing Service at Princeton, in the U.S., as a testing associate under a Fulbright Scholarship before proceeding to Harvard University for graduate studies, leading to a master's degree and a Ph.D. in Education (1960–62).

While Ruth Wong had originally wanted to pursue a career in medicine, as a teacher she was "willing to remain one. In my whole career, I left no post by deliberate choice to further my own ambitions, more particularly because I had no personal resources. With each step upward, God had to equip me first with the wherewithal to cope and His provision was always just where and when it was needed to anticipate His next move." Writing just a few weeks before her death, Ruth Wong reflected that "after a manner of speaking, then, I was shunted into education. . . . If I had not been directed by the Lord into teaching, I would never have imagined I could teach. I was a rather introverted type of person, not always at ease in the presence of others." Although describing herself as "frequently tongue-tied," the educator was a remarkably innovative teacher with great compassion for the weak and disadvantaged. A colleague spoke of her "unique admixture of exemplary qualities that are hard to emulate, for she was simultaneously firm, fair, flexible, friendly and far-sighted." Very articulate at the lectern and much in demand as a speaker in both Malaysia and Singapore, Ruth Wong was also a skilled and prolific writer (a bibliography of her published work lists sixty-eight items, including conference papers, speeches, journal articles, monographs, and chapters in books), with an elegant command of English. She wrote engagingly on a wide range of topics, drawing on the sophisticated intellectual tradition formerly experienced at Harvard.

Ruth Wong taught briefly at the University of Singapore upon her return from Harvard before going up in 1963 to the University of Malaya in Kuala Lumpur to set up its School of Education. This later became the Faculty of Education of which she was the first dean. Inspirational in her idealism, enthusiasm, and dedication to the cause of education, Ruth Wong was well known in the city; a colleague recalls that she was "a dynamic leader in education . . . She had the courage of her convictions and started a school to experiment with multilingual programs at a time when nationalism and the national language [Malay] were being intensely promoted."

In 1969 Ruth Wong returned to Singapore to assume responsibility in the Ministry of Education as director of research overseeing research, statistics, guidance, and counseling. In order to gain first-hand knowledge of the problems being experienced at the grassroots, she spent three months visiting schools. Her purpose was to understand the implemented curriculum, i.e., what was actually happening, as distinct from the intended curriculum as reflected in the subject syllabi. The seminar "Whither the Sacred Cows of Education?" conducted late in 1969 as a result of her tour was designed "to question certain entrenched beliefs about children and classroom teaching and to open a frank dialogue between Ministry officials and those laboring in the field on what they perceived to be urgent problems needing attention." Dr. Wong exercised a strong and enduring influence on the structural planning of Singapore's school curriculum, having been made chair of its Advisory Committee on Curriculum Development in early 1970.

She was also appointed, in mid-1971, as principal of the Teachers' Training College; her brief was "to re-organize the College and see to it that a new breed of teachers, sympathetic to the spirit and objectives of the new [school] curriculum, would be trained." Ruth Wong then became the inaugural director of the Institute of Education, formed in April 1973 to replace the Teachers' Training College, the University School of Education, and the Research Unit of the Ministry of Education. Largely under her leadership, the concept of teacher training evolved into teacher education, and in this field she made her most significant contribution in Singapore. Ruth Wong introduced changes that developed a new curriculum for teacher education; new ways of assessing coursework; a tighter link between theory and practice through the establishment of "experimental and demonstration" schools; educational research, much of it carried out by indigenous researchers; and a mechanism for teaching University of Singapore's graduate candidates.

Having declined to renew her contract with the Institute of Education in 1976, Ruth Wong continued to participate in research projects in education on a voluntary basis. She also worked as a part-time student counselor at the University of Singapore and took an active interest in community and church work. She became very ill in 1981 and died in 1982, at the age of 64.

A former student wrote how Ruth Wong "never retired from education. . . . Indeed, to the very end, even when she was ill and in pain, she did not hold back her advice on educational matters. She was actually writing lesson plans and teaching three monolingual [academically weak] classes while undergoing radiotherapy. She stopped being a school teacher only when she was confined to bed. . . . She was non-partisan in the cause of education, a real beacon to all and sundry."

HO Wah Kam

Ho Wah Kam. *The Educational Legacy of Dr. Ruth Wong Hie King.* Singapore: Centre for Applied Research in Education, 1995.

Lau, Aileen. "A Tribute to Dr. Ruth Wong." *STAS Bulletin,* April 1982, 1.

Librarian, Queen's University Library. Personal communication, 1995.

Lim Kiat Boey. Personal communication, 1995.

Ministry of Education. *The Sacred Cows of Education.* Seminar Report. Singapore: Ministry of Education, 1969.

Sim Wong Kooi. "Foreword." In *Unto Each Child the Best,* ed. Lee Kok Cheong, Singapore: P.G. Publishing, 1990.

Wong, Ruth. "Called to Be a Teacher." Singapore: Singapore Teachers' Christian Fellowship, 1982.

——. "Curriculum Development in Singapore with Special Reference to the Revised Primary Syllabuses." Paper presented at the Singapore Book Publishing Association Seminar on the Role of Educational Materials in Singapore Schools, 14–16 March 1973.

——. *Educational Innovation in Singapore.* Paris, UNESCO, 1974.

Wu, Butterfly: *see* **Hu Die**

Wu, Chien-Shiung

Chien-Shiung Wu [Wu Jianxiong], 1912–1997, was born in Shanghai, although her ancestral home was Taicang County, Jiangsu Province; she was a renowned scientist in atomic and nuclear physics.

Hers was a family of intellectuals who advocated gender equality. Her father, Wu Zhongyi, founded Mingde College in Taicang County, and her mother, Fan Fuhua, encouraged and supported girls in going to school. Chien-Shiung Wu graduated at the age of fifteen from Jiangsu Second Normal School in Suzhou and worked for two years as a primary school teacher before being admitted in 1929 to the Mathematics Department at the National Central University in Nanjing. A year later she transferred to the Physics Department, graduating in 1934 with a bachelor's degree. After a period as an assistant lecturer at the University of Zhejiang, Chien-Shiung Wu worked for a time in Academia Sinica, where she was the only female research associate.

Desiring to further her studies and build upon her excellent academic performance, Chien-Shiung Wu spent her savings on a third-class cabin ticket and sailed in 1936 for the United States. She undertook graduate studies at the University of California, Berkeley, under the famous physicist E.O. Lawrence (1901–1958), inventor of the cyclotron and recipient in 1939 of the Nobel Prize in Physics. Chien-Shiung Wu concentrated on atomic and nuclear physics, achieving outstanding success in her experimental technique. After gaining a Ph.D. in 1940, she was invited to work as an assistant in Lawrence's laboratory.

In 1942 Chien-Shiung Wu married Luke C.L. Yuan (Yuan Jialiu, b. 1912), who had graduated in 1932 from Yen-ching University in Beijing and been awarded a Ph.D. from Caltech (California Institute of Technology) in 1940. Luke Yuan has since made significant contributions to the field of nuclear physics, especially high energy physics, and in 1961 co-edited with Chien-Shiung Wu *Nuclear Physics,* volume 5, of *Methods of Experimental Physics.* Their son, Vincent Yuan, also became a physicist.

Chien-Shiung Wu taught at Smith College and Princeton University before becoming part of the American war effort; she was invited to join the Wartime Research Institute at Columbia University and work on one of the components of the Manhattan Project, which produced the first atomic bomb. Chien-Shiung Wu was involved in radiation monitoring research that led to improvements in the Geiger Counter. With the end of World War II, she remained at Columbia University and continued research into radiation, carrying out with her colleagues systematic experiments on the beta decay of dozens of radioactive atomic elements. Chien-Shiung Wu was considered an authority in the field of beta decay and was appointed to an associate professorship at the university in 1952. With the physicist S.A. Moczkowski, Wu co-authored the book *Beta Decay* (1956).

The most important scientific contribution of Chien-Shiung Wu was to prove the hypothesis proposed in 1956 by Chen Ning Yang (Yang Zhenning, b. 1922) and Tsung-Dao Lee (Li Zhengdao, b. 1926) that the principle of conservation of parity, long regarded as a basic universal law, did not hold for weak interactions of subatomic particles. Chien-Shiung Wu was asked to devise an experiment to prove the claim. Her research team conducted meticulous experiments with the radioactive isotope cobalt 60 cooled to 0.01° above absolute zero (minus 459.67° F). Locating the cobalt 60 in a strong electromagnetic field, Chien-Shiung Wu observed that when the cobalt nuclei broke down in beta decay, the atoms behaved "like a left-handed screw." This confirmed the thesis of Yang and Lee and proved that nature differentiates between left and right. The results of her experiment caused a sensation in the world of physics when they were released at the beginning of 1957. Yang and Lee (but not Chien-Shiung Wu) were awarded that year's Nobel Prize in Physics; Dr. Lee said on hearing of Chien-Shiung Wu's death in 1997 that she was "one of the giants of physics." Chien-Shiung Wu was appointed professor in the Faculty of Physics at Columbia University in 1958 in recognition of her work and the same year was awarded an honorary Doctor of Science from Princeton University and elected to the U.S. National Academy of Sciences.

In 1963 she and her team also verified by experiment the theoretical law of vector current in beta decay put forward in 1958 by Richard Feynman (1918–1988) and Murray Gell-Mann (b. 1929). They thus proved a close connection between electromagnetic and weak interactions and laid the ground for the "grand unified theory" that was advanced in 1974. This was extremely important in beta decay research for nuclear and particle physics.

In the late 1940s, Chien-Shiung Wu carried out with her team research experiments in basic quantum mechanics proving that electrons and positrons had opposite parity. Her team carried out further experiments in 1970 that supported at a more advanced level the formal principles of quantum mechanics. She conducted research in the 1960s and 1970s into muon, mesotron, and antiproton physics, publishing several books and over one hundred research papers on her innovative and highly valued work. Chien-Shiung Wu also researched the application and measurement of the Mössbauer Effect, particularly its application to macromolecular biology, such as determining the structure of blood cell protein.

Chien-Shiung Wu was once called the "Queen of Physics"; she was also said to have "richly earned the right to be called the world's foremost female experimental physicist." Dozens of additional honorary doctorates from famous universities, including Harvard and Yale, were bestowed upon her, and in 1975 Chien-Shiung Wu was elected president of the American Physical Society, the first woman to hold the position. The same year, she was presented with the National Medal of Science, the highest award for achievement in science. In 1978 Chien-Shiung Wu received the inaugural Wolf Prize in Physics.

Although taking out American citizenship (28 June 1954) and living and working for most of her life in America, she retained a concern for the development of science in China. Chien-Shiung Wu visited there several times after 1973 to see relatives, pay official visits, and give talks; she also donated money to Mingde College in her hometown. Chien-Shiung Wu was appointed honorary professor at Nanjing University, Peking University, and the Chinese Science and Technology University and made a member of the Academic Committee of the High Energy Research Institute of the Chinese Academy of Sciences. The Wu Chien-Shiung Physics Award was established in China in 1986, under the sponsorship of a Hong Kong business, for the purpose of rewarding excellent academic achievement in young physicists under the age of forty. Zijinshan Observatory in Nanjing named an asteroid in Chien-Shiung Wu's honor in May 1990 in recognition of her outstanding achievement in atomic physics research and substantial contributions to the development of science education in China. In 1994 the first group of foreign academicians was elected to the Chinese Academy of Sciences: Chien-Shiung Wu was the first foreign female to be admitted.

The following comment attributed to Chien-Shiung Wu provides some insight into her attitude toward her work: "There is only one thing worse than coming home from the lab to a sink full of dirty dishes—and that is not going to the lab at all."

WANG Bing
(Translated by Barbara Law)

Dicke, William. "Chien-Shiung Wu, 84, Dies; Top Experimental Physicist." *The New York Times* Biographical Service, February (1997): 323.
Feng Duan and Lu Yan, eds. *Bange shiji de kexue shengya—Wu Jianxiong, Yuan Jialiu wenji.* Nanjing: Nanjing daxue chubanshe, 1992.
Jiang Caijian. *Wu Jianxiong: Wulikexue de diyi furen.* Taipei: Shibao wenhua chubanqiye, 1996.
"Wu, Chien-Shiung." CWP, at <http://www.physics,ucla.edu/~cwp>, accessed 24 February 2001.
Wu, C.S., and S. A. Moczkowski. *Beta Decay.* New York: Interscience, 1965.
Yang Fujia and Hu Xusheng. "Wu Jianxiong." In *Zhongguo xiandai kexuejia zhuanji,* vol. 4. Beijing: Kexue chubanshe, 1993, 127–42.
Yuan, Luke C.L., and Chien-Shiung Wu, eds. *Nuclear Physics,* vol. 5 of *Methods of Experimental Physics.* New York: Academic Press, 1961–63.

Wu, C.S.: *see* **Wu, Chien-Shiung**

Wu Fulian

Wu Fulian, 1912–1937, born in Shanghang County, Fujian Province, to a peasant family was one of the thirty women who took part in the Chinese communists' Long March of 1934–35.

Given away by her widowed mother as a child bride, Wu Fulian left home at the age of seventeen and traveled about with communist propaganda teams, becoming head of the Young Pioneers and a member of the CCP (1929), head of the local Women's Bureau, a member of the County Committee (1931), and a member of the provincial Fujian-Guangdong-Jiangxi Committee (1932). She worked on this last committee with a man named Liu Xiao, whom she later married, and with fellow Long Marcher Li Jianzhen (*q.v.*). Wu Fulian was sent to the Central Party School in the Jiangxi soviet in 1933 and headed a Provincial Women's Bureau in 1934. After completing military training at the Central School with Wei Xiuying (*q.v.*) and Deng Liujin (*q.v.*), Wu Fulian participated with them in the mass recruitment drive that foreshadowed the Long March. Her duties on the march included political work with its field hospital and Convalescent Company, hiring bearers, buying/confiscating grain and cash, seeking out billets, and placing out direction markers for the marchers. Assigned to Zhang Guotao's Fourth Front Army in August 1935, she was made head of a northwest Women's Bureau, then political commissar of the Women's Anti-Japanese Vanguard Regiment, which was under the leadership of Wang Quanyuan (*q.v.*). Wu Fulian was wounded, captured, and died in prison in April 1937, barely six months after the Western Route Army crossed the Yellow River and was massacred by Moslem cavalry in the Gansu Corridor.

Sue WILES

Guo Chen. *Jinguo liezhuan: Hong yifangmianjun sanshiwei changzheng nühongjun shengping shiji.* Beijing: Nongcun duwu chubanshe, 1986, 190–93.
Xi Jun. *Jinguo beige.* Chengdu: Sichuan remin chubanshe, 1995, 224–35.

Wu Jianxiong: *see* Wu, Chien-Shiung

Wu Ma-li

Wu Ma-li, b. 1957 in Taipei, Taiwan, studied at the Angewandte Kunstakademie, Vienna, from 1980 to 1982, and graduated from the Staatliche Kunstakademie, Düsseldorf, with an M.F.A. in 1986. Fluent in German and English, she is one of the most intellectual artists in Taiwan who, through the practice of installation in "deformed" or "appropriated" objects and situations as well as video, deconstructs both habitual Chinese notions of women and the spectral power of new goods in a consumer society.

Wu Ma-li has exhibited widely internationally, including her plastic encasement of Western philosophy books she had torn up at the 49th Venice Biennale in 1995. Her status was recognized when this work was selected by Najo Fumio for the 1998 Taipei Biennial. At this event, the artist exhibited a life-sized simulacrum of a sex motel together with explanatory texts, metaphors for the nature of Taiwanese society and its male orientation.

John CLARK

Art Taiwan. Biennale Venezia, Palazzo Delle Prigioni: organized by Taipei Fine Arts Museum, 1995.
Ch'ang Fang-wei, Miki Akiko, and Ishigami Mori, eds. *Yü-wang ch'ang-yü / Site of Desire: 1998 Taipei Biennial.* Taipei: Taipei shih-li mei-shu-kuan, 1998.
Ch'en Yü-ling, ed. *I-hsiang yü mei-hsü: Taiwan nü-hsing i-shu-chan.* Taipei: Taipei shih-li mei-shu-kuan, 1998.
Clark, John. "Touch Texture and Concept: Three Woman Artists from Taiwan." In *Art Taiwan,* eds. N. Jose and Yang Wen-i. Sydney: Museum of Contemporary Art, 1995.
Wu Ma-li, *Treasure Island MA-LI WU.* Taipei: I T PARK Gallery, 1998.

Wu Molan: *see* **Wu Mulan**

Wu Mulan
Wu Mulan, 1888?–1939, original name Wu Molan and also known during the late 1930s as Hu Dachang, was a native of Fuzhou County, Jiangxi Province. She was a revolutionary and one of the leading proponents for women's suffrage in China before and after the 1911 Revolution.

Wu Mulan went to Japan in 1904 to pursue her studies, enrolling at Jissen Jogakkō, a girls' school founded by the famous Japanese woman educator Shimoda Utako (1854–1936). From there Wu Mulan went in 1905 to an academy known as Daisei Gakkan; she enjoyed literature. During this period, Wu Mulan joined the revolutionary Tongmenghui and participated in a bomb-making enterprise set up in Yokohama in the same year by Huang Xing (1874–1916) and other Chinese students anxious for the future of their country. Some of those involved in this activity were Qiu Jin, Fang Junying, and Chen Xiefen (for all three, see *Biographical Dictionary of Chinese Women: The Qing Period*), Lin Zongsu (*q.v.*), and Tang Qunying (*q.v.*).

When it appeared that the October 1911 Revolution in China would be successful, Wu Mulan was among the Chinese students still in Japan who attended and spoke at a meeting in November that year celebrating the "establishment of New China." Skilled in oratory, Wu Mulan urged women to pursue education in order to devote themselves to their nation and take an active part in military and political affairs. The following day she announced her intentions to return to China to join the Women's Red Cross Army (Nüzi chishizituan); if it turned out she was not needed on the battlefield, then she would become an active participant in the revolution, not drawing the line at serving as a spy. After returning to China, Wu Mulan helped organize the Women Citizens' Army (Nü guomin jun), upon which women in Shanghai modeled their various military groups. Wu Mulan threw her weight behind the Women's Northern Attack Brigade (Nüzi beifa dui) and in January 1912 set up in Shanghai the Women's United Military Team (Tongmeng nüzi jingwu lianxidui) to promote the ideals of the Women Citizens' Army. Wu Mulan was chair and among the eighty or so who joined were Li Yuanhong (1864–1928), Wu Tingfang (1842–1922), and Cheng Dequan (1860–1930).

Once the Nanjing provisional government had been set up in 1912, the women revolutionaries of Shanghai changed their focus from military activities to gaining political rights and gender equality before the law. Theirs was a short, dramatic, but ultimately fruitless struggle (*vide* Tang Qunying, a Hunan feminist who was involved in seeking suffrage and equality at this time). Wu Mulan became chair of the Alliance for Women's Participation in Politics (Nüzi canzheng tongmenghui) formed on 22 February to fight for the right of women to take part in politics. On 16 March, a sister organization called the Association of Chinese Women for the Promotion of the Republic (Shenzhou nüjie gonghe xiejihui) formed in Shanghai with Zhang Mojun (*q.v.*, also known as Zhang Zhaohan and Sophie Zhang) as chair. Wang Changguo, Tang Qunying, Shen Peizhen, and Lin Zongsu were all vocal in their determination to gain political rights for women. On 19 March, a formal request was submitted to provisional president Dr. Sun Yat-sen (1866–1925) that a statement guaranteeing equal rights for men and women be included in the new Constitution. Dr. Sun, who was in principle sympathetic to the women's demands, was removed from the presidency in April and the seat of government was moved to Beijing, where Yuan Shikai (1859–1916) prepared to assume control of China. Although public opinion largely opposed women's participation in politics, the women continued their campaign.

In April, under the leadership of Tang Qunying, the Alliance for Women's Participation in Politics, which had been formed in February from its Shanghai counterpart (Shanghai nüzi canzheng tongmenghui), along with the Women's Reinforcement Association (Nüzi houyuanhui), the Women's Society for the Esteem of Military Affairs (Nüzi shang wu hui), the Nanjing Women's Revolutionary Alliance (Jinling nüzi tongmenghui), and the Hunan Women's Citizens' Association (Hunan nüguomin hui) published their manifesto. In this declaration, they committed themselves to promoting political knowledge among women, improving women's political skills, and fighting for the right of women to participate in politics. Wu Mulan went with many of the women to Beijing to pursue the goals but the authorities ignored their demands, and by early 1913 women's political organizations had been banned.

.Hardly anything is known of Wu Mulan after this. At some stage, she married Wang Jiannong, whom she later divorced, and she had a son, Wu Zhenqiu (b. 1921), who graduated from Haidong Secondary School in Shanghai during the 1930s. Wu Mulan changed her name to Hu Dachang during the war with Japan (1937–45) and captained a guerrilla unit. She had also joined Wang Jingwei (1883–1944) in his attempt to establish a pro-Japanese central political power but mainly engaged in the activities of the Women's Peace Association (Funü heping hui). Believed to be a traitor to the Chinese people, she was assassinated by persons unknown on 22 December 1939 in Huabei Mansion on Malang Road in Shanghai's French concession. She was fifty-two years old.

Hok-chung LAM

(Translated by Vivian C.T. Fu)

Du Wei. "Shanghai nüzi beifa gansidui." In *Xinhai geming huiyilu*, vol. 4, eds. Zhongguo renmin zhengzhi xieshang huiyi weiyuanhui and Wenshi ziliao yanjiu weiyuanhui. Beijing: Zhonghua shuju, 1962, 59–62.

Fujita Masanori. *Gendai Chūgoku jinbutsu besshosoran.* Tokyo: Kyuko shoin, 1986.

Kojima Yoshio. *Ryunichi gakusei no shingai kakumei.* Tokyo: Aoki shoten, 1989.

Minlibao, 19 November 1911, 3; 14 January 1912, 6; 23 March 1912, 7; 12 April 1912, 1, 8.

Nanjing xinbao, 23 December 1939, 1a; 24 December 1939, 1a.
Shenbao, 22 February 1912, 7.
Shibao, 2 March 1912, 2–3; 10 April 1912, 3–4.
Tokyo asahi shinbun, 12 November 1911, 5; 18 November 1911, 5.

Wu Sheng: *see* **Yan Huizhu**

Wu Shun-wen

Wu Shun-wen [Wu Shunwen], b. 1912, a native of Wu-chin [Wujin], Chiang-su [Jiangsu] Province, is an industrialist. She has been described as a captain of industry in Taiwan for her involvement in the textile, automobile, and shipping industries and is also active in women's organizations in Taiwan.

The daughter of textile industrialist Wu Ching-yüan [Wu Jingyuan], who was based in Ch'ang-chou [Changzhou], Chiang-su, before 1949, Wu Shun-wen received her education in Shanghai, attending McTyeire Girls' School and St. John's University. She then went to the United States to further her studies and received a master's degree from Columbia University.

By the time the Wu family settled in Taiwan in 1952, Wu Shun-wen was married to Yen Ch'ing-ling [Yan Qingling] (1908–1981), whose father, Yen Yü-t'ang [Yan Yutang] (1880–1959), had founded the Ta-lung [Dalong] Workshops in Shanghai. In 1948, Wu Shun-wen and her husband formulated a plan for their future career. Yen Ch'ing-ling had set his mind on heavy industry because of his family's involvement in manufacturing textile machinery. Heavy industry required high levels of investment, however, and because they did not have enough capital to initiate such a project at that time they decided to start with textiles. The two could then use the profits generated from textiles to support heavy industry. Therefore, they brought twenty thousand spindles and five hundred machines made by the Yen family's Shanghai machinery plant to Taiwan and established the T'ai-yüan Textile Company in Hsin-chu.

Wu Shun-wen ran this factory entirely by herself. In its early days, T'ai-yüan aimed at the domestic market, and as the largest textile company in Taiwan it was very profitable. One of Wu Shun-wen's innovations during this early period was to change from two ten-hour shifts to three eight-hour shifts in an effort to protect the health of the women workers and allow them to spend more time at home looking after their children. She received tough opposition from senior administrative staff and the board but through great patience managed to convince these people that the shorter shifts would increase efficiency, reduce sickness in workers, and improve the quality of the products. As she had predicted, the three-shift system saw a rise in profits.

The 1950s was the golden age of the textile industry in Taiwan. Wu Shun-wen nevertheless foresaw tough domestic competition ahead that would require an upgrading of machinery and products so that T'ai-yüan could enter the export market. Through contacts established during her father's time, she was able to buy on credit fifteen thousand brand-new spindles and more than four hundred new machines from a British manufacturer who agreed to accept installment payments. This investment greatly increased the productivity of the company, which in 1962 won the Quality

Award for Cotton Yarn in a competition centered on reforms in production and sales in the private sector, sponsored by the National Industries' Union (Ch'üan-kuo kung-yeh tsung-hui).

With improved products, Wu Shun-wen concentrated on developing export, first to Australia, England, and America and expanded then to Africa, Hong Kong, Southeast Asia, and Canada. For many years from 1969 on, T'ai-yüan was commended by the government for achieving the highest export record. When the United States later decided to restrict the import of Taiwan textile products, many Taiwan companies suffered. They formed a delegation to go to the United States to negotiate with trade officials, and the textile industry elected Wu Shun-wen as their leader in the mission. This move resulted in the United States giving a quota to Taiwan. Because of its high market share before the quota was imposed, T'ai-yüan enjoyed 18.7 percent of this figure and was therefore not too badly affected by the import restriction crisis.

Wu Shun-wen was always one step ahead. At the end of the 1960s, she foresaw that the days of concentration on cotton were over, synthetics and cotton blends being the future of textiles. Wu Shun-wen therefore ordered from England new machinery that could handle blending and embarked on another new operation. She created T'ai-wen Knitting Company when knitwear became popular in the 1960s and 1970s and also planned a successful campaign to enter into the European market in order to expand Taiwan's export market.

The success of Wu Shun-wen's textile business helped nurture her husband's fledgling automobile manufacturing company, Taiwan's first car manufacturer—Yüeh Lung (Yü-lung [Yulong]) Automobile Manufacturing Company. Yen Ch'ing-ling established Yüeh Lung in 1953, and until 1963 it had been Taiwan's only automobile manufacturer. In 1969, T'ai-yüan and Mitsubishi established China Motors (Chung-kuo ch'i-ch'e kung-ssu) to produce light trucks and commercial vehicles. Wu Shun-wen had been on the board of Yüeh Lung from the beginning and after her husband's death in 1981 ran the company as chair of the board. In 1990, she also assumed the position of chief executive officer.

In 1957, Yüeh Lung had established technological transfer relations with the Japanese company Nissan. As the only locally manufactured car, Yüeh Lung had for many years received government protection; with the gradual evolution of the car industry toward a free market, however, the company faced many difficulties. Wu Shun-wen began a series of internal reforms, one being to break off in 1988 an unhappy relationship with its sole agent, thus allowing Yüeh Lung to choose many other dealers and expand its distribution network. She decided to build an engineering center that would make Yüeh Lung more independent in technical matters from its Japanese partner. This center designed and built the Fei-ling car in 1986 to fulfill her husband's dream of building a "Chinese" car.

However, in response to the changing conditions of the marketplace, the philosophy of the company also shifted from being a nationalistic car manufacturer to becoming an internationally successful enterprise through integration into the global market. In 1986, Nissan bought 25 percent of Yüeh Lung's shares from Wu Shun-wen, making her Taiwan's biggest taxpayer that year. Also at that time, 25 percent of

China Motors was transferred to Mitsubishi. Yüeh Lung participated in developing Mitsubishi's Freeca, which was designed for the Asian market, and took on responsibility for the technical side of producing it in Taiwan, the Philippines, and Indonesia to sell in Southeast Asia, Taiwan, and China. With these restructures, Yüeh Lung has remained the most profitable automobile manufacturer on the Taiwan market. The Yüeh Lung group now has thirty enterprises in five diverse areas: automobiles, textiles, financial services, construction, and high technology. Since 1990, her son Yen K'ai-t'ai [Yan Kaitai] (b. 1965) has gradually taken the helm of the family business, starting with the position of deputy general manager and being appointed deputy chair of the board in 1999.

Wu Shun-wen serves Taiwan and its industries in more than one way. In order to improve the speed and costs of shipping her products, she became involved as chair of the Shipping and Consignment Association (T'o-yün hsieh-hui) in negotiating on behalf of Taiwan exporters. Her colleagues praised her work. Wu Shun-wen also sits on the board of the National Industries' Union, the Association for the Promotion of the Information Technology Industry (Tzu-hsün kung-yeh ts'e-chin hui), and the Foundation for Cross-Strait Exchange (Hai-hsia chiao-liu chi-chin-hui).

Apart from being an industrialist, Wu Shun-wen also contributed to education in Taiwan. From the 1950s, she taught at Soochow University (Tung-wu ta-hsüeh) and Cheng-chi University (Cheng-chih ta-hsüeh) in Taipei. Wu Shun-wen also established the Hsin-p'u Technical College (Hsin-p'u kung-chuan) to provide training for industry and is its president as well as chair of its board. From 1961 to 1966, she held the government-appointed post of senior member of the Examination Committee of the Examination Yüan. At the same time, Wu Shun-wen participated in many women's organizations, being elected president of the International Women's Association (1961–62), the first Chinese to win such an honor, and the founding president of the Taipei chapter of the International Zonta Society. She received two honorary doctorates: a Doctor of Law from Kennedy College, Nebraska, and a Doctor of Commerce from St. John's University, New York. Wu Shun-wen was among the first to be honored as one of the "Ten Great Industrialists" of the Republic of China.

As a leader of industry, she not only created several successful businesses of her own but also supported her husband's car business, restructuring it after his death into a stronger and more independent entity. She introduced the three-shift system in the textile industry, which improved the quality of life for women workers; developed exports, and helped ensure the survival of the textile industry in Taiwan; and devoted herself to working tirelessly for the common welfare of Taiwan industries. As an educator, she trained generations of students for industry and society at large. Wu Shun-wen is a shining example of a woman who has excelled in industry, a field generally dominated by men.

Lily Xiao Hong LEE

Chung-hua min-kuo ming-jen lu. Taipei: Chung-yang t'ung-hsün-she, 1999.
Chung-hua min-kuo tang-tai ming-jen lu, vol. 3. Taipei: Taiwan Chung-hua shu-chü, 1978, 1438.

Erh-shih-nien lai ti Taiwan funü. Taipei: Chung-hua min-kuo lien-ho-kuo t'ung-chih-hui. Fu-nü wei-yuan-hui, 1969?, 65–71.

Guiheux, Gilles. "Economic History of Taiwan: The Case of Yan Qingling, from Textile to Automobile Industry." Paper presented at the Thirteenth European Association of Chinese Studies Conference, University of Torino, Italy, 2000.

Li Ta, ed. *Taiwan ti nü-ch'iang-jen,* ti i chi. Hong Kong: Kuang-chiao-ching ch'u-pan-she, 1988, 80–103.

Wu Xiaoheng: *see* Zhong Yuzheng

Wu Xuanwen: *see* Caoming

Wu Yi

Wu Yi, b. 1938 in Wuhan, Hubei Province, devoted more than twenty years to China's petroleum industry. She is better known, however, as China's minister of Foreign Trade and Economic Cooperation.

Biographers remain vague about what work Wu Yi's parents did, simply stating that she was born into a family of intellectuals. Wu Yi is said to have spent her early years reading Chinese and foreign literary works and acknowledges the influence such exposure had on her, claiming it as the source of her idealism. In 1957, she enrolled in the Petroleum Refining Department at Beijing Petroleum Institute. That Wu Yi chose to work in this male-dominated field is evidence of her high aspiration and courage to be different. At the institute, she was a notable figure, leading by example in undertaking student voluntary work. Having been influenced by a Soviet Russian novel that romanticized working in a remote place, Wu Yi chose at graduation in 1962 to work in the northwestern Gansu Province as a technician at Lanzhou Refinery. She was later transferred to a desk job in the Ministry of Petroleum Industry for three years before becoming deputy chief engineer and deputy director of Beijing Dongfanghong Oil Refinery.

In 1967, Wu Yi began what became a twenty-year-long association with Yanshan Petroleum and Chemical Corporation, the nation's biggest petroleum enterprise. When she first joined it, the corporation was nothing but a granite-strewn wasteland. Wu Yi worked alongside the workers constructing the company's premises from scratch and progressed steadily upward, from technician to section chief to assistant manager, and finally to party secretary. For many years, she was the only woman leader in China's petroleum industry and won the love and respect of the people at Yanshan, from truck drivers to cadres, through being the hardest worker of all. Whenever difficulties arose or targets had to be reached, everybody united behind her to complete the task at hand.

Wu Yi had always been a technical worker, but in 1983, when serving as deputy manager of Yanshan, she was seconded to Hunan Province and placed in charge of putting the party of that province in order. This was her first venture into political work and Wu Yi excelled at it, which brought her to the notice of the leaders in the Party's Central Committee. Its Organization Department evaluated Wu Yi five times in 1986 in order to ensure that they thoroughly understood her qualities and abilities.

Her name then appeared as a candidate in 1988 for deputy mayor of Beijing. When she appeared on television before voters, Wu Yi had come straight from Yanshan and wore a work jacket; her straightforward manner and talk also impressed the people of Beijing, who elected her. As deputy mayor, Wu Yi had the double portfolio of industry and external trade, both considered among the "hard" portfolios for deputy mayors and rarely given to one person. When she finally left office, the two portfolios were divided between two separate deputy mayors. As a new deputy mayor, Wu Yi visited more than thirty enterprises, from factories that produced daily necessities to county and township industries in the countryside near Beijing. She did not hesitate to travel to other provinces to buy or try to hasten the delivery of materials. Even after Wu Yi left the municipal government, her superiors continued to cite her as a model.

In 1991, she was transferred to the central government and made executive deputy minister of Foreign Economic and Trade Relations. Only a few months later, Wu Yi was pushed into the international limelight when she replaced the chief negotiator, who had fallen ill, in talks with the United States on intellectual property rights. During these negotiations, which lasted for two years and two months, Wu Yi proved herself to be a formidable opponent who was able to improve China's position considerably with little sacrifice. In 1993, she was promoted to the position of minister of Foreign Trade and Economic Cooperation. Wu Yi has won the recognition and respect of her opponents and the foreign media in several high profile negotiations that she has since participated in, including intellectual property rights (again), most-favored-nation status, and entry into the World Trade Organization.

Wu Yi seems to have created her own personal style of negotiation: to her candor, pragmatism, and quick-wittedness she adds a judicious combination of firmness and softness. Her involvement in foreign trade commenced just after the Tian'anmen Incident, when people in many countries boycotted trade with China. Pragmatism kept her about her business in spite of that, and as time went on the bad feelings were gradually forgotten and trade increased. As minister of Foreign Trade, Wu Yi frequently travels overseas, and her daily schedule is always hectic, an environment in which she seems to thrive. In her early days as minister of Trade, Wu Yi toured the remote and impoverished northwest provinces of Shaanxi, Gansu, Ningxia, Qinghai, and Xinjiang that had little to export and enjoyed the least benefits from foreign cooperation. Her purpose no doubt was to try to find out what could be done to help change this situation. Attracting investors to these areas would have been one of China's targets in economic planning, and Wu Yi would certainly have contributed greatly to this.

She is of slight built, with fair skin and distinctive features, has never married, and often lives in her office, separating her rest area from her work area with just a screen or curtain. While working at Yanshan Petroleum in the countryside not far from Beijing, Wu Yi was not able to enjoy any of the conveniences and comforts a city could offer, yet she considered Yanshan to be her home. She has even said that she would like her ashes to be scattered over the low granite hills behind Yanshan Refinery. Wu Yi has also made known her views on how to cope with the irritations that are often strewn across a single woman's path. When she became deputy mayor of Beijing, it was widely rumored that her promotion foreshadowed a marriage to a high leader who was a widower. Although angry, all Wu Yi said was that time was the best means of removing such rumors. She maintains that it is important to find one's own place in the world and believes that once it is found, no one can shake you loose. "I am rather tenacious. I want to be my own mistress and not be swayed by public opinion. Without this sort of determination, it is awfully hard for a single woman to go on." In reply to a reporter's question, Wu Yi has said that she did not choose to be single but that life had not given her the opportunity to meet the right man.

She leads a rich and happy life, however, and has no regrets. Wu Yi is a woman of courage who has never been afraid to take up new challenges. She has also learned quickly in new jobs, spending long hours on study and investigation. Unlike many other women leaders, Wu Yi enjoys a range of interests and hobbies to complement her love of the party and work: music, literature, dancing, and fishing. Although an aficionado of Western classical music, Wu Yi also appreciates contemporary Chinese popular music and has been known to show off her contralto voice, singing pop songs at karaoke parties. She is also captain of the women ministers' tennis team, which includes the veteran Chen Muhua (*q.v.*) and younger women such as He Luli and Nie Li.

Wu Yi joined the CCP in 1962 after graduating from university. She was party secretary of Yanshan Petroleum and Chemical Corporation in the 1980s and in 1987 was elected as an alternate member to the CCP Central Committee; Wu Yi became a full member in 1992. It is predicted that she will continue to advance in the party hierarchy. Wu Yi represents the generation of CCP women who went to university in the 1950s and matured as cadres in the 1970s. Usually optimistic and idealistic, they were not traumatized by the Cultural Revolution. At the same time, the women have adapted well to the new ideas of the reform and the opening up of China and contributed toward creating a new paradigm both for officials and for women.

Lily Xiao Hong LEE

Li Guoqiang. "Wu Yi yu He Luli." In *Zhongguo dangdai renminglu*, vol. 5. Hong Kong: Guangjiaojing chubanshe, 1988, 103–11.
———. "Zhongguo zhengtan da heima: Wu Yi." In *Zhongguo dangdai renminglu*, vol. 17. Hong Kong: Guangjiaojing chubanshe, 1988, 79–89.
Zhongguo renming dacidian: Xianren dang zheng jun lingdao renwu juan. Beijing: Waiwen chubanshe, 1994, 712.
Zhonghua quanguo funü lianhehui. Zuzhi lianluobu, ed. *Jinri nübuzhang.* Shenyang: Liaoning renmin chubanshe, 1995.

Wu Yifang

Wu Yifang, 1893–1985, was born in Wuchang, Hubei Province, and was one of China's foremost women educators, having the distinction of being China's first woman university president. She was also active in politics in both the KMT and CCP periods, assuming posts in the CPPCC and the NPC. Wu Yifang gained international stature through her work in education, philanthropy, and the Chinese Christian Council. While performing all of these functions, she represented the interests of Chinese women and maintained a strong belief in the inherent equality of the sexes.

Wu Yifang was the third of four children. Her father, Wu Shouxun, although originally from Hangzhou, was a Qing government official stationed in Hubei during most of Wu Yifang's childhood. Until the age of eleven, she received an education at home with her siblings after which time she was sent with her sister to the newly established Hangzhou Girls' School. After completing two years in Hangzhou, the sisters attended Catholic and Methodist schools in Shanghai (Qiming nüzi xuexiao) and Suzhou (Jinghai nüxiao) respectively, for brief periods. This was Wu Yifang's introduction to Christianity, an influence that remained important throughout her life.

In 1910 Wu Shouxun died, the first in a string of tragedies that were to strike the family. By the end of 1911, just after the collapse of the Qing dynasty, Wu Yifang's elder brother, mother, and elder sister also were to die within months of each other. She and her younger sister were cared for by an aunt. Wu Yifang continued schooling, eventually enrolling, in 1916, in the first intake of China's first women's university, Ginling [Jinling] Women's University (Jinling nüzi daxue), in Nanjing. She was soon elected head of the student union. While there, Wu Yifang converted to Christianity and was active in the Methodist Church, which she joined in 1918.

After graduating in 1919, Wu Yifang took up a post at Beijing Higher Normal Girls' College, heading the English Department, staying until 1922. In this year, she took up a Barbour Scholarship at the University of Michigan and there completed an M.S. (1924) and a Ph.D. (1928) in Biology. Wu Yifang assumed a leadership role during her time as a student at Michigan, serving as president of the Chinese Christian Student Association of the United States (1924–25) and as vice-chair of the Chinese Student Alliance (1925–26). The high level of her qualifications and general esteem for her leadership capabilities is evidenced by Wu Yifang's appointment as president of Ginling Women's University on her return to China in 1928. This appointment made her, at the age of thirty-five, the first woman president of a university in China. The Ginling Women's University expanded considerably during her presidency. She promoted the idea of educating students to enrich their own lives by helping others. Recognizing the difficulty women university graduates had in finding work, Wu Yifang tried to make the courses at her university as practical as possible and also placed great importance on physical education and extracurricular activities.

Her university work in Nanjing became disrupted with the start of the war against Japan in 1937. In July, Ginling was forced to close until it could be relocated to the campus of West China Union University in Chongqing. Ginlin functioned there on a reduced war footing for the remainder of the war, not returning to its Nanjing campus until 1945. During her time in Chongqing, Wu Yifang was active in many of the KMT government's political and administrative bodies. In 1938, she assisted Soong Mayling (*q.v.*) with the Women's Advisory Committee of the New Life Movement, a body that coordinated services for war orphans and refugees. That same year, Wu Yifang became a councillor in China's wartime Parliament, the People's Political Council (PPC), sometimes translated as People's Political Participation Conference (Guomin canzhenghui), and in 1941 was appointed to the five-member presidium of the PPC, the only woman to attain this position. During her time in the PPC, she worked to enhance the position of women in politics by campaigning for a set minimum quota of seats for women in Parliament. Her efforts resulted in women being guaranteed 10 percent of the seats in the Republic of China's parliamentary bodies. In the 1946 National Assembly, convened to promulgate the Constitution of the Republic of China, Wu Yifang sat as one of the few women delegates.

International recognition of her position as a prominent educator and philanthropist was forthcoming. On her 1942 visit to the United States, she was awarded an honorary LLD by Smith College, a longtime supporter of Ginling Women's University. In 1945, when attending the San Francisco U.N. Conference on International Cooperation (again as the only woman member of the Chinese delegation), Wu Yifang was awarded honorary degrees from Mills College and the University of Southern California. The University of Michigan also paid homage to her in 1979 with an award for Outstanding Achievements in Knowledge.

Wu Yifang's apparent close relationship with the KMT government, however, did not result in her departure for Taiwan with the victory of the CCP in 1949. Instead, she worked to facilitate a smooth transition to CCP control in Nanjing by heading the Citizens' Protection Committee. Wu Yifang maintained a high profile in education, philanthropic organizations, and politics throughout the remainder of her long life. Initially, she worked to ensure that Gingling's structure and curricula were altered to incorporate Marxist principles of the new government. Eventually, in 1952, Ginling was amalgamated with Nanjing University, and Wu Yifang was appointed vice-president of the new institution, called the National Jinling University. She sat variously on the editorial board of *China Reconstructs*, as commissioner for Education of Jiangsu Province, and was vice-president of Nanjing Normal College. In 1957 Wu Yifang joined the Executive Committee of the ACWF, China's peak body for the mobilization of women. Her long-term enthusiasm for political activism is evident from her participation as vice-president in the Chinese Association for the Advancement of Democracy. These leadership roles in prominent mass organizations facilitated her entrance to national government bodies. She served as a delegate to the first five NPCs and on the Standing Committee of the Third NPC (1965), as member of the CPPCC, and served on the Standing Committee of the Fifth Session (1978).

Wu Yifang was not only preeminent among women in the educational and political scene; she was also a national leader for the Christian churches in China both before and after 1949. In 1935 and again for the decade from 1938 to 1948, Wu Yifang was president of the National Christian Council of China (NCC) and assumed a similar leadership role for the organization under the communist government when she was appointed vice-chair of the NCC in 1956. Her philanthropic interests manifested in the administrative positions she undertook for the Christian movement. In 1933 Wu Yifang was the Chinese delegate to the United Foreign Missions Conference held in America and the International Missionary Council held in England. Her outstanding leadership qualities were recognized in these international meetings, and in 1938 she led the Chinese delegation to the International Missionary Council Assembly in Madras, India, and was elected vice-chair. In the years after 1949, Wu Yifang served as president to the Three Self's Chinese Christian Church Movement, maintaining her dedication to the existence of Christianity within communist China.

Wu Yifang was an outstanding woman, committed to the development of China and particularly the education of China's women. She maintained the difficult role of being a leader in both the KMT and CCP governments and through her participation in many international organizations and bodies brought much prestige to both regimes. Wu Yifang was one of China's preeminent female educators and political leaders in the difficult period of the transition from the KMT to CCP government. She died in 1985 in Nanjing.

Louise EDWARDS

Boorman, Howard L., and Richard C. Howard, eds. *Biographical Dictionary of Republican China*, vol. 3. New York: Columbia University Press, 1967, 460–62.
Gao Kuixiang and Shen Jianguo, eds. *Zhonghua gujin nüjie pu*. Beijing: Zhongguo shehui chubanshe, 1991, 256–57.
Song Ruizhi, ed. *Zhongguo funü wenhua tonglan*. Jinan: Shandong wenyi chubanshe, 1995, 279–80.
Wang Xin, ed. *Zhongguo minzhu dangpai mingrenlu*. Nanjing: Jiangsu renmin chubanshe, 1993, 312–15.
Wu Yi-fang. "The People's Political Council." *China at War*, 6, no. 5 (May 1941): 86.
Yuan Shaoying and Yang Guizhen, eds. *Zhongguo funü mingren cidian*. Changchun: Beifang funü ertong chubanshe, 1989, 241.
Zhongguo xiandai kexuejia zhuanji, vol. 4. Beijing: Kexue chubanshe, 1993, 127–42.

Wu Yuxia

Wu Yuxia, b. 1959 in Shanghai, is one of China's finest exponent of the *pipa*, a stringed instrument with a fretted fingerboard not unlike a guitar, that is plucked.

From a working-class family, she is said to have always been a sensible girl who not only got good results at school but also helped her parents with the housework and in caring for her younger brothers and sisters. At the age of eleven, in 1970, Wu Yuxia was selected to learn the *pipa* after school at the Young People's Palace (Shaoniangong) in the Luwan District of Shanghai. There, she had the opportunity to learn from Wei Zuguang, son of the well-known *pipa* master Wei Zhongle. Because eleven was considered rather late to start learning the instrument, Wu Yuxia had to work extremely hard to keep up with the rest of the class. She did not own a *pipa*, so practiced her fingering on a washing board that had regular indentations like those on the instrument, with rubber bands stretched over it as the strings. This was the only means that Wu Yuxia had for keeping her fingers agile. Just two years after beginning her training, she was given the opportunity of performing with four other girls for the United States's President Richard Nixon when he visited China in 1972.

At about the same time, Shanghai People's Broadcasting Station recruited amateur musicians and Wu Yuxia was selected because of her excellent skills. She became a member of the station's Youth Choir Orchestra and also had the chance to learn from teachers at the Shanghai Academy of Music. Her parents are said to have eschewed their wish for a sewing machine or radio for the family in favor of buying Wu Yuxia her first *pipa*. In 1977, she enrolled at the Central Wuqi Art University in Beijing, now

Beijing Dance and Music Academy, and traveled alone to Beijing. Because there was no practice room at the academy, Wu Yuxia again resorted to unconventional methods, practicing in corridors, the dining hall, and even in the bathroom, for seven or eight hours a day. By then, steel strings had replaced the earlier nylon ones; these cut her fingers until they bled, but still she practiced. After graduating in 1979, Wu Yuxia stayed on as a member of the academy's orchestra to become a professional musician.

The turning point of her professional life occurred when she took part in 1980 in the first national *pipa* competition, held in Shanghai. Her father had just died and the young woman did not intend to enter; at the urging of her teachers, however, Wu Yuxia changed her mind. She came in second; her prize, ironically, was a Red Lamp radio, precisely what her father had given up buying so that he could purchase a *pipa* for her. Her success at the competition prompted six different orchestras to invite the musician to join them. She chose the Central Orchestra of National Music (Zhongyang minzu yuetuan), one that specialized in the study and performance of the music of China's diverse nationalities. As a soloist, Wu Yuxia continued to scale new heights. The piece that won her national fame, "Little Sisters of the Steppes" (Caoyuan xiao jiemei), is difficult to play yet she never puts a finger wrong in the entire ten minutes it takes to perform. Other well-known pieces generally associated with her are "Spring and Autumn" (Chunqiu), "Hymn of Eternity" (Qianqiu song), and "Rhythm" (Lüdong). In 1987, she was assessed by the Ministry of Culture and ranked as a Top Performer.

In October 1997, Wu Yuxia held a recital in Beijing to commemorate the 2545th anniversary of the death of Confucius (551–479 BCE). At this concert, she played her own composition "Rhythm," described as a work of modern music because of its idioms and the way the musical material is used. This new direction in ethnic music attracted a great deal of attention. Besides appearing in concerts and on radio and television in China, Wu Yuxia frequently traveled overseas, to Japan, the U.S., Burma, Pakistan, Finland, Sweden, Singapore, South Korea, Hong Kong, and Macao. Audiences in Japan, where she has appeared nine times, give her an especially warm reception. Wu Yuxia considers her performances overseas as conversing with the world through her *pipa*. Her experience of playing to international audiences has convinced her that the more of an ethnic flavor the music retains, the wider its appeal.

Wu Yuxia is married, and her husband (whose name is not given in sources) works for New China News Agency; they have one son, born in the late 1980s. Wu Yuxia aims to be an outstanding musician as well as a good wife and mother, roles that are to her not mutually exclusive. She does admit, however, that it requires her to work harder. Her only hobby is talking to friends on the telephone, because she rarely has time to see them.

A critic from the journal *Renmin yinyue* commented that Wu Yuxia's playing is not only exquisite and passionate but that she shows great understanding of the music, which she plays in her own distinctive style. Another critic, from overseas, maintains that Wu Yuxia has gone beyond the level of perfecting *pipa* technique and the pursuit of beautiful melodies to reveal the inner world of the musician.

Lily Xiao Hong LEE

Zheng Qunhai. "Zhongguo diyi nü pipashou." *Mochou*, no. 1 (1998): 22–24.

Wu Zhonglian

Wu Zhonglian, 1908–1967, of Yizhang County, Hunan Province, was one of the thirty women who went with the First Front Red Army on the Chinese communists' Long March of 1934–35.

Born into a family classified as "urban poor," Wu Zhonglian attended the County Girls' School and went on in 1927 to Hengyang Third Women's Normal School (Hengyang nü san shi) in southern Hunan. There, she joined the CCP and became involved in underground work and propaganda activities. With the collapse of the KMT-CCP united front in April 1927, Wu Zhonglian and her lover Peng Qi, about whose life and death nothing is known, returned to Yizhang County and set up a local branch of the Communist Youth League. Wu Zhonglian was an extremely active propaganda worker and took part in the Xiangnan Insurrection (also known as the Yizhang Uprising), which swept across southern Hunan in the first three months of 1928 after Zhu De (1886–1976) had retreated there with remnants of his troops from the failed Nanchang Uprising. In autumn 1928, Wu Zhonglian went with Zhu De's troops onto Jinggangshan, where the Red Army was then formed. There, she did organization work with the Youth League and worked under the personal direction of Mao Zedong (1893–1976). Wu Zhonglian also formed at Jinggangshan a lasting friendship with Kang Keqing (*q.v.*).

From Jinggangshan, Wu Zhonglian accompanied the Red Army through Jiangxi and Fujian as a partisan-guerrilla; she became known for her ability to throw a hand grenade further than most men, despite her slender build. When the Soviet Republic of China was established in southern Jiangxi in 1931, Wu Zhonglian was assigned to the Red Army School in Ruijin as an instructor. She was designated as an organizer with the Convalescent Company on the Long March but was weak from malaria and often fell behind. Wu Zhonglian was nevertheless required to act as secretary to the Cadres Unit because of her high level of literacy, and each night would find her writing out sheaves of marching orders for distribution to military personnel.

At some stage, she formed a liaison with Zeng Risan, who later became head of the Enemy Section of the Western Route Army's general headquarters. By July-August 1935, she was pregnant and being cared for in a field hospital in the Tibetan foothills. Wu Zhonglian and her husband were assigned at that time to Zhang Guotao's Fourth Front Army, which hived off from the main body led by Mao Zedong and marched to the southeast. Wu Zhonglian gave birth to a baby boy at Ganzi in Tibet in spring 1936 and was part of the ill-fated Western Route Army that crossed the Yellow River in September. She survived the massacre that followed, leaving her son with a couple in Gansu. Wu Zhonglian and her husband were captured but she escaped; her husband was killed. Recaptured by the Moslems, she escaped again, this time in company with Zhang Qinqiu (*q.v.*), only to be betrayed in Xi'an and captured by the KMT. The CCP negotiated the release of the women from Nanjing after the two parties had agreed to a second united front, and Wu Zhonglian finally reached the comparative safety of Yan'an in August 1937. During the Yan'an period, she acted as head and secretary-general of the Organization Department of the Shandong Column of the Eighth Route Army and then as director of the Political Department and secretary-general of the First Column of the Jiangsu-Anhui Column in east China.

After the establishment of the PRC in 1949, Wu Zhonglian lived in Hangzhou with her husband Jiang Hua (1905–1992?), a prominent member of the Zhejiang Provincial Party Committee and later to become president of the Supreme People's Court, and her son Wu Changzheng (Long March Wu), whom she had sought out and brought back from his foster parents in the northwest. Wu Zhonglian rose to the position of president of Zhejiang Supreme People's Court and sat on the Executive Committee of the ACWF. She came under attack at the very beginning of the Cultural Revolution, however, her imprisonment by the KMT in 1937 being used against her. So severe was the harassment that Wu Zhonglian died in 1967. She was rehabilitated posthumously, in 1978, two years after her son Wu Changzheng was killed in an accident.

Although an educated youth, Wu Zhonglian would never have had the opportunity to fill a position in the judiciary had she not been a member of the Long March generation of women. Nor would she have been persecuted to death had she not been a Long Marcher.

Sue WILES

Dong Hanhe. *Xilujun nüzhanshi mengnan ji*. Beijing: Jiefangjun wenyi chubanshe, 1990, 155–74.

Guo Chen. *Jinguo liezhuan: Hong yifangmianjun sanshiwei changzheng nühongjun shengping shiji*. Beijing: Nongcun duwu chubanshe, 1986, 174–78.

Lee, Lily Xiao Hong, and Sue Wiles. *Women of the Long March*. Sydney: Allen & Unwin, 1999.

Wulan

Wulan, 1923–1987, was born in Beijing, although her native place was Chaoyang County, Liaoning Province, previously known as the Jostu League of Inner Mongolia. She was romanticized as a heroine of Mongolian nationality and known as the "Two-Gun Red Commander."

As a child, Wulan was called Baolige (Spring Water) and, from primary to high school until finally attending university in Yan'an, went at different times by the names Zhang Wei, Zhang Cen, and Lu Lin. She formally took the name Wulan (red, in Mongolian) after 1949. Her father was a low-ranking military officer who had been imprisoned because of his opposition to the imperial pretensions of Yuan Shikai; an uncle who was a staff officer stationed in Inner Mongolia was also implicated. Although Wulan's father was released after the death of Yuan Shikai, his career stagnated, and her father and uncle died about the time she was born. The family fortune declined, and Wulan wandered the steppes with her paternal aunt, whose husband practiced medicine.

After the Japanese occupied China's three northeastern-most provinces (following the September Eighteenth Incident of 1931), Wulan returned to Beijing. There, she lived with her grandmother, mother, the wife of her paternal uncle, female cousin Zhulan, and younger brother; they survived by pawning heirlooms. Wulan was a bright student and a quiet child but harbored a deep sadness about her father's reversal of fortune and unhappy end. She became interested in martial arts, desiring to become a woman warrior who could avenge his loss. At the age of eight, about 1932, Wulan wrote an essay entitled "The Story My Brother Told Me" (Gege jiang de gushi) and it won a prize awarded by a small Beijing newspaper. The story told of a knight-errant who righted wrongs and the writing became a means to express the anger she felt.

Wulan attended several schools in Beijing, including the Mongol-Tibet School (Mengzang xuexiao), Dongbei Technical High School (Dongbei zhiye zhongxue), and the Girls' Normal School of Tongzhou (Tongzhou nüzi shifan xuexiao). Her fellow students at the Mongol-Tibet School, located in Xiaoshihu hutong, belonged to upper-class Mongolian and Tibetan families, but some of the school's teachers were CCP members who spread Marxist-Leninist ideology. Several Mongolians who are now leaders of the People's Republic took their first steps toward revolution there. Wulan's revolutionary path also seems to have begun at this school when she met the famous poet of Mongolian nationality Guo Xiaochuan, who was a member of the CCP. Wulan was expelled after taking part in the December Ninth anti-Japanese student movement of 1935. She was also forced to leave the Girls' Normal School of Tongzhou at the end of 1936 after supporting the anti-Japanese activities of the KMT general Fu Zouyi, who was stationed in Suiyuan. Wulan joined the Chinese Vanguard for National Liberation (Zhonghua minzu jiefang xianfengdui) during this period.

Following the Marco Polo Bridge Incident of July 1937, she marched with the Wartime Service Unit of the Chinese Vanguard to show support for the anti-Japanese activities of the Twenty-ninth Army. Her house was later searched by Japanese soldiers, so she left Beijing with fellow students, some of whom went to Yan'an, some to southern China, and some to Xiangshan, on the outskirts of Beijing, to continue their anti-Japanese activities.

Wulan attempted to join the guerrillas at Fangshan but she did not succeed nor did she tell her family what she was about. The Chinese Vanguard then told her to go to Tianjin to work with anti-Japanese national salvation groups. Before leaving for Tianjin in August 1937, Wulan said farewell to friends and penned a passionate lyric (*ci*) expressing her patriotic anger. Thus, at the age of fourteen, she and several other girls became involved in bombings that targeted the Japanese Zhongyuan Company in Beijing, the Haihe Wharf Warehouse in Tianjin, and the Tanno Trading Company, the latter believed to be a front for a spying organization.

In August 1938, Wulan boarded a ship for Hong Kong with several comrades. From there, they traveled to Guangzhou and received permission through the Eighth Route Army office to go to the communist enclave in Yan'an to study at the Anti-Japanese University (Kangda). It took three months for her to reach Yan'an, however, after traveling through Changsha, Wuhan, and Xi'an, and walking 250 km to get to Luochang in northern Shanxi. In Luochang she received two months of military training and in November led a troop to Yan'an to begin her studies. Wulan enrolled in the sixth intake at Kangda and three months later was assigned to a literary and artistic troupe (*wengong tuan*). Reluctantly, she accepted those orders. Her unhappiness arose from the humiliation that she, a proud Mongolian, felt at being relegated to such a menial duty as acting. In time, however, she became a competent actress.

When, in April 1939, Wulan joined the CCP, she became the first member of the troupe to do so. Wulan remained at Kangda when the troupe was sent to the front in the Taihang Mountains in June, and two months later was sent to the Journalism Department at the Chinese Women's University (Zhongguo nüzi daxue). This move fired her imagination, and she dreamed of being a war correspondent. Not only was Wulan a diligent student, however, she also worked hard at manual labor, carrying bricks, collecting firewood, and harvesting grain. When graduating in 1940, Wulan was recognized as a "Model Student, Model Worker." She refused to join a literary and artistic troupe working in the northwest, asking instead to be sent back to Mongolia to fight the Japanese. Because Wulan was only seventeen years old and had lied about her age, saying she was nineteen, the young woman was finally given permission to join the Northwest Work Committee (Xibei gongzuo weiyuanhui). Wulan was assigned to underground work in Inner Mongolia with the KMT Third Revolutionary Army, which was essentially under communist control. It was not long, however, before she was sent back to Yan'an, after contracting typhoid fever and also because of an affair with a comrade named Keligeng. The young couple reached Yan'an in 1941, and the two were immediately assigned to Mongolian issues in the Research Unit of Minority Nationalities (Shaoshu minzu wenti yanjiushi). They transferred to the Institute for Nationalities when it was established in Yan'an and married on New Year's Day the next year. During this period, Wulan was a teacher of a Mongolian language class. She read closely the few histories of her people then available—*Menggu shi*, *Yuan chao mishi*, and *Menggu yuanliu*—and researched the history of her own native place. Also during this period, Wulan was borrowed by the Northwestern Cultural Troupe to play the role of Suyi in Cao Yu's play *The Beijinger* (Beijing ren).

She did not fare well in the 1942 rectification campaign. Accused of being a Japanese spy sent from Hong Kong, a KMT commando, and a Trotskyite, Wulan was forbidden to live with her husband. He was unable to care for her during her pregnancy and could only occasionally, with great stealth, ask Wulan about her health. She gave birth in 1944 to her son Asileng (Lion) while still under guard, but it was not until 1945 that they were finally able to resume living together. Wulan gave birth to her second son in April but gave him into the care of a villager so that she could continue with her work. Her political problems were soon resolved, however, when the person who had been her group leader in Tianjian arrived in Yan'an and vouched for her.

After the surrender of the Japanese in 1945, Wulan was sent to the northeast. This meant placing her older son in the Yan'an crèche, and for several years after she suffered the pain of separation. The League of Inner Mongolia Self-Rule Movements was formed in Zhangjiakou in November, and Wulan served as head of the Women's Department and a member of the Standing Committee. Then she was ordered to become the political commissar of the Mongolian Armed Workforce stationed at Xiaoheyan in February 1946. This was an ideologically confused local militia, and twenty-three-year-old Wulan had to think quickly to win over the rough elements of recruits comprising its ranks. She displayed great ability in bringing alongside both the upper-class Mongolians and the remnants of the KMT army, maintaining law and order, organizing the peasants, and establishing local administration. The Militia

Workforce increased from thirty-odd to over three hundred individuals and formed the Eleventh Detachment of the Inner Mongolia Self-Defense Army. Wulan then set up a Twelfth and a Thirteenth Detachment and acted as commissar of all three. She displayed great courage both on the battlefield and in the arena of land reform, becoming known at this time as the "Two-Gun Red Commander," and the Hua Mulan of Mongolian nationality.

The Inner Mongolian People's Congress convened its first meeting at the foot of Genghis Khan Mountain in 1947 and established the Inner Mongolia Autonomous Government, now the Inner Mongolian Autonomous People's Government. When the notion of national separation floated at the congress, Wulan pointed out that the Inner Mongolian revolution could not be separated from the Chinese revolution or the leadership of the CCP, and her point of view prevailed. She was elected to the First Provisional Parliament and the Government Committee (Zhengfu weiyuanhui) in April. On 5 May, Wulan rode in full uniform at the front of the Inner Mongolian People's Self-Defense Cavalry. In July, she headed the Work Committee of the Eastern Region of Jostu (present-day Xinhui, Beipian, Fuxin, Chaoyang, and Jianping), Liaoning Province. Wulan was also member of the Rehe-Liaoning Regional Committee and head of the Meng-ming Work Department.

From the end of the Sino-Japanese War in 1945, Wulan had fought at the head of her three detachments in eastern Mongolia and western Liaoning to help bring this area under the rule of the PRC. She also initiated land reform in those areas. Wulan attended an International Democratic Women's Federation Conference in Hungary in December 1948 and served as a member of the Executive Committee at the First Congress of the ACWF in Beijing in 1949.

Wulan removed her military uniform in May 1949 on leaving the army to become head of the ACWF in Inner Mongolia. Her story, however, was told throughout the northeast and Inner Mongolia. Despite her record, she was cruelly persecuted during the Cultural Revolution. Her ankle was smashed, leaving her with some difficulty in walking. Nevertheless, Wulan returned to work in the late 1970s with the Railway Bureau at the Inner Mongolian capital of Huhhote. Transportation at that time was paralyzed, but she succeeded in reviving the railway system and resolving the transportation problem. Wulan was transferred to the All-China Federation of Trade Unions (ACFTU) in 1980 and doubled as secretary to the secretariat and as head of its women workers. She was later made a consultant for the ACFTU and elected to the Executive Committee.

Wulan died in Beijing in April 1987, a heroine to the people of Inner Mongolia.

DING Shoupu
(Translated by Lily Xiao Hong Lee and Sue Wiles)

Liu Huai. "Shuangqiang hongsiling Wulan." *Funü zhinan*, no. 7–12 (1987); no. 1–12 (1988).
Naran Touyaa. "Huainian Wulan tongzhi." *Nei Menggu funü*, no. 11 (1996).
Yingchun. "Shuangqiang siling: Ji quanguo zonggonghui shuji qu shuji, nü gongbu buzhang Wulan." In *Zhongguo Menggzu nüjie*. Huhhote: Nei Menggu renmin chubanshe, 1997.
Yingwen *Zhongguo funü*, ed. *Gujin zhuming funü renwu*, vol. 2. Shijiazhuang: Hebei renmin chubanshe, 1986, 1024.

X

Xia Juhua

Xia Juhua, 1937–1989, born to a family named Xu in Qianshan, Anhui Province, was given the surname Xia when she was "mortgaged" to a circus troupe at the age of five. The following year, Xia Juhua learned acrobatics and performed with the troupe as it traveled around Anhui, Jiangxi, and Hunan, and later in Wuhan in 1951. In 1953 Xia Juhua joined the Wuhan Acrobatic Troupe.

Her specialty acts in acrobatics, such as the Pagoda of Bowls and Flower Biting, required great agility and flexibility. Her most famous act, Pagoda of Bowls, entailed putting twelve slippery bowls on top of her head while simultaneously performing many difficult movements to music. She won a gold medal for the performance, and the act was a sensation in Moscow in 1957. Xia Juhua trained hard at her art and continually developed new skills, taking the traditional Chinese acrobatic act of carrying bowls on the head, known as *dingwan*, to new levels. In 1958, she mastered the skill of "balancing one layer of bowls on the head while assuming the twin flying swallows pose." Two years later she was able to carry water-filled bowls on her head on a revolving rod and then to stand on one hand while rotating bowls with the other. From this, she progressed to balancing bowls on top of a rod while assuming a single flying swallow pose, and finally, by 1966, to carrying two lots of bowls on top of sticks while assuming the twin flying swallows pose.

Between 1954 and 1966, Xia Juhua performed overseas with the troupe, winning medals for performances from both the Afghanistan and Cambodian governments. Nothing is known of Xia Juhua's activities during the Cultural Revolution except that she was appointed deputy director of Wuhan City Cultural Bureau (Wuhanshi wenhuaju fujùzhang) in 1973.

In 1983 Xia Juhua led a Chinese acrobatic troupe to compete in the Sixth World of Tomorrow Acrobatic and Circus Competition in Paris and the Ninth International Circus and Acrobatic Competition in Monte Carlo. She judged competitions and led other delegations to North Korea and Russia and has held various professional posts, including president of the Chinese Acrobatic Artists' Association and executive vice-president of the Chinese Artists' Association. It is not known if she married or had children.

HE Li and Shirley Wai CHAN
(Translated by Yang Jingqing)

Liu Bo, ed. *Zhongguo dangdai wenhua yishu mingren dacidian*. Beijing: Guoji wenhua chubanshe, 1993, 753–54.

Song Ruizhi, ed. *Zhongguo funü wenhua tonglan*. Jinan: Shandong wenyi chubanshe, 1995, 653–54.

Yingwen *Zhongguo funü*, ed. *Gujin zhuming funü renwu*, vol. 2. Shijiazhuang: Hebei renmin chubanshe, 1986, 1184.

Zhongguo renwu nianjian. Beijing: Huayi chubanshe, 1989, 302.

Xia Peisu

Xia Peisu, b. 1923 in Chongqing, Sichuan Province, came from a literary family. She is a specialist in computer science and technology.

Her father, Xia Zhiyu, held a provincial degree (*juren*) and was a progressive scholar of late Qing who took part in the famous Railway Protection Movement to retain provincial ownership of the Sichuan-Wuhan Railroad. Her mother, Huang Xiaoyong, graduated from normal school (*shifan xuexiao*) and placed great importance on the education of her daughter.

Xia Peisu started attending primary school at the age of four and a half and studied at home under a private tutor for six years, from the age of eight. Her excellent academic results gained her admission to senior high school in 1937, and she graduated three years later, in 1940, taking first place. That year, Xia Peisu enrolled in the Department of Electrical Engineering of Central (Zhongyang) University, graduating in 1944. The following year she became a graduate student at the Telecommunications Research Institute of Jiaotong University in Shanghai.

In 1947, Xia Peisu went to Britain to further her studies in the Electrical Engineering Department of Edinburgh University, undertaking doctoral research. She was awarded a Ph.D. in 1950; her dissertation was "(I) On Parametric Oscillations in Electronic Circuits. (II) A Graphical Analysis for Non-Linear Systems." Xia Peisu remained at Edinburgh University to undertake postdoctoral research and that year married fellow student Yang Liming (b. 1919), a postdoctoral researcher in mathematical physics. The couple had two sons who both followed in their parents' footsteps: Yang Yuenian became a computer expert, and Yang Yuemin a physicist.

Motivated by patriotism, Xia Peisu and her husband returned to China in 1951, two years after the founding of the PRC. She embarked on telecommunications network research at Tsinghua University (now known as Qinghua University) and was promoted a year later to associate researcher. Then head of the Institute of Mathematics at the Chinese Academy of Sciences, Hua Luogen (1910–1985), planned to introduce computer technology research, and Xia Peisu was transferred there in 1953. She thus became one of the three founding members of China's first Computer Science Research Unit. When the other two members discontinued work with the research facility several years later, Xia Peisu continued on alone. Working under extremely adverse conditions, she designed the arithmetic logic unit and controller of the first digital computer in general use (model 107) in China. Xia Peisu also compiled at this time the first batch of lecture notes on the principles behind computers.

In 1956, Xia Peisu became actively involved in the planning, preparation, and establishment of the Institute of Computer Technology for the Chinese Academy of Sciences. From the 1960s on, she engaged in enhancing the processing speed of computers and studied the transmission of high-speed signals in them, making a major contribution toward the development of high-speed mainframe computers in the country. Xia Peisu was made a researcher in 1978.

In the late 1970s and early 1980s, she took charge of developing an array processor (150-AP), which was successfully used in petroleum exploration, and a parallel distributed array processor system (GF-10). From the late 1980s, Xia Peisu engaged in the design of parallel computers. In addition to her heavy research load, she devoted time to training computer professionals, both in training classes and lecturing at the Institute of Computer Technology, and cultivated several generations of computer experts, including dozens of Ph.D. and master's students.

Xia Peisu was elected as an academician of the Chinese Academy of Sciences in 1991. She is one of the founders of computer science technology in China and has left her mark on every stage of Chinese computer technology since its inception. She believes strongly in the determination and ability of the country to achieve world-class rank in the field, a goal for which she strove even when facing adversities during the Cultural Revolution. Xia Peisu is a person of great integrity, simple and without affectation, rigorous in her studies, and generous to future scholars.

WANG Bing
(Translated by Lam Hing-hei)

Hsia Pei-Su. "A Graphical Analysis for Non-linear Systems." *Proceedings IEE*, 99, Part 2 (1952): 125–34.
Jiang Guizhen. "Xia Peisu." In *Zhonguo xiandai kexuejia zhuanji*, vol. 1. Beijing: Kexue chubanshe, 1991, 891–98.
Xia Peisu. "Wo guo diyi ge dianzi jisuanji keyan zu." *Zhongguo keji shiliao*, 6, no. 1 (1985): 13–18.
Xia Peisu et al., eds. *Ying-Han jisuanji cidian*. Beijing: Renmin youdian chubanshe, 1984.
"Xia Peisu." Division of Technological Sciences, Chinese Academy of Sciences, on the Internet at <http://www.casad.ac.cn/english/members/technolo/1-91-196.htm>
Zhonghua quanguo fulian, Zuzhi lianluobu, ed. *Zhongguo nüyuanshi*. Shenyang: Liaoning renmin chubanshe, 1995, 247–50.

Xia Yu: *see* **Hsia Yu**

Xian Yuqing

Xian Yuqing, 1895–1965, born in Macao, although her native place was Qiaoshan, Nanhai County, Guangdong Province, was an academic specializing in the study of historical records relating to Guangdong. She was also a respected poet and painter.

Her family had moved to Macao during the Taiping Rebellion in the middle of the nineteenth century, and her father, Xian Zaoyang, was a businessman who started in Guangdong and later invested in several well-known Hong Kong companies. He established the Jianchang Tea and Herbal Trading Company, operating out of Macao as well as Hong Kong. Her mother, Ms. Liu, was from a peasant family. Xian Yuqing was the third of their eight children.

She commenced her formal academic studies in 1907, entering Guangen School (also called Zibao School), and graduated six years later from general high school. In 1913 Xian Yuqing heard a speech given by Dr. Sun Yat-sen (1866–1925) as he passed through Macao on a return to his home village. She studied English at St. Stephen's Girls' School in Hong Kong in 1916 and from 1918 to 1920 attended the high school attached to Lingnan University in Guangzhou, which had been until 1927 an American-run institution. Xian Yuqing graduated from the university's Education Department in June 1924, having in the meantime taught history and Chinese at its high school. In 1930 she was installed by its first Chinese president, Zhong Rongguang, in a university residence that Xian Yuqing named Green Jade Lodge. Hers was a lifelong affiliation with Lingnan University that continued despite geographical relocations necessitated at various times by the vicissitudes of war. She rose through the Chinese Department from being associate lecturer (1925) to lecturer (1928) to associate professor (1935) to professor (1938). When the outbreak of the Sino-Japanese War (1937–45) forced the university to move to Hong Kong in November 1938, she went back to Macao and continued to give lectures. When the university returned to the mainland in 1942, Xian Yuqing undertook the dangerous journey to Qujiang to join the school and, to evade the Japanese, moved constantly around Guangdong and Guangxi with the university until 1945. During this time, she was made a full professor (Grade A, 1943). The university was amalgamated in 1952 with Zhongshan (Sun Yat-sen) University at which time Xian Yuqing became professor of Chinese. She was elected to the Standing Committee of the Guangdong People's Political Consultative Conference in 1954 and formally retired from the university in 1955. Xian Yuqing continued to accept students, however, among them Marshal Chen Yi's wife, Zhang Qian, who studied poetry, and the famous Cantonese Opera star Hongxian Nü (*q.v.*), who studied the *Records of History.*

Xian Yuqing wrote many essays on her special research interest, Guangdong historical studies, and became a major scholar in that area. Among her articles were "A Study of Seals of East Guangdong Artists" (Yuedong yinpu kao), "Theatrical Troupes in Guangdong in the Qing dynasty" (Qingdai liusheng xiban zai Guangdong), and "Guangdong Folksongs and Late Qing Politics" (Yue'ou yu wan Qing zhengzhi). She lectured on the indigenous culture of Hainan Island and the influence of central China on that culture. Xian Yuqing wrote *Art and Literature of Guangdong Women* (Guangdong nüzi yiwen kao), which was published in Hong Kong in 1938; her writing style was praised as being elegant yet accessible. Xian Yuqing was appointed in 1940 as an editor of the ten-volume *Cultural Relics of Guangdong* (Guangdongsheng wenwu). This series came out of an exhibition of Guangdong cultural relics inaugurated by Hong Kong University's Fung Ping Shan Library; she had served as a member of its Preparatory Committee for the exhibition. That same year Xian Yuqing assisted in sorting and editing rare books sent out from enemy-occupied areas to Fung Ping Shan Library by the well-known literary historian Zheng Zhenduo.

Xian Yuqing was also appointed in her capacity as a specialist to a number of projects and committees, including the Guangdong Provincial Gazetteer (as compiler); Guangdong Archives Committee; Guangdong Archives Center (1946); National History Unit in Nanjing (editor, 1947); and the Committee for the Preservation of Cultural Relics (1951). That year, she became curator of the Lingnan University Museum and was appointed in 1956 as deputy director of the Guangdong Research Institute for Literature and History. After several years' work, Xian Yuqing completed her last two books—*A Study of the Works of Guangdong Buddhist and Daoist Writers* (Guangdong shi dao zhushu kao) and *A History of Souzhugang* (Souzhugang zhi)—in 1962.

Possessed with a talent for artistic as well as scholarly expression, Xian Yuqing had been invited early in her career to teach poetics at Tsinghua [Qinghua] University and literary theory at Yen-ching [Yanjing] University. She declined both invitations, but during her time in Beijing met several prominent academics and writers, including the poet Huang Jie, the historian Chen Yuan, and the great book collector Lun Zheru. After reading her *Collected Poems from Green Jade Lodge* (Bilangganguan shiji), the famous poet Chen Sanyuan, whom she visited in Beijing in summer 1937, described Xian Yuqing's style as "plain yet elegant, concise yet lucid, resembling a handsome woman who is slender and graceful, full of wit and charm without having to resort to cosmetics—an ample demonstration of the author's simple life style." Upon painting *Wandering to the Edge of the World* (Haitian zhizhu tu, 1939), which she completed the year Lingnan University moved to Hong Kong, Xian Yuqing inscribed a preface and poem that read in part:

> My soul flies over the Jin River;
> My tears pour into the Ba Mountain.
> My sorrows hang over beautiful flowers.
> Spring arrives with me at the corner of the world.
> The cuckoo's cry follows the broken tracks of a traveler.
> Flowers are in bloom in my home village, yet who is there to appreciate them?
> Scented dust is gone with the East Wind.
> Looking out toward the Central Kingdom
> I can barely see the skyline, thin as a hair in the misty drizzle.

The sincerity with which Xian Yuqing approached poetry can also be seen in the lines she penned when rejecting the Japanese army's 1941 request that she be part of an association for East Asian culture it wished to set up in Hong Kong: "A solitary soul in a far-away land, sorrowing over her country. How can she risk being laughed at by yellow flowers for bending her back?" A collection of poems written while she was a refugee during the Sino-Japanese War was published under the title *One Hundred Poems by a Refugee* (Liuli bai yong) in 1947; these formed part of her *Collected Poems from Green Jade Lodge*. Her six-volume *Records of a Solitary Journey of Ten Thousand Miles* (Wanli guzheng lu) was unfortunately lost during the Sino-Japanese War.

A painter of no little talent, Xian Yuqing did not, however, devote a great deal of time to this art and very few of her works have survived. Her *Spring in the Ancient Capital* (Jiujing chunse tu) carried the poems of many celebrities and men of letters, but only *Wandering to the Edge of the World* and *Daffodils* (Shui xian san tu) were reproduced in the centenary volume *A Collection of Articles Commemorating the Centenary of Xian Yuqing's Birth* (Xian Yuqing dansheng baimian jinianji), published in 1995. *Daffodils* is a series of three paintings of the flower in the style of three early artists: one following Huang Quan's (903–968) outlining and coloring-in method, one following Xu Xi's (d. before 875) ink free hand and one following Zhao Zigu's (1199–1264) outline only method. She also commented on the paintings and calligraphy of Yuan dynasty artists in her essays.

In July 1935, Xian Yuqing had gone to Hong Kong for treatment for a thyroid gland condition. Hong Kong newspapers rumored that she had died after an unsuccessful operation, but Xian Yuqing returned to Guangzhou for treatment and by October had recovered sufficiently to return to Lingnan University. The book she wrote about her experience, *A New Lease on Life* (Gengsheng ji), was published in Shanghai in 1936. Toward the end of her life, the professor also wrote an autobiography. In this, she recounts visiting Beijing in 1953 and becoming so absorbed in copying books at the Beijing Library that she sometimes took her meals there. Xian Yuqing ended up spending more than two months transcribing books instead of the month she had originally planned for seeing the new constructions in the capital. Xian Yuqing succumbed to her fascination with books in much the same way again in 1957, when visiting the Zhejiang Library in Hangzhou during a trip to Lushan and Huangshan. On that occasion she began working on some rare books found there, "making summaries of the books written by people of Guangdong origin. Thus, I stayed there for a month without realizing it."

In 1963, Xian Yuqing was operated on for breast cancer but the treatment was unsuccessful, and she died in October 1965 at the age of seventy. Xian Yuqing chose to remain single, having made up her mind at the age of only sixteen or seventeen to devote herself to education and academic studies and not let herself be distracted by a family. She formed other attachments, however, often helping others financially even though she lived quite frugally on her own. She developed a friendship with Xian Xinghai, for example, when he was a student at Lingnan University high school and provided him with financial assistance. He later became famous as a composer and his "Yiyong jun jinxing qu" was adopted as the national anthem of the PRC. Not long before her death, she donated her considerable savings (HK$100,000) to be distributed to several public institutions, including the Sun Yat-sen Medical College. Xian Yuqing also gave her collections of cultural relics and books to the Guangdong Museum of Folk Art, Guangdong Provincial Research Institute of Culture and History, and Zhongshan University. In May 1965 her book *Studies of Written Material Relating to Guangdong* (Guangdong wenxian congtan) was published in Hong Kong.

People called her Miss Xian or Xian the Philosopher as a mark of respect for her virtue, talent, and scholarship. She was a close friend of the eminent historian Chen Yinke (1890–1969) and gave him great support during his long last illness. He praised her highly in his poem *Inscribed on the Painting "Professor Xian Yuqing Compiling History,"* which read: "Her peers vied to praise her achievements in compiling history. She disdained to produce works similar to others. If we are to compare her women's studies with her Chan Buddhism studies, she would be the successor in Guangdong of Ban Zhao."

LO Fu
(Translated by Wang Nian'en)

Chen Meiyan and Chen Liuqiu, eds. *Chen Yinke shiji.* Beijing: Qinghua daxue chubanshe, 1993.
Chen Shurong, ed. *Xian Yuqing dansheng baimian jinianji.* Macao: Aomen lishi xuehui, 1995.
Huang Binyan and Lai Shiguang, eds. *Xian Yuqing wenji.* Guangzhou: Zhongshan daxue chubanshe, 1995.
Huang Renchao. "Xian Yuqing de shengping ji qi zhuzuo." *Lingnan wenshi,* no. 1 (1983).
Liu Shaotang, ed. "Xian Yuqing." In *Minguo renwu xiaozhuan,* vol. 4. Taipei: Zhuanji wenxue chubanshe, 1989, 135–37.

Qi Mingrong and Xie Wenjie. *Xian Yuqing ji shehui fazhan zhanlüe yanjiu.* Xining: Qinghai renmin chubanshe, 1991.
Zhuan Fuwu. *Xian Yuqing xiansheng nianbiao.* In Supplement to *Xian Yuqing wenji.* Guangdong: Guangdongsheng wenshiguan, 1995.

Xiang Jingyu

Xiang Jingyu, 1895–1928, of Xupu, Hunan Province, was an early member of the CCP and leader of the women's movement in Shanghai during the first united front with the KMT (1922–27). After the communists came to power in 1949, she was enshrined as a revolutionary martyr.

Xiang Jingyu was the ninth child of a local merchant, Xiang Ruiling, and his wife Deng Yugui. Her education and unbound feet attested to the family's progressive views. In 1915, Xiang Jingyu graduated from the privately funded Zhounan Girls' School in Changsha, a center of student activism. One of her classmates at Zhounan was Cai Chang (*q.v.*), who introduced Xiang Jingyu to her brother Cai Hesen (1895–1931) and his friend Mao Zedong (1893–1976). After graduating, Xiang Jingyu was convinced that educating the individual was the way to change China and returned to her hometown where, with the support of her father and brothers, she opened a progressive upper primary school and served as its principal until summer 1919.

Upon returning to Changsha, Xiang Jingyu helped Cai Chang to organize a program for women to participate in a work-study program in France through the Sino-French Education Society. Earlier, in 1918, Mao and Cai Hesen and about thirty other men had founded the New People's Study Society (Xinmin xuehui), which had the same goal. Xiang Jingyu became one of its first women members in November and on 25 December 1919 sailed from Shanghai to France with a group that included Cai Hesen, Cai Chang, and their mother, Ge Jianhao (*q.v.*). In France, these four were sent to Montargis where all except Ge Jianhao were assigned to French language classes at the local secondary school. Ge Jianhao studied close by at a girls' secondary school.

The activities of Xiang Jingyu during her years in France can be pieced together from various sources, including published letters written by her and by others as well as reminiscences of fellow work-study students. The two most important events in her life were closely related: her conversion to Bolshevism as a model for China and her marriage to Cai Hesen. An essay first published in France in 1920 and reprinted in a 1980 collection of her writings shows that Xiang Jingyu had espoused the Bolshevik view of the "woman question." She argued that the family had to be replaced by collective institutions and called upon women with awakened consciousness to form organizations promoting public nurseries and free choice in marriage. In her own life, Xiang Jingyu acted upon these ideas when she and Cai Hesen rejected a traditional form of marriage ceremony and declared the "Xiang-Cai Alliance." Reportedly, their "wedding" photograph, taken on 5 May 1920, showed the two sitting together holding a copy of Karl Marx's *Das Kapital.* To seal their alliance, they published a volume of poetry, *The Upward Alliance* (Xiangshang tongmeng), in which they vowed to fight for the revolution together.

Xiang Jingyu and Cai Hesen joined the CCP in Shanghai after returning from

France in 1922. A 1981 biography and other literature commemorating Xiang Jingyu as a martyr place her on the Central Committee as head of a Women's Department established by the Second Party Congress in July 1922. However, official party histories do not indicate the formation of the department, and they list Xiang Jingyu as an alternate member of the Central Committee, if she is mentioned at all. There is no question about her husband's position: he was elected to the Central Committee that year and re-elected at the Third and Fourth Party Congresses in 1923 and 1925.

Sources are generally vague about exactly what Xiang Jingyu did during her Shanghai years (1922–25). She gave birth to a daughter in 1922 and a son in 1924, leaving both children with her mother-in-law in Hunan. After the CCP approved the first united front at its Third Party Congress in 1923, Xiang Jingyu joined the KMT. Reminiscences of various individuals make reference to her organizing a working-women's movement and participating in strikes in tobacco and textile factories, but her exact roles are unclear. She worked with other women to form the Chinese Women's Alliance (Zhongguo funü xiehui) and spoke at its first meeting held in Shanghai on 1–3 May 1925.

The most concrete record for these years is in her own writings. Beginning in 1922, Xiang Jingyu contributed to various women's publications. In 1923, as a member of the KMT, she became editor of *Women's Weekly* (Funü zhoubao). Certain themes emerge from her writings. Xiang Jingyu held to the communist stance that women's liberation could only take place in the context of the proletarian revolution but accepted the need for separate women's organizations because of the low level of women's consciousness. In theory, Xiang Jingyu pointed out, women participate equally with men, but in practice women are poorly educated (if at all), fearful of speaking in public, and usually dominated by men. Education for women remained a basic concern. Xiang Jingyu advocated separate schools for women but criticized the watered-down curricula at all female institutions, calling them a modern version of the women's quarters. She criticized bourgeois women's organizations for seeking representation in the warlord-imperialist governments of the time and urged these organizations to support working-class women. Xiang Jingyu wrote a number of pieces on the plight of women in Shanghai's spinning mills. Anti-imperialism is another theme, and she condemned America along with Japan and Britain, advocating solidarity with Soviet Russia.

The impression one gains of Xiang Jingyu as a person, even as far back as her school days in Hunan, is of a young woman who was bright, articulate, and energetic. By the time she returned from France, Xiang Jingyu had also become confident that her views were correct. She is said not to have hesitated to correct her comrades on ideological matters. Xiang Jingyu also paid little attention to her appearance, wearing homemade clothes and shoes; the combination of her dress and work style led her Shanghai comrades to dub her "Old Grandma."

Given Xiang Jingyu's talent and commitment, it is easy to understand that by late 1925 there were indications that she was experiencing frustration with the fact that those who were assigned to "women's work" did not hold policy-making positions in the CCP (or the KMT). Xiang Jingyu's experience and writings reflect the ambiguous status of women's issues in the CCP: although the party was ideologically committed to women's equality, male prejudice and limited resources gave it low priority.

There was, however, another side to "Old Grandma," one that appeared when she began an affair with Peng Shuzhi (b. 1895), a protégée of the party chairman Chen Duxiu (1880–1942). Xiang Jingyu's women comrades were delighted with the change in her demeanor until they discovered the reason. Because of the affair, she lost her leadership position in the women's movement; it also served to harden attitudes in a disagreement on the issue of party organization, between Cai Hesen and Qu Qiubai on the one hand and Chen Duxiu and Peng Shuzhi on the other. Shortly after the affair became public, Xiang Jingyu and Cai Hesen left for Moscow, she to study at the Toilers of the East University and he as a delegate to the Sixth Comintern Congress.

Sources emanating from the PRC that commemorate Xiang Jingyu as a martyr do not mention the affair with Peng Shuzhi. Zhang Guotao and his wife Yang Zilie (*q.v.*), however, who both later defected from the CCP, discussed it in their separate memoirs published in the United States and Hong Kong, respectively. Xu Shanfu includes the item in his 1935 article on splits in the CCP, published in Shanghai. Mainland China sources indicate indirectly that the breach between Xiang Jingyu and Cai Hesen was not healed in Moscow; no mention was made of the two as a couple after they returned to China, even though they were, at least briefly, in Wuhan at the same time.

In his biography of Xiang Jingyu published in 1981, Dai Xugong says that she returned to China in March 1927 and went to Guangzhou before stopping in Hunan to see her children. Xiang Jingyu then went to Wuhan, becoming head of the Propaganda Department of the Wuhan General Trade Union. After the left-wing KMT officially expelled the communists from the Wuhan government in July, she went underground but was arrested in Wuhan's French Concession in 1928. Accounts vary as to exactly what happened after her arrest. Apparently the French consul did not immediately extradite her to KMT authorities, and some of her fellow students who had studied in France attempted to find ways to save her. However, a new consul turned her over to the Wuhan garrison command post some time in April 1928; on 1 May she was executed by a firing squad. In works emphasizing her martyr persona, she is described as defiant to the end, shouting the slogans "Long Live the Communist Party" and "Down with the Guomindang" on the way to her death. Although such behavior would have been consistent with her personality, none of the accounts that describe her death are by eyewitnesses.

Xiang Jingyu's early death removed her from the struggles and splits in the CCP. As a martyr, she embodied the virtues of a good communist citizen: dedication to the goals of the party, hard work, study, and love of country. Words written by Peter Nettl about Rosa Luxemburg are equally applicable to Xiang Jingyu: she earned her place in the official pantheon "by dying early and by dying hard."

Andrea McELDERRY

Cai Hesen. "Xiang Jingyu tongzhi zhuan." *Jindai shi yanjiu*, 14, no. 4 (1982): 1–3.
Chang Kuo-t'ao. *The Rise of the Chinese Communist Party, 1921–1927*, vol. 1. Lawrence: University of Kansas Press, 1971, 246–47; 297–316; 404; 487–88.

Dai Xugong. *Xiang Jingyu zhuan*. Beijing: Renmin chubanshe, 1981.

Ding Ling. "Xiang Jingyu tongzhi liugei wo de yinxiang." *Shouhuo*, 2 (1980): 184–86, 232.

He Huzhi. *Xiang Jingyu zhuan*. Shanghai: Shanghai renmin chubanshe, 1990.

Jinian Xiang Jingyu tongzhi yingyong jiuyi wushi zhounian. Beijing: Renmin chubanshe, 1978.

Klein, Donald W., and Anne B. Clark. *Biographic Dictionary of Chinese Communism, 1921–1965*. Cambridge, Mass.: Harvard University Press, 1971, 317–19.

Li Lisan. "Dao Xiang Jingyu tongzhi." *Hongqi piaopiao*, 5 (1957): 28–31.

Li Yichun. "Huiyi Hesen tongzhi." In *Huiyi Cai Hesen*. Beijing: Renmin chubanshe, 1980, 127–34.

Lieshi Xiang Jingyu. Beijing: Zhongguo funü zazhishe, 1958.

McElderry, Andrea. "Woman Revolutionary: Xiang Jingyu." *China Quarterly*, 104 (1986): 95–122.

Meng Zhaozhi, Ning Zhouyang, and Ho Guzhi. *Cai Hesen zhuan*. Changsha: Hunan renmin chubanshe, 1980, 58–59, 64–75, 109.

Peng Shuzhi, with Claude Cadart, and Cheng Yingxiang. *Memoires de Peng Shuzhi, L'envol du communisme en Chine*. Paris: Gallimard, 1983, 386–87; 410–11; 460–61, 470.

Qinghua daxue zhonggongdang shi jiaoyanzu. *Fufa qingong jianxue yundong shiliao*, 2, no. 1 (1980), 115, 155.

Shen Yijia. "Wo suo zhidao de zaoqi zhi Cai Hesen." In *Huiyi Cai Hesen*. Beijing: Renmin chubanshe, 1980, 139–40.

Siao-yu. *Mao Zedong and I Were Beggars*. London: Hutchinson, 1961, 50, 60–62, 165.

Snow, Helen. *Women in Modern China*. The Hague and Paris: Mouton Press, 1967, 199–201, 233–59.

Song Feifu. *Xinmin xuehui*. Changsha: Renmin chubanshe, 1980, 62–70.

Wang Yizhi. "A Great Woman Revolutionary." *Women of China*, 2 (1963): 22–24. Also published in *China Reconstructs*, 14 (March 1965), 24–26.

Xiang Jingyu. *Xiang Jingyu wenji*. Changsha: Hunan renmin chubanshe, 1980.

Xinmin xuehui ziliao. Beijing: Renmin chubanshe, 1979, 7, 75–87, 115–27, 412, 462.

Xu Shangu. "Gongchandang fenlie shi." *Tianhai shiliao*, 2 (1935): 227.

Yang Zilie. *Zhang Guotao furen huiyilu*. Hong Kong: Zhongguo wenti yanjiu zhongxin, 1970, 127–62.

Xiao Han: *see* **Ding Ling**

Xiao Hong

Xiao Hong, 1911–1942, childhood name Ronghua, was born Zhang Naiying to a land-owning family in Hulan County, Heilongjiang Province. She was one of the early modern women writers in China.

Xiao Hong's father was apparently a difficult man. She once described him in the following way: "My father often gave up his humanity due to his own covetousness." Her mother, whom Xiao Hong feared, died when she was nine, leaving Xiao Hong with a grandfather as her only and dear friend. She spent countless hours with him in the garden, where he taught her the basics of Chinese literature. Other members of the household were her grandmother, a stepmother and her son (born after the death of Xiao Hong's mother), and tenants who rented portions of the thirty-room family compound. Stories about the lives of the tenants, the peasants in Hulan, and the time spent with her grandfather in the household garden formed the bulk of Xiao Hong's writings in *The Field of Life and Death* (Sheng si chang, 1935); "The Family Outsider" (Jiazu yiwai de ren, 1936); and *Tales of Hulan River* (Hulan he zhuan, 1941).

Xiao Hong's formal schooling began in 1920 at the Agriculture Elementary School (now called Xiao Hong Elementary School) in Hulan County. In 1925, at the age of fourteen, she attended Harbin First Municipal Girls' High School (now Harbin Seventh High School) and graduated in 1930. Xiao Hong was a quiet, serious student, and perceived as a loner, although she did have friends. Her favorite courses were art and history, and she avidly painted until discovering literature, after being introduced to the May Fourth Literature of Mao Dun and Lu Xun and Western romantic fiction in translation. During this time, Xiao Hong first became involved in the youth movement that had been sweeping across China since 1919. In winter 1928, she and her classmates participated in a demonstration against the Japanese military encroachment in Manchuria. While on winter break in 1929, Xiao Hong returned home to find that her father had arranged a marriage for her with the son of a warlord general. Fearing the marriage and with nothing to keep her in Hulan after the death of her grandfather, Xiao Hong fled her home. In "Early Winter" (Chu dong) she wrote: "I cannot go back to that kind of home. I'm not willing to be supported by a father who stands at the opposite pole from me." Several versions exist about what happened next. According to her friend and biographer Luo Binji and close friend Mei Lin, Xiao Hong had returned to Harbin only to leave for Beijing with a lover, a man named Lin who had been her teacher. However, arriving in Beijing, Xiao Hong learned that Lin already had a family. Briefly attending school in Beijing, Xiao Hong soon returned to Harbin; she was pregnant but did not keep the child. Details of the separation are unknown.

Ding Yanzhao, however, says that Xiao Hong went to Beijing with a male cousin (Lu Zongyu) or was followed there by her betrothed (Wang Dianjia) and returned to Harbin in winter 1931–32 with a man who later left her. Ding Yanzhao writes that Xiao Hong lived with Wang Dianjia for six months in a hotel that is now the Sixteenth Street South Renli Police Substation. In debt to the proprietor, Wang supposedly went home to get money but never returned, leaving Xiao Hong a virtual prisoner in the hotel.

Howard Goldblatt recounts another version: that Xiao Hong returned to Harbin alone and lived as a vagrant, sleeping in friends' houses or wherever she could find a roof. Xiao Hong eventually landed at the Dongxingxun Hotel, which was run by White Russians. According to Sun Ling, she not only incurred food and housing debt but also became addicted to opium. Nevertheless, Xiao Hong wrote to Pei Xingyuan, editor of Harbin's *International Gazette* (Guoji xiebao), seeking assistance. He and several other young writers went to check on her living conditions and settled the outstanding debt. Then, when a flood threatened the hotel, Pei Xingyuan took her in with his family. There, Xiao Hong was introduced to her future common-law husband Xiao Jun and her lasting friend Shu Qun.

Xiao Jun (b. 1908) came from a family of peasant farmers in Liaoning Province; his original name was Liu Honglin. Lacking extended formal education, he spent time in volunteer armies from 1925 to 1931 before arriving in Harbin. Xiao Jun did write, however, and became a regular contributor to the *International Gazette* literary supplement.

Xiao Hong's new friendship with Xiao Jun marked a turning point in her life: she soon left the northeast and began a new life in southern China. Because of her tumultuous relationship with Xiao Jun—he was known as a womanizer and beat her on occasion—Xiao Hong often turned to friends to protect her from his physical abuse. It was becoming evident that Xiao Hong had fallen into a pattern of abusive relationships with men upon whom she was dependent (her father, first lover, and now Xiao Jun). These relationships, combined with her health problems (a stomach ailment, anemia, tuberculosis, and malnutrition), are seen by biographers as the two main factors preventing Xiao Hong from reaching her full creative potential.

She began her writing career by submitting work to the *International Gazette* and *Dagong Newspaper* (Dagong bao). Xiao Hong and Xiao Jun, under the pen names Qiao Yin and San Lang, respectively, jointly published a collection of their writings under the title *Trudging* (Bashe, 1933) and formed a drama club with fellow writers. The collection was banned by the Japanese censors, and participation in the drama club became dangerous. In May 1934, the couple left for Qingdao in Shandong Province at the invitation of their friend Mei Lin; he offered Xiao Jun the post of editor of the literary supplement of his newly founded paper *Qingdao Morning News* (Qingdao chenbao). In Qingdao, she completed the draft of her first novel, *The Field of Life and Death*, an emotionally intense depiction of the poverty of peasant life in northern rural China, where both animals and humans balance on a knife edge between life and death. Xiao Hong was just twenty-three years old. Because of the worsening political situation in the north, however, she, Xiao Jun, and Mei Lin then moved to Shanghai, the culturally vibrant commercial hub of China, far removed from the world of Xiao Hong's fiction.

In Shanghai, she and Xiao Jun struck up a correspondence and eventually a close friendship with the renowned writer Lu Xun. Known for giving patronage to young writers, he was especially supportive of Xiao Hong. With his assistance, the young couple submitted their writings to publishers of various journals throughout Shanghai. Xiao Hong's essays, poetry, and fiction appeared in *Taibai, Zhongxuesheng, Wenxue, Zuojia, Wencong, Wenxue Yuekan,* and *Zhongliu,* many of them submitted under her pen name Qiao Yin.

Despite delays of many months at the Literary Censorship Committee of the Central Propaganda Bureau, Lu Xun eventually published *The Field of Life and Death* in his own Slave Society Series. He wrote a preface for it and Hu Feng an afterword. The novel was eagerly received by the reading public and became even more of a sensation when it was promptly banned by the KMT government. The piece was hailed as an introspective on the burgeoning resistance movement of the peasants massing against the Japanese military invasion of Manchuria, and it exalted Xiao Hong's literary position as part of the politicized Northeast Writers' Group. The work was also noted for what Lu Xun described as its "keen observations and extraordinary writing style." This was the first time Xiao Hong used the pen name by which she is presently known, and it marked the beginning of her popularity.

In 1935 she also completed *Market Street* (Shangshi jie, 1936), which has been read as an autobiographical account of her time with Xiao Jun in Harbin, telling of their struggle to find employment and stave off hunger. *The Bridge* (Qiao), a collection of short stories and sketches, was also well received that same year, and included two memorable and heart-wrenching stories of the tragic lives of two women: "The Bridge" and "Hands" (Shou).

Also in 1936, Xiao Hong left for Tokyo, Japan. Her correspondence with Xiao Jun, who remained in Shanghai, reveals her loneliness and difficulty in writing. Yet it is evident from the 1937 publication of a collection of short stories entitled *On the Oxcart* (Niuche shang) that she did manage to write a few stories there, among them a short piece called "A Lonely Life" (Gudu de shenghuo). The title story, "On the Oxcart," is considered to be one of Xiao Hong's most successful pieces of fiction. It includes several of the elements for which her writings were known: a vivid setting, an impoverished and lonely female protagonist, and autobiography.

Upon receiving news of Lu Xun's death in August 1936, Xiao Hong returned to Shanghai to mourn her mentor. She maintained a close friendship with Lu Xun's lover, Xu Guangping (*q.v.*). Xiao Hong wrote several memorial pieces on her relationship with Lu Xun, including a little-studied pantomime drama called *Lu Xun, the Soul of the People* (Minzu hun Lu Xun, composed in 1940).

Because of growing political hostilities in Shanghai, Xiao Hong left for Wuhan and eventually Wuchang in Hubei Province. In Wuhan, her relationship with Xiao Jun deteriorating, Xiao Hong met the man she was to marry, Duanmu Hongliang. Born Cao Jingping in 1912, he was also a writer from the northeast. Cao adopted the pen name Duanmu Hongliang when his first writings were published in *Wenxue* in 1937. His lack of emotional maturity, however, would later make Xiao Hong's life difficult, as her constant ill health and self-doubt made her dependent on levels of support he could never give her.

Xiao Hong's remaining years were nomadic as she and fellow writer friends moved constantly to avoid encroaching battlelines. Throughout 1937, she sat on the editorial board of Hu Feng's left-wing literary magazine *Qiyue*. Minutes from the meetings reveal how Xiao Hong's stance on the criteria for National Defense Literature differed from her contemporaries. Throughout her writing career, she moved about with central figures in left-wing literary circles but, like Lu Xun, never joined the CCP.

Invited by Li Gongpu (1901–1946) to attend the People's Revolutionary University (Minzu geming daxue), Xiao Hong, Xiao Jun, and Duanmu Hongliang went to Shanxi Province in 1938. There, Xiao Hong met the famous woman writer Ding Ling (*q.v.*) with whom Lu Xun had often compared her. While in Shanxi, Xiao Hong terminated her tumultuous relationship with Xiao Jun and took up with Duanmu Hongliang; they returned to Wuchang and married. Xiao Hong was pregnant at the time of her marriage, but her baby was stillborn shortly after her arrival in Chongqing in 1938. There, Xiao Hong wrote "A Remembrance of Mr. Lu Xun" (Huiyi Lu Xun xiansheng) and several more short pieces. She also completed a draft of her second novel, *Tales of Hulan River*, a series of largely autobiographical sketches based on memories of life in Hulan County. In 1940, in poor physical health and emotionally drained from yet another unsuccessful relationship, Xiao Hong moved with Duanmu Hongliang to Hong Kong. There, she completed her third and final novel, *Ma Bole* (1940), a satirical piece rivaling the humor of the famous Lao She (1898–1966).

Xiao Hong met the respected American journalist Agnes Smedley, who was well known among Chinese left-wing writers, in 1941. Concerned by Xiao Hong's physical deterioration, Smedley accompanied her to Queen Mary's Hospital, where Xiao Hong was diagnosed with tuberculosis. Greatly impoverished, she relied in her final days on the generosity of Smedley, the prominent fiction writer and literary critic Mao Dun, and her friend Luo Binji. Xiao Hong wrote her last piece, "Spring in a Small Town" (Xiaocheng sanyue), while in hospital.

In January 1942, she underwent two unnecessary surgical procedures for a throat ailment and lost the ability to speak. Her health declined rapidly afterward. By 18 January, the Japanese military had taken over the hospital and removed civilian patients to a makeshift ward in a schoolyard, where Duanmu Hongliang and Luo Binji found her. Xiao Hong died on 22 January of a throat infection, pulmonary tuberculosis, and other illnesses. She was thirty-one years old.

Duanmu Hongliang said that he placed part of her remains at Repulse Bay (Qianshuiwan) and part in the grounds of the makeshift hospital in Hong Kong. However, Luo Binji was unable to find any trace of them in the schoolyard the following day. In 1957, some people in Hong Kong helped the Chinese Writers' Association of Guangzhou move Xiao Hong's remains from Repulse Bay to Yinhe gongmu, a cemetery in Guangzhou.

In the last two decades of the twentieth century, Xiao Hong's life and writings became important to contemporary scholars, writers, and feminists within China and beyond. With the legacy of early twentieth-century Chinese women writers being discussed with new vigor in mainland China and Taiwan as socialist literary discourses expand to include discussions of gender and emotions, several contemporary women writers have suggested that their writings were influenced by Xiao Hong, Ding Ling, and Bing Xin (q.v.). Several biographies of her life, as well as collected writings, have also been published. Biographer Ding Yanzhao prefers to see Xiao Hong as a tragic, romantic figure, while a study co-authored by Dai Jinhua and Meng Yue reinterprets Xiao Hong's writings less politically and more personally. They argue that her descriptive abilities deserve closer attention, not simply for revealing peasant life under Japanese occupation but because of the depth of emotional struggle her predominantly female protagonists experienced to survive. In that vein, Lydia Liu demonstrates how Xiao Hong's writings were misunderstood by her contemporary male writers.

Although Xiao Hong's writings were informed by a realist ideology, her art expressed a politics all its own, the subtlety of which was also lost on many of her contemporaries. The author's simple yet lucid portrayal of people suffering poverty, abuse, or abandonment deserves greater attention. The pictographic images and montage-like narrative sequences of her longer pieces imbue Xiao Hong's writings with a filmic quality. The specificity of the rural China she portrayed made her subject material easily translate into the universal.

Translations of Xiao Hong's works can be found in Japanese, Russian, German, and English.

Megan M. FERRY

Ding Yanzhao. *Xiao Hong zhuan*. Nanjing: Jiangsu wenyi chubanshe, 1993.
Du Yibai and Zhang Yumao. *Xiao Hong*. Taipei: Haifeng chubanshe, 1990.
Goldblatt, Howard. *Hsiao Hung*. Boston: Twayne Publishers, 1976.
Keen, Ruth. *Autobiographie und Literatur. Drei Werke der chinesischen Schriftstellerin Xiao Hong*. Munich: Minerva Publikation, 1984.
Liu, Lydia He. *Translingual Practice: Literature, National Culture, and Translated Modernity—China, 1900–1937*. Stanford: Stanford University Press, 1996.
Luo Binji. *Xiao Hong xiaozhuan*. Harbin: Heilongjiang renmin chubanshe, 1981.
Meng Yue and Dai Jinhua. *Fuchu lishi dibiao*. Zhengzhou: Henan renmin chubanshe, 1989.
Shao Feng. *Xiao Hong zhuan*. Tianjin: Baihua wenyi chubanshe, 1980.
Sun Ling. "Xiao Hong de cuowu hunyin." In *Fushi xiaopin*, Sun Ling. Taipei: Zhengzhong shuju, 1961.
Zhang Lin. "Yi nüzuojia Xiao Hong er san shi." In *Huainian Xiao Hong*, ed. Wang Guanquan. Harbin: Heilongjiang renmin chubanshe, 1981.

Xiao Li: *see* **Li Ziyun**

Xiao Qingyu: *see* **Hsiao Sa**

Xiao Sa: *see* **Hsiao Sa**

Xiao Yanhong: *see* **Hongxian Nü**

Xiao Yuehua

Xiao Yuehua, 1913–1983, one of the thirty women who took part in the Chinese communists' Long March of 1934–35, was born in Dabu County, Guangdong Province.

Her poor peasant family gave her away as a child bride, but Xiao Yuehua eventually ran away to Hailufeng, where she became involved in revolutionary activities. While working in western Fujian some time after 1927, Xiao Yuehua and her husband, whose name is not known, fell foul of a witchhunt within the communist ranks. He was killed and she became ostracized by her comrades, with only Li Jianzhen (*q.v.*) standing by her.

Xiao Yuehua joined the Youth League in 1933 and was transferred to the Youth League Office in Ruijin where she worked with Hu Yaobang (1915–1989). That same year, she was chosen by "the organization" (zuzhi shang) to be the sexual partner of the German Comintern agent Otto Braun (Li De, 1900–1974); her initial refusal was countered by threats of dismissal from her job. Apart from this specific obligation, Xiao Yuehua carried out the same duties on the Long March as the other peasant women, hiring bearers, finding food, and caring for the wounded. Ding Ling (*q.v.*) later told Harrison Salisbury, however, that Xiao Yuehua had been an orderly for Dr. Nelson Fu (1894–1968). Xiao Yuehua joined the CCP in May 1937, about the same time that she gave birth to Otto Braun's son and filed for divorce; Xiao Yuehua was employed in Yan'an as a dispatcher in the Central Committee Office.

Little is known about her life after this. She kept her son and apparently remarried. In 1960, Xiao Yuehua was made deputy head of the Road Maintenance Office in the Hunan Communications Bureau. She may also have worked in Changsha. During the

Cultural Revolution, Xiao Yuehua came under suspicion but is said to have coura-geously offered refuge to several unnamed leaders who had been criticized. In 1983 she was diagnosed with cancer. Hu Yaobang, with whom she had worked in Ruijin in 1933 and whose death triggered the demonstrations that were squashed in the Tian'anmen Massacre of 4 June 1989, arranged for Xiao Yuehua to be brought to Beijing for treatment. She died not long after, however. Hu Yaobang ordered that the red flag of China and the flag of the CCP be draped over her coffin in recognition of her contribution over the years.

Sue WILES

Guo Chen. *Jinguo liezhuan: Hong yifangmianjun sanshiwei changzheng nühongjun shengping shiji.* Beijing: Nongcun duwu chubanshe, 1986, 69–71.
Salisbury, Harrison E. *The Long March: The Untold Story.* New York: Harper & Row, 1985, 81–82.

Xiao Yun: *see* **Hiu Wan, Ven.**

Xiaomi: *see* **Li Lihua**

Xie Bingxin: *see* **Bing Xin**

Xie Bingying: *see* **Hsieh Ping-ying**

Xie Fei
Xie Fei, b. 1913, as Xie Qiongxiang, of Wenchang County on Hainan Island, was one of the thirty women who went with the First Front Red Army on the Chinese commu-nists' Long March of 1934–35. She was also known as A Xiang but has been con-fused in some sources with Jin Weiying (*q.v.*, also known as A Jin), whom Helen Foster Snow in Yan'an mistakenly called "Ah Ch'ing (Hsiang)."

Xie Fei's family was not well off, yet she attended school and in 1926 enrolled in Hainan Sixth Normal School. Xie Fei was the youngest student and one of the most active in terms of taking part in various nascent revolutionary groups. She joined the Communist Youth League in 1927, gaining admission to the CCP the same year. When the KMT-CCP united front collapsed in April following a massacre of workers in Shanghai by KMT soldiers, Xie Fei returned home to organize the local women in support of the communists and workers. In 1928 she went to Hong Kong and carried out undercover work with the provincial party organization; her family's home was torched during this period and most of her twenty-three close relatives were killed.

In 1929, Xie Fei was sent to Singapore where she did clerical work with the Provi-sional Nanyang Committee. During her three years there, Xie Fei had little support and often went hungry. She was apprehended only once, however, in 1930. Upon returning to China in 1932, Xie Fei was assigned to the coastal city of Amoy in Fujian Province and continued her undercover work. Several times she ingested sensitive documents, after first boiling them, to prevent them from falling into the hands of the

KMT; Xie Fei had stomach problems for the rest of her life. In July 1934, she was transferred to the Office of National Security in Ruijin, capital of the Jiangxi soviet, and marched out of Ruijin in October with the Red Army. On the Long March, Xie Fei performed similar duties to those of the other women and was officially designated as an organizer with the Convalescent Company.

After the marchers reached the relative safety of Wayaobao in the northwest, Xie Fei married Liu Shaoqi (1898–1969; *vide* Wang Guangmei), then a member of the Politburo, later to become head of state and eventually to become the chief target of the Cultural Revolution. Her marriage to Liu Shaoqi lasted less than six years, from 1936 to approximately 1941. They worked together in Tianjin, spent a short period in Yan'an during which Xie Fei attended the Party School and then in 1939 were assigned to the New Fourth Army in central China. At some point, Xie Fei became separated from Liu Shaoqi while crossing the Yangzi [Yangtze] River and was stranded on the southern bank, unable to make contact with her unit. She remained in the south, becoming secretary of a joint county committee and political commissar of an independent battalion of soldiers. Xie Fei stayed with this battalion for several years, assuming leadership after the commander fell ill; they fought over twenty battles against Japanese and KMT forces. Xie Fei was known locally as Regimental Commander Xie.

In 1945 she and her battalion rejoined the New Fourth Army. Xie Fei was then assigned to the northeast and elected to the Standing Committee of the northeastern Women's Federation and made head of the Organization Department. After the establishment of the PRC in 1949, she was appointed deputy director of Beijing's Huabei Revolutionary University and in 1950 placed in charge of a special training course in the newly established Chinese People's University. Aware of her academic potential, Xie Fei enrolled in a law course at the People's University at the age of thirty-nine. Upon graduation in 1956, she was appointed deputy principal of the Central Cadres' School of Politics and Law (Zhongyang zhengfa ganbu xuexiao).

Xie Fei never remarried. In the political upheavals of the late 1950s, she was targeted as a rightist and sent in 1959 to work on a pig farm; it is unclear how long Xie Fei remained there before being allowed to return to Beijing. She also suffered badly during the Cultural Revolution, largely because of her brief marriage to Liu Shaoqi, who died in prison at the end of 1969. She was physically attacked and imprisoned under frightful conditions from 1968 to 1973. After rehabilitation in 1978, she appeared to bear no grudge against the communist authorities. Xie Fei sat on the CPPCC and the Public Security Consultative Committee; accepted the position of deputy principal at the Central Cadres' School of Politics and Law (later renamed the Central People's Security College); and was director of the Chinese Law Society and deputy director of the Beijing Law Society. The successful academic career Xie Fei carved out in the second half of her life was largely based on her own efforts. However, it would not have been possible had she been entirely without the *guanxi* (connections) of having been a Long Marcher, despite the principle of equal access upon which the new nation was founded. At the time of writing, Xie Fei was believed to be living in Beijing.

Sue WILES

Guo Chen. *Jinguo liezhuan: Hong yifangmianjun sanshiwei changzheng nühongjun shengping shiji*. Beijing: Nongcun duwu chubanshe, 1986, 44–47.
Hu Guohua and Zhuang Jianmin. "Bu pingfande lu." In *Hongjun nüyingxiong zhuan*, eds. Liaowang bianjibu. Beijing: Xinhua chubanshe, 1986, 74–82.
Lee, Lily Xiao Hong, and Sue Wiles. *Women of the Long March*. Sydney: Allen & Unwin, 1999.
Snow, Helen Foster. *Inside Red China*. 1977 reprint [with a new preface and biographical notes by the author]. New York: Da Capo Press, 1939, 175.
Yingwen *Zhongguo funü*, ed. *Gujin zhuming funü renwu*, vol. 2. Shijiazhuang: Hebei renmin chubanshe, 1986, 858–62.

Xie Qiongxiang: *see* **Xie Fei**

Xie Wanying: *see* **Bing Xin**

Xie Xiaomei
Xie Xiaomei, b. 1913, one of the thirty women who went with the First Front Red Army on the Chinese communists' Long March of 1934–35, was born in Longyan County, Fujian Province.

She came from a family of shopkeepers who were deeply involved in revolutionary activities. Xie Xiaomei completed primary school and started work at fifteen with Shimazhen Telephone Company as a wirer. She joined the Communist Youth League in 1929 and the CCP in 1930 at which time she acted as secretary to the Fujian Provincial Party Committee. That same year she met and married Luo Ming, then party secretary of Fujian.

After a short stint with the Central Committee in Shanghai in 1931, the couple returned to the Fujian soviet, where they worked off and on for a year or so. They were demoted to teaching posts and recalled to Ruijin when Luo Ming was criticized for his "pro-Wang Ming line, anti-party attitude" and Xie Xiaomei placed her month-old daughter with a cadre family in Fujian in 1932 so as to continue her guerrilla work.

Ten days before the Long March began in October 1934, Xie Xiaomei gave birth to her second child, whom she placed with a local communist family. Her duties on the Long March involved tending wounded stragglers, buying food, and working with a field hospital. After Luo Ming was seriously wounded in Guizhou, Xie Xiaomei devoted considerable time to caring for him. In March or April 1935, they were ordered to stay behind in Guiyang to agitate among the peasantry. However, they were repeatedly betrayed, arrested, and released over the next few years as they moved from Guiyang to Shanghai to Nanjing. Because of Luo Ming's past connection with the defeated Wang Ming line, the party would not take them back; it nevertheless asked them to continue revolutionary work in Fujian. The two taught school and spread communist and anti-Japanese propaganda in Xie Xiaomei's hometown for several years. In 1947 they went to Singapore to escape the KMT's death throes in southeastern China and in 1949 returned to China.

Xie Xiaomei was appointed to various teaching and library posts but was investigated during the Cultural Revolution because of her numerous arrests in the 1930s;

she was labeled as a traitor. Sent down to cadre school in the countryside, Xie Xiaomei was required to perform manual labor for three years. In 1973 she retired in protest against the policies of the Cultural Revolution and was punished with a pitifully low pension. Finally rehabilitated in 1981, her status of continuous party membership since 1930 was restored along with the privileges and pension appropriate to an old Long March cadre. She was understood to be living in Guangdong at the time of writing (2000).

Sue WILES

Guo Chen. *Jinguo liezhuan: Hong yifangmianjun sanshiwei changzheng nühongjun shengping shiji.* Beijing: Nongcun duwu chubanshe, 1986, 158–65.
Lee, Lily Xiao Hong and Sue Wiles. *Women of the Long March.* Sydney: Allen & Unwin, 1999.
Qi Xiu. "Lijin qianxin zhi yu jian." In *Hongjun nüyingxiong zhuan,* eds. Liaowang bianjibu. Beijing: Xinhua chubanshe, 1986, 175–87.

Xie Xide

Xie Xide, 1921–2000, of Quanzhou, Fujian Province, was a physicist who worked in semi-conductor physics, solid state energy spectrum, and surface physics. She was also one of the few women to become president of a university.

Her mother, Guo Jinyu, died early. Xie Xide's father was the famous physicist Xie Yuming (1893–1986), who gained his doctorate from Chicago University in 1926 and returned to work in the Physics Department at Yanjing [Yen-ching] University in Beijing. Xie Xide and her grandmother moved to the capital with him.

Xie Xide studied in the primary school and high school affiliated with Yanjing University and went on to Bridgeman Girls' High School. Her family moved to Wuchang and Changsha when the Sino-Japanese War erupted in 1937, but her father went by himself to Changting, Fujian Province, to take up a teaching position at Xiamen University. The rest of the family moved to Guiyang to escape the encroaching Japanese presence. In 1938 Xie Xide suspended her studies because of tuberculosis in her right hip, and over the following four years read a great deal, completing part of the mathematics and physics syllabus by self-study. She won the battle with tuberculosis but was left with an immovable hip joint.

The student passed the entrance examination to the Mathematics and Physics Department of Xiamen University in 1942 and spent the next four years in extremely harsh conditions in the western region of Fujian. In summer 1946, Xie Xide traveled to Nanjing to sit an examination for overseas study and in the autumn tutored mathematics and physics at Shanghai (Hujiang) University. She was accepted in 1947 as a self-financed graduate student at Smith College in the United States and also worked there as a tutor. Xie Xide was awarded a master's degree after two years and went on to the Physics Department of the Massachusetts Institute of Technology to study for her doctorate. She researched the wave function of the hydrogen atom under high pressure, receiving her Ph.D. in 1951. For about a year, Xie Xide was a research scientist in the department and worked on the use of a microwave resonant cavity to measure the dielectric constant and the conductivity of the semi-conductor germanium.

Xie Xide married the biochemist Cao Tianqin (b. 1920) in Britain in May 1952; he had gained his Ph.D. in Biochemistry from Cambridge University. In August they returned to China and settled in Shanghai. Xie Xide worked in the Physics Department of Fudan University as a lecturer (1952–56), associate professor (1956–62), and professor (1962–). Her later academic appointments were as head of the Solid Physics Unit (1953–61), head of the Semiconductor Physics Unit (1961–66), deputy director of the Shanghai Research Institute of Technological Physics of the Chinese Academy of Sciences (1958–66), and director of the Contemporary Physics Research Institute of Fudan University (1978–83). She was also vice-president, and then president, of Fudan University from 1983 to 1988. In 1980 Xie Xide was elected as an academician of the Chinese Academy of Sciences and placed on its board. Several famous overseas universities bestowed honorary doctorates on her, and she sat on the editorial committees of international journals. In 1988 Xie Xide was appointed as an academician at the Third World Academy of Sciences.

As a physicist, Xie Xide worked on semi-conductor physics, solid state energy spectrum, and surface physics. In 1960 she mainly researched space groups and semi-conducting energy bands; in 1980 Xie Xide engaged in research on solid surface absorption. She published scores of papers on the electronics of the interior, surface, and interface of solid bodies and reached a high level of academic achievement. Xie Xide taught at both undergraduate and graduate levels for many years and presided over nation-wide seminars on solid physics and surface physics. She devoted a great deal of attention to the quality of teaching and was heavily involved in the preparation of textbooks. Xie Xide contributed significantly to the discipline of surface physics, cultivating semi-conductor physics experts and technicians, as well as developing tertiary education in general.

She worked hard at an extremely busy and important career and yet found time to pursue her hobby of stamp collecting. Xie Xide overcame great obstacles in the early 1950s to return to China from the United States via England. During the Cultural Revolution, she was persecuted but clung to the belief that false accusations would in the end be reversed and justice would prevail. A woman of morality and strong will, in the 1990s Xie Xide continued her studies of the surface and interface of semi-conductors and short-period superlattices phonon spectrum even after being diagnosed with cancer. She supported her husband through his terminal illness; she died in 2000.

WANG Bing
(Translated by Shirley Cai)

Huang Kun and Xie Xide, eds. *Bandaoti wulixue*. Beijing: Kexue chubanshe, 1958.
Wang Zengfan. "Xie Xide." In *Zhongguo xiandai kexuejia zhuanji*, vol. 1. Beijing: Kexue chubanshe, 1994, 171–77.
Xie Xide. "Feijingtai wuzhi." In *Guti wulixue*, vol. 2, eds. Fang Junxin and Lu Dong. Shanghai: Shanghai kexue jishu chubanshe, 1982.
———. ed. *Qunlun ji qi zai wulixue zhong de yingyong*. Beijing: Kexue chubanshe, 1986.
Xie Xide and Fang Junxin, eds. *Guti wulixue*. Shanghai: Shanghai kexue jishu chubanshe, 1962–1963.

"Xie Xide." Chinese Academy of Sciences, on the Internet at <http://www.casad.ac.cn/english/members/physics/1-80-45.htm>

Yanjing Daxue renwuzhi. Beijing: Yanjing yanjiuyuan, 1999, 38–40.

Yingwen *Zhongguo funü*, ed. *Gujin zhuming funü renwu*, vol. 2. Shijiazhuang: Hebei renmin chubanshe, 1986, 1014–18.

Zhonghua quanguo funü lianhehui. Zuzhi lianluobu. *Zhongguo nüyuanshi*. Shenyang: Liaoning renmin chubanshe, 1995, 315–17.

Xie Xuehong

Xie Xuehong [Hsieh Hsüeh-hung], 1901–1970, was a Taiwan revolutionary who opposed the Japanese colonialists and the KMT government that followed it.

She was born in Zhanghua [Chang-hua] (some sources say Taizhong [T'ai-chung] because Zhanghua was at that time part of Taizhong) to a laborer's family, the fourth of seven children. Her original name was Xie Jianü [Hsieh Chia-nü] or Xie Anü [Hsieh Ah-nü], and throughout life Xie Xuehong went by the noms de guerre Xie Feiying [Hsieh Fei-ying], Yamane Yoshiko, and Xie Xuehong, although it is by the latter that she is most commonly known.

Life was hard for her family, and the little girl began selling bananas in the street at the age of six. When twelve years old and after her parents had died, Xie Xuehong was sold to a man named Hong Xi as a child bride for his eldest son, Hong Chunrong. One source says she became his concubine, but at the age of sixteen Xie Xuehong ran away and became a worker at the Imperial Sugar Manufacturing Factory (Diguo zhitang chang). There, she met Zhang Shumin [Chang Shu-min], a member of the factory's Sugarcane Committee. They fell in love but he was already married; because Xie Xuehong had no wish to live in his household as a concubine, they went to Japan. Zhang Shumin then had a shop selling Taiwan-made straw hats. During her three-year sojourn in Nagoya, Japan, Xie Xuehong devoted herself to studying Chinese and Japanese, which enabled her in later years to develop her studies in other subjects.

With Zhang Shumin's hat shop not doing well, Xie Xuehong returned to Taiwan in 1920. She took a position as a saleswoman for the Singer Sewing Machine Company and after two years had saved enough money to open the Nagahaya seamstress shop in the city of Taizhong. At this time, Xie Xuehong gradually was drawn into the anti-Japanese movement. While being economically independent gave her a certain freedom, Xie Xuehong may have been motivated by two factors to change direction. Firstly, her childhood hardship led her to search for a more just society; secondly, she was influenced by the political atmosphere of the time. In 1921, Xie Xuehong joined the Taiwan Culture Association (Taiwan wenhua xiehui [T'ai-wan wen-hua hsieh-hui]) and became involved in their work with women. It is possible that she met young intellectuals at this point from whom she got the idea of going to mainland China for further studies.

Xie Xuehong and Zhang Shumin went to Shanghai in 1924. There, she joined in the activities of the Taiwan Self-Government Association (Taiwan zizhi xiehui) and became a member of the CCP-sponsored Shanghai General Trade Union (Shanghai zong gonghui). Communist leaders noted Xie Xuehong's participation in the May

Thirtieth general strike organized by underground CCP members; at this time, she changed her name to Xie Feiying. In 1925, she enrolled in the CCP-controlled Shanghai University (Shanghai daxue) to study sociology. In her four or five months there, Xie Xuehong learned a great deal about social and political history and became acquainted with many Taiwanese students; they would later become her colleagues in revolutionary work.

In November, the CCP recommended that Xie Xuehong be sent to the Soviet Union to study at the party school, the Toilers of the East University in Moscow. The two years spent there gave her a good opportunity to learn more about socialism and communism as well as the revolutionary history of Russia. The young woman then made her final name change, to Xie Xuehong (Red Snow), to commemorate this often snow-bound country. In Moscow, she also made the acquaintance of the Chinese communist leaders Cai Hesen and Li Lisan, the Japanese Communist Party (JCP) leaders Tokuda Shūichi and Watanabe Masanosuke, and the only other Taiwan student, Lin Mushun. Xie Xuehong thus became one of the very few Taiwanese people then to tread the stage of international politics.

When Xie Xuehong left Moscow in 1927 at the end of her studies, the Comintern charged her with establishing a communist organization in Taiwan. Because the area was then a colony of Japan, however, the Comintern resolution stipulated that the JCP was to assume overall responsibility for planning and establishing a party organization in Taiwan. To liaise with the JCP, the Comintern nominated Xie Xuehong and Lin Mushun, with whom she had formed a romantic relationship, as Taiwan's representatives. However, when they went to Tokyo that year to receive guidelines from Japanese communist leader Watanabe Masanosuke, the two were told instead to seek guidance from the CCP.

Xie Xuehong and Lin Mushun therefore went to Shanghai in early 1928, where the Taiwan Communist Party (TCP) was officially established on 15 April, with Xie Xuehong as chair, at the head of eight leftist activists. Two observers attended, one from the CCP and the other from the Korean communists: one of their goals was to establish a Taiwanese republic. Strangely, Xie Xuehong was not among the twelve full members of the TCP Central Committee. She had worked extremely hard to set up the party, yet three people who were not present were elected full members while she was made only an alternate member. It seems quite possible that Xie Xuehong was discriminated against because of her gender and checkered background. As she prepared to set off for Tokyo to liaise again with the JCP, Xie Xuehong was arrested in April by the Japanese police for having distributed anti-Japanese pamphlets. Her sentence was to be sent back to Taiwan. When she was released in June because of lack of evidence, Xie Xuehong was perfectly placed to lead the TCP on Taiwan.

She found the party in a shambles, its leading cadres either having run away or gone into hiding. Undaunted, Xie Xuehong contacted the New Taiwan Culture Association and the Taiwan Peasants' Union (Taiwan nongmin zuhe [T'ai-wan nung-min tsu-ho]) as well as other members of the TCP who had returned. With their help, she started to organize and train workers. Xie Xuehong attempted to form the Taizhong Association of Organizations for the Liberation of Taiwan, an alliance of leftist organizations, but the Comintern ordered it disbanded, declaring that all branches must bear the name of the Communist Party. She did succeed, however, in influencing the Peasants' Union to accept her organizational structure of establishing youth and women's departments and creating a system by which members could help rescue each other.

Leading members of the Peasants' Union, such as Jian Ji [Chien Chi] and Zhao Gang [Chao Kang], either joined the TCP or turned further left. Xie Xuehong called the first Central Committee meeting of the TCP in Taipei in November 1928. This meeting passed resolutions to elect her to the Central Committee (as ordered by the JCP), to expel those (including Cai Xiaoqian [Ts'ai Hsiao-ch'ien]) who had abandoned their stations and run away from Taiwan in April, and to open the International Bookshop. The following month, under the guidance of Xie Xuehong and another TCP leader, the Peasants' Union agreed at their All-Island Conference to accept the platforms of the TCP, thus becoming an important fringe organization of the party. The International Bookshop opened in 1929 to sell leftist books and served as a meeting place for the intelligentsia as well as a secret contact point for the party.

As the Japanese colonial government focused attention on the Peasants' Union, Xie Xuehong turned to the Culture Association, whose members were mainly from the intelligentsia and middle class. With the help of former Shanghai University students, she gained control of the New Culture Association; through study and youth groups, Xie Xuehong encouraged the study of what was called social science but really was Marxist-Leninist propaganda.

That year, Wang Wande [Wang Wan-te] and Su Xin [Su Hsin], two members of the radical Li Lisan line who had recently returned from the mainland, criticized Xie Xuehong for being too moderate and not achieving enough. At a meeting the following year, her allies were expelled in order to isolate her. In 1931, Wang Wande and Su Xin formed the Reform Union (Gaige tongmeng) of the TCP and expelled Xie Xuehong (in May 1931). Ironically, she was arrested the following month because the radical actions of her political enemies had provoked a large-scale search and arrest by the colonial government. Xie Xuehong was sentenced to thirteen years' imprisonment. She was released on bail in 1939, however, having served only eight years, after contracting tuberculosis. Xie Xuehong changed her name to Yamane Yoshiko and started a small department store in Taizhong.

When the war ended in 1945, Xie Xuehong reverted to her own name and became politically active again. She formed the People's Association (Renmin xiehui) and then the Peasants' Association (Nongmin xiehui), both outlawed by Chen Yi [Ch'en I], whom the KMT had sent to take over Taiwan from the Japanese. Xie Xuehong created the Jianguo Technical School (Jianguo gongyi xuexiao [Chien-kuo kung-i hsüeh-hsiao]) to unite the young, and, through the Taizhong newspaper *Heping ribao* [Ho-p'ing jih-pao], criticized the Chen Yi administration. After the anti-KMT February 28 Incident of 1947, Xie Xuehong chaired a protest rally in Taizhong. She called for an end to KMT one-party rule and demanded a democratic self-government, asking the people of Taizhong to fight for these goals.

They responded to her call by occupying the police station, locking up all of the weapons and ammunition, and forming a committee to maintain order. When it was rumored that Chen Yi was coming with an army to crush them, however, the committee decided to disband. The youth opposed this course of action and asked Xie Xuehong to lead them in a resistance movement. With the weapons confiscated from the police, she organized the young people into an armed militia to maintain order in Taizhong's busy districts and formed a "people's government."

News of these events spread throughout Taiwan. On 3 March, a militia command headquarters was set up, and Xie Xuehong was asked to act as commander-in-chief. Militia had been set up in nearby Jiayi [Chia-i] and Huwei [Hu-wei] with whom the Taizhong groups shared the weapons they had appropriated. Xie Xuehong became known as a resistance leader and rumor had it that she would attack other cities. However, KMT armies landed in Jilong [Chi-lung] on 9 March, and one after another the resistance groups disbanded; Xie Xuehong retreated to the mountains whence she hoped to engage in guerrilla warfare. Unfortunately, Xie Xuehong failed to gain the support of the aboriginal peoples there and, with 200,000 yuan being offered for her arrest, quietly left Taiwan. Ironically, after bribing some KMT officers she sailed aboard a KMT warship to Xiamen [Hsia-men] and then on to Hong Kong.

A new phase then unfolded in Xie Xuehong's life. A British crown colony, Hong Kong was a melting pot of people of all political colors. There, in 1947, she met early advocates of the Taiwan independence movement, leaders of the TCP escaping Chen Yi's Taiwan, and underground CCP workers. In the meantime, her role in the armed resistance in Taiwan had brought her to the attention of the Americans; her story appeared in *Time* magazine, and she became known internationally.

Xie Xuehong realized from reading CCP publications that, as a part of its general anti-KMT push, the party had shifted its support from independence for Taiwan to self-government for Taiwan. She also realized that her destiny was bound up with the CCP and she thus needed to adjust her stance. In a manifesto published in a Singapore newspaper in August, Xie Xuehong reported on the armed struggle earlier in the year, reiterating her belief in socialism and self-government for Taiwan. With the sponsorship of a Singapore Chinese named Chen Jiageng [Ch'en Chia-keng], Xie Xuehong and her colleagues launched the magazine *Xin Taiwan congkan* (Hsin Taiwan ts'ung-k'an), with Su Xin and Yang Kehuang [Yang K'o-huang] as editors. Xie Xuehong wrote several articles on the destiny of the people of Taiwan and the liberation of women. To her, both were intimately connected to the overthrow of the American-supported KMT government and its oppression of the masses, including women.

However, Xie Xuehong's most important achievement during her time in Hong Kong was the creation of the Taiwan Democratic Self-Government League (Taiwan minzhu zizhi tongmeng, or Taimeng). After the failure of the February Twenty-eighth struggle, Taiwanese who had scattered to Hong Kong, China, and Japan felt the need for an organization through which their efforts could be channeled. With the approval of the CCP, during 1947 Xie Xuehong, Yang Kehuang, and Su Xin planned the Taimeng and established it in July 1948, with Xie Xuehong as president and Yang Kehuang and Su Xin as council members.

The Taimeng published its goals in a Hong Kong newspaper: to fight for self-government in Taiwan and support the efforts of the Chinese people to establish a democratic united government under the Central Committee. In May 1947, the members of the nascent Taimeng had responded positively to the CCP's May Day Manifesto (Wuyi xuanyan), calling for all parties to hold a new political consultative conference in order to form a united government. Leaders of the following three organizations met in Hong Kong: the Taimeng; the Taiwan Province Work Committee (Taiwansheng gongzuo weiyuanhui), consisting of underground CCP workers, including Cai Xiaoqian; and the Shanghai Taiwanese Compatriots' Association (Taiwan tongxianghui). The manifesto aimed to integrate the three groups under the supervision of the CCP. During this meeting, Xie Xuehong's CCP membership was recognized and backdated to 1946, when she had originally applied to join. Cai Xiaoqian demanded that Xie Xuehong complete an application form, despite her argument that it would be foolish to leave such a written record in KMT-ruled Taiwan. However, this formal recognition meant that Xie Xuehong was no longer just the leader of a minor party but also a member of the CCP and as such had to accept orders meted out by the party. Indeed, after the Hong Kong meeting Xie Xuehong's press statements showed clear signs of toeing the party line.

In 1948, she was invited to take part in the preparatory meeting for the CCP's First Political Consultative Conference. The paper Xie Xuehong brought with her, setting out suggestions about Taiwan, however, received no response. While in Beijing, she met with the Taiwan community there and received a warm reception. In September 1949, Xie Xuehong published an article that appeared on the front page of the *People's Daily* about America's conspiracy to occupy Taiwan.

On 1 October, at the ceremonial establishment of the PRC, Xie Xuehong stood in Tian'anmen as a member of the presidium alongside Mao Zedong (1893–1976), Zhou Enlai (1898–1976), and other leaders. In the early 1950s, Xie Xuehong was given many high-level positions, although some were in more of an honorary than an executive capacity. These included membership of the Executive Committee of the ACWF, vice-presidency of the Democratic Youth League (Minzhu qingnian lianhehui), and membership of the CPPCC. In addition to two purely honorary positions, she was placed on the Central Committee's Commission of Politics and Law (Zhongyang zhengzhi falü weiyuanhui). In 1951, with the creation of the East China Bureau, whose jurisdiction extended to Taiwan, Xie Xuehong became one of the members of the East China Military and Administrative Committee. The headquarters of the Taimeng also moved to Shanghai.

However, "liberating Taiwan" became less of a priority with the outbreak of the Korean War (1950–53) and the stationing of the U.S. Seventh Fleet in the Taiwan Strait. Xie Xuehong and the Taimeng subsequently lost propaganda value to the government of the PRC. Other factors contributed to her loss of status at this time. She clung stubbornly to views that were not compatible with the CCP, and factionalism was rife in the Taimeng. Xie Xuehong thus became the target of three waves of attacks between 1952 and 1967.

According to her biographer Chen Fangming, members of Cai Xiaoqian's faction attacked Xie Xuehong as a tactic to divert attention away from themselves after Cai was arrested in Taiwan and had revealed a great deal of information. Everything Xie Xuehong was accused of in 1952, however, seems to have been related to her differences of opinion within the CCP. Firstly, she was accused of having impurities in her thought, a reference to her belief that Taiwan should enjoy a high degree of self-government. Secondly, Xie Xuehong was accused of dictatorial leadership and individualistic heroism, a reference to her lack of humility before the CCP. She considered herself the heroine of the February Twenty-eighth Incident and as such was said to have lorded it over other members of the Taimeng. Finally, Xie Xuehong was accused of protecting bad elements. This was a reference to an article she had written, arguing that because Taiwan had suffered under colonialism for fifty years, its people needed special understanding, even those that the mainlanders considered traitors. Xie Xuehong had also stated that mainlanders did not understand the Taiwanese. Clearly, her actions and words had created a rod for her own back. The result of this struggle was that all of her supporters were expelled from the leadership of the Taimeng, leaving her totally isolated. It is known that she wrote her autobiography during this period, but the manuscript has never been found.

The most destructive attack upon Xie Xuehong took place during the Anti-Rightist Movement of 1957. Xu Mengshan, the secretary-general of the Taimeng, wrote an article that was published in *Guangming Daily*, accusing Xie Xuehong of being antisocialist and anti-party. From November to December, in an enlarged meeting of delegates from various branches and members in Beijing, Xie Xuehong endured ten meetings in which she was criticized and attacked. Xie Xuehong was extremely resilient, however; once telling an ally to be like a wild flower that could withstand any amount of trampling. Of the words with which she defended herself, the following are best known: "My value is indelible; destroy me, and you destroy communism." Nevertheless, in January 1958 Xie Xuehong was formally declared a rightist and stripped of her presidency of the Taimeng. The following month she was stripped of all of her other positions and titles, including CCP membership.

Xie Xuehong lived as a recluse for the next few years, but the rightist stigma returned to haunt her as soon as the Cultural Revolution began. In June 1966, young Red Guards ransacked her home, taking away documents and private possessions, including a savings book showing a balance of more than 10,000 yuan. Her enemies fared little better: the Taimeng was declared an anti-revolutionary organization, its premises were destroyed, and work stopped. During this chaotic period, neither Xie Xuehong's nor Xu Mengshan's faction could claim legitimacy. According to the memoirs of a supporter, a rebel group formed—with Xie Xuehong directing it behind the scenes—and retaliated against Xu Mengshan and his faction.

For a time, this rebel group seemed to have the upper hand, but in May 1968 Xu Mengshan made use of the Red Guards; his son led them to Xie Xuehong's home. They took her to Taimeng headquarters, kicked her behind the knees to make her kneel and bent her arms back to make her bow her head. Someone pressed her head down and declared: "Xie Xuehong, who said she would never bow her head, has now done so." Then they beat her until she passed out. Xie Xuehong was sixty-eight years old, and the assault broke her spirit. Her health deteriorated rapidly, and she was diagnosed with pneumonia. Her partner, Yang Kehuang, cared for her in spite of having leg problems himself. Xie Xuehong died of lung cancer in 1970.

It appears that Xie Xuehong and Yang Kehuang had lived together before 1952; from the time of the struggles of that year he admitted to having lived with her as husband and wife. When all her positions were removed in 1958, she asked and received permission to continue to live with Yang. Xie Xuehong never had any children, but the couple adopted his niece, Yang Meizhu. Yang Kehuang left everything to her in his will when he died in 1978.

After the Cultural Revolution, when many people's cases were overturned, Xie Xuehong's was still pending. In the 1980s, as her story spread outside China, many of her Taiwan compatriots became interested in her. Her case was finally reviewed, and an official biography recognizes Xie Xuehong's place in fighting a foreign invasion and confirming her leadership position in the February Twenty-eight struggle. Xie Xuehong's ashes were moved from the cemetery for common people in Babaoshan to the section reserved for revolutionary heroes. Many Taiwanese people will also remember her as one of the greatest of their heroines.

Lily Xiao Hong LEE

Chen Fangming. *Luotu budiao de yuye hua: Xie Xuehong pingzhuan*. Irvine, Calif.: Taiwan chubanshe; Taipei: Qianwei chubanshe, 1991.

Jingsheng and Xiquan, eds. *Xin Zhongguo mingren lu*. Nanchang: Jiangxi renmin chubanshe, 1987, 381–82.

Wang Xin, ed. *Zhongguo minzhu dangpai mingren lu*. Nanjing: Jiangsu renmin chubanshe, 1993, 413–14.

Who's Who in Communist China. Hong Kong: Union Research Institute, 1969, 254.

Xie Dexi [Hsieh Te-hsi]. "Geming nü haojie Xie Xuehong." In *Taiwan jindai mingren zhi*, vol. 5, eds. Zhang Wenxian [Chang Wen-hsien], Li Xiaofeng [Li Hsiao-feng], and Zhuang Rongming [Chuang Jung-ming]. Taipei: Zili wanbaoshe, wenhua chubanshe, 1990, 189–205.

Xin Fengxia

Xin Fengxia, 1927–1998, original name Yang Shumin, was a native of Suzhou, Jiangsu Province; she grew up, however, in the northern city of Tianjin. Xin Fengxia was a *ping* (local opera indigenous to north and northeastern China) opera actress who specialized in *qingyi* (young or middle-aged women of rectitude) and *huadan* (lively young women) roles.

Xin Fengxia was born into a poor family and did not receive a formal education. At the age of six, she started learning *jingju* (Beijing opera) from her paternal cousin and switched to *ping* opera and a new teacher at thirteen. Her new teacher was able to demonstrate for her all the necessary movements, and Xin Fengxia was thus exposed from early childhood to all aspects of the craft: voice, singing technique, stage presentation, and self-discipline. She performed on stage after only four months with the teacher in the play *Beating the Dog to Persuade the Husband* (Da gou quan fu). By the time Xin Fengxia was twenty, the young woman had performed in operas and plays in both traditional and modern dress, as well as in *jingju bangzi* (Hebei opera), and *zhuizi* (Henan opera). She also performed versified storytelling in the Beijing dialect with drum accompaniment (*jingyun dagu*) and storytelling mainly in song with musical accompaniment (*qinshu*). Xin Fengxia toured extensively and became well known as the star of her troupe.

Her fame in *ping* opera circles in Tianjin in the 1940s rivaled such well-established actresses as Liu Cuixia, Bai Yushuang (*q.v.*), and Fu Ronghua, but theatrical venues at that time were controlled by hooligans and ruffians who would intimidate actresses. Nicknamed "opera beggars" (*xihuazi*), actresses had virtually no personal freedom even when they had become famous. Xin Fengxia often went on stage in a state of fear and on the verge of tears.

Not until after 1949, when she and her performing troupe went to Beijing, was Xin Fengxia able to give full rein to her enormous talents. Her first performance of modern *ping* opera was in *Little Er-hei's Marriage* (Xiao Er-hei jiehun), which was staged in Wanshengxuan Theater in Tianqiao. This play, adapted from a novel of the same name written by Zhao Shuli (1906–1970) and published in 1943, tells the story of a young peasant who fought for freedom of choice in marriage. The theater was small and the facilities simple, but the two famous writers Zhao Shuli and Lao She (1899–1966) enjoyed her performance from long wooden benches along with the rest of the audience. Her next performance was in another *ping* opera, *Liu Qiao'er*. So successful was Xin Fengxia that she was soon able to perform in the more prestigious section of Tianqiao, i.e., the northern part, and enjoyed full recognition in artistic circles.

The character Liu Qiao'er was a brand-new female image, profoundly loved by the people: energetic and lovable, showing hatred and love, and daring to pursue freedom of choice in marriage. Xin Fengxia wrote for *Liu Qiao'er* many new tunes, which brought to the play lucidity, rhythm, and vitality and her charming coloratura style (*xiao huaqiang*) made the tunes clear and expressive. *Liu Qiao'er* enjoyed tremendous popularity all over China, as did Xin Fengxia. For the play *A Marriage Proposal Bouquet* (Hua wei mei), she reworked the well-known aria "Four Seasons" (Siji hua kai), using the traditional *ping* opera tune "Peaceful Year" (Taiping nian) so that it became a showcase for her voice. In the process of sorting out old operas and rehearsing new ones, Xin Fengxia transformed the traditionally sorrowful music of *ping* opera into joyous tunes. She created new musical tempi and melodies, particularly the tunes "Fanzi daman ban" and "Fandiao daman ban," for the jubilant "Dragonfly Melody" (Qingting diao), the lyrical "*Jiangxiang* Melody" (Jiangxiang diao), and the melancholy "Seeing Her Son Off Melody" (Song zi diao). These new tempi and melodies significantly enriched the female repertoire for *ping* opera. Both *Liu Qiao'er* (1956) and *A Marriage Proposal Bouquet* (1964) were made into extremely popular films.

In 1951 Xin Fengxia married the famous playwright Wu Zuguang (b. 1917). He encouraged her to read, practice calligraphy, and write in order to cultivate her artistic interests. The following year, the famous traditional painter Qi Baishi (1864–1957) accepted her as his student and passed on to her his freehand brushwork skills and techniques.

Wu Zuguang, however, was labeled a "rightist element" in 1957 and sent to the northeast *Beida huang* (the great northern wilderness) to undergo labor reform. Xin Fengxia refused to listen to those who urged her to divorce her husband, saying:

"Wu is a good man. I will wait for him. [The opera character] Wang Baochuan waited eighteen years for Xue Pinggui, and I will wait twenty-eight years for Wu Zuguang." Xin Fengxia and Wu Zuguang were truly faithful in adversity. Xin Fengxia served seven years of forced labor reform during the Cultural Revolution, and in December 1975 suffered a stroke that left her paralyzed. Wu Zuguang did not let her down. He took extremely good care of her, spending as much time as he could tending to her needs while still completing the *jingju The Red Lady* (Hong niangzi); the three-act drama *Journeying Bravely Out into the World* (Chuang jiang hu, 1979); and two television serials: *The Peony Pavilion* (Mudan ting, 1987) and *Little Feng* (Xiao Feng, 1994).

Unable to return to the stage, Xin Fengxia turned to training the actors of a younger generation from all over China and writing and painting. Her amazingly retentive memory enabled her to piece together an extremely detailed account of her life, complete with evocations of people, occasions, and conversations so vivid that they spring to life on the page. Her prose and essay style is uniquely unadorned and sincere. By 1997, her memoirs, *Xin Fengxia's Collected Memoirs*, had been published in four volumes totaling two million words.

Xin Fengxia's flower-and-plant paintings inscribed with Wu Zuguang's calligraphy have over the years come to be regarded as pieces of "Celebrity Painting and Calligraphy," popular with the public. He inscribed a fitting reflection on Xin Fengxia's life on her *Portrait of Plum Blossoms* (Meihua): "Pure as jade inside, white as snow outside." A legend in her own lifetime, she lived a life of passion and beauty.

HE Li
(Translated by Zhongwei Song)

Li Yuanrong. "Wu Zuguang Xin Fengxia qingshi." *Zhongwai zazhi*, 10 (1989): 32–37.
Wu Zuguang. "Xin Fengxia yu xin pingju." *Yishu de huaduo*. Beijing: Xinwenyi chubanshe, 1956.
Xin Fengxia. "Finding Happiness in Hardship." *Chinese Literature*, no. 5 (1983): 83–105.
———. "Fuqi neng gong baitou buyi: Wo he Wu Zuguang de huannan zhi qing." *Kaifang* (December 1995): 58–59.
———. "Zou guo siwang bianyuan." *Kaifang* (February 1996): 80.
Zhongguo dabaike quanshu: Xiqu quyi. Beijing: Zhongguo dabaike quanshu chubanshe, 1989, 513.
Zhu Qi. "Xinwei—fang pingju yishujia Xin Fengxia." *Renmin ribao* (Haiwaiban), 12 August 1986, 2.

Xiu Zelan: see Hsiu Tse-lan

Xixi

Xixi, b. 1938, as Zhang Yan, is a poet, fiction writer, and essayist well known for her literary innovations. Although born in Shanghai, she is a native of Zhongshan, Guangdong Province; her family moved to Hong Kong in 1950, and that is where Xixi is now based. She adopted the pen name Xixi because the Chinese characters resemble a caricature of a little girl in a skirt playing hopscotch.

Xixi was educated in an English-language high school in Hong Kong but did not attend university, not being able to afford the high tuition fees. She enrolled instead at Grantham College of Education, which charged no fees and also because graduation from the institution almost guaranteed a job. For many years, Xixi worked as an English teacher at a government primary school. She received an early retirement payment from the Hong Kong school system in 1983, and it allowed her to become a professional writer. From her early years, Xixi had loved to read, and living in Hong Kong and being able to read in English as well as Chinese gave her the advantage of exposure to world literatures.

Xixi began her literary career as a poet, contributing in student days to such publications as the Hong Kong student magazine *Zhongguo xuesheng zhoubao* for which she later edited the Poetry Page. Her poetry collection *Lofty Rock* (Shipan) was published in the 1970s, but it is as a writer of fiction that Xixi is most accomplished and best known. She enjoys experimenting with different techniques and subject matter and ventures boldly into the unfamiliar. "Maria" (Maliya), for example, is about a nun in the former Belgian Congo, and *The Hunter Who Whistles to Entrap Deer* (Shaolu) is about Emperor Qianlong's hunting expeditions in Manchuria. Even when Xixi does write about familiar topics, and that are slightly autobiographical, such as *My City* (Wo cheng), the author adopts the magic realism approach favored by Latin American writers. Xixi is attracted by the French "new novel" (*nouveau roman*), and has written stories whose protagonist is an object; "Olympus" (Ao-lin pi-si), for example, is about a young man and the lens of his Olympus camera. One critic has said that Xixi has tried almost all sub-genres of contemporary literature: realism, modernism, post-modernism, magic realism, allegory, reinterpretation of fairy tales, legend, and history.

Despite the variety of subject matter and techniques, the writer has developed her own style. She uses short, simple, almost childish sentences (perhaps influenced by her years as a primary school teacher), keeps up a brisk pace, and avoids lengthy descriptions. Yet, while her style is disarmingly simple, her stories yield up incisive insights and uncanny observations. Her material offers a philosophical side, too, dealing provocatively, in a typically understated way, with such issues as human nature, the environment, life, and death. As a Hong Kong writer, Xixi is clearly indebted to both Chinese and non-Chinese literatures and has little need to be concerned with such pressures as tradition, politics, or literary trends. Unlike others who write in Chinese, Xixi lists as her major influences children's books, the cinema, and contemporary European and Latin American writers.

To date, the author has published more than a dozen novels, collections of short stories and prose, and one collection of poetry. Some of her stories have been translated into English. She received a prize for "Maria" in 1965 from *Zhongguo xuesheng zhoubao* and a prize in 1983 from the Taiwan daily *Lianhebao*. Xixi has also done editing and in the 1980s was editor of the literary magazines *Damuzhi zhoukan* and *Suye wenxue*. Her interests range widely and include art, music, art films, sports, and, of course, reading. In the 1960s, she wrote film scripts and is recognized as a pioneer of Hong Kong short films, having also produced a short documentary. In one interview, Xixi said that she never felt the need for love, considering it a drag and too "old wifely" (*poma*). True to her word, Xixi appears never to have married. She dresses plainly and lives plainly in a not-so-spacious flat; this flat must count, for her, as "a room of her own." Xixi has been quoted as saying that many of her works were written in the kitchen or the bathroom.

She is a pioneer in Hong Kong in two senses. Firstly, Xixi was one of the earliest young writers growing up in Hong Kong to devote her life to serious literature. Secondly, she is one of Hong Kong's earliest women writers; as such, Xixi served as a role model for women who wish to follow a literary path. In an economic and commercial center such as Hong Kong, where money reigns supreme, to be a writer, let alone a serious one, would seem to be an impossible dream. Not surprisingly, most of her works have been published in Taiwan. And yet, Xixi, after working silently for many years, has finally received recognition.

Lily Xiao Hong LEE

Chan, Stephen C.K. "The Cultural Imaginary of a City: Reading Hong Kong through Xi Xi." In *Chinese Literature in the Second Half of the Twentieth Century: A Critical Survey*, eds. Pang-yuan Chi and David Wang. Bloomington: Indiana University Press, 2000, 180–92.

Chung Ling. "Perspective and Spatiality in the Fiction of Three Hong Kong Women Writers." In *Modern Chinese Women Writers: Critical Appraisals*, ed. Michael S. Duke. Armonk, N.Y.: M.E. Sharpe, 1989, 217–35.

Gu Cangwu. "Shamo de qiji." *Xin Wanbao*, 13 October 1981.

Kangfu, ed. "Xixi fangwenji." *Luopan*, no. 1 (December 1976): 3–8; *Xin Wanbao*, 13 October 1981.

Pan Yadun. "Xiandai de Xixi." In *Shijie huawen nüzuojia sumiao*, ed. Pan Yadun. Guangzhou: Jinan daxue chubanshe, 1993, 146–53.

Ren Yiming. "Xianggang nüxing wenxue gaiguan." *Xinjiang shifan daxue xuebao: Zhesheban*, no. 4 (1995): 18–23.

Xi Xi. *A Girl Like Me and Other Stories*. Hong Kong: Chinese University of Hong Kong, 1986.

———. "Piñata," trans. Hannah Cheung and John Minford. *Renditions*, special issue (Spring and Autumn 1987): 113–22.

———. "A Woman Like Me," trans. Howard Goldblatt. In *Worlds of Modern Chinese Fiction: Short Stories and Novellas from the People's Republic, Taiwan and Hong Kong*, ed. Michael S. Duke. Armonk, N.Y.: M.E. Sharpe, 1991, 163–73; also in *Bamboo Shoots after the Rain: Contemporary Stories by Women Writers of Taiwan*, eds. Ann C. Carver and Sung-sheng Yvonne Chang. New York: Feminist Press at the City University of New York, 1990, 134–46.

Xu Chunju: *see* Liang-Hsü Ch'un-chü

Xu Feng: *see* Hsü Feng

Xu Guangping

Xu Guangping, 1898–1968, of Guangzhou, Guangdong Province, was a student and devoted disciple of Lu Xun (1881–1936), the most influential left-wing writer and intellectual leader in modern China. Over a period of many years, she contributed greatly to his studies.

Xu Guangping was born into a declining official family and rebellious from the start. She refused to have her feet bound and rejected an arranged marriage. After her father died in 1917, Xu Guangping went to Tianjin and enrolled in the preparatory course at Zhili First Women's Normal School. She became involved in the Tianjin Women's Patriotic Association (Tianjin nüjie aiguo tongzhi hui) and was one of the editors of its *Enlightening Weekly* (Qingshi zhoukan). Xu Guangping graduated in 1921 and then enrolled in Beijing Women's Higher Normal School (Nüzi gaodeng shifan xuexiao), which in 1924 became Beijing Women's Normal University.

The college became a battlefield between conservatives and progressive intellectuals. Its open-minded president Xu Shoushang (1882–1948) was forced to resign in 1923, and his successor was the conservative Yang Yinyu (d. 1938), who supported the warlord government and had opposed the May Fourth Movement. Yang Yinyu's appointment created further conflict at the college, which culminated in the mass resignation of lecturers and the closure of the institution for two months. Xu Guangping did not agree with Yang Yinyu but was skeptical about the goals of the student protests; out of frustration, she corresponded with Lu Xun.

Xu Guangping eventually decided to become politically involved and was elected as one of the college's six student representatives. Her decision was clearly influenced by Lu Xun's Nietzschean stance because Xu Guangping saw herself not as a student leader but as a lone rebel. The campus unrest intensified after Zhang Shizhao (1881–1973) was appointed minister of Education in April 1925. Backed by him and supported by the *Modern Review* (Xiandai pinglun) circle, Yang Yinyu expelled the student representatives. The struggles in the college spilled over into intellectual circles in Beijing and ignited bitter polemics between the *Modern Review* circle led by Chen Yuan and the *Spinner of Words* (Yusi) circle led by Lu Xun.

Xu Guangping was moved by the latter's devotion to the students' cause and fell in love with him. She expressed her feelings in two essays that in turn inspired Lu Xun to write two short stories: "The Misanthrope" (Guduzhe) and "Regret for the Past" (Shangshi). After the warlord massacre of dozens of students in the March Eighteenth Incident of 1926, Xu Guangping and Lu Xun decided to leave Beijing, each going to a different destination: she went to Guangzhou and he went to Xiamen.

At that time, Guangzhou was the capital of the revolutionary KMT government. Xu Guangping had joined the KMT before going to Guangzhou but for some unknown reason did not declare her membership to the party organization there. She worked and taught at Guangdong First Women's Normal College and became immediately dragged into the struggles between the CCP and its allies within the KMT and its right-wing faction.

Meanwhile, after lecturing at Xiamen University for only a few months, Lu Xun left for Zhongshan University to join Xu Guangping in Guangzhou. They soon became disillusioned with the "revolutionary" government and were further shocked by the massacres during the 12 April 1927 coup d'état launched by the KMT to purge the communists. They resigned their positions, left Guangzhou, and settled down in Shanghai in October.

In Shanghai, Xu Guangping was persuaded to sacrifice herself for Lu Xun's literary movement. She became his secretary and housekeeper and gave birth to his only son, Zhou Haiying, in 1929; Lu Xun had continued to live a bachelor's life after reluctantly honoring a marriage arranged over twenty years previously by his mother, and the marriage did not produce any children. After Lu Xun died in 1936, Xu Guangping continued to promote and protect his legacy and was closely associated with the left-wing literary movement. In 1938, she edited and published the first collected edition of Lu Xun's works. Xu Guangping prevented Lu Xun's younger brother Zhou Zuoren from selling Lu Xun's library in Beijing in 1944. Also during the 1940s, she published dozens of essays about Lu Xun, which were eventually published in two books in 1951 and 1954. Xu Guangping also continued to support Lu Xun's mother and his wife, Zhu An (1878–1947), in Beijing. Xu Guangping was arrested by the Japanese in December 1941 and tortured for almost three months. She published a book about her horrifying experience in 1947.

After the Japanese surrendered, Xu Guangping was actively involved in the anti-KMT and pro-communist women's movement and appointed head of the Shanghai branch of the China Women's Association (Zhongguo funü lianyihui) in 1945. She became editor of the supplement "Friends of Women" (Fu you) of the influential newspaper *Wenhui bao* in 1946. In 1948, Xu Guangping was taken to the communist liberated areas in the northeast to avoid KMT persecution.

She took up several minor positions in the CCP government in 1949 and also became a representative of a minor political organization called the Chinese Association for the Promotion of Democracy (Zhongguo minzhu cujinhui). Her most significant contributions, however, were in establishing the Lu Xun museums and archives. Because of her symbolic importance to the new cultural movement centering on Lu Xun that the CCP gradually built up, Xu Guangping was immune from political troubles when Lu Xun's disciples were purged one after another. She joined the CCP in 1960. Xu Guangping published further reminiscences about Lu Xun in 1961, but the writing of this book was supervised by the Zhou Yang (1908–1989) faction and marred by the ideological guidelines of the time, which included criticism of Lu Xun's disciples. When Zhou Yang fell from power in 1966, Xu Guangping had to re-align herself with the party, which involved publishing an essay in the party journal *Red Flag* (Hongqi) to denounce Zhou Yang.

During the Cultural Revolution, Qi Benyu confiscated some important manuscripts of Lu Xun's in the name of the Cultural Revolution Central Committee. When Qi Benyu lost power the following year (in 1968), Xu Guangping was so worried about the safety of the manuscripts that she suffered a heart attack and died in March.

Chiu-yee CHEUNG

Chen Shuyu. *Xu Guangping de yisheng.* Tianjin: Tianjin renmin chubanshe, 1981.
Cheung, Chiu-yee. "The Love of a Decadent 'Superman': A Re-reading of Lu Xun's 'Regret for the Past.'" *Journal of the Oriental Society of Australia*, 30 (1998): 26–46.

Haiying, ed. *Xu Guangping wenji*, 3 vols. N.p.: Jiangsu wenyi chubanshe, 1998.
Lu Xun bowuguan and Zhongguo minzhu cujinhui zhongyang xuanchuanbu, ed. *Xu Guangping*. Beijing: Kaiming chubanshe, 1995.
Wang Dehou. *Liang di shu yanjiu*. Tianjin: Tianjin renmin chubanshe, 1982.
Zhu Zheng. *Lu Xun huiyilu zheng wu*. Beijing: Renmin wenxue chubanshe, 1986.

Xu Juhua: *see* **Xia Juhua**

Xu Peixuan: *see* **Xu Zonghan**

Xu Qing: *see* **Xu Zonghan**

Xu Shixian: *see* **Hsü Shih-hsien**

Xu Yulan

Xu Yulan, b. 1921 in Xindeng County, Zhejiang Province (present-day Xindeng township, Fuyang city), was a performing artist in the *yue* local opera genre, a form of opera in which all the roles were traditionally played by females. Most recently, she has sat on the Executive Committee of the Chinese Dramatists' Association and as artistic consultant to the Shanghai *Yue* Opera Academy.

In summer 1933, Xu Yulan commenced her training in traditional opera at Dong'an Theater School. Initially, she studied *huadan* (lively young women) roles but later took up the study of the *laosheng* (older male) part. Xu Yulan learned scholarly roles under Yu Chuanhai and martial roles under Yuan Shichang, a famous Anhui (*huiban*) opera performer of scholarly/military *laosheng*. Her studies included martial arts and acrobatics—she could somersault from three-and-a-half tables piled on top of each other—as well as various fighting (*hualian*) skills, such as those employed in playing the role of Monkey. Among her parts were Zhao Yun in *Burning the Long Lines of Tent Camps* (Huoshao lianying zhai), Wu Song in *Yongying Gate* (Yongying men), Monkey in *Sizhou City* (Sizhoucheng), Guan Sheng in *Defeating Guan Sheng with the Broad Sword* (Dadao shou Guan Sheng), and a comedian in *Dragon Pool Temple* (Longtan si).

In December 1941, Xu Yulan started performing *xiaosheng* (young and teenage male) roles with Shi Yinhua at Laozha Theater in Shanghai, which was then under partial Japanese occupation. In summer 1943, she and Fu Quanxiang (*q.v.*) performed together, and during the second half of 1945 she performed with Xiao Dangui. In summer 1947, Xu Yulan was an enthusiastic participant in the benefit performance of *Love for Mountains and Rivers* (Shanhe lian) and in September formed and lent her name to the Yulan Opera Troupe, which employed a number of progressive literary workers as playwright-directors. She engaged many new artists including Wu Chen, Xu Jin, Zhuang Zhi, and Shi Jingshan and held rehearsals for a major new opera entitled *The Land of a Vanquished Nation* (Guopo shan he zai). In late 1948, Xu Yulan began a long period of collaboration with Wang Wenjuan.

In July 1949, Xu Yulan and many other opera performers were required to attend classes organized by the Art Department of the Shanghai government, which was then under military administration, to research folk operas for the *yue* opera group belonging to its cultural troupe. Around the time that the PRC was established later that year, she performed in such operas as *The White-Haired Girl* (Baimao nü), *Prince Xinling* (Xinling gongzi), and *The Jade-Faced Wolf* (Yumian lang). Under her leadership, the troupe joined the *Yue* Opera Troupe of the Art Workers' Unit of the Political Department of the CCP's Central Military Committee in January 1952. Xu Yulan was also at that time awarded First Prize in the first Chinese folk opera festival sponsored by the Ministry of Culture for the portrayal of Scholar Zhang in *The Story of the Western Chamber* (Xixiang ji). In spring 1953, toward the end of the Korean War, she performed for Chinese and Korean soldiers at the frontline with a cultural work troupe and participated in the exchange of prisoners of war. Her contribution was recognized by the Korean Workers' Party when she was awarded a Third-Grade National Flag medal.

Xu Yulan's opera troupe was recalled to Shanghai in spring 1954 and assigned to the second group of the *Yue* Opera Experimental Troupe of the Huadong Opera Research Institute; the Experimental Troupe was itself later assigned to the Shanghai *Yue* Opera Academy. At the competition held by the Huadong Institute in the autumn, Xu Yulan was awarded First Grade Performer for her portrayal of Li Menglong in *The Story of Chunxiang* (Chunxiang zhuan). Xu Yulan made her first trip overseas the following year when she accompanied the troupe on a tour of the Soviet Union and the Democratic Republic of Germany. She performed the part of Scholar Zhang in *The Story of the Western Chamber* during this tour. In 1959, she toured the Democratic People's Republic of Vietnam. When returning to Korea in 1962 to assist in the production of *The Dream of Red Mansions* (Honglou meng), Xu Yulan had an audience with Kim Il-Sung. Her definitive 1958 portrayal of Jia Baoyu in *The Dream of Red Mansions* was transferred to film in July 1962, and in August 1959 she played the role of Zhang Zhen in the film *The Carp Fairy* (Zhui yu).

In all her performances, Xu Yulan displayed a vast array of talents and an uncanny ability to immerse herself in characters that made her performances quite natural. She is acknowledged, however, as being the best in *yue* opera at playing the carefree and elegant roles. Her voice possesses a soaring lingering quality, especially in the middle and high registers, which became known as the Xu technique. Apart from singing arias in the traditional manner, Xu Yulan also incorporated into her repertoire aspects of Beijing, Shaoxing, and Hangzhou opera, to name only the most famous ones. Her best-known roles include Jia Baoyu, Scholar Zhang, Li Menglong, Zhang Zhen, and Liu Chen in *King of the North* (Beidi wang). Some of these operas have been made into films or television series, and Xu Yulan produced an eight-part television series called *Highlights of Xu Yulan's Performances* (Xu Yulan yishu jijin). During the Cultural Revolution, the only operas that could be performed were "reformed Peking opera" (*yangbanxi*). Most performers of other genres were simply sidelined (*kao bianzhan*), although some were attacked.

Xu Yulan serves as a board member for the All-China Federation of Literature and Art Circles (Zhongguo wenxue yishujie lianhehui lishi), a committee member of the *Dream of Red Mansions* Studies Association (Quanguo *Honglou meng* xuehui huiyuan), and a member of the Shanghai People's Congress. With the end of the Cultural Revolution, she threw herself enthusiastically into structural reform of the arts and took the initiative in forming the Red Mansions Opera Company. Xu Yulan has also performed in Singapore, Thailand, Hong Kong, Taiwan, and other countries and regions on cultural exchange programs. In 1989 she received a Gold Record from the Chinese Record Company, and books about her were published in the early 1990s. Xu Yulan currently receives a special allowance from the State Commission.

Having witnessed many unhappy marriages among her *yue* opera sisters, Xu Yulan believed that she preferred to be a "single bird soaring high in the sky" rather than a "small person" (i.e., a wife) anchored to the earth. Yet, Xu Yulan had the good fortune to meet an honest young shipbuilding engineer (whose name is not recorded in sources) in Ningbo in 1943. Before leaving there in 1945 to return to Shanghai to pursue her performing career, she slipped him a letter expressing her feelings for him, but they were not able to marry until 1955. Thus, Xu Yulan, an extremely talented performer of *xiaosheng* (male) roles, went against her professional type to embroil herself in the real-life role of a female in the comedy that is marriage. Hers, fortunately, was a happy one.

HE Li and Shirley Wai CHAN
(Translated by Jennifer Eagleton)

Huaxia funü mingren cidian. Beijing: Huaxia chubanshe, 1988, 86.
Xu Yulan. *Xu Yulan changqiang jicheng.* Shanghai: Shanghai wenyi chubanshe, 1992.
Zhao Xiaosi. *Xu Yulan zhuan.* Shanghai: Shanghai wenyi chubanshe, 1994.

Xu Zonghan

Xu Zonghan, 1876–1944, originally named Peixuan, *zi* Qing, was from Xiangshan County (present-day Zhongshan), Guangdong Province. She was a radical revolutionary who belonged to the Tongmenghui in her youth and in her later years a dedicated philanthropist and social worker.

Her father was a tea merchant and the family was well off, but nothing is known of her mother. Her eldest sister, Xu Mulan (originally named Peilan), and second eldest sister, Xu Peiyao, both joined the revolutionary Tongmenghui. Xu Zonghan adopted the name Zonghan to express her determination to adhere to her Han Chinese origins. All three sisters were educated at home by private tutors.

At the age of eighteen, Xu Zonghan married Li Qishi, also known as Li Jinyi, of Haifeng, Guangdong Province; her sister Mulan married Li Qishi's eldest brother, Li Zishi. The head of the Li family, Li Qingchun, worked on the Foreign Affairs Committee in the Government of the Guangdong and Guangxi Office in Charge of Foreign Affairs and was fluent in English, rich, and politically influential. Xu Zonghan's husband, Li Qishi, was a progressive young man who had also studied English. A few years into their marriage, however, he fell ill and died, leaving his wife the difficult and lonely task of bringing up their son, Li Yingqiang, and daughter, Li Ruohong.

Xu Zonghan's participation in the revolution that brought down the Qing government owed much to the influence of her good friend Zhang Zhujun (see *Biographi-*

cal Dictionary of Chinese Women: The Qing Period). Zhang Zhujun was a medical doctor who graduated in 1900 from the Xiage Women Doctors' Training Institute attached to Rouji Hospital in Guangzhou. A warm-hearted and generous person, Xu Zonghan sponsored Zhang Zhujun's establishment of both Tifu Hospital and Nanfu Hospital in Guangzhou. The cost of building them amounted to the considerable sum of over 10,000 tael (ounces) of silver each, raised entirely by these two young women. The chapels attached to the hospitals also served as a venue for discussing current politics and propagating new learning, attracting quite a number of intellectuals, among them Xu Zonghan. Gradually, she accepted the new ideas and finally became a Christian.

When her sister Xu Peiyao went to Penang in Malaya to teach in a school for overseas Chinese about 1906, Xu Zonghan went to assist her. The Tongmenghui was at that time launching a branch in Penang, and Xu Zonghan joined. Returning to Guangzhou in 1908, she stopped over in Hong Kong to visit Feng Ziyou (1882–1958), then president of the Hong Kong branch of the Tongmenghui and editor-in-chief of *Zhongguo ribao.* In order to carry out covert revolutionary activities and transmit messages, Xu Zonghan and some friends, including Gao Jianfu (1879–1951) and Pan Dawei (1880–1929), opened the Shouzhenge Paintings Mounting Shop in Guangzhou. Xu Zonghan recruited several women, among them Liang Huanzhen, Chen Ruiyun, and Luo Daoying, to undertake communication and delivery work.

Xu Zonghan was a forthright and valiant woman, quick-witted, and not prone to panicking even in the face of grave danger. Her composure was indeed legendary. When, in 1908, the Tongmenghui assigned her to take ammunition to Guangdong, she slept peacefully at night, unlike her very nervous companions—Chen Shuzi, the wife of Hu Hanmin, and Li Ziping, the wife of Feng Ziyou. In preparation for the revolt in Guangzhou on the twenty-ninth of the third lunar month of 1911, Xu Zonghan led a team of close associates to deliver weapons and ammunition from Hong Kong to Guangzhou for distribution to various revolutionary groups. One of the leaders of the revolt, Huang Xing (1874–1916), failed in an attempt to take the Guangdong-Guangxi government office and fled to Guangzhou, where he met Xu Zonghan. She then escorted him to Hong Kong.

In order to maintain revolutionary momentum, Huang Xing set up the Dongfang Assassination Corps, which carried out two assassinations and to which Xu Zonghan pledged wholehearted support. During the successful Wuchang Uprising of late 1911, Xu Zonghan and Huang Xing reached Wuchang undercover with the Red Cross, organized at that time by her friend Zhang Zhujun, and were actively involved in the revolution. Huang Xing was commander in charge of warfare, and Xu Zonghan was his assistant. Their working relationship continued after the provisional president of the Republic, Sun Yat-sen (1866–1925), appointed Huang Xing as commander of the army; Xu Zonghan then became his assistant and secretary.

Huang Xing had married Liao Danru in 1892 and had two sons and a daughter. Xu Zonghan, however, became his constant companion, and the two lived together as man and wife. Xu Zonghan was completely unconcerned at the illegal status of their union and in June 1912 moved to Shanghai with Huang Xing. Their own son Huang Yimei was born the following year; it is not known what happened to Xu Zonghan's children from her first marriage. Disheartened at the miscarriage of the second revolution when Sun Yat-sen failed to regain power, Huang Xing left for the United States in 1914 but soon succumbed to an old stomach ailment. Xu Zonghan joined him in 1915, and they returned to China the following year after armed opposition to the imperial pretender Yuan Shikai erupted. The couple arrived in Shanghai in July 1916, and their younger son, Huang Yiqiu, was born in October. Huang Xing had a relapse of his stomach ailment, however, and died at the end of the month; he was forty-two years old.

After the death of Huang Xing, Xu Zonghan ceased all involvement in politics, concentrating instead on social issues, resuming her work in the Nanjing Poor Children's Home (Nanjing pin'er jiaoyangyuan) that she had founded in 1912. She continued to work there almost until the time of her death. Xu Zonghan wrote in 1936, when war with Japan was imminent, that the most pressing issue for China was the nation's survival and the livelihood of its people. She opposed tactics of chanting slogans and mounting class struggle and was convinced that priority should be given to turning poor children into useful adults. Her belief was that the foundation of China's modernization lay in cultivating hardworking and pragmatic young people. She was indeed the first Chinese woman to promote national modernization through social issues.

Between 1931 and 1932, Xu Zonghan visited North and South America to raise funds from overseas Chinese for the operation of her Poor Children's Home. While she was abroad, the Manchurian Incident of 18 September erupted in China, and Xu Zonghan lost no time in raising money for the anti-Japanese campaign that the event provoked. The money was sent back in batches, over a period of more than two years, to the northeast Anti-Japanese United Army led by Ma Zhanshan and to the Shanghai Nineteenth Route Army led by Cai Tingkai.

Xu Zonghan experienced during her life a major personal change in philosophy, derived from her roles as a radical revolutionary in the last years of the Qing dynasty to the enthusiastic and pragmatic social worker she had become during the early Republican and Nationalist period. She eschewed politics but retained her absolute dedication to the cause of national salvation. Xu Zonghan died of illness in Chongqing on 8 March 1944, at the age of sixty-eight.

Xu Zonghan's life and work are detailed in Li Yu-ning's paper "Xu Zonghan and Huang Xing" on which this biography is mainly based.

Sandra LEE
(Translated by Chan Yuk Ping)

Li Youning [Li Yu-ning]. "Xu Zonghan yu Huang Xing." In *Huang Xing yu jindai Zhongguo xueshu taolunhui lunwenji*. Taipei: Zhengzhi daxue lishi yanjiusuo, 1993, 61–102.
Liu Shaotang, ed. "Xu Zonghan." In *Minguo renwu xiaozhuan*, vol. 7. Taipei: Zhuanji wenxue chubanshe, 1985, 215–19.

Xue Zhao: *see* **Chen Xuezhao**

Y

Yamane Yoshiko: *see* **Xie Xuehong**

Yan Daifeng: *see* **Yan Fengying**

Yan Fengying

Yan Fengying, 1930–1968, born Hongliu and also known as Daifeng, was from Tongcheng in Anhui Province. She was a *huangmei* (local opera performed in the Wu dialect) actress who played *xiaodan* (young maidens), *huadan* (lively young women), *guimendan* (women from good families), and *laodan* (old women) roles.

Born into a poor family, Yan Fengying enjoyed folksongs and *huangmei* tunes, but because this interest ran counter to clan regulations she was obliged to leave her family in order to develop her natural talent. By the age of thirteen, Yan Fengying was a *huangmei* apprentice to Yan Yungao, and her acting ability was noticed in performances given in Congyang, Tongcheng. Yan Fengying also received instruction from an established artist named Ding Yongquan and gradually made a name for herself in and around southern Anhui. Yan Fengying studied *jingju* (Beijing opera) in 1947 with Hu Jintao and Liu Fengyun and after the establishment of the PRC in 1949 studied with Bai Yunsheng, a famous northern *kunqu* (older opera genre) actor. Throughout her career, Yan Fengying assimilated allied genres in order to expand her acting skills. In 1953 she joined the *Huangmei* Company of Anhui Province.

Yan Fengying's voice was clear, crisp, and sweet and she sang beautifully in a simple and mellow manner. Her enunciation was very clear; her manner was refined and sophisticated, with a lucid and lively performance style. She placed great importance on conveying the feelings of a character; the clear, luxuriant sound of her voice and artistic seductiveness remained with audiences long after a performance was finished. Yan Fengying played a great variety of roles, bringing out in each the distinctiveness of the character: she was Tao Jinhua in *Hunting in the Grass* (Dalie cao), Princess Grace in *The Golden Bough* (Dajinzhi), Fifth Auntie Zhao in the modern drama *After the Harvest* (Fengshou zhi hou), the seventh goddess in *Marriage of the Goddess* (Tianxian pei), Feng Suzhen in *The Female Imperial Son-in-law* (Nü fuma), and the weaving maid in *The Cowherd and the Weaving Maid* (Niulang zhi nü). The last three were made into films.

By 1960, at thirty years of age, Yan Fengying had already been a performing artist for two decades and made a significant contribution to *huangmei* performance. She joined the CCP that year and was appointed director of the *Huangmei* Company of Anhui Province. She was also elected to the Committee of the China Federation of Literary and Art Circles (Zhongguo wenxue yishujie lianhehui, or Wenlian; also known as the Federation of Literature) and to the CPPCC.

Yan Fengying was fortunate in making a happy marriage with Wang Guanya, also a well-known *huangmei* performer. Yan Fengying was a loyal friend, mother, and wife, possibly because she herself had been denied parental affection as a child. The performing artist was as frank, outspoken, and passionate as the seventh goddess and weaving maid that she played on stage. Yan Fengying could never have anticipated, however, how cruel real life could be. In 1968 a trumped-up charge of "being opposed to Jiang Qing" (*q.v.*) was laid against her, and she was charged with the crime of "counter-revolutionary activity of a serious nature." She killed herself in protest at the injustice of the accusation. She was thirty-eight years old.

Wang Guanya published Yan Fengying's biography in 1981, and the story of her life became the subject of a nationally broadcast television series in the 1980s.

Shirley Wai CHAN
(Translated by Michael Paton)

Jingsheng and Xiquan, eds. *Xin Zhongguo mingrenlu*. Nanchang: Jiangxi renmin chubanshe, 1987.
Yin Wei and Wang Xiaoying. *Yan Fengying*. Hefei: Huangshan shushe, 1985.
Yingwen *Zhongguo funü*, ed. *Gujin zhuming funü renwu*, vol. 2. Shijiazhuang: Hebei renmin chubanshe, 1986, 1134–37.
Zhongguo dabaike quanshu: Xiqu quyi. Beijing: Zhongguo dabaike quanshu chubanshe, 1989, 524.

Yan Hongliu: see Yan Fengying

Yan Huizhu
Yan Huizhu, 1919–1966, also known as Zhong Ming and Wu Sheng, was of Mongolian nationality. She was a famous *jingju* (Beijing opera) and *kunqu* (an older opera genre popular from the Ming dynasty on in Jiangsu and Beijing) artist.

After her parents divorced when she was a child, Yang Huizhu lived with her father, Yan Jupeng, a famous *laosheng* (the role of a male of integrity) actor in *jingju* and founder of the Yan school of *jingju*. He understood how harsh the vagrant and unstable life of acting was and had experienced the bitterness of belonging to such an inferior social class. Yan Jupeng was determined, therefore, that his children, especially his favorite child Yan Huizhu, should not follow in his footsteps.

Exposed to *jingju* from childhood, however, Yan Huizhu showed early dramatic talent and intelligence. Behind her father's back, she did calisthenics to strengthen her legs and loosen her waist and trained her voice, learning songs from veteran actors while he was away on tour. By this means, she learned a dozen or so roles, *qingyi* (young or middle-aged women of rectitude), *huadan* (lively young women), and *wudan* (woman warrior). At the age of fifteen, Yan Huizhu performed "Nüqijie" (Female prisoner), the first act of the opera *Yutangchun*, at her school, Beijing Chunming Girls' School. She performed so well that Yan Jupeng finally agreed to allow Yan Huizhu to act, stipulating, however, that she was not to consider making a career in *jingju* and would sing only occasionally and then only with him. Yan Huizhu thus began formal singing and acting lessons in 1937, under the stage name Huizhu. When, soon afterward, Hubei Province was hit by severe floods, Yan Huizhu and her father took part in a benefit performance and put on *A Fisherman's Tragedy* (Dayu shajia) and *Empress He Demands an Explanation* (Hehou madian) to warm acclaim. Yan Huizhu's performance convinced her father that she should be allowed to play supporting roles; when he later formed the Yongpingshe Troupe, Yan Jupeng finally gave his daughter permission to go on stage and have her name on the playbill.

Yan Huizhu devoted herself uncomplainingly to practicing basic skills under the several teachers who trained her. The most influential one, however, was the great *jingju* master Mei Lanfang. It had been her father's last wish that Yan Huizhu learn from Mei Lanfang, so Yan Huizhu went to Shanghai to seek him out after her father's death. She was then twenty-four, and Mei Lanfang was not working at that time, the city being under Japanese occupation. Mei Lanfang devoted great care to fostering Yan Huizhu's talent, and she became popular, winning the complimentary epithet "Little Mei Lanfang." Yan Huizhu staged famous *jingju* of the Mei [Lanfang] school; her performance at Queens' Theater in February 1946 in *Regret for Life and Death* (Shengsi hen) won great admiration from the audience. In August that year she was dubbed "Queen of Beijing Opera."

With the establishment of the PRC in 1949, Yan Huizhu continued her involvement with traditional Chinese theater. She was appointed vice-president of the School of Traditional Operas in Shanghai in 1957 and gave classes on the Mei school. Yan Huizhu performed many times with the famous *jingju* and *kunqu* star Yu Zhenfei and together they revised and greatly improved the *kunqu* entitled *Love at First Sight, Atop the Wall* (Qiangtou mashang). Yan and Yu married in 1960 but were temperamentally incompatible, and the marriage was not successful. Both of them were severely criticized at the beginning of the Cultural Revolution; so distraught was Yan Huizhu at the treatment she received that she committed suicide in September 1966.

HE Li and Shirley Wai CHAN
(Translated by Chen Jinlan and Zhang Jinxin)

"Ji yidai hongling Yan Huizhu wenge ziyiqian de pianduan." *Zhuanji wenxue*, 68, no. 4 (1996): 92–97.

Jiang Wei. "Yu Zhenfei de aiqing sanbuqu: Yu Zhenfei, Yan Huizhu, Li Qianghua." *Zhongwai zazhi*, March (1991): 30–35.

Jingsheng and Xiquan, eds. *Xin Zhongguo mingrenlu*. Nanchang: Jiangxi renmin chubanshe, 1987.

Liu Bo, ed. *Zhongguo dangdai wenhua yishu mingren dacidian*. Beijing: Guoji wenhua chuban gongsi, 1993.

Xiao Xin. "Yan Huizhu de yishu shengya." *Baokan ziliao xuanhui: Xiqu yanjiu*, no. 12 (1986): 71–74.

Yang Chengye: *see* **Yang Mo**

Yang Chongrui

Yang Chongrui, 1891–1983, *zi* Xuefeng, of Tongxian County, Hebei Province (present-day Tongxian County of Beijing), was a pioneer in Chinese family planning and dedicated her life to improving the health of women and infants.

Her father, Yang Yunjie, held a provincial degree (*juren*) and taught at the Union Academy in Tongxian County; he also taught Yang Chongrui to read and write at a very young age. She entered Bridgeman Girls' High School in Beijing at thirteen and after graduation enrolled in 1910 at Union University (which later became Yen-ching [Yanjing] University), majoring in chemistry and physics. Upon graduation two years later, Yang Chongrui attended Union Women's Medical College and gained her medical degree in 1917.

Her first postings after graduation were in Boji Hospital at Dezhou in Shandong Province and Tianjin Women's and Children's Hospital. Soon after Union Medical College was founded, Yang Chongrui went to the newly established Public Health Department to further her studies in 1921. Her decision to join the field of public health and devote her life to public service came about after a joint research project carried out by the Public Health and Gynecology Departments revealed tetanus and puerperal fever to be the main causes of the high mortality rate of new-born babies and mothers.

In 1925, Yang Chongrui won a scholarship to the Johns Hopkins University in the United States. She visited Canada, England, Germany, France, Denmark, and Austria either on her way to the United States or on the way home to gather information about their respective public health systems and midwifery education. On her return, Yang Chongrui published many articles promoting education in midwifery and gained the support of prominent people. In 1929, she established the Beiping First Midwifery School (Beiping guoli diyi zhuchan xuexiao) and an affiliated maternity hospital. The motto chosen for the institute was "Serving with the Spirit of Sacrifice."

The school became the wellspring of Chinese midwifery education and teacher training, offering three-year study programs; during its twenty-two years of operation (its doors closed in 1951), the school produced several hundred graduates who formed the backbone of the nation's drive to improve the health of Chinese women and infants. Yang Chongrui also helped found the Central Midwifery School (Zhongyang zhuchan xuexiao) in Nanjing, baby protection centers, midwife training centers, and healthcare centers for mothers and infants in various cities. Her efforts brought about a dramatic drop in the death rates for mothers and infants.

Population surveys, figures revealing high birth and death rates, and information gathered about the number of babies Chinese mothers had and the conditions under which they had them convinced Yang Chongrui of the gravity of the Chinese population crisis and the urgency of birth control. In 1930, she co-founded the Beiping Mothers' Healthcare Committee (Beiping muqin baojian weiyuanhui) in conjunction with Yen-ching University's Sociology Department, the Social Welfare Department, and Union Hospital's Charity and Welfare Department. They instituted a propaganda program—"Limit the Number of Children"—aimed at improving maternal health. In 1932, Yang Chongrui established birth control consulting services in conjunction with the Sociology Departments of Yanjing and Tsinghua [Qinghua] Universities. At conferences and in written articles, she brought attention to the significance of birth control as well as detailing the practical measures to be taken.

After being appointed to the League of Nations' Women's and Infants' Health Section as a specialist at the beginning of 1937, Yang Chongrui researched women and children's health and midwifery education in about a dozen countries in Europe and Asia. By the time she returned to China, the Sino-Japanese War had broken out, and in November Yang Chongrui joined the Anti-Japanese Red Cross medical team. The Ministry of Education assigned her the task of setting up the Guiyang Medical College, and she was appointed professor to its Gynecology Department. In August 1938, Yang Chongrui was appointed supervisor in the Central Health Bureau and in 1941 left to pursue further training in gynecology at the Johns Hopkins Medical College. Upon return to China the following year, she became director of the Women's and Infants' Health Section (Fuyin weisheng zu) of the Central Public Health Research Clinic (Zhongyang weisheng shiyanyuan); at the end of the Sino-Japanese War in 1945, Yang Chongrui traveled widely within China in order to revive work on health programs for women and infants.

After another overseas fact-finding trip in 1947, to the United States and Canada, she was appointed as a specialist the following year to the World Health Organization's International Women's and Infants' Health Section; Yang Chongrui was soon made its deputy director. She attended a conference in Geneva in 1949 and won a European Midwifery Education and Women's and Children's Health Scholarship to visit Switzerland, Finland, Sweden, Denmark, England, and France.

Yang Chongrui accepted the invitation of Health Minister Li Dequan (*q.v.*), extended on behalf of Mao Zedong (1893–1976) and Zhou Enlai (1898–1976), to return to China after the establishment of the PRC in 1949. She gave up her prominent position and high salary in Geneva and returned home to become director of the Women's and Infants' Section of the Ministry of Health. Tragically, Yang Chongrui was denounced as a rightist and severely criticized in 1957 because of her consistent promotion of birth control. She was sent to study in the Academy of Socialism (Shehui zhuyi xueyuan) and assigned in 1959 to catalog foreign language books in the library of the Chinese Medical Association. Yang Chongrui later became editor for *Gynecology* (Fuchan ke zazhi) and an advisor to the Women's and Infants' Health Department. Her rightist label was not rescinded until 1979, however.

Yang Chongrui never married; her life was dedicated to the health of Chinese women and infants and the public welfare. Throughout her years, she was meticulous in her official duties and lived a thrifty and simple life. Yang Chongrui assisted her relatives by nurturing eleven of them through university and in accordance with her father's wish established Yunjie Primary School in her hometown in 1928.

WANG Bing
(Translated by Jennifer Zhang)

Lei Zhifang. "Yang Chongrui." In *Zhongguo xiandai kexuejia zhuanji*, vol. 4. Beijing: Kexue chubanshe, 1993, 552–59.

Yan Renying et al., eds. *Yang Chongrui boshi*. Beijing: Beijing yike daxue, Zhongguo xiehe yike daxue lianhe chubanshe, 1990.

Yang Chongrui. *Diyi zhuchan xuexiao shi zhounian jiniance*. N.p.: Zhongyang weisheng shiyanyuan, 1939.

———. *Fuyin weisheng gangyao*. N.p.: Zhongyang weisheng shiyanyuan, 1939.

Yang Chongrui et al., eds. *Fuyou weisheng*. Beijing: Renmin weisheng chubanshe, 1953.

Yang Fuqing

Yang Fuqing, b. 1932, in Wuxi, Jiangsu Province, is a computer software specialist and computer studies academic.

Her father, Yang Jiechen, was a businessman and industrialist while her mother, Li Wenying, was a housewife. Yang Fuqing is the eldest of three children; she has a brother and sister. From childhood, Yang Fuqing's interests ranged widely, and she obtained outstanding results at school, especially in mathematics. Yang Fuqing graduated from First Girls' High School of Wuxi in 1951 and went on to the Mathematics Department at Peking University. After graduating in 1955, she completed two years of graduate work in the Mathematics and Mechanics Department before going on to graduate study at the Soviet Academy of Sciences and Moscow University (1957–59). Yang Fuqing returned to Peking University in 1962 as a lecturer in the Computer Science and Technology Department. She has remained there until the present, apart from two years (1962–64) at the computer center of the Joint Institute of Nuclear Research in Moscow. Yang Fuqing was appointed associate professor in 1979 and promoted in 1983 to professor and head of the Computer Science and Technology Department at Peking University.

In the 1950s, she studied computing mathematics in her undergraduate years and reverse compiling in graduate years. In the 1960s, Yang Fuqing presented the concept and method of resource sharing and coordinating multiprogram processing. In the early 1970s, she developed the operating system for the first integrated circuit computer in China and subsequently won a National Science Congress Achievement Award (Quanguo kexue dahui chengguo jiang) in 1978. From that year on, Yang Fuqing undertook research into the structure of operating systems and successfully developed the system programming language XCY. She gained First Prize in the Ministry of Education Awards for Advances in Science and Technology (Guojia jiaowei keji jinbu jiang). Under her direction, the operating system DTS200/XT2 was developed, making use of core modularization to reduce the size of the core to the minimum; it was the first large operating system to be written in an advanced language in China. Of great significance in the development of computers in China, this achievement led to the award in 1985 of First Prize in the Ministry of Electronic Industry Awards for Achievement in Science and Technology (Dianzi gongyebu keji chengguo jiang).

Yang Fuqing also pioneered software engineering and organized China's first conference on that subject in 1980. In the foundation research of software engineering, she raised a number of theoretical and practical problems and worked to resolve them. Since the 1980s, Yang Fuqing has been in charge of national key research projects such as the software engineering core supporting environment Beta-85, an integrated software engineering environment, and an intelligent software engineering environment. In the early 1990s, she used object-oriented and environment-building techniques "Jade Bird" CASE to develop an integrated software engineering support environment. These projects represented the most advanced levels in software engineering in the world in their time.

Yang Fuqing contributed greatly to teaching and research in computer studies, especially in the development of software and building China's computer industry.

She has won several national prizes for research and throughout a long academic career educated many advanced software professionals, supervising their master's and doctoral studies. Because of her contribution and achievements, Yang Fuqing was named a member of the Subject Evaluation Section of the State Council Academic Degrees Committee (Guowuyuan xuewei weiyuanhui xueke pingyizu) and deputy director of the China Computer Association (Zhongguo jisuanji xuehui). She also serves on the editorial board of six national academic journals, including *Scientia Sinica* (Zhongguo kexue). Yang Fuqing is a member of the worldwide Institute of Electrical and Electronic Engineers and in 1991 became an academician of the Chinese Academy of Sciences.

She is married to Wang Yangyuan, a specialist in microelectronics; they have a son and daughter.

Lily Xiao Hong LEE

Zhongguo xiandai kexuejia zhuanji, vol. 5. Beijing: Kexue chubanshe, 1994, 893–96.
Zhonghua quanguo funü lianhehui. Zuzhi lianluobu. *Zhongguo nü yuanshi*. Shenyang: Liaoning renmin chubanshe, 1995, 355–58.

Yang Houzhen

Yang Houzhen, 1908–1977, born in Ruijin County, Jiangxi Province was one of the thirty women who took part in the Chinese communists' Long March of 1934–35.

Her father was a teacher, and she attended Lenin Primary School. Yang Houzhen's feet had been bound as a child, but she later "liberated" them. Yang Houzhen married army commander Luo Binghui (1897–1946) in 1926 and went with him after he defected from the KMT during the 1929 Ji'an Uprising to Jinggangshan, where the Red Army had been forged. After joining the CCP in 1931, Yang Houzhen attended the Red Army University in the Jiangxi soviet and undertook various duties, including mimeographing, nursing, administration, and running of cooperative ventures initiated by the army and the Central Committee. Despite the dreadful handicap of her liberated feet, Yang Houzhen walked almost every step of the Long March, although she does not appear to have been assigned duties. In his book *The Long March: The Untold Story*, Harrison Salisbury says that the wife of Luo Binghui gave birth to a child on the Long March but Chinese sources are silent on this point. She was, however, wounded during a bombing raid, as was He Zizhen (*q.v.*) then wife of Mao Zedong (1893–1976). Yang Houzhen was separated from her husband when he was assigned to Zhang Guotao's Fourth Front Army in August 1935. This appears to have signalled the end of their marriage. Luo Binghui told Helen Foster Snow in Yan'an in 1937 that he had three children in Jiangxi and a son in Yunnan. He did not tell her how many wives he had had nor mention Yang Houzhen.

Listed by Helen Snow as "Yang Hu-chen . . . a housewife" in Yan'an, Yang Houzhen was in fact assigned to manage cooperatives and local factories run by families; unfortunately, her health declined before long. She remarried and at some stage gave birth to a child. Yang Houzhen took the child with them when her second husband Liu Zhengming was dismissed from the party (for what reason is unclear) and sent away from Yan'an. She opened a shop in 1940 and, excommunicated from the party, supported the family until Liu Zhengming was cleared and reinstated in 1946. When the communists left Yan'an in 1947, Yang Houzhen and her husband were taken to Shanxi and admitted to a veterans' hospital. After 1949 Yang Houzhen was employed by the Ministry of Culture as head of a sporting goods factory, a most unusual appointment for a woman of her background, possibly made because of her extensive experience with cooperatives and administration. Nothing is known of what happened to her during the Cultural Revolution, and she is said to have died of natural causes in 1977.

Sue WILES

Guo Chen. *Jinguo liezhuan: Hong yifangmianjun sanshiwei changzheng nühongjun shengping shiji.* Beijing: Nongcun duwu chubanshe, 1986, 201–03.

Salisbury, Harrison E. *The Long March: The Untold Story.* New York: Harper & Row, 1985, 167.

Snow, Helen Foster. *Inside Red China,* 1977 reprint [with a new preface and biographical notes by the author]. New York: Da Capo Press, 1939, 125.

Yang Hu-chen: *see* **Yang Houzhen**

Yang Huizhen

Yang Huizhen, ca. 1913–1989, was a Chinese Muslim of Hui nationality. She was born Wang Rong in Zhoukou, Henan Province, a place known among Chinese Muslims as "Little Mecca" because of the strength of its religious tradition. Until very recently, the memory of Yang Huizhen was preserved through oral tradition alone, initially by the Muslim communities of Jiaxing and Shanghai but afterward by those she had saved from starvation, homelessness, the indignities forced upon refugees, and the uncertainties that befell so many orphans during social upheaval.

Unusually so for her time and place, Yang Huizhen was literate in Chinese and educated in Islamic precepts and conduct. During the 1930s, she entered the family of a rich pawnbroker in Kaifeng as a daughter-in-law. Not known is whether she studied at one of the numerous women's mosques (*nüsi*) in Kaifeng at that time, some of which retained the old name of "religious school" (*nüxue*). Yang Huizhen had moved to Shanghai with her husband after he ruined the family through an opium addiction. Her infant daughter died of illness, and her husband died several years later, still addicted. Upon moving there, Yang Huizhen embarked upon the study of Islamic scriptures under the widely revered Shanghai scholar *ahong* (religious leader) Mai Junsan (1888–1967). Her decision accorded with a local tradition that Muslim women of a certain status could choose to enter Islamic schools to prepare themselves for a religious career. This included women of mature age or widowed, married to an *ahong*, or retired from active household duties.

In 1942 Yang Huizhen accepted an invitation from the Muslim community in Jiaxing, near Shanghai, to become the first resident *ahong* at their new women's mosque. Appointed for three years and welcomed with a banquet, she initially followed the traditional path of presiding over the religious affairs of the mosque, teaching and counseling the women who called upon her. Before long, however, Yang Huizhen deviated from conventions when she began to leave the grounds of the mosque to visit the poor in their homes. Yang Huizhen further shocked and alienated the patriarchal leadership of the men's mosque after insisting on ministering to refugees from the Sino-Japanese War.

While to the people she was immensely popular, a woman who was unafraid of opposition and ready to intervene on their behalf to initiate social change, the religious leadership, backed by the China Islamic Association (Zhongguo huijiao xiehui), saw her as a threat. They expelled Yang Huizhen from her duties and place of residence. Her founding of the Muslim Association for the Orphaned and Widowed (Huijiao gu'er guafunü hui) was considered to be a dereliction of her duties as an *ahong*. And her soliciting of donations and alms on the association's behalf so affronted the Muslim establishment that in August 1946 they terminated her contract and issued an expulsion from the Zhejiang Province branch of the Huijiao Association (Zhongguo huijiao xiehui Zhejiang shengzhi) altogether. She was officially accused of improper use of the mosque; unseemly independent action in violation of the proper (i.e., patriarchal) authorities; lack of consultation with the men's mosque; and a general air of defiance inconsistent with the code of conduct of a female *ahong*.

When Yang Huizhen left the women's mosque in mid-year, she took with her all of the refugees in her care. Yang Huizhen then set up a house of refuge and relief for Muslims (Huijiao jiaoyangsuo), subsequently known as the Muslim Emergency Refuge (Huijiao jiujiyuan), and traveled to Nanjing, Shanghai, and Hangzhou soliciting financial support from Hui communities. She provided housing and food and welcomed to her shelter non-Muslim and Han refugees. Yang Huizhen was dogged in her approaches to provincial and county administrations for relief for the growing refugee population, caused now by the civil war between communists and nationalists. She made overtures to the Huijiao Association, reporting on her work and asking permission to enlarge the refuge and even offering to hand control over to them. Her political skill and the high esteem in which she was held in the wider community by Muslim and non-Muslim alike led to the association finally writing to Jiaxing County in June 1947 professing staunch support for her charitable projects.

In 1947 Yang Huizhen set up a charity primary school in which secular and Islamic education was provided by Hui and Han teachers to children of poor families. She not only taught the rudiments of Islam to the children but also set up a small rope factory, taking personal responsibility for selling the rope made there. From an initial enrollment of forty-four children, the refuge expanded by February 1949 to housing fifty orphans and 116 refugees, including twenty-seven children, twenty-one men, fifty women, and nine frail elderly. The charity closed down in the first half of 1950, however. Now that Yang Huizhen's services as an *ahong* were no longer required, she returned to Shanghai. Yang Huizhen nevertheless visited the Jiaxing community frequently, her last visit taking place in 1988 at which time she stayed for over a year. Yang Huizhen died in 1989, not among her people, but in Shanghai.

She remained a popular local hero in Jiaxing Muslim folklore; her name was cited frequently by Muslim women in various localities as a paragon of Islamic piety. The letters and reports testifying to the controversy surrounding her impact on the Muslims of Jiaxing also remained—untouched—in the archives of the Jiaxing branch of the Chinese Islamic Association (Zhongguo huijiao xiehui Jiaxing xianzhi), until the visit in early 1997 of one of the authors of this article. A senior official of the association not only proffered these documents then but collated them and contributed the story of Yang Huizhen's life to a study of women's mosques in central China. This man, Guo Chenmei, was the son of the female *ahong* chosen as Yang Huizhen's successor many years previously. The recent commemoration in print of Yang Huizhen might be seen as public rehabilitation and tacit admission of her place in communal memory, despite continued official caution over the proper appraisal of her charitable work.

Yang Huizhen's significance lies not only in her sharing with other Chinese women the economic and social hardships of China's entry into the twentieth century but also a defiance of patriarchal and religious strictures in performing duties as a resident female *ahong*. Her independence and integrity as much as her compassion inscribed her extraordinary gifts and charisma on the communities with whom she worked. Yang Huizhen is also memorable as a representative of an unusual female tradition of learned and respected religious women. The Ming dynasty Islamic scholar (*nü junshi*) Sumingdashishi was one such, as were the predecessors of female *ahong*, Ba Jinlan (*q.v.*) and Du Shuzhen (*q.v.*). Yang Huizhen's position in her religious community benefited from the established right of women to Islamic education and professional training, but her career also demonstrates the severe punishment meted out to women who dared to think and act outside the social boundaries defined by a patriarchal society.

Maria H.A. JASCHOK and SHUI Jingjun

Alles, Elisabeth. "Une organisation de l'Islam au féminin: Le personnel des mosquées féminines en Chine." *Lettre d'information*. Paris: Programme de Recherches Interdisciplinaires sur le Monde Müsulman Périphérique, 14 (1994): 1–12.

Dai Jianning. "Shilun huizu funü xinyang yisilanjiaode xinli tezheng." *Huizu yanjiu*, 4 (1992): 67–70.

Etudes Orientales, 13/14 (1994). Contributions by Elisabeth Alles, Leila Cherif, and Constance-Hélène Halfon.

Feng Jinyuan. "Shilun yisilanjiaode funüguan." *Zhongguo musilin*, 4 (1995): 19–24.

Jaschok, Maria and Shui Jingjun. *The History of Women's Mosques in Chinese Islam: A Mosque of Their Own*. Richmond, Surrey: Curzon Press, 2000.

Nan Wenyuan. *Yisilanjiao yu xibei musilin shehui shenghuo*. Xining: Qinghai renmin chubanshe, 1994.

Pang Keng-Fong. "Islamic 'Fundamentalism' and Female Empowerment among the Muslims of Hainan Island, PRC." In *Mixed Blessings: Gender and Religious Fundamentalism Cross Culturally*, eds. Judy Brink and Joan Mencher. London: Routledge, 1997, 41–56.

Shui Jingjun. "Lun nüxue nüside xingqi yu fazhan." *Huizu yanjiu*, 1 (1996): 51–59.

Yang Jiang

Yang Jiang, b. 1911, original name Yang Jikang, a native of Wuxi in Jiangsu Province but born in Beijing, is a writer of fiction, drama, and prose, a scholar of comparative literature, and a translator. She is best known in China for her translations into Chinese of major works of Spanish and French literature, including *Don Quixote de la Mancha*, and her Cultural Revolution memoirs. Yang Jiang is less well known outside of China, where her work has received little critical attention.

Yang Jiang's father, Yang Yinhang (1878–1945), a lawyer by profession, worked as a translator, professor, and editor. He was also an early anti-Qing activist and served in a number of government posts in Beijing during the early years of the Republic of China. Her mother, Tang Xuying (1878–1937), ran the Yang household and had ten children; she was also an avid reader of Ming and Qing fiction.

Owing to the nature of her father's work and political instability of the early years of the Republic, Yang Jiang spent her childhood moving back and forth among the cities of Beijing, Shanghai, Suzhou, Hangzhou, and Wuxi before the family finally settled in Suzhou during her early teens. Ten years younger than her next oldest sibling, Yang Jiang was indulged by her parents; they both strongly supported her precocious interests in poetry and fiction. She attended high school at Zhenhua Girls' High School in Suzhou.

In 1928, at the age of seventeen, the young woman enrolled at Soochow University (Dongwu daxue) in Suzhou. The university offered no major in literary subjects, however, and her advisors urged her to study the natural sciences. Yang Jiang considered majoring in pre-law, however, thinking that work as her father's paralegal would provide her with insights into interpersonal relations and human character that she could then incorporate into fiction. Only when her father discouraged her from entering law did she enroll, reluctantly, in the Politics Department. Uninterested in that area as an academic field of study, Yang Jiang did only enough course work to get by and instead spent most of her college years reading literature and teaching herself French and Spanish. She was awarded but declined to accept a fellowship to Wellesley College in the United States during her junior year.

Yang Jiang graduated from Soochow University in 1932 and that autumn enrolled at Tsinghua [Qinghua] University (Qinghua daxue) as a graduate student in the Foreign Languages Department. There, she undertook her first formal study of foreign literature and made a powerful impression on the department's professors for having taught herself Spanish in her spare time. Yang Jiang's graduate studies at Tsinghua, combined with additional graduate-level study in England and France, would prove to be of decisive importance for her subsequent academic career as a literary comparativist and translator of foreign literature. It was also at Tsinghua, however, that she wrote fiction seriously. Her first substantial effort, a short story titled "Lulu, Don't Worry!" (Lulu, buyong chou!), so impressed one professor, the scholar Zhu Ziqing, that he submitted it to the Arts and Literature Supplement (Wenyi fukan) of *Dagongbao*. "Lulu" was first published there in 1935, before being anthologized in 1936 alongside stories by such prominent writers as Lao She and Shen Congwen. During her first year as a graduate student at Tsinghua, Yang Jiang had met Qian Zhongshu, a fellow graduate student; they became engaged, and the two married in summer 1935.

In autumn, Yang Jiang left Tsinghua before completing her graduate program to join her husband in study at Oxford University, where he had been awarded a Boxer Indemnity Scholarship. She also studied at Oxford for two years, earning an M.Phil.

in Literature, before going on to Paris to study Romance languages for one more year. Yang Jiang returned to China in autumn 1938 with her husband and one-year-old daughter and settled in Shanghai, where her family had moved when Suzhou was captured by Japanese forces the previous winter.

Yang Jiang lived in Shanghai for the next eleven years, taking a number of part-time jobs, mostly as a private tutor and substitute primary school teacher, to help support her family. From 1939 to 1941, she also helped establish and run a Shanghai branch of her high school *alma mater*, only to see it close in December, when Japanese forces occupied the city.

During the eleven years in the city, Yang Jiang made a number of outstanding contributions to the city's cultural life, which continued to thrive despite the imposition of Japanese rule and isolation from other parts of China. Urged by Shi Huawen, Li Jianwu, and Huang Zuolin, three close friends who figured prominently in Shanghai's theater circles, Yang Jiang began writing plays in 1942. Her first one, a four-act comedy titled *As You Desire* (Chenxin ruyi), was performed in 1943 by the Shanghai United Arts Theater and greeted with wide critical acclaim. Over the next three years, Yang Jiang wrote three more plays: a five-act comedy titled *The Cheat* (Nongzhen chengjia), performed in 1943 by the Tongmao Theater Company; a farce titled *Sport with the World* (Youxi renjian), performed by the Kugan Players in 1944 but never published; and *Windswept Blossoms* (Fengxu), a four-act tragedy serialized in 1946 but never produced for the stage. Although her first two plays are generally considered comedies (one early reviewer considered *As You Desire* a tragedy), they betray a serious dramatic, and often feminist, vision; a deft use of irony; and lively, deliberate dialogue among large casts of youth on the fringe of bourgeois society. *Windswept Blossoms* depicts three urban youth caught in a love triangle in rural Republican China as they try to come to terms with personal failure. Though generally considered a tragedy, the play has also been read as a highly stylized melodrama (Yang Jiang herself referred to it as a "potboiler"), innovatively sustaining its focus on the psychological dimension of interpersonal relations.

Although Yang Jiang first achieved recognition for dramatic works, by the mid- to late 1940s she had also published a number of short stories, including "Romanesque," which many consider her best-crafted short story, and "Indian Summer" (Xiaoyangchun), focusing on marital strife. By now, however, Yang Jiang had begun to direct the better part of her creative energy to translation, the line of work for which she would subsequently secure her reputation as a scholar. Her early translations were largely of prose, the most substantial being the collection *English Prose since 1939* (Yijiusanjiunian yilai Yingguo sanwen zuopin), published in 1948.

Turning down several opportunities to leave China after the end of the Sino-Japanese War, Yang Jiang moved to Beijing with her husband and daughter on 27 May 1949. There, she first served as a professor in the Western Languages Department at Tsinghua University and in 1953 became a research fellow at the Division of Foreign Literature (later known as the Institute of Foreign Literature) of the Institute of Literature at Peking University. (The institute subsequently relocated twice, first to the

Chinese Academy of Sciences and then to the Chinese Academy of Social Sciences.) Yang Jiang remains (1998) a research fellow at the Institute.

Her first major work of literary translation, a rendition of the Spanish picaresque novel *La Vida de Lazarillo de Tormes*, was published in 1951 as *Xiaolaizi*. This was followed in 1956 with a translation from the French of Alain René Le Sage's eighteenth-century *Histoire de Gil Blas de Santillane*, as *Ji'er Bulasi*. Her third major effort, a Chinese rendition of Miguel de Cervantes's seventeenth-century masterpiece *Don Quixote*, as *Tang Jihede* was the most ambitious project of her career and occupied her attention for well over a decade. The outbreak of the Cultural Revolution interrupted her work on *Don Quixote*, however, and at one point her only copy of the manuscript was seized and lost. By a stroke of great fortune combined with courage, Yang Jiang furtively recovered the manuscript herself, having stumbled across it accidentally in a storeroom that she had been assigned to sweep. The manuscript was finally published in its first edition in March 1978. Her rendition of *Don Quixote* was the first major literary translation into Chinese directly from Spanish (previous translations, including the first edition of her own *Xiaolaizi*, had been rendered indirectly via French, German, or English translations). In 1986, in recognition of an outstanding contribution to the spread of Spanish culture, Yang Jiang was awarded the Alfonso X "the Wise" Award by King Juan Carlos of Spain.

Although Yang Jiang survived the three-antis campaign (1951) and the anti-rightist campaign (1957) relatively unscathed, on 9 August 1966 she was "seized" and dubbed a "bourgeois scholar." Having thus entered the ranks of "cow-demons and snake-spirits," Yang Jiang was reassigned to work as a custodian in charge of cleaning the women's lavatory at her work unit. On and off between August 1966 and July 1970, she was housed with her husband and colleagues in office space known as "ox pens" and subjected to several waves of struggle sessions, public investigation, and public self-criticism. Her formal "re-education" by worker and PLA propaganda teams began in 1969. In July 1970, after having been released from re-education with her husband, owing to provisions implemented for the weak and elderly (she was fifty-nine at the time), Yang Jiang was reassigned to a cadre school in Xi County, Henan Province. At the cadre school, she was responsible for weeding and patroling garden plots tilled by her cadre school colleagues. In early spring 1971, her cadre school moved to Minggang, Henan Province, and the emphasis of re-education shifted from manual labor to study. Yang Jiang returned to Beijing with her husband in March 1972, along with other elderly and sick returnees. For the next three years, she lived with him in office space at the Institute of Foreign Literature and gradually resumed academic work.

Before and after the Cultural Revolution, Yang Jiang wrote a number of essay-length works of literary criticism, including studies of Jane Austen, Miguel de Cervantes, Henry Fielding, Li Yu's theory of dramatic form, and *The Story of the Stone* (Honglou meng). Many of these can be found in her two major essay collections *Spring Soil* (Chunni ji) and *About Fiction* (Guanyu xiaoshuo). Her discourse on the art of translation, "The Experience of Defeat: An Essay on Translation" (Shibai de jingyan: Shitan fanyi), was included in the second printing of *Tang Jihede*. In the late

1970s, she also collaborated on the major committee publication of the Academy of Social Sciences' *Foreign Theorists and Writers on Literary Form* (Waiguo lilunjia zuojia lun xingxiangsiwei), an anthology of essays translated from several European languages.

A series of memoirs published in the 1980s, however, earned Yang Jiang her widest readership. The first one, *Six Chapters of My Life "Downunder"* (Ganxiao liuji, 1984), an account of her own and her husband's cadre school life during the Cultural Revolution, was enthusiastically reviewed and immediately translated into Japanese, English, French, and Russian. Its restrained allegorical style was praised and compared favorably with the genre of "scar literature" that had recently become popular. In 1989 *Six Chapters of My Life "Downunder"* was named an Outstanding Prose Collection of China's New Era by the Chinese Writers' Association. A second Cultural Revolution memoir, two lengthy "recollections" of her father and aunt, and two short reminiscences of her husband and the writing of his popular novel *Fortress Besieged* (Weicheng) followed and coincided with a minor renaissance in the publication of her work. Between 1979 and 1986, much of Yang Jiang's early writings, including two plays, a collection of short stories, and literary essays, were reissued in new editions, and in 1993 the Chinese Academy of Social Sciences published her selected works, *Yang Jiang zuopin ji*, in three volumes. She continues to write and publish short prose essays, many of which are biographical or autobiographical in nature.

In 1988 Yang Jiang published her first and only novel, *Taking a Bath* (Xizao), an unforgiving, if humorous, depiction of three generations of literature scholars undergoing thought reform for the first time, during the three-antis campaign of 1951. The novel highlights how political campaigns intersected with the more mundane aspects of the lives of intellectuals during the early years of the People's Republic, giving special attention to marital strife and extramarital relations. As of this writing, Yang Jiang is collaborating with Lu Wenhu on the publication of her husband's letters. Yang Jiang has recently annotated and published a collection of his poetry.

The writer lives in Beijing with her husband. Their only child died of cancer in 1997. A bibliography of Yang Jiang's publications through 1995, along with a selection of critical essays on her work in Chinese, can be found in Tian et al., cited below.

Mark SWISLOCKI

Dooling, Amy D. "In Search of Laughter: Yang Jiang's Feminist Comedy." *Modern Chinese Literature*, 8 (1994): 41–67.

Gunn, Edward M., Jr. *Unwelcome Muse: Chinese Literature in Shanghai and Peking, 1937–1945*. New York: Columbia University Press, 1980, 231–43.

Kong Qingmao. *Qian Zhongshu yu Yang Jiang*. Haikou, Hainan: Hainan guojixinwen chubanshe, 1997.

———. *Yang Jiang pingzhuan*. Beijing: Huaxia chubanshe, 1998.

Tian Huilan, Ma Guangyu, and Chen Keyu, eds. *Qian Zhongshu Yang Jiang yanjiu ziliao ji*. Wuchang: Huazhong shifan daxue chubanshe, 1990; 2nd edn., 1997, 511–672.

Yang Jiang zuopin ji, 3 vols. Beijing: Chinese Academy of Social Sciences Press, 1993.

Yang Jikang: *see* **Yang Jiang**

Yang Jingqin: *see* **Yang Zilie**

Yang Junmo: *see* **Yang Mo**

Yang Kaihui

Yang Kaihui (*zi* Yunjin or Mingjun, *hao* Xia), 1901–1930, of Bancang, Changsha County, Hunan Province, was the first wife of Mao Zedong (1893–1976). Strictly speaking, Yang Kaihui was his second wife; however, Mao's first, arranged, marriage at the age of thirteen or fourteen to a young woman six years older whose name he never divulged is generally discounted because of his persistent claim that he did not consummate the marriage. Yang Kaihui was not his first sweetheart, either, an honor that is said to belong to Tao Yi (*zi* Siyong, 1896–1930) of Xiangtan, Hunan Province, who had earlier helped Mao organize a group dedicated to spreading literacy.

Yang Kaihui was the daughter of Mao's earliest and beloved ethics teacher, Yang Changji (d. 1919). He had studied in Europe and on his return in 1913 moved his family to Changsha, taking charge of the newly established Hunan First Normal School. Yang Kaihui thus knew Mao and his fellow students from their frequent visits to her home, where she sat on the sidelines and listened to their discussions on philosophy and world affairs with her father. In summer 1918, Yang Kaihui accompanied her father to Beijing when he accepted a position at Peking University. When Mao visited the capital and during the short period of his employment at Peking University Library, he and his friends would, as before, spend time at his old teacher's home. Although Yang Kaihui was by no means uneducated, her father did not encourage his daughter to pursue further education; he remained a traditionalist in many ways, holding the view that "a woman who lacks talent is virtuous." Thus, she did not attend school until after his death in January 1919, which coincided with the revolutionary upsurge that became the May Fourth Movement. Encouraged by Mao, however, Yang Kaihui doubtless read such radical literature as *New Youth* (Xin qingnian) and *New Tide* (Xin chao) and was swept up by the fervor of the times. Returning to Bancang, she enrolled in an American-run missionary school but soon left, challenging tradition by passing the entrance examination and then enrolling in Yueyun Boys' School.

Her period of independence was short-lived, however. Once she married Mao in autumn 1920, Yang Kaihui devoted herself to him as his wife and mother to his children. Although joining the Socialist Youth League (Zhongguo shehuizhuyi qingnian tuan) that year (some sources say 1922) and the CCP in 1921, thus becoming one of its earliest members, she never held official position. Yang Kaihui is described, however, as having carried out "confidential work and liaison" with the communist Xiang Region Committee (Zhonggong Xiang qu weiyuanhui) that Mao established that year and ran from their home in Qingshuitang just outside Changsha. While her commitment to the Chinese revolution is never in question, her duties were apparently confined to assisting Mao. She organized his papers, looked after and kept them in a safe place; fanned her husband on hot summer nights as he worked; made sure he was

warm; and brought food on winter nights as he worked. Yang Kaihui generally remained in Qingshuitang when Mao traveled about but did accompany him at various
times between 1923 and 1927 to Shanghai, Shaoshan, and Wuhan and is said to have
contributed to the nascent labor, peasant, and women's movements.

They quarreled from time to time; a poem believed to have been written by Mao in
December 1923 as he left for Shanghai was addressed to Yang Kaihui and deplores a
lovers' quarrel that had led to their estrangement:

> A wave of the hand, and the moment of parting has come.
> Harder to bear is facing each other dolefully,
> Bitter feelings voiced once more.
> Wrath looks out of your eyes and brows,
> On the verge of tears, you hold them back . . .
> Let us strive to sever those threads of grief and anger,
> Let it be as though the sheer cliffs of Mount Kunlun collapsed,
> And as though a typhoon swept through the whole universe.
> Let us be once again two birds flying side by side,
> Soaring high as the clouds.

Yang Kaihui bore three sons to Mao: Anying (1922–1951), Anqing (b. 1923), and
Anlong (b. 1927 in Wuchang). She took them back to Bancang in late 1927 as Mao
prepared his ill-fated Autumn Harvest Uprising. She never saw him again. While he
retreated to Jinggangshan, built the Red Army, and established a new "revolutionary
marriage" with He Zizhen (*q.v.*), Yang Kaihui lived in Bancang and, later, Changsha.
She and her son Anying were arrested in Changsha by the local warlord, and Yang
Kaihui was executed on 14 November 1930 because she was the wife of Mao Zedong.
He had led an unsuccessful Red Army attack on Changsha just a few weeks earlier.

Yang Kaihui died a tragic death at a young age. However, evaluations such as
Edgar Snow's that she was "a youth leader during the Great Revolution, and one of
the most active women Communists" seem to be informed more by the fact that she
was Mao Zedong's wife than by any hard evidence. Christina Gilmartin's quote from
"an early male member of the party" who said simply that Yang Kaihui undertook
"numerous political tasks" may be more accurate. Her image as a fine young revolutionary was further enhanced in 1957 when, playing on the meaning of her surname
Yang (poplar tree), Mao wrote nostalgically in a poem: "I lost my proud Poplar."
Yang Kaihui's image also became a rallying point to mobilize the nation against Mao's
last wife, Jiang Qing (*q.v.*), when his death brought the Cultural Revolution to a close.

Sue WILES

Gilmartin, Christina K. "The Politics of Gender in the Making of the Party." In *New Perspec-
tives on the Chinese Communist Revolution*, eds. Tony Saich and Hans van de Ven. New
York: M.E. Sharpe, 1995, 49.
Liu Fulang. *The Analysis of Mao Tse-tung's Personality*. Hong Kong: Union Press, 1973, 60.
Mao Tsetung Poems. Beijing: Foreign Languages Press, 1976.
Schram, Stuart R., ed. *Mao's Road to Power: Revolutionary Writings 1912–1949. Vol. 2. Na-*

tional Revolution and Social Revolution, December 1920-June 1927. Armonk, N.Y.: M.E. Sharpe, 1994, 195–96.

Snow, Edgar. *Red Star over China.* London: Victor Gollancz, 1937; 1963 reissue, 147–53, 173.

Yingwen *Zhongguo funü,* ed. *Gujin zhuming funü renwu,* vol. 2. Shijiazhuang: Hebei renmin chubanshe, 1986, 601–06.

Yun Ting and Zhang Sulan. *Mao jia xiongdi yu He jia jiemei.* Jiangsu wenyi chubanshe, 1996.

Yang Liping

Yang Liping, b. 1959, in Xishuang banna, southern Yunnan Province, is a dancer and performer; she is of Bai nationality and her ancestral home is Dali, Yunnan Province. Yang Liping has been awarded the rank of First-Grade Performer.

She was from childhood entranced by the beautiful scenery and fascinating singing and dancing of Xishuang banna; at the age of twelve, Yang Liping joined the Xishuang Banna Autonomous Prefecture Opera Troupe as an actress. She played the leading role in the dance drama *Zhao Tree Village and Nanmu Nuona* (Zhaoshu cun yu Nanmu Nuona) at nineteen. Her dancing is fresh and original, the choreography graceful, and her style distinctive. Imitating the rhythm of a peacock spreading its tail, she creates flashing movements: her long arms and open shoulders enable her to "turn with hands clasped at the back"; artistry is further displayed in the movements and postures of her hand, arms, and shoulders. Each of these joints can move independently, displaying an uncanny likeness to the peacock flapping its wings. Often these movements were performed while the dancer was standing still; "dancing on the spot" is said to embody her unique style. *Spirit of the Peacock* (Que zhi ling), *Fire* (Huo), *Fine Rain* (Yu si), and *Colors of Banna* (Banna sanse) are regarded as her finest works.

In 1986 Yang Liping won First Prize for both performance and choreography of the solo dance *Spirit of the Peacock* and Second Prize for co-choreography of *Love during the Hunt* (Lie zhong qing) at the Second National Dancing Competition. She was the first Chinese dancer since the founding of the People's Republic to perform solo overseas and in 1988 performed at the National Arts Center in the Philippines, where she was awarded life membership into the Philippines Folk Dance Association. Yang Liping performed at the Cultural Palace of the Nationalities in Beijing that same year and also was honored as one of the ten Beijing People of the Year. Her performance at the 1989 Spring Festival CC-TV Special was acclaimed by the Shanghai newspaper *Wenhui bao,* and the hand gestures she created for her peacock dance were used as the emblem for the first Yunnan Arts Festival.

Much of Yang Liping's work, choreographed and directed by herself, is unaffected and marked by spontaneity. Originality and beauty are important qualities in her dance. She has served on the Executive Committee of the Chinese Dancers' Association and is a member of the Foundation for Chinese Minorities' Culture and Arts. Yang Liping is now a solo dancer with the Central Nationalities Singing and Dancing Troupe.

HE Li
(Translated by Yang Jingqing)

Chao Kuocheng. "Yang Liping he tade wudao xin." *Wudao luncong*, no. 4 (1988).
Wang Kefen, Liu Bo'en, and Xu Erchong, eds. *Zhongguo wudaojia dacidian*. Beijing: Wenhua yishu chubanshe, 1994, 502–53.

Yang Mo

Yang Mo, b. 1914, in Beijing, into a landlord family from Xiangyin County, Hunan Province, was influential in mainland China in the 1960s as a novelist. She also went by the names Yang Chengye and Yang Junmo and is the sister of the well-known film actress Bai Yang (*q.v.*).

Yang Mo's father held a Qing dynasty provincial degree and used the family fortune to establish a private university. Yang Mo studied at Xishan Warm Springs Girls' High School (Xishan wenquan nüzi zhongxue) in Beijing for three years (1927–30) but was unable to go on after her family went bankrupt, apparently because her father's private university failed. Her parents wanted to marry Yang Mo off to a rich family when she was only sixteen, threatening to cut off all financial support if she did not cooperate. Yang Mo said later that she had the courage to leave home and become an independent woman after reading the work of Feng Yuanjun (*q.v.*), who opposed arranged marriages.

Yang Mo worked at several jobs to support herself, including primary school teacher, home tutor, and shop assistant in a bookshop. Because she lived close to Peking University, Yang Mo came to know some of the students during the patriotic student movement of January 1935 and from them learned about the work of the CCP, joining the party in 1936. With the outbreak in the following year of the Sino-Japanese War, she became part of the war effort in the CCP-controlled central Hebei area of Shanxi-Chahar-Hebei Border Region (Jin-Cha-Ji bianqu). Her first posts were as director of the Women's National Salvation League (Fujiuhui) in Anguo County and head of the Propaganda Department of the Women's National Salvation League of Central Hebei. In both of these positions, she was required to move from village to village, mobilizing the local women. Yang Mo later became editor of the newspapers *Liming bao*, *Jin-Cha-Ji ribao*, and *Renmin ribao*, also editing their literary supplements from time to time.

With the establishment of the PRC in 1949, Yang Mo moved into the film industry, working as a screenwriter for the Scriptwriting Institute of the Central Film Bureau (Zhongyang dianyingju juben chuangzuosuo) and Beijing Film Studio. In 1963, she became a professional writer with the Beijing Writers' Association (Beijing zuojia xiehui); by 1981 Yang Mo had become its deputy chair. In 1963, she also became an executive member of the national Chinese Writers' Association. Since her first work, a prose piece entitled "Sketches of the Mountain Dwellers of South of Rehe" (Re-nan shandi jumin shenghuo sumiao), was published in 1934 in the Beijing magazine *Heibai*, Yang Mo has written numerous stories and prose pieces. Her novella *It Happened in the Reed Pond* (Weitang jishi, 1950) is about her experiences during the Sino-Japanese War. However, it is for her novel *The Song of Youth* (Qingchun zhi ge) that she is best known. The book has sold more than five million copies and become a modern Chinese bestseller. Yang Mo wrote the screenplay for the film, which served only to add to the book's popularity, in 1959. The heroine, a young intellectual called Lin Daojing, also became a household name. It is said that many youth who were uncertain and pessimistic about the future gained encouragement and inspiration from the novel.

The Song of Youth is semi-autobiographical; Yang Mo has said that the first half is based on her life. She first had the idea of writing it in 1950 while in hospital recuperating from an illness; her thoughts went back to many comrades who had sacrificed their lives in the revolution. Yang Mo had often thought that their deeds should be written down but had never had the time until then. Lying in her hospital bed, she wrote *The Song of Youth*. Despite lacking a complete formal education and never feeling adequate to the task, Yang Mo labored over the manuscript with the tenacity of a veteran revolutionary and by the end of 1952 had finished the second draft. Between then and 1958, when the novel was published, she continued to revise it. Yang Mo also showed the manuscript to many people and listened to what they had to say; in her modest way, she would say it was more appropriate to call the writing a collective creation than all her own work. Even though *The Song of Youth* was severely criticized during the Cultural Revolution by Yao Wenyuan, one of the infamous Gang of Four, for its bourgeois language and sentimentality, Yang Mo was still writing in the mid-1970s.

The writer started another novel—*Dawn Is about to Break in the East* (Dongfang yu xiao)—in 1972, which was published in 1980. In this one, she tried to toe the party line, but the book does not seem to have enjoyed the same kind of popularity as *The Song of Youth*. Although related to it, the second work had a male protagonist who had gone on the Long March and led the fight against the Japanese. After the Cultural Revolution, Yang Mo frequently appeared at literary gatherings and led delegations of writers to foreign countries. She also continued to write. Her works of this period include novels, reportage, and diaries. Her novels are *Fangfei's Song* (Fangfei zhi ge, 1986); *Breaking through Darkness* (Chongpo hei'an); and *Red, Red, the Shandan Flower* (Honghong de shandan hua, 1978). Her work of reportage was "Diary That Is Not a Diary" (Bushi riji de riji, 1980). Her diaries were *Confession—My Diaries* (Zibai—wo de riji, 1985); *Selected Stories of Yang Mo*; and *Selected Prose of Yang Mo* (1981).

In the 1930s, Yang Mo married Ma Jianmin (d. 1985), said to have been second in command at Beijing Normal University in the 1970s. She gave birth to her first child—a daughter named Ma Xuran—in 1937 and the following year had a son—Ma Qingke. Like many communist women of that period, however, Yang Mo often left her children in the care of others so that she would be free to carry on revolutionary work. Yang Mo had at least one other daughter—Ma Huoran—who was murdered not long after graduating from the Institute of Foreign Languages (Waiyu xueyuan) some time after 1960. By 1993, Yang Mo had several grandchildren. She has been troubled by heart disease since 1960 but continued to write into the 1990s. In 1994, Yang Mo coauthored with her daughter Ma Xuran a book on their family and the world of women.

Yang Mo acknowledges the influence on her work of eighteenth- and nineteenth-century Western and revolutionary Russian writers. She mentions Bingxin (*q.v.*) and

Ding Ling (*q.v.*) as the Chinese writers who have influenced her. Yang Mo was one of the most important writers on the Chinese mainland in the 1960s and 1970s. Her *The Song of Youth* was arguably the most influential novel among young people, who loved and emulated its heroine, Lin Daojing. *The Song of Youth* has been translated into more than a dozen foreign languages.

Lily Xiao Hong LEE

Hsu, Kai-yu. *Literature of the PRC*. Bloomington: Indiana University Press, 1980, 329–38.
———. "Yang Mo (1915–)." In *The Chinese Literary Scene: A Writer's Visit to the People's Republic*, Kai-yu Hsu. New York: Vintage Books, 1975, 139–55.
Huaxia funü mingren cidian. Beijing: Huaxia chubanshe, 1988, 423–24.
Nie Zhonglin. *Yang Mo zhi lu*. Huhhot: Nei-Menggu renmin chubanshe, 1988.
Song Ruizhi, ed. *Zhongguo funü wenhua tonglan*. Jinan: Shandong wenyi chubanshe, 1995, 521–22.
Women of China, October (1981): 16–17.
Yang Mo. *The Song of Youth*. Beijing: Foreign Languages Press, 1978.
———. "Liuyin jie." *Xinhua wenzhai*, no. 5 (1994): 114–15.
———. "Proud to Be a Woman." (Speech given at Wellesley College, April 1981.)
———. "Yang Mo zizhuan." *Zhongguo xiandai zuojia zhuanlüe*, vol. 1. Xuzhou: Xuzhou shifan xueyuan, 1981, 340–51.
Yingwen *Zhongguo funü*, ed. *Gujin zhuming funü renwu*, vol. 2. Shijiazhuang: Hebei renmin chubanshe, 1986, 896–900.
Zhongguo funü guanli ganbu xueyuan, ed. *Gujin Zhongwai nümingren cidian*. Beijing: Zhongguo guangbo dianshi chubanshe, 1980, 614–15.

Yang Shumin: *see* **Xin Fengxia**

Yang Tzu-lieh: *see* **Yang Zilie**

Yang Xiaofeng: *see* **Yang Zilie**

Yang Yizhi: *see* **Wang Yizhi**

Yang Zhihua
Yang Zhihua, 1900–1973, of Xiaoshan, Zhejiang Province, was a prominent CCP labor organizer in the 1920s.

The daughter of a silk merchant and landlord, she entered Hangzhou Girls' Normal School in 1917 and became involved in the May Fourth student protests of 1919. After graduation, Yang Zhihua worked at the *Weekly Review* (Xingqi pinglun), a political journal established by the well-known KMT member Shen Xuanlu (also known as Shen Dingyi) in Shanghai that year. Before long, Shen encouraged Yang Zhihua to work at the experimental peasant school he had founded near his family homestead in Yaqian. In late 1920, she married Shen's son, Shen Jianlong, and in 1921 gave birth to a daughter, Qu Duyi.

Yang Zhihua's long-term relationship with the CCP began in 1922 when she joined the Socialist Youth League. Yang Zhihua also wrote articles on women's issues, five of which appeared in *Women's Critic* (Funü pinglun) during 1922. One subject addressed with great intensity was divorce, which she advocated as a legitimate solution not only in the case of arranged marriages but also for free-choice marriages that had gone sour. At this time, her own marriage was already strained because Shen Jianlong had proven to be unreliable and reckless. Yang Zhihua enrolled in the newly established Shanghai University, a collaborative CCP-KMT venture, in 1923, and became more active in the efforts of the CCP to organize women workers. In the second half of 1924, she fell in love with Qu Qiubai (1899–1935), an influential communist who was serving as chairman of the Sociology Department. When the two decided they would like to marry, Yang Zhihua declared her divorce from Shen Jianlong by placing a public notice in a major Shanghai newspaper, the *Republican Daily*, in November, and announced at the same time the couple's marriage. Qu Qiubai adopted Yang Zhihua's daughter, and the couple resolved not to have any more children.

Yang Zhihua distinguished herself as a women's labor leader during the May Thirtieth Movement of 1925. She was elected one of the leaders of the Shanghai General Labor Union when it was founded on 1 June. Her efforts to draw women workers of the British-American Tobacco Company into the general strike that month proved quite successful. In October she became acting director of the communist Women's Bureau when Xiang Jingyu (*q.v.*) stepped down to go to Moscow for further study. At the Fifth Congress in May 1927, Yang Zhihua was elected to the Central Committee of the party and also officially confirmed as director of the Women's Bureau.

In 1928, she went to study in the Soviet Union, where her daughter was educated along with many other children of communist revolutionaries. Yang Zhihua returned to Shanghai in 1930 and worked in the underground. She lost her husband in 1935 when he was captured by KMT forces in Jiangxi and executed. Soon after, Yang Zhihua returned to Moscow where she resided until 1942. Upon returning to China, Yang Zhihua was arrested by the KMT in Xinjiang along with Mao Zemin, the brother of Mao Zedong (1893–1976), and Chen Tanqiu. She was not released from jail until 1946 and then immediately went to the communist revolutionary base area of Yan'an.

With the establishment of the PRC in 1949, Yang Zhihua was appointed to a number of prominent positions, the most significant of which were in the All-China Federation of Trade Unions, first serving on the Executive Committee (1948–66) and later as director of its Women's Department (1953–66). At the same time, Yang Zhihua held several important posts in the ACWF, including vice-chair from 1957 to 1966. She served on the Committee for Implementing the Marriage Law (1953) and on the Sino-Soviet Friendship Association (1949–54) and represented China at various international meetings. When the Cultural Revolution broke out, Yang Zhihua came under heavy attack, particularly because of her imprisonment in Xinjiang where it was alleged by ultra-leftists that she had divulged important information about the CCP. She was also attacked for her association with Qu Qiubai, who had come under harsh criticism, for despairing statements he had written about Marxism before his execution. Yang Zhihua developed cancer while incarcerated but was denied proper medical treatment. She died in the Beijing Medical School Hospital in 1973, having been released from prison three days earlier.

Christina K. GILMARTIN

Gilmartin, Christina K. *Engendering the Chinese Revolution: Radical Women, Communist Politics, and Mass Movements in the 1920s.* Berkeley: University of California Press, 1995.

Huaxia funü mingren cidian. Beijing: Huaxia chubanshe, 1988.

Jingsheng and Xiquan, eds. *Xin Zhongguo mingrenlu.* Nanchang: Jiangxi renmin chubanshe, 1987.

Perry, Elizabeth. *Shanghai on Strike: The Politics of Chinese Labor.* Stanford: Stanford University Press, 1993.

Yang Zhihua nüshi. "Lilun wenti de wojian." *Funü pinglun,* no. 56 (30 August 1922): 1.

Yang Zhiying. "Jiejie Yang Zhihua de zuihou si tian." *Shanghaitan,* no. 4 (1998): 52–53.

Zhonggong dangshi renwu zhuan, vol. 47. Xi'an: Shaanxi renmin chubanshe, 1980–1996, 301–18.

Yang Zilie

Yang Zilie, b. 1902, as Yang Xiaofeng in Zaoyang County, Hubei Province, was an early member of the CCP. She was the wife of Zhang Guotao (1897–1979), one of the founders of the CCP, who later transferred his allegiance to the KMT. During the 1920s and 1930s, Yang Zilie was associated with many well-known communist figures, including Xiang Jingyu (*q.v.*) and Deng Yingchao (*q.v.*).

Yang Zilie's father, Yang Yuda, held traditional feudal attitudes toward women but her mother, née Wang, was sufficiently progressive that she eventually loosened her daughter's bound feet and supported her desire for an education. Yang Zilie's paternal grandfather taught her to read, and she entered Wuchang Girls' Normal School in 1914 to study her great love: art. In autumn 1921, Yang Zilie became one of the earliest communists when she joined the new Hubei regional branch of the CCP. Yang Zilie first met Peking University student activist Zhang Guotao in Beijing in 1922 while studying drama at Fazheng University. The following year, she resigned from her course in protest against the military government and became involved with the KMT magazine *New Republic* (Xin minguo). In February 1924, Yang Zilie and Zhang Guotao entered into a "revolutionary marriage" (in which the couple dispensed with official ceremonies, declaring instead their commitment to each other and the revolution); her first taste of life with a high-ranking communist came three months later, when they were both arrested and imprisoned on a charge of sedition.

The charges against them were reduced to "attempting" sedition and then, inexplicably, their protestations of innocence were accepted; the two were released five months later. They made their separate ways to Shanghai in early 1925, where Zhang had been sent to continue his labor movement work. While he traveled extensively on behalf of the party, Yang Zilie remained in the city. Under the alias Fan Zhenhua, she joined the Women's Department within the Shanghai KMT organization and was also involved with the Shanghai Women's National Salvation Association formed by Song Qingling (*q.v.*).

In October Yang Zilie was sent, alone and seven months pregnant, to Moscow. She gave birth to a son (Haiwei) on 1 December in the port city of Vladivostok and eventually arrived in Moscow in early January 1926. Her sixteen months there were not happy: Yang Zilie was criticized for devoting too much attention to her new baby instead of her studies and was relieved to leave for home in April 1927. After spending some time with family in Hubei, in early 1928 she left her son in their care and returned to Shanghai to be with her husband. They were forced to move several times and then ordered to travel separately to Moscow; Zhang had been appointed the CCP delegate to the Comintern. Yang Zilie later admitted to being unhappy during this period at being ordered about by the party for no apparently good reason. Arriving in Moscow toward the end of that year, she attended Sun Yat-sen University but during a party purge at the end of 1929 was made to spend three months working under observation in a factory (the Seventh Printing Works). Zhang Guotao perceived her "banishment" as a symbol of punishment for him.

After two years in Moscow, the couple eventually managed to extricate themselves from the political strife at the university and traveled back to China under false passports, reaching Shanghai in late January 1931. They were there for only two months when Zhang was ordered in March to the E-yu-wan (Hubei-Henan-Anhui) soviet region in central China to lead guerrilla forces from which the Fourth Front Red Army were formed; permission for Yang Zilie to accompany him was denied. They were not to see one another again for almost seven years.

Yang Zilie described her life over the next few years as extremely difficult. Unable to contact her husband and constantly worried that her identity would be exposed, she moved about between Shanghai and Wuchang, studying English and typing at various times but finally returning to Shanghai. Yang Zilie had lost contact with the party by this time and enrolled as Yang Jingqin in a midwifery school attached to Shanghai Huili Hospital. Soon after the outbreak in July 1937 of the Sino-Japanese War, the city fell to the Japanese. Yang Zilie remained there but managed to contact the Eighth Route Army in Nanjing. She finally received a letter from her family telling her that Zhang Guotao was in Yan'an and wanted her to join him with their son. Yang Zilie arrived in Yan'an in September 1937, and her parents sent her son there the following month.

As was usual at that time, Yang Zilie had been removed from party membership because she had lost contact with the party for several years, from approximately 1931 to 1937 in her case. The Organization Department of the Central Committee refused to readmit her without an investigation into her recent history. Yang Zilie was extremely upset at this insult, given her early revolutionary activity and CCP membership and the fact that her husband was now chairman of the border region government. It must have come as no surprise to Zhang Guotao, however, who was by that time clearly being frozen out of the party leadership: he was considered little more than a traitor to Mao Zedong because of his fractious behavior on the Long March when he disobeyed Central Committee directives. In his autobiography, Zhang recounts his fury on hearing Mao Zedong "cackle maliciously" at how fitting it was that Zhang Guotao's son should play the role of the traitor Zhang Mutao in a school performance. No doubt correctly, Zhang Guotao perceived these "blows" at his wife and son as covert attacks against him.

On 4 April 1938—the traditional annual festival of *qingming* (sweeping of the graves of ancestors)—Zhang Guotao led a small official delegation on a visit to the nearby grave of the Yellow Emperor. To Yang Zilie's surprise, he did not return to Yan'an with the others, and it was a matter of weeks before she discovered that Zhang had in fact fled Yan'an and the CCP. Yang Zilie was then six months pregnant. After several weeks of fruitless requests to the Central Committee, she finally approached Mao Zedong directly and won from him a written note giving her permission to leave Yan'an, ostensibly to have the baby in her native place with family.

Zhang Guotao joined the KMT and was elected to the National Assembly. He played an increasingly less active political role, however, and soon after the Sino-Japanese War ended in 1945 moved to Taiwan as it became clear that a communist victory was imminent. Yang Zilie had been "completely fed up with politics" by the end of her brief stay in Yan'an and was relieved to move to Hong Kong in 1949. After recovering from a broken thigh in 1950, she lived a peaceful life with her husband in Hong Kong, happy to spend time with their grandchildren, well away from the political stage. In late 1968, the couple moved to Toronto, Canada. The eldest and youngest of their three sons—Hai-wei (a mathematician) and Yu-chuan (an engineer)—were still living in Toronto in 1982; their middle son, a doctor, had moved to New York.

Zhang Guotao moved into a nursing home in 1973 and died on 3 December 1979. Yang Zilie moved into a separate nursing home at some stage and according to newspaper reports was still alive when her husband died. Despite extensive searches of public records and newspapers and inquiries at Chinese community groups and nursing homes in Toronto (carried out by Tom Fuller from Washington, D.C.), no further information on Yang Zilie has been unearthed.

In the early 1970s, both Zhang Guotao and Yang Zilie published memoirs of their early years as active members of the Chinese revolution, and these are important sources that provide an alternative view of individuals and events in that period. Yang Zilie wrote of her husband that, at seventy, he was "content with a poor but happy life; and he looks back not with a sense of grief, but with a sense of relief." She, too, appeared content with her life, describing herself as "an ordinary woman who lived through an extraordinary time."

Sue WILES

Chang Kuo-t'ao [Zhang Guotao]. *The Rise of the Chinese Communist Party 1921–1927: The Autobiography of Chang Kuo-t'ao*, 2 vols. Lawrence, Wichita: University Press of Kansas, 1971, 1972.

Price, Jane L. *Cadres, Commanders, and Commissars: The Training of the Chinese Communist Leadership, 1920–1945.* Boulder, Colo.: Westview Press, 1976.

Terrill, Ross. *Madame Mao: The White-Boned Demon: A Biography of Madame Mao Zedong*. New York: A Touchstone Book published by Simon & Schuster, 1984, 1992.

Yang Zilie. *Zhang Guotao furen huiyilu*. Hong Kong: Zilian chubanshe, 1970.

———. "A Biographical Sketch of Chang Kuo-t'ao." In *The Rise of the Chinese Communist Party 1921–1927: The Autobiography of Chang Kuo-t'ao*, vol. 1, Zhang Guotao. Lawrence, Wichita: University Press of Kansas, 1971, xiii–xvii.

Zhang Shujun. *Zhang Guotao*. Shijiazhuang: Hebei renmin chubanshe, 1997.

Ye Gongshao

Ye Gongshao, b. 1908, in Jiujiang, Jiangxi Province, is a medical doctor who has devoted her professional life to children's health and health care education; she is also known in the West as K.S. Yeh.

Her paternal grandfather, Ye Yanlan, held a metropolitan degree (*jinshi*, 1851) and served in late Qing as a Hanlin bachelor (*shujishi*) in the Hanlin Academy. He was appointed as a director (*langzhong*) in the Ministry of Revenue and as secretary to the Council of State (*junji zhangjing*) in the Ministry of Armed Services. Her father, Ye Peiqiang, held a provincial degree (*juren*) and was appointed to the civil service in the prefecture of Jiangxi. An older brother, Ye Gongchuo, was a calligrapher of great note. He was a follower of Sun Yat-sen (1866–1925) and became minister of Communications in the provisional government established immediately after the 1911 Revolution, later serving as undersecretary to the Ministry of Communications in the 1927 KMT government in Nanjing.

Born into a traditional gentry family, Ye Gongshao experienced the usual pro-male–anti-female discrimination of the time in which sons were sent abroad to further their studies and daughters were married out to families of similar social status even before high school was completed. Ye Gongshao was determined to break out of this mold and, after graduating at the age of nineteen from the Tientsin Sino-Anglo Girls' School (Zhongxi nüzi zhongxue), applied to Nankai University, also in Tianjin. Two years later, Ye Gongshao was admitted to the pre-medical course at Yanjing [Yen-ching] University and then in 1930 admitted to Peking Union Medical College (Beiping xiehe yixueyuan), whence she graduated in 1935 with an M.D. That year, she married Huang Zhenxiang (1910–1987), who later became an academician of the Chinese Academy of Sciences; they had two sons and two daughters.

Ye Gongshao remained at Peking Union Medical College after graduation, working in the Faculty of Public Health first as a tutor and then as a lecturer. She also worked part-time in infant and childcare with the Beiping First Office of Public Health (Beiping diyi weisheng shiwusuo), researching the nutritional requirements of children for healthy growth and development. The Medical College was forced to close in 1941, and two years later Ye Gongshao and her husband fled to Chongqing, where she continued her work at the Central Institute of Public Health. Ye Gongshao returned to Beijing at the end of the Sino-Japanese War and established a Gynecology and Pediatrics Center under the auspices of the Beijing branch of the Central Institute of Public Health. She was appointed its director.

The growth and development of children and adolescents and puberty in young adults became the focus of Ye Gongshao's scientific research. In 1947–48, she traveled to the United States, where she studied the growth and development of children. Upon her return, Ye Gongshao compiled a comprehensive review of the work done in China in the previous fifty years in those two related fields. After the founding of the PRC, she became deputy head of the Public Health Department of Beijing Medical School and director of the Research Center in the Children's and Adolescents' Health Care Institute. She compiled and revised the 1960 and 1965 editions of *Health Care Study of Children and Adolescents*, teaching texts that greatly assisted practitioners and those who worked in the field of children's and adolescents' health care education. An extensive study of the growth and development of children and adolescents was launched in Beijing and surrounding rural areas in the 1950s and 1960s, and Ye Gongshao's *Study of Puberty in Students in Beijing* (Beijingshi xuesheng qingchunqi yanjiu) opened a new area of inquiry. This research report was instrumental in promoting the development of health programs related to puberty.

Between 1979 and 1983, Ye Gongshao visited the United States, Britain, Japan, the Philippines, and Malaysia to study children's and adolescents' health care, particularly the psychological and social difficulties associated with puberty. In both 1979 and 1985, she proposed a comprehensive China-wide research study to evaluate children's growth, development, and health. She directed a massive multi-disciplinary scientific investigation that covered 1.2 million students of both sexes ranging in age from seven to twenty-two and from twenty-seven ethnic minorities as well as those of Han ethnicity. She also worked in the field herself. The data gathered in this investigation was invaluable. The Children's and Adolescents' Health Care Research Center set up in 1982 by Beijing Medical School was largely the result of Ye Gongshao's efforts. She was made honorary president, and the center has initiated various studies into children's and adolescents' health care.

Through personal commitment and devotion to her work, Ye Gongshao has been responsible for fostering several generations of health workers in preventive medicine and contributed significantly to science through the several works she has written and compiled.

WANG Bing
(Translated by Li Sheung Yee)

Ye Gongshao. *Ertong shaonian weishengxue.* Beijing: Renmin weisheng chubanshe, 1960, 1965.
———. *Zhongguo yixue baike quanshu: Ertong shaonian weishengxue.* Shanghai: Kexue jishu chubanshe, 1983.
———. *Zhongxiaoxuesheng weisheng baojian shouce.* Beijing: Kexue puji chubanshe, 1987.
———. "Physical Growth of Chinese Children: A Summary of Work Done During the Past Half Century." *Chinese Medical Journal,* 78 (1959): 439–45.
———. "A Study of Beijing Student Adolescents." *Chinese Medical Journal,* 94 (1981): 101–08.
Ye Guangjun. "Ertong shaonian weishengxue jia, yixue jiaoyu jia—Ye Gongshao." *Zhonghua yufang yixue zazhi,* 22 (1988): 193–95.
Ye Guangjun and Lu Zizhi. "Ye Gongshao." In *Zhongguo xiandai kexuejia zhuanji,* vol. 3. Beijing: Kexue chubanshe, 1992, 605–11.
Yeh, K.S. "Peking Diets, I, II, III." *Chinese Medical Journal,* 54 (1938): 201–22; 56 (1939): 99–110; 56 (1939): 225–31.
———. "Soybean Milk as a Food for Young Infants." *Chinese Medical Journal,* 54 (1938): 1–12.

Ye Qu: *see* **Chen Xuezhao**

Ye Qun

Ye Qun, 1917–1971, originally named Ye Yijing, was born into a humble family in Fuzhou, Fujian Province. She rose to become the nation's second most powerful female political figure, after Jiang Qing (*q.v.*), and arguably the de facto commander of the massive Chinese army between the years 1967 and 1971. Her husband, Marshal Lin Biao (1907–1971), was defense minister from 1959 and the "closest comrade-in-arms" and anointed successor of Mao Zedong (1893–1976) during the Cultural Revolution. The mysterious flight and crash in which Ye Qun and Lin Biao died graphically signified the bankruptcy of Mao's Cultural Revolution, which marked the most tumultuous years in the PRC.

When pursuing her higher education in the early 1930s in Beijing, Ye Qun not only distinguished herself as a diligent student but also emerged as an able young leader. She actively participated in the 29 December 1935 student movement that called for a united front against Japanese aggression. Her patriotism and revolutionary fervor as much as her humble background probably predisposed her to the proletarian cause championed by the CCP. Ye Qun soon chose to start her new life in Yan'an, the Mecca of the Chinese communist revolution, despite the obvious dangers and hardship.

Idealism aside, in the down-to-earth world of Yan'an she quickly became a sought-after commodity (one of the "Eight Yan'an Beauties"). Ye Qun was hotly pursued by senior party cadres because it was rare at that time for a young and good-looking female intellectual to join the communists, then still perceived as red bandits. Mao Zedong and Red Army commander-in-chief Zhu De (1886–1976) reportedly played matchmaker for Ye Qun and the legendary Red Army general Lin Biao soon after he returned from medical treatment in Moscow in 1942. As Mao's favorite lieutenant, Lin Biao proved to be the CCP's most brilliant military leader.

Many latter-day critics have dismissed the relationship between Lin and Ye Qun as a marriage of expediency, implying that her motives were simply vanity and a lust for power. However, despite Ye Qun's initial reservations—Lin Biao's two previous marriages had failed—the couple appear to have remained genuinely devoted to each other. When she gave birth to their first child, Lin Liheng (better known as Lin Doudou), in a poverty-stricken Yan'an hospital, Lin Biao sent bowls of chicken soup on stormy nights to show his affection. Almost three decades later, at the height of their political career, he composed a prophetic love poem to his wife: "Though the color of our hair is different, in the same pit we shall rest together." When, on the eve of the Cultural Revolution, after Ye Qun was subjected to repeated innuendo by the wife of then-propaganda chief Lu Dingyi, Lin Biao presented to the Politburo an affidavit stating that his wife had been a virgin when they married. This was a rather bizarre incident in high-level CCP politics.

A gregarious social being, Ye Qun nevertheless struck problems in her marriage. This was largely because of Lin Biao's eccentric nature, but his extremely poor health was also another factor. He had received a gunshot wound to his chest, and his nervous system had been shattered during the Sino-Japanese War. Lin Biao was an aloof statesman who not only loathed the protocol of meeting visiting foreign leaders but also rarely engaged socially with his colleagues. He had a low tolerance to light, wind, and cool temperatures, could not bear the sight of a landscape painting, and the slightest hint of water could bring on diarrhea. Ye Qun sometimes called her husband a "living corpse," and his unsociable, rigid, and puritanical lifestyle, in addition to his chronic illness, certainly suggests that they did not enjoy normal relations in their marriage.

However, her husband's peculiarities left room for Ye Qun to maneuver behind his back. All she needed to do to keep him away and in the dark, for example, was to lower the temperature of her room. Further opportunities for manipulation existed because Lin Biao frequently relied on her to interact on his behalf with the political and military elite. On the other hand, Ye Qun was able to defuse the great tension between Lin Biao and Mao's wife, Jiang Qing, during the Cultural Revolution, and Ye Qun also kept her husband informed about what was happening outside his residential compound, Maojiawan. It is indeed difficult to judge whether Lin Biao's political acuity was handicapped or assisted by his wife.

Apart from her appointment as a junior party functionary, Ye Qun's political career was relatively uneventful in the first twenty or so years of her marriage. This may have been partly because of Lin Biao's choice to remain on the political sidelines despite his high party and military status, albeit without portfolio. It was also partly because of the constraints Lin Biao placed on his wife: his mottoes for her included "never overstep one's mark" and "never ride the political tiger." There had never been any indication up to that point that Ye Qun was a vicious "ambitionist" in the making. Nor was there any evident difference when, against his will, Lin Biao was called upon to assume the exhausting job of defense minister in the wake of Mao's purge of Peng Dehuai in 1959.

However, toward the end of 1965 circumstances started to change for Ye Qun as, increasingly, she became a major player at Mao's court. Freudians may argue that this was a Lady Chatterley turning to politics when opportunities presented themselves (as to Ye Qun's possible loose behavior, the authorities later disclosed material pointing to a flirtation with chief of staff and Lin Biao's right-hand man General Huang Yongsheng). The crucial factor in her rise, however, was undoubtedly Mao's encouragement. With his blessing, Ye Qun was first appointed director of her husband's office. Then Lin Biao's health finally collapsed in autumn 1962, after three hectic years as head of national defense. Instead of allowing him to retire, Mao granted sick leave and encouraged Ye Qun to take on more responsibility, including representing Lin Biao at Politburo meetings. She played the most prominent role in the December 1965 Enlarged Politburo Standing Members Conference that purged Chief of Staff Luo Ruiqing. Whatever their differing intentions, Mao and Ye Qun had clearly drawn first blood in the Cultural Revolution.

Apparently needing the full support of the military, in August 1966 Mao promoted Lin Biao as his successor-designate. At the same time, Mao made Ye Qun one of those responsible for dealing with the Cultural Revolution within the military. A year later, on the recommendation of Premier Zhou Enlai (1898–1976), she was formally appointed to the five-member Central Military Commission in charge of the daily running of military affairs. The other four members were the chief of staff, the air force commander, the navy political commissar, and the head of the Logistics Department. Ye Qun wielded extraordinary clout in her position because the other members of the group had all been her husband's subordinates. She also gained privileged access to Mao and continued to act as the guardian of her husband's office, which handled vital information and decisions. At the Ninth Party Congress in April 1969, Ye Qun was elected to the Central Committee for the first time and, despite her husband's initial disapproval, elevated to full membership of the Politburo.

Although living dangerously in the game of court politics, Ye Qun was hardly a good politician. She may have been a member of the highest policy making body in the land, but her exercise of political duties was, like her husband's, little more than "I circle when the Chairman circles." Both followed and endorsed Mao's policies despite any reservations they might have harbored deep in their hearts, and both were clearly culpable in promoting the cult of Mao. They put a great deal of effort into promoting the interests of the PLA and stabilizing the army during the chaotic years of the Cultural Revolution. However, even these efforts were tainted by a factional concern to boost the representation of the Fourth Field Army, Lin Biao's key "mountaintop" during the revolutionary period. Under their reign, the PLA became the role model for Chinese socialism in the mid-1960s in terms of ideological correctness and state reconstruction. During the Cultural Revolution, the military even took over administrative duties and headed most of the provincial revolutionary committees. Lin Biao and Ye Qun's policy of "politics in command" (*zhengzhi guashuai*) within the army soon placed the military center stage in politics. Ironically, the expansion of the military's influence into politics, though initially occurring with Mao's blessing, led to the demise of its architects as soon as the erratic chairman perceived that the army was overstepping the mark. After the Ninth Party Congress, Mao apparently considered restoring civilian authority over the military. The real trouble for Ye Qun and Lin Biao, however, emerged at Lushan when Mao questioned whether the military was really backing his Cultural Revolution.

At the Lushan Conference in August 1970, the dispute between the military and the radical Cultural Revolution Small Group of which Zhang Chunqiao was a prominent member initially occurred over the state chairmanship. It soon developed into a fierce struggle, with the ranking generals, together with Ye Qun's political ally and fellow provincial Chen Boda, launching a bitter attack on Zhang Chunqiao, who followed Mao closely in opposing the idea of restoring the state chairmanship. While the position would have been of little value to Mao, he quickly sensed that the generals were venting, through their attack on Zhang Chunqiao, their unhappiness with the Cultural Revolution. Once Mao discovered that Ye Qun had masterminded these developments and felt that his Cultural Revolution was at stake, Mao-Lin/Ye relations soured dramatically. Mao demanded self-criticisms from Ye Qun and the generals. They complied, but even after she made repeated self-criticisms Mao would not let the matter rest. Instead, he remarked that Ye Qun "loves gossip and has not learned Marxism-Leninism well." An imperial comment such as this spelled doom for Ye Qun's political life.

Nor was she a good and loving mother. Her manipulations and shrewdness, including privately launching a nationwide campaign to pursue perfect marriage partners for her two children, clearly backfired. Both of them had strong characters and refused to budge, leading to deep mutual distrust and behind-the-scenes maneuvering. Lin Doudou, her father's darling, even attempted suicide to register her protest, while Lin Biao was kept completely in the dark concerning his daughter's trauma. The long-standing mother-daughter feud eventually led Lin Doudou to abandon her family by blowing the whistle on her parents on that fateful night of 12 September

1971, revealing their plan to flee abroad. This action immediately set in motion a chain of events (including the still-secret telephone call from Zhou Enlai that prompted Ye Qun to run for her life) that resulted in the destruction of Lin Doudou's family, including her beloved father. Historians remain puzzled by her apparent betrayal, which was, paradoxically, based on a loyalty to Mao that her father had all along been teaching her and the whole country. On the other hand, Lin Doudou, like the tragic Greek heroine Electra, has since set out to clear her father's name, while not wavering from the belief that her mother was the culprit. Lamentably, the tragic family politics in Ye Qun's household were as complex and astonishing as the larger elite politics in Mao's China.

Ye Qun's son, Lin Liguo (1945–1971), was a clever science student and, like his father, an acute observer of the dark side of Chinese elite politics at the highest level. Lin Liguo quickly established a clique of loyal followers after being catapulted to the position of deputy head of the Air Force's Warfare Department in October 1969. Most of them were mid-ranking officers, and a few had been initially sent by Ye Qun to spy on him. When Mao turned against Lin Liguo's parents, he, once considering Mao the greatest feudal tyrant of modern times, raised with confidants the idea of a military coup (the "571 Program"). Later, sensing that Mao was coming to get his parents, Lin hastily drew up a plot to assassinate the chairman. Probably neither Ye Qun nor Lin Biao had any knowledge of their son's desperate plan until the last minute, when it was abandoned. In any case, the plot could only have added another serious problem to their already difficult struggle for survival. By then, it seemed to Ye Qun that exile was the only way to exit Mao's politics and save her family and herself. The final straw was the premier's mysterious telephone call. Three hours later, Ye Qun, villain and victim of the most radical and violent period of CCP politics, had perished. In the early hours of 13 September 1971, her partly charred body was found near the wreckage of a Chinese Trident in a remote area of the Mongolia desert. However cruel and unjust, this sickening picture has since become the enduring image of Ye Qun.

A three-year national campaign to disgrace her name and Lin Biao's soon began. Both were labeled counterrevolutionary careerists, traitors, and conspirators. These alleged crimes were reaffirmed in a 1980–81 show trial held under the new regime of Deng Xiaoping. To exercise full control of the gun, he decided it was necessary to "whip the dead tiger" and cleanse the military of Lin Biao's lingering influence, especially within the Fourth Field Army. Many of its leaders had not found the official verdict fair or credible.

The political role of Ye Qun and the truth of the whole Lin Biao affair remain cloudy and contentious for many historians. It is worth noting that Chinese elite politics largely took place in a black box and that in the power game at Mao's court few players could afford to be their real self. Who was Ye Qun? What drove this otherwise charming and "well-behaved" lady to such a tragic end? How true are the official accounts depicting her as an evil schemer, a swindler with an unquenchable lust for power, vanity, and conspiracy? We may never know the real Ye Qun. We can only report that as a former student of literature, she seemed to enjoy reading. Among the

Western works she loved were *Henry IV, A Tale of Two Cities, The Count of Monte Cristo*, and, especially, Stendhal's *The Charterhouse of Parma*. Ye Qun also revealed to her staff a great admiration for the Renaissance, a time when individual emancipation and sexual love first became legitimate subjects of humanistic literature after the long darkness of the Middle Ages. All else is hard to tell with certainty.

Warren SUN

Guan Weixun. *Wo suo zhidao de Ye Qun*. Beijing: Zhongguo wenxue chubanshe, 1993.
Huang Yao. *Sanci danan busi de Luo Ruiqing dajiang*. Beijing: Zhonggong dangshi chubanshe, 1994.
Jiao Ye. *Ye Qun zhi mi—yige mishu yanzhong de Ye Qun yu Lin Biao*. Beijing: Zhongguo wenlian chuban gongsi, 1993.
Nan Zhi. *Ye Qun yeshi*. Liaoning: Shenyang chubanshe, 1988.
Teiwes, Frederick, and Warren Sun. *The Tragedy of Lin Biao—Riding the Tiger during the Cultural Revolution*. London: Hurst & Company, 1996.
Wang Nianyi. *1949–1989 nian de Zhongguo: Dadongluan de niandai*. Henan: Henan renmin chubanshe, 1988.
Xiao Sike. *Chaoji shenpan: Shenli Lin Biao fangeming jituan qinliji*. Jinan: Jinan chubanshe, 1992.
Zhang Ning. *Zhang Ning huiyilu*. Hohhot: Neimenggu wenhua chubanshe, 1998.
Zhang Yunsheng. *Maojiawan jishi: Lin Biao mishu huiyilu*. Beijing: Chunqiu chubanshe, 1988.

Ye Shuhua

Ye Shuhua, b. 1927, in Guangzhou, Guangdong Province, is an astronomer who pioneered research into astro-geodynamics in China. She graduated from the Mathematics and Astronomy Department of Zhongshan University in 1949 and in 1951 began working at Xujiahui Observatory, soon to become Shanghai Astronomical Observatory, Chinese Academy of Sciences.

In the 1950s and 1960s, the focus of Ye Shuhua's research was on universal time and Earth's rotation. Universal time, which provides essential information and data for geodetic survey and navigation, has been the subject of international scientific cooperation since the nineteenth century. One of the first priorities of the newly established PRC in the early 1950s was to produce a precise map of the country. The only Chinese observatory working with the universal time project, however, was Xujiahui Observatory, which had been established by French Catholic missionaries in 1872. Despite its long-term involvement in the project, the observatory had only outdated 1930s equipment to work with, and Purple Mountain (Zijinshan) Observatory in Nanjing, under the auspices of the Chinese Academy of Sciences, took over Xujiahui Observatory's administration. The State Council then provided personnel and resources for the universal time project in 1954, instructing the Academy of Sciences to give it top priority. Initially under the direction of Wang Shouguan and Gong Huiren, by 1958 the project had reached the stage where the emission of time signals met basic requirements.

At this time, Ye Shuhua was given the task of developing the Joint Chinese Universal Time System (JCUTS). Starting with two major observatories in Shanghai and

Nanjing, she linked them to observatories in Wuhan, Beijing, Xi'an, and Kunming to observe and process Chinese Universal Time. After much experimentation, Ye Shuhua and her team decided upon an analytical method for system differentiation that was suitable for the country. In 1963, China's universal time jumped in elevation to second in the world in terms of precision; it previously had ranked last. This satisfied domestic needs but, even more, in the eyes of the international community it was a major triumph for China. In 1965, after national appraisal and examination, the JCUTS was set as the basic national standard; in 1978, 1981, and 1982 the project was awarded the National Science Congress Prize, a Chinese Academy of Sciences First Prize, and a National Natural Science Second Prize, respectively.

The field of universal time came to the forefront of science in the 1970s and 1980s along with advances in outer space technology. Ye Shuhua took this opportunity to suggest that the technology and equipment at Shanghai Observatory be upgraded and a comprehensive systematic data processing team be established. She also organized the participation of all Chinese observatories in the 1980–85 joint global observation of Earth's rotation. One result of this joint observation was international confirmation that the precision of China's technology had greatly increased. Another was the founding in 1988 of the International Earth Rotation Service (IERS), which China joined the same year. The IERS replaced the Earth Rotation Section of the Universal Time Bureau (Bureau International de l'Heure) and the International Polar Motion Service. Because of her timely promotion of the need to upgrade technology, Shanghai Observatory won the prestigious opportunity to join this transformed area of research. The Chinese Academy of Sciences awarded a First Prize in Scientific and Technological Advancement to the Joint International Observation of Earth Rotation project.

Shanghai Observatory established a satellite laser ranging (SLR) station and a very long baseline interferometry (VLBI) station and participated in many international projects, thus taking the lead in the SLR and the VLBI networks in China. Its participation in the IERS makes Shanghai Observatory one of only two global information analysis centers in the world applying SLR, lunar laser ranging (LLR), and VLBI technology.

New technology not only improved the IERS but also made it possible to observe the movement of Earth's tectonic plates. In 1982, Ye Shuhua instigated China's participation in international cooperation in geodynamics, solid geodynamics, solid earth, and natural disasters programs, using VLBI and SLR. Over its years of cooperation with various countries, Shanghai Observatory has become a joint observatory base able to use VLBI, SLR, the global positioning system (GPS), and the Precise Range and Range Rate Equipment system (PRARE). It is thus one of only six bases in the world that possess and are able to use these four technologies.

She was appointed in 1991 as chief scientist to a study of China's crustal motion. This Key Basic Research Project, entitled "Contemporary Crustal Motions and Geodynamics Research and Applications," was carried out in collaboration with the relevant research arms of the Chinese Academy of Sciences, the State Bureau of Seismology, the National Bureau of Surveying and Mapping, and the Military Bureau of Surveying and Mapping. The project provided preliminary data on the crustal motion of various tectonic plates and revealed the current state of China's crustal motion. It verified that movement of the Indian Plate, which is to the south of the Eurasian Plate, is causing the land mass of China to move slightly eastward; further research is being undertaken.

Crustal motion is linked to earthquakes, volcanic activity, variations in sea levels, and natural disasters. Asia-Pacific geology is the most complex in the world, and the region, which is densely populated, has been visited by many natural disasters over the centuries. It is for this reason that regional geodynamics is an important area of study. In 1994, Ye Shuhua initiated an international project on the basis of existing cooperation from four Chinese government departments (those involved in her Key Basic Research Project, above) with the National Aeronautics Space Agency, the United States's space authority. Her proposal was called Asia-Pacific Space Geodynamics (APSG) and was supported at the United Nations's Asia Pacific Economic Cooperation (APEC) Conference on the Application of Space Technology to Sustainable Development, held in Beijing in 1994. At the 1995 joint conference of the International Association of Geodesy and the International Association of Geophysics held in the United States, Ye Shuhua's proposal was adopted by the International Association of Geodesy. At the first meeting of the joint project held in Shanghai in 1996, she was elected chair of the inaugural Executive Committee, whose members represented Australia, China, Indonesia, Japan, Russia, South Korea, and the United States.

Ye Shuhua was appointed research professor of Shanghai Astronomical Observatory in 1976 and its director from 1981 to 1993. She has been active throughout her career in professional circles and was vice-president of the Chinese Astronomical Society between 1978 and 1988 and its honorary president since 1989. Ye Shuhua was elected as an academician of the Chinese Academy of Sciences in 1980, a foreign member of the Royal Astronomical Society of Britain in 1985, and vice-president of the International Astronomical Union from 1988 to 1994. Since 1981 she has been a member of the Appraisal Panel for Astronomy of the State Council's Committee for the Conferral of Academic Degrees.

Ye Shuhua has been given another, singular, honor for her pioneering work in astro-geodynamics, however: Purple Mountain Observatory in Nanjing has named a newly discovered asteroid after her.

XI Zezong
(Translated by Zhongwei Song)

Hong Kong Polytechnic University, 29 October 1999, at <http://www.polyu.edu.hk>, accessed 20 May 2000.
Yingwen *Zhongguo funü*, ed. *Gujin zhuming funü renwu*, vol. 2. Shijiazhuang: Hebei renmin chubanshe, 1986, 1079.
Zhongguo xiandai kexuejia zhuanji, vol. 5. Beijing: Kexue chubanshe, 1994, 294–300.
Zhonghua quanguo funü lianhehui, Zuzhi lianluobu. ed. *Zhongguo nüyuanshi*. Shenyang: Liaoning renmin chubanshe, 1995, 81–83.

Ye Tao: *see* **Yeh T'ao**

Ye Yijing: *see* **Ye Qun**

Yeh, K.S.: *see* **Ye Gongshao**

Yeh T'ao

Yeh T'ao [Ye Tao], 1905–1970, of Kao-hsiung, Taiwan, played a leading role in the social movement that arose during the period of Japanese colonial rule. She was a public school teacher but later participated in and became an important cadre in both the Taiwan Peasants' Union (Taiwan nung-min tsu-ho) and the Taiwan Culture Association (Taiwan wen-hua hsieh-hui). Yeh T'ao was married to the famous writer Yang K'uei [Yang Kui] (1905–1985).

Yeh T'ao was born into a middle-class family. Her father was head of a neighborhood (*pao-cheng*). She had her own maid when young because of her mother's bound feet. Yeh T'ao inherited her mother's disposition, being candid, enthusiastic, fond of the pursuit of freedom, and the first to act against the old ways. Although it was in response to pain rather than feminist awareness, her rebellious childhood act of unbinding her feet and throwing the cloth into the sea reveals her resolute and steadfast character. She received a traditional Chinese education from a young age in the *Four Books*, *Five Classics*, T'ang and Sung poetry, and the various schools of Chinese philosophy.

Yeh T'ao also received a Japanese-style modern education when she attended Hop'ing Public School. This, however, symbolized the paradox in which Taiwanese intellectuals found themselves at that time. The modern education they received from their Japanese rulers provided them with new modes of thought and the means to critique tradition and colonialism, even though the education system itself was colonialist in nature. This created an almost irreconcilable tension in the students of that era. As a woman, Yeh T'ao was also subject to the gender strictures of traditional culture, and she therefore felt more strongly than did men the evils of the "old social system." Her background and lot in life thus enabled her to draw from her modern education the critical strength to oppose both tradition and colonialism.

Yeh T'ao studied for three years at a teacher training institute attached to T'ai-nan Women's Public School (T'ai-nan nü-tzu kung-hsüeh-hsiao fu-she chiao-yüan yang-hsi-so) before returning to teach at Ho-p'ing Public School; she was later transferred to Kao-hsiung Third Public School. Yeh T'ao was then about seventeen years old, but her students gave her the nickname "Black Hen" (Wu-chi mu) because she was comparatively dark-skinned and stout, had a loud and sonorous voice, and was bold and generous by nature. A black hen is considered to be more nutritious than other chickens, so the nickname sat well with Yeh T'ao's physique and disposition. According to her descendants, who recall "barbarian" relatives coming to visit, Yeh T'ao had non-Han Chinese blood on the maternal side of her family. Although it is impossible to know much of Yeh T'ao's maternal lineage, given Chinese society's preoccupation with paternal lineage, oral history recollections such as this offer considerable assistance in reconstructing the influences that formed her.

Around the time of World War I, Taiwan felt the impact of several international movements aimed at reclaiming the power of the less powerful—nations, classes and gender alike. The Taiwan Culture Association, which became the vanguard of social and cultural movements, was founded in 1921 in order to address meetings all over the island on cultural issues, both local and international. Taiwan's Japanese rulers had long dictated policy for the sugar industry, and the exploitation of workers and peasants by the colonial government and industrialists gradually stimulated the beginnings of a political movement. The Er Lin Incident of 1925 was a curtain raiser; it led to the Taiwan Peasants' Union (established in 1926), which flourished throughout the late 1920s.

Formed essentially from the Feng-shan and Ta-chia Unions, the Taiwan Peasants' Union was centered on Kao-hsiung, located in the sugar-producing region of Kao-p'ing. Chien Chi, a founder of the Peasants' Union, was a colleague of Yeh T'ao, and they frequently discussed the problems of the sugar farmers and the colonial government. She had been quick to join the union and was one of very few female social agitators at that time. It was through the union that Yeh T'ao met her future husband, Yang K'uei. He had been recruited in 1927, after completing studies at a Japanese university, by people in the community who were eager to have him return and take part in the social and cultural movement in Taiwan. Yeh T'ao noticed him during one of the union's campaigns and invited him to write an inscription on her fan. Yang K'uei first contemplated writing the phrase "Laws to Punish Bandits" (Japanese laws to punish Taiwanese dissidents). Then, because he admired Yeh T'ao's daring in becoming a "bandit" who opposed Japanese rule, Yang K'uei wrote the three characters meaning "Bandit Woman." Their fate was sealed from that moment on.

During the period of Japanese rule, Yeh T'ao was belligerent and uncompromising. An excellent orator, she would visit the fields to discuss her ideas, presenting a sharp image in a simple, long black Taiwanese skirt, her hair combed back in a knot. Yeh T'ao attracted large crowds to street corners as she related historical events and spoke uncompromisingly of ending Japanese rule. Consequently, Yeh T'ao was in and out of Japanese prisons, being arrested twelve times in all.

The Peasants' Union was at its strongest from 1926 to 1928, a period that coincided with Yeh T'ao's involvement in the social movement. In the latter year, after quitting school teaching to concentrate on activism, she was appointed to the union's Special Operations Group and made director of planning for the creation of its Women's Bureau. She became known as one of T'ai-chung's three famous fighters. Because her activities centered there, where the union's headquarters had been set up, Yeh T'ao and Yang K'uei moved to live in the middle of the town, too.

In 1928, the Taiwanese Communist Party (TCP) became involved in the inner sanctum of the Peasants' Union, which led to a split, with Yeh T'ao and Yang K'uei both being removed from the organization's roll. They then lived in Chang-hua, where life was difficult. The activists sought help from Dr. Lai Ho, the "father of new Taiwan literature" and the most important cadre of the Culture Association in the Chang-hua region. Study groups were being organized in Lu Kang and Chang-hua, and Yeh T'ao and Yang K'uei joined in many of the association's activities.

Because their living together as an unmarried couple affronted the traditional marriage system and Confucian ethics in 1920s Taiwan, they agreed, at the urging of their families' elders, to return to Yang K'uei's native place in Hsin-hua on 21 February

1929 to conduct a marriage ceremony. Along the way on the road passing through T'ai-nan, they stopped in the city the night before the ceremony to attend a conference of the Federation of Trade Unions. That evening, the chief cadres of the Federation of Trade Unions, the Culture Association, and the Peasants' Union were all arrested by the Japanese police in what became known as the "February Twenty-first Incident." Yeh T'ao and Yang K'uei were transported to T'ai-nan Prison with their hands and feet in chains; they were later transferred to T'ai-chung Prison to have what they themselves called a "honeymoon at public expense."

After being released, the two settled for a short time in Kao-hsiung, running a home-based clothing manufacture business, which failed. They cut wood in the mountains and then made a very sparse living for a time as street hawkers. Their life was difficult; when their eldest son was born, he suffered from night blindness because of a lack of vitamin A. Yeh T'ao wrote an extremely short novel entitled *Crystal of Love* (Ai-ti chieh-ching) about these experiences.

In 1935, the couple moved to the Mei-chi District (between present-day Wu-huan Road and T'ai-p'ing Road) in T'ai-chung, renting a large plot of land on which to grow flowers. Yeh T'ao also obtained work in Wu-feng as a private tutor for the Wu family. That was the year that Yang K'uei established the magazine *Taiwan New Literature*, with Yeh T'ao responsible for business management. For a time, she became bedridden because of fatigue. In 1937, after the Japanese government proclaimed a law forbidding the publication of Chinese-language magazines, *Taiwan New Literature* folded. Yang K'uei was by that stage suffering from tuberculosis and coughing up blood. The whole family depended on Yeh T'ao for medicines and sustenance. When, after the outbreak of the Sino-Japanese War, the social movement was banned, the entire burden of supporting the family fell on Yeh T'ao; Yang K'uei recuperated as he continued with his writing.

With the Japanese surrender in August 1945, the KMT government prepared to take over Taiwan in accordance with the secret Cairo talks. Yeh T'ao and Yang K'uei set up a group to promote a new life in T'ai-chung and help with post-war reconstruction and sanitation work. Yeh T'ao even swept the streets along with other members of the group. However, not long after the handover in October, Yeh T'ao's enthusiasm for the "motherland" changed to disappointment. One reason for this was the White Terror Uprising, also known as the February Twenty-eighth Incident, an armed revolt on 28 February 1947 against the KMT government.

A people's militia unit, known as the Twenty-seventh Unit, had formed in the T'ai-chung area and for a short while seemed to draw sufficient strength to exist. However, the Twenty-first Division of the KMT army arrived in Taiwan to quell the revolt, and the people's militia did not resist. Because, as usual, Yeh T'ao and Yang K'uei had become rather involved as activists in the country's affairs, the authorities offered a reward of 50,000 yuan each for their arrest. The two thus became fugitives in T'ai-chung, Chang-hua, and Yun-lin; they carried a mimeograph machine with them at all times so as to be prepared for organizational and training work in the countryside. Because the coastline was completely secured, however, there was no way for them to escape. They returned home to be arrested, and both were given the death penalty.

While on death row, Yeh T'ao impressed the judge with her bravery. Yang K'uei and other inmates recall that Yeh T'ao had decided that if she was going to die, it would be with dignity, not by hanging her head in grief. Yeh T'ao therefore sang Taiwanese folksongs, loudly, in her cell, calling on the young to spread socialist thought. As she and seventeen others prepared themselves on the evening before their execution, the new provincial governor, Wei Tao-ming, issued a decree that "it was not for the army, but for the judiciary, to administer justice." When her death sentence, along with that of her comrades, was commuted to imprisonment, Yeh T'ao was suddenly granted a new life, which was to last for another twenty-three years.

Upon their subsequent release, Yeh T'ao and Yang K'uei rented a bit of land in T'ai-chung to grow flowers. On 6 April 1949, however, he was imprisoned again, this time for twelve years. The reason for his arrest was his four hundred-word tract called "Manifesto for Peace." Yeh T'ao was arrested the same day. She was released, but arrested again in September. In the 1950s, while her husband was in Green Island Prison, Yeh T'ao's home was searched sporadically by police. However, because the political atmosphere was so volatile and not wanting to further upset her children, Yeh T'ao refrained from criticizing the government. Instead, she joined in the activities of the local women's movement and became an executive of T'ai-chung Women's Association (T'ai-chung-shih fu-nü-hui) and Taiwan Women's Association (Taiwan-sheng fu-nü-hui). Economically, Yeh T'ao and her family were still desperate; their only means of support was cultivating flowers. Her children dropped out of school for a time, chopping firewood, selling soybean milk, and making soy sauce to supplement family income. Yeh T'ao was adamant, however, that no matter what, her children must not abandon their education. Except for the two oldest children, a son and daughter who had been out of school for so long that they had no way of going back, the remaining three children all resumed attendance and completed high school.

Yang K'uei completed his twelve-year sentence in 1961 and returned to Taiwan proper. With some difficulty, the family borrowed money to buy land in Ta-tu Mountain in the suburbs of T'ai-chung and established the East Sea (Tung-hai hua-yüan) Flower Garden. Yeh T'ao was responsible for both cultivating and selling the flowers. In the last nine years of her life, she lived under great pressure to repay the substantial sum of money the family had borrowed. Yeh T'ao developed heart trouble and kidney disease, which manifested in uremia, and died in 1970 at the age of sixty-five.

Yeh T'ao appeared in many guises throughout her years: "Black Hen" to her students, "Bandit Woman," the mysterious "a woman who appears to be a perch or an eel" to Yang K'uei, and she called herself "The Flower Woman." Yeh T'ao life spanned two epochs, and she took part in the social and cultural transformation of each. As a Taiwanese woman born at the beginning of the twentieth century, Yeh T'ao reflected in her life the changes that took place in Taiwan. Moreover, her social activism reflected the process of emancipation of a traditional woman.

YANG Ts'ui
(Translated by Michael Paton)

Lin Fan. *Yang K'ui hua-hsiang.* Taipei: Pi-chia-shan, 1976.
Taiwan she-hui yün-tung-shih, vols. 1, 3, and 4. Taipei: Ch'uang-tsao, 1989. This is a Chinese
translation of *Taiwan Tsung-tu-fu ching-ch'a yüan-ke-chih: Section 2: Ling-T'ai i-hou ti
chih-an chuang-k'uang.* N.p.: n.d.
Yang Ts'ui. "Hai ti nü-erh Wu-chi-mu." In *A-ma ti ku-shih,* ed. Chiang Wen-yü. Taipei: Yü-
shan she, 1995.
———. *Jih-chü shih-ch'i Taiwan funü chieh-fang yün-tung.* Taipei: Shih-pao, 1993.
———. "Lu-man ch'a-mou—mai-hua a-ma." In *Tao-kuo hsien-ying, ti san chi.* Taipei: Ch'uang-
i-li, 1997.
"Yeh T'ao." *Taiwan min-pao/Taiwan hsin min-pao* (1927–1930).

Yi Xiang: *see* **Wang Dingguo**

Yi-hao: *see* **Deng Yingchao**

Yin Ruizhi: *see* **Lin Zongsu**

Yin Weijun: *see* **Lin Zongsu**

Yishabei: *see* **Yishu**

Yishu
Yishu, b. 1946 in Ningbo, Zhejiang Province, as Ni Yishu, is a writer of popular
fiction.
  She has used many pen names, including Luo Jiang, Lu Guo, Meifeng, Meiqian,
and Yishabei. Yishu has also followed many lines of work: as a journalist for the Hong
Kong newspaper *Ming Pao* and the movie magazine *Nanguo dianying,* a promoter
for the Shaw Brothers Movie Studio, a hotel public relations officer, a television script
writer, and a news spokesperson for the Hong Kong government. The writer is based
in Hong Kong but has readers in Taiwan, mainland China, and throughout the world
among overseas Chinese. Her brother is the famed Hong Kong science fiction writer
Ni Kuang, who is also known by his pen name Wei-si-li.
  Yishu's family moved to Hong Kong when she was a child, and she has lived there
ever since. She is said to have studied in England, but no details are known about this.
Yishu started writing at the age of fifteen and published her work in *Ming Pao* and
Zhongguo xuesheng zhoubao. Cha Liangyong, head of *Ming Pao* and himself a well-
known writer of popular fiction under the pseudonym Jin Yong, enjoyed her stories.
They were initially mainly autobiographical, however, and he took her to task for
this, suggesting that Yishu could not write anything else. Her response was *Xibao,* a
story in which anything sensational that can happen does happen, including suicide,
adultery, terminal illness, and a heroine turning into a nun.
  Yishu then branched into different subjects. Her romantic stories are distinctive,
distinguishable from those of other writers in the genre such as Ch'iung Yao (*q.v.*) and
Eileen Chang (*q.v.*). Unmistakable Hong Kong icons figure in her settings: white
villas, Italian sports cars, and name-brand fashions. For a time, Yishu wrote stories

about mistresses. These were not confined as characters to women from the world of entertainment but included professional women, clerical workers, and students, reflecting the changing values of a changing society. As her writing matured, her attention turned to the people closer to her own experience. No longer content to weave dreams, Yishu instead attempted to portray women who had succeeded in fighting their way through Hong Kong's commercial society. Her women are mature, capable, and independent. Conquering setbacks and failure, they carve out successful careers and live confidently and freely in their personal lives—happy and carefree when single; moving on, discovering rejuvenation, when marriages founder; and retaining a youthful outlook even in middle age.

Critics describe her as a feminine narcissist because of her sometimes over-optimistic belief in women's ability to create their own happiness. Typical in this category is *When Gold Flows* (Liujin suiyue); it is the story of two women in the changing society of Hong Kong as the city is transformed from a small fishing village to a global metropolis. Despite experiencing circumstances of hardship and setback, they go on to embody success, courage, and liberation.

Although her books are mostly romances, Yishu has attempted to avoid repetition of stories by introducing different components into the basic story line. She has brought in supernatural events, people with special powers, as well as detective and sci-fi elements. Examples of this category are *Wish on a Star* (Ziwei yuan), *Asura* (Axiuluo), and *Bureau of Romantic Love* (Chiqingsi). The author has even written pure science fiction.

Yishu's writing is down to earth. Plots, although always in exotic settings, are not overly melodramatic. Characters are pragmatic, sometimes even cool, and let love take its course, never forcing an issue or trying to change a situation. Little sentimentality is exhibited. She keeps up a brisk pace, and while occasionally inserting her own reflections, they are never long-winded but instead are delightfully insightful. Despite the writer's popular success, however, critics point to the narrowness of Yishu's vision and lack of depth in her work. However, others find in Yishu's fiction a realism that exposes the harsh life of the common people of Hong Kong and the gap between rich and poor. Her works reflect the contemporary woman's life, society, and humanity to a degree at times transcending the genre of the romance novel.

Yishu acknowledges being influenced by the classic novel *Honglou meng*, as well as by modern writers as different as Lu Xun and Eileen Chang. Yishu has published more than 168 titles, mainly novels and short stories, also collections of articles, and writes regular columns for newspapers and magazines in Hong Kong. Her fiction is most popular in Hong Kong, where people share the same physical environment and mental attitude. The revival of popular literature in mainland China, however, has sent the romantic novels of Yishu and others like her to the top of the bestseller lists and created a new wave of popularity in the 1980s.

In a survey of students from a Shanghai university conducted around that time she was one of the best-loved Hong Kong authors, second only to the martial arts master Jin Yong. More than twenty of her works have been reprinted in mainland China, where for political and cultural reasons popular fiction had long been frowned upon. People there had been starved for light-reading material until the thaw in political and literary policy early in the decade. Nevertheless, Yishu's popularity showed signs of waning in the 1990s, the cause lying not so much in Yishu and her work perhaps as in the vagaries of history and society.

Lily Xiao Hong LEE

Ren Yiming. "Xianggang nüxing wenxue gaiguan." *Xinjiang shifan daxue xuebao: Zhesheban*, no. 4 (1995): 18–23.

Xiaochun. "Yishu xiao zhuan." *Mingbao yuekan*, no. 364; or 31, no. 4 (April 1996): 46.

Xu Xue. "Qiong Yao Yishu xiaoshuo de shenmei qingqu." *Mingbao yuekan*, no. 364; or 31, no. 4 (April 1996): 38–41.

Yan Chungou. "Yishu shan xie duhui nüzi." *Mingbao yuekan*, no. 364; or 31, no. 4 (April 1996): 45–46.

Yongtzu: *see* **Jung-tzu**

You Wanfen: *see* **Hiu Wan,Ven.**

You Yongkang: *see* **Longlian, Ven.**

You Yunshan: *see* **Hiu Wan, Ven.**

Yu Lihua: *see* **Yü Li-hua**

Yü Li-hua

Yü Li-hua [Yu Lihua], b. 1931 in Shanghai although a native of Chen-hai [Zhenhai] County (present-day Ning-po city), Che-chiang [Zhejiang] Province, is an American Chinese writer.

She came to prominence in Taiwan in the 1950s and went on to become famous in the United States in the 1960s. Yü Li-hua has been called the progenitor of the "Chinese students overseas" genre (*liu-hsüeh-sheng wen-hsüeh*). For many years, she wrote about the experience of Chinese students in America, known as the "rootless generation" (*shih-ken-ti i-tai*). However, other critics consider Yü Li-hua to be an exponent of the Taiwan experience, saying that many other authors were writing, in both Chinese and English, about the lives of students in the United States before she went there. Both schools of thought, however, admire the depth, scope, variety, and quantity of the work the author has produced.

Yü Li-hua's father had gone to France as part of a work-study program and taught at Kuang-hua [Guanghua] University in Shanghai on his return. When he became unemployed, the whole family traveled by a torturous route to Ch'eng-tu [Chengdu], Ssu-ch'uan [Sichuan] Province, via Fu-chien [Fujian] and Hu-nan. Yü Li-hua attended school irregularly during this period. At the end of the Sino-Japanese War, the family returned to Ning-po. When Yü Li-hua was in her second year of high school, her father worked under the famous geologist Weng Wen-hao and through him got an opportunity to work in the sugar industry in Taiwan. In 1947, then, her family moved to Taiwan, and Yü Li-hua accompanied them, albeit reluctantly.

After graduating from high school, she attended Taiwan University. It was fashionable then for young women to study a foreign language at university, so Yü Li-hua took English. Unfortunately, her family's peripatetic existence during her formative years had adversely affected her education, and her English was not very good. Her new language teacher, Yü Ta-ts'ai [Yu Dacai], was the wife of Fu Ssu-nien [Fu Sinian], president of the university, and very demanding. When Yü Li-hua failed the first-year English course, her teacher said Yü Li-hua was "not up to it" (pu-hsing) and suggested a transfer to the History Department. This became a turning point for Yü Li-hua, who subsequently determined that she would work very hard and make a name for herself in the world of literature, proving that she was indeed "up to it." Yü Li-hua later explained that it was her nature, when confronted with something she could not have, to do everything possible to get it. Yü Li-hua therefore did everything she could to prove Yü Ta-ts'ai wrong. Yü Li-hua also wrote in her autobiography: "Ms. Yü [Ta-ts'ai] would often say to her students, 'Yü Li-hua became what she is today because of me.'"

It was also the fashion in Taiwan at that time for young people to go overseas. Those who could afford it sent their children to study in the United States, and some young people left Taiwan even before they completed university. Their letters home were enthusiastic and filled with talk of the fun they were having. Naturally, Yü Li-hua's dream was to go to the United States. Her father, who had studied overseas when he was a young man, was also keen for his children to have that experience, regardless of whether they were suited for it or not. Through his work, he met an American willing to be guarantor for Yü Li-hua and provide free room and board. After graduating from Taiwan University, Yü Li-hua was sent to America in 1953 and enrolled in journalism at the University of California at Los Angeles (UCLA). Two of her heroes had always been Margaret Higgins and Hsü Chung-p'ei [Xu Zhongpei]. Yü Li-hua admired the American Margaret Higgins for her bravery in accompanying the military to the front and writing war reports with human interest; she also admired the Taiwanese Hsü Chung-p'ei for the literary quality of her reportage.

With the help of an American roommate, Yü Li-hua wrote a short story in English for a new writing award a publisher had set up for students at the University of California. Her story, "The Sorrow at the End of the Yangtze River," won First Prize. While at university, she wrote more stories in English, but many were rejected for publication. English was not her first language, and Yü Li-hua did not understand the U.S. literary market.

She completed her master's in 1956 and got married that year as well. Her husband, Sun Chih-jui [Sun Zhirui], taught physics at UCLA but soon got a job at Princeton University. Their first daughter, Sun Hsiao-fan, was born in 1957, their son, Sun Chung-han, two years later. Yü Li-hua stopped writing in order to take care of her children but by 1961 was sick of being a housewife. The young mother wanted to take up writing again. A friend encouraged her to do so, suggesting that she go back to writing in Chinese, so Yü Li-hua did, writing down her memories of childhood and young adulthood. This work was published as Returning to Ch'ing-ho in My Dreams (Meng hui Ch'ing-ho). In 1962 the author gave birth to her youngest daughter, Sun Yen-jan.

Again, the additional responsibilities interfered with Yü Li-hua's writing plans, and she became so frustrated that she took her three children to Taiwan to live with her mother. During that year there, with her mother's help, Yü Li-hua felt as if the creativity she had experienced while studying at Taiwan University had returned. All her energies were put into writing, and Yü Li-hua completed the short-story collection *Homecoming* (Kuei) and the novella *Also Autumn* (Yeh shih ch'iu-t'ien).

By the time she returned to America, Yü Li-hua knew she wanted to live her life as a writer, her role as a mother coming second, her wifely duties, third. Not unexpectedly, her husband was not happy with this scheme. He was a traditional husband devoted to his career and whose model consisted of a husband dealing with the family's public face, while a wife managed its private sphere. After a day's teaching, he expected to enjoy the care and attention of his wife, who should not be spending too much time and energy on writing, which he did not consider to be a career. Cracks appeared in their marriage. Yü Li-hua and her family moved to New York, but she was still not able to put her plan to write into practice. Instead, her husband encouraged her to teach, saying it was good to be in contact with the young.

In 1968, Yü Li-hua gave a course on modern Chinese literature in English translation, and she has continued to teach and write since then. Ten books were produced between that year and 1978, almost all of them about the lives and loves of Taiwanese and Hong Kong students in America. Her underlying theme, however, was people's roots. Regardless of whether her characters succeeded or failed in life, they always experienced such a sense of loss that they had to return to their place of origin to seek personal roots and peace of mind. The books she wrote during this period were *Homecoming*; *Also Autumn*; *Change* (Pien); *Stars on the Snow* (Hsüeh-ti shang ti hsing-hsing); *I See the Palms Again, I See the Palms Again* (Yu chien tsung-lü, yu chien ts'ung-lü); *Flame* (Yen); *White Horse* (Pai-chü chi); *Conference Scenes* (Hui-ch'ang hsien-hsing chi); *Trials* (K'ao-yen); *The Fu Children* (Fu-chia ti erh-nü-men); and *Women of New China and Others* (Hsin Chung-kuo ti nü-hsing chi ch'i-ta).

In 1975, Yü Li-hua journeyed to seek her own roots in China. But speaking of this experience, she said later: "I only saw what I was able to see, not what I wanted to see. But at that time I didn't ask to see other things. I . . . [thought that] what I saw was what I wanted to see." Her sister, who had had only three or four years of primary education, also later told Yü Li-hua of her inability at that time to be outspoken about the real situation there. That visit to her native place was doubtless a disappointment but, because Yü Li-hua satisfied the urge to seek her roots, she refused to analyze the visit too closely. Nor was Yü Li-hua concerned about whether or not she had looked at what was really going on.

Yü Li-hua returned to China in 1977 and in 1979 she went again with a delegation from her university. Finally, Yü Li-hua met the writers she wanted to meet. What saddened and frightened her, however, was to witness the trend in China of "admiring the West." Returning to America, Yü Li-hua wrote a long letter imbued with a strong nationalist consciousness. Entitled "To the Young Friends of the Motherland," it was published in *Jen-min jih-pao* [Renmin ribao] in April 1980. In this letter, she advised the youth of China to respect and value themselves, work hard, and be strong rather than blindly worshipping and imitating everything foreign. Nor, Yü Li-hua wrote, was there any need to be in a rush to accept all foreign values.

Because Sun Chih-jui was unable to accommodate his wife's writing career, the couple divorced in the early 1980s. Not long afterward, Yü Li-hua married Dr. Vincent O'Leary, president of the State University of New York at Albany.

Tung LAM
(Translated by Lily Xiao Hong Lee and Sue Wiles)

Ha Ying-fei [Ha Yingfei] and Lü Jo-han [Lü Ruohan], eds. *Jen tsai lü-t'u—Yü Li-hua tzu-chuan*. Nan-ching [Nanjing]: Chiang-su wen-i ch'u-pan-she, 2000.

Huang Ch'ung-t'ien [Huang Chongtian]. *Taiwan ch'ang-p'ian hsiao-shuo lun*. Fu-chou [Fuzhou]: Hai-hsia wen-i ch'u-pan-she, 1990.

Huang Wen-hsiang [Huang Wenxiang]. *Ou–Mei chieh-ch'u Hua-i nü-hsing*. Hong Kong: Shang-hai shu-chü, 1992, 184–226.

Kao, Hsin-sheng C. "Yu Lihua's Blueprint for the Development of a New Poetics: Chinese Literature Overseas." In *Nativism Overseas: Contemporary Chinese Women Writers*, ed. Hsin-sheng Kao. Albany: State University of New York Press, 1993, 81–107.

Ling Ch'eng-huang [Ling Chenghuang]. "Mei ken i-tai ti hsin-ling chi-mo—Yü Li-hua hsiao-shuo 'Yu chien tsung-lü, yu chien tsung-lü' p'ing-chieh." In *Taiwan Hsiang-kang wen-hsüeh p'ing-lun chi*. Fu-chou [Fuzhou]: Hai-hsia wen-i ch'u-pan-she, 1994.

Lu Shih-ch'ing [Lu Shiqing]. "Yü Li-hua ho t'a ti 'Yu chien tsung-lü, yu chien tsung-lü.'" In *Taiwan wen-hsüeh hsin-lun*. Shanghai: Fu-tan ta-hsüeh ch'u-pan-she, 1993, 198–212.

P'an Ya-tun [Pan Yadun]. *Shih-chieh hua-wen nü-tso-chia su-miao*. Kuang-chou [Guangzhou]: Chi-nan ta-hsüeh ch'u-pan-she, 1993, 343–50.

Wang Chin-min [Wang Jinmin], ed. *T'ai–Kang–Ao wen-hsüeh tso-p'in ching-hsüan*. Kuang-chou [Guangzhou]: Kuang-tung kao-teng chiao-yü ch'u-pan-she, 1998.

"Yü Li-hua." In *Hai-wai hua-wen wen-hsüeh shih*, vol. 4, ed. Ch'en Hsien-mao [Chen Xianmao]. Hsia-men [Xiamen]: Lu-chiang ch'u-pan-she, 1999, 24–36.

"Yü Li-hua: 'Yu chien tsung-lü, yu chien tsung-lü.'" In *T'ai-Kang hsiao-shuo chien-shang tz'u-tien*, eds. Ming Ch'ing [Ming Qing] and Ch'in Jen [Qin Ren]. Beijing: Chung-yang min-tsu hsüeh-yüan ch'u-pan-she, 1994.

Yu Luojin

Yu Luojin, b. 1946 in Beijing, was a controversial protest writer in 1980s China.

Hers had been a comfortable and stable family life, growing up with three brothers, until 1957, when the CCP launched its anti-rightist campaign. Both of her parents had studied in Japan and were labeled "rightist elements": her father was a civil engineer and her mother was a director of a factory that was half privately and half publicly owned. Yu Luojin finished high school in 1961 and continued her studies at Beijing Arts and Crafts School (Beijing gongyi meishu xuexiao). After graduating in 1966, she became a toy designer at Beijing Sixth Toy Factory. That year, however, saw the start of the Cultural Revolution, and this time, political persecution extended beyond her parents.

Yu Luojin was sentenced to three years forced labor after a house search by Red Guards revealed diaries containing remarks critical of the Cultural Revolution. Her elder brother Yu Luoke was also arrested for writing articles criticizing the prevailing theory of blood lineage, the most controversial one being "On Family Background." Even under torture, he refused to renounce his belief that it is wrong to judge people by their family background. In 1970, the year Yu Luojin was sent to Linxi District in Hebei Province to do manual labor, her brother was executed after being publicly humiliated in front of thousands of watchers. Without the knowledge or consent of his parents, his corneas were immediately removed for transplanting to another person. In the wake of the "political crimes" committed by Yu Luojin and her brother, the rest of the family were persecuted and ostracized by the communist government.

As the only daughter, Yu Luojin was expected to alleviate her family's suffering by marrying into a more prosperous region, where the family could also move. She complied with her parents' wishes and married Wang Shijun, who promised the family they could settle in the northeastern countryside where he worked. Their marriage produced a son. However, Yu Luojin's husband constantly humiliated and beat her, and four years later she asked for a divorce. Her family refused to accept her back in Beijing, saying that the political and economic situation was still bleak. Yu Luojin therefore "bought" her way back into the family with 300 yuan and the offer of her own ration coupons (for necessities of food and clothing). She supported herself for a time by working as a maid. Yu Luojin then married Cai Zhongpei, a divorced electrician with a nine-year-old daughter, in 1978. Yu Luojin later admitted that she had not married Cai Zhongpei for love but out of expediency: his daughter lived with a grandmother, Cai did not want another child, had a room, and seemed reliable. This, her second marriage, lasted two years (1978–80); Yu Luojin asked for a divorce after being rehabilitated in April 1979. She was allowed to return to her old work unit, Beijing Sixth Toy Factory. Both Yu Luojin and the presiding judge who ruled in her favor discussed her divorce in the media, and it served as a focus for a wider discussion of the issues of marriage and divorce.

From 1980, she took an active part in the feminist movement, belonging to an unofficial organization called the "Chinese Women's Association" (Zhongguo funü lianhehui; this group is not to be confused with the ACWF, i.e., Quanguo funü lianhehui), which had been active at Beijing University during the 1980–81 election campaigns for district-level People's Congress. Orders were soon issued for it to be dissolved, however. From about this time, Yu Luojin started to write novels. *A Chinese Winter's Tale* (Yige dongtian de tonghua) attracted the most attention and controversy. It described the political persecution, injustice, and cruelty that her brother Yu Luoke and her family suffered during the Cultural Revolution. However, the novel transcended the sentimentalist genre that prevailed in Chinese literature after that era and went on to explore the nature of love, marriage, and family values through the author's own experience.

Her second autobiographical novel, *A Spring Tale* (Chuntian de tonghua), written in 1982, defends her decisions to leave unhappy marriages and courage to pursue true love. This novel caused heated debate on love, marriage, divorce, and morality and was criticized and banned by the government. *Chinese Youth Daily* (Zhongguo qingnian bao) commented that in the novel Yu Luojin pursues not eternal love but "exhibitionism of an egoistic personality." With the launching in 1983 of the government's "anti-spiritual-pollution campaign," she immediately became the target of criticism in all official media. Yu Luojin was dismissed by her employer, Beijing Municipal Council, for one of whose magazines she had worked as an editor since 1982.

In 1985, Yu Luojin traveled to Germany, requesting political asylum, and was naturalized as a German citizen in 1993. She continues to write occasionally for Hong Kong magazines such as *Zhengming* and *Kaifang*. Her latest work, *The Call of Love*, was published in Taiwan.

CUI Zhiying

Minford, John. "Introduction." In *A Chinese Winter's Tale: An Autobiographical Fragment*, Yu Luojin; trans. Rachel May and Zhou Zhiyu. Hong Kong: Research Center for Translation, Chinese University of Hong Kong, 1986.

Nerlich, Jorg Michael. "In Search of the Ideal Man: Yu Luojin's Novel *A Winter's Tale*." In *Women and Literature in China*, eds. Anna Gerstlacher et al. Bochum: Brockmeyer, 1985, 454–72.

Yu Luojin. *A Chinese Winter's Tale: An Autobiographical Fragment*, trans. Rachel May and Zhou Zhiyu. Hong Kong: Research Center for Translation, Chinese University of Hong Kong, 1986.

———. "Chuntian de tonghua." *Huacheng*, no. 1 (1981).

———. "Qizhi shi yige wenge?—Xie zai wenge sanshi zhounian zhi ji." *Kaifang* (May 1996): 52–53.

———. "Wo weishenme yao lihun?" *Minzhu yu fazhi*, no. 1 (1981): 26–29.

———. "Yige dongtian de tonghua." *Dangdai*, no. 3 (1980): 58–107.

Yu Shan

Yu Shan, 1908–1968, of Shanyin (present-day Shaoxing), Zhejiang Province, was an actress; she was born in Japan.

Yu Shan came from a wealthy literati family, which owned properties in Zhejiang, Beijing, Shanghai, and Nanjing. Her paternal grandfather had been a famous poet, educator, and politician, and one of her father's cousins (Yu Dawei) was a missile specialist and high official in the Nanjing KMT government. Her father, Yu Dachun, studied overseas and returned to become a railway engineer. Little is known of her mother, Bian Jiejun.

Yu Shan was the elder of two daughters and publicly disowned by her family, until she became famous. Her sister, Yu Jin, became a medical doctor. Her four brothers pursued different professions: Yu Qixiao studied in the United States and returned to take up a professorship; Yu Qixin studied chemistry and worked in an armaments factory; Yu Qiwei, who was a youthful lover of Jiang Qing (*q.v.*), was the only communist in the family; and Yu Qizhong studied agriculture in the United States and returned to take up a professorship.

Yu Shan attended Nankai Girls' High School (Nankai nüzhong) in Tianjin before enrolling in the Shanghai Public Conservatorium of Music. When the famous director Tian Han (1898–1968) visited the school in 1929 to direct *A Tragedy on the Lake* (Hushang de beiju), he invited her to join the Nanguo Society. In the society's second season that year (July-August), Yu Shan played the leading role in the Chinese version of Oscar Wilde's *Salomé*, creating a stir with her provocative rendition of the "Dance of the Seven Veils." In the third season the following year, she played the fiery lead in *Carmen*, which Tian Han had adapted for the Chinese stage. During this time, Yu Shan also studied *dan* (the lead female role in *jingju*) [Beijing opera] with the well-known *jingju* performer Shuixianhua [Guo Jixiang]), and soon became a star.

About this time, Yu Shan married Zhao Taimei, a professor at Qingdao University (Qingdao daxue) and teacher of Jiang Qing. It is not known whether Yu Shan had children. Having spent the early 1930s in Tianjin and Beijing, she moved to Chongqing during the Sino-Japanese War and performed frequently as an amateur. In 1948 the performer went to the liberated area in Shijiazhuang where, according to one source, Yu Shan had an affair with Mao Zedong (1893–1976). After the establishment of the People's Republic in 1949, she worked firstly with the Jiangsu Drama Troupe (Jiangsu jutuan) and then with the China Institute of Opera Research (Zhongguo xiqu yanjiuyuan).

HE Li
(Translated by Qianbo Xin)

Zhongguo dabaike quanshu: Xiqu quyi. Beijing: Zhongguo dabaike quanshu chubanshe, 1989.

Yu Wan-fen: *see* **Hiu Wan, Ven.**

Yu Yün-shan: *see* **Hiu Wan, Ven.**

Yu Zhihua: *see* **Wang Ying**

Yü-Ch'en Yüeh-ying

Yü-Ch'en Yüeh-ying [Yu-Chen Yueying], b. 1926, in Kao-hsiung, Taiwan, as Ch'en Yüeh-ying, was the first woman to become mayor of a county in Taiwan.

She was the youngest daughter of an influential family; her father, Ch'en Tsai-hsing, was the director of a sugar refinery during the period of Japanese occupation. Ch'en Yüeh-ying had a sheltered childhood, returning home after school to read, play, or practice the piano. She completed her early schooling during this war period, enrolling in Ch'ang-yung Girls' High School in T'ai-nan after completing public-school primary education in 1940. At the end of the war in the Pacific (1945), Yü-Ch'en Yüeh-ying went on to senior high school and graduated.

She entered into an arranged marriage with Yü Jui-yen [Yu Ruiyan], son of a promising new family in the same district, in 1949. Her father-in-law, Yü Teng-fa, was a delegate to the First National Assembly and chair of the local Irrigation Committee; he wielded considerable political influence. As the wife of the eldest son, Yü-Ch'en Yüeh-ying became manager of the household, in charge of organizing all the daily chores and other important matters. This training ground developed her natural ability to accept challenges, make decisions, and assume responsibility.

Determined to frustrate the KMT's plan to field their own candidate under the pretext of establishing a quota system for female candidates, Yü Teng-fa arranged for Yü-Ch'en Yüeh-ying to run in the third session of the Provincial Council elections in 1963. She won easily and established her political career by becoming reelected to the fourth, fifth, and sixth Provincial Councils. Yü-Ch'en Yüeh-ying's personal political success also strengthened the "Kao-hsiung Black Clique," as the Yü family's political faction was known.

She continued to be guided by her father-in-law when, in partnership with her daughter Yü Ling-ya, she ran for mayor of Kao-hsiung County in 1980. She lost by some three thousand votes to Ts'ai Ming-yao, a male KMT candidate. However, her daughter was elected to the Provincial Council. Three years later, Yü-Ch'en Yüeh-ying entered the central government, replacing her sister-in-law Huang-Yü Hsiu-luan as a member of the Legislative Yuan. In 1985 Yü-Ch'en Yüeh-ying again campaigned for mayor of Kao-hsiung, winning this time with the highest number of votes in the country, and thus became the first female county mayor. She ran again in 1989, under the campaign theme "A Mother's Holy War," and won a second term in office, gaining the highest number of votes ever recorded.

The nineteen years during which Yü-Ch'en Yüeh-ying served as an elected representative were a stormy period in Taiwanese politics, and she did not hesitate to make her views known on sensitive issues. In spite of political pressure, Yü-Ch'en Yüeh-ying held firmly to her opinions on the orthodoxy of government and the political assassination of Chiang Nan. Also, her refusal to take an oath while in the Legislative Yuan in 1972 deeply shocked the public. However, in the eight years of being mayor, Yü-Ch'en Yüeh-ying implemented in their entirety all the promises she had made during her campaigns and set many an example for conduct in the county administration. Among the measures she initiated were the County Mayor Service Center, a flexi-plan ensuring that public services were maintained over the Chinese lunar New Year holidays, and a health care scheme for peasants.

Yü-Ch'en Yüeh-ying consolidated the power of her family's "Black Clique" during her nearly thirty years of public service. Her personality and manner were well liked by the people of Kao-hsiung County. Her patience and tenacity in serving her constituents won her the sobriquets of "Iron Lady of T'ai-nan" and "Grandma Matsu." After relinquishing public office, Yü-Ch'en Yüeh-ying was appointed to the Education Reform Committee, under the Executive Yuan, in recognition of her lifelong concern for matters educational. In May 1996, she was appointed national policy consultant to President Li Teng-hui [Li Denghui] and in May 2000 as consultant to the presidential office of President Chen Shui-bian [Chen Shui-pien].

During elections at the end of the twentieth century, the clan politics of the Yü family came under criticism from political rivals, and this created serious division within the family. Members of the family have nevertheless remained in power in public office, some examples being Yü Cheng-hsien (county mayor), Yü Cheng-tao (Kao-hsiung representative in the Legislative Yuan), and Cheng Kuei-lien (delegate to the National Assembly). Yü-Ch'en Yüeh-ying's greatest challenge will be to see whether she can resolve the ills of clan politics while maintaining her position as guardian of the "Black Clique" family.

LIN Ch'ien-ju
(Translated by Li Sheung Yee)

Min-tsu wan-pao, 26 February 1984.
Yü-Ch'en Yüeh-ying. *Yü-Ch'en Yüeh-ying hui-i lu*. Taipei: Shih-pao wen-hua, 1996.

Yu-Chen Yueying: *see* **Yü-Ch'en Yüeh-ying**

Yuan En: *see* **Nieh Hualing**

Yuan Xuefen
Yuan Xuefen, b. 1922, in Dushan village, Shengxian County, Zhejiang Province, is a performing artist of the *yueju* genre, a local opera indigenous to the Shaoxing region of Zhejiang, characterized by romanticism and lyrical melodies; in traditional times, all roles were played by females.

Her father, a private tutor, apprenticed Yuan Xuefen in 1933 to the traditional-style Siji Chun *Yueju* Troupe, where she was trained in the *qingyi* (morally upright female) and *dan* (female lead) roles; she also trained within a larger theatrical group specializing in *huiju* (Anhui opera), playing martial-cum-acrobatic roles. In 1936, Yuan Xuefen traveled to Shanghai with a *yueju* troupe for a performance at the Tongchun Theater; she was also in the cast of the first all-female *yueju* production featured on a sound recording. Yuan Xuefen returned to Shanghai in February 1938 and remained there as a performing artist during the period when the city was called the "lonely island," alone among the surrounding areas not yet under Japanese occupation. For over three years, she collaborated in staging *yueju* performances with the leading female actor Ma Zhanghua, who was a male impersonator. Yuan Xuefen promoted *yueju* melodies, or chants, through concerts broadcast over Shanghai radio and made a name for herself. Underworld triad gangs were extremely powerful in the city at that time, yet the artist was able to maintain her personal integrity. She became a practicing Buddhist, wore a plain blue cotton gown regardless of the season, affected a simple hairdo of two plaits, and went without makeup. Yuan Xuefen also refused to perform at private functions for the rich and famous or to socialize with financial supporters or patrons.

Influenced by progressive Chinese-language spoken drama, from late 1942 Yuan Xuefen initiated important reforms in the performance of *yueju*. Using mostly her own money, she employed professional scriptwriters, directors, stage designers, supervisors, and stage managers. Yuan Xuefen then held rehearsals with a written script rather than following the traditional *yueju* practice of adlibbing and also had historically accurate costumes designed and made for specific characters in the plays, replacing the old "pool" system of generic *yueju* costumes. She used three-dimensional sets instead of the traditional bare stage, incorporated lighting and sound effects, and provided oil-based makeup in place of powder. This "neo-*yueju*" was the start of a comprehensive new standard for performance and became quickly copied by other *yueju* troupes. Certain drama and film techniques were also adapted, particularly the portrayal of character and the realistic expression of feelings, dance, and movement; she also assimilated the bodily aesthetics of the older *kunqu* opera genre.

Yuan Xuefen paid great attention to the expression of feeling in singing. For a

1943 performance of *The Fragrant Concubine* (Xiang Fei), she developed with the *huqin* (a stringed instrument) master Zhou Baocai a new style of singing, somewhat similar to mezzo-soprano and known as *chi diao*. It is characterized by purity of melody, variations in tempo, a mellow tone, and the lengthening of a final syllable by singing it through many notes in order to intensify emotion. Adopted by other troupes, this *chi diao* became famous as the Yuan school's main *yueju* style and has been further refined by such artists as Qi Yaxian and Lu Ruiyin. The Yuan school of singing is unique in its emotiveness. The voice of the female playing a male role is particularly enchanting in its beauty, lyricism and subtlety, and is popular with audiences. Yuan Xuefen herself became famous for the delicacy and emotion of her three wailing chants in *The Fragrant Concubine*, *A Strand of Hemp* (Yi lü ma), and *Liang Shanbo and Zhu Yingtai*.

During the Japanese occupation of Shanghai, Yuan Xuefen performed a series of patriotic *yueju*, including *The Fragrant Concubine*, *Women Warriors* (Hongfen jingge), *Mu Lan Goes to War* (Mu Lan congjun), *An Evil Family* (Hei'an jiating), and *Wang Zhaojun*, which eulogized national heroes. The Sino-Japanese War ended in 1945, and the following year Yuan Xuefen's production of *Xiang Lin's Wife* (Xiang Lin Sao), adapted from Lu Xun's famous story "A New Year's Sacrifice," was acclaimed by such progressive literati and journalists as Tian Han, Xu Guangping (*q.v.*), Ouyang Shanzun, Bai Yang (*q.v.*), and Hu Feng as "a milestone in neo-*yueju*." This production of *Xiang Lin's Wife* was made into a film in 1948. During this period, Yuan Xuefen took part in a benefit performance of *Love for Mountains and Rivers* (Shanhe lian) as one of "Ten Sisters of yueju," that is, the ten most loved performers. She also joined in protests over the death of her colleague Xiao Dangui. Because of this stance, Yuan Xuefen suffered several bouts of persecution by the KMT.

She was required to attend classes to research folk operas, organized in 1949 by the Art Department of the Shanghai government, which was at that time under military administration. Yuan Xuefen was appointed as the corps leader for performance. Together with other well-known performance delegates such as Mei Lanfang, Zhou Xinfang, and Cheng Yanqiu, Yuan Xuefen attended the First CPPCC and was present at the ceremonial inauguration of the People's Republic.

During the 1950s, Yuan Xuefen continued to innovate. She produced *The Love Tree* (Xiangsi shu) as a 16 mm color film in 1950 and created a male-voice style for *yueju*. Yuan Xuefen became director of the East China *Yueju* Experimental Ensemble, which was the first state-run opera troupe in Shanghai. With the establishment in 1951 of the East China Opera Research Institute, she was made vice-director as well as director of its Experimental Troupe. Yuan Xuefen and Fan Ruijuan (*q.v.*) played in *Liang Shanbo and Zhu Yingtai* (also known as *Butterfly Lovers*), which in 1953 was made into China's first color film of opera and won a prize for musical film in an international film festival the following year. This film was also awarded the prize of honor by the Chinese Ministry of Culture as the Best Film of 1949–55. Yuan Xuefen also developed and performed in *Story of the West Chamber* (Xixiang ji), adapted from Wang Shifu's drama, playing the role of Cui Yingying; this opera won First Prize for Performance at the East China Folk Opera Festival in 1954.

With the establishment of the Shanghai *Yueju* Academy in 1955, Yuan Xuefen became its director, and later that year she and Xu Guangping took the Chinese *Yueju* Ensemble overseas for performances in East Germany and the USSR. Yuan Xuefen remained busy with performances for the next few years, improving the script and performance of *Xiang Lin's Wife* and performing in Hong Kong (1960) and North Korea (1961). For the new opera *Huoye Village* (Huoye cun) in which she performed in 1965, Yuan Xuefen and *huqin* master Zhou Boling created a *yueju* song in B-flat.

The Cultural Revolution caused Yuan Xuefen great suffering. During this period, Jiang Qing (*q.v.*) dictated that only a small number of model operas (*yangban xi*, also known as "reformed" operas) were to be performed, and *yueju* disappeared almost completely. In 1966 Yuan Xuefen was asked to step down from the directorship of the Shanghai *Yueju* Academy and then placed in solitary confinement. She had just had a baby, and her "prison," a room in the academy, was only a short distance from her home, but Yuan Xuefen was forbidden to see her infant son. A large number of big character posters were aimed at her, and she was placed under severe scrutiny for five years, being interrogated and suffering physical as well as mental torture. Yuan Xuefen aged so much because of the mistreatment that upon being finally allowed to return home, her son, then six years old, failed to recognize her.

Yuan Xuefen's professional commitment remained, however, and with the end of the Cultural Revolution resumed involvement with *yueju*. Her version of *Xiang Lin's Wife* was made into a wide-screen color film. She was reappointed as director of the Shanghai *Yueju* Academy and responsible for a series of new operas and performances as well as training young actors and actresses. Yuan Xuefen visited several countries, including West Germany (1977), Japan (1979), France (1986), and the United States (1989). At the Fifteenth Art Festival in Paris she was awarded a medal of honor and honorary citizenship of several French cities and received various other international and domestic awards. China Record Company awarded her a Gold Record in 1989, and in 1994 the Baogang Gaoya Art Award was conferred upon her.

Yuan Xuefen is currently vice-chair of the Society of Chinese Dramatists and honorary director and art consultant to the Shanghai *Yueju* Academy. Her outstanding contribution to *yueju* has been acknowledged by the State Council, which has given her the title of Specialist and supports her with an allowance.

Shirley Wai CHAN
(Translated by Li Sheung Yee)

Yingwen *Zhongguo funü*, ed. *Gujin zhuming funü renwu*, vol. 2. Shijiazhuang: Hebei renmin chubanshe, 1986, 1031–33.
Zhongguo dabaike quanshu: Xiqu quyi. Beijing: Zhongguo dabaike quanshu chubanshe, 1989, 558–59.

Yue Daiyun

Yue Daiyun, b. 1931 in Guiyang, the provincial capital of Guizhou, is widely acclaimed for her important pioneering contributions to Chinese literature in the post-Mao period. Her article "Nietzsche in China" (Nicai zai Zhongguo, 1980) and edited book *Collected Essays on Lu Xun by Foreign Scholars* (Guowai Lu Xun yanjiu lunji, 1981) are among the earliest attempts of the period to reassess China's modern literary history. At the time of their publication, these works were courageous statements on behalf of critical literary scholarship, absent in China for three decades.

In 1985, mainly through Yue Daiyun's efforts, the Chinese Comparative Literature Association was established; its affiliation with the International Comparative Literature Association brought Chinese scholars into the international network of cross-cultural exchanges in literature and scholarship. The relationship also alerted the international body itself to the fact that modern Chinese literature could no longer be ignored as an integral part of world literature in comparative literature studies. Yue Daiyun's standing as a senior academic at Peking University facilitated the university's gradual re-opening of studies in modern world literature (at the time still labeled "bourgeois" and "decadent") and the promotion of studies of contemporary Western literature with its new approaches, theories, and methodologies. Thus, the critiques of Habermas, Derrida, and Foucault and cross-disciplinary developments in cultural, gender, and post-colonial studies, first introduced by Yue Daiyun at Peking University, soon spawned similar program developments at all major Chinese universities. She held a joint appointment in both bodies of the comparative literature associations, and encouraged the proliferation of provincial comparative literature associations as affiliates to all major universities.

Strong-minded even as a teenager, Yue Daiyun traveled to Chongqing to sit for the national university examinations and succeeded in being offered places both at Nanjing and Peking. She chose Peking University and after enrolling in 1948 became an active member of the Communist Party Democratic Youth League. In July in the following year, Yue Daiyun joined the CCP. In 1950 she led the students in May Fourth celebrations and was a delegate to the Second World Student Congress held in Prague. During 1951–52, Yue Daiyun took part in a land reform team in Jiangxi Province. On returning to Beijing, she graduated and was retained as a lecturer in Chinese literature and, in the same year, married Tang Yijie (b. 1927), a young professor of Chinese philosophy. Tang Yijie's father was Tang Yongtong (1893–1964), an eminent scholar of Buddhist and Indian studies and president of Peking University from 1949 to 1952. When Yue Daiyun moved into the Tang household, it was her father-in-law who encouraged her to study Chinese classical literature to enrich her understanding of modern literature.

In 1955 a campaign against counter-revolutionaries began, and Yue Daiyun was penalized for taking leave to visit her parent's family in Guizhou: she was suspended from teaching and her position as CCP branch secretary. This was only the beginning of the troubles she would subsequently encounter because of her professed interest in literature that transcended the prescribed boundaries of the time. On 24 January 1958, one month after the birth of her first son, Tang Shuang, Yue Daiyun was criticized and formally declared a rightist. Her party membership was revoked, and she was sentenced to one year of labor at Zhaitang (to the west of Beijing), the first of a number of rural locations near Beijing to which she would be sent over the next two decades.

Although in mid-1960 her rightist label was removed, its stigma remained, and

Yue Daiyun was first sent to work on village history at Lingyuesi before being sent back to Peking University. In February 1961, she was denied teaching and assigned to write commentaries on Tang poetry. Not until autumn 1962 was Yue Daiyun able to resume teaching, and then only in composition and not literature.

Despite her now "blemished" background, when her father-in-law was received by Mao Zedong (1893–1976) at the 1 October celebrations of 1962, Yue Daiyun was included in the small family group that attended and had the honor of shaking the chairman's hand. Nevertheless, by 1964 when a Central Committee work team came to Peking University, she again found herself relieved from teaching and targeted for attack at three meetings during February. In June Yue Daiyun was assigned to gather material for a movement to criticize bourgeois literary viewpoints and in September was sent to Xiaohongmen in the countryside to implement the "Four Clean-Ups."

While her fortunes spiraled downward, Yue Daiyun's husband Tang Yijie was highly regarded by the authorities and an important participant at the national conference on education held at the International Hotel in Beijing in July 1965. However, in 1966, with the unfolding of the Cultural Revolution, a new work team was sent to Peking University. In June, a few days after Yue Daiyun had returned from Xiaohongmen and was assigned to physical labor on campus, violence broke out at the university: Tang Yijie now became a target. Red Guards vandalized the Tang family's books and records and forced family members to give up most of the house.

From 1967 the Peking University campus turned into a battlefield for Red Guard factions, and in January 1968 Yue Daiyun and her husband moved out into a separate house with their children. In February 1969, she was again attacked as a rightist; later in the year, her daughter Tang Dan (b. 1953) was sent to Heilongjiang and Yue Daiyun herself was sent to a cadre school at Liyuzhou in Jiangxi Province. In 1970 this school became a branch campus of Peking University, and she resumed teaching literature there. When the Liyuzhou Cadre School discontinued in 1971, Yue Daiyun returned to the main campus of Peking University.

In 1973, she was sent with students of journalism to Shijiazhuang during which time her husband accompanied Mao Zedong's wife Jiang Qing (q.v.) there on a tour of inspection. In apprehension, Yue Daiyun watched Tang Yijie's continued rise in political prominence as the Jiang Qing faction recruited senior academics to serve on its propaganda team. Tang Yijie subsequently became a member of what was known as the Two Universities Group (Liangxiao, academics from Peking University and Qinghua [Tsinghua] University), which was organized to lead the criticism campaigns against Lin Biao (1907–1971) and Zhou Enlai (1898–1976).

Yue Daiyun returned from Shijiazhuang to Peking University in 1974 only to encounter poster attacks as the Jiang Qing faction on campus led the attack on "right deviationists." During the year, Yue Daiyun accompanied students to a PLA Unit in Changping County, worked with journalism students on the *Beijing Daily*, and taught courses at the university on the Legalists. In the following year, 1975, she was assigned to the university farm in Daxing County, Hebei Province, to work and teach, but returned to Beijing with a severe recurrence of thyroid illness. Yue Daiyun was later assigned to teach a Chinese literature course to a group of foreign students. Deng Xiaoping (1904–1997) then had returned to politics, systematically consolidating his power base by returning many of the senior cadres who had been displaced during the Cultural Revolution. In August that year, Mao Zedong's comments on the historical novel *Water Margin* were used by the Jiang Qing factions to launch an attack on Deng Xiaoping. The Two Universities Group was required to provide the material for these attacks. On 8 January 1976, Premier Zhou Enlai died and in February posters went up at Peking University attacking Deng Xiaoping. The fierce intra-party struggle continued until the end of the year, resolved by the death of Mao Zedong on 26 September and the arrest of the Jiang Qing clique. This naturally had repercussions for Tang Yijie, who was detained as a member of the Two Universities Group. At Peking University, he and other group members were criticized at struggle meetings.

In 1978, at the Third Plenum of the Eleventh Central Committee, Deng Xiaoping and his new policies were endorsed by the party. Tang Yijie was released from detention and resumed teaching philosophy at Peking University, while Yue Daiyun was rehabilitated and her CCP membership restored. With the ascendancy of Deng Xiaoping to political power and the new policies that he engineered—significantly, including the restoration of a voice and role to intellectuals as well as opening up China to the rest of the world—Yue Daiyun and Tang Yijie quickly rose to prominence in their respective fields in the academic world.

In 1982 Yue Daiyun secured a research appointment at the Center for Chinese Studies on the Berkeley Campus at the University of California. Before returning to Peking University in 1984, she completed research on the representation of intellectuals in Chinese fiction and worked on an autobiographical account of her life. This account, written up by Carolyn Wakeman and published as *To the Storm: The Odyssey of a Revolutionary Chinese Woman* (1985), is one of the earliest unbiased documents on the Cultural Revolution.

In November 1984, the International Academy for Chinese Culture had been established through the initiative of a group of eminent professors in the Philosophy Department at Peking University, including Feng Youlan, Zhang Dainian, Zhu Bokun, and Tang Yijie. The group liaised with academics from the Chinese Academy of Social Sciences, the People's University of China, Beijing Normal University, Qinghua University, Beijing Teacher's College, as well as from Hong Kong, Taiwan, and abroad. The importance of the academy lies in the fact that it was the first privately funded, i.e., non-government-funded, academic institution established in China since 1949.

Yue Daiyun's passionate commitment to modern literature has been infectious among her numerous students, many of whom have now become established academics in their own right both within the universities of China and various other countries of the world. Her achievements, especially during the early years of the 1980s, would have foundered but for her veteran credentials as a rightist, persuasiveness, and, most importantly, resolute persistence in dealing with entrenched bureaucratic practices.

Mabel LEE

Poon, Cathy, trans. "Nietzsche in China." *The Journal of the Oriental Society of Australia*, 20
& 21 (1988–89): 199–219.
Yue Daiyun. *Touguo lishi de yanchen*. Beijing: Peking University Press, 1997.
———. *Wo jiu shi wo: Zhe lishi shuyu woziji*. Taipei: Zhengzhong shuju, 1995.
———, ed. *Guowai Lu Xun yanjiu lunji, 1960–1981*. Beijing: Beijing daxue chubanshe, 1981.
———. "Nicai zai Zhongguo." *Beijing daxue xuebao*, 3 (1980): 20–32.
Yue Daiyun and Carolyn Wakeman. *To the Storm: The Odyssey of a Revolutionary Chinese
Woman*. Berkeley: University of California Press, 1985.

Yuen, Susan

Susan Yuen, early 1920s–1980, was born in Manchester, England; neither her maiden
name nor the exact date of her birth has been established. She became an outstanding
community leader in Hong Kong from the 1950s to the 1970s.

Susan Yuen held a vision of what was needed to support the growth of industry and
commerce in Hong Kong and pursued it with energy and organizational ability. She
did so not as the nominal head of the many organizations she founded and ran but as
the second-in-command who actually did the work. At that time, few women were
promoted to leading positions in commerce or government in the Territory of Hong
Kong, and Susan Yuen accepted a subordinate role, wielding power through her influence and forceful personality. Although never serving on Hong Kong's quasi-par-
liament, the Legislative Council, she fed her ideas to council members at various
stages and so guided much of the debate in the chamber. In the words of one contemporary, Susan Yuen was exceptionally able in articulating problems and finding answers
and was "results focused." Thanks largely to her tireless efforts, Hong Kong's post-war
business development and export drive enjoyed spectacular success, making the territory a model for economic development throughout East and Southeast Asia.

No entry exists for Susan Yuen in the Hong Kong *Who's Who*, not because she did
not merit inclusion but because Susan Yuen refused authorization for a note. She
worked for the whole Hong Kong community, not her own personal reward, and
avoided publicity, revealing little of her own background, even to her own children.
This biographical essay is based on the little public information that is available and
on personal communication from former colleagues and friends.

Born and educated in Britain, Susan Yuen took up debating as a hobby. Her English language skills became impeccable, even to the point of her later being able to
prepare briefs for Hong Kong's international negotiations, greatly adding to her ability to contribute to the territory's development. In 1945, she married S.T. Yuen, an
engineer, who was later employed in the Hong Kong government. According to Robin
Hutcheon, former editor-in-chief of *South China Morning Post*, their marriage was a
happy partnership: "Where Susan was outspoken and argumentative, S.T. was retiring and unassuming. Outside of the family home, Susan made the running. Inside,
she deferred to him as the man of the house in the traditional Chinese way."

Susan Yuen arrived in Hong Kong in 1949 and within days had obtained a job as a
secretary at the English-language *Post*. Before long, she became secretary to a leading
Chinese businessman, a job that offered more challenge and interest. Susan Yuen also
threw herself into a campaign for the establishment of the Ruttonjee Hospital, a specialist

tuberculosis institution endowed by a Parsee family. The hospital was originally staffed by Columbian Mission doctors and nurses who had been working in China during the war; it played an important role in monitoring and treating mutations of tuberculosis, which was then endemic in large parts of the country. In Hong Kong in the early 1950s, hundreds of people died every week from this treatable disease. Later, Susan Yuen became vice-chair of the Hong Kong Anti-Tuberculosis and Thoracic Diseases Association.

Her work for Ruttonjee Hospital brought Susan Yuen to the attention of the Hong Kong government, and in 1959 she was invited by then governor Sir Alexander Grantham to become secretary to the working party responsible for setting up the body later known as the Federation of Hong Kong Industries. This group largely embodied her vision to promote Hong Kong industry regionally and internationally. Although a Chinese Manufacturers' Association already existed, it comprised mostly Cantonese business owners involved in traditional trade with overseas Chinese markets and lacked broad representation or promotional capacity. Susan Yuen persuaded recently arrived industrialists from Shanghai, Ningbo, and north China to join with the Cantonese in the new federation to project Hong Kong industry overseas. Bringing together these sectional groups and factions was a great challenge. Many business leaders were recent arrivals and not seeking direction regarding a long-term commitment to their new home; for the most part they saw themselves as temporary refugees from the chaos in China. Susan Yuen convinced them of the benefits of promoting Hong Kong products and in less than one year became the first executive director of the federation, in 1960.

Industrial enterprises in Hong Kong at that time mainly used finance from local banks and drew on the pool of labor provided by the hundreds of thousands of refugees from the civil war in China. Most of this industry was small-scale and labor intensive. Hong Kong products were regarded internationally as being of low quality and dubious reliability, and there was no vehicle for their promotion or regulation.

Extending her interest in promoting Hong Kong industry, Susan Yuen was also instrumental in forming the Hong Kong Management Association. This body was the main provider of the territory's in-service business management training program and provided initial promotion prospects for many aspiring young Chinese. She was chief executive for seventeen years. Sir S.Y. Chung (Zhong Shiyuan) later recalled: "The inception of the Management Association took place one evening in March 1960 in Sydney, when a small delegation of five of us led by Sir Sik-nin Chau [Zhou Xinian] was attending a CIOS [International Council for Scientific Management] world conference on management. Mrs. Yuen was the secretary of that delegation. With the flair for organization and management we have come to recognize as her hallmark, Mrs. Yuen had us drafting the memorandum and articles of association, recruiting the first members and inaugurating the association, all within a matter of months of that Sydney meeting. At the end of its first year of existence, the association's membership was 300."

Susan Yuen also actively participated in the formation of the Hong Kong Export Credit Insurance Corporation, which provided competitive insurance terms against business risks in Hong Kong's world markets for local manufacturers and exporters. In 1961, she helped form the Freight Joint Committee and became its honorary secretary. For over six years, she worked with its members, which included the Chinese

Manufacturers' Association, Federation of Hong Kong Industries, Hong Kong Exporters' Association, Hong Kong Chamber of Commerce, and the Indian Chamber of Commerce, and finally persuaded these bodies to establish the Hong Kong Shippers' Council. This was then joined by the Hong Kong Spinners' Association, the Hong Kong Plastic Manufacturers' Association, Hong Kong Air Freight Agents, the Management Association, Federation of Hong Kong Garment Manufacturers, the Hong Kong Export Credit Insurance Corporation, and the Chinese Chamber of Commerce, making it one of the most powerful business bodies in the territory.

Moving easily between government and business, Susan Yuen was instrumental in setting up a variety of business organizations that provided an effective interface between the two realms. These non-government organizations have been a special feature of Hong Kong development. In 1963, as an observer from the Hong Kong government, she attended the meeting of the governing body of the Asian Productivity Organization (APO), which at that time had nine government representatives and was aiming to raise productivity and living standards in the region. Following this meeting, Susan Yuen recommended that Hong Kong join the international organization, and Hong Kong's decision took effect in the same year, together with the formation of the Hong Kong Productivity Council. She became vice-chair of the APO in 1978. Susan Yuen also helped found the Hong Kong Polytechnic (now the Hong Kong Polytechnic University) to provide technical and vocational education at the tertiary level and support to Hong Kong industry and commerce. She was active in the formation and governorship of the Hong Kong Training Council, catering to industrial training and apprenticeships; the Standards and Testing Center, to enhance the quality and image of Hong Kong products; the Industrial Design Council, to promote product design consciousness and manufacturing standards; and the Packaging Council, to improve promotional and protective packaging.

Perhaps her most significant achievement was in the field of trade promotion. Susan Yuen saw the possibility of Hong Kong copying the example of the Japanese Export Trade Organization (JETRO), which had effectively enhanced the value and reputation of Japanese products. She lobbied the Hong Kong government vigorously on this point. Sir Jack Cater, who was then economic secretary, was convinced by Susan Yuen's arguments and asked her to assist in organizing such a body. Sir Sik-nin Chau, head of the Hong Kong Chinese Bank, became the first chairman of the Hong Kong Trade Development Council in 1965, and Susan Yuen was a council member. She traveled widely with Chau representing Hong Kong export industries.

In recognition of her service to the business community, Susan Yuen was elected as a fellow to the International Academy of Management, one of only a few women to have been so honored. She was secretary-general to the World Packaging Organization, chair of the Export Group on Shipping and Ports of the Economic and Social Commission for Asia and the Pacific, a Hong Kong Justice of the Peace, and was awarded an OBE (Order of the British Empire) in 1976 for her services to industry.

In 1967, Hong Kong experienced serious unrest flowing from the Cultural Revolution in China. Left-wing factions aligned to different interests on the mainland fought running battles on the streets of Hong Kong, and law and order became the top priority of government authorities. Business confidence was at a low ebb, and many foreign companies pulled out of the territory. Susan Yuen assisted the government in many ways and frequently convened meetings with local and foreign business leaders to discuss problems and find solutions. Speaking at her memorial service in 1980, Sir S.Y. Chung recalled that in mid-1967 he was chairing a special meeting of the General Committee of the Federation of Hong Kong Industries to discuss whether they should make a public declaration of support for the Hong Kong government. The meeting had gone on all morning without reaching consensus. During the break for lunch, she was able as executive director to persuade all the committee members to come to an agreement; when they reconvened in the afternoon, they passed unanimously a resolution to declare full and unreserved support.

Susan Yuen's interests were not exclusively commercial and industrial. She also worked with Sir Run Run Shaw (Shao Yifu), a partner in Hong Kong's largest movie company, the Shaw Brothers Film Studio, to start the annual Hong Kong Arts Festival. Susan Yuen was a member of several welfare body boards, including the Ruttonjee Hospital and its sister institution, the Grantham Hospital. The Grantham, which specializes in cardiothoracic and heart diseases, pioneered open-heart surgery in the region.

Having helped set up the Shipping Federation, Susan Yuen was widely expected to assume the position of first chair in 1980. However, she suddenly fell ill, became hospitalized in the Grantham Hospital, and died, probably of cancer. In the same year, she had been on the point of becoming chair of the APO but declined the appointment because of ill health. Susan Yuen retired from full-time work with the Federation of Industries and the Hong Kong Management Association in 1976; at that time, the two bodies had jointly established a foundation in her honor to provide fellowships for industrial and business managers to develop skills and promote industrial and management research.

She has been described by Lady Peggy Cater, a former colleague on several boards and committees, as "highly eloquent, forceful and dedicated, with deep and detailed knowledge of her many interests, combined with a delightful personality and an enviable sense of humour." Susan Yuen's two children, David and Diana, now live in Australia.

Jocelyn CHEY

Cater, Lady Peggy. Personal communication to author, 1998.
"'First Lady' Susan Yuen Passes Away." *Hong Kong Industrial News*, 9 July 1980, 10–11.
Hutcheon, Robin. Personal communication to author, 2000.
"It Takes a Team of Five to Replace Susan Yuen." *South China Morning Post*, 25 June 1976.
"A Last Tribute to Hong Kong's First Lady of Industry." *South China Morning Post*, 24 June 1980.
"Leaders Pay Tribute to Susan Yuen." *Hong Kong Standard*, 27 June 1980.
"Susan Yuen: We Will Not Forget Her." *Shippers Today* (Hong Kong), July 1980.

Yungtze: *see* **Jung-tzu**

Yung-tzu: *see* **Jung-tzu**

Z

Zen, Sophia: *see* Chen Hengzhe

Zen Sun, E-tu: *see* Sun, E-tu Zen

Zeng Baosun: *see* Zheng Zhaoyu

Zeng Zhaoyu

Zeng Zhaoyu, 1909–1964, of Xiangxiang County, Hunan Province, was an archaeologist and museum specialist.

The family into which she was born includes several famous women. Zeng Jifen (see *Biographical Dictionary of Chinese Women: The Qing Period*), the youngest daughter of late Qing reform statesman Zeng Guofan (1811–1872), married into the Nie family of Hengshan, Hunan. Guo Yun (see *Biographical Dictionary of Chinese Women: The Qing Period*) was the wife of Zeng Guofan's third son Zeng Jihong (1848–1881). Zeng Baosun (1893–1978), the great-granddaughter of Zeng Guofan and granddaughter of Guo Yun, was the first Chinese woman to graduate from an English university, obtaining a Master of Science from the University of London in 1916. Zeng Baosun also obtained a diploma in teaching before returning to Changsha where she founded the Yifang Girls' School to honor the memory of her grandmother.

Zeng Zhaoyu was the third of seven children born to Zeng Yongzhou, grandson of Zeng Guofan's younger brother, and his wife Chen Xiuying. Zeng Zhaoyu's older brother Zeng Zhaolun (1899–1967) became famous as a chemist; a younger brother, Zeng Shaojie, achieved fame as an artist and expert on seal inscriptions. Her younger sister Zeng Zhaomei recalled that when she was ill, Zeng Zhaoyu used to tell her stories, make papercuts, and give her medicine. The family was brought up strictly, with an emphasis on the importance of education. A household teacher was recruited to teach all the children as soon as they reached five years of age; when the children were twelve years old, they were sent to high school in Changsha. Zeng Zhaoyu was regarded as the best scholar in the family and showed talent in writing classical poetry.

In 1929 she gained entrance to the Literature Department of Nanjing's Central University, then one of China's top universities. Her professors praised her academic work, and her calligraphy was highly regarded. After graduation, Zeng Zhaoyu entered the National Studies Research Institute of Ginling [Jinling] University. By this time, she had achieved a reputation as a poet, writing in classical Chinese.

In 1933 Zeng Zhaoyu took a teaching position in the high school attached to Ginling Men's University in Nanjing, teaching the national language to senior students. In summer 1935, she went to Britain to study archaeology at her own expense, obtaining a master's degree the following year, before going on to study museum science at the German National Museum in Berlin. There, and in Schleswig-Holstein, Zeng Zhaoyu participated in local archaeological work. In 1938 she obtained a position as an assistant lecturer at the University of London, but instead of pursuing this career returned to China, determined to share in the Chinese people's struggle in the face of the Japanese invasion. The Japanese had already occupied Hunan and Guangdong Provinces, and when Zeng Zhaoyu reached her old home in Xiangxiang she found that her mother had fled to Guilin. Zeng Zhaoyu followed her and placed an advertisement in the local paper in Guilin to find news of her mother's whereabouts before going on with her to Kunming. There, Zeng Zhaoyu was invited by the Preparatory Committee of the National Museum to join its Specialist Design Committee. Her older brother Zeng Zhaolun was teaching at nearby Southwest Union University and two younger sisters also studied there. When her mother died of diabetes in Kunming, Zeng Zhaoyu helped support her sisters through their studies.

In 1939 Zeng Zhaoyu joined an archaeological expedition to Dali in search of new Stone Age sites. This was the first such expedition in Yunnan Province and her first opportunity to apply on a dig in her own country the archaeological techniques she had acquired in Europe. Between March that year and September 1940, the team uncovered five sites—Malong, Foding I and II, Longchuan, and Baiyun I—yielding many objects. In the second half of the year, Zeng Zhaoyu went with the National Museum in its move to Lizhuang village in Nanxi County, Sichuan Province. A two-volume report on the excavations in Yunnan Province, jointly compiled with Wu Jinding, was published in 1942 and greatly enriched the literature on Yunnan archaeology. Zeng Zhaoyu was the sole author of one of these volumes, entitled *Ancient Inscribed Tiles Excavated below Diancangshan* (Diancangshan xia suo chu gudai you zi canwa).

Between 1940 and 1943, the National Museum and the Institute of History and Linguistics at Academia Sinica cooperated in archaeological studies in Sichuan Province, their first objective being to excavate a Han dynasty "hanging tomb" in Pengshan County near Chengdu. Zeng Zhaoyu, then in her thirties and full of energy and enthusiasm, took part in many of the digs, worked in the office, and wrote up reports. She believed that historical work based only on written records was limited and suggested that such theoretical efforts required tangible objects to enrich it, in essence transforming the study by incorporating empirical evidence within the material. This belief lay behind her earlier decision to engage in museum studies. Zeng Zhaoyu and Li Ji, head of the Preparatory Committee for the National Museum, collaborated on a book entitled *The Museum* (Bowuguan). It seems Zeng Zhaoyu was largely responsible for the comprehensive content of the book; although only eighty-four pages in length, it listed reference materials in Chinese, English, and French that made it an important contribution to Chinese museum studies.

After the end of the Sino-Japanese War in 1945, the archaeologist returned to Nanjing with the National Museum as its general manager and continued to serve as a member of its Specialist Design Committee. The museum had been bombed by the Japanese and lay in ruins. Twice, Zeng Zhaoyu borrowed other halls in which to stage exhibitions, one devoted to the Han period and the other to Bronze Age objects. By spring 1948, the museum's exhibition halls were basically restored, and she was able to arrange a large joint exhibition with the Palace Museum.

At the end of 1948 wounded KMT soldiers moved into Nanjing after the battle of Huaihai, and some were accommodated in the museum. Zeng Zhaoyu was not happy about this. She also resisted the plan of Chiang Kai-shek (1887–1975) to remove museum treasures to Taiwan, making ultimately unsuccessful representations to senior KMT officials. According to her younger sister, Zeng Zhaoyu became very depressed, feeling that her mission was to remain in China. The main building of the National Museum was still under construction, and she did not want to abandon efforts mid-stream. Although many of her friends and colleagues left for Taiwan, Zeng Zhaoyu and her older brother Zeng Zhaolun remained on the mainland. The communist government changed the museum's name to the Nanjing Museum, and it formally reopened in March 1950, with Zeng Zhaoyu as deputy director, under Xu Pingyu as director. In January 1955, Zeng Zhaoyu was promoted to director.

In 1950 she had led an excavation of two Southern Tang dynasty royal tombs and authored the report on the dig. During that decade, Zeng Zhaoyu led two archaeological teams, one working on the regulation of the waters of the Huai River and another in East China. Zeng Zhaoyu also edited the report on the ancient painted tomb south of the Yi River, in Shandong Province. Numerous discoveries were made about that time in Jiangsu Province, and she contributed significantly to knowledge about the Stone Age. Zeng Zhaoyu co-authored with Yin Huanzhang two important reports, one on the Hushu culture and the other entitled "Two Problems in the Ancient History of Jiangsu" (Jiangsu gudai lishi shang de liangge wenti). While studying in Europe, Zeng Zhaoyu had become convinced of the importance of ethnographic studies and she arranged training courses for specialists to work in Jiangsu and Zhejiang, combining ethnography and archaeology. Recognizing the importance of Jiangsu and Zhejiang artists in the history of Chinese art, she also took an active interest in Ming and Qing paintings. Thus, by 1960 the Nanjing Museum collection amounted to over thirty thousand pieces and was recognized as the third most important holding in the country.

Great strides were made in archaeological work in China in the 1950s, and Zeng Zhaoyu played an important role in promoting this by then prestigious discipline. She remained unmarried, devoted her time to work and study, and achieved recognition for her contribution. A colleague, Tang Maosong, later wrote this tribute to her:

> Among Chinese archaeologists there used to be a saying: "South Zeng and North Xia," indicating that you and Xia Nai were equally outstanding . . . What people admired was not only your exceptional academic achievements, but also that you never put on an air of authority, that you were always disciplined and serious about correcting your own faults.

This and many other tributes to Zeng Zhaoyu were published in a bulletin of the Nanjing Museum in 1984 on the twentieth anniversary of her death. Other colleagues testified to her generosity even during the difficult war years and to her plain lifestyle, hard work, and dedication to duty. In her leisure hours, Zeng Zhaoyu was known to sometimes recite the older *kunqu* operas but had little time in her busy academic life to attend performances.

She was, however, active in the political movements engineered by the CCP after

1949. During the movement in the early 1950s to criticize the KMT scholar Hu Shi (1891–1962), for instance, Zeng Zhaoyu did not hesitate to hand over to the party a copy of his works that the scholar himself had given her. She played her part in united front work, broadcasting several speeches to relatives in Taiwan. Zeng Zhaoyu joined in demands for the restoration of treasures stolen from the mainland by Chiang Kai-shek. She made repeated unsuccessful applications to join the CCP, despite expressing a willingness to criticize her own past in the process. Zeng Zhaoyu was appointed to the CPPCC and Jiangsu provincial and Nanjing municipal branches of the ACWF; the Foreign Cultural Association; as a council member to the Preparatory Committee for the Chinese Archaeological Association; and as first president of the Jiangsu Provincial Combined Association for Philosophy and the Social Sciences. Her name was even mentioned once by Mao Zedong (1893–1976) in a speech, in reference to Zeng Zhaoyu's being a descendant of Zeng Guofan.

Zeng Zhaoyu's elder brother Zeng Zhaolun became vice-minister for Education in 1957 but was condemned as a rightist and imprisoned. Then, in 1964 many famous scholars, including several she admired, were attacked during the socialist education movement. Deeply traumatized over these events and having no one to share her feelings of anger and fear, Zeng Zhaoyu became depressed, silent, and eventually psychotic, to the extent that she was admitted to the Dingshan Sanatorium in Nanjing. When friends visited, Zeng Zhaoyu told them: "Do not make more allowances for me, I am not capable of anything." On 22 December, it is said that she wished to take her doctor back to his home by car. After accompanying him there, Zeng Zhaoyu then told the driver: "Take me to Linggu temple, I want to cheer myself up." When the car stopped at the temple, she gave the driver apples to eat and asked him to wait. Then she climbed up the pagoda and jumped to her death.

Zeng Zhaoyu belonged to the first generation of Chinese women to gain professional Western qualifications on the same basis as men and the same opportunities to follow a professional career. She made important advances in her chosen fields of archaeology and museum studies. Unfortunately, the political system and atmosphere of China in the late 1950s and 1960s adversely affected her psychological balance and career, preventing her achieving even greater results at a time when unprecedented archaeological discoveries were being made in China. Her death at the age of fifty-five was a tragic loss.

This biography is based on the comprehensive account of Zeng Zhaoyu's life and achievements compiled by Li Yu-ning from written and oral sources.

Jocelyn CHEY

Li Youning [Li Yu-ning]. "Zeng Zhaoyu (1909–1964)—Wo guo zui jiechu de nüxing kaoguxuejia ji bowuguanxuejia." *Jindai Zhongguo funü shi yanjiu.* no. 1 (June 1993), 35–46.

Zeng Zhi

Zeng Zhi, 1911–1998, of Yizhang County, Hunan Province, was one of a small group of women demonstrating outstanding organizational ability within the CCP; she rose to the position of deputy head of the Organization Department of the Central Committee.

Zeng Zhi was born into a wealthy family. Her maternal grandfather was a graduate of Zhengfa University and a well-known local public figure, with fair-sized land holdings of over one hundred *mu* (equivalent to about six hectares). Zeng Zhi was strong willed and rebellious and was said to have been beautiful and wild. She desired above all else to become a "professional revolutionary" instead of remaining the daughter of a bourgeois family or becoming the wife of a prominent man.

Zeng Zhi studied at Hunan Third Normal School in the city of Hengyang and was deeply influenced by classmates such as Mao Zejiang, Xia Mingheng, and Xia Mingyu. These young men belonged to the famous "two revolutionary families" of Mao Zedong (1893–1976) and Xia Minghan. Zeng Zhi also read martial arts novels extensively and longed to be a female hero. Wanting to discard the destiny with which she had been born—a young woman wrapped up in beautiful clothes and hidden under makeup—Zeng Zhi dreamed of disguising herself as a man to sit for examinations at the Whampoa Military Academy. Eventually, she was able to enter Hengyang Peasants' Movement Institute in Hunan, where students followed both military training (30 percent) and political studies (70 percent). Zeng Zhi was the only female student at this kind of institute; most of these schools eventually mutated into mainly military training institutions.

Active in revolutionary work at fifteen, in 1926 she became involved in the peasant's movement in Binzhou and participated in organizing a guerrilla force. Shortly afterward, Zeng Zhi armed herself with a red-tasseled spear and, a red belt at her waist, dressed as a man to lead a guerrilla force in the South Hunan peasants' riot. She also worked as a propaganda agitator. Zeng Zhi fell in love with and married Xia Mingzheng, director of the Peasants' Movement Institute; he was also a younger brother of Xia Minghan. Zeng Zhi's husband was killed within a year after the Hunan riot failed.

In 1927, she went as a propaganda worker with the South Hunan Peasants' Militia into Jinggangshan, where Mao Zedong and Zhu De (1886–1976) had recently established the Red Army base. The militia was initially designated as the Seventh Division of the Red Army but soon became the Thirty-first Regiment. Zeng Zhi was by then married to Cai Xieming, who had been political commissar of the Seventh Division; Zeng Zhi was appointed general party secretary of the Red Army's General Rear Hospital. In early 1929, she placed their infant son in the care of peasants on Jinggangshan and marched southeast with the Fourth Red Army of Mao, Zhu De, and Chen Yi. As team leader of the Women's Section and chief of the Workers' and Peasants' Movement Committee, Zeng Zhi was in charge of the more than one hundred women marching with the Red Army. She also helped establish revolutionary bases in South Jiangxi and South Fujian. Zeng Zhi worked directly under the leadership of Mao and became very friendly with him and other party leaders. After the Red Army gained control of Western Fujian, she left the army and remained in the area as secretary to the special Youth League Committee. Zeng Zhi engaged in long-term underground work and set up local military forces, which led to her being dubbed "Woman Warrior of West Fujian" (Minxi nüjiang).

Because the militia was so short of funds, she sold her second son in order to raise funds for her party membership. During this time, her husband was denounced as a member of the Democratic Socialist Party and persecuted to death. In 1932, Zeng Zhi married her third husband, the famous Tao Zhu (1908–1969), who was then party secretary of Fuzhou Municipality. She herself was wrongfully persecuted by the CCP on four separate occasions while doing underground work in the KMT-controlled region in Xiamen (Amoy). This was because the rectification campaigns of that period became excessive; at one stage, Zeng Zhi was excommunicated from the party. In 1938, during the second KMT-CCP united front, Zeng Zhi was in Hubei Province. In her official capacity as head of the Jingmen Cooperative Restaurant, she arranged transportation for CCP troops designated as the Thirty-third KMT Regiment. In this way, Zeng Zhi also fulfilled her underground responsibilities as party secretary to Jingmen, Dangyang, and Yuan'an Counties.

She reached the communist enclave in Yan'an in 1939; Tao Zhu arrived the following year, and they lived together from then on. Zeng Zhi studied at the Marxist-Leninist College, but, despite a record of courageous devotion to the party, was detained for over a year during the 1941 rectification campaign. Tao Zhu, however, was not criticized. Upon rehabilitation, Zeng Zhi was reelected as an alternate member for the Seventh Plenary Session of the CCP. With the end of the Sino-Japanese War in 1945, she accompanied her husband to the northeast to establish a base there. During the four years in the region, Zeng Zhi was appointed party secretary to Shenyang, a member of the Shenyang Municipal Committee, and head of the Organization Department of Liaoning First Regional Committee.

She attended both the first National Women's Congress in Beijing and the opening ceremony of the founding of the PRC. Zeng Zhi continued to hold high-level posts after 1949 and was appointed party secretary to the city of Guangzhou. Her husband became provincial party secretary of Guangdong. By August 1966, Tao Zhu had been elected to the Standing Committee of the Central Committee of the CCP, which placed him fourth highest in the party hierarchy. At the beginning of the Cultural Revolution, however, he suffered persecution. Zeng Zhi, who was ill at the time, left Guangzhou and traveled to Beijing in September 1966 to be with him. She endured three years of extreme hardship with her husband before he was exiled to Anhui Province, where he died soon after, of cancer. Zeng Zhi was then sent to a village in Guangdong Province. Weak, fragile, and sick, she lived alone in a dilapidated hut for three years. Tao Zhu was posthumously rehabilitated after the Cultural Revolution, and Zeng Zhi's rehabilitation resulted in her becoming deputy head of the Organization Department of the Central Committee. In this capacity, she assisted Hu Yaobang (1915–1989), head of the Department, in the enormous task of rehabilitating the wronged.

Zeng Zhi edited a three-volume work entitled *Women Soldiers of the Long March* (Changzheng nüzhanshi) in 1987 and wrote an autobiography. Although well into her eighties by then, ill and weighing only thirty-seven kilograms, she continued to document the rehabilitation work commenced in 1977. Suffering from cancer and with her health deteriorating, Zeng Zhi dictated to her daughter Tao Siliang (b. 1940) a verbal will, declaring: "As a communist, I should not have anything to bequeath. Therefore, my children cannot inherit my hard-earned money." Her "hard-earned money" included 140,000 yuan of accumulated backpay for the period of the Cultural Revolution and pocket money that she had sorted carefully into eighty envelopes to demonstrate her incorruptibility. After Zeng Zhi's death, 160,000 yuan was given, as instructed, to the Old Cadres Bureau of the Central Committee to build "Hope" primary schools in the remotest and poorest regions of Qiyang and Yizhang Counties in Hunan Province. An amount was also given to the Old Cadres Bureau to cover the cost of publishing her two books. Astonishingly, despite the several serious injustices she and her loved ones had suffered over a period of many years beginning in the 1930s, Zeng Zhi appeared to harbor no bitterness toward the CCP or its leaders.

On 16 June 1998, she slipped into a coma. When Zeng Zhi awoke briefly the following day, her daughter told her that publication of the autobiography had been confirmed to which her mother replied: "Don't praise me too much!" These were her last words. She died in Beijing on 21 June at the age of eighty-seven.

Zeng Zhi once said: "I am most disgusted by being called 'Shouzhang furen' [wife of a leader]. I dislike being just a wife." In accordance with her will, part of her ashes were buried under a tree on Jinggangshan, where her dreams and memories remained, and part under the rock at Tao Zhu's tomb in Baiyunshan in Guangzhou.

GUO Chen
(Translated by Jennifer Zhang)

Quan Yanchi. *Tao Zhu zai wenhua dageming zhong*. Beijing: Zhonggong zhongyang dangxiao chubanshe, 1991.
Zeng Zhi, ed. *Changzheng nüzhanshi*, 3 vols. Changchun: Beifang funü ertong chubanshe, 1987.
———. "Tao Zhu zai Liao Ji zhanhuo zhong." In *Bili Tao Zhu*. Beijing: Renmin chubanshe, 1990, 143.
———. "Yu Mao Zedong de jiaowang." In *Zhongguo nühongjun*. Xi'an: Shanxi renmin chubanshe, 180–96.

Zhai Yongming

Zhai Yongming, b. 1955 in Chengdu, Sichuan Province, is a prominent poet in the PRC.

Her name is first and foremost associated with the emergence in the mid-1980s of a critical discourse on "women's poetry" (*nüxing shige*) in the PRC. While it is true that Zhai Yongming enunciated the idea of "women's consciousness" (*nüxing yishi*) in poetry, her life and writings also bear relevance to other issues in contemporary literature in the country, such as the discourse on distinctive mainland Chinese poetic styles, coexistence of official and unofficial literary circuits, cultural regionalism versus the hegemony of Beijing, and Chinese writers and artists in the diaspora.

Zhai Yongming's family originally hailed from Henan Province. The combination of holding down a demanding job in the army and raising four children became too much for Zhai's mother, and she left her eight-month-old daughter with an elderly Chengdu couple living in traditional Chinese housing (a courtyard surrounded by wooden homes inhabited by a number of families). In raising the baby, Zhai Yongming's foster parents employed less rigorous discipline than her mother might have. By the time she returned to Chengdu from her army postings, her daughter Zhai Yongming was fourteen years old and decidedly a less submissive and obedient teenager than she should have been by orthodox standards. The ensuing conflict between mother and daughter—Zhai Yongming summed up their relationship as "alienating"—never truly resolved itself. The poet's attempts at reconciliation while asserting and preserving her individuality and independence proved fruitless; their relationship is reflected in *Mother* (Muqin), one of Zhai's most famous poems, written during the first phase of her literary career that had commenced in earnest in the early 1980s.

Zhai had written her very first poems more than a decade earlier, in 1969. Like other accomplished contemporary Chinese poets, Zhai Yongming recalls briefly trying her hand at classical Chinese genres but soon discarded the "old forms" (*jiuti shi*). As had happened in the lives of countless urban youths, Yongming's own secondary schooling was interrupted in the late 1960s when the education apparatus ground to a halt with the outbreak of the Cultural Revolution; she did, however, graduate from a Chengdu high school, in 1974. Subsequently, Zhai Yongming and her classmates were "rusticated," in line with a pattern recurrent in the lives of many in her generation of "young intellectuals" (*zhishi qingnian*): the young people were requested to live and work in the countryside or on factory production teams. Zhai Yongming spent close to two years living in a village not far from Chengdu. Again, this episode would later find literary expression in an important part of her early oeuvre, the long poem *Jing'an Village* (Jing'an zhuang). Its twelve sections named after the twelve months of the year dwell in literary fashion on the hard lot of local peasants and, more broadly, on the insignificance and helplessness of human beings in the face of fate.

In 1976 the poet was transferred back to Chengdu. After six months in a city factory, she was among those lucky enough to be admitted to institutes of tertiary education. Zhai Yongming enrolled in the Laser Technology Department of the Chengdu Institute for Telecommunications Engineering (Chengdu dianxun gongcheng xueyuan jiguang jishu xi) and graduated in 1980. In 1981 she found employment at the Number 209 Research Institute of the Military Equipment Industries Department (Bingqi gongye bu 209 yanjiu suo), also located in Chengdu. Her official affiliation with this work unit continued into the 1990s, although by that time most of her professional activities were in literature. In 1984, Zhai Yongming had become a member of the Sichuan branch of the Chinese Writers' Association.

She started writing seriously in 1980 and began to publish in 1982. In that year, two of her poems were included in *Forest Regrown* (Ci shenglin), an early and influential Chengdu-centered anthology of avant-garde poetry also containing the work of such famous authors as Bai Hua, Huang Xiang, Ouyang Jianghe, and Zhong Ming. *Forest Regrown* is a classic example of mainland Chinese "underground" (*dixia*) or "unofficial" (*fei guanfang*) poetry publications, which have been instrumental in the development of post-Mao poetry. The most famous was the Beijing-based magazine *Today* (Jintian), which appeared from 1978 to 1980. These publications were usually tolerated as long as they steered clear of politically sensitive subject matter and were not officially marketed and sold; underground and unofficial channels in different regions of China have thus voiced a wide range of poetic experiments outside the narrow confines of state-sanctioned cultural orthodoxy of the 1980s and 1990s.

Having written and published a number of roughly one-page texts—in PRC literary terminology, classified as "short poems" (*duanshi*)—Zhai Yongming truly found her stride in 1984 when she wrote *Woman* (Nüren), consisting of four sections, each made up of four or five separate, indeed autonomous, poems but displaying clear thematic and stylistic consistency. Through 1990 she continued to produce predominantly long texts, called poem cycles/series (*zushi*) or simply "long poems" (*changshi*), as in the case of the abovementioned *Jing'an Village*. With regular exposure in underground and unofficial circuits from the beginning, Zhai Yongming's official breakthrough came in 1986 when *Woman* appeared in *Poetry News* (Shige bao), accompanied by her manifesto-like piece called *Night Consciousness* (Heiye de yishi), as well as in the authoritative nationwide journal *Poetry* (Shikan). Other mainstream official periodicals that featured her work in the second half of the 1980s were *People's Literature* (Renmin wenxue), *Chinese Writers* (Zhongguo zuojia), and *The Stars Poetry Journal* (Xingxing shikan)—a record indicative of the prominence the poet acquired almost overnight with the appearance of *Woman*. Further publication data underscoring her rapid rise to fame are the substantial selections from her work in all major poetry anthologies covering the late 1980s and after, and the fact that two individual collections of her poetry came out in 1988 and 1989 with respected publishing houses, *Woman*, named after Zhai's *pièce de resistance*, and *Above All Roses* (Zai yiqie meigui zhi shang).

While Zhai Yongming has contributed much to post-Mao poetry, the debate on "women's poetry" sparked by her writings is of special importance, not least because the poet herself has at various times used the prerogative of the instigator-cum-expert to reappraise the discussion. In *Night Consciousness*, she first brings up "women's thinking" (*nüxing sixiang*) and the sublimation in poetry of aspects of womanhood, presenting night as a metaphor for women's consciousness. Zhai Yongming distinguishes three possible qualities to its presence, "feminine, lyrical sentimentality" (*nüzi qi shuqing ganshang*); "unconcealed feminism" (*bu jia yanshi de nüquan zhuyi*); and "women's literature," based on a women's consciousness expressing itself in superficially intangible ways.

Turning to her contemporaries, she points out that several Chinese women poets have yet to realize their subtle powers, hastening to add that she does not consider herself anything like a "typical woman." In tune with not a few of her contemporaries in poetry and criticism, Zhai's tone in the article is positively idealist and solemn. To be sure, post-Mao poetry in China had seen an influential woman poet before Zhai, e.g., the widely read Shu Ting (*q.v.*), who was a resounding name in the "obscure poetry" (*menglong shi*) first canvassed in *Today*. But Shu Ting's foremost accomplishment had lain in balancing the pessimism and despair of her fellow literary iconoclasts in the late 1970s and early 1980s while joining forces with them to reclaim poetry's rightful ground from politics.

Zhai's *Woman* and *Night Consciousness* immediately drew the attention of Tang Xiaodu, a leading poetry critic in 1980s and 1990s China. Early in 1987, he published a review article in *Poetry* called "Women's Poetry: From Night to Day," canonizing the concept of women's poetry as put forward by Zhai's work. Tang acknowledged the dominance of male worldviews in twentieth-century Chinese literature and its extension to the practice of and the discourse on women's literature. He recognized that in spite of many theoretical declarations and creative efforts in women's literature since the New Culture Movement of the 1920s, Zhai's poetry and commentary presented an actual breakthrough: her work successfully freed itself from an image of woman that had been effectively constructed by men. This was especially manifest in Zhai's deconstruction of traditional concepts of (female) beauty (*mei*). In discussing her poetry, Tang pointed out both specific traits of Zhai's "women's poetry" and kinship with foreign women poets such as Sylvia Plath, stressing the striking individuality of Zhai Yongming's poems.

The public dialogue between Tang and Zhai Yongming took place at a time when post-Mao poetry was about to explode into unprecedented abundance and pluriformity. In the late 1980s, "women's poetry" quickly became an active constituent in the bustling mainland Chinese literary scene, as is clear from numerous publications in both unofficial and official circuits. An outstanding example of the latter category is provided by a twenty-page feature in *Poetry*'s June 1989 special issue on "women's poetry," which went to press days before the bloody repression of the Protest Movement in Tian'anmen now remembered as June Fourth (*liu si*). The issue "Notes on 'Women's Poetry'" includes contributions by Zheng Min, Yi Lei, Zhai Yongming, Hai Nan, Wang Xiaoni, Xiao Jun, and Lu Yimin. Alternating between disparagement and support, thoughtfulness and impulse, their writings show that official recognition of the importance of "women's poetry" had not detracted from the genre's controversiality. Zhai Yongming's piece, "'Women's Poetry' versus Women's Consciousness in Poetry" ("Nüxing shige" yu shige zhong de nüxing yishi) is arguably one of the most forceful statements on the topic to date. With a characteristically elegant economy of thinking, she asks a number of pertinent questions: If poetry about women written by women is "women's poetry," then how should poetry about women written by men be classified? Is it right for critics to focus on the contingency of an author's gender rather than on the text itself? Is there a danger of women poets limiting themselves to remain within the boundaries of "common fables about woman" as a result of the debate? Zhai Yongming concludes that "a true 'women's consciousness' in poetry does not find expression through fixed models but is present in the atmosphere created by women poets in their work, whatever they write about and in whatever form. The question is not what one writes, but how one writes it." In sum, her contribution shows a combination of original insight and a drive to initiate serious debate on the one hand and an ability to maintain critical distance on the other.

If the special issue on "women's poetry" of this leading official journal proves Zhai's impact on her contemporary environment—otherwise evident in her popularity among poetry readers—in one sense the significance also marks the end of a stage in her development as an artist. In her work between 1980 and 1989, thematics of womanhood coexist and blend with literary exploration of themes about the individual self and its relationship to the world around it as well as the role of fate and reality of dreams and visions. Stylistically, Zhai Yongming's poem cycles/series and "long poems" delivered in urgent, sometimes eerie, voice remain a trademark of her art. See, for instance, the opening stanzas of *Premonition* (Yugan), one of the constituent poems in *Woman:*

> in the depth of night comes the woman in black / her stealthy glances wear me out /
> / suddenly I realize all fish die in this season / and all roads cross birds / trails //
> darkness tugs at the corpse-like mountain range / faintly, the heartbeat of the undergrowth is heard / giant birds with human eyes / look down upon me from the sky / in savage air kept secret / winter throbs with a cruel, male consciousness.

In 1990–91, however, the poet was to undergo a transition that would eventually lead to a new, albeit recognizably personal, realm of poetics. Arguably, this change may have been catalyzed by the course the poet took in her personal life.

For not a few PRC writers and artists, the events of June Fourth in 1989 presented a rather compelling moment for reflection. Yet, as a poet, Zhai Yongming had not really been socially or politically oriented; it is in fact impossible to identify unequivocal, direct connections between the 1989 sociopolitical upheaval and her literary production. The greatest influence on her writing in those years was her departure from Chengdu in December 1990 to New York, with her husband, the successful painter He Duoling. He had been given an opportunity to live and work in the city for an extended period. While Zhai had for many years quite contentedly been part of the Chengdu avant-garde, she was excited at the prospect of living abroad and widening her horizons. In some ways, however, the couple's move there turned into a disappointment. Zhai quickly realized "she would never be able to express herself in English as well as in Chinese" and subsequently dropped efforts to learn the language of the country in which she then resided. The couple's social contacts largely remained within the circle of the New York PRC Chinese community.

On the whole, Zhai did not feel comfortable in New York and more or less stopped writing poetry. Tellingly, she would later refer to her status there as a visitor, not a resident. At one point in 1991, Zhai and He Duoling decided that indeed they were not in New York to stay and "turned themselves into tourists," bought a car, and set out to travel extensively across the U.S., covering places as far apart as New Mexico and Alaska. Both artists found their journey through North America inspiring but were clearly decided on their next destination: home, not just China but specifically Chengdu.

On their way back in June 1992, the couple traveled to Rotterdam in the Netherlands, where Zhai Yongming became one of many Chinese poets from the PRC, Taiwan, and the diaspora—including Gu Cheng, Lo Fu, and Mang Ke—to participate in that year's edition of the Poetry International Festival alongside such world famous authors as John Ashbery, Miroslav Holub, James Merrill, and Vikram Seth. Before Zhai gave *acte de présence* at the festival, the couple stopped in London, where she also took part in a Conference on Modern Chinese Poetry held at the London University School of Oriental and African Studies. Also around this time, poems by Zhai appeared in translation in Dutch, English, French, German, and Japanese.

After returning to Chengdu, Zhai's poetic production slowly picked up again. If the time spent abroad had reaffirmed that her roots lay in her native language and soil, the experience had also been stimulating intellectually and artistically. Critics consider the 1993 poem *The Café Song* (Kafei guan zhi ge) representative of a change in Zhai's writing coinciding with the turn of the decade and her sojourn in the United States. To be sure, *The Café Song* is more narrative and quasi-objective and less confessional in nature than most of her 1980s poetry, as exemplified in this passage from part 1, "Afternoon" (Xiawu):

> melancholy—lingering in the café / on Fifth Avenue / under the streetlights on the corner / a low iron fence // sit by the window / slowly sipping the bald owner's black coffee / "so many people passing / going to work, going home, and no one's paying attention" // we talk about tasteless love / "yesterday—all my / troubles seemed so far away" / a nostalgic ditty floats through the air.

Zhai Yongming and He Duoling's combined presence in Chengdu art scenes is embodied in the beautifully produced *The Collected Poems of Zhai Yongming* (Zhai Yongming shiji, 1994); its cover features a portrait of the wife-poet expertly done by the husband-painter. The collection contains both Zhai's early work and specimens of poetry written after her 1992 homecoming. Her next book of poetry, *White Songs in the Black Night* (Heiye li de su ge), appeared in 1997 and charted the further unfolding of Zhai's new poetic undertakings. Both the poetry from the 1990s and a 1995 piece entitled *'Night Consciousness' and 'Women's Poetry' Revisited* (Zai tan "Heiye yishi" yu "Nüxing shige") served to make critics realize how much more there is to Zhai Yongming and her poems than can be contained in the label "woman poet," which understandably stuck to her for years after her spectacular 1986 official debut. An extensive and nuanced review article of Zhai Yongming's entire oeuvre, appropriately called "Who Is Zhai Yongming?" was written—once again—by seasoned critic Tang Xiaodu.

In public appearances in China and abroad—in 1997 she participated in poetry festivals in France and Italy—Zhai has consistently positioned herself with great modesty, gracefully declining to become involved in literary rat races outside her individual itinerary. The answer to Tang Xiaodu's question must be sought in Zhai's poems, the occasional interview, and her essays, collected in *Buildings on Paper* (Zhi shang jianzhu, 1997). The writings outline a powerful original personality helping to shape Chinese avant-garde culture in the late twentieth century: the poet reasserts the independence of the creative mind vis-à-vis the formidable, state-sanctioned pressures of ideology in the 1980s and the commercialization of the 1990s.

Maghiel VAN CREVEL

Li Youliang. "'Biran' de quantao—lun Zhai Yongming shi." *Lüliang xuekan*, no. 1/2 (1989): 57–62.

Rospenk, Karl. Introduction to *"Frau: Sechs Gedichte von Zhai Yongming." Orientierungen*, no. 1 (1991): 125–26.

Tang Xiaodu. "Nüxing shige: Cong heiye dao baizhou—du Zhai Yongming de zushi 'Nüren.'" *Shikan*, no. 2 (1987): 50, 58–59.

———. "Shei shi Zhai Yongming?" *Jintian*, no. 2 (1997): 49–64.

Tao, Naikan. "Going Beyond: The Post-*Menglong* Poets, Zhai Yongming and Zhang Zhen." *Journal of the Oriental Society of Australia*, 27 and 28 (1995–1996): 146–64.

van Crevel, Maghiel. Interviews with Zhai Yongming, 1992 and 1997.

———. *Language Shattered: Contemporary Chinese Poetry and Duoduo.* Leiden: Research School CNWS, 1996.

Zhai Yongming. *Heiye li de su ge.* Beijing: Gaige chuban she, 1997.

———. *Nüren.* Guilin: Lijiang chubanshe, 1988.

———. *Zai yiqie meigui zhi shang.* Shenyang: Shenyang chubanshe, 1989.

———. *Zhai Yongming shiji.* Chengdu: Chengdu chubanshe, 1994.

———. *Zhi shang jianzhu.* Shanghai: Shanghai dongfang chuban zhongxin, 1997.

———. "Heiye de yishi," reprinted in *Cichang yu mofang: Xin chao shilun juan*, ed. Wu Sijing. In *Dangdai shige chaoliu huigu*, eds. Xie Mian and Tang Xiaodu, 6 vols. Beijing: Beijing shifan daxue chubanshe, 1993, 140–43.

———. "'Nüxing shige' yu shige zhong de nüxing yishi." *Shikan*, no. 6 (1989): 10–11.

———. "Wancheng zhi hou you zenmoyang—huida Zang Di, Wang Ai de tiwen." In *Zhongguo zuojia fangtan lu*, eds. Shen Wei and Wu Hong. Urumqi: Xinjiang qingshaonian chubanshe, 1997, 325–39.

———. "Zai tan 'Heiye yishi' yu 'nüxing shige.'" *Shi tansuo*, no. 1 (1995): 128–29.

Zhang Ailing: *see* **Chang, Eileen**

Zhang Cen: *see* **Wulan**

Zhang Guiqin
Zhang Guiqin, b. 1941, a native of Liaoning Province, became an entrepreneur when she was in her fifties.

In the mid-1950s, Zhang Guiqin joined the army and worked as a broadcaster. In 1958, she married Zheng Dianfu, an army staff officer, who retired not long afterward and returned to his native village of Sujiatun, accompanied by Zhang Guiqin. With the beginning of economic reform at the end of the 1970s, she became deputy village head of Sujiatun in charge of industrial development. This was a time of rapid growth for village and township enterprises, and within two years, under her leadership, the village came to own over one hundred enterprises with production worth RMB 25 million. In 1979, Zhang Guiqin was assessed as a Model Worker of Liaoning Province and a national March Eighth Red Flag Holder (*sanba hongqishou*).

In the early 1980s, Shenyang Women's Federation asked her to take over and resuscitate a crochet company. The Mulan Handicrafts Company, started by twelve women wanting to help unemployed women, had up until then been profitable. However, sales of its products, which included bedspreads, tablecloths, and the like, suddenly declined. Zhang Guiqin decided to run the company as a contractor and became its sole operator, thus cutting out much red tape. However, the decision also meant that she would have to absorb all losses while still paying 15 percent of any profit to the Women's and Children's Fund of the Women's Federation, the nominal owner of Mulan Handicrafts. In 1984, the company restructured and was renamed Mulan Enterprises, with Zhang Guiqin as general manager. Where previously the company had produced only crocheted goods, a new strategy was adopted of seeking whatever work could be handled. Many small factories were established, and the company further diversified into wool, plastics, dry cleaning, etc. With no premises of its own, Mulan Enterprises leased the air-raid shelter of a local school; Zhang Guiqin had no office and would use her knees as a desk wherever she could find a spot to sit down. Her health suffered; anxiety and overwork caused her eyes to hemorrhage, which in turn blurred her vision. But her hard work paid off, and by 1988 Mulan Enterprises had become one of Shenyang's biggest taxpayers, with eighteen branches and factories. That same year, Zhang Guiqin was voted as the Outstanding Woman Entrepreneur of the nation.

Perhaps the largest and most profitable section of Mulan Enterprises is Mulan Home Appliances, which manufactures small electrical goods. Zhang Guiqin realized that as the economy improved in China more and more people would be able to afford, and want, electrical goods for domestic use. Therefore, when a young army veteran came to see her about establishing Mulan Home Appliances, she immediately agreed. Adopting the operating model of foreign companies, they established a chain of retail stores in Shenyang and plastered posters all over the city to publicize their new jingle: "For home appliances, come to Mulan." Their electrical goods were soon selling in more than six provinces and fifty cities and counties.

Zhang Guiqin also envisaged Mulan as an international enterprise. When Wang Shifang, one of the managers of Mulan Home Appliances, told Zhang Guiqin of a Russian contact interested in a joint venture, she authorized him to go to Moscow to negotiate. Soon after, the joint venture became a reality in 1992. Land worth RMB 1 million was purchased in Manzhouli, Heilongjiang Province, and became the base for Mulan's Russian and East European trade; an added advantage to the site was its geographical position as a border trading town. In the meantime, Zhang Guiqin flew south to Hong Kong and Shenzhen to invest in and develop real estate there as well as to bring in investment capital for projects in mainland China. In the mid-1990s, Mulan was ready for global expansion and deals were negotiated with South Korea, Italy, and France.

Aware of the importance of the company's having healthy relationships with branches and subsidiaries, Zhang Guiqin developed a policy whereby subsidiaries would take the larger share of both profit and liabilities than the mother company. Consequently, operators of subsidiaries have been eager to make their own enterprises successful and assumed responsibility for their own debts.

She and Mulan Enterprises have continued to contribute funds to various projects benefiting women and children. The Palace for Women and Children, for example, has been built with company funds and stands beside South Lake in Shenyang. Funds have also been set aside for kindergartens for intellectually disabled children, career high schools for girls, and a children's fund.

One of the secrets of Zhang Guiqin's success is that she values talent. Extra benefits and understanding have always been offered to those with special skills, even though the individuals might sometimes fail. Such an approach won the hearts of capable people who came to work for her because they knew they would be appreciated.

Lily Xiao Hong LEE

"Shenyangshi de Hua Mulan—Zhang Guiqin." *Zhongguo jiaoyubao*, 8 March 1993, 4.
Xu Guangrong. "Mulan Zhengchun: Ji Shenyang Mulan shiye zonggongsi zongjingli Zhang Guiqin." *Zhongguo funü*, no. 5 (1993): 2–4.

Zhang Jie

Zhang Jie, b. 1937, in Beijing but a native of Liaoning Province, is a well-known writer of novels and essays.

During childhood, she lived only with her mother, of Manchu descent, whose husband appears to have deserted the family when Zhang was only a few months old. Her mother worked as a maid, factory office worker, and primary school teacher to support the two of them. Despite the low income, Zhang Jie was able to go to school and loved literature and music. In 1960, she graduated from the Planning and Statistics Department (Jihua tongji xi) of the People's University (Renmin daxue) in Beijing and worked for many years as a statistician at the First Ministry of Industry (Diyi gongye bu).

During the Cultural Revolution, however, Zhang Jie was sent to Jiangxi to tend pigs and work in the rice paddies. What hurt her more than the menial labor was the four-year separation from her mother. After the Cultural Revolution, Zhang Jie returned to her job. In the comparatively open atmosphere of the late 1970s that gave rise to a flourishing new literature, she was tempted to try her hand at writing. Zhang Jie began to write comparatively late in life, when she was already forty-one, in 1978.

In her early works, Zhang Jie focused on portraying the positive side of human nature that not even catastrophic experience could extinguish. Her style was gentle and her mood hopeful, tinged with sadness, and reflected the sense of reawakening that prevailed at the end of the Cultural Revolution. Her best works of this period are "Love Must Not Be Forgotten" (Ai shi bu neng wangji de) and "A Child from the Forest" (Cong senlin li lai de haizi). The former is an especially influential piece that provoked a great deal of praise, some criticism, and much analysis. It was the first work in post-Mao China to emphasize romantic love, and it touched on the taboo of extramarital love.

Zhang Jie soon moved on from the virginal first phase of her writing to a concern with social conditions and institutions in which she revealed tragic identity conflicts of a variety of characters, many of them women. "The Ark" (Fangzhou) and *Emerald* (Zumulü) are thought to be the earliest Chinese works possessing a feminist consciousness, although Zhang Jie strongly denies being a feminist. In *Heavy Wings* (Chenzhong de chibang, 1981), recognized as one of the first political satires in post-Mao China, she raises the problem of how to carry on economic reform without political reform. This was followed by several works on a similar theme. "Angry" (Shanghuo) first published in October 1991 in the literary magazine *Zhongshan*, based in Nanjing, raised controversy from the start. The Ministry of Propaganda demanded that the magazine investigate the ideological leanings of the story, which allegedly was a thinly disguised vilification of undesirable characters in the PRC literary establishment. Zhang Jie's style during this period played to a passionate exposé of social malaise and the seedy side of humanity.

After her mother's death in 1991, however, the writer's style changed yet again. She had been exceptionally close to her mother and became ill for quite a long time. Eventually, Zhang Jie wrote the autobiographical *The Person Who Loved Me Most in the World Has Gone* (Shijie shang zui teng wo de ren qule, 1994). Her only other works of this period were short prose and essays, many of which were collected in *Wordless Is My Heart* (Wuzi woxin, 1995). The turbulent storm of grief passed with time, however, although Zhang Jie's style retains a quiet sadness, often informed by nostalgia. Since 1990, she has been planning her magnum opus, an epic of the twentieth century covering the lives of a number of people. The first volume of this projected four-volume work, *Without Words* (Wuzi), was published at the end of 1999, and the rest is expected to appear by the end of 2001.

Zhang Jie received many honors, both in China and abroad. Her short stories "A Child from the Forest," "Who Can Live Better" (Shei shenghuo de geng meihao), and "Conditions Are Not Yet Ripe" (Tiaojian shang wei chengshou) won the National Outstanding Short Story Award (Quanguo youxiu duanpian xiaoshuo jiang) in 1978, 1979, and 1983, respectively. Her novella *Emerald* won the National Outstanding Novella Award of 1983–84, and her novel *Heavy Wings* won the second Mao Dun Literature Award in 1985. In spite of this, the novel was criticized by conservative elements in the Chinese literary establishment as being anti-party and anti-socialist.

Zhang Jie has frequently been criticized for having been poisoned by eighteenth- and nineteenth-century Western novels, an influence she herself proudly acknowledges. Perhaps this led to her being well received in Europe and the United States. She is reputedly one of the most translated of modern Chinese writers; *Heavy Wings*, for example, has been translated into at least fourteen languages. In 1989, Zhang Jie won an Italian Literary Prize and was appointed in 1992 as an honorary member of the American Academy of Arts and Letters in New York. Like most writers from the Chinese mainland, Zhang Jie acknowledges her indebtedness to Russian literature.

In the early 1960s, she married a colleague from the First Ministry of Industry, giving birth to a daughter Tang Di in 1963. It is not known when this marriage ended, but in the 1980s Zhang Jie married a high-level official of the PRC. She has maintained her independence as a dedicated writer, however. More than a few articles in *Wordless Is My Heart* are about her husband, whom she reveals in "I Love My Husband" to be Sun Youyu, former executive vice-minister of the First Ministry of Machinery (Diyi jixie bu). Her daughter Tang Di studied in the United States, graduating from university in 1989.

Zhang Jie has traveled a long road in both thematic choice and stylistic development. Thematically, she began with intimate sketches, expanded to social concern and social criticism, and returned to sound a more personal note. Stylistically, she developed from invoking pure and gentle descriptions of beautiful and bright people and objects to a sharply sarcastic, passionate cursing of the darker side of life. Eventually, however, her writing returned to a calmer harbor from which she regards the world more coolly and wisely. Zhang Jie can indeed be said to have reached perfection in her art. Dai Jinhua's rereading of Zhang Jie's works perceives that the author sees love as human salvation. Xiaomei Chen, on the other hand, points out that, because women's texts such as Zhang Jie's critique cultural values, they are subversive in pointing to the possibilities of cultural liberation and renewal. It is to be hoped that Zhang Jie will continue to produce works that probe humanity and the social institutions that attempt constantly to restrain and stifle it.

GAO Yuanbao
(Translated by Lily Xiao Hong Lee)

Bailey, Allison. "Traveling Together: Narrative Technique in Zhang Jie's 'The Ark.'" In *Chinese Women Writers: Critical Appraisals*, ed. Michael S. Duke. Armonk, N.Y.: M.E. Sharpe, 1989, 96–111.

Chen Xiaomei. "Reading Mother's Tale—Reconstructing Women's Space in Amy Tan and Zhang Jie." *Chinese Literature: Essays, Articles, Reviews*, 16 (1994): 111–32.

Dai Jinhua. "Shiji de zhongjie: Chong du Zhang Jie." *Wenyi zhengming*, no. 4 (1994): 35–56.

"The Life and Literature of Zhang Jie." *Beijing Scene*, 7, no. 13 (April 2000), at <http://www.beijingscene.com/feature.html>.

Liu Huiying. "Zhang Jie de 'waiguo xuanfeng.'" *Mingbao yuekan* (June 1992): 100–02.

Lü Zhenghui. "Xujia de nüxing zhuyi xiaoshuo—Zhang Jie de 'Fangzhou' yu 'Zumulü.'" *Wenxing*, no. 111 (1987): 80–85.

Zhang Jie. *As Long as Nothing Happens, Nothing Will*. London: Virago, 1987.

———. *Heavy Wings*, trans. Howard Goldblatt. New York: Grove Weidenfeld, 1989.

———. *Love Must Not Be Forgotten*. Beijing: Chinese Literature Press, 1987.

———. *Wu zi*. Shanghai: Shanghai wenyi chubanshe, 1998.

———. *Zhang Jie wenji*. Beijing: Zuojia chubanshe, 1997.

———. *Zhang Jie xuanji*. Beijing: Renmin wenxue chubanshe, 1993.

———. "The Boat I Steer: A Study in Perseverance." In *Modern Chinese Writers' Self-Portrayals*, eds. Helmut Martin and Jeffrey Kinkley. Armonk, N.Y.: M.E. Sharpe, 1992, 118–22.

———. "What's Wrong With Him?" trans. Gladys Yang. *Renditions*, special issue (Spring and Autumn 1987): 141–57.

Zhang Kangkang

Zhang Kangkang, b. 1950 in Hangzhou, Zhejiang Province, is a writer of novels, novellas, and short stories.

Her father, Zhang Kaizhi, a native of Guangdong Province, worked as a journalist for several left-wing newspapers in Shanghai and Hangzhou under the KMT government in the 1930s and 1940s; he secretly joined the CCP before 1949. After the communists came to power, however, Zhang Kaizhi was suspected of being a double agent, lost his job, and was sent to a labor camp. Zhang Kangkang thus grew up in considerable poverty but was fortunate in having a well-read mother who nurtured her daughter's youthful imagination with fairy tales selected from the canon of world literature. Her mother's name is not known. Zhang Kangkang was a bright student at school and showed considerable literary talent at an early age.

During the Cultural Revolution, she was sent to work on a state farm, as were millions of other high school students; her assignment was in Heilongjiang Province. The year after the death of Mao Zedong (1893–1976), which signaled the end of the Cultural Revolution, Zhang Kangkang was admitted to the Heilongjiang College of Arts. Upon graduation in 1979, she became a professional writer, i.e., a writer on the state payroll. Zhang Kangkang now sits as vice-chair of the Heilongjiang Writers' Association and serves on the Executive Council of the national Writers' Association and as a member of the Heilongjiang Provincial Political Consultative Conference.

She writes prolifically: in the two decades of her literary career to date, Zhang Kangkang has produced three novels, eighteen novellas, and numerous short stories and literary essays (*san wen, sui bi*). A number of the fictional works, including *The Invisible Companion* (Yinxing banlü, 1986), have been translated into English and other foreign languages.

Her first novel, the little-known *Boundaries* (Fenjie xian), was published in 1972, but the short stories, particularly the novellas, published between 1979 and 1982, gained her recognition as an important writer. The short story "Summer" (Xia, 1980) and her first novella, *Morning Mist* (Dandande chenwu, 1980), were both awarded national prizes. However, while such attention usually signifies more of an official certification of a work's political soundness than an indication of literary excellence, Zhang Kangkang cannot be said to be a purveyor of official propaganda.

Most of the protagonists in the stories written in the 1980s belong to her own peer group; they lived similar experiences during the Cultural Revolution, ones leaving deep scars on minds and sometimes even bodies. Her early works, typified by *Morning Mist*, owed their tremendous success to their explicitly political themes rather than artistic achievement. Their message invariably condemned Maoist extremism and called for humanism and liberalism, a voice common to nearly all fictional works published at that time. What distinguishes Zhang Kangkang's fiction is probably her residual idealism. Her positive characters—usually female—in spite of their painful pasts maintain moral integrity and retain a measure of faith in the future of their country and humanity, if not in socialism. She is fond of integrating moral-political values within the private, romantic lives of her characters. The plots of the major works in this period—the novellas *Morning Mist* and *Aurora Borealis* (Beiji guang, 1982) and the novel *The Invisible Companion*—revolve around the emotional turmoil of a heroine whose husband or boyfriend fails to live up to her ideals.

Of the better-known novels and novellas, *The Invisible Companion* is probably the most successful. Depicting as it does the life of young students exiled to a state farm in Heilongjiang Province, the material contains autobiographical elements. Also evinced is a more mature understanding of human nature and sophisticated psychological presentations of the protagonists, which are not as evident in her earlier work. Technically, too, the writing displays more innovation; conventions and realism are now modified by borrowings from modernist techniques. More attention is paid to consciousness in the reflections and reverie of the characters, and a straight chronological ordering of external events is eschewed in favor of a more fluid treatment of temporality, allowing for backward and forward cross-referencing of action.

In the latter half of the 1980s, social-realist literature went out of fashion at the same time as highbrow literature lost out to popular literature. To meet the expectations of a much smaller but more select readership, Zhang Kangkang experimented in several of her shorter pieces with new styles and techniques. "The Yintuolo Net" (Yintuolo de wang, 1987) and "The Leaning Building" (Xie xia, 1992), for example, show strongly the influence of Latin American magical realism and the theater of the absurd. She nevertheless continued to write realist fiction of social criticism, a style in which Zhang Kangkang is clearly more at home.

Of these writings, the novella *Blue Collar* (Lan Ling, 1991) deserves special mention. The story deals with the taboo subject of a workers' strike in a state-owned enterprise, exposing the weakness and irrelevance of a state-sponsored trade union. The piece apparently reflects the experience of her husband, Lü Jiamin. An academic, he was arrested after the 1989 Tian'anmen Incident because of involvement in the independent trade union movement. Zhang Kangkang showed considerable courage in publishing the work, as this was a sensitive issue after the crackdown following June Fourth.

Her next novel, *The Scarlet and the Red* (Chi tong dan zhu), published in 1995, is a slightly fictionalized version of the real-life story of her parents. Their colorful adventures while working as underground communist agents under KMT rule and the unjust treatment received at the hands of the CCP, to which they had dedicated their lives, are told in an engaging and moving style.

Her latest novel, *Gallery of Eros* (Qing'ai hualang, 1996), was an instant hit. It tells the love story of two too-good-to-be-true individuals: a beautiful, tender, and talented academic and a handsome, loving, and talented painter. She has an unbelievably generous husband; he has an unbelievably generous ex-girlfriend. The academic's betrayed but rich husband is happy to see to it that the lovers live comfortably with nothing to do except enjoy each other; meanwhile, the painter's jilted girlfriend takes it upon herself to look after the academic's distraught teenage daughter, who has fallen in love with the painter. The selling power of this blatantly absurd, poorly executed story probably lies in its erotic passages, which are couched in pretentious lyricism, thus enabling the book to be marketed as serious literature rather than as soft pornography.

Sylvia CHAN

Bryant, Daniel. "Making It Happen: Aspects of Narrative Method in Zhang Kangkang's *Northern Lights*." In *Modern Chinese Women Writers: Critical Appraisals*, ed. Michael S. Duke. Armonk, N.Y.: M.E. Sharpe, 1989, 112–34.

Leung, Laifong. "Zhang Kangkang: Sensing the Trends." In *Morning Sun: Interviews with Chinese Writers of the Lost Generation*. Armonk, N.Y.: M.E. Sharpe, 1994, 229–39.

Zhang Kangkang. *Chi tong dan zhu*. Beijing: Renmin wenxue chubanshe, 1995.

———. *Feng guo wu hen*. Nanjing: Jiangsu renmin chubanshe, 1998.

———. *Hong Yingsu*. Harbin: Beifang wenyi chubanshe, 1986.

———. *The Invisible Companion*, trans. Daniel Bryant. Beijing: New World Publishing House, 1996.

———. *Kongju de pingheng*. Beijing: Huayi chubanshe, 1994.

———. *Nüren de jidi*. Taipei: Yeqiang chubanshe, 1998.

———. *Qing'ai hualang*. Shenyang: Liaoning chunfeng wenyi chubanshe, 1996.

———. *Tuoluo xia*. Beijing: Huayi chubanshe, 1992.
———. *Yin he*. Wuhan: Changjiang wenyi chubanshe, 1997.
———. *Yinxing banlü*. Beijing: Zuojia chubanshe, 1986.
———. *Yong bu qianhui*. Hong Kong: Tiandi tushu chuban gongsi, 1994.
———. *Zhang Kangkang daibiao zuo*. Harbin: Beifang wenyi chubanshe, 1991.
———. *Zhang Kangkang zixuan ji*, 5 vols. Guiyang: Guizhou renmin chubanshe, 1996–1997.
———. *Zhang Kangkang zuopin ji*. Beijing: Renmin wenxue chubanshe, 1998.

Zhang Mojun

Zhang Mojun, 1883–1965, original name Zhang Zhaohan, also known as Sophie Zhang and Luo Feiya, *zi* Shu Fang, was a native of Xiangxiang in Hunan Province. Failing to realize the singular identity of Zhang Mojun and Zhang Zhaohan, one source (*Zhongguo funü mingren cidian*) mistakenly gives Zhang Zhaohan's year of birth as 1888 and goes on to say that she died during the liberation war. Zhang Mojun was one of the most prominent advocates of women's education and rights during the Republican period.

An active supporter of the anti-Qing Tongmenghui and the KMT, she performed various functions for both the KMT and the KMT government. Her work promoting women's education and equal political rights through the magazines and newspapers that she edited and contributed to has ensured her a significant place in the history of the women's movement in China.

Her father, Zhang Tongdian (a Hanlin scholar and official), was active in the anti-Qing revolutionary movement around the Jiangnan region. He gave his daughter a sound classical education in history, philosophy, and literature, and she excelled in calligraphy and poetry. Zhang Mojun published three volumes of her work over the course of her life: *Poems of Mojun* (Mojun shicun), *Poems from the Baihua Caotang* (Baihua caotang shi), and *Lyrics from the Jiang Shu Bao Yun Shanguan* (Jiang shu bao yun shanguan ci). Her father also transmitted his revolutionary fervor to his daughter who, as a young woman during the last few years of imperial rule, engaged in underground anti-Qing activities in Jiangsu and Zhejiang. (One source writes admiringly but erroneously of her being only sixteen years old in 1911 when she was an activist in the underground movement in Suzhou; that year Zhang Mojun was twenty-eight years old.) In September, she became responsible for the publication of the Jiangsu newspaper *Great Han News* (Da Han bao) that, during the few brief months of its existence, advocated republicanism and military uprising. That same month, Zhang Mojun and her father were the secret revolutionary coordinators responsible for Suzhou declaring its independence from the Qing.

In the first few months of 1912, Zhang Mojun was quick to place women's issues in the forefront of national debate when she established the Shenzhou United Women's Assistance Society (Shenzhou nüjie gonghe xiejishe). It aimed to promote women's education and industry, its underlying premise being that women should possess sufficient political knowledge to participate as full citizens in the new Republic. Fundamental to the Shenzhou United Women's Assistance Society's platform was gender equality in legal, social, and political realms. In November the society set up a newspaper called the *Shenzhou Women's News* (Shenzhou nübao): until February 1913 this came out every ten days, then changed to a monthly under the leadership of Yang Jiwei and Tan Sheying, and finally ceased publication mid-year after producing four monthly issues. The society's manifesto declared a commitment to debating social issues important to women, promoting knowledge on citizenship among women, and enhancing women's participation in the literary field. The society also established the Shenzhou School for Girls (Shenzhou nüxue) in 1914, with Zhang Mojun as its principal. This school was her first venture into education. Throughout the remainder of a long and productive life, her major concern was the education of women. She achieved recognition for being one of the most important women educationists of this period in China's history.

Early on, the Shenzhou Women's United Assistance Society agitated for women's equal political rights with men. Toward this end, Zhang Mojun's society briefly allied with the Women's Northern Attack Brigade (Nüzi beifa dui), led by Tang Qunying (*q.v.*), Zhang Hanying (see *Biographical Dictionary of Chinese Women: The Qing Period*), and Wang Changguo. During this time, the women raised funds to cover the costs of the war against the remnants of the Qing army, amounting to more than 15,000 yuan (in two batches, of 5,000 and 10,000), which was presented to Sun Yat-sen on 1 and 10 February 1912.

The two groups differed in their methods of activism, with Tang Qunying's advocating radical change and Zhang Mojun's preferring a more gradual, conciliatory approach. Nevertheless, the two major wings of the women's movement sustained their alliance during the crucial period of February and March 1912 when constitutional debates took place; they were able to lobby Sun Yat-sen on the issue of women's suffrage as a unified force. On 3 March, for example, on behalf of the Shenzhou United Women's Assistance Society, Zhang Mojun sent a memorial to Sun Yat-sen about the importance of women's suffrage. In his reply, Sun Yat-sen expressed support for the fullest possible role for women in the new Republic.

His and other prominent Tongmenghui political figures' responsiveness inspired Zhang Mojun to reinvigorate her group. On 16 March, she announced a change of name for the organization to the slightly shorter Shenzhou Women's Society (Shenzhou nüjie xiejishe). Song Qingling (*q.v.*), the young wife of Sun Yat-sen, became its patron while Zhang Mojun remained its driving force. The society's membership included such prominent figures as He Miaoling (wife of Wu Tingfang), Liu Qingxia (see *Biographical Dictionary of Chinese Women: The Qing Period*), and Yang Jiwei. The goals of the society were explicitly moderate: a gradualist approach to the question of women's suffrage, including the promotion of women's education, industry, and laws in order to nurture women's more effective participation in politics. Initially, the society requested that women be granted observer status in the Parliament in order to cultivate political knowledge and skills. This orientation was clearly supported and advocated by Sun Yat-sen. By December, however, when it was clear that the Parliament was no longer willing to consider the question of women's suffrage, moderate activists like Zhang Mojun felt prompted to focus instead on providing girls with educational opportunities that had long been denied.

In 1918, at the age of thirty-six, Zhang Mojun was funded by the Education Department to research women's education internationally. She enrolled at Columbia University in New York and was elected president of the New York Students' Association. Once her studies were completed, she traveled to Europe to survey women's education there; Zhang Mojun also represented one of the patriotic groups protesting against the signing of the Versailles Treaty by the Chinese in May 1919.

Upon return to China in 1920, she resumed work with the Shenzhou School for Girls and its publication *Shenzhou Daily* (Shenzhou ribao). In acknowledgment of her expertise, the Jiangsu government appointed her as principal of the First Women's Normal College. In 1927 she served as education member of the Shanghai branch of the Central Political Council and also headed the Hangzhou city Education Department. The KMT government appointed Zhang Mojun a member of the Higher Examinations Standards Committee of the Examination Yuan (1929) and councillor of the Legislative Yuan (1930).

After returning from her brief overseas sojourn, she married Shao Yuanchong (1888–1936), Sun Yat-sen's private secretary. The couple first met in 1912 when Zhang Mojun headed the Publications Section (wenshubu) of the Communications Department of the newly formed KMT. They did not marry until 1924 by which time she was forty-one years old and Shao Yuanchong thirty-four. They had two children, a boy (Shao Fuyi) and girl (Shao Yingduo). Shao Yuanchong was a native of Shaoxing in Zhejiang Province and variously held the posts of vice-president of the KMT government's Legislative Yuan, KMT foreign secretary, lecturer in politics at Whampoa Military Academy, and private secretary, mentioned above. Zhang Mojun's marriage was brief: Shao Yuanchong was fatally wounded in the 1936 Xi'an Incident during which Chiang Kai-shek was captured. Tragically, her son Shao Fuyi also died prematurely, in a car accident in 1951.

Zhang Mojun worked for the KMT government throughout the 1930s and 1940s. In addition to holding positions with the Legislative and Examination Yuans, she was elected to the KMT Central Committee, the only woman to serve in this elite group. One of her major initiatives in government was to argue for the establishment of the Chinese navy; because of this, she is known in the Republic of China as the "Mother of China's Navy."

In 1948, at the age of sixty-five, Zhang Mojun left the mainland and settled in Taiwan, continuing to work with the Examination Yuan and becoming a member of the KMT's Central Control Committee. In later years, she grew interested in the National History Museum, making several personal donations of ancient jade artifacts to improve the collection. Zhang Mojun died at the age of eighty-two in January 1965.

Louise EDWARDS

Boorman, Howard L., and Richard C. Howard, eds. *Biographical Dictionary of Republican China*, vol. 1. New York: Columbia University Press, 1967, 85–87.
Gao Kuixiang and Shen Jianguo, eds. *Zhonghua gujin nüjie pu*. Beijing: Zhongguo shehui chubanshe, 1991, 143–44.
Huang Jilu, ed. *Geming renwu zhi*. Taipei: Zhongyang wenwu gongying she, 1969, 124–26.
Lin Guanghao. "San Xiang cainü Zhang Mojun." *Zhongwai zazhi*, February (1991): 88–90.

Lin Weihong. "Tongmenghui shidai nügeming zhishi de huodong." In *Zhongguo funüshi lunwenji*, eds. Li Youning and Zhang Yufa. Taipei: Shangwu yinshuguan, 1981, 129–78. Also in Bao Jialin, *Zhongguo funüshilunji*. Taipei: Daoxiang chubanshe, 1979.

Lü Meiyi and Zheng Yongfu. *Zhongguo funüyundong (1840–1921)*. Zhengzhou: Henan renmin chubanshe, 1990.

Shang Hai et al., eds. *Minguo shi da cidian*. Beijing: Zhongguo guangbo dianshi chubanshe, 1991.

Tan Sheying. *Zhongguo funüyundong tongshi*. Nanjing: Funügongwu she, 1936.

Wei Shishuang. "Huainian Zhang Mojun nüshi." *Zhongwai zazhi*, 20, no. 6 (December 1976): 105.

Wu Zhimei. "San Xiang nüjie Zhang Mojun." *Zhongwai zazhi*, 37, no. 9 (1984): 19–21.

Yao Guliang. "Weida de Zhang Mojun xiansheng." *Zhongguo yizhou*, no. 355 (1957): 3–4.

Yuan Shaoying and Yang Guizhen, eds. *Zhongguo funü mingren cidian*. Changchun: Beifang funüertong chubanshe, 1989, 329, 339.

Zhang Naiying: *see* **Xiao Hong**

Zhang Qinqiu

Zhang Qinqiu, 1904–1968, born as Zhang Wu in Tongxiang County, Zhejiang Province, was an active CCP member from the 1920s and one of the first women to receive an appointment at ministerial level in the government of the PRC.

She was born into a literati family. Her father, Zhang Dianqing, was editor of the newspaper *Sanjiang ribao* in Jiaxing; however, after losing his job he went back to Tongxiang to become a farmer and trader in farm-related businesses, such as egg distribution and a mulberry seedling nursery. Zhang Qinqiu was the fourth of seven children and one of the three who survived; the two others were an elder brother, Zhang Tong, and a younger sister, Zhang Lan.

Zhang Qinqiu was the most intelligent and hardworking of her siblings and, with the support of her mother, given an advanced education. Zhang Qinqiu entered Zhenhua Girls' School at the age of nine and after graduating in 1921 studied at the Hangzhou Women's Normal School (Hangzhou nüzi shifan xuexiao). She was one of the few students there who advocated cutting their hair short as a defiant gesture against tradition; this she did herself to set an example. In 1923, Zhang Qinqiu transferred to the Patriotic Women's School (Aiguo nüxiao) in Shanghai. One of her classmates there, Kong Dezhi, was the wife of the famous writer Mao Dun (the nom de plume of Shen Yanbing); through Kong, Zhang Qinqiu thus met Shen and his younger brother Shen Zemin, who at that time was already a youth with progressive ideas. Under their influence, Zhang Qinqiu read widely on social reform and revolution. Later that year, she was accepted by the Nanjing Fine Arts Institute but withdrew not long afterward because of ill health.

Zhang Qinqiu enrolled in 1924 at the communist-supported Shanghai University of which she had learned through Shen Zemin. This proved to be a crucial period in her life. In that one year, Zhang Qinqiu joined the Communist Youth League, transferred to full membership in the CCP, and married Shen Zemin. With many of the early communist intellectuals, such as Qu Qiubai, on the faculty of Shanghai University, Zhang Qinqiu was able to study Marxism and Leninism, as well as the various paths that were being proposed for the Chinese revolution.

Her student life over the next two years was characterized by political activism. Xiang Jingyu (*q.v.*), already a CCP member, was active in the women's movement in Shanghai at that time and encouraged educated women to operate night schools for women workers. One of these was set up by Zhang Qinqiu, Yang Zhihua (*q.v.*), and others on Pingliang Road; their school attracted two hundred to three hundred pupils. These young women activists would visit women workers at home, observing their lives, assessing needs, and even teaching them revolutionary songs. Zhang Qinqiu helped organize successful workers' strikes and raised financial support for the strikers and their families. She was thus instrumental in the rise of trade unions in Shanghai and during the May Thirtieth Movement of 1925 also participated in anti-Japanese rallies and demonstrations, making speeches in the streets.

Zhang Qinqiu and her husband were sent to the Soviet Union to study in 1926; they embarked one October night on a Soviet coal ship with more than one hundred other Chinese youths. From that year to 1930, she studied at Sun Yat-sen University in Moscow. Zhang Qinqiu revealed a flair for languages and after only two years was sufficiently proficient in Russian to be able to act as an interpreter for the CCP. During holidays, she worked in textile mills in order to learn techniques and management methods, knowledge that would prove useful to her later in life.

Throughout the 1930s, Zhang Qinqiu displayed ability in political work and also proved to be a decisive and brilliant commander on the battlefield. Upon returning to China in 1930, she worked for a time in Shanghai before being sent with Shen Zemin to the Hubei-Henan-Anhui base area (E-Yu-Wan genjudi) to work under the leadership of Zhang Guotao. For a year, she was political commissar to the Peng Yang Cadre School, responsible not only for drilling staff and students in ideology and running the teaching program of the school but for taking the students to military drill and teaching revolutionary songs and dances; she also acted in plays with them. In July 1932, Chiang Kai-shek began his fourth "encirclement and extermination" of the base and in October Zhang Guotao decided to retreat to the west. Shen Zemin, who held the post of provincial party secretary, was ordered to remain behind. He died in November 1933 as a result of a recurrence of his tuberculosis, brought on by the harsh conditions at the base, and malaria.

From 1932 to 1933, Zhang Qinqiu progressed from being commissar of the Seventy-third Division to commissar of the Fourth Front Army. After she and others doubted the wisdom of Zhang Guotao's decision to move west with no apparent destination, they forced him to hold a meeting at Xiaohekou (Shaanxi Province) in 1932 during which Zhang Guotao agreed to consult his comrades in future when making decisions. In December that year, the Fourth Front Army took advantage of warlord infighting in Sichuan Province to occupy the northern region, where they created the Sichuan-Shaanxi base area. As commissar, Zhang Qinqiu led a team of women propaganda workers, promoting party policies and carrying out recruitment for the Red Army by means of posters and slogans, songs, and dances. She also trained a group of actors for a newly established drama troupe. However, because Zhang Guotao bore a grudge against her, presumably for forcing him to act more democratically, Zhang Qinqiu was demoted at the end of that year from head of the army's Political Department to acting county secretary of Hongjiang. Her exceptional leadership, however, soon made Hongjiang a model county in the Sichuan-Shaanxi base area.

In 1933, she was transferred to head the Political Department of the Fourth Front Army's General Hospital. This proved to be a demanding job but not beyond her abilities. The hospital was responsible for a number of subordinate institutions; its Political Department was in charge of the Security Section, transportation team, medical school, Lenin School, Party School, new drama troupe, and the *Flower of Blood* magazine. In order to adapt to the "three-sides surrounding attack" employed by the army, the hospital established five mobile branches; even the hospital itself moved three times during this period. Lack of anesthetics forced medical staff to experiment and develop their own drugs, and Zhang Qinqiu recruited many experienced traditional herbal doctors for other medical problems, without concern for their political stance. Staff and patients alike praised her initiative in overcoming many difficulties.

At one point during a transfer of the General Hospital from Tongjiang to Chibei County, she and her party were ambushed at Kucaoba (one source gives this as Kushuba) by KMT soldiers. Zhang Qinqiu took to the field, leading the five hundred women soldiers of the Red Defense Battalion (Chiweiying) and a small armed convoy to protect the sick and wounded. When the KMT soldiers showed a reluctance to shoot females, Zhang Qinqiu realized that the moment was crucial. She told the women to shout, "We welcome you to come over to the Red Army!" and "The Red Army is the vanguard for fighting the Japanese!" so that when KMT officers ordered their men to shoot, the men turned their guns on the commanding officers and arrested them instead. During this battle, Zhang Qinqiu captured the whole regiment as well as their weapons and ammunition. The incident was written up in a Chengdu newsletter under the heading "Five Hundred Peasant Women Disarm a Regiment of White [KMT] Soldiers" and was later republished by *China Forum* (Zhongguo luntan).

In January 1934, Zhang Qinqiu was elected to the Executive Committee of the Central Committee of the Chinese Soviet. A year later, in February 1935, in preparation for the Fourth Front Army's participation in what is celebrated as the Long March, Zhang Guotao transferred women cadres and workers to the Women's Independent Regiment. This sudden increase in numbers led to a change in the unit's name, i.e., the Women's Independent Division, which split into two regiments. Zhang Qinqiu was appointed commander of the division and head of the first regiment. Her command was taken from her three months later, when she was transferred to head the Provincial Women's Department of Sichuan and Shaanxi. Zhang Qinqiu was then sent to study at the Party School.

The Fourth Front Army arrived at Maogong in June 1935 to unite with the First Front Army, then under the command of Mao Zedong (1893–1976), who had marched out from the Jiangxi soviet in October 1934. In the euphoria of their "victorious meeting," it was agreed that the two armies should be integrated under the common banner of the party and divided into two columns. The Left Column was headed by Zhang Guotao and the Right Column by Mao Zedong; part of the First Front Army was then placed under Zhang's command and part of the Fourth Front Army transferred to Mao. However, as the euphoria wore off, disagreements between the two commanders soon surfaced, and each went his own way: Mao marched north while Zhang Guotao turned back toward the southeast. During this period, in 1936, Zhang Qinqiu married Chen Changhao (b. 1910), who then held the post of Zhang Guotao's political commissar.

When the forces of He Long and Ren Bishi joined up with Zhang Guotao's Fourth Front Army in Ganzi, Sichuan, in 1936, they took him to task for not abiding by the CCP Central Committee's decision to go north. Zhang Qinqiu herself again came into conflict with Zhang Guotao during a meeting attended by He Long (commander of the Second Regiment) and Xiao Ke (commander of the Sixth Regiment) in July. At this meeting, she spoke up in support of Zhu De (1886–1976), who criticized Zhang Guotao for not joining Mao in northern Shaanxi. Zhang Guotao subsequently agreed to march northward.

However, the Fourth Front Army was stopped by KMT troops before it had completed its crossing of the Yellow River in late 1936, and only two-thirds of the army crossed to the western side. Thus cut off from the main force, the troops were renamed the Western Route Army (Xilujun), with Zhang Qinqiu head of its Organization Department within the Political Department. In January 1937 after the army had been ambushed and scattered in the frigid northwestern desert, Zhang Qinqiu directed the soldiers to break out and then went into labor, giving birth to a baby girl, who probably died. The cavalry of the Ma Clan from Gansu and Qinghai massacred the ill-fated Western Route Army and, their ammunition and strength exhausted, Zhang Qinqiu and her comrades were captured. Fellow prisoners kept her identity secret from their captors. She dressed as a cook and, despite being widely publicized as one of the most wanted communists, lived unrecognized among the women prisoners for some time. Later, Zhang Qinqiu was eventually betrayed by a young woman from her own side and taken to Xiaozhuang, a prison for political prisoners in Nanjing. This occurred after the Xi'an Incident of December 1936, marking the second alliance of the KMT and CCP. Zhang Qinqiu was among the political prisoners exchanged at the intercession of Zhou Enlai (1898–1976) and Ye Jianying.

She was sent to Yan'an and there entered the struggle between Zhang Guotao and Mao Zedong, criticizing Zhang for his erroneous policies and thinking. As an important eyewitness from the Fourth Front Army, her testimony carried considerable weight. During the late 1930s and also later in the 1940s, Zhang Qinqiu did what is known as women's work and trained cadres, initially heading the Women Students' Brigade of the Anti-Japanese University (Kangda), whose seven hundred to eight hundred students mainly came from KMT areas. Under continual threat of air-raids, classes met in gullies and moved about as the situation demanded. Staff and students packed their lunch every morning and returned in the evening so that classes could be conducted safely. In 1939, in response to the increasing number of students arriving in Yan'an, the Chinese Women's University was established from the Women Students' Brigade, expanding to a student population of fifteen hundred. Zhang Qinqiu became dean of studies of this new university, was in charge of the teaching program, and taught political theory. Answering Mao Zedong's call for self-sufficiency during this period, Zhang Qinqiu led staff and students to clear wasteland to grow their own food. In the

1940s, she was a member of the Women's Committee of the CCP Central Committee and one of the delegates representing the CCP-controlled areas at the Second International Federation of Democratic Women in Budapest in 1948.

At about the same time that Zhang Qinqiu arrived in Yan'an in 1937, her husband Chen Changhao also arrived after a period of recuperation in his native Hubei. The two were happily reunited, but six months later, in April 1938, Chen was sent to Russia for medical attention. Five years after that, in 1943, Zhang heard that he was living with a Russian woman. She applied to the party for a divorce. Su Jingguan (d. 1964), a medical doctor with the Fourth Front Army and whom Zhang Qinqiu had known while working as political commissar of the General Hospital, then declared his love for her. They married in 1943.

With the establishment of the People's Republic in 1949, Zhang Qinqiu was appointed vice-minister in the Ministry of Textile Industry. Su Jingguan was appointed vice-minister in the Ministry of Public Health. Zhang Qinqiu was elected to the Executive Committee of the ACWF, and during the first two decades of the new republic was elected both to the CPPCC and the NPC.

In her capacity as vice-minister, she led a delegation from the Ministry of Textile Industry to visit the Soviet Union in 1953. Zhang Qinqiu paid a great deal of attention to technical advances and reforms carried out in the industry and was responsible for recognizing and making widely available in China a number of new methods, such as the "Fine Thread Method" of Hao Jianxiu (*q.v.*) and the 1951 Cotton Weaving Method. Zhang Qinqiu set up an experimental workshop in Shanghai to test innovations. During the Great Leap Forward (1958–60), some mills increased the speed of their looms without achieving higher production, creating instead much wastage. An Ren, the deputy director of the Northwest Textile Bureau, had spoken out on this issue but was portrayed in a play in a negative light. When Zhang Qinqiu was invited to comment after seeing the play, she candidly expressed her disagreement with how An Ren had been smeared in the play. Zhang Qinqiu did this in full knowledge that it might attract criticism to herself. This kind of pragmatism later earned her the name of a "rightist." In 1966, she held a large-scale exhibition of new achievements nationwide in the textile industry.

During her two decades at the Textile Industry Ministry, Zhang Qinqiu traveled all over China to inspect textile mills and devoted time and resources to research and development. She is thus credited with having provided a good foundation for China's textile industry. Zhang Qinqiu is also said to have been a caring minister concerned with the working and living conditions of textile workers. An example often given by her biographers reveals a concern about the marriage prospects of women working in mills in remote areas: she is said to have asked those in charge to arrange social events so that the women could meet male workers.

During the Cultural Revolution, Zhang Qinqiu endured severe persecution, which led to suicide in April 1968 at the age of sixty-four: she jumped to her death from the balcony of her office, where she had been imprisoned. Su Jingguan had died in 1964 from cancer, but her previous husband, Chen Changhao, was accused of opposing Mao Zedong and also committed suicide, in 1976. The daughter Zhang Qinqiu had

had with her first husband, Shen Zemin, also died that year: unable to endure the torture and humiliation meted out to her by Red Guards for being sympathetic to the April Fifth Movement—mourning the death of Zhou Enlai—she committed suicide by taking an overdose of sleeping pills.

In 1979, Zhang Qinqiu was reevaluated by the Central Committee and praised as an "outstanding communist who was loyal to the party and the people."

Lily Xiao Hong LEE

Klein, Donald W., and Anne B. Clark. *Biographic Dictionary of Chinese Communism, 1921–65.* Cambridge, Mass.: Harvard University Press, 1971, 21–22.
Qian Qing. "Hongjun nüjiangling Zhang Qinqiu xiaozhuan." *Renwu,* no. 1 (1984): 100–02.
Qiu Zhizhuo, ed. *Zhonggong dangshi renminglu.* Chongqing: Chongqing chubanshe, 1986, 228.
Song Ruizhi, ed. *Zhongguo funüwenhua tonglan.* Jinan: Shandong wenyi chubanshe, 1995, 241–43.
Yuan Shaoying and Yang Guizhen, eds. *Zhongguo funü mingren cidian.* Changchun: Beifang funüertong chubanshe, 1989, 335–37.
Zhonggong dangshi renwu zhuan, vol. 17. Xi'an: Shaanxi renmin chubanshe, 1984, 229–61.
"Zhongguo geming de yiwei weida nüxing: Shenqie huainian Zhang Qinqiu." *Zhongguo funübao,* 17 June 1988, 2.

Zhang Quan

Zhang Quan, 1919–1993, of Yixing, Jiangsu Province, was a famous soprano.

She was the seventh child in her family; two older sisters and a brother died at a young age. Her father was a teacher in a traditional private school, while her mother kept house. At the age of seventeen and against her family's wishes, Zhang Quan sat for and passed the entrance examination for piano performance studies at the Hangzhou Institute of the Arts (Hangzhou yishu zhuanke xuexiao). However, she studied voice at the school instead with a Russian professor (who was given the Chinese name Ma Xun). In 1937 (some sources say 1940), Zhang Quan enrolled in the Voice Department at the Institute of Music of Shanghai (Shanghai yinzhuan), where she studied with Zhou Shu'an (*q.v.*) and Huang Youkui. Zhang Quan gave her first solo recital in 1942.

About then, she married Mo Guixin (d. 1957) with whom she had three children. With his encouragement and support, in 1947 Zhang Quan went to the United States to pursue further study. She enrolled at Nazareth College (Rochester, N.Y.) and studied piano, music appreciation, conducting, music analysis, French, philosophy, psychology, literature, and theology. Zhang Quan was awarded a scholarship to study at the Eastman School of Music, also in Rochester, and gained a Concert Soloist Certificate, a Vocal Performance Artist Certificate, and a master's in Music, 1951. After returning to China that year, she performed with the Central Experimental Opera Company (Zhongyang shiyan gejuyuan).

Zhang Quan knew little of Chinese music and art, and, with the new official policy of promoting Chinese culture—especially music and dance—devoted herself to familiarizing herself with the country's repertoire. During this period, she sang in the operas *La Traviata* and *Orchid Blossom* (Lanhuahua), performed in Chinese for the first time. In 1957, however, Zhang Quan was denounced as a rightist, and her husband was exiled to the far north for labor reform; he died the same year. In 1961 she returned to the theater after being assigned to the Harbin Performance Theater (Harbin gewu juyuan) and later expressed deep gratitude for the special care Premier Zhou Enlai (1898–1976) had managed to provide her at this time. During the Cultural Revolution, however, Zhang Quan experienced further hardship.

In 1978 she was recalled to Beijing and made chair of the Beijing Musicians' and Dancers' Association, art director of the Beijing Singing and Dancing Troupe, and vice-president of the China Conservatorium of Music. Zhang Quan was also made a professor. Her contribution to music in China was publicly acknowledged with a seminar celebrating the fortieth anniversary of her return to China, held in Beijing by the Conservatorium of Music on 16 October 1991.

Shirley WAI CHAN and HE Li
(Translated by Qianbo Xin)

"I Sing for the People." *Women of China*, November 1981.
Liu Bo, ed. *Zhongguo dangdai wenhua yishu mingren da cidian*. Beijing: Guoji wenhua chuban gongsi, 1993.
"Qiusuozhe zhi ge—Nügaoyin gechangjia Zhang Quan zishu." *Renwu*, no. 3 (1990): 98–112.
Zhongguo renwu nianjian. 1992. Beijing: Beijing huayi chubanshe, 1992.

Zhang Ruoming

Zhang Ruoming, 1902–1958, of Baoding, Hebei Province, was the first Chinese woman to be awarded a doctorate in France and a pioneer in the women's movement and patriotic causes of modern China. She made a major contribution to the dissemination of Marxism and national reform.

In 1916 Zhang Ruoming entered the First Tianjin Women's Normal School in Zhili, Hebei Province, where she enrolled in the same year as Deng Yingchao (*q.v.*). These two young students became the radical reformists of the school. In 1919 during the May Fourth Movement, along with Guo Longzhen (1894–1932) and Liu Qingyang (*q.v.*), they initiated and led the Tianjin Women's Patriotic Association (Tianjin nüjie aiguo tongzhi hui) in which more than six hundred women participated. Together with Zhou Enlai (1898–1976), Ma Jun, and Chen Zhidu, the four women also formed the backbone of the Awakened Society (Juewushe), which constituted the core leadership of the May Fourth Movement in Tianjin. In the same month, Zhang Ruoming, Guo Longzhen, Zhou Enlai, Yu Fangzhou, Ma Jun, Ma Qianli, and more than twenty other young intellectuals were arrested in Tianjin in connection with this movement and imprisoned until July. While incarcerated, Zhang Ruoming experienced her first taste of Marxism when Zhou Enlai gave several talks on that subject as part of an inmates group devoted to the study of social issues.

In November 1920, Zhang Ruoming, Zhou Enlai, Guo Longzhen, and Liu Qingyang went to France to study. While there, Zhang Ruoming worked as a special correspondent for the Beijing publication *Morning News* (Chenbao) for which she wrote many articles on political analysis. Zhang Ruoming also joined the Communist Group in Paris in early 1922 and became chair of this organization but resigned in 1924 to pursue studies.

Zhang Ruoming's thinking on the women's movement was both innovative and profoundly influential. Her major works in the field were "Vanguard Women" (Jixian feng de nüzi)—published under the pen name Three-six (Sanliu), edited by Zhou Enlai, and appearing in the inaugural issue of *Awakening* (20 January 1920)—and "What Form of Liberation Will Satisfy Modern Women?" (Xiandai de nüzi yi zenyangde jiefang wei manyi)—edited by Deng Yingchao and appearing in the 18 March 1924 issue of Tianjin *Women's Daily* (Funü ribao). Zhang Ruoming believed twentieth-century women had to develop a revolutionary spirit to forge the values of independence and autonomy. A prerequisite to creating a women's movement, however, was toppling the three traditional concepts: a "double standard in male-female morality," "psychological and physiological gender differences," and "gender inequality in vocations." She also encouraged women to participate in politics so as to further their liberation and particularly emphasized women's participation in government.

In thinking about national reform, Zhang Ruoming was deeply influenced by the patriotic ideas that prevailed during the May Fourth Movement. She opposed imperialism and capitalism and believed that in order to reform China, it was essential "intellectuals turn their hands to manual work." Her anti-imperialist and anti-capitalist viewpoint, as well as intense patriotism, is explicit in the political articles she wrote in France and published in *Morning News*: "Britain's Devious Foreign Strategy" (Ying jili zhi guimi de waijiao celüe), "Notes on the English Coalminers' Strike" (Yingguo meikuang bagong yeji), "The Turko-Greek War and the German Situation" (Tu-Xi zhanzheng yu Deguo xingshi), "A Lay Guide to Imperialism" (Diguozhuyi qianshuo), "Surplus Value" (Shengyu jiazhi), and "Class Struggle" (Jieji douzheng). The last two were the earliest articles written by a Chinese woman promoting Marxism.

In a 1921 article entitled "The Fear of Work-Study Program Chinese Students in France and Sino-French Education" (Liu Fa jianxuesheng zhi konghuang yu Hua Fa jiaoyu) published in *Morning News*, Zhang Ruoming pointed out:

> What the present cultural movement in China is disseminating is dazzling in its variety, with seemingly no holds barred. People talk of new-isms, of democracy, of Marxist studies and of Bolshevism—all sorts of things. But when you put it all together, what they are doing is seeking security for the livelihood of all . . . From now on, it is essential that those who do manual labor be awakened and intellectualized, and that intellectuals do manual labor.

In her eyes, both Chinese men and women of the twentieth century had to stand on their own two feet with genuine conviction. To be Chinese was to use one's abilities to serve society in order to implement wholeheartedly the "intellectualization of the laborer" and "laborization of the intellectual" and to make the nation wealthy and powerful.

In 1924, Zhang Ruoming enrolled at the Université de Lyon. In 1930, she undertook research on French literary history from a psychological perspective and on the literary theorist André Gide. Zhang Ruoming was awarded a doctorate for her dissertation "L'Attitude d'André Gide." In the same year, she married Yang Kun (b. 1901), a fellow Chinese student at the university and later to become a renowned ethnologist; their son Yang Zaidao was born in China in 1931.

The couple returned to China that year and taught at Beiping Sino-French University (Beiping Zhong–Fa daxue). In 1937 Zhang Ruoming published her other major work *Three Great French Symbolist Poets: Baudelaire, Verlaine, and Rimbaud* (Faguo xiang zheng pai sanda shiren: Baodelai'er, Wei'erlainuo yu Lanbao). In this scholarly work on French literature, she discussed the works and lives of the three poets, particularly introducing their unique system of symbolism. Zhang Ruoming was instrumental in introducing French literature and intellectual trends to the Chinese literary world, annotating a large quantity of French poetry and prose, e.g., "An Annotated Selection of the Writings of Proust" (Proust: Textes Choisis; Pulusite wenxuan zhu).

In 1948, Zhang Ruoming and her husband moved to Yunnan University in Kunming, where he became professor and head of the Sociology Department, while she became professor of the Chinese Department. Zhang Ruoming also taught Marxism and in 1953 founded the Literary Criticism Unit. Apart from teaching and research, she did editing work for the *French Language Monthly* (Fawen yuekan) and translated many famous Chinese works into French, including those of Lu Xun and Yu Dafu. Zhang Ruoming thus contributed significantly to cultural exchange between the two countries. It was a great loss when she died in 1958 at the age of fifty-six.

WONG Yin Lee
(Translated by Martin Williams)

Chenbao (Beijing). 15–19 June 1921; 29–30 June 1921; 1–5 July 1921.

Lin Rulian. Personal communication with the author.

Qinghua daxue Zhonggong dang shi jioayan shi, ed. *Fu Fa Qin gong jianxue yundong shi liao*. Beijing: Beijing chubanshe, 1980.

Quanguo fulian fuyun shi, ed. *Zhongguo funüyundong lishi ziliao*. Beijing: Zhongguo funüchubanshe, 1991.

Tianjin lishi bowuguan, Nankai daxue lishixi, eds. *Wusi yundong zai Tianjin—Lishi ziliao xuanji*. Tianjin: Tianjin renmin chubanshe, 1979.

Yang Kun. Personal communication with the author.

Yang Zaidao. Personal communication with the author.

Yishibao (Tianjin). 3 December 1919.

Zhang Ruoming. "André Chenier: Poèmes" (In French). *Fawen yanjiu* (Beiping), 4, no. 4 (July 1943).

———. "Francis Jammes: Poèmes." (In French.) *Fawen yanjiu* (Beiping), 3, no. 7 (May 1942).

———. "Jide de jieshao." *Xin sichao* (Beiping), 1, no. 4 (November 1946).

———. "Paul Valery: Le Retour de Hollande." (In French.) *Fawen yanjiu* (Beiping), 3, no. 8 (June 1942).

———. "Shilun wenxue zhong dianxingxing de chuangzuo guocheng." *Renwen kexue* (Yunnan University), 1 (1957).

Zhong-Fa daxue yuekan. 11:4/5 (August 1937).

Zhonggong Tianjinshi wei dangshi ziliao zhengji weiyuanhui, Tianjinshi funülianhehui, eds.

Deng Yingchao yu Tianjin zaoqi funüyundong. Beijing: Zhongguo funüchubanshe, 1987.
Zhongguo kexueyuan lishi yanjiu suo, ed. *Wusi yundong huiyilu.* Beijing: Zhonghua shuju, 1959.
Zhongguo shehui kexueyuan jindaishi yanjiu suo, ed. *Wusi yundong huiyilu,* vol. 2. Beijing: Zhongguo shehui kexue chubanshe, 1979.
Zhou Enlai. *"Juewu," "Jueyou": Zhou Enlai shi wenji.* Tianjin: Nankai daxue, 1980.

Zhang, Sophie: *see* **Zhang Mojun**

Zhang Wei: *see* **Wulan**

Zhang Wu: *see* **Zhang Qinqiu**

Zhang Xinxin
Zhang Xinxin, b. 1953 in the city of Nanjing, was one of the most talented writers of the first decade of the post-Mao era.

As with many young urban dwellers born shortly after the establishment of the PRC in 1949, her schooling in Beijing was interrupted by the outbreak of the Cultural Revolution. In 1969, she was dispatched to the countryside to do farm work. Because of ill health, however, Zhang Xinxin was removed from the farm and worked first as an army nurse and then in a factory as a Communist Youth League administrator. In 1979, she was admitted to the Central Drama Institute in Beijing, training as a stage director.

Zhang Xinxin started publishing short stories in 1978 and catapulted to national fame with the publication of her controversial novella *On the Same Horizon* (Zai tongyi dipingxian shang, 1981). The novella abandoned the by then hackneyed theme of the disastrous consequences of the Cultural Revolution, dealing instead with the more universal problem of how females construct an identity in a male-dominated society. She gives a sympathetic and sensitive portrayal of a woman character who struggles to be her own person, pursuing a career in the face of social prejudice and male chauvinism, particularly her husband's.

Often regarded as one of the most daring pieces of feminist writing in post-1949 Chinese literature, the novella probably contains autobiographical elements, for, like the heroine, Zhang Xinxin had left her first husband. Predictably, the story was not well received by the male-dominated establishment, and Zhang Xinxin was attacked for promoting what was described as "bourgeois individualism." Undaunted, she continued to write from a feminist perspective. *The Dreams of My Age Group* (Women zhege nianji de meng, 1982) is about a young woman married to a dull man; she tries to escape through daydreams the banality and meaningless existence of her life. The story ends with the devastating discovery that the white knight of her fantasies may be none other than her despised petty-minded neighbor. *The Last Anchorage* (Zuihoude tingpodi, 1985) portrays the heartache of an intelligent career woman who seeks but cannot find romantic fulfillment. *Which Parental Role Are You Playing This Time?* (Zheci ni yan na yiban, 1988) is a touching story about relationships among three females sharing a flat: the roommates are a single woman, divorced mother, and the latter's sensitive and precocious daughter. The young single woman assumes some of the responsibility of caring for the little girl and playfully asks the child to call her "Father," warning her not to do so in public. Ironically, the daughter comes to accept the simulated "father" in place of a biological one.

Zhang Xinxin's less than flattering depiction of Chinese males in these writings was unconventional and disconcerting to say the least. The authorities were apparently so angered by her attitude that they did not assign her a job when she graduated from the Central Drama Institute in 1984. A change in the political wind later that year, however, brought with it a period of moderation, and Zhang Xinxin found work in the Chinese Youth Art Theater and the Beijing People's Art Theater. She also hosted several television programs.

In later works, Zhang Xinxin experimented with a variety of styles, abandoning psychological realism in favor of intricate plots. The novella *Philately* (Feng, pian, lian, 1985), which is reminiscent of a detective story, is most representative of this style, while *Clivia Craze* (Fengkuangde junzilan, 1983), a social satire on money worship, incorporates Latin American magical realism. However, the writer's next book, *Beijing People* (Beijing ren, 1986), brought international fame. The novel was conceived in 1984 when she and journalist Sang Ye traveled all over China, interviewing hundreds of individuals from all social strata and occupations. Over one hundred stories based on these interviews were published at different times between 1984 and 1986 under the collective title *Beijing People*; the pieces were collected into a volume bearing the same name in 1986. The book was clearly inspired by the oral history tradition exemplified in Studs Terkel's *American Dreams: Lost and Found*; its Chinese translation had been popular with Chinese readers. *Beijing People* has been translated into many foreign languages. It is mainly read by Western readers for its sociological content as truthfully representing a cross-section of post-Mao Chinese society. The collection is not without literary merit, however. Many stories are told in a lively colloquial style, reproducing speech rhythm and mannerisms, and vividly capture the nuances of mood and individuality in the gamut of speakers. The initial success of *Beijing People* must have inspired a second collaboration by the same authors. This was a piece of reportage on what went on in an eye hospital, a fire brigade and a crematorium during a Chinese New Year break. Entitled *Disasters* (Zaibian, 1986), there is no apparent rhyme or reason for bringing these disparate episodes together, which makes the long report somewhat rambling and tedious.

Zhang Xinxin's linguistic virtuosity, already evident in early works, reached its apogee in *On the Road* (Zai lu shang, 1986). This is a slightly fictionalized account of her three-month solo bicycle ride of some 2,500 km along China's Grand Canal; it skillfully blends history with fiction, facts with imagination, and jokes with serious reflection. A mixture of high literary style and vulgar and facetious expressions match its wide-ranging subject matter. The narrative was made into the television series *People along the Grand Canal* (Yunhe ren), featuring Zhang Xinxin herself as the narrator. Its popularity so overshadowed the script that the latter has not received due recognition for its literary merit.

During a short and very productive career as a writer in China, Zhang Xinxin was invited to visit many Western countries. She left China in 1988 to take up a position at

Cornell University as a writer-in-residence. Zhang Xinxin met her second husband in the United States and has made her home there; it is not known whether she has children. It is a pity that her name has disappeared from the literary scene.

Sylvia CHAN

Gunn, Edward, Donna Jung, and Patricia Farr, eds. and trans. *The Dreams of Our Generation and Selections from Beijing's People*. Cornell East Asia Series. Ithaca, N.Y.: Cornell University, 1993.
Huang Dewei, ed. *Women zhege nianji de meng*. Taipei: Xindi wenxue chubanshe, 1988.
Kinkley, Jeffrey C. "The Cultural Choices of Zhang Xinxin: A Young Writer of the 1980s." In *Ideas Across Cultures: Essays on Chinese Thought in Honor of Benjamin Schwartz*, eds. Paul A. Cohen and Merle Goldman. Cambridge, Mass.: Harvard University Press, 1990, 137–62.
Roberts, Rosemary A. "Images of Women in the Fiction of Zhang Jie and Zhang Xinxin." *China Quarterly*, 120 (December 1989): 800–13.
Wakeman, Carolyn, and Yue Daiyun. "Fiction's End: Zhang Xinxin's New Approaches to Creativity." In *Modern Chinese Women Writers: Critical Appraisals*, ed. Michael S. Duke. Armonk, N.Y.: M.E. Sharpe, 1989, 196–216.
Wang Fei, ed. *Zhang Xinxin daibiao zuo*. Zhengzhou: Huanghe wenyi chubanshe, 1988.
Zhang Xinxin. *Jie hou jie*. Hong Kong: Boyi chuban jituan, 1986.
———. *Women zhege nianji de meng, Zhang Xinxin zhong duan pian xiaoshuo ji*. Chengdu: Sichuan wenyi chubanshe, 1985.
———. *Zai tongyi dipingxian shang*. Taipei: Sanmin shuju, 1988.
———. *Zheci ni yan na yiban*. Taipei: Sanmin shuju, 1989.
Zhang Xinxin and Sang Ye. *Beijing ren*. Shanghai: Shanghai wenyi chubanshe, 1986.
———. *Chinese Lives: An Oral History of Contemporary China*, eds. W.J.F. Jenner and Dellia Davin. London: Macmillan, 1987.

Zhang Yan: *see* **Xixi**

Zhang Yuliang: *see* **Pan Yuliang**

Zhang Yun
Zhang Yun, 1905–1995, of Changsha, Hunan Province, became famous as a leader of the women's movement; her original name was Du Runzhang and one source gives her year of birth as 1916.

Zhang Yun attended school in Changsha and in 1925 joined the CCP in Hankou, where she had gone to study. Zhang Yun was assigned during that period of KMT-CCP alliance to such tasks as heading the KMT Hankou Municipality Women's Department, organizing the women's reception work for the Northern Expeditionary Army, and heading the Qiaokou District Committee's Organization and Women's Departments. In 1925 she married fellow communist Li Yunsheng with whom she had two children, a son and daughter.

After the failure of the National Revolution of 1924–27, Zhang Yun engaged in underground work in Wuchang, Nanjing, and elsewhere. After her husband was martyred and young son (Li Xiaolin) arrested, along with his teenage paternal aunt, in 1931 or 1932, Zhang Yun continued to work and to care for her daughter (Li Zaoli).

Zhang Yun lost contact with the CCP for a time yet never sought employment within the KMT or government organizations. She moved from Changsha to Wuhan to Nanjing and met an acquaintance who told her that Li Yunsheng had written a note while in jail, asking his wife to "shoulder the hundred catty load alone."

In 1936 Zhang Yun became county secretary to the CCP Xiangtan Committee and served during the Sino-Japanese War as leading cadre of the Southeastern Branch Office's Women's Committee. She also served in other party positions in various parts of Jiangsu, including as secretary to the local area's Central Jiangsu Committee (Su zhong erfenqu diwei shuji). Zhang Yun was one of the few women placed in sole charge of an entire area. From 1945, she served as a committee member of the CCP central China branch, concurrently holding the position of head of the Women's Department (Zhonggong Huazhongju weiyuan funübuzhang) and head of the East China Division Women's Department (Huadongju funübuzhang). Subsequently, Zhang Yun became vice-secretary of the Henan-Anhui-Jiangsu Party Committee (Yu-Wan-Su qu dangwei fu shuji), head of the Henan-Anhui-Jiangsu Branch Office's Propaganda Department, and principal of the Third Field Army Women Cadres' School.

Zhang Yun's son, Li Xiaolin, was redeemed from KMT imprisonment about 1937 by his paternal grandfather and from then on worked on the family farm. His mother did not find him until he was fifteen, about 1945, but then ensured that her son gained an education. He went overseas to study science, and Zhang Yun was said to have been proud of him. Her daughter, Li Zaoli, is also said to have studied abroad and become a senior engineer with the Department of Space Industry.

In 1949 with the founding of the People's Republic, Zhang Yun served on the CCP East China Bureau's Women's Committee, as secretary to the Women's Committee of the Shanghai Municipal Party Committee, director of the East China Region's Women's Federation, director of Shanghai Municipal Women's Federation, third secretary to the CCP Women's Committee (1952), and secretary-general (1952) and vice-chair (1953) of the ACWF. She thus became one of the leaders of the women's movement in China. In that capacity, Zhang Yun was elected to the First, Second, and Third NPCs as well as to the Second, Third, and Fourth CPPCC of whose Standing Committee she was also a member. Zhang Yun was elected in 1956 as an alternate member of the Central Committee and represented China at international women's conferences in Denmark, France, the USSR, and Vietnam.

She was persecuted by Kang Sheng during the Cultural Revolution after he accused her of being a traitor to the party. Zhang Yun remained essentially unbowed, however, despite being sent to cadre school and enduring hard labor; she was not rehabilitated until 1975. Elected as a deputy secretary to the Central Committee Discipline and Inspection Commission, she supervised matters arising from the Cultural Revolution with extraordinary courage, insight, and boldness. Zhang Yun was responsible for many who had suffered injustice being exonerated and rehabilitated without undue delay. She also dared take responsibility to act impartially while investigating and judging serious economic crimes and during campaigns against corruption.

Her book *Zhang Yun on the Construction of the Party* ran to sixty thousand copies and became an approved teaching text for the party. As a long-time participant in women's work, Zhang Yun emphasized that female cadres should "sink into and master the essential points; create and accumulate experience and promote communality: in doing this, they themselves will be able to work, to lead others in a realistic manner and to educate other cadres." She was known for her innovative recommendations throughout her period of work with the ACWF. Zhang Yun died on 25 December 1995.

ZHAO Jinping
(Translated by Malcolm Robertson)

Chen Min. "'Ta shi womende nüzhong haojie'—Ji Zhongyang guwen weiyuanhui weiyuan Zhang Yun." In *Tawukui yu Gongchandang de chenghao.* Shanghai: Shanghai renmin chubanshe, 1984, 1–8.
Feng Yuehua. "'Tiedajie' Zhang Yun." In *Nübing liezhuan,* vol. 2, ed. Han Zi. Shanghai: Shanghai wenyi chubanshe, 1986, 146–56.
Klein, Donald W., and Anne B. Clark. *Biographic Dictionary of Chinese Communism, 1921– 1965.* Cambridge, Mass.: Harvard University Press, 1971, 71–73.
Lamb, Malcolm. *Directory of Officials and Organizations in China.* Armonk, N.Y.: M.E. Sharpe, 1994.
Yingwen *Zhongguo funü,* ed. *Gujin zhuming funürenwu,* vol. 2. Shijiazhuang: Hebei renmin chubanshe, 1986, 705–09.
Zhang Yun. *Zhang Yun wenji,* ed. Zhonghua quanguo funülianhehui. Beijing: Zhongguo funüchubanshe, 1996.
Zhongguo funüwushinian. CD-ROM.

Zhang Zhaohan: *see* **Zhang Mojun**

Zhang Zhixin
Zhang Zhixin, 1931?–1975, of Tianjin, was a political dissident who became one of the martyrs of the Cultural Revolution when she was killed after being held in prison for over five years.

Although Zhang Zhixin's parents were both teachers, her father was unemployed. Thus, she stayed at home helping her mother with housework and taking care of her younger sister. Her parents were finally able to afford to send Zhang Zhixin to school when she was eleven. However, her mother taught her to read, and her father taught her the violin. The most important lesson they gave her, though, was to think for herself.

When the Liberation Army of the CCP marched into Tianjin in January 1949, Zhang Zhixin welcomed them. She was then in her final year of high school and rapidly absorbing Marxist-Leninist ideology. Zhang Zhixin was inspired by the party's exemplary heroes and heroines, real and fictional, and dedicated herself to communism and the creation of the new China. In 1950, she entered the Education Department of the Normal College of Hebei (Hebei shifan xueyuan). Upon the outbreak of the Korean War that year, she immediately applied to join the army and was accepted. Instead of being sent to the front, however, Zhang Zhixin was enrolled in the PLA College for Military Cadres (Junshi ganbu xueyuan). Later, she was sent to the Russian Department of the People's University in Beijing. What Zhang Zhixin learned there about revolutionary theory framed her outlook on life and worldview. In 1955, she joined the CCP and two years later was appointed to a position in the Propaganda Department of the Liaoning Provincial Committee. Zhang Zhixin performed well at her job but continued to study and seek "truth" because she believed it to be both a right and a sacred duty of party members.

Initially, Zhang Zhixin had nothing but praise for the Cultural Revolution and participated wholeheartedly. However, as increasing numbers of cadres and leaders were attacked and the graves of revolutionary martyrs exhumed in order to purge those heroes in public, she began to harbor doubts. Zhang Zhixin is said to have expressed skepticism to a friend about the correctness of canceling out the achievements of old leaders such as Liu Shaoqi (1898–1969); because of this, Zhang Zhixin was sent to a May Seventh Cadre School for labor reform. There, she still continued her search for what she thought was the truth, undertaking further study of revolutionary writings. Zhang Zhixin became even more convinced, however, that what was happening in the nation was wrong. This led to her arrest in September 1969 by supporters of the Gang of Four, who held power in Liaoning; Zhang Zhixin was labeled as a "current anti-revolutionary," a crime of a most serious nature. While in jail, she wrote diaries, notes, letters, and self-criticisms as well as lyrics and music for several songs, the most famous possibly being "Whose Crime?" In this piece, Zhang Zhixin declared her innocence: "If I am guilty, then the more guilty people like me there are, the less the people will suffer." Her best-known work is the fifty-thousand-word "Manifesto of a Communist Party Member" (Yige gongchandangyuan de xuanyan), written in response to a demand for a confession. In the manifesto, she related the process of her maturity as a party member and expressed her understanding of the Cultural Revolution. Not only was she certain that it was a great mistake, she also believed it was not a sudden occurrence, that it had been building up for seventeen years, since 1949. She even declared that, despite the greatness of his thought, Mao Zedong (1893–1976) had made mistakes and blind worship of him was wrong.

Zhang Zhixin was killed by the Gang of Four in April 1975; she was only forty-four years old. Zhang Zhixin was survived by her husband, Zeng Zhen, their two children (a daughter and son), and her sick mother. The last letter she wrote to her husband did not reach him but was placed in her personal file as evidence of anti-revolutionary crimes. In the letter, Zhang Zhixin expressed regret at not having been a better mother and wife, apologizing to her husband for having to leave him with the responsibility of bringing up their children. Finally, she asked him to use her savings to care for her sick mother. True to the tradition of revolutionary martyrs, Zhang Zhixin ended with the words: "Long live the Chinese Communist Party! Long live our great motherland! Long live Chairman Mao."

She was posthumously rehabilitated after the Eleventh Congress of the CCP in 1978. Named a revolutionary martyr by Liaoning Province, her image appeared in newspapers and magazines all over China as a heroine who resisted the "evil Gang of Four and their lackeys."

Zhang Zhixin was not the only person to realize the damage of the ten-year-long Cultural Revolution. In higher positions than hers, people who were older, with longer party histories, and sitting closer to the power center of the CCP knew, yet not one of them denounced the Cultural Revolution as publicly and as uncompromisingly as did she. Far removed from power politics, Zhang Zhixin spoke out clear-eyed and honestly, fully aware of the danger in which it placed her. She is an example of a fine individual who fought for truth as she saw it and against a relentless political system that valued obedience over honesty.

Lily Xiao Hong LEE

Song Ruizhi, ed. *Zhongguo funüwenhua tonglan*. Jinan: Shangdong wenyi chubanshe, 1995, 168–70.
Wei zhenli er douzheng youxiu Gongchandangyuan Zhang Zhixin de yingxiong shiji. Shenyang: Liaoning renmin chubanshe, 1979.
Yingwen *Zhongguo funü*, ed. *Gujin zhuming funü renwu*, vol. 2. Shijiazhuang: Hebei renmin chubanshe, 1986, 1124–28.
Yuan Shaoying and Yang Guizhen, eds. *Zhongguo funü mingren cidian*. Changchun: Beifang funüertong chubanshe, 1989, 325.
Zhang Zhixin. Shenyang: Liaoning renmin chubanshe, 1985.
Zhang Zhixin and Liu Shaorong. *Guoqu, xianzai, jianglai*. Shenyang: Liaoning renmin chubanshe, 1985.
Zhongguo funüguanli ganbu xueyuan, ed. *Gujin Zhongwai nümingren cidian*. Beijing: Zhongguo guangbo dianshi chubanshe, 1980, 582.

Zhao Moya: *see* **Chao Mo-ya**

Zhao Yanxia

Zhao Yanxia, b. 1928, in Hebei Province, is a singer in *jingju* (Beijing opera).

Performing with her father, Zhao Xiaolou, in Hangzhou, Shanghai, and Hankou by the time she was seven, Zhao Yanxia at the age of fourteen learned from Zhu Ruxiang the *qingyi* (young or middle-aged women of rectitude) and *huadan* (lively young women) roles. Zhao Yanxia also received instruction from Xun Huisheng. Zhao's talent first showed itself when she performed in *Outstanding Heroes* (Da ying jielie) at the age of fifteen. Zhao Yanxia then co-starred with Yang Baoshen in *Wu's Hillside* (Wujiapo), with Jin Shaoshan in *The General and the Concubine* (Bawang bie ji), with Ma Lianliang in *The Upstairs Murder of Yan Poxi* (Zuolou sha Xi), and with Hou Xirui in *Woman Warrior Shisanmei* (Shisanmei).

Known for her clear enunciation, smooth singing, and an easy, graceful style, Zhao Yanxia led the Yanming *Jingju* Troupe on tour around Beijing in 1947, giving performances of *Hongniang*, *Huatian cuo*, *Xin'an Station* (Xin'an yi), *Xun Guanniang*, and *Interrogating the Husband and Seeking the Husband* (Panfu suofu). The troupe's distinguishing feature was that they made the best use possible of individual talent in singing, movement, dialogue, and martial arts and pushed performance to its limit, in this way developing the *jingju* tradition. Yet, the troupe also adhered to the principle that performances should spring from real life. Zhao Yanxia once pointed out that the main quality of her style was that the clarity in the performers' technical repertoire allowed the audience to understand fully the plot and characters in the story. Her performances aimed to achieve artistic integrity and a heightened dramatic effect.

When, for example, Li Huiniang in *Red Plum Pavilion* (Hongmei ge) is rebuked for enraging the cruel Jia Sidao by an unrestrained show of affection for Pei Sheng, the character asks forgiveness, singing "I beg you, Venerable Grand Tutor, to show mercy and pardon me" (*Hai wang qiu Lao Taishi faluo congkuan*). In playing the role of Li Huiniang, Zhao Yanxia conveyed immense sorrow and earnestness as she sang the words. Further, she created a new movement instead of following the tradition of either singing, then kneeling, or kneeling, then singing. As Li Huiniang, Zhao Yanxia faced the audience so that Jia Sidao saw only a profile and the flick of her right sleeve outward. Trembling, she adopted a pose of supplication with hands in her sleeves, singing *fa* ... *luo* ... *cong* ... *kuan*, she slowly sank down on her right leg, dragging the words out so that as her knee touched the stage she sang the word *kuan*. The gesture never failed to profoundly move her audience.

Another example is Zhao Yanxia's innovative interpretation of the role of Zhang Cuiluan in *Night Rain in Xiaoxiang* (Xiaoxiang yeyu). Having been convicted of a crime, the character unexpectedly runs into her long-lost father. At this point, Zhao Yanxia executed a *huadan* movement instead of the traditional *qingyi* movement, stamping her feet with great force to express the character's complex emotions of surprise and deep grief. Again, her performance in this part never failed to move her audience to tears.

Zhao Yanxia joined the Beijing *Jingju* Troupe in 1960 as deputy director, a position retained until she became director of the first troupe of the Beijing Opera Institute in 1979. Zhao Yanxia played the leading role in *The White Snake* (Baishe zhuan) and *Red Plum Pavilion* many times and in 1964 took the part of Aqing sao in the modern *jing* opera *The Sha's Beach* (Shajia bang), one of only a few approved by Jiang Qing (*q.v.*) for staging.

Shirley Wai CHAN
(Translated by Cui Zhiying)

Liu Bo, ed. *Zhongguo dangdai wenhua yishu mingren dacidian*. Beijing: Guoji wenhua chubanshe, 1993, 505–06.
Zhu Cheng. "Chuangxin shi yishu de linghun—Zhao Yanxia jiu xiqu liupai yixitan." *Renmin daxue baokan ziliao xuanhui*, no. 11 (1986): 81–83.

Zhao Yiman

Zhao Yiman, 1905–1936, a native of Yibin County, Sichuan Province, was a CCP martyr who worked with the anti-Japanese partisans known as the People's Revolutionary Army of the Northeast (Dongbei renmin gemingjun). Originally named Li Kuntai, she went by many other names, including Li Yijie, but chose Zhao Yiman as her nom de guerre when she went to the northeast to work in Japanese-occupied areas.

Zhao Yiman was from a landlord family but, influenced by her brother-in-law, read many progressive books and periodicals and became receptive to revolutionary ideas. She joined the Socialist Youth League of China in 1924 at nineteen and immediately embarked upon revolutionary activities in her own county. In 1926, Zhao Yiman attended Yibin Women's High School in Yibin's county seat and there became active in the student movement as a student leader. She joined the CCP that year, and the party sent her to study at the Central Political and Military School at Wuhan, generally known as the Wuhan Branch of Whampoa Military Academy. In 1927 Zhao

Yiman was sent to Dongfang University in the Soviet Union to further her studies. There, she married a former Whampoa student named Chen Dabang. One source says Zhao Yiman decided to leave the Soviet Union to take up secret work in China when she was five months pregnant. Certainly, upon her return to China in 1928 Zhao Yiman did underground work for the CCP in Hubei, Jiangxi, and Shanghai; while in Hubei, she gave birth to a boy.

In 1931, Zhao Yiman was sent to the Japanese-occupied northeast where at first she worked with women workers in Harbin. The following year, Zhao Yiman was appointed acting secretary to the General Workers' Union of Harbin. But when the party organization in Harbin was smashed soon afterward by the Japanese, she and her colleagues were forced to retreat to the countryside. From 1932 to 1934, Zhao Yiman held various party positions at provincial and county levels. In the last year, she was sent as a special commissioner (*tepaiyuan*) to develop the work of the party in the anti-Japanese guerrilla area of Zhuhe (present-day Shangzhi County in Heilongjiang Province), where she won local fame as a guerrilla leader. In 1935, Zhao Yiman became political commissar of the Second Regiment of the Third Army of the People's Revolutionary Army of the Northeast. As the Third Army retreated eastward before the Japanese army, the Second Regiment was left to fight along the railway, engaging the enemy to cover the retreat. In November, however, the Japanese army surrounded the Second Regiment. Zhao Yiman told its commander to break out while she and one squad of soldiers covered him. During the ensuing fierce fighting, Zhao Yiman was hit in the right eye and left arm and lost consciousness from loss of blood. She was taken prisoner by the Japanese.

The Japanese are said to have first tried a soft approach in prison, praising her courage and fighting prowess. When that did not work, they took a hard line. After nine months of imprisonment and torture during which Zhao Yiman revealed no information whatsoever, the Japanese decided to send her back to Zhuhe. There, she was captured again and sent to be executed. On the way to execution, Zhao Yiman wrote a letter to her young son telling him to remember that she died for her country. The martyr is said to have sung a revolutionary song as she approached the execution ground and died shouting anti-Japanese slogans.

The story of Zhao Yiman was widely told after 1949, and a film (*Zhao Yiman*) was made in 1951. A memorial museum in the northeast mounted an exhibition about her; in her native Yibin, a memorial stele was built for which the famous poet Guo Moruo composed a poem in Zhao Yiman's memory. The Shanghai opera (*huju*) artist Gu Yuezhen (*q.v.*) also created a modern opera based on Zhao Yiman's life.

She was survived by her husband Chen Dabang and their son Chen Yexian. He was only two years old when Zhao Yiman had left him with his uncle so that she could go to the northeast; he grew up not knowing the true identity of his mother. After 1949, Zhao Yiman's husband, son, and sister (Li Kunjie) tried to find her. With the help of an old photograph, a journalist finally identified Zhao Yiman as Li Yijie or Li Kuntai.

Lily Xiao Hong LEE

Qiu Zhizhuo, ed. *Zhonggong dangshi renminglu*. Chongqing: Chongqing chubanshe, 1986, 328.
Song Ruizhi, ed. *Zhongguo funüwenhua tonglan*. Jinan: Shandong wenyi chubanshe, 1995, 230–31.
Yang Zitian. "Zhao Yiman he tade erzi Chen Yexian." *Renwu*, no. 3 (1993): 154–59.
Yuan Shaoying and Yang Guizhen, eds. *Zhongguo funü mingren cidian*. Changchun: Beifang funüertong chubanshe, 1989, 405–06.

Zhao Zhiwen: *see* **Zhong Yuzheng**

Zheng Jie: *see* **Liu Ying**

Zhengyan fashi: *see* **Cheng Yen, Master**

Zhengyan, Ven.: *see* **Cheng Yen, Master**

Zhenhua fashi: *see* **Zhenhua, Ven.**

Zhenhua, Ven.
Ven. Zhenhua [Zhenhua fashi], 1909–1947, a native of Xinghua County, Jiangsu Province, was a Buddhist nun; her family name was Tang. She was the abbess of the Jade Buddha Temple (Yufo si) in Shanghai. The only information we have about her is culled from a "Publisher's Note" of *Gaoseng zhuan heji* in which her *Sequel to the Biographies of Eminent Nuns* (Xu Biqiuni zhuan) is found, along with two prefaces and a postscript to her *Sequel to the Biographies of Eminent Nuns* (published in 1991).

Yushan Tuiyin's preface maintains that Ven. Zhenhua possessed outstanding perception and knowledge before the age of thirty (*nian wei zi li, shi yi guo ren*). She apparently had at least one disciple by the name of Chaochen, who wrote the postscript for her *Sequel to the Biographies of Eminent Nuns*. In the abbess's own preface, she expressed the idea that in the Buddhist world, all beings are equal, and thus, no difference should exist between the genders among human beings and that vast ignorance kept women discriminated against in Chinese society. In Ven. Zhenhua's view, the lives of eminent monks had been well recorded but only the *Biographies of Eminent Nuns* (Biqiuni zhuan) by Baochang was available as a record for the lives of eminent nuns up until some time in the Liang dynasty (502–557). She herself thus wished to maintain a continuous record about these religious women from the Liang period where Baochang's work stopped, extending it up to the 1930s.

The *Sequel to the Biographies of Eminent Nuns* contains 201 biographies, and another forty-seven nuns are briefly mentioned. Completed before the Japanese attack on Shanghai in 1932, her first manuscript was lost and all of her books burned during the subsequent Sino-Japanese War. However, with the help of her disciple Chaochen, who had committed to memory much of the lost manuscript, the abbess reconstructed it. As an aide-memoire, they borrowed books and checked details with friends and colleagues by mail. The manuscript's reconstruction was completed in 1939 and a preface was added, recounting the story of the book.

Although our knowledge of Ven. Zhenhua's life is confined to these sparse details, what she achieved needs to be recorded. Firstly, Ven. Zhenhua was the abbess of the distinguished Jade Buddha Temple, an important temple built in 1882 to house a sitting and reclining jade Buddha from Sri Lanka. The temple also held a rich collection of sutras and is presently the site of the Buddhist Academy of Shanghai. More importantly, thanks to Ven. Zhenhua, the recorded history of Chinese nuns is unbroken from the time that the first nuns were ordained in the fourth century up until the twentieth century. Critics say that because some biographies quote only the poetry of the nuns they do not conform to the format of the biography genre. However, it is indeed fortunate that Ven. Zhenhua did include them, for otherwise posterity would not even have known their names. To be able to read their poetry at least helps us to imagine their personalities.

Lily Xiao Hong LEE

Chaochen, Ven. "[Ba]," *Xu Biqiuni zhuan*. In *Gaoseng zhuan heji*. Shanghai: Shanghai guji chubanshe, 1991, 1019–20.
"Chuban shuoming." *Gaoseng zhuan heji*. Shanghai: Shanghai guji chubanshe, 1991, v–vi.
Yushan Tuiyin (pseud.). "Xu Biqiuni zhuan xu," *Xu Biqiuni zhuan*. In *Gaoseng zhuan heji*. Shanghai: Shanghai guji chubanshe, 1991, 981.
Zhenhua, Ven. "Zi xu," *Xu Biqiuni zhuan*. In *Gaoseng zhuan heji*. Shanghai: Shanghai guji, 1991, 982.

Zhong Ling: *see* **Chung Ling**

Zhong Ming: *see* **Yan Huizhu**

Zhong Weiluo: *see* **Gong Peng**

Zhong Xiaoyang

Zhong Xiaoyang, b. 1962, is a Hong Kong writer of novels and short stories.

Her origins are complex. A native of Meixian, Guangdong Province, she was born in Guangzhou. Her father is an overseas Chinese from Indonesia whose patriotic sentiments led him to go to China in his youth, while her mother is from the northeastern Chinese city of Shenyang. Her family moved to Hong Kong when Zhong Xiaoyang was five months old, and so she grew up there. After finishing high school at Maryknoll Girls' School, in 1983 Zhong Xiaoyang went to Michigan University in the United States to study film. She now lives in Sydney, Australia. Her mother's native place in northeast China considerably influenced her writing.

Zhong Xiaoyang began writing in her teens and excelled in the many genres attempted: classical *shi* and *ci* poems, modern poetry, prose, and fiction. Her early works were published in Hong Kong magazines such as *Damuzhi banyuekan*, *Suye wenxue*, *Dangdai wenyi*, *Xianggang shibao*, and Taiwan's *Sansan jikan* and *Lianhebao*. Between 1979 and 1981, she won Hong Kong Youth Literature Awards (Xianggang qingnian wenxue jiang) in the categories of poetry, prose, and fiction. Zhong Xiaoyang became a "Double Champion" in the latter year, also winning a Literary Prize given by Hong Kong's City Hall. When her novella *Halt the Carriage and Ask Directions*

(Tingche zan wenlu), created after a visit to northeast China and published that year, appeared, she was widely recognized as a fully-fledged writer, even though Zhong Xiaoyang was still only nineteen years old. The novella about Shenyang and Fushun in the 1940s successfully captured the sights, sounds, smells, and details of that place and time and seemingly relived her mother's life. Short stories and novellas followed, including *Telling in Detail* (Xishuo), *Fleeting Years* (Liunian), *Ordinary Lives* (Putong de shenghuo), *After Burning* (Ranshao zhi hou), and the novel *A Strange Tale of Lingering Remorse* (Yihen chuanqi).

Zhong Xiaoyang's style is characterized by sensitivity and intimacy, adapting a tone in between modern and classical, and her plots take many twists and turns. She deals incisively with profound questions, searching for the meaning of love and hate, life and death; the yearning for an ideal life, whatever it might be; and one's helplessness in failing to achieve it. Combining feelings with ideas, Zhong Xiaoyang shows the influence of the classical Chinese novel *Dream of the Red Chamber* (Honglou meng) and the works of Eileen Chang (*q.v.*), readily acknowledging her indebtedness to both. Yet, in adapting Western literary ideas, Zhong Xiaoyang created her own unique style as she probes the psyche of her characters.

In 1998, Zhong Xiaoyang published four volumes of poetry *Dead Tree and Extinguished Ashes* (Gaomu sihui ji): *Change Color* (Bianse), *Love Lost* (Shilian), *The Study* (Shuzhai), and *Seed* (Zhongzi). *Change Color* is about her past. *Love Lost* is about the fading of love, love no longer in favor, and what is not love. *The Study* is about books, ink-stones, paper, and pens or writing brushes. *Seed* is about freedom and joy. These four volumes encompass her everyday life, feelings and thoughts, desires, and what has been discarded. Influenced by the long narrative poetry and drama pieces of the West, along with the technique of stream of consciousness, Zhong Xiaoyang creates in her work a profound and vivid world.

To date, she has published more than a dozen titles of fiction and prose in Hong Kong and Taiwan. Zhong Xiaoyang is loved by readers in both places; *Halt the Carriage and Ask Directions* was a bestseller in Taiwan, and recently Zhong Xiaoyang has become the focus of attention of university students in mainland China. Critics laud her literary technique, especially the sensitivity with which she treats human relationships. Some, however, speak of Zhong Xiaoyang's need to come out from the shadow of Eileen Chang and create her own world of fiction.

SUN Ailing
(Translated by Lily Xiao Hong Lee)

Chung Ling. "Perspective and Spatiality in the Fiction of Three Hong Kong Women Writers." In *Modern Chinese Women Writers: Critical Appraisals*, ed. Michael S. Duke. Armonk, N.Y.: M.E. Sharpe, 1989, 217–35.

Liu Yichang, ed. *Xianggang zuojia zhuanlüe*. Hong Kong: Xianggang shizhengju gonggong tushuguan, 1996, 875–76.

Pan Yadun. "Zhongguo daxuesheng xi'ai de Zhong Xiaoyang." In *Shijie huawen nüzuojia Sumiao*, ed. Pan Yadun. Guangzhou: Jinan daxue chubanshe, 1993, 162–72.

Zhong Xiaoyang. "Green Sleeves," trans. Michael S. Duke. In *Worlds of Modern Chinese Fiction*, ed. Michael S. Duke. Armonk, N.Y.: M.E. Sharpe, 1991, 206–20.

Zhong Yuzheng

Zhong Yuzheng, b. 1930 in Hong Kong but a native of Shunde, Guangdong Province, is a leading figure in the field of chemical disarmament in China. She was the first practicing woman scientist promoted to the rank of general in the Chinese military. At the time of her appointment (1993), Zhong Yuzheng was one of only twelve women—out of over three million military personnel—to have held the rank of general.

Zhong Yuzheng's father was born into a merchant family. He studied at an unspecified institution for two years in Shanghai before being recalled, to his regret, to enter the family business; he was also required to honor an arranged marriage to the daughter of a landlord family. Zhong Yuzheng's mother, however, was from an enlightened family, one that did not forcibly bind her feet and believed in the value of education for girls.

Zhong Yuzheng was the second of three children; she has an older sister and a younger brother. At some stage, her family moved to Hong Kong, where Zhong Yuzheng spent her early years. She was deeply influenced in spiritual matters by her paternal grandmother and aunt. Her grandmother was a strong-minded woman and a fervent Buddhist. Her aunt was a Christian and, because she was unwilling to marry, was sent by her own father to live with a younger brother—Zhong Yuzheng's father. The paternal aunt was therefore a constant presence in Zhong Yuzheng's young life. Despite spending her adult life in communist China and becoming a member of the CCP in the early 1960s, Zhong Yuzheng was clearly fortified by these two influences—Buddhist and Christian—in difficult times. Her devotion to the cause of world peace, evident in her career decisions, echoes Buddhist belief. She has said, however, that although appreciating the benefits and comfort that religion bestows on its believers, the more important work one should do is to create a better world in the present.

Zhong Yuzheng's father insisted that all three of his children receive a good education, and she spent fourteen years attending Christian schools in China, returning home to Hong Kong for holidays. The first one attended was a Peizheng primary school, which had been moved from Guangzhou to Amoy because of the Sino-Japanese War. After attending Union Girls' High School (Xiehe nüzhong) in Shanghai, she went on to Ginling [Jinling] Women's University in Nanjing (Jinling nüzi daxue). Apart from receiving an excellent education at these institutions, Zhong Yuzheng became fluent in English, which proved to be invaluable in her later career.

For most of her young life, until the age of nineteen, she had known nothing but war. Zhong Yuzheng was studying physics at Ginling University when the People's Republic was established in 1949 and in the following year joined the volunteer forces in response to the national recruitment drive for the Korean War (1950–53). Her family remained in Hong Kong and appears to have opposed the decision; she never saw either of her parents again. After her mother's death, her father remarried; he and his second wife died in quick succession in 1980.

Zhong Yuzheng said later that newspaper reports of the use of bacteriological and chemical weapons against Korean civilians motivated her to join the anti-chemical warfare corps, a special combat arm of the military. As a member of the first generation of students trained in this field, she frequently stepped forward in stifling protective clothing and gas mask when volunteers were required. Zhong Yuzheng refused to allow her gender to hold her back, requesting to be allocated even more duties than her male colleagues so as to gain more experience.

China had relied entirely on the Soviet Union for anti-chemical knowledge and techniques in the 1950s. By the early 1960s, however, the anti-chemical warfare corps began to step out from the shadow of the Soviet Union. While not having studied overseas, she learned from returning students about overseas developments in analytical chemistry and read English-language materials available in China. At that time, Zhong Yuzheng was an associate professor at Harbin Military Engineering Academy (Harbin junshi gongcheng xueyuan).

With the onset of the Cultural Revolution, Zhong Yuzheng's class background came against her. She was already married by this time (her husband's name is not given in sources), and she and her husband suffered severe beatings. Even her only child, a son, was persecuted because his mother had been born into the landlord class. Zhong Yuzheng was banished to the countryside for six years. One source says she spent ten years at the May Seventh Cadre School. Zhong Yuzheng returned to her unit, then stationed some forty km from Beijing, in spring 1975.

Setting aside any resentment she may have felt, Zhong Yuzheng turned her thoughts to what she could do for her country. Zhong Yuzheng realized that the past ten years had been a wasted period for keeping abreast in her field of study. She immediately embarked upon intensive reading in analytical chemistry in an effort to catch up with developments in the rest of the world, reading her way through the major libraries in Beijing, going through *Chemical Abstracts* from 1917 to 1979 in just over a year, and devouring vast quantities of specialist material from overseas. Zhong Yuzheng took copious notes, laying a solid foundation for the development of analytical chemistry in the service of the anti-chemical warfare corps.

Building upon this knowledge, she became known in the field of international chemical disarmament. Zhong Yuzheng has given dozens of papers on analytical chemistry at conferences in China and overseas and published papers in international chemistry journals. Two books on which she collaborated—*Analytical Chemistry for Studying Toxins* (Duji zhencha fenxi huaxue) and *Scientific and Technical Documents* (Keji wenxian jiansuo)—have become standard texts in China. After dedicating decades to analytical chemistry research, Zhong Yuzheng gained preeminence as an educator in the military's anti-chemical warfare system. She also gained respect in a related field of chemistry in acting as an interpreter for the well-known Polish chemist Professor M. Mikolajczyk at the International Conference on Phosphorus Chemistry held in China in March 1985.

As a professor at the General Staff Anti-Chemical Command Engineering College (Zongcan fanghua zhihui gongcheng xueyuan), Zhong Yuzheng was appointed in 1990 to head a Chinese team taking part in an international competition in Geneva. This was the second in a round-robin series of tests related to chemical disarmament. In November, the Australian Defence Laboratory distributed to all participating countries twenty-nine samples of unidentified toxic materials. Each laboratory had one month in which to identify them and submit a report. After her team had analyzed the samples, she was left with the task of writing the work report.

Over a period of two weeks, Zhong Yuzheng wrote 206 pages, in English, and typed it up on an ancient German typewriter that her father had bequeathed to the family but no one else wanted. The Chinese team were placed sixth in these round-robin tests when the results were announced in March 1991. One of Zhong Yuzheng's water management models was recommended to participating laboratories in the final report, published as *International Interlaboratory Comparison (Round-Robin) Test for the Verification of Chemical Disarmament, F2: Testing of Procedures on Simulated Industry Samples* (Helsinki: Verifin, 1991). She also guided the Chinese team in the next two round-robin tests, in 1992 and 1993. They managed to find everything that was to be found in the 1992 samples, winning praise from the United States's laboratory chief for their separation skills. The 1993 samples were prepared by the United States, and again the Chinese team won praise, this time for their quality assurance and subsequent report.

Despite the size of China's military and the active part women played in the revolutionary years before the establishment of the People's Republic, few have made their way into the upper echelons of the military hierarchy. Li Zhen (*q.v.*) had spent a lifetime with the Red Army before she became the first female general in the Chinese military in 1955. Thirty-three years later (1988), five other women rose to that rank. All of them ranged in age from their middle to late fifties and, like Zhong Yuzheng, had been educated in the military from the early 1950s and suffered in the Cultural Revolution.

Lieutenant-General Nie Li (b. 1930 in Shanghai) is the daughter of the famous general Nie Rongzhen (1899–1992), one of the founding fathers of the communist military. Nie Li had studied precision machining and optics in the Soviet Union in the late 1950s and then worked for some years with the Ministry of National Defense in the field of guided missiles. Major-General Li Xikai (b. 1932 in Beijing) trained in medicine but made her career in the military as an academic, rising to the position of deputy head of the PLA Third Military Medical University. Major-General Wu Xiaoheng (b. 1932 in Wuhan) also followed an academic career within the military medical system, becoming deputy head of the PLA First Military Medical University. Major-General Liao Wenhai (b. 1934 in Shanghai) had medical training, worked in military hospitals after graduating in 1956, and rose to become head of the PLA General Military Hospital. Major-General Professor Hu Feipei (b. 1930 in the United States) was deputy head of the PLA Foreign Languages College and head of its English Department.

The PLA's reputation suffered badly when it responded with sickening violence to mass demonstrations during the Tian'anmen Incident of 4 June 1989. Whether as a public relations exercise or part of an ongoing series of promotions, eight women of whom Zhong Yuzheng was one were elevated to the rank of major-general in the early 1990s. Again, all but one had been born before 1940; most had joined up in the early 1950s, receiving their education through the PLA. Four were involved in scientific or technical fields: Peng Gang (b. 1939) in telecommunications, Chao Fuhuan (b.

1940) as deputy head of the Academy of Medical Sciences, Deng Xianqun (b. 1935) in wireless, and Zhong Yuzheng. Zhao Zhiwen (b. 1935) was an English professor; He Jiesheng (b. 1935) was a political editor. Two were active in arts units within the military: Wang Xiaotang (b. 1934) as head of a film studio and Qiao Peijuan (b. 1932) as a stage performer. It is interesting to note the family connections of three of these women. Peng Gang is the niece of the famous Red Army general Peng Dehuai; Deng Xianqun is the half-sister of Deng Xiaoping; and He Jiesheng is the daughter of another famous Red Army general, He Long.

In the early 1990s, when her husband worked in Japan, Zhong Yuzheng lived with her son and his wife in Beijing. She long ago adopted the military ethic of simplicity: in order to save time and effort, she would prepare two-days' worth of food in advance and wore her uniform at all times, even to overseas conferences. In her acceptance speech at the Geneva round-robin chemical disarmament competition in March 1991, she said that it was the bound duty of those present to work toward peace. Zhong Yuzheng has also been quoted as saying that she has worked hard throughout her career because "to make a contribution to humanity is the most beautiful thing." One source describes her as "an ordinary female general, female professor, mother, and wife."

Sue WILES

Bai Lingling. "Yige jiangjun de ceying." In Zhongguo nüjiangjun, ed. Cui Xianghua et al. Beijing: Jiefangjun wenyi chubanshe, 1995, 428–64.
Li Weiping. "Zhongguo nüjiangjun." Zhongguo funü, no. 3 (1990): 12–17.
Tan Zhongying and Zhang Dongwen. "Chicheng guoji huaxuejie de Zhongguo nüjiangjun: Ji wojun weiyi jishu nüjiangjun Zhong Yuzheng jiaoshou." Zhongguo funü, no. 9 (1994): 10–11.
Wiles, Sue. "Red Army Heroines? Or Women Warriors?" Paper presented at the Women, Modernity, and Opportunity in Twentieth-century China Workshop, The University of Sydney, 27–28 April 2000.

Zhou Lüyun: *see* **Chou, Irene**

Zhou Meiyu: *see* **Chou Mei-yü**

Zhou Shu'an
Zhou Shu'an, 1894–1974, of Xiamen (Amoy) city in Fujian Province, was a music educator and composer.

She was born into a Protestant missionary family. Zhou Shu'an graduated from Xiamen Women's Higher Normal School in 1911 and in 1914 went to study in the United States. She studied music and art theory at Harvard University, piano at the New England College of Music, and obtained a B.A. from Harvard.

Zhou Shu'an returned home in 1921 and taught at both McTyeire Girls' School in Shanghai and Xiamen University. In 1927, she went to New York to undertake advanced studies in voice. After returning to China in 1928, Zhou Shu'an became director of the Voice Department of the Institute of Music in Shanghai, a position held until 1937. Unfortunately, no information at all appears to be available on her activities from that year until 1959, when she was appointed professor of voice at Shenyang Music School. Nor is it known what happened to her during the Cultural Revolution.

Zhou Shu'an was one of the first Chinese music educators to devote herself to the study of traditional European vocal music. She strove to cultivate outstanding musicians of both general and specialized talent and sought to change national vocal music education to the extent that her contribution to and influence on music education had ramifications in China and overseas.

Besides this substantial contribution to voice, Zhou Shu'an also conducted, played, and wrote music. At the end of the 1920s, she founded the Shanghai Women's Choral Group and acted as its conductor, thus becoming known as China's first female choirmaster. In the 1920s and 1930s, Zhou Shu'an wrote a great variety of songs. The ones about democracy included "False Friends and False Teachers" (Jia pengyou, jia shisheng) and "The Spinner's Song" (Fangshage). Two of her nationalistic anti-Japanese songs were "Compatriots" (Tongbaomen) and "Don't Buy Japanese Goods" (Bu mai Ri huo). She also wrote choral pieces—"A Buddhist Song" (Foge)—and children's songs—"Lullaby" (Anmiange) and "The Song of the Resolute" (Jianjingge). Spoken Chinese is a tonal language, and Zhou Shu'an attached great importance to matching the music she wrote for songs with the tones of the words (Standard Chinese has four tones). Zhou Shu'an also drew on the tunes of the various nationalities within China and made preliminary attempts to impart Chinese characteristics to their harmony and instrumentation.

"A Buddhist Song" and some of her children's songs were made into recordings, and her published song collections include "A Collection of Lyrical Songs" (Shuqinggequ ji), "A Collection of Love Songs" (Liange ji), and "A Collection of Children's Songs" (Ertongge ji). She also wrote *My Experiences in Teaching Voice* (Wode shengyue jiaoxue jingyan).

HE Li and Shirley Wai CHAN
(Translated by Michael Paton)

Liu Bo, ed. *Zhongguo dangdai wenhua yishu mingren da cidian.* Beijing: Guoji wenhua chubangongsi, 1993, 75.

Zhou Sicong

Zhou Sicong, 1939–1996, of Hebei Province, was a leading artist in the PRC and one of its most influential painters from the 1980s on.

She entered the Central Academy of Fine Arts (Zhongyang meishu xueyuan) in 1958, graduating in 1963, and then attended the Beijing Painting Academy (Beijing huayuan). Strongly influenced by Jiang Zhaohe, who was well known for his everyday life subjects, especially people and their emotions, Zhou Sicong emerged as a public artist in the mid-1970s. Her drawings and paintings figuring such popular subjects as children, workers, and soldiers were stronger and clearly different from those of other artists. The figures seemed less posed than required by the vapid conventional social-realist style, and she invested her individuals with a dignity that transcended representation as mere types.

Zhou Sicong attempted to deal in her paintings with both cultural and aesthetic issues. Her large historical pieces on the theme of social consciousness, such as the Miner Series, are strongly humanistic and expressionistic. Expressionism was not new to her, however. While still a middle-school student in 1957, she had seen an exhibition in Beijing of the Hiroshima Murals of Maruki Iri and his wife Toshi, depicting the horrors visited on the people of Hiroshima and Nagasaki by the 1945 atomic bombs. Zhou Sicong wrote afterward that these harrowing images raging against harshness and violence "shook her to the bone" and she had not realized until then how painting could be such a force for peace and humanism. With the new "open door" policy of 1980, Zhou Sicong visited Japan and met the Marukis, who visited China the following year. From this interchange came Zhou Sicong's 1980–83 Miners Series of figure compositions painted with ink on large sheets of fibrous paper: *Land of Joy*, *Hell on Earth*, *Orphan*, and *Compatriot, Traitor, and Dog*. The series depicts the suffering of coal miners and their families in Manchuria under Japanese occupation. Zhou Sicong even went there to talk to survivors so as to gain a greater sense of their experience and literally see where the tragic events of those years had taken place. The inky darkness of the paintings gives them a heavy power that conveys the blackness of the mines and the miners and recreates a cold, fireless hell.

The tortured distortion of the figures in the Miners Series extends Zhou Sicong's earlier expressionistic portrayal of ordinary people, a technique adopted partly from German artists, especially Käthe Kollwitz. Zhou Sicong's expressionist poignancy and power was completely new in Chinese painting, and the intense qualities of patriotism, humanism, and expressionism in her work reflected the melancholic state of mind of the Chinese people undergoing a process of social transformation. This series remained unfinished because of an illness that sapped much of Zhou Sicong's strength.

During the 1980s, her figure paintings depicted ordinary life, most of them in this period being devoted to the two themes of the life of women of a particular ethnic group in Sichuan and lotuses, especially lotuses in fog and rain. The Yi Women Series (1980–92) reveals with fine and sensitive brushstrokes the tranquil life-style of the Yi minority of Liangshan. Its stolid women dressed in colorful national costumes are typically shown carrying heavy loads; in this portrayal, Zhou Sicong explored the enormous physical and psychological burdens that people bear. She faced the dilemma of many normal Chinese citizens in mid-life, balancing the glamour of socialist ideology and the reality of tough living conditions. As a working woman, Zhou Sicong had to confront the problem of holding down a responsible administrative job (as deputy chair of the Chinese National Arts Association) and family obligations, both of which kept her from painting.

In her last years, the artist's work predominantly focused on lotuses, an ancient symbol of purity and spiritual transcendence. The various images of the flowers conveyed contrasts between death and life, solitude and passion, sorrow and joy. She suffered from severe arthritis from the late 1980s and painting lotuses became a means of finding a measure of peace. Zhou Sicong hoped to turn her pain and loneliness into a sense of balance in her soul through artistic sensibility. After a long and painful illness, she died in 1996, at the age of fifty-seven, from complications of pancreatitis.

Her work underwent a great shift in the last twenty years of her life, reflecting the political situation in China and the radical changes in the conditions under which artists worked, as well as the expectations placed upon them. The artist tried to remain aloof from political commitment and the traditional convention in China of artists imitating one another and conforming to approved trends. Her entire output has, in different ways, the ring of authenticity and a personal voice. Zhou Sicong's major breakthrough was to reinterpret traditional subjects in a modern format and visual language. In this, her painting achieved great individual and distinctive style.

SHAO Yiyang

Shao Yiyang. "Lun Zhou Sicong de huihua chuangzuo." *Zhongguo hua*, no. 1 (1993).
"Zhou Sicong." *Mei shujia tongxun*, 7 (1981): 20.
Zhou Sicong. "Autobiography." In *Zhou Sicong huaji*. Tianjin: Tianjin renmin meishu chubanshe, n.d.

Zhou Xiaohong: *see* **Zhou Xuan**

Zhou Xuan

Zhou Xuan, 1919–1957, was one of the most famous actresses in the Chinese film world of the 1930s and 1940s, known especially for her sweet voice. She starred or appeared in over forty-four films produced by a variety of studios. Songs that she sang in films, totaling over two hundred, were among the most popular of the time and continue to be sung today. As the result of an extremely difficult personal life, Zhou Xuan suffered psychological problems in her later years.

She was born into the Su family of Changzhou in Jiangsu Province. Her father was a pastor and her mother a nurse. For reasons that are not clear, when Zhou Xuan was three or four she was sold to the Zhou family of Shanghai, who gave her the name Xiaohong. She grew up never really having known her biological parents. Her adoptive father was an interpreter in the *gongbu ju*, a government department in the English Concession, and her mother performed Cantonese opera. The family slipped into poverty as the father developed an opium habit, and the mother was forced to abandon her singing career to become a servant. When Zhou Xuan was eight, her father tried to sell her into prostitution, but an aunt intervened and placed her with a dance troupe run by a Mr. Sun. The troupe failed, however, and Zhou Xuan became for a time a servant girl in the Sun family.

At the age of twelve, she joined the Bright Moon Song and Dance Troupe (Mingyue gewu tuan) and eagerly and diligently studied piano, singing, and music with the help of Zhang Jinwen, the troupe's piano player. Zhou Xuan also practiced Mandarin Chinese with a teacher named Yan Hua with whom she fell in love and later married. As in the classic Hollywood musicals, Zhou Xuan's hard work paid off: when the lead was unable to perform one night, she took over and became a big hit. In 1934 Zhou

Xuan took First Place in a Shanghai citywide singing competition, earning from the audience the sobriquet "Golden Voice" (*jin sangzi*).

Shortly thereafter, the Mingyue Troupe disbanded for financial reasons (this form of entertainment was threatened by the bourgeoning film industry), and she joined the Yihua Film Studio in 1935. Yihua had been under the influence of leftist writers such as Tian Han (1898–1968) and Yang Hansheng (b. 1902) until KMT Blueshirts destroyed it in 1933. When the studio resumed production in 1934, its films were less "progressive" and became associated with the term "soft film" (*ruan dianying*), entertainment films promoted by the likes of the writer Liu Na'ou (1900–40). Zhou Xuan's first role for the studio was in *Wedding Night* (Huazhu zhi ye, 1936), a love story and the first of Yihua's soft films. She also starred in several other Yihua films, including *Happiness Knocks on the Door* (Xi lin men, 1936); *Hundred Treasures Map* (Bai bao tu, 1936); *Goddess of Wealth* (Nücaishen, 1937); *Garden of Love* (Manyuan chunse, 1937); and *Three Stars Accompany the Moon* (Sanxing banyue, 1937). In her early roles, Zhou Xuan often played innocent, lively young women involved in love affairs. These films were criticized in the leftist press for being a dangerous "opiate" for their audiences.

Impressed with her performance in *Goddess of Wealth*, the leftist director Yuan Muzhi (1909–78) sought out the actress for a role in a film he was making with Mingxing Film Studio. This studio had in the 1920s produced primarily entertainment films, in a variety of genres; under the influence of leftist writers sent by the League of Left-wing Writers, however, it began to produce in the 1930s socially and politically engaged films. With her performance in *Street Angels* (Malu tianshi, 1937), Zhou Xuan emerged as a true star in the Shanghai entertainment world. *Street Angels* is her most famous film, deservedly so.

In it she plays Xiaohong, a young singer who performs in teahouses with a cruel *erhu* player cum pimp. Xiaohong, however, is in love with Xiao Chen, played by the brilliant Zhao Dan (1915–80), a poor trumpet player and leader of a small group of friends who are all social misfits. The *erhu* player arranges for Xiaohong to meet with a customer, the sleazy Lao Gu. She is tempted by his lavish gifts, and this leads to a quarrel with the ever-idealistic Xiao Chen, who is disgusted by her behavior. The lovers eventually flee and set up home together, though they are soon discovered by the *erhu* player and Lao Gu. In the process, Xiaoyun, Xiaohong's "sister" in prostitution, is murdered trying to protect Xiaohong. What is remarkable in this film is not its plot, which is rather conventional leftist fare, but its brilliant pastiche of scenes whose purpose is to entertain rather than to teach. The band of misfit friends creates a world of fantasy through shadowplays, magic tricks, songs, jokes, and storytelling. There are many comedic, even slapstick, moments that raise this film above mere political melodrama and show a clear Hollywood influence. Outstanding also are the two songs performed in the film by Zhou Xuan: "Four Seasons" (Siji ge) and "Songstress at the End of the World" (Tianya genü), with lyrics by Tian Han. These beautiful songs were extremely popular at the time and remain Zhou Xuan's most famous. She is, in fact, credited with helping foster a new kind of Chinese folk-style popular song, both natural and expressive.

After the outbreak of the war with Japan in 1937, she and Yan Hua went to Beijing, his hometown, where they married. Zhou Xuan spent most of the war years in Shanghai, however, making "costume drama" films, with traditional themes and settings, mostly for the Guohua Studio; she starred in such films as *Meng Lijun*, *Meng Jiangnü*, *Three Smiles* (San xiao), and *Story of the Western Chamber* (Xixiang ji). Although some of these costume films were allegories carrying anti-Japanese sentiment, most were simply a form of diversion that became extremely popular with the *xiao shimin* (petty urbanites) of the Shanghai "island" population, orphaned from the rest of China by Japanese occupation. The films were made quickly—(*Meng Lijun* was shot in a record fifty-six hours)—as studios competed aggressively for audiences. (Yihua and Guohua, for example, came out with their own versions of the "Three Smiles" story within weeks of each other.) The edge that Guohua had over other studios though was Zhou Xuan's voice; nearly every one of her films contained at least a few songs, many of them becoming among the most popular of the day.

Plagued by marital troubles (Yan Hua seems to have been jealous of her growing fame and friendship with male actors) and exhausted from a miscarriage and grueling filming schedule, Zhou Xuan seems to have begun to suffer from psychological problems that would dog her until her death. She and her husband divorced in 1941 after Zhou Xuan attempted suicide.

The actress continued making films in Shanghai, although for the Huaying Studio; her films during this period include *Fisherman's Daughter* (Yujia nü), *Marital Bliss* (Luanfeng heming), *Dream of the Red Chamber* (Honglou meng), and *Phoenix Flies* (Fenghuang yufei). Zhou Xuan performed in a few films in Hong Kong in 1946, the exodus of filmmakers from Shanghai during the war with Japan having led to a thriving film industry there. Returning to Shanghai in 1947, she starred in *Remembering the South* (Yi Jiangnan, 1947), a film written by Tian Han in which Zhou Xuan played two roles, and *Night Lodgings* (Yedian, 1947), loosely based on Gorky's play *The Lower Depths*. These were two of her more memorable performances. She returned to Hong Kong and starred in *Secret History of the Qing Court* (Qinggong mishi), a film about late Qing imperial intrigue, and *Flower Street* (Hua jie), about prostitutes.

In 1948, Zhou Xuan married Zhu Huaide, a Shanghai businessman who had been pursuing her for years. Pregnant with his child, she learned that on a trip to Shanghai he had fled with all of her hard-earned savings to live with another woman. Zhou Xuan became very depressed and was hospitalized with "schizophrenia" but gave birth to his son, Zhou Min, her first child. With the help of friends in the film world, Zhou Xuan returned to Shanghai in 1950. During the shooting of *Dove of Peace* (Heping ge), a film that was never completed, she was introduced to the portrait artist Tang Di. They fell in love and began living together. Zhou Xuan was pregnant when, in 1952, her friends accused Tang Di also of swindling and marrying her under false pretenses (it emerged during the ensuing trial that he had lived during the war with another woman, a single mother of three). Zhou Xuan defended him during the trial, but nonetheless the artist was sentenced to three years in prison. She bore him a son, Zhou Wei, but by the time Tang Di was released a few months later Zhou Xuan had suffered a relapse and been placed in a psychiatric hospital. The actress spent the next five years in and out of these institutions. On the verge of recovery, Zhou Xuan is said to have contracted encephalitis and died in 1957 at the age of thirty-nine.

Kirk A. DENTON

Shen Ji. *Yidai gexing Zhou Xuan*. Xi'an: Shaanxi renmin chubanshe, 1986.
Tu Guangqi. *Zhou Xuan de zhenshi gushi*. Taipei: Zhuanji wenxue chubanshe, 1987.
Wang Xueren. *Zhou Xuan yichan fengbo*. Beijing: Falü, 1990.
Yu Yonghe. *Zhou Xuan wai zhuan*. Beijing: Zhongguo wenlian, 1985.
————. *Zhou Xuan zhuan*. Hong Kong: Dong Xi wenhua shiye, 1987.
Zhan Hongzhi. *Zhou Xuan xiaozhuan*. Taipei: Gunshi zazhi she, 1987.
Zhou Wei. *Wo de mama Zhou Xuan*. Taiyuan: Shanxi renmin chubanshe, 1987.
Zhou Xuan. *Zhou Xuan zishu*. Shanghai: Shanghai sanlian, 1995.
Zhou Xuan yanjiu ziliao ji. Hong Kong: Xianggang dianying ziliao yanjiu she, 1982.

Zhou Yuebin: *see* **Han Suyin**

Zhou Yuehua

Zhou Yuehua, 1904–1977, one of the thirty women who took part in the Chinese communists' Long March of 1934–35, was born in Guangji County, Hubei Province. Her father was a peasant who became successful as a tailor; he taught his daughter to read and write and sent her to Wuhan Free Normal School. Her mother had bound feet, and Zhou Yuehua's feet were also bound but she liberated them, possibly during her teens.

Zhou Yuehua joined the CCP in 1926 and the following year studied military subjects at the Wuhan branch of Whampoa Military Academy with another Long Marcher, Wei Gongzhi (*q.v.*). Zhou Yuehua worked as a nurse during the famous Canton Commune uprising of December 1927 and in the first Chinese soviet in Hailufeng in Guangdong Province, which was crushed in February 1928. During this period, she met He Cheng (1901–1992), a medical doctor whom she married. They worked together from then on; they had at least one child. Zhou Yuehua and her husband set up clinics in Wuhan and Shanghai, which acted as covers for their underground work. She was arrested several times over the next few years. Each time though Zhou Yuehua managed to walk free, protesting: "I don't know what you are talking about, I am an illiterate housewife." She worked as a nurse on the Long March but was assigned, with her husband, to Zhang Guotao's Fourth Front Red Army in August 1935. From Yan'an, He Cheng went to Russia for several years, while Zhou Yuehua undertook further study in Yan'an; she was placed in charge of investigating security with regard to posts and telecommunications. Zhou Yuehua worked with He Cheng in public health in the northeast in 1945 and after 1949 was a leading member in the Ministry of Public Health. Her health gave out, however, and she retired in 1960. Zhou Yuehua was "struggled" during the Cultural Revolution and beaten because she would neither confess to political crimes she had not committed nor write confessions accusing others. Zhou Yuehua died on 17 September 1977, of illness.

Sue WILES

Guo Chen. *Jinguo liezhuan: Hong yifangmianjun sanshiwei changzheng nühongjun shengping shiji.* Beijing: Nongcun duwu chubanshe, 1986, 167–74.

Zhu Lian

Zhu Lian, 1909–1978, *zi* Jingyu, of Liyang County, Jiangsu Province, was an acupuncturist, and a medical administrator and educator.

She studied midwifery at Zhihua Midwifery Hospital in Suzhou, graduating in 1931. After joining the CCP in 1935, Zhu Lian went to Shijiazhuang in Hebei to work at Zhengtai Railway Hospital. She later started her own Zhu Lian Clinic as a cover for underground CCP activities. In 1936, when General Feng Yuxiang was fighting the Japanese in the Chahar and Suiyuan areas, Zhu Lian organized the local women into support groups to help with the medical treatment and nursing care of soldiers. At the same time, she was active in the women's movement, attempting to mobilize women in patriotic activities and for national salvation. In addition, Zhu Lian edited supplements for a number of newspapers, such as *Shimen zhengyanbao* and *Huabei minbao*. She was part of the CCP leadership in Shijiazhuang, holding positions on the Party's Municipal Committee and the Beiping-Hankou Railway Line Committee. Zhu Lian was appointed head of the Health Department of the 129th Army and director of its field hospital in 1937, when the Red Army was reorganized into the Eighth Route Army during the second KMT-CCP coalition.

In the late 1930s or early 1940s, she went to Yan'an to study at the Marxist-Leninist Academy (Ma-Lie xueyuan) and afterward was appointed vice-president of Yan'an China Medical University (Yan'an Zhongguo yike daxue). During the latter decade, Zhu Lian became head (or deputy head) of the Health Departments in the regional governments in Shanxi-Hebei-Shangdong-Henan Border Region and Huabei Region. It is probably during this period that she studied acupuncture because she compiled *Notes on Acupuncture* (Zhenjiuxue jiangyi) and *New Acupuncture* (Xin zhenjiuxue) in 1948; no mention had been made before this of any association with the medical technique. Quite possibly she may have become involved with this old Chinese treatment and prepared notes for classes on acupuncture while at Yan'an China Medical University. One source relates how top CCP leaders showed their support for Zhu Lian's work: Red Army General Zhu De (1886–1976) did the calligraphy for the title of *New Acupuncture*, while Dong Biwu (1886–1975) wrote its preface.

With the establishment of the PRC in 1949, Zhu Lian was appointed to a series of official positions related to health, including head of the Department of Women and Children's Health (Fu you weisheng si) and deputy director of the Ministry of Health's Academy of Traditional Chinese Medicine (Zhongyi yanjiuyuan), where she also acted as head of its Acupuncture Research Institute (Zhenjiu yanjiusuo). Later in life, Zhu Lian spent some time in Nanning, Guangxi Province, was vice-mayor of Nanning, and head of the city's Acupuncture Research Institute. The last position she is recorded as holding was president of the July Twenty-first Acupuncture University (Qi eryi zhenjiu daxue).

Zhu Lian was one of the earliest Western-trained medical workers to pay attention to the ancient Chinese art of acupuncture. Her books wielded considerable influence in China, while her *New Acupuncture* has been translated into several languages and sold well throughout the world.

Lily Xiao Hong LEE

Huaxia funü mingren cidian. Beijing: Huaxia chubanshe, 1988, 219.
Jingsheng and Xiquan, eds. *Xin Zhongguo mingrenlu*. Nanchang: Jiangxi renmin chubanshe, 1987, 604–5.
Zhongguo funüguanli ganbu xueyuan, ed. *Gujin Zhongwai nümingren cidian*. Beijing: Zhongguo guangbo dianshi chubanshe, 1980, 617.

Zhu Lin (actress)

Zhu Lin, b. 1923, in Meizhou, Jiangsu Province, was a spoken drama (*huaju*) actress.

She commenced her education at the age of seven at a Catholic primary school attached to Huaiyin Normal School, which had a reputation for providing good musical training. There was a *jingju* (Beijing opera) ensemble near her home, and the young Zhu Lin loved to go and watch it, learning many operas by heart. These were the two major influences on her early musical development. In 1938, she passed the entrance examination for Wuchang Performing Arts College (Wuchang yishu zhuanke xuexiao) and majored in music.

That year, just after the outbreak of the Sino-Japanese War, Zhu Lin joined the Changhong Drama Group (Changhong jushe) and performed in *Storm* (Baofengyu) and *Put Down Your Whip* (Fangxia nide bianzi). She also played an active role in the wartime propaganda effort and performed in anti-Japanese plays such as *A Family Destroyed, All in It Gone or Dead* (Jiapo renwang), *Mulan Goes to War* (Mulan congjun), and *One Year* (Yinianjian). In 1941, Zhu Lin joined the playwright Tian Han (1898–1968) with the New China Drama Group (Xin Zhongguo jushe) in Guilin and played leading roles in *Song of Autumn* (Qiusheng fu), *Thunderstorm* (Leiyu), *Sunrise* (Richu), and *Death of a Famous Star* (Mingyou zhi si). Critics hailed her performance as Katarina in *The Thunderstorm*, by Russian playwright A.N. Ostrovsky.

After the Sino-Japanese War, she performed in *The Peacock's Gall* (Kongque dan), *Rhapsody for the Common Man* (Xiaoren wu kuangxiang qu), *Spring Chill* (Chun han), and *Song of the Beauties* (Liren xing). Zhu Lin also starred in the films *Weakling, Your Name Is Woman* (Ruozhe, nide mingzi shi nüren) and *Gusts of Wind and Rain* (Jifan fengyu). She moved to Beijing in 1950 and there joined the Chinese Youth Art Theater (Zhongguo qingnian yishu juyuan), performing in *The Inspector-General* (Qinchai dachen) and *Confronting New Things* (Zai xinshiwu mianqian). In 1953, Zhu Lin transferred to Beijing People's Art Theater (Renmin yishu juyuan) and played more than twenty characters, including Mother Lu in *Thunderstorm*. Two Russian plays she performed in at that time were *Yegor Bulychov and Others* (Gorky) and *Man with a Gun* (N. Pogodin).

From 1949 on, the famous performing artist and director of Beijing People's Art Theater Jiao Juying blended modern dramatic theory with traditional Chinese drama technique, thus creating a Chinese school of drama. Zhu Lin was an enthusiastic and integral part of this new movement and, under Jiao Juying's guidance, made bold attempts to achieve its aims. Zhu Lin applied traditional Chinese opera performing skills to modern drama, and also adopted the performing art theory of the Russian master Konstantin Stanislavsky (upon whose work the American Method School is also based), turning to real life for inspiration. Her experiments in establishing a Chinese school of performing arts thus combined "traditional," "foreign," and "real life" elements, especially as embodied in the plays *Thunderstorm*, *The Tiger Tally* (Hu fu), and *Yegor Bulychov and Others*.

In 1956, Zhu Lin performed in the historical drama *The Tiger Tally*, spending more than six months in rehearsal. Blending the three methods, she created with great success the character Ruji, a righteous concubine. Zhu Lin imbued the role with depth, incorporating the concepts and skills of traditional opera ("hands, eyes, body, style, steps") with modern drama theory. In her next study, playing the servant girl in Gorky's *Yegor Bulychov and Others*, she used Stanislavsky's theory of performance, first discerning the emotional state of the character and then manifesting it in the character's physical movements.

Her 1959 portrayal of Natasha in Chekhov's *Three Sisters* was also a triumph. One Soviet film director exclaimed after seeing the performance: "I don't believe this was a Chinese actress playing that part! Actresses such as Zhu Lin can play serious, simple or typical Chinese females, but in this play she has portrayed a giddy, vigorous and vulgar Russian woman so vividly and realistically it is unbelievable!"

That same year, Zhu Lin played the lead in the historical play *Cai Wenji*, written by the modern playwright Guo Moruo. Zhu Lin played to perfection the character of Cai Wenji, an emotional, noble, and talented female poet of old, expressing her misery and sadness, strength of character, and extraordinary courage. Zhu Lin immersed herself fully in the character. Guo Moruo was so impressed with her performance that he wrote a poem for her:

> Child prodigy of music
> unfortunately had to play a tribal flute;
> in the cold winds of the barren north,
> still she made a beautiful melody.
> —For Zhu Lin's brilliant performance in *Cai Wenji*.

Zhu Lin took great care with her lines. Her speaking voice was clear and expressive, with a beautiful tone and rhythm, but she also knew the value of silence, adeptly applying stresses and pauses. Her earlier musical training had given the actress an understanding of the relationship between sound and breathing technique, and it allowed her to make the best use of her voice in delivering lines powerfully, yet musically. In the play *Eighteen Songs, with Barbarian's Flute* (Hujia shi-ba pai), Zhu Lin's chanting was rich and emotional, rhythmic, and touching. This was not simply because she was musically gifted but also because of her ability to combine her experience in traditional opera with modern music.

In 1962, after playing Cai Wenji, Zhu Lin accepted an offer to perform in *Wu Zetian*, another of Guo Moruo's historical plays. This role was livelier than the ones in *The Tiger Tally* and *Cai Wenji*, with a closer identity between physical movement and the character's personality and emotions. Zhu Lin portrayed the Tang dynasty empress as an ambitious, successful, poised, talented, and enlightened female politician, a totally different image from Cai Wenji's. The play was well received by the public.

Benefiting from the advice of Jiao Juying, Zhu Lin successfully created a series of characters perfect in both spirit and form and dominated the drama scene to reach the first peak of her performing career. In 1978 after the Cultural Revolution and at the age of fifty-five, she played Cai Wenji again, evincing her own maturity and an even greater depth of feeling. In the 1980s, Zhu Lin played Claire in *The Visit* (Der Besuch der alten Dame, Friedrich Dürrenmatt), Linda in *Death of a Salesman* (Arthur Miller), and Fang Xiya in *Foreign Mah-jong*. Zhu Lin had almost turned seventy years old when she performed in *Death of a Salesman* in 1992 to great acclaim; on this occasion she had clearly reached a second peak in her career.

Zhu Lin had a successful marriage lasting nearly fifty years to the famous dramatist Diao Guangtan. He had been a drama student and joined a wartime anti-Japanese propaganda team; their passion for performing arts brought the two together. Although both were eager to go to the revolutionary base of Yan'an, they obeyed the decision of their underground leaders to remain in KMT-occupied areas to participate in wartime propaganda activities. Their performance skills grew alongside their love in the difficult and tense time they spent with the Propaganda Performance Team. Diao Guangtan loved Zhu Lin for her artistic qualities and talent, and Zhu Lin fell in love with him because of his cleverness, simplicity, and honesty. Nor did the harshness of wartime deprive their love of romance. When Diao Guangtan, star of the basketball team, was on the court, Zhu Lin was his most vocal supporter, and her presence made him play at his best. On social occasions, Diao Guangtan always volunteered to be Zhu Lin's "bodyguard," drinking her toasts for her. The real matchmaker of their marriage, however, was performing art. Early on in their assignment with the performance team, they had played together in the anti-Japanese play *Misty Reed Port* (Yan wei gang). Diao Guangtan played the fisherman to Zhu Lin's Jinhua. The scene where they swear a blood oath to one another seems to have forged their first link. Later, the two played together in Gogol's *The Inspector-General*. In discussing plays and roles, their shared interest brought them close as both friends and lovers, in life and art.

Zhu Lin and Diao Guangtan married in Changsha in 1942. They moved to Beijing after the founding of the People's Republic in 1949 and commenced working at Beijing People's Art Theater, bringing to life their dream of performing for the people. Over the next ten years, the couple performed in the plays already mentioned above as well as *Bright Day* (Minglang de tian), *You Have to Live Like This* (Fei zheyang shenghuo buke), *Guan Hanqing*, *Li Guorui*, and *Courage and the Sword* (Danjianpian). In the 1960s, their performance together in *Cai Wenji* caused a sensation in Chinese drama circles; both Zhu Lin and Diao Guangtan were at their best, and their dreams had been realized.

Shirley Wai CHAN
(Translated by Laura Long)

Huaxia funü mingren cidian. Beijing: Huaxia chubanshe, 1988, 219–20.
Zhongguo funü guanli ganbu xueyuan. *Gujin Zhongwai nümingren cidian.* Beijing: Zhongguo guangbo dianshi chubanshe, 1980, 617.

Zhu Lin (writer)

Zhu Lin, b. 1949 in Shanghai as Wang Zuling, is a writer of novels, novellas, short stories, and children's fiction.

When her mother broke off all contact with the family, Zhu Lin was left as a new-born baby with her father, a remote and eccentric academic. The pain of abandonment, doubts about her paternity, and the cold domestic environment of her childhood contributed to the melancholy and mistrustful nature of the themes present in her work. Her family suffered in the Cultural Revolution, both because of its intellectual background and overseas connections. To escape the disgrace, and to get away from home, Zhu Lin was among the first to leave Shanghai for the countryside in the mass rustication of urban youth of the late 1960s. She spent six years in Fengyang County, one of the poorest parts of Anhui Province, before returning to the city in 1975.

Her first short stories were published in those years in the countryside but, more importantly, the hardships experienced and witnessed in Anhui resulted in the book *The Path of Life* (Shenghuo de lu), begun after her return to the city; it was released in the post-Mao thaw at the end of the 1970s. This novel was the first to reveal the hardship suffered by urban youth, especially young women, in the countryside. Setting the tone for her later fiction, the story follows a beautiful girl, out of place in cruel surroundings, denied higher education because of her class background, abused by officialdom, and failed by the man she trusts, a combination of disasters that results in her suicide. The author's manuscript initially received a hostile reception from the literary authorities, and only with the support of the veteran novelist Mao Dun, and a sympathetic editor who made judicious cuts, did it become published at all.

Mistreated and unhappy women appear frequently in Zhu Lin's fiction; rape serves as a recurrent metaphor for the relations between men with power and women without it. On occasion, the plight of young women is recounted by analogy to myths drawn from the natural world. At the end of the short story "Snake's Pillow" (She zhentou hua, 1983), the victim-protagonist tells the story of the good-hearted flower who takes pity on the snake, only to suffer a lifetime of cruelty. The flower stands not only for the young woman but also for womanhood, abused by the powerful phallic image of the snake, a figure that also recalls the serpent of the biblical myth of Eden. Like the women in much of Zhu Lin's fiction, the flower is unable to protect itself because, the tale concludes, it has no thorns.

The physical setting for most of her work is Jiangnan, the area south of the Yangzi [Yangtze] River that includes villages, suburbs, and the great metropolis of Shanghai. The lush physical beauty of the rural part of the region stands in ironic contrast to the cruelty of the human society that her characters encounter there. In a departure from this location, *The Sobbing Lancang River* (Wuye de Lancang jiang, first published as *Women Are Human* [Nüxing—ren], 1989) follows a group of rusticated youth from Shanghai southwest of Yunnan (a place the author had never been when she wrote the novel); it is a bitter tale that takes its young protagonist through disillusion, malnutrition, and paralysis before she is able to return to the city and regain her health and self-worth.

It is tempting to read much of Zhu Lin's work as autobiographical, a repeated attempt to come to terms with the traumas of childhood and youth. In response to a question about personal experience and *The Path of Life*, the author asserted that if she had described the horrors witnessed in her years in Anhui, no press would have published the novel and no reader would have believed it. Material for some of her other novels is drawn from lives witnessed and heard about, the protagonist of *The Sobbing Lancang River*, for example, being based on the life of a neighbor in the Shanghai suburb of Jiading. By her own admission, *Everlasting Love* (Zhi'ai zai renjian) is the most autobiographical of all her novels; it is a lightly fictionalized account of a father-daughter relationship that developed between the author and a publisher from Taiwan before his sudden death robbed them both of a deeper understanding.

Zhu Lin claims to write from the heart rather than consciously, seldom discusses her work, and is reluctant to hear any evaluation of it. It took a persistent interviewer to make the writer admit what is obvious to any reader, that "thinking back, I've been writing from a woman's perspective all along." The nearest Zhu Lin has come to describing the creative impulse is in an essay entitled "Summoning Souls" ('Jiao hun' zhongzhong), which followed the first publication of *The Sobbing Lancang River*. In this essay, she reveals the custom still followed in village Jiangnan of calling back the spirits of departed loved ones. Her own realization was that similarly it was her task as a writer to reunite people with the souls they had lost and thereby make them complete.

The publication in 1998 of the five-volume *Collected Works of Zhu Lin* (Zhu Lin wenji) provided the material for a review of the author's literary career, spanning twenty-five years to that date. The first three volumes contain five novels written for adult readers: *The Path of Life* (1979); *The Chinaberry Tree* (Kulianshu, 1985); *The Sobbing Lancang River* (1989); *The Shamaness* (Nüwu, 1993); and *Everlasting Love* (1994). The fourth volume has selected short stories and novellas, and the final volume contains fiction written for children. The first anthology of Zhu Lin's short fiction in English translation, *Snake's Pillow and Other Stories*, appeared in 1998.

Richard KING

Zhu Lin. *Snake's Pillow and Other Stories*, trans. Richard King. Honolulu: University of Hawaii Press, 1998.
———. *Zhu Lin wenji*, 5 vols. Beijing: Huaxia chubanshe, 1998.

Zong Pu

Zong Pu, b. 1928 as Feng Zhongpu, is a contemporary Chinese writer.

Zong Pu was born in Beijing, but her ancestral home is Nanyang County, Henan Province. Her family had produced several generations of noted scholars and writers. Her father, Feng Youlan (1895–1990), was one of the greatest philosophers of his generation. Her aunt Feng Yuanjun (*q.v.*), a specialist in classical literature, was a pioneer of the New Literature Movement and as well known during the May Fourth period as Bing Xin (*q.v.*), Luyin (*q.v.*), and Ling Shuhua (*q.v.*).

Zong Pu was deeply influenced by the literary and scholarly atmosphere of her family life. She was already being tutored in Tang poetry by her mother by the time she was ten years old; every morning the young girl would be summoned to her mother's bedside to recite several poems before setting off for primary school. Zong Pu started reading the classics *Dream of the Red Chamber* (Honglou meng) and *Water Margin* (Shuihuzhuan) also around then and greatly enjoyed them. It was her father, however, whom Zong Pu credits for introducing her to literature. While Feng Youlan is best known as a philosopher, he was also a gifted writer of classical-style poetry and frequently shared his views on literature with his daughter.

Also at that time, Zong Pu's entire family moved to a village outside Kunming because of the Sino-Japanese War. They lived close to Peking University's Foreign Literature Research Institute, which also relocated during the war, and she went there often to read. Besides classical literature, Zong Pu also dipped into philosophy and scientific books, finding them all interesting. Zong Pu has a great fondness for nature. What she remembers most about those youthful years spent in the countryside was the unspoiled beauty of the region. Zong Pu often walked the twenty-nine li (about fifteen km) to the city with her brothers, and as they admired the beauty surrounding them they all took turns telling stories, letting their imaginations run wild. This was an extremely happy and fulfilling time for Zong Pu. She attended the high school attached to Southwest Union University (Xinan lianda fu zhong), and during this period her first work was published. When Zong Pu was sixteen, she took a trip to the scenic Dian Lake with school friends and wrote about her feelings for this charming place; the essay later appeared in a magazine.

In 1948 Zong Pu entered the Foreign Languages Department at Tsinghua [Qinghua] University, majoring in English literature. That same year, her first story, "AKC," was published in the Tianjin newspaper *Tianjin Dagong bao* under the pen name Lü Fan. Zong Pu was then studying French, and "AKC" appears to be her transliteration of the French " . . . ai cassé . . ." (broken). The story tells how a young girl puts a letter in a bottle, which she then asks a boy to break. The boy cannot fathom why she wants him to do this, and he misses his opportunity with her, something regretted for the rest of his life. Although the fictional story is rather immature artistically, it does reveal the writer's innate ability to describe love intimately and naturally.

While conducting propaganda work in factories during the movement to resist America and support Korea at the time of the Korean War, Zong Pu wrote the short story "Accusation" (Su, 1950), centering on an accusation made by a woman worker, and it recounts the dark side of society before 1949. In September 1953, the Second Conference on Literature decreed that literature and art must be used ideologically as tools to promote socialism, educate the people about communism, and create proletarian heroes rendered as capable of smashing the enemy; "socialist realism" became the hard and fast rule for writers and artists. The formula turned literature into a propaganda arm of the government and drastically restricted the range of subjects that could be discussed. Believing that writing to this kind of formula was worse than not writing at all, Zong Pu basically stopped writing.

After graduating from university that year, she was assigned as an editor to the magazine *World Literature* at the Foreign Literature Research Institute at the Chinese Academy of Social Sciences. Zong Pu worked there for twenty years, greatly broadening her understanding of Western literature. Her work was also influenced by Western realism and contemporary literature.

In 1956, Mao Zedong (1893–1976) had declared a new policy toward literature under the slogan of "Letting One Hundred Flowers Bloom and the Hundred Schools of Thoughts Contend." While ostensibly an invitation to intellectuals, such as Zong Pu, to at last say and write what they wanted, this new movement really was part of Mao's "struggle against rightists." His aim really was to "entice the snakes out of the cave," in other words, to round up the critics of communism.

Zong Pu wrote the novel *Red Beans* (Hong dou) that year, publishing the piece in *People's Literature* (Renmin wenxue). The work received widespread attention and made the author famous. The novel was acclaimed for showing the talent and erudition of an educated female writer. Taking love as its theme, the story unfolds to tell about the life of a young Christian couple in 1949. The heroine, Jiang Mei, and her boyfriend have always loved each other and had much in common. When she decides to adopt a revolutionary way of life, however, conflicts arise over their views on life and the value of love, leading to a rupture in their relationship. Love, the novel explains, does not last forever.

The story is multilayered, linking emotions within a complex social background, exposing clashes between personal feelings and social responsibilities. Zong Pu eulogizes the spiritual dimension to this conflict, coming down on the side of righteousness, that emotions, not society, should be sacrificed. *Red Beans* broke with the wooden style of writing that had flourished after the establishment of the People's Republic, and Zong Pu can be said to have been the first mainland author brave enough to write openly about love. The characters in this novel are typical Zong Pu personages in that they are true to life: *Red Beans* describes in meticulous detail the agonizing dilemma experienced by the heroine when she has to choose between first love and revolution. Zong Pu deals openly and honestly with human feelings and morality as she reveals the layers of emotional and psychological changes that Jiang Mei goes through.

Red Beans so clearly broke with current fiction that the novel came in for heavy criticism. The book was declared to insinuate that "love is persecuted by revolution" and for depicting "unhealthy petty bourgeois feelings" that "undermined the foundations of socialism." Zong Pu was forced to make repeated self-criticisms. Several other writers who used realism in their work—Wang Meng, Ding Ling (*q.v.*), Liu Shaotang, and Zhang Xianliang—also came under attack at that time. They were accused of criticizing the bureaucratism of the CCP and revealing the moral decline of party cadres when they moved to the cities from the countryside. Because they wrote of people's inner lives, engaging in deep reflections on human life, these writers were also accused of deviating from the accepted proletarian view. Many were labeled counter-revolutionary rightists and dispatched in 1957 to border areas for reform through labor. In 1978, however, Shanghai Literature and Art Press (Shanghai wenyi chubanshe) published the novels that had been written by "rightists" and criticized in 1957, including *Red Beans*, as a collection, significantly titled *Flowers Blossoming Anew* (Chongfang de xianhua).

In 1959 the CCP attempted to "reform" intellectuals by demoting them to the level of workers and peasants with whom they were to eat, live, and work. Zong Pu was "sent down to the countryside" in Sanggan River, Hebei Province, the area made famous by Ding Ling in her *The Sun Shines on Sanggan River* (Taiyang zhao zai Sangganhe shang). Adapting to her changed political circumstances, Zong Pu demonstrated self-reform by writing the novel *The Daughter of the Peach Garden Goes in Marriage to Guwo* (Taoyuan nü'er jia Guwo). This novel, set in the period of the collectivization of agriculture, tells of a young woman from a prosperous production brigade who is prepared to marry into a poor one. It extols the noble ideals of the mountain people who were working to change the face of their destitute region. Although the subject with which she deals reeks of political propaganda, Zong Pu still managed to paint a realistic picture of the environment of the villages and the psyche of the peasants. Through this novel, Zong Pu became known as a model intellectual who had successfully "reformed."

Zong Pu considers that her understanding of workers and peasants did become broadened and her experience enriched when she had to leave her cloistered study and go to the factories and farms. She regrets, however, the prohibitions imposed on writers by the new policy of literature serving the proletariat. Its effect was to inhibit authors from unreservedly expressing their understanding of the actual circumstances and inner world of the people and also shackled writers to formulaic creative concepts.

Between the late 1950s and the early 1960s, Zong Pu wrote many outstanding literary essays; "Notes on West Lake" (Xihu manbi) is the one for which she is best known. Zong Pu began writing essays as travel diaries and was clearly influenced in this by classical essayists such as Li Daoyuan and Xu Xiake. Her prose style is simple and highly expressive. Zong Pu describes the minutiae of life carefully, while carrying on the classical literature tradition of using landscape to express emotion. The feelings expressed are subtle, evoking a profound philosophical ambience; the pieces reveal her solid foundation in classical literature.

Zong Pu's father came under repeated attack by the CCP from 1949 on as a "typical bourgeois idealist." When the Cultural Revolution began at Peking University where he held a professorship, Feng Youlan was one of many famous scholars pilloried as "reactionary scholarly authorities" and "running dogs of the Guomindang." His house was ransacked by the Red Guards, and Feng was subjected to humiliation. Zong Pu herself was paraded through the streets wearing a dunce's cap labeled "Daughter of Feng Youlan." The hardships she endured during this decade of upheaval led to a new maturity in her understanding of human nature and society, which was subsequently reflected in her work. In 1978 Zong Pu published the novella *Dream on a Bowstring* (Xian shang de meng) about the Cultural Revolution. Her first work of fiction in fifteen years won a national prize for Best Novella. From this time on, she wrote "scar literature," focusing on the experience of intellectuals she knew. In a dark and tragic style, she conducted a thorough re-evaluation of the tragedy that was the Cultural Revolution.

Between the end of 1979 and the beginning of 1980, Zong Pu published in quick succession the novellas *Who Am I?* (Wo shi shei) and *My Humble Abode* (Wo ju), which created quite a stir in literary circles. Critics see these stories, along with the works of Wang Meng, as opening the floodgates on a new period of realism. Zong Pu's long association with the Foreign Literature Research Institute of the Academy of Social Sciences influenced her greatly. On the eve of the Cultural Revolution, she had been assigned to study the work of Franz Kafka in order to criticize it; after the Cultural Revolution, Zong Pu realized that the best way to express the bitter experiences of that time was through Kafkaesque exaggeration and mockery. In the novella *Who Am I?*, a female biologist returns to China after studying abroad, only to be labeled as a counter-revolutionary in the Cultural Revolution; she is transformed into an insect. *My Humble Abode* is about a mysterious city of spirits that appears spontaneously in the human world. Zong Pu uses this surreal realm to reflect that preposterous era when the slightest incident could turn people into ox, devil, and snake spirits, and to throw light on the inhumane politics of the Cultural Revolution. She clearly borrowed from Kafka's *Metamorphosis* in her concepts and techniques. In the novel *Sacrifice of the Heart* (Xin ji), Zong Pu allows the story to unfold by means of the main character's psychological and emotional stream of consciousness, interweaving memory and reality. Clearly influenced by modern Western psychology, Zong Pu also strives to link the novel with traditional Chinese art, utilizing Western realism to realize the deeper meaning of classical Chinese songs and poems.

Zong Pu retired from the Foreign Literature Research Institute in 1988 but continued to write, completing the first part, "Record of a Southern Crossing" (Nan du ji), of a long novel called *The Wild Gourd Prelude* (Ye hulu yin). This historical novel spans the year or so from the 1937 Lugouqiao (Marco Polo Bridge) Incident when Japan invaded China; it describes the life of senior intellectuals in Beijing. "Record of a Southern Crossing" is a moving segment that reveals the deep impression the period had on Zong Pu during childhood. In drawing the setting and speech of her characters, she utilizes classical verses in the introduction and intersperses them throughout the text, each poem appropriately placed and following a correct rhyme scheme. The writing is complex and nuanced and reflects her in-depth training in classical Chinese literature

During retirement, Zong Pu wrote many memoirs. Contrasting the poetic-prose style that she applied in the 1960s, these pieces take on a more austere quality and lift her writing to a new height of professionalism. She had lived for several decades with her father in Yanyuan on the campus of Peking University and witnessed in this famous courtyard many scenes. In "Mist Falls on Yanyuan" (Xia luo Yanyuan), Zong Pu reminisced about a dozen or so famous scholars who lived there, graphically recording in grave brushstrokes and straightforward description their individual traits and the tragedies that befell them. Her own agony and deep understanding is palpable throughout.

During a writing career that bridged more than three decades, Zong Pu crafted an artistic world built upon the principles of "sincerity" and "elegance." Her solid cultural background in both traditional Chinese culture and Western literature deeply influenced her literary work, ideologically blending an Eastern striving for traditional morality and a Western humanism. Artistically, she grafted Western realism onto classical Chinese literature, thereby creating in her own accomplishment a traditional and contemporary flavor as well as a national character open to outside influences. Zong Pu's literary achievements are unique in contemporary Chinese literature.

She has never married. Zong Pu visited Australia at the invitation of the Australia-China Council in the early 1980s on what may have been her only overseas trip.

Rubing HONG
(Translated by Yuen Kwan Veronica Ngok and Jennifer Eagleton)

Chen Suyan. "Lun Zong Pu de sanwen." *Xuzhou shifan xueyuan xuebao, zhesheban*, no. 3 (1994): 100–05.

Lang Baodong, ed. *Zong Pu daibiao zuo*. Zhengzhou: Henan renmin chubanshe, 1987.

Li Zhenxia, ed. *Dangdai Zhongguo shi zhe*. Beijing: Huaxia chubanshe, 1991.

Shi Shuqing. "You gudian you xiandai—yu dalu nüzuojia Zong Pu de duihua." In *Wentan fansi yu qianzhan*. Hong Kong: Mingchuang chubanshe, 1989.

Tang Shaodan. "Zong Pu xiaoshuo lun." *Dangdai zuojia pinglun*, no. 4 (1994): 63–75.

Yin Ding. *Feng Youlan*. Taipei: Dongda tushu gufen youxian gongsi, 1991.

Zong Pu. "Huojiang gan yan." *Dangdai*, no. 1 (1995): 183.

Zou Yixin

Zou Yixin, b. 1911 in Guangzhou city, Guangdong Province, is an internationally recognized astronomer.

Born into a family of intellectuals, from a young age Zou Yixin devoted herself to studies in an effort to fulfill vicariously her father's own dream of studying overseas. Despite passing the entrance examination to a preparatory school, family difficulties had once forced him to step aside so that a brother could go in his place. Although physically rather frail, from the beginning Zou Yixin was academically gifted; after graduating from junior high school, she passed the entrance examination to the preparatory school of Zhongshan University. Zou Yixin was eighteen when she enrolled and the only female studying mathematics and astronomy. Soon after, her father died, and Zou Yixin helped support her family by taking part-time work, including teaching. She won scholarships with great regularity and was invited to remain with Zhongshan University as a teacher after graduating in 1932. The university authorities decided to send her to study in Japan and also gave special consideration to her financial difficulties; the president promoted Zou Yixin ahead of time so that she would take the opportunity offered.

Zou Yixin married in 1935 and three months later went to study at Tokyo Imperial University. She was fortunate enough to be there when the total solar eclipse of 19 June 1936 took place, a spectacular astronomical phenomenon occurring only once every twelve years. Observation teams from many countries traveled to Hokkaido to observe the eclipse, and Zou Yixin attended as part of the Chinese team. She photographed the entire event, using up-to-date technology. Mentioned in the Japanese newspaper *Asahi shimbun* and the Japanese journal *Fujin koron*, Zou Yixin was referred to as "the only female to successfully record" the phenomenon and "the first female astronomer in East Asia."

She returned home in 1937 to a China in the early stages of the Sino-Japanese War and found it almost impossible to do research work. When Zhongshan University took refuge from the war in the north of Guangdong Province, she moved with it, taking her astronomical instruments and books but leaving her personal belongings behind. When Zou Yixin's husband went to France to continue his studies in 1940, she remained to take care of their daughter and pursued a career as a professor in astronomy.

The outstanding work Zou Yixin accomplished was highly recommended by the Exchange Scholar Committee of the International Astronomical Union, and in 1948 she was offered a handsome scholarship for research and study at Greenwich Observatory in Britain. Zou Yixin was the first Asian female scholar to win such a scholarship. The following year, she was awarded considerable financial support, which allowed her to go to Edinburgh Observatory and Cambridge Observatory of Solar Physics. Zou Yixin canceled her scholarship, however, and declined further invitations from the University of Malaysia and Hong Kong Observatory when news came of the founding of the PRC. In 1950 she headed home with boxes of materials and notes to take up a position with Purple Mountain Observatory in Nanjing.

During his visit there in 1957, the Russian astronomer Fedorov was so impressed by Zou Yixin's work on accurately measuring the positions of large sets of stars that he invited her to study in the Soviet Union. While there, she devised a new method of measuring precisely the screw value of a zenith telescope, thereby doubling the efficiency of the measurement. On her return to China the following year, Zou Yixin chose latitude $39° 8'$ N as the site for an international stellar positioning observatory in Caocun, Tianjin; she then planned and took charge of the observatory. This international stellar positioning observatory was the country's only polar motion center and marked the start of polar migration measurement in China. More importantly, however, the establishment of the observatory allowed her to continue internationally recognized work on the accurate measurement of the positions of large sets of stars.

During the early years of the Cultural Revolution, Zou Yixin came under attack and was forced to abandon research. In 1970, however, she was called back to Beijing to undertake research into solar activity prediction. In the 1980s, the Chinese Academy of Sciences awarded her First Prize for Scientific Progress for her contribution in research on sudden interference in short-wave communication and sunspot prediction. She supplemented her technologically advanced work with extensive research into a wealth of early Chinese records of solar activity in an effort to deduce evidence for characteristics and patterns. This material led to a series of treatises that were received with great enthusiasm by the international astronomical community.

WANG Bing
(Translated by Yang Yi)

Liu Dongping and Wang Fan. "Ji dangdai Zhongguo diyiwei nütianwenxuejia Zou Yixin." *Renwu*, no. 3 (1992): 5–17.

Glossary of Chinese Names

A Jin: *see* Jin Weiying

A Xiang: *see* Xie Fei

Ah Ch'ing (Hsiang): *see* Jin Weiying

Aw, Sally   胡仙

Aw Sian: *see* Aw, Sally

Ba Jinlan   巴金蘭   巴金兰

Bai Fengxi   白峰谿

Bai Shuxiang   白淑湘

Bai Wei   白薇

Bai Yang   白楊   白杨

Bai Yushuang   白玉霜

Baolian: *see* Lü Bicheng

Baolige: *see* Wulan

Bin Zhi: *see* Ding Ling

Bing Xin   冰心

Bingxin: *see* Bing Xin

Cai Chang   蔡暢   蔡畅

Cai Lanying	蔡蘭英	蔡兰英

Cai Xianxi: *see* Cai Chang

Cai Yanci: *see* Choi Yan Chi

Can Xue	殘雪	残雪
Cao Mengjun	曹孟君	

Cao Shuying: *see* Cao Yi'ou

Cao Yi'ou	曹軼歐	曹轶欧
Caoming	草明	
Chan, Anson	陳方安生	陈方安生

Chang Ai-ling: *see* Chang, Eileen

Chang, C.H.: *see* Lu Shijia

Chang, C.S. Wang: *see* Wang Chengshu

Chang, Eileen	張愛玲	张爱玲

Chang Hsiu-Chen: *see* Lu Shijia

Chang Hsui-Chen: *see* Lu Shijia

Chao Fuhuan 晁福寰: *see* Zhong Yuzheng

Chao Mo-ya	趙默雅	赵默雅

Chee, Irene Kwong: *see* Moss, Irene

Ch'en Ai-chu	陳愛珠	陈爱珠

Chen Aizhu: *see* Ch'en Ai-chu

Chen Bijun	陳璧君	陈璧君
Chen Bingru: *see* Chen Bijun		
Ch'en Che: *see* Ch'iung Yao		
Ch'en Chin	陳進	陈进
Chen Chin: *see* Ch'en Chin		
Chen Congying	陳琮英	陈琮英
Chen Derong: *see* Shen Rong		
Chen, Georgette	張荔英	张荔英
Chen Hengzhe	陳衡哲	陈衡哲
Ch'en Hsiang-mei: *see* Chen Xiangmei		
Ch'en Hsing-wan	陳幸婉	陈幸婉
Ch'en Hsiu-hsi	陳秀喜	陈秀喜
Chen Huiqing	陳慧清	陈慧清
Chen Jin: *see* Ch'en Chin		
Ch'en Jo-hsi: *see* Chen Ruoxi		
Chen Liying: *see* Chen, Georgette		
Ch'en Mei-ch'üan	陳湄泉	陈湄泉
Chen Meiquan: *see* Ch'en Mei-ch'üan		
Chen Muhua	陳慕華	陈慕华
Ch'en P'ing: *see* San Mao		

Chen Ping: *see* San Mao

Chen Ran   陳染   陈染

Chen Rong   陳顒   陈顒

Chen Rong, writer: 諶容 *see* Shen Rong

Chen Ruoxi   陳若曦   陈若曦

Chen Shamin: *see* Chen Shaomin

Chen Shaomin   陳少敏   陈少敏

Chen Shiman: *see* Ch'en–Shih Man

Chen Shuying: *see* Chen Xuezhao

Chen Shuzhang: *see* Chen Xuezhao

Chen, Sophia Hung-che: *see* Chen Hengzhe

Chen Xiangmei   陳香梅   陈香梅

Chen Xingwan: *see* Ch'en Hsing-wan

Chen Xiuqing: *see* Pan Yuliang

Chen Xiuxi: *see* Ch'en Hsiu-hsi

Chen Xuezhao   陳學昭   陈学昭

Chen Yong: *see* Chen Rong

Ch'en Yüeh-ying: *see* Yü–Ch'en Yüeh-ying

Chen Yueying: *see* Yü–Ch'en Yüeh-ying

Chen Zen, Sophia: *see* Chen Hengzhe

Chen Zhe: *see* Ch'iung Yao

Chen–Shi Man: *see* Ch'en–Shih Man

Ch'en–Shih Man   陳石滿   陈石满

Ch'eng Hsiao-kuei   程曉桂   程晓桂

Cheng Naishan   程乃珊   程乃珊

Cheng Xiaogui: *see* Ch'eng Hsiao-kuei

Cheng Yen, Master   證嚴法師   证严法师

Cheng Yueru: *see* Lin Dai

Cheng-yen Shih: *see* Cheng Yen, Master

Cheng-yen, Ven.: *see* Cheng Yen, Master

Chennault, Anna: *see* Chen Xiangmei

Chi Cheng   紀政   纪政

Chi Cheng, Reel: *see* Chi Cheng

Chi Jishang   池際尚   池际尚

Chi Li   池莉

Chia Fu-ming   賈馥茗   贾馥茗

Chiang Kai-shek, Madame: *see* Soong Mayling

Ch'i-chün   琦君

Ch'ien Chien-ch'iu   錢劍秋   钱剑秋

Chien O   簡娥   简娥

Chi-oang   芝苑

Ch'iu Yüan-yang	邱鴛鴦	邱鸳鸯
Ch'iung Yao	瓊瑤	琼瑶
Choi Yan Chi	蔡仞姿	
Chou Guanghu: *see* Han Suyin		
Chou, Irene	周綠雲	周绿云
Chou Mei-yü	周美玉	
Chou, Rosalie: *see* Han Suyin		
Chu Yaming: *see* Caoming		
Chung Ling	鍾玲	钟玲
Ciwang Iwal: *see* Chi-oang		
Cong Xuan: *see* Ding Ling		
Cui Xiaoping: *see* Ts'ui Hsiao-p'ing		
Dai Ailian	戴愛蓮	戴爱莲
Dai Houying	戴厚英	
Dai Jinhua	戴錦華	戴锦华
Dai Qing	戴晴	
Dbyangs-can Lha-mo: *see* Dbyangs-dgav		
Dbyangs-dgav	央嘎	
Deng Lianru: *see* Dunn, Dame Lydia Selina		
Deng Lijun: *see* Teng Li-chün		

Deng Liujin   鄧六金   邓六金

Deng Liyun: *see* Teng Li-chün

Deng Wenshu: *see* Deng Yingchao

Deng Xiangjun : *see* Deng Yingchao

Deng Xianqun 鄧先群 : *see* Zhong Yuzheng

Deng Xiaohua: *see* Can Xue

Deng Yingchao   鄧穎超   邓颖超

Deng Yongtong: *see* Deng Yingchao

Deng Yuzhi   鄧裕志   邓裕志

Dengzhu Lamu: *see* Don-grub Lha-mo

Ding Guoxian   ·   丁果仙

Ding Ling   丁玲

Ding Xuesong   丁雪松

Dong Huang: *see* Dong Zhujun

Dong Maoyuan: *see* Dong Zhujun

Dong Pu: *see* Wang Guangmei

Dong Yuying: *see* Dong Zhujun

Dong Zhujun   董竹君

Don-grub Lha-mo   鄧珠拉姆   邓珠拉姆

Du Runzhang: *see* Zhang Yun

Du Shuzhen   杜淑真

Duan Anlin: *see* Siqin Gaowa

Dunn, Dame Lydia Selina 鄧蓮如 邓莲如

Echo: *see* San Mao

Fan Ruijuan 范瑞娟

Fan Tchun-pi 方君璧

Fan Zhenhua: *see* Yang Zilie

Fan Zhushan: *see* Fan Ruijuan

Fang Ansheng: *see* Chan, Anson

Fang Chao-lin: *see* Fang Zhaolin

Fang Fang 方方

Fang Junbi: *see* Fan Tchun-pi

Fang Xiao: *see* Han Zi

Fang Zhaolin 方召麐

Feng Kai: *see* Ke Yan

Feng Yuanjun 馮沅君 冯沅君

Feng Zhongpu: *see* Zong Pu

Fu Ning: *see* Dai Qing

Fu Quanxiang 傅全香

Fu Xiaoqing: *see* Dai Qing

Gan Tang: *see* Kan Shiying

Ge Hua: *see* Dai Jinhua

Ge Jianhao   葛健豪

Ge Lanying: *see* Ge Jianhao

Gong Li   鞏俐   巩俐

Gong Peiyu: *see* Shu Ting

Gong Peng   龔澎   龚澎

Gong Pusheng   龔普生   龚普生

Gong Shuting: *see* Shu Ting

Gong Weihang: *see* Gong Peng

Gu Mei: *see* Koo Mei

Gu Shengying   顧聖嬰   顾圣婴

Gu Xiulian   顧秀蓮   顾秀莲

Gu Yuezhen   顧月珍   顾月珍

Guo Jian   郭建

Guo Jian'en: *see* Guo Jian

Guo Wanrong: *see* Kuo Wan-jung

Guo Xiaozhuang: *see* Kuo Hsiao-chuang

Guozi Hong: *see* Ding Guoxian

Han Shiying: *see* Kan Shiying

Han Suyin   漢素音   汉素音

Han Youtong   韓幽桐   韩幽桐

Han Zi	菡子	
Hang Ying	航鷹	航鹰
Hao Jianxiu	郝建秀	
He Jiesheng 賀捷生: *see* Zhong Yuzheng		
He Ruijian: *see* He Xiangning		
He Xiangning	何香凝	
He Zehui	何澤慧	何泽慧
He Zizhen	賀子貞	贺子贞
Hiu Wan, Ven.	曉雲法師	晓云法师
Ho Zah-Wei: *see* He Zehui		
Hong, Maxine Ting Ting: *see* Kingston, Maxine Hong		
Hongxian Nü	紅線女	红线女
Hou Bo	侯波	
Hsia Pei-Su: *see* Xia Peisu		
Hsia Yu	夏宇	
Hsia Yü: *see* Hsia Yu		
Hsiao Ch'ing-yü: *see* Hsiao Sa		
Hsiao Hung: *see* Xiao Hong		
Hsiao Sa	蕭颯	萧飒
Hsiao Yün: *see* Hiu Wan, Ven.		

Hsiao-yün fa-shih: *see* Hiu Wan, Ven.

Hsieh Ah-nü: *see* Xie Xuehong

Hsieh Chia-nü: *see* Xie Xuehong

Hsieh Fei-ying: *see* Xie Xuehong

Hsieh Hsi-teh: *see* Xie Xide

Hsieh Hsüeh-hung: *see* Xie Xuehong

Hsieh Ping-ying	謝冰瑩	谢冰莹
Hsiu Tse-lan	修澤蘭	修泽兰

Hsü Ch'un-chü: *see* Liang–Hsü Ch'un-chü

Hsü Feng	徐楓	徐枫
Hsü Shih-hsien	許世賢	许世贤

Hu Baojuan: *see* Hu Die

Hu Dachang: *see* Wu Mulan

Hu Die	胡蝶

Hu Feipei 胡斐佩: *see* Zhong Yuzheng

Hu Jieqing	胡絜清

Hu Ruihua: *see* Hu Die

Hu Xian: *see* Aw, Sally

Huang Dianxian	黃典賢	黄典贤
Huang Liang	黃量	

Huang Luyin: *see* Luyin

Huang Ying: *see* Luyin

Huang Zhang: *see* Bai Wei

Huang Zonghan: *see* Xu Zonghan

Huang Zongying   黃宗英

Hui: *see* Chen Xuezhao

Hui Wan: *see* Hiu Wan, Ven.

Huizhu: *see* Yan Huizhu

Jen I-tu: *see* Sun, E-tu Zen

Ji Zheng: *see* Chi Cheng

Jia Fuming: *see* Chia Fu-ming

Jian E: *see* Chien O

Jiang Bingzhi: *see* Ding Ling

Jiang Biwei   蔣碧微   蔣碧微

Jiang Lijin   蔣麗金   蔣丽金

Jiang Qing   江青

Jiang Tangzhen: *see* Jiang Biwei

Jiang Wei: *see* Ding Ling

Jin Weiying   金維映   金维映

June-Nikel, Renée: *see* Wang Henei

Jung-tzu   蓉子

Kan Shiying   闞士穎   阚士颖

Kan Siying: *see* Kan Shiying

Kan Tang: *see* Kan Shiying

Kang Keqing   康克清

Kang Tongbi   康同璧

Kang Tongwei   康同薇

Ke Yan   柯岩

Kingston, Maxine Hong

Koo Mei   顧媚   顾媚

Kou Chen Ying: *see* Gu Shengying

Kuang Jianlian: *see* Hongxian Nü

Kuo Hsiao-chuang   郭小莊   郭小庄

Kuo, Shirley: *see* Kuo Wan-jung

Kuo Wan-jung   郭婉容

Kuo Wanyong: *see* Kuo Wan-jung

Kwong Wai Lin: *see* Moss, Irene

Lai Chunchun: *see* Lai, Jun T.

Lai, Jun T.   賴純純   赖纯纯

Lan Ping: *see* Jiang Qing

Lang Ping   郎平

Lau, Emily   劉慧卿   刘慧卿

Lau Wai-hing: *see* Lau, Emily

Lee Ang: *see* Li Ang

Lei Jieqiong	雷潔瓊	雷洁琼
Li Ang	李昂	
Li Bozhao	李伯釗	李伯钊

Li Chün-chen: *see* Li Jianzhen

Li Chung-kuei: *see* Li Chung-kui

Li Chung-kui	李鍾桂	李钟桂
Li Dequan	李德全	
Li Guiying	李桂英	

Li Guizhen: *see* Bai Yushuang

Li Huimin: *see* Bai Yushuang

Li Jianhua	李建華	李建华
Li Jianzhen	李堅真	李坚真

Li Jin: *see* Jiang Qing

Li Kuntai: *see* Zhao Yiman

Li Li Hua: *see* Li Lihua

Li Li-chüan	李莉娟	
Li Lihua	李麗華	李丽华

Li Lijuan: *see* Li Li-chüan

Li Shude: *see* Li Shu-te

Li Shumeng: *see* Jiang Qing

Li Shu-te 李淑德

Li Shuzheng 李淑靜 李淑诤

Li Xikai 李希楷: *see* Zhong Yuzheng

Li Yijie: *see* Zhao Yiman

Li Yunhe: *see* Jiang Qing

Li Zhen 李貞 李贞

Li Zhonggui: *see* Li Chung-kui

Li Ziyun 李子雲 李子云

Liang Danfeng: *see* Liang Tan-feng

Liang Jing: *see* Chang, Eileen

Liang Tan-feng 梁丹丰 梁丹丰

Liang–Hsü Ch'un-chü 梁許春菊 梁许春菊

Liang–Xu Chunju: *see* Liang–Hsü Ch'un-chü

Liao Mengxing 廖夢醒 廖梦醒

Liao Shaofen: *see* Liao Mengxing

Liao Siguang 廖似光

Liao Wenhai 廖文海: *see* Zhong Yuzheng

Liao Xianlin: *see* Liao Mengxing

Lin Bai 林白

Lin Baiwei: *see* Lin Bai

Lin Chin-chih   林金枝

Lin Ch'iu-chin   林秋錦   林秋锦

Lin Dai   林黛

Lin Hai-yin   林海音

Lin Han-ying: *see* Lin Hai-yin

Lin Huiyin   林徽因

Lin Jinzhi: *see* Lin Chin-chih

Lin Lanying   林蘭英   林兰英

Lin Qiaozhi   林巧稚

Lin Qiujin: *see* Lin Ch'iu-chin

Lin Zongsu   林宗素

Lin Zongxue 林宗雪: *see* Lin Zongsu

Lin–Cai Sunü: *see* Lin–Ts'ai Su-nü

Lin–Ts'ai Su-nü   林蔡素女

Linda: *see* Lin Dai

Ling Ruitang: *see* Ling Shuhua

Ling Shuhua   凌淑華   凌淑华

Ling Yü   零雨

Liu Chien-hsien: *see* Liu Qunxian

Liu Fulan: *see* Liu Hulan

Liu Huiqing: *see* Lau, Emily

Liu Hulan | 劉胡蘭 | 刘胡兰

Liu Lianqing: *see* Liu Zhen

Liu Qingyang | 劉清揚 | 刘清扬

Liu Qunxian | 劉群先 | 刘群先

Liu Sola: *see* Liu Suola

Liu Suola | 劉索拉 | 刘索拉

Liu Xiaoqing | 劉曉慶 | 刘晓庆

Liu Yaxiong | 劉亞雄 | 刘亚雄

Liu Ying | 劉英 | 刘英

Liu Zhen | 劉真 | 刘真

Liu Zhihua | 劉志華 | 刘志华

Liu–Wang Liming | 劉王立明 | 刘王立明

Longlian fashi: *see* Longlian, Ven.

Longlian, Ven. | 隆蓮法師 | 隆莲法师

Lu, Annette: *see* Lü Hsiu-lien

Lü, Annette: *see* Lü Hsiu-lien

Lü Bicheng | 呂碧城

Lü Duntian: *see* Lü Bicheng

Lü Fan: *see* Zong Pu

Lu Guizhen: *see* Lu Gwei-Djen

Lu Guo: *see* Yishu

Lu Gwei-Djen   魯桂珍   鲁桂珍

Lu Hsih-Chia: *see* Lu Shijia

Lü Hsiu-lien   呂秀蓮   吕秀莲

Lu Hsui-Chen: *see* Lu Shijia

Lü Lanqing: *see* Lü Bicheng

Lu Lin: *see* Wulan

Lu Mei: *see* Lu Xiaoman

Lü Mingyin: *see* Lü Bicheng

Lu Ni: *see* Dai Jinhua

Lü Shengyin: *see* Lü Bicheng

Lu Shih-Chia: *see* Lu Shijia

Lu Shijia   陸士嘉   陆士嘉

Lu Xiaoman   陸小曼   陆小曼

Lu Xiaomei: *see* Lu Xiaoman

Lu Xing'er   陸星兒   陆星儿

Lü Xiulian: *see* Lü Hsiu-lien

Lu Xiuzhen: *see* Lu Shijia

Lü-i: *see* Su Hsüeh-lin

Luo Caoming: *see* Caoming

Luo Feiya: *see* Zhang Mojun

Luo Jiang: *see* Yishu

Luo Shuzhang   羅叔章   罗叔章

Luyin   廬隱   庐隐

Man Jia: *see* Ding Ling

Mao Yanwen: *see* Mao Yen-wen

Mao Yen-wen   毛彥文

Meifeng: *see* Yishu

Meiqian: *see* Yishu

Mingzhu: *see* Don-grub Lha-mo

Modegemaa   莫德格瑪   莫德格玛

Moss, Irene

Mo-te-ko-ma: *see* Modegemaa

Ni Yishu: *see* Yishu

Nie Hualing: *see* Nieh Hualing

Nie Li 聶力: *see* Zhong Yuzheng

Nie Ou   聶鷗   聂鸥

Nie Yuanzi   聶元梓   聂元梓

Nie Yuchan   聶毓禪   聂毓禅

Nieh Hualing   聶華苓   聂华苓

Ouyang Quanyuan: *see* Wang Quanyuan

Pan Baojuan: *see* Hu Die

Pan Duo: *see* Pan-thogs

P'an Hsi-chen: *see* Ch'i-chün

Pan Xizhen: *see* Ch'i-chün

Pan Yuliang   潘玉良

Pang Tao   龐濤   庞涛

Pan-thogs   潘多

Peng Gang 彭鋼: *see* Zhong Yuzheng

Peng Peiyun   彭珮雲   彭珮云

Peng Xuezhen: *see* Peng Zigang

Peng Zigang   彭子岡   彭子冈

Phantog: *see* Pan-thogs

Ping-hsin: *see* Bing Xin

Qian Jianqiu:*see* Ch'ien Chien-ch'iu

Qian Xijun   錢希鈞   钱希钧

Qian Ying   錢瑛   钱瑛

Qian Zhengying   錢正英   钱正英

Qiao Peijuan 喬佩娟: *see* Zhong Yuzheng

Qiao Yin: *see* Xiao Hong

Qijun: *see* Ch'i-chün

Qiong Yao: *see* Ch'iung Yao

Qiu Yihan   丘一涵

Qiu Yuanyang: *see* Ch'iu Yüan-yang

Ren Yidu: *see* Sun, E-tu Zen

Reyher, Eileen Chang: *see* Chang, Eileen

Rongzi: *see* Jung-tzu

Ru Zhijuan   茹志鵑   茹志鹃

Ruan Fenggen: *see* Ruan Lingyu

Ruan Lingyu   阮玲玉

Ruan Ruolin   阮若琳

San Mao   三毛

Shao Meng-lan   邵夢蘭   邵梦兰

Shen Rong   諶容   谌容

Shen Zijiu   沈茲九

Shi Liang   史良

Shi Wei: *see* Chen Xuezhao

Shih Man: *see* Ch'en–Shih Man

Shih Shu-tuan: *see* Li Ang

Shu Ting   舒婷

Shu Xiuwen   舒繡文   舒绣文

Shuai Mengqi	帥孟奇	
Shuangqing Louzhu: *see* He Xiangning		
Shuhua: *see* Ling Shuhua		
Siqin Gaowa	斯琴高娃	
Song Ailing: *see* Soong Ailing		
Song Meiling: *see* Soong Mayling		
Song Qingling	宋慶齡	宋庆龄
Soong Ailing	宋藹齡	宋蔼龄
Soong Ching-ling: *see* Song Qingling		
Soong E-ling: *see* Soong Ailing		
Soong Mayling	宋美齡	宋美龄
Soong Mei-ling: *see* Soong Mayling		
Su Hsüeh-lin	蘇雪林	苏雪林
Su Mei: *see* Su Hsüeh-lin		
Su Xuelin: *see* Su Hsüeh-lin		
Sun, E-tu Zen	任以都	
Sun Quanxiang: *see* Fu Quanxiang		
Sun Shamin: *see* Chen Shaomin		
Sun Weishi	孫維世	孙维世
Sun Yat-sen, Madame: *see* Song Qingling		
Sun Yumei: *see* Chen Shaomin		

Sun Zhaoxiu: *see* Chen Shaomin

Sung Ai-ling: *see* Soong Ailing

Sung Ch'ing-ling: *see* Song Qingling

Sung Mei-ling: *see* Soong Mayling

Suxin: *see* Ling Shuhua

Tai Ai-lien: *see* Dai Ailian

Tan, Amy

Tan An-mei: *see* Tan, Amy

Tang Qunying   唐群英

Tang Tingting: *see* Kingston, Maxine Hong

Tang Tiyin   湯蒂因   汤蒂因

Tao Shufan   陶淑範   陶淑范

Teng Li-chün   鄧麗君   邓丽君

Teng, Li-yun: *see* Teng Li-chün

Teng, Teresa: *see* Teng Li-chün

Teng Ying-ch'ao: *see* Deng Yingchao

Tie Ning   鐵凝   铁凝

Ts'ai Su-nü: *see* Lin–Ts'ai Su-nü

Ts'ui Hsiao-p'ing   崔小萍

Tsui Hsiao-ping: *see* Ts'ui Hsiao-p'ing

Wan Shaofen   萬紹芬   万绍芬

Wang Anyi	王安憶	王安忆
Wang Chengshu	王承書	王承书
Wang, C.S. Chang: *see* Wang Chengshu		
Wang Dingguo	王定國	王定国
Wang Fang: *see* Fang Fang		
Wang Guangmei	王光美	
Wang Henei	王合內	
Wang Huiwu	王會悟	王会悟
Wang Jinyun: *see* Cheng Yen, Master		
Wang Jung-chih: *see* Jung-tzu		
Wang Keqin: *see* Wang Ying		
Wang Liming: *see* Liu–Wang Liming		
Wang Quanyuan	王泉媛	
Wang Rong: *see* Yang Huizhen		
Wang Rongzhi: *see* Jung-tzu		
Wang Xiaotang 王曉棠: *see* Zhong Yuzheng		
Wang Ying	王瑩	王莹
Wang Yingchun	王迎春	
Wang Yizhi	王一知	
Wang Zhiying: *see* Li Shuzheng		
Wang Zuling: *see* Zhu Lin (writer)		

Wei Fengying	尉鳳英	尉凤英
Wei Gongzhi	危拱之	
Wei Xiuying	危秀英	
Wong, Ruth Hie King		
Wu, Butterfly: *see* Hu Die		
Wu, Chien-Shiung	吳健雄	吴健雄
Wu, C.S.: *see* Wu, Chien-Shiung		
Wu Fulian	吳富蓮	吴富莲
Wu Jianxiong: *see* Wu, Chien-Shiung		
Wu Ma-li	吳瑪琍	吴玛利
Wu Molan: *see* Wu Mulan		
Wu Mulan	吳木蘭	吴木兰
Wu Sheng: *see* Yan Huizhu		
Wu Shun-wen	吳舜文	吴舜文
Wu Xiaoheng 吳曉恆: *see* Zhong Yuzheng		
Wu Xuanwen: *see* Caoming		
Wu Yi	吳儀	吴仪
Wu Yifang	吳貽芳	吴贻芳
Wu Yuxia	吳玉霞	吴玉霞
Wu Zhonglian	吳仲廉	吴仲廉

Wulan	烏蘭	乌兰
Xia Juhua	夏菊花	
Xia Peisu	夏培肅	夏培肃
Xia Yu: *see* Hsia Yu		
Xian Yuqing	冼玉清	
Xiang Jingyu	向警予	
Xiao Han: *see* Ding Ling		
Xiao Hong	蕭紅	萧红
Xiao Li: *see* Li Ziyun		
Xiao Qingyu: *see* Hsiao Sa		
Xiao Sa: *see* Hsiao Sa		
Xiao Yanhong: *see* Hongxian Nü		
Xiao Yuehua	蕭月華	萧月华
Xiao Yun: *see* Hiu Wan, Ven.		
Xiaomi: *see* Li Lihua		
Xie Bingxin: *see* Bing Xin		
Xie Bingying: *see* Hsieh Ping-ying		
Xie Fei	謝飛	谢飞
Xie Qiongxiang: *see* Xie Fei		
Xie Wanying: *see* Bing Xin		
Xie Xiaomei	謝小梅	谢小梅

Xie Xide	謝希德	谢希德
Xie Xuehong	謝雪紅	谢雪红
Xin Fengxia	新鳳霞	新凤霞
Xiu Zelan: *see* Hsiu Tse-lan		
Xixi	西西	
Xu Chunju: *see* Liang–Hsü Ch'un-chü		
Xu Feng: *see* Hsü Feng		
Xu Guangping	許廣平	许广平
Xu Juhua: *see* Xia Juhua		
Xu Peixuan: *see* Xu Zonghan		
Xu Qing: *see* Xu Zonghan		
Xu Shixian: *see* Hsü Shih-hsien		
Xu Yulan	徐玉蘭	徐玉兰
Xu Zonghan	徐宗漢	徐宗汉
Xue Zhao: *see* Chen Xuezhao		
Yamane Yoshiko: *see* Xie Xuehong		
Yan Daifeng: *see* Yan Fengying		
Yan Fengying	嚴鳳英	严凤英
Yan Hongliu: *see* Yan Fengying		
Yan Huizhu	言慧珠	

Yang Chengye: *see* Yang Mo

Yang Chongrui	楊崇瑞	杨崇瑞
Yang Fuqing	楊芙清	杨芙清
Yang Houzhen	楊厚珍	杨厚珍

Yang Hu-chen: *see* Yang Houzhen

Yang Huizhen	楊慧貞	杨慧贞
Yang Jiang	楊絳	杨绛

Yang Jikang: *see* Yang Jiang

Yang Jingqin: *see* Yang Zilie

Yang Junmo: *see* Yang Mo

Yang Kaihui	楊開慧	杨开慧
Yang Liping	楊麗萍	杨丽萍
Yang Mo	楊沫	杨沫

Yang Shumin: *see* Xin Fengxia

Yang Tzu-lieh: *see* Yang Zilie

Yang Xiaofeng: *see* Yang Zilie

Yang Yizhi: *see* Wang Yizhi

Yang Zhihua	楊之華	杨之华
Yang Zilie	楊子烈	杨子烈
Ye Gongshao	葉恭紹	叶恭绍

Ye Qu: *see* Chen Xuezhao

Ye Qun   葉群   叶群

Ye Shuhua   葉叔華   叶叔华

Ye Tao: *see* Yeh T'ao

Ye Yijing: *see* Ye Qun

Yeh, K.S.: *see* Ye Gongshao

Yeh T'ao   葉陶   叶陶

Yi Xiang: *see* Wang Dingguo

Yi-hao: *see* Deng Yingchao

Yin Ruizhi 尹銳志: *see* Lin Zongsu

Yin Weijun 尹維俊: *see* Lin Zongsu

Yishabei: *see* Yishu

Yishu   亦舒

Yongtzu: *see* Jung-tzu

You Wanfen: *see* Hiu Wan, Ven.

You Yongkang: *see* Longlian, Ven.

You Yunshan: *see* Hiu Wan, Ven.

Yu Lihua: *see* Yü Li-hua

Yü Li-hua   於梨華   於梨华

Yu Luojin   遇羅錦   遇罗锦

Yu Shan   俞珊

Yu Wan-fen: *see* Hiu Wan, Ven.

Yu Yün-shan: *see* Hiu Wan, Ven.

Yu Zhihua: *see* Wang Ying

Yü–Ch'en Yüeh-ying   余陳月瑛   余陈月瑛

Yu–Chen Yueying: *see* Yü–Ch'en Yüeh-ying

Yuan En: *see* Nieh Hualing

Yuan Xuefen   袁雪芬

Yue Daiyun   樂黛雲   乐黛云

Yuen, Susan

Yungtze: *see* Jung-tzu

Yung-tzu: *see* Jung-tzu

Zen, Sophia: *see* Chen Hengzhe

Zen Sun, E-tu: *see* Sun, E-tu Zen

Zeng Baosun: *see* Zeng Zhaoyu

Zeng Zhaoyu   曾昭燏

Zeng Zhi   曾志

Zhai Yongming   翟永明

Zhang Ailing: *see* Chang, Eileen

Zhang Cen: *see* Wulan

Zhang Guiqin   張桂琴   张桂琴

Zhang Jie   張潔   张洁

Zhang Kangkang   張抗抗   张抗抗

Zhang Mojun	張默君	张默君
Zhang Naiying: *see* Xiao Hong		
Zhang Qinqiu	張琴秋	张琴秋
Zhang Quan	張權	张权
Zhang Ruoming	張若名	张若名
Zhang, Sophie: *see* Zhang Mojun		
Zhang Wei: *see* Wulan		
Zhang Wu: *see* Zhang Qinqiu		
Zhang Xinxin	張欣欣	张欣欣
Zhang Yan: *see* Xixi		
Zhang Yuliang: *see* Pan Yuliang		
Zhang Yun	章蘊	章蕴
Zhang Zhaohan: *see* Zhang Mojun		
Zhang Zhixin	張志新	张志新
Zhao Moya: *see* Chao Mo-ya		
Zhao Yanxia	趙燕俠	赵燕侠
Zhao Yiman	趙一曼	赵一曼
Zhao Zhiwen 趙織雯: *see* Zhong Yuzheng		
Zheng Jie: *see* Liu Ying		
Zhengyan fashi: *see* Cheng Yen, Master		

Zhengyan, Ven.: *see* Cheng Yen, Master

Zhenhua fashi: *see* Zhenhua, Ven.

Zhenhua, Ven.   振華法師   振华法师

Zhong Ling: *see* Chung Ling

Zhong Ming: *see* Yan Huizhu

Zhong Weiluo: *see* Gong Peng

Zhong Xiaoyang   鍾曉陽   钟晓阳

Zhong Yuzheng   鍾玉徵   钟玉征

Zhou Lüyun: *see* Chou, Irene

Zhou Meiyu: *see* Chou Mei-yü

Zhou Shu'an   周淑安

Zhou Sicong   周思聰   周思聪

Zhou Xiaohong: *see* Zhou Xuan

Zhou Xuan   周璇

Zhou Yuebin: *see* Han Suyin

Zhou Yuehua   周越華   周越华

Zhu Lian   朱璉   朱琏

Zhu Lin (actress)   朱琳

Zhu Lin (writer)   竹林

Zong Pu   宗璞

Zou Yixin   鄒儀新   邹仪新